Living in the Environment

An Introduction to Environmental Science/Sixth Edition

G. Tyler Miller, Jr.

Wadsworth Publishing Company
Belmont, California
A Division of Wadsworth, Inc.

Science Editor: Jack Carey
Editorial Assistant: Olivia Wirthman
Signing Representative: Charles O. Delmar
Production Editor: Michael Oates
Managing Designer: Andrew H. Ogus
Print Buyers: Barbara Britton, Karen Hunt
Copy Editors: Noel Deeley, Lura S. Harrison
Art Editor: Donna Kalal
Compositor: Graphic Typesetting Service
Color Separator: Color Response
Make-up Artist: Edie Williams
Photo Researcher: Stephen Forsling
Technical Illustrators: Darwin and Vally Hennings, John
and Judith Waller, Raychel Ciemma, Jeanne M.
Schreiber, Joan Carol, Susan Breitbard, Shirley Bortoli,
Salinda Tyson, Florence Fujimoto, Victor Royer, and
Linda Harris-Sweeney
Cover photograph © 1989 David Muench

Printed in the United States of America   48

3 4 5 6 7 8 9 10——94 93 92 91 90

Library of Congress Cataloging-in-Publication Data
Miller, G. Tyler (George Tyler), 1931–
      Living in the environment: an introduction to environmental
      science / G. Tyler Miller, Jr.—6th ed.
          p.   cm.
      Includes bibliographical references.
      ISBN 0-534-12222-1
      1. Human ecology.   2. Environmental policy.   I. Title.
GF41.M54   1990
363.7——dc20   89-37025
                                                    CIP

Preface:
To the Instructor

Goals This book is designed to be used in introductory courses on environmental science. My goals for the book are to

- cover the diverse materials of an introductory course on environmental science in an accurate, balanced, and interesting way without the use of mathematics or complex chemical and biological information

- help your students discover that dealing with environmental and resource issues is fun, interesting, and important to their lives

- allow you to use the material in a flexible manner to meet your needs depending on course length and what you believe are the important topics

- introduce students to key concepts and principles that govern how nature works and apply them to possible solutions to environmental and resource problems

- show how environmental and resource problems are interrelated and must be understood and dealt with on local, regional, national, and global bases

- give a realistic but hopeful view of how much has been done and what remains to be done in sustaining the earth

- indicate what students can do in their personal lives and life-styles to help sustain rather than degrade the earth's life-support systems

A Well-Tested Book The material in this textbook has been used and class-tested by well over 1 million students at over two-thirds of the country's colleges and universities. It has been the most widely used environmental science textbook in the United States since 1975, when the first edition was published.

Concept Centered The text was the first to use basic principles and concepts to help students understand environmental and resource problems and possible solutions to these problems. This approach gives students a way to tie together and evaluate the massive amount of information in the field. I have introduced only the concepts and principles necessary to understand material in this book, and have tried to present them simply but accurately.

Three Different Textbooks Available This book is one of a series of three textbooks designed for different introductory courses on environmental science and resource conservation.

- This book, *Living in the Environment* (6th ed., Wadsworth 1990, 620 pages), gives broad and fairly detailed discussions of environmental and resource issues.

- *Environmental Science: An Introduction* (2d ed., Wadsworth, 1988, 406 pages) is a brief version of *Living in the Environment* that omits detailed discussions of many topics.

- *Resource Conservation and Management* (Wadsworth, 1990, 546 pages) has a different organizational pattern and content than the other two textbooks. It includes more detailed discussions of living resources. It has separate chapters on food, fishery, forest (two chapters), and wildlife (two chapters) resources and their management and less detailed discussions of ecological concepts, population, and pollution than *Living in the Environment*.

Readability Students often complain that textbooks are difficult and boring. I have tried to overcome this problem by writing this book in a clear, interesting, and informal style and relating the information in the book to the real world and to the student's own life. My goal has been to keep sentences and paragraphs short and avoid the use of a long word when a short one can express an idea just as well.

Flexibility I have designed this book to be flexible enough to be used in many different ways by dividing it into six major parts:

- Humans and Nature: An Overview (two chapters)
- Basic Concepts (four chapters)
- The Human Population (three chapters)
- Resources (eight chapters)

- Pollution (four chapters)
- Environment and Society (three chapters)

After you have covered all or most of Parts One and Two, you can cover the rest of the book in almost any order. For example, after covering the concepts in Part Two some of you may wish to then cover pollution in Part Four or you may wish to cover environmental economics, politics, and ethics in Part Six. These and other rearrangements of the course content can easily be done. Also most chapters within parts and many sections within these chapters can be moved around or omitted to accommodate courses with different lengths and emphases.

Other Major Features

- *Balanced discussions of opposing views* on major environmental and resource issues, especially in the 26 boxed *Pro/Con* discussions found throughout the book.

- *Emphasis on what individuals can do.* Most chapters end with a section on *What Can You Do?* Also see the suggestions for conserving water and energy inside the back cover.

- Content based on an *extensive review of the professional literature* (from more than 10,000 research sources); key readings for each chapter are listed on pp. A10-A35.

- *Extensive manuscript review* by 217 experts and teachers (see list on p. x) to help make the material accurate and up-to-date. Several experts reviewed each chapter. Teachers of environmental science courses or related types of courses reviewed most or all of the manuscript.

- 18 *Guest Essays* to provide more information and expose the reader to various points of view.

- 51 *Case Studies* to give in-depth information about key issues and to apply concepts.

- 52 *Spotlights* to highlight and give further insights into environmental and resource problems

- 419 *diagrams and carefully selected photographs* to illustrate complex ideas in a simple manner and to show how topics in the book relate to the real world.

- *Summary of key ideas* inside the front cover.

Learning Aids
To help students learn more effectively, I have included a number of aids.

- *General Questions and Issues:* Each chapter begins with several simple questions (see p. 158). They give the student an overview of the chapter and can also be used as review questions after the chapter is completed.

can also be used as review questions after the chapter is completed.

- *Chapter Summaries*
- *Key Terms:* When any new term is defined it is shown in **boldfaced** type.
- *Discussion Topics:* Each chapter has several discussion questions designed to encourage students to think about and apply what they have learned.
- *Glossary:* All key terms are defined in a glossary near the end of the book.

Major Changes in This Edition   Despite the success of this textbook, the publisher and I feel obligated to improve each edition to meet changing needs indicated by the extensive reviews and surveys of users. *This new edition is a major revision.* The major changes in this edition include:

- Material throughout the book has been updated and rewritten to make this an even better textbook. Since the information and many of the problems in this diverse field change on an almost yearly basis, frequent updating (ideally every two years) is more important than in most introductory courses.

- The number of chapters has been reduced from 26 to 24 by editing and rearranging of topics. The number of chapters on energy resources in Part Four has been reduced from three to two. Hazardous waste and risk analysis have been placed in Chapter 18 on Environment, Health, and Risk.

- The chapters on Environment, Health, and Risk (Chapter 18), Environmental Economics (Chapter 22), and Environmental Politics (Chapter 23), have been completely rewritten with the help of a number of experts in these fields. There is also expanded treatment of tropical deforestation, ozone depletion, and global warming.

- 51 Case Studies and 216 Pro/Con discussions of controversial issues have been added.

- Many new topics have been added including: jobs and environment (pp. 16 and 524), agenda for the future (p. 46), Gaia hypothesis (p. 143), importance of wetlands (pp. 122 and 128), nature of science and technology (p. 72), genetic engineering (p. 148), ecosystem restoration and rehabilitation (p. 151), the birth dearth controversy (p. 174), AIDS (p. 481), water rights (p. 254), home gardening and lawn care (p. 232), polyculture (p. 266), environmental impact of agriculture (p. 271), sustainable agriculture (p. 281), fires in Yellowstone National Park (p. 302), animal rights (p. 319), Arctic National Wildlife Refuge (p. 333), rock cycle and plate tectonics (p. 334), recycling of plastics (p. 367), safety at nuclear weapons facilities (p. 399), nuclear power as a solution to global warming (p. 405), determining toxicity levels (p. 450), risk assessment and risk management (p. 458), international toxic waste trade (p. 478), asbestos (p. 491), and the Valdez oil spill (p. 534).

- Special emphasis has been placed on improving readability by reducing sentence and paragraph length, omitting unnecessary details, and writing in a more personal style.

- Ten new guest essays have been added to eight used in earlier editions.

- 146 new illustrations and photographs have been added.

- A two-page summary of key ideas has been placed inside the front cover.

Help Me Improve This Book   I need your help in improving this book in future editions. Writing and publishing a textbook is an extremely complex process. Thus, any textbook is almost certain to have some typographical and other errors. To minimize errors, I have had all or parts of the manuscript reviewed by a large number of teachers and experts.

If you find any errors, please write them down and send them to me. Most errors can be corrected in subsequent printings of this edition, rather than waiting for a new edition.

I would also like to know how you think this book can be improved. We all have the same goal: finding the best way to teach students about this field. Helping me do this helps you and your students. I also hope you will encourage your students to evaluate the book and send me their suggestions for improvement.

Send any errors you find and your suggestions for improvement to Jack Carey, Science Editor, Wadsworth Publishing Company, 10 Davis Drive, Belmont, CA 94002. He will send them on to me.

Supplementary Materials   Dr. David Cotter at Georgia College has written an excellent Instructor's Manual and Test Items Booklet for use with this text. It contains sample multiple-choice test questions with answers, suggested projects, field trips, experiments, and a list of topics suitable for term papers and reports for each chapter. Master sheets for making overhead transparencies of many key diagrams are also available from the publisher.

Annenberg/CPB Television Course   This textbook is being offered as part of the Annenberg/CPB television course *Race to Save the Planet*, to be broadcast on PBS beginning in the fall of 1990.

Race to Save the Planet is a ten-part public television series and a college-level television course examining the major environmental questions facing the world today, ranging from population growth to soil erosion, from the destruction of forests to climate changes induced by human activity. The series will take into account the wide spectrum of opinion about what constitutes an environmental problem, as well as the controversies about appropriate remedial measures. It will analyze problems and emphasize the successful search for solutions. The course will develop a number of key themes that cut across a broad range of environmental issues including sustainability, the interconnection of the economy and the ecosystem, short-term versus long-term gains, and the tradeoffs involved in balancing problems and solutions.

In addition to my books (*Environmental Science* and *Living in the Environment*) and the video programs, the course will include a study guide and faculty guide available from Wadsworth Publishing Company. The television course is being developed as part of the Annenberg/CPB collection.

For further information about available television course licenses and off-air taping licenses contact: PBS Adult Learning Service, 1320 Braddock Place, Alexandria, VA 22314-1698, 1-800-ALS-ALS-8.

For supplementary audiovisual use, videocassettes and off-air taping licenses are available. For information, contact: The Annenberg/CPB project at PO Box 1922, Santa Barbara, CA 93166-1922, 1-800-LEARNER.

Acknowledgments   I wish to thank the many students and teachers who responded so favorably to the first five editions of *Living in the Environment* and the two editions of *Environmental Science* and offered many helpful suggestions for improvement.

I am also deeply indebted to the 217 reviewers of this and previous editions who pointed out errors and suggested many important improvements and to those who wrote guest essays. Any errors and deficiencies left are mine, not theirs.

Others have also made important contributions. They include production editors Michael Oates and Hal Humphrey, copy editors Noel Deeley and Lura S. Harrison, art editor Donna Kalal, photo researcher Stephen Forsling, designer Andrew Ogus, dummier Edie Williams, print buyers Karen Hunt and Barbara Britton, editorial assistant Olivia Wirthman, and artists Darwin and Vally Hennings, John and Judith Waller, Linda Harris-Sweeney, Raychel Ciemma, Victor Royer, Joan Carol, Salinda Tyson, Jeanne M. Schreiber, Susan Breitbard, Shirley Bortoli, and Florence Fujimoto.

Above all I wish to thank Jack Carey, science editor at Wadsworth, for his encouragement, help, friendship, and superb reviewing system. It helps immensely to work with the best and most experienced editor in college textbook publishing.

G. Tyler Miller, Jr.

Preface:
To the Student

Why Study About Resource and Environmental Issues? This is not just another college course to be passed for credit. It is an introduction to how nature works, how the environment has been and is being used and abused, and what you can do to protect and improve it for yourself and other people, future generations, and other living things. I am convinced that nothing else deserves more of your energy, time, concern, and personal involvement.

Studying environmental and resource problems is different than studying most courses like chemistry, biology, economics, or psychology. Why? Because it is an *interdisciplinary* study. It involves combining ideas and information from physical sciences such as biology, chemistry, and geology and social sciences such as economics, politics, and ethics to get a general idea of how the world works and what our role in the world should be.

What Is the Purpose of Learning? *The purpose of education is not to learn as much as you can. It is to learn as little as you can.* The goal of education is to learn how to sift through mountains of information and ideas and find the small amount that is really useful and worth knowing.

Inside the front cover of this book you will find a list of key principles that summarizes what I have learned so far about how the world works and what my role in it should be. These ideas are not original. They are the result of over 40 years of reading books and articles, tens of thousands of conversations with others, letters from students like you, and direct observations of nature.

I use these principles to evaluate other ideas and to make decisions about what to buy or not buy and how to live my life with increased joy. I am also constantly striving to improve this list by modifying or removing some ideas and adding new ones. I make no claims about whether these ideas are true. They are merely what I have found to be useful.

Trying to discover the knowledge that is really worth knowing is an exciting and never-ending process. It's great fun. As you draw up your own list, please send me any ideas you have. We are all in this together and we need all the help we can get.

How I Became Involved I feel you are entitled to know how I became involved in environmental and resource concerns and to what degree I try to put what I write about into practice in my own life and lifestyle. In 1966, when what we now know as the environmental movement began in the United States, I heard a scientist give a lecture on the problems of overpopulation and environmental abuse. Afterwards I went to him and said, "If even a fraction of what you have said is true, I will feel ethically obligated to give up my present scientific research on the corrosion of metals and devote the rest of my life to environmental issues. Frankly, I don't want to believe a word you have said, and I'm going into the literature to try to prove what you have said is either untrue or grossly distorted."

After six months of study I was convinced of the seriousness of these problems. Since then I have been studying, teaching, and writing about them. I have also attempted to live my life in an ecologically sound way—with varying degrees of success—by treading as lightly as possible on the earth. Working toward this goal has involved making more compromises and trade-offs than I have liked. But I continue the effort (see p. 444 for a summary of my own progress in attempting to work with nature).

Readability Students often complain that textbooks are difficult and boring. They are usually right, although some are unwilling to put in the time and hard work that reading and understanding always take.

I have tried to overcome this problem by writing this book in a clear, interesting, and informal style. I keep sentences and paragraphs fairly short. I try not to use long words when short ones can express an idea just as well. My goal is to communicate with you, not confuse you.

I also relate the information in the book to the real world and to your own lifestyle, in the main text and in boxed Spotlight, Case Studies, and Pro/Con discussions of issues sprinkled throughout the book.

A Realistic but Hopeful Local, National, and Global Outlook We face many environmental and resource problems. But a problem is an opportunity for change.

Pessimists who think we are doomed and optimists who blindly think everything will be all right regardless of what we do are dangerous people. These extreme positions are mind games that people use to avoid thinking about problems and becoming involved in bringing about change. This book is written for doers who care about the earth, not bench-sitters and toe dippers who care only about themselves.

In this book I offer a realistic but hopeful view of the future. Much has been done since 1965, when many people first became aware of the resource and environmental problems we face today. But much more needs to be done to protect the earth, which keeps you and all other forms of life alive. This book suggests ways that you can help sustain—not degrade—the earth.

As you will learn, most environmental and resource problems and their possible solutions are interrelated. Treating them in isolation is a recipe for disaster. They must also be considered on a local, national, and global scale—as this book does.

How the Book Is Organized This book is divided into six major parts:

- Humans and Nature: An Overview (two chapters)
- Basic Concepts (four chapters)
- The Human Population (three chapters)
- Resources (eight chapters)
- Pollution (four chapters)
- Environment and Society (three chapters)

Look at the Brief Contents on p. xiii to see the topics covered in each part. Before studying each chapter, I also suggest that you look over its detailed contents given on pp. xiv–xviii. This gives you a road map of where you will be going.

This Book Is Flexible I have designed the book so that it can be used in courses with different lengths and emphases. This gives your instructor great flexibility in designing the course you are taking.

The material in Parts One and Two gives you the background, basic definitions, and concepts needed to understand the rest of the book. Once you have studied most or all of Parts One and Two, you can cover the other four parts in any order your instructor assigns. Chapters in these parts and many sections within chapters can be rearranged or omitted. So don't be concerned if your instructor skips around and omits material.

General Questions and Issues and Chapter Summaries I believe in the old writing and teaching adage: Tell people where you are going, go there, and then remind them of where they have been. Each chapter begins with a few general questions to give you an idea of what you will be learning in each chapter. After you finish a chapter you can go back and try to answer these questions to review what you have learned.

You will also find a brief summary at the end of each chapter. Reading the summary should not replace reading the entire chapter. The summary is a review that omits much of the information needed for adequate understanding of the material.

Frankly, I have some misgivings about chapter summaries. They tempt people to read the summary and not read the chapter. Also my gut feeling is that you should be making your own summaries. But many instructors and students want them so I have provided them.

Vocabulary Each chapter will introduce new terms, whose meanings you need to know and understand. When a term is introduced and defined, it is printed in **boldfaced** type. There is also a glossary of all key terms at the end of the book.

Visual Aids Learning requires verbal and visual inputs. I have developed a number of diagrams to illustrate concepts and complex ideas in a simple manner. I have also used a number of carefully selected photos to give you a better picture of how topics discussed in this book relate to the real world.

Discussion Topics Each chapter ends with a set of discussion questions designed to encourage you to think and to apply what you have learned to your personal lifestyle. They also ask you to take sides on controversial issues and to back up your conclusions and beliefs.

I have not provided questions that test your recall of facts. This important but mechanical task is left to you and your instructor. As a college student you should know how to learn definitions and facts on your own. It is done the old-fashioned way—reading, marking key passages, making notes and summaries, and writing and studying flash cards.

Further Readings If you become especially interested in some of the topics in this book, you can get more information by reading other books and articles. A list of suggested readings for the material in each chapter is given in the back of this book beginning on p. A10. Also, Appendix 1 is a list of publications you can use to keep up to date on the material in this book.

Interact with the Book When I read something, I interact with it. I mark sentences and paragraphs with a highlighter or pen. I put an asterisk in the margin next to something I think is important and double asterisks next to something that I think is really important. I write comments in the margins, such as *Beautiful, Confusing, Bull, Wrong,* and so on.

I fold down the top corner of pages with highlighted passages and the top and bottom corners of especially important pages. This way I can flip through a book and quickly review the key passages. I hope you will interact in such ways with this book. You will learn more and have more fun. I hope you will often disagree with what I have written and take the time to think about or write down why.

Save This Book   After you finish this course, you may be tempted to discard this book or resell it to the bookstore. But learning is a lifelong process and you will have to deal with the vital issues discussed here for the rest of your life. Therefore, I hope you will keep this book in your personal library for future use. Or at least pass it on to someone whom you want to learn about the earth.

Help Me Improve the Book   I need your help in improving future editions. Writing and publishing a book is an incredibly complex process. That means that this or any other book is likely to have some typographical and factual errors. If you find an error, write it down and send it to me.

I would also appreciate learning from you what you like and dislike about the book. This information helps me make the book better. Some of the things you will read here were suggested by students like you.

Send any errors you find and any suggestions for improvement to Jack Carey, Science Editor, Wadsworth Publishing Company, 10 Davis Drive, Belmont, CA 94002. He will send them on to me.

Your input helps me, students who take this course in the future, and the earth.

And Now   Relax and enjoy yourself as you learn more about the exciting and challenging issues we all face in sustaining the earth's life-support systems.

G. Tyler Miller, Jr.

Guest Essayists

Donald G. Barnes, Staff Director, Science Advisory Board, Environmental Protection Agency

Kenneth E. Boulding, Institute of Behavioral Science, University of Colorado at Boulder

Herman E. Daly, Senior Environmental Economist, World Bank and Alumni Professor of Economics, Louisiana State University

John H. Gibbons, Director, Congressional Office of Technology Assessment

Garrett Hardin, Professor Emeritus of Human Ecology, University of California, Santa Barbara

Carl Haub, Director Demographic Analysis and Public Information, Population Reference Bureau

Edward J. Kormondy, Chancellor and Professor of Biology, University of Hawaii–Hilo/West Oahu College

Richard D. Lamm, Professor and Director of Center for Public Policy and Contemporary Issues, University of Denver

Amory B. Lovins, Energy policy consultant and Director of Research, Rocky Mountain Institute

Norman Myers, Consultant in environment and development

David Pimentel, Professor of Entomology, Cornell University

Philip R. Pryde, Department of Geography, San Diego State University

Neil Seldman, President, Institute for Local Self Reliance

George Sessions, Professor of Philosophy, Sierra College

Julian L. Simon, Professor of Economics and Business Administration, University of Maryland

Robert Leo Smith, Professor of Wildlife Biology, Division of Forestry, West Virginia University

Gus Speth, President, World Resources Institute

Alvin M. Weinberg, Distinguished Fellow, Institute of Energy Analysis

Reviewers

Barbara J. Abraham, Hampton College

Donald D. Adams, Plattsburgh State University of New York

Larry G. Allen, California State University, Northridge

James R. Anderson, U.S. Geological Survey

Kenneth B. Armitage, University of Kansas

Gary J. Atchison, Iowa State University

Marvin W. Baker, Jr., University of Oklahoma

Virgil R. Baker, Arizona State University

Ian G. Barbour, Carleton College

Albert J. Beck, California State University, Chico

W. Behan, Northern Arizona University

Keith L. Bildstein, Winthrop College

Jeff Bland, University of Puget Sound

Roger G. Bland, Central Michigan University

Georg Borgstrom, Michigan State University

Arthur C. Borror, University of New Hampshire

John H. Bounds, Sam Houston State University

Leon F. Bouvier, Population Reference Bureau

Michael F. Brewer, Resources for the Future, Inc.

Mark M. Brinson, East Carolina University

Patrick E. Brunelle, Contra Costa College

Terrence J. Burgess, Saddleback College North

David Byman, Pennsylvania State University, Worthington Scranton

Lynton K. Caldwell, Indiana University

Faith Thompson Campbell, Natural Resources Defense Council, Inc.

Ray Canterbery, Florida State University

Ted J. Case, University of San Diego

Ann Causey, Auburn University

Richard A. Cellarius, Evergreen State University

William U. Chandler, Worldwatch Institute

F. Christman, University of North Carolina, Chapel Hill

Preston Cloud, University of California, Santa Barbara

Bernard C. Cohen, University of Pittsburgh

Richard A. Cooley, University of California, Santa Cruz

Dennis J. Corrigan

George W. Cox, San Diego State University

John D. Cunningham, Keene State College

Herman E. Daly, The World Bank

Raymond F. Dasmann, University of California, Santa Cruz

Kingsley Davis, Hoover Institution

Edward E. DeMartini, University of California, Santa Barbara

Thomas R. Detwyler, University of Wisconsin

Peter H. Diage, University of California, Riverside

Lon D. Drake, University of Iowa

T. Edmonson, University of Washington

Thomas Eisner, Cornell University

David E. Fairbrothers, Rutgers University

Paul P. Feeny, Cornell University

Nancy Field, Bellevue Community College

Allan Fitzsimmons, University of Kentucky

George L. Fouke

Kenneth O. Fulgham, Humboldt State University

Lowell L. Getz, University of Illinois at Urbana-Champaign

Frederick F. Gilbert, Washington State University

Jay Glassman, Los Angeles Valley College

Harold Goetz, North Dakota State University

Jeffery J. Gordon, Bowling Green State University

Eville Gorham, University of Minnesota

Ernest M. Gould, Jr., Harvard University

Michael Gough, Resources for the Future, Inc.

Peter Green, Golden West College

Katharine B. Gregg, West Virginia Wesleyan College

Paul K. Grogger, University of Colorado at Colorado Springs

James L. Guernsey, Indiana State University

Ralph Guzman, University of California, Santa Cruz

Raymond Hames, University of Nebraska Lincoln

Raymond E. Hampton, Central Michigan University

Ted L. Hanes, California State University, Fullerton

William S. Hardenbergh, Southern Illinois University at Carbondale

John P. Harley, Eastern Kentucky University

Neil A. Harrimam, University of Wisconsin-Oshkosh

Grant A. Harris, Washington State University

Harry S. Hass, San Jose City College

Arthur N. Haupt, Population Reference Bureau

Denis A. Hayes, Environmental consultant

John G. Hewston, Humboldt State University

David L. Hicks, Whitworth College

Eric Hirst, Oak Ridge National Laboratory

S. Holling, University of British Columbia

Donald Holtgrieve, California State University, Hayward

Michael H. Horn, University of California, Fullerton

Mark A. Hornberger, Bloomsberg University

Marilyn Houck, Pennsylvania State University
Richard D. Houk, Winthrop College
Robert J. Huggett, College of William and Mary
Donald Huisingh, North Carolina State University
Marlene K. Hutt, IBM
David R. Inglis, University of Massachusetts
William Irons, Northwestern University
Robert Janiskee, University of South Carolina
Hugo H. John, University of Connecticut
Brian A. Johnson, University of Pennsylvania
  Bloomsburg
David I. Johnson, Michigan State University
Agnes Kadar, Nassau Community College
Thomas L. Keefe, Eastern Kentucky University
Nathan Keyfitz, Harvard University
David Kidd, University of New Mexico
Edward J. Kormondy, University of Hawaii-Hilo/
  West Oahu College
Judith Kunofsky, Sierra Club
Edwin B. Kurtz, University of Texas–Permian Basin
Theodore Kury, State University College at Buffalo
John V. Krutilla, Resources for the Future, Inc.
Steve Ladochy, University of Winnepeg
Mark B. Lapping, Kansas State University
Tom Leege, Idaho Department of Fish and Game
William S. Lindsay, Monterey Peninsula College
E. S. Lindstrom, Pennsylvania State University
Valerie A. Liston, University of Minnesota
Dennis Livingston, Rensselaer Polytechnic Institute
James P. Lodge, Air pollution consultant
Ruth Logan, Santa Monica City College
Robert D. Loring, DePauw University
Thomas Lovering, University of California, Santa
  Barbara
Paul F. Love, Angelo State University
Amory B. Lovins, Rocky Mountain Institute
Hunter Lovins, Rocky Mountain Institute
Gene A. Lucas, Drake University
David Lynn
Timothy F. Lyon, Ball State University
Melvin G. Marcus, Arizona State University
Stuart A. Marks
Gordon E. Matzke, Oregon State University
Parker Mauldin, Rockefeller Foundation
Theodore R. McDowell, California State University,
  San Bernadino
Vincent E. McKelvey, U.S. Geological Survey
John G. Merriam, Bowling Green State University
A. Steven Messenger, Northern Illinois University
John Meyers, Middlesex Community College
Norman Myers, Environmental consultant
Raymond W. Miller, Utah State University
Rolf Monteen, California Polytechnic State
  University
Ralph Morris, Brock University, St. Catherines,
  Ont., Canada
William W. Murdoch, University of California,
  Santa Barbara
Brian C. Myres, Cypress College
A. Neale, Illinois State University
Duane Nellis, Kansas State University
Jan Newhouse, University of Hawaii, Manoa

John E. Oliver, Indiana State University
Eric Pallant, Allegheny College
Charles F. Park, Stanford University
Richard J. Pedersen, U.S. Department of
  Agriculture, Forest Service
Robert A. Pedigo, Callaway Gardens
Harry Perry, Library of Congress
David Pelliam, Bureau of Land Management, U.S.
  Department of Interior
Rodney Peterson, Colorado State University
William S. Pierce, Case Western Reserve University
David Pimentel, Cornell University
Peter Pizor, Northwest Community College
Robert B. Platt, Emory University
Mark D. Plunkett, Bellevue Community College
Grace L. Powell, University of Akron
James H. Price, Oklahoma College
Marian E. Reeve, Merritt College
Carl H. Reidel, University of Vermont
Roger Revelle, California State University, San Diego
L. Reynolds, University of Central Arkansas
Ronald R. Rhein, Kutztown University of
  Pennsylvania
Charles Rhyne, Jackson State University
Robert A. Richardson, University of Wisconsin
Benjamin F. Richason III, St. Cloud State University
Ronald Robberecht, University of Idaho
William Van B. Robertson, School of Medicine,
  Stanford University
C. Lee Rockett, Bowling Green State University
Terry D. Roelofs, Humboldt State University
Richard G. Rose, West Valley College
Stephen T. Ross, University of Southern Mississippi
Robert E. Roth, The Ohio State University
David Satterthwaite, I.E.E.D., London
Stephen W. Sawyer, University of Maryland
Arnold Schecter, State University of New York
  Syracuse
Frank Schiavo, San Jose State University
William H. Schlesinger, Duke University
Stephen H. Schneider, National Center for
  Atmospheric Research
Clarence A. Schoenfeld, University of Wisconsin,
  Madison
Henry A. Schroeder, Dartmouth Medical School
Lauren A. Schroeder, Youngstown State University
Norman B. Schwartz, University of Delaware
George Sessions, Sierra College
David J. Severn, Clement Associates
Paul Shepard, Pitzer College and Claremont
  Graduate School
Michael P. Shields, Southern Illinois University at
  Carbondale
Kenneth Shiovitz,
F. Siewert, Ball State University
Ellen K. Silbergold, Environmental Defense Fund
Joseph L. Simon, University of South Florida
William E. Sloey, University of Wisconsin-Oshkosh
Robert L. Smith, West Virginia University
Howard M. Smolkin, U.S. Environmental
  Protection Agency
Patricia M. Sparks, Glassboro State College

Brief Contents

Detailed Contents

Humans and Nature:
An Overview

USDA/Soil Conservation Service

It is only in the most recent, and brief, period of their tenure that human beings have developed in sufficient numbers, and acquired enough power, to become one of the most potentially dangerous organisms that the planet has ever hosted.

John McHale

The environmental crisis is an outward manifestation of a crisis of mind and spirit. There could be no greater misconception of its meaning than to believe it is concerned only with endangered wildlife, human-made ugliness, and pollution. These are part of it, but more importantly, the crisis is concerned with the kind of creatures we are and what we must become in order to survive.

Lynton K. Caldwell

CHAPTER 1

Population, Resources, Environmental Degradation, and Pollution

General Questions and Issues

1. How rapidly is the human population increasing?
2. What are the major types of resources, and how can they be depleted or degraded?
3. What are the major types of pollution?
4. What are the relationships among human population size, resource use, technology, environmental degradation, and pollution?
5. What are the two major schools of thought about how to solve present and future resource and environmental problems?

We must stop mortgaging the future to the present. We must stop destroying the air we breathe, the water we drink, the food we eat, and the forests that inspire awe in our hearts. . . . We need to prevent pollution at the source, not try to clean it up later. . . . It's time to remember that conservation is the cheapest and least polluting form of energy. . . . We need to come together and choose a new direction. We need to transform our society into one in which people live in true harmony—harmony among nations, harmony among the races of humankind, and harmony with nature. . . . We will either reduce, reuse, recycle, and restore—or we will perish.

Rev. Jesse Jackson

W e are at a critical turning point. We have spent billions to send a handful of people to the moon, only to learn the importance of protecting the diversity of life on the beautiful blue planet that is our home. While technological optimists promise a life of abundance for everyone, conservationists and environmentalists warn that the earth's life-support systems are being strained and degraded.

We face a complex mix of interrelated problems. One is population growth: World population has almost doubled—from 2.5 billion to 1950 to 5.2 billion in 1989. If present trends continue, by 2100 the world's population will double to 10.4 billion and may reach 14 billion. This will put severe stress on the earth's already strained life-support systems.

Another problem is the way we use resources. The resources that keep us alive and drive the world's economies come from the sun and from the earth's air, water, soil, plants, animals, and decomposers (fungi and bacteria). Energy cannot be recycled, but the earth recycles and reuses chemicals needed to sustain life.

The earth is remarkably resilient. It can dilute, break down, and recycle many of the chemicals we add to the air, water, and soil as long as we don't overload these natural processes. It can replenish topsoil, water, air, forests, grasslands, and wildlife as long as we don't use these resources faster than they are renewed.

Think of the earth's resources as our savings account—our natural capital. As long as we live off the interest on this capital, we and most other species can be sustained. But we are depleting this natural capital by recycling and reusing little of what we extract from the earth and change into products. Instead, we dump into the air, water, and soil most of the chemicals produced by resource extraction and use, hoping these chemicals won't build up to harmful levels. We also produce products that the earth's natural processes can't recycle. Each day we "throw out" mountains of garbage and other solid waste instead of thinking of the refuse as potential resources.

Think of the earth's life-support systems as a gigantic network of interconnected rubber bands that can be stretched a long way without breaking. Growing evidence indicates that we are stretching some of these rubber bands close to, and in some cases beyond, their breaking points. The numerous links between the air, water, land, and living organisms in this web are often regional and global. Disturbing any one of them can have unexpected results in other places now and in the future.

PART ONE

Humans and Nature:
An Overview

It is only in the most recent, and brief, period of their tenure that human beings have developed in sufficient numbers, and acquired enough power, to become one of the most potentially dangerous organisms that the planet has ever hosted.

John McHale

The environmental crisis is an outward manifestation of a crisis of mind and spirit. There could be no greater misconception of its meaning than to believe it is concerned only with endangered wildlife, human-made ugliness, and pollution. These are part of it, but more importantly, the crisis is concerned with the kind of creatures we are and what we must become in order to survive.

Lynton K. Caldwell

Population, Resources, Environmental Degradation, and Pollution

General Questions and Issues

1. How rapidly is the human population increasing?

2. What are the major types of resources, and how can they be depleted or degraded?

3. What are the major types of pollution?

4. What are the relationships among human population size, resource use, technology, environmental degradation, and pollution?

5. What are the two major schools of thought about how to solve present and future resource and environmental problems?

We must stop mortgaging the future to the present. We must stop destroying the air we breathe, the water we drink, the food we eat, and the forests that inspire awe in our hearts. . . . We need to prevent pollution at the source, not try to clean it up later. . . . It's time to remember that conservation is the cheapest and least polluting form of energy. . . . We need to come together and choose a new direction. We need to transform our society into one in which people live in true harmony—harmony among nations, harmony among the races of humankind, and harmony with nature. . . . We will either reduce, reuse, recycle, and restore—or we will perish.

Rev. Jesse Jackson

We are at a critical turning point. We have spent billions to send a handful of people to the moon, only to learn the importance of protecting the diversity of life on the beautiful blue planet that is our home. While technological optimists promise a life of abundance for everyone, conservationists and environmentalists warn that the earth's life-support systems are being strained and degraded.

We face a complex mix of interrelated problems. One is population growth: World population has almost doubled—from 2.5 billion to 1950 to 5.2 billion in 1989. If present trends continue, by 2100 the world's population will double to 10.4 billion and may reach 14 billion. This will put severe stress on the earth's already strained life-support systems.

Another problem is the way we use resources. The resources that keep us alive and drive the world's economies come from the sun and from the earth's air, water, soil, plants, animals, and decomposers (fungi and bacteria). Energy cannot be recycled, but the earth recycles and reuses chemicals needed to sustain life.

The earth is remarkably resilient. It can dilute, break down, and recycle many of the chemicals we add to the air, water, and soil as long as we don't overload these natural processes. It can replenish topsoil, water, air, forests, grasslands, and wildlife as long as we don't use these resources faster than they are renewed.

Think of the earth's resources as our savings account—our natural capital. As long as we live off the interest on this capital, we and most other species can be sustained. But we are depleting this natural capital by recycling and reusing little of what we extract from the earth and change into products. Instead, we dump into the air, water, and soil most of the chemicals produced by resource extraction and use, hoping these chemicals won't build up to harmful levels. We also produce products that the earth's natural processes can't recycle. Each day we "throw out" mountains of garbage and other solid waste instead of thinking of the refuse as potential resources.

Think of the earth's life-support systems as a gigantic network of interconnected rubber bands that can be stretched a long way without breaking. Growing evidence indicates that we are stretching some of these rubber bands close to, and in some cases beyond, their breaking points. The numerous links between the air, water, land, and living organisms in this web are often regional and global. Disturbing any one of them can have unexpected results in other places now and in the future.

Each year more of the world's forests, grasslands, and wetlands disappear, and deserts grow in size. Vital topsoil is washed or blown away from farmland (see photo on p. 1) and chokes rivers with sediment. Water is withdrawn from underground deposits faster than it is replenished. The oil that runs cars and heats homes and that is used to produce food and most of the products we use will probably be depleted in your lifetime.

Toxic wastes produced by factories and homes are accumulating and poisoning soil and water resources. Agricultural pesticides contaminate the groundwater that many of us drink and some of the food we eat.

As levels of carbon dioxide and several other gases we are adding to the atmosphere rise, the earth's lower atmosphere is expected to become warmer. Such a change in the earth's climate will disrupt our ability to grow food by making some areas much drier and other areas much wetter. Higher temperatures will also expand the oceans which will flood low-lying coastal cities and cropland. Scientists warn that these changes can't be stopped, but they can be slowed if we take emergency action over the next two decades.

A thin layer of ozone gas in the upper atmosphere protects you and most other forms of life by filtering the sun's harmful ultraviolet radiation. Chlorofluorocarbons (CFCs) are chemicals we use as coolants in refrigerators and air conditioners and as propellants in spray cans, as well as to make styrofoam insulation and fast-food containers. These and other uses emit CFCs into the lower atmosphere. They then drift into the upper atmosphere and react with and deplete ozone gas faster than it is produced; they also contribute to atmospheric warming.

Burning coal, oil, and gasoline increases the amount of ozone, acids, and other pollutants in the earth's lower atmosphere. These chemicals are harming and killing trees, fish, and people. As forests and grassland disappear, as soils erode, as deserts and cities expand, and as soils and lakes acidify, an increasing number of the earth's plant and animal species are disappearing forever.

Why are we fouling our own life-support systems? The answer is a combination of survival, greed, apathy, and ignorance about our ultimate dependence on the sun and earth for everything we have or will have. To survive, poor people cut trees and deplete soil faster than those resources can be renewed. More affluent people deplete and degrade the earth's resources to support short-term economic growth and throwaway lifestyles.

The bad news is that we are doing this. The good news is that we know how to sustain the earth for human beings and other species by protecting the earth's resources and by using them in sustainable ways. That is what this book is about.

1-1 HUMAN POPULATION GROWTH

The J-Shaped Curve of Human Population Growth

Plotting the estimated number of people on earth over time gives us a curve with the shape of the letter J (Figure 1-1). This increase in the size of the human population is an example of **exponential growth.** Such growth occurs when some factor—such as population size—grows by a constant percentage of the whole during each unit of time. One of the greatest shortcomings of the human race is our failure to understand the implications of exponential growth (see Spotlight on p. 4).

For the first several million years of human history, people lived in small groups and survived mostly by hunting wild game and gathering wild plants. During this period the earth's population grew exponentially at a slow average rate of only 0.002% a year. This slow, early phase of exponential growth is represented by the long horizontal part of the curve plotted in Figure 1-1. Since then, the average annual exponential growth rate of the human population has increased. It reached an all-time high of 2.06% in 1970, before dropping somewhat to 1.75% between 1980 and 1988 and then rising to 1.8% in 1989. Because of this large increase, the curve of population growth has rounded the bend of the J and is heading almost straight up from the horizontal axis (Figure 1-1).

With this increase in the rate of exponential growth, it has taken less time to add each billion people. It took 2 million years to add the first billion people; 130 years to add the second billion; 30 years to add the third billion; 15 years to add the fourth billion; and only 12 years to add the fifth billion. With present growth rates, the sixth billion will be added during the 10-year period between 1987 and 1997, and the seventh billion 10 years later in 2007. This rapid increase in population size has had severe effects on other species and on the air, water, and soil upon which we and other forms of life depend.

In 1989 the earth's population increased by 90 million—more than now live in Canada and West Germany combined. This amounted to an average increase of 1.7 million people a week, 247,000 a day, or 10,270 an hour. At this rate, it takes

- less than 5 days to replace people equal in number to the Americans killed in all U.S. wars

- 10 months to add 75 million people—the number killed in the bubonic plague epidemic of the fourteenth century, the world's greatest disaster

- less than 2 years to add 165 million people—the number of people killed in all wars fought during the past 200 years

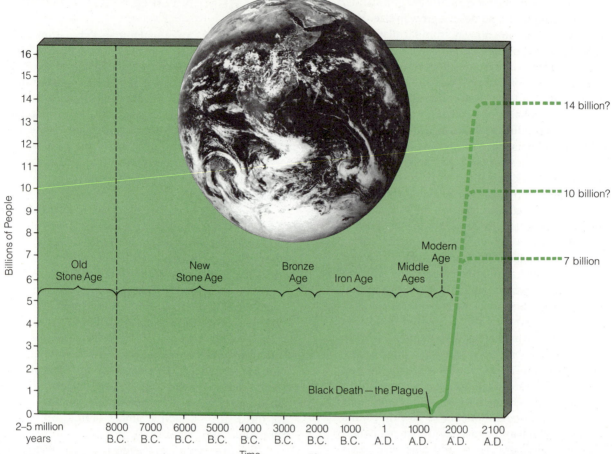

Figure 1-1 J-shaped curve of past exponential world population growth with projections to 2100. (Data from World Bank and United Nations)

SPOTLIGHT The Nature of Exponential Growth

An example of *arithmetic growth* is 1, 2, 3, 4, 5, and so on. *Exponential growth* means a quantity increases by doubling: 2, 4, 8, 16, 32, and so on. We can use a fable to help understand exponential growth:

Once there were two kings who enjoyed playing chess, with various prizes going to the winner. After one of their matches the winner asked for a new type of prize. He asked that the losing king place a grain of wheat on the first square of the chessboard, two on the second, four on the third, and so on. The number of wheat grains was to double each time until all 64 squares were filled.

The losing king didn't understand the nature of exponential growth and was delighted to get off so easy. He agreed to the proposal. It was the biggest mistake he ever made.

The winning king wanted to start with one grain of wheat and double it 63 times. This amounts to one less than 2^{64} grains of wheat, which still doesn't seem like much. But it is actually more than 500 times all the wheat harvested in the world this year. It is probably larger than all the wheat that has ever been harvested!

From this example we can understand some of the properties of exponential growth. It is deceptive because it starts off slowly. But a few doublings lead quickly to enormous numbers. Why? Because after the second doubling each additional doubling is more than the total of all preceding growth.

The time it takes in years for doubling to occur depends on the annual percentage growth rate. You can calculate doubling time by dividing the annual percentage

growth rate into 70 (70 ÷ percentage growth rate = doubling time in years). In 1989 the world's population grew by 1.8%. If this rate continues, the earth's population will double in 39 years (70 ÷ 1.8 = 39 years).

You can also use this rule of 70 to estimate how long it will take to double an amount of money put into a savings account or an investment that grows exponentially at some annual rate. For example, suppose you put $1,000 into a savings account with an annual interest rate of 10%. Your money would double every seven years (70 ÷ 10% = 7 years). At the end of 7 years you would have $2,000 in your account. At the end of 100 years you would have $22,026,465!

Figure 1-2 One-sixth of the people in the world don't have adequate housing. Lean-to sidewalk shelters such as these are homes for many families in Dacca, Bangladesh.

UNICEF/Bernard Wolff

These figures give you an idea of what it means to go around the bend of the J curve of exponential growth. This massive increase in population is happening when:

- At least half the adults on this planet cannot read or write.

- One out of five people is hungry or malnourished, and one out of six does not have adequate housing (Figure 1-2).

- One out of four lacks clean drinking water.

- One out of three does not have adequate sewage disposal, health care, and fuel to keep warm and cook food.

Population Growth in the More Developed and Less Developed Countries

The world's 175 countries can be divided into two groups based on the average annual per capita gross national product (GNP)—the average market value of all goods and services produced per year per person in each country (Figures 1-3 and 1-5).

The world's 33 **more developed countries (MDCs)** are highly industrialized and have high average GNPs per person. Most are in the temperate (or middle) latitudes and have generally favorable climates and fertile soils. MDCs include Japan, the Soviet Union, Australia, New Zealand, and all countries in Europe and North America. These MDCs, with 1.2 billion people (23% of the world's population), use about 80% of the world's mineral and energy resources.

The 142 **less developed countries (LDCs)** have low to moderate industrialization and low to moderate average GNPs per person. Most are located in the tropical (or low) latitudes in Africa, Asia, and Latin America. Many of these countries have less favorable climates and less fertile soils than most MDCs. The LDCs contain 4.0 billion people or 77% of the world's population, but LDCs use only about 20% of the world's mineral and energy resources. Nine of every ten babies are born in LDCs, but 98% of all infant and childhood deaths also occur in these countries (see Spotlight on p. 8).

Two examples of LDCs are China and India. China, the world's most populous country, has a population of 1.1 billion and a doubling time of 49 years. India, the world's second most populous country, has a population of 835 million and a doubling time of 32 years.

Population experts forecast that unless we have a global nuclear war or widespread famine and disease, by 2100 the earth's population will be 10.4 billion—

Figure 1-3 Classification of countries based on their degree of industrial development and average GNP per person. (Data from Population Reference Bureau. Map based on a modified Goode's projection, copyright by the University of Chicago, Department of Geography, and used by their permission)

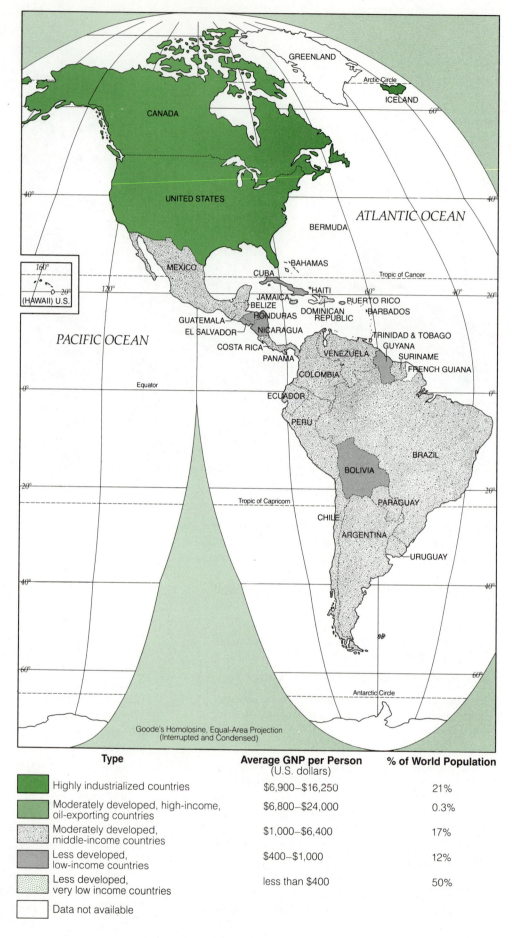

Type		Average GNP per Person (U.S. dollars)	% of World Population
■	Highly industrialized countries	$6,900–$16,250	21%
■	Moderately developed, high-income, oil-exporting countries	$6,800–$24,000	0.3%
▦	Moderately developed, middle-income countries	$1,000–$6,400	17%
▩	Less developed, low-income countries	$400–$1,000	12%
▨	Less developed, very low income countries	less than $400	50%
□	Data not available		

Figure 1-2 One-sixth of the people in the world don't have adequate housing. Lean-to sidewalk shelters such as these are homes for many families in Dacca, Bangladesh.

UNICEF/Bernard Wolff

These figures give you an idea of what it means to go around the bend of the J curve of exponential growth. This massive increase in population is happening when:

- At least half the adults on this planet cannot read or write.

- One out of five people is hungry or malnourished, and one out of six does not have adequate housing (Figure 1-2).

- One out of four lacks clean drinking water.

- One out of three does not have adequate sewage disposal, health care, and fuel to keep warm and cook food.

Population Growth in the More Developed and Less Developed Countries

The world's 175 countries can be divided into two groups based on the average annual per capita gross national product (GNP)—the average market value of all goods and services produced per year per person in each country (Figures 1-3 and 1-5).

The world's 33 **more developed countries (MDCs)** are highly industrialized and have high average GNPs per person. Most are in the temperate (or middle) latitudes and have generally favorable climates and fer-

tile soils. MDCs include Japan, the Soviet Union, Australia, New Zealand, and all countries in Europe and North America. These MDCs, with 1.2 billion people (23% of the world's population), use about 80% of the world's mineral and energy resources.

The 142 **less developed countries (LDCs)** have low to moderate industrialization and low to moderate average GNPs per person. Most are located in the tropical (or low) latitudes in Africa, Asia, and Latin America. Many of these countries have less favorable climates and less fertile soils than most MDCs. The LDCs contain 4.0 billion people or 77% of the world's population, but LDCs use only about 20% of the world's mineral and energy resources. Nine of every ten babies are born in LDCs, but 98% of all infant and childhood deaths also occur in these countries (see Spotlight on p. 8).

Two examples of LDCs are China and India. China, the world's most populous country, has a population of 1.1 billion and a doubling time of 49 years. India, the world's second most populous country, has a population of 835 million and a doubling time of 32 years.

Population experts forecast that unless we have a global nuclear war or widespread famine and disease, by 2100 the earth's population will be 10.4 billion—

Figure 1-3 Classification of countries based on their degree of industrial development and average GNP per person. (Data from Population Reference Bureau. Map based on a modified Goode's projection, copyright by the University of Chicago, Department of Geography, and used by their permission)

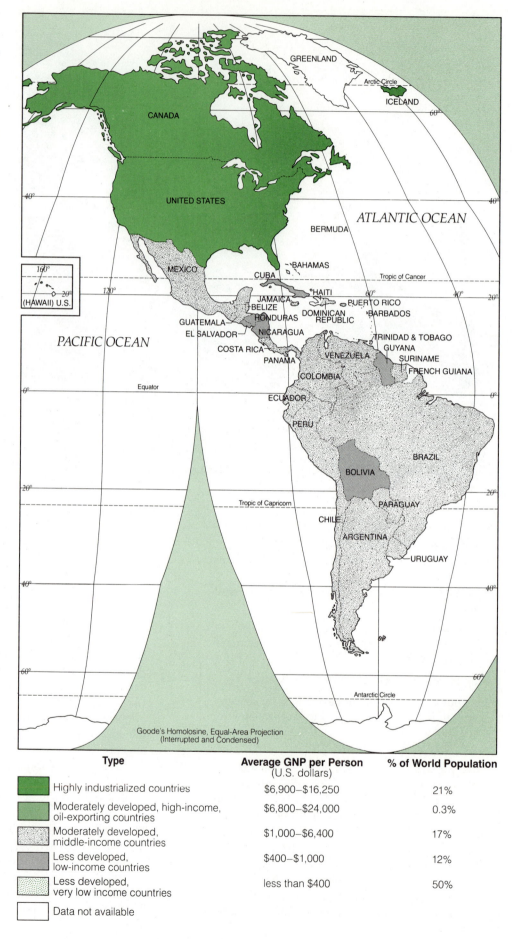

Type	Average GNP per Person (U.S. dollars)	% of World Population
Highly industrialized countries	$6,900–$16,250	21%
Moderately developed, high-income, oil-exporting countries	$6,800–$24,000	0.3%
Moderately developed, middle-income countries	$1,000–$6,400	17%
Less developed, low-income countries	$400–$1,000	12%
Less developed, very low income countries	less than $400	50%
Data not available		

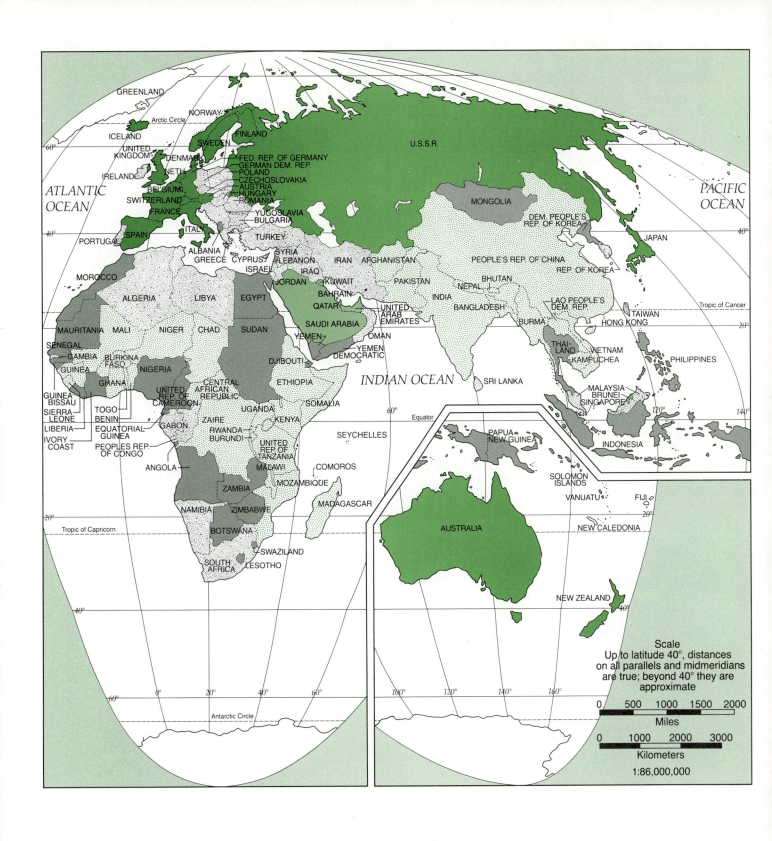

We are feeding more people than ever before. Yet more people are hungry and poor today than at any time during human history. One of every five people on earth is desperately poor. These 1 billion people live mostly in 79 low-income and very low income countries (Figure 1-3).

They are too poor to buy or grow enough food and to buy the fuel they need for heating and cooking. At least 20 million (and probably 40 million) of these people die unnecessarily each year from preventable malnutrition (lack of enough protein and other nutrients needed for good health) and diseases. Half of those who die are children under age 5 (Figure 1-4). Most of these children die from diarrhea and measles, deadly diseases for people weakened by malnutrition. During the last 10 years average per capita spending on health in the world's 37 poorest countries decreased by 50% mostly because of economic decline and rising debt.

During your lunch hour, at least 2,300 (probably 4,600) people died prematurely from starvation, malnutrition, and/or poverty-related diseases. By the time you eat lunch tomorrow, at least 55,000 (probably 110,000) more will have died. This death toll is equivalent to 137 to 275 jumbo jet planes, each carrying 400 passengers, crashing every day with no survivors.

Yet this tragic news is rarely covered by the media. Why? Because it happens every day. Because it happens most in rural areas and urban slums in LDCs away from the glare of TV cameras and reporters. And because most people don't want to hear about it.

Life for the world's poor is a harsh, daily struggle for survival. In typical rural villages or urban slums, groups of malnourished children sit around wood or dung (dried manure) fires eating breakfasts of bread and coffee. The air is filled with the stench of refuse and open sewers.

Figure 1-4 This Ethiopian child is one of the estimated 1 billion people on earth who suffer malnutrition caused by a diet without enough protein and other nutrients needed for good health.

Children and women carry heavy jars or cans of water, often for long distances, from muddy, microbe-infested rivers, canals, or village water faucets. Some people sleep on the street in the open, under makeshift canopies (Figure 1-2). Others sleep on dirt floors in crowded single-room shacks, often made from straw, cardboard, rusting metal, or drainage pipes.

Parents—some with seven to nine children—are lucky to have an annual income of $300—an average of 82 cents a day. Some people in affluent countries consider poor people ignorant for having so many children. To most poor parents, however, having many children, especially boys, makes good sense: They know that three or four of their children will probably die of hunger or child-

hood diseases, such as diarrhea or measles, that rarely kill in affluent countries. They must have many children so that two or three survive to adulthood.

Poor parents need children to help grow food or to beg in the streets. Surviving children are also a form of social security to help their parents survive in old age (typically their forties). For people living near the edge of survival, having too many children may cause problems. But having too few children can contribute to premature death.

The bad news is that so many of the world's poor are dying every day. The good news is that most of these premature deaths could be prevented at little cost—if enough of us really cared.

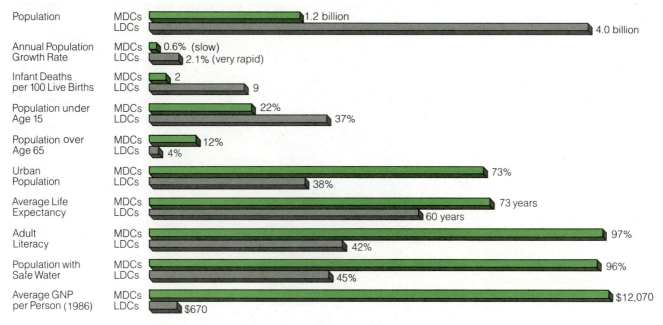

Figure 1-5 Some characteristics of more developed countries (MDCs and less developed countries (LDCs) in 1989. (Data from United Nations and Population Reference Bureau)

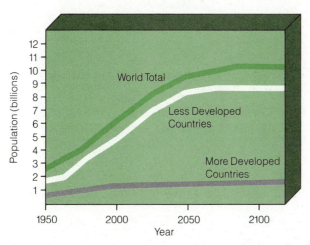

Figure 1-6 Past and projected population size for MDCs, LDCs, and the world, 1950–2120. (Data from United Nations)

twice that in 1989. Most of this increase will take place in the LDCs (Figure 1-6).

During the past 90 years the global economic output has increased 20-fold. But this increase in output and wealth has not been shared very equally. Since 1960 the gap between rich and poor countries has been widening (Figure 1-7). Today, perhaps one in five people on earth enjoys a high level of affluence. Three others get by, and the fifth is desperately poor and must constantly struggle to survive (see Spotlight on p. 8). Leaders in LDCs are concerned that depletion and degradation of resources by their own people and for export to MDCs may not leave enough resources for many LDCs to become MDCs.

Dividing the world into MDCs and LDCs can be misleading. Some MDCs are richer and more industrialized than others, and some LDCs are poorer than others (Figure 1-3). And poverty is found in the richest countries.

1-2 RESOURCES AND ENVIRONMENTAL DEGRADATION

What Is a Resource? A **resource** is anything we get from the physical environment to meet our needs and wants. Some resources are directly available for use. Examples are fresh air, fresh water in rivers and lakes, and naturally growing edible plants. But most resources, such as oil, iron, groundwater (water found in underground deposits), and modern crops, aren't directly available. They become resources only because of our ingenuity, economic systems, and cultural beliefs.

We have used science and technology to find, extract, process, and convert some of the earth's materials into resources and products that can be bought at reasonable prices. For example, groundwater below the earth's surface wasn't a resource until we developed the technology for drilling a well and installing pumps to bring it to the surface. Petroleum was a mysterious fluid until we learned how to find it, extract it, and refine it into gasoline, home heating oil, road tar, and other products at affordable prices. Cars, television sets, tractors, and other manufactured objects are available only because people have developed methods for converting an array of once-useless raw materials from the earth's crust into useful forms.

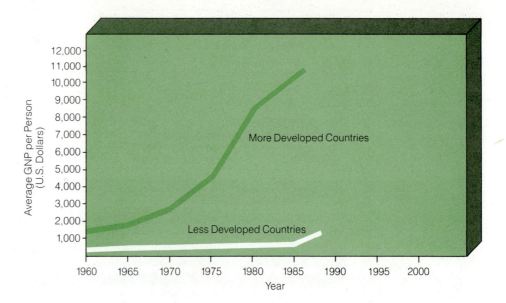

Figure 1-7 The gap in average GNP per person between MDCs and LDCs has been widening since 1960, raising fears that many LDCs might become never-developed countries. Adjusting for inflation, the average GNP per person in LDCs has decreased since 1960. (Data from United Nations)

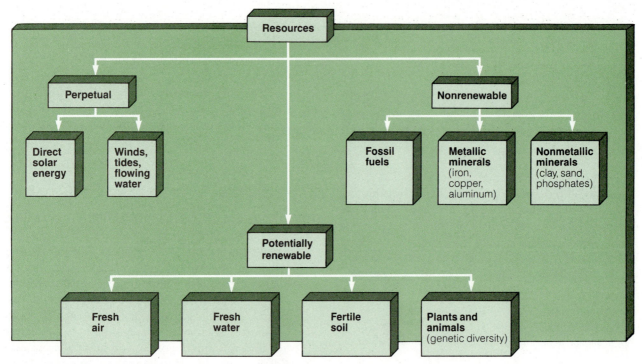

Figure 1-8 Major types of resources. This scheme, however, isn't fixed; potentially renewable resources can be converted to nonrenewable resources if used for a prolonged time faster than they are renewed by natural processes.

Cultural beliefs also determine what is classified as a resource. For example, fried grasshoppers are a delicacy and a useful source of protein for some people in Africa. To most people in affluent countries, however, grasshoppers are a revolting source of food.

People differ in the resources they need and want. The resource needs of the poor are minimal but represent absolute needs, not merely wants. The affluent use much larger quantities of resources to satisfy a range of wants far beyond basic survival needs.

Take a few minutes to make a list of the resources you truly need. Then make another list of the resources that you use each day only because you want them. Then make a third list of resources you want and hope to use in the future.

Types of Resources Resources can be classified as perpetual, nonrenewable, and renewable (Figure 1-8). A **perpetual resource,** such as solar energy, is virtually inexhaustible on a human time scale. **Nonrenewable,**

Everything runs on energy. For most people in MDCs and an increasing number in LDCs, oil is the key source of energy. It is used to heat homes, grow food, run vehicles, and produce most of the products we use. It is also used to find, extract, and process more oil, coal, natural gas, and other sources of energy. When the price of oil rises, so do the prices of other forms of energy and most things we use.

So far, oil has been cheap in spite of its importance and low estimated remaining supplies. Its low price has encouraged MDCs and LDCs undergoing economic growth to become heavily depen-dent—indeed, addicted—to this important resource.

Since 1950, cheap oil has fueled remarkable economic growth in many countries. Between 1950 and 1979 a fivefold increase in oil use by farmers helped double world food production. During the same period, world auto production increased fourfold and gasoline consumption fivefold.

Low prices have also encour-aged waste of oil and discouraged the search for other sources of energy. Most resource analysts expect the price of oil to rise sharply some time between 1995 and 2010, when the world's oil demand exceeds the rate at which remaining supplies can be extracted.

Many analysts believe that over the next 50 years the world must gradually withdraw from its pres-ent oil addiction and find replace-ments—or face economic turmoil. They also believe that conventional and nuclear wars will become more likely as countries fight for control over the world's dwindling oil.

So far, much too little is being done to stretch the world's remain-ing supply of oil and to find and phase in substitutes. In what ways are you addicted to oil? What do you think should be done?

---

or **exhaustible, resources** exist in a fixed amount (stock) in various places in the earth's crust. Examples are copper, aluminum, coal, and oil. They can be exhausted either because they are not replaced by natural processes (copper and aluminum) or because they are replaced more slowly than they are used (oil and coal). The world's supply of oil took millions of years to form. However, affordable supplies of oil will probably be gone by 2059, two hundred years after the first oil well was drilled in Titusville, Pennsylvania.

When nonrenewable resources are used, they are converted to a less useful form (rusted abandoned automobiles) or a useless form (heat and exhaust gases from burning a fossil fuel). Some supplies of nonre-newable resources will always be left in the earth's crust. Instead of being physically exhausted, they become economically depleted when it's too expen-sive to extract and process what is left.

Typically, a nonrenewable resource is considered **economically depleted** when 80% of its total esti-mated supply has been removed and used. At that point finding, extracting, and processing the rest usu-ally costs more than it's worth. Why? Because the remaining supply is too dilute (low-grade copper ore, for example) or is found only in remote and difficult-to-tap deposits (deep oil wells in the Antarctic).

Some nonrenewable resources can be recycled or reused to extend supplies—copper, aluminum, iron, and glass, for example. **Recycling** involves collecting and remelting or reprocessing a resource so that it can be made into a new product. For example, aluminum beverage cans can be collected, melted, and converted into new beverage cans or other aluminum products.

Reuse involves using a resource over and over in the same form. For example, refillable beverage bottles can be collected, washed, and refilled.

Other nonrenewable resources, such as fossil fuels (coal, oil, and natural gas), can't be recycled or reused. When burned, the high-quality, useful energy in these fuels is converted to low-quality waste heat and vir-tually useless exhaust gases (see Spotlight above).

Sometimes we can find a substitute or replacement for a scarce or expensive nonrenewable resource. Some resource economists believe we can use our ingenuity to find a substitute for any nonrenewable resource. But substitution isn't always possible. Some materials have properties that can't easily be matched. In other cases, replacements may be inferior, too costly, or too scarce. Economic disruption can occur while a substi-tute for a widely used renewable resource is being found and phased into manufacturing processes.

A **potentially renewable resource** is one that can be depleted in the short run if used or polluted too rapidly but ultimately is replaced through natural processes. Examples are trees in forests, grasses in grasslands, wild animals, fresh surface water in lakes and rivers, most deposits of groundwater, fresh air, and fertile soil.

Classifying something as a renewable resource, however, doesn't mean that it can't be depleted and that it will always be renewable. The highest rate at which a renewable resource can be used without decreasing its potential for renewal throughout the world or in a particular area is called its natural replacement rate or **sustainable yield.** If this yield is exceeded, the base supply of a renewable resource

Several types of environmental degradation can change potentially renewable resources into nonrenewable or permanently extinct resources:

- covering productive land with water, silt, concrete, asphalt, or buildings to such an extent that crop growth declines and places for wildlife to live (habitats) are lost
- cultivating land without proper soil management so that crop growth is reduced by soil erosion and depletion of a plant nutrients
- irrigating cropland without sufficient drainage so that excessive buildup of water (waterlogging) or salts (salinization) in the soil decreases crop growth
- removing trees from large areas (deforestation) without adequate replanting so that wildlife habitats are destroyed and long-term timber growth is decreased
- depletion of grass by livestock (overgrazing) so that soil is

eroded to the point where grasslands are converted into deserts (desertification)

- killing various forms (species) of wild plant and animal life through destruction of habitat, commercial hunting, pest control, and pollution to the point where these species no longer exist (extinction)

In many parts of the world sustainable yields of potentially renewable resources are being exceeded, sometimes to an alarming degree. Table 1-1 summarizes the status of key life-sustaining resources.

One situation that can cause environmental degradation is the use of **common-property resources.** These are resources to which people have virtually free and unmanaged access. Most are potentially renewable. Examples are clean air, fish in parts of the ocean not under the control of a coastal country, migratory birds, wildlife in areas with no effective

controls on hunting and harvesting, gases of the lower atmosphere, and the ozone content of the upper atmosphere.

Because anyone has a right to use or abuse these resources, they can easily be polluted or overharvested and converted from renewable to slowly renewable or nonrenewable resources. Abuse or depletion of common-property resources is called the **tragedy of the commons.** It occurs because each user reasons, "If I don't use this resource, someone else will. The little bit I use or the little bit of pollution I create is not enough to matter."

When the number of users is small, there is no problem. But eventually the cumulative effect of many people trying to maximize their use of a common-property resource depletes or degrades the usable supply. Then no one can make a profit or otherwise benefit from the resource.

begins to shrink—a process known as **environmental degradation** (see Spotlight above). If such unsustainable use continues, the resource can become nonrenewable on a human time scale or nonexistent. The key to maintaining the supply of a nonrenewable resource is to keep its rate of use at or below its sustainable yield.

Some resource experts define another type of resource: **aesthetic** or **amenity resources.** Solitude, scenic beauty, and peaceful surroundings are examples. As population levels rise and the need to "get away from it all" increases, aesthetic resources become more scarce and important.

Conserving Resources **Resource conservation** involves using, managing, and protecting resources so that they will be available on a sustainable basis for present and future generations. People who actively support this effort are called **conservationists.** Sometimes they are also known as **environmentalists,** although this term is more often used to describe those who are primarily concerned with preventing polluting of the air, water, and soil.

Most people are in favor of conserving resources. But they often disagree over which resources are essential and how much of each resource should be conserved for future generations.

Some conservationists, known as **preservationists,** stress the need to limit human uses of important resources such as wilderness, estuaries (where rivers and oceans meet), and wetlands (coastal and inland areas normally covered with water). Preservationists emphasize protection of such resources from development and human activities, except for nondestructive recreation, education, and research.

Others, known as **scientific conservationists,** stress using the findings of science and technology to manage resources in ways that don't damage them for future generations. They believe that publicly owned land resources such as national forests should be used for a mixture of human purposes including timbering, mining, recreation, grazing, hunting, construction, and water conservation. This guideline for resource management is known as the **principle of multiple use.** Scientific conservationists also believe that potentially renewable resources such as trees and wildlife should

Table 1-1 Health Report for Some of the Earth's Vital Resources

Productive Land	About 8.1 million square kilometers (3.1 million square miles) of once-productive land (cropland, forest, grassland) have become desert in the last 50 years. Each year almost 61,000 square kilometers (23,500 square miles) of new desert are formed.
Cropland Topsoil	Topsoil is eroding faster than it forms on about 35% of the world's cropland—a loss of about 24 billion metric tons (26 billion tons) of topsoil a year (see photo on p. 1). Crop productivity on one-third of the earth's irrigated cropland has been reduced by salt buildup in topsoil. Topsoil waterlogging has reduced productivity on at least one-tenth of the world's cropland.
Forest Cover	Almost half of the world's original expanse of tropical forests has been cleared. Each year 62,000 square kilometers (24,000 square miles) and perhaps 155,400 square kilometers (60,000 square miles) of tropical forest are cleared and 155,400 square kilometers (60,000 square miles) are degraded. Within 50 years there may be little of these forests left. One-third of the people on earth cannot get enough fuelwood to meet their basic needs, and many are forced to meet their needs by cutting trees faster than they are being replenished. In MDCs 312,000 square kilometers (120,400 square miles) of forest have been damaged by air pollution.
Grasslands	Millions of acres of grasslands have been overgrazed; some, especially in Africa and the Middle East, have been converted to desert. Almost two-thirds of U.S. rangeland is in fair to poor condition.
Coastal and Inland Wetlands	Between 25% and 50% of the world's wetlands have been drained, built upon, or seriously polluted. Worldwide, millions of acres of wetlands are lost each year. The United States has lost 54% of its wetlands.
Oceans	Most of the wastes we dump into the air, water, and land eventually end up in the oceans. Oil slicks, floating plastic debris, polluted estuaries and beaches, contaminated fish and shellfish are visible signs that we are using the oceans as the world's largest trash dump.
Lakes	Thousands of lakes in eastern North America and in Scandinavia have become so acidic that they contain no fish; thousands of other lakes are dying; thousands are depleted of much of their oxygen because of inputs of various chemicals produced by human activities.
Drinking Water	In LDCs 61% of the people living in rural areas and 26% of urban dwellers do not have access to safe drinking water. Each year 5 million die from preventable waterborne diseases. In parts of China, India, Africa, and North America water is withdrawn from underground deposits (aquifers) faster than it is replenished by precipitation. In the United States one-fourth of the groundwater withdrawn each year is not replenished. Pesticides contaminate some groundwater deposits in 38 states. In MDCs hundreds of thousands of industrial and municipal landfills and settling ponds, several million underground storage tanks for gasoline and other chemicals, and thousands of abandoned toxic waste dumps threaten groundwater supplies.
Climate	Emissions of carbon dioxide and other gases into the atmosphere from fossil fuel burning and other human activities may raise the average temperature of the earth's lower atmosphere several degrees between now and 2050. This would disrupt food production, flood low-lying coastal cities and croplands, and wipe out many forms of wildlife.
Atmosphere	Chlorofluorocarbons released into the lower atmosphere are drifting into the upper atmosphere and reacting with and gradually depleting ozone faster than it is being formed. The thinner ozone layer will let in more ultraviolet radiation from the sun. As results, skin cancer and eye cataracts will increase and our immune-system defenses against many infectious diseases will be weakened. Levels of eye-burning smog, damaging ozone gas, and acid rain in the lower atmosphere will increase, and yields of some important food crops will decrease.
Wildlife	Several thousand species of plants and animals become extinct each year because of human activities; if deforestation (especially of tropical forests), desertification, and destruction of wetlands and coral reefs continue at present rates, at least 500,000 and perhaps 1 million species will become extinct over the next 20 years.
Environmental Refugees	More than 10 million people worldwide have lost their homes and land because of environmental degradation. These people are now the world's single largest class of refugees.

Data from Worldwatch Institute and World Resources Institute

The relative scarcity of oil between 1973 and 1979 was caused by several factors. One was rapid economic growth during the 1960s, stimulated by low oil prices. Another factor was the growing dependence of the United States and many of the MDCs on imported oil.

A third factor was that between 1973 and 1979 the Organization of Petroleum Exporting Countries (OPEC)* was able to control the world's supply, distribution, and

*OPEC was formed in 1960 so that LDCs with much of the world's known and projected oil supplies could get a higher price for this resource and stretch remaining supplies by forcing the world to reduce oil use and waste. Today its 13 members are Algeria, Ecuador, Gabon, Indonesia, Iran, Iraq, Kuwait, Libya, Nigeria, Qatar, Saudi Arabia, United Arab Emirates, and Venezuela.

price of oil. About 63% of the world's proven oil reserves are in the OPEC countries, compared to only 3% in the United States. In 1973 OPEC produced 56% of the world's oil and supplied about 84% of all oil imported by other countries.

During 1973 the United States imported about 30% of its oil (Figure 1-9), almost half from OPEC countries. Other MDCs, such as Japan and most western European countries, have little or no domestic oil supplies. They were and still are more dependent on imported oil than the United States.

This dependence of most MDCs on OPEC countries for oil set the stage for the two phases of the relative oil scarcity crisis of the 1970s. First, in 1973 Arab members of OPEC reduced oil exports to West-

ern industrial countries and banned all shipments of their oil to the United States because of its support of Israel in its 18-day war with Egypt and Syria.

This embargo lasted until March 1974 and caused a fivefold increase in the average world price of crude oil (Figure 1-10). The increase contributed to double-digit inflation in the United States and many other countries, high interest rates, soaring international debt, and a global economic recession. Americans, accustomed to cheap and plentiful fuel, waited for hours to buy gasoline and turned down thermostats in homes and offices.

Despite the sharp price increase, U.S. dependence on imported oil increased from 30% to 48% between 1973 and 1977. OPEC imports increased from 48% to 67% during the same period (Figure 1-9). This increasing dependence was caused mostly by the government's failure to lift controls that kept oil prices artificially low and discouraged energy conservation.

The artificially low prices sent a false message to consumers and set the stage for the second phase of the oil distribution crisis. Available world oil supplies decreased when the 1979 revolution in Iran shut down most of that country's production. Gasoline waiting lines became even longer, and by 1981 the average world price of crude oil rose to about $35 a barrel.

A combination of energy conservation, substitution of other

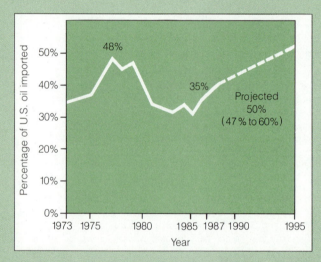

Figure 1-9 Percentage of U.S. oil imported between 1973 and 1988 with projections to 1995. (Data from U.S. Department of Energy and Spears and Associates, Tulsa, Oklahoma)

be managed so that they are not removed faster than they are replaced by natural processes. This guideline for use of renewable resources is known as the **principle of sustainable yield.**

Still others, known as **sustainable-earth conservationists,** go further. They believe that nature exists for all the earth's living species, not just for us. They view humans as no more important than any other species. This life-centered approach sees human beings as part of nature—not apart from nature and not conquerors of nature. To them conservation means

- working with—not against—nature
- interfering with nonhuman species only to meet important needs
- not wasting resources
- seeing that resource use doesn't seriously degrade the earth's life-support systems for people and other species now and in the future

Types of Resource Scarcity Resource scarcity can be absolute or relative. Both types lead to a rapid rise in

energy sources for oil, and increased oil production by non-OPEC countries led to a drop in world oil consumption between 1979 and 1988. The drop in demand and the inability of OPEC countries to reduce their oil production enough to sustain relative resource scarcity and high prices led to a glut of oil. In 1988 OPEC produced only about 27% of the world's oil.

Because supply exceeded demand, the price of oil dropped from $35 to around $17 per barrel between 1981 and 1988. This meant that the inflation-adjusted price of crude oil in 1988 was about the same as it was in 1974 (Figure 1-10).

The oil glut has had some good effects for MDCs such as the United States and for LDCs heavily dependent on imported oil. It has stimulated economic growth and created new jobs (except in the oil industry), and it has reduced the rate of inflation.

At the same time, the price drop has had a number of undesirable effects:

- a sharp decrease in the search for new oil in the United States and most other countries
- economic chaos in many oil-producing countries, especially those with large international debts (such as Mexico), and in major oil-producing states (such as Texas, Oklahoma, Louisiana, and Alaska)
- loss of many jobs in oil and related industries

- failure or near-failure of many U.S. banks with massive outstanding loans to oil companies and oil-producing LDCs such as Mexico
- decreased rate of improvement in energy efficiency and decreased development of energy alternatives to replace oil
- increased dependence on imported oil from a low of 31% in 1985 to 42% in 1988, draining $208 billion from the U.S. economy in 1988 (Figure 1-9)

Most energy analysts believe that the oil glut of the 1980s is only temporary. They expect that sometime between 1995 and 2010 the world will enter a period of increasing absolute scarcity of oil. They project that OPEC countries will increase their share of the world's oil market from 27% in 1988 to 60% sometime between 1995 and 2010. OPEC will domi-

nate world oil markets and raise prices even more than in the 1970s. The price of a barrel of oil is projected to rise to at least $32 and perhaps as high as $98.

The U.S. Department of Energy and most major oil companies project that by 1995 the United States could be dependent on imported oil for 60% of its oil consumption—much higher than in 1977 (Figure 1-9). This would drain the already debt-ridden United States of vast amounts of money, leading to severe inflation and widespread economic recession, perhaps even a major depression. It would also increase the chances of war as the world's MDCs compete for greater control over dwindling oil supplies to avoid economic collapse. Since 1981 the United States has done little to prepare for such a possibility. What do you think should be done?

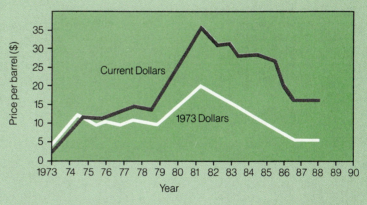

Figure 1-10 Average world crude oil prices between 1973 and 1988. (Data from Department of Energy and Department of Commerce)

the prices of raw materials, goods, and services, economic disruption, and an attempt to find and phase in substitute resources.

Absolute resource scarcity occurs when there aren't enough actual or affordable supplies of a resource left to meet present or future demand. A period of absolute resource scarcity begins when the demand for a resource exceeds the supply. It continues until the resource becomes economically depleted. For example, the world's affordable supplies of nonrenewable oil may be used up within your lifetime. The period

of absolute scarcity and increasing cost of oil may begin between 1995 and 2010.

Relative resource scarcity occurs when enough of a resource is still available to meet the demand but its distribution is imbalanced. For example, between 1973 and 1979 the world had enough oil to meet demand. But not enough oil was produced and distributed to meet the needs and wants of the United States, Japan, and many western European countries. During this period of relative resource scarcity, the price of oil rose from $3 to $35 a barrel (see Case Study on p. 14).

1-3 POLLUTION

What Is Pollution?   Any change in air, water, soil, or food that can affect the health, survival, or activities of human beings in an unwanted way is called **pollution.** When pollution occurs, a resource is no longer fit for its intended use. Usually pollution is defined in terms of harmful effects on human life. But some expand the term to include harmful effects on other forms of life as well. Today pollution is occurring on a vast and unprecedented scale worldwide.

Most pollutants are unwanted solid, liquid, or gaseous chemicals produced as by-products or wastes when a resource is extracted, processed, made into products, and used. Pollution can also take the form of unwanted energy emissions such as excessive heat, noise, or radiation.

A major problem is that people differ in what they consider an acceptable level of pollution, especially if they have to choose between pollution control and losing their jobs (see Case Study below). As philosopher Georg Hegel pointed out, the nature of tragedy is not the conflict between right and wrong but between right and right.

Sources and Types of Pollution   Pollutants can enter the environment naturally (for example, from volcanic eruptions) or through human activities (burning coal).

CASE STUDY Pollution and Jobs in Front Royal, Virginia

I was born and spent the first 14 years of my life in Front Royal, Virginia. It is a small town nestled in a valley at the beginning of the Skyline Drive, which runs through the mountains of Shenandoah National Park.

In 1940 the American Viscose Corporation built the world's largest rayon plant a few miles outside the town. The plant provided jobs for almost half the residents of Front Royal and nearby Warren County. I worked at the plant during two summer vacations while I was in college.

The plant caused problems, however. When the wind blew in a certain direction the air smelled like rotten eggs because of the hydrogen sulfide and carbon disulfide gases emitted by the plant. Hydrogen sulfide is more toxic than hydrogen cyanide, but when it reaches dangerous levels, your nose can no longer detect its awful smell. Hydrogen sulfide also reacts with metals such as silver and lead to form black metal sulfides. If you polished silver in Front Royal, it usually turned black overnight. It was foolish to paint your house white or a light color using the lead-based paints available in the 1940's. Within a few days the paint started turning black.

No one paid much attention to these problems in the 1940s. The plant supported the area's economy, and it was not until the 1970s that people in the United States became concerned enough to pass effective air pollution laws.

Today the plant, still the country's largest rayon producer, is run by Avtex Fiber. It is now the sole supplier of critical materials used in rocket engines. Although air pollution emissions from the plant have been sharply reduced, in December 1988 Virginia's attorney general charged Avtex with repeated air pollution violations. And in 1989, it was revealed that Avtex was at the top of the list in total emissions of toxic materials by American industries.

In the 1980s, federal and state environmental officials also charged the company with severely polluting the Shenandoah River and groundwater on both sides of the river. Avtex was forced to spend $750,000 to buy 23 properties with severely polluted wells.

In 1984 the Environmental Protection Agency (EPA) designated the plant's chemical disposal area a Superfund site containing high levels of hazardous waste. The EPA intends to charge Avtex's current and previous owners for the multimillion-dollar cleanup.

State officials have charged Avtex with repeatedly discharging untreated wastewater into the Shenandoah and violating the company's water discharge permit almost 2,000 times between 1980 and 1987. In November 1988 the state attorney general sued Avtex, seeking $19.7 million for environment damage caused by river and groundwater pollution.

In September 1988 the EPA held a public meeting to discuss ways of cleaning up the plant and contaminated water supplies. The meeting turned into a confrontation between local residents who complained about the pollution and workers who opposed cleanup. "We've got to eat first. We'll die second," said one worker. When one resident, barely holding back tears, urged that the plant be closed "for the sake of our children," a worker stood up and yelled, "What about our jobs and my children who have to eat."

In November 1988 Avtex announced that it would close down because of financial troubles, throwing 1,300 people out of work with only three days' notice. A week later plant officials reopened the plant after getting new orders from the Pentagon and the National Aeronautics and Space Administration.

Cleanup of the area will cost millions of dollars, taking at least a decade and possibly up to 30 years. Environmentalists are concerned that the company does not have enough money for the cleanup and fear it may shut down in the future to avoid facing up to the environmental problems it has created. If you worked at this plant, would you want the owners to spend money for cleanup even if this forced them to shut the plant down?

Most natural pollution is dispersed over a large area and is often diluted or broken down to harmless levels by natural processes.

In contrast, most serious pollution from human activities occurs in or near urban and industrial areas, where large amounts of pollutants are concentrated in small volumes of air, water, and soil. Some pollutants contaminate the areas where they are produced. Others are carried by winds or flowing water to other areas. Agriculture in MDCs is also a major source of pollution. Soil particles, fertilizers, pesticides, animal wastes, and other substances wash into streams. Some of these agricultural chemicals also contaminate underground water and blow into the air, contaminating faraway land and water.

Some of the pollutants we add to the environment come from single, identifiable sources, such as the smokestack of a power plant, the sewer pipe of a meat-packing plant, the chimney of a house, or the exhaust pipe of an automobile. These are called **point sources.** Other pollutants enter the air, water, or soil from spread-out and often hard-to-identify sources called **nonpoint sources.** Examples are the runoff of fertilizers and pesticides from farmlands and of numerous types of chemicals from urban areas and suburban lawns into rivers and streams.

Most potential pollutants added to the environment by natural processes and many of those we produce are broken down into harmless chemicals or acceptable levels by natural processes and recycled. In nature there are virtually no wastes. The waste products and dead bodies of one organism are resources for others.

But human beings often overload the earth's dilution and degradation processes. We have learned how to put together some of the earth's raw materials in new ways. Thousands of synthetic chemicals and products have replaced natural products (Figure 1-11). Worldwide, about 70,000 different synthetic chemicals are in everyday use. About 1,500 new ones are added each year. In the United States between 1950 and 1988 the production of synthetic chemicals rose tenfold.

We know little about the potential harmful effects of 80% of these chemicals on people, other animals, and plants. According to the Environmental Protection Agency, as many as 35,000 of the 70,000 chemicals in commercial use may be definitely or potentially harmful to human health. Many of these products, such as DDT (a pesticide), PCBs (oily chemicals used in electrical transformers), and most plastics, are broken down slowly in the environment. Others, such as toxic compounds of mercury and lead, don't break down at all.

Effects of Pollution   Pollution can have a number of unwanted effects:

- *nuisance and aesthetic insult:* unpleasant smells and tastes, reduced atmospheric visibility, and soiling of buildings and monuments

- *property damage:* corrosion of metals, weathering or dissolution of building and monument materials, and soiling of clothes, buildings, and monuments

- *damage to plant and nonhuman animal life:* decreased tree and crop production, harmful health effects on animals, and extinction

- *damage to human health:* spread of infectious diseases, respiratory system irritation and diseases, genetic and reproductive harm, and cancers

- *disruption of natural life-support systems at local, regional, and global levels:* climate change and decreased natural recycling of chemicals and energy inputs needed for good health and survival of people and other forms of life

Three factors determine how severe the effects of a pollutant will be. One is its *chemical nature*—how active and harmful it is to specific types of plants and animals. Another is its *concentration*—the amount per volume unit of air, water, or soil. A third factor is its *persistence*—how long it stays in the air, water, or soil.

During its lifetime a particular plant or animal is typically exposed to many different types and concentrations of pollutants with different degrees of persistence. This explains why it's rarely possible to show that a particular pollutant caused a particular effect such as the premature death of a specific plant or animal.

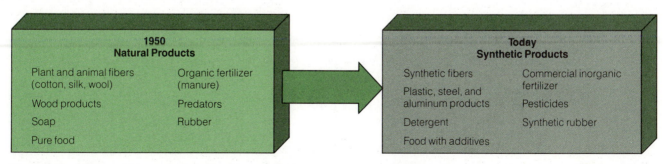

Figure 1-11 Some synthetic products that have been substituted for natural products in industrialized countries since 1945. Some of these synthetic products take a long time to break down in the environment.

Pollution Control We can control pollution in two ways: input control and output control. **Input pollution control** prevents potential pollutants from entering the environment or sharply reduces the amounts released. For example, sulfur impurities can be removed from coal before it's burned. This stops or sharply reduces emissions of the air pollutant sulfur dioxide, a chemical that damages plants and our respiratory systems.

Reducing unnecessary use and waste of matter and energy resources is another way to reduce harmful inputs of chemicals and excessive heat into the environment. We can also recycle or reuse chemical outputs from human activities instead of discarding them. We can impose taxes, penalties, or use other economic and political devices to make the resource inputs of a process so expensive that people will use these resources more efficiently. Efficient use decreases inputs of waste materials into the environment and makes recycling and reuse more profitable.

So far most attempts to control pollution have been output approaches, based on treating rather than preventing the problem. **Output pollution control** deals with wastes after they've entered the environment.

CASE STUDY Poland: The World's Most Polluted Country

In 1985 the Polish Academy of Sciences described Poland, a heavily industrialized country, as the most polluted country in the world. Air, water, and soil pollution are so severe that at least one-third of the country's people are likely to acquire environmentally induced cancers, respiratory illnesses, and a host of other diseases.

Less than half of Poland's 813 cities have sewage treatment plants, and none of its large cities have proper sewage treatment facilities. In the capital city of Warsaw only 5% of the sewage is treated. The rest is simply dumped into the Vistula River, which flows through the country and empties into the Baltic Sea.

Nearly half of the country's water is classified as unfit even for industrial use. About 90% of the water in the country's rivers is too polluted to drink, and most of the water in its biggest river, the Vistula, is too polluted for industrial use. Fish and other types of aquatic life are not found in 90% of Poland's rivers.

This widespread water pollution has caused a shortage of drinking water in most of Poland's large cities. People in large apartment buildings store water they get from reasonably safe sources in buckets and bathtubs. Private home owners often build water storage tanks. The Polish Academy of Sciences projects that by the year 2000, the country will have no safe drinking water.

Four areas of the country have been declared ecological disaster areas by the Polish parliament. They are Gdansk Bay, where the Vistula River empties into the Baltic Sea; the heavily industrialized district of Upper Silesia; the area in and around the city of Krakow; and the copper mining and smelting basin of Glascow. By Poland's own lax environmental standards, these regions are so contaminated that the 30% of the country's people living there should be evacuated.

A quarter of Poland's soil is believed to be too contaminated to grow food safe for consumption by livestock or people. In 1988 the government declared five villages in the industrial region of Silesia unfit to live in because of high levels of toxic metals in the soil and water. The government took over the villages and paid villagers to relocate. It is also considering a ban on growing vegetables in the Silesia area.

Gdansk's sandy beaches have been closed for years. Children cannot even play in the wet sand due to dangerous bacteria counts. Many of the bay's fish contain excessive levels of mercury and have open sores.

Air pollution control is grossly inadequate. Satellite photographs show that the biggest clouds of smoke in Europe hang over Poland, partly because large coal-burning power and industrial plants have shut down their air pollution control equipment to save power and money. Some of these pollutants are carried by prevailing winds to West Germany.

Air pollution in nearly every major city is reportedly 50 times above government-set limits. In the Krakow district infant mortality is more than three times the national average. Today 60% of the country's forests have been damaged, and at least 15% have virtually disappeared after decades of exposure to high levels of air pollutants.

Since the mid-1980s Polish citizens have organized to demand better environmental protection. In 1986 a group born out of the Solidarity trade union movement organized three public protests against a steel mill that was endangering the drinking water in the city of Wroclaw. The government agreed to shut down the plant by 1992.

But generally the government has been slow to act to prevent continuing pollution and environmental degradation and has saddled itself with a $40 billion debt to western MDCs. It spends only 1% of its gross national product on environmental protection—a much lower percentage than even most LDCs.

The costs of cleaning up the damage already done and minimizing future damage will be high. But the costs will be much higher if the government fails to act. Estimated economic losses due to pollution equal at least 10% of the country's annual GNP.

The problem is that output approaches often remove a pollutant from one part of the environment and cause pollution in another part.

For example, air pollution control equipment in smokestacks can remove most of the sulfur dioxide, solid particles, and other chemicals produced by burning coal and other fossil fuels. But this equipment leaves us with mountains of toxic ash or gooey liquids formed by removing the pollutants. What do we do with these chemicals? We could use our ingenuity to recycle or reuse most of them. But mostly we bury them and hope they won't contaminate underground water supplies used for drinking water.

Most of the improvements in environmental quality in the United States, Japan, and many western European countries since 1965 have been based on output control instead of pollution prevention. Unfortunately, the Soviet Union, many eastern European countries, and most LDCs near the bottom of the economic ladder are far behind in any kind of pollution control (see Case Study on p. 18).

Pollution is rising rapidly in many LDCs. For example, an estimated 70% of the rivers and lakes in India are polluted. The air in many cities in LDCs is more polluted than the air in most cities in MDCs. What may be the worst industrial accident in history occurred at a pesticide plant in Bhopal, India, in 1984. More than 3,300 people were killed and tens of thousands were injured.

Often both input and output controls are needed. But environmentalists urge that where possible we place primary emphasis on pollution prevention. As Benjamin Franklin reminded us long ago: "An ounce of prevention is worth a pound of cure."

1-4 RELATIONSHIPS AMONG POPULATION, RESOURCE USE, TECHNOLOGY, ENVIRONMENTAL DEGRADATION, AND POLLUTION

One Model of Environmental Degradation and Pollution Who pollutes and degrades resources? You, me, everybody. Some of us pollute and degrade resources more than others, but we all do it.

We do it directly when we consume resources and indirectly when these resources are extracted and transformed to products we need or want. According to one simple model, the total environmental degradation and pollution—that is, the environmental impact of population—in a given area depend on three factors: **(1)** the number of people, **(2)** the average number of units of resources each person uses, and **(3)** how these resources are used—the environmental degradation and pollution caused when each unit of resource is used (Figure 1-12).

Overpopulation occurs when the people in a country, a region, or the world use resources to such an extent that the resulting degradation or depletion of the resource base and pollution of the air, water, and soil are damaging their life-support systems. The data in Table 1-1 suggest that the planet is already overpopulated. Overpopulation is a result of growing numbers of people, growing affluence (resource consumption), or both.

Differences in the importance of the factors shown in Figure 1-12 lead to two types of overpopulation: people overpopulation and consumption overpopulation (Figure 1-13). **People overpopulation** exists where there are more people than the available supplies of food, water, and other important resources can support. It can also happen when the rate of population growth so exceeds the rate of economic growth that an increasing number of people are too poor to grow or buy enough food, fuel, and other important resources.

In this type of overpopulation, population size and the resulting degradation of potentially renewable soil, grasslands, forests, and wildlife are the key factors determining total environmental impact (Figure 1-13). In the world's poorest LDCs, people overpopulation causes premature death for at least 20 million and perhaps 40 million people each year and bare survival for hundreds of millions more. Many analysts fear the plight of these countries will get worse unless population growth is brought under control and improved management is used to restore degraded resources.

Industrialized countries have the second type of overpopulation: **consumption overpopulation.** It exists when a small number of people use resources at such a high rate that significant pollution, environmental degradation, and resource depletion occur. With this type of overpopulation, high rates of resource use per person and the resulting high levels of pollution per person are the key factors determining overall environmental impact (Figure 1-13).

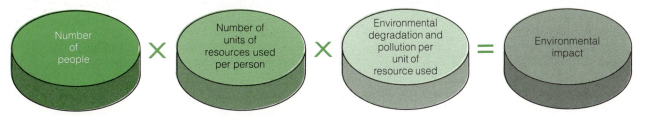

Figure 1-12 Simplified model of how three factors affect overall environmental degradation and pollution, or the environmental impact of population.

People Overpopulation

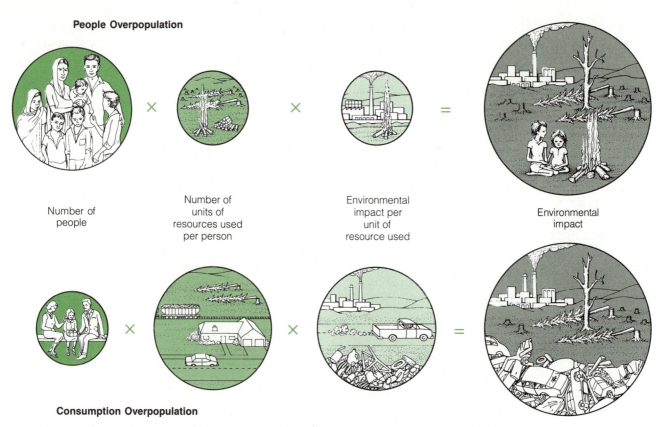

Number of people × Number of units of resources used per person × Environmental impact per unit of resource used = Environmental impact

Consumption Overpopulation

Figure 1-13   Two types of overpopulation based on the relative importance of the factors in the model shown in Figure 1-12. Circle size shows relative importance of each factor. People overpopulation is caused mostly by growing numbers of people. Consumption overpopulation is caused mostly by growing affluence (resource consumption).

According to the model in Figure 1-13, the United States has the world's highest level of consumption overpopulation. With only 4.8% of the world's population, it produces about 21% of all goods and services and uses about one-third of the world's processed nonrenewable energy and mineral resources. It also produces at least one-third of the world's pollution. The United States has 17 times the environmental impact of India with 16% of the world's population and 11 times the impact of China with 21% of the world's people. It has twice the impact of the Soviet Union and Japan, the U.S.'s closest competitors in depleting the earth's natural savings account. According to biologist Paul Ehrlich: "While overpopulation in poor nations tends to keep them poverty stricken, overpopulation in rich nations tends to undermine the life-support capacity of the entire planet."

Multiple-Factor Model   The three-factor model shown in Figure 1-12, though useful, is too simple. The major causes of the environmental, resource, and social problems we face are more complex. They include the following:

- *People overpopulation and consumption overpopulation* (Figure 1-13).

- *Population distribution*—the population implosion or urban crisis. The most severe air and water pol-

lution problems occur when large numbers of people and industrial activities are concentrated in an urban area. Winds blow many of these pollutants over smaller cities and rural areas.

- *Overconsumption and wasteful patterns of resource use, especially in industrialized countries*—throwaway mentality, planned obsolescence, producing unnecessary and harmful items, and very little recycling and reuse of essential resources.

- *Blind faith that technology will solve our problems*—failure to distinguish between appropriate forms of technology that reduce pollution and unnecessary resource waste and help sustain the earth's life-support systems and those that without proper control can degrade the earth's life-support systems.

- *Oversimplification of the earth's life-support systems*—excessive reduction of the diversity of plant and animal life in forests, oceans, grasslands, and other parts of the earth's life-support system, resulting in increased soil erosion, flooding, accelerated extinction of plant and animal species, and damage to crops from insects and diseases (Table 1-1).

- *Crisis in political and economic management*—overemphasis on all types of economic growth (growthmania) instead of encouraging desirable

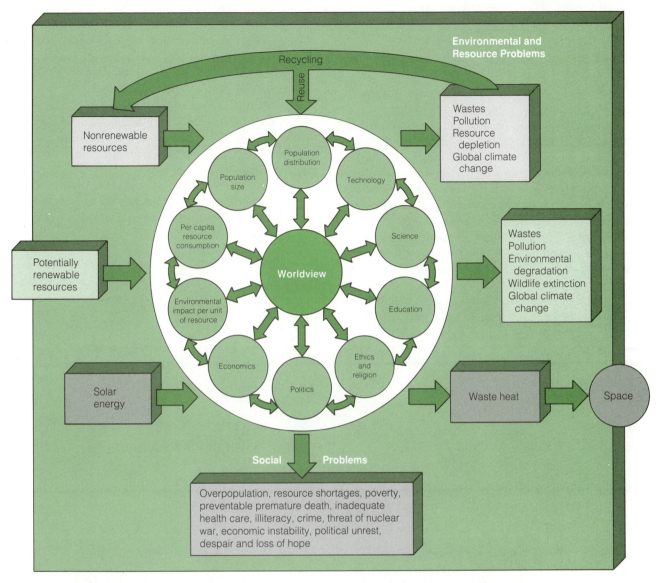

Figure 1-14 Environmental, resource, and social problems are caused by a complex, poorly understood mix of interacting factors, as illustrated by this simplified model.

forms of economic growth such as pollution control, recycling, and resource conservation and discouraging polluting and resource-wasting forms of economic growth; short-term outlook that leads governments to lurch from crisis to crisis instead of trying to anticipate problems and prevent them from reaching crisis levels; short-term band-aids instead of long-term cures.

■ *Failure to have market prices represent the overall environmental cost of an economic good or service to society and the earth's life-support systems*—not knowing the harmful effects of the products we buy because most of the costs of pollution, environmental degradation, and resource depletion caused by their production and use are not included in their market prices.

■ *Ignorance of how the earth works*—not understanding that everything we have or will have ultimately depends on the sun and the earth and that

protecting this base must be our most important goal; thinking that our cleverness and technology will allow us to escape the physical and biological processes that govern the sustainability of the earth's life-support systems.

■ *Me-first and human-centered (anthropocentric) worldview and behavior instead of we-first and earth-centered (biocentric) world view and behavior*—tragedy of the commons; emphasis on immediate satisfaction of many frivolous wants instead of basic needs; thinking that we are above and in charge of nature instead of just another part of nature; working against rather than with nature.

These and other factors interact in complex and largely unknown ways to produce the major environmental, resource, and social problems the world faces (Figure 1-14). One of our most important needs is to understand more about these interactions.

1-5 WHAT SHOULD BE DONE? NEO-MALTHUSIANS VERSUS CORNUCOPIANS

Two Opposing Views There are conflicting views about what the role of people in the world should be, how serious the world's present and projected environmental and resource problems really are, and what should be done about them. **Neo-Malthusians** (called "gloom-and-doom pessimists" by their opponents) believe that if present trends continue, the world will become more crowded and more polluted, and many resources will be depleted or degraded. They believe that this situation will lead to greater political and economic turmoil and increase the threat of nuclear and conventional wars as the rich get richer and the poor get poorer.

The term *neo-Malthusian* refers to an updated and expanded version of a hypothesis proposed in 1789 by Thomas Robert Malthus (1766–1834), an English clergyman and economist. He believed that human population growing exponentially will eventually outgrow food supplies and will be reduced in size by starvation, disease, and war.

Members of an opposing group are called **cornucopians** (or "unrealistic technological optimists" by their opponents). The term *cornucopian* comes from *cornucopia*, the horn of plenty, a symbol of abundance. Most cornucopians are economists. They believe that if present trends continue, economic growth and technological advances will produce a less crowded, less polluted, and more resource-rich world. It will also be a world in which most people will be healthier, will live longer, and will have greater material wealth.

Major differences between these two schools of thought are summarized in the Pro/Con box on pp. 22–23 and are reflected in the two Guest Essays ending this chapter.

PRO/CON Cornucopians Versus Neo-Malthusians

Cornucopians	Neo-Malthusians
Role of Humans on Earth	
Conquer nature to promote increasing economic growth.	Work with nature to promote kinds of economic growth that sustain the earth's life-support systems.
Seriousness of Environmental Problems	
Exaggerated; can be cured by increased economic growth and technological innovations.	Serious now and could become more serious without a shift to sustainable forms of economic growth.
Population Growth and Control	
Should not be controlled; people are our most vital source for solving the world's problems.	Should be controlled to prevent disruption of local, regional, and global life-support systems.
People should be free to have as many children as they want.	People should be free to have as many children as they want only if this freedom does not infringe on the rights of others to survive

Cornucopians	Neo-Malthusians
Resource Depletion and Degradation	
We will not run out of potentially renewable resources because we will learn to manage them better or switch to substitutes.	In many areas potentially renewable resources are already seriously degraded (Table 1-1). There are no substitutes for the earth's topsoil grasslands, forests, fisheries, and wildlife.
We will not run out of nonrenewable resources because we can find more, mine less concentrated deposits, or find substitutes.	We may not find substitutes for some nonrenewable resources, and substitutes may take too long to phase in without causing economic hardship.
Increases in economic growth and technological innovation can reduce resource depletion, pollution, and environmental degradation to acceptable levels.	Because of high rates of resource use and unnecessary waste, MDCs are causing unacceptable regional and global resource depletion, pollution, and environmental degradation.
Energy Resources	
Emphasize nuclear power and nonrenewable oil, coal, and natural gas.	Emphasize using energy conservation, perpetual solar, wind, and flowing water, and sustainable use of potentially renewable biomass (wood, crop wastes).

Throwaway and Sustainable-Earth Worldviews The debate between cornucopians and neo-Malthusians has been going on for decades. But it's more than an intellectual debate between people who often use the same data and trends to reach quite different conclusions. Members of these opposing groups have sharply different views of how the world works and what our role in the world should be.

Cornucopians usually have a **throwaway worldview**, also known as a **frontier worldview**. They see the earth as a place of unlimited resources, where any type of resource conservation that hampers short-term economic growth is unnecessary. If we deplete or pollute the resources in one area, they believe, we will find substitutes and control the pollution through technology. If resources become scarce or a substitute can't be found, we can get materials from the moon and asteroids in the "new frontier" of space. This worldview is based on two beliefs: We are more impor-

tant than any other species, and through science and technology we can conquer, control, and change nature to meet our present and future needs and wants.

In contrast, most neo-Malthusians have a **sustainable-earth worldview.*** They believe that the earth does not have infinite resources and that ever-increasing production and consumption will put severe stress on the natural processes that renew and maintain the air, water, and soil and support the earth's varie[] potentially renewable plant and animal life. The[] believe that present and future resource and env[] mental problems are caused by our ignorance of[] nature works, our attempts to dominate nature[]

---

*Others have used the terms *sustainable worldview* and *co[] worldview* to describe this idea. I add the word *earth* to[] clear that it's all the earth's life-support systems and li[] just human beings and their societies, that must be sust[]

Resource Conservation

Recycling, reuse, and reducing unnecessary resource waste are desirable but not if they decrease economic growth for the present generation.	Reducing unnecessary resource waste is vital for sustaining the earth's life-support systems and long-term economic productivity. It stretches supplies of nonrenewable resources, sustains supplies of potentially renewable resources, and reduces the environmental impact of resource extraction and use.
We can find a substitute for any scarce resource, so resource conservation is not necessary unless it promotes economic growth.	Substitutes may not be found or may be inferior or too costly.

Wildlife

The earth's wild plant and animal species are here to serve our needs.	Premature extinction of any wild species by human activities is wrong. These potentially renewable resources should be used only on a sustainable basis to meet vital needs, not frivolous wants.

Pollution Control

Pollution control should not be increased at the expense of short-term economic growth, which provides funds for pollution control.	Inadequate pollution control damages people and other forms of life and reduces long-term economic productivity.
Polluters should be given government subsidies and tax breaks to install pollution control equipment.	Polluters should pay for reducing pollution to acceptable levels. Goods and services should include the costs of pollution control so that consumers will know the effects of what they buy and use. Using the taxpayer-pays approach hides the harmful costs of goods and services.
Emphasize output control to reduce pollution once it has entered the environment.	Emphasize input control to prevent pollution from entering the environment.
Burn, dump, or bury waste materials.	Think of waste materials as resources that should be recycled or reused.

What do you think?

our failure to recognize that we're part of, not apart from and superior to nature.

Some neo-Malthusians have used the term *Spaceship Earth* to help people see the need to protect the earth's life-support systems. However, other neo-Malthusians have criticized this image. They believe that the spaceship analogy reinforces the idea that our role is to dominate and control nature. Thinking of the earth as a spaceship encourages us to view the earth merely as a machine that we can change and manage at will and to believe that we understand how nature works.

We must recognize that the earth's resource and environmental problems and their possible solutions

GUEST ESSAY The Global Environmental Challenge

Gus Speth

Since 1982 Gus Speth has served as president of the World Resources Institute, a center for policy research on global resource and environmental issues. He served as head of the President's Council on Environmental Quality (CEQ) between 1979 and 1981, after serving as a member of the council from 1977 to 1979. In 1980 he chaired the President's Task Force on Global Resources and Environment. Before his appointment to the CEQ, he was a senior attorney for the Natural Resources Defense Council, an environmental organization he helped found in 1970.

Writing recently in *Foreign Affairs*, George F. Kennan observed that "our world is at present faced with two unprecedented and supreme dangers:" any major war at all among great industrial powers and "the devastating effect of modern industrialization and overpopulation on the world's natural environment."

The deterioration of the global environment to which Kennan refers has a scale that encompasses the great life-supporting systems of the planet's biosphere. It includes the alteration of the earth's climate and biogeochemical cycles, the accumulation of wastes, the exhaustion of soils, loss of forests, and the decline of ecological communities (Table 1-1).

Since World War II, growth in human population and economic activity has been unprecedented. The world's population has doubled and now exceeds five billion, and another billion will be added by 1997. The gross world product has increased fourfold since

1950. With these increases in population and economic activity have come large increases in both pollution and pressure on natural resources (Figure 1-13).

Air pollution today poses problems for all countries. As use of fossil fuels has increased, so have emissions of sulfur and nitrogen oxides and other harmful gases. Acid rain, ozone, and other ills born of this pollution are now damaging public health and harming forests, fish, and crops over large areas of the globe.

Another gas emitted when fossil fuels burn is carbon dioxide, the chief culprit among the greenhouse gases, which trap heat in the atmosphere. If the buildup of greenhouse gases in the atmosphere is not halted, the global warming now apparently under way will bring about major climate changes. Regional impacts are difficult to predict accurately, but rainfall and monsoon patterns could shift, disrupting agriculture in many areas. Sea levels could rise, flooding coastal areas. Ocean currents could shift, further altering the climate and fisheries. Fewer plant and animal species could survive as favorable habitats are reduced. Heat waves, droughts, hurricanes, and other weather anomalies could harm susceptible people, crops, and forests.

Depletion of the stratosphere's ozone layer also threatens human health and natural systems. In 1987 an international treaty was negotiated to address this problem by reducing the use of chlorofluorocarbons (CFCs). This treaty, however, is already considered inadequate since scientists recently discovered more ozone depletion than expected.

These interrelated atmospheric issues constitute the most serious pollution threat in history. Simultaneous and gradual, their effects will be hard to reverse. Because pollutants react with other substances, with each other, and with the sun's energy, a well-planned response has to take all these factors into account. These air pollution issues are also linked to the use of fossil fuels. In the future, energy policy and environmental policy should be made together.

The United States can take some pride in actions to improve air quality. But the country still emits about 15% of the world's sulfur dioxide, about 25% of all

are interconnected in complex ways that we're only beginning to understand and will never understand completely. We should be guided by the motto of philosopher and mathematician Alfred North Whitehead, "Seek simplicity and distrust it," and by writer and social critic H. L. Mencken, who warned, "For every problem there is a solution—simple, neat, and wrong."

What's the use of a house if you don't have a decent planet to put it on?

Henry David Thoreau

---

nitrogen oxides, and 25% of the carbon dioxide, and it sill manufactures about 30% of all CFCs.

Improvements in U.S. energy efficiency have been considerable. Per capita energy use dropped by 12% between 1973 and 1985—a period when per capita gross domestic product grew 17%. Yet the United States is still consuming one-fourth of the world's energy annually and producing only half as much GNP per unit of energy as its world market competitors such as West Germany and Japan.

Our national concern for the atmosphere must be matched by a growing awareness of the steady deterioration of forests, soils, and water in much of the developing world. The UN Food and Agriculture Organization predicts that without corrective action rainfed crops in the Third World will become 30% less productive by the end of this century because the soil is depleted or eroded.

In developing countries, 10 trees are cut down for every one replanted—30 trees for one in Africa—and every minute about 22 hectares (54 acres) of tropical forests disappear, as do uncounted species that inhabit them. Fuelwood shortages affect an estimated 1.5 billion people in 63 countries. Most people in developing countries lack access to basic sanitary facilities, and 80% of all illness is due to unsafe water supplies. People in LDCs now rank high among those exposed to toxic chemicals—from lead in Mexico to DDT in China.

In 1988 the World Commission on Environment and Development described a new consensus, supported by nations north and south. The old notion that environmental loss was the price of economic progress was rejected. Far from bringing about broad-based development, overexploitation or mismanagement of natural resources has contributed to famines and floods, dam reservoirs that fill with silt within a decade, irrigation schemes that salt the soil, and conversion of grasslands and tropical forests into unproductive wastelands. The commission's report, *Our Common Future*, stated: "Many forms of development erode the natural resources upon which they must be based, and environmental degradation can undermine economic development. Poverty is a major cause and effect of global environmental problems."

Fighting requires diffusing the underlying pressures on the world's resource base. While many complex factors are involved, the LDCs must deal with:

- Rapid population growth. Of the one billion people to be added to the world's population between 1987 and 1997, nine out of ten will be born in developing countries.

- Shortsighted economic policies pursued by governments of both industrial and developing countries. These include direct and indirect subsidies that encourage the wasteful use of energy, water, and forests, and policies that favor city dwellers over the rural poor.

- Misguided development and aid programs. Many large-scale development projects have neglected environmental factors and local needs.

The United States is directly affected by these LDC concerns. Twenty percent of the carbon dioxide contributing to the greenhouse effect is estimated to come from tropical deforestation. A wide range of biological resources—species yet to be analyzed for their agricultural, industrial, or pharmaceutical value—is being lost.

The growth of developing economies expands global U.S. trade and job opportunities at home; already more than a third of U.S. trade is with LDCs. With economic recovery, the developing countries could absorb up to half of all U.S. exports by the year 2000. But sustained growth in much of the developing world requires better management of natural resources.

"Sustainable development" is the widely accepted answer—development that meets today's needs without compromising the ability of future generations to meet theirs. U.S. leadership in applying this approach requires both vigorous evaluation of environmental consequences of development assistance programs and also support for national development strategies that conserve and restore the land's productive capacity.

It means helping developing countries invest in reforestation, agroforestry (growing crops and trees together), water conservation, and energy efficiency.

(continued)

It also means reducing debt and other pressures that force LDCs to cash in their natural resources to earn foreign exchange. Family planning, primary health services, and better sanitation all deserve a high priority since they reduce child mortality and slow birth rates.

In the 1990s industrialized and developing countries will have to face these challenges together. Nations north and south, east and west must act in concert to sustain the earth and its people.

Twenty years ago, the United States responded vigorously to the serious environmental concerns then emerging. New national policies were declared, new agencies created, and major pollution cleanup and resource management initiatives launched.

Today, as we enter the 1990s, the Bush administration and members of Congress face a new agenda of

environmental concerns that are more serious and challenging than the problems of the 1970s.

These concerns are not the ones to which the United States addressed itself when environmental concerns emerged forcefully 20 years ago. They present us with new policy challenges that are more global in scope and international in implication.

The 1990s will be the crucial decade for action on these pressing concerns. If major national and international efforts are not pursued in this period, irreparable damage will be done to the world's environment, and the problems will prove increasingly intractable, expensive, and dominated by crises.

If the United States and other countries do respond, however, tropical deforestation can be arrested and disappearing species saved; poverty can be alleviated and human populations stabilized; soils

---

Julian L. Simon

Julian L. Simon is professor of economics and business administration at the University of Maryland. He has effectively presented and defended the cornucopian position in many articles and books, including The Ultimate Resource *and* The Resourceful Earth *(see Further Readings).*

This book and most others discussing environmental and resource problems begin with the proposition that there is an environmental and resource crisis. If this means that the situation of humanity is worse now than in the past, then the idea of a crisis—and all that follows from it—is dead wrong. In almost every respect important to humanity, the trends have been improving, not deteriorating.

Our world now supports 5.2 billion people. In the nineteenth century the earth could sustain only 1 billion. And 10,000 years ago, only 1 million people could keep themselves alive. People are living more healthily than ever before, too.

One would expect lovers of humanity—people who hate war and worry about famine in Africa—to jump with joy at this extraordinary triumph of the human mind and human organization over the raw forces of nature. Instead, they lament that there are so many human beings and wring their hands about the problems that more people inevitably bring.

The recent extraordinary decrease in the death rate—to my mind, the greatest miracle in history—accounts for the bumper crop of humanity. Recall that it took thousands of years to increase life expectancy at birth from the 20s to the 30s. Then in just the last 200 years, life expectancy in the advanced countries jumped from the mid-30s to the 70s. And starting well after World War II, life expectancy at birth in the poor countries, even the very poorest, has leaped upward (averaging 60 in 1989) because of progress in agriculture, sanitation, and medicine. Average life expectancy at birth in China, the world's most populous country, was 66 in 1989, an increase of 22 years since the 1950s. Is this not an astounding triumph?

In the short run, another baby reduces income per person by causing output to be divided among more people. And as the British economist Thomas Malthus argued in 1798, more workers laboring with existing capital results in less output per worker. However, if resources are not fixed, then the Malthusian doctrine of diminishing resources, resurrected by

can be conserved and more food provided; climate change can be contained; regional and global pollution can be reduced.

These and other things can be done with means within our grasp. But success hinges on concerted effort made with some urgency to change many current policies, to strengthen and multiply successful programs, and to launch bold initiatives where they are needed.

There are ample grounds in the experience of the last two decades for both optimistic and pessimistic assumptions about the future. The gaps between success and failure in addressing resource, environmental, and population problems have been enormous. The good news is that these divergent outcomes are primarily the result of differences in policies and programs pursued by governments, the private sector,

and others. In short, leadership and new initiatives can make a world of difference.

Guest Essay Discussion

1. How serious are the problems cited in this essay and throughout this chapter? How do these problems affect your life and lifestyle, now and in the future?

2. What is sustainable development? Is it being practiced in the United States? How could it be implemented in MDCs and LDCs?

3. Compare the viewpoint in this essay with the one presented by Julian Simon in the essay that follows. Which viewpoint more closely matches your own?

today's neo-Malthusians, does not apply. Given some time to adjust to shortages with known methods and new inventions, free people create additional resources.

It is amazing but true that a resource shortage due to population or income growth usually leaves us better off than if the shortage had never arisen. If firewood had not become scarce in seventeenth-century England, coal would not have been developed. If coal and whale oil shortages hadn't loomed, oil wells would not have been dug.

The prices of food, metals, and other raw materials have been declining by every measure since the beginning of the nineteenth century and as far back as we know. That is, raw materials have been getting less scarce instead of more scarce throughout history, defying the commonsense notion that if one begins with an inventory of a resource and uses some up, there will be less left. This is despite, and indirectly because of, increasing population.

All statistical studies show that population growth doesn't lead to slower economic growth, though this defies common sense. Nor is a high population density a drag on economic development. Statistical comparison across nations reveals that higher population density is associated with faster instead of slower growth. Drive around on Hong Kong's smooth-flowing highways for an hour or two. You will then realize that a large concentration of human beings in a small area does not make impossible comfortable existence and exciting economic expansion, if the system gives individuals the freedom to exercise their talents and pursue economic opportunities. The experience of

densely populated Singapore makes clear that Hong Kong is not unique either.

In 1983 a blue-ribbon panel of scientists summarized their wisdom in *The Resourceful Earth*. Among the findings, besides those I have noted above, were:

- Many people are still hungry, but the food supply has been improving since at least World War II, as measured by grain prices, production per consumer, and the famine death rate.

- Land availability won't increasingly constrain world agriculture in coming decades.

- In the U.S., the trend is toward higher-quality cropland, suffering less from erosion than in the past.

- The widely published report of increasingly rapid urbanization of U.S. farmland was based on faulty data.

- Trends in world forests are not worrying, though in some places deforestation is troubling.

- There is no statistical evidence for rapid loss of plant and animal wildlife species in the next two decades. An increased rate of extinction cannot be ruled out if tropical deforestation is severe, but no evidence about linkage has yet been demonstrated.

- Water does not pose a problem of physical scarcity or disappearance, although the world and U.S. situations do call for better institutional management through more rational systems of property rights.

- There is no persuasive reason to believe that the world oil price will rise in coming decades. The price may fall well below what it has been.

(continued)

- Compared to coal, nuclear power is no more expensive and is probably much cheaper under most circumstances. It is also much cheaper than oil.
- Nuclear power gives every evidence of costing fewer lives per unit of energy produced than does coal or oil.
- Solar energy sources (including wind and wave power) are too dilute to compete economically for much of humankind's energy needs, though for specialized uses and certain climates they can make a valuable contribution.
- Threats of air and water pollution have been vastly overblown. The air and water in the United States have been getting cleaner, rather than dirtier.

We don't say that all is well everywhere, and we don't predict that all will be rosy in the future. Children are hungry and sick; people live out lives of physical or intellectual poverty and lack of opportunity; war or some other pollution may do us in. *The Resourceful Earth* does show that for most relevant matters we've examined, total global and U.S. trends are improving instead of deteriorating.

Also, we do not say that a better future happens automatically or without effect. It will happen because men and women—sometimes as individuals, sometimes as enterprises working for profit, sometimes as voluntary nonprofit-making groups, and sometimes as governmental agencies—will address problems with muscle and mind, and will probably overcome, as has been usual through history.

We are confident that the nature of the physical world permits continued improvement in humankind's economic lot in the long run, indefinitely. Of course, there are always newly arising local problems, shortages, and pollutions, due to climate or to increased population and income. Sometimes temporary large-scale problems arise. But the world's physical conditions and the resilience in a well-functioning economic and social system enable us to overcome such problems, and the solutions usually leave us better off than if the problem had never arisen; that is the great lesson to be learned from human history.

Guest Essay Discussion

1. Do you agree with the author's contention that there is no environmental, population, or resource crisis? Explain. How is it compatible with the data presented in Table 1-1 and in Gus Speth's essay? After you've finished this course, come back and answer this question again to see if your views have changed.

2. In effect, the authors of this essay and the one that preceded it have taken the same general trends, projected them into the future, and come to quite different conclusions. How can this happen? What criteria can we use to decide who's more likely to be correct?

3. In 1967, Herman Kahn (now deceased), a leading cornucopian and Julian Simon's coeditor of *The Resourceful Earth*, wrote a book using existing trends to project the future from 1967 to 2000. In his book Kahn said that the problems of pollution, environmental degradation, and population growth were not problems. Yet shortly after that, in the 1970s, they became major societal concerns. Environmentalists and conservationists contend that Kahn's attitude shows the tendency of cornucopians to ignore problems or declare them not serious, despite clear evidence to the contrary. Do you agree with this analysis? Explain.

CHAPTER SUMMARY

Throughout human history the number of people on earth has been growing *exponentially* at some constant annual percentage. After averaging about 0.002% a year for several million years, the exponential population growth rate accelerated. It reached an all-time high of 2.06% in 1970 before dropping slightly to 1.8% in 1989. This means that 90 million people will have been added to the 5.2 billion people on earth in 1989.

About 1.2 billion of these people live in the 33 richer, *more developed countries (MDCs)* that are highly industrialized and have moderate population growth rates. The other 4.0 billion live in 142 poorer, *less developed countries (LDCs)* that have low to moderate industrialization and high population growth rates. In these countries at least 20 million and probably 40 million poor people—half of them

children—die prematurely each year from malnutrition and disease. Most of these deaths could be prevented at little cost.

Another billion people, most in LDCs, are expected to be added between 1987 and 1997. The world's population is not expected to level off until 2100 at around 10.4 billion.

Resources are anything we obtain from the environment to meet our needs. They can be classified as *nonrenewable* (exhaustible resources with a fixed supply, such as fossil fuels that can't be recycled or reused and metals that can be recycled and reused), *potentially renewable* (forests, grasslands, animals, fresh water, fresh air, and fertile soil, which are regenerated by natural processes if not used faster than they are replenished), and *perpetual* (virtually inexhaustible resources such as solar energy and wind).

Resource conservation involves using, managing, and protecting resources so that they will be available on a sustainable basis for present and future generations. Nonrenewable fossil fuel and mineral resources are *economically depleted* when what is left is too expensive to find, extract, process, and use. *Environmental degradation* occurs when a potentially renewable resource is harvested or used faster than it is replenished by natural processes. If such unsustainable use continues, such resources can become nonrenewable on a human time scale or nonexistent (wildlife extinction).

Pollution is a change in air, water, soil, or food that can affect the health, survival, or activities of people in an unwanted way. Most pollutants can be viewed as wasted resources or potential resources that are in the wrong place.

Most potential pollutants added to the environment by natural events (such as volcanic eruptions) and many of those we add are broken down into harmless chemicals or acceptable levels by natural processes and recycled. But we often overload the earth's dilution and degradation processes. We also produce thousands of chemicals that are only slowly degraded or not degraded at all by these processes.

We can control pollution in two ways. *Input pollution control* prevents potential pollutants from entering the environment or sharply reduces the amounts released. *Output pollution control* attempts to reduce potential pollutants to acceptable levels after they have entered the environment.

Environmental problems are caused by a complex, poorly understood set of interrelated population, resource use, technological, economic, political, social, and ethical factors. Groups known as *neo-Malthusians* and *cornucopians* disagree over how serious these problems are and what should be done about them. Generally these two groups have different worldviews—how we think the world works and what our role should be. Neo-Malthusians believe we should use our ingenuity and technology to work with nature to sustain rather than deplete and degrade the earth. Cornucopians believe that our role is to use our ingenuity and technology to conquer the earth to sustain economic growth and make the planet a better place to live.

DISCUSSION TOPICS

1. Is the world overpopulated? Explain. Is the United States suffering from consumption overpopulation? Explain.

2. Do you favor instituting policies designed to reduce population growth and stabilize **(a)** the size of the world's population as soon as possible and **(b)** the size of the U.S. population as soon as possible? Explain.

3. Explain why you agree or disagree with the following proposition: High levels of resource use by the United States and other MDCs is beneficial. MDCs stimulate the economic growth of LDCs by buying their raw materials. High levels of resource use also stimulate economic growth in MDCs. Economic growth provides money for more financial aid to LDCs and for reducing pollution and environmental degradation.

4. Explain why you agree or disagree with the following proposition: The world will never run out of resources because technological innovations will produce substitutes or allow use of lower grades of scarce resources.

5. Do your own views more closely resemble those [of a] neo-Malthusian or a cornucopian? Does your life[style] show that you're acting as a cornucopian or a ne[o-Mal]thusian? Compare your views with those of othe[rs in] your class.

6. What are the major resource and environmental [prob]lems in **(a)** the city, town, or rural area where yo[u live] and **(b)** the state where you live? Which of these [prob]lems affect you directly?

7. Assume you have been appointed to a new-tech[nology] assessment board. What environmental drawba[cks and] advantages would you list for the following: **(a)** [auto]mobiles, **(b)** trash compactors, **(c)** television set[s, **(d)**] electric cars, **(e)** computers, **(f)** nuclear power plants, **(g)** a drug that a woman could take to cause a medically safe abortion, **(h)** effective sex stimulants, **(i)** drugs that would retard the human aging process, **(j)** electrical or chemical methods that would stimulate the brain to remove anxiety, fear, unhappiness, and aggression, and **(k)** genetic engineering (manipulation of human genes) that would produce people with superior intelligence, strength, health, and other attributes? In each case, would you recommend that the technology be introduced?

CHAPTER 2

Brief History of Resource Exploitation and Conservation

General Questions and Issues

1. How did early and advanced hunter-gatherer societies affect the environment, and what was their relationship to nature?

2. What major impacts have early agricultural societies and today's nonindustrialized agricultural societies had on the environment, and what is the relationship of these societies to nature?

3. How do present-day industrialized societies affect the environment, and what is their relationship to nature?

4. What are the major phases in the history of resource exploitation, resource conservation, and environmental protection in the United States?

5. What major environmental protection and resource conservation problems do we face during the 1990s and beyond?

A continent ages quickly once we come.

Ernest Hemingway

O ur species, *Homo sapiens sapiens*, has lived on earth for about 40,000 years. During most of this time we, like several other species of humans that lived on the earth 1.7 million to 2 million years before us, have been hunter-gatherers.

About 10,000 years ago some people began breeding wild animals and cultivating wild plants. This marked the beginning of a cultural change from hunters and gatherers of wild plants and animals to farmers and herders of domesticated plants and animals. About 275 years ago some people invented various machines that led to a new cultural change known as the Industrial Revolution.

The J-shaped curves of exponentially increasing population, resource use, pollution, and environmental degradation are symptoms of these cultural changes from hunting-gathering to agricultural to industrial societies. To see where we might be headed and how we can influence our path, it is useful to learn about how we have used and abused the earth during these cultural changes.

2-1 HUNTING-AND-GATHERING SOCIETIES

Our Early Ancestors You are a member of a human species called *Homo sapiens sapiens*, which evolved from other human (*Homo*) species. Members of the earliest human species, known as *Homo habilis*, are believed to have lived in southern Africa about 1.7 to 2 million years ago. They probably survived by scavenging meat from the bodies of dead animals and gathering and eating wild plants. They also learned to make simple stone tools and weapons and may have done some hunting for meat.

They were followed by two other human species, *Homo erectus* about 1.5 million years ago and *Homo sapiens* somewhere between 100,000 and 300,000 years ago. The latter species led to our species, *Homo sapiens sapiens*, about 40,000 years ago. Evidence indicates that *Homo erectus*, *Homo sapiens*, and, for about 30,000 years, our own species were **hunter-gatherers**, who got food by gathering edible wild plants and hunting wild game from the nearby environment.

Cultural Change Since the emergence of *Homo sapiens sapiens*, humans have spread out across the world and adapted to a broad range of environmental conditions. They did so not through biological evolution but through a series of rapid cultural changes. Two human characteristics have been largely responsible for those changes: a large brain relative to overall body size and the ability to exchange ideas and information by speaking and writing. These traits have allowed us

Figure 2-1 Most people who have lived on earth have survived by hunting wild game and gathering wild plants.

to develop increasingly sophisticated tools and other technological inventions to adapt to and modify nature. Many animals use simple tools and a few even make them. But only human beings use tools to make other tools.

Today we are by far the most numerous large animals that have ever lived. The growth of our population and our increasing ability to manipulate nature to meet our needs and wants are unprecedented in the history of life on this planet. We now have the power to wipe out our own species and at least half the world's other species. Indeed, there is increasing evidence that we have gone too far in simplifying and modifying nature to suit our purposes (Table 1-1, p. 13). Our survival as a species and the survival of many of the world's other forms of life will probably depend on our willingness and ability to undergo another profound cultural change over the next few decades. It will involve using our brain power to recognize that we must start working with rather than against nature.

Early Hunter-Gatherers Archaeological findings and anthropological studies indicate that most hunter-gatherers lived in small groups of rarely more than 50 people, who worked together to get enough food to survive. Men did the hunting and women did the gathering (Figure 2-1).

Many of these widely scattered bands were nomadic. They moved with the seasons and migrations of game animals to get enough food and to minimize work effort. Sometimes a group became so large that its members could not find enough food within reasonable walking distances. Then the entire group moved to a different area or split up and moved to different areas. Sometimes a group split up in the dry season, when food was scarce, and reassembled in the wet season, when food was more abundant.

These hunter-gatherers were experts in survival. Their knowledge of nature enabled them to predict the weather and find water even in the desert. They discovered a variety of plants and animals that could be eaten and used as medicines. By using stones to chip sticks, other stones, and animal bones, they made primitive weapons for killing animals and tools for cutting plants and scraping hides for clothing and shelter.

Although women typically gave birth to four or five children, usually only one or two children survived to adulthood. Infant deaths from infectious diseases and infanticide (killing the newborn) led to an average life expectancy of about 30 years. This helped keep population size in balance with available food supplies.

Early hunter-gatherers exploited their environment for food and other resources—as do all forms of life. But their numbers were small, most moved from place to place, and they used only their own muscle energy to modify the environment. Their environmental impact was small and localized.

Advanced Hunter-Gatherers Archaeological evidence indicates that hunter-gatherers gradually developed improved tools and hunting weapons. Examples are spears with sharp-edged stone points mounted on wooden shafts and later the bow and arrow (about 12,000 years ago). Some people learned to work together to hunt herds of reindeer, woolly mammoths, European bison, and other big game. They used fire to flush game from thickets toward hunters lying in wait and to stampede herds of animals into traps or over cliffs. Some also learned to burn vegetation to promote the growth of food plants and plants favored by the animals they hunted.

Advanced hunter-gatherers had a greater impact on their environment than early hunter-gatherers, especially in using fire to convert forests into grasslands. There is also evidence that they contributed to the extinction of some large game animals in different parts of the world.

But because of their small numbers, nomadic behavior, and dependence on their own muscle power to modify the environment, their environmental impact was still fairly small and localized. Both early and advanced hunter-gatherers were examples of *people in nature*, who learned to survive by understanding nature.

2-2 AGRICULTURAL SOCIETIES

Domestication of Wild Animals and Plants One of the most significant changes in human history began about 10,000 years ago, when groups of people in several parts of the world began domesticating—herding, taming, and breeding—wild game for food, clothing, and carrying loads. They also began domesticating selected wild food plants, planting and growing them close to home instead of gathering them over a large area.

Archaeological evidence indicates that plant cultivation, which we now call horticulture, probably began in tropical forest areas. People discovered they could grow yam, taro, arrowroot, and other wild food plants by digging holes with a stick (a primitive hoe) and placing roots or tubers of these plants in the holes.

To prepare for planting, they cleared small patches of forests by **slash-and-burn cultivation**—cutting down trees and other vegetation, leaving the cut vegetation on the ground to dry, and then burning it (Figure 2-2). The ashes that were left added plant nutrients to the nutrient-poor soils found in most tropical forest

areas. Roots and tubers were then planted in holes dug between tree stumps.

These early growers also used **shifting cultivation** as part of their horticultural system (Figure 2-2). After a plot had been planted and harvested for two to five years, few if any crops could be grown. By then either the soil was depleted of nutrients or the patch had been invaded by a dense growth of vegetation from the surrounding forest. When yields dropped, the growers shifted to a new area of forest and cleared a new plot for planting. The growers learned that each abandoned patch had to be left fallow (unplanted) for 10 to 30 years before the soil became fertile enough to grow crops again.

These growers practiced **subsistence farming,** growing only enough food to feed their families. Their dependence on human muscle power and crude stone or stick tools meant that they could cultivate only small plots; thus, they had relatively little impact on their environment.

True agriculture (as opposed to horticulture) began about 7,000 years ago with the invention of the metal plow, pulled by domesticated animals and steered by the farmer. Animal-pulled plows allowed farmers to cultivate larger plots of land and to break up fertile grassland soils, which previously couldn't be cultivated because of their thick and widespread root systems.

In some arid (dry) regions early farmers further increased crop output by diverting nearby water into hand-dug ditches and canals to irrigate crops. With this animal- and irrigation-assisted agriculture, families usually grew enough food to survive. Sometimes they had enough left over for sale or for storage to provide food when flooding, prolonged dry spells, insect infestation, or other natural disasters reduced crop productivity.

Emergence of Agriculture–Based Urban Societies The gradual shift from hunting and gathering to farming had four major effects:

- Population began to increase because of a larger, more constant supply of food.

- People cleared increasingly larger areas of land and began to control and shape the surface of the earth to suit their needs.

- Urbanization—the formation of cities—began because a small number of farmers could produce enough food to feed their families plus a surplus that could be traded to other people. Many former farmers moved into permanent villages. Some villages gradually grew into towns and cities, which served as centers for trade, government, and religion.

- Specialized occupations and long-distance trade developed as former farmers in villages and

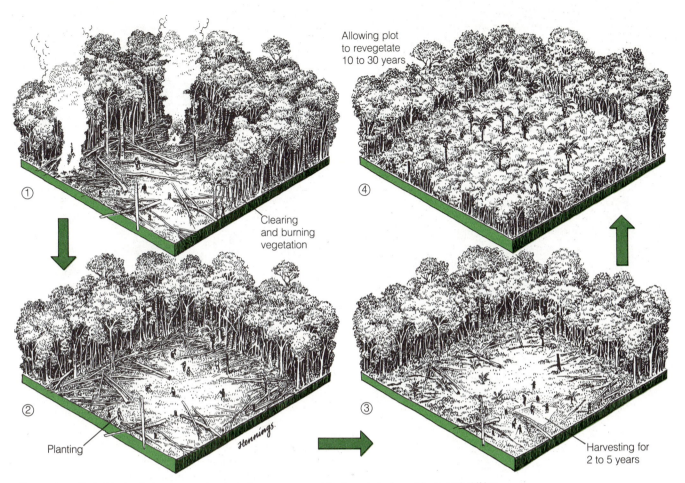

Figure 2-2 Probably the first crop-growing technique was a combination of slash-and-burn and shifting cultivation in tropical forests. This is a sustainable method if only a small portion of the forest is cleared. Soil fertility will not be restored unless each abandoned plot is left unplanted for 10 to 30 years.

towns learned crafts such as weaving, toolmaking, and pottery to produce handmade goods that could be exchanged for food.

About 5,500 years ago, the trade interdependence of rural farmers and urban dwellers led to the gradual development of a number of agriculture-based urban societies near early agricultural settlements. The trade in food and manufactured goods created wealth and the need for a managerial class to regulate the distribution of goods, services, and land.

As ownership of land and water rights became a valuable economic resource, conflict increased. Armies and their leaders rose to power and took over large areas of land. These rulers forced powerless people—slaves and landless peasants—to do the hard, disagreeable work of producing food and constructing irrigation systems, temples, and other projects. Male leaders dominated most of these societies.

Environmental Impact The growing populations of these emerging civilizations needed more food and

more wood for fuel and buildings. To meet these needs, people cut down areas of forest and plowed up vast areas of grasslands. Such massive land clearing destroyed and degraded the habitats of many forms of plant and animal wildlife, causing or hastening their extinction.

Poor management of many of the cleared areas led to greatly increased deforestation, soil erosion, and overgrazing of grasslands by huge herds of sheep, goats, and cattle. These abuses helped convert fertile land to desert. The topsoil that washed off these barren areas polluted streams, rivers, lakes, and irrigation canals, making them useless. The gradual degradation of the vital resource base of soil, water, forests, grazing land, and wildlife was a major factor in the downfall of many great civilizations (see Spotlight on p. 34).

The gradual spread of agriculture meant that most of the earth's population shifted from hunter-gatherers *in nature* to shepherds, farmers, and urban dwellers *against nature*. This change in how people viewed their relationship to nature is a major cause of today's resource and environmental problems.

Archaeological evidence and historical records show that a number of agriculture-based urban societies in the Middle East, North Africa, and the Mediterranean area prospered economically between 3500 B.C. and 500 A.D. But they did so by degrading their land resource base so severely that they eventually helped bring about their own downfall.

As late as 7000 B.C., sites of the great Sumerian and Babylonian civilizations were covered with productive forests and grasslands. But with each generation, the elaborate network of irrigation canals that supported these civilizations became filled with more silt from deforestation, soil erosion, and overgrazing. More and more slaves and laborers were needed to keep the irrigation channels free of silt.

By 3000 B.C. much of this once-productive land had been converted into the barren desert that makes up much of Iran and Iraq today. A combination of environmental degradation, climate change, periodic drought, and a series of invading armies eventually led to the downfall of the Sumerian and Babylonian civilizations.

Severe environmental degradation also took place in other areas around the Mediterranean Sea and in Saharan Africa, where the remains of great cities are now buried in the sand. Some analysts argue that unless we learn from these past environmental lessons and use our knowledge and technology to work with rather than against nature, we will repeat these mistakes on a regional and global scale. What do you think?

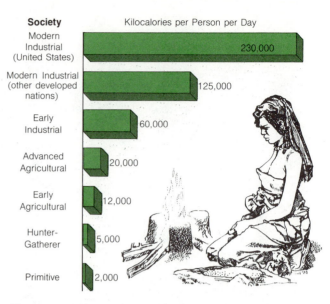

Figure 2-3 Average direct and indirect daily energy use per person at various stages of human cultural development.

2-3 INDUSTRIAL SOCIETIES: THE INDUSTRIAL REVOLUTION

Early Industrial Societies The next major cultural change, the Industrial Revolution, began in England in the mid-1700s and spread to the United States in the 1800s. It involved a shift from small-scale production of goods by hand to large-scale production of goods by machines. Horse-drawn wagons, plows, and grain reapers, and wind-powered ships were replaced by fossil-fuel-powered locomotives, cars, trucks, tractors, reapers, and ships.

Within a few decades these innovations changed agriculture-based urban societies in western Europe and North America into even more urbanized early industrial societies. These societies and the more advanced ones that followed were based on using human ingenuity to increase the average amount of energy used per person (Figure 2-3). This led to greatly increased production, trade, and distribution of goods.

The growth in industries increased the flow of mineral raw materials, fuel, timber, and food into the cities that served as industrial centers. As a result, environmental degradation increased in nonurban areas supplying these resources. Industrialization also produced greater outputs of smoke, ash, garbage, and other wastes in urban areas.

Fossil-fuel-powered farm machines, commercial fertilizers, and new plant-breeding techniques greatly increased the amount of crops that could be grown per acre of cultivated land. Greater agricultural productivity reduced the number of people needed to produce food and increased the number of former farmers migrating from rural to urban areas. Many found jobs in the growing number of mechanized factories. There they worked long hours for low pay in boring assembly line jobs. Most factories were noisy, dirty, and dangerous places to work.

Advanced Industrial Societies After World War I (1914–18), more efficient machines and mass production techniques were developed, forming the basis of today's advanced industrial societies in the United States, Japan, and other MDCs. These societies are characterized by

- greatly increased production and consumption of goods, stimulated by mass advertising to create artificial wants

- greatly increased dependence on nonrenewable resources such as oil, natural gas, coal, and various metals

Figure 2-4 Chief Sealth of the Duwamish tribe of the state of Washington. His 1855 letter to President Franklin Pierce criticized the country's white settlers for exploiting and degrading the earth's resources. (Courtesy of Thomas Burke Memorial Washington State Museum, Catalog No. L 4772)

- a shift from dependence on natural materials, which are degradable, to synthetic materials, many of which break down slowly in the environment (Figure 1-11, p. 17)

- a sharp rise in the amount of energy used per person for transportation, manufacturing, agriculture, lighting, heating and cooling (Figure 2-3)

Advanced industrial societies benefit most people living in them. These benefits include

- creation and mass production of many useful and economically affordable products

- a sharp increase in average agricultural productivity per person because of advanced industrialized agriculture, in which a small number of farmers produce large amounts of food

- a sharp rise in average life expectancy from improvements in sanitation, hygiene, nutrition, medicine, and birth control

- a gradual decline in the rate of population growth because of improvements in health, birth control, education, average income, and old-age security

Environmental Impact Along with their many benefits, advanced industrialized societies have intensi-

fied many existing resource and environmental problems and created new ones. These problems now threaten human well-being at several levels:

- *local level:* contamination of groundwater with toxic pollutants

- *regional level:* damage to forests and degradation of lakes from air pollutants

- *global level:* possible climate change from the atmospheric buildup of carbon dioxide and other gases and depletion of the ozone layer

The combination of industrialized agriculture, increased mining, and urbanization has increased the degradation of potentially renewable topsoil, forests and grasslands, and wildlife populations (Table 1-1, p. 13)—the same problems that contributed to the downfall of earlier civilizations (see Spotlight on p. 34).

Industrialization has given people much greater control over nature and has decreased the number of people living close to the land. As a result, people, especially in MDCs and urban areas, have intensified the view that their role is to conquer nature. Many analysts believe that as long as we have this worldview, we will continue to abuse the earth's life-support systems.

2-4 HISTORICAL OVERVIEW OF RESOURCE EXPLOITATION, RESOURCE CONSERVATION, AND ENVIRONMENTAL PROTECTION IN THE UNITED STATES

America's First Conservationists When Europeans discovered North America in the fifteenth and sixteenth centuries, they found that it had a diverse network of families, clans, tribes, and nations of aboriginal people—called Indians by the Europeans and now often referred to as Native Americans.

Although there were exceptions, most Native Americans had cultures based on a deep respect for the land and its animals. In 1855 Chief Sealth (Figure 2-4) of the Duwamish tribe of the state of Washington wrote a letter to President Franklin Pierce about the U.S. government's offer to buy the tribe's land, the heart of which is now occupied by Seattle. The following passage from his letter shows the respect that most early Native Americans had for wild animals:

If I decide to accept your offer, I will make one condition. The white man must treat the beasts of this land as his brothers. I am a savage and do not understand any other way. I have seen a thousand rotting buffaloes on the prairies left by the white man who shot them from a passing train. I am a savage and I do not understand how the smoking iron horse can be more

Figure 2-5 Thousands of snow geese in a national wildlife refuge near Albuquerque, New Mexico. When European settlers arrived in North America, such sights were common.

Figure 2-6 California redwood forest.

important than the buffalo that we kill only to stay alive. What is man without beasts? If all the beasts were gone, men would die from great loneliness of spirit, for whatever happens to the beasts also happens to man. All things are connected.

Frontier Expansion and Resource Exploitation (1607–1900)

When European colonists began settling in North America in 1607, they found a vast continent. It appeared to have abundant and inexhaustible supplies of timber, fertile soil, wildlife, water, minerals, and other resources for their own use and for export to Europe. Seventy-pound turkeys roamed through the woods. Enormous flocks of geese (Figure 2-5), ducks, and passenger pigeons blotted out the sun. Streams overflowed with so many fish that horses could not cross. Lakes contained 4-meter (12-foot) long sturgeon that could be killed only with axes. Remarkably diverse forests seemed to stretch almost endlessly from the Atlantic coast to the Great Plains. Forests beyond the Great Plains were even more dramatic (Figure 2-6).

American settlers viewed the continent as a hostile wilderness to be conquered, opened up, cleared, and exploited as quickly as possible. This attitude led to enormous resource waste and little regard for future resource needs.

After the Civil War ended in 1865, the government turned its attention to expanding the frontier west-

ward. This meant taming the Native American tribes and eliminating the American bison, which were obstacles to settling the plains (see Case Study on p. 38). In the late 1800s hunters also killed large numbers of herons, snowy egrets (Figure 2-7), and other exotically plumed birds to supply feathers for women's fashions.

After the Civil War, cattle and sheep ranchers began a period of rapid expansion on western rangelands. Federal land-use policies encouraged the use of most public rangelands by any and all livestock operators at no charge. By 1900, after more than 50 years of continuous close grazing by cattle, sheep, and horses, much of this rangeland had been severely overgrazed.

In 1850 about 80% of the total land area of the United States was government owned. Most of this land had been taken from Native American tribes and nations, whose people had lived on it for centuries. In 1891 an old Sioux Indian summarized the behavior of the American government: "They made us many promises, more than I can remember, but they never kept but one; they promised to take our land and they took it."

By 1900 more than half of the public land had been given away or sold at low cost to railroad, timber, and mining companies, land developers, states, schools, universities, and homesteaders. By artificially lowering the prices of resources, these land transfers

Figure 2-7 The snowy egret was hunted to near extinction in the late 1800s because its feathers were used to adorn women's hats. Since being protected, it is no longer threatened with extinction.

Henry David Thoreau
1817–1862

Library of Congress

George P. Marsh
1801–1882

Engraving by Henry B. Hall, Jr.

John Muir
1838–1914

Sierra Club

Gifford Pinchot
1865–1946

Library of Congress

Theodore Roosevelt
1858–1919

Theodore Roosevelt Association

Aldo Leopold
1886–1948

AP/Wide World Photos

Figure 2-8 Some early American conservationists.

encouraged widespread exploitation, waste, and degradation of much of the country's forests, grasslands, and minerals. Most of this land was obtained and exploited by speculators and large corporations.

Early Conservation Warnings (1832–70) Between 1832 and 1870 a number of people warned that America's forest, grassland, and wildlife resources were being depleted and degraded at an alarming rate. These early conservationists included George Catlin, Horace Greeley, Ralph Waldo Emerson, Frederick Law Olmsted, Charles W. Eliot, Henry David Thoreau, and George Perkins Marsh (Figure 2-8). They proposed that part of the unspoiled wilderness owned by the government be protected from resource exploitation.

These warnings were either ignored or vigorously opposed by many citizens and politicians. They believed that the country's forests and wildlife would last forever and that people had the right to do with private and public land as they pleased.

In 1864 George Perkins Marsh, a scientist and congressman from Vermont, published a book, *Man and Nature* (see Further Readings), that helped legislators and influential citizens see the need for resource conservation. Marsh questioned the idea that the coun-

try's resources were inexhaustible and showed how the rise and fall of past civilizations were linked to the misuse of their resource bases. He also set forth basic resource conservation principles still used today.

Beginnings of the Federal Government's Role in Resource Conservation (1870–1916) In the late 1800s the American conservation movement emerged as a number of citizens and government officials began realizing the extent of deforestation and wildlife depletion throughout the country. The federal role in forest and wildlife resource conservation began in 1872, when the government set aside over 809 thousand hectares (2 million acres) of forest mostly in northwestern Wyoming as Yellowstone National Park and banned all hunting in the area.

Congress protected this land mostly because it was viewed as essentially useless for resource exploitation. However, this action marked the beginning of the *first wave of resource conservation* in the United States.

In 1890 the Census Bureau and historian Frederick J. Turner declared that the United States had been settled to the point that its geographic frontier was closed. This helped federal officials recognize the need to conserve resources on lands still under federal ownership.

In 1891 Congress passed the Forest Reserve Act. It set aside Yellowstone Timberland Reserve as the first federal forest reserve. The act also authorized the president to set aside additional federal lands to ensure future supplies of timber and to protect water resources. This was a turning point in establishing the responsibility of the federal government for protecting public lands from resource exploitation.

Between 1891 and 1897, Presidents Benjamin Harrison and Grover Cleveland withdrew millions of acres of public land, located mostly in the West, from timber cutting. Powerful and wealthy political foes—especially Westerners accustomed to using these public lands as they pleased—called these actions undemocratic and un-American.

In 1892 California nature writer John Muir (Figure 2-8) founded the Sierra Club to help protect public lands from resource exploitation. By the turn of the century, however, American forests were still being cut down faster than they were being replaced by natural regrowth and tree-planting efforts (Figure 2-10).

More effective protection of forests and wildlife didn't occur until Theodore Roosevelt, an ardent conservationist, became president. The period of his pres-

CASE STUDY The Near Extinction of the American Bison

When European explorers discovered North America in the late 1400s, various tribes of Native Americans depended heavily on bison for survival. The meat was their staple diet. The skin was used for tepees, moccasins, and clothes. The gut made their bowstrings, and the horns their spoons. Even the dried feces, called buffalo chips by English-speaking settlers, were used for fuel.

In 1500, before European settlers came to North America, between 60 million and 125 million grass-eating American bison roamed the plains, prairies, and woodlands over most of the continent (Figure 2-9). Their numbers were so large that they were thought to be inexhaustible. By 1906, however, the once-massive range of the American bison was reduced to a tiny area, and the species was nearly driven to extinction, mostly because of overhunting and loss of habitat.

By the late 1600s some Plains Native American tribes had begun hunting bison using horses descended from those brought earlier by Spanish explorers. They hunted on foot and on horseback, armed only with lances and bows and arrows. Occasionally they drove bison over cliffs. This hunting hardly made a dent in the vast bison population.

As settlers moved west after the Civil War, the sustainable balance between Native Americans and bison was upset. Plains Native Americans traded bison skins to settlers for steel knives and firearms and began killing bison in larger numbers.

But much more severe depletion of this resource was caused by other factors. First, as railroads spread westward in the late 1860s, railroad companies hired professional bison hunters to supply construction crews with meat. The well-known railroad bison hunter "Buffalo Bill" Cody killed an estimated 4,280 bison in only 18 months—surely a world record. Passengers also gunned down bison from train windows purely for the "joy" of killing, leaving the carcasses to rot.

As farmers settled the plains, they shot bison because the animals destroyed crops. Ranchers killed them because they competed with cattle and sheep for grass and knocked over fences, telegraph poles, and sod houses.

An army of commercial hunters shot millions of bison for their hides and for their tongues, which were considered a delicacy. Instead of being eaten, however, most of the meat was left to rot. "Bone pickers" then collected the bleached bones that whitened the prairies and shipped them east for use as fertilizer.

A final major factor in the near extinction of the bison occurred after the Civil War. The U.S. Army killed millions of bison to subdue plains tribes of Native Americans and take over their lands by killing off their major source of food. Between 1870 and 1875 at least 2.5 million bison were slaughtered each year.

By 1890 only one herd of about 1 million bison was left. Commercial hunters and skinners descended on this herd, and by 1892 only 85

idency from 1901 to 1909 is regarded by many as the country's golden age of conservation.

Roosevelt's first step was to convince Congress to grant him executive powers to establish federal wildlife refuges. In 1903 he established the first federal refuge at Pelican Island off the east coast of Florida for preservation of the endangered brown pelican (Figure 2-11). Roosevelt also tripled the size of the forest reserves and transferred administration of them from the Department of the Interior, which had a reputation for lax enforcement, to the Department of Agriculture.

In 1905 a group of private citizens founded the National Audubon Society to protect wildlife. During the same year, Congress created the U.S. Forest Service to manage and protect the forest reserves. Roosevelt appointed Gifford Pinchot as its chief (Figure 2-8). Pinchot pioneered efforts to manage potentially renewable forest resources scientifically according to the principles of sustainable yield and multiple use.

In 1907, Congress, upset over Roosevelt's addition of vast tracts to the forest reserves, amended the Forest Reserve Act of 1891 to ban further withdrawals of public forests by the president. This amendment also changed the name of the reserves to national forests—implying that these lands should not be preserved from all types of development. On the day before the amendment became law, Roosevelt defiantly reserved another 16 million acres of national forests.

Early in this century conservationists disagreed over how the beautiful Hetch Hetchy Valley in what is now Yosemite National Park was to be used. This controversy split the American conservation movement into two schools of thought, the preservationists and the scientific conservationists.

Scientific conservationists, led by Gifford Pinchot, wanted to build a dam and flood the valley to create a reservoir to supply drinking water for San Francisco. Preservationists, led by John Muir, wanted to keep this beautiful spot from being flooded. After a long and highly publicized battle, the dam was built and the valley was flooded. The controversy between these two schools of thought continues today (see Spotlight on p. 41).

bison were left. These were given refuge in Yellowstone National Park and protected by an 1893 law against the killing of wild animals in national parks.

In 1905 sixteen people formed the American Bison Society to protect and rebuild the captive population of the animal. In the early 1900s the federal government established the National Bison Range near Missoula, Montana. Since then, captive herds on this federal land and other herds mostly on privately owned land scattered throughout the West have been protected by law.

Today there are about 75,000 bison in the United States—one-fifth of them on the National Bison Range. Some captive bison are crossbred with cattle to produce hybrids, called beefalo. They have a tasty meal, grow faster and are easier to raise than cattle, and need no expensive grain feed.

Ranchers have complained that bison straying from Yellowstone National Park were damaging their fences and depleting grass needed by cattle. Since 1985 the Montana state legislature has allowed hunters to shoot stray bison. Conservationists have protested and urged federal authorities to provide feeding spots for the animals inside the park.

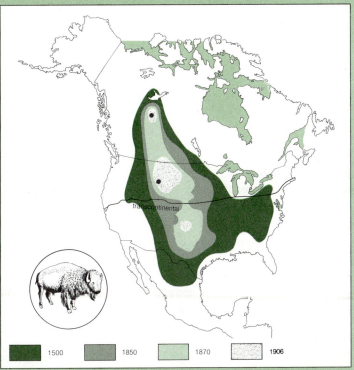

| | 1500 | | 1850 | | 1870 | | 1906 |

Figure 2-9 Severe shrinkage of the range of the bison between 1500 and 1906, primarily as a result of overhunting and settlement.

Figure 2-10 In 1900, Pacific Coast loggers were cutting gigantic trees such as this Douglas fir. Teams of horses, mules, or oxen dragged the logs from the forests.

Figure 2-11 The first national wildlife refuge was set up off the coast of Florida in 1903 to protect the brown pelican from extinction.

In 1912 Congress created the U.S. National Park System, and in 1916 it passed the National Park System Organic Act. This law declared that national parks are to be set aside to conserve and preserve scenery, wildlife, and natural and historic objects for the use, observation, health, and pleasure of people. The parks are to be maintained in a manner that leaves them unimpaired for future generations.

The law also established the National Park Service within the Department of the Interior to manage the system. The Park Service's first director, Stephen Mather, recruited a corps of professional park rangers to manage the parks.

During the Republican administrations of 1921–33, the government increased emphasis on using public resources to favor big business and promote economic growth. Indeed, while Herbert Hoover was president between 1929 and 1933, he proposed that the federal government return all remaining federal lands to the states or sell them to private interests so that they could make money out of them. The economic depression of the 1930s, however, made the financial burden of owning such lands unattractive to state governments and private interests.

Expanding Federal Role in Wildlife and Public Land Management (1933–60) The *second wave of national resource conservation* began in the early 1930s, as President Franklin D. Roosevelt attempted to get the country out of the Great Depression (1929–41). Conser-

vation of resources benefited because financially strapped landowners were eager to sell vast tracts of land at low prices to the government.

To provide jobs for 2 million unemployed young men, Roosevelt established the Civilian Conservation Corps. The CCC planted trees, developed parks and recreation areas, restored silted waterways, provided flood control, controlled soil erosion, protected wildlife, and carried out other conservation projects.

During the Depression the federal government built and operated many large dams in the arid western states, such as Hoover Dam on the Colorado River. These projects stimulated the economy by providing jobs, irrigation water, flood control, and cheap electricity.

In 1933 the Soil Erosion Service under the Department of Agriculture was created. Its mission was to correct some of the massive erosion problems that had ruined many of the farms of the Great Plains states. This erosion, brought about by prolonged drought and lack of soil conservation, contributed to the Great Depression. It forced large numbers of bankrupt farmers in the Midwest to migrate to eastern and western cities in search of nonexistent jobs, as described in John Steinbeck's novel *The Grapes of Wrath*. In 1935 the Soil Erosion Service was renamed the Soil Conservation Service, and Hugh H. Bennett became its first director.

The passage of the Taylor Grazing Act in 1934 marked the beginning of the regulation of grazing of

Past and present preservationists emphasize protecting large areas of public lands from mining, timbering and other forms of development so they can be enjoyed by present generations and passed on unspoiled to future generations. They would do this by establishing protected parks, wilderness areas, and wildlife refuges to prevent potentially renewable public resources from being degraded by short-term, "quick-buck" economic development.

The preservationists were led by naturalist John Muir and, after Muir's death in 1914, by forester Aldo Leopold (Figure 2-8). According to Leopold, the role of the human species should be that of a member and protector of nature—not its conqueror.

Another effective supporter of wilderness preservation was Robert Marshall, an officer in the U.S. Forest Service. In 1935 he and Leopold founded the Wilderness Society. Others, who have led preservationist efforts in recent years, include David Brower (former head of the Sierra Club and founder of Friends of the Earth), Ernest Swift, and Stewart L. Udall.

In contrast, scientific conservationists see public lands as resources to be used now to enhance economic growth and national strength. The government protected these lands from degradation by managing them efficiently and scientifically for sustainable yield and multiple use. Early scientific conservationists were led by Theodore Roosevelt, Gifford Pinchot, John Wesley Powell, Charles Van Hise, and others.

According to Roosevelt and Pinchot, conservation experts would form an elite corps of resource managers in the federal bureaucracy. They would be protected from excessive political pressure and could design and implement management strategies based on scientific criteria. Pinchot angered Muir and other preservationists, who had been active allies in Roosevelt's conservation efforts, when he stated his principle of the wise use of resources:

The first great fact about conservation is that it stands for development. There has been a fundamental misconception that conservation means nothing but the husbanding of resources for future generations. There could be no

more serious mistake. . . . The first principle of conservation is the use of the natural resources now existing on this continent for the benefit of the people who live here now.

Although they differed on how resources should be used, most early preservationists and scientific conservationists called for equitable (fair) use of publicly owned resources. Both schools felt that such resources belonged to all the people and should be managed by the federal government for widespread and fair use by everyone. They were against letting these public resources fall into the hands of a few for private profit.

The goal of equity has not been achieved. Since 1910 the rights to much of the forest and mineral resources on public lands and the water resources supplied by federally financed dam and irrigation projects in the West have gone to large, privately owned farms, ranching operations, mining companies, and timber companies. Often the resource rights on public lands have been sold to these influential private interests at below normal market prices.

---

domesticated livestock on public lands, especially in the West, which for many decades had been overgrazed by ranchers. This law required permits and fees for the use of federal grazing lands and placed limits on the number of animals that could be grazed.

From the start, ranchers resented government interferences with their long-established, unregulated use of public land. Since 1934 they have led repeated efforts to have these lands removed from government ownership and turned over to private ranching, mining, timber, and development interests.

In 1935 Paul B. Sears wrote *Deserts on the March.* In this book he warned that continuing abuse of western rangeland could convert much of it to desert, as earlier civilizations had learned the hard way. This warning was largely ignored.

Until passage of the Federal Land Policy and Management Act in 1976, western congressional delegations kept the Grazing Service (which in 1946 became the Bureau of Land Management, or BLM) poorly

funded, and understaffed, and without enforcement authority. This allowed many ranchers and mining and timber companies to continue abusing western public lands.

In 1937 the Federal Aid in Wildlife Restoration Act (also known as the Pittman-Robertson Act) levied a federal tax on all sales of guns and ammunition. This tax plus matching state funds have provided more than $2.1 billion for states to buy land for wildlife conservation (mostly for game species), to support wildlife research, and to reintroduce wildlife in depleted areas.

Between 1940 and 1960, there were few new developments in federal resource conservation policy because of preoccupation with World War II (1941–1945) and economic recovery after the war. In 1948 the United States had its first major air pollution disaster, when pollutants from a steel mill, zinc smelter, and sulfuric acid plant stagnated over the town of Donora, Pennsylvania. About 6,000 of the town's 14,000 inhabitants fell ill and 20 died from breathing the polluted air. The incident caused some people to question the sight of belching smokestacks as an acceptable nuisance and a sign of economic progress.

In 1948 William Voight warned about the dangers of rapid population growth and overpopulation in his book *The Road to Survival*. The same year, Fairfield Osborn wrote about the need to increase efforts to protect and conserve the country's natural resources during the period of rapid economic growth after World War II. Few people took either of these warnings seriously until the 1960s.

Rise of the Environmental Movement (1960–80)
The *third wave of national resource conservation* began during the short administration of John F. Kennedy (1961–63). These efforts were expanded under the administration of Lyndon B. Johnson (1963–68).

In 1962 biologist Rachel Carson (Figure 2-12) published *Silent Spring* (see Further Readings). This book described the pollution of air, water, and wildlife from the widespread use of slowly degradable pesticides such as DDT. It helped broaden the concept of resource conservation to include the preservation of the *quality* of the air, water, and soil, which were under assault by a country experiencing rapid economic growth. She pointed out that "for the first time in the history of the world, every human being is now subjected to dangerous chemicals, from the moment of conception until death." The public's unprecedented response to Carson's book was the beginning of what is now known as the environmental movement in the United States.

In 1964 Congress passed the Wilderness Act. It authorizes the government to protect undeveloped tracts of public land as part of the National Wilderness System unless Congress later decides they are needed for the national good. Land in this system is to be protected from development and used only for nondestructive forms of recreation such as hiking and camping.

Between 1965 and 1970 the emerging science of ecology received widespread media coverage. At the same time, the popular writings of biologists such as Paul Ehrlich, Barry Commoner, and Garrett Hardin helped the public become aware of the interlocking relationships between population growth, resource use, and pollution (Figure 1-12, p. 19).

During this period a number of events covered by the media increased public awareness of pollution:

- In 1963 high concentrations of air pollutants accumulated in the air above New York City, killing about 300 people and injuring thousands.

- In the mid-1960s foam caused by widespread use of nonbiodegradable substances in synthetic laundry and cleaning detergents began appearing on creeks and rivers (Figure 2-13).

Figure 2-12 Biologist Rachel Carson (1907–1964) was a pioneer in increasing public awareness of pollution. She died without knowing that her efforts were a key in starting today's environmental movement.

- In 1969 the oil-polluted Cuyahoga River running through Cleveland, Ohio, caught fire. Two bridges were burned by the five-story-high flames (Figure 2-14).

- In 1969 oil leaking from an offshore well near Santa Barbara, California, coated beaches and wildlife (Figure 2-15).

- By the late 1960s Lake Erie had become severely polluted. Large numbers of fish died, numbers of desirable species of commercial and game fish dropped sharply, and many bathing beaches had to be closed.

- During the late 1960s and early 1970s several well-known species of wildlife, including the American bald eagle (Figure 2-16), the grizzly bear, the whooping crane, and the peregrine falcon, were threatened with extinction from pollution and loss of habitat.

On April 22, 1970, the first annual Earth Day took place in the United States. About 20 million people in more than 2,000 communities took to the streets to demand better environmental quality. Elected officials got the message. Between 1969 and 1980 Congress

Figure 2-13 Foam on a creek caused by nondegradable components in synthetic laundry detergents in 1966.

Figure 2-14 The oil-polluted Cuyahoga River, which runs through Cleveland, Ohio, caught fire in 1969.

Figure 2-15 Straw being used to soak up oil released by rupture of an oil well off the coast of Santa Barbara, California, in 1969.

Figure 2-16 There were an estimated 250,000 American bald eagles when this bird became the national symbol in 1782. During the late 1960s and early 1970s the number of American bald eagles in the lower 48 states declined because of loss of habitat, illegal hunting, and reproductive failure caused by pesticides in its primary diet of fish. Federal protection has led to recovery in many areas. In 1988 there were about 11,800 bald eagles in the wild.

passed more than two dozen separate pieces of legislation to protect the air, water, land, and wildlife (see Appendix 3). These laws provide environmental protection and resource conservation by

- Setting pollution level standards or limiting emissions or effluents of various types of pollutants Examples are the Federal Water Pollution Control Act of 1972 and the Clean Air Acts of 1965, 1970, and 1977.

- Screening new substances to determine their safety before they are widely used. An example is the Toxic Substances Control Act of 1976.

- Requiring that any project to be undertaken by a government agency be evaluated to project its

environmental impact before it is started. An example is the National Environmental Policy Act of 1969.

- Setting aside or protecting various natural systems, resources, or species from harm. Examples are the Wilderness Act of 1964 and the Endangered Species Act of 1973.

- Encouraging resource conservation. Examples are the Resource Conservation and Recovery Act of 1976 and to some extent the National Energy Act of 1978.

Between 1965 and 1980, people became aware that the country's environmental frontier was closed. They began to realize that there is no infinite "away"—no place to get rid of the wastes produced by a heavily industrialized society whose economy runs on converting the earth's resources to wastes as fast as possible. The accomplishments during this period by government and by citizen-supported, private environmental and conservation groups were the *fourth wave of national resource conservation.*

The 1973 OPEC oil embargo and the shutdown of oil production in Iran in 1979 led to oil shortages and sharp rises in the price of oil between 1973 and 1981 (see Case Study on p. 14). This period of relative oil scarcity showed the need for effective conservation of energy resources, especially oil.

In 1977 President Jimmy Carter created the Department of Energy to help the country deal with shortages of oil. He, along with most conservationists, realized that the United States and other industrialized countries must develop a long-range energy strategy.

But most efforts to make the United States face up to the end of the cheap oil era were undermined by Carter's political defeat and the temporary oil glut of the 1980s. These events sent a false message to many consumers and elected officials that energy conservation and a search for oil substitutes were no longer high priorities.

During his term Carter appointed a number of competent and experienced administrators to key posts in the Environmental Protection Agency, the Department of the Interior, and the Department of Energy. He drew heavily on established environmental and conservation organizations for such appointees and for advice on environmental and resource policy. He also created the Superfund to clean up abandoned hazardous waste sites such as the Love Canal suburb in Niagara Falls, New York (see later Case Study).

Just before leaving office, Carter used the Antiquities Act of 1906 to increase public lands protected from development. He tripled the amount of land in the National Wilderness System, primarily by adding vast tracts of public land in Alaska. This also doubled the area under the administration of the National Park Service.

Continuing Controversy and Some Retrenchment (the 1980s) The Federal Land Policy and Management Act of 1976 gave the Bureau of Land Management its first real authority to manage the public lands, mostly in the West, under its control. This angered ranchers, farmers, miners, users of off-road motorized vehicles, and others, who had been doing pretty much as they pleased on these public lands.

In the late 1970s, western ranchers, who had been paying low fees for grazing rights that encouraged overgrazing, launched a political campaign known as the sagebrush rebellion. Its major goal, like that of earlier efforts, was to remove most western public lands from public ownership and turn them over to the states. Then these campaigners planned to persuade state legislatures to sell or lease the resource-rich lands at low prices to ranching, mining, timber, land development, and other private interests.

In 1981 Ronald Reagan, a self-declared sagebrush rebel, became president, having won the election by a large margin. He had campaigned as a champion of strong national defense, less federal government control, and reduced government spending to lower the national debt and combat the economic recession that had followed the sharp rises in oil prices during the 1970s.

During his eight years in office Reagan mounted a massive attack on the country's major conservation and environmental laws. He

- Appointed people who came from industries or legal firms that opposed existing federal environmental, resource conservation, and land use legislation and policies to key positions in the Interior Department, BLM, and EPA. President Harry S. Truman had recognized the dangers of such appointments when he said, "You don't set foxes to watching the chickens just because they have a lot of experience in the hen house."

- Barred established environmental and conservation organizations and leaders from having input into such appointments and into the administration's environmental and resource policies.

- Made the enforcement of existing environmental and resource conservation laws difficult by encouraging drastic budget and staff cuts in enforcement agencies.

- Greatly increased energy and mineral development and timber cutting by private enterprise on public lands. Often the government sold these resources at giveaway prices to private corporations, shortchanging the citizens, who jointly own the resources.

- Increased the federal budget for nuclear power. This way of producing electricity is still not economically competitive with most other energy alternatives even though taxpayers have given the nuclear industry over $40 billion in subsidies.

- Cut federal funding for energy conservation by 70%, lowered automobile gas mileage standards, and relaxed air- and water-quality standards.

- Eliminated tax incentives for encouraging residential solar energy and energy conservation.

- Drastically cut funding for programs to provide energy conservation and fuel aid for the poor.

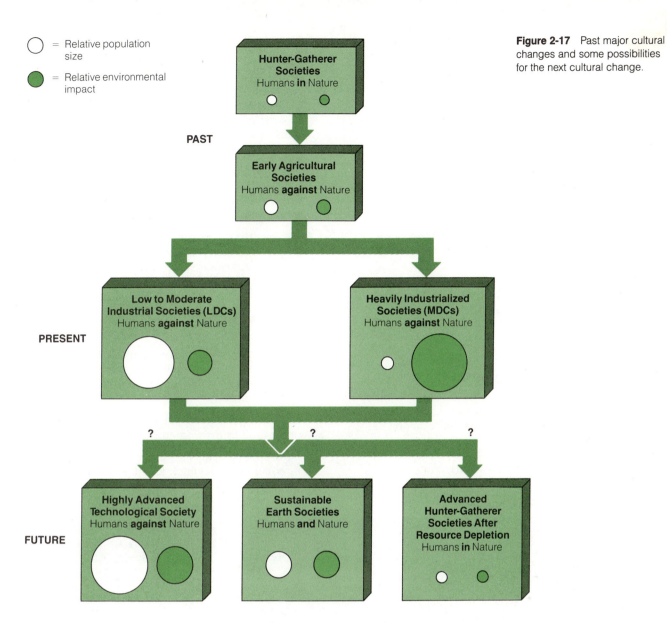

○ = Relative population size

● = Relative environmental impact

PAST

Hunter-Gatherer Societies
Humans **in** Nature

Early Agricultural Societies
Humans **against** Nature

PRESENT

Low to Moderate Industrial Societies (LDCs)
Humans **against** Nature

Heavily Industrialized Societies (MDCs)
Humans **against** Nature

FUTURE

?   ?   ?

Highly Advanced Technological Society
Humans **against** Nature

Sustainable Earth Societies
Humans **and** Nature

Advanced Hunter-Gatherer Societies After Resource Depletion
Humans **in** Nature

- Reduced funding for research and development on perpetual and renewable energy resources by 85%.

Although Reagan was an immensely popular president, most of the public strongly opposed his environmental and resource policies. These policies were blunted by strong opposition by Congress, public outrage, and legal challenges by environmental and conservation organizations, whose memberships soared in this period.

The net effect of the Reagan years was to slow down the momentum of environmental protection and resource conservation built up in the 1970s. Instead of moving forward, environmental and conservation organizations had to spend much of their time and money fighting off a vigorous attempt to move backwards.

2-5 SOME POSSIBLE FUTURES

The Next Cultural Change Some futurists project that over the next 50 to 75 years we will undergo another major cultural change, resulting in one of several possibilities (Figure 2-17):

- a series of *sustainable-earth societies* throughout the world, consisting of people working with nature to sustain the earth's life-support systems for humans and other species

- a series of *superindustrialized societies* based on major advances in technology that allow people even greater control over nature

- a small number of people in scattered bands trying to survive as *modern hunter-gatherers* in a world polluted and depleted of resources by global nuclear war or by excessive industrialization and population growth without adequate resource conservation and environmental protection

An Agenda for the 1990s and Beyond The easy part of the drive to protect the environment and conserve resources is over. In the 1990s and beyond we are faced with a set of complex, less visible, widely dispersed, long-term environmental and resource problems. Many of these are global and regional problems such as global warming, ozone depletion, ocean pollution, acid deposition, and the shift from nonrenewable fossil fuels to energy efficiency and renewable energy.

In the 1990s and beyond, our efforts to protect the environment and conserve resources must include the following:

- Demand that world leaders hold an annual summit meeting to review environmental and resource problems and progress and to establish treaties and action plans.

- Deal with long-term global and regional environmental threats by international agreements and cooperation.

- Develop integrated national, regional, and global environmental protection, resource conservation, urban and rural development, agricultural, economic development, and population strategies that treat problems as interrelated and not in a piecemeal fashion.

- Demand that countries treat environmental protection and resource conservation as vital foreign policy and national and global security issues.

- Shift much of the foreign assistance by the United States and other MDCs to LDCs from military aid to sustainable development of natural resources, which are the ultimate basis of military and economic security for everyone.

- Shift some of the funds devoted to maintaining military forces to development of an Earth Conservation Corps at the global, national, state, and local levels (see Spotlight below).

- Redirect the energy and creativity of most of the world's scientists, engineers, business leaders, and political leaders from the development of military weapons and strategies to sustaining the earth.

- Establish the goal of cutting the rate of world population growth in half by the year 2000.

- Make birth control information and devices available to every man and woman and increase funding for research and development of new methods of birth control.

- Greatly expand educational and paid employment opportunities for women.

- Slow down global warming by negotiating an international agreement to cut global carbon dioxide emission by 20% within a decade, sharply

---

SPOTLIGHT Creating an Earth Conservation Corps

We need to create an Earth Conservation Corps (ECC), an expanded version of the Peace Corps. It could be an alternative to military service for young people and a source of jobs and satisfaction for people of all ages. People could work full time in the ECC or part time in local Earth Guards similar to National Guard units.

Corps of people at the international, national, state, and local levels could be trained to

- restore degraded forests, grassland, cropland, rangeland, watersheds, wetlands, and strip-mined lands
- plant trees in rural and urban areas
- create and maintain national, state, and local parks and trails

- reduce soil erosion
- help establish and maintain wildlife refuges for endangered plants and animals
- help the poor restore abandoned or degraded urban housing
- help the poor insulate and weatherize housing
- build new energy-efficient and resource-efficient housing for the poor
- convert abandoned urban lots to community gardens, playgrounds, and vest-pocket parks

The ECC could be supplemented by using part of the armed forces for earth conservation—the most important form of national and global security. Up to one-fourth of military forces and resources could be used to

- restore degraded land, plant trees, and create and maintain national parks, trails, and wildlife refuges
- transport endangered animals and natural predators by helicopter or trucks to national parks, wildlife refuges, and other public land
- detect illegal fishing and ocean dumping, illegal toxic dumping, air pollution, and oil spills
- clean up oil spills, toxic spills, and toxic dumps

What do you think?

---

reduce emissions of other gases that contribute to atmospheric warming, use energy more efficiently, shift from fossil fuels to renewable energy resources, and reduce tropical deforestation.

- Ban all use of chlorofluorocarbons, which deplete the earth's ozone layer and warm the earth's atmosphere.

- Maintain a world grain reserve equivalent to 80 days of consumption as a buffer against unpredictable climate change and natural disasters.

- Slow down the present rapid degradation and depletion of the world's remaining tropical forests, wetlands, and other natural systems by developing and enforcing an international tropical forest preservation treaty and an international treaty to protect biological diversity.

- Launch an international tree-planting program to be carried out at the local level.

- Require the World Bank and other international lending and aid agencies to fund only projects that minimize pollution and environmental degradation.

- Encourage banks, international lending agencies, and the governments of MDCs to forgive much of the debt owed them by LDCs if the debtor countries agree to set aside funds and establish policies to protect tropical forests, wetlands, wildlife, and other natural resources from degradation or to use them on a sustainable basis.

- Encourage countries to establish national zoning plans to protect unique areas and to promote sustainable development of areas used to supply food, wood, water, minerals, and other resources. Countries with such plans and with plans for reducing population growth should have priority in getting international development aid.

- Protect wildlife by increasing emphasis on protection or sustainable use of wildlife habitats instead of protecting a few individuals of endangered animal or plant species in zoos, botanical gardens, and other expensive sanctuaries.

- Greatly increase research and financial support for restoration or rehabitation of degraded natural areas.

- Increase recycling and reuse of nonrenewable mineral resources, increase energy efficiency, and use a mix of perpetual and renewable energy resources to get us unhooked from our present addiction to oil.

- Greatly reduce or eliminate government subsidies that encourage waste by keeping prices of resources, such as fossil fuels, nuclear power, water, and food, artificially low. The market prices of goods and services should include their social and environmental costs.

- Require new automobiles produced or sold in the United States to average 19 kilometers per liter (45 miles per gallon) and light trucks 15 kilometers per liter (35 miles per gallon) by the year 2000.

- Phase in a $1-a-gallon gasoline tax by 1995 to improve fuel efficiency and provide funds for improving energy efficiency, development of renewable energy resources, and environmental protection. This should be coupled with a fuel rebate or aid programs for the poor.

- Use most of the Department of Energy (DOE) budget for improving energy efficiency and increased use of solar, wind, and other perpetual and renewable energy resources instead of on fossil fuels, commercial nuclear power, and military expenditures. The nuclear weapons program, which now absorbs almost two-thirds of the DOE budget, should be transferred to the Department of Defense.

- Require all nuclear weapons facilities to meet the same safety standards as commercial nuclear power plants.

- Develop a national energy policy that allows all energy alternatives to compete in the marketplace on a fair economic basis. Present policy distorts the marketplace by giving massive subsidies to fossil fuels and nuclear power and minute subsidies to energy efficiency and renewable energy resources. Either withdraw all subsidies or distribute them more equally and fairly.

- Shift emphasis from pollution control (output control) to pollution prevention (input control).

- Shift emphasis from waste disposal to waste prevention and reduction. Think of waste materials resources that should be recycled, reused, or reformulated, and develop laws and economic rewards that encourage this approach.

- Ban exports of toxic waste from one country another by international agreement and law.

- Ban ocean dumping and vigorously protect remaining coastal and inland wetlands from degradation.

- Decrease acid deposition by sharply decreasing emissions of sulfur dioxide and nitrogen oxides by fossil-fuel-burning power plants, industrial plants, and motor vehicles.

- Control emissions of thousands of difficult-to-detect hazardous chemicals into the environment from millions of widely dispersed, hard-to-identify, hard-to-control nonpoint sources.

- Greatly increase funding for environmental monitoring and scientific research on how the earth works, methods for sustainable use of resources, improving energy efficiency, and pollution prevention.

- Develop effective educational programs from kindergarten through college about nature and how to work with the earth. Require all high school and college students to take at least one interdisciplinary course on local, national, and global environmental protection and resource conservation.

- Demand that current and future presidents rebuild the morale and expertise of the EPA and the Interior, Agriculture, and Energy departments. Presidents with vision can draw from the vast reservoir of support for environmental protection and resource conservation found in the American public. A 1988 *New York Times*-CBS News poll showed that two-thirds of the public agree that "continuing environmental improvement must be made regardless of cost."

- Create a cabinet-level Department of Environmental Protection by combining the EPA and the National Oceanic and Atmospheric Administration.

- Have a senior White House coordinator for environmental and resource policy and elevate the President's Council on Environmental Quality to the same status as that of the Council of Economic Advisors.

- Change our individual consumption habits and lifestyles to reduce environmental impact and resource depletion and degradation (see Spotlight below).

Dealing with the environmental and resource problems we face will not be easy or cheap. It will

SPOTLIGHT Everyone Wants Clean Air and Water, but . . .

Everyone wants to breathe clean air and drink uncontaminated water. But how much are you willing to pay in taxes to protect the environment and conserve resources? What changes in your lifestyle would you really be willing to make?

These are crucial questions. Why? Because each of us must recognize the truth in Pogo's statement, "We have met the enemy, and it is us," and begin to change our lifestyles accordingly.

Most people want factories to be inspected and required by the government to install air and water pollution control equipment. Most also want companies that violate pollution control laws to be fined and the responsible corporate executives jailed.

But how many people want the same types of laws and standards to apply to their own activities? For example, recent measurements have shown that the air inside most of today's houses, offices, and stores—where people spend most of their time—is more polluted and hazardous than the outside air.

How many people want the nuisance and expense of annual inspections of their homes for indoor air pollution? How many favor being forced to install indoor air pollution control systems? How

many want to be told that they cannot use certain types of building materials and common household chemicals? How many favor laws requiring fireplaces, wood stoves, and oil furnaces to have air pollution controls?

How many people favor much stricter semiannual inspections of air pollution control equipment on their motor vehicles and tough fines for not keeping these systems in good working order? In the United States almost 60% of such equipment on cars and trucks has either been dismantled or is not working properly.

People want clean water. But how many city dwellers support the sharp increases in monthly sewage treatment bills this will require. How many rural dwellers support mandatory annual testing of their well water and septic tank systems? How many want to be told they have to install purification systems when their drinking water is found to be contaminated?

People know that the growing volume of trash is a major problem. But how many support laws that would require them to separate their trash into paper, bottles and cans for recycling and food wastes for composting? How many insist that we pass laws banning throwaway bottles and cans and

that we recycle and reuse our containers?

Everyone is against hazardous waste. Thousands of abandoned leaking hazardous-waste dumps, hundreds of thousands of underground storage tanks, and tens of thousands of unlined settling ponds and landfills can contaminate groundwater supplies providing 96% of the drinking water in U.S. rural areas and 20% in urban areas. But how many people support the large increase in federal and state taxes needed to clean up these potential sources of pollution?

People also want proper management of radioactive nuclear waste industrial hazardous waste produced in supplying the electricity, products, and services they use. But how many oppose locating a nuclear waste dump, a hazardous waste incinerator, a landfill, or a recycling plant anywhere near them? How many want to be told that they will be heavily fined if they put a partially filled container of paint thinner, pesticide, cleaning product, or other hazardous waste in their trash or pour it down their drain?

These are the questions and issues we must now face up to if we really care about the earth. How would you answer these questions?

involve much controversy and require us to make some trade-offs and changes in lifestyle.

The estimated worldwide cost of restoring tree cover and soil, managing water supplies, halting species extinctions, protecting the earth's ozone shield, and slowing down the greenhouse effect is about $150 billion per year for at least the next decade. But failure to take these steps during the 1990s will cost much more in money, ecological disruption, and human suffering in your lifetime and your children's. We must recognize that short-term economic greed eventually leads to long-term economic and environmental grief.

We found our house—the planet—with drinkable, potable water, with good soil to grow food, with clean air to breathe. We at least must leave it in as good as shape as we found it, if not better.

Rev. Jesse Jackson

CHAPTER SUMMARY

Humans have gained increasing control over nature through a series of major *cultural changes*. For several million years a small number of humans lived in small scattered groups of *hunters and gatherers*. Their environmental impact was fairly small and localized because of their small numbers, dependence on their own muscle power, and limited technology. They were examples of *humans in nature* who learned to survive by cooperating with nature and with one another.

About 10,000 years ago people in various parts of the world began learning how to domesticate wild animals and to cultivate wild plants. This was the beginning of a cultural change from hunter-gatherers to farmers and herders. The spread of this new way of life meant an increase in food production and a decrease in the number of people needed to supply the food. This led to significant population growth, urbanization, specialized occupations, trade between farmers and city people, and the rise of armies and war leaders to acquire and protect land and water resources.

The growth and spread of these *agriculture-based urban societies* led to massive clearing of forests, plowing of grasslands, soil erosion, and diversion of surface waters for irrigation and urban water supplies. People began viewing nature as something to conquer and subdue for their purposes. They became *humans against nature*.

The next major cultural change, known as the *Industrial Revolution*, began in England around 1760 when people invented machines that could harness large amounts of energy from the burning of coal and later oil, natural gas, and uranium.

Since then, the gradual transformation of *early industrialized societies* to the *advanced industrialized societies* in today's MDCs has led to significant increases in average energy use, agricultural productivity, life expectancy, and GNP per person, a decline in the rate of population growth, and increased urbanization. It also has led to a greatly increased environmental impact as *humans against*

nature have gained increasing control over the physical world.

The history of resource exploitation, resource conservation, and environmental protection in the United States has taken place in several phases:

- frontier expansion and resource exploitation with little regard for resource conservation (1607–1870)

- early warnings about the need for resource conservation (1830–1870)

- beginning of the government's role in resource conservation by setting aside and protecting some forests held as public lands (1870–1910)

- split of resource conservationists into *preservationists*, who wanted to protect more publicly owned lands from resource exploitation, and *scientific conservationists*, who believed that resources on public lands could be used now and also protected for future generations through the principles of sustainable yield and multiple use (1911–1932)

- expanding role of the federal government in the management of pubic lands by scientific conservation (1933–1960)

- rise of the environmental and conservation movement to provide increased scientific conservation and preservation of public forests, grasslands, and soil as well as air and water (1960–1980)

- loss of momentum in environmental protection and resource conservation (1981–1989)

There are growing signs that over the next 50 to 75 years we will undergo another major cultural change to one of several possibilities:

- a series of sustainable-earth societies based on humans learning to work and cooperate with nature to preserve the earth's resource base for all species

- a superindustrialized world based on major advances in technology that allow humans even greater control over nature

- a small number of humans in scattered bands trying to survive as modern hunter-gatherers in a world polluted and depleted of resources from nuclear war or excessive industrialization without sufficient resource conservation and environmental protection

In the 1990s and beyond we will have to greatly increase efforts to protect the environment and con resources. Individuals, especially in MDCs, will hav change their lifestyles to reduce waste, environmen radation, and pollution.

Governments will have to cooperate to deal wit global and regional problems such as global warmin ozone depletion, ocean pollution, acid deposition, population growth, tropical deforestation, and the from nonrenewable fossil fuels to energy efficiency renewable energy.

Economic development, population growth, environmental protection, and resource conservation are interrelated and must be dealt with through integrated strategies at local, national, regional, and global levels. Emphasis will have to shift from pollution control to pollution prevention, waste disposal to waste prevention and reduction, species protection to habitat protection, and increased resource use to increased resource conservation.

DISCUSSION TOPICS

1. Those wishing to avoid dealing with environmental and resource problems sometimes argue: "People have always polluted and despoiled this planet, so why all the fuss over pollution and resource conservation? We've survived so far, and for most people things have gotten better, not worse." Identify the core of truth in this position and then discuss its serious deficiencies.

2. Explain how in one sense the roots of our present environmental and resource problems and our increased alienation from nature began with the invention of agriculture about 10,000 years ago.

3. Do you think we would be better off if agriculture had never been discovered and we were still hunters and gatherers today? Explain.

4. Make a list of the major benefits and drawbacks of an advanced industrial society such as the United States. Do you feel that the benefits outweigh the drawbacks? Explain. What are the alternatives?

5. Cornucopians believe that continued economic growth and technological innovation in today's industrial societies offer the best way to solve the environmental and resource problems we face. Neo-Malthusians believe that these problems can be effectively dealt with only by changing from a predominantly industrial society to a sustainable-earth society over the next 50 to 75 years. Which position do you support? Why?

6. Do you believe that a cultural change to a sustainable-earth society is possible over the next 50 to 75 years? What changes, if any, have you made and what changes do you plan to make in your lifestyle to help bring about such a change?

Basic Concepts

Animal and vegetable life is too complicated a problem for human intelligence to solve, and we can never know how wide a circle of disturbance we produce in the harmonies of nature when we throw the smallest pebble into the ocean of organic life.

George Perkins Marsh

CHAPTER 3

Matter and Energy Resources: Types and Concepts

General Questions and Issues

1. What are the major forms of matter, what is matter made of, and what makes matter useful to us as a resource?

2. What are the major forms of energy, what major energy resources do we rely on, and what makes energy useful to us as a resource?

3. What are physical and chemical changes, and what scientific law governs changes of matter from one physical or chemical form to another?

4. What are the three major types of nuclear changes that matter can undergo?

5. What two scientific laws govern changes of energy from one form to another?

6. How can we waste less energy, and how much useful energy is available from different energy resources?

7. How are the scientific laws governing changes of matter and energy from one form to another related to resource use and environmental disruption?

8. What is science and how does it differ from technology?

The laws of thermodynamics control the rise and fall of political systems, the freedom or bondage of nations, the movements of commerce and industry, the origins of wealth and poverty, and the general physical welfare of the human race.

Frederick Soddy, Nobel laureate, chemistry

T his book, your hand, the water you drink, and the air you breathe are all samples of *matter*—the stuff all things are made of. The light and heat streaming from a burning lump of coal and the work you must do to lift this book are examples of *energy*. It is what you and all living things use to move matter around, change its form, or cause a heat transfer between two objects at different temperatures.

This chapter is a brief introduction to what is going on in the world from a physical and chemical standpoint. It describes the major types of matter and energy and the scientific laws governing all changes of matter and energy from one form to another.

The next three chapters are an introduction to what is going on in the world from an ecological standpoint, based on how key physical and chemical processes are integrated into the biological systems we call life.

3-1 MATTER: FORMS, STRUCTURE, AND QUALITY

Physical and Chemical Forms of Matter Anything that has mass (or weight on the earth's surface) and takes up space is **matter**. **Mass** is the amount of "stuff" in an object. All matter found in nature can be viewed as being organized in identifiable patterns, or *levels of organization,* according to size and function (Figure 3-1).

This section is devoted to a discussion of the three lowest levels of organization of matter—subatomic particles, atoms, and molecules—which make up the basic components of all higher levels. Chapter 4 discusses the five higher levels of organization of matter—organisms, populations, communities, ecosystems, and the ecosphere—the major concerns of ecology.

Any matter, such as water, can be found in three *physical forms:* solid (ice), liquid (liquid water), and gas (water vapor). All matter also consists of *chemical forms:* elements, compounds, or mixtures of elements and compounds.

Elements The 92 **elements** that occur naturally on earth are distinctive forms of matter that make up every material substance. Another 15 elements have been artificially synthesized in laboratories. Examples of these basic building blocks of all matter are hydrogen (represented by the symbol H), carbon (C), oxygen (O), nitrogen (N), phosphorus (P), sulfur (S), chlorine (Cl), fluorine (F), sodium (Na), and uranium (U).

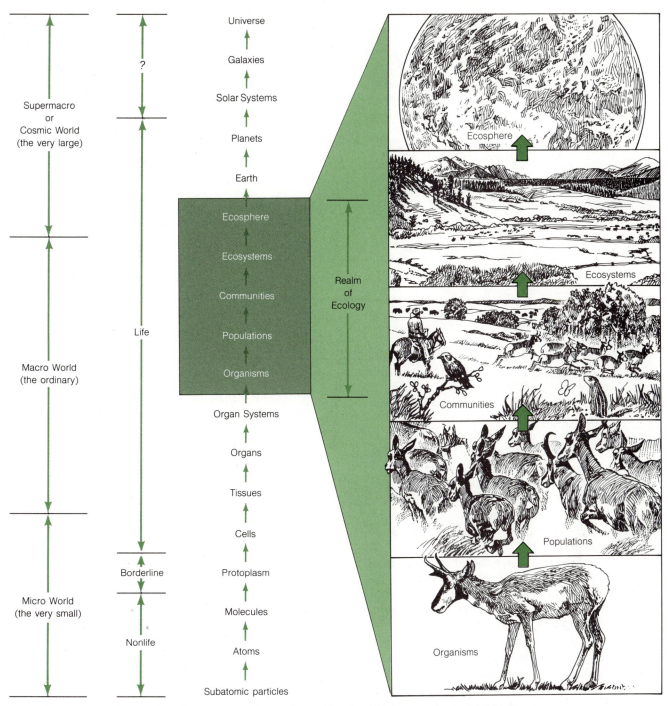

Figure 3-1 Levels of organization of matter, according to size and function. This is one way scientists classify patterns of matter found in nature.

All elements are composed of an incredibly large number of particular types of minute particles called **atoms.** Two or more atoms of the same or different elements can combine to form **molecules.** A few elements are found in nature as molecules. Examples are the nitrogen and oxygen gases making up about 99% of the volume of air we breathe. Two atoms of nitrogen (N) combine to form a nitrogen gas molecule with the shorthand formula N_2 (read as "N-two"). The subscript after the symbol of the element gives the number of atoms of that element in a molecule. Similarly,

most of the oxygen gas in the atmosphere exists as O_2 (read as "O-two") molecules. A small amount of oxygen, found mostly in the upper atmosphere (stratosphere), exists as ozone molecules with the formula O_3 (read as "O-three").

All atoms are made up of even smaller **subatomic particles**: protons, neutrons, and electrons. Each atom of an element has a tiny center, or **nucleus,** which contains almost all of an atom's mass. Each nucleus has a certain number of **protons** (represented by the symbol p), each with a positive (+) electrical charge,

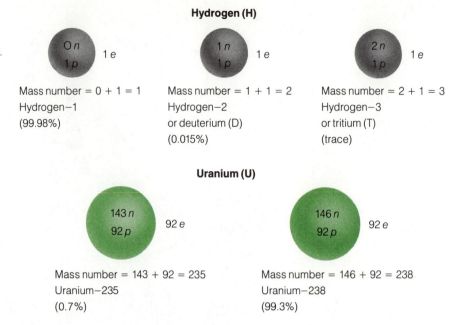

Figure 3-2 Isotopes of hydrogen and uranium. Figures in parentheses show the percent abundance by weight of each isotope in a natural sample of each element.

Hydrogen (H)

$0\,n$
$1\,p$ $1\,e$

Mass number = 0 + 1 = 1
Hydrogen−1
(99.98%)

$1\,n$
$1\,p$ $1\,e$

Mass number = 1 + 1 = 2
Hydrogen−2
or deuterium (D)
(0.015%)

$2\,n$
$1\,p$ $1\,e$

Mass number = 2 + 1 = 3
Hydrogen−3
or tritium (T)
(trace)

Uranium (U)

$143\,n$
$92\,p$ $92\,e$

Mass number = 143 + 92 = 235
Uranium−235
(0.7%)

$146\,n$
$92\,p$ $92\,e$

Mass number = 146 + 92 = 238
Uranium−238
(99.3%)

and uncharged **neutrons** (n). One or more **electrons** (e), each with a negative ($-$) electrical charge, whiz around somewhere outside each nucleus.

Each atom of the same element always has the same number of positively charged protons inside its nucleus and an equal number of negatively charged electrons outside its nucleus. Because of this electrical balance, each atom as a whole has no net electrical charge. For example, each atom of the lightest element, hydrogen, has one positively charged proton in its nucleus and one negatively charged electron outside. Each atom of a much heavier element, uranium, has 92 protons and 92 electrons (Figure 3-2).

Because an electron has an almost negligible mass (or weight) compared to a proton and a neutron, the approximate mass of an atom is determined by the number of neutrons plus the number of protons in its nucleus. This number is called its **mass number**.

Atoms of the same element must have the same number of protons and electrons. However, they may have different numbers of uncharged neutrons in their nuclei, and thus different mass numbers. These different forms of the same element are called **isotopes**.

Isotopes of the same element are identified by attaching the mass number to the name or symbol of the element: hydrogen-1, or H-1; hydrogen-2, or H-2 (common name, deuterium); and hydrogen-3, or H-3 (common name, tritium). A natural sample of an element contains a mixture of its isotopes in a fixed proportion or percent abundance by weight (Figure 3-2).

Atoms of some elements can lose or gain one or more electrons to form **ions**: atoms or groups of atoms with one or more net positive ($+$) or negative ($-$) electrical charges. The number of positive or negative charges is shown as a superscript after the symbol for an atom or group of atoms. Examples of positive ions

are sodium ions (Na^+) and ammonium ions (NH_4^+). Common negative ions are chloride ions (Cl^-), nitrate ions (NO_3^-), and phosphate ions (PO_4^{3-}).

Compounds Most matter exists as **compounds**—combinations of atoms or oppositely charged ions of two or more different elements held together in fixed proportions by attractive forces called chemical bonds. Water, for example, is made up of H_2O (read as "H-two-O") molecules, each consisting of two hydrogen atoms chemically bonded to an oxygen atom. Sodium chloride, or table salt, consists of a network of oppositely charged ions (Na^+Cl^-) held together by the forces of attraction that exist between opposite electric charges.

Compounds can be classified as organic or inorganic. Skin, blood, food, vitamins, oil, gasoline, natural gas, cotton, wool, paper, plastics, detergents, aspirin, penicillin, and many other materials important to you and your lifestyle have one thing in common. They all are **organic compounds,** containing atoms of the element carbon, usually combined with itself and with atoms of one or more other elements such as hydrogen, oxygen, nitrogen, sulfur, phosphorus, chlorine, and fluorine.

The following are examples of the more than 7 million known organic compounds:

- *Hydrocarbons:* compounds of carbon and hydrogen atoms. An example is methane (CH_4), the major component of natural gas.

- *Chlorinated hydrocarbons:* compounds of carbon, hydrogen, and chlorine atoms. Examples are DDT ($C_{14}H_9Cl_5$), an insecticide, and toxic PCBs (such as $C_{12}H_5Cl_5$), used as insulating materials in electric transformers.

- *Chlorofluorocarbons (CFCs):* compounds of carbon, chlorine, and fluorine atoms. An example is Freon-12 (CCl_2F_2), used as a coolant in refrigerators and air conditioners and in making plastics such as styrofoam.

- *Simple sugars:* certain types of compounds of carbon, hydrogen, and oxygen atoms. An example is glucose ($C_6H_{12}O_6$), which most plants and animals break down in their cells to obtain energy.

Larger and more complex organic compounds, called *polymers,* consist of a number of basic structural units (monomers) linked together by chemical bonds. Some important types of organic polymers are

- *Carbohydrates:* made up by linking together a number of simple-sugar molecules such as glucose. Examples are the complex starches in rice and potato plants.

- *Proteins:* produced in plant and animal cells by linking together different numbers and sequences of about 20 different building-block units, or monomers, known as *amino acids.* Most animals, including humans, can make about 10 of these amino acids in their cells. Sufficient quantities of the other 10, known as essential amino acids, must be obtained from food intake to prevent protein deficiency diseases.

- *Nucleic acids:* made by linking together hundreds to thousands of four different types of building-block monomers, called nucleotides, in different numbers and sequences. Examples are various types of DNA and RNA in plant and animal cells. Genetic information coded in the structure of DNA molecules is what makes you different from an oak leaf, a dog, an alligator, or a flea and from your mother and father. This information is contained in sequences of nucleotides in parts of various cellular DNA molecules known as **genes.** Various genes and associated proteins in plant and animal cells are grouped together in **chromosomes,** which carry certain types of genetic information.

Inorganic compounds are combinations of two or more elements other than those used to form organic compounds. Some inorganic compounds you will encounter in this book are sodium chloride (NaCl), water (H_2O), nitric oxide (NO), carbon monoxide (CO), carbon dioxide (CO_2), nitrogen dioxide (NO_2), sulfur dioxide (SO_2), ammonia (NH_3), sulfuric acid (H_2SO_4), and nitric acid (HNO_3).

Matter Quality When does a type of matter become a human resource? There are three requirements. First, it must be available in a useful physical or chemical form, or we must discover a way to convert it to a useful form. Second, it must be concentrated enough to be useful, or we must use energy to concentrate it.

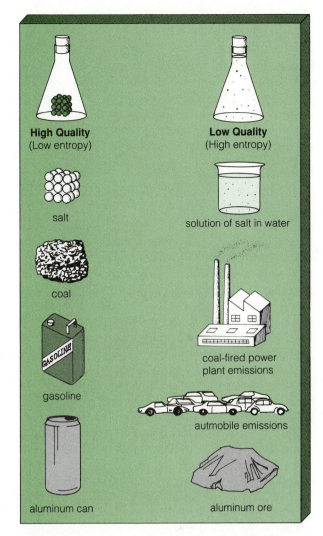

Figure 3-3 Examples of difference in matter quality. High-quality matter is fairly easy to get and is concentrated. It is ordered and thus has low entropy. Low-quality matter is hard to get and is dispersed. It is disorganized and has high entropy.

Third, it must not cost too much to make the resource available. Otherwise, few people could afford to use it.

There are two keys to resource availability: human ingenuity and an ample supply of affordable energy. **Matter quality** is a measure of how useful a matter resource is, based on its availability and concentration (Figure 3–3). **High-quality matter** is organized, concentrated, and usually found near the earth's surface. It has great potential for use as a matter resource. **Low-quality matter** is disorganized, dilute or dispersed, and often found deep underground. It usually has little potential for use as a matter resource.

Scientists use the term **entropy** as a measure of disorder or randomness. High-quality matter, which is organized and concentrated, such as concentrated aluminum ore, has low entropy. Low-quality matter, which is disorganized and dispersed, such as dilute aluminum ore, has high entropy.

An aluminum can is a more concentrated, higher-quality form of aluminum than aluminum ore with the same amount of aluminum. That is why it usually takes less energy, water, and money to recycle an aluminum can than to get new aluminum from ore. This assumes that the government doesn't distort the effects of this physical principle by giving aluminum mining and processing companies tax breaks or other subsidies to make up the difference in cost.

3-2 ENERGY: TYPES, FORMS, AND QUALITY

Types of Energy Energy, not money, is the real "currency" of the world. We depend on it to grow our food, keep us and other living things alive, and to warm and cool our bodies and the buildings where we work and live. We also use it to move people and other forms of matter from one place to another and to change matter from one physical or chemical form to another.

Energy is the ability to do work or to cause a heat transfer between two objects at different temperatures. **Work** is what happens when a force is used to push, pull, pump, or lift a sample of matter, such as this book, over some distance. Everything going on in and around us is based on work in which one form of energy is transformed into one or more other forms of energy.

Scientists classify most forms of energy as either potential or kinetic. **Kinetic energy** is the energy that matter has because of its motion and mass. Examples include a moving car, a falling rock, a speeding bullet, and the flow of water or charged particles (electrical energy). **Potential energy** is stored energy that is potentially available for use. A rock held in your hand, a stick of dynamite, still water behind a dam, and nuclear energy stored in the nuclei of atoms all have potential energy. Other examples are the chemical energy stored in molecules of gasoline and in the carbohydrates, proteins, and fats of the food you eat.

Heat refers to the total energy of all the moving atoms or molecules in a given substance. **Temperature** is a measure of the average speed of motion of the atoms or molecules in a substance at a given moment. A substance can have a high content (much mass and many moving atoms or molecules) but a low temperature (low average molecular speed). For example, the total heat content of a lake or an ocean is enormous, but its average temperature is low. Other samples of matter can have a low heat content and a high temperature. For example, a cup of hot coffee or a burning match have a much lower heat content than an ocean or a lake but have a much higher temperature.

We use fairly dilute, moderate-temperature heat energy for heating enclosed spaces or buildings (space heating) to between 20°C and 26°C (65°F and 78°F). We use more concentrated, higher-temperature heat at one hundred to several hundred degrees to boil water, cook food, and carry out some industrial processes. Highly concentrated, high-temperature heat at several thousand degrees is used to melt metals, produce superheated steam to spin turbines that produce electricity, and carry out various industrial processes.

Energy Resources Used by People We talk about heating buildings by burning oil, gasoline, coal, or wood or by fissioning uranium nuclei to produce electricity. But the truth is that *the direct input of essentially inexhaustible solar energy alone supplies 99% of the energy used to heat the earth and all buildings free of charge.* Were it not for this direct input of energy from the sun, the average temperature would be −240°C (−400°F) and life as we know it would not have arisen. This input of solar energy also continuously recycles the carbon, oxygen, water, and other chemicals we and other organisms need to stay alive and healthy and to reproduce.

Most people think of solar energy in terms of direct heat from the sun. But, broadly defined, **solar energy** includes *direct* energy from the sun and a number of *indirect* forms of energy produced by the direct input. Major indirect forms of solar energy include wind, falling and flowing water (hydropower), and biomass (solar energy converted to chemical energy in trees and other plants).

We have learned how to capture and use some of these direct and indirect forms of solar energy. Passive solar energy systems capture and store direct solar energy and use it to heat buildings and water without the use of mechanical devices. Examples are a well-insulated, airtight house with large triple-paned windows that face the sun and the use of rock, cement, or water to store and release heat slowly.

Direct solar energy can also be captured by active solar energy systems. For example, specially designed roof-mounted collectors concentrate direct solar energy; pumps transfer this heat to water, to the interior of a building, or to insulated storage tanks of stone or water. We have also developed wind turbines and hydroelectric power plants to convert indirect solar energy in the form of wind and falling or flowing water into electricity. Solar cells convert solar energy directly into electricity in one simple, nonpolluting step.

We have discovered a number of ways to use various forms of perpetual, renewable, and nonrenewable energy resources to supplement the direct input of solar energy and sell this energy to users. This *supplemental commercial energy* makes up the remaining 1% of the energy we use on earth (Figure 3–4).

Worldwide, three-fourths of the commercial energy used to supplement direct solar energy comes from burning nonrenewable fossil fuels (oil, coal, natural gas) to provide heat and to produce electricity and from burning gasoline processed from crude oil to move vehicles. A moderate amount comes from burning potentially renewable biomass (wood, dung, crop residues, and trash) to produce heat. A small amount comes from using falling or flowing water (hydropower) and controlled nuclear fission to produce electricity. A very small amount (less than 1%) comes from using heat from the earth's interior (geothermal energy) and wind to produce electricity and from using solar energy (passive and active systems) to heat buildings and water.

Not wasting any form of energy and improving energy efficiency save money and make nonrenewable energy resources such as oil, coal, natural gas, and uranium last longer. This also reduces the environmental impact of using any form of energy.

At one extreme, the United States, with 4.8% of the world's population, uses 25% of the world's commercial energy. At the other extreme, India, with about 16% of the world's people, uses only about 1.5% of the world's commercial energy. In 1989 the 249 million Americans used more energy for air conditioning alone than the 1.1 billion Chinese used for all purposes.

The most important supplemental source of energy for LDCs is potentially renewable biomass—especially fuelwood—the main source of energy for heating and cooking for roughly half the world's population. One-fourth of the world's population in MDCs may soon face shortages of oil (see Case Study on p. 14), but half the world's population in LDCs already faces a fuelwood shortage.

In 1850 the United States and most other MDCs had a decentralized energy system based on locally available renewable resources, primarily wood. Today they have centralized energy systems based on nonrenewable fossil fuels, especially oil and natural gas, increasingly produced in one part of the world and transported to and used in another part. By 1986 about 87% of the commercial energy used in the United States was provided by burning oil, coal, and natural gas, with the largest percentage (41%) coming from oil (Figure 3–5).

This shift fueled the rapid economic development of the MDCs, especially since the 1950s. But it has also caused most MDCs to become addicted to oil—a nonrenewable resource that is being rapidly depleted. Before this shift, countries, communities, and individuals got most of the energy they needed from local resources. Today they are dependent on large national and multinational energy companies, government policies, and other countries for most of their energy as well for the prices they pay for such energy.

Energy Quality Energy varies in its quality, or ability to do useful work. **Energy quality** is a measure of

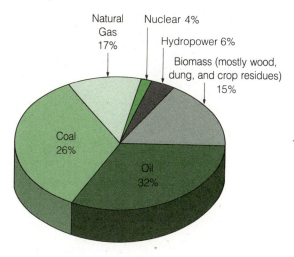

Figure 3-4 World consumption of commercial energy by source in 1987. (Sources: U.S. Department of Energy and Worldwatch Institute)

energy usefulness (Figure 3–6). **High-quality energy** is organized or concentrated and has great ability to perform useful work. It has low entropy. Examples of these useful forms of energy are electricity, coal, gasoline, concentrated sunlight, nuclei of uranium-235, and high-temperature heat.

By contrast, **low-quality energy** is disorganized or dilute and has little ability to do useful work. It has high entropy. An example is the low-temperature heat in the air around you or in a river, lake, or ocean. For instance, the total amount of low-temperature heat stored in the Atlantic Ocean is greater than the amount of high-quality chemical energy stored in all the oil deposits in Saudi Arabia. But heat is so widely dispersed in the ocean that we can't do much with it. This dispersed heat, like that in the air around us, can't be used to move things and to heat things to high temperatures.

We use energy to accomplish certain tasks, each requiring a certain minimum energy quality (Figure 3–7). Very high-quality electrical energy is needed to run lights, electric motors, and electronic devices. We need high-quality mechanical energy to move a car. But we need only low-temperature heat (less than 100°C) to heat homes and other buildings.

Unfortunately, many forms of high-quality energy, such as high-temperature heat, electricity, gasoline, hydrogen gas (a useful fuel that can be produced by heating or passing electricity through water), and concentrated sunlight, do not occur naturally. We must use other forms of high-quality energy such as fossil, wood, and nuclear fuels to produce, concentrate, and store them, or to upgrade their quality so that they can be used to perform certain tasks.

Figure 3-5 Changes in U.S. consumption of commercial nonrenewable fossil fuel and nuclear energy and renewable energy resources between 1850 and 1986. Relative circle diameter indicates the total annual amount of energy used. (Data from U.S Department of Energy)

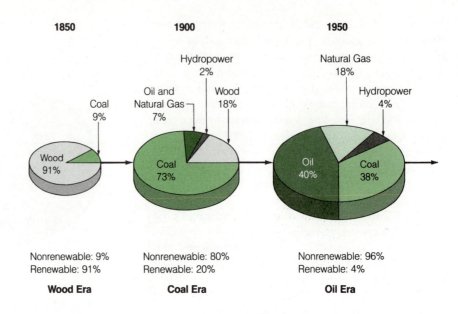

1850

Wood
91%

Coal
9%

Nonrenewable: 9%
Renewable: 91%

Wood Era

1900

Hydropower
2%

Oil and
Natural Gas
7%

Wood
18%

Coal
73%

Nonrenewable: 80%
Renewable: 20%

Coal Era

1950

Natural Gas
18%

Hydropower
4%

Oil
40%

Coal
38%

Nonrenewable: 96%
Renewable: 4%

Oil Era

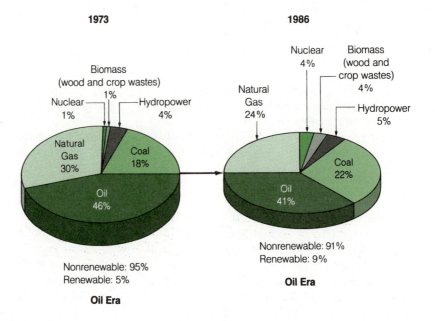

1973

Biomass
(wood and crop wastes)
1%

Nuclear
1%

Hydropower
4%

Natural
Gas
30%

Coal
18%

Oil
46%

Nonrenewable: 95%
Renewable: 5%

Oil Era

1986

Nuclear
4%

Biomass
(wood and
crop wastes)
4%

Natural
Gas
24%

Hydropower
5%

Coal
22%

Oil
41%

Nonrenewable: 91%
Renewable: 9%

Oil Era

3-3 PHYSICAL AND CHEMICAL CHANGES AND THE LAW OF CONSERVATION OF MATTER

Physical Changes Elements and compounds can undergo physical and chemical changes; each change either gives off or requires energy, usually in the form of heat. A **physical change** is one that involves no change in chemical composition. For example, cutting a piece of aluminum foil into small pieces is a physical change. Each cut piece is still aluminum.

Changing a substance from one physical state to another is also a physical change. For example, when solid water, or ice, is melted or liquid water is boiled,

none of the H_2O molecules involved is altered; instead they are organized in different spatial patterns. In ice the water molecules are held close together in an ordered (low-entropy) pattern. In liquid water the molecules are fairly close together but are moving around in a fairly disorganized (moderate-entropy) pattern. Molecules of water vapor are relatively far apart and are moving in a highly chaotic (high-entropy) manner (Figure 3-3).

Chemical Changes In a **chemical change**, or **chemical reaction**, a change takes place in the chemical composition of the elements or compounds involved. Like physical changes, some chemical changes won't

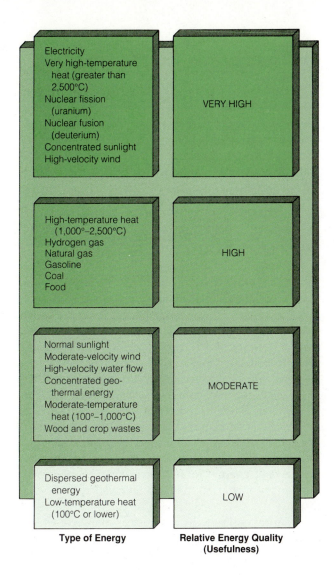

Type of Energy — **Relative Energy Quality (Usefulness)**

VERY HIGH
- Electricity
- Very high-temperature heat (greater than 2,500°C)
- Nuclear fission (uranium)
- Nuclear fusion (deuterium)
- Concentrated sunlight
- High-velocity wind

HIGH
- High-temperature heat (1,000°–2,500°C)
- Hydrogen gas
- Natural gas
- Gasoline
- Coal
- Food

MODERATE
- Normal sunlight
- Moderate-velocity wind
- High-velocity water flow
- Concentrated geothermal energy
- Moderate-temperature heat (100°–1,000°C)
- Wood and crop wastes

LOW
- Dispersed geothermal energy
- Low-temperature heat (100°C or lower)

Figure 3-6 Generalized ranking of quality or usefulness of different types of energy.

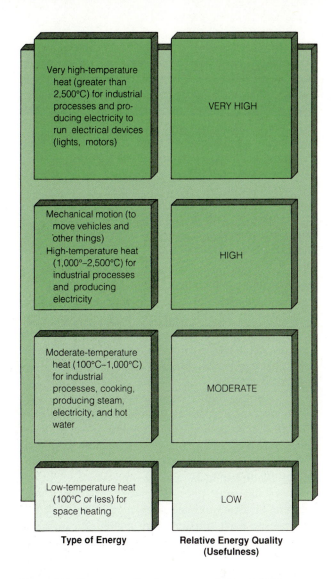

Type of Energy — **Relative Energy Quality (Usefulness)**

VERY HIGH
- Very high-temperature heat (greater than 2,500°C) for industrial processes and producing electricity to run electrical devices (lights, motors)

HIGH
- Mechanical motion (to move vehicles and other things)
- High-temperature heat (1,000°–2,500°C) for industrial processes and producing electricity

MODERATE
- Moderate-temperature heat (100°C–1,000°C) for industrial processes, cooking, producing steam, electricity, and hot water

LOW
- Low-temperature heat (100°C or less) for space heating

Figure 3-7 General quality of energy needed to perform various energy tasks. To avoid unnecessary energy waste, it is best to match the quality of an energy source (Figure 3-6) to the quality of energy needed to perform a task—that is, not to use energy of a higher quality than necessary. This saves energy and usually saves money.

happen without an input of energy and others give off energy.

For example, when coal (which is mostly carbon, or C) burns, it combines with oxygen gas (O_2) from the atmosphere to form the gaseous compound carbon dioxide (CO_2). In this case energy is given off, explaining why coal is a useful fuel.

A chemical change can be represented in shorthand form by a chemical equation using the chemical formulas for the elements and compounds involved. Formulas of the original chemicals, called *reactants*, are placed to the left. Formulas of the new chemicals produced, called *products*, are placed to the right. An arrow, indicating that a chemical change has taken place, is placed between the reactants and products. For example, the burning of coal can be represented as follows:

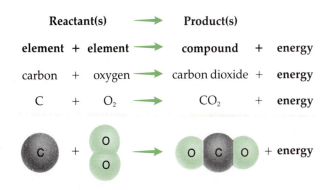

Reactant(s)	$\longrightarrow$	Product(s)
element + element	$\longrightarrow$	compound + energy
carbon + oxygen	$\longrightarrow$	carbon dioxide + energy
C + O_2	$\longrightarrow$	CO_2 + energy

The equation for this reaction shows how the burning of coal or any carbon-containing compounds, such as those in wood, natural gas, oil, and gasoline, adds carbon dioxide gas to the atmosphere. This can cause warming of the atmosphere by intensifying the greenhouse effect.

When complex, solid and liquid organic compounds in carbon-containing fuels are burned, they release simple gaseous molecules such as carbon dioxide into the atmosphere. This conversion of complex, solid or liquid ordered forms of matter to less complex, more disordered gaseous forms of matter increases the entropy of the environment.

The Law of Conservation of Matter: There Is No Away The earth loses some gaseous molecules to space and it gains small amounts of matter from space, mostly in the form of stony or metallic bodies (meteorites). However, these losses and gains of matter are minute compared to the earth's total mass—somewhat like the world's beaches losing or adding a few grains of sand.

This means that *the earth has essentially all the matter it will ever have.* Fortunately, over billions of years nature has developed systems for continuously recycling key chemicals back and forth between the nonliving environment (soil, air, and water) and the living environment (plants, animals, and decomposers).

You, like most people, probably talk about consuming or using up material resources. But the truth is that we don't consume any matter. We only use some of the earth's resources for a while. We take materials from the earth, carry them to another part of the globe, and process them into products. These products are used and then discarded, reused, or recycled.

In making and using products, we may change various elements and compounds from one physical or chemical form to another, but we neither create from nothing nor destroy to nothingness any measurable amount of matter. This fact, based on many thousands of measurements of matter undergoing physical and chemical changes, is known as the **law of conservation of matter**. In other words, *in all physical and chemical changes we can't create or destroy any of the atoms involved. All we can do is rearrange them into different spatial patterns (physical changes) or different combinations (chemical changes).*

The law of conservation of matter means that there is no "away." *Everything we think we have thrown away is still here with us in one form or another.* We can collect dust and soot from the smokestacks of industrial plants, but these solid wastes must then go somewhere. We can collect garbage and remove solid grease and sludge from sewage, but these substances must be burned (perhaps causing air pollution), dumped into rivers, lakes, and oceans (perhaps causing water pollution),

deposited on the land (perhaps causing soil and groundwater pollution), recycled, or reused. *There is no away.*

We can make the environment cleaner and convert some potentially harmful chemicals to less harmful or even harmless physical or chemical forms. But the law of conservation of matter means that we will always be faced with the problem of what to do with some quantity of wastes—although we don't have to create nearly as much as we presently do.

3-4   NUCLEAR CHANGES

Natural Radioactivity In addition to physical and chemical changes, matter can undergo a third type of change known as a **nuclear change**. It occurs when nuclei of certain isotopes spontaneously change or are forced to change into one or more different isotopes. The three major types of nuclear change are natural radioactivity, nuclear fission, and nuclear fusion.

Unlike chemical and physical changes, nuclear changes involve conversion of a small amount of mass in a nucleus into energy. The law of conservation of matter does not apply to nuclear changes. This type of change is governed by the **law of conservation of matter and energy**: In any nuclear change the total amount of matter and energy involved remains the same.

Natural radioactivity is a nuclear change in which unstable nuclei spontaneously shoot out "chunks" of mass (usually alpha or beta particles), energy (gamma rays), or both at a fixed rate. An isotope of an atom whose unstable nucleus spontaneously emits fast-moving particles, high-energy radiation, or both is called a **radioactive isotope**, or **radioisotope**.

Radiation emitted by radioisotopes is called **ionizing radiation**. It has enough energy to dislodge one or more electrons from atoms it hits to form positively charged ions, which can react with and damage living tissue. The two most common types of particles emitted by radioactive isotopes are high-speed **alpha particles** (positively charged chunks of matter that consist of two protons and two neutrons) and **beta particles** (negatively charged electrons). The most common form of ionizing electromagnetic radiation released from radioisotopes is high-energy **gamma rays**. Figure 3-8 shows the relative penetrating power of alpha, beta, and gamma ionizing radiation. Any exposure to ionizing radiation can damage tissue in your body.

Nuclear Fission: Splitting Nuclei **Nuclear fission** is a nuclear change in which nuclei of certain isotopes with large mass numbers (such as uranium-235) are split apart into lighter nuclei when struck by slow- or fast-moving neutrons; this process releases more neu-

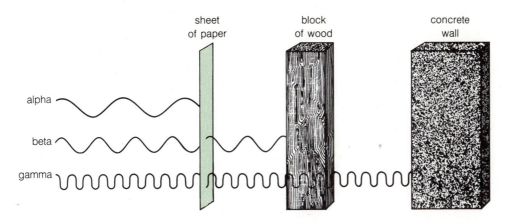

Figure 3-8 The three major types of ionizing radiation emitted by radioactive isotopes vary considerably in their penetrating power.

sheet of paper

block of wood

concrete wall

alpha

beta

gamma

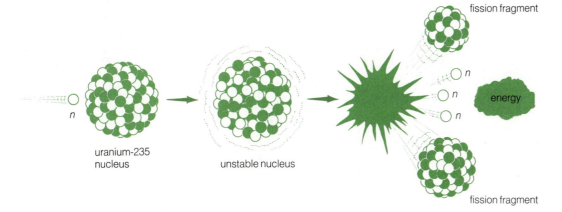

Figure 3-9 Fission of a uranium-235 nucleus by a slow-moving neutron.

fission fragment

n

energy

n

n

uranium-235 nucleus

unstable nucleus

fission fragment

trons and energy (Figure 3-9). The two or three neutrons produced by each fission can be used to split many additional uranium-235 nuclei if enough nuclei are present to provide the **critical mass** needed for efficient capture of these neutrons.

These multiple fissions taking place within the critical mass represent a **chain reaction** that releases an enormous amount of energy (Figure 3-10). Living cells can be damaged by the ionizing radiation released by the radioactive lighter nuclei and the neutrons produced by nuclear fission.

In an atomic or nuclear fission bomb, a massive amount of energy is released in a fraction of a second in an uncontrolled nuclear fission chain reaction. This reaction is initiated by an explosive charge, which suddenly pushes a mass of fissionable fuel together from all sides, causing the fuel to reach the critical mass needed for a massive chain reaction.

In the nuclear reactor of a nuclear electric power plant, the rate at which the nuclear fission chain reaction takes place is controlled so that only one of each two or three neutrons released is used to split another nucleus. In conventional nuclear fission reactors, nuclei of uranium-235 are split apart and release energy. The heat released is used to produce high-pressure steam, which spins generators to produce electricity. Another fissionable radioisotope is plutonium-239, formed from

nonfissionable uranium-238 in breeder nuclear fission reactors, which may be developed in the future to extend supplies of uranium.

Nuclear Fusion: Forcing Nuclei to Combine

Nuclear fusion is a nuclear change in which two nuclei of isotopes of light elements such as hydrogen are forced together at extremely high temperatures until they fuse to form a heavier nucleus, releasing energy in the process. Temperatures of 100 million°C to 1 billion°C are usually needed to force the positively charged nuclei (which strongly repel one another) to join together. High-temperature fusion is much harder to initiate than fission, but once started, it releases far more energy per gram of fuel than fission. Fusion of hydrogen atoms to form helium atoms is the source of energy in the sun and other stars. Some controversial evidence indicates that it may be possible to carry out nuclear fusion near room temperature. Even if so, it is not clear whether the energy output will be large enough to yield high-temperature heat.

After World War II the principle of uncontrolled nuclear fusion was used to develop extremely powerful hydrogen, or thermonuclear, bombs and missile warheads. These weapons involve the D-T fusion reaction, in which a hydrogen-2, or deuterium (D), nucleus and a hydrogen-3, or tritium (T), nucleus are

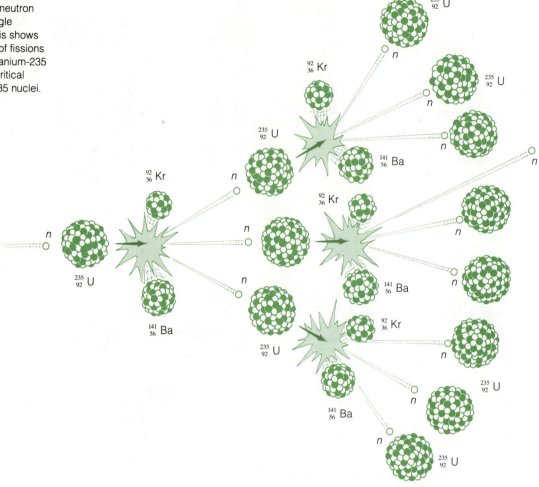

Figure 3-10 A nuclear chain reaction initiated by one neutron triggering fission in a single uranium-235 nucleus. This shows only a few of the trillions of fissions caused when a single uranium-235 nucleus is split within a critical mass of other uranium-235 nuclei.

fused to form a larger, helium-4 nucleus, a neutron, and energy (Figure 3-11).

Scientists have also tried to develop controlled nuclear fusion, in which the D-T reaction is used to produce heat that can be converted into electricity. However, this process is still at the laboratory stage despite 40 years of research. If it ever becomes technologically and economically feasible—a big *if*—it is not projected to be a commercially important source of energy until 2050 or later, if ever.

3-5 THE FIRST AND SECOND LAWS OF ENERGY

First Law of Energy: You Can't Get Something for Nothing In studying millions of falling objects, physical and chemical changes, and changes of temperature in living and nonliving systems, scientists have observed and measured energy being changed from one form to another. However, they have never been able to detect any creation or destruction of energy in any chemical or physical change.

This information is summarized in the **law of conservation of energy**, also known as the **first law of energy or thermodynamics**. According to this scientific law, in any physical or chemical change, in any movement of matter from one place to another, and in any change in temperature, energy is neither created nor destroyed but merely transformed from one form to another. In other words, the energy gained or lost by any living or nonliving *system*—any collection of matter under study—must equal the energy lost or gained by its *surroundings* or *environment*—everything outside the system.

This law means that we can never get more energy out of an energy transformation process than we put in: *Energy input always equals energy output; we can't get something for nothing (there is no free lunch).*

Second Law of Energy: You Can't Break Even
Because the first law of energy states that energy can neither be created nor destroyed, you might think that there will always be enough energy. Yet if you fill a car's tank with gasoline and drive around or if you use a flashlight battery until it is dead, you have lost

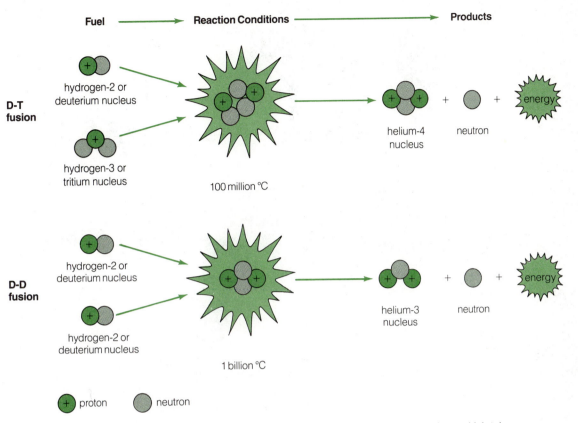

Fuel → Reaction Conditions → Products

D-T fusion

hydrogen-2 or deuterium nucleus

hydrogen-3 or tritium nucleus

100 million °C

helium-4 nucleus + neutron + energy

D-D fusion

hydrogen-2 or deuterium nucleus

hydrogen-2 or deuterium nucleus

1 billion °C

helium-3 nucleus + neutron + energy

+ proton   ⬤ neutron

Figure 3-11 The deuterium-tritium (D-T) and deuterium-deuterium (D-D) nuclear fusion reactions, which take place at extremely high temperatures. Some unconfirmed experiments in 1989 suggested that some type of nuclear fusion of deuterium nuclei may be possible at room temperature.

something. If it isn't energy, what is it? The answer is energy quality.

Millions of measurements by scientists have shown that in any conversion of energy from one form to another, there is always a decrease in energy quality or the amount of useful energy. This summary of what we always find occurring in nature is known as the **second law of energy**: In any conversion of energy from one form to another some of the initial energy input is always degraded to lower-quality, less-useful energy, usually low-temperature heat that flows into the environment. This low-quality, high-entropy energy is so disordered and dispersed that it is unable to perform useful work. This law of energy quality degradation is also known as the **second law of thermodynamics**. No one has ever found a violation of this fundamental scientific law.

Consider three examples of the second energy law in action. First, when a car is driven, only about 10% of the high-quality chemical energy available in its gasoline fuel is converted to mechanical energy to propel the vehicle and electrical energy to run its electrical systems. The remaining 90% is degraded to low-quality heat that is released into the environment and eventually lost into space. Second, when electrical energy flows through filament wires in an incandes-

cent light bulb, it is changed into a mixture of about 5% useful radiant energy, or light, and 95% low-quality heat that flows into the environment.

A third example of the degradation of energy quality is illustrated in Figure 3-12: a green plant converts solar energy to high-quality chemical energy stored in molecules of glucose and low-quality heat given off to the environment. When you eat a plant food, such as an apple, its high-quality chemical energy is transformed within your body to high-quality electrical and mechanical energy (used to move your body and perform other life processes) and low-quality heat.

According to the first energy law, we will never run out of energy because energy can neither be created nor destroyed. But according to the second energy law, the overall supply of concentrated, high-quality energy available to us from all sources is being continually depleted as it is converted to low-quality energy. *Not only can we not get something for nothing in terms of energy quantity (the first energy law), we can't break even in terms of energy quality (the second energy law).* In using energy, we always decrease the amount of useful energy and increase entropy in the environment.

The second energy law also means that *we can never recycle or reuse high-quality energy to perform useful work.* Once the concentrated, high-quality energy in a piece

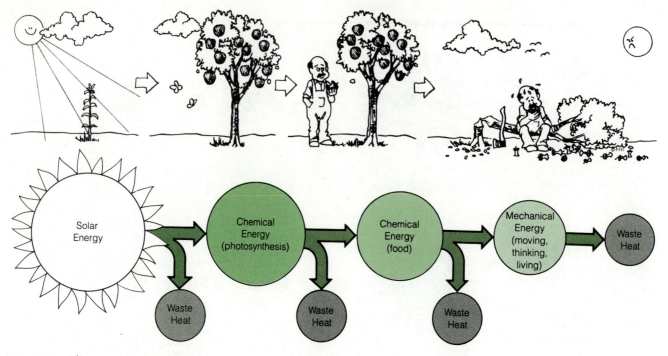

Figure 3-12 The second energy law in action in living systems. When energy is changed from one form to another, some of the initial input of high-quality energy is degraded, usually to low-quality heat, which is added to the environment.

of food, a gallon of gasoline, a lump of coal, or a piece of uranium is released, it is degraded into dispersed, low-quality heat that flows into the environment. We can heat up air or water at a low temperature and upgrade it to high-quality energy. But the second energy law tells us that it will take more high-quality energy to do this than we get.

Life and the Second Energy Law To form and preserve the highly ordered arrangement of molecules and the organized network of chemical changes in your body, you must continually get and use high-quality matter resources and energy resources from your surroundings. As you use these resources, you add disordered, low-quality heat and low-quality waste matter to your surroundings.

For example, your body continuously gives off heat equal to that of a 100-watt light bulb—the reason a closed room full of people gets warm. You also continuously give off molecules of carbon dioxide gas and water vapor that become dispersed in the atmosphere.

Planting, growing, processing, and cooking the foods you eat all require high-quality energy and matter resources that add low-quality heat and waste materials to the environment. In addition, enormous amounts of low-quality heat and waste matter are added to the environment when concentrated deposits of minerals and fuels are extracted from the earth, processed, and used or burned to heat and cool the buildings you use, to transport you, and to make roads, clothes, shelter, and other items you use.

Some of these processes create order in the form of complex organic molecules and living organisms. But, at the same time, these processes require an increase in disorder, or entropy, in the sun and in the earth's environment. Measurements show that the total amount of entropy, in the form of low-quality heat and low-quality matter, added to the environment to keep you (or any living thing) alive and to provide the items you use is much greater than the order maintained in your body.

Thus, *all forms of life are tiny pockets of order maintained by creating a sea of disorder in their environment. The primary characteristic of any advanced industrial society is an ever-increasing flow of high-quality energy and matter resources to maintain the order in human bodies and the larger pockets of order we call civilization.* As a result, today's advanced industrial societies are increasing the entropy of the environment more than at any other time in human history.

This is the entropy trap. The second energy law tells us that we can't avoid increasing the entropy of the environment, but we can reduce or minimize the amount we add.

3-6 ENERGY EFFICIENCY AND NET USEFUL ENERGY

Increasing Energy Efficiency The two energy laws are important tools in helping us decide how to reduce unnecessary energy waste by improving energy effi-

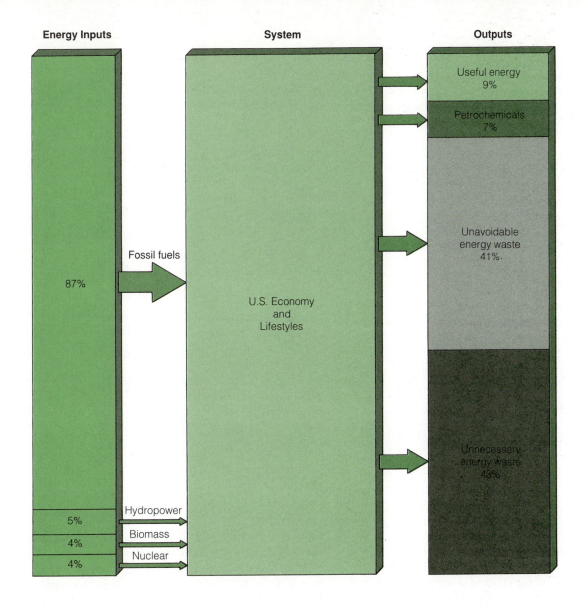

Energy Inputs

87%

5%

4%

4%

Fossil fuels

Hydropower

Biomass

Nuclear

System

U.S. Economy
and
Lifestyles

Outputs

Useful energy
9%

Petrochemicals
7%

Unavoidable
energy waste
41%

Unnecessary
energy waste
43%

Figure 3-13 Flow of commercial supplemental energy through the U.S. economy. Note that only 16% of all commercial energy used in the United States ends up performing useful tasks or is converted to petrochemicals. The rest is automatically wasted because of the second law of energy (41%) or is wasted unnecessarily (43%).

ciency and in evaluating the net useful energy available from various energy resources. For example, only 16% of all the commercially produced energy that flows through the U.S. economy performs useful work or is used to make petrochemicals, which are used to produce plastics, drugs, and many other products (Figure 3-13). *This means that 84% of all energy used in the United States is wasted.* About 41% of this energy is wasted automatically because of the energy quality tax imposed by the second energy law. But 43% of the commercial energy used in the United States is unnecessarily wasted.

One way to cut much of this energy waste and save money, at least in the long run, is to increase **energy efficiency.** This is the percentage of total energy input that does useful work and is not converted to low-quality, essentially useless heat in an energy conversion system. The energy conversion devices we use

vary considerably in their energy efficiencies (Figure 3-14). We can reduce waste by using the most efficient processes or devices available and by trying to make them more efficient.

We can save energy and money by buying the most energy-efficient home heating systems, water heaters, cars, air conditioners, refrigerators, and other household appliances available. The initial cost of the most energy efficient models is usually higher, but in the long run they usually save money by having a lower **life-cycle cost:** the initial cost plus lifetime operating costs.

The net efficiency of the entire energy delivery process of a heating system, water heater, or car is determined by finding the efficiency of each energy conversion step in the process. These steps include extracting the fuel, purifying and upgrading it to a useful form, transporting it, and finally using it.

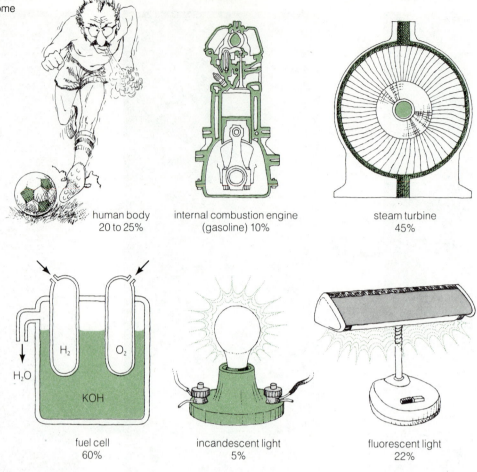

Figure 3-14 Energy efficiency of some common energy conversion devices.

human body
20 to 25%

internal combustion engine
(gasoline) 10%

steam turbine
45%

fuel cell
60%

incandescent light
5%

fluorescent light
22%

Figure 3-15 shows how net energy efficiencies are determined for heating a well-insulated home **(1)** passively with an input of direct solar energy through windows facing the sun and **(2)** with electricity produced at a nuclear power plant, transported by wire to the home, and converted to heat (electric resistance heating). This analysis shows that the process of converting the high-quality nuclear energy in nuclear fuel to high-quality heat at several thousand degrees, converting this heat to high-quality electricity, and then using the electricity to provide low-quality heat for warming a house to only about 20°C (68°F) is extremely wasteful of high-quality energy. By contrast, it is much less wasteful to use a passive or active solar heating system to obtain low-quality heat from the environment and, if necessary, raise its temperature slightly to supply space heating.

Using high-quality energy to provide low-quality heat is like using a chain saw to cut butter or a sledgehammer to kill a fly. A general rule of energy use is the *principle of matching energy quality to energy tasks*: Don't use high-quality energy to do something that can be done with using lower-quality energy (Figures 3-6, 3-7).

Figure 3-16 lists the net energy efficiencies for a variety of space-heating systems. It shows that the most energy-efficient way to provide heating, espe-

cially in a cold climate, is to build a superinsulated house. Such a house is so heavily insulated and airtight that even in areas where winter temperatures fall to −40°C (−40°F), all of its space heating can usually be supplied by a combination of passive solar gain (about 59%), waste heat from appliances (33%), and body heat from occupants (8%).

Passive solar heating, which has been used for thousands of years, is the next most efficient and cheapest method of heating a house, followed by one of the new, high-efficiency, natural gas furnaces. The least efficient, most expensive way to heat a house is with electricity produced by nuclear power plants. For example, in 1988 the average price of obtaining 250,000 kilocalories (1 million British thermal units, or Btus) for heating space or water in the United States was $5.34 using natural gas, $5.87 using fuel oil, and $22.83 using electricity.

Utility companies often run advertisements urging people to buy heat pumps, mostly because their combined heating and air conditioning systems run on electricity. A heat pump is an efficient way to heat a house as long as the outside temperature does not fall below −15°C (4.5°F). But when it does, these devices begin using electric resistance heating, the most expensive, energy-wasting way to heat any space. Heat pumps are useful in areas with warm climates. But in

Passive Solar

Electricity from Nuclear Power Plant

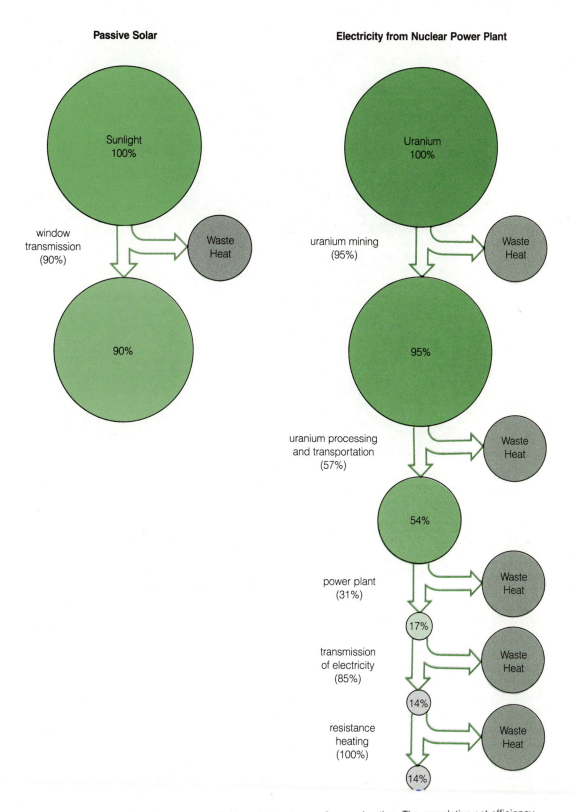

Figure 3-15 Comparison of net energy efficiency for two types of space heating. The cumulative net efficiency is obtained by multiplying the percentage shown inside the circle for each step by the energy efficiency for that step (shown in parentheses). Usually, the greater the number of steps in an energy conversion process, the lower its net energy efficiency.

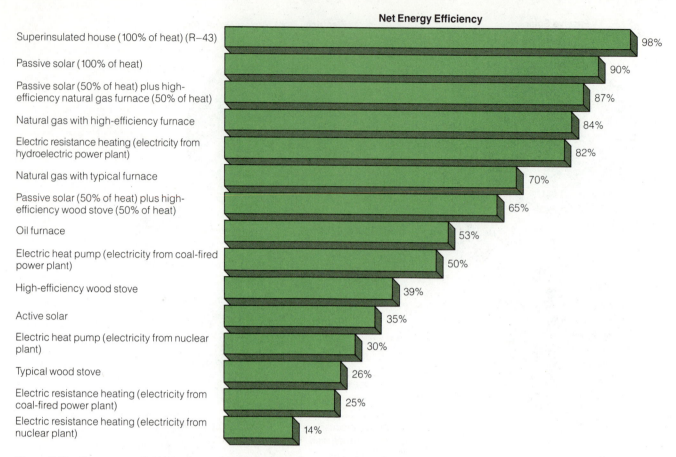

Net Energy Efficiency

Superinsulated house (100% of heat) (R–43)	98%
Passive solar (100% of heat)	90%
Passive solar (50% of heat) plus high-efficiency natural gas furnace (50% of heat)	87%
Natural gas with high-efficiency furnace	84%
Electric resistance heating (electricity from hydroelectric power plant)	82%
Natural gas with typical furnace	70%
Passive solar (50% of heat) plus high-efficiency wood stove (50% of heat)	65%
Oil furnace	53%
Electric heat pump (electricity from coal-fired power plant)	50%
High-efficiency wood stove	39%
Active solar	35%
Electric heat pump (electricity from nuclear plant)	30%
Typical wood stove	26%
Electric resistance heating (electricity from coal-fired power plant)	25%
Electric resistance heating (electricity from nuclear plant)	14%

Figure 3-16 Net energy efficiencies for various ways to heat an enclosed space such as a house.

such areas their main use is for air conditioning. The air conditioning units with most heat pumps are much less energy-efficient than many stand-alone units.

A similar analysis of net energy efficiency shows that the least efficient and most expensive way to heat water for washing and bathing is to use electricity produced by nuclear power plants. The most efficient method is to use a tankless, instant water heater fired by natural gas or liquefied petroleum gas (LPG). Such heaters fit under a sink and burn fuel only when the hot water faucet is turned on, heating the water instantly as it flows through a small burner chamber and providing hot water only when and as long as it is needed. In contrast, conventional natural gas and electric resistance heaters keep a large tank of water hot all day and night and can run out after a long shower or two. Tankless heaters are widely used in many parts of Europe and are slowly beginning to appear in the United States. A well-insulated, conventional natural gas or LPG water heater is also efficient.

As mentioned earlier, the net energy efficiency of a car powered with a conventional internal combustion engine is only about 10%. An electric engine with batteries recharged by electricity from a hydroelectric power plant has a net efficiency almost three times that of a gasoline-burning internal combustion engine. But a hydroelectric-powered system cannot be widely used in the United States because favorable hydroelectric sites are found only in certain areas and most have already been developed. In addition, electric cars will not be cost-effective unless scientists can develop cheaper, longer-lasting batteries.

The second most efficient nonelectric automobile system is a gasoline-burning turbine engine. American, Japanese, and European carmakers have built prototype turbine engines, but so far we don't know whether they are cost-effective. Thus, for the time being, the best way to save money and gasoline is to drive a fuel-efficient car (at least 35 to 50 miles per gallon) and whenever possible use mass transportation, ride a bicycle, or walk.

If engineers were asked to sit down and invent three devices that would waste enormous amounts of energy, they would probably come up with (1) the incandescent light bulb (which wastes 95% of its energy input), (2) a car or truck with an internal combustion engine (which wastes 90% of the energy in its fuel), and (3) a nuclear power plant with its electricity used to heat space or water (which wastes 86% of the energy in its fuel). These devices were developed and widely used during a time when energy was cheap and plentiful. As this era draws to a close, we will have to replace or greatly improve the energy efficiency of these three items, so important to modern society.

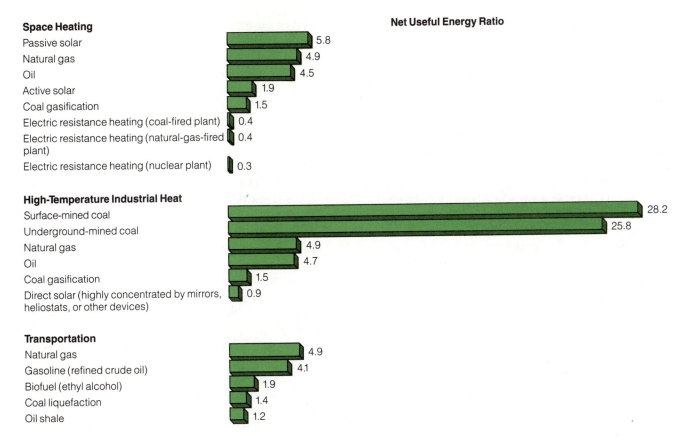

Space Heating

	Net Useful Energy Ratio
Passive solar	5.8
Natural gas	4.9
Oil	4.5
Active solar	1.9
Coal gasification	1.5
Electric resistance heating (coal-fired plant)	0.4
Electric resistance heating (natural-gas-fired plant)	0.4
Electric resistance heating (nuclear plant)	0.3

High-Temperature Industrial Heat

Surface-mined coal	28.2
Underground-mined coal	25.8
Natural gas	4.9
Oil	4.7
Coal gasification	1.5
Direct solar (highly concentrated by mirrors, heliostats, or other devices)	0.9

Transportation

Natural gas	4.9
Gasoline (refined crude oil)	4.1
Biofuel (ethyl alcohol)	1.9
Coal liquefaction	1.4
Oil shale	1.2

Figure 3-17 Net useful energy ratios for various energy systems over their estimated lifetimes. (Data from Colorado Energy Research Institute, *Net Energy Analysis*, 1976, and Howard T. Odum and Elisabeth C. Odum, *Energy Basis for Man and Nature*, 3rd ed., McGraw-Hill, 1981)

Using Waste Heat We cannot recycle high-quality energy. But we can slow the rate at which waste heat flows into the environment when high-quality energy is degraded. For instance, in cold weather an uninsulated, leaky house loses heat almost as fast as it is produced. By contrast, a well-insulated, airtight house can retain most of its heat for five to ten hours, and a well-designed, superinsulated house can retain most of its heat up to four days.

In some office buildings, waste heat from lights, computers, and other machines is collected and distributed to reduce heating bills during cold weather and exhausted to reduce cooling bills during hot weather. Waste heat from industrial plants and electrical power plants can be distributed through insulated pipes and used as a district heating system for nearby buildings, greenhouses, and fish ponds, as is done in some parts of Europe.

Waste heat from coal-fired and other industrial boilers can be used to produce electricity at half the cost of buying it from a utility company. The electricity can be used by the plant or sold to the local power company for general use. This combined production of high-temperature heat and electricity, known as **cogeneration**, is widely used in industrial plants throughout Europe.

If all large industrial boilers in the United States used cogeneration, they could produce electricity equal to that of 30 to 200 large nuclear or coal-fired power plants (depending on the technology used) at about half the cost. This would reduce the average price of electricity and essentially eliminate the need to build any large electric power plants through the year 2020.

Net Useful Energy: It Takes Energy to Get Energy The usable amount of high-quality energy obtainable from a given quantity of an energy resource is its **net useful energy**. It is the total energy available from the resource over its lifetime minus the amount of energy used (the first energy law), automatically wasted (the second energy law), and unnecessarily wasted in finding, processing, concentrating, and transporting it to a user. For example, if nine units of fossil fuel energy are needed to supply ten units of nuclear, solar, or additional fossil fuel energy (perhaps from a deep well at sea), the net useful energy gain is only one unit of energy.

We can express this relationship as the ratio of useful energy produced to the useful energy used to produce it. In the example just given, the net energy ratio would be 10/9, or 1.1. The higher the ratio, the greater the net useful energy yield. When the ratio is less than 1, there is a net energy loss over the lifetime of the system. Figure 3-17 lists estimated net useful energy ratios for various alternatives for space heating, high-temperature heat for industrial processes, and gaseous and liquid fuels for vehicles.

Currently, oil has a relatively high net useful energy ratio because much of it comes from rich, accessible deposits such as those in Saudi Arabia and other parts of the Middle East. When these sources are depleted, however, the net useful energy ratio of oil will decline and prices will rise. Then more money and high-quality fossil fuel will be needed to find, process, and deliver new oil from poorer deposits found deeper in the earth and in remote, hostile areas like Alaska, the Arctic, and the North Sea—far from where the energy is to be used.

Conventional nuclear fission energy has a low net energy ratio because large amounts of energy are required to build and operate power plants. Additional energy is needed to take them apart after their 25 to 30 years of useful life and to store the resulting highly radioactive wastes.

Large-scale solar energy plants for producing electricity or high-temperature heat for industrial processes also have low net useful energy ratios. The small flow of high-quality solar energy in a particular area must be collected and concentrated to provide the necessary high temperatures. Large amounts of money and high-quality energy are necessary to mine, process, and transport the materials used in vast arrays of solar collectors, focusing mirrors, pipes, and other equipment. On the other hand, passive and active solar energy systems for heating individual buildings and for heating water have relatively high net useful energy

ratios because they supply relatively small amounts of heat at moderate temperatures.

The scientific laws discussed in this chapter tell us what we can and cannot do in using matter and energy resources. People who don't know these laws and understand their implications often come up with or fall for some ridiculous ideas (see Spotlight below).

3-7 MATTER AND ENERGY LAWS AND ENVIRONMENTAL AND RESOURCE PROBLEMS

Throwaway Societies Because of the law of conservation of matter and the second law of energy, resource use by each of us automatically adds some waste heat and waste matter to the environment, thus increasing its entropy. The more energy and matter resources we use and waste, the greater the entropy increase in the environment.

Your individual use of matter and energy resources and your addition of waste heat, waste matter, and entropy to the environment may seem small and insignificant. But you are only one of the 1.2 billion individuals in industrialized countries using large quantities of the earth's matter and energy resources at a rapid rate. Meanwhile, the 4.0 billion people in less developed countries hope to be able to use more of these resources.

Today's advanced industrialized countries are **throwaway societies**, sustaining ever-increasing economic growth by maximizing the rate at which matter

---

SPOTLIGHT Scientific Ignorance Can Cost You Money

Some of the key ideas proposed by cornucopian economist Julian Simon (see Guest Essay on p. 26) reveal a considerable lack of scientific knowledge about natural resources. He once stated that we will never run out of energy because it can be partially recycled. When he was questioned, it turned out that he was talking about making use of waste heat before it flows into the environment. This is an excellent way to save some money and energy. But it is not a source of *any* high-quality energy, much less an infinite supply.

Another time Simon made the following statement:

Copper can be made from other metals. . . . Even the total weight of the

earth is not a theoretical limit to the amount of copper that might be available to earthlings in the future. Only the total weight of the universe . . . would be such a theoretical limit.

He based this statement on the fact that nuclear reactions can change isotopes of some elements into isotopes of other elements. For example, an isotope of nickel can be converted to an isotope of copper. But such conversions would be incredibly difficult and expensive. Using extremely optimistic assumptions, two physicists calculated that to produce copper from nickel would cost at least a billion dollars a pound!

Since the 1800s people have invented a variety of so-called perpetual-motion machines. These

machines are supposed to put out more high-quality energy than they take in—violating both the first and second energy laws. Con artists, who rely on people's greedy desire to get something for nothing, have made lots of money selling such devices to uninformed people.

Such schemes illustrate why it is important for everyone to have at least a basic knowledge of science. Otherwise, we can be duped by people with stupid, costly, even dangerous, ideas. Remember, anytime someone says you can get something for nothing, hold on to your pocketbook and run.

---

and energy resources are used and wasted (Figure 3-18). The scientific laws of matter and energy tell us that if more and more people continue to use and waste resources at an increasing rate, sooner or later the capacity of the local, regional, and global environments to dilute and degrade waste matter and absorb waste heat will be exceeded.

Matter-Recycling Societies   A stopgap solution to this problem is to convert from a throwaway society to a **matter-recycling society**. The goal of such a shift would be to allow economic growth to continue without depleting matter resources and without producing excessive pollution and environmental degradation.

But as we have seen already, there is no free lunch. The two laws of energy tell us that *recycling matter resources always requires high-quality energy, which cannot be recycled*. However, if a matter resource such as aluminum or paper is not too widely scattered, recycling often requires less high-quality energy than that needed to find, extract, and process virgin resources. It usually adds less entropy to the environment than using virgin resources.

Resource recycling should be guided by four principles:

- High-quality energy cannot be recycled.

- Recycling matter always requires high-quality energy, but efficient recycling usually takes less high-quality energy than producing new products by mining or harvesting and processing virgin materials.

- Don't dilute, disperse, or mix products that contain recyclable matter resources.

- To promote matter recycling, give government tax breaks and other subsidies to manufacturers that use recycled materials; give few if any subsidies to industries that extract virgin resources. If funds are limited, eliminate all subsidies and let the resource extraction and recycling industries compete in the open marketplace.

In the long run, a matter-recycling society based on indefinitely increasing economic growth must have an inexhaustible supply of affordable high-quality energy. And the environment must have an infinite capacity to absorb and disperse waste heat and to dilute and degrade waste matter.

Experts disagree on how much usable high-quality energy we have. However, supplies of coal, oil, natural gas, and uranium are clearly finite. And affordable supplies of oil, the most widely used supplementary energy resource, may be used up in several decades.

"Ah," you say, "but don't we have a virtually inexhaustible supply of solar energy flowing to the earth?" The problem is that the amount of solar energy reaching a particular small area of the earth's surface each minute or hour is low, and nonexistent at night.

With a proper collection and storage system, concentrating solar energy slightly to provide hot water and to heat a house to moderate temperatures makes good thermodynamic and economic sense. But to provide the high temperatures needed to melt metals or to produce electricity in a power plant, solar energy may not be cost-effective. Why? Because it has a very low net useful energy ratio (Figure 3-17). It takes a lot of energy to concentrate and raise its quality to a high level.

Suppose that cheap solar cells, nuclear fusion at room temperature, or some other breakthrough were to supply an essentially infinite supply of affordable useful energy. Would this solve our environmental problems? No.

Such a breakthrough would be important and useful. But the second energy law tells us that the faster we use energy to transform matter into products and to recycle these products, the faster low-quality heat and waste matter are dumped into the environment.

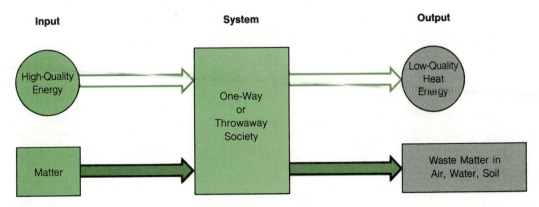

Figure 3-18   The one-way, or throwaway, society of most industrialized countries is based on maximizing the rates of energy flow and matter flow, rapidly converting the world's high-quality matter and energy resources to trash, pollution, and low-quality heat.

What Is Science?

Which of the following statements are true?

- Science emphasizes facts or data.
- Science has a method—a how-to-scheme—for learning about nature.
- Science establishes absolute truth or proof about nature.
- Science emphasizes the use of logic, not creativity, imagination, and intuition.

The answer is that they are all false or mostly false. Let's see why.

Science is an attempt to discover order in nature and then use this knowledge to make predictions about what will happen in nature. In this search for order, scientists try to answer two basic questions: *What happens in nature over and over with the same results? How or why do things happen this way?*

What Do Scientists Do?

To find out what is happening, scientists collect **scientific data** or facts by making observations and measurements. But collecting data is not the main purpose of science. As the French scientist Henri Poincaré put it, "Science is built up of facts. But a collection of facts is no more science than a heap of stones is a house."

Data are the stepping stones to **scientific laws,** which summarize what happens in nature over and over in the same way. Examples are the law of conservation of matter and the two energy laws discussed in this chapter.

Once a scientific law has been formulated, scientists try to explain how or why things happen this way. They make a **scientific hypothesis,** an educated guess that attempts to explain a scientific law or certain scientific facts.

Then they test the hypothesis by making more observations and measurements. If many experiments by different scientists support the hypothesis, it can become a scientific theory. In other words, a **scientific theory** is a well-tested and widely accepted scientific hypothesis.

Are Scientific Theories and Laws True?

A favorite debating and advertising trick is to claim that something "has not been scientifically proved." But scientists don't establish absolute proof or truth.

Scientists are concerned only with how *useful* a theory or law is in describing, explaining, and predicting what happens in nature. Science is the acceptance of what works and the rejection of what does not. That is why scientific theories may be modified, or even discarded, because of new data or more useful explanations of the data.

Someone once described scientists as professional skeptics. They challenge any idea about how nature works and insist that its usefulness be verified by observation and experiment. Advances in scientific knowledge are often based on vigorous disagreement, speculation, and controversy.

Scientific laws and theories are based on circumstantial evidence and statistical probabilities, not certainties. A scientist trying to find out how oak trees grow cannot study any more than a minute fraction of the earth's oak trees. Oak tree growth is affected by numerous variables—factors that vary from site to site. Examples are climate, soil, genetic composition, competition from other plants, insect damage, and diseases. A scientist can study only a small number of the thousands, perhaps millions, of possible interactions of these and other variables.

Scientific Methods

The ways scientists gather data and formulate and test scientific laws and theories are called **scientific methods**. Using scientific methods may require logical reasoning, but it also requires imagination and intuition. Albert Einstein, the famous physicist, once said, "Imagination is more important than knowledge, and there is no completely logical way to a new scientific idea."

Thus, intuition, imagination, and creativity are as important in science as in poetry, art, music, and other great adventures of the human spirit. However, there are only a few truly creative or great scientists, just as there are only a few great artists or poets.

Scientists must have a lot of patience, be willing to tolerate uncertainty and controversy, and be able to live with repeated failures. Experiments have to be tediously repeated, and often things go wrong.

But some of the most important scientific discoveries have been made when the results of an experiment were unexpected and the experimenter insisted on trying to find out why instead of tossing the results into the wastebasket. The English chemist Sir Humphrey Davy once remarked, "The most important of my discoveries has been suggested to me by my failures." That is why science is sometimes described as "the art of intelligent failure."

So why do scientists put up with all this? Because it is challenging, fun, and beautiful. Because when they discover something new, the joy of that moment makes up for all the past failures and tedious hard work. Science, like climbing a mountain, is an adventure. Science at its best helps awaken us to the wonder, mystery, and beauty of the universe, the earth, and life.

What Is Technology?

Technology is the creation of new products and processes to improve our survival, comfort, and quality of life. In many cases technology develops from known scientific laws and theories. Scientists invented the laser, for example, by applying knowledge about the internal structure of atoms. Applied scientific knowledge about chemistry has given us nylon, pesticides, laundry detergents, ways to control some types of pollution, and countless other products. Scientific knowledge of genetics has been used to develop new strains of crops and livestock.

But some technologies were developed long before anyone understood the scientific principles on which they were based. Aspirin, originally derived from a chemical found in the bark of a tropical willow tree, relieved pain and fever long before anyone found out how it did this. Photography was invented by people who had no knowledge of its chemistry.

Science and technology differ in the way the information and ideas they produce are shared. Most of the results of scientific research are published and passed around freely so they can be evaluated, verified, and perhaps challenged. This process strengthens the validity of scientific knowledge and helps expose cheaters. In contrast, technological discoveries are often kept secret until the inventor or company can get a patent for the new process or product.

Science, Technology, and the Future

Advances in science and technology have clearly improved the lives of many people. This progress, however, has also produced many unforeseen effects, such as pollution, that diminish the quality of our lives and threaten some of the earth's life-support systems.

In many cases we can discover new scientific ideas and invent new technologies to reduce pollution and unnecessary resource waste. But this is not always possible.

For the past 250 years science has studied nature primarily by examining increasingly lower levels of organization (Figure 3-1). This approach is called *reductionism*. It is based on the belief that if we can understand subatomic particles, then we can go back up the ladder of organizational levels and understand atoms, then molecules, and so on to organisms, communities, ecosystems, the ecosphere, and eventually the universe.

The reductionist approach has been useful in learning much about nature. But in the last few decades we have learned that it has a basic flaw. Each higher level of organization has properties that cannot be predicted or understood merely by understanding the lower levels that make up its structure. Even if you learn all there is to know about a particular tree, this will tell you only a small part of how a forest works.

The science of ecology has shown the need for combining reductionism with *holism* (sometimes spelled *wholism*)—an attempt to look at the properties of wholes, not just parts. A holistic approach attempts to describe all properties of a level of organization, not merely those based on the lower levels of organization that make up its underlying structure. This approach also attempts to understand and describe how the various levels interact with one another and with their constantly changing environments. This requires interdisciplinary research and cooperation.

Is Science Good or Bad?

Scientific knowledge itself is neither good nor bad. Only the ways we choose to use such knowledge can be judged good or bad. Thus, our real challenge is to learn how to use scientific knowledge and technology to sustain the earth for humans and other species and to improve the quality of life for all people, not just the affluent. The real purposes of our science and technology should be to understand, preserve, and improve our existence on a truly marvelous planet—not to plunder the planet for short-term economic gain.

This means that some forms of technology must be eliminated or rigidly controlled—for example, production of hazardous chemicals that don't break down in nature and nuclear, chemical, and biological weapons. It also means discovering and using technologies that greatly reduce the harmful impacts we have on the environment.

Most decisions about how to use science and technology are made by nonscientists—usually with advice from scientists. That is why it's important for nonscientists to have a basic knowledge of how nature works. Science must not be for scientists alone. Decision makers in business and government must have enough general knowledge of science to ask tough questions of scientists. They must also know enough about science to evaluate the answers and make decisions without having enough information.

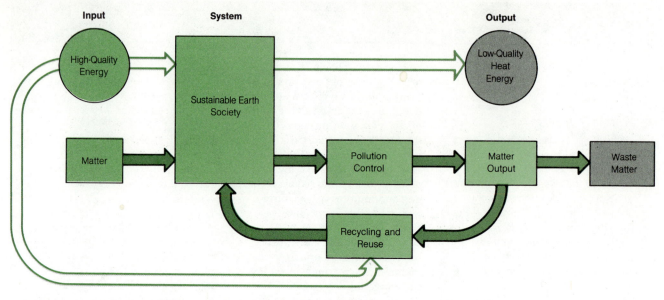

Figure 3-19 A sustainable-earth society, based on energy flow and matter recycling, reuses and recycles renewable matter resources, wastes less matter and energy, reduces unnecessary consumption, and controls population growth.

Thus, the more we attempt to "conquer" the earth, the more stress we put on the environment. Although experts argue over how close we are to reaching overload limits, the scientific laws of matter and energy indicate that such limits do exist.

Sustainable-Earth Societies   The three scientific laws governing matter and energy changes indicate that the best long-term solution to our environmental and resource problems is to shift from a throwaway society based on maximizing matter and energy flow (and in the process wasting an unnecessarily large portion of the earth's resources) to a **sustainable-earth society** (Figure 3-19).

The goal of a sustainable-earth society would be to minimize production of entropy. It would be modeled after what nature does to sustain us and other species. Such a society would go a step further than a matter-recycling society. In addition to recycling and reusing much of the matter we now discard as trash, it would use energy more efficiently, not use high-quality energy to do things that require moderate-quality energy, and use energy primarily to provide vital needs instead of frivolous wants.

Another goal of a sustainable-earth society would be to reduce use and waste of matter resources by making things that last longer and are easier to recycle, reuse, and repair. Just as important, a sustainable-earth society would cut down on the use of resources by regulating population growth.

Finally, a sustainable-earth society would not exceed the local, regional, and global limits of the environment ability to absorb low-quality heat and to dilute and degrade waste matter because it would use input approaches to reduce resource waste and prevent pollution. The matter and energy laws show us why input or prevention approaches make more sense thermodynamically and economically than output approaches. For example, preventing a toxic chemical from reaching underground supplies of drinking water is much easier and cheaper than trying to remove the chemical once it has contaminated a groundwater deposit.

Because of the three basic scientific laws of matter and energy, we are all dependent on each other and on the other living and nonliving parts of nature for our survival. We are all in it together. In the next chapter we will apply these laws to living systems and look at some biological principles that can teach us how to work with the rest of nature.

The second law of thermodynamics holds, I think, the supreme position among laws of nature. . . . If your theory is found to be against the second law of thermodynamics, I can give you no hope.

Arthur S. Eddington (1882–1944)

CHAPTER SUMMARY

Matter is found in various *physical forms*—solid, liquid, and gas—and *chemical forms*—elements, compounds (combinations of elements), and mixtures of elements and compounds. All matter is composed of uncombined or combined *atoms*. Atoms contain certain numbers of *protons* and *neutrons* in a tiny *nucleus* and *electrons* outside the nucleus.

High-quality matter is organized (low entropy), concentrated, and usually found near the earth's surface. It has great potential for use as a resource. *Low-quality matter* is disorganized (high entropy), dispersed, and often found deep underground. It usually has little potential for use as a resource.

Energy is the ability to do work by pushing or pulling matter or to cause a heat transfer between two objects at different temperatures. Its many forms can be classified as either *potential energy* (stored energy) or *kinetic energy* (energy of motion).

High-quality energy is organized (high entropy) or concentrated and has great ability to perform useful work. *Low-quality energy* is disorganized (high entropy) or dilute and has little ability to do useful work.

Elements and compounds can undergo *physical changes*, in which their chemical composition is not changed, and *chemical changes*, in which a change occurs in the chemical composition of the elements and compounds involved. According to the *law of conservation of matter*, in any physical or chemical change matter is neither created nor destroyed but merely changed from one physical or chemical form to another. This means that everything we think we have thrown away is still here with us in one form of another. *There is no away.*

The nuclei of certain types of atoms can undergo three major types of nuclear changes. One is *natural radioactivity*, in which unstable nuclei of atoms spontaneously emit one or more forms of ionizing radiation as high-speed alpha or beta particles or high-energy gamma rays. The other two are *nuclear fission*, in which the nuclei of certain types of atoms are split apart by a neutron, and *nuclear fusion*, in which the nuclei of certain atoms are combined at extremely high temperatures and pressures.

The *first law of energy*, or the *law of conservation of energy*, states that in any physical or chemical change, any movement of matter from one place to another, or any change in temperature, energy is neither created nor destroyed but merely changed from one form to another.

The *second law of energy* states that in any conversion of one form of energy to another some of the initial input of energy is always degraded to lower quality, less-useful energy, usually low-temperature heat that flows into the environment. This means that high-quality (low-entropy) energy, unlike matter, cannot be recycled or reused.

Energy conversion devices and processes differ in their *energy efficiency:* the percentage of energy input that does useful work. We waste less energy by using the most efficient energy conversion furnaces, motors, and appliances available and by not using high-quality energy to perform tasks that can be done with lower-quality energy. We can slow down the inevitable loss of degraded, low-quality heat to the environment by insulating and sealing buildings and by using the high-temperature waste heat produced by burning fossil fuels to generate electricity (*cogeneration*).

Net useful energy is the amount of useful energy produced by using an energy resource minus the useful energy used to produce it, often expressed as a ratio. Energy resources differ widely in their net useful energy for performing various tasks. It is important to consider net useful energy in deciding which energy resources to use.

The primary characteristic of any advanced industrial society is an ever-increasing flow, or throughput, of high-quality energy and matter resources to maintain the order in human bodies and the larger pockets of order we call civilization. As a result, today's advanced industrial societies, or *throwaway societies*, are increasing the disorder (entropy) of the environment more than at any other time in history.

Scientists project that because of the law of conservation of matter and the two energy laws, sooner or later we will have to make a transition to various *sustainable-earth societies* throughout the world. Such societies will be based on improving energy efficiency, reducing unnecessary use and waste of energy, recycling and reusing matter resources, and reducing unnecessary use and waste of matter resources.

Science is an attempt to discover order in nature and then use this knowledge to make predictions about what will happen in nature. Scientists do this by making observations and measurements to collect *scientific data or facts.* Data are the stepping stones to *scientific laws* that summarize what happens in nature over and over in the same way and *scientific theories* that explain how or why things happen that way.

Scientists don't establish absolute proof or truth. Instead, they are concerned only with how *useful* a theory or law is in describing, explaining, and predicting what happens in nature. The ways scientists gather data and formulate and test scientific laws and theories are called *scientific methods.*

Technology is the creation of new products and processes to improve our survival, comfort, and quality of life. Often technology is based on the application of known scientific laws and theories. Scientific or technological knowledge itself is neither good nor bad. Only the ways we choose to use such knowledge can be judged as good or bad. Our challenge is to use such knowledge to sustain the earth for humans and other species.

DISCUSSION TOPICS

1. Explain why we don't really consume anything and why we can never really throw matter away.

2. A tree grows and increases its mass. Explain why this isn't a violation of the law of conservation of matter.

3. If there is no away, why isn't the world filled with waste matter?

4. Use the second energy law to explain why a barrel of oil can be used only once as a fuel.

5. Explain why most energy analysts urge that improving energy efficiency forms the basis of any individual, corporate, or national energy plan. Is it an important part of your personal energy plan or lifestyle? Why or why not?

6. Explain why using electricity to heat a house and to supply household hot water is expensive and wasteful of energy. What energy tasks can be done best by electricity?

7. You are about to build a house. What energy supply (oil, gas, coal, or other) would you use for space heating, cooking food, refrigerating food, and heating water? Consider the long-term economic and environmental impact. Would you decide differently if you planned to live in the house for only 5 years instead of 25 years? If so, how?

8. (a) Use the law of conservation of matter to explain why a matter-recycling society will sooner or later be necessary. (b) Use the first and second laws of energy to explain why in the long run a sustainable-earth society, not just a matter-recycling society, will be necessary.

9. Why is it important for you to have a basic knowledge of science?

CHAPTER 4

Ecosystems:
What Are They and
How Do They Work?

General Questions and Issues

1. What two major natural processes keep us and other organisms alive?
2. What is an ecosystem and what are its major living and nonliving components?
3. What happens to energy in an ecosystem as a result of the first and second laws of energy?
4. What happens to matter in an ecosystem as a result of the law of conservation of matter?

5. What roles do different organisms play in ecosystems, and how do organisms interact?

If we love our children, we must love the earth with tender care and pass it on, diverse and beautiful, so that on a warm spring day 10,000 years hence they can feel peace in a sea of grass, can watch a bee visit a flower, can hear a sandpiper call in the sky, and can find joy in being alive.

Hugh H. Iltis

What organisms live in a forest or a pond? How do they get enough matter and energy resources to stay alive? How do these organisms interact with one another and with their physical and chemical environment? What changes will this forest or pond undergo through time?

Ecology is the science that attempts to answer such questions about how nature works. In 1869 German biologist Ernst Haeckel coined the term *ecology* from two Greek words: *oikos*, meaning "house" or "place to live," and *logos*, meaning "study of."

Ecology is the study of living things in their home or **environment**: all the external conditions and factors, living and nonliving, that affect an organism. In other words, **ecology** is the study of the interactions between organisms and their living (biotic) and nonliving (abiotic) environment. The key word is *interactions*. Scientists usually carry out this study by examining different **ecosystems**: forests, deserts, grasslands, rivers, lakes, oceans, or any set of organisms interacting with one another and with their nonliving environment.

This chapter will consider the major nonliving and living components of ecosystems and how they interact. The next two chapters will consider major types of ecosystems and the changes they can undergo because of natural events and human activities.

4-1 THE EARTH'S LIFE-SUPPORT SYSTEMS: AN OVERVIEW

The Biosphere and the Ecosphere The earth has several major parts that play a role in sustaining life (Figure 4-1). You are part of what ecologists call the **biosphere**—the living and dead organisms found near the earth's surface in parts of the atmosphere, hydrosphere, and lithosphere. Virtually all life on earth exists in a thin film of air, water, and rock in a zone extending from about 61 meters (200 feet) below the ocean's surface to about 61,000 meters (20,000 feet) above sea level.

The living organisms that make up the biosphere interact with one another, with energy from the sun, and with various chemicals in the atmosphere, hydrosphere, and lithosphere (Figure 4-1). This collection of living and dead organisms (the biosphere) interacting with one another and their nonliving environment (energy and chemicals) throughout the world is called the **ecosphere**. If the earth were an apple, the ecosphere would be no thicker than the apple's skin. *The goal of ecology is to learn how the ecosphere works.*

Energy Flow and Matter Recycling What keeps you, me, and most other organisms alive on this tiny planet? The answer is that life on earth depends largely on two fundamental processes (Figure 4-2):

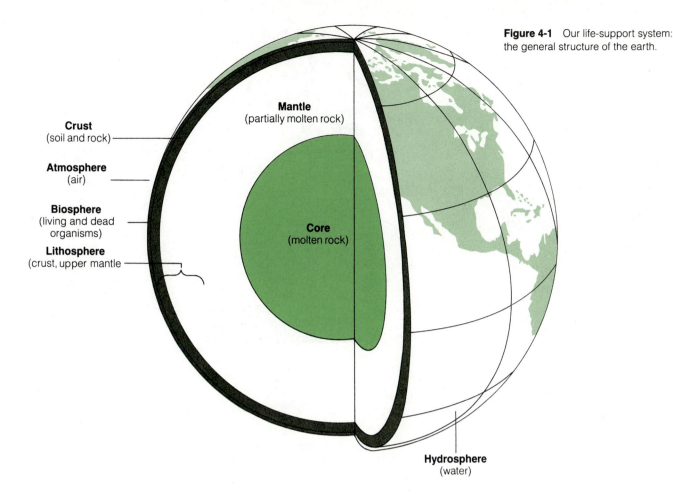

Figure 4-1 Our life-support system: the general structure of the earth.

Crust
(soil and rock)

Mantle
(partially molten rock)

Atmosphere
(air)

Biosphere
(living and dead
organisms)

Core
(molten rock)

Lithosphere
(crust, upper mantle

Hydrosphere
(water)

- *the one-way flow of high-quality energy from the sun,* through materials and living things on or near the earth's surface, then into the atmosphere, and eventually into space as low-quality heat

- *the recycling of chemicals* required by living organisms through parts of the ecosphere

The Sun: Source of Energy for Life The source of the energy that sustains life on earth is the sun. It lights and warms the earth and supplies the energy used by green plants to synthesize the compounds that keep them alive and serve as food for almost all other organisms. Solar energy also powers the recycling of key chemicals and drives the climate and weather systems that distribute heat and fresh water over the earth's surface.

The sun is a gigantic fireball composed mostly of hydrogen (72%) and helium (28%) gases. Temperatures and pressures in its inner core are so high that the hydrogen nuclei found there are compressed and fused to form helium gas. This nuclear fusion reaction (Figure 3-11, p. 63) taking place at the center of the sun continually releases massive amounts of energy.

This energy is radiated into space as a spectrum of ultraviolet light, visible light, infrared radiation, and

other forms of radiant, or electromagnetic, energy (Figure 4-3). These forms of energy travel outward in all directions through space and make the 150-million-kilometer (93-million-mile) trip to the earth in about eight minutes.

Figure 4-4 shows what happens to the solar radiant energy reaching the earth. About 34% is immediately reflected back to space by clouds, chemicals, and dust in the atmosphere and by the earth's surface. Most of the remaining 66% warms the atmosphere and land, evaporates water and cycles it through the ecosphere, and generates winds. A tiny fraction (0.023%) is captured by green plants and used in the process of photosynthesis to make organic compounds that organisms need to survive.

Most of the radiant energy reaching the earth's surface is in the form of light and near-infrared radiation (Figure 4-3). Most of the harmful forms of ionizing radiation emitted by the sun, especially ultraviolet radiation, are absorbed by molecules of ozone (O_3) in the upper atmosphere (stratosphere) and water vapor in the lower atmosphere. Without this screening effect, most present forms of life on earth could not exist.

Most of the incoming solar radiation not reflected away is degraded into low-quality heat (far-infrared radiation) in accordance with the second law of energy, and flows into space. The amount of energy returning

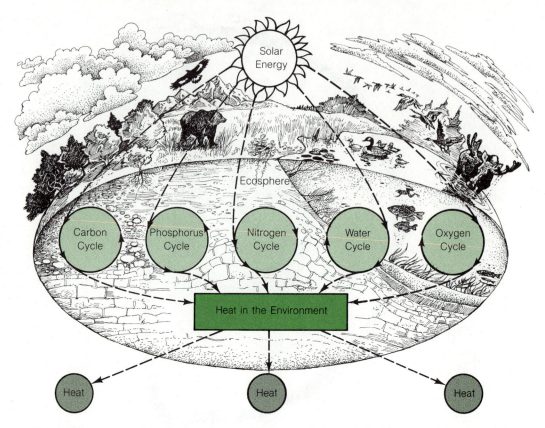

Figure 4-2 Life on earth depends on the recycling of critical chemicals (solid lines) and the one-way flow of energy through the ecosphere (dashed lines). This greatly simplified overview shows only a few of the many chemicals that are recycled.

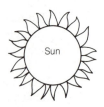

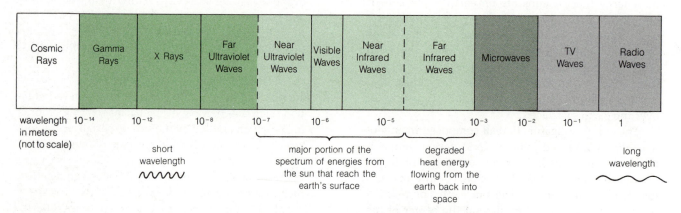

Figure 4-3 The sun is a gigantic nuclear fusion reactor that gives off a wide spectrum of radiant energy into space. When this energy reaches the earth, much of it is either reflected or absorbed by the atmosphere, which prevents most of the harmful, high-energy cosmic rays, gamma rays, X rays, and far-ultraviolet ionizing radiation from reaching the earth's surface.

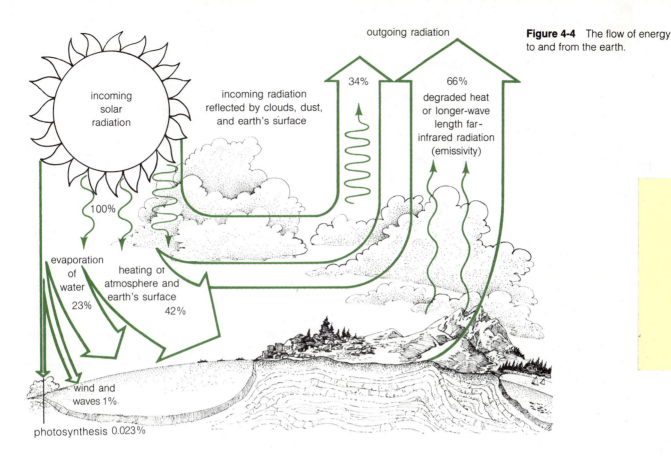

outgoing radiation

Figure 4-4 The flow of energy to and from the earth.

incoming solar radiation

incoming radiation reflected by clouds, dust, and earth's surface

34%

66% degraded heat or longer-wave length far-infrared radiation (emissivity)

100%

evaporation of water 23%

heating of atmosphere and earth's surface 42%

wind and waves 1%

photosynthesis 0.023%

to space as low-quality heat is affected by the presence of molecules such as water, carbon dioxide, methane, nitrous oxide, and ozone and by some forms of solid particulate matter in the atmosphere. These substances, acting as gatekeepers, allow some high-quality forms of radiant energy from the sun to pass through the atmosphere. They also absorb and reradiate some of the resulting low-quality heat back toward the earth's surface.

Scientists are becoming increasingly concerned that human activities are changing global climate patterns by disrupting the rate at which incoming solar energy flows through the ecosphere and returns to space as low-quality heat. Some possible effects of our activities on climate are discussed in Section 19-5.

Biogeochemical Cycles Any element or compound an organism needs to live, grow, and reproduce is called a **nutrient**. Nutrients include organic compounds such as sugars and proteins and inorganic materials such as water, carbon dioxide, oxygen gas, nitrate ions, phosphate ions, and ions of elements such as iron and copper.

About 40 elements and some of their compounds are essential to living organisms. Those required by organisms in large amounts are called **macronutrients**. Examples are carbon, oxygen, hydrogen, nitrogen, phosphorus, sulfur, calcium, magnesium, and potassium. These elements and their compounds

make up 97% of the mass of your body and more than 95% of the mass of all living organisms. The 30 or so other nutrients required by organisms in small, or trace, amounts are called **micronutrients**. Examples are iron, copper, zinc, chlorine, and iodine.

Most of the earth's chemicals do not occur naturally in forms useful to the organisms that make up the biosphere. Fortunately, elements and compounds required as nutrients for life on earth are continuously recycled through the ecosphere and converted to useful forms by a combination of biological, geological, and chemical processes.

This recycling of nutrients from the nonliving environment (reservoirs in the atmosphere, hydrosphere, and earth's crust), to living organisms, and back to the nonliving environment takes place in **biogeochemical cycles** (*bio* meaning "life," *geo* for "earth," and *chemical* for the changing of matter from one form to another). These cycles, driven directly or indirectly by incoming energy from the sun, include the carbon, oxygen, nitrogen, phosphorus, sulfur, and hydrologic (water) cycles (Figure 4-2).

Thus, a chemical may be part of an organism at one moment and part of its nonliving environment at another moment. For example, one of the oxygen molecules you just inhaled may be one inhaled previously by you, your grandmother, King Tut thousands of years ago, or a dinosaur millions of years ago. Similarly, some of the carbon atoms in the skin covering your right hand may once have been part of a leaf, a dinosaur hide, or a limestone rock.

There are two basic types of biogeochemical cycles: gaseous and sedimentary. Gaseous cycles primarily move nutrients back and forth between reservoirs in the atmosphere and hydrosphere and living organisms. Most of these cycles recycle elements rapidly, often within hours or days. The major gaseous cycles are the carbon, oxygen, hydrogen, and nitrogen cycles.

Sedimentary cycles cycle nutrients, mostly back and forth between reservoirs in the earth's crust (soil and rocks) and hydrosphere (water) and living organisms. Elements in these cycles are usually recycled much more slowly than those in gaseous cycles because the elements are tied up in sedimentary rocks for long periods of time, often thousands to millions of years. Phosphorus and sulfur are two of the 36 or so elements recycled in this manner.

4-2 ECOSYSTEMS: TYPES AND COMPONENTS

The Realm of Ecology Ecology is primarily concerned with interactions among five of the levels of organization of matter shown in Figure 3-1 (page 53): organisms, populations, communities, ecosystems, and the ecosphere. An **organism** is any form of life. Biologists classify the earth's organisms in anywhere from 3 to 20 categories. But to understand the key ideas in this introductory book, we will broadly classify organisms as *plants*, *animals*, and *decomposers*.

Plants range from microscopic, one-celled, floating and drifting plants known as phytoplankton to the largest of all living things, the giant sequoia trees of western North America. Animals range in size from floating and moving zooplankton (which feed on phytoplankton) to the 4-meter- (14-foot-) high, male African elephant and the 30-meter- (100-foot-) long blue whale. Decomposers range from microscopic bacteria to large fungi such as mushrooms.

A **population** is a group of organisms of the same kind living in a particular region. Examples of populations are all the sunfish in a pond, gray squirrels in a forest, white oak trees in a forest, people in a country, or people in the world. Populations are dynamic groups of organisms that adapt to changes in environmental conditions by changing their size, distribution of various age groups (age structure), and genetic makeup.

For organisms that reproduce sexually, a **species** is one or more populations whose members actually or potentially interbreed under natural conditions. Worldwide, it's estimated that 5 million to 30 million different species exist. Some biologists put the estimate as high as 50 million species, 30 million of them insects. So far, about 1.7 million of the earth's species

have been described and named, and about 10,000 new species are added to the list each year.

Each organism and population has a **habitat**: the place or type of place where it naturally lives. When several populations of different species live together and interact with one another in a particular place, they make up what is called a **community**, or **biological community**. Examples are all the plants, animals, and decomposers found in a forest, a pond, a desert, a dead log, and an aquarium.

An **ecosystem** is the combination of a community and the chemical and physical factors making up its nonliving environment. It is an ever-changing (dynamic) network of biological, chemical, and physical interactions that sustain a community and allow it to respond to changes in environmental conditions. All the earth's ecosystems together make up the ecosphere.

Major Terrestrial and Aquatic Ecosystems
Although no two are exactly alike, ecosystems can be classified into general types that contain similar types of organisms. The ecosphere's major land ecosystems such as forests, grasslands, and deserts are called **terrestrial ecosystems**, or **biomes**. The differences among these land ecosystems in various parts of the world are caused mostly by differences in average temperature and average precipitation (Figure 4-5).

Major ecosystems in the hydrosphere are called **aquatic ecosystems**. Examples include ponds, lakes, rivers, open ocean, coral reefs, estuaries (mouths of rivers or ocean inlets where salt water and fresh water mix), and coastal and inland wetlands (such as swamps, marshes, and prairie potholes that are covered with water all or part of the time). The major differences between these ecosystems are the result of differences in the amount of various nutrients dissolved in the water (salinity), differences in the depth of sunlight penetration, and differences in average water temperature. Major terrestrial and aquatic ecosystems are discussed in more detail in Chapter 5.

Whether large or small, ecosystems normally don't have distinct boundaries. An ecosystem blends into an adjacent one through a transition zone, called an **ecotone**. An ecotone contains many of the plant, animal, and decomposer species found in both adjacent ecosystems and often has species not found in either of them. As a result, an ecotone usually has a greater diversity of species than its surrounding areas.

Abiotic Components of Ecosystems
Ecosystems consist of various nonliving and living components. Figures 4-6 and 4-7 are greatly simplified diagrams showing a few of the components of ecosystems in a freshwater pond and in a field.

The nonliving, or **abiotic**, components of an ecosystem include various physical and chemical factors. Important physical factors are sunlight, shade, precipitation, wind, temperature, and water currents. The

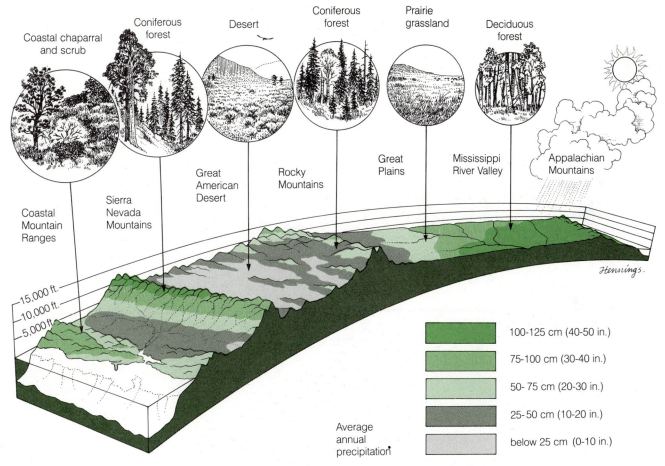

Coastal chaparral and scrub

Coniferous forest

Desert

Coniferous forest

Prairie grassland

Deciduous forest

Coastal Mountain Ranges

Sierra Nevada Mountains

Great American Desert

Rocky Mountains

Great Plains

Mississippi River Valley

Appalachian Mountains

Hennings.

—15,000 ft.
—10,000 ft.
—5,000 ft.

	Average annual precipitation
	100-125 cm (40-50 in.)
	75-100 cm (30-40 in.)
	50-75 cm (20-30 in.)
	25-50 cm (10-20 in.)
	below 25 cm (0-10 in.)

Figure 4-5 Gradual transition from one major biome to another along the 39th parallel crossing the United States. The major factors causing these transitions are changes in average temperature and precipitation.

major chemical factors are the nutrient elements and compounds in the atmosphere, hydrosphere, and earth's crust, which are required in large or small amounts for the survival, growth, and reproduction of organisms.

Biotic Components of Ecosystems   The major types of organisms that make up the living, or **biotic,** components of an ecosystem are usually classified as producers, consumers, and decomposers. This classification is based on organisms' general nutritional habits.

Producers—sometimes called **autotrophs** (self-feeders)—are organisms that can manufacture the organic compounds they use as sources of energy and nutrients. Most producers are green plants that make the organic nutrients they require through **photosynthesis.** This process begins when sunlight is absorbed by pigments such as chlorophyll, which gives the plants their green color. The plants use this energy to combine carbon dioxide (which they get from the atmosphere or from water) with water (which they get from the soil or aquatic surroundings) to make carbohydrates—sugars (such as glucose), starches, and celluloses. Oxygen gas is given off as a by-product of photosynthesis. Photosynthesis can be represented as follows:

$$\text{carbon dioxide} + \text{water} + \textbf{solar energy} \rightarrow \text{glucose} + \text{oxygen}$$

$$6CO_2 + 6H_2O + \textbf{solar energy} \rightarrow C_6H_{12}O_6 + 6O_2$$

In essence this complex process converts radiant energy from the sun into chemical energy stored in the chemical bonds that hold glucose and other carbohydrates together. This stored chemical energy produced by photosynthesis is the direct or indirect source of food for most organisms. The vast majority of the oxygen in the atmosphere is also a product of photosynthesis.

Some producer organisms, mostly specialized bacteria, can extract inorganic compounds from their environment and convert them to organic nutrients without the presence of sunlight. This process is called **chemosynthesis.** For example, hydrothermal vents in some parts of the ocean floor spew forth large amounts of superheated ocean water and rotten-egg-smelling hydrogen sulfide gas. In this pitch-dark, hot environment, specialized producer bacteria carry out chemosynthesis to convert inorganic hydrogen sulfide to nutrients they require.

Only producers can make their own food. In addition, they provide food directly or indirectly for

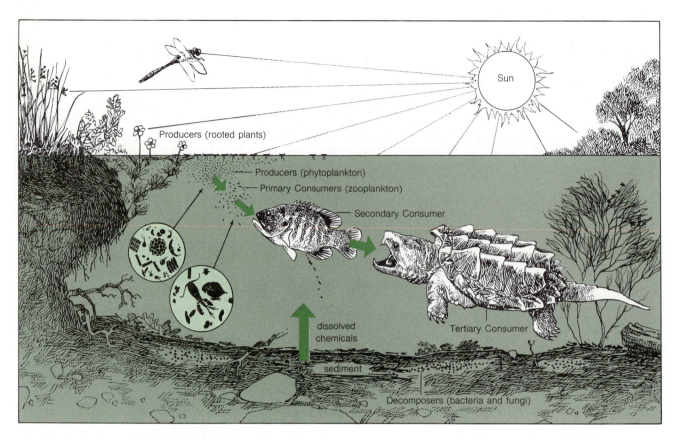

Figure 4-6   The major components of a freshwater pond ecosystem.

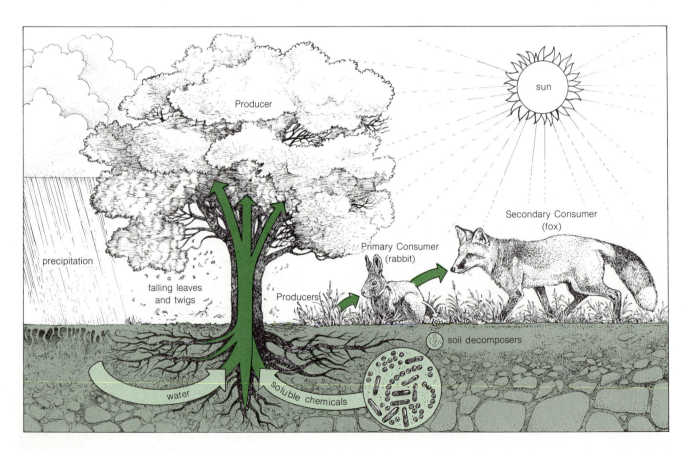

Figure 4-7   The major components of an ecosystem in a field.

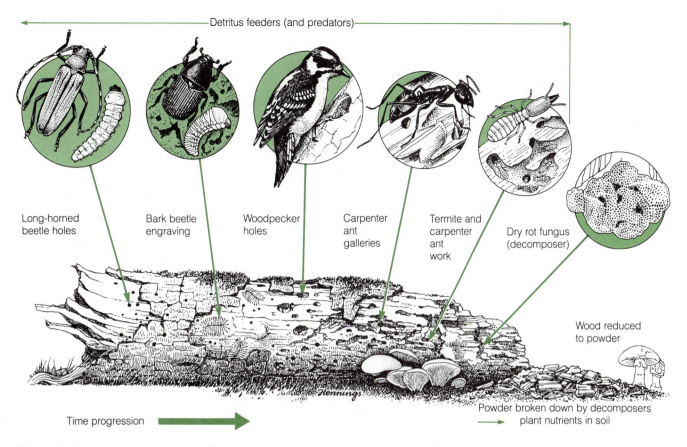

Long-horned beetle holes

Bark beetle engraving

Woodpecker holes

Carpenter ant galleries

Termite and carpenter ant work

Dry rot fungus (decomposer)

Detritus feeders (and predators)

Time progression

Wood reduced to powder

Powder broken down by decomposers plant nutrients in soil

Figure 4-8 Some detritivores, called detritus feeders, directly consume dead organic matter in a fallen tree. Other detritivores, called decomposers, break down complex organic chemicals in the dead wood into simpler nutrient chemicals that are returned to the soil for reuse by plants.

animals and decomposers. You, I, and most other animals get nutrients either by eating plants or by eating animals that feed on plants; all flesh is grass, so to speak.

Organisms that get the nutrients and energy they require by feeding either directly or indirectly on producers are called **consumers,** or **heterotrophs** (other-feeders). Some consumers feed on living plants and animals, and others feed on dead plant and animal matter, called **detritus.**

Depending on their food sources, consumers that feed on living organisms fall into three major classes:

■ **herbivores** (plant eaters), *primary consumers* which feed directly and only on all or part of living plants. Birds eat seeds, buds, and foliage. Deer and rabbits eat twigs and leaves. Gophers attack plant roots. Grasshoppers and many other kinds of insects eat all parts of plants. In aquatic ecosystems, zooplankton feed on phytoplankton.

■ **carnivores** (flesh eaters), *secondary consumers,* which feed only on plant-eating animals (herbivores), and *tertiary or higher-level consumers,* which feed only on animal-eating animals. Spiders and birds that eat plant-eating insects and tuna, which feed on herrings and anchovies, are secondary consumers. Hawks, which eat snakes and weasels, and sharks, which eat other fish, are tertiary or higher-level consumers.

■ **omnivores** ("everything eaters"), which can eat both plants and animals. Examples are pigs, rats, foxes, cockroaches, and humans.

Consumer organisms that feed on detritus, or dead organic plant and animal matter are known as **detritivores** (Figure 4-8). There are two major classes of detritivores: detritus feeders and decomposers. **Detritus feeders** directly consume dead organisms and their cast-off parts and organic wastes. Examples are crabs, jackals, termites, earthworms, millipedes, ants, and vultures.

Much of the detritus in ecosystems—especially dead wood and leaves—undergoes decay, rot, or decomposition, in which its complex organic molecules are broken into simpler inorganic compounds containing nutrient elements. This decomposition process is brought about by the feeding activity of the other type of detritus consumer, **decomposers.** Decomposers consist of two classes of organisms: *fungi* (mostly molds and mushrooms) and microscopic, single-celled *bacteria.* Bacteria and fungi decomposers in turn are an important source of food for organisms such as worms and insects living in the soil and water.

The chemical energy stored in glucose and other carbohydrates is used by producers, consumers, and decomposers to drive their life processes. This is part of the one-way flow of energy through organisms and

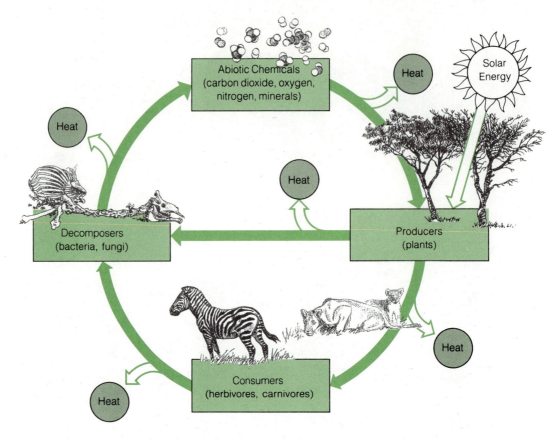

Figure 4-9 The major structural components (energy, chemicals, and organisms) of an ecosystem are connected through the functions of energy flow (open arrows) and matter recycling (solid arrows). There is a one-way flow of energy from the sun through producer organisms (mostly plants), through consumers (mostly animals), through decomposers (bacteria and fungi), and back into the environment as low-quality heat. Because of the second energy law, the quality of this energy is degraded as it flows through the ecosystem. Nutrients are transferred from one organism to another and modified as needed. Decomposers break down the complex organic chemicals in dead organisms and in their wastes to simpler inorganic chemicals for use by producers to begin the cycle again.

ecosystems governed by the second law of energy. Aerobic (oxygen-consuming) organisms change part of the glucose and other, more complex organic compounds they synthesize (producers), eat (consumers), or decompose (decomposers) back into carbon dioxide and water by the process of **cellular aerobic respiration**:

glucose + oxygen → carbon dioxide + water + **energy**

$$C_6H_{12}O_6 + 6O_2 \rightarrow 6CO_2 + 6H_2O + \textbf{energy}$$

This process is not the same as the breathing process, which is also called respiration. Aerobic respiration is a carefully controlled, slow burning of organic compounds that takes place in the cells of living organisms. The chemical energy released in this process is stored in other molecules and released as needed to drive the life processes of organisms. As it is used, most of this chemical energy is degraded to low-temperature heat that flows into the environment, as required by the second law of energy.

The survival of any individual organism depends on matter flow and energy flow through its body. However, the community of organisms in an ecosys-

tem survives primarily by a combination of matter recycling and a one-way flow of energy (Figure 4-9).

Figure 4-9 shows that decomposers are responsible for completing the cycle of matter. They carry out waste disposal in nature by breaking down organic compounds in organic wastes and dead organisms into inorganic nutrients for producers so that the cycle of life can begin again. Without decomposers, the entire world would soon be knee-deep in plant litter, dead animal bodies, animal wastes, and garbage. Figure 4-9 also shows that an ecosystem can exist without consumers because chemicals can be cycled directly from producers to decomposers and back to producers.

Tolerance Ranges of Species to Abiotic Factors

The spread of organisms from one type of ecosystem to another and from one part of an ecosystem to another is limited by various factors. The reason that organisms don't spread everywhere is that each species and each individual organism of a species has a particular **range of tolerance** to variations in chemical and physical factors in its environment, such as temperature (Figure 4-10). A plant, such as the magnolia tree, that

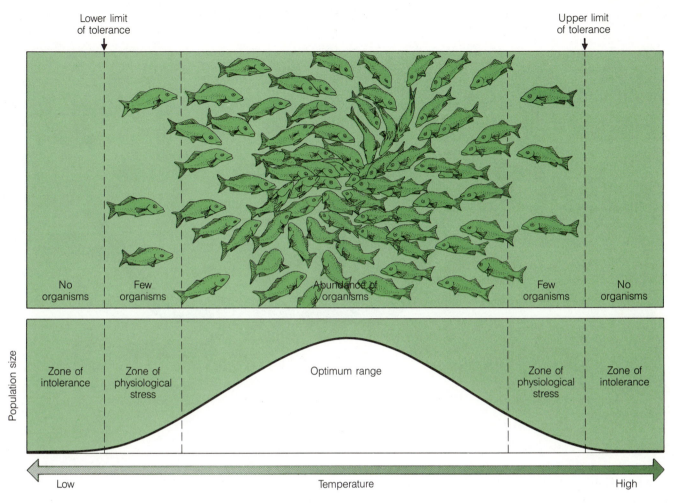

Figure 4-10 Range of tolerance for a population of organisms of the same species to an abiotic environmental factor—in this case temperature.

is killed by freezing temperatures will not be found in the far north. And you won't find plants that need lots of water in a desert.

The tolerance range includes an optimum range of values, within which populations of a species thrive and operate most efficiently (Figure 4-10). This range also includes values slightly above or below the optimum level of each abiotic factor—values that usually support a smaller population size. When values exceed the upper or lower limits of tolerance, few if any organisms of a particular species survive.

Some organisms survive only within narrow temperature ranges. For example, tropical fish such as angelfish and neon tetras will die if the water in their natural habitat or aquarium drops below about 16°C (60°F). Other species can survive in a wide range of temperatures but cannot endure sudden or extreme changes in temperature. Goldfish, for example, can live in water as warm as 24°C (75°F). They can also survive if the water temperature decreases to near freezing, as long as the decrease is gradual.

These observations are summarized in the **law of tolerance**: The existence, abundance, and distribution of a species in an ecosystem are determined by whether the levels of one or more physical or chemical factors fall above or below the levels tolerated by the species.

Individual organisms within a large population of a species may have slightly different tolerance ranges because of small differences in their genetic makeup. For example, it may take a little more heat or a little more of a poisonous chemical to kill one frog or one person than another. That is why the tolerance curve shown in Figure 4-10 represents the response of a population composed of many individuals of the same species to changes in an environmental factor such as temperature.

Usually the range of tolerance to a particular stress varies with the physical condition and life cycle of the individuals making up a species. Individuals already weakened by fatigue or disease are normally more sensitive to stresses than healthy ones. For most animal species, tolerance levels are much lower in juveniles (where body defense mechanisms may not be fully developed) than in adults.

Many types of organisms can change their tolerance to physical factors such as temperature if exposed to gradually changing conditions. For example, you can tolerate a higher water temperature by getting into

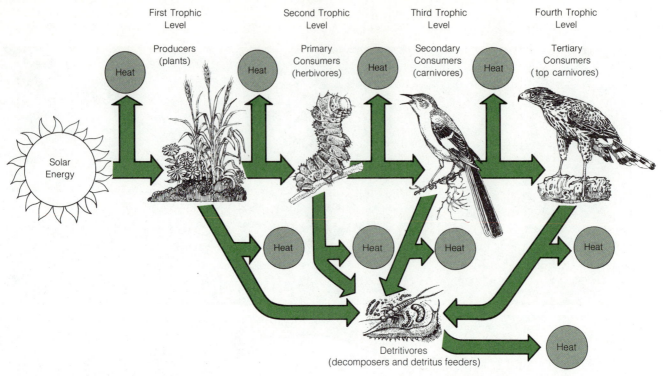

First Trophic Level — Producers (plants)

Second Trophic Level — Primary Consumers (herbivores)

Third Trophic Level — Secondary Consumers (carnivores)

Fourth Trophic Level — Tertiary Consumers (top carnivores)

Solar Energy

Heat

Detritivores (decomposers and detritus feeders)

Figure 4-11 A food chain. The arrows show how chemical energy in food flows through various trophic levels, with most of the high-quality chemical energy being degraded to low-quality heat in accordance with the second law of energy.

a tub of fairly hot water and then slowly adding hotter and hotter water.

This adaptation to slowly changing new conditions, or acclimation, is a useful protective device, but it can also be dangerous. With each change, the organism comes closer to its limit of tolerance. Suddenly, without any warning signals, the next small change triggers a **threshold effect**—a harmful or even fatal reaction as the tolerance limit is exceeded—much like adding the single straw that breaks an already overloaded camel's back.

The threshold effect partly explains why many environmental problems seem to arise suddenly even though they have been building for a long time. For example, trees in certain forests begin dying in large numbers after prolonged exposure to numerous air pollutants. We usually notice the problem only when entire forests die, as is happening in parts of Europe and North America. By then we are 10 to 20 years too late to prevent the damage.

Some species live in changeable environments such as terrestrial areas with changing seasons and estuaries with changing water levels and temperatures. Usually such species can tolerate a wide range of physical and chemical conditions. On the other hand, species that live in fairly constant environments, such as tropical rain forests and deep seas, usually are able to survive only within a narrow range of physical and chemical conditions.

Limiting Factors in Ecosystems Another ecological principle related to the law of tolerance is the **limiting factor principle**: Too much or too little of any abiotic factor can limit or prevent growth of a population of a species in an ecosystem even if all other factors are at or near the optimum range of tolerance for the species. A single factor found to be limiting the population growth of a species in an ecosystem is called the **limiting factor.**

Examples of limiting factors in terrestrial ecosystems are temperature, water, light, and soil nutrients. For example, suppose a farmer plants corn in a field where the soil has too little phosphorus. Even if the corn's needs for water, nitrogen, potassium, and other nutrients are met, the corn will stop growing when it has used up the available phosphorus. In this case, availability of phosphorus is the limiting factor that determines how much corn will grow in the field. Growth can also be limited by the presence of too much of a particular abiotic factor. For example, plants can be killed by too much water or by too much fertilizer.

In aquatic ecosystems, **salinity** (the amounts of various salts dissolved in a given volume of water) is a limiting factor. It determines the species found in marine ecosystems, such as oceans, and freshwater ecosystems, such as rivers and lakes. Three major limiting factors determining the numbers and types of organisms at various layers in aquatic ecosystems are temperature, sunlight, and **dissolved oxygen content**

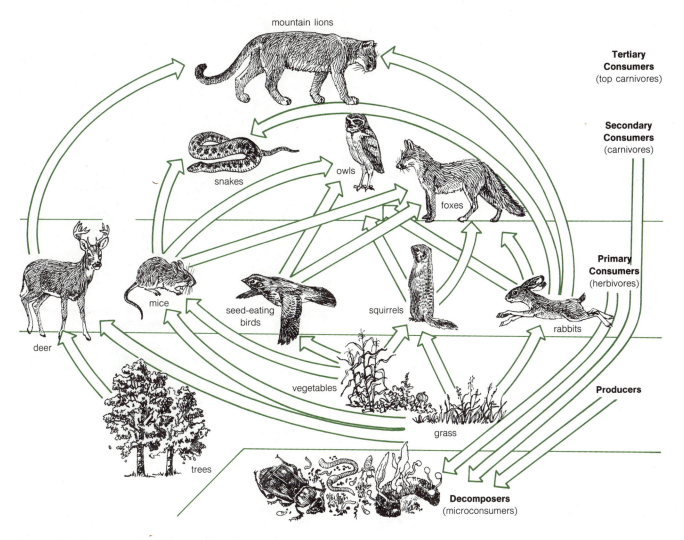

Figure 4-12 Greatly simplified food web for a terrestrial ecosystem.

(the amount of oxygen gas dissolved in a given volume of water at a particular temperature), as discussed in Chapter 5.

4-3 ENERGY FLOW IN ECOSYSTEMS

Food Chains and Food Webs *There is no waste in functioning natural ecosystems.* All organisms, dead or alive, are potential sources of food for other organisms. A caterpillar eats a leaf; a robin eats the caterpillar; a hawk eats the robin. When the plant, caterpillar, robin, and hawk die, they are in turn consumed by decomposers.

A series of organisms, each eating or decomposing the preceding one, is called a **food chain** (Figure 4-11). Food chains are channels for the one-way flow of a tiny part of the sun's high-quality energy captured by photosynthesis, through the living components of ecosystems, and into the environment as low-quality heat. Food chains are also pathways for the recycling of nutrients from producers, consumers (herbivores, carnivores, and omnivores), and decomposers back to producers (Figure 4-9).

All organisms that share the same general types of food in a food chain are said to be at the same **trophic level** (from the Greek *trophos*, "feeder"). As shown in Figure 4-11, all producers belong to the first trophic level; all primary consumers, whether feeding on living or dead producers, belong to the second trophic level; and so on.

The food chain concept is useful for tracing chemical recycling and energy flow in an ecosystem, but simple food chains like the one shown in Figure 4-11 rarely exist by themselves in nature. Few herbivores or primary consumers feed on just one kind of plant, nor are they eaten by only one type of carnivore or secondary consumer. In addition, omnivores eat several different kinds of plants and animals at several trophic levels.

This means that the organisms in a natural ecosystem are involved in a complex network of many interconnected food chains, called a **food web.** A simplified food web in a terrestrial ecosystem is diagrammed in Figure 4-12, which shows that trophic levels can be assigned in food webs just as in food chains.

Figure 4-13 Generalized model of the main pathways for the one-way flow of energy through ecosystems via grazing and detritus food webs.

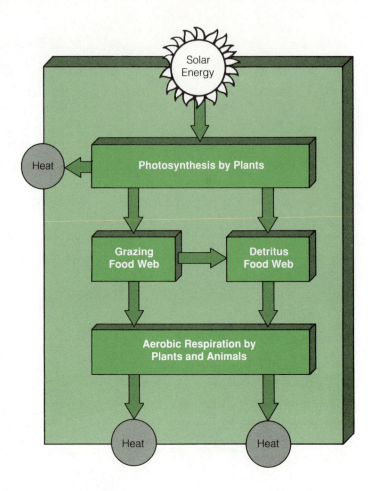

Energy flows through ecosystems by means of two interconnected types of food webs: grazing and detritus (Figure 4-13). In **grazing food webs** herbivores consume living plant tissue and are then consumed by an array of carnivores and omnivores. In **detritus food webs** detritus feeders and decomposers break down organic waste products and the remains of dead plants and animals to simple inorganic compounds for reuse by plants.

Energy Flow Pyramids At each transfer from one trophic level to another in a food chain or web, work is done, low-quality heat is given off to the environment, and the availability of high-quality energy to organisms at the next trophic level is reduced. This reduction in high-quality energy available at each trophic level is the result of the inevitable energy quality tax imposed by the second law of energy.

The percentage of available high-quality energy transferred from one trophic level to another varies from 2% to 30%, depending on the types of species involved and the ecosystem in which the transfer takes place. In the wild, ecologists estimate that an average of about 10% of the high-quality chemical energy available at one trophic level is transferred and stored in usable form as chemical energy in the bodies of the

organisms at the next level. The rest of the energy is used to keep the organisms alive, and most is eventually degraded and lost to the environment as low-quality heat in compliance with the second law of energy. Some of it is transferred to decomposers, which use a small amount to stay alive and degrade the rest to low-quality heat.

Figure 4-14 illustrates this loss of usable high-quality energy at each step in a simple food chain. The **pyramids of energy flow and energy loss** in this diagram show that the greater the number of trophic levels or steps in a food chain or web, the greater the cumulative loss of usable high-quality energy. Figure 4-15 shows the actual annual energy flow through an ecosystem.

The energy flow pyramid explains why a larger population of people can be supported if people shorten the food chain by eating grains directly (for example, rice → human) rather than eating animals that feed on grains (grain → steer → human). To prevent protein malnutrition, a vegetarian diet must include a variety of plants that provide enough of the 10 nitrogen-containing amino acid molecules used to make proteins that our bodies cannot synthesize. Poor people surviving on a plant diet often don't have enough money to grow or purchase the variety of plants needed to avoid protein malnutrition.

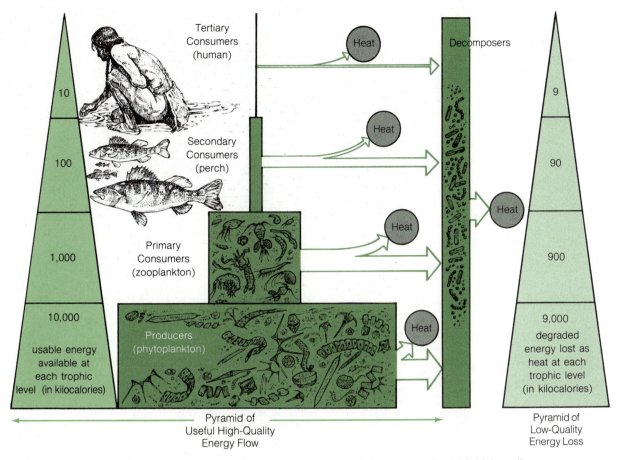

Tertiary
Consumers
(human)

Secondary
Consumers
(perch)

Primary
Consumers
(zooplankton)

Producers
(phytoplankton)

10
100
1,000
10,000

usable energy
available at
each trophic
level (in kilocalories)

Heat

Heat

Heat

Heat

Decomposers

9
90
900

9,000
degraded
energy lost as
heat at each
trophic level
(in kilocalories)

Pyramid of
Useful High-Quality
Energy Flow

Pyramid of
Low-Quality
Energy Loss

Figure 4-14 Generalized pyramids of energy flow and energy loss, showing the decrease in usable high-quality energy available at each succeeding trophic level in a food chain or web.

Pyramids of Numbers and Biomass We can collect samples of organisms in ecosystems and count the number of each type found at each trophic level. This information can then be used to construct **pyramids of numbers** for ecosystems (Figure 4-16). For example, a million phytoplankton in a small pond may support 10,000 zooplankton, which in turn may support 100 perch, which might feed one person for a month or so.

Pyramids of numbers for a grassland and many other ecosystems taper off in going from the producer level to the higher trophic levels (Figure 4-16, left). But for some ecosystems the number pyramids have different shapes and can take on an inverted form. For example, in a forest a small number of large trees, such as redwoods (the producers), support a larger number of mostly small, herbivorous insects and birds (the primary consumers) that feed on and from the trees (Figure 4-16, right).

The dried weight of all organic matter contained in the organisms in an ecosystem is called its **biomass.** Each trophic level in a food chain or web contains a certain amount of biomass. This can be estimated by harvesting several randomly selected patches or narrow strips in an ecosystem. The organisms in the sam-

ples are then sorted according to known trophic levels, dried, and weighed. These data are then used to plot a **pyramid of biomass** for the ecosystem (Figure 4-17).

For most land ecosystems the total biomass at each successive trophic level of a food chain or web usually decreases. This yields a pyramid of biomass with a large base of producers, topped by a series of increasingly smaller trophic levels of consumers (Figure 4-17, left).

In aquatic ecosystems, however, the pyramid of biomass can be upside down, with the biomass of consumers exceeding that of producers (Figure 4-17, right). Here the producers are tiny phytoplankton that grow and reproduce rapidly, not large plants that grow and reproduce slowly.

Net Primary Productivity of Plants The rate at which the plants in an ecosystem produce usable chemical energy or biomass is called **net primary productivity.** It is equal to the rate at which plants use photosynthesis to store chemical energy in biomass minus the rate at which they use some of this chemical energy in aerobic cellular respiration to live, grow, and reproduce.

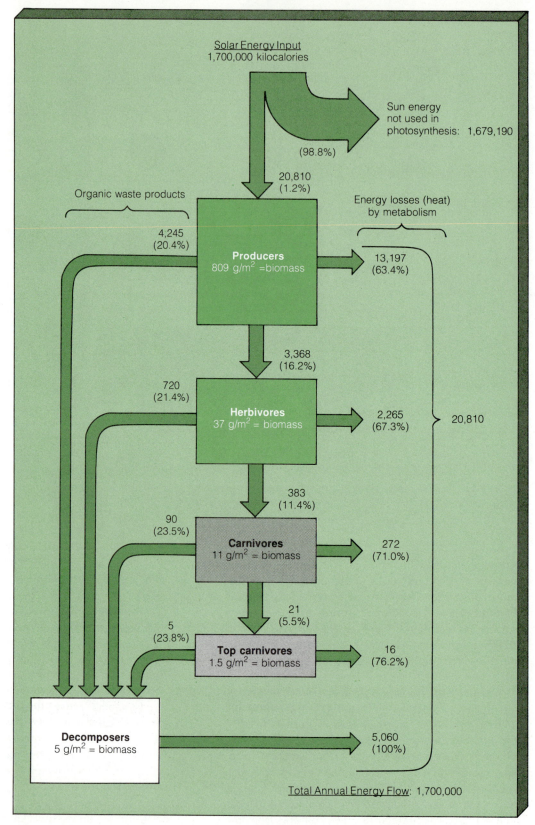

Figure 4-15 Simplified summary of the annual energy flow measured in kilocalories per square meter per year for an aquatic ecosystem in Silver Springs, Florida. (Adapted with permission from Cecie Starr and Ralph Taggart, *Biology: The Unity and Diversity of Life*, 5th ed., Belmont, Calif.: Wadsworth, 1989)

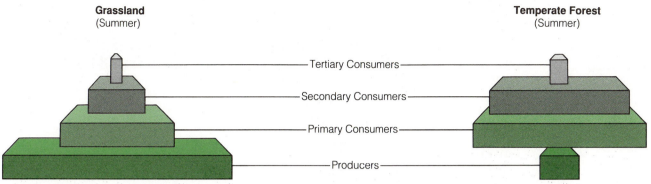

Figure 4-16 Generalized pyramids of numbers in ecosystems.

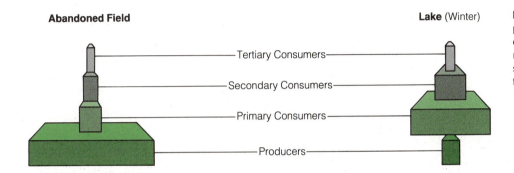

Figure 4-17 Generalized pyramids of biomass in ecosystems. The size of each tier represents the dry weight per square meter of all organisms at that trophic level.

| net primary productivity | = | rate at which plants produce chemical energy through photosynthesis | − | rate at which plants use chemical energy through aerobic cellular respiration |

Net primary productivity is usually reported as the amount of energy produced by the plant material in a specified area of land over a given time. Typical units are kilocalories or kilojoules of energy produced per square meter of area per year (Appendix 2).

Net primary productivity can be thought of as the basic food source or "income" of animals. We can use it to evaluate the potential of various ecosystems for producing plant material that forms the base of the food supply for humans and other animals. Ecologists have estimated the average annual net primary production per square meter for the major terrestrial and aquatic ecosystems. Figure 4-18 shows that ecosystems with the highest average net primary productivities are estuaries, swamps and marshes, and tropical rain forests; the lowest are tundra (Arctic grasslands), open ocean, and desert.

You might conclude that we should clear tropical forests to grow crops and that we should harvest plants growing in estuaries, swamps, and marshes to help feed the growing human population. That conclusion is incorrect. One reason is that the plants—mostly grasses—in estuaries, swamps, and marshes cannot be eaten by people. But they are extremely important as food sources and spawning areas for fish, shrimp, and other forms of aquatic life that provide us with protein. So we should protect, not destroy, these plants.

In tropical forests most of the nutrients are stored in the trees and other vegetation rather than in the soil. When the trees are cleared, the low levels of nutrients in the exposed soil are rapidly depleted by frequent rains and by growing crops. Thus, food crops can be grown only for a short time without massive, expensive inputs of commercial fertilizers.

Figure 4-19 shows the total world net primary productivity for major types of ecosystems. Because their total area is small, estuaries are low on the list. On the other hand, because about 71% of the world's surface is covered with oceans, the world's open ocean ecosystems head the list.

But this can be misleading. The world net primary productivity is high for oceans because they cover so much of the globe, not because they have a high average productivity per square meter per year. Also, harvesting widely dispersed (high-entropy) algae and seaweeds from the ocean requires enormous amounts of energy—more than the chemical energy available from the food that would be harvested.

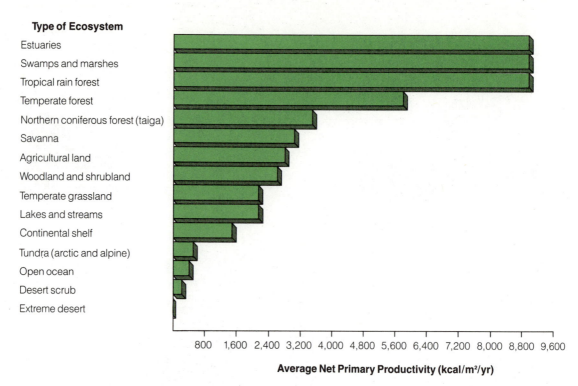

Figure 4-18 Estimated annual average net productivity of plants per square meter in major types of ecosystems.

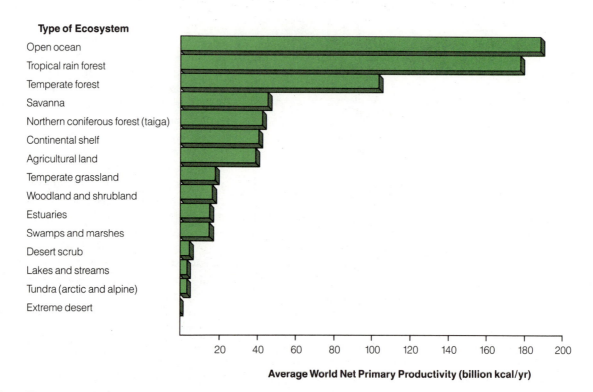

Figure 4-19 Estimated annual total world net primary productivity of plants in major types of ecosystems.

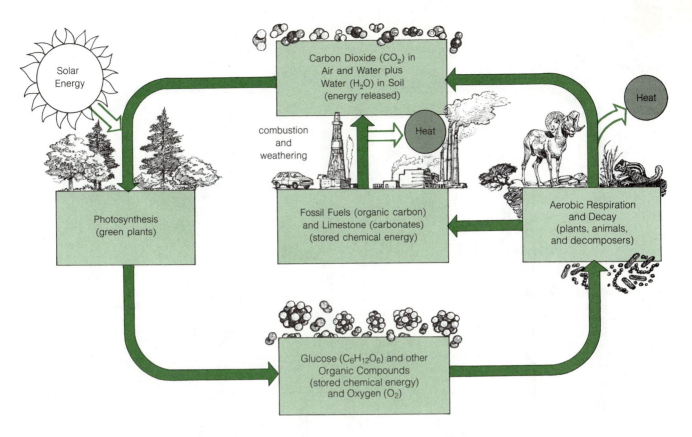

Figure 4-20 Simplified diagram of a portion of the carbon cycle, showing matter recycling (solid arrows) and one-way energy flow (open arrows) through the processes of photosynthesis and aerobic respiration. This cyclical movement of matter through ecosystems and the ecosphere is also an important part of the oxygen and hydrogen cycles.

4-4 MATTER RECYCLING IN ECOSYSTEMS

Carbon Cycle Carbon is the basic building block of the carbohydrates, fats, proteins, nucleic acids such as DNA and RNA, and other organic compounds necessary for life. Most land plants get their carbon by absorbing carbon dioxide gas, which makes up about 0.04% of the gaseous atmosphere, through pores in their leaves. Phytoplankton, the microscopic plants that float in aquatic ecosystems, get their carbon from atmospheric carbon dioxide that has dissolved in water.

These producer plants then carry out photosynthesis, which converts the carbon in carbon dioxide to carbon in complex organic compounds such as glucose:

$$\text{carbon dioxide} + \text{water} + \textbf{solar energy} \rightarrow \text{glucose} + \text{oxygen}$$

Then the cells in oxygen-consuming plants, animals, and decomposers carry out aerobic cellular respiration, which breaks down glucose and other complex organic compounds and converts the carbon back to carbon dioxide for reuse by producers:

$$\text{glucose} + \text{oxygen} \rightarrow \text{carbon dioxide} + \text{water} + \textbf{energy}$$

This linkage between photosynthesis and aerobic respiration circulates carbon in the ecosphere and is a major part of the **carbon cycle.** This part of the gaseous cycle is shown in greatly simplified form in Figure 4-20. The diagram shows some of the ways plants, animals, and decomposers in the biosphere depend on one another for survival. Oxygen and hydrogen, the other elements in glucose and other carbohydrates, cycle almost in step with carbon.

Carbon cycles rapidly between the atmosphere and hydrosphere and living organisms. Figure 4-21 shows some other parts of the carbon cycle. It shows that some of the earth's carbon is tied up for long periods in fossil fuels—coal, petroleum, natural gas, peat, oil shale, tar sands, and lignite—formed over millions of years in the lithosphere. The carbon in these mineral deposits remains locked up until it is released to the atmosphere as carbon dioxide when fossil fuels are extracted and burned.

In aquatic ecosystems carbon and oxygen combine with calcium to form insoluble calcium carbonate in shells and rocks. When shelled organisms die, they sink and their shells are buried in bottom sediments (Figure 4-21). Carbon in these sediment deposits reenters the cycle as carbon dioxide very slowly, over millions of years, by dissolution into ocean water, form-

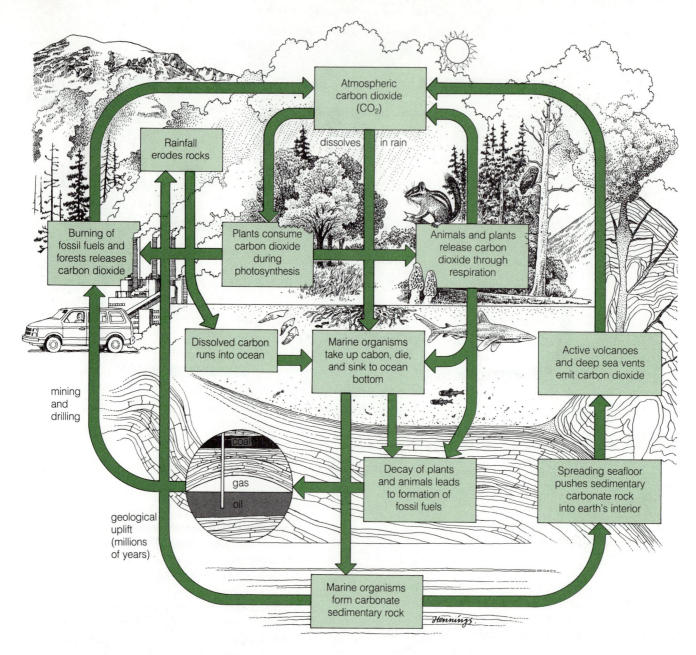

Figure 4-21 Simplified diagram of other parts of the carbon cycle, including the effects of human activities.

ing dissolved carbon dioxide gas that can enter the atmosphere. The melting of rocks in long-term geological processes and volcanic eruptions also release carbon dioxide to the air or water. And movements of the earth's crust uplift sediment deposits to form an island or a continent, exposing the carbonate rock to chemical attack and conversion to carbon dioxide gas.

Another part of the carbon cycle (not shown in Figures 4-20 and 4-21) is anaerobic respiration, which takes place without the presence of oxygen. In this process, various types of anaerobic bacteria convert organic compounds to methane (CH_4) gas and other compounds. This type of respiration takes place mostly in swamps and bogs. It also occurs in landfills, where we bury trash.

We have intervened in the carbon cycle mainly in two ways, especially since 1950, as world population and resource use have increased rapidly:

- Removal of forests and other vegetation without sufficient replanting, which leaves less vegetation to absorb CO_2. Also, carbon dioxide is added to the atmosphere when unharvested wood and plant debris decay and organic matter and roots in the exposed soil react with oxygen in the atmosphere.
- Burning carbon-containing fossil fuels and wood (Figure 4-21). This produces carbon dioxide that flows into the atmosphere. Scientists project that this carbon dioxide, along with other chemicals

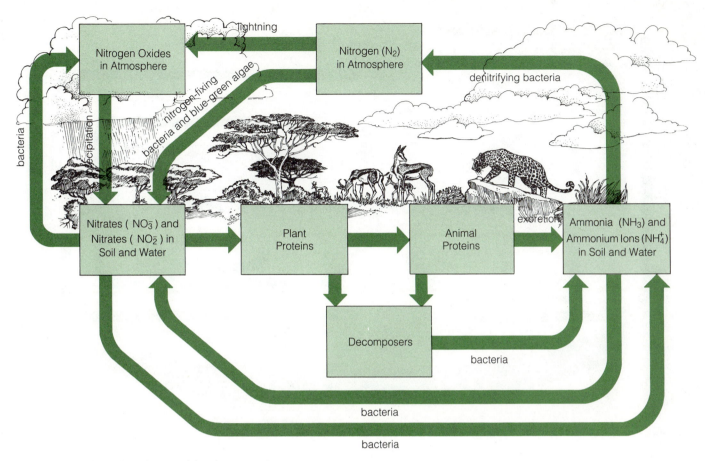

Figure 4-22 Simplified diagram of the nitrogen cycle.

we are adding to the atmosphere, will warm the earth's atmosphere in coming decades and disrupt global food production.

Nitrogen Cycle   Organisms require nitrogen in various chemical forms to make proteins and genetically important nucleic acids such as DNA. Most green plants need nitrogen in the form of nitrate ions (NO_3^-) and ammonium ions (NH_4^+). The nitrogen gas (N_2) that makes up about 78% of the volume of the earth's atmosphere is useless to such plants, people, and most other organisms. Fortunately, nitrogen gas is converted into water-soluble ionic compounds containing nitrate ions and ammonium ions, which are taken up by plant roots as part of the **nitrogen cycle.** This gaseous cycle is shown in simplified form in Figure 4-22.

The conversion of atmospheric nitrogen gas into other chemical forms useful to plants is called **nitrogen fixation.** It is carried out mostly by blue-green algae and certain kinds of bacteria in soil and water and by rhizobium bacteria living in small swellings called nodules on the roots of alfalfa, clover, peas, beans, and other legume plants. Also playing a role in nitrogen fixation, lightning converts nitrogen gas and oxygen gas in the atmosphere to nitric oxide and

nitrogen dioxide gas. These gases react with water vapor in the atmosphere and are converted to nitrate ions that return to the earth as nitric acid dissolved in precipitation and as particles of nitrate salts.

Plants convert inorganic nitrate ions and ammonium ions obtained from soil water into proteins, DNA, and other large, nitrogen-containing organic compounds they require. Animals get most of their nitrogen-containing nutrients by eating plants or other animals that have eaten plants.

Specialized decomposer bacteria convert the nitrogen-containing organic compounds found in detritus (wastes and dead bodies of organisms) into inorganic compounds such as ammonia gas (NH_3) and water-soluble salts containing ammonium ions (NH_4^+). Other specialized groups of bacteria then convert these inorganic forms of nitrogen back into nitrate ions in the soil and into nitrogen gas, which is released to the atmosphere to begin the cycle again.

We intervene in the nitrogen cycle in several ways:

■ Emission of large quantities of nitric oxide (NO) into the atmosphere when wood or any fossil fuel is burned. The nitric oxide then combines with oxygen gas in the atmosphere to form nitrogen dioxide (NO_2) gas, which can react with water

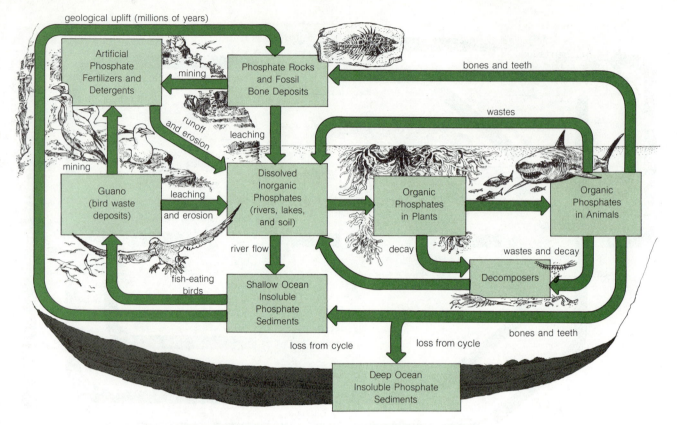

Figure 4-23 Simplified diagram of the phosphorus cycle.

vapor in the atmosphere to form nitric acid (HNO_3). This acid is a component of acid deposition, which is damaging trees and killing fish in parts of the world.

- Emission of the greenhouse gas nitrous oxide (N_2O) into the atmosphere by the action of certain bacteria on fertilizers and livestock wastes.

- Mining mineral deposits of compounds containing nitrate and ammonium ions for use as commercial fertilizers.

- Depleting nitrate ions and ammonium ions from soil by harvesting nitrogen-rich crops.

- Adding excess nitrate ions and ammonium ions to aquatic ecosystems in runoff of animal wastes from livestock feedlots, runoff of commercial nitrate fertilizers from cropland, and discharge of untreated and treated municipal sewage. This excess supply of plant nutrients stimulates rapid growth of algae and other aquatic plants. The breakdown of dead algae by aerobic decomposers depletes the water of dissolved oxygen gas, causing massive fish kills.

Phosphorus Cycle Phosphorus, mainly in the form of certain types of phosphate ions (PO_4^{3-} and HPO_4^{2-}), is an essential nutrient of both plants and animals. It is a part of DNA molecules, which carry genetic infor-

mation; ATP and ADP molecules, which store chemical energy for use by organisms in cellular respiration; certain fats in the membranes that encase plant and animal cells; and bones and teeth in animals.

Various forms of phosphorus are cycled mostly through the water, soil, and living organisms by the **phosphorus cycle,** shown in simplified form in Figure 4-23. In this sedimentary cycle, phosphorus moves slowly from phosphate deposits on land and shallow ocean sediments to living organisms and back to the land and ocean. Bacteria are less important in the phosphorus cycle than in the nitrogen cycle.

Phosphorus released by the slow breakdown, or weathering, of phosphate rock deposits is dissolved in soil water and taken up by plant roots. However, most soils contain only small amounts of phosphorus because phosphate compounds are fairly insoluble in water and are found only in certain kinds of rocks. Thus, phosphorus is the limiting factor for plant growth in many soils and aquatic ecosystems.

Animals get their phosphorus by eating plants or by eating animals that have eaten plants. Animal wastes and the decay products of dead animals and plants return much of this phosphorus to the soil, to rivers, and eventually to the ocean bottom as insoluble deposits of phosphate rock.

Some phosphate is returned to the land as guano— the phosphate-rich manure produced by fish-eating birds such as pelicans, gannets, and cormorants. But this return is small compared to the much larger amounts of phosphate eroded from the land to the oceans each year by natural processes and human activities.

Over millions of years geologic processes may push up and expose the seafloor, forming islands and other land surfaces. Weathering then slowly releases phosphorus from the exposed rocks and allows the cycle to begin again.

We intervene in the phosphorus cycle chiefly in two ways:

■ Mining large quantities of phosphate rock to produce commercial inorganic fertilizers and detergent compounds.

■ Adding excess phosphate ions to aquatic ecosystems in runoff of animal wastes from livestock feedlots, runoff of commercial phosphate fertilizers from cropland, and discharge of untreated and treated municipal sewage. As with nitrate and ammonium ions, an excessive supply of this plant nutrient causes explosive growth of blue-green algae and other aquatic plants that disrupt life in aquatic ecosystems.

Sulfur Cycle Sulfur is transformed to various compounds and circulated through the ecosphere in the **sulfur cycle** (Figure 4-24). It enters the atmosphere from natural sources as

■ hydrogen sulfide (H_2S), a colorless, highly poisonous gas with a rotten-egg smell, from active volcanoes and the decay of organic matter in swamps, bogs, and tidal flats

■ sulfur dioxide (SO_2), a colorless, suffocating gas, from active volcanoes

■ particles of sulfate salts, such as ammonium sulfate, from sea spray

About one-third of all sulfur compounds and 99% of the sulfur dioxide reaching the atmosphere from all sources come from human activities. Burning sulfur-containing coal and oil to produce electric power accounts for about two-thirds of the human-related input of sulfur dioxide into the atmosphere. The remaining third comes from industrial processes such as petroleum refining and the smelting of sulfur-containing ore compounds of metals such as copper, lead, and zinc.

In the atmosphere sulfur dioxide reacts with oxygen to produce sulfur trioxide gas, which reacts with water vapor to produce tiny droplets of sulfuric acid (H_2SO_4). It also reacts with other chemicals in the atmosphere to produce tiny particles of sulfate salts. These droplets of sulfuric acid and particles of sulfate salts fall to the earth as components of acid deposition, which harms trees and aquatic life.

Hydrologic Cycle The **hydrologic cycle**, or **water cycle**, which collects, purifies, and distributes the earth's fixed supply of water, is shown in simplified form in Figure 4-25. Solar energy and gravity continuously move water among the ocean, air, land, and living organisms. The main processes in this cycle are *evaporation* (conversion of water to water vapor), *condensation* (conversion of water vapor to droplets of liquid water), *precipitation* (rain, sleet, hail, snow), and *runoff* back to the sea to begin the cycle again.

Incoming solar energy evaporates water from oceans, rivers, lakes, soil, and vegetation into the atmosphere. Winds and air masses transport this water vapor over various parts of the earth's surface. Decreases in temperature in parts of the atmosphere cause the water vapor to condense and form tiny droplets of water in the form of clouds or fog. Eventually these droplets combine and become heavy enough to fall to the land and bodies of water as precipitation. The average water molecule remains in the air about 10 days before falling back to the earth as precipitation. About half of the earth's precipitation falls on tropical forests.

Some of the fresh water returning to the earth's surface as precipitation becomes locked in glaciers. Much of it collects in puddles and ditches and runs off into nearby lakes, streams, and rivers, which carry water back to the oceans, completing the cycle. This runoff of fresh water from the land also causes soil erosion, which moves various chemicals through portions of other biogeochemical cycles.

A large portion of the water returning to the land seeps deep into the ground. There it is stored as groundwater in aquifers—spaces in and between rock formations. Underground springs and streams eventually return this water to the surface and to rivers, lakes, and surface streams, from which it evaporates or returns to the ocean. Fresh water percolates downward through the soil to replenish aquifers. However, the underground circulation of water is extremely slow compared to that on the surface and in the atmosphere.

We intervene in the water cycle in two main ways:

■ Withdrawing large quantities of fresh water from rivers, lakes, and aquifers. In heavily populated or heavily irrigated areas, withdrawals have led to groundwater depletion or intrusion of ocean salt water into underground water supplies.

■ Clearing vegetation from land for agriculture, mining, roads, parking lots, construction, and other activities. This reduces seepage that recharges groundwater supplies, increases the risk of flooding, and increases the rate of surface runoff, which increases soil erosion.

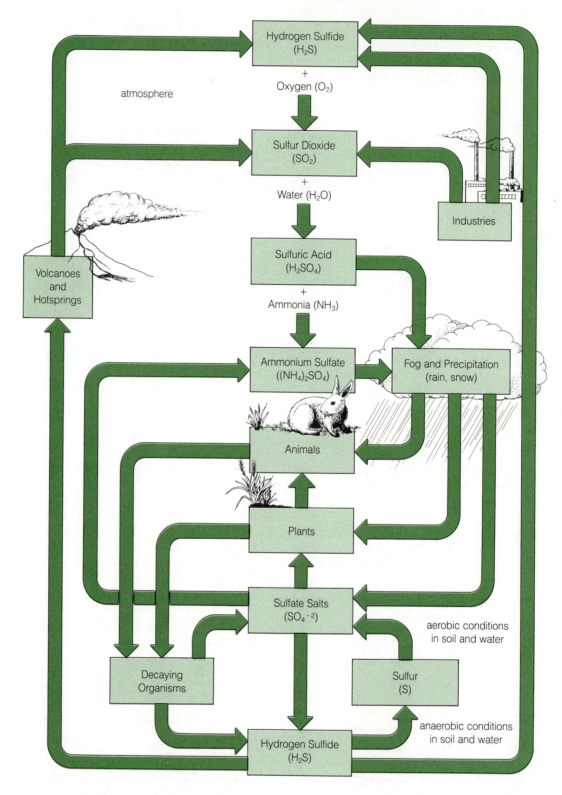

Figure 4-24 Simplified diagram of the sulfur cycle.

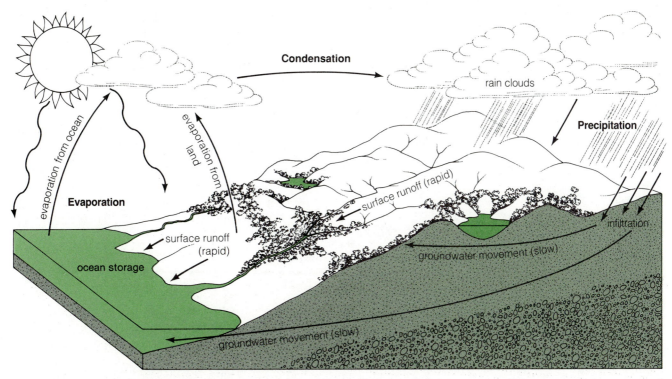

Figure 4-25 Simplified diagram of the hydrologic cycle.

4-5 ROLES AND INTERACTIONS OF SPECIES IN ECOSYSTEMS

Ecological Niche An **ecological niche** (pronounced "nitch") is a description of all the physical, chemical, and biological factors that a species needs to live, grow, and reproduce in an ecosystem. It describes an organism's role in an ecosystem.

A common analogy is that an organism's habitat is its "address" in an ecosystem, while its ecological niche is its "occupation" and "lifestyle." For example, the habitat of a robin includes woodlands, forests, parks, pasture lands, meadows, orchards, gardens, and yards. Its ecological niche includes factors such as nesting and roosting in trees, eating insects, earthworms, and fruit, and dispersing fruit and berry seeds in its droppings.

Each species has important roles to play in its ecosystem. Ecologists have found evidence that certain species, called *keystone species*, play roles that affect many other organisms in an ecosystem. The demise of a keystone species may trigger a cascade of sharp population drops and extinctions of other species that depend on it for certain services. Many keystone species are little known and not cute, cuddly, or glamorous like those that get the lion's share of wildlife conservation funds.

Two keystone species are the gopher tortoise and the alligator (see Case Study on p. 100). The gopher tortoise is found in sandhill areas of Florida and other southern states. Each of these slow-moving, dinner-plate-size animals digs a 9-meter (30-foot) deep burrow. In the hot, inhospitable ecosystems of the South, these holes become cool refuges for some 40 other species, including the gray fox, the opossum, the indigo snake, and many insects. In areas where the gopher tortoise has been hunted to extinction or near extinction for its tasty meat, many species depending on the tortoise no longer exist.

Information about ecological niches helps people manage domesticated and wild plant and animal species as sources of food and other resources. It also helps us predict the effects of either adding or removing a species to or from an ecosystem. But determining the interacting factors that make up an organism's ecological niche is very difficult.

Specialist and Generalist Niches The niche of an organism can be classified as specialized or generalized, depending primarily on its major sources of food, the extent of its habitat, and its tolerance to temperature and other physical and chemical factors. Most species of plants and animals can tolerate only a narrow range of climatic and other environmental conditions and feed on a limited number of different plants or animals. Such species have a specialized niche, which limits them to specific habitats in the ecosphere.

The giant panda, for example, has a highly specialized niche because it obtains 99% of its food by consuming bamboo plants. The destruction and mass

People tend to divide plants and animals into "good" and "bad" species and to assume that we have a duty to wipe out the villains or use them up to satisfy our needs and wants. One species that we drove to near extinction in many of its marsh and swamp habitats is the American alligator (Figure 4-26).

Alligators have no natural predators, except people. Hunters once killed large numbers of these animals for their exotic meat and supple belly skin, used to make shoes, belts, and other items. Between 1950 and 1960, hunters wiped out 90% of the alligators in Louisiana. The alligator population in the Florida Everglades also was threatened.

Many people might say, "So what?" But they are overlooking the key role the alligator plays in subtropical, wetland ecosystems such as the Everglades. Alligators dig deep depressions, or "gator holes," which collect fresh water during dry spells. These holes are refuges for aquatic life and supply fresh water and food for birds and other animals.

Large alligator nesting mounds also serve as nest sites for birds such as herons and egrets. As alligators move from gator holes to nesting mounds, they help keep waterways open. They also eat large numbers of gar, a fish that preys on other fish. This means that alligators help maintain populations of game fish such as bass and bream.

In 1967 the U.S. government placed the American alligator on the endangered species list. Averaging about 40 eggs per nest and protected from hunters, by 1975 the alligator population had made a strong comeback in many areas—too strong, according to some people, who found alligators in their backyards and swimming pools.

The problem is that both human and alligator populations are increasing rapidly, and people are taking over the natural habitats of the alligator. A gator's main diet is snails, apples, sick fish, ducks, raccoons, and turtles. But if a pet or a person falls into or swims in a canal, pond, or other area where a gator lives, the reptile's jaws will shut by reflex on just about anything it encounters.

Many people encourage gators to hang around houses by feeding them. In Florida 71 people were attacked and 2 were killed by gators between 1978 and 1988. But this is more of a people problem than a gator problem.

In 1977 the U.S. Fish and Wildlife Service reclassified the American alligator from endangered to threatened in Florida, Louisiana, and Texas, where 90% of the animals live. In 1987 this reclassification was extended to seven other states.

As a threatened species, alligators are still protected from excessive harvesting by hunters. However, limited hunting is allowed in some areas to keep the population from growing too large. Florida, with at least 1 million alligators, permits 7,000 kills a year. Another 1 million live in southern states extending from Texas to South Carolina. The comeback of the American alligator is an important success story in wildlife conservation.

U.S. Fish and Wildlife Service

Figure 4-26 In 1967 the American alligator was classified as an endangered species in the United States. This protection allowed the population of the species to recover to the point that its status has been changed from endangered to threatened.

die-off of several species of bamboo in parts of China, where the panda is found, have led to the animal's near extinction.

In a tropical rain forest, an incredibly diverse array of plant and animal life survives by occupying a variety of specialized ecological niches in distinct layers of the forest's vegetation (Figure 4-27). The widespread clearing of such forests is dooming millions of specialized plant and animal species to extinction. Figure 4-28 shows various feeding niches of different bird species in a wetland.

Species with a generalist niche are very adaptable. They can live in many different places, eat a wide variety of foods, and tolerate a wide range of environmental conditions. This explains why they are usually in less danger of extinction than species with a specialized niche. Examples of generalist species include flies, cockroaches, mice, rats, and human beings.

The ecological niches of species include interaction with other species in an ecosystem. The major species interaction are interspecific competition, predation, parasitism, mutualism, and commensalism.

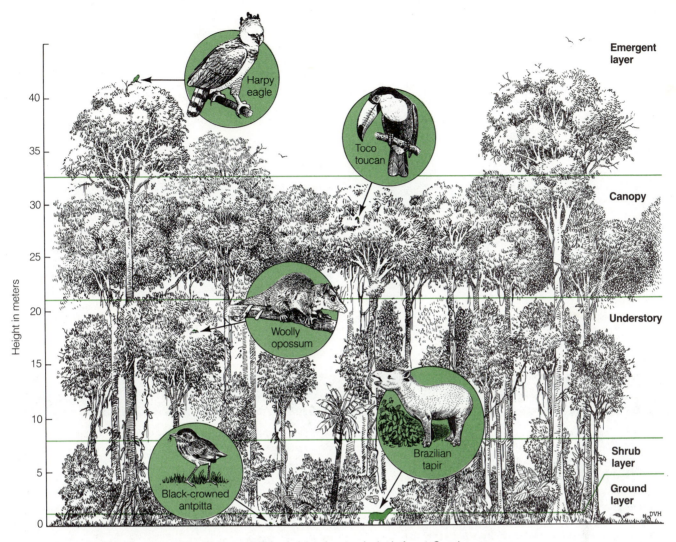

Figure 4-27 Stratification of specialized plant and animal niches in a tropical rain forest. Species occupy specialized niches in the various layers of vegetation.

Competition Between Species   As long as commonly used resources are abundant, different species can share them. But when two or more species in the same ecosystem attempt to use the same scarce resources, they are said to be engaging in **interspecific competition.** At least part of their ecological niches overlap. The scarce resource may be food, water, carbon dioxide, sunlight, soil nutrients, space, shelter, or anything required for survival.

In some cases individuals in two species have equal access to a common resource, but they differ in how fast or efficiently they can exploit it. One competing species may gain an advantage over the other species by producing more young, getting more food or solar energy, or defending itself better. It may also have an advantage by being able to tolerate a wider range of temperature, light, water salinity, or concentrations of certain poisons.

Other species gain greater access to a scarce resource by preventing competing species from using the resource. For example, hummingbirds chase bees and other hummingbird species away from clumps of flowers.

Populations of some animal species avoid or reduce competition with more dominant species by moving to another area, switching to a less accessible or less readily digestible food source, or hunting for the same food source at different times of the day or in different places. For example, hawks and owls feed on similar prey, but hawks hunt during the day and owls hunt at night. Where lions and leopards occur together, lions take mostly larger animals as prey and leopards take smaller ones.

Predation and Parasitism   The most obvious form of species interaction in food chains and webs is **predation**: An individual organism of one species, known as the **predator,** feeds on parts or all of an organism of another species, the **prey,** but does not live on or in the prey. Together, the two kinds of organisms

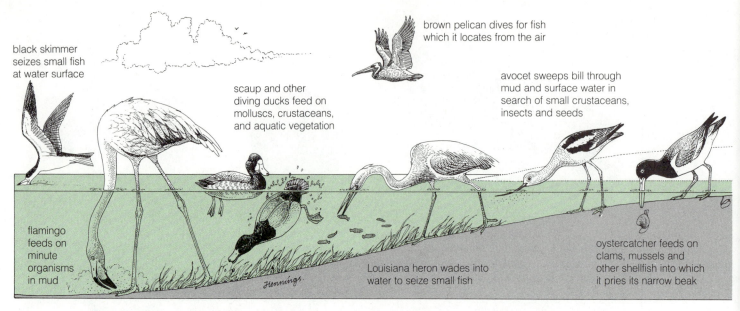

black skimmer seizes small fish at water surface

scaup and other diving ducks feed on molluscs, crustaceans, and aquatic vegetation

brown pelican dives for fish which it locates from the air

avocet sweeps bill through mud and surface water in search of small crustaceans, insects and seeds

flamingo feeds on minute organisms in mud

Louisiana heron wades into water to seize small fish

oystercatcher feeds on clams, mussels and other shellfish into which it pries its narrow beak

Hennings

Figure 4-28 Specialized feeding methods that are part of the ecological niches of various types of birds in a wetland.

CASE STUDY Sharks: The Oceans' Most Important Predator

Sharks have lived in the oceans for over 400 million years, long before dinosaurs appeared. Sharks have evolved into more than 350 species, whose size, behavior, and other characteristics differ widely.

The smallest species, the cigar shark, is only a foot long at maturity. Another species, called "cookie cutters," is also about a foot long. Cookie cutters survive by taking bites out of the sides of porpoises, whales, and large fish such as bluefin tuna. At the other end of the scale is the whale shark, the world's biggest fish. It can grow to 18 meters (60 feet).

Sharks have extremely sensitive sense organs. They can detect the scent of decaying fish or blood even when it is diluted to only one part per million parts of seawater. They have superb hearing and better night vision than we do. They also sense the electrical impulses radiated by the muscles of animals, making it difficult for their prey to escape detection. They are powerful and rapid swimmers. Because their bodies are denser than seawater, they must always keep moving in order not to sink.

Sharks are the key predators in the world's oceans, helping control the number of many other ocean predators. Without sharks the oceans would be overcrowded with dead and dying fish and depleted of many healthy ones that we rely on for food. Eliminating sharks would upset the balance of ocean ecosystems.

Yet this is precisely what we are in danger of doing. Every year we catch over 100 million sharks, mostly for food and for their fins, which are sent to Asia for shark-fin soup. Since 1986, the demand for sharks has increased dramatically. Others are killed for sport and out of fear. Some shark species, such as edible thresher and mako sharks, are being commercially exploited and could face extinction. Sharks are vulnerable to overfishing because members of most species don't produce pups until about the twelfth year, and then produce only a few at a time.

Influenced by movies and popular novels, most people see sharks as people-eating monsters. This is far from the truth. Each year a few types of shark—great white, bull, tiger, and oceanic white tip—injure about 100 people

and kill perhaps 25. Most attacks are by great white sharks, which often feed on sea lions and other marine mammals and sometimes mistake human swimmers for their normal prey. Nevertheless, with hundreds of millions of people swimming in the ocean each year, the chances of being killed by a shark are minute—about 1 in 5 million. You are thousands of times more likely to get killed when you drive a car.

Furthermore, sharks help save lives. In addition to providing people with food, they are helping us learn how to fight cancer, bacteria, and viruses. Sharks are very healthy and have aging processes similar to ours. Their highly effective immune system allows wounds to heal quickly without becoming infected. A chemical extracted from shark cartilage is being used as an artificial skin for burn victims. Sharks are among the few animals in the world that almost never get cancer and eye cataracts. Understanding why can help us improve human health.

Sharks are needed in the world's ocean ecosystems. Although they don't need us, we need them.

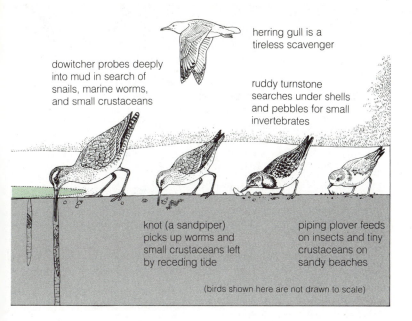

herring gull is a tireless scavenger

dowitcher probes deeply into mud in search of snails, marine worms, and small crustaceans

ruddy turnstone searches under shells and pebbles for small invertebrates

knot (a sandpiper) picks up worms and small crustaceans left by receding tide

piping plover feeds on insects and tiny crustaceans on sandy beaches

(birds shown here are not drawn to scale)

involved are said to have a **predator-prey relationship.** Sharks are one of the most important predators in the world's oceans (see Case Study on p. 102).

Prey species have various protective mechanisms. Otherwise, they would easily be captured and eaten. Some can run or fly fast. Others have thick skins or shells. Still others have camouflage colorings or the ability to change color so that they can hide by blending into their environment. Others give off chemicals that smell or taste bad to their predators or poison them.

Predators have several methods of capturing their prey. A carnivore generally has to chase and catch its food; a herbivore doesn't. One way a carnivore can get enough food is to run fast, as the cheetah does. Another way is to cooperate by hunting in packs, as spotted hyenas, African lions, wolves, and Cape hunting dogs do. Under natural conditions such species are often more abundant than those, such as leopards, tigers, and cougars, that do not cooperate in hunting prey.

A third way many predators get enough to eat is to look for prey individuals that appear to be sick, crippled, or in some way disabled. This natural weeding out of diseased and weak individuals also benefits the prey species by preventing the spread of disease and leaving stronger and healthier individuals for breeding. A fourth way to capture prey is to invent weapons and traps and learn how to domesticate animals as humans have done.

Another type of species interaction is **parasitism. Parasites** feed off another organism, called their **host,** but unlike predators, they live on or in the host for a good part of its life cycle. The parasite draws nourishment from and gradually weakens its host. This may or may not kill the host.

Both plants and animals can be attacked by parasites, and both plants and animals may be parasites. Tapeworms, disease-causing bacteria, and other parasites live inside their hosts. Lice, ticks, and mistletoe plants attach themselves to the outside of their hosts.

Some parasites can move from one host to another, as dog fleas do. Others spend their adult lives attached to a single host. Examples are mistletoe, which feeds on oak tree branches, and tapeworms, which feed in the intestines of humans and other animals. Fleas and ticks may have internal parasites even smaller than they are.

Mutualism and Commensalism   In some cases two different types of organisms interact directly in ways that benefit each species. Such a mutually beneficial interaction between species is called **mutualism.** One example is the interaction of the yucca plant and the yucca moth in the desert of the southwestern United States. The yucca plant is fertilized only by the female yucca moth when she carries pollen from one yucca plant to another as she lays her eggs in seed pods of the plant. When the eggs hatch, the moth larvae eat some, but not all, of the yucca seeds. Neither organism could survive without the other.

Another mutualistic interaction occurs between conifer (cone-bearing) trees and certain kinds of fungi that grow on the tree roots. The fungi survive by extracting nutrient-rich fluids from the roots. The conifers benefit because the fungi help draw water and minerals from the soil into the tree roots.

In another type of species interaction, called **commensalism,** one type of organism benefits, while the other is neither helped nor harmed to any great degree. For example, in the open sea certain types of barnacles live on the jawbones of whales. The barnacles benefit by having a safe place to live and a steady food supply. The whale apparently gets no benefit from this relationship, but it suffers no harm from it either.

This chapter has shown that the essential feature of the living and nonliving parts of individual terrestrial and aquatic ecosystems and of the global ecosystem, or ecosphere, is interdependence and connectedness, as summarized in the Guest Essay on p. 104. Without the services performed by diverse communities of plants, animals, and decomposers, we would be starving, gasping for breath, and drowning in our own wastes. The next two chapters show how this interdependence is the key to understanding the earth's major types of ecosystems and how ecosystems change in response to natural and human stresses.

We sang the songs that carried in their melodies all the sounds of nature—the running waters, the sighing of winds, and the calls of the animals. Teach these to your children that they may come to love nature as we love it.

Grand Council Fire of American Indians

Edward J. Kormondy

Edward J. Kormondy is chancellor and professor of biology at the University of Hawaii-Hilo/West Oahu College. He has taught at the California State University at Los Angeles, the University of Southern Maine, the University of Michigan, Oberlin College, and Evergreen State College. Among his many research articles and books are Concepts of Ecology *and* Readings in Ecology *(both published by Prentice-Hall). He has been a major force in biological education and for several years was director of the Commission on Undergraduate Education in the Biological Sciences.*

Energy flows—but downhill only in terms of its quality; chemical nutrients circulate—but some stagnate; populations stabilize—but some go wild; communities age—but some age faster. These dynamic and relentless processes are as characteristic of ecosystems as are thermonuclear fusion reactions in the sun.

Thinking one can escape the operation of these and other laws of nature is like thinking one can stop the earth from revolving or make rain fall up. Yet we have consciously peopled the earth only for hundreds of millions to endure starvation and malnutrition, deliberately dumped wastes only to ensure contamination, purposefully simplified agricultural systems only to cause widespread crop losses from pest invasions. Such actions suggest that we believe that energy and food automatically increase as people multiply, that things stay where they are put, that simplification of ecosystems aids in their productivity. Such actions indicate that we have ignored basic, inexorable and unbreakable physical laws of ecosystems. We have proposed, but nature has disposed, often in unexpected ways counter to our intent.

We proposed more people, more mouths to be fed, more space to be occupied. Nature disposed by placing an upper limit on the rate at which the earth's plants can produce organic nutrients for themselves and for the people and other animals that feed on them. It also disposed by using and degrading energy quality at and between all trophic levels in the biosphere's intricate food webs and by imposing an upper limit on the total space that is available and can be occupied by humans and other species.

Ultimately, the only way there can be more and more people is for each person to have less and less food and fuel energy and less and less physical space. Absolute limits to growth are imposed both by thermodynamics and space. We may argue about what these limits are and when they will be reached, but there are limits and, if present trends continue, they will be reached. The more timely question then

CHAPTER SUMMARY

Ecology is the study of interactions between organisms and their living (biotic) and nonliving (abiotic) environment. This study is based on examining different *ecosystems*, communities of organisms interacting with one another and with their nonliving chemical environment (the elements and compounds needed by organisms to remain alive and reproduce) and physical environment (solar energy, wind, moisture, and other factors).

The living and dead organisms found near the earth's surface in parts of the atmosphere, hydrosphere, and lithosphere make up what is called the *biosphere*. This collection of living and dead organisms interacting with one another and their nonliving environment (energy and chemicals) throughout the world is called the *ecosphere*.

Life on earth depends on the *one-way flow of high-quality energy* from the sun through the ecosphere and back into space as degraded, low-quality heat and on the *recycling* of *nutrients*—chemicals required by living organisms—through parts of the ecosphere. This recycling of nutrients from the nonliving environment to living organisms and back to the nonliving environment takes place in *biogeochemical cycles*.

Ecology is primarily concerned with interactions among *organisms* (any form of life), *populations* (a group of organisms of the same kind living in a particular area or habitat), *communities* (populations of different species living and interacting in a particular place), *ecosystems*, and the *ecosphere*.

Major land ecosystems (deserts, grasslands, and forests) are called *biomes*, and major ecosystems found in the hydrosphere (oceans, rivers, lakes) are called *aquatic ecosystems*. The major types of living (biotic) components of ecosystems are **(1)** *producers* (mostly green plants that can make the organic nutrients they need through photosynthesis), **(2)** *consumers* (herbivores, carnivores, and omnivores) that feed on living organisms, and **(3)** *detritivores* that feed directly on dead organisms and organic wastes (*detritus feeders*) or that break down the remains of dead animals and plants or the waste products of living organisms into simpler chemicals for reuse by producers (*decom-*

becomes a qualitative one. What quality of life will we have within these limits? What kind of life do you want? What quality of life will future generations have?

We proposed exploitative use of resources and indiscriminate disposal of human and technological wastes. Nature disposed, and like a boomerang, the consequences of our acts came back to hit us. On the one hand, finite oil, coal, and mineral resource supplies are significantly depleted—some nearing exhaustion. On the other hand, air, water, and land are contaminated, some beyond restoring.

Nature's laws limit each resource; some limits are more confining than others, some more critical than others. The earth is finite, and its resources are therefore finite. Yet another of nature's laws is that fundamental resources—elements and compounds—circulate, some fully and some partially. They don't stay where they are put. They move from the land to the water and the air, just as they move from the air and water to the land. Must not our proposals for using resources and discharging wastes be mindful of ultimate limits and the earth's chemical recycling processes? What about your own patterns of resource use and waste disposal?

We proposed simplification of our agricultural systems to ease the admittedly heavy burden of cultivation and harvest. Nature has disposed otherwise, however. Simple ecosystems such as a cornfield are youthful ones, and like our own youth, are volatile, unpredictable, and unstable. Young ecosystems do not conserve nutrients, and agricultural systems in such a stage must have their nutrients replaced artificially and expensively by adding commercial inor-

ganic fertilizers. Young agricultural systems essentially lack resistance to pests and disease and have to be protected artificially and expensively by pesticides and other chemicals. These systems are also more subject to the whims of climate and often have to be expensively irrigated. Must not our proposals for managing agricultural systems be mindful of nature's managerial strategy of providing biological diversity to help sustain most complex ecosystems? What of your own manicured lawn?

The take-home lesson is a rather straightforward one: We cannot propose without recognizing how nature disposes of our attempts to manage the earth's resources for human use. We are shackled by basic ecological laws of energy flow, chemical recycling, population growth, and community aging processes. We have plenty of freedom within these laws, but like it or not we are bounded by them. You are bounded by them. What do you propose to do? And what might nature dispose in return?

Guest Essay Discussion

1. List the patterns of your life that are in harmony with the laws of energy flow and chemical recycling and those that are not.

2. Can you think of other examples of "we propose" and "nature disposes"?

3. Set up a chart with examples of "we propose" and "nature disposes," but add a third column titled "we repropose," based on using ecological principles to work with nature.

posers, mostly bacteria and fungi). Oxygen-consuming organisms break down the organic nutrients they make or consume by *cellular aerobic respiration*.

Each individual organism of a species has a particular *range of tolerance* to variations in chemical and physical factors in its environment. The existence, abundance, and distribution of an organism is determined by whether one or more physical or chemical factors in its environment fall above or below the levels most individuals in the population of a species can tolerate (*law of tolerance*). Too much or too little of any abiotic factor can limit or prevent growth of a population of a species in an ecosystem even if all other factors are at or near the optimum range of tolerance for the species (*limiting factor principle*).

The one-way flow of energy from producers to consumers of plants and animals and eventually to decomposers in a particular ecosystem can be described in terms of *food chains* and *food webs*. An average of only about 10% of the high-quality chemical energy available at one trophic level is typically transferred and stored in usable form as chemical energy in the bodies of the organisms at the next

level. The rest of this energy is used to keep the organisms alive, and most is eventually degraded and lost as low-quality heat to the environment.

This loss of usable high-quality energy at each step in a food chain can be diagrammed as a *pyramid of energy flow.* *Pyramids of numbers* and *pyramids of biomass* can also be used to describe what happens in ecosystems. The rate at which the plants in a particular ecosystem produce usable chemical energy or biomass is called *net primary productivity*.

The *carbon, oxygen, nitrogen, phosphorus, sulfur, and water cycles* are the major ways that the key elements and compounds needed for life are recycled within the ecosphere in forms usable by plant and animal life. Human activities are increasingly intruding into these cycles.

An *ecological niche* describes the physical, chemical, and biological factors that a species needs to live, grow, and reproduce in an ecosystem. It describes an organism's role in an ecosystem. *Interspecific competition, predation, parasitism, mutualism,* and *commensalism* are the main ways that different species interact in ecosystems as part of their ecological niches. The key message of ecology is that all forms of life on earth are either directly or indirectly dependent on one another and on their nonliving environment.

DISCUSSION TOPICS

1. **a.** A bumper sticker asks, "Have you thanked a green plant today?" Give two reasons for appreciating a green plant.
   b. Trace the sources of the materials that make up the sticker and see whether the sticker itself is a sound application of the slogan.
   c. Explain how decomposers help keep you alive.

2. **a.** How would you set up a self-sustaining aquarium for tropical fish?
   b. Suppose you have a balanced aquarium sealed with a clear glass top. Can life continue in the aquarium indefinitely as long as the sun shines regularly on it?
   c. A friend cleans out your aquarium and removes all the soil and plants, leaving only the fish and water. What will happen?

3. Using the second law of energy, explain why there is such a sharp decrease in high-quality energy as energy flows through a food chain or web. Doesn't an energy loss at each step violate the first law of energy? Explain.

4. Using the second law of energy, explain why many poor people in less developed countries exist mostly on a vegetarian diet. How can people on such a diet avoid malnutrition? Why are many poor people on a plant diet unable to avoid malnutrition?

5. Using the second law of energy, explain why a pound of steak costs more than a pound of corn.

6. Why are there fewer lions than mice in an African ecosystem supporting both types of animals?

Ecosystems:
What Are the Major Types?

General Questions and Issues

1. Why do different parts of the world have different climates?

2. What are the major types of terrestrial ecosystems (biomes), and how does climate influence the type found in a given area?

3. What are the major types of aquatic ecosystems, and what major factors influence the kinds of life they contain?

When we try to pick out anything by itself, we find it hitched to everything else in the universe.

John Muir

The ecosphere, in which all organisms are found, contains an astonishing variety of terrestrial ecosystems, such as deserts, grasslands, and forests, and aquatic ecosystems, such as lakes, reservoirs, ponds, rivers, and oceans. Each ecosystem has a characteristic plant and animal community adapted to certain environmental conditions—especially climate.

5-1 CLIMATE: A BRIEF INTRODUCTION

Weather and Climate We live at the bottom of an ocean of invisible gases that make up the earth's atmosphere. Every moment and every day, there are changes in temperature, barometric pressure, humidity, precipitation, sunshine (solar radiation), cloudiness, wind direction and speed, and other conditions in the lower part of the atmosphere called the **troposphere.** These short-term changes in the properties of the troposphere are what we call **weather.**

Climate, in contrast, is the general pattern of atmospheric or weather conditions, seasonal variations, and weather extremes in a region over a long period—at least 30 years. Climate is the weather you might expect to occur at a particular time and place on the basis of past experience. Weather is the atmospheric conditions you actually experience at a given moment.

The physical properties and chemical composition of the atmosphere, along with the daily input of energy from the sun, are the major factors determining the weather and climate of different parts of the earth. A raindrop, a breeze, a tornado—all can be ultimately traced to the effect of the sun's energy upon the earth's atmosphere. Climate in turn is a key factor determining the types and numbers of plants and animals in various ecosystems, especially on land.

The two most important factors determining the climate of an area are its average temperature and average precipitation. Figure 5-1 shows the global distribution of the major types of climate based on these two factors.

Climate and the Global Circulation of Air Five major factors determine the uneven patterns of average temperature and average precipitation shown in Figure 5-1 and thus the climates of the world:

- variations in the amount of incoming solar energy striking different parts of the earth

- the earth's annual orbit around the sun and its daily rotation around its axis—the imaginary line connecting the North and South poles

- chemical content of the atmosphere

- distribution of the continents and oceans

- topographical features such as mountains

The amount of incoming solar energy reaching the earth's surface varies with latitude—the distance north or south from the equator. Air in the troposphere is heated more at the equator (zero latitude), where the sun is almost directly overhead, than at the high-latitude poles, where the sun is lower in the sky and strikes the earth at a low angle (Figure 5-2).

The large input of heat at and near the equator warms large masses of air, which rise because warm air has a lower density (mass per unit of volume) than cold air. As these warm air masses rise, they spread northward and southward, carrying heat from the equator toward the poles.

At the poles the warm air cools and sinks downward because cool air is denser than warm air. These cool air masses then flow back near ground level toward the equator to fill the void left by rising warm air masses. This general global air circulation pattern in the troposphere leads to warm average temperatures near the equator, cold average temperatures near the poles, and

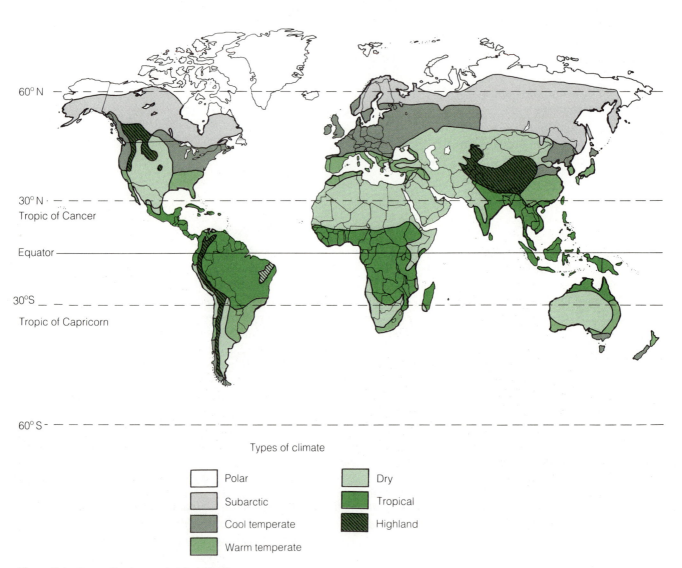

Types of climate

- Polar
- Subarctic
- Cool temperate
- Warm temperate
- Dry
- Tropical
- Highland

Figure 5-1 Generalized map of global climates.

moderate or temperate average temperatures at the middle latitudes between the two regions (Figure 5-1).

However, general average temperature patterns vary with the seasons in all parts of the world away from the equator. Seasonal changes in climate are caused by two major factors. One is the earth's annual orbit around the sun. The other is the earth's daily, eastward rotation around its axis, which is tilted 23.5 degrees from its plane of revolution around the sun. When the North Pole leans toward the sun, the sun's rays strike the Northern Hemisphere in a more direct and concentrated manner per unit of area, bringing summer to the northern half of the earth. At the same time, the South Pole is angled away from the sun; thus, winter conditions prevail over the Southern Hemisphere (Figure 5-3). As the earth makes its annual

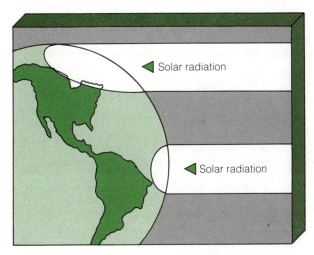

Figure 5-2 During certain times of the year the sun's rays are almost perpendicular to the earth's equatorial zones, concentrating heat on this part of the earth. The sun's rays strike the earth's poles at a slanted angle, spreading the incoming solar energy over a larger area and diluting the heat input.

rotation around the sun, these conditions shift and cause seasonal changes.

Forces created on the atmosphere as the earth spins around its tilted axis break up the general air circulation pattern from the equator to the poles and back. This creates three separate belts of moving air, or prevailing surface winds, north and south of the equator (Figure 5-4).

The general circulation of air masses in the troposphere and the prevailing surface winds also affect the distribution of precipitation over the earth. The larger input of solar energy near the equator evaporates huge amounts of water from the oceans, inland water sources, soil, and vegetation in this region into the troposphere. The moisture-holding capacity of air (humidity) increases when it is warmed and decreases when it is cooled. As warm, humid tropical air rises, it cools rapidly and loses most of its moisture as rain near the equator. This abundant rainfall and the constant warm temperatures give rise to the world's tropical rain forests (see color insert Figures 1 and 2.).

By the time these air masses have moved 30 degrees in latitude north and south of the equator (around the Tropic of Cancer and the Tropic of Capricorn), they have lost most of their moisture. The low precipitation in these regions explains why most of the world's large deserts are found there (see color insert Figures 1 and 2).

In flowing over these desert and semiarid areas, the air is warmed again. As it continues northward and southward, this warm air picks up some moisture. By the time it reaches latitudes about 60 degrees north and south of the equator, it begins rising and cooling again. Enough moisture is released in these mid-latitudes to support temperate forests and grasslands (see color insert Figure 2). The fairly dry air then flows toward the poles and cools even more, producing zones with low precipitation, mostly snow.

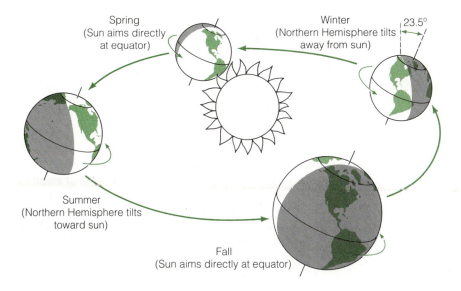

Spring
(Sun aims directly at equator)

Winter
(Northern Hemisphere tilts away from sun)

23.5°

Summer
(Northern Hemisphere tilts toward sun)

Fall
(Sun aims directly at equator)

Figure 5-3 The seasons (shown here for the Northern Hemisphere only) are caused by variations in the amount of incoming solar energy as the earth makes its annual rotation around the sun on an axis tilted by 23.5 degrees.

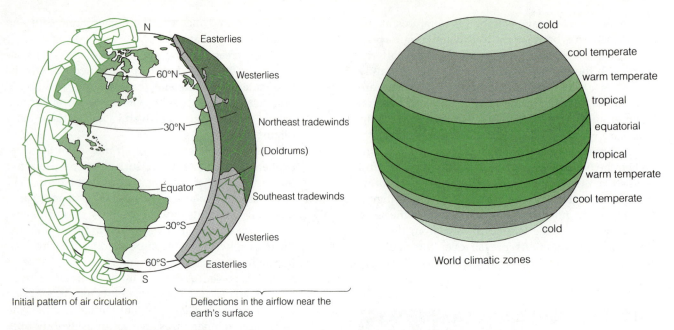

Initial pattern of air circulation
Deflections in the airflow near the earth's surface

World climatic zones

Figure 5-4 Formation of prevailing surface winds. The twisting motion caused by the earth's rotation on its axis causes the airflow in each hemisphere to break up into three separate belts of winds. Prevailing winds affect the types of climate found in different areas.

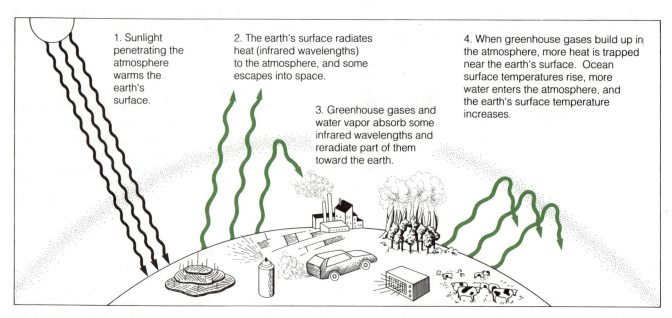

1. Sunlight penetrating the atmosphere warms the earth's surface.

2. The earth's surface radiates heat (infrared wavelengths) to the atmosphere, and some escapes into space.

3. Greenhouse gases and water vapor absorb some infrared wavelengths and reradiate part of them toward the earth.

4. When greenhouse gases build up in the atmosphere, more heat is trapped near the earth's surface. Ocean surface temperatures rise, more water enters the atmosphere, and the earth's surface temperature increases.

Figure 5-5 The greenhouse effect. (Adapted with permission from Cecie Starr and Ralph Taggart, *Biology: The Unity and Diversity of Life*, 5th ed., Belmont, Calif.: Wadsworth, 1989)

Climate and the Chemical Content of the Atmosphere The chemical content of the troposphere and stratosphere is another factor determining the earth's average temperatures and thus its climates. In the troposphere, carbon dioxide, water vapor, and trace amounts of ozone, methane, nitrous oxide, and chlorofluorocarbons play a key role in this temperature regulation process.

These gases, known as **greenhouse gases,** act somewhat like a pane of glass in a greenhouse. They let in visible light from the sun but prevent some of the degraded infrared radiation, or heat, from escaping back into space. They reradiate it back toward the earth's surface (Figure 5-5). The resulting heat buildup raises the temperature of the air in the troposphere, a warming action called the **greenhouse effect.**

The Earth's Major Ecosystems

The ecosphere contains a variety of major terrestrial ecosystems (biomes), such as deserts, grasslands, and forests, and aquatic ecosystems such as lakes, rivers, and oceans. These ecosystems are the life-support systems for us and other species. Each ecosystem has a characteristic community of plants, animals, and decomposers adapted to certain environmental conditions, especially climate. For example, differences in average precipitation and average temperature are the major factors leading to tropical, temperate, and polar deserts, grasslands, and forests.

The world's ecosystems are dynamic, not static. As environmental conditions change because of natural processes or as a result of our activities, the biological communities found in the world's ecosystems undergo changes in response to these stresses. However, there are limits to how rapidly such adaptations to stress can occur. Understanding how the world's ecosystems work and change can help guide us in sustaining them rather than degrading and destroying them.

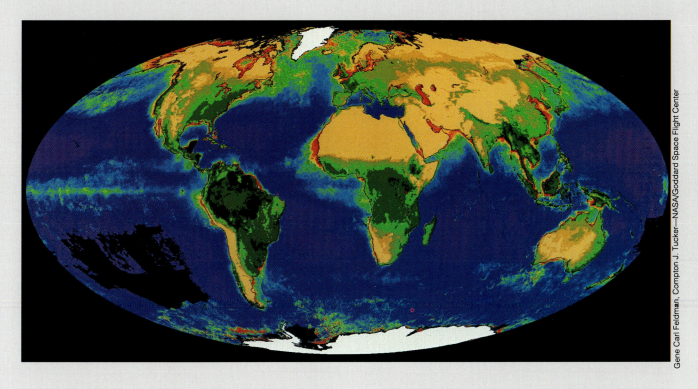

Gene Carl Feldman, Compton J. Tucker—NASA/Goddard Space Flight Center

1. The biosphere. Three years of satellite data were combined to produce this picture of earth's biological productivity. Rain forests and other highly productive land areas appear as dark green, deserts yellow. The concentration of phytoplankton, a primary indicator of ocean productivity, is represented by a scale that runs from red (highest) to orange, yellow, green, and blue (lowest).

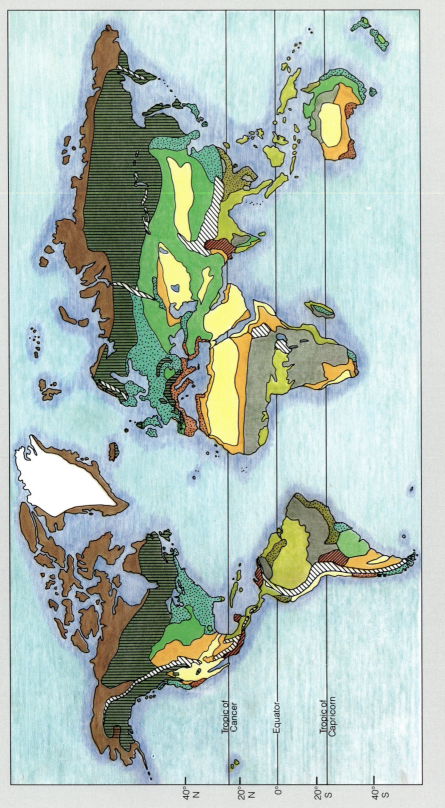

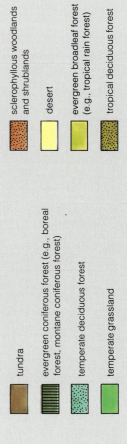

tropical scrub forest

tropical savanna, thorn forest

semidesert, arid grassland

mountains (complex zonation)

sclerophyllous woodlands and shrublands

desert

evergreen broadleaf forest (e.g., tropical rain forest)

tropical deciduous forest

tundra

evergreen coniferous forest (e.g., boreal forest, montane coniferous forest)

temperate deciduous forest

temperate grassland

40° N

20° N

0°

20° S

40° S

Tropic of Cancer

Equator

Tropic of Capricorn

2. The world's major terrestrial ecosystems.

From Cecie Starr and Ralph Taggert, *Biology: The Unity and Diversity of Life, Fourth Edition* (Belmont, California: Wadsworth). © 1987 by Wadsworth, Inc.

Koene/Explorer/Photo Researchers

3. Tropical desert,
Sahara dunes in Algeria.

Harlo H. Hadow

4. Temperate desert
near Tuscon, Arizona.
The vegetation includes
cresote bushes, ocotillo,
saguaro cacti, and
prickly pear cacti.

5. (Bottom left)Tropical
grassland (savanna),
Serengeti Plain in
Tanzania, in Africa.

6. (Bottom right) Tem-
perate grassland (short-
grass prairie) in the
Rocky Mountains.

E.E. Kingsley/Photo Researchers, Inc.

Kenneth W. Fink/Ardea, London

7. (Left) Temperate grassland (patch of tall grass prairie) in Illinois.

8. (Right) Replacement of a temperate grassland with wheatfields, north of Johnstown, Colorado.

9. (Bottom) Polar grassland (Arctic tundra) in Alaska in summer.

10. Tropical rain forest in Costa Rica. These forests are the world's most diverse biomes.

11. (Left) Cleared and burned tropical rain forest in the Amazon Basin, Rondonia, Brazil. The world's remaining tropical rain forests are being cleared and degraded at an alarming rate.

12. (Top left) Temperate deciduous forest south of Nashville, Tennessee, during summer.

13. (Top right) Temperate deciduous forest south of Nashville, Tennessee, during winter.

14. (Lower left) Tree farm of southern pine in North Carolina.

15. (Lower right) Northern coniferous forest (taiga, or boreal forest) in the Sierra Nevada of California.

16. (Top left) Salt marsh (coastal wetland) in New England.

17. (Top right) Rocky shore beach, Big Sur, California.

18. (Left) Developed barrier beach in Seaside Park, New Jersey. Protective dunes have been removed, making the beach and houes subject to flooding and erosion.

19. (Above) Developed barrier island. Human developments on barrier islands are highly vulnerable to storms, hurricanes, and severe beach erosion.

20. (Above) Coral reef
    in the Red Sea.

21. (Top right) Oligotro-
    phic lake in Canadian
    Rockies.

Carl Roessler/Animals, Animals

D.W. MacManiman

Vic Cox/Peter Arnold, Inc.

John M. Coffman/National Audubon Society

22. (Lower left) Eutrophic lake in northeastern Oregon.

23. (Lower right) Mountain stream in George
    Washington National Forest, Virginia.

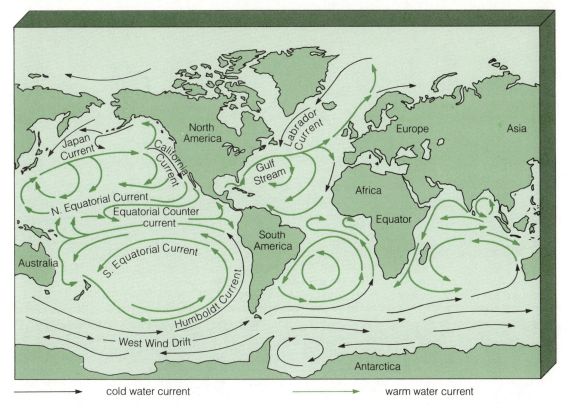

| cold water current | warm water current |

Figure 5-6 Major warm and cold surface currents and drifts of the world's oceans. These water movements are produced by the earth's winds and modified by its rotational forces. They circulate water in the oceans in great surface gyres and have major effects on the climate on adjacent lands.

If there were no greenhouse gases in the atmosphere, the earth would be a cold and lifeless planet with an average atmospheric temperature of −18°C (0°F). Now, however, scientists expect increases in levels of carbon dioxide and other greenhouse gases from human activities to raise the average temperature of the troposphere and thus change global climate and food-producing patterns within your lifetime.

The ozone content of the stratosphere also affects climate. Absorption of UV radiation by ozone molecules creates warm layers high in the **stratosphere**—the portion of the atmosphere above the troposphere. These layers prevent churning gases in the troposphere from entering the stratosphere. This thermal cap is an important factor in determining the average temperature of the troposphere and thus the earth's climates. Any human activities that decrease the average amount of ozone in the stratosphere can have far-reaching effects on climate, human health, and wildlife.

Climate and Ocean Currents The earth's rotation, inclination, prevailing winds, and differences in water density cause ocean currents and surface drifts that generally move parallel with the equator (Figure 5-6). Trade winds, blowing almost continuously in an easterly direction toward the equator, push surface ocean waters westward in the Atlantic, Pacific, and Indian

oceans until these waters bounce off the nearest continent. This causes two large, circular water movements, called *gyres*, that turn clockwise in the Northern Hemisphere and counterclockwise in the Southern Hemisphere. These gyres move warm waters to the north and south of the equator.

Warm and cold currents and surface drifts in the world's oceans affect the climates of nearby coastal areas. For instance, without the warm Gulf Stream, which transports 25 times more water than all the world's rivers, the climate of northwestern Europe would be more like that of the sub-Arctic. Ocean currents and drifts also help mix ocean waters and distribute the nutrients and dissolved oxygen needed by aquatic organisms. Recurring changes in global climate and weather can change water temperatures and currents (see Case Study on p. 112).

Climate and Topography Mountains, valleys, and other topographical features of the earth's surface also affect the climates of areas. Because of their higher elevation, mountain highlands tend to be cooler, windier, and wetter than bordering valleys. For instance, although Mount Kilimanjaro, Africa's highest peak, stands just south of the equator, its summit is always covered with snow.

Mountains interrupt the flow of prevailing surface winds and the movement of storms. When prevailing

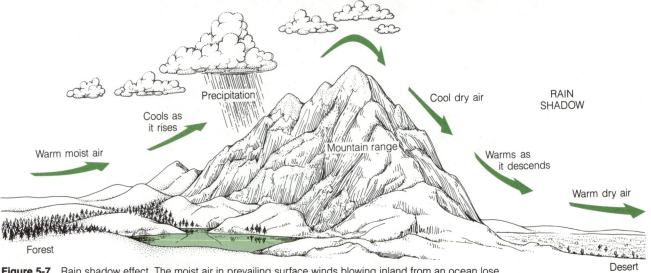

Figure 5-7 Rain shadow effect. The moist air in prevailing surface winds blowing inland from an ocean lose most of their moisture as rain and snow on the windward (wind facing) slopes of mountains. This leads to semiarid and arid conditions on the leeward side of the mountain range and the land beyond.

CASE STUDY Climate Oscillations, Fish Populations, and the El Niño–Southern Oscillation

High atmospheric pressure in the eastern Pacific and low pressure in the western Pacific drive trade winds. As these winds blow along the coast of South America and then westward along the equator, they drag surface water away from the coast. The warm water removed by these westward-flowing currents is replaced by cooler water upwelling from below the *thermocline*—the rapid drop in water temperature that takes place between warm surface water and frigid deep water (Figure 5-8, left).

The resulting upwelling off the coast of Peru is one of the largest in the world. These nutrient-rich waters produce massive blooms of phytoplankton, which support large numbers of zooplankton. The zooplankton in turn provide enough food for large populations of anchovy and other fish. Large populations of seabirds then dive into the surface waters and feed on the fish.

Much of the warm surface water transported from the western Pacific evaporates and feeds torrential rains. High above, the air slowly returns to the east (Figure 5-8, left). This air and water loop is called the Walker Circulation.

Every two to seven years, near the end of December, winds push a warm current southward along the coasts of Ecuador and Peru. The current mixes with the upwelling cold water, warming it slightly and depressing the thermocline (Figure 5-8, right). The warmer water no longer cools the air above it as effectively. The westward surface winds stop or even reverse, disrupting the Walker Circulation.

This irregular increase in water temperature is called *El Niño* (Christ child) because it usually takes place during the Christmas season. It acts jointly with the Southern Oscillation, a periodic change in atmospheric pressure at the earth's surface in Indonesia, northern Australia, and the southeastern Pacific. This change in atmospheric pressure causes prevailing surface winds in the western equatorial Pacific to pick up speed.

The outcome of the combined *El Niño*–Southern Oscillation (ENSO) is that warm surface waters in the western equatorial Pacific move eastward. Sometimes the ENSO is mild and ceases in a few months, when there's no longer enough warm water to sustain the shift. Once in a while—at least 9 times in the last 40 years—the combined effect is severe and lasts 1 to 2 years.

When this happens, there's not enough cold, nutrient-rich water to sustain large plankton populations in upwellings like the one off the coast of Peru. The fish that feed on them either die or migrate to colder, deep water. Seabirds that feed on the anchovy and other fish in the surface waters then starve or migrate to other areas.

During such times massive numbers of fish, squid, sea turtles, and seabirds die. As the creatures decay, they release hydrogen sulfide into the water. This triggers another effect, called *El Pintor* (the painter) by people in South America, but known elsewhere as red tide. The water turns shades of yellow, brown, and red when it becomes filled with microscopic plants called dinoflagellates. Dense blooms of these plankton give off chemicals that kill many kinds of fish and shellfish.

A strong *El Niño*–Southern Oscillation combination can also trigger massive weather changes over at least two-thirds of the globe, especially in the Pacific and Indian Ocean regions. During 1982 and 1983 there was a destructive ENSO—maybe the worst in recorded history. Peru and Ecuador were drenched with the heaviest rains in their history, and some of their rivers were 1,000 times winds blowing inland from an ocean reach a mountain range, the moist air cools as it is forced to rise and expand. This causes the air to lose most of its moisture as rain and snow on the windward (wind-facing) slopes. As the drier air mass flows down the leeward slopes (not facing the wind), it is compressed and becomes warmer. Then it flows over the arid and semiarid land beyond.

This drop in air moisture and the resulting semi-arid and arid conditions on the leeward side of high mountains and the land beyond is called the **rain shadow effect** (Figure 5-7). The Mojave Desert east of the Sierra Nevada mountains parallel to the coast of California is the result of the rain shadow effect. Rain shadows also produce arid and semiarid lands near the Himalayan mountain range of Asia and the Andes of South America.

5-2 MAJOR TYPES OF TERRESTRIAL ECOSYSTEMS: DESERTS, GRASSLANDS, AND FORESTS

Effects of Precipitation and Temperature on Plant Types

Why is one area of the earth a desert, another a grass-land, and another a forest? Why are there different types of deserts, grasslands, and forests? What determines the types of life found in these biomes? The general answer to these questions is differences in climate—primarily average temperature and average precipitation (Figure 5-9).

With respect to plants, *precipitation generally is the limiting factor that determines whether the biomes of most of the world's land areas are desert, grassland, or forest.* A **desert** is an area where evaporation exceeds precipitation and the average amount of precipitation is less

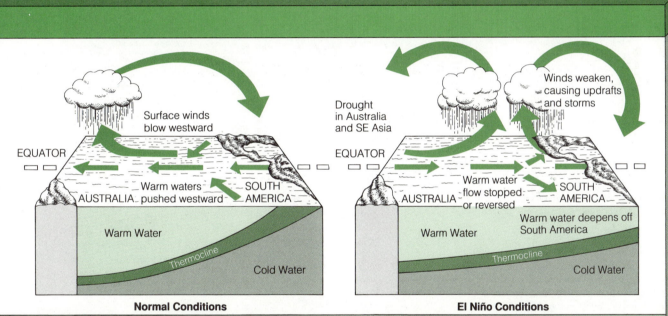

Figure 5-8 Normal surface water temperature and currents in upwellings of nutrient-rich bottom water near the coast of Peru (left) and warming of these surface waters by a periodic change in climate patterns called the El Niño-Southern Oscillation (ENSO). When an ENSO lasts one or two years, it severely disrupts populations of plankton, fish, and seabirds in upwelling areas. A strong ENSO can also trigger massive weather changes over at least two-thirds of the globe, especially in the countries along the Pacific and Indian oceans. Some areas receive abnormally high rainfall; others experience severe droughts.

higher than normal. Parts of the western coast of the United States were also heavily flooded.

Meanwhile, India got little of its vital monsoon rains. Australia, Africa, and Indonesia suffered from severe droughts, brush fires, and dust storms. Many typhoons occurred in the western Pacific. These severe weather shifts caused 1,300 to 2,000 deaths and $8 billion in property damage and job losses.

Another major ENSO took place between 1986 and 1988. It dried out India by weakening the monsoon rains. The ENSO, coupled with the greenhouse effect from rising carbon dioxide levels, made 1987 the warmest year, on average around the globe, during the past 100 years that temperatures have been measured.

After climatic conditions return to normal, fish and seabird populations normally recover. However,

if a species of fish is harvested in excessive numbers before a severe ENSO hits, its population may take a long time to recover.

Sometimes an ENSO warming of Pacific waters is followed by a cooling effect called *La Niña*. It leads to a dry winter in the south-eastern United States and a slight cooling of global atmospheric temperatures. Such an effect occurred in late 1988 and early 1989.

Figure 5-9 Average precipitation and average temperature act together over a period of 30 years or more as limiting factors that determine the type of desert, grassland, or forest ecosystem found in a particular area.

Figure 5-10 Generalized effects of latitude and altitude on climate and biomes. Biomes with similar types of vegetation occur primarily as a result of similarities in climate in traveling from the equator toward the earth's poles or up mountain slopes. Similar types of animals live in each vegetation belt or life zone by adapting to similar environmental conditions.

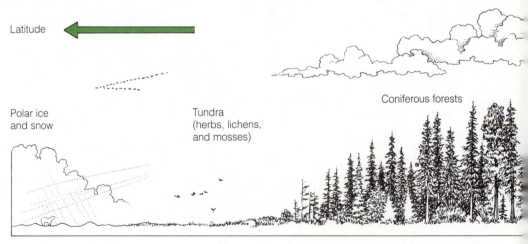

than 25 centimeters (10 inches) a year. Such areas have little vegetation or have widely spaced, mostly low vegetation. Because vegetation is sparse and skies are usually clear, the heat stored in desert soil during the day is quickly lost at night. Thus, deserts undergo large changes in temperature between day and night.

Grasslands are regions where the average annual precipitation is great enough to allow grass to prosper yet so erratic that periodic drought and fire prevent large stands of trees from growing. Undisturbed areas with moderate to high average annual precipitation tend to be covered with **forest,** containing various species of trees and smaller forms of vegetation.

Average precipitation and average temperature, along with soil type (Section 10-1), are the major factors determining the particular type of desert, grassland, or forest in a particular area. Acting together, these factors lead to tropical, temperate, and polar deserts, grasslands, and forests (Figure 5-9).

Climate changes with latitude and altitude. If you travel from the equator to either of the earth's poles, you will encounter increasingly cold and wet climates and zones of vegetation adapted to each climate (see color insert Figure 2 and Figure 5-10). Similarly, as elevation, or altitude, above sea level increases, the climate becomes wetter and colder. That is why high mountains with permanent ice or snow exist in the tropics. If you climb a tall mountain from its base to its summit, you will find changes in plant life similar to those you would find in traveling from the equator to one of the earth's poles (Figure 5-10).

Major Types of Deserts   Deserts cover around 16% of the earth's land surface and are located mainly between the tropical and subtropical regions (see color insert Figures 1 and 2). You may think that all deserts are hot during the day and consist of vast expanses of sand dunes dotted with a few oases. Such deserts do exist. But they are only one of three major types of deserts that occur because of combinations of low average precipitation with different average temperatures: tropical, temperate, and cold. (Figure 5-9).

Tropical deserts, such as the southern Sahara, make up about one-fifth of the world's desert area (see color insert Figure 3). They typically have few plants and a hard, windblown surface strewn with rocks and some sand. Sand dunes cover about 10% of these deserts. Temperatures are hot year-round. In *temperate deserts*, such as the Mojave in southern California, daytime temperatures are hot in summer and cool in winter (see color insert Figure 4). In *cold deserts*, such as the Gobi lying south of Siberia, winters are cold and summers are warm or hot.

Plants and animals in all deserts are adapted to capture and conserve scarce water. Plants in temperate and cold deserts usually are widely spaced, minimizing competition for water. Thorny bushes and shrubs such as mesquite and salt cedar have roots reaching deep into the soil to tap groundwater. Others, such as the evergreen creosote bush, have wax-coated leaves, which reduce the amount of water lost by evaporation. Ocotillo shrubs drop their leaves and

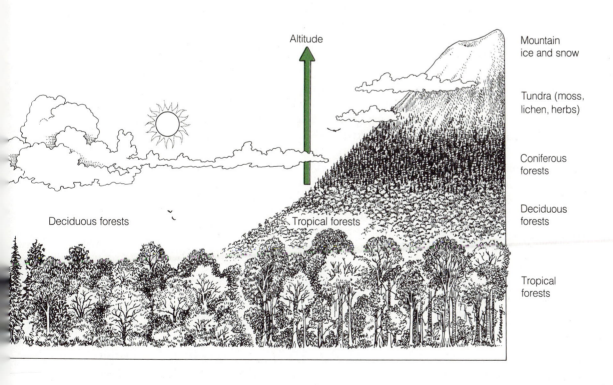

Altitude

Mountain ice and snow

Tundra (moss, lichen, herbs)

Coniferous forests

Deciduous forests

Tropical forests

Deciduous forests

Tropical forests

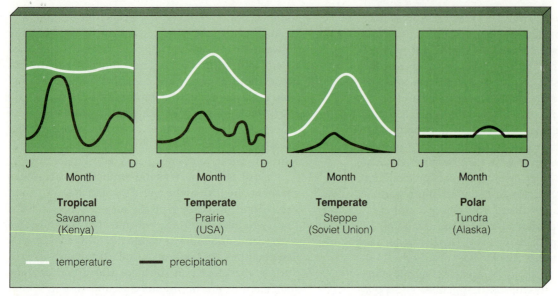

J　Month　D　　J　Month　D　　J　Month　D　　J　Month　D

Tropical　　　**Temperate**　　　**Temperate**　　　**Polar**
Savanna　　　Prairie　　　　Steppe　　　　Tundra
(Kenya)　　　(USA)　　　(Soviet Union)　　(Alaska)

—— temperature　　　—— precipitation

Figure 5-11 Typical annual variations in temperature and precipitation for different types of grasslands.

survive in a dormant state during long dry spells and then grow new leaves within a week after a rain.

Fleshy-stemmed cacti are either short (prickly pear) or tall (saguaro) and have shallow but widespread root systems that absorb water quickly. They store water in their succulent tissues and have thick, waxy skins that prevent water loss. After a brief spring rain, desert wildflowers and grasses grow swiftly, produce seed, and die within a few weeks. Their seeds lie in the sand awaiting the next spring rain.

Most desert animals escape the daytime heat by staying underground in burrows during the day and being active at night. If you visit an Arizona or California desert during the day, you will probably see only a few insects, lizards, and birds, such as hawks and roadrunners, that prey on lizards. At night, however, the desert is alive with rodents and their predators, such as rattlesnakes and owls.

Desert animals also have special adaptations to help them conserve water. The nocturnal kangaroo rat, for example, doesn't drink water. It gets the water it needs from its food and cellular respiration. It also conserves water by excreting dry feces and thick, nearly solid urine. Insects and reptiles have thick outer coverings to minimize water loss through evaporation. Some desert animals become dormant during periods of extreme heat or drought.

In some desert areas the soil is low in nutrients, and in other areas it is fairly rich in nutrients. In these areas, only the lack of water prevents the growth of plants found in wetter biomes. Humans have converted desert into productive farmland by bringing in water for irrigation from other areas or by drawing on deep pools of groundwater underneath the desert surface.

The slow growth rate of plants, low species diversity, and shortages of water make deserts fragile biomes.

For example, vegetation destroyed by activities such as livestock grazing and off-road driving may take decades to grow back. Vehicles can also collapse burrows that are key habitats for many desert animals.

Major Types of Grasslands *Tropical grasslands,* or *savannas,* are found in areas with high average temperatures, two prolonged dry seasons (during winter and summer) and abundant rain the rest of the year (Figure 5-11). They occur in a wide belt on either side of the equator beyond the tropical rain forests (see color insert Figure 2).

Some of these biomes, such as Africa's Serengeti Plain, consist mostly of open plains covered with grasses (see color insert Figure 5). Others contain grasses along with widely spaced, small, mostly deciduous trees and shrubs, such as palms, acacias, and baobab. These plants shed their leaves during the dry season and avoid excessive water loss.

Savanna herbivores have specialized eating habits. Giraffes eat leaves and twigs found high on the scattered trees. Elephants eat leaves and branches further down, and gazelles, antelopes, and zebras graze on grasses of different heights and coarseness. Grasses grow from the bottom instead of the top so that their stems can grow again after being nibbled off by grazing animals.

Savannas have a larger number and variety of hoofed animal species than any other biome. In African savannas vast herds of wildebeests, gazelles, zebras, giraffes, antelopes, and other large herbivores graze in different areas, depending on water and soil conditions. During the dry season, fires often sweep savannas, and the herds migrate in search of food. Some of these herbivores and their large predators, such as lions, leopards, and cheetahs, are disappearing rapidly except in a few protected areas because of ranching, farming, hunting, poaching, and other human activities.

Temperate grasslands are found in the large, interior areas of continents, especially North America, South America, Europe, and Asia (see color insert Figure 2). Types of temperate grasslands are the *tall-grass prairies* (see color insert Figure 7) and *short-grass prairies* (see color insert Figure 6) of the midwestern and western United States and Canada, the *pampas* of South America, the *veld* of southern Africa, and the *steppes* that stretch from central Europe into Siberia. Figure 5-11 shows typical annual changes in temperature and precipitation for a prairie and a steppe. In these biomes winds blow almost continuously and evaporation is rapid. As long as it is not plowed up, the soil is held in place by the thick network of grass roots.

The soil of temperate grassland is highly fertile and supports large populations of decomposers. Beetles, spiders, grasshoppers, and other insects live in the grasses in huge numbers and varieties. Prairie dogs, pocket gophers, deer mice, ground squirrels, prairie chickens, and other small herbivores live in the American grasslands, mostly in underground burrows.

Temperate grasslands are often populated by herds of grazing animals. At one time, for example, vast herds of bison and pronghorn antelope roamed the prairies of North America. But these wild herbivores have been replaced by domesticated herbivores such as cattle and sheep. Wolves, cougars, coyotes and other animals that preyed on wild herbivores have largely been killed or driven away because they are a threat to livestock.

Of the original tall-grass prairies that once thrived in the midwestern United States and Canada, only about 1% remains. Because of their highly fertile soils, most of these prairies have been cleared for crops such as corn, wheat (see color insert Figure 8), and soybeans and for hog farming.

The short-grass prairies of the western United States are covered with low perennial grasses. They have too little precipitation and soils too low in some plant nutrients to support taller grasses. They are widely used to graze unfenced cattle and in some areas to grow wheat and irrigated crops. Mismanagement and periodic, prolonged droughts led to severe erosion and loss of topsoil in the 1930s—a condition called the Dust Bowl (see Case Study on p. 226).

Polar grassland, or *Arctic tundra*, is found in areas just below the Arctic ice region (see color insert Figure 2). During most of the year this biome is bitterly cold with icy, galelike winds and is covered with ice and snow. Winters are long and dark; average annual precipitation is low and occurs mostly as snow (Figure 5-11). The Arctic tundra is an enormous biome, covering a fifth of the earth's land surface. It is carpeted with a thick, spongy mat of low-growing plants such as lichens (growths of algae and fungi), sedges (grasslike plants

often growing in dense tufts in marshy places), mosses, grasses, and low shrubs (see color insert Figure 9). These hardy plants are adapted to the lack of sunlight and water, freezing temperatures, and constant high winds in this harsh environment. Because of the cold temperatures, decomposition is slow. Partially decomposed organic matter accumulates as soggy masses of peat.

One effect of this biome's extreme cold is **permafrost**—water permanently frozen in thick, underground layers of soil. During the six-to-eight-week summer, when sunlight persists almost around the clock, the surface layer of soil thaws. But the layer of permanent ice a few feet below the surface prevents the water from seeping deep into the ground. As a result, during summer the tundra turns into a soggy landscape dotted with shallow lakes, marshes, bogs, and ponds. Hordes of mosquitoes, deerflies, blackflies, and other insects thrive in the shallow surface pools. They serve as food for large colonies of migratory birds, especially waterfowl, which migrate from the south to nest and breed in the bogs and ponds.

Most of the tundra's permanent animal residents are small herbivores such as lemmings, hares, voles, and ground squirrels, which burrow under the ground to escape the cold. Few species are present in large numbers. Musk-oxen are the only large herbivores that live all year in the tundra. Caribou in North America and reindeer, a similar species in Eurasia, spend the summer in the Arctic tundra but migrate south into northern coniferous forests for the rest of the year.

Populations of lemmings in the tundra rise and fall depending on how good the summer season is for plants they eat. The lemming populations, in turn, regulate the numbers of their predators, such as the lynx, arctic fox, arctic wolf, weasel, and snowy owl. Many of these animals have white coats in winter, which makes them hard to see against the winter snow.

Laplanders in northern Finland and Scandinavia are the only people who live in the harsh tundra. However, discoveries of oil and gas have led to the building of pipelines through the North American tundra. The low rate of decomposition, shallow soil, and slow growth rate of plants make the Arctic tundra perhaps the earth's most fragile biome. Wheel ruts left by a single wagon crossing over tundra soil 100 years ago are still visible. Vegetation destroyed by this and other human activities can take decades to grow back. Buildings, roads, pipelines, and railroads must be built over bedrock, on insulating layers of gravel, or on deep-seated pilings. Otherwise, the structures melt the upper layer of permafrost and tilt or crack as the land beneath them shifts and settles.

Major Types of Forests *Tropical rain forests*, found in certain areas near the equator (see color insert Figures 1 and 2), have a warm but not hot annual mean tem-

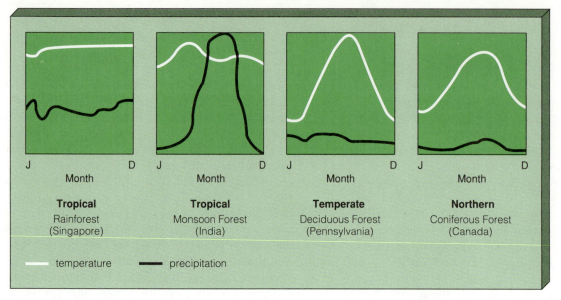

Figure 5-12 Typical annual variations in temperature and precipitation for different types of forests.

perature that varies little daily or seasonally (Figure 5-12). They have high humidity and heavy rainfall almost daily. These biomes are dominated by evergreen trees, which keep most of their leaves or needles throughout the year and thus can use photosynthesis to produce organic nutrients all year (see color insert Figure 10).

The almost unchanging climate in rain forests means that water and temperature are not limiting factors as they are in other biomes. In this biome, nutrients from the often nutrient-poor soils are the major limiting factors.

A mature rain forest has a greater diversity of plant and animal species per unit of area than any other biome. More species of animals can be found in a single tree in a tropical forest than in an entire forest at higher latitudes. Although tropical forests cover only about 7% of the earth's land surface, they contain almost half of the world's growing wood and at least half of its different wildlife species.

These diverse forms of plant and animal life occupy a variety of ecological niches in distinct layers (Figure 4-27, p. 101). Much of the animal life, particularly insects, bats, and birds, is found in the sunny canopy layer with its abundance of shelter, fruits, and other foods. The tangled vegetation and the leaves on the lower canopy of smaller trees block out most of the sunlight so that the forest floor is dark, humid, and relatively free of vegetation.

Monkeys, geckos, iguanas, snakes, chameleons, and other animals move up and down the trunks and vines to feed on insects and fruits. A great variety of tiny animals live on the ground, where there are also vast populations of termites and other decomposers. Because of the warm, moist conditions, decomposition is very rapid; that is why there is little litter on the ground.

Most of the nutrients in this biome are in the vegetation, not in the upper layers of soil as in most other biomes. Once the vegetation is removed, the soils rapidly lose the few nutrients they have and cannot grow crops for more than a few years without large-scale use of commercial fertilizers. Furthermore, when vegetation is cleared, the heavy rainfall washes away most of the thin layer of topsoil. This means that regenerating a mature rain forest on large cleared areas is almost impossible.

These unique and valuable forests are being cleared at an alarming rate to harvest timber and to plant crops and graze livestock on unsustainable soils (see color insert Figure 11). Some ecologists project that if the clearing of tropical rain forests continues at the present rate, within 50 years only a few of these diverse ecosystems will remain. Many thousands of animal and plant species with highly specialized niches in these forests will vanish. Also gone will be millions of trees and other plants, which by absorbing carbon dioxide, help prevent further warming of the earth's atmosphere as a result of the greenhouse effect.

Other types of tropical forests (see color insert Figure 2) get most of their rainfall during monsoon periods (Figure 5-12). During the annual dry period most of the trees in these monsoon forests shed their leaves.

Temperate deciduous forests grow in areas with moderate average temperatures that change significantly during four distinct seasons (see color insert Figure 2). These areas have long summers, not very severe winters, and abundant precipitation often spread fairly evenly throughout the year (Figure 5-12).

These biomes are dominated by a few species of broadleaf deciduous trees such as oak, hickory, maple, poplar, sycamore, and beech. These plants survive during winter by dropping their leaves and going into an inactive state. Each spring they sprout buds that grow into deep green leaves that change in the fall into a beautiful array of colors before dropping (see color insert Figures 12 and 13). In most mature deciduous forests, as in tropical forests, the vegetation is found in distinct layers: a canopy of leaves in the tops of the tallest trees, an understory of shorter, shade-tolerant trees, a layer of shrubs, and a layer of ferns and other low-growing plants on the forest floor.

This layering of vegetation supplies a diversity of ecological niches for animal life. Hawks and owls nest in the canopy. They play an important ecological role by keeping down populations of mice and other small rodents, which would otherwise destroy much of the vegetation on the forest floor. Woodcocks and black bears nest and feed on the ground, and squirrels regularly commute between the canopy and the forest floor.

Once the deciduous forests in the eastern United States were home for many large predators such as bears, wolves, foxes, and mountain lions. Today most of the predators have been killed or displaced, and large numbers of plant-eating whitetail deer live in these forests. Warblers, robins, and other bird species migrate to the forests during the summer to feed and breed.

Temperate forests have nutrient-rich soil (helped by the annual fall of leaves) and valuable timber and are located near settled areas. Thus, all but about 0.1% of the original stands of temperate forests in North America have been cleared for farms, orchards, timber, and urban development. Some have been converted to intensely managed *tree farms*, where a single species is grown for timber or pulpwood (see color insert Figure 14).

Unlike tropical forests, many temperate forests are resistant to disturbance and recover fairly quickly after being cleared. In recent years, however, many temperate forests in Europe, southeastern Canada, and the northeastern United States have been damaged and weakened by prolonged exposure to air pollutants produced by the burning of fossil fuels.

Northern coniferous forests, also called *boreal forests* and *taigas*, are found in regions with a subarctic climate. Winters are long and dry with light snowfall and short days, and temperatures range from cool to extremely cold (Figure 5-12). Summers are short with mild to warm temperatures, but the sun typically shines for 19 hours each day.

These coniferous forests form an almost unbroken belt just south of the Arctic tundra across North America, Asia, and Europe (see color insert Figure 2). They are dominated by a few species of coniferous (cone-bearing) evergreen trees such as spruce, fir, cedar, and pine (see color insert Figure 15). The needle-shaped, waxy-coated leaves of these trees conserve heat and water during the long, cold, dry winters. Plant diver-

sity is low in these forests because few species can survive the winters, when soil moisture is frozen. Parts of the forests are dotted with wet bogs, or *muskegs*.

The crowded needles of the evergreen trees block out much of the light. Beneath the dense stands of trees, a carpet of fallen needles and leaf litter covers the nutrient-poor soil, making the soil acidic and preventing most other plants from growing on the forest floor. During the brief summer the soil becomes waterlogged.

For all or part of the year, taigas are home for large herbivores such as mule deer, elk, caribou, and moose and small herbivores such as porcupines, snowshoe hares, squirrels, and chipmunks. Taigas also contain medium to large predators such as grizzly bears, black bears, wolverines, foxes, lynxes, martens, and wolves. Insect pests thrive during the warm summer months. They are fed upon by birds that migrate from the south for the breeding season.

In settled areas of this biome in North America, farmers and ranchers have essentially eliminated large predators, such as timber wolves, which can prey on livestock. As a result, however, populations of moose, caribou, and mule deer have increased, devastating taiga vegetation. In the long run this reduces the ability of the land to support grazing livestock. Loggers have cut the trees from large areas of taiga in North America. Much fur trapping has also taken place in this biome.

5-3   AQUATIC ECOSYSTEMS

Limiting Factors of Aquatic Ecosystems   Five main factors affect the types and numbers of organisms in aquatic ecosystems. One is **salinity:** the concentration of dissolved salts, especially sodium chloride, in a body of water. The other factors are the depth to which sunlight penetrates, the amount of dissolved oxygen, the availability of plant nutrients, and the water temperature. Fresh water freezes at 0°C (32°F), but the dissolved salts in seawater change its properties so that it freezes at temperatures below 0°C (32°F).

Salinity levels are used to divide aquatic ecosystems into two major classes. Those with high salinity levels are marine or saltwater ecosystems. They include oceans, estuaries (where fresh water from rivers and streams mixes with seawater), coastal wetlands, and coral reefs. Freshwater ecosystems have low salinity. Examples are inland bodies of standing water (lakes, reservoirs, ponds, and inland wetlands) and flowing water (streams and rivers).

Most producers need sunlight to carry out photosynthesis. Thus, the depth to which sunlight penetrates determines the abundance of plant life (and thus animal life) found in various parts of aquatic ecosystems. Phytoplankton producers, for example, are found near the surface.

On land oxygen is easily available from the atmosphere to oxygen-consuming animals. In aquatic ecosystems, however, oxygen is dissolved by exposure of the water to the atmosphere and through photosynthesis in aquatic plants. Oxygen is often scarce in the bottom layers of nonflowing aquatic ecosystems, which are not exposed to the atmosphere and sunlight. Thus, species requiring lots of oxygen are generally found near the surface.

Aquatic plants require nutrients. That is why most plant productivity in aquatic ecosystems occurs near shore, where plant nutrients run off the land and are also available from bottom sediments. In deep waters plant productivity is limited, except in upwellings, where nutrients from the ocean bottom are transported to surface waters (Figure 5-8, left).

Marine Aquatic Ecosystems: Why Are the Oceans Important?

As landlubbers, we tend to think of the earth in terms of land. It is more accurately described, however, as the "water planet" because 71% of its surface is covered by water (Figure 5-13). The oceans make up 97% of that water, and they play key roles in the survival of life on earth.

The oceans are the ultimate receptacle of terrestrial water flowing from rivers. Because of their size, and currents, the oceans mix and dilute many human-produced wastes to less harmful or harmless levels. They play a major role in regulating the climate of the earth by distributing solar heat through ocean currents and evaporation as part of the hydrologic cycle. They also participate in other major biogeochemical cycles.

In addition, by serving as a gigantic reservoir for carbon dioxide, the oceans help regulate the temperature of the atmosphere. Oceans provide habitats for about 250,000 species of marine plants and animals, which are food for many organisms, including human beings. They also serve as a source of iron, sand, gravel, phosphates, lime, magnesium, oil, natural gas, and many other valuable resources.

Major Ocean Zones

Each of the world's oceans can be divided into two major zones: coastal and open sea (Figure 5-14). The **coastal zone** is the relatively warm, nutrient-rich, shallow water that extends from the high-tide mark on land to the edge of a shelflike extension of the continental land mass known as the *continental shelf*. The coastal zone, representing less than 10% of the total ocean area, contains 90% of all ocean plant and animal life and is the site of most of the major commercial marine fisheries. It contains some of the earth's most important ecosystems (see Spotlight on p. 122).

The sharp increase in water depth at the edge of the continental shelf marks the separation of the coastal zone from the **open sea** (Figure 5-14). This marine

Ocean Hemisphere   Land-Ocean Hemisphere

Figure 5-13 The ocean planet. About 71% of the earth's surface is covered with water. About 97% of this water is in the interconnected oceans that cover 90% of the planet's ocean hemisphere (left) and 50% of its land-ocean hemisphere (right).

zone contains about 90% of the total surface area of the ocean but only about 10% of its plant and animal life. However, because of its massive surface area, the open ocean is the largest contributor to the earth's total net primary productivity (Figure 4-19, p. 92). The open sea is divided into three zones based primarily on the ability of sunlight to penetrate to various depths (Figure 5-14).

The Coastal Zone: A Closer Look

The coastal zone includes a number of different habitats. **Estuaries** are coastal areas where fresh water from rivers, streams, and land runoff mixes with salty seawater. Estuaries provide aquatic habitats with a lower average salinity than the waters of the open ocean. Along, with inland swamps and marshes and tropical rain forests, estuaries produce more plant biomass per square meter each year than any of the world's other ecosystems (Figure 4-18, p. 92).

Land that is flooded all or part of the year with fresh or salt water is called a **wetland**. Wetlands extending inland from estuaries and covered all or part of the year with salt water are known as **coastal wetlands**. In temperate areas coastal wetlands usually consist of a mix of bays, lagoons, and salt marshes, where grasses are the dominant vegetation (see color insert Figure 16). In areas with warm tropical climates, we find swamps dominated by mangrove trees.

These nutrient-rich areas are among the world's most productive ecosystems (see Spotlight on p. 122). Only about 5% of all wetlands in the United States are coastal wetlands. The other 95% are inland wetlands covered with fresh water during all or part of the year.

Some coasts have steep rocky shores pounded by waves (see color insert Figure 17). Many organisms live in the numerous intertidal pools in the rocks. Other coasts have gently sloping barrier beaches at the water's edge, which are prime sites for human developments (see color insert Figure 18). Strings of thin barrier islands in some coastal areas (such as portions of North America's Atlantic and Gulf coasts) help protect the mainland, estuaries, lagoons, and coastal wetlands by dispersing the energy of approaching storm waves.

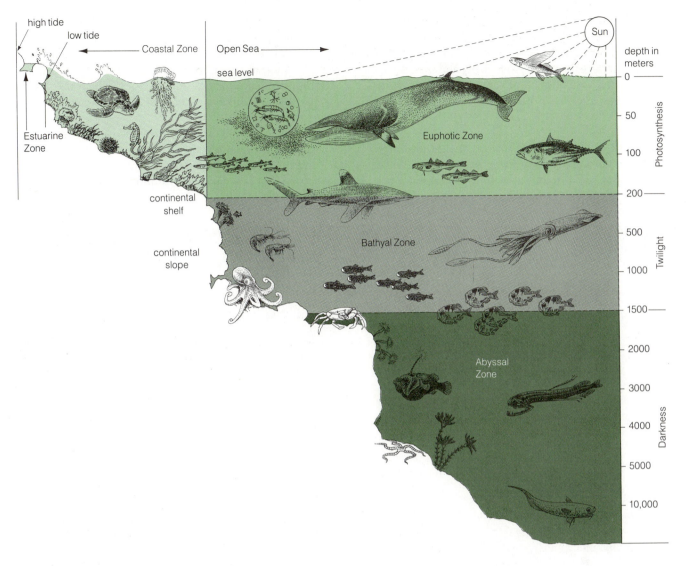

Figure 5-14 Major zones of life in an ocean ecosystem. Actual depths of zones may vary. The lighted upper zone, where photosynthesis takes place, supports scattered populations of microscopic, drifting producers (mostly algae and bacteria) called phytoplankton (plant plankton). They are fed upon by slightly larger, more mobile zooplankton (animal plankton). These herbivores in turn are eaten by commercially important herrings, sardines, anchovies, and other small fish that feed in the surface layer. These secondary consumers are then eaten by larger predators such as tuna, mackerel, and swordfish.

People build cottages and other structures on these slender ribbons of sand with water on all sides (see color insert Figure 19), but sooner or later most of these structures are damaged or destroyed. These islands are flooded and eroded by major storms and hurricanes and are slowly but continually moved toward the mainland by currents and winds. As they move, the islands relocate with no net loss of beach. But human structures built near the original high-tide line are gradually undermined. There is an urgent need to improve the protection and management of coastal zones (see Enrichment Study on p. 129).

The coastal zones of warm tropical and subtropical oceans, with water temperatures above 20°C (68°F), often contain *coral reefs* (see color insert Figure 20).

They consist mostly of deposits of insoluble calcium compounds secreted by photosynthesizing red and green algae and small coral animals. Because of their complexity and diversity, coral reefs support at least one-third of all marine fish species as well as numerous other marine organisms. They are also believed to be important in maintaining ocean salinity levels.

Along some steep, western coasts of continents, almost constant trade winds blow offshore and push surface water away from the shore. This outwardly moving surface water is replaced by an **upwelling** of cold, nutrient-rich bottom water (Figure 5-8, left). An upwelling brings plant nutrients from the deeper parts of the ocean to the surface and supports large populations of plankton, fish, and fish-eating seabirds.

Although they make up only about 0.1% of the world's total ocean area, upwellings are highly productive. However, periodic changes in climate and ocean currents can reduce their high productivity and cause sharp drops in the annual catch of some important marine fish species, such as anchovies (see Spotlight below).

Freshwater Lakes and Reservoirs **Lakes** are large natural bodies of standing fresh water formed when precipitation, land runoff, or flowing groundwater fills

depressions in the earth. Causes of such depressions include glaciation (the Great Lakes of North America), earthquakes (Lake Nyasa in East Africa), and volcanic activity (Lake Kivu in Africa). Lakes normally consist of four distinct zones (Figure 5-16), which provide a variety of habitats and ecological niches for different species.

Lakes can be divided into three categories, based on their supply of plant nutrients. A lake with a small supply of plant nutrients (mostly nitrates and phosphates) is called an **oligotrophic lake** (Figure 5-17).

SPOTLIGHT Why Is the Coastal Zone So Important?

Many people view estuaries and coastal wetlands as desolate, mosquito-infested, worthless lands. They believe these ecosystems should be drained, dredged, filled in, built on, or used as depositories for human-generated waste materials.

Nothing could be further from the truth. These highly productive areas provide us and other species with a remarkable variety of benefits. They supply food and serve as spawning and nursery grounds for many species of marine fish and shellfish (Figure 5-15). They are also breeding grounds and habitats for waterfowl and other wildlife, including many endangered species. Each year millions of people visit coastal zones for whale or bird watching, waterfowl hunting, and other recreational activities.

In the United States, estuaries and coastal wetlands are spawning grounds for 70% of the country's seafood, including shrimp, salmon, oysters, clams, and haddock. The $15-billion-a-year commercial and recreational marine fishing industry, taking place mostly in the coastal zone, provides jobs for millions of people.

Coastal areas also dilute and filter out large amounts of waterborne pollutants, helping protect the quality of waters used for swimming, fishing, and wildlife habitats. It is estimated that one acre of tidal estuary substitutes for a $75,000 waste treatment plant and has a total land value of $83,000 when its production of fish for food and recreation is included. By comparison, one acre of prime farmland in Kansas has a top

value of $1,200 and an annual production value of $600.

Estuaries and coastal wetlands help protect coastal areas. They absorb damaging waves caused by violent storms and hurricanes and serve as giant sponges to absorb floodwaters.

Clearly, estuaries and coastal wetlands are among our most productive and important natural ecosystems. But they are also among our most intensely populated, used, and stressed ecosystems. Human activities are increasingly impairing or destroying some of the important, free services these ecosystems provide (see Enrichment Study on p. 129).

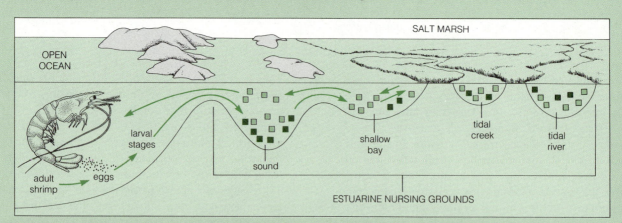

Figure 5-15 Life history of shrimp that use the coastal zone as nursery grounds. Adult shrimp spawn offshore and the larva of their offspring move into semi-enclosed estuaries. There they find the food and protection they need for rapid growth during their young and adolescent stages. As they mature, the shrimp move into deeper coastal waters and then into the open ocean. (Adapted with permission from Cecie Starr and Ralph Taggart, *Biology: The Unity and Diversity of Life*, 5th ed., 1989, Belmont, Calif.: Wadsworth)

Such a lake is usually deep and has crystal-clear water with cool to cold temperatures (see color insert Figure 21). It has small populations of phytoplankton and fish such as smallmouth bass and lake trout. Lake Tahoe, high in the Sierra Nevada on the border between Nevada and California, is an oligotrophic lake.

A lake with a large or excessive supply of plant nutrients is called a **eutrophic lake** (Figure 5-17 and color insert Figure 22). This type of lake is usually shallow and has cloudy, warm water. It has large populations of phytoplankton (especially algae) and zooplankton, and diverse populations of fish, particularly bullhead, catfish, and carp. In warm summer months the bottom layer of a eutrophic lake is often depleted of dissolved oxygen. Lake Erie is a eutrophic lake. Many lakes fall somewhere between the two extremes of nutrient enrichment and are called **mesotrophic lakes.**

Eutrophication is the physical, chemical, and biological changes that take place after a lake receives inputs of plant nutrients from the surrounding land basin from natural erosion and runoff over a long period of time. Near urban or agricultural centers the natural input of plant nutrients to a lake can be greatly accelerated by human activities. This **accelerated,** or **cultural, eutrophication** is caused mostly by nitrate- and phosphate-containing effluents from sewage treatment plants, runoff of fertilizers and animal wastes, and accelerated soil erosion.

All substances, including water, have a certain density, or mass per unit of volume. The density of most substances increases as they go from gaseous to liquid to solid physical states. But water doesn't follow this normal behavior. It reaches its maximum density as liquid water at 4°C (39°F). In other words, the density of solid ice at 0°C (32°F) is less than that of liquid

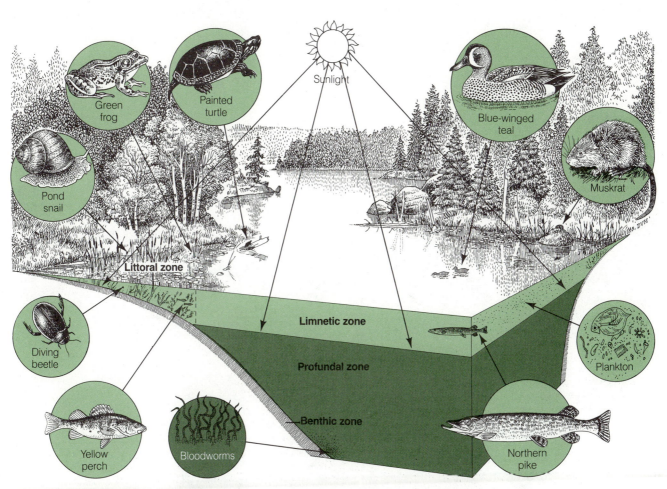

Figure 5-16 Four major zones of life in a lake. The *littoral zone* includes the shore and the shallow, nutrient-rich waters near the shore, in which sunlight penetrates to the lake bottom. It contains a variety of free-floating producers, rooted aquatic plants, and other forms of aquatic life such as frogs, snails, and snakes. The *limnetic zone* is the open-water surface layer, which gets enough sunlight for photosynthesis. It contains varying amounts of floating phytoplankton, plant-eating zooplankton, and fish, depending on the supply of plant nutrients. The *profundal zone* is the deep open water, where it is too dark for photosynthesis. It is inhabited by fish adapted to its cooler, darker water. The *benthic zone* at the bottom of a lake is inhabited mostly by large numbers of decomposers, detritus-feeding clams, and wormlike insect larvae. These detritivores feed on dead plant debris, animal remains, and animal wastes that descend from above.

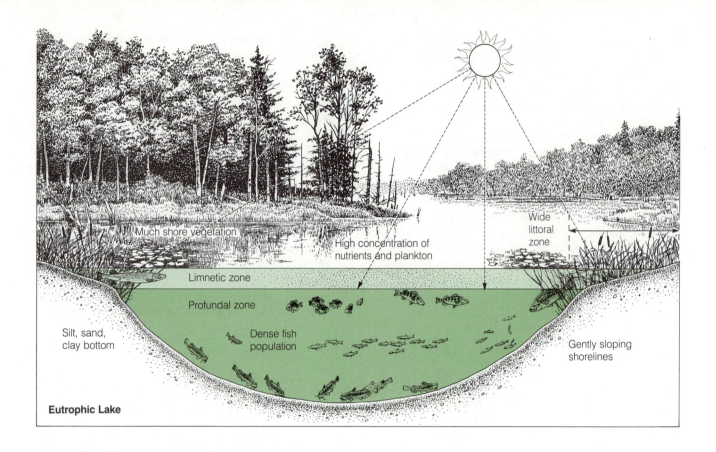

Much shore vegetation

High concentration of nutrients and plankton

Wide littoral zone

Limnetic zone

Profundal zone

Silt, sand, clay bottom

Dense fish population

Gently sloping shorelines

Eutrophic Lake

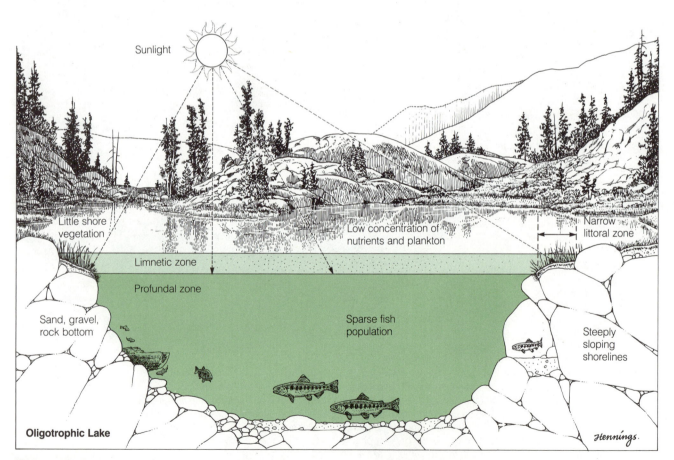

Sunlight

Little shore vegetation

Low concentration of nutrients and plankton

Narrow littoral zone

Limnetic zone

Profundal zone

Sand, gravel, rock bottom

Sparse fish population

Steeply sloping shorelines

Oligotrophic Lake

Hennings.

Figure 5-17 Eutrophic, or nutrient-rich lake, and oligotrophic, or nutrient-poor lake. Mesotrophic lakes fall between these two extremes of nutrient enrichment.

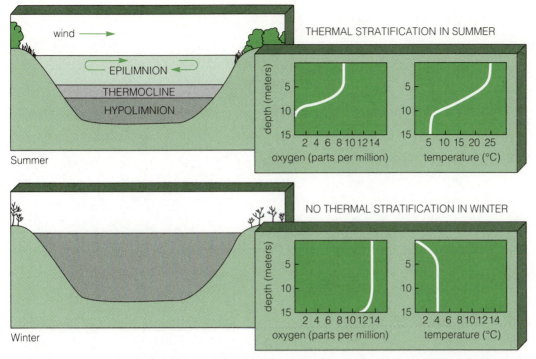

Figure 5-18 Thermal stratification in a northern temperate lake during summer prevents the bottom and top layers of water from mixing. In summer the colder, denser, oxygen-poor water in the bottom layer (the hypolimnion) is separated from the upper layer (the epilimnion) of warmer, less dense, oxygen-rich water by a broad zone, the thermocline. In this zone temperature and oxygen levels change rapidly with depth. During the spring and fall the top and bottom layers circulate and allow replenishment of oxygen in the bottom layer. During winter such lakes are not thermally stratified. (Adapted with permission from Cecie Starr and Ralph Taggart, *Biology: The Unity and Diversity of Life*, 5th ed., Belmont, Calif.: Wadsworth, 1989.)

water at 4°C (39°F). That is why ice floats on water. This is fortunate for us and most freshwater organisms. Otherwise, lakes and other bodies of fresh water in cold climates would freeze from the bottom up instead of from the surface down.

This unusual property of water causes seasonal changes in density and temperature from surface to bottom of large, deep lakes in northern temperate areas with cold winters and warm summers (Figure 5-18). Because water is densest at about 4°C (39°F), water at that temperature sinks beneath water that is either cooler or warmer. In winter the surface water falls to about 0°C (39°F). Below it lies less dense, warmer water. This allows aquatic organisms to survive even if the surface layer freezes.

In spring when the atmosphere warms, the lake's surface water warms to 4°C (39°F), reaches maximum density, and sinks through and below the cooler, less dense water. This brings the bottom water to the surface. During this spring overturn, dissolved oxygen in the surface layer is moved downward and nutrients released by decomposition on the lake bottom are moved toward the surface.

By midsummer the lake becomes thermally stratified into a surface layer of warm water separated from a denser, cooler bottom layer by a thermocline, in which temperature falls rapidly (Figure 5-18). This gradient prevents the surface and bottom waters from mixing. In fall when temperatures begin to drop, the surface layer sinks to the bottom when it cools to 4°C (39°F) and the thermocline disappears. This second annual mixing of the lake's surface and bottom layers is called the fall overturn.

Reservoirs are normally large, deep, human-created bodies of standing fresh water. They are often built behind dams to collect water running down from mountains in streams and rivers (Figure 5-19). Often reservoirs are incorrectly called lakes. For example, I live not too far from a massive reservoir in central North Carolina called Jordan Lake. In northern temperate regions, large reservoirs may become thermally stratified during summer as lakes do (Figure 5-18).

Reservoirs are built primarily to store and release water in a controlled manner. The released water may be used for hydroelectric power production at the dam site. Water can also be released over the dam and diverted into irrigation canals to grow crops on dry land. It can be stored and released slowly to prevent flooding, and it can be carried by aqueduct to towns and cities for use by homes, businesses, and industries. Reservoirs are also used for recreation such as swimming, fishing, and boating.

Figure 5-19 Reservoir formed behind Shasta Dam on the Sacramento River north of Redding, California. This reservoir and dam are used to produce electricity (hydropower) and to help control flooding in areas below the dam by storing and releasing water slowly. The reservoir is also used for recreation.

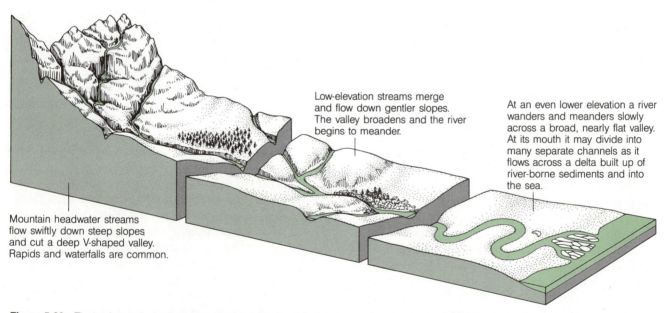

Low-elevation streams merge and flow down gentler slopes. The valley broadens and the river begins to meander.

At an even lower elevation a river wanders and meanders slowly across a broad, nearly flat valley. At its mouth it may divide into many separate channels as it flows across a delta built up of river-borne sediments and into the sea.

Mountain headwater streams flow swiftly down steep slopes and cut a deep V-shaped valley. Rapids and waterfalls are common.

Figure 5-20 Three phases in the flow of water downhill from mountain headwater streams to wider, lower-elevation streams to rivers, which empty into the ocean.

Freshwater Streams and Rivers Precipitation that doesn't infiltrate into the ground or evaporate remains on the earth's surface as **surface water.** This water becomes **runoff,** which flows into streams and rivers and eventually downhill to the oceans for reuse in the hydrologic cycle (Figure 4-25, p. 99). The entire land area that delivers the water, sediment, and dissolved substances via streams to a major river, and ultimately

Figure 5-21 Prairie potholes and cropland in Minnesota.

to the sea, is called a **watershed,** or **drainage basin.** Some streams are fed mostly by groundwater flow instead of surface runoff.

The downward flow of water from mountain highlands to the sea takes place in three phases (Figure 5-20). First, narrow headwater or mountain highland streams with cold, clear water rush down steep slopes (see color insert Figure 23). As this turbulent water flows and tumbles downward over waterfalls and rapids, it dissolves large amounts of oxygen from the air. Most plants in this flow survive because they are attached to rocks. Most fish that thrive in this environment are cold-water fish, such as trout, which require a high level of dissolved oxygen.

In the second phase the headwater streams merge to form wider, deeper, lower-elevation streams that flow down gentler slopes and meander through wider valleys. Here the water is warmer and usually less turbulent. It can support a variety of cold-water and warm-water fish species with slightly lower oxygen requirements.

Gradually these streams coalesce into wider and deeper rivers that meander across broad, flat valleys. The main channels of these rivers support a distinctive variety of fish, whereas their backwaters support species similar to those found in lakes. At its mouth

a river may divide into many channels as it flows across a delta—a built-up deposit of river-borne sediments—and coastal wetlands and estuaries, where river water mixes with ocean water.

As rivers flow downhill, they are powerful shapers of land. Over millions and billions of years the friction of moving water wears away mountains and cuts deep canyons. Rivers also build hills and mountains by depositing sediment in low-lying areas.

Inland Wetlands Lands covered with fresh water all or part of the year and located away from coastal areas are called **inland wetlands.** They include inland bogs, marshes, swamps, mud flats, river-overflow lands, prairie potholes (Figure 5-21), and the wet tundra during summer. Shallow marshes and swamps are among the most productive ecosystems in the world.

In the United States, inland wetlands in the lower 48 states are roughly equivalent in total area to the state of California. Almost twice this area of inland wetlands is found in Alaska—58% of the state is covered with wetlands. Most of the waterfowl harvested in North America are produced in wetland habitats of Canada. Inland wetlands are important ecosystems that are being rapidly destroyed and degraded (see Spotlight on p. 128).

Connections Between Terrestrial and Aquatic Ecosystems Distinguishing between land and water ecosystems is useful. At the same time, understanding how these ecosystems are linked together is also important.

One important connection is the runoff of plant nutrients, mostly as nitrates and phosphates, from the land into aquatic ecosystems. These nutrients help support plant life in rivers, lakes, and estuaries, which in turn support aquatic animal life. The runoff of decaying organic matter into aquatic ecosystems is a source of food for aquatic detritivores. When soil erodes into lakes and slow-moving rivers, it builds up bottom sediments. These sediments gradually change the types of aquatic life that can thrive; eventually they convert an aquatic ecosystem to a terrestrial ecosystem.

Natural events and human activities can drastically change the rates at which plant nutrients, detritus, and soil are transferred from land to water. For example, flooding and land clearing increase the rate at which materials move to aquatic ecosystems, often overloading them with plant nutrients. This can cause explosive growth, or blooms, of algae. When the algae die and are broken down by oxygen-consuming decomposers, the water is depleted of dissolved oxygen, killing fish and other organisms.

Conversely, matter resources also flow from aquatic to terrestrial ecosystems. Fish and shellfish are sources of food for many land-dwelling animals such as seabirds, bears, eagles, and people. When seabirds deposit their wastes on land, they return some of these nutrients from the sea to the land as part of the nitrogen and phosphorous cycles.

Earth and water, if not too blatantly abused, can produce again and again for the benefit of all.
Stewart L. Udall

SPOTLIGHT Why Are Inland Wetlands So Important?

Inland wetlands provide habitats for a variety of fish, waterfowl, and other wildlife, including many rare and endangered species. Wetlands near rivers help regulate stream flow by storing water during periods of heavy rainfall and releasing it slowly. Thus, they reduce the frequency, level, and velocity of floods and riverbank erosion. Wetlands also improve water quality by trapping stream sediments and absorbing, diluting, and degrading many toxic pollutants. By holding water, many wetlands allow increased ground infiltration, thus helping recharge groundwater supplies. Wetlands are used for recreation, especially waterfowl hunting, and to grow crops such as blueberries, cranberries, and rice—which feeds half the world's people. Wetlands also play significant roles in the global cycles of carbon, nitrogen, and sulfur.

Because people are unaware of their ecological importance, inland wetlands often are dredged or filled in and used as croplands, garbage dumps, and sites for urban and industrial development. They are viewed as wastelands.

Altogether, about 56% of the original coastal and inland wetland acreage in the lower 48 states has been destroyed—enough to cover an area four times the size of Ohio. About 80% of this loss was due to draining and clearing of wetlands for agriculture. Most of the rest was used for real estate development and highways. Wetland destruction has greatly reduced the habitat of birds and other wildlife that live on or near these ecosystems, threatening some species with extinction.

Iowa has lost 95% of its natural marshes and California has lost 90% of its wetlands. Almost all southern bottomland hardwood wetlands are gone. It is estimated that each year the United States is losing 121,000 to 182,000 hectares (300,000 to 450,000 acres) of wetlands.

Attempts have been made to slow the rate of wetland loss. The Farm Act of 1985 has a "swampbuster" provision that withholds agricultural subsidies from landowners who convert wetlands to croplands. The Emergency Wetlands Resource Act raises about $20 million a year for federal wetland acquisition. A federal permit is now required to fill wetlands or deposit polluting material in them. The North American Waterfowl Management Plan should help the Canadian and American governments and conservation organizations acquire and restore massive wetland areas in the next 15 years.

A major problem is that only about 8% of inland wetlands is under federal protection, and federal, state, and local protection of wetlands are weak. Existing laws are poorly enforced and subsidies and tax incentives are still given to developers who drain, dredge, fill, and destroy wetlands.

The United States urgently needs a better system for protecting and managing its wetlands, both coastal and inland. The immediate goal of such a program should be to prevent further loss of the country's wetlands. The long-term goal should be to restore the quantity and quality of the country's wetlands.

About 55% of the U.S. population lives along the coastlines of the Atlantic Ocean (see color insert Figure 18), the Pacific Ocean, and the Great Lakes. Two out of three Americans live within an hour's drive of these shores. By 1995, three out of four will live in or near the country's coastal zones.

Nine of the country's largest cities, most major ports, about 40% of the manufacturing plants, and two out of three nuclear and coal-fired power plants are located in coastal counties. The coasts are also the sites of large numbers of motels, hotels, condominiums, beach cottages, and other developments (Figure 5-22). To meet energy, irrigation, and flood control needs, most of the country's major rivers have been dammed or diverted. This changes the normal flow of fresh water into estuaries and modifies their nutrient supplies and food webs.

Because of these multiple uses and stresses, nearly 50% of the estuaries and coastal wetlands in the United States have been destroyed or damaged, primarily by dredging and filling and contamination by wastes. For example, garbage slicks laden with harmful bacteria and viruses and toxic chemicals have caused massive fish kills and closed beaches in New Jersey. Only about 58% of

U.S. shellfish waters are now clean enough to produce edible seafood.

Fortunately, about half of the country's estuaries and coastal wetlands remain undeveloped, but each year additional areas are developed. Some coastal areas have been purchased by federal and state governments and by private conservation agencies. Such purchases are designed to help protect key areas from development and to allow most of them to be used as parks and wildlife habitats.

The National Coastal Zone Management Acts of 1972 and 1980 gave federal aid to the 37 coastal and Great Lakes states and territories to help them develop voluntary programs for protecting and managing coastlines not under federal protection. By 1988, more than 90% of the country's coastal areas in all but six of the eligible states had federally approved state coastal management plans.

These plans, however, are voluntary, and many are vague and don't provide enough enforcement authority. Since 1981 their implementation has also been hindered by federal budget cutbacks. California and North Carolina are considered to have the strongest programs, but developers and other interests make continuing efforts to weaken them.

A major problem is that more than 70% of the country's shoreline (excluding Alaska) is privately owned. Unless they are given much larger tax breaks for preserving undeveloped coastal areas, most private owners find it hard to resist lucrative offers from developers.

The Water Quality Act of 1987 is a step in the right direction. It established the National Estuary Program with the goal of identifying nationally significant estuaries, protecting and improving their water quality, and enhancing their living resources. It also identified 11 estuaries for "priority consideration" by the EPA. The EPA's role is to provide technical assistance and an organizational umbrella under which federal, state, and local interests work together to develop long-term protection and management plans.

Barrier islands and the sand dunes of barrier beaches help protect coastal areas from hurricanes and violent storms. For more effective flood protection, buildings should be constructed only behind the secondary dunes on such beaches (Figure 5-23). Walkways should be built over both dunes to keep them intact. But this is rarely done because of the high economic value of oceanfront land (see color insert Figure 19).

Figure 5-22 Development of the Port of Los Angeles between 1972 (above) and 1988 (below).

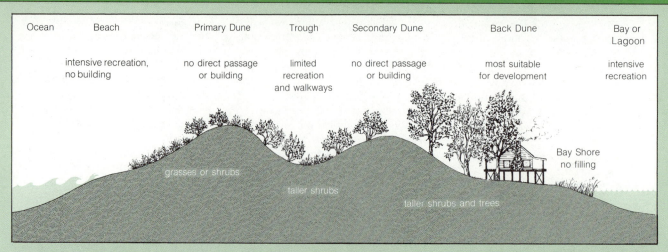

Ocean	Beach	Primary Dune	Trough	Secondary Dune	Back Dune	Bay or Lagoon
	intensive recreation, no building	no direct passage or building	limited recreation and walkways	no direct passage or building	most suitable for development	intensive recreation

grasses or shrubs

taller shrubs

taller shrubs and trees

Bay Shore no filling

Figure 5-23 Primary and secondary dunes on a barrier beach. Ideally, construction should be allowed only behind the second strip of dunes, with walkways to the beach built over the dunes to keep them intact. This helps protect structures from being damaged and washed away by wind, high tides, beach erosion, and flooding from storm surges. Protection of barrier beaches is rare, however, because the short-term economic value of limited oceanfront land is considered much higher than its long-term ecological and economic values.

Little if any development should be allowed on still undeveloped barrier islands. But the barrier areas rarely receive such protection (see color insert Figure 19). When coastal developers remove the dunes or build behind the first set of dunes, minor hurricanes and sea storms flood and even sweep away houses and other buildings (Figure 5-24). Coastal dwellers mistakenly call these human-assisted disasters natural disasters.

Beach erosion is a serious problem undermining development along 80% to 90% of the barrier beaches and barrier islands in the United States. The main cause of this problem is that sea levels have been rising gradually ever since the last ice age ended and the earth began to warm.

Many states require that oceanfront structures be elevated and built of concrete. But such struc-

Figure 5-24 Damage to beachfront property caused by Hurricane Elena in Florida, 1985. Note that buildings were not built behind protective dunes as shown in Figure 5-23.

tures can still be toppled by beach erosion and wind and wave damage as the average high-tide mark gradually moves inland.

Several methods have been used in attempts to halt or reduce beach erosion (Figure 5-25), but they either make matters worse or

are only temporary solutions. The movement of sand from one place to another along a coastline is a natural process that cannot be stopped. Seawalls eventually lead to increased erosion. Building groins that extend outward from the shore to trap sand can slow

CHAPTER SUMMARY

Climate is an average of the various day-to-day weather conditions, seasonal variations, and weather extremes in a region over at least a 30-year period. The two most impor-

tant factors determining the climate of an area are its *average temperature* and *average precipitation*.

Differences in these and other climatic factors in various parts of the world are caused primarily by **(1)** variations in the amount of incoming solar energy striking different parts of the earth, **(2)** the earth's annual orbit

Groin

Groins are structures that extend from the beach into the water. They help counter erosion by trapping sand from the current. Groins accumulate sand on their updrift side; but erosion is worse on the downdrift side which is deprived of sand.

Seawall

Seawalls protect property temporarily, but they also increase beach erosion by deflecting wave energy onto the sand in front of and beside them. High waves can wash over seawalls and destroy them and property.

Importing sand

Imported sand on a beach is considered the best response to erosion. The new sand is often dredged from offshore and can cost tens of millions of dollars. Because it is often finer than beach sand, dredged sand erodes more quickly.

Figure 5-25 Why beach erosion can't be stop[...]

beach erosion in one area but greatly increase erosion in down-current areas—sometimes setting off "sand-rustling" controversies between various beach communities. New sand can be brought in to restore an eroded beach, but this is a very expensive operation that must be repeated every few years.

No human interventions are ever going to stop the perpetual movement of sand from one area to another by the actions of waves and storms. The best solution is to prevent development on remain-ing beach areas or to allow such development only behind protec-tive dunes (Figure 5-23). Areas already developed in an environ-mentally unsound manner will continue to experience erosion and considerable damage to beachfront property.

around the sun and its daily rotation around its axis, which is tilted away from the sun, **(3)** chemical content of the atmosphere, **(4)** distribution of the continents and oceans, and **(5)** topographical features such as mountains.

Average annual precipitation generally is the limiting factor that determines whether the biomes of most of the world's land areas are *desert, grassland,* or *forest*. This factor combined with *average annual temperature* and *soil type* leads to various types of *tropical, temperate,* and *polar* deserts, grasslands, and forests with different characteristics and different types of plants and animals.

The major limiting factors in aquatic ecosystems are

salinity, light, dissolved oxygen, dissolved nutrient concentrations, and water temperature. Major aquatic ecosystems include (1) *freshwater ecosystems* consisting of inland bodies of standing water (lakes, reservoirs, and wetlands) and flowing water (streams and rivers) with low salinity, and (2) *marine*, or *saltwater*, *ecosystems* (the oceans) with high to very high salinity levels.

Large, deep aquatic ecosystems, such as lakes, reservoirs, and oceans, usually have several layers: a shallow, sunlit, *shore zone*; a sunlit *surface layer of open water*, where photosynthesis can take place; a colder, deeper level of *open water*; and a nutrient-rich *bottom layer*, where sunlight is absent. Because of ample sunlight and nutrients, the shallow shore zone usually contains the largest numbers of species of aquatic plant and animal life.

The coastal zones of the world's oceans represent less than 10% of the total ocean area, but contain 90% of all ocean plant and animal life (including most of the commercially important marine fish and shellfish). Barrier beaches and barrier islands protect low-lying coastal areas from flooding and other damaging effects of storms and hurricanes. However, these and other important ecological services are being threatened by large-scale human development on scarce, economically valuable coastal land.

DISCUSSION TOPICS

1. List a limiting factor for each of the following ecosystems: (a) a desert, (b) the surface layer of the open sea, (c) the Arctic tundra, (d) the floor of a tropical rain forest, and (e) the bottom of a deep lake.

2. What type of biome do you live in or near? What effects have human activities had on the characteristic vegetation and animal life normally found in this biome? How is your own lifestyle affecting this biome?

3. If possible, visit a nearby lake. Would you classify it as oligotrophic, mesotrophic, or eutrophic? What are the major factors contributing to its nutrient enrichment? Which of these are related to human activities?

4. Since the deep oceans are vast, self-sustaining ecosystems located far away from human habitats, why not use them as a depository for essentially all of our radioactive and other hazardous wastes? Give your reasons for agreeing or disagreeing with this proposal.

5. Why are coastal and inland wetlands considered to be some of the planet's most important ecosystems? Why have so many of these vital ecosystems been destroyed by human activities? What factors in your lifestyle contribute to the destruction and degradation of wetlands?

Changes in Populations, Communities, and Ecosystems

General Questions and Issues

1. What are the major effects of environmental stress on organisms, populations, communities, and ecosystems?

2. How can populations of species change and adapt to natural and human-induced stresses?

3. How can communities and ecosystems adapt to small- and large-scale, natural and human-induced stresses?

4. What major impacts do human activities have on populations, communities, and ecosystems?

5. What efforts are being made to restore ecosystems damaged by human activities?

We cannot command nature except by obeying her.

Sir Francis Bacon

I f you observe the living world, two things should stand out: the diversity and adaptability of living organisms. Organisms are immensely diversified in the structures and functions of their bodies, in the places where they live, and in the ways they interact with other species and with their nonliving environments.

At the same time, at least some members of most populations have the ability to adapt to changes in environmental conditions so that they continue to survive and reproduce. Some environmental changes occur because of natural events such as climate changes, floods, and volcanic eruptions. Others are caused by land clearing, emissions of various pollutants, and other human activities.

6-1 RESPONSES OF LIVING SYSTEMS TO ENVIRONMENTAL STRESS

Stability of Living Systems The organisms that make up the populations of various biological communities and ecosystems have some ability to withstand or recover from externally imposed changes or stresses—provided these external stresses are not too severe. In other words, organisms have some degree of *stability*.

This stability is maintained, however, only by constant dynamic change.

Although an organism maintains a fairly stable structure over its life span, it is continually gaining and losing matter and energy. Similarly, in a mature tropical rain forest some trees will die, others will take their place. Some species may disappear, and the number of individual species in the forest may change. But unless it is cut, burned, or blown down, you will recognize it as a tropical rain forest 50 years from now.

It is useful to distinguish between three aspects of stability in living systems. **Inertia,** or **persistence,** is the ability of a living system to resist being disturbed or altered. **Constancy** is the ability of a living system, such as a population, to maintain a certain size. **Resilience** is the ability of a living system to restore itself to an original condition after being exposed to an outside disturbance that is not too drastic.

Nature is remarkably resilient. For example, human societies have survived natural disasters, plagues, and devastating wars. Changes in the genetic makeup of rapidly producing insect populations enable many individual insects to survive massive doses of deadly pesticides and ionizing radiation. Plants recolonize areas devastated by volcanoes, retreating glaciers, mining, bombing, and farming, although such natural restoration usually takes a long time on a human time scale.

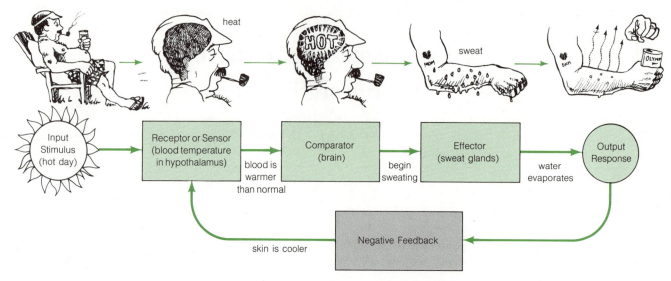

Figure 6-1 Keeping cool on a hot day—a human temperature control system based on negative feedback of information to counteract a change in environmental conditions (arrows show flow of information).

Stability and Information Feedback Living organisms have various systems that maintain certain internal conditions within some tolerable range when external conditions fluctuate, provided these external stresses are not too severe. For instance, your body has systems that maintain a fairly constant blood pressure and temperature. These regulatory processes in a living organism are called *homeostasis*, from the Greek word for "equilibrium."

Homeostatic systems control various conditions by means of the flow of information along the network of interconnected parts in the system. **Information feedback** is the process by which information is fed back into a system and causes it to change to maintain a particular equilibrium state. There are two types of information feedback: negative and positive.

Negative feedback is a flow of information into a system that counteracts the effects of change in external conditions. The thermostat on a home furnace is an example of control of temperature by negative feedback of information. If the room temperature drops below the temperature set on the thermostat, this information (in the form of an electrical signal) is fed back into the system to turn the furnace on. When the desired room temperature is reached, information is fed back to cut the furnace off.

Negative feedback also keeps your body temperature around 37°C (98°F), as shown in Figure 6-1. Note that such homeostatic systems have three essential elements: a *receptor* or *sensor*, which detects when the system is not at equilibrium, a *comparator*, which receives and evaluates information from the sensor and transmits information to an *effector*, which has the ability to change the condition being monitored.

For example, if you go outdoors on a hot day, sensors in your skin detect the high temperature and send

this information as a nerve signal to your brain (comparator). Your brain then sends information as a nerve impulse to sweat glands in your skin (effectors) to activate sweating, a cooling mechanism. Evaporation requires energy. Thus, as sweat evaporates, it removes heat from your skin. When your body has cooled down, this new information (output response) is fed back to your skin sensors. Then your brain sends a new message to your skin effectors to slow or stop the sweating process. *You and all living systems are self-regulating homeostatic systems maintained at the equilibrium state we call life primarily by negative feedback.*

There are also systems in which the feedback of information is positive. **Positive feedback**—also known as runaway feedback—occurs when a change in the system in one direction provides information that causes the system to change further in the same direction. For example, suppose the wires on a furnace thermostat were accidentally hooked up backwards. Then a positive feedback of information from the thermostat would turn the furnace on when the room got too hot and off when it got too cold.

Generally, negative feedback tends to keep a system in a fairly constant or stable state, while positive feedback tends to disrupt a system's stability—worse gets worser. In social systems the arms race is an example of positive feedback. When country A produces more weapons, this causes country B to produce more weapons, which causes country A to make more weapons, which leads country B to increase its weapons, and so on. Such a process can continue until one or both countries go bankrupt or blow each other (and a lot of other countries and organisms) up (see Guest Essay on p. 000).

But positive feedback is not always harmful. Falling in love is an example of a positive feedback situ-

Table 6-1 Some Effects of Environmental Stress

Organism Level

Physiological and biochemical changes

Psychological disorders

Behavioral changes

Fewer or no offspring

Genetic defects in offspring (mutagenic effects)

Birth defects (teratogenic effects)

Cancers (carcinogenic effects)

Death

Population Level

Population increase or decrease

Change in age structure (old, young, and weak may die)

Survival of strains genetically resistant to stress

Loss of genetic diversity and adaptability

Extinction

Community-Ecosystem Level

Disruption of energy flow

    Decrease or increase in solar energy input

    Changes in heat output

    Changes in trophic structure in food chains and food webs

Disruption of chemical cycles

    Depletion of essential nutrients

    Excessive addition of nutrients

Simplification

    Reduction in species diversity

    Reduction or elimination of habitats and filled ecological niches

    Less complex food webs

    Possibility of lowered stability

    Possibility of ecosystem collapse

---

ation in which beneficial feelings and actions are amplified. You take an interest in and do something nice for your partner, and then your partner reciprocates. This leads you to do more, your partner to do more, and so on.

Time Delays Another characteristic of systems regulated by information feedback is **time delay**—the delay between the time a stimulus is received and the time when the system makes a corrective action by negative feedback.

Time delays can protect a system from information overload and prevent hasty responses until more information is received. But a long delay between a cause and its effect often means that corrective action is not effective by the time symptoms of harm appear. For example, cigarette smoking is a time delay trap. A heavy smoker exposed to cancer-causing (carcinogenic) chemicals in inhaled cigarette smoke may not get lung cancer for 20 to 30 years. By then it is too late for a corrective response (not to smoke) through negative feedback.

The longer the time between an action and the harmful effects of that action, the less likely we are to respond before serious damage occurs. Most of the world's economic systems and our individual economic behavior are based on trying to maximize short-term economic gain even though this can lead to long-term economic and environmental pain and grief. The pleasurable effects—more money, more things—of borrowing money and depleting nature's capital show up now. But the ultimate financial and environmental

bankruptcy from borrowing too much money and depleting nature's capital don't show up until much later. By then the harm has been done, and correcting the situation, if possible, is incredibly expensive.

Additional examples of the harmful effects of prolonged delays are toxic dumps that have been lying around as chemical time bombs for decades, depletion of the ozone layer, and global warming and climate change from an enhanced greenhouse effect. Similarly, when we discover that our actions have reduced the population of a species to the point where it is in danger of becoming extinct, it is often too late to restore the species.

Synergistic Effects You were taught that 1 plus 1 always equals 2. But in complex systems, 1 plus 1 may sometimes be greater than 2 because of synergistic effects. A **synergistic effect** occurs when two or more factors interact so that the net effect is greater than that expected from adding together their independent effects (1 plus 1 is greater than 2).

For example, separately, either cigarette smoke or tiny particles of asbestos fibers inhaled into the lungs over a prolonged period can cause lung cancer. Acting together, however, they greatly increase one's chances of contracting lung cancer. Workers who are exposed to asbestos and who smoke are 10 times more likely to contract lung cancer than asbestos workers who do not smoke.

Effects of Environmental Stress Table 6-1 summarizes what can happen to organisms, populations,

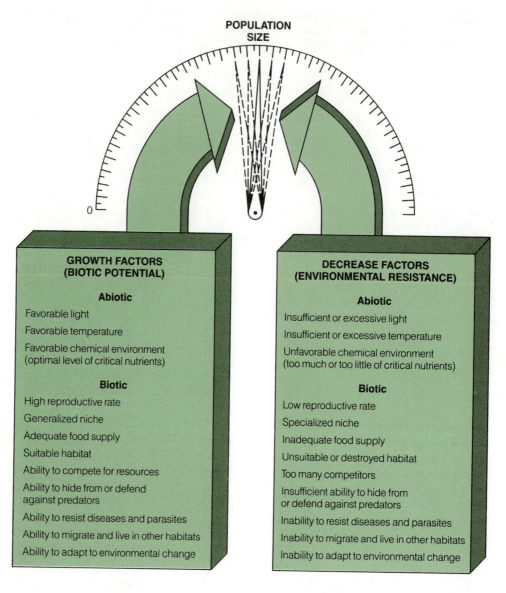

Figure 6-2 Population size is a balance between factors that increase numbers and factors that decrease numbers.

POPULATION SIZE

GROWTH FACTORS (BIOTIC POTENTIAL)

Abiotic

Favorable light

Favorable temperature

Favorable chemical environment (optimal level of critical nutrients)

Biotic

High reproductive rate

Generalized niche

Adequate food supply

Suitable habitat

Ability to compete for resources

Ability to hide from or defend against predators

Ability to resist diseases and parasites

Ability to migrate and live in other habitats

Ability to adapt to environmental change

DECREASE FACTORS (ENVIRONMENTAL RESISTANCE)

Abiotic

Insufficient or excessive light

Insufficient or excessive temperature

Unfavorable chemical environment (too much or too little of critical nutrients)

Biotic

Low reproductive rate

Specialized niche

Inadequate food supply

Unsuitable or destroyed habitat

Too many competitors

Insufficient ability to hide from or defend against predators

Inability to resist diseases and parasites

Inability to migrate and live in other habitats

Inability to adapt to environmental change

communities, and ecosystems as a result of environmental stress—that is, if one or more environmental factors fall above or below the levels tolerated by various species (Figure 4-10, p. 85). The stresses that can cause the changes shown in Table 6-1 may result from natural hazards (such as earthquakes, volcanic eruptions, hurricanes, drought, floods, and fires) or from human activities (industrialization, warfare, transportation, and agriculture).

6-2 POPULATION RESPONSES TO STRESS

Changes in Population Size, Structure, and Distribution Populations of organisms that make up ecosystems respond in various ways to changes in environmental conditions, such as an excess or a shortage of food or other critical nutrients. Changes in the size, structure, and distribution of a population

in response to changes in environmental conditions are called **population dynamics**.

A change in the birth rate or death rate is the major way that populations of most species respond to changes in resource availability or other environmental changes (Figure 6-2). Favorable changes usually cause an increase in population size through more births than deaths. Unfavorable changes usually cause a drop in population size through more deaths than births.

Members of some animal species can avoid or reduce the effects of an environmental stress by leaving one area (emigration) and migrating to an area (immigration) with more favorable environmental conditions and resource supplies. Thus, four variables—births, deaths, immigration, and emigration—determine the rate of change in the number of individuals in a population over a period of time:

population change rate =
(births + immigration) − (deaths + emigration)

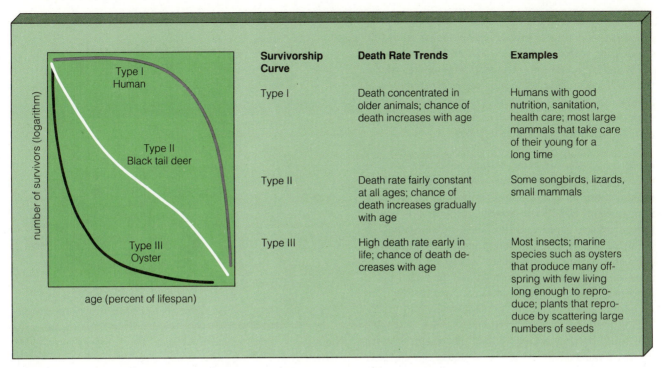

Survivorship Curve	Death Rate Trends	Examples
Type I	Death concentrated in older animals; chance of death increases with age	Humans with good nutrition, sanitation, health care; most large mammals that take care of their young for a long time
Type II	Death rate fairly constant at all ages; chance of death increases gradually with age	Some songbirds, lizards, small mammals
Type III	High death rate early in life; chance of death decreases with age	Most insects; marine species such as oysters that produce many offspring with few living long enough to reproduce; plants that reproduce by scattering large numbers of seeds

Figure 6-3 The three general types of survivorship curves for populations of different species.

The structure of the population in terms of the numbers of individuals of different ages and sex may change. Old, very young, and weak members may die when exposed to an environmental stress. The remaining population is then better equipped to survive such stresses as a more severe climate, an increase in predators, or an increase in disease organisms.

Populations of various species are also distributed in their habitats in different ways to take better advantage of food supplies, shelter, and other resources and to escape or defend themselves against predators or to find prey. Often members of a population are clumped together in small groups throughout their habitat. Why? One reason is that resources needed for survival and reproduction are rarely distributed uniformly. Also, some parts of a habitat offer more protection for prey or better hunting conditions for predators. These population distribution patterns often change in response to changes in environmental conditions.

Factors Influencing Birth Rate Several major characteristics of an animal species affect its birth rate. One is the number of live young hatched or born to a female at the end of the birthing period. For example, female California condors lay only 1 or 2 eggs during each breeding period. This makes the species more vulnerable to extinction than birds, such as ducks and grouse, that lay and incubate 8 to 15 eggs at one time.

Some fish produce thousands or even millions of eggs per female each year. Rats and mice produce about four litters of young each year, with about six young in each litter.

The birth rate of a species is also affected by the number of times a female goes through a complete breeding cycle each year and by the length of the gestation period before hatching or birth occurs. The meadow vole (a small rodent), with a gestation period of only 21 days, can produce large numbers of young in a short period. In contrast, the African elephant has a gestation period of almost two years and does not breed while its offspring is nursing heavily. Thus, it produces at most one young every 2.5 years or longer.

When the density (number of individuals per unit of area) of a population living in a particular area falls below a certain level, individuals may have trouble finding mates. As a result, the birth rate may be lower than normal. The birth rate can also decline when population density becomes too high for available food supplies and the health of breeding individuals suffers. Under overcrowded and stressful conditions some species, such as rats, have a drop in birth rate even when plenty of food is available.

Factors Influencing Death Rate A major characteristic that affects the death rate and age structure of a species is the chances individuals in various age groups have for survival. We can construct a survivorship curve for a particular species by plotting the number or percentage of individuals in a particular population still alive at various ages. Studies have shown that most species tend to have one of three general types of survivorship curves (Figure 6-3).

Other factors can affect the death rate of a species. One is *interspecific competition*: competition between members of two or more different species for scarce food and other resources. Another is *intraspecific competition*: competition between members of the same species for scarce resources. Death rates can also be increased by predation, diseases and parasites, stress from overcrowded conditions, loss or degradation of habitat as a result of human activities, and catastrophic natural events such as droughts, earthquakes, hurricanes, fires, and floods.

J and S Curves: Idealized Model of Population Dynamics

With unlimited resources and ideal environmental conditions, a species can produce offspring at its maximum rate. Such growth starts off slowly and then increases rapidly to produce an exponential, or J-shaped, curve of population growth (Figure 6-4). Almost any kind of organism would be capable of increasing its population to crowd out the entire world if given ample food, water, space, and protection from its enemies. With unlimited resources, rapidly producing species such as bacteria, insects, mice, and some fish could do this in a short time. For example, with no restrictions a single species of bacteria could cover the earth in only 29.5 days.

Why doesn't this happen? Because environmental conditions are less than ideal and resources are normally limited. Factors such as predation, competition within and between species, food shortages, disease, adverse climatic conditions, and lack of suitable habitat usually act to keep the growth rate of a population below its maximum rate. The maximum species population size that a natural ecosystem can support indefinitely under a given set of environmental conditions is called that ecosystem's **carrying capacity** for that species.

Without unlimited resources the population size of a species is limited, and its death rate begins to rise as it reaches or temporarily exceeds its ecosystem's carrying capacity. When this happens, the J-shaped curve of population growth bends away from its steep incline and eventually levels off to form an S-shaped curve (Figure 6-4). Then the population size typically fluctuates slightly above and below the carrying capacity of the environment.

This transition can be fairly smooth, or it can be a sharp drop in population size known as a population crash (Figure 6-4). A crash occurs when a reproducing population of a species overshoots the carrying capacity of its environment or when a change in conditions suddenly lowers the carrying capacity. Large numbers of individuals then die if they cannot migrate to other areas.

Crashes have occurred in the human populations of various countries throughout history. Ireland, for example, experienced a population crash after a fungus infection ruined the potato crop in 1845. Dependent on the potato for a major portion of their diet,

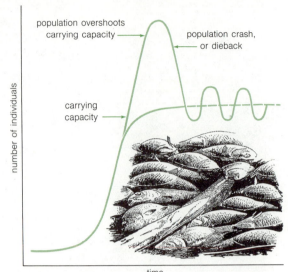

Figure 6-4 Conversion of a J-shaped curve of population growth of a species to an S-shaped curve when its population is limited by one or more environmental factors.

by 1900 half of Ireland's 8 million people had died of starvation or emigrated to other countries.

In spite of such local and regional disasters, the overall human population on earth has continued to grow. Human beings have made technological, social, and other cultural changes that have extended the earth's carrying capacity for their species (Figure 6-5). The human species has been able to alter its ecological niche by increasing food production, controlling disease, and using large amounts of energy and matter resources to make normally uninhabitable areas of the earth inhabitable.

Patterns of Population Dynamics in Nature

The idealized J-shaped to S-shaped mathematical model of population dynamics shown in Figure 6-4 can be observed in laboratory experiments. In nature, however, we find that species have three general types of population growth curves: relatively stable, irruptive, and cyclic (Figure 6-6).

Species whose numbers remain about the same from year to year once they have reached the environmental carrying capacity have *relatively stable populations*. Such constancy of population size is characteristic of many species of wildlife found in undisturbed tropical rain forests, where average temperature and rainfall don't change much from day to day and year to year (Figure 5-12, p. 118).

Some species, such as the raccoon, normally have a fairly stable population. But occasionally their numbers rise sharply, or irrupt, to a high peak and then crash to a relatively stable lower level. Such species have *irruptive populations* (Figure 6-6). The sudden

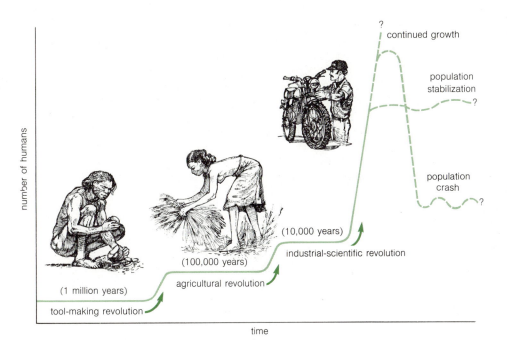

Figure 6-5 Human beings have expanded the earth's carrying capacity for their species through technological innovation, leading to several major cultural changes. Dashed lines represent possible future changes in human population size: continued growth, population stabilization, and continued growth followed by a crash and stabilization at a much lower level. This generalized curve is plotted by a different mathematical method (a plot of the logarithm of population size versus the logarithm of time) from the method (a plot of population size versus time) used in Figure 1-1, p. 4.

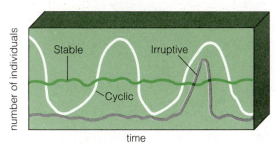

Figure 6-6 Basic types of population curves for living species.

population rise is due to some factor that temporarily increases the carrying capacity for the population, such as a favorable change in weather, an increase in the food supply, or a sharp reduction of predators, including human hunters and trappers. After soaring past its new, higher carrying capacity, the population experiences high death rates and decreases its size.

Some species undergo sharp increases in their numbers followed by crashes every 3 to 4 years, every 10 years, or at other regular intervals. These species have *cyclic populations* (Figure 6-6). The factor or mix of factors responsible for this pattern is still poorly understood.

Natural Selection and Biological Evolution A population of a particular species can undergo changes in its genetic composition, or gene pool, that enable it to better adapt to changes in environmental conditions. All individuals of a population do not have exactly the same genes. This genetic diversity helps protect a species from extinction.

Individuals with a protective genetic composition generally produce more offspring than those that don't have these traits. This ability of individuals with adaptive genetic traits to reproduce more offspring than individuals without such traits is called **differential reproduction.** Individuals with adaptive genetic traits pass these favorable traits to their offspring.

The process by which some genes and gene combinations in a population are reproduced more than others is called **natural selection.** Charles Darwin, who proposed this idea in 1858, described natural selection as meaning "survival of the fittest." This phrase has often been misinterpreted to mean survival of the strongest, biggest, or most aggressive. Instead, *fittest* means that individuals with the genetic traits best adapted to existing environmental conditions on the average produce the most offspring in a given generation. Those types that reproduce more often and more successfully tend to replace the less successful ones.

Species differ widely in how rapidly they can undergo natural selection. Some species have many offspring and short generation times. Others have few offspring and long generation times. Those that can quickly produce a large number of tiny offspring with short average life spans (weeds, insects, rodents, bacteria) can adapt to a change in environmental conditions through natural selection in a short time.

For example, individual members of a large insect population have slightly different genetic makeups. This means that a few will have built-in genetic resistance to a normally toxic chemical. When that chemical is used as a pesticide to reduce the insect population, the small number of resistant individuals

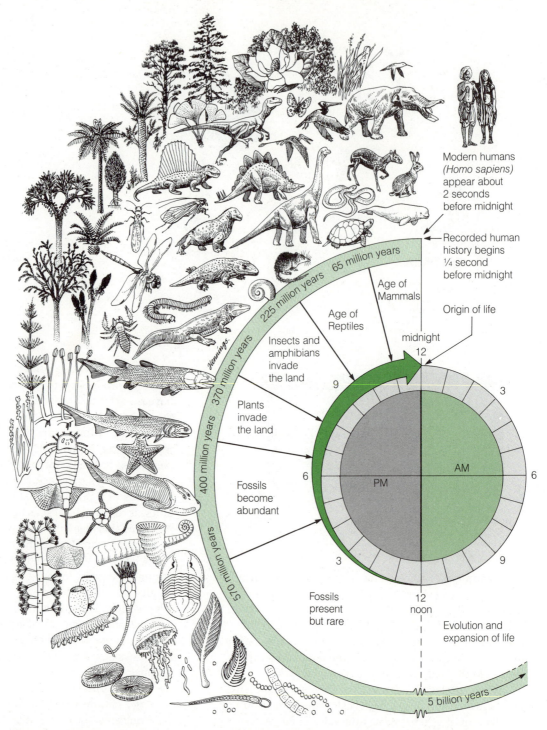

Figure 6-7 Greatly simplified history of the development of different forms of life on earth through biological evolution compared to a 24-hour time scale. The human species developed only about 2 seconds before the end of this 24 hours. But despite our brief time on earth, we are now in the process of hastening the extinction of more of the earth's species in a shorter time than at any other time in the earth's 5-billion-year history. (Adapted from George Gaylord Simpson and William S. Beck, *Life: An Introduction to Biology*, 2nd ed., New York: Harcourt Brace Jovanovich, 1965)

survive. They can then rapidly breed new populations with a larger number of individuals genetically resistant to the toxic effects of the chemical. The more an insect population is exposed to a particular pesticide, the more genetically resistant its members become to that chemical.

Experience has shown that in the long run our present chemical approach to pest control usually increases, not decreases, the populations of species we consider pests. It is an example of a harmful positive or runaway feedback system. As one observer put it, "I hope that when the insects take over the

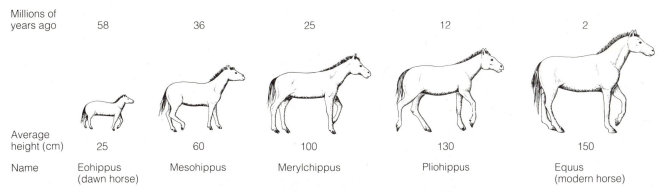

Millions of years ago	58	36	25	12	2
Average height (cm)	25	60	100	130	150
Name	Eohippus (dawn horse)	Mesohippus	Merylchippus	Pliohippus	Equus (modern horse)

Figure 6-8 Speciation of the horse through natural selection along the same genetic line into different equine species.

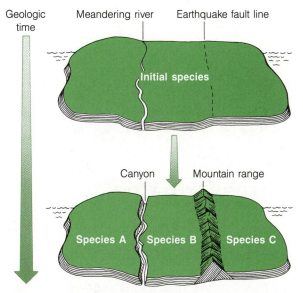

Figure 6-9 Speciation of a single species into three species as a result of prolonged geographic and reproductive isolation.

world, they will remember that we always took them along on our picnics."

Other species, such as elephants, horses, tigers, white sharks, and humans, have long generation times and a small number in each litter. This means that they cannot reproduce a large number of offspring rapidly. For such species, adaptation to an environmental stress by natural selection typically takes thousands to millions of years.

The resulting change in the genetic composition of a population exposed to new environmental conditions because of differential reproduction and natural selection is called **biological evolution** or simply **evolution.** Thus, evolution operates mainly through natural selection.

Speciation and Extinction The earth's present inventory of 5 to 30 million species is believed to be the result of a combination of two processes taking

place over billions of years (Figure 6-7). One is **speciation:** A new species, adapted to changes in environmental conditions, originates as a result of natural selection. The other is **extinction:** A species ceases to exist because it cannot genetically adapt and successfully reproduce under new environmental conditions.

Biologists estimate that 94% to 99% of all the species that have ever lived are now extinct. But the fact that we have 5 to 30 million species on earth today means that speciation, on average, has kept ahead of extinction.

Speciation can occur from changes within a single genetic line over a long period of time, often because of long-term changes in climate (Figure 6-8). It can also take place by the gradual splitting of lines of descent into two or more new species in response to new environmental conditions. This type of speciation is believed to occur when a population of a particular species becomes distributed over areas with different climates, food sources, soils, and other environmental conditions for long periods—typically for 1,000 to 100,000 generations. For example, different populations of the same species may be isolated when geological processes break up a single land mass into separate islands, change a river's course, thrust mountains upward from the seafloor, or submerge parts of dry land (Figure 6-9).

Populations of some animal species also split up when part of the group migrates in search of food (Figure 6-10). Eventually, the isolated populations in two different physical habitats diverge in their genetic makeup due to different selection pressures. If they remain separated under different conditions long enough, members of the two populations will be unable to interbreed if they occupy the same area again. Thus, one species has become two different species.

Some speciation is influenced by adaptations of different types of organisms to each other through a process called *coevolution.* In coevolutionary associations, each species exerts selective pressures on the other. For example, a carnivore species may become

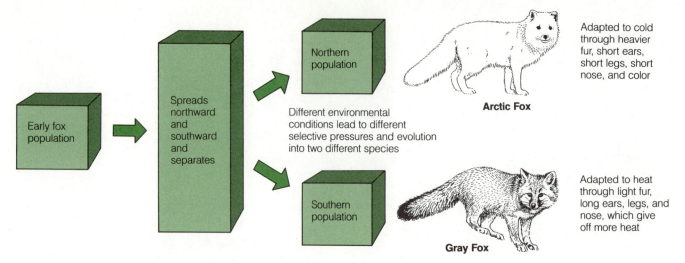

Figure 6-10 Speciation of an early species of fox into two different species as a result of migration of portions of the original fox population into areas with different climates.

increasingly efficient at hunting and capturing its prey. If certain individuals in the prey population have traits that allow them to elude the predator species, they pass these adaptive traits on to their offspring. These coevolutionary changes may eventually be enough to form new predator and prey species. Similarly, plants may evolve defenses such as camouflage or unpleasant or poisonous chemicals as defenses against efficient herbivores.

In some rapidly producing organisms, speciation may take place in thousands or even hundreds of years. In most cases, however, it takes from tens of thousands to millions of years.

Biological Diversity Over billions of years the combination of speciation and extinction operating through natural selection have produced the planet's most valuable resource: **biological diversity,** or **biodiversity.** It is made up of two related concepts: genetic diversity and species diversity. **Genetic diversity** is the genetic variability among individuals within a single species. **Species diversity** is the number of different species within a community of organisms.

The diversity within and among species has provided us with new sources of food, energy, raw materials, industrial chemicals, and medicines. This gigantic genetic library also helps provide us and other species with free resource recycling and purification services through the earth's biogeochemical cycles. Every species here today represents stored genetic information that allows the species to adapt to certain changes in environmental conditions. This biodiversity is nature's "insurance policy" against disasters. It must be preserved and sustained.

Some scientists have proposed that the entire earth is a gigantic living organism that regulates environmental conditions over millions and billions of years so that life can continue (see Pro/Con on p. 143).

6-3 COMMUNITY-ECOSYSTEM RESPONSES TO STRESS

Responses to Slight and Moderate Stress

Communities and ecosystems are so complex and variable that ecologists have little understanding of how they maintain their inertia and resilience. One major problem is the difficulty of conducting controlled experiments. Identifying and observing even a tiny fraction of the interacting variables in simple communities and ecosystems are virtually impossible.

In addition, ecologists cannot run long-term experiments in which only one variable in a natural community or ecosystem is allowed to change. Greatly simplified ecosystems can be set up and observed under laboratory conditions. But extrapolating the results of such experiments to much more complex, natural communities and ecosystems is difficult if not impossible.

At one time it was believed that the higher the species diversity in an ecosystem, the greater its stability. According to this idea, an ecosystem with a diversity of species has more ways to respond to most environmental stresses because it does not "have all its eggs in one basket." However, research indicates many exceptions to this intuitively appealing idea. Part of the problem is that there are many different ways to define stability and diversity.

In the early 1970s, British chemist and inventor James Lovelock and American biologist Lynn Margulis proposed that the biosphere—the earth's living organisms—creates and maintains the conditions necessary for its own existence. According to this idea, the biosphere is a gigantic, complex living organism—a superorganism that interacts with nonliving parts of the earth to keep environmental conditions within rather narrow limits that allow most forms of life to continue.

This proposal, based on a scientific analysis of the long-term changes in the earth's climate, atmospheric composition, and ocean salinity levels, is called the **Gaia** (pronounced guy' uh) **hypothesis.** Actually the idea that the earth is alive is not new. The ancient Greeks recognized this in their mythology describing the earth goddess, whom they named Gaia. Lovelock and Margulis's hypothesis is a modernized version of this old intuition.

You might think that this more scientific version of the ancient Gaia hypothesis would strengthen the idea that we need to protect the life-support systems that keep the earth and its living species alive and functioning well. If the earth is alive, then people might be more inclined to protect and sustain it.

Instead, Lovelock, who has ridiculed most environmentalists and conservationists, has used his hypothesis to undermine many environmental and resource conservation concerns. Lovelock is unconcerned about forms of pollution and environmental degradation such as acid deposition, ozone depletion, possible climate change from rising carbon dioxide levels, and even global nuclear war. He has argued that the earth as a living organism is so resilient and adaptable that it eventually adjusts to such changes.

Lovelock argues that Gaia, like other organisms, has certain vital organs—wetlands, the coastal zones of the oceans, and tropical forests—that must be protected from destruction and degradation. But Lovelock does not view the deep oceans, grasslands, temperate forests, rivers, lakes, and other lands and waters that make up the rest of Gaia as vital to the long-term existence of the earth as a living organism over millions and billions of years.

On this extremely long time frame, Lovelock argues that all individuals and most species are irrelevant to the long-term sustainability of Gaia. He points out that at least 99% of the species believed to have existed on earth have already become extinct and have been replaced by other species that maintain Gaia.

Cornucopians have used these aspects of the Gaia hypothesis to justify the continued human domination and exploitation of the earth. They propose that we gain even greater human domination over Gaia's corrective systems and evolutionary processes.

Environmentalists agree with Lovelock and Margulis that in the long run the earth is resilient and adaptable and that no single species—including the human species—is important to its long-term sustainability. However, they point out that the human species has amassed enough power to seriously damage some of the earth's life-support systems. Indeed, human activities, especially the wide-scale clearing of tropical forests, are bringing about the premature extinction of more species in a shorter period of time than ever before in the earth's history.

Corrective feedback mechanisms may eventually help absorb and correct these abuses, but such changes typically take millions to billions of years. Thus, continuing our present abuse of the earth will doom billions of people to premature death and miserable life quality during these long corrective periods. The present extinction epidemic also means premature extinction for millions of the earth's species, possibly including the human species.

Biologists point out that although the earth does have corrective feedback mechanisms, it does not metabolize, reproduce, or mutate as living systems do. To such critics, the Gaia concept is primarily a useful, even inspiring, poetic image, not a scientific reality. There is considerable evidence that life influences the environment through corrective feedback mechanisms and that life controls the earth's environmental conditions. But this does not mean that the earth itself is alive.

In 1987 Lovelock conceded that his original hypothesis that the earth was a superorganism striving to create and maintain conditions suitable to the flourishing of life went too far. He now believes that the earth is a homeostatic system, not a true living system.

Now the argument is primarily about how much influence the biosphere has on the earth's physical and chemical processes. Most biologists agree that living organisms affect the earth's environment. But Lovelock and his supporters believe that living organisms not only affect the environment but also regulate it.

Lovelock's critics agree with him that we need to carry out much more research to find out how much the earth's living organisms influence the environmental conditions needed for life. Do you believe that the earth is alive?

Malaria once infected 9 out of 10 people in North Borneo, now known as Brunei. In 1955 the World Health Organization (WHO) began spraying dieldrin (a pesticide similar to DDT) to kill malaria-carrying mosquitoes. The program was so successful that the dreaded disease was almost eliminated from the island.

But other, unexpected things happened. The dieldrin killed other insects, including flies and cockroaches, living in houses. The islanders applauded. But then small lizards that also lived in the houses died after gorging themselves on dead insects. Then cats began dying after feeding on the dead lizards. Without cats, rats flourished and overran the villages. Now people were threatened by sylvatic plague carried by the fleas on the rats. The situation was brought under control when WHO parachuted healthy cats onto the island.

Then roofs began to fall in. The dieldrin had killed wasps and other insects that fed on a type of caterpillar that either avoided or was not affected by the insecticide. With most of its predators eliminated, the caterpillar population exploded. The larvae munched their way through one of their favorite foods, the leaves used in thatching roofs.

In the end, the Borneo episode was a success story; both malaria and the unexpected effects of the spraying program were brought under control. But it shows the unpredictable results of interfering in an ecosystem.

Does an ecosystem need both high inertia and high resilience to be considered stable? Evidence indicates that some ecosystems have one of these properties but not the other. For example, California redwood forests and tropical rain forests have high species diversity and high inertia. This means that they are hard to alter significantly or destroy through natural processes. However, once large tracts of these diverse ecosystems are completely cleared, they have such low resilience that restoring them is nearly impossible.

On the other hand, grasslands, with much lower species diversity, burn easily and thus have low inertia. However, because most of their plant matter consists of roots beneath the ground surface, these ecosystems have high resilience, which allows them to recover quickly. A grassland can be destroyed only if its roots are plowed up and wheat or some other crop is planted in its soil.

Clearly, we have a long way to go in understanding how the factors involved in natural communities and ecosystems interact. But considerable evidence indicates that simplifying a natural community or ecosystem by the intentional or accidental removal of a species often has unpredictable short- and long-term harmful effects (see Spotlight on p. 144).

Responses to Large-Scale Stress: Ecological Succession The organisms in most communities and ecosystems can adapt not only to small and moderate changes in environmental conditions but also to quite severe changes. Sometimes, for example, little vegetation and soil are left as a result of a natural environmental change (retreating glaciers, fires, floods, volcanic eruptions, earthquakes) or a human-induced change (fires, land clearing, surface mining, flooding to create a pond or reservoir, pollution).

After such a large-scale disturbance, life usually begins to recolonize a site in a series of stages. First, a few hardy **pioneer species** invade the environment and start creating soil or, in aquatic ecosystems, sediment. Eventually the species that make up the pioneer community change the soil or bottom sediments and other conditions so much that the area is less suitable for them and more suitable for a new group of plants and animals with different ecological niche requirements. This process, in which communities of plant, animal, and decomposer species change into at least partially different and usually more complex communities, is called **ecological succession** or **biotic development.**

If not severely disrupted, ecological succession often continues until the community becomes more self-sustaining than the preceding ones. When this happens, what ecologists call the **mature community** occupies the site. Depending primarily on the climate, these terrestrial communities may be various types of mature grasslands, forests, or deserts (Figure 5-9, p. 114).

Ecologists recognize two types of ecological succession: primary and secondary. Which type takes place depends on the conditions at a particular site at the beginning of the process. **Primary succession** is the sequential development of biotic communities in a bare area. Examples of such areas include the rock or mud exposed by a retreating glacier or mudslide, cooled volcanic lava, a new sandbar deposited by a shift in ocean currents, and surface-mined areas from which all topsoil has been removed. On such barren surfaces, primary succession from bare rock to a mature forest may take hundreds to thousands of years.

The more common type of succession is **secondary succession**. This is the sequential development of communities in an area where the natural vegetation has been removed or destroyed, but the soil or bottom

canopy

lower canopy trees

tall shrub understory

annual weeds

perennial weeds and grasses

shrubs

young pine forest

mature oak forest

Time——→

Figure 6-11 Secondary ecological succession of plant communities on an abandoned farm field in North Carolina over about 150 years. Succession of animal communities is not shown.

sediment has not been destroyed. Examples of areas that can undergo secondary succession include abandoned farmlands, burned or cut forests, land stripped of vegetation for surface mining, heavily polluted streams, and land that has been flooded naturally or to produce a reservoir or pond. Because some soil or sediment is present, new vegetation can usually sprout within only a few weeks.

In the central (Piedmont) region of North Carolina, European settlers cleared away the native oak and hickory climax forests and planted the land in crops. Figure 6-11 shows how this abandoned farmland, covered with a thick layer of soil, has undergone secondary succession over a period of about 150 years until the area is again covered with a mature oak and hickory forest.

Newly created lakes, reservoirs, and ponds also undergo secondary succession (Figure 6-12). They gradually fill up with bottom sediments and eventually become terrestrial ecosystems, which then undergo secondary ecological succession.

Comparison of Immature and Mature
Immature ecosystems and mature ecosystems have strikingly different characteristics, as summarized in Table

6-2. Immature communities at the early stages of biotic development have low species diversity—that is, they consist of only a few species. They also have fairly simple food webs, made up mostly of producers fed upon by herbivores and relatively few decomposers.

Most of the plants in a pioneer community are small annuals that grow close to the ground. They use most of their energy to produce large numbers of small seeds for reproduction rather than to develop large root, stem, and leaf systems. They receive some matter resources from other ecosystems for example, as runoff, because they are too simple to hold and recycle many of the nutrients they receive.

In contrast, the community in a mature ecosystem has high species diversity, relatively stable populations, and complex food webs dominated by decomposers that feed on the large amount of dead vegetation and animal wastes. Most plants in mature ecosystems are larger herbs and trees that produce a small number of large seeds. They use most of their energy and matter resources to maintain their large root, trunk, and leaf systems rather than to produce large numbers of new plants. They also have the complexity necessary to entrap, hold, and recycle most of the nutrients they need.

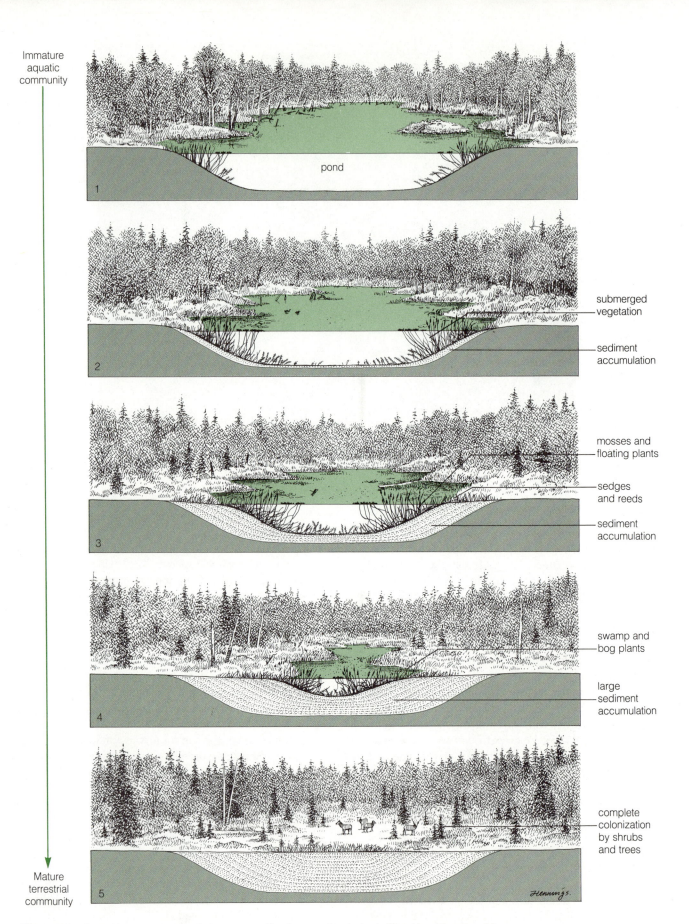

Immature aquatic community

pond

submerged vegetation

sediment accumulation

mosses and floating plants

sedges and reeds

sediment accumulation

swamp and bog plants

large sediment accumulation

complete colonization by shrubs and trees

Mature terrestrial community

Hennings.

Figure 6-12 Secondary succession of plant communities in a pond as it slowly fills with sediment and is eventually converted to a mature forest community.

Table 6-2 Ecosystem Characteristics of Communities at Immature and Mature Stages of Ecological Succession or Biotic Development

Characteristic	Immature Ecosystem	Mature Ecosystem
Ecosystem Structure		
Plant size	Small	Large
Species diversity	Low	High
Trophic structure	Mostly producers, few decomposers	Mixture of producers, consumers, and decomposers
Ecological niches	Few, mostly generalized	Many, mostly specialized
Community organization (number of interconnecting links)	Low	High
Ecosystem Function		
Food chains and webs	Simple, mostly plant → herbivore with few decomposers	Complex, dominated by decomposers
Efficiency of nutrient recycling	Low	High
Efficiency of energy use	Low	High

6-4 HUMAN IMPACTS ON ECOSYSTEMS

Human Beings and Ecosystems In modifying ecosystems for our use, we simplify them. For example, we bulldoze and plow grasslands and forests. Then we replace the thousands of interrelated plant and animal species in these ecosystems with greatly simplified, single-crop ecosystems, or monocultures, or with structures such as buildings, highways, and parking lots.

Modern agriculture is based on the practice of deliberately keeping ecosystems in early stages of succession, in which the biomass productivity of one or a few plant species (such as corn or wheat) is high (Figure 6-13). But such simplified ecosystems are highly vulnerable.

A major problem is the continual invasion of crop fields by unwanted pioneer species, which we call *weeds* if they are plants, *pests* if they are insects or other animals, and *diseases* if they are harmful microorganisms such as bacteria, fungi, and viruses. Weeds, pests, or diseases can wipe out an entire monoculture crop unless it is artificially protected with pesticides such as insecticides (insect-killing chemicals) and herbicides (plant-killing chemicals) or by some form of biological control.

When quickly breeding species develop genetic resistance to these chemicals, farmers must use ever-stronger doses or switch to a new product. Thus, every pesticide increases the rate of natural selection of the pests to the point that the effectiveness of the chemical is eventually lost. This illustrates biologist Garrett Hardin's **first law of ecology:** We can never do merely

EPA Documerica (Charles O'Rear)

Figure 6-13 Modern, industrialized agriculture uses large inputs of fossil fuels—mostly oil—to plant, protect, and harvest vast fields of one crop (monoculture). These greatly simplified ecosystems are highly vulnerable to disruption from weeds, insects, and crop diseases.

one thing. Any intrusion into nature has numerous effects, many of which are unpredictable.

Cultivation is not the only way people simplify ecosystems. Ranchers, who don't want bison or prairie dogs competing with sheep for grass, eradicate these species as well as wolves, coyotes, eagles, and other predators that occasionally kill sheep. Far too often, ranchers allow livestock to overgraze grasslands until excessive soil erosion converts these ecosystems to simpler and less productive deserts.

The cutting of vast areas of diverse tropical rain forests is causing the irreversible loss of many plant and animal species. People also tend to overfish and overhunt some species to extinction or near extinction, another way of simplifying ecosystems. The burning of fossil fuels in industrial plants, homes, and vehicles creates atmospheric pollutants that fall to the earth as acidic compounds. These chemicals simplify forest ecosystems by killing trees, and aquatic ecosystems by killing fish.

It is becoming increasingly clear that the price we pay for simplifying, maintaining, and protecting such stripped-down ecosystems is high: It includes time, money, increased use of matter and energy resources, loss of genetic diversity, and loss of natural landscape (Table 6-3). There is also the danger that as the human population grows, we will convert too many of the world's mature ecosystems to simple, young, productive, but highly vulnerable forms. The challenge is to maintain a balance between simplified, human ecosystems and the neighboring, more complex, natural ecosystems our simplified systems depend on.

During the last 40,000 years or so, the human species used its intelligence to develop cultural mechanisms or changes for controlling and adapting to environmental stresses (Figure 6-5). We have also learned to speed up genetic change in other species—first through crossbreeding and recently through genetic engineering (see Pro/Con below).

PRO/CON Do Benefits of Genetic Engineering Outweigh the Risks?

For many decades humans have selected and crossbred different genetic varieties of plants and animals to develop new varieties with certain desired qualities. Today "genetic engineers" have learned how to splice genes and recombine sequences of existing DNA molecules in organisms to produce DNA with new genetic characteristics (recombinant DNA).

In other words, they use laboratory techniques to transfer traits from one species to another to make new genetic combinations instead of waiting for nature to evolve new genetic combinations through natural selection. We are already using this biotechnology to produce new forms of life, which are then patented and sold in the marketplace. Genetic engineering may give us greatly increased control over the course of evolution of the earth's living species.

This developing technology excites some scientists. They see it as a way to increase crop and livestock yields and to produce plants and livestock that have greater resistance to diseases, pests, frost, and drought and that provide greater quantities of nutrients such as proteins. They hope to develop bacteria that can destroy oil spills and degrade toxic wastes and to

develop new vaccines, drugs, and therapeutic hormones. Gene therapy would also be used to eliminate certain genetic diseases and other genetic afflictions.

Already genetic engineering has produced a drug to arrest heart attacks and agents to fight diabetes, hemophilia, and some forms of cancer. It has also been used to diagnose AIDS and cancer. Genetically altered viruses have been used to manufacture more effective vaccines.

In agriculture, gene transfer has been used to develop strawberries that resist frost and smaller cows that produce more milk. Toxin-producing genes have been transferred from bacteria to plants, increasing the plants' immunity to insect attack. Genetic technology has also produced edible fish that grow faster and bigger than conventional varieties.

But some people are horrified by the prospect of biotechnology running amok. Most of these critics recognize that it is essentially impossible to stop the development of genetic engineering, which is already well under way. But they believe that this technology should be kept under strict control.

They are particularly concerned that it may be used to reduce the

natural genetic diversity among individuals of a single species. It could also reduce the biological diversity represented by the world's variety of species. Genetic and species diversity are essential to the long-term functioning and adaptability of ecosystems and the ecosphere. These critics do not believe that people have enough understanding of how nature works to be trusted with such great control over the genetic characteristics of humans and other species.

Critics also fear that unregulated biotechnology could lead to the development of "superorganisms." If such organisms were released deliberately or accidentally into the environment, they could cause unpredictable, possibly harmful health and ecological effects. Most would probably be safe, but some would inevitably turn out to be dangerous.

Critics are especially concerned with increasing military control over the development of biotechnology in the United States and other countries. These highly secret activities are not subject to the normal scientific review that controls the direction of technology. Also, the military is likely to use genetic engineering to develop

Table 6-3 Comparison of a Natural Ecosystem and a Simplified Human System	
Natural Ecosystem (marsh, grassland, forest)	Simplified Human System (cornfield, factory, house)
Captures, converts, and stores energy from the sun	Consumes energy from fossil or nuclear fuels
Produces oxygen and consumes carbon dioxide	Consumes oxygen and produces carbon dioxide from the burning of fossil fuels
Creates fertile soil	Depletes or covers fertile soil
Stores, purifies, and releases water gradually	Often uses and contaminates water and releases it rapidly
Provides wildlife habitats	Destroys some wildlife habitats
Filters and detoxifies pollutants and waste products free of charge	Produces pollutants and waste, which must be cleaned up at our expense
Usually capable of self-maintenance and self-renewal	Requires continual maintenance and renewal at great cost

harmful organisms for biological warfare. The history of grossly inadequate control over the safety of nuclear weapons facilities in the United States and in the Soviet Union over the past 45 years heightens public fears about safety in government biological warfare facilities.

Since many organisms, especially bacteria, are capable of rapidly reproducing and spreading to new locations, any problems they cause would be widespread. For example, genetically altered bacteria designed to clean up ocean oil spills by degrading the oil might multiply rapidly and eventually degrade the world's remaining oil supplies—including the oil in cars and trucks.

In addition to reproducing rapidly, genetically engineered organisms might also mutate and change their form and behavior. Unlike defective cars and other products, living organisms can't be recalled once they are in the environment.

The risks of this or other catastrophic events resulting from biotechnology are small. But critics contend that biotechnology is a potential source of such enormous profits that without strict controls greed—not ecological wisdom and restraint—will take over. They

contend that rules proposed by the EPA in 1988 for regulation of biotechnology are wholly inadequate. A major problem is that regulatory authority would be delegated to committees dominated—if not fully controlled—by industries proposing releases of bioengineered organisms into the environment.

Genetic scientists answer, however, that it is highly unlikely that the release of genetically engineered species would cause serious and widespread ecological problems. To have a serious effect, such organisms would have to be outstanding competitors and resistant to predation. In addition, they would have to be capable of becoming dominant in ecosystems and in the ecosphere. But critics point out that this has happened many times when we have accidentally or deliberately introduced alien organisms into biological communities.

In 1989 a committee of prominent ecologists appointed by the Ecological Society of America released a report stating that many of the assertions about the inherent safety of genetically engineered organisms are not true. They point out that the risk posed by a bioengineered organism

released or escaping into the environment depends on whether it survives and reproduces, its potential for spread, its interactions with other organisms, and its affects on the physical environment. No sweeping statements about safety can be valid until there are answers to these important questions.

Generally adding a gene or genes tends to reduce the fitness of an organism to survive and thrive in the environment. But the committee warns that it might take hundreds of thousands of generations before the trait is eliminated. Meanwhile, natural selection will tend to increase the fitness of the organism. If the organism passes on the new gene to other organisms in the environment, that trait could persist even after the original modified organism has died out.

The committee calls for a case-by case review of any proposed environmental releases. It also calls for carefully regulated, small-scale field tests before any bioengineered organism is put into commercial use.

This controversy illustrates the difficulty of balancing the actual and potential benefits of a technology with its actual and potential risks of harm. What do you think?

Nuclear War: The Ultimate Ecological Catastrophe

Most people believe that the greatest threat to human and other life on this planet is global nuclear war. The nuclear age began in August 1945, when the United States exploded a single nuclear fission atomic bomb over Hiroshima and another over Nagasaki. These blasts killed an estimated 110,000 to 140,000 and severely injured tens of thousands more people.

By the end of the year another 100,000 had died, mostly from exposure to radioactive fallout: dirt and debris sucked up and made radioactive by the blast and dropped back to earth near ground zero and on downwind areas hundreds and even thousands of miles away. Other people, exposed to nonlethal doses of ionizing radiation, developed cataracts, leukemia, and other forms of lethal cancer decades later. This shows us what a small nuclear bomb can do.

Today the world's nuclear arsenals have an explosive power equal to more than 952,000 Hiroshima-type bombs or 3,333 times all the explosives detonated during World War II. A single U.S. Trident I nuclear submarine carries nuclear missles with an explosive power equal to the power of 914 Hiroshima bombs or over six times all the explosives detonated in World War II. Each Trident II submarine that began coming on line in 1989 carries warheads with five times the explosive power of the Trident I, and thus has the firepower of 30 World War IIs and the radioactive fallout of 1,885 Chernobyl nuclear accidents.

Some U.S. and Soviet military strategists have talked about the concept of "limited nuclear war." In this scenario, combatants would direct nuclear weapons only at military targets rather than launching an all-out nuclear attack on both military targets and major cities. According to these strategists, most people in the United States and the Soviet Union could survive a limited nuclear war and the effects on most other countries not involved in the exchange would not be drastic.

Since 1982, however, evaluation of previously overlooked calculations has suggested that even a limited nuclear war could kill 1 billion to 4 billion people—20% to 80% of the world's population. Such an exchange would probably take place in the Northern Hemisphere, presumably between the United States and the Soviet Union. If this happened, the direct effects of the explosions would kill an estimated 1 billion people, mostly in the Northern Hemisphere. Tens of millions more would suffer injuries.

Within the next two years, another 1 billion to 3 billion might die from starvation caused by disruption of world agricultural production, first in the Northern Hemisphere and later in the Southern Hemisphere. Computer models have been used to project what might happen in the mid-latitudes of the Northern Hemisphere, where most of the world's food is grown. These models indicate that if a nuclear war took place in summer, these areas in the Northern Hemisphere would experience what is called the *nuclear winter* or *nuclear autumn effect*.

Depending on the extent of the explosions, average temperatures in the middle Northern Hemisphere would probably drop rapidly to temperatures typical of fall or early winter. This atmospheric cooling would happen because of a reverse greenhouse effect. Massive amounts of smoke, soot, dust, and other debris, lifted into the atmosphere as a result of the nuclear explosions and subsequent fires, would coalesce into huge smoke clouds. Within two weeks these dense clouds would cover large portions of the Northern Hemisphere and prevent 20% to 90% of all sunlight from reaching these areas.

During the weeks or months while the dark, patchy clouds persisted, regions under them would be subjected to varying periods of darkness or semidarkness during normally daylight periods. Without the sun's warmth, continental surface temperatures would drop below freezing, even in midsummer. For example, large clouds of smoke produced by devastating northern California forest fires in 1987 caused summer temperatures in the Klamath River Canyon to plummet an average of −2.7°C (27°F) for a week. This small-scale effect indicates what could happen on a much larger scale, if much of the Northern Hemisphere were covered with massive smoke clouds.

The abnormally cold temperatures and reduction of sunlight would cause a sharp drop in food production in the growing season following the war. This would cause widespread starvation in the Northern Hemisphere and in African and Asian countries dependent on food imports from countries such as the United States and Canada.

Food production in the Southern Hemisphere might also be affected as the smoke clouds gradually became less dense and spread southward. Drops in temperature and sunlight would be less severe than in the Northern Hemisphere. But even a slight reduction in temperature could be disastrous to agriculture in tropical and subtropical forest areas and could lead to the extinction of numerous plant and animal species. Subtropical grasslands and savannas in Africa and South America might be the least affected of the world's biomes because their plants are more cold-tolerant and drought-resistant.

Loss of sunlight and freezing temperatures would not be the only cause of food scarcity. Plagues of rapidly producing insects and rodents—the life forms best equipped to survive nuclear war—would damage stored food and spread disease. In areas where crops could still be grown, farmers would be isolated from supplies of seeds, fertilizer, pesticides, and fuel. People hoping to subsist on seafood would find many surviving aquatic species contaminated with radioactivity, runoff from ruptured tanks of industrial liquids, and oil pouring out of damaged offshore rigs.

Incineration of oil in tanks and refineries, storage tanks of hazardous chemicals, rubber tires, and other materials would produce toxic smog, which would cover much of the Northern Hemisphere. Large areas might also be assaulted with extremely acid rains. High levels of radioactivity from fallout would contaminate most remaining food and water supplies, kill many people and other warm-blooded animals, some crops, and certain coniferous trees, especially pines.

Thus, people not killed outright by the nuclear explosions would find themselves choking and freezing in a smoggy, radioactive darkness with contaminated water supplies and little chance of growing food for a year or perhaps several years. Most people who survived in underground bunkers would die slowly rather than quickly.

The computer models used to make these calculations are not perfect and may overestimate or underestimate the effects of a nuclear explosion. But scientists agree that even if the effects are less than the models suggest, they would still cause serious disruptions in regional and global climate.

Thus, the idea that anyone would win in even a limited nuclear war is clearly insane (see Guest Essay on p. 153). Some have wondered whether there is intelligent life in other parts of the universe. The more important question may be "Is there intelligent life on earth?"

Some Environmental Lessons It should be clear from the brief discussion of principles in this and the preceding three chapters that living systems have six major features: *interdependence, diversity, resilience, adaptability, unpredictability,* and *limits.* Understanding this does not mean that we should stop growing food, building cities, and making other changes that affect the earth's biological communities. But we do need to recognize that such human-induced changes have far-reaching and unpredictable consequences. We need wisdom, care, and restraint as we alter the ecosphere.

In addition to the first law of ecology, our actions should take into account the **second law of ecology** or principle of interrelatedness: Everything is connected to and intermingled with everything else; we are all in it together. Another cardinal rule is the **third law of ecology:** Any compound that we produce should not interfere with any of the earth's natural biogeochemical cycles.

We also have an obligation to work with nature to repair many of the wounds we have already inflicted. This is the goal of the emerging science and art of *rehabilitation and restoration ecology* (see Enrichment Study below). We must tune our senses to how nature really works and sustains itself, sensing in nature fundamental rhythms we can trust and cooperate with even though we will never fully understand them.

What has gone wrong, probably, is that we have failed to see ourselves as part of a large and indivisible whole. For too long we have based our lives on a primitive feeling that our "God-given" role was to have "dominion over the fish of the sea and over the fowl of the air and over every living thing that moveth upon the earth." We have failed to understand that the earth does not belong to us, but we to the earth.

Rolf Edberg

ENRICHMENT STUDY Ecosystem Rehabilitation and Restoration

Rehabilitation Versus Restoration

Researchers are creating a new discipline of rehabilitation and restoration ecology. When a degraded ecosystem is abandoned, in most cases it will eventually restore itself, at least partially, through ecological succession. But this process takes a long time. For example, it typically takes more than a century for a slash-and-burn site in a tropical forest (Figure 2-2, p. 00) to be fully reforested. If such a site is cleared by

bulldozer, natural recovery will take at least 1,000 years.

By studying how natural ecosystems recover from severe stresses, scientists are learning how to speed up the repair of environments that have been damaged by human activities. Environmentally degraded ecosystems can either be rehabilitated or restored. *Rehabilitation* involves making degraded land useful for humans again on a sustainable basis. It is particularly useful for stopping soil

erosion and desertification and allowing degraded land to be used again to produce food or fuel.

Restoration is more ambitious. Its goal is to take a degraded site and reestablish a community of organisms close to what would be found naturally. It is used primarily to reestablish unique or rare ecosystems in parts of the world where most ecosystems have been degraded or destroyed. Often you

(continued)

don't have to plant anything. Instead, you find the strongest types of natural growth, protect it, and remove all plant and animal species not native to the area to be restored.

A number of scientists, with the aid of dedicated volunteers, have been successful in restoring or rehabilitating various types of damaged ecosystems to reasonably good health. The costs of such projects are high, but the long-term costs of doing nothing are much higher.

Rehabilitating Degraded Mountainous Areas and Forestlands

Mountainous areas that are farmed or cleared of trees for fuelwood or lumber are particularly vulnerable to erosion of topsoil. The land cannot sustain crops or trees, and rivers and streams in the valleys below are filled with silt as the soil washes down. This increases the severity of flooding.

Other forestlands in need of rehabilitation are overlogged forests, cut forests with poor species composition, damaged agricultural lands, drained forested wetlands, and severely burned areas.

Several things can be done to rehabilitate such lands. Terraces can be built across slopes to help retain water and hold crops. Small walls of stone (check dams) can be built across gullies. Planting rapidly growing vegetation can help hold soil in place and fruit trees can be planted to provide food and hold soil in place. Some areas can also be reforested with fast-growing fuelwood trees.

Rehabilitating Degraded Drylands

Drylands in areas with arid or semiarid climates cover almost one-fifth of the land area in LDCs. More than 300 million people try to survive on these drylands by growing food, grazing livestock, and cutting trees for fuelwood and lumber. This has led to increased degradation of cropland and rangeland. In some cases land that could once be used for dryland farming or livestock grazing has been converted to desert. An estimated 60% of the croplands and 80% of the rangelands in dryland regions of LDCs are declining in productivity because of environmental degradation.

The usual way to rehabilitate degraded rangeland is to reseed it with perennial grasses, legumes, and other plants and then prohibit or restrict grazing until the plants are established. Because the net productivity of drylands is low, rehabilitation techniques must be inexpensive or they will not be profitable.

Instead of plowing and disking the soil, it is much cheaper to prepare the soil for planting by land imprinting. Rolling cylinders with angle-iron teeth welded onto them are rolled over the soil. This mimics the role that the hoof prints of grazing and browsing livestock play in seedbed preparation. A large herd of livestock can also be driven over a degraded area once to give a similar effect.

With rainfed cropland in semiarid areas, windbreaks of trees can be planted along degraded fields to keep soil and seeds from blowing away and to provide habitats for natural predators of crop pests. Degraded dryland can also be planted with tree plantations of fast-growing fuelwood trees.

Tallgrass Prairie Restoration

One of the most extensive restoration projects has focused on restoring areas of tallgrass prairie that once blanketed the midwestern United States. Since 1936, scientists at the University of Wisconsin-Madison's Arboretum have worked to restore the Curtis Prairie, a project conceived by Aldo Leopold in 1934. After over 50 years of painstaking work and research, parts of the Curtis Prairie are now almost comparable to the native prairie once found on the site.

Another pioneering example of prairie restoration is near Chicago. In 1962 Ray Schulenberg, curator of Plant Collections for the Morton Arboretum at Lisle, Illinois, began reestablishing a prairie on a plot of land at the arboretum. He collected seeds from remnants of prairie in the area, raised seedlings in a greenhouse, and then broadcast them on the plot.

For two years teams of workers removed weeds by hand. After the prairie grasses became established, they used controlled burning each spring to remove weeds and encourage the growth of perennial prairie plants. Today this site is covered with healthy prairie plants. It is used for educational purposes and as a refuge for endangered species of local plants and insects.

The largest prairie restoration project is being carried out at the Fermi National Accelerator Laboratory in Illinois by Schulenberg and Robert Betz, a biology professor at Northeastern Illinois University in Chicago. Schulenberg and Betz found remnants of virgin Illinois prairie in old cemeteries, on embankments, and on other patches of land. In 1972 they transplanted these by hand on a four-hectare patch at the Fermi Laboratory site.

Each year volunteers carefully prepared 10 to 20 more hectares of land, sowed it with virgin prairie plants, and weeded it manually. Today more than 180 hectares of the plot have been restored with prairie plants. New species are introduced each year, with the goal of eventually establishing the 150 to 200 species that once flourished on the 240-hectare site.

Wetlands Restoration

There are also numerous examples of restoration of coastal and freshwater wetlands, especially in the eastern United States. Ed Garbisch, formerly a professor of chemistry, has spent the last two decades

(continued)

developing techniques to restore saltwater marshes in Florida. The rate of such wetlands restoration, however, is much slower than the rate at which thesevital ecosystems are being destroyed (see Spotlight on p. 128).

Forest Restoration

Some attempts to restore degraded forests are also being made. But restoring forests is difficult because forests take a long time to mature and are more complex in structure and composition than most other ecosystems.

One project involves efforts to reestablish a redwood forest on 14,500 hectares (35,630 acres) of logged land next to Redwood National Forest near San Francisco. The most ambitious forest restoration project is being carried out in a dry tropical forest in Guancaste National Park in northwest Costa Rica under the leadership of Daniel Janzen, professor of biology at the University of Pennsylvania. His vision is to make the nearly 40,000 people who live near the area an integral part of the restoration of 70,000 hectares (270 square miles) of forest—a concept he calls *biocultural restoration*. By actively

participating in the project, local residents will reap enormous educational, economic, and environmental benefits.

The essence of the program is to make the park a living classroom. Students in grade schools, high schools, and universities will study the ecology of the park in the classroom and go on annual field trips in the park itself. There will also be educational programs for civic groups and tourists from Costa Rica and elsewhere. These visitors and activities will stimulate the local economy.

The project will also serve as a training ground in tropical forest restoration for scientists throughout the world. Research scientists working on the project will give guest lectures in classrooms and lead some of the field trips.

Already dozens of students in the region visit the park each day. Plans call for several thousand elementary and high school students in the region to visit the park for a full day of field biology at least once a year.

Janzen recognizes that in 20 to 40 years these children will be running the park and the local political system. If they understand the importance of their local environment, they are more likely

to protect and sustain its biological resources.

Preservation of Biodiversity

Restoration of damaged ecosystems, coupled with preservation of natural areas, is a key to conserving much of the earth's vital biological diversity. But ecosystem restoration isn't easy. It takes lots of money and decades of hard work.

The dedicated scientists who are carrying out such projects and the many volunteers who help them are important and inspiring examples of people caring for the earth. Expanding and supporting this emerging field designed to heal rather than hurt the earth must become a major priority.

It is arrogant to think that we can rebuild damaged systems completely. But we can repair much of the damage we have done. Anyone can become involved in such earth healing. Volunteers can get together and revitalize a creek or revegetate a small plot of land in a city. Restoring parts of the earth's damaged fabric will also help show that it is easier and cheaper not to hurt the earth in the first place.

GUEST ESSAY The Abolition of War as a Condition for Human Survival

Kenneth E. Boulding

Kenneth E. Boulding is Distinguished Professor of Economic Emeritus and director of the Program of Research and General Social and Economic Dynamics at the Institute

of Behavioral Sciences, University of Colorado at Boulder. During his long and distinguished career as an economist and social thinker he has served as president of the American Economic Association and the American Association for the Advancement of Science. He has engaged in research on peace, systems analysis, economic theory, economics and ethics, and economics and environment. He was the first leading economist to propose in the late 1960s that we move from our present throwaway or frontier economy to a sustainable earth economy.

Perhaps the most profound change in the state of the Planet Earth in the last 100 years has been the development of more destructive forms of warfare. The first major development was aerial warfare and the

(continued)

bombing of cities. The second was the development of the nuclear weapon, especially the hydrogen bomb with its enormous destructive power, and the long-range missile which can deliver it to virtually any point on the earth's surface. This massive increase in destructive power has created a totally unprecedented situation in regard to the nature of war and what we might call the "unilateral national defense organizations," like the U.S. Department of Defense and the corresponding organizations in other countries.

Something like this, however, though on a smaller scale, has happened before in human history. A good example is the development of gunpowder and the effective cannon in the 15th and 16th centuries, which really brought the feudal system to an end and created national states the size of England or France. As long as the means of destruction were spears and arrows, there was some sense in having a castle or a city wall. With the coming of the effective cannon, these made no sense. The baron who stayed in his castle got blown up. Some attempt was made to save the city wall by building longer triangular projections from them, with cannon on them, a little reminiscent of the Strategic Defense Initiative (SDI) or "Star Wars" defense now being pursued by the United States. But this turned out to be ineffective. City walls were torn down and became boulevards, castles became tourist attractions.

The nuclear weapon and the long-range missile has done for unilateral national defense precisely what the cannon did for the feudal baron and the city wall, but we haven't caught on to this yet. We delude ourselves by thinking that we have a stable deterrence. Deterrence says "You do something nasty to me and I'll do something nasty to you." Deterrence can work over short periods and in specific places, but it cannot be stable in the long run, otherwise it would not deter in the short run. If the probability of nuclear weapons going off were zero, that would be the same as not having them. They would deter nobody.

Deterrence always has a positive probability of breaking down. Before the nuclear weapon the probability of deterrence breaking down seems to have been something like 4% per year, rather like the probability of a flood every 25 years. The probability of nuclear war may be a little less than this, perhaps more like a flood every 50 years or perhaps every 100 years. However, it is a fundamental principle that if there is a positive probability of anything, if we wait long enough it will happen. When one reflects that the Chernobyl nuclear power plant was carefully designed not to go off and that nuclear weapons are carefully designed to go off, the possibility of even accidental nuclear war may be alarmingly high. Strategists talk about limited nuclear war without coming up with any organization whatever to limit it. For the

first time in human history the fate of the planet is in the hands of a very few decision makers. There is always a positive probability that one or more of them will make a fatal decision.

There is some uncertainty about the consequences of nuclear war. There is some probability it might create a nuclear winter or autumn, which could cause at least a billion, perhaps several billion, human beings to starve to death. We know very little about the long-run effects of massive radiation fallout from a major nuclear war, and there may even be some small probability that it would bring the whole evolutionary process on earth to an end. What is more probable is that it would be a disaster that would distort and in some sense cripple the whole process of evolutionary development on earth for a very long time to come. This is also a threat to the environment which exceeds anything else that the human race is doing, whether in terms of the "greenhouse effect," depletion of the ozone layer, tropical forest destruction, or chemical pollution.

The only way to remove this dire threat to the planet is through the abolition of war. This too has a noticeable probability. Again there are historical parallels. We abolished dueling when it went from swords to pistols and often both parties were getting killed. We abolished slavery when it became economically and morally unacceptable.

Now the great task of the human race is to abolish national defense and transform the military into a means of production rather than a means of destruction. Some of this may come from the military themselves. There are intelligent people among them—and they are not very different from the rest of us—who recognize that in some sense the old system has come to an end, that the traditional military ethic and military culture of courage, sacrifice, and "fighting" have become of minor significance. These individuals recognize that the military forces of the world are now a single united system designed, we might say, though not intended, to destroy the human race and perhaps render the planet uninhabitable, a position that no human being should be in.

We have to learn that military victory is something that has disappeared from the earth, that we have to live without enemies. The great problem of the military is that they have to have enemies in order to justify their budgets. Hence they are designed to be very ineffective at conflict management, the most important skill we need on this planet today. Somehow we must catch onto this and recognize that the greatest conflict in the world at the moment is between the united military of the world and the human race, which of course includes those in the military system. Once we recognize this, things can happen.

(continued)

Peace is not something exotic and improbable. In the last 150 years we have seen the rise of stable peace among many nations, beginning perhaps in Scandinavia, spreading to North American by about 1870, now to Western Europe and the Pacific, where we now have perhaps 18 nations in a great triangle from Australia to Japan to Finland who have no plans whatever to go to war with each other.

The next step is to establish stable peace between the Soviet bloc and the rest of the world. With the extraordinary things that have been happening in the communist countries, this peace has risen above the horizon as a real possibility if the West can respond positively to it. Then, of course, the next step is to spread stable peace to the tropics and the Third World.

It is a fundamental principle that what exists must be possible. Stable peace has existed now in many nations for at least 150 years. It must clearly be possible. In that there is great hope for the human race and this incredibly beautiful planet.

Guest Essay Discussion

1. Do you think or talk about the possibility of nuclear war? Why or why not? What causes most people to largely ignore this greatest threat to their survival and the survival of their children and grandchildren?

2. The history of warfare has shown that any advance in military technology is countered by another advance in military technology and that the pace of this process is increasing. In light of this, do you believe that the United States should pour hundreds of billions of dollars into a "Star Wars" defense system against nuclear attack? Explain.

3. Do you agree that the most urgent task on this planet is to abolish war? Why? Do you believe that this is possible? Explain. If you agree that it is the most urgent task, then what are you doing as an individual to convert this possibility into reality?

CHAPTER SUMMARY

Living systems have some ability to withstand stress. They tend to resist being disturbed or altered (*inertia*) and to restore themselves to their original condition (*persistence*) if not disturbed too drastically. Organisms, populations, and ecosystems maintain themselves within a tolerable range of conditions through *homeostasis*. They do this primarily through negative feedback of information into the system to counteract the effects of a change in environmental conditions.

Populations of a species respond to changes in environmental conditions in several ways. Population size is altered by changes in birth rates and death rates and for some species by moving to another area. Population structure may also change, with fewer old, very young, or weak members.

Without unlimited resources, the population size of a species is limited. The maximum population size of each species that a natural ecosystem can support indefinitely under a given set of environmental conditions is called that ecosystem's *carrying capacity* for that species.

A population of a particular species can also undergo changes in its genetic composition, or gene pool, that enable it to adapt to changes in environmental conditions. Individuals with genetic traits that allow them to resist or adapt to a new environmental condition reproduce more offspring than individuals without such traits (*differential reproduction*).

The process by which some genes and gene combinations in a population are reproduced more than others is called *natural selection*. The change in the genetic composition of a population exposed to new environmental conditions because of differential reproduction and natural selection is called *biological evolution*.

The earth's present inventory of different species is believed to be the result of two processes—*speciation* and *extinction*. Over billions of years the combination of speciation and extinction operating through natural selection has produced the planet's most valuable resource: *biological diversity*.

When severe natural or human-induced environmental changes destroy or severely degrade an area, it can be gradually recolonized by a series of increasingly complex communities. This process, involving a change from a simple, immature community to a more complex, mature community, is called *ecological succession*.

Humans greatly simplify natural ecosystems in order to build habitats, grow food, and remove or extract resources. Increasing amounts of money, time, and energy and matter resources are being used to maintain such simplified systems and to protect them from pests, drought, floods, and other disturbances. The challenge is to maintain a balance between simplified human ecosystems and the neighboring, more complex, natural ecosystems upon which the simplified systems depend.

Another challenge is to prevent nuclear war, the ultimate ecological catastrophe. Even a limited nuclear war would kill 20% to 80% of the world's population directly from the explosions and indirectly from a loss of food production when the sun is partially blotted out for weeks or longer after the explosions. Millions of wild species would also become extinct. We also have an obligation to work with nature to repair many of the ecological wounds we have inflicted through the emerging science and art of *rehabilitation and restoration ecology*.

DISCUSSION TOPICS

1. Explain how 1 plus 1 does not always equal 2 in an organism or ecosystem.

2. Give two examples of time delays not discussed in this chapter. How can time delays be harmful? How can they be helpful?

3. Someone tells you not to worry about air pollution because through natural selection the human species will develop lungs that can detoxify pollutants. How would you reply?

4. Are human beings or insects such as flies and mosquitoes better able to adapt to environmental change? Defend your choice and give the major way each of these species can adapt to environmental change.

5. Explain how a species brings about changes in local conditions so that the species becomes extinct in a given ecosystem. Could human beings do this to themselves? Explain.

6. Explain why a simplified ecosystem such as a cornfield is much more vulnerable to harm from insects, plant diseases, and fungi than a more complex, natural ecosystem such as a grassland. Why are natural ecosystems less vulnerable?

7. Do you believe that most of the survivors of a global nuclear war would envy the dead. Why? Would you want to be one of the survivors? Why or why not?

8. Do you think that nuclear war is preventable? How?

9. Do you believe that genetic engineering should be widely used? Explain. What restrictions, if any, would you place on its use? How would you enforce such restrictions, especially in secret biological warfare facilities?

CHAPTER 7

Population Dynamics

eneral Questions and Issues

. How is population size affected by birth rates, death rates, and migration?

2. How is population size affected by the average number of children women have during their reproductive years?

3. How is population size affected by the percentage of men and women at each age level?

The population of most less developed countries is doubling every twenty to thirty years. Trying to develop into a modern industrial state under these conditions is like trying to work out the choreography for a new ballet in a crowded subway car.

Garrett Hardin

I n the late 1970s, newspaper headlines such as "Population Time Bomb Fizzles," "Another Non-Crisis," and "Population Growth May Have Turned Historic Corner" falsely implied that world population growth had almost stopped. What actually happened was not a halt in net population growth. Instead, the annual rate at which the world's population was growing decreased from a high of 2% in the late 1960s to around 1.7% in the mid-1980s.

This slowdown in the annual growth rate is encouraging. But it is like learning that a truck heading straight at you has slowed down from 100 to 85 miles per hour. Indeed, by 1989 the annual growth rate had risen to 1.8% (see Guest Essay on p. 168).

In 1969, when the world's population was growing at 2%, it increased by 70 million people (150 a minute). But since then the population base has increased to 5.2 billion people. In 1989 the 1.8% growth rate of this bigger population base added 90 million people (179 a minute)—more than in any year in human history. We are now adding a billion more people about every 10 years. This is the nature of exponential growth (see Spotlight on p. 4). Most of this rapid growth is taking place in LDCs, where food and many other resources are already stretched.

This chapter is devoted to an overview of the major factors that affect the size of the human population. In Chapter 8 you will learn about methods that can be used to bring about changes in population size. In Chapter 9 you will learn about how the world's people are distributed between urban and rural areas and about major urban problems.

7-1 BIRTHS, DEATHS, AND CHANGES IN HUMAN POPULATION SIZE

Net Population Change The study of population characteristics and changes in the world and parts of the world is called **demography**. In a country experiencing little or no migration, annual changes in population size are determined by the difference between the number of people born and the number that die.

World population grows as long as the number of live births is greater than the number of deaths. In 1989 there were about 2.8 live births for each death throughout the world. About 92% of the 90 million people added in 1989 were born in the less developed countries of Africa, Asia, and Latin America, which already contained 77% of the world's population.

Crude Birth Rates and Death Rates Demographers, or population specialists, normally use the annual crude birth rate and crude death rate rather than total live births and deaths to describe population change. The **crude birth rate** is the annual number of live births per 1,000 persons in a population at the midpoint of a given year (July 1). The **crude death rate** is the annual

The Human Population

United Nations

We need the size of population in which human beings can fulfill their potentialities; in my opinion we are already overpopulated from that point of view; not just in places like India and China and Puerto Rico, but also in the United States and Western Europe.

George Wald, Nobel laureate, biology

Population Dynamics

General Questions and Issues

1. How is population size affected by birth rates, death rates, and migration?

2. How is population size affected by the average number of children women have during their reproductive years?

3. How is population size affected by the percentage of men and women at each age level?

The population of most less developed countries is doubling every twenty to thirty years. Trying to develop into a modern industrial state under these conditions is like trying to work out the choreography for a new ballet in a crowded subway car.

Garrett Hardin

I n the late 1970s, newspaper headlines such as "Population Time Bomb Fizzles," "Another Non-Crisis," and "Population Growth May Have Turned Historic Corner" falsely implied that world population growth had almost stopped. What actually happened was not a halt in net population growth. Instead, the annual rate at which the world's population was growing decreased from a high of 2% in the late 1960s to around 1.7% in the mid-1980s.

This slowdown in the annual growth rate is encouraging. But it is like learning that a truck heading straight at you has slowed down from 100 to 85 miles per hour. Indeed, by 1989 the annual growth rate had risen to 1.8% (see Guest Essay on p. 168).

In 1969, when the world's population was growing at 2%, it increased by 70 million people (150 a minute). But since then the population base has increased to 5.2 billion people. In 1989 the 1.8% growth rate of this bigger population base added 90 million people (179 a minute)—more than in any year in human history. We are now adding a billion more people about every 10 years. This is the nature of exponential growth (see Spotlight on p. 4). Most of this rapid growth is taking place in LDCs, where food and many other resources are already stretched.

This chapter is devoted to an overview of the major factors that affect the size of the human population. In Chapter 8 you will learn about methods that can be used to bring about changes in population size. In Chapter 9 you will learn about how the world's people are distributed between urban and rural areas and about major urban problems.

7-1 BIRTHS, DEATHS, AND CHANGES IN HUMAN POPULATION SIZE

Net Population Change The study of population characteristics and changes in the world and parts of the world is called **demography.** In a country experiencing little or no migration, annual changes in population size are determined by the difference between the number of people born and the number that die.

World population grows as long as the number of live births is greater than the number of deaths. In 1989 there were about 2.8 live births for each death throughout the world. About 92% of the 90 million people added in 1989 were born in the less developed countries of Africa, Asia, and Latin America, which already contained 77% of the world's population.

Crude Birth Rates and Death Rates Demographers, or population specialists, normally use the annual crude birth rate and crude death rate rather than total live births and deaths to describe population change. The **crude birth rate** is the annual number of live births per 1,000 persons in a population at the midpoint of a given year (July 1). The **crude death rate** is the annual

The Human Population

United Nations

We need the size of population in which human beings can fulfill their potentialities; in my opinion we are already overpopulated from that point of view; not just in places like India and China and Puerto Rico, but also in the United States and Western Europe.

George Wald, Nobel laureate, biology

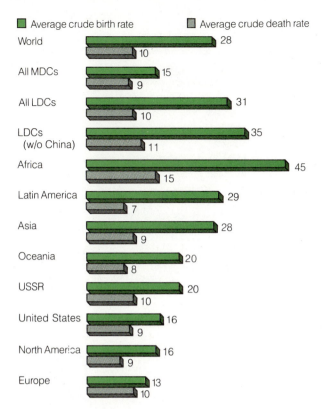

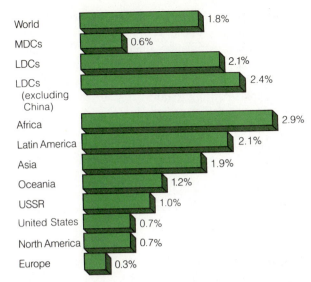

Figure 7-2 Average annual population change rate in various groups of countries in 1989. (Data from Population Reference Bureau)

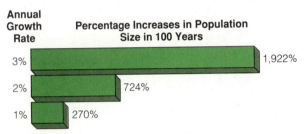

Figure 7-3 Effects of various growth rates on population size over 100 years.

Figure 7-1 Average crude birth rates and crude death rates of various groups of countries in 1989. (Data from Population Reference Bureau)

number of deaths per 1,000 persons in a population at the midpoint of a given year.

$$\text{crude birth rate} = \frac{\text{live births per year}}{\text{midyear population}} \times 1,000$$

$$\text{crude death rate} = \frac{\text{deaths per year}}{\text{midyear population}} \times 1,000$$

Figure 7-1 shows the crude birth rates and death rates for the world and various groups of countries in 1989.

The annual rate at which the size of a population changes is called the **annual rate of natural population change.** It is usually expressed as a percentage representing the difference between the crude birth rate and the crude death rate divided by 10:

$$\begin{array}{l}\text{annual rate}\\ \text{of population} \\ \text{change (\%)}\end{array} = \frac{\text{crude birth rate} - \text{crude death rate}}{10}$$

For example, in 1989 the crude birth rate for the world was 28, and the death rate 10. Thus, the world's population grew exponentially in 1989 at a rate of 1.8%:

$$\frac{28 - 10}{10} = \frac{18}{10} = 1.8\%$$

When the crude death rate equals the crude birth rate, the population size remains stable (assuming no migration). This condition is known as **zero population growth (ZPG).** When the crude death rate is higher than the crude birth rate, population size decreases.

Figure 7-2 gives the annual population change rates in major parts of the world. In 1989 population change rates ranged from a growth rate of 4.1% in Kenya in eastern Africa and in Gaza in eastern Asia to a decline rate of −0.2% in Hungary. At their present growth rates the populations of Kenya and Gaza will double in only 17 years.

An annual population growth rate of 1% to 3% may seem small, but such exponential rates lead to enormous increases in population size over a 100-year period (Figure 7-3). For example, Nigeria, the most populous country in Africa, had 115 million people and a growth rate of 2.9% in 1989. By the end of the next century its population is projected to grow to more than half a billion. A sharp increase in death rates, however, may prevent such a long-range projection from becoming a reality.

The impact of exponential population growth on population size is much greater in countries with a large existing population base. In sheer numbers, China and India dwarf all other countries, making up 37% of the world's population (Figure 7-4). Five countries—China, India, Brazil, Indonesia, and Mexico—will account for 37% of the world's projected population increase during the next 20 years.

Rapid population growth in LDCs creates pressures on their physical and financial resources, making it difficult to raise living standards. It has also helped widen the differences in average income between rich and poor countries (Figure 1-7, p. 10). And in both LDCs and MDCs population growth contributes to resource depletion and degradation (Table 1-1, p. 13).

Factors Affecting Birth Rates A number of socioeconomic and cultural factors affect a country's average birth rate. The following are the most significant factors:

- *Average levels of education and affluence:* Birth rates are usually lower in MDCs, where both of these factors are high.

- *Importance of children as a part of the family labor force:* Birth rates tend to be high in LDCs (especially in rural areas). They are lower in countries where a compulsory mass education system removes children from the family labor force during most of the year.

- *Urbanization:* People living in urban areas tend to have lower birth rates than those living in rural areas, where children are needed to help in growing food, collecting firewood and water, and other survival tasks.

- *High costs of raising and educating children:* Birth rates tend to be low in MDCs and other countries where school is mandatory and child labor is generally illegal. In these countries raising children is much more costly because they don't enter the labor force until their late teens or early twenties.

- *Educational and employment opportunities for women:* Birth rates tend to be high when women have little or no access to education and to paid employment outside the home.

- *Infant mortality rates:* Birth rates tend to be very high in areas with high infant mortality rates. Because children in such areas are often an important part of the family labor force, parents have a strong incentive to replace those that have died.

- *Average marriage age* (or, more precisely, the average age at which women give birth to their first child): Birth rates tend to be much lower in countries where the average marriage age of women is at least 25. This reduces the typical childbearing years (ages 15–44) by 10 years and cuts the prime reproductive period (ages 20–29), when most women have children, by about half.

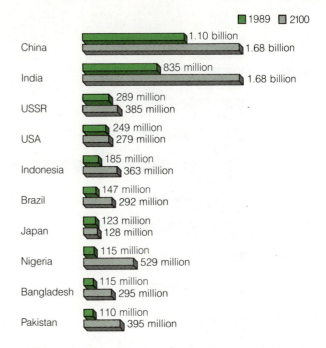

Figure 7-4 The world's 10 most populous countries in 1989, with projections of their population size in 2100. (Data from World Bank)

- *Availability of private and public pension systems*: In MDCs with pension systems birth rates tend to be low. Pensions eliminate the need for parents to have many children to support them in old age.

- *Availability of reliable methods of contraception* (Figure 8-3, p. 182): Widespread availability tends to reduce birth rates. However, this factor can be counteracted by religious beliefs that prohibit or discourage the use of abortion or certain forms of contraception.

- *Cultural norms that influence the number of children couples want to have:* Examples are religious beliefs and past tradition.

Factors Affecting Death Rates The rapid growth of the world's population over the past 100 years was not caused by a rise in crude birth rates. Rather, it is due largely to a decline in crude death rates, especially in the LDCs (Figure 7-5).

The major reasons for this general drop in death rates are

- better nutrition because of increased food production and better distribution

- reduced incidence and spread of infectious diseases because of improved personal hygiene and improved sanitation and water supplies

- improvements in medical and public health technology, including antibiotics, immunization, and insecticides

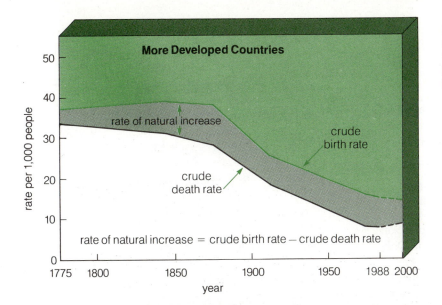

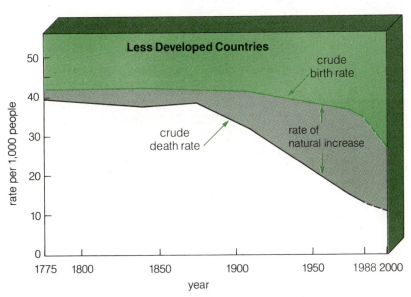

Figure 7-5 Changes in crude birth and death rates for MDCs and LDCs between 1775 and 1989 and projected rates (dashed lines) to 2000. (Data from Population Reference Bureau and United Nations)

Two useful indicators of overall health in a country or region are **life expectancy**—the average number of years a newborn infant can be expected to live—and the **infant mortality rate**—the number of babies out of every 1,000 born that die before their first birthday (Figure 7-6).

In 1989, average life expectancy at birth ranged from a low of 35 years in Sierra Leone in western Africa to a high of 78 years in Japan and Iceland. In the world's 41 poorest countries, mainly in Asia and Africa, average life expectancy is only 47 years.

Between 1900 and 1989, average life expectancy at birth increased sharply in the United States from 42 to 75 (78.3 for females and 71.3 for males). But in 1989, people in 15 countries and colonies had an average life expectancy at birth one to three years higher than people in the United States.

A high infant mortality rate usually indicates insufficient food (undernutrition), poor diet (malnu-

trition), and a high incidence of infectious disease (usually from contaminated drinking water). In 1989 infant mortality rates ranged from a low of 3.4 deaths per 1,000 live births in Finland to a high of 175 deaths per 1,000 live births in Mali in western Africa.

The United States has an infant mortality rate of 9.9 deaths per 1,000 (18 for blacks and 9 for whites), compared to 25 deaths per 1,000 in the USSR. Babies born in the United States today are four times less likely to die in their first year than babies born in 1940. But the average infant mortality rate in the United States is still much higher than it should be in a country with such wealth and medical technology. In 1989, in fact, 23 other countries had lower infant mortality rates than the United States.

Why is the infant mortality rate in the United States higher than in many other MDCs? One reason is lack of adequate health care for poor women during pregnancy and for their babies after birth. By contrast, such care is encouraged and subsidized in Canada and in most western European countries. Another reason is the high birth rate for teenage women (see Case Study on p. 163).

Migration The annual rate of population change for a particular country, city, or other area is also affected by the movement of people into (immigration) and out of (emigration) that area:

population change rate = (births + immigration)
                        − (deaths + emigration)

Most countries control their rates of population growth to some extent by restricting immigration. Only a few countries annually accept a large number of immigrants and refugees. This means that population change for most countries is determined mainly by the differences between their birth rates and death rates.

However, migration within countries, especially from rural to urban areas, plays an important role in the population dynamics of cities, towns, and rural areas. This migration affects the way population is distributed within countries, as discussed in Chapter 9.

7-2 FERTILITY

Replacement Level Fertility and Total Fertility Rate In addition to the crude birth rate, two types of fertility rates affect the population of a country.

Replacement level fertility is the number of children a couple must have to replace themselves. You might think that two parents need have only two children to replace themselves. The actual average replacement level fertility rate, however, is slightly higher, primarily because some female children die before reaching their reproductive years. In MDCs the average replacement level fertility is 2.1 children per couple or woman. In LDCs with high infant mortality rates, the replacement level may be as high as 2.5 children per couple or woman.

The most useful measure of fertility for projecting future population change is the **total fertility rate (TFR).** This is an estimate of the number of live children the average woman will bear if she passes through all her childbearing years (ages 15 to 44) conforming to age-specific birth rates of a given year. In 1989 the average TFR was 3.6 children per woman for the world as a whole, 1.9 in MDCs, and 4.1 in LDCs. These rates ranged from a low of 1.3 in Hong Kong and in Italy to a high of 8.5 in Rwanda in eastern Africa.

Total fertility rates are influenced by the same factors that affect birth rates. In LDCs average TFRs dropped from about 6 births per woman in the mid-1960s to 4.1 by 1989, or 4.7 excluding China. Much of

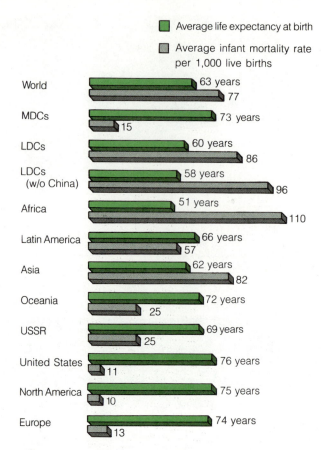

Figure 7-6 Life expectancy at birth and average infant mortality rate for various groups of countries in 1989. (Data from Population Reference Bureau)

the large drop in Asia was the result of massive family-planning efforts by China. But during the same period, the average TFR in the 41 poorest LDCs remained at around 6.5.

Fertility and Population Stabilization Since 1972 the United States has had a total fertility rate of around 1.8—below the replacement level (Figure 7-7). But a TFR below replacement level doesn't necessarily mean that a country's population has stabilized or is declining. The U.S. population, for example, continues to grow, although its rate of growth has decreased (see Case Study on p. 164).

Figure 1-1, p. 4, shows three projections of world population growth through the next century. Each projection is based on a different set of assumptions about fertility rates, death rates, and international migration patterns.

Figure 7-8 shows UN projections of the size and year of population stabilization for different groups of countries, based on the medium projection shown in Figure 1-1. These projections assume that the worldwide average fertility rate will drop to replacement-level fertility of 2.1 births per woman by 2035. Most demographers see little chance that this will happen.

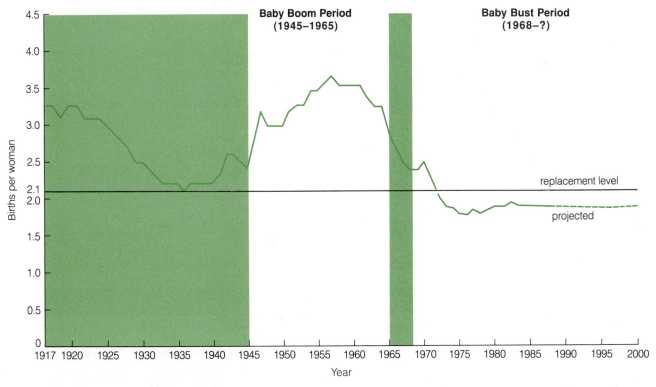

Figure 7-7 Total fertility rate for the United States between 1917 and 1989 and projected rate (dashed line) to 2000. (Data from Population Reference Bureau and U.S. Census Bureau)

CASE STUDY Teenage Pregnancy in the United States

The United States has the highest teenage pregnancy rate of any industrialized country, ten times higher than Japan's and three times higher than most European countries. Every year in the United States about 900,000 teenage women—one in every ten— become pregnant. About 470,000 of these young women give birth. The remaining 430,000 have abortions, accounting for almost one of every four abortions performed in the United States.

Almost half of the babies born to teenage mothers in the United States depend on welfare to survive. Each of these babies costs taxpayers an average of $15,600 over the 20 years following its birth.

Babies born to teenagers are more likely to have a low birth weight—the most important factor in infant deaths. The large number of births to teenage women is one reason the infant mortality is higher in the United States than in most other industrialized countries.

The United States has developed the medical technology for saving low-weight babies. But babies of poor teenage women with no health insurance often do not have access to these expensive, life-saving procedures.

Why is the teenage pregnancy rate in the United States so high? UN studies show that U.S. teenagers aren't more sexually active than those in other countries. But they are less likely to take precautions to prevent pregnancy. They aren't getting effective sex education at home or at school. Only about one-fifth of U.S. teenagers learn about the risks of pregnancy and how to prevent it from their parents.

In Sweden, which has a much lower teenage pregnancy rate than the United States, every child receives a thorough grounding in basic reproductive biology by age 7. By age 12, each child has been told about the various types of contraceptives.

Polls show that 75% of Americans favor sex education in the schools, including information about birth control, and school clinics that dispense contraceptives with parental consent. Yet effective sex education is not widely available and is not given at an early enough age. Only about 100 U.S. high schools have health clinics where students can get contraceptives with parental consent. Why? Mostly because of strong opposition to sex education by small but highly vocal religious groups who fear that such education will increase sexual activity and abortions.

UN studies have shown that teenage pregnancy rates are lowest in countries where birth control and sex education are easily available. Providing earlier sex education and contraceptives is also the best way to reduce teenage abortions. What do you think should be done about teenage pregnancy?

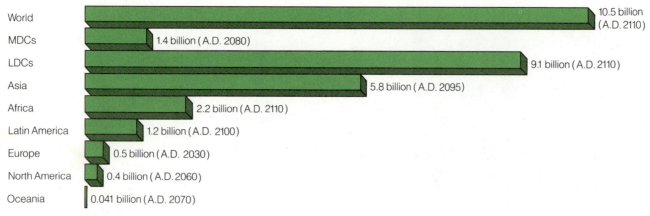

Figure 7-8   United Nations medium projections for stable population size and year of stabilization (shown in parentheses) of various groups of countries.

U.S. Population Stabilization

The population of the United States has grown from 4 million in 1790 to 249 million in 1989—a 62-fold increase. The total fertility rate in the United States has oscillated wildly (Figure 7-7). At the peak of the post–World War II baby boom (1945–65) in 1957, the TFR averaged 3.7 children per woman. Since then it has generally declined and has been at or below replacement level since 1972.

Various factors contributed to this decline:

■ Widespread use of effective birth control methods.

■ Availability of legal abortions.

■ Social attitudes favoring smaller families.

■ Greater social acceptance of childless couples.

■ Rising costs of raising a family ($125,000 to $175,000 to raise one child born in 1987 to age 18).

■ Increases in the average marriage age between 1950 and 1986 from 20.3 to 23.6 for women and from 22.8 to 25.8 for men.

■ An increasing number of women working outside the home. By 1987 more than 70% of American women of childbearing age worked outside the home and had a childbearing rate one-third the rate of those not in the paid labor force.

The decline in the total fertility rate since 1969 has led to a decline in the annual rate of population growth in the United States. The United States has not reached zero population growth in spite of the dramatic drop of the average TFR to below the replacement level. The major reasons:

■ the large number of women still moving through their childbearing years

■ high levels of annual legal and illegal immigration

■ an increase in the number of unmarried young women (including teenagers) having children

In 1989 the U.S. population grew by 0.7%. This added 2.5 million people: 1.7 million more births than deaths, 0.6 million legal immigrants, and an estimated 0.2 million illegal immigrants.

Given the erratic history of the U.S. TFR (Figure 7-7), no one knows whether or how long it will remain below replacement level. The Census Bureau and the World Bank have made various projections of future U.S. population growth, assuming different average total fertility rates, life expectancies, and net legal immigration rates (Figure 7-9).

The medium projection made by the Census Bureau in 1989 showed the U.S. population peaking at around 302 million by 2038 and then declining slowly to a stable size of 292 million by 2080. This projection assumes that the TFR will remain at 1.8 live births per woman and that the average annual immigration of 600,000 will drop to 500,000 by 1998. If so, legal and illegal immigration will account for all U.S. population growth by the 2030s. The projected growth in U.S. population between 1987 and 2038 is equal to the combined populations of the country's three most populous states—California, New York, and Texas—in 1987.

But no one knows whether these assumptions will hold up. Fertility could rise unexpectedly as it did in the 1950s. New medical discoveries could extend average life expectancy. New laws and more effective enforcement could sharply reduce illegal and legal immigration.

Some demographers project a stable population size even larger than 292 million. They believe that an annual net migration rate (including both legal and illegal immigration) of 800,000 to 1 million is more likely than the 500,000 used by the Census Bureau. Still others project a higher population

Indeed, by 1988 the loss of momentum in population control programs in some LDCs indicated that future growth may be closer to the high UN projection of about 1 billion more people every 10 years.

No one really knows whether any of these projections will prove accurate. Demography, like economics, is a notoriously inexact social science. Demographic projections are not predictions of what will necessarily take place. Instead, they represent possibilities based on present trends and certain assumptions about people's future reproductive behavior. Despite their uncertainty, demographic projections help us focus our energies on converting the most desirable possibilities into reality.

7-3 POPULATION AGE STRUCTURE

Age Structure Diagrams Why will world population probably keep growing for at least 60 years after the average world total fertility rate has reached or dropped below replacement-level fertility of 2.1? The answer to this question lies in an understanding of the **age structure,** or age distribution, of a population. The age structure is the percentage of the population, or the number of people of each sex, at each age level.

Demographers make a population age structure diagram by plotting the percentages or numbers of males and females in the total population in three age categories: *preproductive* (ages 0–14), *reproductive* (ages

size because of a future rise of the total fertility rate.

You and all other Americans will play a role in determining which of these and other demographic possibilities becomes a reality. Assuming you are able to have children, you will decide whether or not to have children and how many to have.

You will also play a key role in

determining how long you live; thus, you will influence average death rates. To increase their life spans, many Americans have given up smoking, reduced or eliminated alcohol use, and reduced their exposure to sun. Many also exercise more frequently, pay more attention to what they eat, and fasten their seat belts while driving.

On average, Americans move 13 times in their lives. How many times people move and where they move determine what areas gain or lose people. The migrations of people also affect demands on air, water, soil, recreation, and other resources. What role do you intend to play in determining the country's future demographic history?

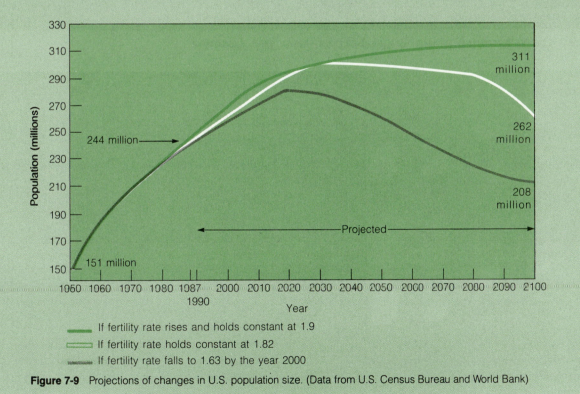

Figure 7-9 Projections of changes in U.S. population size. (Data from U.S. Census Bureau and World Bank)

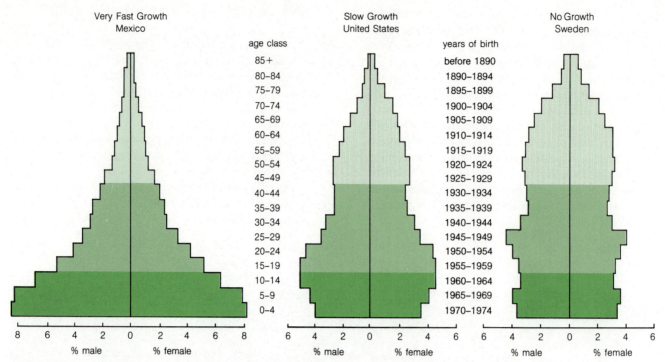

Figure 7-10 Population age structure diagrams for countries with rapid, slow, and zero population growth rates. Dark portions represent preproductive years (0–14), medium portions represent reproductive years (15–44), and light portions represent postproductive years (45–85+). (Data from U.S. Census Bureau and Population Reference Bureau)

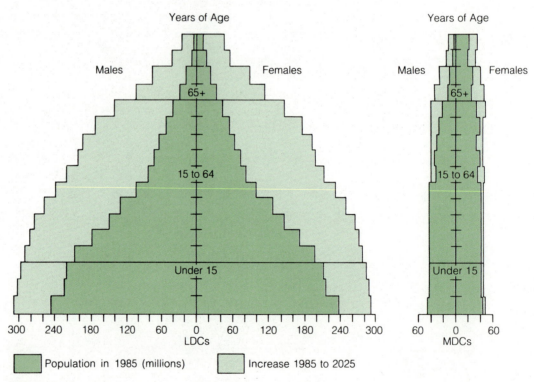

Figure 7-11 Age structure diagrams of LDCs and MDCs, 1985–2025. (Data from Population Reference Bureau)

15–44), and *postproductive* (ages 45–85+). Figure 7-10 shows the age structure diagrams for countries with rapid, slow, and zero growth rates.

Mexico and most LDCs with rapidly growing pop-

ulations have pyramid-shaped age structure diagrams. This indicates a high ratio of children under age 15 to adults over age 65. In contrast, the diagrams for the United States, Sweden, and most MDCs

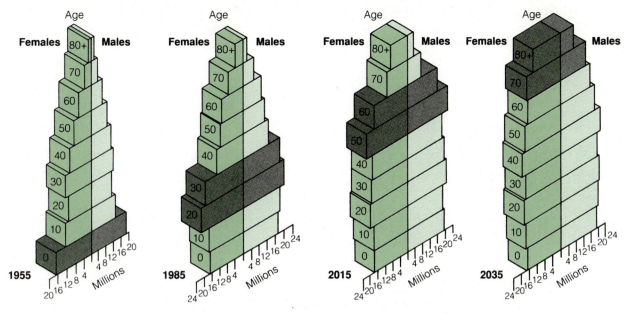

Figure 7-12 Tracking the baby boom. Age structure of the U.S. population in 1955, 1985, 2015, and 2035. (Data from Population Reference Bureau and U.S. Census Bureau)

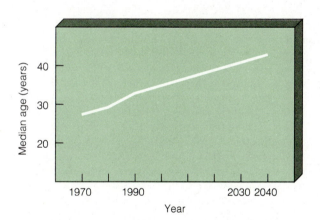

Figure 7-13 Median age of the U.S. population, 1970–2040. (Data from U.S. Census Bureau)

undergoing slow or no population growth have a narrower base. This shows that such countries have a much smaller percentage of population under age 15 and a larger percentage above age 65 than countries experiencing rapid population growth.

MDCs, such as Sweden, that have achieved zero population growth have roughly equal numbers of people at each age level (Figure 7-10). Hungary, West Germany, and Denmark, which are experiencing a slow population decline, have roughly equal numbers of people at most age levels but lower numbers under age 5.

Age Structure and Population Growth Momentum
Any country with a large number of people below age 15 has a powerful built-in momentum to increase its population size unless death rates rise sharply. The number of births rises even if women have only one or two children. This happens because the number of women who can have children increases greatly as girls reach their reproductive years. The population of a country with a large number of people under 15 continues to grow for one average lifetime—roughly 60 to 70 years—after the average total fertility rate of its women has dropped to replacement level or lower.

In 1989 one of every three persons on this planet was under 15 years of age. In LDCs the number is even higher—37%, compared to 22% in MDCs. Figure 7-11 shows the massive momentum for population growth in LDCs because of their large number of people under age 15. This powerful force for continued population growth in LDCs will be slowed only by a crash program to reduce birth rates or a catastrophic rise in death rates.

Making Projections from Age Structure Diagrams
A baby boom took place in the United States between 1945 and 1965. This 75-million-person bulge will move upward through the country's age structure during the 80-year period between 1945 and 2025 as baby boomers move through their youth, young adulthood, middle-age, and old age (Figure 7-12).

This means that the median age of the U.S. population is rising (Figure 7-13). The U.S. population is getting older for three reasons. One is that the large baby boom generation is now approaching middle age. In 1985 the first baby boomers reached age 40, and all baby boomers will have passed that milestone by 2005.

Second, U.S. fertility is so low that the proportion of children in the population is declining. Third, the proportion of the elderly is increasing, in part due to increased longevity. By 2030, when all living members of the baby boom generation are senior citizens, about 21% of the projected population will consist of people 65 and older, compared to 12% in 1985 (Figure 7-14).

Today baby boomers make up nearly half of all adult Americans. In sheer numbers they dominate the population's demand for goods and services. Later they will put strains on the Social Security System and elderly health care services. Between 1970 and 1984, large numbers of baby boomers flooded the job market, raising unemployment rates of teenagers and young adults. Baby boomers, who made up an estimated 60% of registered voters in 1989, will play an increasingly important role in deciding who gets elected and what laws are passed between 1989 and 2030.

During their working years baby boomers will create a large surplus of money in the Social Security trust fund. However, even if elected officials resist the

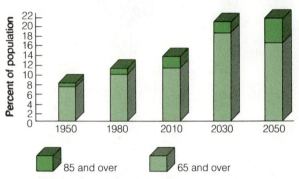

Figure 7-14 Projected growth in the number and percentage of people age 65 and older in the United States between 1985 and 2080. (Data from U.S. Census Bureau)

GUEST ESSAY The Population Bomb: A Perspective After Two Decades

Carl Haub

Carl Haub is a demographer and has been associated with the Population Reference Bureau, Inc. in Washington, D.C. since 1979. He serves as Director of Demographic Information and Education and, with Mary M. Kent, prepares the annual World Population Data Sheet *and responds to thousands of requests each year for population information.*

The publication of Paul Ehrlich's landmark book in 1968, *The Population Bomb*, raised public awareness of rapid world population growth. When the book was written, the world headcount stood at about 3.6 billion. Human population had first passed the billion mark about 1800 and grew to 2 billion by 1930. By the 1960s it was clear that an acceleration in growth was taking place (Figure 1-1, p. 4). In 1975 the fourth billion was achieved. A scant 12 years later, the United Nations marked the Day of the Five Billion on July 11, 1987.

Although birth rates have declined in many countries, it is astounding to consider the current projec- tions for global population growth in the next few decades. Each of the next three billions are projected by the United Nations to arrive only about ten or eleven years apart: the sixth billion about 1997, the seventh by 2008, and the eighth in 2019. But these projections assume that observed declines in death rates will continue or that, where no decline has taken place, rates will soon begin to fall.

In terms of sheer numbers the earth is, without question, right in the middle of an unprecedented expansion in population. This fact is made even more compelling when we consider that virtually all of the projected growth will take place in the developing countries which can least afford it. Despite this seemingly alarming situation, a debate of sorts has risen over the precise impact such growth will have. In the past it was simply enough to point out the facts of rapid growth; the conclusion that such growth would lead to disaster would stand unquestioned. But no more, as some of the disastrous predictions appear to have been nimbly avoided.

What caused this subtle shift in attitude? Before we consider that, it is best to keep in mind that we are speaking primarily about attitudes of many of those in industrialized countries. Most of those in the poorer countries have few misconceptions about the link between rapid population growth and economic and societal problems.

In part, the problem may lie in the anticipation that population, described as a "bomb," appears not to have "exploded." Events in poor countries have lit tle effect on the daily lives of those in the industrialized countries. Also newspaper headlines can leave lasting effects on our consciousness, so that a story on agricultural success in India may tend to set one's

temptation to dip into these funds for balancing the budget or other purposes, the large number of retired baby boomers will quickly use up this surplus. Unless changes in funding are made, the Social Security fund will be depleted by 2048.

The economic burden of supporting so many retired people will be on the baby bust generation, the much smaller group of people born between 1968 and 1989, when average fertility rates fell sharply (Figure 7-7). Retired baby boomers may use their political clout to force members of the baby bust generation to pay greatly increased income and Social Security taxes.

In many respects, the baby bust generation should have an easier time than the baby boom generation. Much smaller numbers of people will be competing for education, jobs, and services. Labor shortages should also drive up their wages. But three out of four new jobs available between 1990 and 2010 will require education or technical training beyond high school. People without such training may face economic hard times. With a shortage of young adults, the armed forces might find it hard to meet recruiting levels. This could lead the baby boom generation to use its political power to reinstate the draft.

Although they will probably have no trouble getting entry-level jobs, the baby bust group may find it hard to get job promotions as they reach middle age because most upper-level positions will be occupied by the much larger baby boom group. Many baby boomers may delay retirement because of improved health and the need to build up adequate retirement funds. From these few projections, we see that any baby boom bulge or baby bust indentation in the age structure of a population creates a number of social and economic changes that ripple through a society for decades.

mind at ease. Also we naturally don't like to hear bad news. A final difficulty in understanding the effects of population growth is the simple fact that the links between demographic change and economic affairs, environmental conditions, and human welfare are quite complex.

While these debates continue, another form of demographic change has entered the scene—population decline due to very low birth rates. Many European countries, the United States, Japan, and other developed countries are recording historic lows in their fertility. For a few, such as West Germany, Denmark, and Hungary, population decline has already begun.

This decrease leads not only to smaller numbers, but also to older populations with larger proportions of society requiring health care and being dependent on pensions. As the number of youth available for the work force begins to dwindle, countries are faced with novel choices. Should immigration be encouraged? If so, of what kind? Should families be persuaded to have more children? In fact, to what extent is population good or bad? Good for the environment? Bad for the economy?

Thus, as the 20th century draws to a close, a growing range of demographic issues compete for our attention. A satisfactory understanding must begin with the recognition that world demographic issues are multifaceted. Today, India has made sufficient progress so that the country is able to produce enough to feed itself, although at levels not typically acceptable to a citizen of an industrialized country. But even that self-sufficiency is placed in jeopardy during times of drought or flood, such as those in recent years. For the future, the real question is: If India has coped, to a degree, with rapid growth for 300 million in the 1940s to 835 million people today, does that mean that all will be well when the population rises to the 1.6 billion projected by the middle of the next century?

The extent to which we perceive world population growth to be a true concern or crisis depends, to an extent, upon our view of the world as a "global village." From a strictly humanitarian viewpoint, is it tolerable that living standards, nutrition, and health conditions vary so widely on this planet? If the populations of the Western nations begin to shrink, will their attitudes on new immigrants undergo some relaxation?

Today, the possibility of global warming and the realities of ozone depletion and acid rain forces more international cooperation, along with a rising tension between national interest and global welfare. But, no matter what paths we choose, one thing is certain: there will be billions more of us.

Guest Essay Discussion

1. Do you think that population growth is good or bad? Explain. What about population decline?

2. Should immigration into the United States be encouraged? Explain.

3. Should families in the United States be given financial incentives and persuaded to have more children to prevent population decline? Explain.

Rapid population growth is contributing to an expansion of poverty that is a moral outrage.

Barber Conable, President, The World Bank

CHAPTER SUMMARY

Four major factors affect the size and the rate of change in size of the human population: difference between birth rate and death rate, migration, fertility, and the number of people at each age level. As long as the *birth rate* is greater than the *death rate*, the world's population size will grow at a rate that depends on the positive difference between these two rates. The annual rate of population change for a particular country, city, or other area is equal to (births + immigration) − (deaths + emigration).

The population size of the world and of a particular country can level off or stabilize only after the *total fertility rate*—the average number of children born to women during their reproductive years—stays at or below an average *replacement-level fertility* of 2.1 children per woman. Once replacement-level fertility is achieved, the length of time required before population size levels off depends primarily on the number of women in their reproductive years (ages 15–44) and the number below age 15, who will soon be entering their reproductive years.

The time before world population or that of a particular country stabilizes after the average total fertility rate has reached or fallen below replacement level also depends on the population's *age structure*—the percentage of females and males at each age level. The larger the number and percentage of women in their reproductive years (15—44) and preproductive years (under 15), the longer it will take for population size to reach zero population growth (ZPG). Major changes in the age structure of a population because of a period of high fertility or low fertility have demographic, social, and economic effects that last a generation or more.

DISCUSSION TOPICS

1. Why are falling birth rates not necessarily a reliable indicator of future population growth trends?

2. Suppose modern medicine finds cures for cancer and heart disease. What effects would this have on population growth in MDCs and LDCs? On their population age structures?

3. Explain the difference between achieving replacement-level fertility and achieving zero population growth.

4. How many children do you plan to have? Why?

5. Why is it rational for a poor couple in India to have six or seven children? What changes might induce such a couple to think of their behavior as irrational?

6. Project what your own life may be like at ages 25, 45, and 65 on the basis of the present population age structure of the country in which you live. What changes, if any, do such projections make in your career choice and in your plans for children?

7. Do you believe that a comprehensive sex education program like that in Sweden should be instituted in all U.S. schools, beginning at the elementary grade levels? Explain.

8. Do you believe that all U.S. high schools should have health clinics that make contraceptives available to students and provide prenatal care for pregnant teenage women? Explain. Should such services be available at the junior high school age level, when many teenagers first become sexually active? Explain.

CHAPTER 8

Population Regulation

General Questions and Issues

1. How can economic growth be used to lower birth rates?

2. How can family planning be used to lower birth rates?

3. What other methods can be used to lower birth rates?

4. How is migration restriction used to control population size in various countries?

5. What success have the world's two most populous countries, China and India, had in trying to control the rate of growth of their populations?

6. What birth control methods are available now and what methods might be available in the future?

Short of thermonuclear war itself, rampant population growth is the gravest issue the world faces over the decades immediately ahead.

Robert S. McNamara

ount slowly to 60. During the minute it took you to do this, there were 179 more people in the world to feed, clothe, educate, and house. By this time tomorrow there will be 254,000 more people on our only home. We are now adding more people each day than at any other time in human history.

The reason that the world's population continues to grow rapidly is simple. There are 2.8 births for each death. We have brought average death rates and birth rates down, but death rates have fallen more sharply than birth rates (Figure 7-5, p. 161).

One of every three persons on earth is under age 15. These young people in the broad base of the population age structure pyramid (Figure 7-11, p. 166) are moving into their reproductive years. Even if each female in this group has only two children, world population will still grow for 60 years unless deaths rise sharply. But instead of having two children, women in LDCs now have an average of 4.1 children.

That explains why we are adding about 1 billion more people every 10 years. If this continues, one of two things will happen during your lifetime: the number of people on earth will double or the world will experience an unprecedented population crash with billions of people dying prematurely.

Some say that such talk is alarmist and that the world can support billions more people. But others point out that we are not adequately supporting one of five people here today. They believe that the world is already overpopulated and that slowing world population growth is one of the most urgent issues we face (see Guest Essay near the end of this chapter). Many analysts argue that we are faced with two population problems: people overpopulation in LDCs and consumption overpopulation in MDCs (Figure 1-13, p. 20).

Basically there are two ways to deal with population growth: the death rate solution or the birth rate solution. The first option is to do little to slow population growth and let billions die as we shoot way past the earth's carrying capacity for people. The other option is to mount a global crash program to bring birth rates down, preventing a catastrophic and unnecessary loss of life. If we don't sharply lower birth rates, we are deciding by default to raise death rates. Not to decide is to decide.

This chapter is about how we can bring about a birth rate solution to this crisis.

8–1 POPULATION REGULATION BY ECONOMIC DEVELOPMENT

Ways to Regulate Population Size and Growth A government can influence the size and rate of growth or decline of its population by encouraging a change

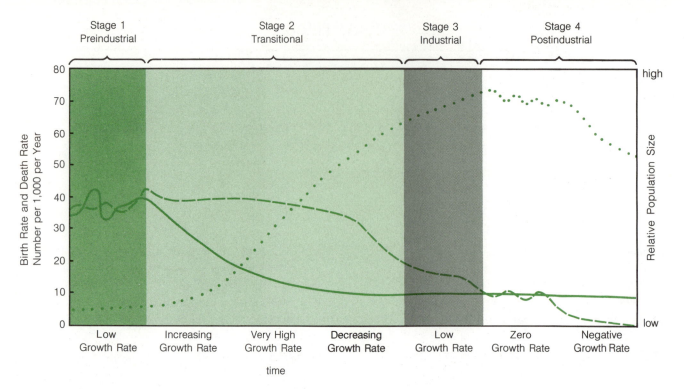

Figure 8-1 Generalized model of the demographic transition.

in any of the three basic demographic variables: births, deaths, and migration. All but a few countries slow down population growth by restricting immigration and in some cases encouraging emigration to other countries. Increasing the death rate is not an acceptable alternative. Thus, decreasing the birth rate is the focus of most efforts to slow population growth.

In 1960 only two countries, India and Pakistan, had official policies to reduce their birth rates. Today about 93% of the world's population and 91% of the people in LDCs live in countries with fertility reduction programs. However, the effectiveness and funding of these programs vary widely from country to country. Few governments spend more than 1% of the national budget on them.

Three general approaches to decreasing birth rates are *economic development, family planning,* and *socioeconomic change.* There is controversy over which approach is best. But increasing evidence shows that a combination of economic development and family planning, and in some cases of all three methods, offers a country the best way to reduce its birth rate and thus its rate of population growth.

Economic Development and the Demographic Transition Demographers examined the birth and death rates of western European countries that industrialized during the nineteenth century. On the basis of these data they developed a hypothesis of population change known as the **demographic transition.**

Its basic idea is that as countries become industrialized, they have declines in death rates followed by declines in birth rates. As a result, they move from fast growth, to slow growth, to zero growth, and eventually to a slow decline in population.

This transition takes place in four distinct phases (Figure 8-1). In the *preindustrial stage* harsh living conditions lead to a high birth rate (to compensate for high infant mortality) and a high death rate, and the population grows slowly, if at all. The *transitional stage* begins shortly after industrialization begins. In this phase the death rate drops, mostly because of increased food production and improved sanitation and health. But the birth rate remains high and the population grows rapidly (typically 2.5% to 3% a year).

In the *industrial stage* industrialization is widespread. The birth rate drops and eventually approaches the death rate. The major reason for this is that couples in cities realize that children are expensive to raise and that having too many children hinders them from taking advantage of job opportunities in an expanding economy. Population growth continues but at a slower and perhaps fluctuating rate, depending on economic conditions. Most MDCs are now in this third phase.

A fourth phase, the *postindustrial stage,* takes place when the birth rate declines even further to equal the death rate, thus reaching zero population growth. Then the birth rate falls below the death rate, and total population size slowly decreases. By 1989, Austria, Belgium, Bulgaria, Czechoslovakia, Denmark, East Germany, Finland, Greece, Hungary, Italy, Luxembourg, Norway, Portugal, Spain, Sweden, Switzerland, the United Kingdom, and West Germany had reached or were close to ZPG. Together these 18 European countries have 6.3% of the world's population.

Two of these countries—Hungary and West Germany—are experiencing slow population declines. When the number of people under age 15 in a population is less than the number at higher age levels, we can expect the population to decline for 60 years or so. The only ways to prevent this is for the women in their childbearing years to have more children or for the number of immigrants to increase.

Can Most of Today's LDCs Make the Demographic Transition? In most LDCs, death rates have fallen much more than birth rates (Figure 7-5, p. 161). In other words, these LDCs are still in the transitional phase, halfway up the economic ladder, with high population growth rates. Some economists believe that LDCs will make the demographic transition over the next few decades without increased family planning efforts.

But many population analysts fear that the rate of economic growth in many LDCs will never exceed their high rates of population growth. Without rapid and sustained economic growth, LDCs could become stuck in the transitional stage of the demographic transition.

Furthermore, some of the conditions that allowed today's MDCs to develop are not available to today's LDCs. Even with large and growing populations, many LDCs do not have enough skilled workers to produce the high-technology products needed to compete in today's economic environment. Most low- and middle-income LDCs also lack the capital and resources needed for rapid economic development. And the amount of money being given or lent to LDCs—struggling under tremendous debt burdens—has been decreasing since 1980. LDCs face stiff competition from MDCs and recently industrialized LDCs in selling the products on which their economic growth depends.

A country that gets stuck in the transitional phase won't stay there. If population growth continues to outstrip economic growth, death rates may rise. This slows down population growth, but by then the country will have slipped back into the preindustrial phase.

Should MDCs Be Concerned About Population Decline? Slowing the population growth rate is a major concern of leaders in most of the world's countries. But in a few countries, such as West Germany and Hungary, now undergoing a slow population decline, leaders are trying to find ways to raise birth rates.

For example, if West Germany maintains its pres-ent total fertility rate of 1.4 and does not allow significant immigration, its population will decrease from 61.5 million in 1989 to 45 million by 2050. West German leaders fear that there will be too few workers to support continued economic growth and to pay taxes to support the increasing portion of the population over age 65. An alternative is to increase the immigration of workers from other countries.

As other MDCs enter the postindustrial stage, some may become concerned with increasing their birth and fertility rates to reduce their rate of population decline (see Pro/Con on p. 174). For example, France and Great Britain are expected to experience slow population declines after 2000, and the United States is expected to begin a slow decline in population size after 2038.

8–2 POPULATION REGULATION BY FAMILY PLANNING

What Is Family Planning? Recent evidence suggests that improved and expanded family planning programs may bring about a more rapid decline in the birth rate and at a lower cost than economic development alone. **Family planning** programs provide educational and clinical services that help couples choose how many children to have and when to have them.

Such programs vary from culture to culture. But most provide information on birth spacing, birth control, breast-feeding, and prenatal care and distribute contraceptives. In some cases they also perform abortions and sterilizations, often without charge or at low rates. Present and future methods of birth control are discussed in the Enrichment Study on p. 182. With the exception of China (discussed in Section 8-4), family planning programs in most countries have not tried to persuade or coerce couples to have fewer children.

In MDCs about 70% of women in their reproductive period use some form of birth control. In LDCs only about 50% of women in their reproductive period practice birth control, with the figure dropping to 39% if China is excluded.

Family planning services were first introduced in LDCs in the 1940s and 1950s by private physicians and women's groups. Since then the International Planned Parenthood Federation, the Planned Parenthood Federation of America, the United Nations Fund for Population Activities, the U.S. Agency for International Development, the Ford Foundation, the World Bank, and other organizations have been helping countries carry out family planning by providing technical assistance, funding, or both.

Family planning saves a government money by reducing the need for various social services. A cost-benefit analysis of Thailand's program showed that between 1972 and 1980 the government saved an average of $7 for each $1 invested in family planning. Thailand's projected savings through 2010 amount to $16 for each $1 invested in the program.

Family planning also has health benefits. In LDCs about 1 million women die from pregnancy-related causes. Half of these deaths could be prevented by effective family planning and health care programs. Such programs also help control the spread of AIDS and other sexually transmitted diseases (see Enrichment Study on p. 182).

How Successful Has It Been? Family planning has been a major factor in reducing birth and fertility rates in highly populous China and Indonesia and in some LDCs with moderate to small populations. Examples include Barbados, Cuba, Colombia, Costa Rica, Fiji, Hong Kong, Jamaica, Mauritius, Mexico, Thailand, Singapore, South Korea, Sri Lanka, Taiwan, and Venezuela. These successful programs have been based on committed leadership, local implementation, and wide availability of contraceptive services.

But family planning has had moderate to poor results in more populous LDCs such as India, Brazil, Bangladesh, Pakistan, and Nigeria. Results have also been poor in 79 less populous LDCs—especially in Africa and Latin America—where population growth rates are usually very high. For example, only 3% to 10% of couples in most African countries use contraception.

The Population Crisis Committee estimates that between 1978 and 1983, family planning programs reduced world population by 130 million and saved at least $175 billion in government expenditures for food, shelter, clothing, education, and health care. Despite these efforts, the delivery of family planning services in much of the less developed world is still woefully inadequate, particularly in rural areas. The momentum of family planning in many major LDCs has slowed in recent years.

An estimated 400 million women in LDCs want to limit the number and determine the spacing of their children but lack access to such services. Extending family planning services to these women and those who will soon be entering their reproductive years could prevent an estimated 5.8 million births a year and more than 130,000 abortions a day. By 2100 this would mean 2.7 billion fewer people—over half of the world's present population—needing food, water, shelter, and health services.

PRO/CON Is a Birth Dearth Good or Bad?

In 1987 social thinker and cornucopian Ben J. Wattenberg wrote a book titled *The Birth Dearth* (see Further Readings). He warned that if present fertility rates remain below replacement level as projected, the share of the world's population in the United States and other western democracies will decline from 15% in 1985 to 9% in 2025.

Wattenberg and other cornucopians, such as Julian Simon (see Guest Essay on p. 26), urge the United States and other MDCs to increase their populations to maintain their economic growth and power. Wattenberg believes that the U.S. government should encourage more births by paying each couple $2,000 a year for 16 years for each child they have.

Without more babies, he believes, the country will face a shortage of workers, taxpayers, scientists and engineers, consumers, and soldiers needed to maintain healthy economic growth, national security, and global power and influence. He also contends that an aging U.S. society will be less innovative and dynamic.

Critics of the proposal counter that the influence of democratic ideals is not based on numbers of people but on the effectiveness of democracies making life better for people. Critics also point out that technological innovation—not sheer numbers of people—is the key to military and economic power in today's world. Using Wattenberg's reasoning, England and Japan, with fairly small populations, should have little global power and China should rule the world.

History does not show that an older society is necessarily more conservative and less innovative than one dominated by younger people. A society with a higher average age tends to have a larger pool of collective wisdom based on experience. Indeed, the most conservative and least innovative societies in the world today are LDCs with a large portion of their populations under age 29.

Critics also argue that adding millions to the U.S. population will intensify many environmental and social problems by increasing resource use, environmental degradation, and pollution. Instead of encouraging more births, they believe that the United States should establish an official goal of stabilizing its population by 2025. This would help reduce environmental stress in the United States and throughout the world. It would also set a good example for other countries, especially LDCs. What do you think?

Family planning could be provided in LDCs to all couples who want it for about $7 billion a year—less than three days of world military spending. Currently only about $3 billion is being spent. If MDCs provided half of the $7 billion, each person in the MDCs would spend only 34 cents a year (compared to 3 cents now) to help reduce world population by 2.7 billion.

But even the present inadequate level of expenditure for family planning is decreasing. The United States has sharply curtailed its funding of international family planning agencies since 1985, mostly as a result of political pressure by pro-life activists. Instead of cutting back on international family planning assistance, the United States and other MDCs need to increase contributions. This will prevent an unnecessary loss of life.

8–3 POPULATION REGULATION BY SOCIOECONOMIC CHANGE AND MIGRATION RESTRICTION

Are Family Planning and Economic Development Enough? Some population experts argue that family planning, even coupled with economic development, cannot lower birth and fertility rates fast enough to avoid a sharp rise in death rates in many LDCs. Why? Because most couples in LDCs want 3 or 4 children—well above the 2.1 fertility rate needed to bring about eventual population stabilization.

These experts call for increased emphasis on bringing about socioeconomic change to help regulate population size. Governments can discourage births by using economic rewards and penalties. And increased rights, education, and work opportunities for women would reduce fertility rates.

Economic Rewards and Penalties About 20 countries offer small payments to individuals who agree to use contraceptives or to be sterilized. They also pay doctors and family planning workers for each sterilization they perform and each IUD they insert. In India a person receives about $15 for being sterilized, the equivalent of about two weeks' pay for an agricultural worker.

Such payments, however, are most likely to attract people who already have all the children they want. Although payments are not physically coercive, they have been criticized as being psychologically coercive. In some cases the poor feel they have to accept them in order to survive.

Some countries, such as China, penalize couples who have more than a certain number of children— usually one or two. Penalties may be extra taxes and other costs or not allowing income tax deductions for a couple's third child (as in Singapore, Hong Kong,

Ghana, and Malaysia). Families who have more children than the desired limit may also suffer reduced free health care, decreased food allotments, and loss of job choice.

Like economic rewards, economic penalties can be psychologically coercive for the poor. Programs that withhold food or increase the cost of raising children punish innocent children for the actions of their parents.

Experience has shown that economic rewards and penalties designed to reduce fertility work best if they

- nudge rather than push people to have fewer children
- reinforce existing customs and trends toward smaller families
- do not penalize people who produced large families before the programs were established
- increase a poor family's income or land

However, once population growth is out of control, a country may be forced to use coercive methods to prevent mass starvation and hardship. This is what China has had to do (Section 8–4).

Some countries have tried to use economic incentives to increase the birth rate. Since the 1930s France has had vigorous pro-birth policies. All parents get substantial subsidies and services to help with child raising. Despite these efforts, France's total fertility rate has fallen from 2.7 children per woman in 1960 to 1.8 today.

Changes in Women's Roles Another socioeconomic method of population regulation is to improve the condition of women. Today women do almost all of the world's domestic work and child care, mostly without pay. They also do more than half the work associated with growing food, gathering fuelwood, and hauling water. In LDCs women account for at least half the food production and as much as 80% in Africa. Women also provide more health care with little or no pay than all the world's organized health services put together.

The economic value of women's work at home is estimated at $4 trillion annually. This unpaid work is not included in the GNP of countries, so the central role of women in an economy is unrecognized and unrewarded.

Women also make up one-third of the world's paid labor force and 44% of the U.S. work force. But they have many of the lowest-paid jobs and earn about 75% less than men who do similar work. The 57% of U.S. working-age women who have a job outside the home earn an average of 30% less than men doing similar work, with women workers ages 21 to 29 earning 17% less.

Despite their vital economic and social contributions, most women in LDCs don't have a legal right to own land or to borrow money to increase agricultural productivity. Although women work two-thirds of all the hours worked in the world, they get only one-tenth of the world's income and own a mere one-hundredth of the world's land.

At the same time, women make up about 60% of the world's almost 900 million adults who can neither read nor write. Women also suffer the most malnutrition, because men and children are fed first where food supplies are limited.

Numerous studies have shown that increased education is a strong factor leading women to have fewer children. Educated women are more likely than uneducated women to be employed outside the home rather than to stay home and raise children. They marry later, thus reducing their prime reproductive years, and lose fewer infants to death, a major factor in reducing fertility rates.

According to Worldwatch Institute researcher Jodi Jacobson,

Improving the status of women—more specifically, reducing their economic dependence on men—is a crucial aspect of economic development. Until female education is widespread, until women gain at least partial control over the resources that shape their economic lives, high fertility, poverty, and environmental degradation will persist in many regions of the world.

Achieving these important goals will require some major social changes. But making these changes will be difficult because of the long-standing political and economic domination of society by men throughout the world. In addition, in many countries competition between men and women for already scarce jobs should become even more intense by 2000, when another billion people will be looking for work.

Restricting Migration The governments of most countries achieve some degree of population regula-

---

CASE STUDY Immigration and Population Growth in the United States

The United States, founded by immigrants and their children, has admitted more immigrants and refugees than any other country in the world. Between 1820 and 1989 the United States admitted almost twice as many immigrants as all other countries combined.

The number of legal immigrants entering the United States has varied during different periods as a result of changes in immigration laws and economic growth (Figure 8-2). Between 1820 and 1960 most legal immigrants came from Europe. Since then, most have come from Asia and Latin America.

Between 1960 and 1989 the number of legal immigrants admitted per year more than doubled from 250,000 to 610,000. Each year another 200,000 to 500,000 enter the country illegally, most from Mexico and other Latin American countries. This means that in 1989 legal and illegal immigrants increased the U.S. population by 800,000 to 1.1 million people, accounting for almost 40% of the country's population growth. If

birth and death rates and immigration rates continue at present levels, soon immigration will be the major factor increasing the population of the United States.

Some analysts have called for an annual ceiling of no more than

450,000 for all categories of legal immigration, including refugees, to reduce the intensity of some of the country's social, economic, and environmental problems and to reach zero population growth sooner. In polls taken in 1985, half

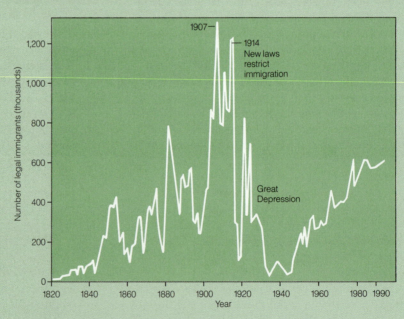

Figure 8-2 Legal immigration to the United States: 1820–1988. (Data from U.S. Immigration and Naturalization Service)

tion by allowing little immigration from other countries. Some governments also encourage emigration to other countries to reduce population pressures. Only a few countries, chiefly Canada, Australia, and the United States (see Case Study on p. 176), allow large annual increases in their population from immigration.

8–4 CASE STUDIES: POPULATION REGULATION IN INDIA AND CHINA

India India started the world's first national family planning program in 1952, when its population was nearly 400 million. In 1989, after 37 years of population control effort, India was the world's second most populous country, with a population of 835 million.

In 1952 India was adding 5 million people to its population each year. In 1989 it added 18 million. India is expected to become the world's most populous country around 2015. Its population is projected to more than double to 1.6 billion before leveling off early in the twenty-second century.

In 1989 India's average per capita income was about $300 a year. At least one-third of its population had an annual income per person of less than $100 a year, and 10 out of every 100 babies born died before their first birthday. To add to the problem, nearly half of India's labor force is unemployed or can find only occasional work. Each week 100,000 more people enter the job market, and for most of them jobs do not exist.

Without its long-standing family planning program, India's numbers would be growing even faster. But the results of the program have been disappointing. Factors contributing to this failure have been poor planning, bureaucratic inefficiency, the low status of women (despite constitutional guarantees of equality), extreme poverty, and too little administrative and financial support.

the people surveyed favored lower legal immigration levels.

Other analysts favor increasing the number of immigrants and changing immigration law to give preference to those with valuable professional skills, high levels of education, and a knowledge of English. This could help offset the projected decrease in skilled younger workers as U.S. population growth slows (Figure 7-9, p. 165) and the U.S. median age increases (Figure 7-13, p. 167).

Today only about 5% of all legal immigrants enter the United States on the basis of their skills. A typical working immigrant will add about $3,000 a year to the Social Security trust fund. As workers and consumers, trained immigrants also contribute to economic growth.

But some people oppose a policy of immigration based primarily on skills. They argue that it amounts to a brain drain of educated and talented people from LDCs that need these important human resources. It would also diminish the historic role of the United States in serving as a place of opportunity for the world's poor and oppressed.

In 1986 Congress passed a new immigration law designed to help control illegal immigration. This law included an amnesty program for some illegal immigrants. Those who entered the United States before January 1, 1982, and who could provide evidence that they have lived here continuously since then were eligible to become temporary residents and to apply for citizenship after 6.5 years. By the May 4, 1988, deadline, about 2.1 million of the estimated 5 million illegal aliens had signed up for the amnesty program.

The 1986 law also prohibits the hiring of illegal immigrants. Employers must examine the identity documents of all new employees. Employers who knowingly hire illegal aliens are subject to fines of $250 to $10,000 per violation, and repeat offenders can be sentenced to prison for up to six months. The bill also authorized funds to beef up the border patrol staff by 50%, to increase efforts to detect employers violating the new law, and to deport illegal aliens.

According to the Immigration and Naturalization Service, apprehensions of illegal immigrants at the U.S. Mexico border declined sharply between 1986 and 1988. Two-thirds of the 18,000 employers checked by the INS in 1988 were in compliance with the law.

But critics charge that illegal immigrants can get around the law with readily available fake documents. Employers are not responsible for verifying the authenticity of documents or for keeping copies. Also, the INS does not have enough money or staff to check most employers, prosecute repeated violators, or effectively patrol more than a fraction of the 3,140-kilometer (1,950-mile) U.S.–Mexico border. With nearly 60% of Mexico's labor force unemployed or underemployed, many Mexicans think being caught and sent back is a minor risk compared to remaining in poverty. What, if anything, do you think should be done about legal and illegal immigration into the United States?

But the roots of the problem are deeper. More than 3 out of every 4 people in India live in 560,000 rural villages, where crude birth rates are still close to 40 births per 1,000 people. The overwhelming economic and administrative task of delivering contraceptive services and education to the mostly rural population is complicated by an illiteracy rate of about 71%, with 80% to 90% of the illiterate people being rural women.

For years the government has provided information about the advantages of small families. Yet Indian women still have an average of 4.3 children because most couples believe they need many children as a source of cheap labor and old-age survival insurance. This belief is reinforced by the fact that almost one-third of all Indian children die before age 5.

In 1976 Indira Gandhi's government started a mass sterilization program, primarily for men in the civil service who already had two or more children. The program was supposed to be voluntary, with financial incentives given to those who volunteered to be sterilized. But officials allegedly used coercion to meet sterilization quotas in a few rural areas. The resulting backlash played a role in Gandhi's election defeat in 1977.

In 1978 the government took a new approach, raising the legal minimum age for marriage from 18 to 21 for men and from 15 to 18 for women. The 1981 census, however, showed that there was no drop in the population growth rate between 1971 and 1981. Since then the government has increased family planning efforts and funding, with the goal of achieving replacement-level fertility by 2000. Whether these efforts will succeed remains to be seen.

The United Nations projects that 2015 is the earliest India can expect to reach replacement-level fertility. Even then, its population will still grow significantly for 60 to 70 years because there are so many people under age 15.

Although effective population control still lags behind, India's agricultural production has improved dramatically since the mid-1960s. Today it can feed its population without foreign aid, even in years when the harvest is bad. But widespread poverty means that about 37% of its people have an inadequate diet. There is a good chance that by the end of this century India's population growth will again outstrip its food production.

China Between 1958 and 1962 an estimated 30 million people died from famine in China. Since 1970, however, China has made impressive efforts to feed its people and bring its population growth under control.

Today China has enough grain both to export and to feed its population of 1.1 billion. Between 1972 and 1985, China achieved a remarkable drop in its crude birth rate, from 32 to 18 per 1,000 people, and its average total fertility rate dropped from 5.7 to 2.1 children per woman. Since 1985 China's infant mortality has been less than one-half the rate in India.

To accomplish a sharp drop in fertility, China has established the most extensive and strictest population control program in the world, with an outlay of about $1 per person annually. The following are its major features:

- strongly encouraging couples to postpone marriage

- expanding educational opportunities

- providing married couples with easy access to free sterilization, contraceptives, and abortion

- giving couples who sign pledges to have no more than one child economic rewards such as salary bonuses, extra food, larger pensions, better housing, free medical care and school tuition for their child, and preferential treatment in employment when the child grows up

- requiring those who break the pledge to return all benefits

- exerting pressure on women pregnant with a third child to have abortions

- requiring one of the parents in a two-child family to be sterilized

- using mobile units and paramedics to bring sterilization, family planning, health care, and education to rural areas

- training local people to carry on the family planning program

- expecting all leaders to set an example with their own family size

By 1987, however, China's birth rate had risen slightly, to 21, and its total fertility rate had increased to 2.4. These rates have remained at these levels. The major reasons for these increases were the large number of women moving into their childbearing years, some relaxation of the government's stringent policies, and a strong preference for male children. Most couples who have a female child are eager to try again for a son, who by custom helps support his parents as they grow old.

China's leaders have a goal of reaching zero population growth by 2000 with a population 1.2 billion, followed by a slow decline to a population of 0.6 billion to 1 billion by 2100. Achieving this goal will be very difficult, because 34% of the Chinese people are under age 15. As a result, the United Nations projects that the population of China may be around 1.5 billion by 2020.

Most countries cannot or do not want to use the coercive elements of China's program. Other parts of this program, however, could be used in many LDCs. Especially useful is the practice of localizing the program, rather than asking the people to go to distant centers. Perhaps the best lesson that other countries can learn from China's experience is not to wait to curb population growth until the choice is between mass starvation and coercive measures.

8–5 GLOBAL AND U.S. POPULATION POLICY

Cutting Global Population Growth   Regulating population growth will not solve the world's resource, environmental, and social problems. But most analysts believe that reducing population growth will reduce the intensity of these problems.

Lester Brown, president of the Worldwatch Institute, urges the leaders of countries to adopt a goal of cutting world population growth in half by the year 2000. Assuming that the average world death rate remains at 10 per 1,000 people, this would require reducing the average global birth rate from 28 to 19 per 1,000 people. This would cut world population growth from 1.8% in 1989 to 1% by the year 2000.

The experience of some countries indicates that this is a possible goal. Japan cut its birth rate and population growth rate in half between 1949 and 1956 by legalizing abortion and creating a national family planning program. Between 1970 and 1976 China was able to cut its birth rate and population growth rate in half.

Cutting the global birth rate in half as soon as possible will require a combination of family planning, sustainable economic development, economic rewards and penalties, and changes in women's roles. The mix of these factors must be carefully designed to work with the culture of each country. The following are the important steps governments around the world should take to accomplish this goal:

- Increase the $3 billion now spent annually on family planning services to $8 billion by the year 2000.

- Make birth control information and devices available to every man and woman.

- Expand educational and employment opportunities for women.

- Provide LDCs with aid for sustainable development and resource conservation in return for forgiveness of their debts to MDCs.

- Increase funding for development of new methods of birth control that are culturally acceptable

and easier to use (see Enrichment Study on p. 182).

- Shift from unsustainable to sustainable development in MDCs to reduce consumption overpopulation, which is undermining the planet's life-support capacity. (Figure 1-13, p. 20)

The U.S. Role   The United States has an important role to play in bringing about a slowdown in world population growth. Key actions include the following:

- Set an example by adopting a national goal of a two-child family and zero population growth.

- Introduce the principles and issues of demography, family planning, and population regulation in all high school curricula.

- Shift to sustainable-earth economic development and resource conservation to reduce the massive effects of U.S. consumption overpopulation on the earth's life-support systems.

- Assist LDCs in making population, environmental, and economic policies.

- Provide LDCs with aid for sustainable development and resource conservation in return for debt forgiveness.

- Restore and increase financial support for the UN Fund for Population Activities and the International Planned Parenthood Federation.

By taking these steps, the United States would show that it wants to see world population growth slowed by the humane process of reducing birth rates instead of the chaotic and inhumane process of raising death rates.

Population programs aren't simply a matter of promoting smaller families. They also mean guaranteeing that our children are given the fullest opportunities to be educated, to get good health care, and to have access to the jobs and careers they eventually want. It is really a matter of increasing the value of every birth, of expanding the potential of every child to the fullest, and of improving the life of a community.

Pranay Gupte

Garrett Hardin

As professor of human ecology at the University of California at Santa Barbara for many years, Garrett Hardin made important contributions to the joining of ethics and biology. He has raised hard ethical questions, sometimes taken unpopular stands, and forced people to think deeply about environmental problems and their possible solutions. He is best known for his 1968 essay "The Tragedy of the Commons," which has had significant impact on economics, political science, and the management of potentially renewable resources. His many books include Promethean Ethics *and* Filters Against Folly: How to Survive Despite Economists, Ecologists, and the Merely Eloquent.

For many years Angel Island in San Francisco Bay was plagued with too many deer. A few animals transplanted there early in this century lacked predators and rapidly increased to nearly 300 deer—far beyond the carrying capacity of the island. Scrawny, underfed animals tugged at the heartstrings of Californians, who carried extra plant food from the mainland to the island.

Such charity worsened the plight of the deer. Excess animals trampled the soil, ate the bark off of small trees, and destroyed seedlings of all kinds. The net effect was a lowering of the carrying capacity, year by year, as the deer continued to multiply in a deteriorating habitat.

State game managers proposed that the excess deer be shot by skilled hunters. "How cruel! " some people protested. Then the managers proposed that coyotes be imported to the island. Though not big enough to kill adult deer, coyotes can kill defenseless young fawns, thus reducing the size of the herd. But the Society for the Prevention of Cruelty to Animals was adamantly opposed to such human introduction of predators.

In the end it was agreed to export deer to some other area suitable for deer life. A total of 203 animals were caught and trucked many miles away. From the fate of a sample of animals fitted with radio collars, it was estimated that 85% of the transported deer died within a year (most of them within two months) from various causes: predation by coyotes, bobcats, and domestic dogs; shooting by poachers and legal hunters; and being run over by automobiles.

The net cost (in 1982 dollars) for relocating each animal that survived for a year was $2,876. The state refused to finance the continuation of the program, and no volunteers stepped forward to pay future bills. Even if funding had been forthcoming, managers would soon have run out of areas suitable for deer life. Organisms reproduce exponentially like compound interest (see Spotlight on p. 4), but the environment doesn't increase at all. The moral is a simple ecological commandment: *Thou shalt not transgress the carrying capacity.*

Now let's look at the human situation. A competent physicist has placed the human carrying capacity of the globe at 50 billion—about 10 times the present world population. Before you are tempted to urge women to have more babies, consider what Robert Malthus said nearly 200 years ago: "There should be no more people in a country than could enjoy daily a glass of wine and piece of beef for dinner."

A diet of grain or bread is symbolic of minimum living standards; wine and beef are symbolic of all forms of higher living standards that make greater demands on the environment. When land used for the direct production of plants for human consumption is converted to growing crops for wine or corn for cattle, fewer calories get to the human population. Since carrying capacity is defined as the *maximum* number of animals (humans) an area can support, using part of the area to support such cultural luxuries as wine and beef reduces the carrying capacity. This reduced capacity is called the *cultural carrying capacity.* Cultural carrying capacity is always less than simple carrying capacity.

Energy is the common coin in which all competing demands on the environment can be measured. Energy saved by giving up a luxury can be used to produce more bread and support more people. We could increase the simple carrying capacity of the earth by giving up any (or all) of the following luxuries: street lighting; vacations; most private cars; air conditioning; and artistic performances of all sorts—drama, dancing, music, and lectures. Since the heating of buildings is not as efficient as multiple layers of clothing, space heating would be forbidden.

Is that all? By no means: to come closer to home, Look at this book. The production and distribution of such an expensive treatise consume a great deal of energy. In fact, the energy bill for the whole of higher education is very high (which is one reason tuition costs so much). By giving up all education beyond the eighth grade, we could free enough energy to sustain millions more human lives.

At this point a skeptic might well ask: Does God give a prize for the maximum population? From this brief analysis we can see that there are two choices. We can maximize the number of human beings living at the lowest possible level of comfort, or we can try to optimize the quality of life for a much smaller population.

What is the carrying capacity of the earth? is a scientific question. Scientifically, it may be possible to support 50 billion people at a "bread" level. But is this what we want? What is the cultural carrying capacity? requires that we debate questions of value, about which opinions differ.

An even greater difficulty must be faced. So far we have been treating the capacity question as a *global* question, as if there were a global sovereignty to enforce a solution on all people. But there is no global sovereignty ("one world"), nor is there any prospect of one in the foreseeable future. We must make do with nearly 200 different national sovereignties. That means, as concerns the capacity problem, we must ask how nations are to coexist in a finite global environment if different sovereignties adopt different standards of living.

Consider a redwood forest (Figure 2-6, p. 36). It produces no human food. Protected in a park, the trees do not even produce lumber for houses. Since people have to travel many miles to visit it, the forest is a net loss in the national energy budget. But those who are fortunate enough to wander quietly through the cathedral-like aisles of soaring trees report that the forest does something precious for the human spirit.

Now comes an appeal from a distant land where millions are starving because their population has overshot the carrying capacity. We are asked to save lives by sending food. So long as we have surpluses we may safely indulge in the pleasures of philanthropy. But the typical population in such poor countries increases by 2.5% a year—*or more;* that is, the country's population doubles every 28 years—*or less.* After we have run out of our surpluses, then what?

A spokesperson for the needy makes a proposal: "If you would only cut down your redwood forests, you could use the lumber to build houses and then grow potatoes on the land, shipping the food to us. Since we are all passengers together on Spaceship Earth, are you not duty bound to do so? Which is more precious, trees or human beings?"

The last question may sound ethically compelling, but let's look at the consequences of assigning a preemptive and supreme value to human lives. There are at least 2 billion people in the world who are poorer than the 32 million legally "poor" in America, and they are increasing by about 40 million per year. Unless this increase is brought to a halt, sharing food

and energy on the basis of need would require the sacrifice of one amenity after another in rich countries. The final result of sharing would be complete poverty everywhere on the face of the earth to maintain the earth's simple carrying capacity. Is that the best humanity can do?

To date, there has been overwhelmingly negative reaction to all proposals to make international philanthropy conditional upon the stopping of population growth by the poor, overpopulated recipient nations. Foreign aid is governed by two apparently inflexible assumptions:

- The right to produce children is a universal, irrevocable right of every nation, no matter how hard it presses against the carrying capacity of its territory.
- When lives are in danger, the moral obligations of rich countries to save human lives is absolute and undeniable.

Considered separately each of these two well-meaning doctrines might be defended; together they constitute a fatal recipe. If humanity gives maximum carrying capacity questions precedence over problems of cultural carrying capacity, the result will be universal poverty and environmental ruin.

Or do you see an escape from this harsh dilemma?

Guest Essay Discussion

1. What items would you include as essential in maintaining your own quality of life? Do you feel that everyone in the world should have or should strive for that quality of life? Explain.

2. What population size do you believe would allow the world's people to have the quality of life you described in the previous question? What do you believe is the cultural carrying capacity of the United States? Should the United States have a national policy to establish this population size as soon as possible? Explain.

3. Do you agree with the two principles the author of this essay says are the basis of foreign aid to needy countries? If not, what changes would you make in the requirements for receiving such aid?

4. Do you believe that the United States and other MDCs indulge in consumption overpopulation that threatens to reduce the global carrying capacity for everyone (Figure 1-13, p. 20)? If so, what luxury items should be eliminated or discouraged to protect the earth? Which items in the list you made in answer to question 1 would you be willing to delete from your lifestyle?

Extremely Effective

Total abstinence	100%
Abortion	100%
Sterilization	99.6%

Highly Effective

IUD with slow-release hormones	98%
IUD plus spermicide	98%
IUD	95%
Condom (good brand) plus spermicide	95%
Oral contraceptive	94%

Effective

Condom (good brand)	86%
Diaphragm plus spermicide	84%
Rhythm method (daily temperature readings)	84%
Vaginal sponge impregnated with spermicide	83%
Cervical cap	83%
Spermicide (foam)	82%

Moderately Effective

Spermicide (creams, jellies, suppositories)	74%
Withdrawal	74%
Condom (cheap brand)	70%

Unreliable

Douche	40%
Chance (no method)	10%

Figure 8-3 Typical effectiveness of birth control methods in the United States. Percent effectiveness is based on the number of undesired pregnancies per 100 couples using a method as their sole form of birth control for a year. A 98% effectiveness for oral contraceptives means that for every 100 women using the pill regularly for one year, two are likely to get pregnant. (Data from Allan Guttmacher Institute)

Present Methods The ideal form of birth control would be effective, safe, inexpensive, convenient, and free of side effects. It would also be compatible with one's cultural, religious, and sexual attitudes. Available methods either prevent pregnancy or terminate pregnancy before birth. These methods vary widely in their typical effectiveness (Figure 8-3) and use throughout the world and the United States (Figure 8-4). No one method can fit the needs of every couple.

The failure rates shown in Figure 8-3 are for the United States. Failure rates tend to be higher in LDCs because of lack of education and human error. For example, although oral contraceptives have a failure rate of only 2% in the United States, worldwide failure rates range from 4% to 10%.

Preventing Pregnancy The most common form of birth control in the world is *sterilization* of females and males, mostly because of its widespread use in three populous

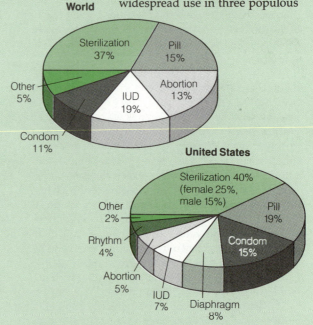

Figure 8-4 Estimated use of various birth control methods by couples of reproductive age in the world and the United States in 1986. (Data from UN Population Division, Population Crisis Committee, and U.S. National Center for Health Statistics)

countries—China, India, and the United States. It involves relatively simple surgical procedures that can be done under local anesthetic in a doctor's office. Sometimes sterilization can be reversed surgically. But reversal procedures presently have a success rate of only 30% to 40% for women and 50% to 60% for men.

The *intrauterine device (IUD)* is the second most used method of preventing pregnancy in the world. Three-fourths of the world's IUD users are in China. It is particularly useful for women who can't take the pill, don't want to undergo sterilization, and don't want to settle for less effective and less convenient methods. The IUD has few health risks for women who have only one sex partner. However, for childless young women with several sexual partners, the device poses a greater than normal risk of pelvic inflammatory disease, which often leads to sterility.

In the United States an earlier type of IUD, the Dalkon shield, caused thousands of cases of sterility and miscarriages and was implicated in the deaths of 20 women. Other versions of the IUD are considered safe, but only one company is now making IUDs in the United States. Other manufacturers quit making them to avoid liability suits. This narrows the choice for American women who don't want to be sterilized and who cannot take the pill.

The IUD terminates a pregnancy by preventing a fertilized egg from implanting on the uterine walls. For this reason, this method of birth control is considered by some pro-life groups as an unacceptable method.

Oral contraceptives are the third most used method for preventing pregnancy in the world and the second most used method in the United States. New formulations of the pill decrease the risk of ovarian and uterine cancer by 40%

to 50% but can increase the risk of breast cancer by 43% or more in women who use them for more than three years. Pill users also experience a lower than normal incidence of benign breast and ovarian cysts, pelvic infections, iron-deficiency anemia, premenstrual tension, and menstrual cramps. However, they have increased risk of stroke and heart attack if they smoke or if they are over age 35. Women with diabetes and those with a family history of breast cancer should be especially wary about using the pill.

The use of *condoms* is increasing, especially in the United States. In addition to birth prevention, latex condoms offer the best protection against sexually transmitted diseases such as herpes, AIDS, and gonorrhea, especially if used with a spermicide. Condoms made from animal skins prevent births but do not offer protection against AIDS and most sexually transmitted diseases. However, despite heavy AIDS education efforts, condom use among people 18 to 24 years old in the United States dropped in 1987.

Since 1989 condoms for females have been available in the United States. They consist of a loose-fitting polyethylene sheath and two diaphragm-like flexible rings. The condom is inserted into the vagina like a tampon. The sheath protects the vagina and the inner ring covers the cervix. The other ring remains outside.

Other birth control methods such as *diaphragms, spermicides, and spermicide-impregnated sponges* are less widely used. They are less effective (Figure 8-3), messy, inconvenient, and effective only for a limited period of time, usually for just one act of intercourse.

The *rhythm method*, in which couples abstain from sex during the woman's fertile period, is normally only moderately effective (Figure 8-3). However, certain variations of the rhythm method, such

as the Billings method and Sympto-Thermal methods, are said to have a failure rate of only 2% to 5% if practiced very carefully.

In 1988 the U.S. Food and Drug Administration approved the use of the *cervical cap*—a thimble-shaped latex dome that fits over the cervix. Like the diaphragm, it is a barrier contraceptive that blocks sperm from passing from the vagina into the uterus. When used with a spermicide, it has a failure rate of about 17%—the same as a diaphragm plus spermicide. But it is less likely to tear than a diaphragm and can be worn for up to two days, compared to one day for the diaphragm.

There is no reliable evidence of harm from the use of spermicides. However, spermicides are low-profit items, and one or two lawsuits might be enough to convince U.S. companies to discontinue production.

Breastfeeding can play an important role in controlling fertility. Some women who regularly nurse a baby do not ovulate and thus cannot conceive for at least a year. But breast-feeding is not a reliable method of birth control. Breast-feeding also helps reduce infant mortality rates because mother's milk provides a baby with antibodies to help prevent disease and is usually the most nutritious food available for infants in poor families.

Unfortunately, breastfeeding is declining in many LDCs, mostly because large U.S.-based international companies have promoted the use of infant formulas instead of mother's milk. Buying infant formula when free breast milk is available is an unnecessary expense for a poor family struggling to survive. Using formula can lead to infant illnesses and deaths. Poor people, lacking fuel, often prepare formula with

(continued)

unboiled, contaminated water and use unsterilized bottles.

Highly effective *injectable contraceptives* have been on the market for over two decades. An injection of Depo-Provera is virtually 100% effective in preventing pregnancy for three months. It has been used by more than 11 million women in 90 countries for over 20 years with no reported deaths or serious side effects. However, it has not been approved for use in the United States. The FDA says more research is needed to establish its long-term safety, and its use has been opposed by groups that generally oppose contraception.

One-month injectable contraceptives are also used, mostly in China and Latin America. A vaccine that prevents pregnancy for three months is being tested in several countries and could be available within a decade.

Hormonal implants, such as Norplant, have been approved for use in 12 countries and are undergoing evaluation in 24 others and may be available in the United States by 1991. After being implanted under the skin of the upper arm in a simple surgical procedure, they release small amounts of hormones that prevent pregnancy for two to five years. Their low cost, about $3 a year, makes them particularly useful for low-income women in LDCs. So far their only known drawback is that they cause irregular menstrual bleeding in about 20% to 25% of users.

A more easily reversible sterilization device, the Filshie clip, has been used by half a million women worldwide but is not approved in the United States.

Terminating Pregnancy:
Abortion Spontaneous abortion, or miscarriage, is nature's way of preventing the development of most genetically impaired embryos and fetuses. It ends far more pregnancies than induced abortion. About one-third of all fetuses three months or older are terminated by spontaneous abortion. Miscarriage rates tend to be highest among women who are ill or malnourished.

Worldwide, induced abortion is the fourth most widely used method of birth control (Figure 8-4). According to the Alan Gutmacher Institute each year an estimated 54 million induced abortions—an average of 140,000 a day—are performed in the world. About 28 million are performed in LDCs and 26 million in MDCs. The Soviet Union has the world's highest abortion rate with 204 abortions for every 100 live births. It is followed by Bulgaria (93 abortions per 100 live births), China (76), Hungary (69), and the United States (42). In 1989 there were about 1.6 million legal abortions in the United States, about 30% of all pregnancies, excluding still births and miscarriages. About 91% of these abortions were performed during the first three months of pregnancy.

Worldwide, it is estimated by the Alan Gutmacher Institute that one-third to one-half of all abortions are illegal. Most illegal abortions are performed under unsanitary conditions by unskilled attendants or by the woman herself.

Illegal abortions often cause hemorrhaging, and pelvic inflam-matory disease. It is estimated that illegal abortions are responsible for the premature deaths of 250,000 women each year.

About 39% of the world's population lives in countries where abortion on request is legal. But hundreds of millions of women in such countries are too poor to pay for an abortion or live in rural areas where such services are not available. Only 8% of the world's population, mostly in Latin America, live in countries where abortion is totally prohibited. For the remaining 59% of the world's people, abortion is available under certain circumstances.

The widespread use of abortion indicates that governments around the world have failed to meet the need for family planning. At least half of all abortions could be prevented at little cost by making family planning services readily available to all people, especially the poor.

Abortion is a highly emotional issue that does not lend itself to compromise or cool debate. On one side are pro-lifers, who believe that abortion is an act of murder and should be illegal under all circumstances. On the other side are pro-choicers, who believe that a woman should have the freedom to decide whether or not to have a legal abortion.

Between these two extremes are people who believe that a legal abortion should be allowed if a woman's health is seriously endangered, the pregnancy is due to rape or incest, or there is strong evidence that the baby has a serious health defect.

CHAPTER SUMMARY

Governments of most LDCs favor reducing birth and fertility rates in their countries through a combination of economic development and family planning. According to a model known as the *demographic transition,* as countries become industrialized they move from fast population growth, to slow growth, to zero growth, and eventually to a slow decline in population. But without rapid and sustained economic growth, many LDCs may not be able to undergo the demographic transition.

Family planning programs provide educational and clinical services that help couples choose how many children to have and when to have them. It has been a major factor in reducing birth and fertility rates in China and Indonesia, with large populations, and in some LDCs with mod-

Some analysts hope that pro-life and pro-choice supporters will be able to join together in an abortion prevention program. This would be done by expanding sex education in the schools, providing a nationwide network of free or low-cost maternity homes for pregnant women who agree to put their babies up for adoption, and greatly increasing the availability of family planning services, especially for the poor.

Abortion Pills In 1988 an abortion pill (called RU-486 or Mifepristone) was approved for use in France and China. It causes an abortion by blocking the action of the hormone progesterone, thus provoking the uterine lining to slough off the embryo. Used alone it is about 80% effective in preventing implantation of a fertilized egg if taken within five weeks after a missed period. If taken with a small dose of a prostaglandin, a substance that makes the uterus contract, it is 95% effective up to five weeks after a missed period. After seven weeks it is not very effective. After counseling and at least a week waiting period, a pregnant woman gets a dose of RU-486 at a clinic and returns two days later for a dose of a prostaglandin. She makes a final visit a few days later to make sure the abortion has occurred.

This drug is a safer, less expensive way to end unwanted pregnancies than existing abortion methods. Tests on 8,000 women have shown that the drug has no harmful physical side effects, except a very small risk of excessive bleeding.

It is unlikely that this drug will be legally available to women in the United States in the foreseeable future because of intense opposition from pro-life groups fearing that it will make abortions commonplace. Government-funded researchers are not allowed to test it or to develop other abortion drugs. So far no company has expressed an interest in marketing RU-486 in the United States because of such pressure and the fear of liability suits.

Future Methods of Birth Control Researchers throughout the world are at work trying to develop new and better methods of fertility control. Examples include biodegradable implants that don't require surgical removal, a two-year pregnancy vaccine, a contraceptive for men that reduces sperm count, and chemicals for nonsurgical sterilization. Attempts are also being made to develop female and male sterilization techniques that can be more easily reversed.

How soon these methods become available depends mostly on the amount of money invested in research and development and safety testing. To develop, test, and evaluate the safety of a new contraceptive takes 15 years or more and $50 million or more. Despite the importance of population control, annual worldwide expenditures on reproductive research and contraceptive development have declined from a high of $250 million a year to $200 million a year today—an average of only 25 cents per person.

In the United States contraceptive research and development by

private drug firms has virtually stopped, mostly because of the difficulty and expense of getting FDA approval of a new contraceptive. Other factors are changes in patent protection laws that have reduced company profits, fear of liability suits, and the high cost of liability insurance. Drug companies also make more money by selling birth control pills that have to be taken daily than in selling a contraceptive pill, vaccine, or implant that prevents conception for a month to five years.

Since 1979 federal funding for research has decreased by 25% (adjusted for inflation) because of budget cuts and pressure from pro-life groups. Most population experts fear that unless government and private funding of contraceptive research is at least doubled, few if any of the possible improved forms of birth control will be available in the United States.

The range of birth control choices for Americans is becoming narrower at a time when it is widening for most other people in the world. For Americans this will probably mean more sterilizations, more abortions (including illegal ones if abortion is outlawed or restricted), and more unwanted children.

erate to small populations. But family planning has had moderate to poor results in India and several other populous LDCs and in 79 less populous LDCs, especially in Africa and Latin America.

Some population experts believe that family planning, even coupled with economic development, cannot lower birth and fertility rates fast enough to avoid a sharp rise in death rates in many LDCs. They call for increased empha-

sis on discouraging births by means of economic rewards and penalties and reducing fertility by increasing rights, education, and work opportunities for women.

Most governments control population growth to some extent by restricting *immigration* to their countries. A major exception is the United States, which continues to admit significant numbers of legal immigrants and refugees each year. There is growing pressure, however, to reduce the annual level of legal immigrants and to stem the large number of illegal immigrants entering the United States.

Although India has had a national family planning program since 1952, it has had disappointing results. Reasons for this are poor planning, insufficient funding, bureaucratic inefficiency, low status of women, cultural and religious diversity, extreme poverty, widespread illiteracy, and a high infant death rate.

In contrast, China, with the world's largest population, has been able to sharply reduce its birth rate and total fertility rate since 1972. It also now produces enough food to feed its people with some left over for export. China achieved this remarkable drop in fertility by establishing the world's most extensive and strictest population control program in order to avoid massive famine.

Effective family planning depends primarily on providing couples with information about and access to various forms of birth control, which either *prevent pregnancy* or *terminate pregnancy before birth*. The four most widely used methods for preventing pregnancy are sterilization, IUDs, oral contraceptives, and condoms. Injectable contraceptives and hormonal implants are also being used in some LDCs.

Preventing pregnancy by legal or illegal abortion is the fourth most used method of birth control in the world. Most of the world's people now live in countries where abortions are legal during the first three months of pregnancy. Abortion, however, is a highly controversial way to end a pregnancy.

DISCUSSION TOPICS

1. Should world population growth be controlled? Explain.

2. How can population growth intensify environmental and social problems even if it is not the root cause of them? Give three examples.

3. Debate the following resolution: The United States has a serious consumption overpopulation problem and should adopt an official policy to stabilize its population and reduce unnecessary resource waste and consumption as rapidly as possible.

4. Do you believe that the demographic transition hypothesis applies to most of today's LDCs? Explain.

5. Why is the low status of women in terms of education, employment, legal rights, and self-esteem a major factor contributing to high fertility and poverty?

6. What are some ways in which women are discriminated against in the United States? On your campus?

7. a. Should the number of legal immigrants and refugees allowed into the United States each year be sharply reduced? Explain.

   b. Should illegal immigration into the United States be sharply decreased? Explain. If so, how would you go about achieving this?

8. Why has China been more successful than India in reducing its rate of population growth? Do you agree with China's present population control policies? Explain. What alternatives, if any, would you suggest?

9. a. Do you believe that each woman should be free to use abortion as a means of birth control? Explain.

   b. Do you believe that a woman who has been raped, who has AIDs or some other disease that can be passed on to a baby, or whose health is threatened by pregnancy should be allowed to have an abortion? Explain.

10. a. Should federal and state funds be used to provide free or low-cost abortions for the poor in the United States? Explain.

    b. Should U.S. family planning clinics that are supported partially by federal funds be allowed to tell pregnant clients that abortion is one of their options? Explain.

    c. Should federal aid be withheld from any international family planning agency that informs clients that abortion is one of their options? Explain.

CHAPTER 9

Population Distribution: Urbanization and Urban Problems

General Questions and Issues

1. How is the world's population distributed between rural and urban areas?

2. What factors determine how urban areas develop?

3. What are the major benefits and problems associated with living in an urban area?

4. How do transportation systems affect population distribution and urban growth?

5. What methods are used to decide and regulate how different parcels of land in urban areas are used?

6. How can cities be made more livable and sustainable?

The test of the quality of life in an advanced economic society is now largely in the quality of urban life. Romance may still belong to the countryside—but the present reality of life abides in the city.

John Kenneth Galbraith

Economic, environmental, and social conditions are affected not only by population growth and age structure but also by how population is distributed geographically in rural or urban areas. In 1900 only 14% of the world's population lived in an **urban area**, often defined as a village, town, or city with a population of more than 2,500 people. Today 41% of the world's people are urban dwellers—73% in MDCs and 32% in LDCs. Jobs pull many people to cities. In LDCs the rural poor, without enough land or income to survive in the country, migrate to cities to seek their livelihoods.

Supplying the resources needed to support urban areas is a major cause of degradation of forests, farmlands, rangelands, watersheds, and other nonurban areas. How we deal with these problems will be the major factor determining the well-being and health of urban and rural dwellers and the environment upon which all people and other living things depend.

9-1 URBANIZATION AND URBAN GROWTH

The World Situation   It is important to distinguish between urbanization and urban growth. A country's **urbanization** is the percentage of its population living in an urban area. **Urban growth** is the rate of growth of urban populations. Three things lead to both urbanization and urban growth: rapid population growth, economic development, and rural poverty.

Several trends are important in understanding the problems and challenges of urbanization and urban growth:

- The percentage of the population living in urban areas has increased significantly since 1900, with almost two out of three people projected to be living in such areas by 2020 (Figure 9-1).

- Urbanization varies in different parts of the world but is increasing almost everywhere (Figure 9-2).

- LDCs, with 32% urbanization, are simultaneously experiencing high rates of natural population increase and rapid and increasing urban growth.

- In MDCs, with 73% urbanization, urban growth is increasing at lower and declining rates.

- The distribution of people living in absolute poverty is shifting from rural to urban areas at an increasing rate.

Unprecedented urban growth in MDCs and LDCs has given rise to a new concept—the *megacity*, an urban area with a population of more than 10 million. In 1985 there were 10 megacities, most of them in MDCs (Table

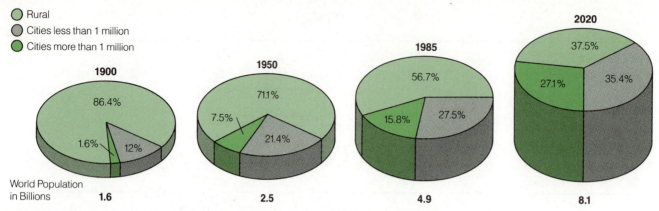

Figure 9-1 Patterns of world urbanization from 1900 to 1985, with projections to 2020. (Data from United Nations and Population Reference Bureau)

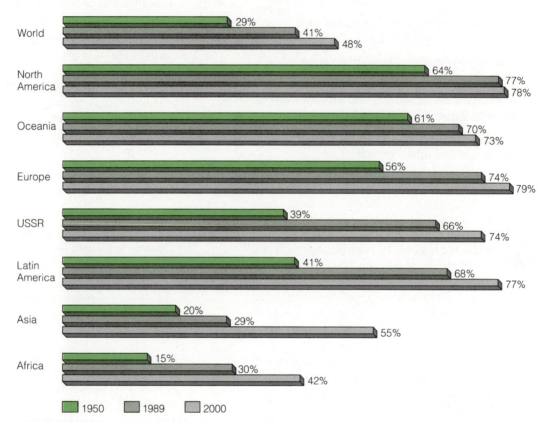

Figure 9-2 Urbanization of various groups of countries, 1950-2000. (Data from United Nations and Population Reference Bureau)

9-1). The United Nations projects that by 2000 there will be 26 megacities, more than two-thirds of them in LDCs (Table 9-1).

The Situation in LDCs In LDCs more than 20 million rural people migrate to cities each year. Several factors are responsible for this population shift (see Case Study on p. 189). Part is caused by the pull of urban job opportunities. But much of this migration is caused by rural poverty, which pushes people into cities. Modern, mechanized agriculture decreases the need for farm labor and allows large landowners to buy out small-scale, subsistence farmers who cannot afford to modernize. Without jobs or land these people are forced to move to cities.

For most of these migrants, as well as the urban poor in MDCs, the city becomes a poverty trap, not an oasis of economic opportunity and cultural diversity (see Case Study on p. 190). Those few fortunate enough to get a job must work long hours for low wages. To survive they often have to take jobs that expose them to dust, hazardous chemicals, excessive noise, and dangerous machinery.

Table 9-1 The Ten Largest Megacity Urban Areas in the World in 1985 and 2000 (Data from United Nations)

	1985		2000	
Urban Area	Population (millions)		Urban Area	Projected Population (millions)
Tokyo-Yokohama	18.8		Mexico City	25.8
Mexico City	17.3		São Paulo	24.0
São Paulo	15.9		Tokyo-Yokohama	20.2
New York-N.E. New Jersey	15.6		Calcutta	16.5
Shanghai	12.0		Greater Bombay	16.0
Calcutta	11.0		New York-N.E. New Jersey	15.8
Greater Buenos Aires	10.9		Shanghai	14.3
Rio de Janeiro	10.4		Seoul	13.8
London	10.4		Tehran	13.6
Seoul	10.2		Rio de Janeiro	13.3

CASE STUDY Brazil

Between 1950 and 1989 the urban population in Brazil increased from 34% to 71%. Brazil is a notable example of a two-tiered society: most of the wealth is concentrated in the hands of a small fraction of the population, and most other people are poor. The country is also divided geographically into a largely impoverished tropical north and a temperate south, where most industry and wealth are concentrated.

Attracted by the prospect of jobs, many of the rural poor in the north and northeast have flooded into Rio de Janeiro and São Paulo in the south (Table 9-1). There they build shantytowns near apartment towers and wealthy suburbs.

Overpopulation is one factor increasing the ranks of the unemployed and underemployed in rural and urban Brazil. Many poor people have been displaced from the land by the conversion of small farms in the south to industrialized agriculture for export crops. Deforestation and desertification in the extremely poor northeast have also helped push environmental refugees to southern cities and to development projects in the tropical forests of the Amazon basin.

As a safety valve for its exploding population, the Brazilian government has encouraged migration to the Amazon basin, with economic aid from international lending agencies such as the World

Bank. This policy is supported by wealthy Brazilians, who want to diffuse pressures for more equitable land distribution and by ranchers who receive government subsidies to establish cattle ranches by clearing tropical forests.

This policy, however, is leading to widespread deforestation and degradation of tropical forests, one of the world's most diverse and important ecosystems. In effect, the country is mortgaging its environmental future for short-term economic gain by the wealthy few.

Urban growth in LDCs is also caused by government policies that distribute most income and social services to urban dwellers at the expense of rural dwellers. For example, in many LDCs where 70% of the population is rural, only about 20% of the national budget goes to the rural sector. This inequity encourages rural-to-urban migration, which further intensifies the need for services in cities and decreases resources in rural areas.

Many of the urban poor in LDCs are forced to live on the streets (Figure 1-2, p. 5). Others crowd into slums and shantytowns, made from corrugated steel, plastic sheets, tin cans, and packing boxes, which ring the outskirts of most cities in these countries. In most large cities in LDCs, shantytown populations double every five to seven years—four to five times the population growth rate of the entire city. Because it is impossible to get an accurate count of the number of squatters, they are rarely included in urban population estimates like those given in Table 9-1.

Probably between a third and a half of the residents of cities in LDCs live on public or private lands illegally. The people in these settlements live in constant fear of eviction or of having their makeshift shelters destroyed by bulldozers. Many shantytowns are also located on land subject to landslides, floods, or tidal waves or in the most polluted districts of inner cities. Fires are common because most residents use kerosene stoves, fuelwood, or charcoal for heating and cooking.

Most cities refuse to provide shantytowns and slums with adequate drinking water, sanitation, food, health care, housing, schools, and jobs. Not only lacking the money, officials also fear that improving services will attract even more of the rural poor.

Despite joblessness and squalor, shantytown residents cling to life with resourcefulness, tenacity, and hope. Most are convinced that the city offers, possibly for themselves and certainly for their children, the only chance of a better life.

Most urban migrants do have more opportunities and are better off than the rural poor they left behind. With better access to family planning programs, they tend to have fewer children. Children in most cities have better access to schools than do rural dwellers. Even so, nearly half of all school-age children in urban areas of LDCs drop out before they finish the fourth grade to work or take care of younger children.

A few squatter communities have organized to improve conditions. One example is Rio de Janeiro's Santa Marta slum, home for 11,500 of the city's 2 million squatters. Residents organized to establish a day-care program and to bring in water lines, electricity, health clinics, and drainage systems to prevent mud slides. In the town of Lima's Villa, El Salvador, a network of women's groups and neighborhood associa-tions planted half a million trees, trained hundreds of door-to-door health workers, and built 300 commu-nity kitchens, 150 day-care centers, and 26 schools. In this town of 300,000 people, illiteracy has fallen to 3%—one of the lowest rates in Latin America—and infant mortality is 40% below the national average. Such self-help success stories are rare, but they show what can be done.

The U.S. Situation In 1800 only 5% of Americans lived in cities. Since then three major internal population shifts have taken place in the United States. They are migration from rural to urban areas, from central cities to suburbs and smaller cities, and from the North and East to the South and West.

The major shift was from rural to urban areas as the country industrialized and needed fewer farmers to produce sufficient food. Currently about three out of four Americans live in the nation's 281 urban areas and two out of three live in the country's 28 largest urban regions (Figure 9-3).* Nearly half (48%) of the American people live in metropolitan areas of 1 mil-

---

*Each of these areas, known as a Metropolitan Statistical Area (MSA), is a county or group of counties that contains either a city of at least 50,000 people or an urbanized area with 50,000 or more people and a total population of 100,000 or more. A Consolidated Metropolitan Area (CMSA) is a large urban area with a population of 1 million or more.

CASE STUDY Mexico City, Mexico

In 1969 the population of Mexico City, the capital of Mexico, was 9 million. In 1989 it had 20 million residents, making it the world's most populous urban area. Every day another 2,000 poverty-stricken rural peasants pour into the city, hoping to find a better life.

Today the city suffers from severe air pollution, massive unemployment (close to 50%), and a soaring crime rate. One-third of the city's people live in crowded slums, or barrios, without running water or electricity.

The overpowering stench of garbage and sewage fills the air of the barrios. With at least 5 million people living without sewer facilities, tons of human waste are left in gutters and vacant lots every day. About half of the city's garbage is left in the open to rot, attracting armies of rats and swarms of flies.

Over 3 million cars, 7,000 diesel buses, and 130,000 factories spew pollutants into the atmosphere. Air pollution is intensified because the city lies in a basin surrounded by mountains and has frequent thermal inversions that trap pollut-ants near ground level. Breathing the city's air is like smoking two packs of cigarettes a day from birth. The city's air and water pol-lution cause an estimated 100,000 premature deaths a year.

These problems, already at cri-sis levels, will become even worse if this urban area, as projected, grows to 25.8 million people by the end of this century. The Mexi-can government is industrializing other parts of the country in an attempt to stop or at least slow migration to Mexico City.

One thing may prevent the pro-jected population increase: a lack of water. Because of its elevated site and lack of nearby water, since 1982 the city has pumped water 336 meters (1,100 feet) uphill from a site 100 kilometers (62 miles) away. In the 1990s the city will have to pump additional water 672 meters (2,200 feet) uphill from a site 200 kilometers (124 miles) away. This pumping will require electricity equal to that from six large power plants—prohibitively expensive if energy costs rise as projected.

lion or more. Urbanization in states ranges from a high of 91% in California to a low of 34% in Vermont.

Since 1970 many people have moved from large central cities to suburbs and to smaller cities and rural areas, primarily because of the large numbers of new jobs in such areas. Today about 41% of the country's urban dwellers live in central cities and 59% live in suburbs.

Since 1980 about 80% of the population increase in the United States has occurred in the South and West (Figure 9-4), particularly near the coasts. Most of this increase is due to migration from the North

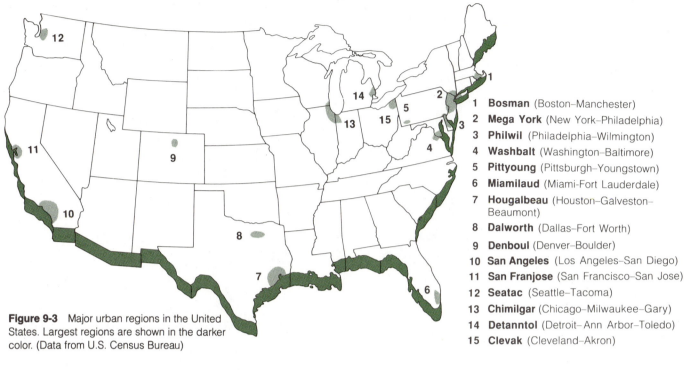

1 **Bosman** (Boston–Manchester)
2 **Mega York** (New York–Philadelphia)
3 **Philwil** (Philadelphia–Wilmington)
4 **Washbalt** (Washington–Baltimore)
5 **Pittyoung** (Pittsburgh–Youngstown)
6 **Miamilaud** (Miami-Fort Lauderdale)
7 **Hougalbeau** (Houston–Galveston–Beaumont)
8 **Dalworth** (Dallas–Fort Worth)
9 **Denboul** (Denver–Boulder)
10 **San Angeles** (Los Angeles–San Diego)
11 **San Franjose** (San Francisco–San Jose)
12 **Seatac** (Seattle–Tacoma)
13 **Chimilgar** (Chicago–Milwaukee–Gary)
14 **Detanntol** (Detroit–Ann Arbor–Toledo)
15 **Clevak** (Cleveland–Akron)

Figure 9-3 Major urban regions in the United States. Largest regions are shown in the darker color. (Data from U.S. Census Bureau)

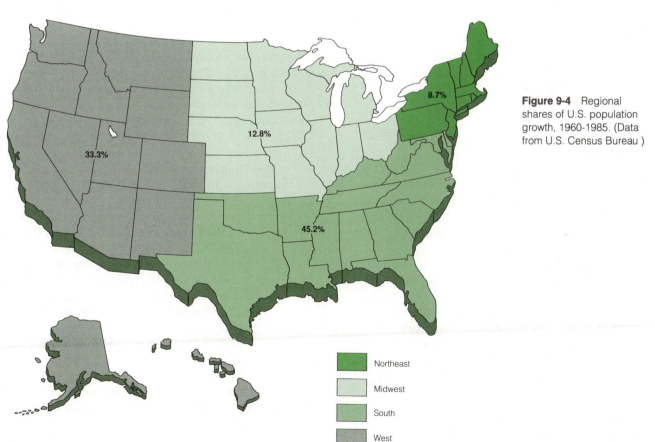

Figure 9-4 Regional shares of U.S. population growth, 1960-1985. (Data from U.S. Census Bureau)

Northeast

Midwest

South

West

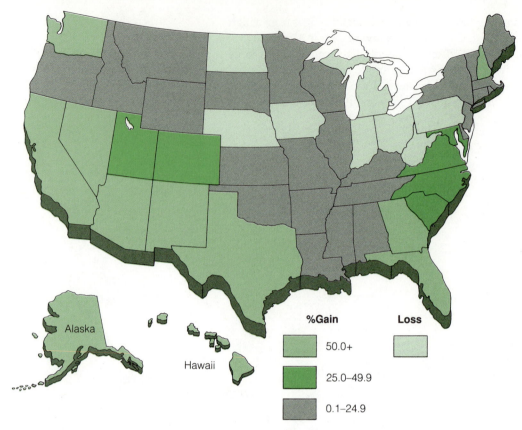

Figure 9-5 Projected percent change in population size by state, 1980–2010. (Data from U.S. Census Bureau and Population Reference Bureau)

%Gain		Loss	
	50.0+		(light green)
	25.0–49.9		
	0.1–24.9		

and East. This shift is projected to continue, with the South having the largest population increase between 1987 and 2010, followed by the West (Figure 9-5).

9-2 PATTERNS OF URBAN GROWTH AND DEVELOPMENT

The Rise of Towns and Cities Towns and cities are a fairly recent phenomenon. The first settlements evolved about 5,500 years ago in Asia when food production from agriculture increased to the point where everyone did not need to be a farmer.

Environmental factors strongly influence where cities are built. Most of the earliest cities were built along the banks of large rivers or near ocean harbors. Rivers were an abundant and dependable source of water and were used for disposal of sewage and other wastes. They also served as transportation routes for trade and for bringing in resources from other areas. Other early cities were built on sites that could easily be defended or near important mineral deposits.

The size of early cities was restricted by the ability of primitive transportation methods to bring food and other necessary resources into the city and to remove wastes. Increasing use of boats, harbors, barges, canals, roads, horses, and wagons allowed the development of larger cities. But these cities never had a population of more than 1 million, and there were few cities of this size. Early cities were compact because the most common mode of transportation was walking. The city could be no larger than the distance a worker could walk to work.

The Industrial Revolution changed this. Factories created jobs in cities, and industrialized agriculture meant that food could be produced by fewer farmers. Rivers near cities were tapped to supply water power for running machinery and producing electricity. Trains, motor-powered ships, trolleys, trucks, and cars allowed a larger inflow of resources. New cities sprang up along railroad lines and later along major highways. Populations of large cities increased, but so did pollution.

Because of modern transportation, construction, and communications, there are fewer limitations on urban growth and location than there were in the early stages of the Industrial Revolution. Today, terrain can be flattened, wetlands and shallow coastal waters filled, and dikes and bulkheads constructed. Water can be brought in from distant lakes and rivers and pumped up from deep underground deposits. Increasingly, large cities develop in areas with warm climates (for example, Florida and California) and near coastlines and lakes.

During the past 100 years new modes of transportation and construction have enabled cities with suitable surrounding land to expand outward. Workers can commute from the suburbs to the central city and within and between suburbs. Because of trucks, factories don't have to be near railroad tracks and warehouses don't have to be near docks. Most people living in cities experiencing urban sprawl are dependent on the automobile for transportation.

The invention of the elevator and new construction methods made taller buildings practical, allowing cities to expand upward and to have higher population densities. Upward expansion is the only way that cities such as New York, Tokyo, and Hong Kong, without room to expand outward, can increase in population size. A leading example of this upward trend is New York City's World Trade Center. This office complex, designed to accommodate 50,000 workers, consumes as much electricity as a typical American city with 100,000 inhabitants.

Spatial Patterns of Urban Development   Cities have various recognizable spatial structures. Major factors determining the spatial character of a city are its historical development, land availability (especially nearby flat agricultural land that can be converted to urban land), topography, rate of population growth, transportation and utility systems, economic development, and political system. A good city site includes a firm rock base, well-drained land for buildings, good nearby agricultural land and water supplies, and a benign local climate.

Three models of urban structure are shown in Figure 9-6. Although no city perfectly matches any of them, these simplified models can be used to identify key patterns of urban development.

A city resembling the *concentric-circle model* develops outward from its central business district (CBD) in a series of rings. Typically, industries and businesses in the CBD are surrounded by circular zones of housing that become more affluent as one moves outward into the suburbs. In many LDCs, however, the affluent live mostly in the central city and many of the poor live in squatter settlements that spring up around the central core.

A city resembling the *sector model* grows in a system of pie-shaped wedges, or ribbons. These growth sectors develop when commercial, industrial, and housing districts push outward from the central business district along major transportation routes. In the *multiple-nuclei model* a large city develops around a number of independent centers, or nuclei, rather than a single center.

Some cities develop in a combination of these patterns. Today many urban areas are spreading out and merging with other urban areas to form a large urban area, or megalopolis. For example, the remaining open space between Boston and Washington, D.C., is being rapidly urbanized and merged. The giant urban area, sometimes called Bowash, is becoming a sprawling megalopolis with almost 50 million people. This and other megalopolises forming as major U.S. cities spread out and merge are shown in Figure 9-3.

If suitable rural land is not available for conversion to urban land, a city grows upward, not outward; it occupies a relatively small area and develops a high population density. Most people living in such compact cities walk, ride bicycles, or use energy-efficient mass transit. Most residents live in multistory apartment buildings with shared walls that have an insulating effect, reducing heating and cooling costs. Because of the lack of land, many European cities are compact and tend to be more energy efficient than the dispersed cities of the United States.

A combination of cheap gasoline, a large supply of rural land suitable for urban development, and a network of highways usually results in a dispersed city with a low population density. Most people living in such a city rely on cars with low energy efficiencies for transportation within the central city, to and from the central city, and within and between suburbs. Most people live in single-family houses, whose unshared walls lose and gain heat rapidly unless they are well insulated.

Another key factor determining whether a city is compact or dispersed is a society's political economy. For example, in socialist countries of eastern Europe, which generally have centralized government planning, cities tend to be compact and energy efficient. But in capitalistic MDCs and LDCs, which have little centralized planning and control, cities tend to be dispersed and energy inefficient. The transportation systems and growth patterns in such cities develop primarily to serve the accumulation of private capital.

9-3   ENVIRONMENTAL AND RESOURCE PROBLEMS OF URBAN AREAS

Effects of Urban Areas on Resources and Environment   Cities give the illusion of self-sufficiency, efficiency, and independence from natural processes. But urban areas are not self-sustaining, and most use resources inefficiently compared to natural communities. An urban area must take in air, water, energy, food, and other resources, and produce wastes as these resources are used to sustain life (Figures 9-7 and 9-8). Cities survive only by importing large quantities of food, water, energy, minerals, and other resources

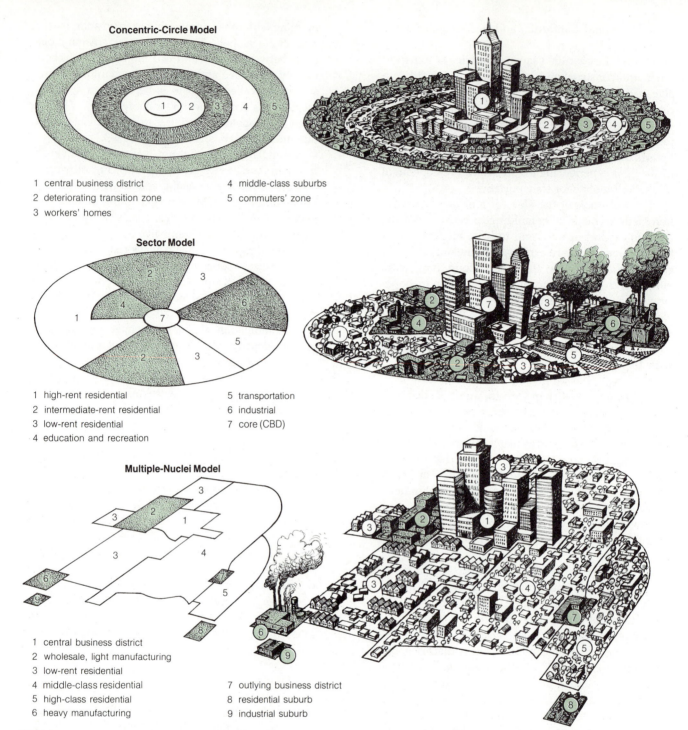

Concentric-Circle Model

1 central business district
2 deteriorating transition zone
3 workers' homes
4 middle-class suburbs
5 commuters' zone

Sector Model

1 high-rent residential
2 intermediate-rent residential
3 low-rent residential
4 education and recreation
5 transportation
6 industrial
7 core (CBD)

Multiple-Nuclei Model

1 central business district
2 wholesale, light manufacturing
3 low-rent residential
4 middle-class residential
5 high-class residential
6 heavy manufacturing
7 outlying business district
8 residential suburb
9 industrial suburb

Figure 9-6 Three models of urban spatial structure. (Modified with permission from Harm J. deBlij, *Human Geography*, New York: John Wiley, 1977)

from near and distant farmlands, forests, mines, and watersheds. Most cities produce only a small fraction of the food their populations consume. Instead of being recycled, most of the solid, liquid, and gaseous wastes of cities are discharged into or eventually end up in air, water, and land outside their boundaries.

As urban areas grow, their resource input needs and pollution outputs place increasing stress on distant aquifers, wetlands, estuaries, forests, croplands, rangelands, wilderness, and other ecosystems. Water and land scarcity, pollution, waste disposal, and inefficient energy use contribute to the escalating economic and ecological costs of supporting modern cities. In the words of Theodore Roszak:

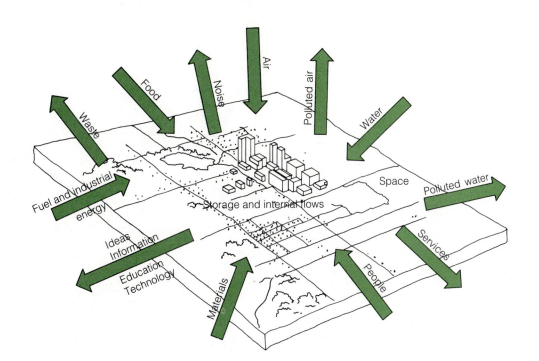

Figure 9-7 Crude model of major inputs and outputs of an urban area. (Modified with permission from T. R. Detwyler and M. G. Marcus, *Urbanization and Environment: The Physical Geography of the City;* Belmont, Calif.: Wadsworth, 1972).

Figure 9-8 Typical daily input and output of matter and energy for a U.S. city of I million people.

U.S. city of
1 million people

Daily Inputs

Daily Outputs

water
568 million kilograms
(625,000 tons)

fuel
8.6 million kilograms
(9,500 tons)

food
1.8 million kilograms
(2,000 tons)

sewage
454 million kilograms
(500,000 tons)

air pollutants
864 thousand kilograms
(950 tons)

refuse
8.6 million kilograms
(9,500 tons)

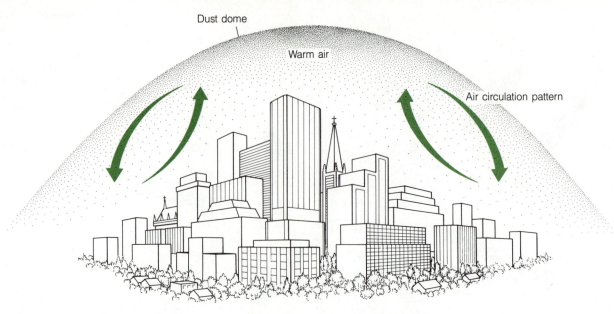

Figure 9-9 An urban heat island causes air circulation patterns that create a dust dome over the city. Winds elongate the dome toward downwind areas. A strong cold front can blow the dome away and lower urban pollution levels.

The supercity . . . stretches out tentacles of influence that reach thousands of miles beyond its already sprawling parameters. It sucks every hinterland and wilderness into its technological metabolism. It forces rural populations off the land and replaces them with vast agroindustrial combines. Its investments and technicians bring the roar of the bulldozer and oil derrick into the most uncharted quarters. It runs its conduits of transport and communication, its lines of supply and distribution through the wildest landscapes. It flushes its wastes into every nearby river, lake, and ocean or trucks them away into desert areas. The world becomes its garbage can.

Vegetation   Urban areas generally have a scarcity of trees, shrubs, and other natural vegetation. As one observer remarked, "Cities are places where they cut down the trees and then name the streets after them." This is unfortunate because urban plants absorb air pollutants, give off oxygen, and help cool the air as water evaporates from their leaves. Three well-placed trees can cut home air conditioning bills as much as 50%. Urban trees and other vegetation muffle noise, provide habitats for wildlife such as birds and squirrels, and satisfy the important psychological need of city dwellers to experience natural surroundings.

Urban Microclimate   Urbanization alters local and sometimes regional climate. Average temperatures, precipitation, fog, and cloudiness are generally higher in cities than in suburbs and nearby rural areas.

The cars, factories, furnaces, air conditioners, and people in cities generate enormous amounts of heat. In the United States, for example, energy use is so high that at any given moment each of the 249 million Americans is directly and indirectly injecting heat into the atmosphere equal to the heat of one hundred 100-watt light bulbs. The tall buildings, paved streets, and parking areas in cities absorb heat and obstruct cooling winds. Rainfall runs off quickly so that little standing water is available to cool the air through evaporation.

The effect of this atmospheric heating is felt in large cities, which are typically like islands of heat surrounded by cooler suburban and rural areas. This microclimatic effect is known as an **urban heat island** (Figure 9-9). As cities grow and merge into vast urban regions, the heat from the cities forms regional heat islands, which affect regional climates and prevent polluted air from being effectively diluted and cleansed.

This dome of heat also traps pollutants, especially tiny solid particles (suspended particulate matter), creating a **dust dome** above urban areas. As a result, concentrations of suspended particulate matter over urban-industrial areas may be 10 to 1,000 times higher than those over rural areas. If wind speeds increase, the dust dome elongates downwind to form a dust plume, which spreads the city's pollutants to rural areas and other urban areas up to hundreds of miles away.

Urban heat islands increase the use of air conditioners, which spew even more waste heat into the atmosphere. The situation will get worse if the greenhouse effect continues unabated, causing warmer temperatures, droughts, falling reservoirs, and the dieback of urban vegetation.

Water, Runoff, and Flooding As cities grow and their water demands increase, expensive reservoirs, aqueducts, and deeper wells must be built. The transfer of water to urban areas decreases water supplies in rural and wild areas and sometimes depletes underground aquifers faster than they are replenished (Chapter 11).

Covering land with buildings, asphalt, and concrete means that precipitation cannot soak into the earth. Instead, it runs off quickly and can overload sewers and storm drains, contributing to water pollution and flooding in cities and downstream areas. Moreover, many cities are built on floodplains, areas subject to periodic natural flooding. Floodplains are considered prime land for urbanization because they are flat, accessible, usually near rivers, and easy to develop. Besides being susceptible to flooding, urban areas generally suffer more flood damage than rural areas because they have greater concentrations of people and buildings.

Cities built in areas with high water tables (the upper levels of underground water) also have problems. Buildings settle and water can seep into basements. Some cities, especially near coasts, have been expanded by draining and filling swamps and marshes. These areas sometimes slowly sink and are susceptible to flooding from a storm or a slight rise in sea level. Many of the world's largest cities are in coastal areas. If the greenhouse effect is not abated, a rise in average sea level of even a meter or so could flood many of *these costal cities*

Solid Waste and Air and Water Pollution Cities produce and concentrate large quantities of garbage, other solid waste, and air and water pollution. Thus, urban residents are generally subjected to much higher concentrations of pollutants than people in rural areas. However, some of the air and water pollutants produced in urban areas are transported by winds and flowing water to other cities and to rural and wild areas.

From 50% to 85% of urban air pollution is caused by motor vehicles, depending on the city. Smog is now a virtually unavoidable aspect of urban life in most of the world. In 1988 the World Health Organization warned that nearly 1 billion city dwellers are being exposed to health hazards from air pollutants. Air pollution is discussed in more detail in Chapter 19, water pollution in Chapter 20, solid waste in Chapter 15, and hazardous waste in Chapter 18.

Noise According to the Environmental Protection Agency, nearly half of all Americans, mostly urban residents, are regularly exposed in their neighborhoods and jobs to levels of noise—unwanted or harmful sound—that interfere with communication or sleep. Every day 1 of every 10 Americans lives, works, or

plays around noise of sufficient duration and intensity to cause some permanent loss of hearing, and this number is rising rapidly.

Industrial workers head the list, with 19 million hearing-damaged people in an industrial work force of 75 million. Each day 5 million U.S. workers are exposed to unsafe noise levels for eight hours. Millions of people who listen to music at loud levels using home stereos, portable stereos ("jam boxes") held close to the ear, and earphones are also damaging their hearing. Studies have shown that 60% of the incoming students at the University of Tennessee have significant hearing loss in the high frequency range. In effect,

Table 9-2 Effects of Common Sounds

Example	Sound Pressure (dbA)	Effect from Prolonged Exposure
Jet takeoff (25 meters away*)	150	Eardrum rupture
Aircraft carrier deck	140	
Armored personnel carrier, jet takeoff (100 meters away), earphones at loud level	130	
Thunderclap, textile loom, live rock music, jet takeoff (161 meters away), siren (close range), chain saw	120	Human pain threshold
Steel mill, riveting, automobile horn at 1 meter, "jam box" stereo held close to ear	110	
Jet takeoff (305 meters away), subway, outboard motor, power lawn mower, motorcycle at 8 meters, farm tractor, printing plant, jackhammer, garbage truck	100	Serious hearing damage (8 hours)
Busy urban street, diesel truck, food blender, cotton spinning machine	90	Hearing damage (8 hours), speech interference
Garbage disposal, clothes washer, average factory, freight train at 15 meters, dishwasher, blender	80	Possible hearing damage
Freeway traffic at 15 meters, vacuum cleaner, noisy office or party, TV audio	70	Annoying
Conversation in restaurant, average office, background music, chirping bird	60	Intrusive
Quiet suburb (daytime), conversation in living room	50	Quiet
Library, soft background music	40	
Quiet rural area (nighttime)	30	
Whisper, rustling leaves	20	Very quiet
Breathing	10	
	0	Threshold of hearing

*To convert meters to feet, multiply by 3.3

these and many other young people are entering their twenties with the hearing capability of people in their sixties.

To determine harmful levels of noise, sound pressure is measured in decibels (db) with a decibel meter. Sounds also have pitch (frequency), and high-pitched sounds seem louder and more annoying than low-pitched sounds at the same intensity. Normally, sound pressure is weighted for high-pitched sounds to which people are more sensitive and expressed in the decibel-A (dbA) scale, in dbA units, as shown in Table 9-2.

Sound pressure becomes damaging at about 75 dbA, painful at around 120 dbA, and deadly at 180 dbA. Because the db and dbA sound pressure scales are logarithmic, a tenfold increase in sound pressure occurs with each 10-decibel rise. Thus, a rise from 30 dbA (quiet rural area) to 60 dbA (normal restaurant conversation) represents a 1,000-fold increase in sound pressure on the ear.

Harmful effects from excessive noise include permanent hearing loss, high blood pressure, tense muscles, migraine headaches, an increase in cholesterol levels, gastric ulcers, and psychological stress. You are being exposed to a sound level high enough to cause permanent hearing damage if you need to raise your voice to be heard above the racket, a noise causes your ears to ring, or nearby speech seems muffled. Noise can be reduced in several ways (see Spotlight on p. 197).

Land Conversion As urban areas expand, they swallow up rural land, especially flat or gently rolling land with well-drained, fertile soil. Once farmland is paved over or built upon, it is permanently lost for food production. This loss forces farmers to produce food on marginal land with poor and easily erodible soils, often in regions that require irrigation. Farming such land increases soil erosion, water pollution (from sediment

Water, Runoff, and Flooding As cities grow and their water demands increase, expensive reservoirs, aqueducts, and deeper wells must be built. The transfer of water to urban areas decreases water supplies in rural and wild areas and sometimes depletes underground aquifers faster than they are replenished (Chapter 11).

Covering land with buildings, asphalt, and concrete means that precipitation cannot soak into the earth. Instead, it runs off quickly and can overload sewers and storm drains, contributing to water pollution and flooding in cities and downstream areas. Moreover, many cities are built on floodplains, areas subject to periodic natural flooding. Floodplains are considered prime land for urbanization because they are flat, accessible, usually near rivers, and easy to develop. Besides being susceptible to flooding, urban areas generally suffer more flood damage than rural areas because they have greater concentrations of people and buildings.

Cities built in areas with high water tables (the upper levels of underground water) also have problems. Buildings settle and water can seep into basements. Some cities, especially near coasts, have been expanded by draining and filling swamps and marshes. These areas sometimes slowly sink and are susceptible to flooding from a storm or a slight rise in sea level. Many of the world's largest cities are in coastal areas. If the greenhouse effect is not abated, a rise in average sea level of even a meter or so could flood many of these coastal cities

Solid Waste and Air and Water Pollution Cities produce and concentrate large quantities of garbage, other solid waste, and air and water pollution. Thus, urban residents are generally subjected to much higher concentrations of pollutants than people in rural areas. However, some of the air and water pollutants produced in urban areas are transported by winds and flowing water to other cities and to rural and wild areas.

From 50% to 85% of urban air pollution is caused by motor vehicles, depending on the city. Smog is now a virtually unavoidable aspect of urban life in most of the world. In 1988 the World Health Organization warned that nearly 1 billion city dwellers are being exposed to health hazards from air pollutants. Air pollution is discussed in more detail in Chapter 19, water pollution in Chapter 20, solid waste in Chapter 15, and hazardous waste in Chapter 18.

Noise According to the Environmental Protection Agency, nearly half of all Americans, mostly urban residents, are regularly exposed in their neighborhoods and jobs to levels of noise—unwanted or harmful sound—that interfere with communication or sleep. Every day 1 of every 10 Americans lives, works, or

---

SPOTLIGHT Controlling Noise

Modern urban societies can reduce excessive noise by building and using quieter industrial machinery, jackhammers, airplane and vehicle motors, vacuum cleaners, and other noisy machines. Automobiles today are quieter than ever before. Commercial airliners are 50% to 70% quieter than those of the 1960s and 1970s, but they could be made much quieter.

Workers can wear protective devices to reduce the amount of noise entering their ears. Noisy factory operations can be totally or partially enclosed by walls. Houses and other buildings can be insulated to reduce sound transfer (and energy waste). Governments can set noise control standards for equipment, and cities can enact and strictly enforce noise control laws.

The control of noise pollution in the United States has lagged behind that in the Soviet Union and many western European and Scandinavian countries. Noise is not effectively controlled in the United States because of industry pressure against establishing stricter workplace noise standards, the virtual elimination of the EPA's budget for noise pollution control since 1981, and lax enforcement of noise control laws.

Europeans have developed quieter jackhammers, pile drivers, and air compressors that do not cost much more than their noisy counterparts. Most European countries also require that small sheds and tents be used to muffle construction noise. Some countries reduce the clanging associated with garbage collection by using rubberized collection trucks. Subway systems in Montreal and Mexico City have rubberized wheels to reduce noise. In France, cars are required to have separate highway and city horns, the latter much quieter than the former.

---

plays around noise of sufficient duration and intensity to cause some permanent loss of hearing, and this number is rising rapidly.

Industrial workers head the list, with 19 million hearing-damaged people in an industrial work force of 75 million. Each day 5 million U.S. workers are exposed to unsafe noise levels for eight hours. Millions of people who listen to music at loud levels using home stereos, portable stereos ("jam boxes") held close to the ear, and earphones are also damaging their hearing. Studies have shown that 60% of the incoming students at the University of Tennessee have significant hearing loss in the high frequency range. In effect,

Table 9-2 Effects of Common Sounds

Example	Sound Pressure (dbA)	Effect from Prolonged Exposure
Jet takeoff (25 meters away*)	150	Eardrum rupture
Aircraft carrier deck	140	
Armored personnel carrier, jet takeoff (100 meters away), earphones at loud level	130	
Thunderclap, textile loom, live rock music, jet takeoff (161 meters away), siren (close range), chain saw	120	Human pain threshold
Steel mill, riveting, automobile horn at 1 meter, "jam box" stereo held close to ear	110	
Jet takeoff (305 meters away), subway, outboard motor, power lawn mower, motorcycle at 8 meters, farm tractor, printing plant, jackhammer, garbage truck	100	Serious hearing damage (8 hours)
Busy urban street, diesel truck, food blender, cotton spinning machine	90	Hearing damage (8 hours), speech interference
Garbage disposal, clothes washer, average factory, freight train at 15 meters, dishwasher, blender	80	Possible hearing damage
Freeway traffic at 15 meters, vacuum cleaner, noisy office or party, TV audio	70	Annoying
Conversation in restaurant, average office, background music, chirping bird	60	Intrusive
Quiet suburb (daytime), conversation in living room	50	Quiet
Library, soft background music	40	
Quiet rural area (nighttime)	30	
Whisper, rustling leaves	20	Very quiet
Breathing	10	
	0	Threshold of hearing

*To convert meters to feet, multiply by 3.3

these and many other young people are entering their twenties with the hearing capability of people in their sixties.

To determine harmful levels of noise, sound pressure is measured in decibels (db) with a decibel meter. Sounds also have pitch (frequency), and high-pitched sounds seem louder and more annoying than low-pitched sounds at the same intensity. Normally, sound pressure is weighted for high-pitched sounds to which people are more sensitive and expressed in the decibel-A (dbA) scale, in dbA units, as shown in Table 9-2.

Sound pressure becomes damaging at about 75 dbA, painful at around 120 dbA, and deadly at 180 dbA. Because the db and dbA sound pressure scales are logarithmic, a tenfold increase in sound pressure occurs with each 10-decibel rise. Thus, a rise from 30 dbA (quiet rural area) to 60 dbA (normal restaurant conversation) represents a 1,000-fold increase in sound pressure on the ear.

Harmful effects from excessive noise include permanent hearing loss, high blood pressure, tense muscles, migraine headaches, an increase in cholesterol levels, gastric ulcers, and psychological stress. You are being exposed to a sound level high enough to cause permanent hearing damage if you need to raise your voice to be heard above the racket, a noise causes your ears to ring, or nearby speech seems muffled. Noise can be reduced in several ways (see Spotlight on p. 197).

Land Conversion As urban areas expand, they swallow up rural land, especially flat or gently rolling land with well-drained, fertile soil. Once farmland is paved over or built upon, it is permanently lost for food production. This loss forces farmers to produce food on marginal land with poor and easily erodible soils, often in regions that require irrigation. Farming such land increases soil erosion, water pollution (from sediment

Figure 9-10 Every year, about 364,000 hectares (900,000 acres) of rural land—mostly cropland—are converted to urban development, rights-of-way, highways, and airports in the United States.

runoff), and air pollution (from dust) and requires high energy inputs.

The UN Food and Agriculture Organization estimates that worldwide about 1.4 billion hectares (3.5 billion acres) of land will be removed from agricultural use between 1980 and 2000 because of urban growth. The United States has some of the earth's best agricultural lands. But each year about 364,000 hectares (900,000 acres) of rural land—mostly cropland—is converted to urban and transportation uses (Figure 9-10). This is equivalent in area to a half-mile-wide highway stretching from New York City to Los Angeles.

The total land involved is small compared to the total land area or the total cropland of the United States. But the impact at local and regional levels can be significant. In the country's top 100 agricultural counties, urban development is twice the national rate.

The Quality of Urban Life   Centuries ago the Greek philosopher Aristotle said that people go to cities "to lead the good life." Many, especially the affluent, do find the good life in cities. But for many urban residents the good life is getting harder and harder to find.

Many cities, especially large ones, are too congested with cars, too noisy, and too frustrating. Crime rates are high and many people are afraid to go outdoors at night. The number of homeless people is increasing. Neighborhood sidewalks used to be social gathering places and neighbors knew and helped one another. Today few people in most neighborhoods and high-rise buildings know one another. For many, a city is a place of loneliness and fear. They are surrounded with concrete and asphalt monotony instead of open space, green landscapes, and clear sky.

9-4   URBAN TRANSPORTATION

Transportation Options   An urban area's transportation system is a major factor affecting its economic activity, spatial pattern, and quality of life. People in urban areas move from one place to another by three major types of transportation:

- individual transit by private automobile, taxi, motorcycle, moped, scooter, bicycle, and walking

- mass transit by railroad, subway, trolley, and bus

- paratransit involving car pools, van pools, jitneys or van taxis traveling along fixed routes, and dial-a-ride systems

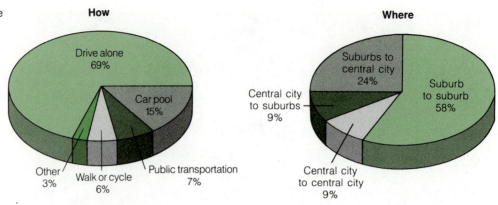

Figure 9-11 How people in the United States go to and from work. (Data from U.S. Census Bureau)

How

Drive alone 69%

Car pool 15%

Other 3%

Walk or cycle 6%

Public transportation 7%

Where

Suburbs to central city 24%

Suburb to suburb 58%

Central city to suburbs 9%

Central city to central city 9%

Automobiles Cars have reshaped our geographic and cultural landscape. They offer us many advantages, but the price we pay for these advantages is becoming increasingly high (see Pro/Con on p. 201).

In the United States the car is now used for about 98% of all urban transportation, 85% of all travel between cities, and 84% of all travel to and from work (Figure 9-11). In widely dispersed American cities like Los Angeles, Detroit, Denver, Phoenix, and Houston, 88% to 94% of the people drive to and from work. Instead of using car or van pools, most people commute alone. The average occupancy per passenger vehicle in the United States is 1.2.

The original interstate highway system was designed to carry motorists primarily from city to city, and its beltways were built mainly as city bypasses for long-distance travelers. Instead, these highways allowed the rapid growth of suburban areas, which now have 60% of urban jobs and 67% of all new ones. So many people and businesses have moved to the suburbs that the number of commuters within or between suburbs has grown twice as fast as the number commuting to a central city. These commuters now jam the beltways, a problem not anticipated by most urban planners.

Some cities have tried to deal with the problem of traffic gridlock. By the mid-1970s commuter traffic in Atlanta, Georgia, was jammed. In 1978 the city responded with a $1.4 billion plan for "freeing the freeways." Traffic engineers used computer models to learn where to expand existing roads and where to streamline the system by eliminating bottleneck entrances and exits and expanding the number of lanes. Today the system can handle four times as much traffic as the old system. But at least $7 billion must be spent on highway and transit improvements between 1989 and 2010 to keep the projected level of congestion from rising.

Another way to reduce traffic gridlock is to control traffic flow with computer-adjusted stoplights on freeway on-ramps. Observers can use remote TV cameras to spot vehicle breakdowns and immediately dispatch tow trucks. Freeway express lanes reserved for buses, van pools, and car pools would discourage car use and encourage bus and car pool ridership. The tax write-off for businesses that subsidize their employees' parking could be eliminated and replaced with a subsidy for employees using mass transit, bicycles, and car pools.

Average per capita gasoline consumption in dispersed U.S. cities is four times that of more compact European cities, where only 40% of urban residents drive to and from work. It is over ten times that of the highly compact cities Hong Kong, Tokyo, and Singapore, where only 15% of the people commute to work by car.

Bicycles The bicycle is fast becoming the best way to move quickly through congested urban traffic. In LDCs it is the most affordable way to get around because a car may cost more than a worker earns in a decade.

Worldwide, there are twice as many bicycles as cars, and annual bicycle sales exceed automobile sales. A bicycle is 98% less expensive to buy and operate than a car, uses no fossil fuels, produces no pollution or carbon dioxide, and takes few resources to make. A bicycle requires less energy per passenger mile than any other form of transportation, including walking.

In urban traffic, cars and bicycles move at about the same average speed. Using separate bike paths running along roads, bicycle riders can make most trips under five miles (which make up about 43% percent of all urban travel in the United States) faster than a car. Bike paths also improve safety for riders. Bicycle accidents can cause injuries, but they are unlikely to kill people unless motor vehicles are involved. For longer trips, secure bike parking spaces can be provided at mass transit stations or buses and trains can be equipped to carry bicycles. Such systems are very popular in Japan, West Germany, the Netherlands (which has more miles of bicycle paths than any other country), and Denmark.

In the United States the number of cars and trucks is growing twice as fast as the number of people. With only 4.8% of the world's people, the United States has one-third of the world's cars. By contrast, China and India, with 37% of the world's people, have only 0.5% of its cars.

In America's dispersed cities cars are not just a necessity, they are a way of life. The average number of miles each U.S. motorist travels has doubled since 1960. No wonder British author J. B. Priestly remarked, "In America, the cars have become the people."

The automobile has many advantages. Above all, it offers people freedom to go where they want to go, when they want to go there. The basic purpose of a motor vehicle is to get one from point A to point B. But to most people cars are also personal fantasy machines that serve as symbols of power, speed, excitement, sexiness, spontaneity, and adventure.

In addition, much of the world's economy is built around producing and supplying roads, services, and repairs for the world's motor vehicles. Half of the world's paychecks and resource use are auto related.

In the United States one of every six dollars spent and one of every six nonfarm jobs are connected to the automobile or related industries such as oil, steel, rubber, plastics, automobile services, and highway construction. This industrial complex accounts for 20% of the annual GNP and provides about 18% of all federal taxes.

In spite of their advantages, motor vehicles have many harmful effects on human lives and on air, water, and land resources. Since 1885 when Karl Benz built the first automobile, about 17 million people have been killed by motor vehicles—130 times the number killed at Hiroshima. Though we tend to deny it, riding in cars is one of the most dangerous things we do in our daily lives.

Worldwide, cars and trucks kill an average of 200,000 people, maim 500,000, and injure 10 million a year. On the average an automobile-related death occurs about every 3 minutes and a disabling injury occurs every 20 seconds. Half of the world's people will be involved in an auto accident at some time during their lives.

Each year in the United States motor vehicle accidents kill around 48,000 people and seriously injure at least 300,000. Since the automobile was introduced, almost 2 million Americans have been killed on the highways—about twice the number of Americans killed in all U.S. wars. Like war, highway fatalities and injuries take their toll disproportionately on the young. If present trends continue, 1 out of 60 American babies born today will die in an automobile accident before the age of 21. Each year the number of Americans killed in motor vehicle accidents is over twice the number killed by violent crime. These accidents cost society about $60 billion annually in lost income and in insurance, administrative, and legal expenses. In addition, local, state, and federal governments use tax revenues to provide $400 billion a year in automobile subsidies—an average of $2,350 a year for every car and truck in the United States.

By providing almost unlimited mobility, automobiles and highways have been a major factor in urban sprawl. This dispersal of cities has made it increasingly difficult for subways, trolleys, and buses to be economically feasible alternatives to the private car.

Motor vehicles use up large areas of land. The automobile has laced U.S. cities and countryside with almost 6.4 million kilometers (4 million miles) of roads. Roads and parking space take up two-thirds of the total land area of Los Angeles, more than half of Dallas, and more than one-third of New York City and Washington, D.C. Worldwide, at least a third of the average city's land is devoted to roads and parking.

Instead of reducing automobile congestion, the construction of roads has encouraged more automobiles and travel, causing even more congestion (Figure 9-12). As economist Robert Samuelson put it, "Cars expand to fill available concrete."

The freedom we associate with the automobile is largely an illusion. If present trends continue, U.S. motorists will spend an average of two years of their lifetimes in traffic jams.

Companies are losing billions of dollars because many of their employees can't get to work on time or arrive at work tired and irritated. Nationwide traffic congestion wasted an estimated 3 billion gallons of gasoline in 1987—4% of annual U.S. consumption. Such energy waste is projected to soar to 7.3 billion gallons by 2005.

In 1907 the average speed of horse-drawn vehicles through the borough of Manhattan was 11.5 miles per hour. Today, cars and trucks with the potential power of 100 to 300 horses creep along Manhattan streets at an average speed of 5.2 miles per hour. In Los Angeles, traffic on the Hollywood Freeway slows to 20 miles per hour for about 14 hours every day. By 2010 the average speed on this freeway is projected to drop to about 7 miles per hour. In London average auto speeds are about 8 miles per hour, and even lower in Tokyo, where everyday traffic is called *tsukin jigoku*, or commuting hell. In the United States motor vehicles travel almost 2 trillion miles a year and account for 63% of the country's oil consumption (up from 50% in 1973). They produce at least 50% of the country's air pollution, *(continued)*

In most MDCs bicycles are used mainly for recreation. But they are the major means of short-distance transportation in Asia, where bicycles transport more people than do automobiles in all other countries combined. Cycle rickshaws are the taxis of Southeast Asia, and sturdy tricycles serve as light trucks that haul loads of up to half a ton. China has about 300 million bicycles—one for every four people, and in cities one for every two. India has 25 times more bicycles than motor vehicles.

The bicycle won't replace cars in the dispersed urban areas of the United States. (It's ironic that many people in the United States drive their cars to health clubs to ride exercise bicycles.) But between 1977 and 1988 the number of Americans using bicycles to commute to and from work regularly rose from approximately 500,000 to 2.7 million. This is an encouraging trend, but it still represents only 2% of all commuters. If 10% of the Americans who commute by car switched to bicycles, they would save money and reduce the U.S. oil import bill by $1.3 trillion.

We could increase bicycle use in the United States, especially in areas with warm climate and flat terrain, by building bike paths along major streets and highways and establishing bike-and-ride mass transit stations and bike-carrying buses and trains. Businesses could reduce car use, congestion, and the need for parking space by providing secure bike parking areas for employees and customers. Employers could also provide showers so that bicycle riders could freshen

even though U.S. emission standards are as strict as any in the world. Motor vehicle use is also responsible for devastating water pollution from oil spills, gasoline spills, and the dumping of used engine oil.

Most people need cars for much of their travel. But we should demand that cars be made much safer. We should also demand better urban planning to reduce traffic gridlock, and we must be willing to pay the higher taxes this will require. We should also support development of transportation alternatives—bicycle paths and flexible mass transit.

Instead of pushing for higher speed limits on rural interstate highways, we should be lobbying to maintain 55 mph limits. This would save energy and lives. Between 1986 and 1988, deaths on rural interstate highways rose 21% in the 38 states that raised the speed limit from 55 mph to 65 mph. What do you think should be done?

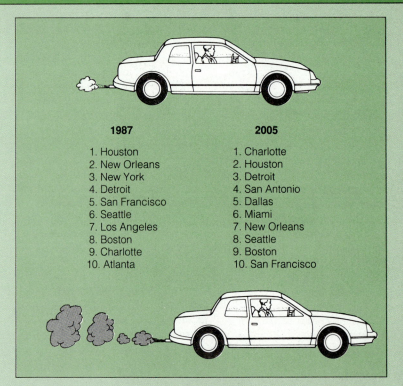

1987	2005
1. Houston	1. Charlotte
2. New Orleans	2. Houston
3. New York	3. Detroit
4. Detroit	4. San Antonio
5. San Francisco	5. Dallas
6. Seattle	6. Miami
7. Los Angeles	7. New Orleans
8. Boston	8. Seattle
9. Charlotte	9. Boston
10. Atlanta	10. San Francisco

Figure 9-12 The 10 U.S. urban areas where traffic congestion was the worst in 1987, with a projection to 2005. (Data from U.S. Department of Transportation)

up before beginning a day's work. But so far only a handful of U.S. cities such as Davis, California (see Case Study on p. 209) have extensive bike paths and secure bike parking facilities.

Mass Transit Although the total population has increased, the number of riders on all forms of mass transit in the United States has dropped drastically from 24 million in 1945 to about 8 million since 1980. This decline generally parallels the increased use of the automobile and the resulting development of increasingly dispersed cities. These interrelated social changes were stimulated by cheap gasoline and the provision of funds from federal gasoline taxes to build highways.

Only a penny of the nine cent federal gas tax goes to mass transit, with the rest going to building highways. This encourages cities to invest in highways instead of mass transit. The federal tax code also discriminates against mass transit. An employer can provide free parking to auto commuters, a tax-free benefit worth $200 to $400 a month in major cities, but can only reimburse $15 a month to those who use public transit.

Since 1970, transit system costs have increased tenfold, and in most cases their survival depends on federal, state, and local subsidies. Mass transit advocates argue that the country needs to increase its support of mass transit to help reduce dependence on imported oil, unnecessary oil waste, highway congestion, and air pollution. They also argue that mass transit systems stimulate new business development and revitalization in central cities, offsetting the federal, state, and local subsidies usually needed for their construction and operation.

European countries and cities are noted for their efficient trains and subways. But even there, rail service is gradually losing customers because increased prosperity since 1980 has enabled so many people to buy cars.

Subways, Trains, and Trolleys Mass transit systems, such as subways and urban commuter trains, have the greatest capacity to transport large numbers of people at high speed. But they are useful only where many people live along a narrow corridor. Such systems also have high construction and operating costs.

Some U.S. cities have built successful subway systems. Since Atlanta's system opened in 1979, it has steadily added riders and opened new stations. Baltimore's state-owned Metro System is also increasing service, routes, and ridership. Pittsburgh has cleaner air and renewed business vitality partly because of its new subway system, opened in 1985. Washington, D.C.'s subway system carries almost 500,000 riders a day.

Other cities, such as San Diego (see Case Study above), Sacramento, Buffalo, Portland, and Toronto,

CASE STUDY San Diego's Successful Trolley System

In the United States the trolley approach got its biggest boost in recent years from the remarkable success of San Diego's "Tijuana Trolley," running between downtown San Diego and the Mexican border city of Tijuana. Two new routes have been added since the system opened in 1981.

This system was funded by California state sales tax revenue and built at a cost per mile almost one-fourth that of San Francisco's subway system (BART). The system now has an average of 23,000 riders each weekday.

Fares pay 87% of the system's operating costs, compared to an average of 48% for all public transportation. System managers keep operating costs low by cutting out red tape, hiring a nonunion work force (possible because no federal funds were involved), and reducing the number of workers by collecting fares on the honor system. More than a dozen other U.S. cities are building trolley systems.

have built trolley systems. These are modernized versions of the streetcar systems running in most major U.S. cities in the 1930s and 1940s, before they were purchased and torn up by General Motors, Firestone Tire, and Standard Oil to increase sales of motor vehicles and buses.[*]

Trolley systems cost 5 to 20 times less per mile to build than subway systems. Although the start-up cost of a trolley system is higher than that of a bus system carrying a comparable number of passengers, a trolley system's operating costs are much lower. Trolleys are also cleaner and quieter than buses.

A possible future alternative to the automobile and the airplane for medium- and long-distance is the magnetic-levitation train, often called the bullet train. Supported and propelled by the force of powerful electromagnets, these trains could reach speeds of 300 mph or more. West Germany and Japan have prototypes in operation. A proposed bullet train line between Los Angeles and Las Vegas would make the trip, usually five hours by auto, in 70 minutes. The estimated cost would be $32, compared to $89 by commercial airline, $61 by conventional train, and $51 by automobile.

---

[*]The courts found the three companies guilty of conspiracy to eliminate about 90% of the country's light-rail system, but the damage had already been done. The corporate executive officers responsible were fined $1 each and each company paid a fine of $5,000. General Motors alone had made $25 million in additional bus and car sales by the time the case was tried.

In the 1970s Houston's public bus service was one of the most unreliable in the United States. Many buses broke down because of poor maintenance, and as many as half of those on the road ran late.

In 1978 Houston voters approved a special 1% tax on retail sales to upgrade service. Since then the city has added 789 new buses, 20 park-and-ride lots, 750 sheltered bus stops, and 5 new maintenance shops.

Houston now has a highly efficient transit system, which the American Public Transit Association ranks as the safest in the U.S. Its buses are now on schedule 98% of the time.

The city plans to expand its system of freeway express lanes and by 1991 should have more bus and carpool express lanes than any other U.S. city. Houston still has very serious traffic problems (Figure 9–12), but its citizens have supported efforts to ease traffic gridlock.

Buses and Paratransit Buses are cheaper and more flexible than rail systems. They can be routed to almost any area in widely dispersed cities and rerouted overnight to meet changing transportation patterns. Buses can zip along freeways in lanes restricted to buses, van pools, and car pools. They also require less capital and have lower operating costs than heavy rail systems.

But by offering low fares to attract riders, bus systems usually lose money. To make up for losses, bus companies tend to cut service and maintenance and seek federal, state, and local subsidies. Some cities, however, have rejuvenated their bus transit systems (see Case Study above).

Because full-sized buses are cost-effective only when full, they are being supplemented by car pools, van pools, jitneys, and dial-a-ride systems. These paratransit systems are a practical solution to some of the transportation problems of today's dispersed urban areas.

Dial-a-ride systems operate in an increasing number of American cities. Passengers call for a van, minibus, or tax-subsidized taxi, which comes by to pick them up at the doorstep, usually in about 20 to 50 minutes. Two-way radios and computerized routing can increase the efficiency of these systems. Dial-a-ride systems are fairly expensive to operate, but compared with most large-scale mass transit systems, they are a bargain.

In cities such as Mexico City, Caracas, Venezuela, and Cairo, large fleets of jitneys—small vans or minibuses that travel relatively fixed routes but stop on demand—carry millions of passengers each day. Laws banning jitney service in the United States were repealed in 1979, despite objections by taxi and transit companies. Since then privately owned jitney service has flourished in San Diego, San Francisco, and Los Angeles and may spread to other cities.

9-5 URBAN LAND-USE PLANNING AND CONTROL

Methods of Land-Use Planning Most urban areas, some rural areas, and some states (for example, Hawaii, Oregon, and Florida) practice some form of **land-use planning** to decide the best present and future use of each parcel of land in the area. Land-use planning involves mapping out suitable locations for houses, industries, businesses, open space, parks, roads, water lines, sewer lines, reservoirs, hospitals, schools, waste treatment plants, and so on. Then zoning regulations or other devices are used to control how land is used.

Many experts believe that Oregon has the best statewide land-use plan, established by law in 1973. Because of the plan, more than 6.1 million hectares (15 million acres) of farmland have been placed in farm-use-only zones and 4.9 million hectares (12 million acres) of forest have been protected. Plans to protect some rivers and streams, however, have been delayed by legal challenges from the timber industry.

Unfortunately, most land-use planners and elected officials assume that existing trends in population growth, economic growth, and other factors will continue, or they wait until a crisis occurs before doing much. These approaches rarely anticipate, prevent, or reduce the severity of long-term urban problems.

Ecological land-use planning, in which all major variables are considered and integrated into a model designed to anticipate present and future needs, is a much better method (see Spotlight on p. 205). The goal of ecological planning is to strike a balance among four major types of ecosystems: *unmanaged natural areas* (wilderness, deserts, and mountains), *managed multiple-use areas* (parks, estuaries, lakes, rivers, and some forests), *managed productive areas* (farms, cattle ranches, tree farms, and strip mines), and managed urban areas (cities and towns).

Ecological land-use planning sounds good on paper, but it is not widely used for several reasons:

- Because land is such a valuable economic resource, there is intense pressure by economically and politically powerful people to develop urban land for short-term economic gain, with little regard for long-term ecological and economic losses.

- Officials seeking reelection every few years usually focus on short-term rather than long-term problems and can often be influenced by economically powerful developers.

- Officials are unwilling to pay for costly ecological land-use planning and implementation even though a well-designed plan can prevent or ease many urban problems and save lots of money in the long run.

- It's difficult to get municipalities in the same general area to cooperate in planning efforts. Thus, an ecologically sound development plan in one area may be disrupted by unsound development in nearby areas.

Methods of Land-Use Control Once a plan is developed, governments control the uses of various parcels of land by legal and economic methods. The most widely used approach is **zoning**, in which various parcels of land are designated for certain uses. Major categories include commercial, residential, industrial, utilities, transport, recreation, and wildlife preserves.

Zoning can be used to protect areas from certain types of development and to control growth. Wealthy Marin County, California, requires that 88% of the land be used for farming, open space, and recreation. Sarasota County, Florida, is using zoning to limit most growth to four urban centers.

Zoning is useful, but it can be influenced or modified by developers because local governments depend on property taxes for revenue. Thus, zoning often favors high-priced housing, and factories, hotels, and other businesses.

In addition to zoning, local governments can control the rate of growth and development of urban areas by limiting the number of building permits, sewer hookups, roads, and other services. State and federal governments can take any of the following measures to protect cropland, forestland, wetlands, and other nonurban lands near expanding urban areas from degradation and ecologically unsound development:

- Give tax breaks to landowners who agree to use land only for specified purposes such as agriculture, wilderness, wildlife habitat, or nondestructive forms of recreation. Such agreements are called conservation easements.

- Tax land on the basis of its use as agricultural land or forestland rather than its fair market value based on its economically highest potential use. This prevents farmers and other landowners from being forced to sell land to pay their tax bills.

- Purchase and protect ecologically valuable land. Such purchases (land trusts) can be made by private groups such as the Nature Conservancy, the Audubon Society, and local and regional nonprofit, tax-exempt, charitable organizations, as well as by public agencies.

- Purchase land development rights that restrict the way land can be used (for example, to preserve prime farmland near cities from development).

- Assign a limited number of transferable development rights to a given area of land.

- Require environmental impact analysis for proposed private and public projects such as roads, industrial parks, shopping centers, and suburban developments; cancel harmful projects unless they are revised to minimize harmful environmental impact.

SPOTLIGHT Steps in Ecological Land-Use Planning

1. *Make an environmental and social inventory.* Experts make a survey of geologic factors (such as soil type, earthquake fault lines, floodplains, and water availability), ecological factors (forest types and quality, wildlife habitats, stream quality, and pollution), economic factors (housing, transportation, utilities, and industrial development), and health and social factors (disease and crime rates, ethnic distribution, and illiteracy).

2. *Determine goals and their relative importance.* Experts, public officials, and the general public decide on goals and rank them in order of importance. For example, is the primary goal to encourage or to discourage further economic development and population growth? To preserve prime cropland from development? To reduce soil erosion?

3. *Develop individual and composite maps.* Data for each factor obtained in step 1 are plotted on separate transparent plastic maps. The transparencies are then superimposed on one another or combined by computer to give three composite maps—one each for geological, ecological, and socioeconomic factors.

4. *Develop a master composite.* The three composite maps are combined to form a master composite, which shows how the variables interact and indicates the suitability of various areas for different types of land use.

5. *Develop a master plan.* The master composite (or a series of alternative master composites) is evaluated by experts, public officials, and the general public, and a final master plan is drawn up and approved.

6. *Implement the master plan.* The plan is set in motion and monitored by the appropriate governmental, legal, environmental, and social agencies.

Figure 9-13 Riverwalk area in downtown San Antonio, Texas, is a focus of the city's tourist and convention trade. It took 30 years to develop.

- Give subsidies to farmers for taking highly erodible cropland out of production or eliminate subsidies for farmers who farm such land or who convert wetlands to cropland.

9-6 MAKING URBAN AREAS MORE LIVABLE AND SUSTAINABLE

Humanizing the Urban Environment Most of our present patterns of urban development are unnecessarily stressful to natural systems and to people. Instead of planning urban development primarily to meet the physical needs of cars, urban areas should be designed to meet the basic needs of people. The human needs that should be at the heart of all urban planning are the need for diversity, for pleasant surroundings, and for economic and physical security. These needs are most likely to be met when citizens participate in planning and design.

Repairing Existing Cities As philosopher-longshoreman Eric Hoffer observed, "History shows that the level achieved by a civilization can be measured by the degree to which it performs maintenance." America's older cities have massive maintenance and repair problems—most of them aggravated by decades of neglect.

Most of the sewers in New Orleans, some of which were purchased secondhand from Philadelphia in 1896, need replacement. When it rains in Chicago, sewage backs up into basements of about one-fourth of the homes. An estimated 46% of Boston's water supply and 25% of Pittsburgh's are lost through leaky pipes.

Forty-two percent of America's bridges are in unsafe condition or are too narrow to handle their traffic loads. New York leads all states with 67% of its bridges in need of replacement or major repairs. Other states with a high percentage (55% to 63%) of deficient bridges are Connecticut, Missouri, Montana, West Virginia, Nebraska, North Carolina, and Oklahoma. About 62% of the paved highways in the United States needs repairs and 13% is in very poor condition.

Maintenance, repair, and replacement of existing U.S. bridges, roads, mass transit systems, water supply systems, sewers, and sewage treatment plants during the 1990s could cost a staggering $1.2 trillion or more—an average expenditure of $1.4 million a minute during the next 10 years. These massive bills from neglect are coming due in a time of record budget deficits, cutbacks in federal funds for building and maintaining public works, and strong citizen opposition to increases in federal, state, and local taxes. Only a small fraction of the funds needed for maintenance and repair will be made available. As a result, the public works infrastructure of the United States will continue to crumble.

Revitalizing Existing Cities Billions of dollars have been spent in decaying downtown areas to build new civic centers, museums, office buildings, parking garages, high-rise luxury hotels, and shopping centers. The city of Montreal in Canada has built a massive underground mall or "minicity" serviced by its subway system. Pittsburgh has rejuvenated its central-city area, and Boston; Baltimore; San Francisco; Long Beach, California; Norfolk, Virginia; and New Orleans have revitalized their urban waterfront areas. San Antonio, Texas, has improved its environment by planting trees and building shops along a river canal (Figure 9-13).

These projects add beauty, preserve and reuse historic buildings, and help revive downtown areas. They provide white-collar jobs for suburbanites and safe and secure shopping and cultural facilities for urban residents and tourists. Downtown revitalization can indirectly benefit the poor by providing additional tax revenues. But such projects are of little direct benefit to the poor, and sometimes they displace much-needed low-cost housing.

In many U.S. cities, older neighborhoods are being revitalized by middle- and high-income residents who buy run-down houses at low prices, renovate them, and either live in them or sell them at high prices—a process called gentrification. This benefits the city economically by increasing property tax values and slowing the flight of businesses and people to the suburbs. But it also displaces low-income residents.

A number of cities have set up urban homesteading programs to help middle- and low-income people purchase houses and apartment buildings abandoned by their owners or acquired by a city because of failure to pay taxes. The city sells these buildings to individuals or to cooperatives of low-income renters for $1 to $100 or provides buyers with low-interest, long-term loans. The new owners must agree to renovate the buildings and live in them for at least three years. This approach has been particularly successful in Wilmington, Delaware, and in Baltimore, Maryland.

Revitalizing Public Housing America is increasingly becoming a nation of housing haves and have-nots. Poor and middle-income families in the United States are facing a housing crisis. Of the 13 million families with incomes under $10,000 a year, nearly half pay more than 50% of their income for housing. Many middle-income families cannot afford to buy a home.

Jobless rates in many central cities are often 30% to 40%. Federal support for subsidized low-income housing was slashed 81% between 1981 and 1988. During this period 2.5 million units of low-income housing and single-room occupancy hotels were torn down, abandoned, or converted to high-rent apartments, luxury condominiums, and office buildings.

Between 1988 and 1993 another 200,000 units of low-income housing could disappear and 864,000 poor families will lose their rent subsidies. By 2003 the gap between the number of people needing low-income housing and the number of available units is expected to be 7.8 million.

By 1989 between 300,000 and 4 million people in the U.S. were homeless. The estimates vary because of the difficulty in counting the homeless. Almost one-fourth of the homeless counted in surveys are children (40% to 50% in some areas), and about one-third are families with children. An estimated one-third of homeless adults are mentally ill (most released from state institutions in the 1970s and 1980s) and one-third are alcoholics or abusers of other drugs. About one-fourth of the people living in shelters have jobs but cannot find an affordable place to live. Regardless of the figures, the number of homeless is expected to rise sharply in the 1990s.

One way to help some of the poor would be to provide aid for low-income tenants to renovate and manage many of the country's 1.3 million public housing units and the 70,000 abandoned units (see Case Study below). Also, the government could provide more aid and lower interest rates to help low- and middle-income families buy homes.

CASE STUDY Tenant-Owned Public Housing

In 1981 the 3,500 tenants of the Kenilworth-Parkside public housing project in Washington, D.C., lived in a crime-ridden, drug-infested neighborhood. For three years they had no heat or hot water and the roofs of their apartments were caving in. Today residents have turned the once squalid project into safe, well-kept buildings.

Things began turning around in 1982, when Kimi Gray, an unemployed welfare mother of five, persuaded housing authorities to let her and other tenants run the project. Gray was also able to get $23 million in federal aid for renovation of all 464 units. Under her leadership the tenants evicted drug dealers, and at least one member of each family was required to take six weeks of training in home repairs, pest control,

and personal budgeting. Residents took turns as hall and building captains.

Within a few years residents had cleaned up the area, made repairs, and restored utilities. Crime has dropped sharply, rent collections have risen by 77%, administrative costs have been reduced by 66%, welfare dependency has fallen from 85% to 2%, and teenage pregnancies have been cut in half.

With aid from the federal government, the tenants have established a day-care center (only for tenants who are working or actively looking for work), a food co-op, barber and beauty shops, a moving company, a construction-management firm, a treatment center for residents addicted to alcohol or other drugs, and a van shuttle that takes residents to jobs

in the suburbs. The tenant-run management corporation now employs more than 100 people, 80% of them residents.

The government sold the project to the management corporation for $1. In 1990, tenants were allowed to apply money they formerly paid in rent to buy their units at discounted prices.

This project required $23 million in federal aid. But in the long run this money will be recouped by the lower administrative costs (already saving the government $5.7 million in operating expenses), elimination of most welfare payments, and taxes paid by tenants who now have jobs. Kimi Gray, who now has a college degree, has successfully trained tenant leaders in St. Louis; Montgomery County, Maryland; and other urban areas.

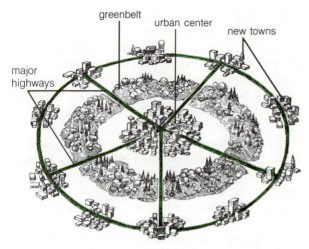

Figure 9-14 Urban growth can be controlled and open space provided by surrounding a large city with a greenbelt used for recreation and sustainable forestry and building satellite towns outside the belt. This approach has been used in London, England.

Creating Urban Enterprise Zones Some analysts call for increased federal aid to help revitalize poor urban areas. Others argue that federal aid is often wasted because it is controlled by distant bureaucrats who have little knowledge of the needs of local people. These analysts favor a program in which federal, state, and local tax breaks and other benefits are given to private companies that locate or expand in economically depressed urban areas, hire the unemployed or disadvantaged, or build or rehabilitate low-income housing. Neighborhoods that qualify for such tax breaks are called urban enterprise zones.

Since 1978, urban enterprise zones have been established in 70 cities. Results have been mixed. Some zones have been successful and some have not. In most cases it is difficult to tell whether an increase in jobs is due to normal economic growth or the lure of the zone. Some companies lay off workers in one part of an urban area and hire new ones in an enterprise zone to qualify for tax breaks. Moreover, tax breaks rarely are enough to attract businesses to the worst urban neighborhoods with high crime rates and few trained workers.

Building New Cities and Towns Most urban problems will have to be solved in existing cities. But we could ease some of these problems by building new cities and towns to take the pressure off overpopulated and stressed urban areas.

Great Britain has built 16 new towns and is building 15 more. New towns have also been built in Singapore, Hong Kong, Finland, Sweden, France, the Netherlands, Venezuela, Brazil, and the United States. There are three types: *satellite towns*, located fairly close to an existing large city (Figure 9-14); *freestanding new towns*, located far from any major city; and *in-town new*

towns, located in existing urban areas. Typically, new towns are designed for populations of 20,000 to 100,000 people.

The most widely acclaimed new town is Tapiola, Finland, a satellite town not far from Helsinki. Designed in 1952, it is being built gradually in seven sections with an ultimate projected population of 80,000. Today many of its 40,000 residents work in Helsinki, but the long-range goal is industrial and commercial independence. Tapiola is divided into several villages separated by greenbelts. Each village consists of several neighborhoods clustered around a shopping and cultural center. Each neighborhood has a social center and contains a mix of high-rise apartments and single-family houses. Finland plans to build six more new satellite towns around Helsinki.

Unfortunately, new towns rarely succeed without massive financial support from the government. Some don't succeed even then, primarily because of poor planning and management. In 1971 the Department of Housing and Urban Development (HUD) provided more than $300 million in federally guaranteed loans for developers to build 13 new towns in the United States. By 1980 HUD had to take title to nine of these projects, which had gone bankrupt, and HUD no longer funds new towns.

Private developers of new towns must put up large amounts of money to buy the land and install facilities and must pay heavy taxes and interest charges for decades before they see profit. In the United States two privately developed new towns—Reston, Virginia, and Columbia, Maryland—have been in financial difficulty since they were established almost two decades ago. However, their situations are gradually improving.

Recently a successful new town called Las Colinas has been built 8 kilometers (5 miles) from the Dallas-Fort Worth Airport on land that was once a ranch. The community is built around an urban center, with a lake and water taxis to carry passengers between buildings. The town is laced with greenbelts and open spaces to separate high-rise office buildings, warehouses, and residential buildings. People working in high-rise buildings park their cars outside the core and take a computer-controlled personal transit system.

Sustainable Urban Design and Revitalization An important goal in coming decades should be to make existing and new urban areas more self-sufficient, sustainable, and enjoyable places to live (see Case Study on p. 209). Ways to do this include the following:

- Bring home, workplace, and services closer together to cut down on energy use, transportation, and the land devoted to accommodating cars.
- Build biological sewage treatment plants in parks and other vegetated areas.

- Establish urban composting centers to convert yard and food wastes to soil conditioner for use on parks and other public lands.

- Recycle food wastes and effluents and sludge from sewage treatment plants as fertilizer for parks, roadsides, flower gardens, and recreation areas.

- Encourage water conservation by installing water meters in all buildings and raising the price of water to reflect its true cost.

- Establish small neighborhood water-recycling plants.

- Restore shorefronts, marshes, springs, creeks, and rivers (Figure 9-13).

- Recycle and reuse solid waste and some types of hazardous waste.

- Plant public areas with wildflowers and natural ground cover vegetation instead of lawns that must be drenched with water, fertilizer, and pesticides.

- Grow food in abandoned lots, community garden plots, small fruit orchards, rooftop gardens and greenhouses, apartment window boxes, and solar-heated fish ponds and tanks.

- Establish ecological land-use planning and control (see Spotlight on p. 205).

- Design buildings that are energy efficient and responsive to climate.

- Establish greenbelts of undeveloped forestland and open space within and around urban areas (see Spotlight on p. 210) and preserve nearby wetlands and agricultural land.

- Plant large numbers of trees in greenbelts, on unused lots, and along streets to reduce air pollution and noise and to provide recreational areas and wildlife habitat.

- Discourage excessive dependence on motor vehicles within urban areas by providing efficient bus and trolley service and bike lanes, charging car commuters fees to enter cities and to park their vehicles, and establishing express lanes for buses and car pools.

- Get more energy from locally available resources. Many cities can increase the energy they get from perpetual and renewable energy resources by relying more on firewood (with adequate reforestation and pollution control for wood stoves), solar energy, small-scale hydroelectric plants, farms of wind turbines, geothermal deposits, methane gas from landfills, and cogeneration of electricity and heat at industrial plants (Chapter 17).

- Enact building codes that require energy conservation and water conservation in new and existing buildings.

CASE STUDY Sustainable Living in Davis, California

Davis, California, has ample sunshine, a flat terrain, and about 38,000 people. Its citizens and elected officials have committed themselves to making it an ecologically sustainable city.

The city's building codes encourage the use of solar energy to provide space heating and hot water and require all new homes to meet high standards of energy efficiency. When any existing home is sold, the buyer must bring it up to the energy conservation standards for new homes. The community also has a master plan for planting deciduous trees, which provide shade and reduce heat gain in the summer and allow solar gain in the winter.

Davis discourages the use of automobiles and encourages the use of bicycles. Some streets are closed to automobiles, and people are encouraged to work at home. The city has built 64 kilometers (40 miles) of bicycle paths and bicycle lanes and provides some city employees with bikes. Any new housing tract must have a separate bicycle lane. As results of these measures, 28,000 bikes account for 40% of all transportation in the city, and much less land is needed for parking. This heavy dependence on the bicycle is made possible by the city's warm climate and flat terrain.

Davis also limits the type and rate of growth and maintains a mix of homes for people with low, medium, and high incomes. Development of the fertile farmland surrounding the city for residential or commercial use is restricted. What things are being done to make the area where you live more sustainable?

- Enact and enforce strict noise control laws to reduce stress from rising levels of urban noise.

- Discourage industries that produce large quantities of pollution and use large amounts of water or energy.

- Balance urban and rural needs by increasing investments and social services in rural areas.

- Do not keep urban food prices artificially low. Fixed low prices discourage food production in rural areas and eventually cause urban food shortages, greater dependence on imported food, external debts, and rural-to-urban migration.

- Legalize shantytowns and provide residents with support and low-cost loans to develop housing, water, sanitation, and utility systems, and to plant community gardens and trees for fruit, shade, and fuel.

- Stimulate sustainable growth of medium-size cities and new towns to take the pressure off overpopulated and overstressed large urban areas.

- Reduce national population growth rates.

Urban areas that fail to become more ecologically sustainable are inviting economic depression and increased unemployment, pollution, and social ten-sion. We can make urban areas better places to live and work, with less stress on natural systems and people. Each of us has an important role in converting this dream to reality.

The city is not an ecological monstrosity. It is rather the place where both the problems and the opportunities of

Some cities have had the foresight to preserve moderate amounts of open space in the form of municipal parks. Each acre of parkland in a crowded urban area yields more benefits for people than 40 hectares (100 acres) of parkland in more remote areas. Central Park in New York City (Figure 9-15), Golden Gate Park in San Francisco, Fairmont Park in Philadelphia, and Lake Front Park in Chicago are examples of large urban parks in the United States. Unfortunately, mature cities that did not plan for such parks early in their development have little or no chance of getting them now. However, as newer cities expand, they can develop large and medium-size parks.

Since World War II, the typical pattern of suburban housing development in the United States has been to bulldoze a tract of woods or farmland and build rows of houses, each standard house on a standard lot (Figure 9-10). Many of these developments and their streets are named after the trees and wildlife that they displaced: Oak Lane, Cedar Drive, Pheasant Run, Fox Fields.

In recent years, builders have made increased use of a new pattern, known as cluster development, which provides areas of open space within housing developments. Houses, town houses,

Figure 9-15   Central Park in New York City.

modern technological civilization are most potent and visible.
Peter Self

CHAPTER SUMMARY

In both MDCs and LDCs the percentage of the population living in urban areas has been increasing. The rate of growth of urban areas has also been increasing in all countries. But it is increasing more rapidly in most LDCs because they are simultaneously experiencing high rates of natural population growth and rapid internal migration of people from rural to urban areas. As a result, many cities in LDCs are flooded with people living in squalid conditions in slums and shantytowns.

Major factors determining the spatial character of a city are historical development, land availability (especially

condominiums, and garden apartments are built on only part of the tract. The rest of the area is left as open space, either in its natural state or modified for recreation (Figure 9-16).

The most overlooked open spaces are the small strips and odd-shaped patches of unused land that dot urban areas. Some cities have converted abandoned railroad track lines and dry creek beds into bicycle, hiking, and jogging paths. In Seattle 8,000 people walk, bike, roller-skate, and run every day on one of the 150 "rail trails" in the United States.

Abandoned lots can be developed as community gardens, small plazas, and vest-pocket parks (Figure 9-17). Research by William H. Whyte, director of the Street Life Project in New York City, has shown that the most widely used small urban plazas and miniparks are located just a few steps from busy streets so that people can easily see and enter them. Ideally, the people who will use these spaces should be involved in their design, construction, and management. And even for the smallest parks, planning must set up systems for daily maintenance and security.

Undeveloped Land — creek — marsh

Typical Housing Development

Cluster Housing Development — swim and tennis club — cluster — creek — cluster — pond

Figure 9-16 Conventional and cluster development as they would appear if constructed on the same land area.

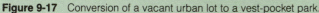

U.S. Department of Housing and Urban Development

Figure 9-17 Conversion of a vacant urban lot to a vest-pocket park.

nearby flat agricultural land that can be converted to urban land), topography, rate of population growth, transportation and utility systems, economic development, and the political system. Three general patterns of urban spatial structure are *concentric-circle cities*, *sector cities*, and *multiple-nuclei cities*. Cities also tend to be either *compact and energy efficient* or *dispersed and energy inefficient*.

Cities are centers of economic growth, population, and culture. But they are also concentrators of solid waste, air pollution, water pollution, noise, disease, and stress. Urban areas are not self-sustaining. They depend on ecosystems outside their boundaries for inputs of food, water, energy, minerals, and other resources and for absorbing some of the concentrated wastes they produce.

Most individual transit in and between urban areas in MDCs is by automobile. The car provides individuals with freedom of movement, and the automaking and related industries are a major component of economic growth in industrialized countries. However, the widespread use of cars and trucks kills and injures large numbers of people, requires large amounts of land for roads and parking space, causes considerable pollution, and encourages development of energy-inefficient, dispersed urban areas.

In most LDCs most individual transit is by bicycle. The bicycle is the best way to move quickly through congested urban car traffic. Cities could increase bicycle use by building bike paths along roads, providing secure bike parking, and establishing bike-and-ride mass transit stations and bike-carrying buses and trains.

Mass transit is more energy efficient, requires less land, and produces far less pollution than individual motor vehicles. However, subway and trolley mass transit systems are too expensive to build and operate in most dispersed urban areas. Bus systems are more flexible than rail systems in providing mass transportation within widely dispersed urban areas and have lower start-up and operating costs. Car pools, van pools, jitneys, and dial-a-ride services are also useful in dispersed urban areas.

Most urban areas use some form of *land-use planning* to decide the best present and future use for each parcel of land in the area. Most land-use planning is based on extrapolating existing trends or reacting to crisis; both methods are ineffective in anticipating and preventing long-term conflicts and problems. *Ecological land-use planning*, in which all major variables are considered and integrated into a model designed to anticipate present and future needs, is a much better method. However, it is not widely used, mostly because of political and economic conflicts over valuable pieces of land.

Methods for controlling land use include zoning, direct public or private purchase, buying development rights, giving tax breaks to owners, and controlling urban growth by limiting building permits, sewer hookups, roads, and other services. More emphasis needs to be placed on designing cities and urban growth for people instead of cars.

Most older cities are in severe need of repairs of roads, bridges, water supply and sewage systems, and other public works. Some cities have revitalized decaying downtown areas, but such projects often displace poor people from increasingly scarce housing. Some of the urban poor are being given aid to repair, manage, and eventually buy public housing units. Also, businesses are being given tax deductions for locating in economically depressed areas.

Some countries build *new towns* near or within existing cities to stimulate economic activity, improve living conditions, and reduce pressures on crowded urban areas. Our major challenge is to make existing and new urban areas more self-sufficient, sustainable, and enjoyable places to live by working with nature.

DISCUSSION TOPICS

1. Give advantages and disadvantages of emphasizing rural rather than urban development in LDCs. Why do most LDCs emphasize urban development even though most of their population is rural?

2. List the advantages and disadvantages of living in (a) the downtown area of a large city, (b) suburbia, (c) a small town in a rural area, (d) a small town near a large city, and (e) a rural area. Which would you prefer to live in? Why? Which will you probably end up living in? Why?

3. Which, if any, of the models shown in Figure 9-6 best describes the spatial form of the city you live in or near?

4. What life-support resources in your community are the most vulnerable to interruption or destruction? What alternate or backup resources, if any, exist?

5. If you live in a city, try to identify the downwind zones that receive air pollution produced by the city. If you live in a rural area, try to determine which city or cities pollute the air you receive. Consult the nearest weather bureau for information on prevailing wind patterns and airshed regions.

6. Consult local officials to identify any floodplain areas in your community. How are these areas used?

7. As a class or group project, try to borrow one or more sound pressure decibel meters from the physics or engineering department or from a local stereo or electronics repair shop. Make a survey of sound pressure levels at various times of day and at several locations and plot the results on a map. Also measure sound levels in a room with a stereo and from earphones at several different volume settings. If possible, measure sound levels at an indoor concert or nightclub at various distances from the sound system speakers. Correlate your findings with those in Table 9-2.

8. What conditions, if any, would encourage you to rely less on the automobile? Would you regularly travel to school or work in a car pool, on a bicycle or moped, on foot, or by mass transit? Explain.

9. What types of mass transit and paratransit systems are available where you live? What systems were available 20 years ago? Has this change been beneficial or harmful? Explain.

10. How is land use decided in your community? What roles do citizens have in this process?

11. Evaluate land use and land-use planning by your college or university.

12. About how many homeless people are there in your community? What is being done to help them and to provide better housing for the poor?

13. Draw a map identifying small, medium-size, and large open spaces in your area and label their current uses. Redraw the map showing how these spaces could be used more beneficially, and consider presenting this information to local officials.

PART FOUR

Resources

Baryett Gallagher/Animals Animals

Our entire society rests upon—and is dependent upon—our water, our land, our forests, and our minerals. How we use these resources influences our health, security, economy, and well-being.

John F. Kennedy

CHAPTER 10

Soil Resources

General Questions and Issues

1. What are the major components and types of soil, and what properties make a soil best suited for growing crops?

2. How serious is the problem of soil erosion in the world and in the United States?

3. What are the major methods for reducing erosion and nutrient depletion in topsoil?

4. How is soil degraded by excessive salt buildup (salinization), waterlogging, and hazardous chemicals?

Below that thin layer comprising the delicate organism known as the soil is a planet as lifeless as the moon.

G. Y. Jacks and R. O. Whyte

Unless you are a farmer you probably think of soil as dirt—something you don't want on your hands, clothes, or carpet. You are acutely aware of your need for air and water. But you may be unaware that your life and that of other organisms depend on soil, especially the upper portion known as topsoil.

The nutrients in the food you eat come from soil. A more accurate version of the saying "All flesh is grass" is "All flesh is soil nutrients." Soil also provides you with wood, paper, cotton, gravel, and many other vital materials and helps purify the water you drink.

As long as soil is held in place by vegetation, it stores water and releases it in a nourishing trickle instead of a devastating flood. Soil's decomposer organisms recycle the key chemicals we and most other forms of life need. Bacteria in soil decompose degradable forms of garbage you throw away. The buildings, roads, utility lines, and waste treatment plants you use are all built upon and supported by soil. Soil is truly the base of life and civilization.

Yet since the beginning of agriculture we have abused this vital, potentially renewable resource. Entire civilizations have collapsed because they mismanaged the topsoil that supported their populations (see Case Study on p. 34).

Today we have escalated soil abuse to an all-time high. You, I, everyone must become involved in pro- tecting the life-giving resource we call soil. In saving the soil, we save ourselves and other forms of life.

10-1 SOIL COMPONENTS, TYPES, AND PROPERTIES

Soil Layers and Components   Pick up a handful of soil and notice how it feels and looks. The **soil** you hold in your hand is a complex mixture of inorganic minerals (mostly clay, silt, and sand), decaying organic matter, water, air, and billions of living organisms.

The components of mature soils are arranged in a series of layers called **soil horizons** (Figure 10-1). Each horizon has a distinct thickness, color, texture, and composition that vary with different types of soils. A cross-sectional view of the horizons in a soil is called a *soil profile*. Most mature soils have at least three of the six possible horizons. But some new or poorly-developed soils don't have horizons.

The top layer, the *surface-litter layer*, or *O-horizon*, consists mostly of freshly fallen and partially decomposed leaves, twigs, animal waste, fungi, and other organic materials. It is usually brown to black in color. The underlying *topsoil layer*, or *A-horizon*, is usually a porous mixture of partially decomposed organic matter (humus), living organisms, and some inorganic mineral particles. It is usually darker and looser than

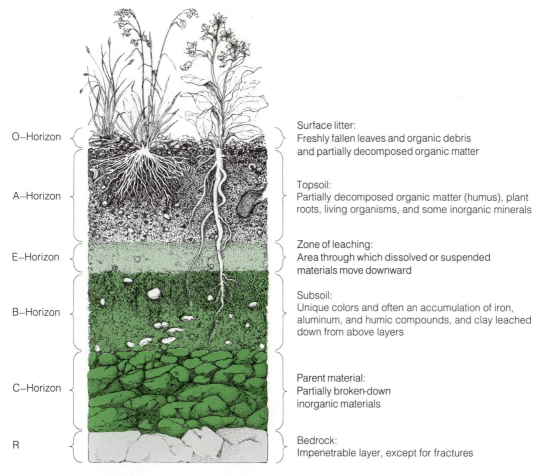

O–Horizon — Surface litter:
Freshly fallen leaves and organic debris
and partially decomposed organic matter

A–Horizon — Topsoil:
Partially decomposed organic matter (humus), plant
roots, living organisms, and some inorganic minerals

E–Horizon — Zone of leaching:
Area through which dissolved or suspended
materials move downward

B–Horizon — Subsoil:
Unique colors and often an accumulation of iron,
aluminum, and humic compounds, and clay leached
down from above layers

C–Horizon — Parent material:
Partially broken-down
inorganic materials

R — Bedrock:
Impenetrable layer, except for fractures

Figure 10-1 Generalized profile of soil. Layers vary in number, composition, and thickness, depending on the type of soil.

deeper layers. The roots of most plants and most of a soil's organic matter are concentrated in these two upper soil layers (Figure 10-1).

The two top layers of most well-developed soils are also teeming with bacteria, fungi, earthworms, and small insects. These layers are also home for larger, burrowing animals such as moles and gophers. All these soil organisms interact in complex food webs (Figure 10-2). Most are bacteria and other decomposer microorganisms—billions in every handful of soil. They partially or completely break down some of the complex inorganic and organic compounds in the upper layers of soil into simpler, nutrient compounds that dissolve in soil water. Soil water carrying these dissolved nutrients is drawn up by the roots of plants and transported through stems and into leaves (Figure 10-3).

Some organic compounds in the two upper layers are broken down slowly and form a dark-colored mixture of organic matter called **humus.** Much of the humus is not soluble in water and it remains in the topsoil layer. It helps retain water and water-soluble plant

nutrients so that they can be taken up by plant roots. A fertile soil, useful for growing high yields of crops, has a thick topsoil layer containing a high content of humus. When soil is eroded, it is the vital surface litter and topsoil layers that are lost.

The color of the topsoil layer tells us a lot about how useful a soil is for growing crops. For example, dark brown or black topsoil has a large amount of organic matter and is nitrogen rich. Gray, bright yellow, or red topsoils are low in organic matter and require nitrogen fertilizer to increase their crop-growing ability.

The B- and C-horizons contain most of a soil's inorganic matter. Most of this is broken-down rock in the form of varying mixtures of sand, silt, clay, and gravel. These and other soil layers lie on a base of bedrock (Figure 10-1).

The spaces, or pores, between the solid organic and inorganic particles in the upper and lower soil layers contain varying amounts of two other key inorganic components: air (mostly oxygen and nitrogen gas) and water. The oxygen gas, highly concentrated in the topsoil, is used by the cells in plant roots to

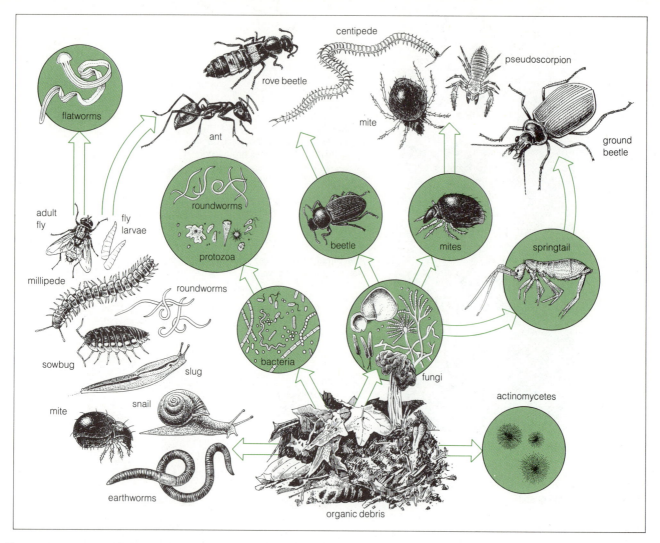

Figure 10-2 Greatly simplified food web of living organisms found in soil.

carry out cellular respiration. Some nitrogen gas is also produced from nitrates in soil by specialized bacteria as part of the nitrogen cycle (Figure 4-22, p. 95).

Some of the rain falling on the soil surface percolates downward through the soil layers and occupies some of the pores. As this water seeps downward, it dissolves and picks up various soil components in upper layers and carries them to lower layers—a process called **leaching**. Most materials leached from upper layers accumulate in the B-horizon, if one has developed.

Major Types of Soil Mature soils in different biomes of the world vary widely in color, content, pore space, acidity (pH), and depth. These differences can be used to classify soils throughout the world into 10 major types, or orders. Five important soil orders are mollisols, alfisols, spodosols, oxisols, and aridisols, each with a distinct soil profile (Figure 10-4). Figure 10-5 is a generalized map of the major soil orders in the lower 48 states.

Most of the world's crops are grown on fertile grassland mollisols and on alfisols exposed when deciduous forests are cleared. After a temperate deciduous forest with an alfisol soil is cleared, it will lose most of its fertility after several years of crop harvests unless key plant nutrients in the A-horizon are replaced by fertilizers.

Oxisols are fairly infertile soils with a thin A-horizon containing little organic matter. They underlie large areas of tropical rain forests and some subtropical humid forests of Central America, Africa, and Asia. Their B-horizons contain iron and aluminum compounds. When a large area of tropical rain forest is cleared, torrential seasonal rains leach most of the remaining nutrients and minerals from the thin A-horizon. After exposure to air and sun, the iron oxide that remains in some oxisols can form red rock called laterite or ironstone, which is so hard it is used for paving highways. Once laterite forms, the land is useless for cultivation. It is estimated that laterite-forming oxisols are found close to the surface on about 7% of

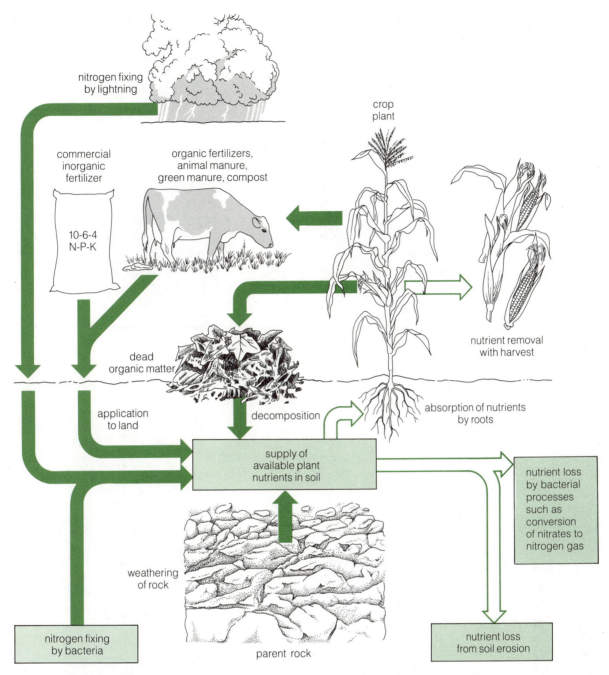

Figure 10-3 Addition and loss of plant nutrients in soils.

the total land area of the tropics, including 2% of tropical America, 11% of tropical Africa, and 15% of sub-Saharan West Africa.

Aridisols are fairly infertile with little accumulation of organic matter in their thin A-horizon. These soils are often covered by rock or a mineral crust called desert pavement. Aridisols are found in the hot, arid deserts of Africa, South America, and western North America. About one-third of the area covered by aridisols is useless for growing crops because it lacks rainfall or irrigation water. In general, land with aridisol soil is better used as grazing land for livestock

(rangeland) than for growing crops. But overgrazing can severely degrade the soil.

Soil Formation Most soil begins as bedrock. Exposure of this rock to the elements gradually breaks it down into small bits and pieces that make up most of the soil's parent inorganic material. These physical and chemical processes are called **weathering.** Other soils develop from the weathering of sediments that have been deposited on bedrock by wind, water (alluvial soils), volcanic eruptions, or melting glaciers.

The slope of the land affects the type of soil and

Figure 10-4 Soil profiles of the major soil orders typically found in five different biomes.

Grassland Soil
(Mollisol)
Semiarid climate

A — alkaline, dark, and rich in humus
B — accumulation of clay and calcium compounds
C

Deciduous Forest Soil
(Alfisol)
Humid mild climate

O — forest litter
A — leaf mold
E — humus-mineral mixture
B — light, grayish-brown, silt loam
   — dark brown firm clay
C — calcareous loam glacial till

Coniferous Forest Soil
(Spodosol)
Humid cold climate

O — acid litter and humus
E — light-colored and acidic
B — humus and iron and aluminum compounds
C

Desert
(Aridisol)
Hot dry climate

A — desert pavement
   — weak humus-mineral mixture
B — dry, brown to reddish-brown with variable accumulations of clay, calcium carbonate and soluble salts
C — old alluvium from eroded uplands

Tropical Rain Forest Soil
(Oxisol)
Humid tropical climate

A — acidic light-colored humus
B — iron and aluminum compounds mixed with clay
C

the rate at which it forms. When the slope is steep, the actions of wind, flowing water, and gravity quickly erode the soil. That is why soils on steep slopes often are thin and infertile. By contrast, valley soils, which receive mineral particles, nutrients, water, and organic matter from adjacent slopes, are fertile and highly productive if not too wet.

Soil Texture and Porosity Soils vary in their content of clay (very fine particles), silt (fine particles), sand (coarse particles), and gravel (large particles). The relative amounts of the different sizes and types of particles determine **soil texture.** Figure 10-6 shows how soils can be grouped into textural classes according to clay, silt, and sand content.

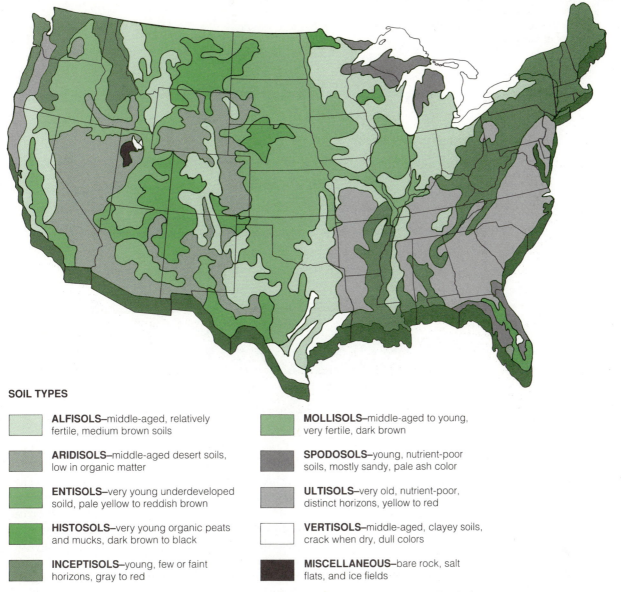

SOIL TYPES

ALFISOLS—middle-aged, relatively fertile, medium brown soils

ARIDISOLS—middle-aged desert soils, low in organic matter

ENTISOLS—very young underdeveloped soild, pale yellow to reddish brown

HISTOSOLS—very young organic peats and mucks, dark brown to black

INCEPTISOLS—young, few or faint horizons, gray to red

MOLLISOLS—middle-aged to young, very fertile, dark brown

SPODOSOLS—young, nutrient-poor soils, mostly sandy, pale ash color

ULTISOLS—very old, nutrient-poor, distinct horizons, yellow to red

VERTISOLS—middle-aged, clayey soils, crack when dry, dull colors

MISCELLANEOUS—bare rock, salt flats, and ice fields

Figure 10-5 Generalized soil map of the lower 48 states. (Data from USDA Soil Conservation Service)

Soil texture helps determine **soil porosity,** a measure of the volume of pores a volume of soil has and the average distance between these spaces. A soil with a high porosity can hold more water and air than one with a lower porosity. The average pore size determines soil permeability: the rate at which soil transmits water and air from upper to lower layers. Soil porosity is also influenced by soil structure: how the particles that make up a soil are organized and clumped together.

Soils fall into three broad textural classes: loam, sandy, and clay. Loams contain almost equal amounts of sand and silt and somewhat less clay. They are the best soils for growing most crops because they retain a large amount of water that is not held too tightly for plant roots to absorb.

Sandy soils are easy to work and have less pore space per volume (lower porosity) than other soils.

However, sandy soils have a high permeability because their pores are larger than those in most other soils. That is why water flows rapidly through sandy soils. They are useful for growing irrigated crops or crops without large water requirements, such as peanuts and strawberries.

The particles in clay soils are very small and easily compacted. When these soils get wet, they form large, dense clumps. That is why wet clay is so easy to mold into bricks and pottery. Clay soils have more pore space per volume and a greater water-holding capacity than sandy soils. But the pore spaces are so small that these soils have a low permeability. Because little water can infiltrate to lower levels, the upper layers of these soils easily become too waterlogged to grow most crops.

To get a general idea of a soil's texture, take a small amount of topsoil, moisten it, and rub it between your fingers and thumb. A gritty feel means that it contains

Figure 10-6 Soil texture depends on the percentages of clay, silt, and sand particles in the soil. Soil texture affects soil porosity—the average number and spacing of pores in a volume of soil. Loams are the best soils for growing most crops. (Data from USDA Soil Conservation Service)

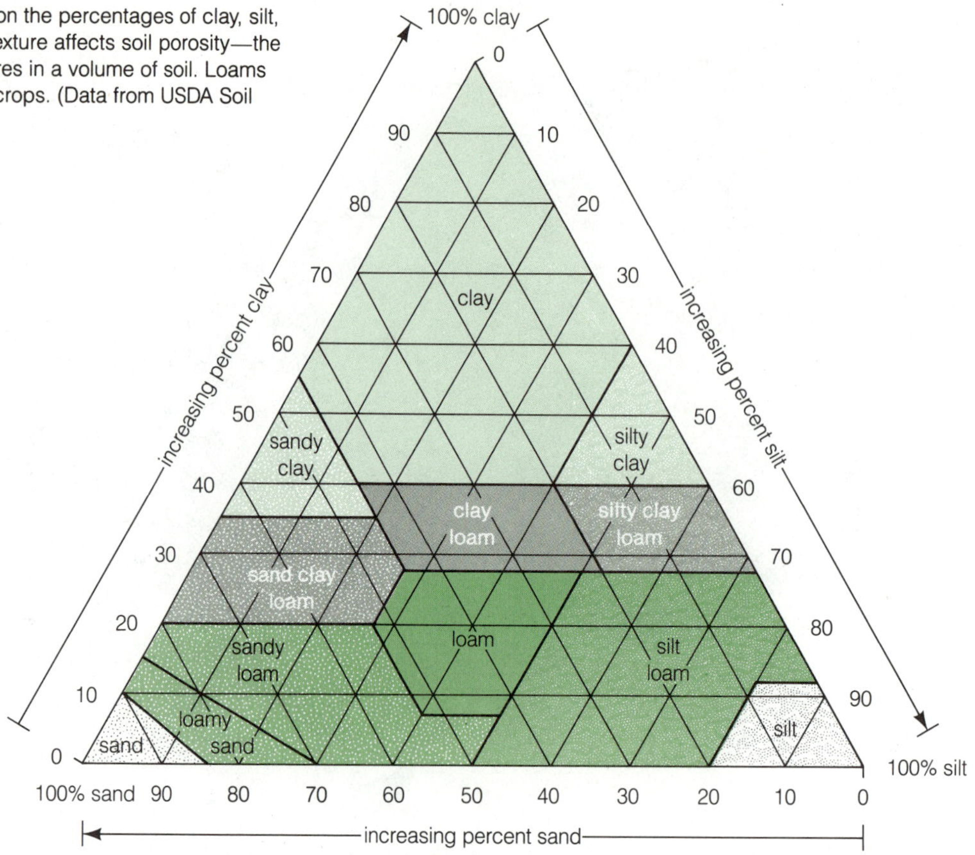

a lot of sand. A sticky feel means that it has a high clay content, and you should be able to roll it into a clump. Silt-laden soil feels smooth like flour. A loam topsoil, best suited for plant growth, has a texture between these extremes. It has a crumbly, spongy feeling, and many of its particles are clumped loosely together.

Soil Acidity (pH) The acidity or alkalinity of a soil is another factor determining the types of plants it can support. Scientists use **pH** as a measure of the degree of acidity or alkalinity of a solution. A solution with a pH of less than 7 is acidic; one with a pH of 7 is neutral; and one with a pH greater than 7 is basic, or alkaline (Figure 10-7). The lower the pH below 7, the more acidic the solution. Each whole number change in pH represents a 10-fold increase or decrease in acidity.

Soil types vary in acidity (Figure 10-4). The pH of a soil influences the uptake of soil nutrients by plants (Figure 10-8). Crops vary in the pH ranges they can tolerate. For example, wheat, spinach, peas, corn, and tomatoes grow best in slightly acidic soils; potatoes and berries do best in very acidic soils; and alfalfa and asparagus, in neutral soils.

When soils are too acidic for the desired crops, the acids can be partially neutralized by an alkaline substance such as lime. But adding lime speeds up the undesirable decomposition of organic matter in the soil, so manure or another organic fertilizer should also be added to maintain soil fertility.

In areas of low rainfall, such as the semiarid valleys in the western and southwestern United States, calcium and other alkaline compounds are not leached away. Soils in the region may be too alkaline (pH above 7.5) for some crops. If drainage is good, irrigation can reduce the alkalinity by leaching the alkaline compounds away. Adding sulfur, which is gradually converted to sulfuric acid by soil bacteria, is another way to reduce soil alkalinity. Soils in areas affected by acid deposition of air pollution are becoming increasingly acidic (Section 17-3).

10-2 SOIL EROSION

Natural and Human-Accelerated Soil Erosion Soil does not stay in one place indefinitely. **Soil erosion** is the movement of soil components, especially topsoil, from one place to another. The two main forces causing soil erosion are wind (Figure 10-9) and flowing water (Figure 10-10).

Some soil erosion always takes place because of natural water flow and winds. But the roots of plants generally protect soil from excessive erosion. Agriculture, logging, construction, and other human activities that remove plant cover greatly accelerate the rate at which soil erodes.

Soil scientists distinguish between three types of erosion by water: sheet, rill, and gully. **Sheet erosion** occurs when surface water moves down a slope or

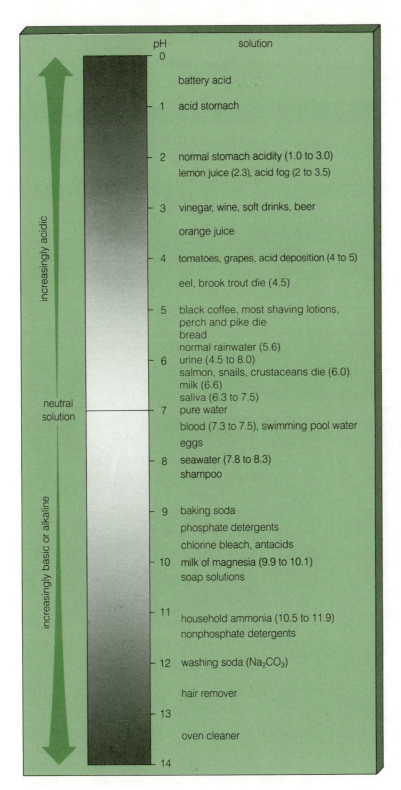

Figure 10-7 Scale of pH, used to measure acidity and basicity (alkalinity) of water solutions. Values shown are approximate.

across a field in a wide flow. Because it erodes topsoil evenly, sheet erosion may not be noticeable until much damage has been done. In **rill erosion** the surface water forms rivulets that flow at high velocities through miniature valleys (Figure 10-10). In **gully erosion** the rivulets join together, forming large, high velocity flows (Figure 10-11).

Excessive erosion of topsoil reduces both the fertility and the water-holding capacity of soil. The resulting sediment, the largest single source of water pollution, clogs irrigation ditches, navigable waterways, and reservoirs.

Soil, especially topsoil, is classified as a renewable resource because it is continually regenerated by natural processes. In tropical and temperate areas, the renewal of 2.54 centimeters (1 inch) of soil takes from 200 to 1,000 years, depending on climate and soil type. However, if the average rate of topsoil erosion exceeds

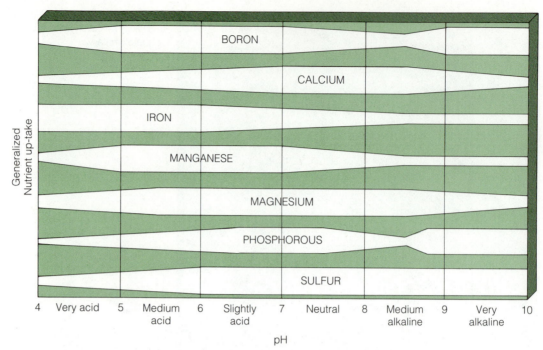

Figure 10-8 Effect of soil pH on availability of plant nutrients.

Figure 10-9 Wind eroding soil from Iowa farmland in 1930.

Figure 10-10 Rill erosion by flowing water on a farm in Oakesdale, Washington.

the rate of topsoil formation on a piece of land, the topsoil on that land becomes a nonrenewable resource being depleted. Annual erosion rates for agricultural land throughout the world are 18 to 100 times the natural renewal rate. Table 10-1 compares the major properties that affect soil nutrient accumulation and soil renewability in natural and cultivated ecosystems. Soil erosion on forestland and rangeland is not as severe as erosion on cropland (Figure 10-12), but forest soil takes two to three times longer to restore itself.

Construction sites usually have the highest erosion rates by far. After bulldozers remove all or most of the vegetation from a site, most builders do little to prevent erosion of the bare soil.

The World Situation Today topsoil is eroding faster than it forms on about one-third of the world's cropland. The amount of topsoil washing and blowing into the world's rivers, lakes, and oceans each year would fill a train of freight cars long enough to encircle the planet 150 times. At this rate the world is losing about 7% of its topsoil from potential cropland each decade. The situation is worsening as farmers cultivate areas unsuited for agriculture to feed the world's growing population. Such mining of the soil converts a potentially renewable resource into a nonrenewable resource.

In mountainous areas, such as the Himalayas on the border between India and Tibet and the Andes

Figure 10-11 Severe soil erosion and gully formation caused by flowing water on a North Carolina farm.

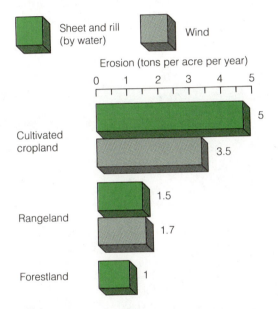

Sheet and rill (by water) Wind

Erosion (tons per acre per year)

Cultivated cropland
5
3.5

Rangeland
1.5
1.7

Forestland
1

Figure 10-12 Average annual erosion rates on various types of land in the United States. These average values mask much higher rates on many parcels of heavily used land. An erosion rate of five tons per acre per year amounts to a loss of about 2.54 centimeters (one inch) every 30 years. Natural replacement of an inch of topsoil in temperate areas typically takes 500 years. (Data from USDA Soil Conservation Service)

Table 10-1 **Characteristics That Affect Soil Nutrient Content and Soil Erosion in Natural and Cultivated Terrestrial Ecosystems**

Factor	Natural	Cultivated
Abiotic		
Water infiltration rate	High	Low
Water runoff rate	Low	High
Soil erosion rate	Low	High
Leaching losses	Low	High
Mineral loss rate	Low	High
Soil organic matter	High	Low
Soil temperature	Low	High
Biotic		
Structural diversity of plants	High	Low
Plant and animal species diversity	High	Low
Plant reproductive potential	High	Low

near the west coast of South America, farmers traditionally built elaborate systems of terraces (Figure 10-13). Terracing allowed them to cultivate steeply sloping land that would otherwise rapidly lose its topsoil. Today farmers in some areas cultivate steep slopes without terraces, causing a total loss of topsoil in 10 to 40 years. Although most poor farmers know that cultivating a steep slope without terracing causes a rapid loss of topsoil, they often have too little time and too few workers to build terraces.

Since the beginning of agriculture, people in tropical forests have successfully used slash-and-burn, shifting cultivation (Figure 2-2, p. 33) to provide food

Figure 10-13 Terraces on cropland in Pisac, Peru, reduce soil erosion. They also increase the amount of usable land on steep terrain.

for relatively small populations. In recent decades, however, growing population and poverty have caused farmers in many tropical forest areas to reduce the fallow period of their fields to as little as 2 years, instead of the 10 to 30 years needed to allow the soil to regain its fertility. The result has been a sharp increase in the rate of topsoil erosion and nutrient depletion.

Overgrazing and poor logging practices also cause heavy losses of topsoil. Intense grazing has turned many areas of North Africa from grassland to desert (see Spotlight below). Once-forested hills in many LDCs have been stripped bare of trees by poor people for firewood and by timber companies for use in MDCs. Because new trees are seldom planted, the topsoil quickly erodes away.

In MDCs, where large-scale industrialized agriculture is practiced, many farmers have replaced traditional soil conservation practices with massive inputs of commercial inorganic fertilizers and irrigation water. But the 10-fold increase in fertilizer use and the tri-pling of the world's irrigated cropland between 1950 and 1989 have only temporarily masked the effects of erosion and nutrient depletion.

Commercial inorganic fertilizer is not a complete substitute for naturally fertile topsoil; it merely hides for a time the gradual depletion of this vital resource. Nor is irrigation a long-term solution. Repeated irrigation of cropland without sufficient drainage eventually decreases or destroys its crop productivity as a result of waterlogging and salt buildup.

Severe erosion accelerated by human activities is most widespread in India, China, the Soviet Union, and the United States, which together account for over half the world's food production and contain almost half the world's people. In China, for example, at least 34% of the land is severely eroded, and river siltation is now a nationally recognized threat. Soil erosion and river siltation are also major problems in India, with erosion and salinization affecting 35% of the country's land area. The Worldwatch Institute estimates that the

CASE STUDY Desertification: A Serious and Growing Problem

According to the UN Environment Program, about 35% of the earth's land surface on which about one-fifth of the world's people try to survive is classified as arid or semiarid desert (see color insert, Figure 2). In drier parts of the world, desert areas are increasing at an alarming rate from a combination of natural processes and human activities.

The conversion of rangeland (uncultivated land used for animal grazing), rain-fed cropland, or irrigated cropland to desertlike land, with a drop in agricultural productivity of 10% or more, is called **desertification.**

Moderate desertification causes a 10% to 25% drop in productivity, and severe desertification causes a 25% to 50% drop. Very severe desertification causes a drop of 50% or more and usually results in the formation of massive gullies and sand dunes.

Most desertification occurs naturally near the edges of existing deserts. It is caused by dehydration of the top layers of soil during prolonged drought and increased evaporation because of hot temperatures and high winds.

However, natural desertification is greatly accelerated by practices that leave the soil vulnerable to erosion by water and wind:

- overgrazing of rangeland as a result of too many livestock on too little land area (the major cause of desertification)
- improper soil and water resource management that leads to increased erosion, salinization, and waterlogging of soil
- cultivation of land with unsuitable terrain or soils
- deforestation and surface mining without adequate replanting

These destructive practices are intensified by rapid population growth, high population density, poverty, and poor land management. The consequences of desertification include intensified drought and famine, declining living standards, and swelling numbers of environmental refugees.

It is estimated that about 810 million hectares (2 billion acres)—an area the size of Brazil and 12 times the size of Texas—have become desertified during the past

50 years (Figure 10-14). Each year an estimated 6 million hectares (15 million acres)—an area the size of West Virginia—of new desert are formed. Most of it is in sub-Saharan Africa, between North Africa's barren Sahara desert and the plant-rich land to its south.

In 1977 government representatives from around the world gathered at Nairobi for the United Nations Conference on Desertification. Out of this conference came a plan of action to halt or sharply reduce the spread of desertification and to reclaim desertified land.

The total cost of such prevention and rehabilitation would be about $141 billion—only five and one-half times the estimated $26 billion annual loss in agricultural productivity from desertified land. Thus, once this potential productivity is restored, the costs of the program could be recouped in 5 to 10 years.

However, by 1989 little had been done because of inadequate funding (about one-tenth the amount needed) and lack of commitment by governments. What do you think should be done?

Soviet Union, which has the world's largest cropland area, may be losing more topsoil than any other country.

The U.S. Situation According to surveys by the Soil Conservation Service, about one-third of the original topsoil on U.S. croplands in use today has already been washed or blown into rivers, lakes, and oceans. Surveys also show that the average rate of erosion on cultivated land in the United States is about seven times the rate of natural soil formation.

But the average rate masks much higher erosion in heavily farmed regions, especially the corn belt and Great Plains. Some of the country's most productive agricultural lands, such as those in Iowa, have lost about half their topsoil.

Enough topsoil erodes away each day in the United States to fill a line of dump trucks 5,600 kilometers (3,500 miles) long. Two-thirds of this soil comes from less than one-fourth of the country's cropland. The plant nutrient losses from this erosion are worth at least $18 billion a year. Erosion also causes $4 billion a year in damages from silt, plant nutrients, and pesticides that are carried into rivers, lakes, and reservoirs.

Soil erosion is also bad for wildlife. A drop in soil fertility means less food, affecting the size and health of animal populations. Excessive silt washing into lakes and streams can reduce—even eliminate—some fish populations.

Unless soil conservation efforts are increased, projected soil erosion may destroy U.S. cropland equal to the combined areas of the states of New York, New Jersey, Maine, New Hampshire, Massachusetts, and Connecticut over the next 50 years.

At present, soil conservation is practiced on only about half of all U.S. farmland and on less than half of the country's most erodible cropland. Increased soil conservation is particularly important in the fertile midwestern plains, which are subject to high rates of erosion from continuous high winds and periodic prolonged drought (see Case Study on p. 226).

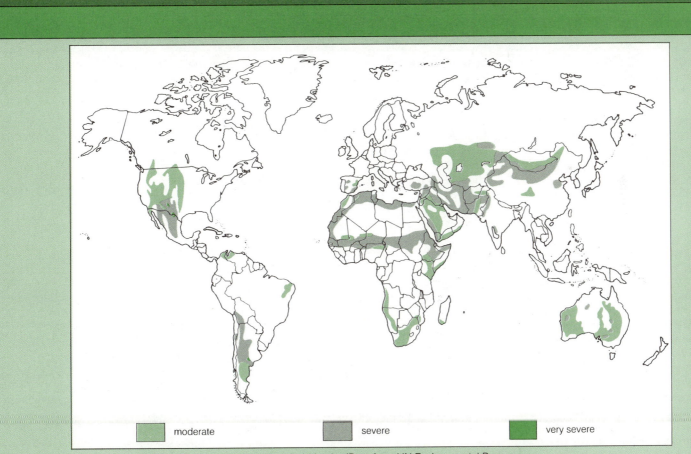

moderate   severe   very severe

Figure 10-14 Desertification of arid and semiarid lands. (Data from UN Environmental Program and Harold E. Dregnue)

10-3 SOIL CONSERVATION

Conservation Tillage The practice of **soil conservation** involves using various methods to reduce soil erosion, to prevent depletion of soil nutrients, and to restore nutrients already lost by erosion, leaching, and excessive crop harvesting. Most methods used to control soil erosion involve keeping the soil covered with vegetation.

In **conventional-tillage farming,** the land is plowed, disked several times, and smoothed to make a planting surface. If plowed in the fall so that crops can be planted in the spring, the soil is left bare during the winter and early spring months—a practice that makes it vulnerable to erosion.

To lower labor costs, save energy, and reduce erosion, an increasing number of U.S. farmers are using **conservation-tillage farming,** also known as minimum-tillage or no-till farming, depending on the degree to which the soil is disturbed. Farmers using this method disturb the soil as little as possible in planting crops.

For the minimum-tillage method, special tillers break up and loosen the subsurface soil without turning over the topsoil, previous crop residues, and any cover vegetation. For no-till farming, special planting machines inject seeds, fertilizers, and weed killers (herbicides) into slits made in the unplowed soil (Figure 10-17).

In addition to reducing soil erosion, conservation tillage reduces fuel and tillage costs, water loss from the soil, and soil compaction, and it increases the number of crops that can be grown during a season (multiple cropping). Yields are as high as or higher than yields from conventional tillage. Depending on the soil type, this approach can be used for three to seven years before more extensive soil cultivation is needed to prevent crop yields from declining. But conservation tillage is no cure-all. It requires increased use of herbicides to control weeds that compete with crops for soil nutrients (see Chapter 21).

Today conservation tillage is used on almost one-third of U.S. cropland and is projected to be used on over half by 2000. The USDA estimates that using con-

---

CASE STUDY The Dust Bowl: Will It Happen Again?

The Great Plains of the United States stretch through 10 states, from Texas through Montana and the Dakotas. The region is normally dry and very windy and periodically experiences long, severe droughts.

Before settlers began grazing livestock and planting crops in the 1870s, the extensive root systems of prairie grasses held the topsoil of these mollisol soils in place (Figure 10-4). When the land was planted in crops, these perennial grasses were replaced by annual crops with less extensive root systems. In addition, the land was plowed up after each harvest and left bare part of the year. Overgrazing also destroyed large areas of grass, leaving the ground bare. The stage was set for crop failures during prolonged droughts, followed by severe wind erosion.

The droughts arrived in 1890 and 1910 and again with even greater severity between 1926 and 1934, the driest year in this century. In 1934, hot, dry windstorms created dust clouds thick enough to cause darkness at midday in some areas (Figure 10-15). The

danger of breathing this dust-laden air was revealed by the dead rabbits and birds left in its wake.

During May 1934 the entire eastern half of the United States was blanketed with a massive dust cloud of topsoil blown off the Great Plains from as far as 2,400 kilometers (1,500 miles) away. Ships 322 kilometers (200 miles) out in the Atlantic Ocean received deposits of midwestern topsoil. These events gave a portion of the Great Plains a tragic new name: the Dust Bowl (Figure 10-16).

An area of cropland equal in size to the combined areas of Connecticut and Maryland was destroyed and additional cropland equal in area to New Mexico was severely damaged. Thousands of displaced farm families from Oklahoma, Texas, Kansas, and other states migrated to California or to the industrial cities of the Midwest and East. Most found no jobs because the country was in the midst of the Great Depression.

In May 1934 Hugh Bennett of the U.S. Department of Agriculture addressed a congressional hearing in Washington, pleading

for new programs to protect the country's topsoil. Lawmakers took action when dust blown from the Great Plains began seeping into the hearing room.

In 1935 the United States established the Soil Conservation Service as part of the Department of Agriculture. With Bennett as its first head, the SCS began promoting good conservation practices in the Great Plains and later in every state. Soil conservation districts were established throughout the country, and farmers and ranchers were given technical assistance in setting up soil conservation programs.

These efforts, however, did not completely stop human-accelerated erosion in the Great Plains. The basic problem is that the climate of much of the region makes it better suited for grazing than for farming. Farmers in the Great Plains have had to relearn this ecological lesson several times since the 1930s. For example, because of severe drought and soil erosion in the 1950s, the federal government had to provide emergency relief funds to many Great Plains farmers.

servation tillage on 80% of U.S. cropland would reduce soil erosion by at least half. So far the practice is not widely used in other parts of the world.

Contour Farming, Terracing, Strip Cropping, and Alley Cropping

Soil erosion can be reduced 30% to 50% on gently sloping land by means of **contour farming**—plowing and planting across rather than up and down the sloped contour of the land (Figure 10-18). Each row planted at a right angle to the slope of the land acts as a small dam to help hold soil and slow the runoff of water.

Terracing can be used on steeper slopes. The slope is converted into a series of broad, nearly level terraces with short vertical drops from one to another (Figure 10-13). Some of the water running down the vegetated slope is retained by each terrace. Thus, terracing provides water for crops at all levels and decreases soil erosion by reducing the amount and speed of water runoff. In areas of high rainfall, diversion ditches must be built behind each terrace to permit adequate drainage.

Figure 10-17 No-till farming. A specially designed machine plants seeds and adds fertilizers and weed killers at the same time with almost no disturbance of the soil.

In 1975 the Council of Agricultural Science and Technology warned that severe drought could again create a dust bowl in the Great Plains. The council pointed out that despite large expenditures for erosion control, topsoil losses in the 1970s were 2.5% worse than in the 1930s.

So far, these warnings have been ignored. Great Plains farmers, many of them debt-ridden, have continued to stave off bankruptcy by maximizing production and minimizing expenditures for soil conservation. If the enhanced greenhouse effect makes this region even drier, farming will have to be abandoned. What do you think should be done about this situation?

Figure 10-15 Dust storm approaching Prowers County, Colorado, in 1934.

Figure 10-16 The Dust Bowl, the Great Plains area where a combination of severe drought and poor soil conservation practices led to massive erosion of topsoil in the 1930s.

Figure 10-18 On this gently sloping land, contoured rows planted with alternating crops (strip cropping) reduce soil erosion.

Strips of dense, deep-rooted vetiver grass can be planted along the contours of sloping cropland to slow sheet erosion. This grass, native to India, can survive in all climates. It requires no maintenance, won't spread, and can be established at 1% to 10% of the cost of other measures. Applying a thick mulch of crop residue can also prevent most erosion on slopes of up to 15%.

In **strip cropping,** a series of rows of one row crop, such as corn or soybeans, is planted in a wide strip; the next strip is planted with a cover crop, such as alfalfa, which completely covers the soil and thus reduces erosion (Figure 10-18). The alternating strips of row crops and cover crops reduce water runoff and help prevent the spread of pests and plant diseases from one strip to another. They also help restore soil fertility if nitrogen-rich legumes such as soybeans or alfalfa are planted in some of the strips. On sloping land, strip cropping can reduce soil losses up to 75% when combined with terracing or contour farming.

Erosion can also be reduced by **alley cropping,** in which crops are planted in alleys between hedgerows of trees or shrubs that can be used as sources of fruits and fuelwood. The hedgerow trimmings can be used as mulch for the crop and fodder for livestock.

Gully Reclamation and Windbreaks Water runoff quickly creates gullies in sloping land not covered by vegetation (Figure 10-11). Such land can be restored by **gully reclamation** (Figure 10-19). Small gullies can be seeded with quick-growing plants such as oats, barley, and wheat to reduce erosion. In deeper gullies, small dams can be built to collect silt and gradually fill in the channels. Rapidly growing shrubs, vines, and trees can be planted to stabilize the soil. Channels built to divert water away from the gully will prevent further erosion.

Erosion caused by exposure of cultivated lands to high winds can be reduced by **windbreaks,** or **shelterbelts,** long rows of trees planted to partially block wind (Figure 10-20). They are especially effective if land not under cultivation is kept covered with vegetation. Windbreaks also provide habitats for birds, pest-eating and pollinating insects, and other animals. Unfortunately, many of the windbreaks planted in the upper Great Plains following the Dust Bowl disaster of the 1930s have been destroyed to make way for large irrigation systems and farm machinery.

Land-Use Classification and Control To encourage wise land use and reduce erosion, the Soil Conservation Service has set up the classification system summarized in Table 10-2 and illustrated in Figure 10-21. An obvious land-use approach to reducing erosion is to prohibit the planting of crops or the clearing of vegetation on marginal land (classes V through VIII in Table 10-2). Such land is highly erodible because of a steep slope, shallow soil structure, high winds, periodic drought, or other factors. Since 1985 U.S. farmers who take highly erodible cropland out of production have been given government subsidies (see Spotlight on p. 231).

Maintaining and Restoring Soil Fertility Organic fertilizers and commercial inorganic fertilizers can be applied to soil to partially restore and maintain plant nutrients lost by erosion, leaching, and crop harvesting and to increase crop yields (Figure 10-3). Three major types of **organic fertilizer** are animal manure, green manure, and compost. **Animal manure** includes the dung and urine of cattle, horses, poultry, and other farm animals. In some LDCs human manure, sometimes called night soil, is used to fertilize crops.

Figure 10-19 Gully reclamation on a farm in Gilmore County, Minnesota. The severely eroded gully (left) was planted with vegetation, primarily locust trees. After five growing seasons the trees had grown enough to control erosion (right) and provide habitats for wildlife.

Figure 10-20 Windbreaks, or shelterbelts, reduce erosion on this farm in Trail County, North Dakota. They also reduce wind damage, help hold soil moisture in place, supply some wood for fuel, and provide a habitat for wildlife.

Application of animal manure improves soil structure, increases organic nitrogen content, and stimulates the growth and reproduction of soil bacteria and fungi. It is particularly useful on crops of corn, cotton, potatoes, cabbage, and tobacco.

Despite its effectiveness, the use of animal manure in the United States has decreased. One reason is that separate farms for growing crops and animals have replaced most mixed animal- and crop-farming operations. Animal manure is available at feedlots near urban areas, but transporting it to distant rural crop-growing areas usually costs too much. In addition, tractors and other motorized farm machinery have replaced horses and other draft animals that naturally added manure to the soil.

Green manure is fresh or growing green vegeta-

tion plowed into the soil to increase the organic matter and humus available to the next crop. It may consist of weeds in an uncultivated field, grasses and clover in a field previously used for pasture, or legumes such as alfalfa or soybeans grown for use as fertilizer to build up soil nitrogen.

Compost is a rich natural fertilizer; farmers and homeowners produce it by piling up alternating layers of carbohydrate-rich plant wastes (such as cuttings and leaves), animal manure, and topsoil. This mixture provides a home for microorganisms that aid the decomposition of the plant and manure layers.

Today, especially in the United States and other industrialized countries, farmers partially restore and maintain soil fertility by applying **commercial inorganic fertilizers.** The most common plant nutrients in

Table 10-2 Land Capability Classification According to the Soil Conservation Service

Land Class	Characteristics	Primary Uses	Secondary Uses	Conservation Measures
Land Suitable for Cultivation				
I	Excellent flat, well-drained land	Agriculture	Recreation Wildlife Pasture	None
II	Good land has minor limitations such as slight slope, sandy soil, or poor drainage	Agriculture Pasture	Recreation Wildlife	Strip cropping Contour farming
III	Moderately good land with important limitations of soil, slope, or drainage	Agriculture Pasture Watershed	Recreation Wildlife Urban industry	Contour farming Strip cropping Waterways Terraces
IV	Fair land, severe limitations of soil, slope, or drainage	Pasture Orchards Limited agriculture Urban industry	Pasture Wildlife	Farming on a limited basis Contour farming Strip cropping Waterways Terraces
Land Not Suitable for Cultivation				
V	Rockiness, shallow soil, wetness or slope prevents farming	Grazing Forestry Watershed	Recreation Wildlife	No special precautions if properly grazed or logged; must not be plowed
VI	Moderate limitations for grazing and forestry	Grazing Forestry Watershed Urban industry	Recreation Wildlife	Grazing or logging should be limited at times
VII	Severe limitations for grazing and forestry	Grazing Forestry Watershed Recreation-Aesthetics Wildlife Urban industry		Careful management required when used for grazing or logging
VIII	Unsuitable for grazing and forestry because of steep slope, shallow soil, lack of water, too much water	Recreation-Aesthetics Watershed Wildlife Urban industry		Not to be used for grazing or logging

these products are nitrogen (as ammonium ions, nitrate ions, or urea), phosphorus (as phosphate ions), and potassium. Other plant nutrients may also be present in low or trace amounts. Farmers can have their soil and harvested crops chemically analyzed to determine the mix of nutrients that should be added.

Inorganic commercial fertilizers are easily transported, stored, and applied. Throughout the world their use increased almost 10-fold between 1950 and 1989. By 1989 the additional food they helped produce fed one of every three persons in the world.

Commercial inorganic fertilizers, however, have some disadvantages. They do not add humus to the soil. Unless animal manure and green manure are added to the soil along with commercial inorganic fertilizers, the soil's content of organic matter and thus its ability to hold water will decrease. If not supplemented by organic fertilizers, inorganic fertilizers cause the soil to become compacted and less suitable for crop growth. By decreasing its porosity, inorganic fertilizers also lower the oxygen content of soil and prevent added fertilizer from being taken up as efficiently. In addition, most commercial fertilizers do not contain many of the nutrients needed in trace amounts by plants.

Water pollution is another problem caused by the widespread use of commercial inorganic fertilizers, especially on sloped land near rivers, streams, and lakes. Some of the plant nutrients in the fertilizers are washed into nearby bodies of surface water, where they cause excessive growth of algae, deplete dissolved oxygen, and kill fish. Rainwater seeping through soil can leach nitrates in commercial fertilizers into groundwater. High levels of nitrate ions make drink-

LAND CAPABILITY CLASSES

	SUITABLE FOR CULTIVATION		NO CULTIVATION-PASTURE, HAY, WOODLAND AND WILDLIFE
I	REQUIRES GOOD SOIL MANAGEMENT PRACTICES ONLY	V	NO RESTRICTIONS IN USE
II	MODERATE CONSERVATION PRACTICES NECESSARY	VI	MODERATE RESTRICTIONS IN USE
III	INTENSIVE CONSERVATION PRACTICES NECESSARY	VII	SEVERE RESTRICTIONS IN USE
IV	PERENNIAL VEGETATION – INFREQUENT CULTIVATION	VIII	BEST SUITED FOR WILDLIFE AND RECREATION

Figure 10-21 Classification of land according to capability; see Table 10-2 for description of each class.

SPOTLIGHT U. S. Policies to Protect Highly Erodible Cropland

The 1985 Farm Act authorized the government to create a conservation reserve by paying farmers for each acre of highly erodible land that they take out of production and replant with soil-saving grass or trees for 10 years. During this period the land cannot be farmed, grazed, or cut for hay.

To be eligible, land must be eroding at three times the rate of natural soil formation. Farmers who violate their contracts must pay back all government payments with interest.

The goals of the program are to reduce erosion, improve water quality, and enhance wildlife habitats by removing about 11% of

U.S. cropland from production by 1990. If the program is adequately enforced, it should reduce excessive soil loss from U.S. cropland by 80%.

The Farm Act also requires all farmers to have five-year soil conservation plans for their entire farms by 1990. Otherwise, they become ineligible for any federal agricultural subsidies and loans. This makes putting land into the conservation reserve more financially attractive.

A third provision of the Farm Act authorizes the government to forgive all or part of debts farmers owe the Farmers Home Administration if they agree not to farm

highly erodible cropland or wetlands for 50 years. Farmers are required to plant trees or grass on this land or convert it back to wetland.

Since 1987, however, the Soil Conservation Service has eased the standards that farmers' soil conservation plans must meet to keep farmers eligible for other subsidies. Conservationists have also accused the Soil Conservation Service of laxity in enforcing the farm bill's "swampbuster" provisions, which deny federal funds to farmers who drain or destroy wetlands on their property.

Unless instructed otherwise, most builders remove the topsoil from a homesite and sell it to increase their profits. This leaves the home owner with a hard subsoil that contains little organic matter and is not fertile enough to support most plants.

The home owner can rebuild topsoil gradually by planting a crop of grass or other ground cover, plowing it up, turning it into the soil as green manure, and then repeating the process with another crop. Another option is to buy enough good-quality topsoil (examine it carefully before purchase) to cover the ground with 10 to 13 centimeters (4 to 5 inches) of soil.

If you are building a home, you can avoid this problem by requiring the contractor not to disturb any topsoil unless necessary, to save and replace any topsoil that must be removed, and to set up barriers to catch any soil eroded during construction. Some type of rapidly growing grass or ground cover should be planted on all areas of exposed soil as soon as possible after construction is complete.

After moving into a new or existing home, you need to determine the site's soil type and its suitability for growing various types of vegetation such as crops, grass, flowers, and trees. Use a spade, soil auger, or posthole digger to dig down 0.9 to 1.2 meters (3 or 4 feet) a few centimeters at a time at several locations. Examine each layer for texture, color, and rock content, using information in Section 10-1 to determine the soil's generalized mixture of clay, sand, and silt.

A dark brown or red soil usually indicates good drainage. A black top layer indicates a high content of organic matter. Pale soil may mean that the topsoil was removed. Soil containing patches of different colors usually means that the water table is near the surface during certain times of the

year. Gray, mixed with yellow or red, indicates that drainage is probably poor.

You can also ask the county agricultural extension agent to have the soil analyzed to determine what type of organic or inorganic fertilizers are needed and whether the soil acidity needs to be adjusted. An inexpensive home kit for testing soil acidity is also available.

You can improve and maintain soil fertility by covering the ground around plants with a mulch of animal manure or other organic materials. You can use leaves, grass clippings, shredded bark, sawdust, straw, peanut hulls, food scraps (not meat), egg shells, black-and-white newspaper (colored paper contains harmful dyes and sometimes toxic lead compounds) as mulch. Don't use pine needles because they decay too slowly. Mulch also retains soil moisture, reduces soil erosion, suppresses weed growth, and keeps soil from getting too hot under intense sunlight.

The best way to produce high-quality mulch is to build a simple compost bin (Figure 10-22). A layer or two of cat litter or alfalfa meal can be used to cut down on odors. Leave a depression at the

top center of the pile to collect rainwater. Turn the pile over every month or so and cover it with a tarp during winter months.

Seriously consider not planting grass on the land around your house. Instead, landscape the area not used for gardening with a mix of wildflowers, herbs (for cooking and to repel many insect pests), low-growing ground cover, small bushes, and other forms of vegetation natural to the area. Paths covered with wood chips, stones, or strips of discarded carpet can be run through the area so that little if any cutting by a lawn mower is needed.

This landscaping method is based on natural biodiversity rather than the traditional grass monoculture. It saves time, water, energy, and money (no lawn mower, gasoline, or mower repairs).

This type of yard also reduces infestations of mosquitoes and other damaging insects by providing a diversity of habitats for their natural predators. If you must have a lawn, never cut it below 7.6 centimeters (3 inches) so that it is tall enough to provide habitats for natural predators of common insect pests.

Figure 10-22 A simple home compost bin used to make mulch.

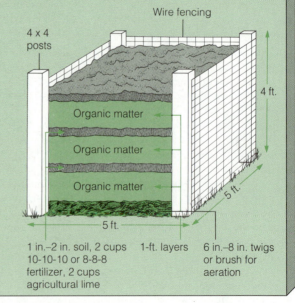

Wire fencing

4 x 4 posts

Organic matter

Organic matter

Organic matter

4 ft.

5 ft.

5 ft.

1 in.–2 in. soil, 2 cups 10-10-10 or 8-8-8 fertilizer, 2 cups agricultural lime

1-ft. layers

6 in.–8 in. twigs or brush for aeration

Figure 10-21 Classification of land according to capability; see Table 10-2 for description of each class.

The following table appears within the figure:

LAND CAPABILITY CLASSES		
SUITABLE FOR CULTIVATION		**NO CULTIVATION – PASTURE, HAY, WOODLAND AND WILDLIFE**
I	REQUIRES GOOD SOIL MANAGEMENT PRACTICES ONLY	V	NO RESTRICTIONS IN USE
II	MODERATE CONSERVATION PRACTICES NECESSARY	VI	MODERATE RESTRICTIONS IN USE
III	INTENSIVE CONSERVATION PRACTICES NECESSARY	VII	SEVERE RESTRICTIONS IN USE
IV	PERENNIAL VEGETATION – INFREQUENT CULTIVATION	VIII	BEST SUITED FOR WILDLIFE AND RECREATION

SPOTLIGHT U. S. Policies to Protect Highly Erodible Cropland

The 1985 Farm Act authorized the government to create a conservation reserve by paying farmers for each acre of highly erodible land that they take out of production and replant with soil-saving grass or trees for 10 years. During this period the land cannot be farmed, grazed, or cut for hay.

To be eligible, land must be eroding at three times the rate of natural soil formation. Farmers who violate their contracts must pay back all government payments with interest.

The goals of the program are to reduce erosion, improve water quality, and enhance wildlife habitats by removing about 11% of U.S. cropland from production by 1990. If the program is adequately enforced, it should reduce excessive soil loss from U.S. cropland by 80%.

The Farm Act also requires all farmers to have five-year soil conservation plans for their entire farms by 1990. Otherwise, they become ineligible for any federal agricultural subsidies and loans. This makes putting land into the conservation reserve more financially attractive.

A third provision of the Farm Act authorizes the government to forgive all or part of debts farmers owe the Farmers Home Administration if they agree not to farm highly erodible cropland or wetlands for 50 years. Farmers are required to plant trees or grass on this land or convert it back to wetland.

Since 1987, however, the Soil Conservation Service has eased the standards that farmers' soil conservation plans must meet to keep farmers eligible for other subsidies. Conservationists have also accused the Soil Conservation Service of laxity in enforcing the farm bill's "swampbuster" provisions, which deny federal funds to farmers who drain or destroy wetlands on their property.

Unless instructed otherwise, most builders remove the topsoil from a homesite and sell it to increase their profits. This leaves the home owner with a hard subsoil that contains little organic matter and is not fertile enough to support most plants.

The home owner can rebuild topsoil gradually by planting a crop of grass or other ground cover, plowing it up, turning it into the soil as green manure, and then repeating the process with another crop. Another option is to buy enough good-quality topsoil (examine it carefully before purchase) to cover the ground with 10 to 13 centimeters (4 to 5 inches) of soil.

If you are building a home, you can avoid this problem by requiring the contractor not to disturb any topsoil unless necessary, to save and replace any topsoil that must be removed, and to set up barriers to catch any soil eroded during construction. Some type of rapidly growing grass or ground cover should be planted on all areas of exposed soil as soon as possible after construction is complete.

After moving into a new or existing home, you need to determine the site's soil type and its suitability for growing various types of vegetation such as crops, grass, flowers, and trees. Use a spade, soil auger, or posthole digger to dig down 0.9 to 1.2 meters (3 or 4 feet) a few centimeters at a time at several locations. Examine each layer for texture, color, and rock content, using information in Section 10-1 to determine the soil's generalized mixture of clay, sand, and silt.

A dark brown or red soil usually indicates good drainage. A black top layer indicates a high content of organic matter. Pale soil may mean that the topsoil was removed. Soil containing patches of different colors usually means that the water table is near the surface during certain times of the

year. Gray, mixed with yellow or red, indicates that drainage is probably poor.

You can also ask the county agricultural extension agent to have the soil analyzed to determine what type of organic or inorganic fertilizers are needed and whether the soil acidity needs to be adjusted. An inexpensive home kit for testing soil acidity is also available.

You can improve and maintain soil fertility by covering the ground around plants with a mulch of animal manure or other organic materials. You can use leaves, grass clippings, shredded bark, sawdust, straw, peanut hulls, food scraps (not meat), egg shells, black-and-white newspaper (colored paper contains harmful dyes and sometimes toxic lead compounds) as mulch. Don't use pine needles because they decay too slowly. Mulch also retains soil moisture, reduces soil erosion, suppresses weed growth, and keeps soil from getting too hot under intense sunlight.

The best way to produce high-quality mulch is to build a simple compost bin (Figure 10-22). A layer or two of cat litter or alfalfa meal can be used to cut down on odors. Leave a depression at the

top center of the pile to collect rainwater. Turn the pile over every month or so and cover it with a tarp during winter months.

Seriously consider not planting grass on the land around your house. Instead, landscape the area not used for gardening with a mix of wildflowers, herbs (for cooking and to repel many insect pests), low-growing ground cover, small bushes, and other forms of vegetation natural to the area. Paths covered with wood chips, stones, or strips of discarded carpet can be run through the area so that little if any cutting by a lawn mower is needed.

This landscaping method is based on natural biodiversity rather than the traditional grass monoculture. It saves time, water, energy, and money (no lawn mower, gasoline, or mower repairs).

This type of yard also reduces infestations of mosquitoes and other damaging insects by providing a diversity of habitats for their natural predators. If you must have a lawn, never cut it below 7.6 centimeters (3 inches) so that it is tall enough to provide habitats for natural predators of common insect pests.

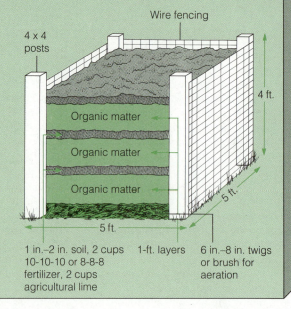

Figure 10-22 A simple home compost bin used to make mulch.

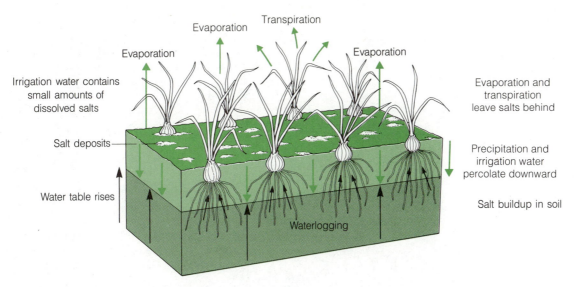

Evaporation   Transpiration

Evaporation   Evaporation

Irrigation water contains
small amounts of
dissolved salts

Salt deposits

Water table rises

Waterlogging

Evaporation and
transpiration
leave salts behind

Precipitation and
irrigation water
percolate downward

Salt buildup in soil

Figure 10-23 Salinization and waterlogging of soil on irrigated land without adequate drainage lead to decreased crop yields.

ing water drawn from wells toxic, especially for infants.

A third method for preventing depletion of soil nutrients is **crop rotation**. Crops such as corn, tobacco, and cotton remove large amounts of nutrients (especially nitrogen) from the soil and can deplete the topsoil of nutrients if planted on the same land several years in a row. Farmers using crop rotation plant areas or strips with corn, tobacco, and cotton one year. The next year they plant the same areas with legumes, which add nitrogen to the soil, or other crops such as oats, barley, and rye. This method helps restore soil nutrients, reduces erosion by keeping the soil covered, and reduces pest infestation and plant diseases.

Concern about soil erosion should not be limited to farmers. At least 40% of soil erosion in the United States is caused by forestry, mining, and urban development carried out without proper regard for soil conservation. Individual home owners also have an important role to play in soil conservation (see Case Study on p. 232).

10-4   SOIL CONTAMINATION

Soil Pollution: A Growing Threat   Like air and water, soil is also vulnerable to pollution from several sources. One source is the atmosphere. Harmful air pollutants settle out on soils. Some of these pollutants are leached into groundwater supplies, and some are blown back into the air as suspended particulate matter when soil erodes. Another source of soil contamination is hazardous waste, the often deadly by-products of industrial processes, buried in landfills or dumped in fields, as discussed in Section 18-6.

Although irrigation helps increase crop productivity in the short run, it can lead to sharp drops in crop productivity in the long run by causing excessive salt buildup (salinization) and rising water tables (waterlogging). Pesticides also temporarily increase crop productivity—until insects develop genetic resistance to them (Section 21-3). But traces of these chemicals appear in many foods grown on pesticide-treated soils, in the groundwater that many people drink, and in the air we breathe.

Irrigation Problems: Salinization and Waterlogging
About 18% of the world's cropland is now irrigated, producing about one-third of the world's food. Irrigated cropland is projected to at least double by 2020.

Irrigation can increase crop yields per hectare two to three times the yields of land watered only by rain. But irrigation also has some harmful side effects. As irrigation water flows over and through the ground, it dissolves salts, increasing the salinity of the water. Much of the water in this saline solution is lost to the atmosphere by evaporation, leaving behind high concentrations of salts such as sodium chloride in the topsoil. The accumulation of salts in soils is called **salinization** (Figure 10-23). Unless the salts are flushed or drained from the soil, their buildup promotes excessive water use, increases capital and operating costs, stunts crop growth, decreases yields, eventually kills crop plants, and makes the land unproductive.

An estimated one-fourth of the world's irrigated cropland is now affected by salt buildup. About half of this area is in Pakistan and India. In the United States salinization has already reduced agricultural productivity on 25% to 35% of all irrigated land in 17 western states (Figure 10-24) and may soon affect half

Figure 10-24 Because of high evaporation, poor drainage, and severe salinization, white alkaline salts have replaced crops that once grew in heavily irrigated Paradise Valley, Wyoming.

USDA Bureau of Reclamation/Lyle C. Axhelm

of this land. Worldwide, it is projected that 50% to 65% of all currently irrigated cropland will suffer reduced productivity from excess soil salinity by 2000.

When irrigation water is repeatedly withdrawn from and returned to a river as it flows from its mountain headwaters to the ocean, the salinity of the river increases in downstream areas. Using this more saline water for irrigation accelerates the rate of soil salinization.

Eventually the water in a river can become so saline that it is useless for irrigation. For example, by the time the Colorado River makes its way from its headwaters in the Rocky Mountains and reaches Mexico, its salt concentration has increased 20-fold, making it essentially useless for crop irrigation. This has led to a long-standing dispute between Mexico and the United States, which may be partially resolved by the recent opening of the Yuma Desalting Plant in Arizona.

One way to reduce salinization is to flush salts out of the soil by applying much more irrigation water than is needed for crop growth. But this increases pumping and crop production costs and wastes enormous amounts of water. Another method is to pump groundwater from a central well and apply it with a sprinkler system that pivots around the well. This method maintains downward drainage and is especially effective at preventing salinization, but at least 30% of the water is consumed by evaporation. Also, groundwater in unconfined aquifers eventually becomes too saline for irrigation and other human uses unless expensive drainage systems are installed.

In theory, once topsoil has become heavily salinized, the farmer can renew it by taking the land out of production for two to five years, installing an underground network of perforated drainage pipe, and flushing the soil with large quantities of low-salt water. This scheme, however, is very expensive and only slows down the buildup of soil salinity—it does not stop the process. Flushing salts from the soil also increases the salinity of irrigation water delivered to farmers further downstream, unless the saline water can be drained into evaporation ponds rather than returned to the river or canal.

In the Indian state of Ultar Pradesh, farmers are rehabilitating tracts of salinized land by planting a saline-tolerant tree that lowers the water table by taking up water through its roots. Tube wells can also be used to lower water tables. But they are useful only in areas with an adequate groundwater supply.

A problem often accompanying salinization in dry regions is **waterlogging** (Figure 10-23). To keep salts from accumulating and destroying fragile root systems, farmers often apply heavy amounts of irrigation water to leach salts deeper into the soil. If drainage isn't provided, water accumulating underground gradually raises the water table closer to the surface. Saline water envelops the roots of plants and kills them, converting once fertile fields to wet deserts. This is a particularly serious problem in the heavily irrigated San Joaquin Valley in California, where soils contain a clay layer impermeable to water. Worldwide, at least one-tenth of all irrigated land suffers from waterlogging, and the problem is getting worse.

Because soil is the base of life, we must demand that soil abuse halt and be replaced with soil healing and soil protection. This transformation in the way we think and act is not idealistic. It is absolutely necessary.

Civilization can survive the exhaustion of oil reserves, but not the continuing wholesale loss of topsoil.
Lester R. Brown

David Pimentel

David Pimentel is a professor of insect ecology and agricultural sciences in the College of Agriculture and Life Sciences at Cornell University. He has chaired the Board on Environmental Studies in the National Academy of Sciences (1979-1981); the Panel on Soil and Land Degradation, Office of Technology Assessment (1978-1981), and the Biomass Panel, U.S. Department of Energy (1976-1985). He has published over 300 scientific papers and 12 books on environmental topics including land degradation, agricultural pollution and energy use, biomass energy, and pesticides. He was one of the first ecologists to employ an interdisciplinary, holistic approach in investigating complex environmental problems.

At a time when the world's human population is rapidly expanding and its need for more land to produce food, fiber, and fuelwood is also escalating, valuable land is being degraded through erosion and other means at an alarming rate. Soil degradation is of great concern because soil reformation is extremely slow. Under tropical and temperate agricultural conditions, an average of 500 years (with a range of 220 to 1,000 years) are required for the renewal of 2.5 cm (1 inch)—a renewal rate of about 1 metric ton (t) of topsoil per hectare (ha) of land per year (1t/ha per year). Worldwide annual erosion rates for agricultural land are 18 to 100 times this natural renewal rate.

Erosion rates vary in different regions because of topography, rainfall, wind intensity, and the type of agricultural practices used. In China, for example, the average annual soil loss is reported to be about 40t/ha, while the U.S. average is 18t/ha. In states like Iowa and Missouri, however, annual soil erosion averages are greater than 35t/ha.

Worldwide, each year about 6 million hectares (about the size of West Virginia) of land are degraded by erosion and other factors. In addition, according to the UN Environmental Program, each year crop productivity becomes uneconomic on about 20 million hectares (about the size of Nebraska) because soil quality has been severely degraded.

Soil erosion also occurs in forestland but is not as severe as that in the more exposed soil of agricultural land. However, soil erosion in managed forests is a major concern because the soil reformation rate in forests is about two to three times slower than that in agricultural land. To compound this erosion problem, at least 12 million hectares (about the size of Pennsylvania) of forest are being cleared each year throughout the world. More than half of this is being used to compensate for loss of agricultural land caused by erosion. Average soil erosion per hectare increases when trees are removed and the land is planted with crops.

The effects of agriculture and forestry are interrelated in many other ways. Large-scale removal of forests without adequate replanting reduces fuelwood supplies and forces the poor in LDCs to substitute crop residue and manure for fuelwood. When these plant and animal wastes are burned instead of being returned to the land as ground cover and organic fertilizer, erosion is intensified and productivity of the land is decreased. These factors, in turn, increase pressure to convert more forestland into agricultural land—further intensifying soil erosion.

One reason that soil erosion does not receive high priority among many governments and farmers is that it usually occurs at such a slow rate that its cumulative effects may take decades to become apparent. For example, the removal of 1 millimeter (1/25 inch) of soil is so small that it goes undetected. But the accumulated soil loss at this rate over a 25-year period would amount to 25 mm (1 inch)—an amount that would take about 500 years to replace by natural processes.

Although reduced soil depth is a serious concern because it is cumulative, other factors associated with erosion also reduce productivity. These are losses of water, organic matter, and soil nutrients. Water is the major limiting factor for all natural and agricultural plants and trees. When some of the vegetation on land is removed, most water is lost to remaining plants because it runs off rapidly and does not penetrate the soil. In addition, soil erosion reduces the water-holding capacity of soil because it removes organic matter and fine soil particles that hold water. When this happens, water infiltration into soil can be reduced as much as 90%.

Organic matter in soil plays an important role in holding water and in decreasing removal of plant nutrients. Thus, it is not surprising that a 50% reduction of soil organic matter on a plot of land has been found to reduce corn yields as much as 25%. When soil erodes, there is also a loss of vital plant nutrients such as nitrogen, phosphorus, potassium, and calcium. With U.S. annual cropland erosion rates of about 18t/ha, estimates are that about half of the 45 million metric tons (49.5 million tons) of commercial fertilizers that are applied annually are replacing soil nutrients lost by erosion. This use of fertilizers substantially adds to the cost of crop production.

(continued)

Some analysts who are unaware of the numerous and complex effects of soil erosion have falsely concluded that the damages are relatively minor. For example, they report that an average soil loss in the United States of 18t/ha per year causes an annual reduction in crop productivity of only 0.1% to 0.5%. However, we need to consider all the ecological effects caused by erosion, including a reduction in soil depth, reduced water availability for crops, and reduction in soil organic matter and nutrients. When this is done, agronomists and ecologists report a 15% to 30% reduction in crop productivity—a key factor in increased levels of costly fertilizer and declining yields on some land despite high levels of fertilization. Because fertilizers are not a substitute for fertile soil, they can only be applied up to certain levels before crop yields begin to decline.

Reduced agricultural productivity is only one of the effects and costs of soil erosion. In the United States, water runoff is responsible for transporting about 3 billion metric tons (3.3 billion tons) of sediment each year to waterways in the 48 contiguous states. About 60% of these sediments come from agricultural lands. Estimates show that off-site damages to U.S. water storage capacity, wildlife, and navigable waterways from these sediments cost an estimated $6 billion each year. Dredging sediments from U.S. rivers, harbors, and reservoirs alone costs about $570 million each year. About 25% of new water storage capacity in U.S. reservoirs is built solely to compensate for sediment buildup.

When soil sediments that include pesticides and other agricultural chemicals are carried into rivers, lakes, and reservoirs, fish production is adversely affected. These contaminated sediments interfere with fish spawning, increase predation on fish, and destroy fisheries in estuarine and coastal areas.

Increased erosion and water runoff on mountain slopes flood agricultural land in the valleys below, further decreasing agricultural productivity. Eroded land also does not hold water well, further decreasing crop productivity. This effect is magnified in the 80 countries (with nearly 40% of the world's population) that experience frequent droughts. The rapid growth in the world's population, accompanied by the need for more crops and a projected doubling of water needs in the next 20 years, will only intensify water shortages, particularly if soil erosion is not contained.

Thus, soil erosion is one of the world's critical problems and if not slowed will seriously reduce agricultural and forestry production and degrade the quality of aquatic ecosystems. Solutions are not particularly difficult but are often not implemented because erosion occurs so gradually that we fail to acknowledge its cumulative impact until damage is irreversible. Many farmers have also been conditioned to believe that losses in soil fertility can be remedied by applying increasingly higher levels of fertilizer.

The principal method of controlling soil erosion and its accompanying runoff of sediment is to maintain adequate vegetative coverage on soils by various methods discussed in Section 10-3. These methods are also cost effective in preventing erosion, especially when off-site costs of erosion are included. Scientists, policymakers, and agriculturists need to work together to implement soil and water conservation practices before world soils lose most of their productivity.

Guest Essay Discussion

1. Some cornucopians contend that average soil erosion rates in the United States and the world are low and that this problem has been overblown by environmentalists and can easily be solved by improved agricultural technology such as no-till cultivation and increased fertilizer use. Do you agree or disagree with this position? Explain.

2. What specific things do you believe elected officials should do to decrease soil erosion and the resulting sediment water pollution in the United States?

3. What specific things can individual citizens, home owners, and home gardeners do to reduce their contribution to soil erosion?

CHAPTER SUMMARY

Soil is a complex mixture of inorganic materials (mostly clay, silt, and sand) and decaying organic matter (humus), water, air, and living organisms (mostly bacteria and other decomposers). These components are arranged in layers with a distinct thickness, color, texture, and composition that vary with different types of soils.

Most soils are formed from the breakdown, or weathering, of underlying bedrock (parent material). Others develop from sediments deposited on bedrock by wind, water, volcanoes, or melting glaciers.

The proportion of very fine clay particles, fine silt particles, and coarse sand particles determines a soil's texture. Soil texture helps determine the number of pores a volume of soil has and the average distances between these spaces (soil porosity). A soil with a high porosity can hold more water and air than one with a lower porosity. Average pore size determines soil permeability, the rate at which the soil transmits water and air from upper to lower layers. Soil porosity is also influenced by soil structure, how the particles that make up a soil are organized and clumped together. The acidity or alkalinity of a soil (measured by pH) is a factor determining the types of crops it can support.

Soil erosion occurs primarily when rain and wind move soil components, especially topsoil, from one place to another. Throughout much of the world the rate at which soil is being eroded as a result of farming, logging, mining, construction, and overgrazing greatly exceeds the natural rate of soil regeneration. Excessive erosion reduces both the fertility and water-holding capacity of soil. When the productivity of rangeland or cropland drops more than 10%, the process is called *desertification*.

In much of the world, including the United States, potentially renewable topsoil is being converted into a nonrenewable resource that is being depleted at alarming rates. Much of the soil eroded from land ends up as sediment in rivers and other bodies of water. This sediment clogs navigable waterways, fills up reservoirs, and harms fish and other forms of aquatic life.

Commercial inorganic fertilizer is not a complete substitute for naturally fertile topsoil; it merely hides for a time the gradual depletion of this vital resource. Nor is irrigation a long-term solution. Repeated irrigation of cropland without sufficient drainage eventually decreases or destroys its crop productivity as a result of *waterlogging* and salt buildup (*salinization*).

Soil conservation involves using various methods to reduce soil erosion, to prevent depletion of soil nutrients, and to restore nutrients already lost by erosion, leaching, and excessive crop harvesting. Most methods used to control soil erosion involve keeping the soil covered with vegetation.

Methods used to reduce erosion include *conservation tillage* (disturbing the topsoil little if any during planting), *contour farming, terracing, strip cropping, gully reclamation, windbreaks,* and *land-use classification and control.*

Organic fertilizers (animal and crop wastes) and commercial inorganic fertilizers can be applied to soil to partially restore and maintain plant nutrients lost by erosion, leaching, and crop harvesting and to increase crop yields. *Crop rotation* also prevents depletion of soil nutrients.

Soil is polluted by the settling out of chemicals from the atmosphere, application of some pesticides, and the dumping or burying of hazardous waste. Irrigation helps increase crop productivity in the short run, but it can lead to sharp drops in crop productivity in the long run by causing excessive salt buildup (salinization) and rising water tables (waterlogging).

Preserving soil—the irreplaceable base that provides us with food, fiber, fuelwood, and numerous other materials—must become one of the major priorities for policymakers and ordinary citizens in rich and poor countries.

DISCUSSION TOPICS

1. Why should everyone, not just farmers, be concerned with soil conservation?

2. Explain how a plant can have ample supplies of nitrogen, phosphorus, potassium, and other essential nutrients and still have stunted growth.

3. What are the key properties of a soil that is good for growing most crops?

4. Describe briefly the Dust Bowl phenomenon of the 1930s and explain how and where it could happen again. How would you try to prevent a recurrence?

5. Explain how contour farming, terracing, strip cropping, and conservation tillage can reduce soil erosion.

6. Visit rural or mostly undeveloped areas near your campus and classify the lands according to the system shown in Figure 10-21 and Table 10-2. Look for examples of land being used for purposes to which it is not best suited.

7. What are the major advantages and disadvantages of using commercial inorganic fertilizers to help restore and maintain soil fertility? Why should organic fertilizers also be used on land treated with inorganic fertilizers?

8. Visit several homesites in your community and evaluate their use of natural vegetation to reduce soil erosion and enhance natural biological diversity as discussed in the Case Study on p. 232. Also, evaluate the planting of your own homesite and various areas of your campus.

CHAPTER 11

Water Resources

General Questions and Issues

1. How much usable fresh water is available for human use and how much of this supply are we using?
2. What are the major water resource problems in the world and in the United States?

3. How can water resources be managed to increase the supply and reduce unnecessary waste?

If there is magic on this planet, it is in water.

Loren Eisley

W ater is our most abundant resource, covering about 71% of the earth's surface. This precious film of water—about 97% salt water and the remainder fresh—helps maintain the earth's climate and dilutes environmental pollutants. Essential to all life, water makes up 50% to 97% of the weight of all plants and animals and about 70% of your body. Water is also a vital resource for agriculture, manufacturing, transportation, and countless other human activities.

Because of differences in average annual precipitation, some areas of the world have too little fresh water and others too much. With varying degrees of success, we have attempted to correct some of these imbalances. We have captured fresh water in reservoirs behind dams, transferred fresh water in rivers and streams from one area to another, tapped underground supplies, and attempted to reduce water use, waste, and contamination.

Despite these efforts, water is one of the most poorly managed resources on earth. We waste it and pollute it. We also charge too little for making it available, encouraging even greater waste and pollution of this potentially renewable resource.

11-1 SUPPLY, RENEWAL, AND USE OF WATER RESOURCES

Worldwide Supply and Renewal The world's fixed supply of water in all forms (vapor, liquid, and solid) is enormous. If we could distribute it equally, every person on earth would have 280 billion liters (74 billion gallons). However, about 97% of the earth's water is found in the oceans (Figure 5-14, p. 121) and is too salty for drinking, growing crops, and most industrial uses except cooling.

The remaining 3% is fresh water. However, all but 0.003% of this supply is highly polluted, lies too far under the earth's surface to be extracted at an affordable cost, or is locked up in glaciers, polar ice caps, atmosphere, and soil. To put this in measurements that we can understand, if the world's water supply were only 100 liters (26 gallons), our usable supply of fresh water would be only about 0.003 liter (one-half teaspoon) (Figure 11-1).

That tiny fraction of usable fresh water still amounts to an average of 8.4 million liters (2.2 million gallons) for each person on earth. This supply is continually collected, purified, and distributed in the natural hydrologic (water) cycle (Figure 4-25, p. 99). This natural recycling and purification process works as long as we don't use water faster than it is replenished and as long as we don't overload it with slowly degradable and nondegradable wastes.

Surface-Water Runoff The fresh water we use comes from two sources: groundwater and surface-water runoff (Figure 11-2). Precipitation that does not infiltrate into the ground or return to the atmosphere by evaporation or transpiration is called **surface water** and becomes **runoff**—fresh water that flows on the earth's surface into streams, rivers, lakes, wetlands, and res-

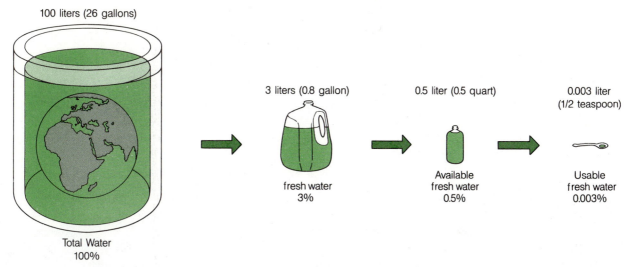

Figure 11-1 Only a tiny fraction of the world's water supply is available as fresh water for human use.

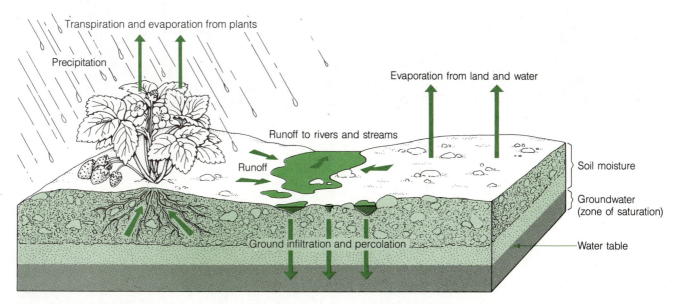

Figure 11-2 Major routes of local precipitation: runoff into surface waters, ground infiltration and percolation into aquifers, and evaporation and transpiration into the atmosphere.

ervoirs. The land area that delivers runoff, sediment, and water-soluble substances to a major river and its tributaries is called a **watershed,** or **drainage basin.**

Surface water can be withdrawn from streams, rivers, lakes, and reservoirs for human activities, but only part of the total annual runoff is available for use. Some of it flows in rivers to the sea too rapidly to be captured, and some must be left in streams for wildlife and to supply downstream areas. In some years the amount of runoff is reduced by below-average precipitation.

Groundwater Some precipitation seeps into the ground, where it accumulates as **soil water** and partially fills pores between soil particles and rocks in the upper layers of the earth's crust (Figure 11-2). Most of this water is eventually lost to the atmosphere by evaporation from the upper layers of soil and by transpiration from leaves.

Under the influence of gravity, some infiltrating water slowly percolates through porous materials deeper into the earth. There it fills pores and fractures in spongelike, or permeable, layers of sand, gravel, and porous rock such as sandstone. This area, where all available pore spaces are filled by water, is called the zone of saturation. These porous, water-bearing layers of underground rock are called **aquifers,** and the water in them is **groundwater** (Figure 11-3).

Aquifers are recharged or replenished naturally by precipitation, which percolates downward through soil and rock in what is called a **recharge area.** The recharge process is usually quite slow (decades to hundreds of

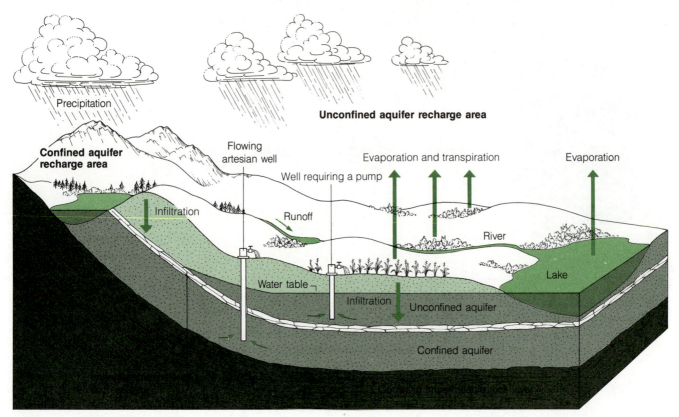

Figure 11-3 The groundwater system.

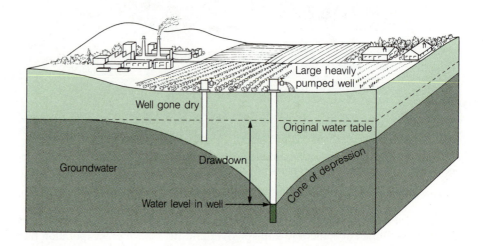

Figure 11-4 Drawdown of water table and cone of depression produced when wells remove groundwater faster than it is recharged, a process known as overdrafting.

years) compared to the more rapid replenishment of surface water supplies. If the withdrawal rate of an aquifer exceeds its recharge rate, the aquifer is converted from a slowly renewable resource to a nonrenewable resource on a human time scale.

There are two types of aquifers: confined and unconfined. An **unconfined aquifer,** or **water table aquifer,** forms when groundwater collects above a layer of impermeable rock or compacted clay. The top of the water-saturated portion of an unconfined aquifer is called the **water table** (Figures 11-2 and 11-3). Groundwater is the part of underground water in the zone of

saturation below the water table. Soil water is the part of underground water above the water table, sometimes called the zone of aeration. A shallow, unconfined aquifer is recharged by water percolating downward from soils and materials directly above the aquifer.

To get water from an unconfined aquifer, a well is drilled below the water table and into the unconfined aquifer. Then a pump must be used to bring water to the surface. The height of the water table in an area rises during prolonged wet periods and falls during prolonged drought. The water table also falls when water is pumped out by wells faster than the natural

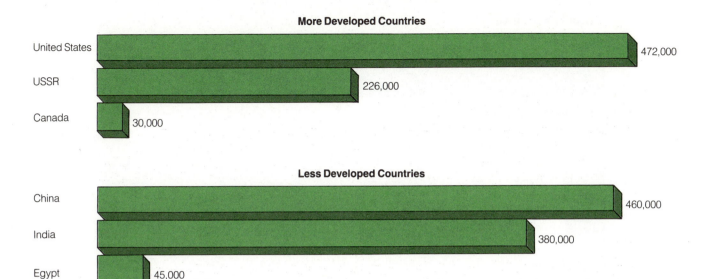

More Developed Countries

United States — 472,000
USSR — 226,000
Canada — 30,000

Less Developed Countries

China — 460,000
India — 380,000
Egypt — 45,000

Figure 11-5 Total water withdrawal in selected countries in 1984 in billions of liters. (Data from Worldwatch Institute and World Resources Institute)

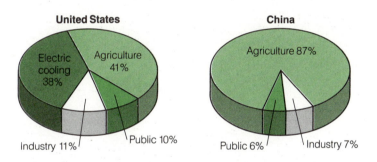

United States

Electric cooling 38%
Agriculture 41%
Industry 11%
Public 10%

China

Agriculture 87%
Public 6%
Industry 7%

Figure 11-6 Use of water in the United States and China. (Data from Worldwatch Institute and World Resources Institute)

rate of recharge. This overdrafting creates a waterless volume known as a cone of depression (Figure 11-4).

A **confined aquifer** forms when groundwater is sandwiched between two layers of impermeable rock, such as clay or shale (Figure 11-3). This type of aquifer is saturated with water under a pressure greater than that of the atmosphere. In some cases pressure from the weight of water higher in the aquifer is so great that when a well is drilled into the confined aquifer, water is pushed to the surface without the aid of a pump. Such a well is called a flowing artesian well. With other confined-aquifer wells, called nonflowing artesian wells, pumps must be used because there isn't enough pressure to force the water all the way to the surface.

The recharge areas for confined aquifers can be hundreds of miles away from wells where water is withdrawn. Thus, the rate of natural recharge for such aquifers may not be based on local precipitation at the point of withdrawal as it is for unconfined aquifers.

World and U.S. Water Use Two common measures of water use are withdrawal and consumption. **Water withdrawal** involves taking water from a groundwater

or surface-water source and transporting it to a place of use. **Water consumption** occurs when water that has been withdrawn is not available for reuse in the area from which it is withdrawn. Some seeps into the ground. Some evaporates into the atmosphere. Some becomes contaminated with salts dissolved from the soil or with other pollutants.

Annual total water withdrawal varies considerably among various MDCs and LDCs (Figure 11-5). Worldwide, almost three-fourths of the water withdrawn each year is used for irrigation. The rest is used in industrial processing, in cooling electric power plants, and in homes and businesses (public use). However, the uses of withdrawn water vary widely from one country to another (Figure 11-6).

In the United States about three-fourths of the fresh water withdrawn each year comes from rivers, lakes, and reservoirs. The rest comes from groundwater aquifers. Almost 80% of the water withdrawn in the United States is used for cooling electric power plants and for irrigation. Producing food and manufacturing various products require large amounts of water (Figure 11-7), although in most cases much of this water could be conserved and reused.

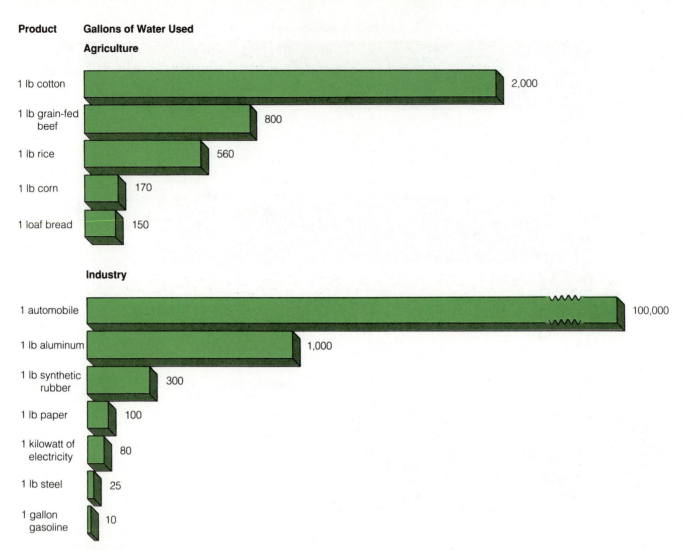

Product   Gallons of Water Used

Agriculture

1 lb cotton	2,000
1 lb grain-fed beef	800
1 lb rice	560
1 lb corn	170
1 loaf bread	150

Industry

1 automobile	100,000
1 lb aluminum	1,000
1 lb synthetic rubber	300
1 lb paper	100
1 kilowatt of electricity	80
1 lb steel	25
1 gallon gasoline	10

Figure 11-7 Amount of water typically used to produce various foods and products in the United States. (Data from U.S. Geological Survey)

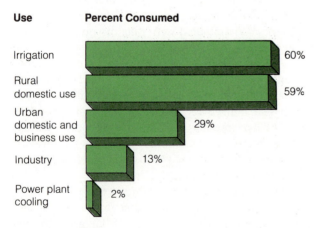

Use   Percent Consumed

Irrigation	60%
Rural domestic use	59%
Urban domestic and business use	29%
Industry	13%
Power plant cooling	2%

Figure 11-8 Percentage of water consumed by different uses in the United States. (Data from U.S. Geological Survey)

Since 1950 total water withdrawal in the United States has more than doubled. This increase was caused by increases in population, urbanization, and eco-nomic activity, and by government-subsidized, low water prices that discourage conservation and reuse.

About one-fourth of the water withdrawn in the United States is consumed. The other three-fourths returns to surface-water or groundwater supplies. Water consumption varies with different types of use (Figure 11-8). It also varies in different regions. For example, the average consumption per person in the mostly arid and semiarid West is 10 times that in the East.

Worldwide, up to 90% of all water withdrawn from rivers and lakes is returned to them for potential reuse. However, about 75% of the water supplied for irrigation is consumed. Between 1985 and 2020 the world-wide withdrawal of water for irrigation is projected to double, primarily because of increasing population in LDCs. Withdrawal for industrial processing and cooling electric power plants is projected to increase 20-fold because of increasing industrialization in LDCs. Withdrawal for public use in homes and businesses is expected to increase fivefold.

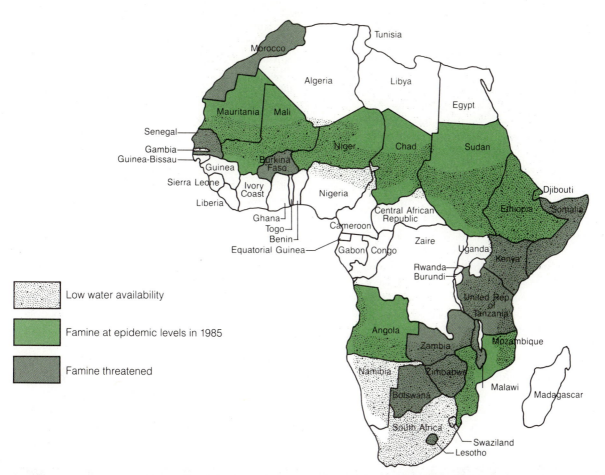

Figure 11-9 African countries suffering from low per capita food production, famine, and poor water availability. These conditions are caused by a combination of rapid population growth, prolonged drought, land misuse, war, and ineffective water and soil resource management. (Data from UN Food and Agriculture Organization)

Legend:
- Low water availability
- Famine at epidemic levels in 1985
- Famine threatened

11-2 WATER RESOURCE PROBLEMS

Too Little Water A number of experts consider the availability of enough fresh water to meet human needs one of the most serious long-range problems confronting many parts of the world and the United States. During the 1970s, major droughts affected an average of 24.4 million people and killed over 23,000 a year—a trend continuing in the 1980s. A **drought** occurs when an area does not get enough water because of lower than normal precipitation, higher than normal temperatures that increase evaporation, or both.

At least 80 arid and semiarid countries, where nearly 40% of the world's people live, have serious periodic droughts. These countries, mostly in Asia and Africa, have great difficulty growing enough food to support their populations. A prolonged drought affected much of Africa between 1982 and 1986 (Figure 11-9). It led to widespread starvation and disease and forced at least 10 million people to abandon their homes in a desperate search for food and water.

Between 1984 and 1988 there were major droughts in parts of China, India, and North America. In the summer of 1988, about 43% of the continental United States experienced severe droughts, comparable to those that created the Dust Bowl in the Midwest in the 1930s (see Case Study on p. 226). The grain harvest dropped by 31% and crop losses amounted to about $15 billion, one of the costliest natural disasters in U.S. history.

Reduced precipitation, higher than normal temperatures, or both usually trigger a drought. But rapid population growth and poor land use intensify its effects. In many LDCs large numbers of poor people have no choice but to try to survive on drought-prone land. To get enough food and fuelwood, they strip the land of trees, cultivate poor soils, let their livestock overgraze grasslands, and grow crops at higher, more erosion-prone elevations. This land degradation increases the severity of long-term drought by reducing the amount of rainfall absorbed and slowly released by vegetation and soils. Each new drought can lead to a downward spiral of further land degradation and desertification (see Case Study on p. 224), lower food and fuelwood productivity, and more poverty.

In arid and semiarid parts of MDCs, where

periodic drought is to be expected, networks of canals and tunnels are often used to withdraw water from rivers and transport it to urban and industrial areas. However, during prolonged drought the flow of water in the rivers is sharply reduced. The resulting water supply crisis is often viewed as a natural disaster. But it is actually a human-caused disaster—the result of trying to support too many people and livestock in areas that normally have droughts.

Almost 150 of the world's 214 major river systems are shared by at least two countries and 12 of these waterways are shared by five or more countries. Together these countries contain 40% of the world's population, and they often clash over water rights. Water scarcity is a source of conflict between countries, especially in the arid Middle East. Israel went to war in 1967 partly because Arabian countries were trying to divert water from the Jordan River. One reason that Israel continues to occupy the Golan Heights and the West Bank is to ensure its access to water from this river.

Too Much Water   Some countries have enough annual precipitation but get most of it at one time of the year. In India, for example, 90% of the annual precipitation falls between June and September, the monsoon season. This downpour runs off so rapidly that most of it cannot be captured and used. The massive runoff also causes periodic flooding.

During the 1970s, major flood disasters affected 15.4 million people, killed an average of 4,700 people a year, and caused tens of billions of dollars in property damages. This trend continued in the 1980s.

Floods, like droughts, are usually called natural disasters. But human activities have contributed to the sharp rise in flood deaths and damages since the 1960s. Cultivation of land, deforestation, overgrazing, and mining have removed water-absorbing vegetation and soil (see Case Study below). Urbanization also increases flooding, even with moderate rainfall. It replaces vegetation and soil with highways, parking lots, shopping centers, office buildings, homes, and other structures that lead to rapid runoff of rainwater.

Many poor people have little choice but to live on land subject to severe flooding. Many other people in LDCs and MDCs believe that the benefits of living in flood-prone areas outweigh the risks. Urban areas and croplands often are located on **floodplains**—flat areas along the banks of rivers naturally subject to periodic flooding. Floodplains usually have highly fertile topsoil deposited by the rivers. They are also close to water supplies and water transportation routes.

CASE STUDY   Natural and Unnatural Flooding in Bangladesh

Bangladesh is one of the world's most densely populated countries. More than 115 million people—almost half the population of the United States—are packed into a country roughly the size of Wisconsin. It is also one of the world's poorest countries, with an average per capita income of about $160.

The country is located on a vast, low-lying delta of shifting islands of silt at the mouths of the Ganges, Brahmaputra, and Meghna rivers. Its people are accustomed to flooding after water deposited by annual monsoon rains in the Himalayan mountain ranges of India, Nepal, Bhutan, and Tibet flows downward through rivers to Bangladesh and into the Bay of Bengal.

Bangladesh depends on this annual flooding to grow rice, its major source of food. The annual deposit of silt in the delta basin also helps maintain soil fertility. Thus, the people of this country

are used to moderate annual flooding and need it for their survival.

But massive flooding is disastrous. In the past, major floods occurred only once every 50 years or so. But since 1950 the number of large-scale floods has increased sharply. During the 1970s and 1980s Bangladesh had major floods on average every four years. After a flood in 1974, an estimated 300,000 people died in a famine.

In the 1980s floods have become even more severe. In 1988 a massive flood covered 80% of the country's land mass after the heaviest monsoon rains in 70 years. At least 1,500 people were killed by drowning and snakebite and 30 million people—one out of four—were left homeless. Hundreds of thousands more contracted diseases such as cholera and typhoid fever from contaminated water and food supplies. At least a quarter of the country's crops were destroyed. Hundreds of thousands

of people will probably die from famine, even with massive international aid.

We usually think of such floods as unpreventable natural disasters. But the increased severity of flooding in Bangladesh is primarily an unnatural disaster caused by human activities.

Bangladesh's flooding problems begin in the Himalayan watershed, where people depend on wood for fuel. There a combination of rapid population growth, deforestation, overgrazing, and unsustainable farming on easily erodible, steep mountain slopes have greatly diminished the ability of the soil to absorb water. Instead of being absorbed and released slowly, water from the annual monsoon runs off mountainsides rapidly and causes massive flooding in Bangladesh. This deluge of water also carries with it the soil vital to the survival of people in the Himalayas._____

Most of the more than 2,000 U.S. cities (including New Orleans, Louisiana; Phoenix, Arizona; Tallahassee, Florida; and Harrisburg, Pennsylvania) located completely or partially on floodplains suffer flooding on an average of once every 2 to 3 years. Other areas are classified as 18-, 25-, 50-, or 100-year floodplains, according to the average interval between major floods. But this is a statistical average; major floods may occur three times within a month, annually for 5 consecutive years, or not for several hundred years. Projected rises in sea levels from atmospheric warming over the next 50 years could flood many low-lying coastal cities and wetlands.

Since 1925 the U.S. Army Corps of Engineers, the Soil Conservation Service, and the Bureau of Reclamation have spent more than $8 billion on flood control projects. They have straightened and deepened stream channels and built dams, reservoirs, levees, and seawalls. These projects stimulate development on flood-prone land. As a result, property damage from floods in the United States has increased from about $0.5 billion a year in the 1960s to about $3 billion a year in the 1980s.

There are a number of effective ways to prevent or reduce flood damage. Vegetation can be replanted in disturbed areas to reduce runoff. In urban areas ponds can be built to retain rainwater and release it slowly to rivers. Rainwater can be diverted through storm sewers to holding tanks and ponds for use by industry.

Governments should identify floodplains, and zoning regulations should prohibit their use for certain types of development. Sellers of property in these areas should be required to provide prospective buyers with information about average flood frequency. In the United States floodplain zoning is now a national policy.

Water in the Wrong Place In some countries the largest rivers, which carry most of the runoff, are far from agricultural and population centers where the water is needed. South America has the largest average annual runoff of any continent. But 60% of this runoff flows through the Amazon, the world's largest river, in areas far from where most people live.

In many LDCs poor people must spend a good part of their waking hours fetching water, often from polluted streams and rivers. Many women and children walk 16 to 24 kilometers (10 to 14 miles) a day, carrying heavy, water-filled jars.

Contaminated Drinking Water Drinking contaminated water is the most common hazard to people in much of the world. In 1983 the World Health Organization estimated that in LDCs 61% of the people living in rural areas and 26% of the urban dwellers did not have access to safe drinking water (Figure 11-10). This means that 1.5 billion people do not have

Figure 11-10 About two out of three rural people and one out of four city dwellers in LDCs lack ready access to uncontaminated water. These children in Lima, Peru, are scooping up drinking water from a puddle.

a safe supply of drinking water. WHO estimated that at least 5 million people die every year from cholera, dysentery, diarrhea, and other preventable waterborne diseases. Every day these diseases prematurely kill an average of 13,700 people. Most of these deaths could be prevented at little cost.

In 1980 the United Nations proclaimed this the International Drinking Water Supply and Sanitation Decade. UN officials called for MDCs and LDCs to spend $300 billion over 10 years to supply all the world's people with clean drinking water and adequate sanitation by 1990. The $30-billion-a-year cost of this program would be roughly equal to what the world spends every 10 days for military purposes. Some progress has been made. But by 1989 the program had fallen far short of its goal because of lack of funding and lack of commitment by MDCs and LDCs.

The U.S. Situation Overall, the United States has plenty of fresh water. But much of the country's annual runoff is not in the desired place, occurs at the wrong time, or is contaminated from agricultural and industrial activities. Average annual precipitation throughout the United States varies widely. Most of the eastern half of the country usually has ample precipitation, while much of the western half has too little (Figure 11-11).

Many major urban centers in the United States are located in areas that don't have enough water or are projected to have water shortages by 2000 (Figure 11-12). Several of the fastest growing states, especially California and Arizona, have severe periodic water shortages.

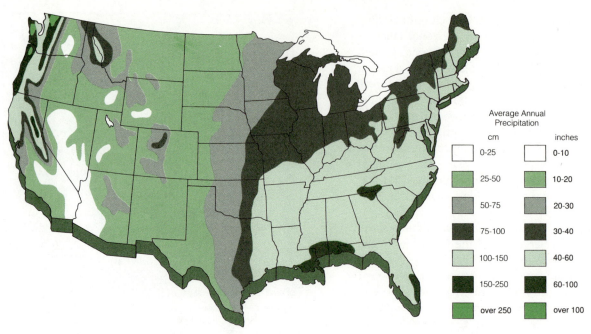

Figure 11-11 Average annual precipitation in the continental United States. (Data from Water Resources Council)

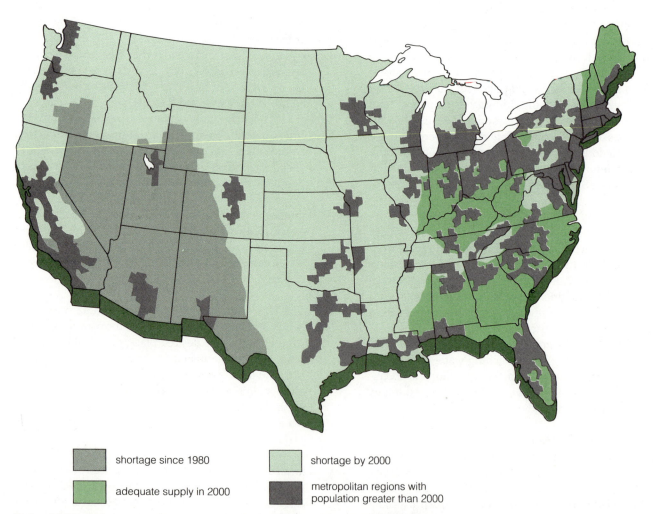

Figure 11-12 Present and projected water deficit regions in the United States compared with present metropolitan regions with populations greater than 1 million. (Data from U.S. Water Resources Council and U.S. Geological Survey)

Most of the more than 2,000 U.S. cities (including New Orleans, Louisiana; Phoenix, Arizona; Tallahassee, Florida; and Harrisburg, Pennsylvania) located completely or partially on floodplains suffer flooding on an average of once every 2 to 3 years. Other areas are classified as 18-, 25-, 50-, or 100-year floodplains, according to the average interval between major floods. But this is a statistical average; major floods may occur three times within a month, annually for 5 consecutive years, or not for several hundred years. Projected rises in sea levels from atmospheric warming over the next 50 years could flood many low-lying coastal cities and wetlands.

Since 1925 the U.S. Army Corps of Engineers, the Soil Conservation Service, and the Bureau of Reclamation have spent more than $8 billion on flood control projects. They have straightened and deepened stream channels and built dams, reservoirs, levees, and seawalls. These projects stimulate development on flood-prone land. As a result, property damage from floods in the United States has increased from about $0.5 billion a year in the 1960s to about $3 billion a year in the 1980s.

There are a number of effective ways to prevent or reduce flood damage. Vegetation can be replanted in disturbed areas to reduce runoff. In urban areas ponds can be built to retain rainwater and release it slowly to rivers. Rainwater can be diverted through storm sewers to holding tanks and ponds for use by industry.

Governments should identify floodplains, and zoning regulations should prohibit their use for certain types of development. Sellers of property in these areas should be required to provide prospective buyers with information about average flood frequency. In the United States floodplain zoning is now a national policy.

Water in the Wrong Place In some countries the largest rivers, which carry most of the runoff, are far from agricultural and population centers where the water is needed. South America has the largest average annual runoff of any continent. But 60% of this runoff flows through the Amazon, the world's largest river, in areas far from where most people live.

In many LDCs poor people must spend a good part of their waking hours fetching water, often from polluted streams and rivers. Many women and children walk 16 to 24 kilometers (10 to 14 miles) a day, carrying heavy, water-filled jars.

Contaminated Drinking Water Drinking contaminated water is the most common hazard to people in much of the world. In 1983 the World Health Organization estimated that in LDCs 61% of the people living in rural areas and 26% of the urban dwellers did not have access to safe drinking water (Figure 11-10). This means that 1.5 billion people do not have

Figure 11-10 About two out of three rural people and one out of four city dwellers in LDCs lack ready access to uncontaminated water. These children in Lima, Peru, are scooping up drinking water from a puddle.

a safe supply of drinking water. WHO estimated that at least 5 million people die every year from cholera, dysentery, diarrhea, and other preventable water-borne diseases. Every day these diseases prematurely kill an average of 13,700 people. Most of these deaths could be prevented at little cost.

In 1980 the United Nations proclaimed this the International Drinking Water Supply and Sanitation Decade. UN officials called for MDCs and LDCs to spend $300 billion over 10 years to supply all the world's people with clean drinking water and adequate sanitation by 1990. The $30-billion-a-year cost of this program would be roughly equal to what the world spends every 10 days for military purposes. Some progress has been made. But by 1989 the program had fallen far short of its goal because of lack of funding and lack of commitment by MDCs and LDCs.

The U.S. Situation Overall, the United States has plenty of fresh water. But much of the country's annual runoff is not in the desired place, occurs at the wrong time, or is contaminated from agricultural and industrial activities. Average annual precipitation throughout the United States varies widely. Most of the eastern half of the country usually has ample precipitation, while much of the western half has too little (Figure 11-11).

Many major urban centers in the United States are located in areas that don't have enough water or are projected to have water shortages by 2000 (Figure 11-12). Several of the fastest growing states, especially California and Arizona, have severe periodic water shortages.

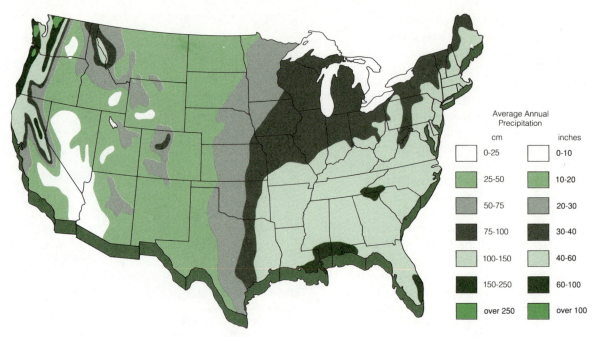

Average Annual Precipitation

cm		inches	
	0-25		0-10
	25-50		10-20
	50-75		20-30
	75-100		30-40
	100-150		40-60
	150-250		60-100
	over 250		over 100

Figure 11-11 Average annual precipitation in the continental United States. (Data from Water Resources Council)

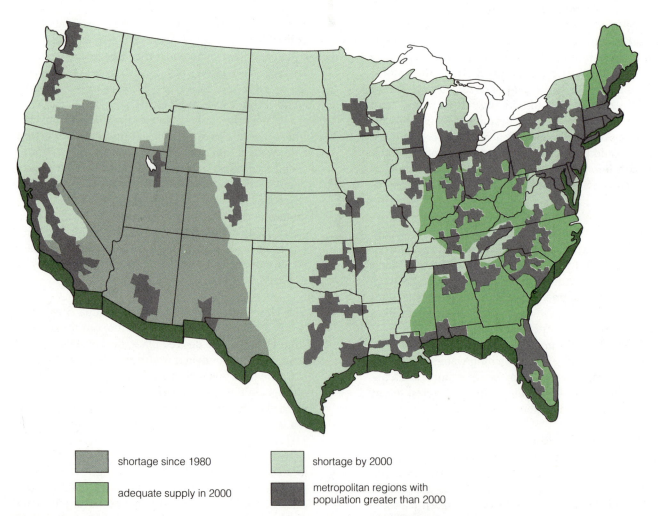

	shortage since 1980		shortage by 2000
	adequate supply in 2000		metropolitan regions with population greater than 2000

Figure 11-12 Present and projected water deficit regions in the United States compared with present metropolitan regions with populations greater than 1 million. (Data from U.S. Water Resources Council and U.S. Geological Survey)

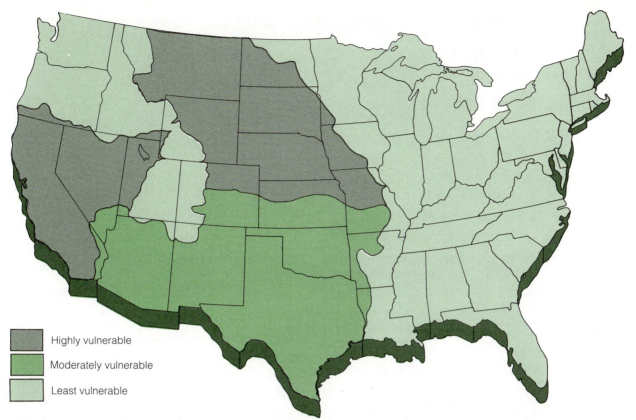

Figure 11-13 Areas in the United States where water supplies may be reduced as the world's climate warms up from the greenhouse effect. (Data from American Association for the Advancement of Science)

- ◻ Highly vulnerable
- ◻ Moderately vulnerable
- ◻ Least vulnerable

Water scarcity and clashes over water rights will intensify in many areas if the world's climate warms up as a result of an enhanced greenhouse effect. Figure 11-13 shows areas in the United States where water supplies may be threatened if this happens. Because water is such a vital resource, you might find Figures 11-12 and 11-13 useful in deciding where to live in coming decades.

In many parts of the eastern United States the major water problems are flooding, inability to supply enough water to some large urban areas, and increasing pollution of rivers, lakes, and groundwater. For example, 3 million residents of Long Island, New York, must draw all their water from an underground aquifer. This aquifer is becoming severely contaminated by industrial wastes, leaking septic tanks and landfills, and ocean salt water, which is drawn into the aquifer when fresh water is withdrawn faster than it is naturally recharged.

The major water problem in the arid and semiarid areas of the western half of the country is a shortage of runoff caused by low and variable average annual precipitation, high rates of evaporation, and prolonged periodic drought. As a result, water tables are dropping rapidly as farmers and cities deplete groundwater aquifers faster than they are recharged.

Because most areas in the region have too little precipitation to grow crops without irrigation, 85% of the western water supply is used in agriculture. Federally subsidized dams, reservoirs, and water transfer projects provide water to farms and cities at such low prices that there is little incentive for conservation. Experts project that present shortages and conflicts will get much worse as more industries and people migrate west and compete with farmers for scarce water.

11-3 WATER RESOURCE MANAGEMENT

Methods for Managing Water Resources   Although we can't increase the earth's supply of water, we can reduce the impact and spread of water resource problems by managing the supply better. The two major approaches to water resource management are to increase the usable supply and to decrease unnecessary loss and waste (Table 11-1). Most water resource experts believe that any effective plan for water management should combine these approaches.

Water problems and available solutions often differ between MDCs and LDCs. LDCs may or may not have enough water, but they rarely have the money needed to develop water storage and distribution systems. Their people must settle where the water is.

In MDCs people tend to live where the climate is favorable and bring in water through expensive water diversion systems. Some settle in a desert and expect water to be brought to them at a low price. Others settle on a floodplain and expect the government to keep flood waters away.

Table 11-1 Methods for Managing Water Resources

Increase the Supply	Reduce Unnecessary Loss and Waste
Build dams and reservoirs	Decrease evaporation of irrigation water
Divert water from one region to another	Redesign mining and industrial processes to use less water
Tap more groundwater	
Convert salt water to fresh water (desalination)	Encourage the public to reduce unnecessary water waste and use
Tow freshwater icebergs from the Antarctic to water-short coastal regions	Increase the price of water to encourage water conservation
Seed clouds to increase precipitation	Purify polluted water for reuse

CASE STUDY Benefits and Costs of Egypt's Aswan High Dam

The billion-dollar Aswan High Dam on the Nile River in Egypt shows what can happen when a large-scale dam and reservoir project is built without adequate consideration of long-term environmental effects and costs. The dam was built in the 1960s to provide flood control and irrigation water for the lower Nile basin and electricity for Cairo and other parts of Egypt. This water was badly needed because only 5% of Egypt is arable land. The rest is desert.

These goals have been partially achieved. Today the dam supplies about one-third of Egypt's electrical power. The dam saved Egypt's rice and cotton crops during the droughts of 1972 and 1973. Year-round irrigation has increased food production. It allows farmers below the dam to harvest crops three times a year on land that was previously harvested only once a year. Irrigation has also brought about 405,000 hectares (1 million acres) of desert land under cultivation.

Since the dam opened in 1964, it has also had a number of undesirable ecological effects. The dam ended the yearly flooding that had fertilized the Nile basin with silt, had flushed mineral salts from the soil, and had swept away snails that infect humans with schistosomiasis, a disease that causes pain, weakness, and premature death (Section 18-2). Cropland in the Nile basin now has to be treated with commercial fertilizer at a cost of over $100 million a year

to make up for plant nutrients once available at no cost. The country's new fertilizer plants use up much of the electrical power produced by the dam.

Salts have built up in the soil of this once-productive cropland. Salinization has offset three-fourths of the gain in food production from new, less productive land irrigated by water from the reservoir. Today 90% of the irrigated land in Egypt is affected by salinization. Since the dam opened, cases of schistosomiasis among farmers wading in irrigation ditches has risen somewhat but not as much as expected due to increased education and sanitation measures.

The dam was expected to increase the amount of cropland. However, because of rapid population growth, the country now has less arable land than when the dam was built. Urbanization has taken over much of Egypt's short supply of arable land.

Because it contains less sediment, the Nile has eroded its bed and undermined numerous bridges and smaller dams downstream. To remedy this problem, the government proposes to build 10 barrier dams. The projected cost is $250 million—one-fourth of what the dam cost. Also, without the Nile's annual discharge of sediment, the sea is eroding the delta and advancing inland, reducing productivity on many acres of agricultural land.

Now that the nutrient-rich silt no longer reaches the waters at the

river's mouth, Egypt's sardine, mackerel, shrimp, and lobster industries have all but disappeared. This has led to losses of approximately 30,000 jobs, millions of dollars annually, and an important source of protein for Egyptians. Eventually, these losses are expected to be recovered by a new fishing industry based on taking bass, catfish, and carp from the massive reservoir, called Lake Nasser, behind the dam.

The reservoir uprooted 125,000 people. It was supposed to be full by 1970 and to have enough water to meet the needs of Egypt and the Sudan during a prolonged drought. But seepage of water into the underlying sandstone and evaporation have been much greater than projected. Today the reservoir is only about half full. Most authorities believe that the level will not rise much more in the next 100 years.

Excessive siltation due to high rates of soil erosion from deforested highlands supplying water to the Nile River has cut the dam's projected life span in half. In 1981 the area around the dam suffered a fairly severe earthquake, despite being a low-risk area. Scientists believe the quake was triggered by the weight of the water in Lake Nasser.

Some analysts believe that in the long run the benefits of the Aswan Dam will outweigh its costs. Others consider it an economic and ecological disaster. What do you think?

Constructing Dams and Reservoirs Rainwater and water from melting snow that would otherwise be lost can be captured and stored in large reservoirs behind dams built across rivers (Figure 5-19, p. 126). Damming increases the annual supply by collecting fresh surface water during wet periods and storing it for use during dry periods.

By controlling river flow, dams reduce the danger of flooding in downstream areas and allow people to live on the fertile floodplains of major rivers below the dam. They also provide a controllable supply of water for irrigating arid and semiarid land below the dam. Hydroelectric power plants, which use the energy of water flowing from dam reservoirs, generate more than 20% of the world's electricity. This is a renewable, non-polluting source of electricity. Reservoirs behind large dams can also be used for outdoor recreation such as swimming, boating, and fishing.

But the benefits of dams and reservoirs must be weighed against their costs (see Case Study on p. 248). Dams are expensive to build and may give developers and residents in a floodplain a false sense of safety from major floods that can overwhelm the ability of a dam to control flood waters. The reservoirs fill up with silt and become useless in 20 to 200 years, depending on local climate and land-use practices. The permanent flooding of land behind dams to form reservoirs displaces people and destroys vast areas of valuable agricultural land, wildlife habitat, white-water rapids, and scenic natural beauty. China's massive Three Gorges Dam project will submerge 10 cities and partially flood another 8. Over 3.3 million people will have to be resettled.

The storage of water behind a dam also raises the water table. The higher water table often waterlogs the soil on nearby land, decreasing its crop or forest productivity. A dam can decrease rather than increase the available supply of fresh water, especially in semiarid areas. This happens because water that would normally flow in an undammed river evaporates from the reservoir's surface or seeps into the ground below the reservoir. Evaporation also increases the salinity of reservoir water by leaving salts behind, decreasing its usefulness for irrigation. The sheer weight of the water impounded in reservoirs increases the likelihood of fault movements, which cause earthquakes.

By interrupting the natural flow of a river, a dam disrupts the migration and spawning of fish. Dams have been a major factor in the 90% drop in the salmon population in the northwestern United States. By trapping silt that would normally be carried downstream, dams deprive downstream areas and estuaries of vital nutrients and decrease their productivity. In the opinion of some outdoor-sports enthusiasts, a dam replaces more desirable forms of water recreation (white-water canoeing, kayaking, rafting, stream fishing) with less desirable, more "artificial" forms (motorboating, sailboating, lake fishing).

Faulty construction, earthquakes, sabotage, or war can cause dams to fail, taking a terrible toll in lives and property. In 1972 a dam failure in Buffalo Creek, West Virginia, killed 125 people. Another in Rapid City, South Dakota, killed 237 and caused more than $1 billion in damages. According to a 1986 study by the Federal Emergency Management Agency, the United States has 1,900 unsafe dams in populated areas. The agency reported that the dam safety programs of most states are inadequate because of weak laws and budget cuts.

Water Diversion Projects In MDCs local governments often increase the supply of fresh water in water-poor populated areas by transferring water from water-rich areas. One such project in the United States is the California Water Plan—the world's largest reservoir and distribution system. It transports water from water-rich parts of northern California to heavily populated parts of northern California and to mostly arid and semiarid, heavily populated southern California (Figure 11-14).

Although several large urban areas use lots of water, about 85% of the water withdrawn in California is used by agriculture. The basic problem is that two-thirds of all the precipitation in California falls in the northern mountains, while 80% of the water is used in central and southern California. For decades, northern and southern Californians have been feuding over how the state's water should be allocated under the California Water Plan (see Case Study on p. 252).

Another example of large-scale water diversion is in Soviet Central Asia, where so much water has been diverted from the Aral Sea for irrigation that the lake bed has dried up. Now massive amounts of salt and sand are blown into the air by winds, disrupting agriculture as far away as India. According to Soviet scientists, this water project may be one of the world's greatest human-caused ecological disasters.

There have been proposals to tow massive icebergs to arid coastal areas (such as Saudi Arabia and southern California) and pump the fresh water from the melting berg ashore. But the technology for doing this is not available and the costs may be too high.

Tapping Groundwater Another solution to water supply problems is to rely on groundwater. In the United States about half of the drinking water (96% in rural areas and 20% in urban areas), 40% of the irrigation water, and 23% of all fresh water used is withdrawn from underground aquifers. In Florida, Hawaii, Idaho, Mississippi, Nebraska, and New Mexico, more than 90% of the population depends on groundwater for drinking water supplies. The only part of the United States in which no one is dependent on groundwater is the District of Columbia.

Overuse of groundwater can cause or intensify several problems: aquifer depletion, subsidence (sink-

Figure 11-14 California Water Plan and Central Arizona Project for large-scale transfer of water from one area to another. Arrows show general direction of water flow.

ing of land when groundwater is withdrawn), intrusion of salt water into aquifers, and groundwater contamination (Figure 11-15). **Aquifer depletion** occurs when groundwater is withdrawn faster than it is recharged by precipitation. Currently, about one-fourth of the groundwater withdrawn in the United States is not replenished. In the arid and semiarid Texas Gulf region up to 77% of the groundwater withdrawn is not replenished. The major groundwater overdraft problem is in parts of the huge Ogallala Aquifer, extending under the farm belt from northern Nebraska to northwestern Texas (see Case Study on p. 253). Groundwater levels often slowly recover when withdrawals are reduced.

Aquifer depletion is also a serious problem in northern China, Mexico City, and parts of India. The most effective solution is to reduce the amount of groundwater withdrawn by wasting less irrigation water and by not growing crops in dry areas.

When groundwater in an unconfined aquifer is withdrawn faster than it is replenished, the soil of the aquifer becomes compacted and the land overlying the aquifer sinks, or subsides. Widespread subsidence in the San Joaquin Valley of California has damaged houses, factories, pipelines, highways, and railroad beds. Some areas have sunk almost 9 meters (30 feet).

When fresh water is withdrawn from an aquifer near a coast or near an inland deposit of salt water faster than it is recharged, salt water intrudes into the aquifer (Figure 11-16). Saltwater intrusion threatens to contaminate the drinking water of many towns and cities along the Atlantic and Gulf coasts (Figure 11-15) and in the coastal areas of Israel, Syria, and the Ara-

bian Gulf states. Another growing problem in the United States and many other MDCs is groundwater contamination from agricultural and industrial activities, septic tanks, underground injection wells, and other sources, as discussed in Section 20-4.

Desalination Removing dissolved salts from ocean water or brackish (slightly salty) groundwater is an appealing way to increase freshwater supplies. Distillation and reverse osmosis are the two most widely used desalination methods. Two other methods are to freeze salt water or to pass electric current through it.

Distillation involves heating salt water until it evaporates and condenses as fresh water, leaving salts behind in solid form. In reverse osmosis, high pressure is used to force salt water through a thin membrane, which allows water molecules but not dissolved salts to pass through its pores. Desalination plants in arid parts of the Middle East and North Africa produce about two-thirds of the world's desalinated water. Desalinization is also used in parts of Florida.

The basic problem with all desalination methods is that they use large amounts of energy and therefore are expensive. Desalination can provide fresh water for coastal cities in arid regions, where the cost of getting fresh water by any method is high. But desalinated water will probably never be cheap enough to irrigate conventional crops or to meet much of the world's demand for fresh water. It might be useful, however, for irrigating genetically engineered strains of crops that can grow in partially salty water.

Another problem is that even more energy and money would be needed to pump desalinated water

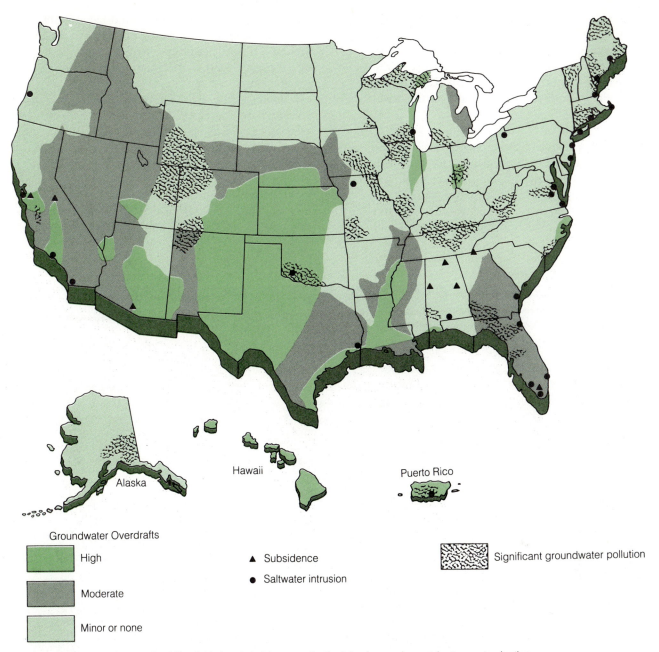

Groundwater Overdrafts

- High
- Moderate
- Minor or none

▲ Subsidence
● Saltwater intrusion

Significant groundwater pollution

Alaska

Hawaii

Puerto Rico

Figure 11-15 Major areas of aquifer depletion, subsidence, saltwater intrusion, and groundwater contamination in the United States. (Data from U.S. Water Resources Council and U.S. Geological Survey)

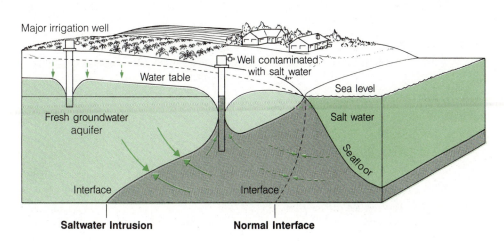

Major irrigation well

Well contaminated with salt water

Water table

Sea level

Fresh groundwater aquifer

Salt water

Seafloor

Interface

Interface

Saltwater Intrusion

Normal Interface

Figure 11-16 Saltwater intrusion along a coastal region. When the water table is lowered from overpumping, the normal interface (dotted line) between fresh and saline groundwater moves inland (solid line).

uphill and inland from coastal desalination plants. Also, a vast network of desalination plants would produce mountains of salt to be disposed of. The easiest and cheapest solution would be to dump the salt in the ocean near the plants. But this would increase the salt concentration and threaten food resources in coastal waters (Figure 5–15, p. 122).

Cloud Seeding Several countries, particularly the United States, have been experimenting for years with seeding clouds with chemicals to produce more rain over dry regions and snow over mountains. Cloud seeding involves finding a large, suitable cloud and injecting it with a powdered chemical such as silver

iodide from a plane or from ground-mounted burners. Small water droplets in the cloud clump together around tiny particles of the chemical and form drops or ice particles large enough to fall to the earth as precipitation.

Cloud seeding, however, is not useful in very dry areas, where it is most needed, because rain clouds are rarely available. Large-scale use could also change snowfall and rainfall patterns and alter regional or even global climate patterns in unknown and perhaps undesirable ways. And widespread cloud seeding would also introduce large amounts of silver iodide into soil and water systems, possibly with harmful effects on people, wildlife, and agricultural productivity.

CASE STUDY Conflict Over Water Supplies in California

In 1982 California voters rejected a proposal to expand the state's water system by building a $1 billion canal to divert to southern California much of the water that now flows into San Francisco Bay. Supporters of this proposal contended that without more water a prolonged drought could bring economic ruin to much of southern California.

Opponents of this proposal called it a costly and unnecessary boondoggle that would degrade the Sacramento River, threaten fishing, and reduce the flushing action that helps clean San Francisco Bay of pollutants. They also argued that much of the water already sent south is wasted and that an increase of only 10% in irrigation efficiency would provide enough water for domestic and industrial uses in southern California. They pointed out that agriculture accounts for only 2.5% of the state's economy and that water used in other ways contributes more to economic growth.

Opponents also contend that too many corporate farms get taxpayer-subsidized water at low prices to grow crops on desert land that could be grown without irrigation in other parts of the country. In California, the number-one crop in terms of water consumption is irrigated pasture—grass and hay for cows and sheep.

This use alone equals the amount of water consumed by all of the state's 27 million inhabitants and provides income equal to only one five-thousandth of the state's economy. Irrigation of alfalfa, the second-most water-consumptive crop, requires as much water as used in the San Francisco and Los Angeles metropolitan areas combined, while providing less economic income than that from a few blocks of downtown Los Angeles.

Conservationists believe that the government should not award new long-term water contracts that give farmers and ranchers federally subsidized water without an assessment of the long-term environmental and economic impact of using so much water for irrigating crops that could be grown more cheaply in rain-fed areas. They also believe that much of farming in arid central and southern California—especially grass for cows, rice, alfalfa, and cotton—should be phased out and transferred to other areas with more water. Cities needing more water would be required to pay farmers to install water-saving irrigation technology and then have the right to use the water saved.

These changes in water policy would provide enough water for California's large and growing urban population, save taxpayers money, and reduce the harmful

environmental impacts of large-scale farming, livestock grazing, and irrigation in an area that does not have enough rainfall for such purposes. But bringing about these changes is difficult because the political power of California's taxpayer-subsidized farmers greatly exceeds their contribution to the state's economy.

A related project is the federally financed $3.9 billion Central Arizona Project. It began pumping water from the Colorado River uphill to Phoenix in 1985 and is expected to deliver water to Tucson by 1991 (Figure 11-14). When the first part of this project was completed in 1985, southern California, especially the arid and booming San Diego region, began losing up to one-fifth of its water. Until then this water had been diverted from the Colorado River to southern California by the Colorado River Aqueduct.

Since 1922 Arizona has been legally entitled to one-fifth of the Colorado River's annual flow. However, until the Central Arizona Project was in place, the state had no way to get more than half its share. The surface water diverted from the Colorado will partially replace groundwater overdrafts that have led to falling water tables in many parts of Arizona during the past 50 years.

Another obstacle to cloud seeding is legal disputes over the ownership of water in clouds. For example, during the 1977 drought in the western United States, the attorney general of Idaho accused officials in neighboring Washington of "cloud rustling" and threatened to file suit in federal court.

Unnecessary Water Waste *An estimated 30% to 50% of the water used in the United States is unnecessarily wasted.* This explains why many water resource experts consider water conservation the quickest and cheapest way to provide much of the additional water needed in dry areas.

A major cause of water waste in the United States is that elected officials have kept water prices artificially low, hoping to stimulate economic growth and get reelected by keeping consumers happy. Until the late 1970s, federal funds were used to build large dams and water transfer projects, especially in the West. These subsidized projects provide low-cost water for farms, industries, and homes. Outdated laws governing access and use of water resources also encourage unnecessary waste (see Spotlight on p. 254).

Low-cost water is the only reason that farmers in Arizona can grow thirsty crops like alfalfa and cotton in the middle of the desert. It also allows people in Palm Springs, California, to keep their lawns and 74 golf courses green.

However, there is no free lunch. Water subsidies are paid for by all taxpayers in the form of higher taxes. Because these indirect costs don't show up on monthly water bills, consumers have little incentive to conserve. Raising the price of water to reflect its true cost would provide powerful incentives for water conservation.

Another reason that water waste in the United States is greater than necessary is that the responsibility for water resource management in a particular water basin is divided among many state and local governments rather than being held by one authority. For example, the Chicago metropolitan area has 349 separate water supply systems, divided among some 2,000 local units of government over a six-county area.

In sharp contrast is the regional approach to water management used in England and Wales. The British Water Act of 1973 replaced more than 1,600 separate agencies with 10 regional water authorities based on

CASE STUDY Depletion of the Ogallala Aquifer

Water withdrawn from the vast Ogallala Aquifer (Figure 11-17) is used to irrigate one-fifth of all U.S. cropland in an area too dry for rainfall farming. The aquifer supports $32 billion of agricultural production a year—mostly wheat, sorghum, cotton, corn, and 40% of the country's grain-fed beef cattle.

The Ogallala Aquifer contains a massive amount of water, but it has an extremely low natural recharge rate because it underlies a region with low average annual precipitation (Figure 11-11). Today the overall rate of withdrawal from this aquifer is eight times its natural recharge rate. Even higher withdrawal rates, sometimes 100 times the recharge rate, are taking place in parts of the aquifer that lie beneath Texas, New Mexico, Oklahoma, and Colorado. Water resource experts project that at the present rate of withdrawal, much of this aquifer will be dry by 2020, and much sooner in areas where it is only a few meters deep.

Long before this happens, however, the high energy cost of pumping water from rapidly dropping water tables will force many farmers to grow crops that need much less water, such as wheat and cotton, instead of profitable but thirsty crops such as corn and sugar beets. Some farmers will have to go out of business. The amount of irrigated land already is declining in five of the seven states using this aquifer because of the high cost of pumping water from depths as great as 1,830 meters (6,000 feet).

If farmers in the Ogallala region began using water conservation measures and switched to crops with low water needs, depletion of the aquifer would be delayed—but not prevented in the long run. Unfortunately, the tragedy of the commons shows us that most farmers are likely to continue withdrawing as much water as possible from this shared resource to increase short-term profits.

To prevent depletion of the

Ogallala Aquifer and still allow the growing of crops, some people have called for diversion of surface water from the Great Lakes. But this could lower water levels in the lakes and reduce their usefulness for nearby heavily populated urban areas. What do you think should be done?

Ogallala Aquifer

Figure 11-17 Ogallala Aquifer.

natural watershed boundaries. In this integrated approach, each water authority owns, finances, and manages all water supply and waste treatment facilities in its region. The responsibilities of each authority include water pollution control, water-based recreation, land drainage and flood control, inland navigation, and inland fisheries. Each water authority is managed by a group of elected local officials and a smaller number of officials appointed by the national government.

Reducing Irrigation Losses Since irrigation accounts for the largest fraction (70% worldwide) of water use and waste, more efficient use of even a small amount of irrigation water frees water for other uses. Worldwide, only about 37% of the water used for irrigation contributes to crop growth; the other 63% is wasted.

Most irrigation systems distribute water from a groundwater well or a surface canal by gravity flow through unlined field ditches (Figure 11-19). This method is cheap as long as farmers in water-short areas don't have to pay the real cost of making this water available. But it provides far more water than needed for crop growth, and at least 50% of the water is lost by evaporation and seepage. Such overwatering with inadequate drainage causes land-degrading salinization and waterlogging (Figure 10-23, p. 233). Farmers could prevent seepage by placing plastic, concrete, or tile liners in irrigation canals. But as long as government-subsidized water is available at low cost, they have little incentive to conserve it or to switch to crops that need less water.

Many farmers served by the dwindling Ogallala Aquifer have switched from gravity flow canal

---

SPOTLIGHT Water Rights in the United States

Laws regulating water access and use differ in the eastern and western parts of the United States (Figure 11-18). In most of the East water use is based on the doctrine of **riparian rights**. Basically this system of water law gives anyone whose land adjoins a flowing stream the right to use water from the stream as long as some is left for downstream landowners.

This approach works well in regions where there are numerous surface streams and rivers with reliable supplies of water. However, as population and water-intensive land uses grow, there is often not enough water to meet the needs of all the people along a stream.

In the arid and semiarid West the riparian system does not work because large amounts of water are needed in areas far from major surface-water sources. In most of the West the principle of **prior appropriation** regulates water use. In this first-come-first-served approach, the first user of water from a stream establishes a legal right for continued use of the amount originally withdrawn. Some areas of the United States have a combination of riparian and prior appropriation water rights (Figure 11-18).

One problem with the prior appropriation system is that later water users have little access to the resource, especially during droughts. Another problem is that it causes unnecessary use and waste. To hold on to their rights, users must keep on withdrawing and using a certain amount of water even if they don't need it—a use-it-or-lose-it approach. This penalizes farmers who use water–conserving irrigation methods.

Different laws also apply to the allocation of groundwater resources. Most groundwater use is based on common law, which holds that subsurface water belongs to whoever owns the land above such water. This means that landowners can withdraw as much as they want to use on their land.

When many users tap the same aquifer, that aquifer becomes a common-property resource. The multiple users remove water at a faster rate than it is replaced by natural recharge. The largest users have little incentive to conserve. Large withdrawals by a few users deplete supplies for other users. This has led to legal disputes over groundwater rights. In recent years courts in some areas have tended to restrict massive with-

drawals by a few users and have distributed groundwater supplies among various landowners using the same aquifer.

Conservationists and many economists call for a change in laws allocating rights to surface and groundwater supplies. They believe that farmers and other users should be free to sell or lease their water rights. Farmers who save water through conservation or by switching to less thirsty crops should be able to sell the water they save rather than losing their rights to this water. Profit motives would then raise the price of scarce water and provide a powerful incentive for water conservation. In parts of Arizona and Colorado such buying and selling of water rights has made some farmers rich, raised water prices, encouraged conservation, and made more water available for cities and industries.

Conservationists also propose that users of water provided by federal and state projects be charged a much higher price for this water. In addition to a higher base price, charges should rise sharply with the amount of water used. What do you think should be done?

Figure 11-19 Gravity flow systems like this one in California's San Joaquin Valley irrigate most of the world's irrigated cropland. About half the water applied is consumed by seepage and evaporation.

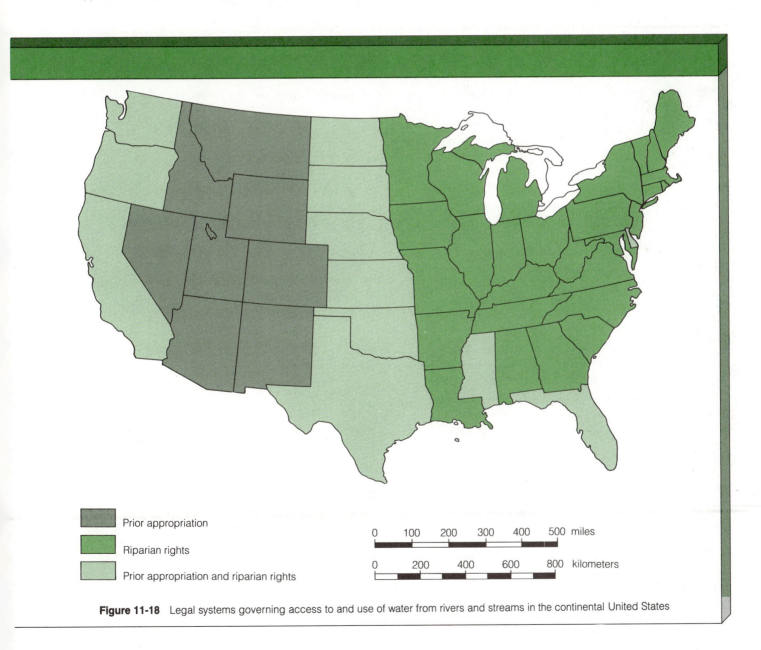

Prior appropriation

Riparian rights

Prior appropriation and riparian rights

| 0 | 100 | 200 | 300 | 400 | 500 | miles |

| 0 | 200 | 400 | 600 | 800 | kilometers |

Figure 11-18 Legal systems governing access to and use of water from rivers and streams in the continental United States

Figure 11-20 Center-pivot irrigation systems like this one in the Ogallala Aquifer area can reduce water consumed by seepage and evaporation to about 30%.

systems to center-pivot sprinkler systems (Figure 11-20), which reduce water waste from 50% or more to 30%. Some farmers are switching to new, precision-application sprinkler systems, which spray water downward, closer to crops, rather than high into the air. These systems cut water waste by 2% to 5% and energy use by 20% to 30%.

Another way to irrigate more efficiently is to bury small plaster-of-Paris (gypsum) blocks in the soil with two wires leading to the surface. As the soil loses or gains water, the electrical resistance between the electrodes changes. A simple clip-on electrical meter can then be used to determine soil moisture. This enables farmers and ranchers to schedule irrigation based on precise measurements of soil moisture rather than on guesses.

In the 1960s highly efficient trickle or drip irrigation systems were developed in arid Israel. A network of perforated piping, installed at or below the ground surface, releases a small volume of water and fertilizer close to the roots of plants, minimizing evaporation and seepage. These systems are expensive to install but are economically feasible for high-profit fruit, vegetable, and orchard crops. But as long as farmers can get water at an abnormally low cost, they don't find it profitable to invest in drip irrigation systems.

Irrigation efficiency can also be improved by computer-controlled systems that set water flow rates, detect leaks, and adjust the amount of water to soil moisture and weather conditions. Farmers can switch to new, hybrid crop varieties that need less water or that tolerate irrigation with saline water. Also, organic gardening techniques produce higher crop yields per acre and require only one quarter of the water and

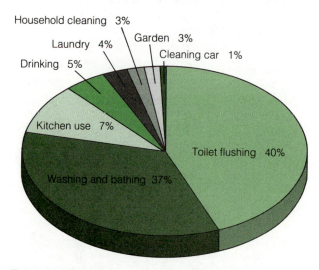

Figure 11-21 Domestic uses of water. (Data from U.S. Geological Survey)

fertilizer used by conventional farming. Since 1950, Israel has used many of these techniques to decrease waste of irrigation water by about 84%, while expanding the country's irrigated land by 44%.

Wasting Less Water in Industry Most manufacturing processes can use recycled water or can be redesigned to use and waste less water. For example, depending on the process used, manufacturing 0.9 metric ton (1 ton) of steel can use as much as 199,250 liters (52,800 gallons) or as little as 4,980 liters (1,320 gallons) of water. To produce 0.9 metric ton (1 ton) of paper, a paper mill in Hadera, Israel, uses one-tenth as much water as most paper mills. Manufacturing aluminum

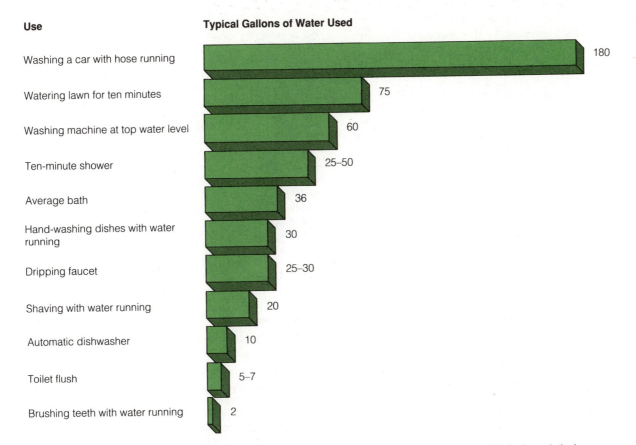

Use

Typical Gallons of Water Used

Use	Gallons
Washing a car with hose running	180
Watering lawn for ten minutes	75
Washing machine at top water level	60
Ten-minute shower	25–50
Average bath	36
Hand-washing dishes with water running	30
Dripping faucet	25–30
Shaving with water running	20
Automatic dishwasher	10
Toilet flush	5–7
Brushing teeth with water running	2

Figure 11-22 Some ways domestic water is wasted in the United States. (Data from American Water Works Association)

from recycled scrap rather than virgin ores can reduce water needs by 97% percent.

Industry is the largest conserver of water. But the potential for water recycling in U.S. manufacturing has hardly been tapped because the cost of water to many industries is subsidized by taxpayers through federally financed water projects. Thus, industries have little incentive to recycle water, which typically accounts for only about 3% of total manufacturing costs. A higher, more realistic price would greatly stimulate water reuse and conservation in industry.

Wasting Less Water in Homes and Businesses

Flushing toilets, washing hands, and bathing account for about 78% of the water used in a typical home in the United States (Figure 11-21). Much of this water is unnecessarily wasted (Figure 11-22). Leaks in pipes, water mains, toilets, bathtubs, and faucets waste an estimated 20% to 35% of water withdrawn from public supplies.

Because water costs so little, in most places leaking water faucets are not repaired and large quantities of water are used to clean sidewalks and streets and to irrigate lawns and golf courses. Instead of being a status symbol, a green lawn in an arid or semiarid area should be viewed as a major ecological and economic

wrong and replaced with types of natural vegetation adapted to a dry climate.

Many cities offer no incentive to reduce leaks and waste. In New York, for example, 95% of the residential units don't have water meters. Users are charged flat rates, with the average family paying less than $100 a year for virtually unlimited use of high-quality water. In Boulder, Colorado, the introduction of water meters reduced water use by more than one-third. Ways that each of us can conserve water and save money are listed inside the back cover.

The city of Glendale, Arizona offers a $100 rebate to homeowners who replace a conventional toilet (3.5 to 6 gallons per flush) with a more efficient model (1.6 or fewer gallons per flush). They also give a $100 rebate to anyone who converts from a conventional water-intensive lawn to a landscape of plants that require little water.

Commercially available systems can be used to purify and completely recycle wastewater from houses, apartments, and office buildings. Such a system can be installed in a small shed outside a residence and serviced for a monthly fee about equal to that charged by most city water and sewer systems. In Japan recycled water costs users less than freshwater. In Tokyo all the water used in Mitsubishi's 60-story office building is purified for reuse by an automated recycling system. Israel treats and reuses about 40% of its waste-water, primarily for irrigation. By the year 2000, the country plans to recycle 80% of its wastewater.

Water is more critical than energy. We have alternative sources of energy. But with water, there is no other choice.

Eugene Odum

CHAPTER SUMMARY

Only about 0.003% of the world's fresh water is available for human use in the forms of *surface water* and *groundwater*, which are collected, purified, and distributed to various parts of the world in an uneven pattern by the hydrologic cycle. Groundwater is found in *unconfined* and *confined aquifers*, which are recharged very slowly compared to the fairly rapid replenishment of surface water in streams, rivers, lakes, wetlands, and reservoirs.

Worldwide, most water withdrawn from surface or ground sources is used and returned to rivers and lakes for reuse. However, about 75% of the water withdrawn for irrigation, the largest use of water throughout the world, is consumed through evaporation and seepage and lost for reuse as surface water in the area from which it is withdrawn. Total and average per capita withdrawal and consumption of surface and groundwater for human use have been increasing rapidly and are projected to increase significantly in the future.

The major water resource problems in various parts of the world are **(1)** *water shortages* as a result of low average annual precipitation, prolonged periodic drought, land degradation by human activities that increase the severity of drought, and population growth; **(2)** *periodic flooding* caused by high precipitation during a short period, removal of vegetative cover that absorbs water and reduces flood damage, and imperfect dams and flood control projects; **(3)** *water in the wrong place* in countries where ample annual precipitation flows away in remote rivers far from population and agricultural centers; **(4)** *lack of sanitary drinking water*; and **(5)** *salinization and waterlogging of soil* from improper irrigation.

The usable supply of fresh water in many areas can be increased by **(1)** *building dams and reservoirs* to catch and store surface-water runoff, **(2)** *transferring water from water-rich to water-poor regions*, and **(3)** *tapping groundwater supplies*. Each of these approaches has certain advantages and disadvantages: Increasing use of groundwater has led to depletion of aquifers, subsidence (land sinking), intrusion of salt water into freshwater aquifers near coastal areas, and aquifer contamination. Desalination of seawater can also be used to produce fresh water but is too expensive except in areas with acute water shortages.

More fresh water can be made available through *water conservation*—reducing unnecessary waste of water used for irrigation (the largest source of waste) and in industry and homes. But water conservation techniques are not widely used in many countries, including the United States, mostly because water prices are kept artificially low and water resources are managed by a maze of conflicting political units and laws that discourage conservation.

DISCUSSION TOPICS

1. How do human activities increase the harmful effects of prolonged drought? How can these effects be reduced?

2. How do human activities contribute to flooding? How can flooding be reduced?

3. In your community:
   a. What are the major sources of the water supply?
   b. How is water use divided among agricultural, industrial, power plant cooling, and public uses? Who are the biggest consumers of water?
   c. What has happened to water prices during the past 20 years? Are they too low to encourage water conservation and reuse?
   d. What water supply problems are projected?
   e. How is water being wasted?

4. Explain why dams and reservoirs may lead to more flood damage than would have occurred if they had not been built. Should all proposed large dam and reservoir projects be scrapped? What criteria would you use in determining desirable projects?

5. Should the price of water for all uses in the United States be increased sharply to encourage water conservation? Explain. What effects might this have on the economy, on you, on the poor, on the environment?

6. List 10 major ways to conserve water on a personal level. Which, if any, of these practices do you now use or intend to use (see inside back cover)?

CHAPTER 12

Food Resources

General Questions and Issues

1. How is food produced throughout the world?

2. What are the world's major food problems?

3. Can increasing crop yields and cultivating more land solve the world's major food problems?

4. What government policies can increase food production?

5. What can giving food aid and redistributing land to the poor do to help solve world food problems?

6. How much food can we get from catching more fish and cultivating fish in aquaculture farms?

7. How can agricultural systems in MDCs and LDCs be designed to be ecologically and economically sustainable?

Hunger is a curious thing: At first it is with you all the time, working and sleeping and in your dreams, and your belly cries out insistently, and there is a gnawing and a pain as if your very vitals were being devoured, and you must stop it at any cost. . . . Then the pain is no longer sharp, but dull, and this too is with you always.

Kamala Markandaya

Agriculture uses more of the earth's land, water, soil, plant, animal, and energy resources and causes more pollution and environmental degradation than any other human activity. Each day the world has 247,000 more people to feed, clothe, and house. By 2020 the world's population is expected to reach at least 8 billion. To feed these people, we must produce as much food during the next 30 years as we have produced since the dawn of agriculture about 10,000 years ago.

Producing enough food to feed the world's population, however, is only one of a number of complex, interrelated food resource problems. Another major problem is food quality—eating food with enough proteins, vitamins, and minerals to avoid malnutrition. We must also have enough storage facilities to keep food from rotting or being eaten by pests after it is harvested. An adequate transportation and retail outlet system must be available to distribute and sell food throughout a country and the world.

Poverty is the leading cause of hunger and premature death from lack of food quantity and quality. It is the main reason that one-fifth of the people on earth today are not adequately fed. Making sure the poor have enough land or income to grow or buy enough food is the key to reducing deaths from malnutrition. Farmers must also have economic incentives to grow enough food to meet the world's needs. Finally, the world's agricultural systems must be managed to minimize the harmful environmental impacts of producing and distributing food.

12-1 WORLD AGRICULTURAL SYSTEMS: HOW IS FOOD PRODUCED?

Plants and Animals That Feed the World Although about 80,000 species of plants are edible, only about 30 crops feed the world. Four crops—wheat, rice, corn, and potato—make up more of the world's total food production than all others combined.

The rest of the food people eat is mainly fish, meat, and animal products such as milk, eggs, and cheese from domesticated livestock. Meat and animal products are too expensive for most people, primarily because of the loss of usable energy when an animal trophic level is added to a food chain (Figure 12-1).

However, as incomes rise, people consume more grain *indirectly,* in the form of meat and products from grain-fed domesticated animals. In MDCs, almost half of the world's annual grain production (especially corn

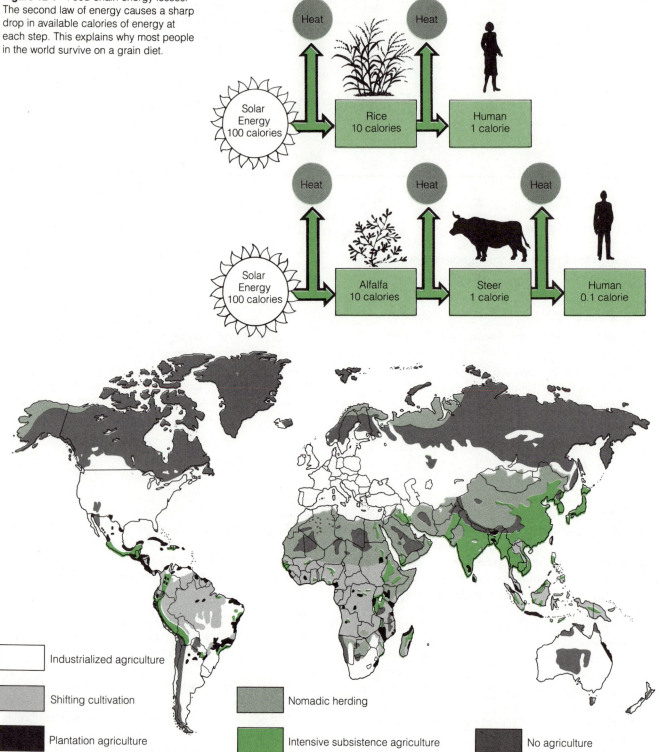

Figure 12-1 Food chain energy losses. The second law of energy causes a sharp drop in available calories of energy at each step. This explains why most people in the world survive on a grain diet.

Solar Energy 100 calories → Rice 10 calories → Human 1 calorie

Solar Energy 100 calories → Alfalfa 10 calories → Steer 1 calorie → Human 0.1 calorie

☐ Industrialized agriculture

☐ Shifting cultivation

■ Plantation agriculture

☐ Nomadic herding

■ Intensive subsistence agriculture

■ No agriculture

Figure 12-2 Generalized location of the world's major types of agriculture.

and soybeans) is fed to livestock. Also, about one-third of the world's annual fish catch is converted to fish meal and fed to livestock.

Major Types of Agriculture   Two major types of agricultural systems are used to grow crops and raise livestock throughout the world: industrialized agriculture

and subsistence agriculture (see Spotlight on p. 262). **Industrialized agriculture** produces large quantities of a single type of crop or livestock for sale within the country where it is grown and to other countries. Farmers carry out industrialized agriculture by supplementing solar energy with large amounts of energy from fossil fuels, mostly oil and natural gas.

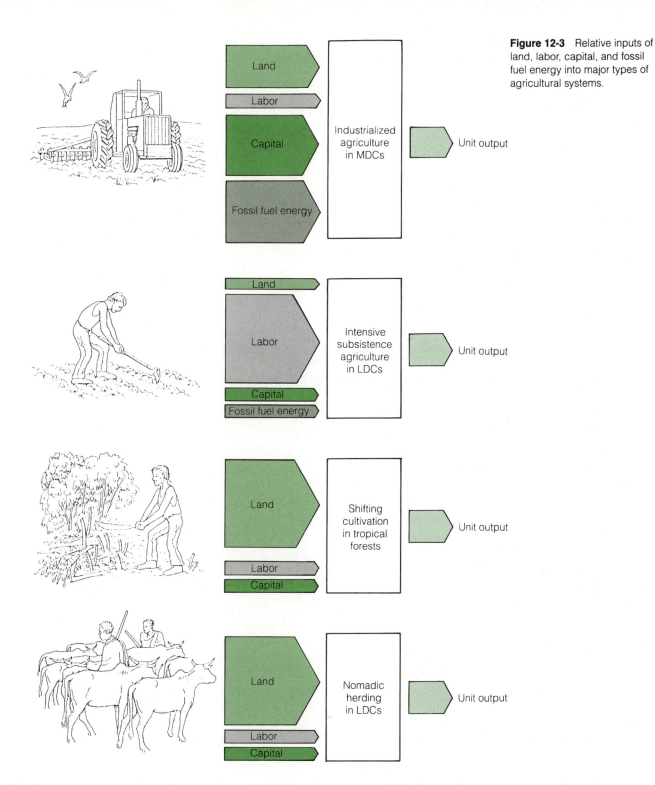

Figure 12-3 Relative inputs of land, labor, capital, and fossil fuel energy into major types of agricultural systems.

Industrialized agriculture is widely used in MDCs and since the mid-1960s has spread to parts of some LDCs (Figure 12-2). It is supplemented by **plantation agriculture,** in which specialized crops such as bananas, coffee, and cacao are grown in tropical LDCs primarily for sale to MDCs.

Traditional **subsistence agriculture** produces enough crops or livestock for the farm family's survival and in good years enough to have some left over to sell or put aside for hard times. Subsistence farmers supplement solar energy with energy from human labor

and draft animals. The three major types of subsistence agriculture are shifting cultivation of small plots in tropical forests (Figure 2-2, p. 33), intensive crop cultivation on relatively small plots of land, and nomadic herding of livestock. These forms of agriculture are practiced by about 2.6 billion people—half the people on earth—who live in rural areas in LDCs.

The relative inputs of land, human and animal labor, fossil fuel energy, and capital (money) needed to produce one unit of food energy by various types of agriculture are shown in Figure 12-3. Industrialized agriculture is capital- and energy-intensive, whereas subsistence agriculture is labor-intensive, and shifting cultivation and nomadic herding are land-intensive. An average of 63% of the people in LDCs work in agriculture, compared to only 10% in MDCs.

Industrialized Agriculture and Green Revolutions

Food production is increased either by cultivating more land or by getting higher yields from existing cropland. Since 1950 most of the increase in world food production has come from increasing the yield per acre in what is called a **green revolution.** This involves planting monocultures of scientifically bred plant varieties and applying large amounts of inorganic fertilizer, irrigation water, and pesticides.

Between 1950 and 1970 this approach led to dramatic increases in yields of major crops in the United States and most other industrialized countries, a phenomenon sometimes known as the first green revolution (Figure 12-5). In 1967, after 30 years of genetic research and trials, a modified version of the first green revolution began spreading to many LDCs. High-yield, fast-growing, dwarf varieties of rice and wheat, specially bred for tropical and subtropical climates, were introduced into several LDCs in what is known as the second green revolution.

The shorter, stronger, and stiffer stalks of the new varieties allow them to support larger heads of grain without toppling over (Figure 12-6). With large inputs of fertilizer, water, and pesticides, their wheat and rice yields can be two to five times those of traditional varieties. The fast-growing varieties allow farmers to grow two and even three consecutive crops a year (multiple cropping) on the same parcel of land.

SPOTLIGHT **Comparison of Industrialized and Subsistence Agriculture**

INDUSTRIAL FARMERS   **SUBSISTENCE FARMERS**

Crop Production

INDUSTRIAL FARMERS	SUBSISTENCE FARMERS
Grow large quantities of food for sale by investing a large amount of money, usually borrowed.	Grow enough food to feed their families, investing little, if any money.
Buy scientifically bred hybrid seeds of a single crop variety and plant as a monoculture on a large field (Figure 6-13, p. 147).	Plant a diversity of naturally available crop seeds on a small plot (Figure 2-2, p. 33).
Buy expensive equipment that is costly to operate, repair, or replace.	Make or buy simple equipment that costs little to run, repair, or replace.
Often farm on flat, easily cultivated fields with fertile soil.	Often farm on easily erodible, hard-to-cultivate, mountainous highlands, drylands with fragile soils, and tropical forests with low-fertility soils.
Increase crop yields by using irrigation and commercial inorganic fertilizers.	Increase crop yields by making efficient use of natural inputs of water and organic fertilizers.
Plant one crop and use chemicals to kill pest species along with a variety of predators of pest species.	Plant a diversity of crops to provide numerous habitats for natural predators of pest species.
Work against nature by using large amounts of fossil fuel energy to keep a monoculture at an early stage of ecological succession.	Work with nature by allowing a diversity of crops to undergo guided ecological succession.
Do most work with fossil-fuel-powered farm machinery.	Do work by hand or with help from draft animals.

Meat and Animal Product Production

INDUSTRIAL FARMERS	SUBSISTENCE FARMERS
Produce large quantities of a single type of meat or animal product for sale by investing a large amount of money, usually borrowed.	Produce enough meat and animal products to feed their families, investing little money.
Use animal feedlots to raise hundreds to thousands of domesticated livestock in a small space (Figure 12-4). Give animals antibiotics and growth hormones to encourage rapid weight gain and to achieve efficient, factorylike production.	Use natural grassland and forests as sources of food and water for small groups of livestock. Often move flocks from one place to another to provide enough food and water.

Nearly 90% of the increase in world grain output in the 1960s and about 70% of that in the 1970s were the result of the second green revolution. In the 1980s and 1990s at least 80% of the additional production of grains is expected to be based on improved yields of existing cropland through the use of green revolution techniques.

These increases, however, depend heavily on fossil fuel inputs. On average it now takes 1.2 barrels of oil to produce a ton of grain, twice the amount needed in 1960. Since 1950, agriculture's use of fossil fuels has increased sevenfold, the number of tractors has quadrupled, irrigated area has tripled, and fertilizer use has risen tenfold. Agriculture, like other parts of industrialized societies, has become addicted to oil, now using about one-twelfth of the world oil output.

Industrialized Agriculture in the United States

Since 1940, U.S. farmers have more than doubled crop production while cultivating about the same amount of land. They have done this through industrialized agriculture coupled with a favorable climate and fertile soils.

Less than 1% of the U.S. work force is engaged in farming. Yet the country's 2.1 million farmers—with only 650,000 working full time at farming—produce enough food to feed most of their fellow citizens better and at a lower percentage of their income than do farmers in any other country. Americans spend an average of 11% to 15% of their disposable income on food, while people in much of the world spend 40% or more. In addition, U.S. farmers produce large amounts of food for export to other countries. About one-third of U.S. cropland is planted for export.

INDUSTRIAL FARMERS

Produce fatty meat that most consumers like but is considered unhealthful in large amounts.

Use massive inputs of energy by burning fossil fuels for heating, cooling, pumping water, producing feed, and transporting supplies and livestock.

Produce large concentrations of animal wastes, which can wash into nearby surface water and contaminate it with disease-causing bacteria and excess plant nutrients (cultural eutrophication).

SUBSISTENCE FARMERS

Produce lean meat that is more healthful than fatty meat.

Use human and animal labor with no inputs of fossil fuels.

Return nutrient-rich animal wastes to the soil where animals roam, or collect it and use it as organic fertilizer for growing crops, or dry it and burn it as a fuel for heating and cooking.

Figure 12-4 Feedlots like this huge one for cattle near Greeley, Colorado, increase production efficiency. However, they concentrate massive amounts of animal wastes, which, without proper controls, can pollute groundwater with excessive levels of nitrates and contribute to cultural eutrophication of nearby lakes and slow-moving rivers. Beef cattle are usually moved to feedlots to be fattened a few weeks before slaughter. Other types of livestock, such as chickens and pigs, are kept in automated feedlots from birth to death.

Environmental Protection Agency

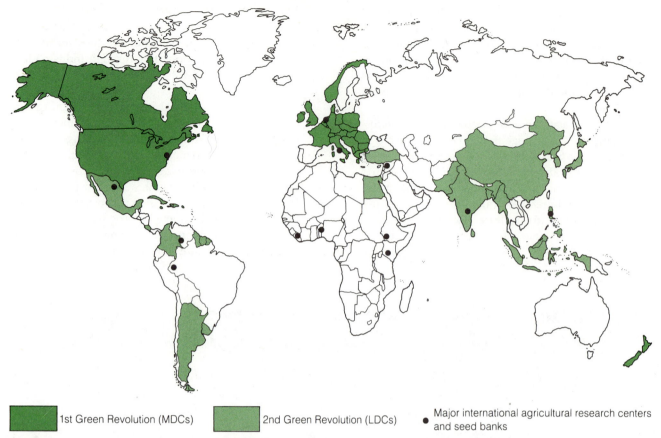

■ 1st Green Revolution (MDCs)	■ 2nd Green Revolution (LDCs)	● Major international agricultural research centers and seed banks

Figure 12-5 Countries achieving increases in crop yields per unit of land area during the two green revolutions. The first took place in MDCs between 1950 and 1970 and the second in LDCs with enough rainfall or irrigation capacity between 1967 and 1988. Thirteen agricultural research centers and genetic storage banks play a key role in developing high-yield crop varieties.

Figure 12-6 Scientists and two Indian farmers compare an older, full-size variety of rice (left) and a new, high-yield, dwarf variety, grown in the second green revolution.

Rockefeller Foundation/Marc and Evelyn Bernheim

About 23 million people—20% of the work force—are involved in the U.S. agricultural system in activities ranging from growing and processing food to selling it at the supermarket. In terms of total annual sales, the agricultural system is the biggest industry in the United States—bigger than the automotive, steel, and housing industries combined. It generates about 18% of the country's GNP. Farmers, however, get an aver-

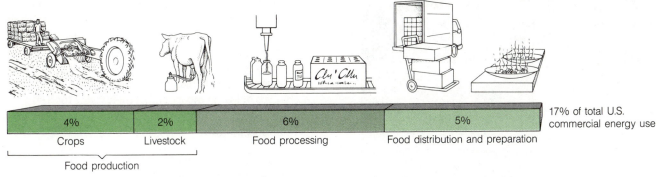

| 4% | 2% | 6% | 5% | 17% of total U.S. commercial energy use |
| Crops | Livestock | Food processing | Food distribution and preparation | |

Food production

Figure 12-7 Commercial energy use by the U.S. industrialized agriculture system.

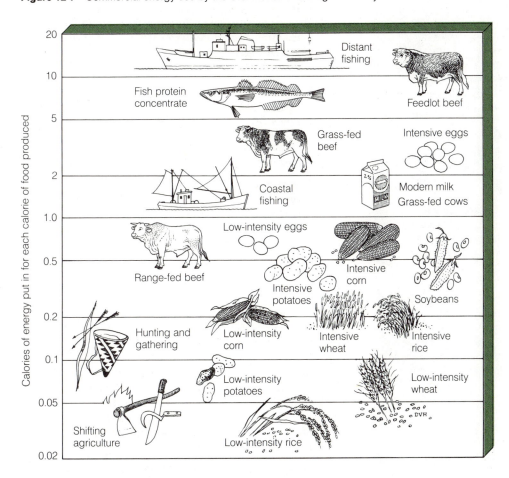

Figure 12-8 Energy input needed to produce one unit of food energy in different types of food production.

age of only 25 cents of every dollar spent on food in the United States. Farming itself accounts for only about 2% of the GNP.

The gigantic agricultural system consumes about 17% of all commercial energy used in the United States each year (Figure 12-7). Most of this energy comes from oil. Most plant crops in the United States provide more food energy than the energy (mostly from fossil fuels) used to grow them. But raising animals for food requires much more fossil fuel energy than the animals provide as food energy (Figure 12-8).

Energy efficiency is much worse if we look at the entire U.S. food system. Counting fossil fuel energy inputs used to grow, store, process, package, trans-

port, refrigerate, and cook all plant and animal food, *an average of about 10 units of nonrenewable fossil fuel energy is needed to put one unit of food energy on the table—an energy loss of nine units per unit of food energy produced.* By comparison, every unit of energy from the human labor of subsistence farmers may provide 10 units of food energy.

Suppose everyone in the world ate a typical American diet consisting of food produced by industrialized agriculture. If the world's known oil reserves were used only for producing this food, these reserves would be depleted in only 13 years.

Suppose that fossil fuel, especially oil, suddenly becomes and remains scarce or much more expensive,

In the Philippines many subsistence-farming families use small-scale polyculture to feed themselves. Typically, they harvest crops throughout the year by planting a small plot with a mixture of fast-maturing grains and vegetables, slow-maturing perennials such as papayas and bananas, and slow-maturing tubers such as cassavas, taros, and sweet potatoes.

The diverse root systems at different depths beneath the ground capture soil nutrients and soil moisture efficiently and reduce the need for supplemental organic fertilizer (usually home-generated chicken manure) and irrigation water. Year-round coverage with plants protects the soil from wind and water erosion.

The diversity of habitats for natural predators means that crops don't need to be sprayed with insecticides to control pests. Weeding is reduced and herbicides are unnecessary because weeds have difficulty in competing for plant nutrients with the multitude of crop plants.

The various crops are harvested all year, so there is always something to eat or sell. Crop diversity also provides insurance against unexpected weather changes. If one crop fails because of too much or too little rain, another crop may survive or even thrive. This approach also spreads the need for labor throughout the growing season.

Most of the crops produced in this particular system have little market value because they are high in starch and low in protein. Nevertheless, using their own hand labor, a typical Filipino farming family can supply most of the food they need with this system without borrowing any money.

Although small-scale farmers using mechanized, green revolution agriculture can sell their crops, many of them have such large debts that they go bankrupt. They then lose their land and can no longer feed their families by farming.

*The information in this case study is based on research carried out by geographer David L. Clawson at the University of New Orleans, New Orleans, Louisiana (see Further Readings).

as most energy experts believe will happen sometime between 1995 and 2010. The present industrialized agricultural system in MDCs would collapse, with a sharp drop in world food production and a rise in food prices, malnutrition, and famine.

Examples of Subsistence Agriculture Farmers in LDCs use various forms of subsistence agriculture to grow crops on about 60% of the world's cultivated land (Figure 12-2). Many subsistence farmers imitate nature by simultaneously growing a variety of crops on the same plot. This biological diversity reduces their chances of losing most or all of their year's food supply from pests, flooding, drought, or other disasters. Common planting strategies include

- **polyvarietal cultivation,** in which a plot of land is planted with several varieties of the same crop

- **intercropping,** in which two or several different crops are grown at the same time on a plot—for example, a carbohydrate-rich grain that depletes soil nitrogen and a protein-rich legume that adds nitrogen to the soil

- **agroforestry,** a variation of intercropping in which crops and trees are planted together—for example, a grain or legume crop planted around fruit-bearing orchard trees or in rows between fast-growing trees that can be used for fuelwood or to add nitrogen to the soil

- **polyculture,** a more complex form of intercropping in which a large number of different plants maturing at different times are planted together (see Case Study at left)

12-2 MAJOR WORLD FOOD PROBLEMS

The Good News About Food Production World food production more than doubled between 1950 and 1984, and average per capita production rose by 40%. During the same period, average food prices adjusted for inflation dropped by 25%, and the amount of food traded in the world market quadrupled. Most of the increase in food production since 1950 came from increases in crop yields per acre by means of improved labor-intensive subsistence agriculture in LDCs and energy-intensive industrialized agriculture in North America, Europe, Australia, New Zealand, and parts of Asia.

The Bad News About Food Production The impressive improvements in world food production disguise the fact that average food production per person declined between 1950 and 1988 in 43 LDCs (22 in Africa) containing one of every seven people on earth. The largest declines have occurred in Africa, where average food production per person dropped 21% between 1960 and 1988 and is projected to drop another 30% during the next 25 years (see Case Study on p. 267).

When China, which produces 35% of the world's food, is removed from the calculation, food production gains in most other LDCs since 1950 barely matched their population growth. Average per capita food production has been falling in Africa since 1967 and in Latin America since 1982.

Another disturbing trend is that the rate of increase in world average food production per person has been steadily declining during each of the past three decades. It rose 15% between 1950 and 1960, 7% between 1960 and 1970, and only 4% between 1970 and 1980. Between 1984 and 1988, average per capita food production fell by 14%. This trend is caused by a combination of population increase, a decrease in yields per unit of land area for some crops cultivated by industrialized agriculture, a leveling off or a drop in food production in some countries, unsustainable use of soil and water, and widespread drought in 1987 and 1988.

Food Quantity and Quality: Undernutrition, Malnutrition, and Overnutrition Poor people who cannot grow or buy enough food for good health and survival suffer from **undernutrition.** Survival and good health also require that people consume food containing the proper amounts of protein, carbohydrates, fats, vitamins, and minerals. Most poor people are forced to live on a low-protein, high-starch diet of grains such as wheat, rice, or corn. As a result, they often suffer from **malnutrition,** or deficiencies of protein and other key nutrients.

Many of the world's desperately poor people suffer from both undernutrition and malnutrition. Such people barely survive on just two bowls of boiled rice (150 calories) and boiled green vegetables (10 calories) a day. They become weak, confused, listless, and unable to work. Disease kills most before they starve.

Each year 20 million to 40 million people—half of them children under age 5—die prematurely from undernutrition, malnutrition, or normally nonfatal infections and diseases, such as diarrhea, measles, and flu, worsened by these nutritional deficiencies. The World Health Organization estimates that diarrhea alone kills at least 5 million children under age 5 a year.

CASE STUDY Africa: A Continent in Crisis

A tragic breakdown of life-support systems has been taking place in Africa, where thousands die each day from malnutrition or hunger-related diseases. Since 1985 one of every four Africans has been fed with grain imported from abroad—a dependence likely to increase. Still the World Bank estimates that 100 million Africans don't have enough food for normal health and physical activity.

Average per capita food production is lowest in most of the African countries south of the Sahara desert, an area known as sub-Saharan Africa (Figure 11-9, p. 243). Famine has been especially severe in a zone known as the *Sahel* (an Arabic word meaning edge of desert), which runs horizontally through the seven countries nearest the desert.

This worsening situation in much of Africa is caused by a number of interacting factors:

- the fastest population growth rate of any continent (Figure 7-2, p. 159), with 1 million more mouths to feed every three weeks
- a 17-year drought. Rainfall can vary by as much as 40% from year to year and prolonged droughts are common.
- poor natural endowment of productive soils in many areas. Three-tenths of the continent is covered by desert or is too sandy for crops.
- overgrazing, deforestation, soil erosion, and desertification in many areas (Figure 10-14, p. 225)
- depletion of fuelwood which provides 80% of Africa's energy
- poor food distribution systems
- governments that often keep food prices low to prevent urban unrest, giving rural farmers little incentive to grow more crops
- frequent wars within and between countries
- increasing dependence on food imports that has helped raise Africa's foreign debt eightfold between 1974 and 1988 to $200 billion—equal to nearly half the continent's annual income
- severe underinvestment and lack of interest by African governments, MDCs, and international aid agencies in rural agriculture and family planning
- government policies designed to subsidize urban dwellers at the expense of the rural poor, who make up 75% of Africa's population
- lack of legal rights to land or access to credit for women who raise most of Africa's food, thus giving them little incentive or ability to increase food productivity
- poor use of foreign aid with funds traditionally used to raise cash crops on irrigated land rather than for improving dryland farming, growing food for domestic use, conserving soil and water resources, and replanting trees

Unless African governments and donors of foreign aid address this complex mix of environmental, political, and economic problems, the likelihood of reducing famine is slight. This will require investments in population regulation, debt forgiveness, sustainable agriculture, soil and water conservation, sustainable forestry, rural development improvement of conditions for women, and allowing local people to participate in the planning and execution of aid projects.

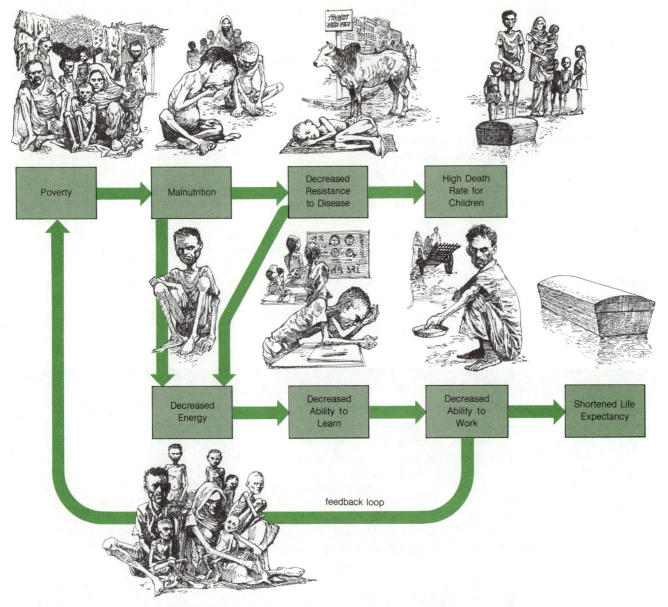

Figure 12-9 Interactions among poverty, malnutrition, and disease form a tragic cycle that perpetuates such conditions in succeeding generations of families.

Adults suffering from chronic undernutrition and malnutrition are vulnerable to diseases and are too weak to work productively or think clearly. As a result, their children are also underfed and malnourished (see Spotlight on p. 269). In Lima, Peru, for example, malnutrition now stunts the growth of one in four children. If these children survive to adulthood, many are locked in a tragic malnutrition-poverty cycle that continues these conditions in each succeeding generation (Figure 12-9).

Each of us must have a daily intake of small amounts of vitamins that cannot be made in the human body. Otherwise we will suffer from various effects of vitamin deficiencies. Although balanced diets, vitamin-fortified foods, and vitamin supplements have greatly reduced the number of vitamin deficiency diseases in MDCs, millions of cases occur each year in LDCs. For example, each year more than 500,000 children in LDCs are partially or totally blinded because their diet lacks vitamin A.

Other nutritional-deficiency diseases are caused by the lack of certain minerals, such as iron and iodine. Too little iron causes anemia. Anemia causes fatigue, makes infection more likely, increases a woman's chance of dying in childbirth, and increases an infant's chances of dying from infection during its first year of life. In tropical regions of Asia, Africa, and Latin America, iron-deficiency anemia affects about 10% of the men, more than half of the children, two-thirds of the pregnant women, and about half of the other women.

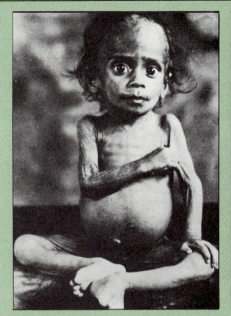

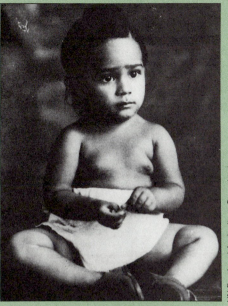

UN Food and Agriculture Organization

Figure 12-10 Most effects of severe marasmus can be corrected if victims are treated in time. This 2-year-old Venezuelan girl suffered from marasmus but recovered after 10 months of treatment and proper nutrition.

The two most widespread nutritional-deficiency diseases are marasmus and kwashiorkor. **Marasmus** (from the Greek "to waste away") occurs when a diet is low in both total energy (calories) and protein. Most victims of marasmus are infants in poor families in which children are not breast-fed or in which food quantity and quality are insufficient after the children are weaned.

A child suffering from marasmus typically has a bloated belly, a thin body, shriveled skin, wide eyes, and an old-looking face (Figure 12-10, left). If the child is treated in time with a balanced diet, most of these effects can be reversed (Figure 12-10, right).

Kwashiorkor (meaning "displaced child" in a West African dialect) occurs in infants and children 1 to 3 years old who suffer from severe protein deficiency. Typically, kwashiorkor afflicts a child whose mother has a younger child to nurse and whose diet changes from highly nutritious breast milk to grain or sweet potatoes, which provide enough calories but not enough protein.

Children suffering from kwashiorkor have skin swollen with fluids, a bloated abdomen, leth-

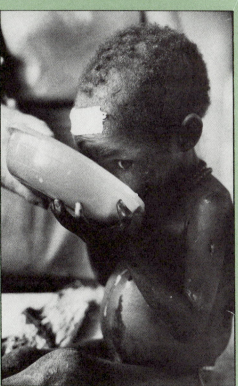

Magnum/Chris Steele Perkins

Figure 12-11 Child suffering from kwashiorkor in Uganda, Africa.

argy, liver damage, hair loss, diarrhea, stunted growth, possible mental retardation, and irritability (Figure 12-11). If such malnutrition is not prolonged, most of the effects can be cured with a balanced diet.

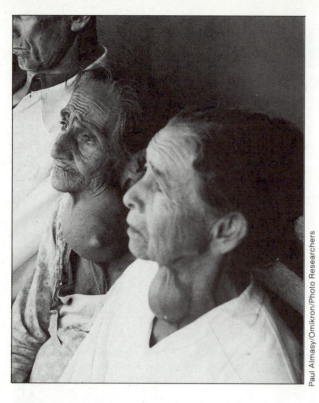

Figure 12-12 People with goiter, an enlargement of the thyroid gland, caused by insufficient dietary iodine.

Too little iodine in the diet can cause goiter, an abnormal enlargement of the thyroid gland in the neck (Figure 12-12), a condition that leads to deafness if untreated. It affects up to 80% of the population in the mountainous areas of Latin America, Asia, and Africa, where soils are deficient in iodine.

Officials of the United Nations Children's Fund (UNICEF) estimate that between half and two-thirds of the worldwide annual childhood deaths from undernutrition, malnutrition, and associated infections and diseases could be prevented at an average annual cost of only $5 to $10 per child. This life-saving program would involve the following simple measures:

- immunization against childhood diseases such as measles

- encouraging breast-feeding

- preventing dehydration from diarrhea by giving infants a solution of a fistful of sugar and a pinch of salt in a glass of water

- preventing blindness by giving people a small vitamin A capsule twice a year at a cost of about 75 cents per person

- providing family planning services to help mothers space births at least two years apart

- increasing female education with emphasis on nutrition, sterilization of drinking water, and child care

While 15% of the people in LDCs suffer from undernutrition and malnutrition, about 15% of the people in MDCs suffer from **overnutrition.** This is an excessive intake of food that can cause obesity, or excess body fat, in people who do not suffer from glandular or other disorders that promote obesity. Overnourished people exist on diets high in calories, cholesterol-containing saturated fats, salt, sugar, and processed foods, and low in unprocessed fresh vegetables, fruits, and fiber. Partly because of these dietary choices, overweight people have significantly higher than normal risks of diabetes, high blood pressure, stroke, and heart disease.

Poverty: The Geography of Hunger If all the food currently produced in the world were divided equally among the earth's people, there would be enough to keep 6 billion people alive. However, if this food were used to give everyone the typical diet of a person in a developed country, it would support only 2.5 billion people—half the present world population. The world's supply of food, however, is not now distributed equally among the world's people, nor will it be, because of differences in soil, climate, and average income throughout the world.

Poverty—not lack of food production—is the chief cause of hunger, malnutrition, and premature death throughout the world. The world's 1 billion desperately poor people do not have access to land where they can grow enough food of the right kind, and they do not have the money to buy enough food of the right kind no matter how much is available. About two-thirds of these people live in Asia and one-fifth in sub-Saharan Africa.

Increases in worldwide total food production and average food production per person often hide widespread differences in food supply and quality between and within countries. For example, about one-third of the world's hungry live in India, even though it is self-sufficient in food production. And although total and per person food supplies have increased in Latin America, much of this gain has been confined to Argentina and Brazil. In more fertile and urbanized southern Brazil, the average daily food supply per person is high. However, in Brazil's semiarid, less fertile northeastern interior many people are severely underfed. Overall almost two out of three Brazilians suffer from malnutrition.

Food is also unevenly distributed within families. In poor families the largest part of the food supply goes to men working outside the home. Children (ages 1–5) and women (especially pregnant women and nursing mothers) are the most likely to be underfed and malnourished.

MDCs also have pockets of poverty and hunger. For example, a 1985 report by a task force of doctors estimated that at least 20 million people—1 out of every

11 Americans—were hungry, mostly because of cuts in food stamps and other forms of government aid since 1980. Half of these people were children.

Without a widespread increase in income and access to land, the number of chronically hungry and malnourished people in the world could increase to at least 1.5 billion by 2000—one out of every four people in the world's projected population at that time.

Environmental Effects of Producing More Food

Both industrialized agriculture and subsistence agriculture have a number of harmful impacts on the air, soil, and water resources that sustain all life (see Spotlight below).

12-3 METHODS OF INCREASING WORLD FOOD PRODUCTION

Increasing Crop Yields Agricultural experts expect most future increases in crop production to come from increased yields per acre on existing cropland and from expansion of green revolution technology to other parts of the world. Agricultural scientists are working to create new green revolutions—or gene revolutions—by using genetic engineering and other forms of biotechnology. Over the next 20 to 40 years they hope to breed high-yield plant strains that have greater resistance to insects and disease, thrive on less fertilizer, make their own nitrogen fertilizer, do well in slightly

---

SPOTLIGHT Major Environmental Impacts of Industrialized and Subsistence Agriculture

Industrialized Agriculture

- soil erosion and loss of soil fertility through poor land use, failure to practice soil conservation techniques, and too little use of organic fertilizers (Section 10-3)
- salinization and waterlogging of heavily irrigated soils (Figure 10-23, p. 233)
- reduction in the number and diversity of nutrient-recycling soil microorganisms due to heavy use of pesticides and commercial inorganic fertilizers and soil compaction by large tractors and other farm machinery
- air pollution by dust blown off cropland that is not kept covered with vegetation and from overgrazed rangeland
- air pollution from droplets of pesticide sprayed from planes or by ground sprayers and blown into the air from plants and soil
- air pollution caused by the extraction, processing, transportation, and combustion of massive amounts of fossil fuels used in industrialized agriculture
- pollution of estuaries and deep ocean zones with oil from offshore wells and tankers and from improper disposal of oil, the main fossil fuel used in industrialized agriculture
- pollution of rivers, lakes, and estuaries and killing of fish and shellfish from pesticide runoff

- depletion of groundwater aquifers by excessive withdrawals for irrigation (Figure 11-15, p. 251)
- pollution of groundwater caused by leaching of water-soluble pesticides, nitrates from commercial inorganic fertilizers, and salts from irrigation water
- overfertilization of lakes and slow-moving rivers caused by runoff of nitrates and phosphates in commercial inorganic fertilizers, livestock animal wastes, and food processing wastes (Section 20-2)
- sediment pollution of surface waters caused by erosion and runoff from farm fields and animal feedlots
- loss of genetic diversity of plants caused by clearing biologically diverse grasslands and forests and replacing them with monocultures of single crop varieties (Figure 6-13, p. 147)
- endangered and extinct animal wildlife from loss of habitat when grasslands and forests are cleared, and wetlands drained, for farming (Chapter 14)
- depletion and extinction of commercially important species of fish caused by overfishing
- threats to human health from nitrates in drinking water and pesticides in drinking water, food, and the atmosphere

Subsistence Agriculture

- soil erosion and rapid loss of soil fertility caused by clearing and cultivating steep mountain highlands without terracing, using shifting cultivation in tropical forests without leaving the land fallow long enough to restore soil fertility, overgrazing of rangeland (Section 13-5), and deforestation to provide cropland or fuelwood (Section 13-4)
- increased frequency and severity of flooding in lowlands when mountainsides are deforested
- desertification caused by cultivation of marginal land with unsuitable soil or terrain, overgrazing, deforestation, and failure to use soil conservation techniques (see Case Study, p. 224)
- air pollution by dust blown from cropland not kept covered with vegetation and from overgrazed rangeland
- sediment pollution of surface waters caused by erosion and runoff from farm fields and overgrazed rangeland
- endangered and extinct animal wildlife caused by loss of habitat when grasslands and forests are cleared for farming
- threats to human health from flooding intensified by poor land use and from human and animal wastes discharged or washed into irrigation ditches and sources of drinking water

salty soils, withstand drought, and make more efficient use of solar energy during photosynthesis.

If even a small fraction of this research and development is successful, the world could experience rapid and enormous increases in crop production in the early part of the next century. But some analysts point to several factors that have limited the spread and long-term success of the green revolutions:

- Without massive doses of fertilizer and water, green revolution crop varieties produce yields no higher and often lower than those from traditional strains.

- Areas without enough rainfall or irrigation water or with poor soils cannot benefit from the new varieties; that is why the second green revolution has not spread to many arid and semiarid areas (Figure 12-5).

- Increasingly greater and thus more expensive inputs of fertilizer, water, and pesticides eventually produce little or no increase in crop yields, as has happened to sorghum and corn in the United States. This diminishing-returns effect, however, typically takes 20 to 30 years to develop, so yields in LDCs using second-green-revolution varieties are projected to increase for some time. Scientists hope to overcome this limitation by developing new and improved varieties through crossbreeding and genetic engineering (see Pro/Con on p. 148)

- Without careful land use and environmental controls, degradation of water and soil can limit the long-term ecological and economic sustainability of green revolutions.

- The cost of genetically engineered crop strains is too high for most of the world's subsistence farmers in LDCs.

The loss of genetic diversity caused when a diverse mixture of natural varieties is replaced with monoculture crops limits the ability of plant scientists to use crossbreeding or genetic engineering to develop new strains for future green revolutions. For example, a perennial variety of wild corn that replants itself each year, is resistant to a number of viruses, and grows well on wet soils was discovered several years ago. Unfortunately, the few thousand plants known to exist were growing on a Mexican hillside that was plowed up. By the year 2000, the Food and Agriculture Organization estimates that two-thirds of all seed planted in LDCs will be of uniform strains. To help preserve genetic variety, some of the world's native plants and native strains of food crops are being collected and stored in 13 genetic storage banks and agricultural research centers around the world (see Figure 12-5 and Spotlight below).

Cultivating More Land Some agricultural experts have suggested that farmers could more than double the world's cropland by clearing tropical forests and irrigating arid lands, mostly in Africa, South America, and Australia (Figure 12-13). Others believe only a small portion of these lands can be cultivated because most are too dry or too remote or lack productive soils. Even if more cropland were developed, much of the increase would offset the projected loss of almost one-third of today's cultivated cropland and rangeland from erosion, overgrazing, waterlogging, salinization, mining, and urbanization.

Location, Soil, and Insects as Limiting Factors About 83% of the world's potential new cropland is in the remote rain forests of the Amazon and Orinoco river basins in South America and in Africa's rain for-

---

SPOTLIGHT Are Gene Banks the Solution to Preserving the World's Plant Diversity?

Specimens of most of the world's native plants and food crops are kept in a series of gene banks. Most plants are stored in the form of seeds. The seeds are usually stored dry and at cold temperatures. Warming them up and adding moisture makes them ready for use.

Despite their importance, plant gene banks are only a stopgap measure for preserving genetic diversity. One problem is that existing banks contain only a small portion of the world's known and

potential varieties of agricultural crops and other plants.

Many species, such as potatoes, fruit trees, orchids, and many tropical plants, cannot be successfully stored. Many seeds rot and must periodically be replaced. Accidents such as power failures, fires, and unintentional disposal of seeds can cause irrecoverable losses.

Furthermore, stored plant species do not continue to evolve. Thus, they are less fit for reintroduction to their native habitats,

which may have undergone various environmental changes.

Because of these limitations, ecologists and plant scientists warn that the best way to preserve the genetic diversity of the world's plant and animal species is to protect large areas of representative ecosystems throughout the world from agriculture and other forms of development. So far financial and political efforts by governments to accomplish this essential goal lag far behind the need. What do you think should be done?

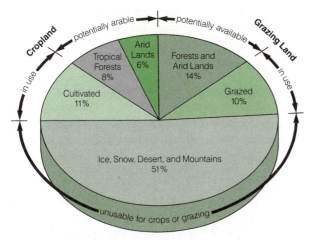

Figure 12-13 Classification of the earth's land. Theoretically, we could double the world's cropland in size by clearing tropical forests and irrigating arid lands. But converting this marginal land to cropland would destroy valuable forest resources, cause serious environmental problems, and usually not be cost-effective.

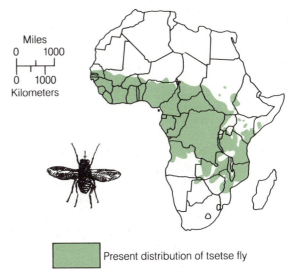

Figure 12-14 Region of Africa infested by the tsetse fly. Its bite can infect livestock and people with incurable sleeping sickness.

ests (see color insert, Figure 2). Most of the land is located in just two countries, Brazil and Zaire.

Cultivation would require massive capital and energy investments to clear the land and to transport the harvested crops to distant populated areas. The resulting deforestation would greatly increase soil erosion. It would also reduce the world's precious genetic diversity by eliminating vast numbers of unique plant and animal species found only in these biomes.

Tropical rain forests have plentiful rainfall and long or continuous growing seasons. However, their soils often are not suitable for intensive cultivation. About 90% of the plant nutrient supply is in ground litter and vegetation above the ground rather than in the soil (Figure 10-4, p. 218). By comparison, as little as 3% of the nutrients in temperate-zone forests are stored above the ground.

Nearly 75% of the Amazon basin, roughly one-third of the world's potential new cropland, has highly acidic and infertile soils. In addition, an estimated 5% to 15% of tropical soils (4% of those in the Amazon basin), if cleared, would bake under the tropical sun into a brick-hard surface called laterite, useless for farming.

Some tropical soils can produce up to three crops of grain per year if massive quantities of fertilizer are applied at the right time, but costs are high. The warm temperatures, high moisture, and year-round growing season also support large populations of pests and diseases that can devastate monoculture crops. Research has shown that crops grown in the tropics are attacked by up to 10 times more species of insects and plant diseases than crops grown in temperate zones. Weeds are especially troublesome, sometimes

reducing monoculture crop yields to zero. Massive doses of pesticides could be used, but the same conditions that favor crop growth also favor rapid development of genetic resistance in pest species.

In Africa potential cropland larger in area than the United States cannot be used for farming or livestock grazing because it is infested by 22 species of the tsetse fly, whose bite can give both people and livestock incurable sleeping sickness (Figure 12-14). A $120 million eradication program has been proposed, but many scientists doubt it can succeed.

Researchers hope to develop new methods of intensive cultivation in tropical areas. Some scientists, however, argue that it makes more ecological and economic sense not to use intensive cultivation in the tropics. Instead, farmers should use shifting cultivation with fallow periods long enough to restore soil fertility. Scientists also recommend plantation cultivation of rubber trees, oil palms, and banana trees, which are adapted to tropical climates and soils.

Water as Limiting Factor Much of the world's potentially arable land lies in dry areas, where water shortages limit crop growth. Large-scale irrigation in these areas would be very expensive, requiring large inputs of fossil fuel to pump water long distances. Irrigation systems would deplete many groundwater supplies and require constant and expensive maintenance to prevent seepage, salinization, and waterlogging. Unfortunately, Africa, the continent that needs irrigation the most, has the lowest potential for irrigation because of the remote locations of its major rivers and its unfavorable topography and rainfall patterns.

Do the Poor Benefit? Whether present and future green or gene revolutions reduce hunger among the world's poor depends on how new technology is applied. In LDCs the major resource available to agriculture is human labor. When green revolution techniques are used to increase yields of labor-intensive subsistence agriculture on existing or new cropland in countries with equitable land distribution, the poor benefit, as has occurred in China.

In most LDCs, however, farmers have been encouraged to combine green revolution techniques with a shift from small-scale, labor-intensive subsistence cultivation to larger-scale, machine-intensive industrialized agriculture. Most poor farmers, however, don't have enough land, money, or credit to buy the seed, fertilizer, irrigation water, pesticides, equipment, and fuel that the new plant varieties need. This means that the second green revolution has bypassed more than 1 billion poor people in LDCs.

Switching to industrialized agriculture makes LDCs heavily dependent on large, MDC-based multinational companies for expensive supplies, increasing the LDCs' foreign debts. It also makes their agricultural and economic systems more vulnerable to collapse from increases in oil and fertilizer prices and reduces their rates of economic growth by diverting much of their capital to pay for imported oil and other agricultural inputs. Finally, mechanization displaces many farm workers, thus increasing rural-to-urban migration and overburdening the cities.

Unconventional Foods Some analysts recommend greatly increased cultivation of various nontraditional plants in LDCs to supplement or replace traditional foods such as wheat, rice, and corn. One little-known crop is the winged bean, a protein-rich legume presently used extensively only in New Guinea and Southeast Asia. Its edible winged pods, leaves, tendrils, and seeds contain as much protein as soybeans, and its edible roots contain more than four times the protein of potatoes. Indeed, this plant yields so many different edible parts that it has been called a "supermarket on a stalk."

Scientists have identified dozens of other plants that could be used as sources of food. The problem is getting farmers to cultivate such crops and convincing consumers to try new foods.

12-4 CATCHING MORE FISH AND FISH FARMING

The World's Fisheries We get an average of 24% of the animal protein in our food directly from fish and shellfish and another 5% indirectly from fish meal fed to livestock. The animal protein we get from these sources is more than that from beef, twice as much as from eggs, and three times the amount from poultry. In most Asian coastal and island countries, fish and shellfish supply 30% to 90% of the animal protein eaten by people.

About 87% of the annual commercial catch of fish and shellfish comes from the ocean and the rest from fresh water. Concentrations of particular aquatic species suitable for commercial harvesting in a given ocean area or inland body of water are called **fisheries.** The world's major commercial marine fisheries are shown in Figure 12-15.

About 99% of the world marine catch is taken from plankton-rich waters within 370 kilometers (200 nautical miles) of the coast. Most of this catch comes from estuaries and upwellings where deep, nutrient-rich waters are swept up to the surface. However, this vital coastal zone is being disrupted and polluted at an alarming rate (see Enrichment Study on p. 129).

Only about 40 of the world's 30,000 known species of fish are harvested in large quantities. Some of the important species of fish in marine habitats are shown in Figure 12-16. Almost half of the world's commercial marine catch is taken by only five countries: Japan (16% of the catch), the USSR (13%), China (7%), the United States (6%), and Chile (6%).

Using small and large fishing boats to catch fish and shellfish is essentially a hunting-and-gathering procedure taking place over a large area. Because 30% to 40% of the operating costs of fishing boats is spent on fuel, energy inputs for each unit of food energy obtained from most marine species are enormous (Figure 12-17).

Trends in the World Fish Catch Between 1950 and 1970 the annual commercial fish catch increased over threefold (Figure 12-18). This increase was larger than that of any other human food source during the same period. This led to widespread optimism that the catch soon could be expanded to 100 million metric tons a year, the estimated maximum sustainable harvest.

That hasn't happened, however. Meanwhile, world population continued to grow. This meant that between 1970 and 1986 the average fish catch per person declined in spite of slight increases in the annual harvest (Figure 12-19). Because of overfishing, pollution, population growth, and increased demand, the average catch per person is projected to drop back to the 1960 level by the year 2000.

Overfishing occurs when so many fish are taken that too little breeding stock is left to prevent a drop in numbers. Overfishing rarely causes biological extinction because commercial fishing becomes unprofitable before that point. That is, prolonged overfishing leads to **commercial extinction**, the point at

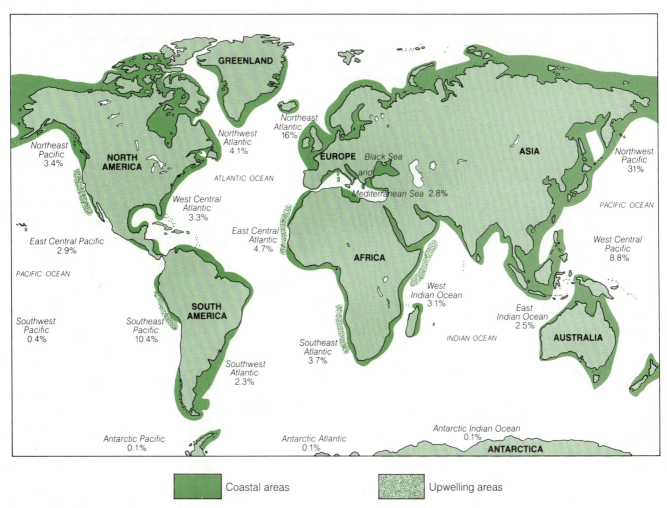

Figure 12-15 Location of the world's major commercial fisheries and distribution of the catch by fishery in 1984. (Data from UN Food and Agriculture Organization)

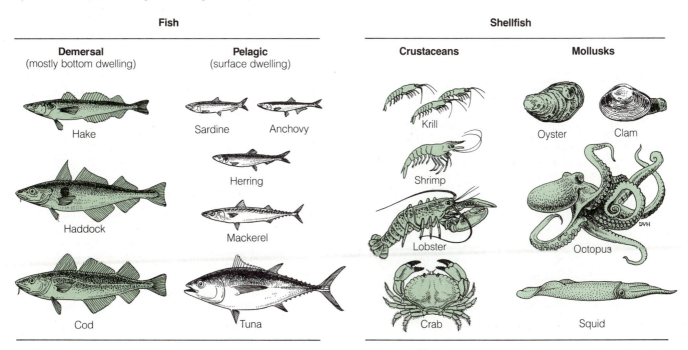

Figure 12-16 Some major types of commercially harvested marine fish and shellfish.

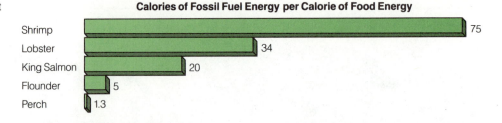

Figure 12-17 Average energy input needed to produce one unit of food energy from some commercially desirable types of fish and shellfish.

Calories of Fossil Fuel Energy per Calorie of Food Energy

Shrimp 75
Lobster 34
King Salmon 20
Flounder 5
Perch 1.3

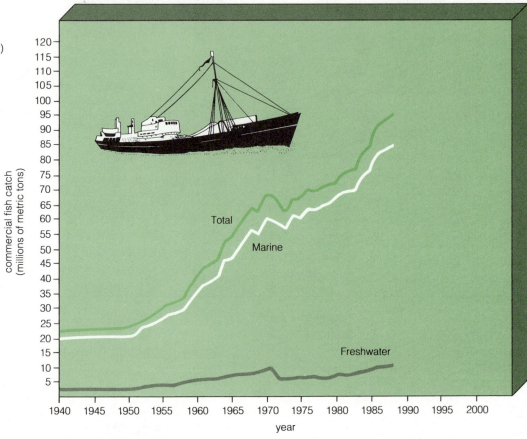

Figure 12-18 World fish catch. (Data from UN Food and Agriculture Organization)

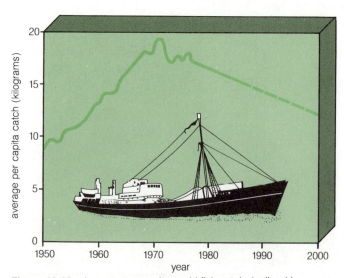

Figure 12-19 Average per capita world fish catch declined in most years since 1970. It's projected to drop further by the end of this century. (Data from United Nations and Worldwatch Institute)

which the stock of a species is so low that it's no longer profitable to hunt and gather the remaining individuals in a specific fishery. Fishing fleets then move to a new species or to a new region, hoping that the overfished species will eventually recover.

By the early 1980s overfishing had depleted stocks of 42 valuable fisheries. Examples include cod and herring in the North Atlantic, salmon and the Alaska king crab in the northwest Pacific, and Peruvian anchovy in the southeast Pacific (see Case Study on p. 278).

Aquaculture Aquaculture supplies about 8% of the world's commercial fish harvest. There are two major types of aquaculture. **Fish farming** involves cultivating fish in a controlled environment and harvesting them when they reach the desired size (Figure 12-20). **Fish ranching** involves holding species in captivity for the first few years of their lives and then harvesting the adults when they return to spawn. Ranching is useful for anadromous species, such as salmon and ocean trout, which after birth move from fresh water to the ocean and then back to fresh water to spawn.

Aquaculture of inexpensive species is a major source of low-cost animal protein for the poor in many LDCs, especially in Asia. Almost three-fourths of the world's annual aquaculture catch comes from 71 LDCs. Species cultivated in LDCs include carp, tilapia, milkfish, clams, and oysters, which feed low in food webs on phytoplankton and other forms of aquatic plants.

In MDCs aquaculture is used mostly to raise expensive fish and shellfish and to stock lakes and rivers with game fish. This benefits anglers who fish for sport and is highly profitable for aquaculture farmers and companies. But it does little to increase food and protein supplies for the poor. In the United States, fish farms supply 40% of the oysters and most of the catfish, crawfish, and rainbow trout consumed as food.

Aquaculture has a number of advantages. It can produce high yields per unit of area. Large amounts of fuel are not required, so yields and profits are not closely tied to the price of oil, as they are in commercial fishing.

One problem, however, is that the fish can be killed by pesticide runoff from nearby croplands. Bacterial and viral infections of aquatic species can also limit aquaculture yields. Without adequate pollution control, waste outputs from shrimp farming and other large-scale aquaculture operations can also pollute nearby surface water and groundwater.

Can the Annual Catch Be Increased Significantly? Some scientists believe that the world's annual commercial catch of fish and shellfish can be increased to at least 100 million metric tons a year. One hopeful sign was the signing of the 1982 United Nations Convention on the Law of the Sea by 159 countries. This treaty gives all coastal countries the legal right to control fishing by their own fishing fleets and by foreign ships within 364 kilometers (200 nautical miles) of their coasts. If enforced, this treaty can sharply reduce overfishing.

By 1987, however, fishery scientists found little recovery of many heavily exploited fish stocks. By 1989 only 40 countries had ratified the treaty, leaving 20 to go before the treaty becomes international law. Furthermore, 22 countries, including the Soviet Union, the United States, West Germany, and the United Kingdom, have refused to sign or ratify this treaty.

The world fish catch can also be expanded by harvesting more squid, octopus, lantern fish, Antarctic krill, and other unconventional species. Greatly expanded harvesting of krill, however, could lead to sharp declines in the populations of certain whales and other species dependent on krill. Also, food scientists haven't been able to process krill into foods that taste good enough for people to eat.

Additional increases could be brought about by a sharp decrease in the one-fifth of the annual catch now wasted, mainly from throwing back potentially useful fish taken along with desired species. More refrigerated storage at sea to prevent spoilage would also increase the catch. Experts project that annual freshwater and saltwater aquaculture production could be increased more than threefold between 1986 and 2000.

Other fishery experts believe that further increases in the annual marine catch are limited by overfishing and by pollution and destruction of estuaries and aquaculture ponds. Another factor that may limit the commercial fish catch from the world's oceans is the projected rise in the price of oil—and thus of boat fuel—between 1995 and 2015. Unless more seafood is produced by aquaculture, consumers may find seafood prices too high.

12-5 MAKING FOOD PRODUCTION PROFITABLE, GIVING FOOD AID, AND DISTRIBUTING LAND TO THE POOR

Government Agricultural Policies Governments can influence crop and livestock prices, and thus the supply of food, in several ways:

- Keep food prices artificially low. This makes consumers happy but can decrease food production by reducing profits for farmers.

- Give farmers subsidies to keep them in business and encourage them to increase food production.

- Eliminate price controls and subsidies, allowing market competition to determine food prices and thus the amount of food produced.

Governments in many LDCs keep food prices in cities low to prevent political unrest. But low prices discourage farmers from producing enough to feed the country's population, and the government must use limited funds or go into debt to buy imported food. With food prices higher in rural areas than in cities, more rural people migrate to urban areas, aggravating urban problems and unemployment. These conditions increase the chances of political unrest, which the price control policy was supposed to prevent.

LDCs with large foreign debts often encourage farmers to produce various crops for export instead of food crops for their own people. About 14% of all cropland in LDCs is used to grow export crops such as coffee, cocoa, rubber, tea, tobacco, and fibers. Increases in the production of such crops has led to

---

CASE STUDY Collapse of the Peruvian Anchovy Fishery

In 1953, Peru began fishing for anchovy in nutrient-rich upwellings off its western coast. The size of the fishing fleet increased rapidly. Factories were built to convert the small fish to fish meal for sale to MDCs for use as livestock feed. Between 1965 and 1971, harvests of the Peruvian anchovy made up about 20% of the world's annual commercial fish catch (Figure 12-21).

Between 1971 and 1978, however, the Peruvian anchovy became commercially extinct and did not begin recovering slightly until 1983. The collapse of this fishery is an example of how biology, geography, economics, and politics interact and often clash in fishery management.

At unpredictable intervals the productivity of the upwellings off the coast of Peru drops sharply because of a natural weather change, called the El Niño–Southern Oscillation, or ENSO (see Case Study on p. 112). The numbers of anchovy, other fish, seabirds, and marine mammals in food webs based on phytoplankton then drop sharply.

UN Food and Agriculture Organization biologists warned that during seven of the eight years between 1964 and 1971 the anchovy harvest exceeded the estimated sustainable yield. Peruvian fishery officials ignored these warnings. Government officials decided to risk the collapse of the fishery to pay off these loans and avoid putting thousands of people out of work. They also believed that a slight drop in the anchovy catch would cause shortages and raise the price of fish meal.

Disaster struck in 1972, when a strong ENSO arrived. The anchovy population, already at dangerously low levels due to overfishing, could not recover from the effects of the ENSO. By putting short-term economics above biology, Peru lost a major source of income and jobs and had to increase its foreign debt.

The country has made some economic recovery by harvesting the Peruvian sardine, which took over the niche once occupied by the anchovy. The catches of mackerel, bonita, and hake have also increased. Since 1983 the Peruvian anchovy fishery has been making a slow recovery.

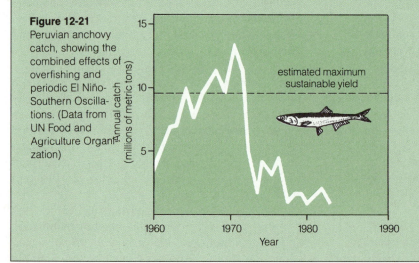

Figure 12-21 Peruvian anchovy catch, showing the combined effects of overfishing and periodic El Niño-Southern Oscillations. (Data from UN Food and Agriculture Organization)

lower prices and reduced the income of LDCs depending on these sales.

Governments can stimulate crop and livestock production by guaranteeing farmers a certain minimum yearly return on their investment. If governments offer adequate but not excessive financial incentives, production will increase, and in LDCs the rate of migration of displaced farmers to urban areas will decrease.

However, if government price supports are too generous and the weather is good, farmers may produce more food than can be sold. Food prices and profits then drop because of the oversupply. The resulting availability of large amounts of food for export or food aid to LDCs depresses world food prices. The low prices reduce the financial incentive for farmers to increase domestic food production. Unless even higher government subsidies are provided to prop up farm income by buying unsold crops or paying farmers not to grow crops on some of their land, a number of debt-ridden farmers go bankrupt. This is what happened in the United States during the 1980s. Excessive subsidies can also promote cultivation of marginal land, resulting in increased soil erosion, nutrient depletion, salinization, waterlogging, desertification, and water pollution.

Government price supports and other subsidies make farmers and agribusiness executives happy. They are also popular with most consumers because they make food prices seem low. Politicians like this approach because it increases their chances of staying in office. What most consumers don't realize is that they are paying higher prices for their food indirectly in the form of higher taxes to provide the subsidies. There is no free lunch.

Eliminating all price controls and agricultural subsidies and allowing market competition to determine food prices and production is a great idea on paper. In practice, however, individuals and companies with excessive economic and political influence use such power to avoid true competition (Section 22-2).

The U.S. Farm Situation The farm debt crisis of the 1980s has torn the social and economic fabric of middle-class rural America. Between 1980 and 1988 over 500,000 part-time and full-time U.S. farmers quit farming or went bankrupt. Today at least another 100,000 are still in trouble.

Farm supply and farm machinery businesses in farm towns have also suffered severe economic losses. Many went bankrupt. Many rural towns and counties have suffered sharp drops in population and tax revenues, causing school closings and reductions in services.

The U.S. farm crisis occurred because the government encouraged farmers to grow food to help fight world hunger and to increase food exports to offset the mounting bill for imported oil after the 1973 OPEC oil embargo. Most farmers responded by expanding their operations. Many borrowed heavily at high interest rates to buy more land and equipment. Their greatly increased debt was backed by the rapid rise in the value of their cropland and the belief that farm income would increase sharply. Many farmers also began farming marginal land with highly erodible soils.

In the 1980s, however, the bottom dropped out for farmers who had borrowed heavily and gambled on increased food demand to keep cropland values and crop prices high. Between 1981 and 1987 the average value per acre of farmland dropped by 33% (40% to 55% in some midwestern states), and net farm income and exports fluctuated. Tax-supported federal subsidies to farmers rose from $7 billion in 1980 to a record $26.5 billion in 1986. To keep even more farmers from going bankrupt, the government used these funds to buy up surplus production and to pay farmers not to grow food.

Two major factors contributed to the drop in the value of cropland. First, overproduction lowered crop prices, reducing the income farmers needed to pay off their debts and plant a new crop. Second, U.S. food exports declined due to increases in food production in many countries because of the second green revolution and cheap farm labor. Also many debt-ridden LDCs were unable to buy the food they needed. Many other countries were able to sell surplus crops for less because a stronger dollar and high federal price supports made U.S. crop exports more expensive.

By 1988 the U.S. farm system had recovered somewhat. Overextended farmers were no longer in business, average cropland prices rose by 32%, and food exports and farm income increased. Government farm subsidies had dropped but were still $16 billion.

According to many food experts, the U.S. agricultural system is too successful for its own good. It produces so much food that the government must pay farmers not to produce or must buy up and store the unneeded crops. This encourages farmers to produce even more.

A number of analysts believe that the only way out of this dilemma is to gradually wean U.S. farmers from all federal subsidies and let them respond to market demand. Only those who were good farmers and financial managers would be able to stay in business. The elimination of subsidies would decrease the environmental impact of agriculture by limiting production to only what can be sold and by discouraging farmers from growing crops on marginal land.

The first step would be to see that federal subsidies go only to poor and middle-class farmers in financial trouble who have the experience and managerial skills to stay in the farming business. Next the government would phase out farm subsidies over several years. Some of the money saved would be used to help needy but capable farmers pay off their debts. However, they would be eligible for such subsidies only if they agreed to use an approved soil and water conservation program or to use new, sustainable-earth agricultural methods on some or all of their land (Section 12-6).

However, phasing out all farm subsidies is not easy. Large corporate farmers, whose profits are higher and financial risks are lower because of subsidies, use their considerable political influence to maintain them. In addition, many small- and medium-size farmers have become dependent on federal subsidies that now provide one-third to one-half of their income regardless of how much they grow. Farmers and owners of farm-related businesses usually have enough votes to elect congressional representatives opposed to phasing out all farm subsidies.

International Aid   Between 1945 and 1985 the United States was the world's largest donor of nonmilitary foreign aid to LDCs. Since 1986, however, Japan has been the larger donor of such aid. Some of this, known as bilateral aid, is donated directly to countries. Some, known as multilateral aid, is given to international institutions such as the World Bank for distribution to countries. These forms of aid are used mostly for agriculture and rural development, food relief, population planning, health, and economic development. Private charity organizations such as CARE and Catholic Relief Services and funds from benefit music concerts and record sales provide over $3 billion a year of additional foreign aid.

In addition to helping other countries, foreign aid stimulates U.S. economic growth and provides Americans with jobs. Seventy cents of every dollar the U.S. gives directly to other countries is used to purchase American goods and services. Today 21 of the 50 largest buyers of U.S. farm goods are countries that once received free U.S. food.

Despite the humanitarian benefits and economic returns of such aid, the percentage of the U.S. gross national product used for nonmilitary foreign aid to LDCs has dropped from a high of 1.6% in the 1950s to only 0.20% in 1988—an average of only $30 per American. Sixteen other MDCs used a higher percentage of their GNP for nonmilitary foreign aid to LDCs in 1988 with Norway (1.12%), the Netherlands (0.98%), Denmark (0.89%), and Sweden (0.87%) leading the way. Some people call for greatly increased food relief from government and private sources, while others question the value of such aid (see Pro/Con below).

Distributing Land to the Poor   An important step in reducing world hunger, malnutrition, poverty, and land degradation is land reform. Land reform involves giving the landless rural poor in LDCs ownership or free use of enough arable land to produce at least enough food for their survival and ideally to produce a surplus for emergencies and for sale. China and Taiwan have had the most successful land reforms.

Such reform would increase agricultural productivity in LDCs and reduce the need to farm and degrade

---

PRO/CON Is Food Relief Helpful or Harmful?

Most people view food relief as a humanitarian effort to prevent people from dying prematurely. However, some analysts contend that giving food to starving people in countries where population growth rates are high does more harm than good in the long run. By encouraging population growth and not helping people grow their own food, food relief condemns even greater numbers to premature death in the future.

Biologist Garrett Hardin (see Guest Essay on p. 18) has suggested that we use the concept of *lifeboat ethics* to decide which countries get food aid. He starts with the belief that there are already too many people in the lifeboat we call earth. If food aid is given to coun-

tries that are not reducing their population, this adds more people to an already overcrowded lifeboat. Sooner or later the boat will sink and kill most of the passengers.

Massive food aid can also depress local food prices, decrease food production, and stimulate mass migration from farms to already overburdened cities. It discourages the government from investing in rural agricultural development to enable the country to grow enough food for its population on a sustainable basis.

Another problem is that much food aid does not reach hunger victims. Transportation networks and storage facilities are inadequate, so that some of the food

rots or is devoured by pests before it can reach the hungry. Typically, some of the food is stolen by officials and sold for personal profit. Some must often be given to officials as bribes for approving the unloading and transporting of the remaining food to the hungry.

Critics of food relief are not against foreign aid. Instead, they believe that such aid should be given to help countries control population growth, grow enough food to feed their population, or develop export crops to help pay for food they can't grow. Temporary food aid should be given only when there is a complete breakdown of an area's food supply because of natural disaster. What do you think?

marginal land. It would also help reduce the flow of poor people to overcrowded urban areas by creating employment in rural areas.

Many of the countries with the most unequal land distribution are in Latin America, especially Brazil and Guatemala. Unfortunately, land reform is difficult to institute in countries where government leaders are unduly influenced by wealthy and powerful landowners.

The emphasis should be on land redistribution rather than land resettlement. To defuse pressure for land distribution, Brazilian officials have encouraged the landless poor to migrate to tropical forests and clear land for agriculture. This resettlement policy is causing severe deforestation and other ecological problems (Section 13-2).

12-6 SUSTAINABLE-EARTH AGRICULTURE

Sustainable-Earth Agricultural Systems The key to reducing world hunger and the harmful environmental impacts of industrialized and traditional subsistence agriculture (see Spotlight on p. 27) is to develop a variety of **sustainable-earth agricultural systems.** In these systems appropriate parts of existing industrialized and subsistence agricultural systems and new agricultural techniques would be combined to take advantage of local climates, soils, resources, and cultural systems.

A sustainable-earth agricultural system does not require large inputs of fossil fuels, promotes polyculture instead of monoculture, conserves topsoil and builds new topsoil with organic fertilizer, conserves irrigation water, and controls pests with little, if any, use of pesticides. The following are general guidelines for sustainable-earth agriculture:

- *Place primary emphasis on preserving and renewing the soil. Long-term sustainability of the soil, not short-term agricultural productivity, must always come first.*

- *Emphasize small- to medium-scale intensive production of a diverse mix of fruit, vegetable, and fuelwood crops and livestock animals, rather than large-scale monoculture production of a single crop or livestock animal.* Such biologically diverse food-producing systems can be used at a number of levels: window box planters and rooftop gardens in urban apartment and office buildings, raised-bed gardens on unused urban lots and in backyards, small or large greenhouses, small to medium farms using low-till and no-till cultivation, organic fertilizers, and minimal use of pesticides (Section 21-5).

- *Whenever possible, matter inputs should be obtained from locally available, renewable biological resources and used in ways that preserve their renewability.* Exam-

ples include using organic fertilizers from animal and crop wastes, planting fast-growing trees to supply fuelwood and add nitrogen to the soil, and building simple devices for capturing and storing rainwater for irrigating crops. Commercially produced inputs such as inorganic fertilizers and pesticides should be used only when needed and in the smallest amount possible.

- *Minimize use of fossil fuels; use locally available perpetual and renewable energy resources such as sun, wind, flowing water, and animal and crop wastes to perform as many functions as possible.*

- *Governments must develop agricultural development policies that include economic incentives to encourage farmers to grow enough food to meet the demand using sustainable-earth agricultural systems.*

In MDCs, such as the United States, a shift from industrialized agriculture to sustainable-earth agriculture is difficult. It would be strongly opposed by agribusiness companies, by farmers with large investments in industrialized agriculture, and by farmers unwilling to learn the necessary managerial skills and knowledge.

In 1989 the National Academy of Sciences recommended that U.S. farmers begin shifting to sustainable agriculture. The shift could be brought about gradually over 10 to 20 years by:

- greatly increased government support of research and development of sustainable-earth agricultural methods and equipment

- setting up demonstration projects in each county so that farmers can see how sustainable systems work

- establishing training programs for farmers, county farm agents, and most Department of Agriculture personnel

- establishing college curricula for sustainable-earth agriculture

- giving subsidies and tax breaks to farmers using sustainable agriculture and to agribusiness companies developing products for this type of farming

The good news is that 50,000 to 100,000 of the 650,000 full-time farmers in the United States have shifted partially or completely away from conventional industrialized agriculture to forms of sustainable agriculture. In 1989 only about 5% of U.S. produce was organically grown, but experts project that with proper incentives this could easily increase to 10% by the year 2000.

What Can You Do? The first step you can take to achieve a sustainable-earth agricultural system is to look at your lifestyle to find ways to reduce your unnecessary use and waste of food, fertilizers, and pesticides. Today about one-third of all U.S. households grow some of their own food, worth about $10 billion. However, most of this food is grown with larger amounts of commercial fertilizers and pesticides per unit of land than are used on most commercial cropland.

You can use sustainable-earth cultivation techniques to grow some of your own food in a backyard plot, a window planter, a rooftop garden, or a cooperative community garden. Spending $31 to plant a living-room size garden can give you vegetables worth about $250—a better return than almost any financial investment you can make. Fertilize your crops primarily with organic fertilizer produced in a compost bin (Figure 10-22, p. 232). Use small amounts of commercial inorganic fertilizer only when supplies of certain plant nutrients are inadequate.

Control pests by a combination of cultivation and biological methods (see Section 21-5). Use carefully selected chemical pesticides in small amounts only when absolutely necessary. Don't use electricity-wasting and noisy electronic zappers to kill bugs. Cut down on insect attacks by not wearing colognes and perfumes outdoors during summer. Rub Avon's Skin-So-Soft on your skin to keep bugs away.

Help reduce the use of pesticides on agricultural products by asking grocery stores to stock fresh produce and meat produced by organic methods (without the use of commercial fertilizers and pesticides). Organically grown fruits and vegetables may have a few holes, blemishes, or frayed leaves. But they taste just as good and are just as nutritious as more perfect-looking products (on which pesticides were used). Eating organically grown food is also a form of health insurance. You won't be ingesting small amounts of pesticides, whose long-term potential threats to your health are still largely unknown (Section 21-3).

Reduce unnecessary waste of food and fertilizer resources. An estimated 25% of all food produced in the United States is wasted; it rots in the supermarket or refrigerator or is thrown away off the plate. Put no more food on your plate than you intend to eat, and ask for smaller portions in restaurants. Eat lower on the food chain by eliminating or reducing meat consumption.

Exert pressure on candidates for public office and elected officials to improve and strictly enforce laws designed to protect the public and the environment from the harmful effects of pesticides. Also support policies designed to develop and encourage sustainable-earth agricultural systems in the United States and throughout the world.

The most important fact of all is not that people are dying from hunger, but that people are dying unnecessarily. . . . We have the resources to end it; we have proven solutions for ending it. . . . What is missing is the commitment.

World Hunger Project

CHAPTER SUMMARY

The small number of different types of plants and animals that feed the world are produced by energy-intensive *industrialized agriculture* in MDCs and labor- and land-intensive forms of *subsistence cultivation and herding* in LDCs. The major world food problems are food quantity, food quality, food storage and distribution, poverty, economic incentives for growing food, and the harmful environmental effects of agriculture.

An estimated 20 million to 40 million people, half of them under 5 years old, die prematurely each year from *undernutrition, malnutrition, and diseases related to or worsened by these conditions.* The chief cause of hunger, malnutrition, and preventable deaths from these conditions is *poverty*—not lack of food production.

Since 1950, most increases in food production in MDCs and a number of LDCs are the result of two major *green revolutions,* in which the yield per unit of cropland was increased by planting new, *hybrid crop varieties* that make increased use of fertilizer, water, and pesticides. However, the spread and effectiveness of the green revolutions have been limited by the lack of water, the displacement of protein-rich legumes by low-protein crops, the eventual leveling off of yields regardless of the level of fertilizer and water inputs, loss of genetic diversity needed to produce new varieties, and inequitable land distribution.

Some have suggested that the total amount of cultivated land throughout the world could be doubled, primarily by clearing tropical forests and irrigating arid lands, mostly in Africa, South America, and Australia. Others believe this is unrealistic because most of these potentially cultivatable (arable) lands are too dry or remote or lack productive soils. Massive inputs of fertilizer and irrigation water could be used to overcome these limitations but in most cases would be too expensive compared to increasing productivity on existing cropland.

Fish and shellfish are important sources of animal protein for many of the world's people, especially in Asia and Africa. Some experts believe that the present annual fish and shellfish catch can be doubled or tripled by increased fishing efforts, increased fish farming and ranching (*aquaculture*), and decreased waste of the annual catch. But other analysts point out that because of *overfishing* and *pollution of estuaries,* there has been only a slight increase in the annual catch since 1971, and the average fish catch per person has declined steadily.

Governments can increase food production by distributing land to the rural poor, making credit available to small farmers, providing farmers with price supports and subsidies, and controlling import and export food prices. MDCs can also provide LDCs with money and technical assistance that enhance their ability to become self-sufficient in food.

Many analysts believe the key to reducing world hunger and decreasing the pollution and environmental degradation caused by agriculture is to shift to *sustainable-earth agricultural systems* that work with nature in both LDCs and MDCs. Such systems would emphasize use of organic fertilizers, soil and water conservation, polyculture cultivation of perennial crops, and biological control of pests.

DISCUSSION TOPICS

1. What are the major advantages and disadvantages of (a) labor-intensive subsistence agriculture, (b) energy-intensive industrialized agriculture, and (c) sustainable-earth agriculture?

2. Explain why you agree or disagree with the following statement: There really isn't a severe world food problem because we already produce enough food to provide everyone on earth more than the minimum amount needed to stay alive.

3. What specific actions should the following groups take to reduce the poverty that is the leading cause of hunger, malnutrition, and greatly increased chances of premature death for one out of five people living in LDCs: (a) governments of LDCs, (b) the U.S. government, (c) private international aid organizations, (d) individuals such as yourself, and (e) the poor?

4. Summarize the advantages and limitations of each of the following proposals for increasing world food supplies and reducing hunger over the next 30 years: (a) cultivating more land by clearing tropical jungles and irrigating arid lands, (b) catching more fish in the open sea, (c) producing fish and shellfish with aquaculture, and (d) increasing the yield per area of cropland.

5. Should price supports and other federal subsidies paid to U.S. farmers out of tax revenues be eliminated? Explain. Try to have one or more farmers discuss this problem with your class.

6. Is sending food to famine victims helpful or harmful? Explain. Are there any conditions you would attach to sending such aid? Explain.

7. Should tax breaks and subsidies be used to encourage more farmers in the United States and other MDCs to switch to sustainable-earth farming? Explain.

CHAPTER 13

Land Resources:
Forests, Rangelands,
Parks, Wilderness

General Questions and Issues

1. How are the world's forests distributed and used, and why are forests such important resources?

2. Why are tropical deforestation and fuelwood shortages two of the world's most serious environmental and resource problems, and how should we deal with these problems?

3. How are forests and public lands used in the United States?

4. How should forest resources be managed and conserved?

5. Why are rangelands important and how should they be managed?

6. What problems do parks face and how should parks be managed?

7. Why is wilderness important and how much should be preserved?

We abuse land because we regard it as a commodity belonging to us. When we see land as a community to which we belong, we may begin to use it with love and respect.

Aldo Leopold

F our important types of land resources are forests, rangelands, parks, and wilderness. As population and economic development grow, these vital biological resources are coming under increasing stress (Table 1-1, p. 13). For example, every second an area of tropical forest the size of a football field is cleared and another area the same size is degraded.

Much of the world's rangeland is degraded by overgrazing. Some forests and other types of ecosystems have been protected from development and degradation by being set aside as wilderness areas and parks. However, these small oases of biological diversity are being threatened by overuse, nearby development, and air pollution. Protecting and managing forest, rangeland, wilderness, and park resources so that they can be used on a sustainable basis is one of our most important challenges.

13-1 FORESTS: TYPES, DISTRIBUTION, AND IMPORTANCE

Types of Forests A forest where the crowns of trees touch and form a closed canopy during all or part of the year is called a **closed forest.** Closed forests make up about 62% of the earth's forested area. An area where trees are abundant but their crowns don't form a closed canopy is known as an **open forest**, or **woodland.**

It's also useful to distinguish between secondary and old-growth forests. **Secondary forests** are stands of trees resulting from secondary ecological succession (Figure 6-11, p. 145). Most forests in the United States and other temperate areas are secondary forests that developed after the logging of virgin forests (forests not altered by human activity) or the abandonment of agricultural lands.

Old-growth forests are virgin forests containing massive trees that are often hundreds, sometimes thousands, of years old. Examples include forests of Douglas fir, western hemlock, giant sequoia, and coastal redwoods in the western United States (Figure 2-6, p. 36); loblolly pine in the Southeast; and most tropical forests. Generally, old-growth forests have a greater diversity of plant and animal life than secondary forests.

Distribution of the World's Forests Potentially renewable, open and closed forests cover about 34% of the earth's land surface (Figure 13-1). Most of Africa and Asia and some parts of Central and South Amer-

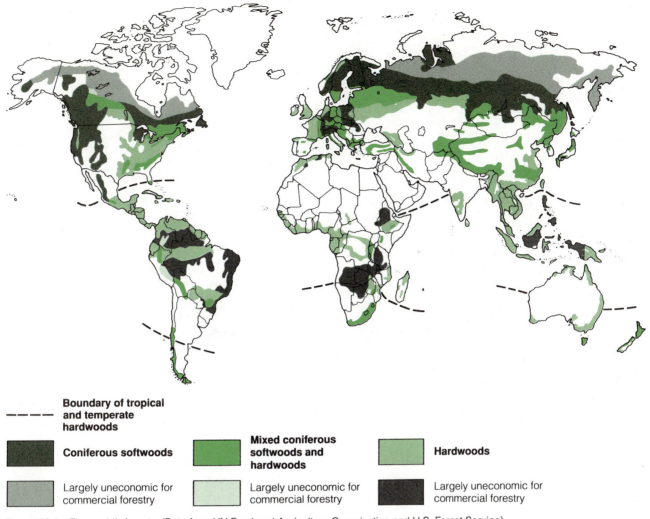

Figure 13-1 The world's forests. (Data from UN Food and Agriculture Organization and U.S. Forest Service)

Legend:

- - - - Boundary of tropical and temperate hardwoods

Coniferous softwoods

Mixed coniferous softwoods and hardwoods

Hardwoods

Largely uneconomic for commercial forestry

Largely uneconomic for commercial forestry

Largely uneconomic for commercial forestry

ica have little forest. Figure 13-2 shows the major types of forests in the lower 48 states of the United States. Worldwide, forests, especially tropical forests, are disappearing faster than any other biome.

Commercial and Ecological Importance of Forests

Forests supply us with lumber, fuelwood, paper pulp, medicines, and many other products, worth over $150 billion a year. Many forestlands are also used for mining, grazing livestock, and recreation.

Worldwide, about one-half the timber cut each year is used as fuel for heating and cooking, especially in LDCs. Some of this is burned directly as firewood, and some is distilled to make charcoal fuel. One-third of the world's annual harvest is sawlogs that are converted to lumber, veneer, panels, plywood, hardboard, particleboard, and chipboard. One-sixth is converted to pulp used in a variety of paper products. Sawlogs and wood pulp are the major uses of timber in MDCs.

Forests have vital ecological functions that many people are unaware of. Forested watersheds act as giant sponges, absorbing, holding, and gradually releasing water that recharges springs, streams, and aquifers. Thus they regulate the flow of water from mountain highlands to croplands and urban areas and help control soil erosion, the severity of flooding, and the amount of sediment washing into rivers, lakes, and reservoirs.

Forests also play an important role in the global carbon and oxygen cycles. Through photosynthesis trees help cleanse the air by removing carbon dioxide and adding oxygen. When trees are harvested and burned, the carbon they contain is released to the atmosphere as carbon dioxide. Removing tree cover also leads to the release of some of the carbon stored in the exposed soil. Thus, large-scale deforestation contributes to the greenhouse warming (Figure 5-5, p. 110), which will probably alter global climate, food production, and average sea levels within your lifetime (Section 19-4).

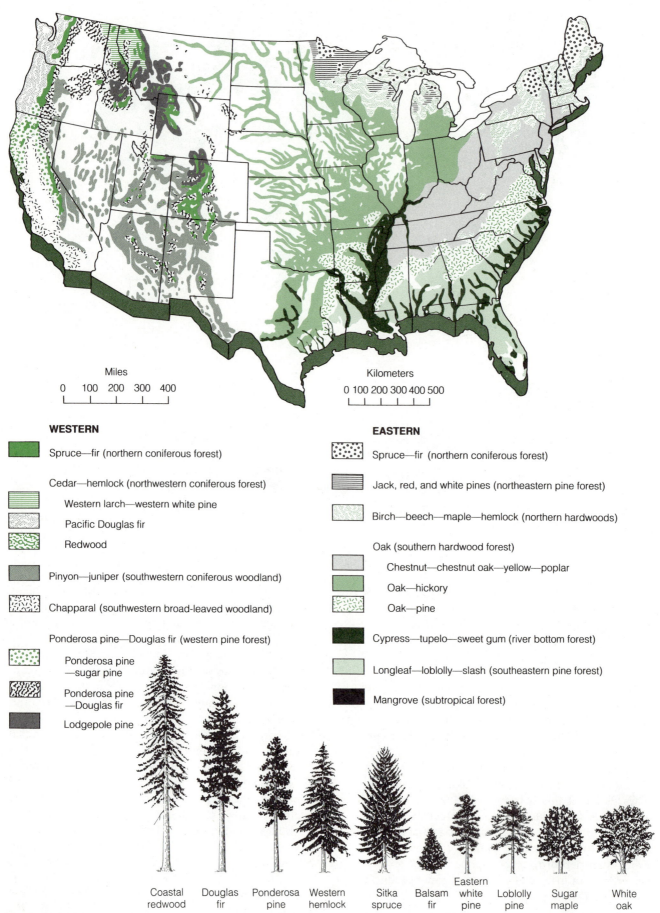

WESTERN

Spruce—fir (northern coniferous forest)

Cedar—hemlock (northwestern coniferous forest)

    Western larch—western white pine

    Pacific Douglas fir

    Redwood

Pinyon—juniper (southwestern coniferous woodland)

Chapparal (southwestern broad-leaved woodland)

Ponderosa pine—Douglas fir (western pine forest)

    Ponderosa pine —sugar pine

    Ponderosa pine —Douglas fir

    Lodgepole pine

EASTERN

Spruce—fir (northern coniferous forest)

Jack, red, and white pines (northeastern pine forest)

Birch—beech—maple—hemlock (northern hardwoods)

Oak (southern hardwood forest)

    Chestnut—chestnut oak—yellow—poplar

    Oak—hickory

    Oak—pine

Cypress—tupelo—sweet gum (river bottom forest)

Longleaf—loblolly—slash (southeastern pine forest)

Mangrove (subtropical forest)

Coastal redwood   Douglas fir   Ponderosa pine   Western hemlock   Sitka spruce   Balsam fir   Eastern white pine   Loblolly pine   Sugar maple   White oak

Figure 13-2 Forest vegetation in the lower 48 states of the United States. (Data from U.S. Forest Service)

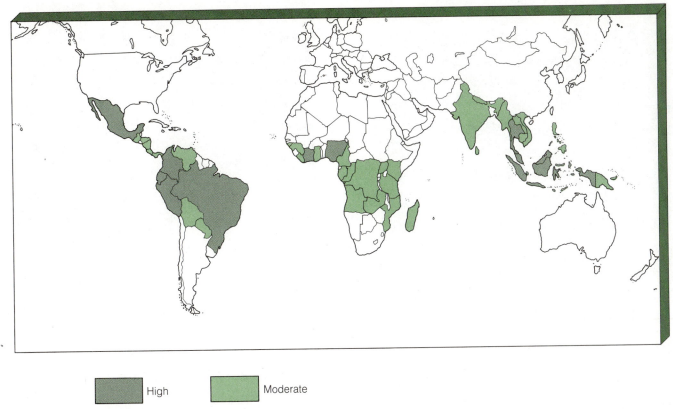

High   Moderate

Figure 13-3 Countries experiencing large annual destruction of tropical forests. (Data from UN Food and Agriculture Organization)

Forests provide habitats for a larger number of wildlife species than any other biome, making them the planet's major reservoir of biological diversity. They also absorb noise and some air pollutants and nourish the human spirit by providing solitude and beauty.

According to one calculation, during its 50-year lifetime a typical tree provides $196,250 worth of ecological benefits of oxygen, air pollution reduction, soil fertility and erosion control, water recycling and humidity control, wildlife habitat, and protein. Sold as timber, this tree is worth only about $590.

13-2 TROPICAL DEFORESTATION AND THE FUELWOOD CRISIS

Deforestation and Degradation of Tropical Forests
Tropical forests cover about 7% of the earth's land surface (see map in Figure 2 of color insert)—an area about three-quarters the size of the United States (excluding Alaska). Tropical rain forests, which account for about two-thirds of all tropical forests, provide homes for at least 50% of the earth's species.

About 55% of the world's original area of tropical moist forests has been cleared for timber, cattle grazing, fuelwood, and farming. Since the 1970s the rate at which the remaining forests are being cleared or

degraded has increased sharply. Surveys made by remote-sensing satellites indicate that at least 62,200 square kilometers—an area about the size of West Virginia or Ireland—and perhaps as many as 155,400 square kilometers—an area about the size of Georgia or Bangladesh—are completely cleared each year. About 99% of all tropical deforestation is taking place in 42 tropical LDCs (Figure 13-3). Almost half of this deforestation is taking place in Indonesia, Colombia, Mexico, and Brazil (Figures 13-4, 13-5, and Figure 11 in color insert). It is estimated that at least another 155,500 square kilometers of tropical forest is degraded each year when more than 30% of the canopy is removed by selective cutting of trees.

If clearing and degradation continue at the current rate, almost all tropical forests will be gone or severely damaged in 30 years or so. Some experts estimate that the rate of removal and degradation of tropical forests is almost two times higher than these estimates. In any case, the loss is staggering.

Why Should You Care About Tropical Forests?
Conservationists and ecologists consider the present destruction and degradation of tropical forests one of the world's most serious environmental and resource problems. Why? One reason is that these incredibly diverse forests are of immense economic and ecological importance to you and everyone else on earth (see

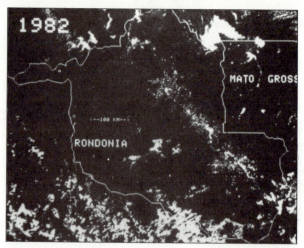

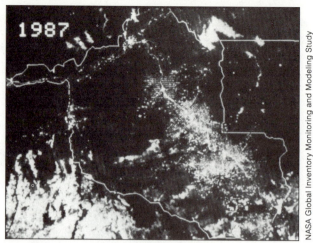

NASA Global Inventory Monitoring and Modeling Study

Figure 13-4 Satellite photos of increasing destruction of the Amazon rain forest in Brazil between 1982 and 1987. The white dots are fires. Such photographs show that 170,000 to 350,000 fires burned over 195,000 square kilometers (77,000 square miles) of the Amazon basin in 1987, an area one and one-half times the size of New York state. These fires may have accounted for as much as 10% of the global input of carbon dioxide to the atmosphere during 1987. The fires closely follow the route of the newly constructed Cuiaba-Port Velho highway, part of a development project financed by the World Bank for the Brazilian state of Rondonia. An estimated 20% of Rondonia's forest is gone, and at present rates of destruction it will be totally wiped out in 25 years.

World Wildlife Fund/Russell A. Mittermeier

Figure 13-5 Ground level view of tropical forest destruction in the Amazon basin in Brazil.

Guest Essay near the end of this chapter). The other reason is ethical. Regardless of the importance of tropical forests to us, sustainable-earth conservationists believe that this destruction must be stopped because it is *wrong*. These and other natural ecosystems should be protected from destruction and degradation because their species have an inherent right to exist (Section 24-2).

Two-thirds of the plant and animal species and as much as 80% of the plant nutrients in a tropical rain forest are in the canopy (Figure 4-27, p. 101). Hence, removing all or most trees in a forest destroys the habitat and food supply of most of its plant and animal life. The loss of tropical habitat is also causing declines in the populations of North American songbird species that migrate to the tropics during cold months. In addition, tropical deforestation exposes the land's nutrient-poor soil (Figure 10-4, p. 218) to drying by the hot sun and to erosion by torrential rains.

Tropical forests supply half of the world's annual harvest of hardwood. Food products derived from tropical forests include coffee, cocoa, spices, sweeteners, Brazil nuts, and tropical fruits. Latexes, gums, resins, dyes, waxes, tannins, and essential oils are among the many industrial materials we get from these forests. These substances are used in ice cream, toothpaste, shampoo, lipstick, deodorant, sunscreen lotion, perfume, varnish, phonograph records, glossy magazines, tires, tennis rackets, jogging shoes, and hundreds of other products.

The raw materials in one-fourth of the prescription and nonprescription drugs we use come from plants growing in tropical rain forests. Aspirin, probably the world's most widely used drug, is made according to a chemical "blueprint" supplied by a compound extracted from the leaves of tropical willow trees.

According to scientists at the National Cancer Institute, 70% of the promising anticancer drugs come from plants in tropical rain forests. Only a few of the millions of plant species found in these forests have been evaluated for their potential as medicines. While you are reading this page, a plant species that can cure a type of cancer that might kill you or someone you love could be wiped out forever.

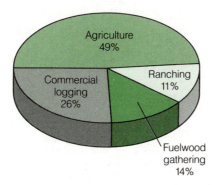

Figure 13-6 Major direct causes of deforestation and degradation of tropical forests. (Data from Norman Myers)

Ecologists warn that the degradation and loss of these extremely diverse biomes could cause the premature extinction of 1 million plant and animal species by the beginning of the next century. This massive reduction in species diversity—one of the world's most important and irreplaceable resources for us and other species—will create a biodiversity crisis.

From 50% to 80% of the moisture in the air above tropical forests comes from trees through transpiration and evaporation. If large areas of these forests are cleared, average annual precipitation decreases and the region's climate gets hotter and drier. Any rain that does fall runs off the bare soil rapidly instead of being absorbed and slowly released by vegetation. As the climate gets even hotter and drier, soil moisture and fertility drop further. Eventually these changes can convert a diverse tropical forest into a sparse grassland or even a desert. The carbon dioxide emitted by deforestation and burning can also affect global climate, food production, and sea levels by making the earth warmer (Section 19-4).

This gives you a glimpse of how tropical forests help support the lifestyle and help protect the health of people in MDCs. But tropical forests are even more important to people living in LDCs. They are home for 250 million people who survive by means of slash-and-burn and shifting cultivation (Figure 2-2, p. 33).

These forests also protect watersheds and regulate water flow for farmers, who grow food for over 1 billion people in LDCs. Unless the destruction of tropical forests stops, the Environmental Policy Institute estimates that as many as 1 billion people will starve to death during the next 30 years.

Causes of Tropical Deforestation Major direct causes of tropical deforestation and degradation are clearing for crop production; commercial logging, mostly for export to MDCs; fuelwood gathering; and livestock grazing, mostly to produce beef for export to MDCs (Figure 13-6). These forests are also cleared or degraded

to mine ores and to build dams and roads. Indirect causes include rapid population growth, widespread poverty, ownership of much of the arable land by a few wealthy people, and government failure to prevent destructive commercial logging and fuelwood gathering.

Rapid population growth and poverty push landless people to clear and cultivate forestland and to cut trees for fuelwood. In Latin America wealthy landowners influence the government to encourage landless peasants to clear tropical forests for cultivation. This helps defuse political pressures for equitable land distribution.

Policies of MDCs and international lending and aid agencies also encourage tropical deforestation. The mass migration of poor people to tropical forests would not be possible without the highway, logging, mining, ranching, and dam-building projects that open up these usually inaccessible areas. Many of these projects have been financed by loans from the World Bank and other international lending agencies whose policies are dictated by MDCs. Not until 1987, for example, did the World Bank set up a department to review the environmental impacts of its projects. How influential this department will be remains to be seen.

Driven by poverty and political forces beyond their control, landless peasants flood into tropical forest areas. Upon arrival they clear patches of forest to grow enough food to survive by shifting slash-and-burn cultivation. Many of the migrants clear and replant abandoned plots after only a few years instead of waiting the 10 to 25 years needed for restoration of soil fertility. This overcropping exhausts soil nutrients and eventually converts the land to shrubland, often used by wealthy ranchers to graze livestock until the land is degraded further.

Governments of most tropical LDCs have failed to regulate timber cutting by multinational and national timber companies and to require these companies to replant cleared areas. Since 1950 the consumption of tropical lumber has risen 15-fold, with Japan accounting for 60% of the consumption. Other major importers are the United States and Great Britain.

This increased demand has encouraged governments of many tropical LDCs to deplete their forests for short-term economic gain. For example, in 1960 Nigeria was a leading exporter of tropical logs. By 1985 its forests had been so depleted that it was a net importer of forest products. Malaysia, currently the world's leading exporter of tropical logs, is cutting down trees four times faster than they are being replenished and has lost half its forests during the past 20 years. As the remaining supply of tropical timber in Asia is depleted in the 1990s, timber cutting in tropical forests will shift to Latin America and Africa.

Between 1965 and 1983, satellite photos showed that cattle ranches were responsible for 30% of the total deforestation in the Amazon basin. Hawaii has only 10% of its rainforests left, and much of these lands are being threatened by urbanization and geothermal energy wells (see Pro/Con below).

Reducing the Destruction and Degradation of Tropical Forests

In 1985 the World Resources Institute, several international economic aid organizations, and representatives from most tropical countries developed a global Tropical Forestry Action Plan. The plan called for $8 billion to be spent over five years to help tropical LDCs protect and renew their forests. The funds would be used to achieve several goals:

- Provide financial incentives to villagers and village organizations for establishment of fuelwood trees and tree farms on abandoned and degraded land with suitable soil.

- Improve management practices in natural forests to increase yields and reduce forest degradation.

- Set aside 14% of the world's tropical forests as reserves and parks protected from unsustainable development; participating tropical countries would act as custodians for the reserves in return for foreign aid.

- Restore degraded tropical forests and watersheds.

- Strengthen forestry research, training, and extension services in tropical LDCs.

So far progress toward these goals has been slow and funding has lagged far behind the need.

Conservation groups have urged that several other approaches be added to the plan:

- Encourage debt-for-nature swaps that allow LDCs to exchange some of their foreign debt for agreeing to protect large areas of their tropical forests and other threatened biomes from destruction and degradation.

- Launch a mammoth international tree-planting program to restore degraded tropical and other

---

PRO/CON Should the United States Stop Importing Beef from Tropical Countries?

During the past 25 years almost two-thirds of Central America's tropical forests and woodlands have been cleared and converted to cropland and pastureland. In the 1970s about 40% of the low-cost beef raised on this land was exported to the United States.

This range-fed beef is cheaper, tougher, and leaner than the feed-lot-finished beef produced in the United States. The imported beef is sold mostly to fast-food chains for hamburger meat and to food-processing companies for use in pet foods, baby foods, luncheon meats, chili, stews, and frozen dinners. For each quarter-pound hamburger made from meat imported from Central America, an area of tropical forest roughly the size of a small kitchen (55 square feet) has been lost.

As tropical-forest expert Norman Myers (see Guest Essay near the end of this chapter) points out, Americans eating hamburgers from fast-food outlets that import beef from tropical countries "indirectly have their hands on the chain saws and bulldozers that are clearing many tropical forests."

After being grazed for 5 to 10 years, these tropical pastures can no longer be used for cattle. Often the land is so depleted of soil nutrients that it can no longer naturally regenerate as forest. Ranchers then move to another area and repeat the process. This destructive "shifting ranching" is often encouraged by government tax subsidies.

By 1985 only 19% of the beef produced in Central America was exported to the United States. This decline in beef imports resulted from a drop in U.S. beef consumption, declining production in Central America caused by pasture degradation, escalating warfare in El Salvador and Nicaragua, and pressure from environmental and consumer groups.

Some conservationists believe that the United States should phase out imports of all beef produced on cleared tropical forest-land. Because such beef makes up only 6% of the country's beef imports, a ban would have no noticeable effect on beef supplies.

In the 1980s, environmental and consumer groups (especially the Rainforest Action Network in San Francisco) have organized boycotts of hamburger chains buying beef imported from Latin America. Because of these efforts, many large chains claim they no longer buy beef from tropical countries. However, such claims are impossible to verify.

The basic question is whether importing beef from tropical countries to cut the cost of a pound of hamburger by a nickel is worth the destruction and degradation of the planet's greatest storehouse of biological diversity.

The best solution would be for Central American governments to permit ranchers to produce beef only on already deforested pastureland and to prohibit the clearing of forestland for cattle raising. Numerous studies have shown that with improved management the sustainable output of beef from a typical Central American ranch could be doubled or tripled. This solution would provide low-cost beef for export to other countries without causing any deforestation. What do you think?

---

forests and to help reduce the rate of global greenhouse warming.

- Phase out dams, plantations, ranches, roads, and colonization programs that threaten tropical forests.

- Include indigenous tribal peoples, women, and private local conservation organizations in the planning and execution of tropical forestry plans.

- Recognize the right of indigenous tribal peoples to have control over their land and natural resources.

- Develop national zoning plans to achieve a sustainable mix of preservation and sustainable economic development.

- Prevent banks and international lending agencies from lending money for environmentally destructive projects.

- Ban imports of tropical lumber because sustainable logging of tropical forests is mostly a myth. Using selection or shelter wood harvesting methods (Section 13-4) in dense tropical forests almost always causes serious degradation of many other trees and wildlife habitats.

- Encourage governments of tropical countries to greatly increase prices for exported wood to provide more income and reduce deforestation and degradation.

- Support effective family planning and sustainable development programs that attack the root causes of poverty, including maldistribution of farmland.

The Fuelwood Crisis in LDCs   Almost 70% of the people in LDCs rely on wood or charcoal produced from wood for heating and cooking. By 1985 about 1.5 billion people—almost one out of every three persons on earth—in 63 LDCs faced a fuelwood crisis (Figure 13-7). They couldn't get enough fuelwood to meet their basic needs, or they were forced to meet their needs by consuming wood faster than it was being replenished. In some areas people have caused shortages of fuelwood by clearing forests to raise cattle and plantation crops for export to MDCs. The UN Food and Agriculture Organization projects that by the end of this century 3 billion people in 77 LDCs will experience a fuelwood crisis.

Fuelwood scarcity has several harmful effects. It places an additional burden on the poor, especially women. Often, they must walk long distances to find and carry home small bundles of fuelwood. Buying fuelwood or charcoal can take 40% of a poor family's meager income.

City dwellers rely more on charcoal than wood because charcoal's light weight makes it easier to transport from the countryside to the city. But when wood is converted to charcoal, more than half the original energy content is lost. This means that villagers who move to a city and switch from wood to charcoal double their consumption of wood—if they can afford it.

Poor families who can't get enough fuelwood often burn dried animal dung and crop residues for cooking

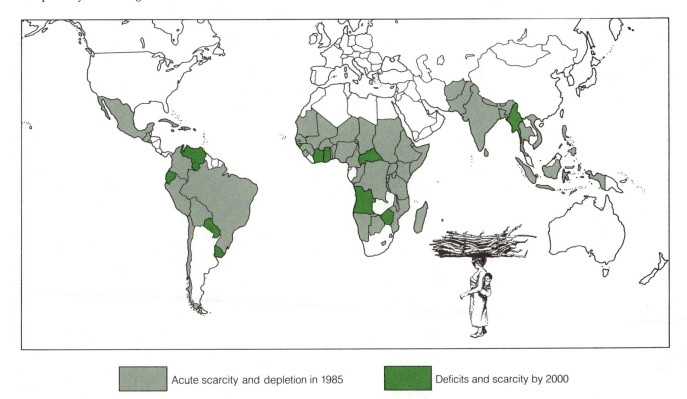

Acute scarcity and depletion in 1985   Deficits and scarcity by 2000

Figure 13-7   Generalized areas of the world experiencing fuelwood scarcity and deficits, 1985 and 2000 (projected). (Data from UN Food and Agriculture Organization)

Figure 13-8 Making fuel briquettes from cow dung in India.

Figure 13-9 The leucaena, which can grow 6 meters (20 feet) in its first year, can be used for fuelwood and reforestation in the tropics. Its leaves are excellent fodder for livestock; the seed pods are a nutritious food; its wood is clean burning and hard enough for furniture and construction; and its roots fertilize the soil with nitrogen.

and heating (Figure 13-8). This keeps these natural fertilizers from reaching the soil and reduces cropland productivity.

Reducing the Fuelwood Crisis LDCs can reduce the severity of the fuelwood crisis by planting more trees, burning wood more efficiently, and switching to other fuels.

The governments of China, Nepal, Senegal, and South Korea have established successful tree-planting programs at the village level in selected areas. Experience has shown that planting projects are most successful when local people, including women, are involved in their planning and implementation. Many reforestation projects have failed because women, who do most of the firewood gathering, were excluded. Programs work best when village farmers own the land or are given ownership of any trees grown on common resource land. This gives them a strong incentive to plant and protect trees for their own use and for sale.

Typically, government foresters supply villagers with seed or seedlings of fast-growing fuelwood trees (Figure 13-9) and shrubs and provide advice on the planting and care of the trees. Villagers are encouraged to plant these species in fields along with crops (agroforestry), on unused patches of land around homes and farmland, and along roads and waterways.

Another promising method is to encourage villagers to use the sun-dried roots of various common gourds and squashes as cooking fuel. These rootfuel plants produce two times the dry biomass of trees per unit of area on dry deforested lands. These plants, which regenerate themselves each year, help reduce soil erosion and produce an edible seed high in protein.

Several countries have started programs to encourage rural and urban people to switch from energy-wasting open fires to more-efficient cook stoves and to other fuels. Villagers in Burkina Faso in West

Africa have been shown how to make a stove from mud and dung that cuts wood use by 30% to 70%. It can be made by villagers in half a day at virtually no cost. New types of stoves must be designed to make use of locally available materials and to provide both heat and light like the open fires they replace.

Despite encouraging success in some countries, most LDCs suffering from fuelwood shortages have inadequate forestry policies and budgets and lack trained foresters. Such countries are planting 10 to 20 times fewer trees than needed to offset forest losses and meet increased demands for fuelwood and other forest products.

13-3 PUBLIC LANDS AND FOREST RESOURCES IN THE U.S.

U.S. Public Lands: An Overview About 42% of all U.S. land consists of public lands owned jointly by all citizens and managed for them by federal, state, and local governments. Over one-third (35%) of the country's land is managed by the federal government (Figure 13-10). About 95% of this federal public land is in Alaska (73%) and in western states (22%).

These public lands have been divided by Congress into different units administered by several federal

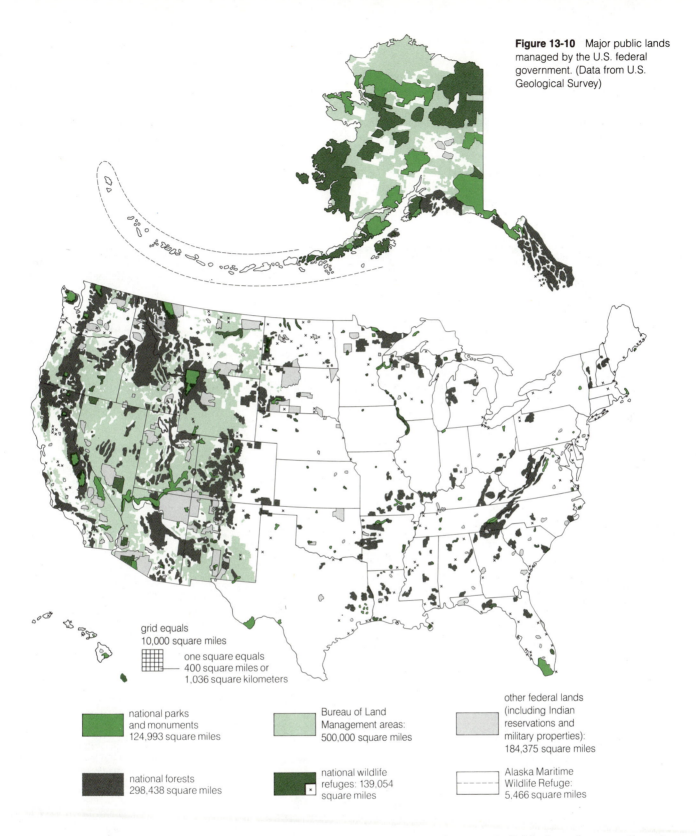

Figure 13-10 Major public lands managed by the U.S. federal government. (Data from U.S. Geological Survey)

grid equals
10,000 square miles

one square equals
400 square miles or
1,036 square kilometers

national parks
and monuments
124,993 square miles

Bureau of Land
Management areas:
500,000 square miles

other federal lands
(including Indian
reservations and
military properties):
184,375 square miles

national forests
298,438 square miles

national wildlife
refuges: 139,054
square miles

Alaska Maritime
Wildlife Refuge:
5,466 square miles

agencies. The allowed uses of these lands vary (see Spotlight on p. 294).

Federally administered public lands contain a large portion of the country's timber, grazing land, and energy resources (Figure 13-11) and most of its copper, silver, asbestos, lead, molybdenum, beryllium, phosphate, and potash. Through various laws Congress has allowed private individuals and corporations to harvest or extract many of these resources—often at below market prices. Because of the economic value of these resources, there has been a long and continuing history of conflict between various groups over management and use of these public lands, as discussed in Section 2-4.

Extent of U.S. Forests Today forests cover about one-third of the land area in the lower 48 states (Figure 13-2). They provide habitats for more than 80% of the country's wildlife species and are the prime setting for outdoor recreation.

Nearly two-thirds of this land is classified as commercial forestland. About three-fourths of it is privately owned. Much of it consists of small plots that are poorly managed. Each year the sale of U.S. lumber and wood products totals more than $54 billion, and the industry provides employment for 600,000 peo-ple. Most of the remaining one-third of U.S. forestland is not capable of producing commercially valuable timber or is set aside as parks, wildlife refuges, or wilderness.

Since 1950 the United States has kept up with the demand for wood and wood products without serious depletion of its commercial forestlands. But according to the U.S. Forest Service, domestic consumption of forest products is projected to double between 1980 and 2030.

SPOTLIGHT Major Components of Federal Public Lands

Multiple-Use Lands

National Forests The forest system includes 156 national forests and 19 national grasslands managed by the Forest Service. Excluding the 15% protected as wilderness areas, this land is managed according to the principles of *sustained yield* and *multiple use*. The lands are used for timbering, grazing, agriculture, mining, oil and gas leasing, recreation, sport hunting, sport and commercial fishing, and conservation of watershed, soil, and wildlife resources. Off-road vehicles are usually restricted to designated routes.

National Resource Lands These lands are mostly grassland, prairie, desert, scrub forest, and other open spaces located in the western states and Alaska. They are managed by the Bureau of Land Management under the principle of *multiple use*. Emphasis is on providing a secure domestic supply of energy and strategically important nonenergy minerals and on preserving the renewability of rangelands for livestock grazing under a permit system. About 10% of these lands is being evaluated for possible designation as wilderness areas.

Moderately-Restricted-Use Lands

National Wildlife Refuges This system includes 437 refuges and various ranges managed by the Fish and Wildlife Service. About 24% of this land is protected as wilderness areas. The purpose of most refuges is to protect habitats and breeding areas for waterfowl and big-game animals in order to provide a harvestable supply for hunters. A few refuges have been set aside to save specific endangered species from extinction. These lands are not officially managed under the principles of multiple use and sustained yield. Nevertheless, sport hunting, trapping, sport and commercial fishing, oil and gas development, mining (old claims only), timber cutting, livestock grazing, and farming are permitted as long as the Secretary of the Interior finds such uses compatible with the purposes of each unit.

Restricted-Use Lands

National Parks This system consists of 354 units. They include 49 major parks (mostly in the West) and 292 national recreation areas, monuments, memorials, battlefields, historic sites, parkways, trails, rivers, seashores, and lakeshores. All are managed by the National Park Service. Its management goals are to preserve scenic and unique natural landscapes, preserve and interpret the country's historic and cultural heritage, provide protected wildlife habitats, protect wilderness areas within the parks, and provide certain types of recreation. National parks can be used only for camping, hiking, sport fishing, and motorized and nonmotorized boating. Motor vehicles are permitted only on roads, and off-road vehicles are not allowed. In addition to the activities permitted in the parks, national recreation areas can be used for sport hunting, new mining claims, and new oil and gas leasing. About 49% of the land in the National Park System is protected as wilderness areas.

National Wilderness Preservation System This system includes 474 roadless areas within the national parks, national wildlife refuges, and national forests. They are managed, respectively, by the National Park Service, the Forest Service, and the Fish and Wildlife Service. These areas are to be preserved in their essentially untouched condition "for the use and enjoyment of the American people in such a manner as will leave them unimpaired for future use and enjoyment as wilderness." Wilderness areas are open only for recreational activities such as hiking, sport fishing, camping, non-motorized boating, and in some areas sport hunting and horseback riding. Roads, timber harvesting, grazing, mining, commercial activities, and human-made structures are prohibited, except where such activities occurred before an area's designation as wilderness. Motorized vehicles, boats, and equipment are banned except for emergency uses such as fire control and rescue operations. However, aircraft are allowed to land in Alaskan wilderness areas.

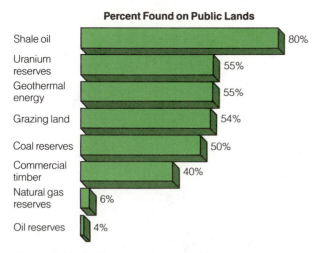

Percent Found on Public Lands

Shale oil — 80%
Uranium reserves — 55%
Geothermal energy — 55%
Grazing land — 54%
Coal reserves — 50%
Commercial timber — 40%
Natural gas reserves — 6%
Oil reserves — 4%

Figure 13-11 Estimated percentages of key resources on U.S. public lands. (Data from U.S. Geological Survey)

Figure 13-12 Monoculture tree farm of white pine near Asheville, North Carolina.

13-4 FOREST MANAGEMENT AND CONSERVATION

Types of Forest Management Managing forests to produce a sustainable supply of timber is not easy. Whereas other crops can be harvested annually, trees take 20 to 1,000 years to mature.

There are two basic forest management systems: even-aged management and uneven-aged management. With **even-aged management,** trees in a given stand are maintained at about the same age and size, harvested all at once, and replanted naturally or artificially so that a new even-aged stand will grow. Growers emphasize mass production of low-quality wood with the goal of maximizing economic return on investment in as short a time as possible.

Even-aged management begins with the cutting of all or most trees from a diverse, old-growth or secondary forest. Then the site is replanted with an even-aged stand of a single species (monoculture) of faster growing softwoods (Figure 13-12 and Figure 14 in color insert). Such stands of one or only a few tree species are called **tree farms.** They need close supervision and usually require expensive inputs of fertilizers and pesticides to protect the monoculture species from diseases and insects. Once the trees reach maturity, the entire stand is harvested and the area is replanted with seeds or seedlings. Genetic crossbreeding and genetic engineering can be used to improve both the quality and quantity of wood produced from tree farms.

With **uneven-aged management,** trees in a given stand are maintained at many ages and sizes to permit continuous natural regeneration. Here the goals are to sustain biological diversity, sustain long-term production of high-quality timber, provide a reasonable economic return, and allow multiple use of a forest stand.

The Forest Management Process Forest management consists of a cycle of decisions and events (Figure 13-13). Each cycle of management between planting and harvesting is called a *rotation.* The major steps in this cycle include making an inventory of the site, developing a forest management plan, preparing the site for harvest, harvesting commercially valuable timber, and regenerating and managing the site before the next harvest.

Tree Harvesting The method chosen for harvesting depends on whether uneven-aged or even-aged forest management is being used. It also depends on the tree species involved, the nature of the site, and the objectives and resources of the owner.

In **selective cutting,** intermediate-aged or mature trees in an uneven-aged forest are cut singly or in small groups (Figure 13-14). This reduces crowding, encourages the growth of younger trees, and maintains an uneven-aged stand with trees of different species, ages, and sizes. Over time the stand will regenerate itself.

Selective cutting of individual trees is used primarily in mixed northern and tropical hardwood forests. Selective cutting of small groups of trees can be used to harvest ponderosa pine, Douglas fir, oak, hickory, and loblolly pine.

If done properly, selective cutting helps protect the site from soil erosion and tree damage by the wind. This harvesting method is favored by those who wish to use forests for multiple uses and wish to preserve biological diversity.

Figure 13-13 Rotation cycle of forest management.

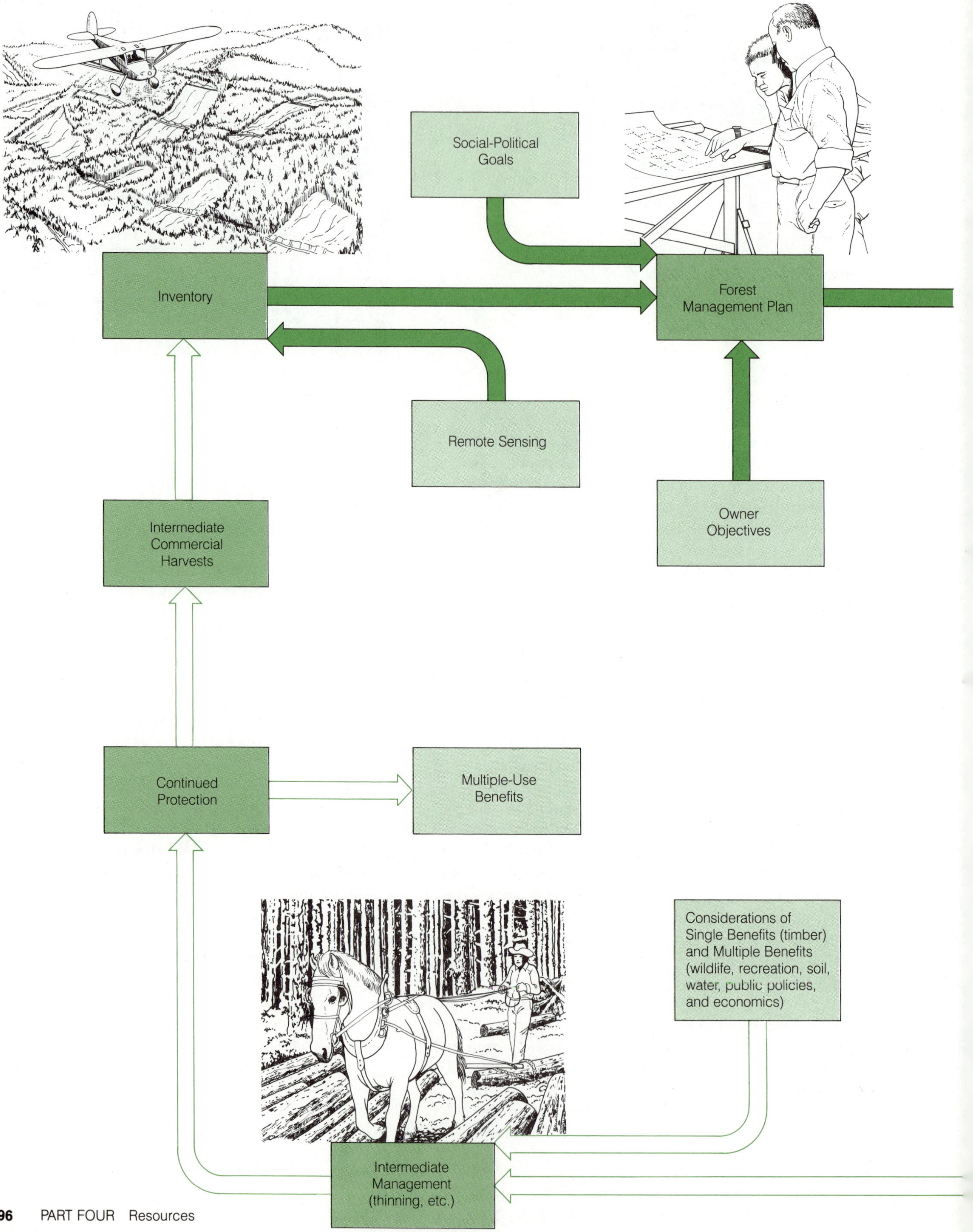

Social-Political Goals

Inventory

Forest Management Plan

Remote Sensing

Owner Objectives

Intermediate Commercial Harvests

Continued Protection

Multiple-Use Benefits

Considerations of Single Benefits (timber) and Multiple Benefits (wildlife, recreation, soil, water, public policies, and economics)

Intermediate Management (thinning, etc.)

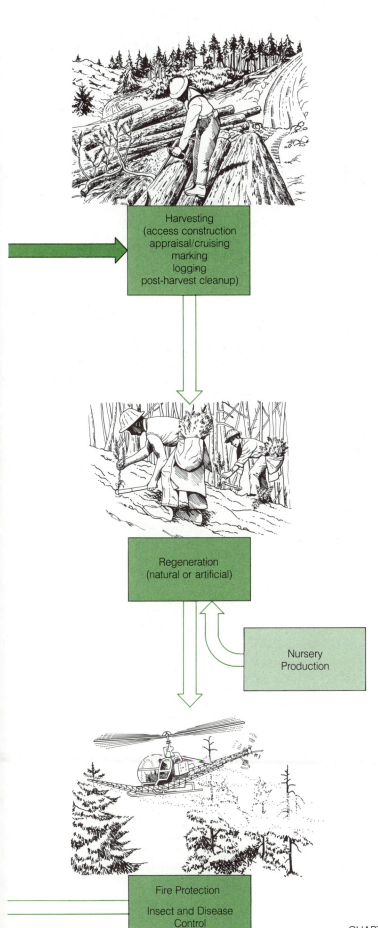

Harvesting
(access construction
appraisal/cruising
marking
logging
post-harvest cleanup)

Regeneration
(natural or artificial)

Nursery
Production

Fire Protection

Insect and Disease
Control

U.S. Forest Service/Ray M. Filloon

Figure 13-14 Selective cutting of ponderosa pine in Deschutes National Forest, an old-growth forest near Sisters, Oregon.

But selective cutting is costly unless the value of the trees removed is high. It's not useful for shade-intolerant species, which require full sunlight for seedling growth. The need to reopen roads and trails periodically for selective harvests can cause erosion of certain soils. Maintaining a good mixture of tree ages and sizes takes considerable planning and skill.

One type of selective cutting, not considered a sound forestry practice, is high grading, or creaming—removing the most valuable trees without considering the quality or distribution of the remaining trees needed for regeneration. Many loggers in tropical forests in LDCs use this destructive form of selective cutting.

Some tree species do best when grown in full or moderate sunlight in forest openings or in large cleared and seeded areas. Even-aged stands or tree farms of such shade-intolerant species are usually harvested by shelterwood cutting, seed-tree cutting, or clearcutting.

Shelterwood cutting is the removal of all mature trees in an area in a series of cuttings typically over a period of 10 years. This technique can be applied to even-aged or uneven-aged stands. In the first harvest, selected mature trees, unwanted tree species, and dying, defective, and diseased trees are removed. This cut opens up the forest floor to light and leaves the

Figure 13-15 First stage of shelterwood
cutting of red pine in a 140-year-old stand
in Minnesota.

best trees to cast seed and provide shelter for growing
seedlings (Figure 13-15).

After a number of seedlings have taken hold, a
second cutting removes more of the remaining mature
trees. Some of the best mature trees are left to provide
shelter for the growing young trees. After the young
trees are well established, a third cutting removes the
remaining mature trees and allows the even-aged stand
of young trees to grow to maturity.

This method allows natural reseeding from the best
seed trees and protects seedlings from being crowded
out. It leaves a fairly natural-looking forest that can be
used for a variety of purposes. It also helps reduce soil
erosion and provides good habitat for wildlife.

Without careful planning and supervision, however, loggers may take too many trees in the initial
cutting, especially the most valuable trees. Shelterwood cutting is also more costly and takes more skill
and planning than clearcutting.

Seed-tree cutting harvests nearly all the trees on
a site in one cutting, leaving a few seed-producing,
wind-resistant trees uniformly distributed as a source
of seed to regenerate a new crop of trees (Figure
13-16). After the new trees have become established,
the seed trees are sometimes harvested.

By allowing a variety of species to grow at one
time, seed-tree cutting leaves an aesthetically pleasing
forest useful for recreation, deer hunting, erosion control, and wildlife conservation. Leaving the best trees
for seed can also lead to genetic improvement in the
new stand.

Clearcutting is the removal of all trees from a given
area in a single cutting to establish a new, even-aged
stand or tree farm. Usually these are stands of only
one or two fast-growing species that need large or

Figure 13-16 Seed trees left after the seed-tree cutting of a
stand of longleaf pine in Florida. About 10 trees per hectare
are left to reseed the area.

moderate amounts of sunlight for germination of seed
and development of seedlings.

The clearcut area may consist of a whole stand
(Figure 13-17), a group, a strip, or a series of patches
(Figure 13-18). After all trees are cut, the site is reforested naturally from seed released by the harvest, or
foresters broadcast seed over the site or plant genetically superior seedlings raised in a nursery.

Currently, almost two-thirds of the annual U.S.
timber production is harvested by clearcutting. Clearcutting increases the volume of timber harvested per
acre, reduces road building, often permits reforesting
with genetically improved stock, and shortens the time
needed to establish a new stand of trees. Timber companies prefer this method because it requires much
less skill and planning than other harvesting methods
and usually gives them the maximum economic return.

Figure 13-17 Forest Service clearcut on Prince of Wales Island, Alaska. All trees in the area are removed and the area is reseeded.

Figure 13-18 Patch clearcutting in Kootenai National Forest, Montana.

However, large-scale clearcutting on steeply sloped land leads to severe soil erosion, sediment water pollution, flooding from melting snow and heavy rains, and landslides when the exposed roots decay. The heavy logging equipment compacts the soil and reduces its productivity.

Clearcutting leaves ugly, unnatural forest openings that take decades to regenerate (Figures 13-17 and 13-18) and reduces the recreational value of the forest. It also reduces the number and types of wildlife habitats and thus reduces biological diversity. Once a site has been clearcut, it is hard to break the cycle and wait 100 to 400 years for an uneven-aged stand to regrow through secondary ecological succession.

Clearcutting can be useful for some species if it's properly done. This means not clearcutting large areas or steeply sloped sites and making sure that the area is reseeded or replanted and protected until the next harvest. The problem is that timber companies have a built-in economic incentive to use large-scale clearcutting, often on species that could be harvested by less environmentally destructive methods.

A variation of clearcutting is **whole-tree harvesting,** in which a machine cuts each tree at ground level. In some cases the entire tree is then transported to a chipping machine, in which massive blades reduce the wood to small chips in about one minute. Some whole-tree harvesting machines pull up the entire tree so that roots are also converted to wood chips.

This approach is used primarily to harvest stands for use as pulpwood or fuelwood chips. By removing all wood materials from a stand, it can increase the yield of wood materials per acre from a temperate forest by as much as 300%.

Many foresters and ecologists, however, oppose this method because the periodic removal of all tree materials eventually depletes the soil of plant nutrients. The removal of standing dead timber and fallen logs also removes numerous wildlife habitats. Research is under way to determine how whole-tree harvesting methods might be modified to reduce such harmful environmental effects.

Protecting Forests from Diseases and Insects

Protecting stands from damage by fire, disease, insects, and air pollution is also an important part of forest management. Throughout the world, diseases and insects cause more losses of commercial timber than do fires. In a healthy, diverse forest, tree diseases and insect populations rarely get out of control and seldom destroy many trees. But a tree farm of one species has few natural defenses and is vulnerable to attack by diseases and insects.

The most destructive tree diseases are caused by parasitic fungi. These diseases can be accidentally introduced into forest communities where natural controls don't exist. In the United States three highly damaging tree diseases were introduced accidentally from other countries: chestnut blight (from China), Dutch elm disease (from Asia via Europe), and white pine blister rust (from Europe). Chestnut blight has almost eliminated the once-abundant and valuable chestnut tree from eastern hardwood forests. Dutch elm disease has killed more than two-thirds of the elm trees in the United States.

Most of the thousands of insect species that can damage trees are kept under control by other species. However, a few insect species can cause severe damage, especially in tree farms or ecosystems where natural controls don't exist. For example, bark beetles bore channels through the layer beneath the bark of spruce, fir, and pine trees. The numerous channels loosen the bark. These insects have killed large areas of forest in the western and southern United States. The larvae of leaf eaters, such as spruce budworm and gypsy moth, eat the needles or leaves of trees. Repeated attacks over several years can kill trees by eliminating the foliage they need to carry out photosynthesis and produce food.

The best and cheapest way to prevent excessive damage to trees from diseases and insects is to preserve forest biological diversity. Other methods include

- banning imported timber that might carry harmful parasites
- removing infected trees and vegetation
- clearcutting infected areas and removing or burning all debris
- treating diseased trees with antibiotics
- developing disease-resistant tree species
- applying insecticides and fungicides (Section 21-1)
- using integrated pest management (Section 21-5)

Protecting Forests from Fires

Today scientists recognize that periodic natural fires set by lightning are an important part of the ecological cycle of many forests. Some species, especially conifers such as pines and redwoods, have thick, fire-resistant bark and benefit from periodic fires. For example, the seeds of some conifers, such as the giant sequoia and the jack pine, are released or germinate only after being exposed to intense heat.

In evaluating the effects of fire on forest ecosystems, it's important to distinguish between three kinds of forest fires: surface, crown, and ground. **Surface fires** are low-level fires that usually burn only undergrowth and leaf litter on the forest floor (Figure 13-19). These fires kill seedlings and small trees but don't kill most mature trees. Animal wildlife can usually escape from these fairly slow-burning fires.

In forests where ground litter accumulates rapidly, a surface fire every five years or so burns away flammable material and helps prevent more destructive crown and ground fires. Surface fires also release and recycle valuable mineral nutrients tied up in slowly decomposing litter and undergrowth, increase the activity of nitrogen-fixing bacteria, stimulate the germination of certain tree seeds, and help control diseases and insects. Some wildlife species, such as deer, moose, elk, muskrat, woodcock, and quail, depend on periodic surface fires to maintain their habitats and to provide food in the form of vegetation that sprouts after fires.

Most surface fires burn themselves out or can be put out if caught in time. However, a combination of dry weather, high winds, and a large buildup of surface litter can convert a surface fire into a more damaging crown or ground fire.

Crown fires are extremely hot fires that burn ground vegetation and tree tops (Figure 13-20). They usually occur in forests where all fire has been prevented for several decades, allowing the buildup of dead wood, leaves, and other flammable ground litter. In such forests an intense surface fire driven by a strong wind can spread to tree tops. These rapidly burning fires can destroy all vegetation, kill wildlife, and accelerate erosion.

Sometimes surface fires become **ground fires,** which burn decayed leaves, or peat, below the ground surface. Such fires, common in northern bogs, may smoulder for days or weeks before being detected. They are very difficult to put out.

The protection of forest resources from fire involves four phases: prevention, prescribed burning, presuppression, and suppression. Prevention of forest fires, the most important and cheapest method, is primarily an educational process. Other methods of fire prevention include requiring burning permits and closing all or parts of a forest to travel and camping during periods of drought and high fire danger.

Figure 13-19 Surface fire in a California forest.

Figure 13-20 Effects of a highly destructive crown fire in Hunts Gulch, Idaho.

The Smokey-the-Bear educational campaign of the Forest Service and the National Advertising Council has been successful in preventing many forest fires in U.S. forests, saving many lives, and avoiding losses of billions of dollars. Ecologists, however, contend that it also caused harm by allowing litter buildup in some forests, increasing the likelihood of highly destructive crown fires. For this reason, many fires in national parks and wilderness areas are allowed to burn as part of the natural ecological cycle in forests (see Pro/Con on p. 302).

Prescribed surface fires can be an effective method for preventing crown fires by reducing litter buildup. They are also used to control outbreaks of tree diseases and pests. These fires are started only by well-trained personnel when weather and forest conditions are ideal for control and proper intensity of burning. Prescribed fires are also timed to keep levels of air pollution as low as possible.

Presuppression involves trying to detect a fire at an early stage and reducing its spread and damage. To help confine fires and allow access by fire-fighting equipment, vegetation is cleared to form fire breaks and fire roads, and brush and trees are cleared along existing roads. Helicopters and small airplanes are used to detect small fires before they get out of control. Helicopters are also used to carry fire fighters to remote fires within minutes of detection.

Once a wildfire starts, fire fighters have a number of methods for fire suppression. They use specially designed bulldozers and breaker plows to quickly establish fire breaks. They pump water onto the fire from tank trucks, and they drop water or fire retardant chemicals from aircraft. Trained personnel use controlled backfires to create burned areas to confine fires.

Protecting Forests from Air Pollution and Global Warming Air pollution is a growing threat to many forests, especially in MDCs. Forests at high elevations and forests downwind from urban and industrial centers are exposed to a variety of air pollutants that can harm trees, especially conifers (Section 19-4). In addition to direct harm, prolonged exposure to multiple air pollutants makes trees much more vulnerable to diseases, drought, and insects.

Large-scale forest degradation from air pollution has occurred in Poland, Czechoslovakia, Great Britain, France, East Germany, West Germany, Switzerland, Scandinavia, and eastern North America. The only solution is to sharply reduce emissions of the offending pollutants from coal-burning power plants, industrial plants, and cars (Section 19-5).

In coming decades an even greater threat to forests, especially temperate and boreal forests, is expected to be changes in regional climate brought about by global warming. By causing changes in the types of vegetation growing in forests, these climate changes will disrupt their economic and ecological values and result in mass extinction of many forms of wildlife. These effects and possible ways to slow down global warming are discussed in Section 19-5.

Management and Conservation of U.S. National Forests About 18% of the country's commercial forest area is located within 156 national forests, managed by the U.S. Forest Service. They contain 84% of the wilderness areas in the lower 48 states. More than 3 million cattle and sheep graze on national forestlands each year. National forests receive more recreational visits than any other federal public lands—more than twice as many as the National Park System.

Almost half of national forest lands are open to commercial logging. They supply about 15% of the country's total annual timber harvest—enough wood to build about 1 million homes. Each year private timber companies bid for rights to cut a certain amount of timber from areas designated by the Forest Service.

The Forest Service is required by law to manage national forests according to the principles of sustained yield and multiple use. **Sustained yield** involves harvesting potentially renewable forest resources in a way that preserves their output for present and future generations. **Multiple use** means that public forests are to be managed to allow timber harvesting, outdoor recreation, livestock grazing, watershed protection, and protection of wildlife and fish habitat *on the same land, at the same time.*

But managing a public forest for balanced multiple use is difficult and sometimes impossible. It usually involves making trade-offs that don't satisfy all the special-interest groups wanting different things from the forest.

Conflicting Demands on National Forests Since 1950 there have been greatly increased demands on national forests for timber sales, development of mineral and energy resources, recreation, wilderness protection, and wildlife conservation. Because of these growing and often conflicting demands on national forest resources, the management policies of the Forest Ser-

---

In U.S. national forests all fires are fought immediately (except in wilderness areas) because these forests are used for logging, energy development, hunting, and other uses. Between 1920 and 1972 the Park Service had the same policy of fighting all fires in national parks. But this allowed the buildup of ground litter and small plants, greatly increasing the chance of destructive crown fires (Figure 13-21).

Since 1972 Park Service policy has been to allow most lightning-caused fires to burn themselves out, as long as they don't threaten human lives, park facilities, private property, or endangered wildlife. The Park Service's intention is to allow fire to play its important role in forest succession and regeneration.

This policy was put to a severe test during the hot, dry summer of 1988. In western states 50,000 fire fighters tried to contain major fires that burned 2 million hectares (5 million acres) of forests. Severe drought plus high winds made

Figure 13-21 A grove of trees in Yosemite National Park. Left photo shows area in 1890, before the government had a policy of suppressing all fires. Right photo shows buildup of ground litter and small plants at the site in 1970, after 50 years of fire suppression. This greatly increases the chances of highly destructive crown fires.

vice have been the subject of heated controversy since the 1960s. Timber company officials complain that they aren't allowed to buy and cut enough timber on public lands, especially in remaining old-growth forests in California and the Pacific Northwest.

Conservationists charge that the Forest Service has bowed to political pressure. Increasingly it has replaced multiple use and uneven-aged management of national forests with dominant use and even-aged management based on excessive clearcutting. They argue that this policy violates the principle of balanced multiple use required by law.

Congress eased the controversy by passing the National Forest Management Act (NFMA) of 1976, after conservation and environmental groups had won several key court decisions. This law sets certain limitations on clearcutting and other timber-harvesting methods in national forests. These restrictions, however, are weakened by numerous exemptions and exceptions written into the law at the urging of timber company interests.

In 1987 the controversy was renewed when a report by the Wilderness Society charged the Forest Service with widespread and regular violations of the NFMA. Violations included excessive clearcutting, logging on physically and economically unsuitable lands, and failure to maintain biological diversity in many national forests, especially in the Pacific Northwest. Aerial surveys by the Wilderness Society of the 19 national forests in the Pacific Northwest showed that the Forest Service had greatly overestimated the amount of old-growth forest still left, had underreported the amount of clearcutting, and had counted mature second-growth forest as old-growth virgin forest.

Conservationists are fighting to save the rapidly disappearing old-growth stands in national and state forests in the Pacific Northwest and timber companies want to clearcut them and replace them with tree farms.

---

fighting the fires a losing battle. At best all the fire fighters could do was slightly alter the paths of the major fires and put out small fires.

Fires raged in parts of Yellowstone National Park. The media gave the impression that most of Yellowstone was devastated. But infrared photographs taken from 1305NASA aircraft revealed that fire affected only about 20% of the park. Less than 1% of the area burned so intensely hot that the soil was severely damaged. Less than 0.1% of the park's area was affected so badly that it won't recover. The bulldozers used to fight the fires did more damage to the park's delicate soils than the searing heat.

Angry residents criticized the Park Service for not fighting the fires earlier. Many in nearby towns feared they would lose money from a drop in tourism. Nearby ranchers and farmers were concerned that bison and elk without enough winter forage would seek food on their lands. Overblown media reports of devastation led many people to call for a reversal of the park policy of letting natural fires burn unless they threaten human life, park facilities, private property, or endangered wildlife.

Park officials insisted that they fought the major fires vigorously from the beginning to protect park property and nearby private property. But the record drought and high winds meant they could not put out the fires. Biologists contend that damage was more widespread than it should have been because the earlier park policy of fighting all fires had allowed the buildup of flammable ground litter and small plants. A return to that policy, they say, would eventually cause a far greater ecological disaster than the fires of 1988.

The dry and cold climate of the park dramatically slows the decomposition of dead plants and leaf litter. With this type of climate, major fires every 200 to 300 years play an important role in maintaining the park's plant and animal life. Without such fires, growing plants would deplete the soil faster than decaying plants could replenish it. Biologists estimate that the 1988 fire will lead to a 30-fold increase in Yellowstone's plant species. The ash provides mineral nutrients for new plant growth. A few weeks after the fire, grasses and other small pioneer plants began coming up.

The fire did reduce vegetation for elk and bison to feed on during the winter after the fire. But ecologists pointed out that the drought had a much greater effect on vegetation than the fires had. As a beneficial result, the elk herd will decrease from about 20,000 to 15,000, the area's estimated carrying capacity.

Tourism will increase as people visit the park to see how this ecosystem regenerates itself, just as tourists flocked to see Mount St. Helens after its volcanic eruption. In 1989 park visits rose by about 20%, and business was booming in surrounding towns. In three to five years the burned areas will be covered with a lush mat of grasses, flowers, and shrubs. Aspen, fir, pine, and spruce trees will be well established, and deer, elk, bear, and most bird populations will be abundant. Indeed, the abundance of new vegetation may help preserve some threatened animal species. Under public pressure, however, the National Park Service decreed that it would fight all fires in national parks immediately. Do you believe that all or only some fires (present policy) should be fought in U.S. national parks?

By law the Forest Service must sell timber for no less than the cost of reforesting the land it was harvested from. The cost of building roads to make the timber accessible is not included in this price. Most of these roads are built by the timber purchaser, and the road-building costs are deducted from the price of the timber. In essence, the government exchanges timber for roads, with taxpayers paying for the roads used by private timber companies.

Studies have shown that between 1975 and 1985 timber from 79 national forests was sold below the amount the Forest Service spent on roads and preparing the trees for sale. During this period Forest Service timber sales lost $2.1 billion.

The Wilderness Society projects that losses from harvests in the national forests could reach another $2 billion between 1985 and 1995. Conservationists oppose these subsidies for private timber companies at taxpayers' expense.

Industry representatives argue that such subsidies help taxpayers by keeping lumber prices down. But conservationists note that each year taxpayers already give the lumber industry tax breaks almost equal to the cost of managing the entire National Forest System.

Forest Service officials argue that timber harvesting shouldn't be subject to strict cost-accounting requirements. They point out that some expenses, such as road building, help prevent forest fires and provide more opportunities for hiking, hunting, and other recreational activities by the general public. Conservationists respond that most people using national forests for recreation would rather hike woodland trails than logging roads. What do you think?

Conservationists point out that the United States is telling Brazil not to cut down its tropical forests while the U.S. is cutting down its remaining old-growth forests at an unprecedented rate.

Only 15% of the country's old-growth forests are left. At current cutting rates most of these ancient, irreplaceable forests will be gone within 15 to 25 years. Conservationists believe that the destruction of these forests and replacing them with short-rotation tree farms will go down as one of the great ecological crimes and blunders of this century.

How Much Timber Should Be Harvested from National Forests? The National Forest Management Act requires the Forest Service to prepare 50-year management plans for each national forest region, with active participation by local citizens and conservation organizations. But conservationists charge that such participation has not been able to offset the influence of the timber industry on the way national forests are managed by the Forest Service.

Conservationists are alarmed at proposals by the Forest Service to double the timber harvest on national forests between 1986 and 2030 at the urging of the Reagan administration and the timber industry. To accomplish this, the Forest Service has proposed the building of 386,500 kilometers (240,000 miles) of new roads in the national forests over the next 50 years—six times the length of roads in the entire interstate highway system. Conservationists charge that plans to build roads in inaccessible areas (about one-fifth of the proposed new roads) are designed to disqualify those areas from inclusion in the National Wilderness Preservation System.

Conservationists have also accused the Forest Service of poor financial management of public forests (see Pro/Con at left).

Forestry experts and conservationists have suggested several ways to reduce exploitation of publicly owned timber resources and provide true multiple use of national forests as required by law:

- Cut the present annual harvest of timber from national forests in half instead of doubling it as proposed by the timber industry and the Forest Service.

- Keep 15% to 25% of remaining old-growth timber in any national forest from being cut.

- Require that timber from national forests be sold at a price that includes the costs of roads, site preparation, and site regeneration.

- Require that all timber sales in national forests yield a profit for taxpayers based on the fair market value of any timber harvested.

- Use a much larger portion of the Forest Service budget to improve management and increase timber yields of the country's privately owned commercial forestland to take pressure off the national forests.

Personal Action People throughout the world have engaged in efforts to reduce deforestation and forest degradation. For two decades women and children in parts of India have gone into nearby forests, linked their hands together, and encircled trees to prevent commercial loggers from cutting them down. Today women and children in this Chipko (an Indian word for "hug" or "cling to") movement also plant trees, prepare village forestry plans, and build walls to stop soil erosion.

In Malaysia, Penan tribesmen armed with blowguns have joined forces with environmentalists in an effort

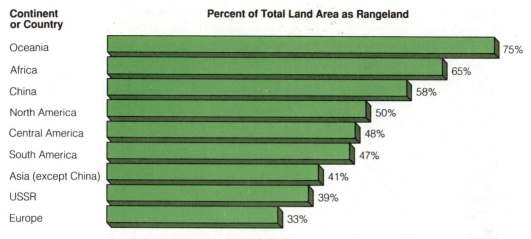

Continent or Country — **Percent of Total Land Area as Rangeland**

Continent or Country	Percent
Oceania	75%
Africa	65%
China	58%
North America	50%
Central America	48%
South America	47%
Asia (except China)	41%
USSR	39%
Europe	33%

Figure 13-22 Distribution of the world's rangelands. (Data from UN Food and Agriculture Organization)

to halt destructive logging. In Brazil 500 conservation organizations have organized a coalition to preserve the country's remaining tropical forests. In the United States members of Earth First! have perched in the tops of giant Douglas firs and put their bodies in front of logging trucks and bulldozers to prevent trees in national forests from being cut down.

You also have an important role to play. If you or your loved ones own forested land, develop a management and conservation plan for the sustainable use of these resources. Above all, try to plant and nurture several trees a year and encourage others to do so. But planting trees is not enough. We also need to pressure leaders to mount a global effort to protect remaining diverse forest ecosystems and to restore those that have been degraded.

Cut down on the use of wood and paper products you don't really need and recycle paper products. Contribute time, money, or both to organizations devoted to forest conservation, especially of the world's rapidly disappearing tropical forests and old-growth forests in the United States (see Appendix 1). Deforestation can be stopped and degraded forestlands can be restored—if you and enough other people care.

13-5 RANGELANDS

The World's Rangeland Resources   Almost half of the earth's ice-free land is **rangeland**—land that supplies forage or vegetation (grasses, grasslike plants, and shrubs) for grazing and browsing animals. Most rangelands are grasslands in semiarid areas too dry for rainfed cropland. Other types of rangeland are desert shrublands, shrub woodlands such as chaparral, temperate forests, and tropical forests.

Figure 13-22 shows the uneven distribution of rangeland throughout the world. Only about 42% of the world's rangeland is used for grazing livestock. Much of the rest is too dry, cold, or remote.

About 29% of the total land area of the United States is rangeland. Most of this is short-grass prairies in the arid and semiarid western half of the country. About two-thirds of this rangeland is privately owned. The remaining one-third of U.S. rangeland is owned by the general public and managed by the federal government, mostly by the Forest Service and the Bureau of Land Management.

Range Livestock Production   Some grazing and browsing animals, called **ruminant animals,** have three- or four-chambered stomachs, which digest the cellulose in grasses and other vegetation. Their bodies convert this carbohydrate into protein-rich meat and milk that other animals and most people can digest. Ruminant animals are also a major source of the greenhouse gas—methane (Section 19-4). Nonruminant livestock animals, such as pigs and chickens, can't feed on rangeland vegetation.

Worldwide, there are about 10 billion ruminant and nonruminant domesticated animals—twice the number of people on earth. About 3 billion of these animals are cattle, sheep, goats, buffalo, and other ruminants. Three-fourths of these ruminants forage on rangeland vegetation. The rest are fed mostly in feedlots (Figure 12-4, p. 263). Seven billion pigs, chickens, and other nonruminant livestock animals feed mostly on cereal grains grown on cropland.

Characteristics of Rangeland Vegetation   Most of the grasses on rangelands have deep, complex root systems. The multiple branches of their roots make these grasses hard to uproot, helping prevent soil erosion. By contrast, many rangeland forbs (herbs) and shrubs have a single taproot, which makes them easier to uproot.

When the leaf tip of most plants is eaten, the leaf stops growing. But each leaf of rangeland grass grows from its base, not its tip. When the upper half of the shoot and leaves of grass is eaten, the plant can grow

Figure 13-23 Lightly grazed (left) and severely overgrazed rangeland.

back quickly. However, the lower half of the plant, known as the **metabolic reserve,** must remain if the plant is to survive and grow new leaves. As long as only the upper half is eaten, rangeland grass is a renewable resource that can be grazed again and again.

Rangeland Carrying Capacity, Overgrazing, and Undergrazing Each type of grassland has a herbivore **carrying capacity**—the maximum number of herbivores a given area can support without consuming the metabolic reserve needed for grass renewal. Carrying capacity is influenced by season, range condition, annual climatic conditions, past grazing use, soil type, kinds of grazing animals, and how long animals graze in an area.

Light to moderate grazing is necessary for the health of grasslands. It maintains water and nutrient cycling needed for healthy grass growth and healthy root systems, hinders soil erosion, and encourages buildup of organic soil matter.

Overgrazing occurs when too many grazing animals feed too long and exceed the carrying capacity of a grassland area. Large populations of wild herbivores can overgraze range in prolonged dry periods. But most overgrazing is caused by excessive numbers of livestock feeding too long in a particular area.

Figure 13-23 compares normally grazed and severely overgrazed grassland. Heavy overgrazing converts continuous grass cover to patches of grass and makes the soil more vulnerable to erosion, especially by wind. Then forbs and woody shrubs such as mesquite and prickly cactus invade and take over.

Sometimes overgrazing is so severe that all vegetation disappears, leaving the land barren and highly vulnerable to erosion. Severe overgrazing combined with prolonged drought can convert potentially productive rangeland to desert (see Case Study on p. 224). Dune buggies, motorcycles, and other off-road vehicles also damage or destroy rangeland vegetation.

Undergrazing can also damage rangeland as a source of food for livestock and many wild herbivores. Undergrazing leaves much leaf and stem to become old. This chokes off grass growth and shifts succession from grasses to woody plants and forbs. Undergrazing, like overgrazing, leads to reduced nutrient and water cycling and increased soil erosion and degradation.

Condition of the World's Rangelands An estimate of how close a particular rangeland is to its productive potential for forage vegetation is called **range condition.** Range condition is usually classified as excellent (more than 80% of its potential forage production), good (50% to 80%), fair (21% to 49%), and poor (less than 21%).

Except in North America, no comprehensive survey of rangeland conditions has been made. However, data from surveys in various countries indicate that most of the world's rangelands have been degraded to some degree.

Since 1936, evaluations of public and private rangelands in the United States have shown that general range conditions have improved. For example, public rangeland in excellent and good condition increased from 16% to 36% between 1936 and 1986. During the same period, public rangeland in fair and poor condition decreased from 84% to 64%, with 20% in poor condition. Privately owned rangeland showed similar improvements. Despite this improvement, there's a long way to go with almost two-thirds of the country's rangeland in poor and fair condition.

Rangeland Management The major goal of range management is to maximize livestock productivity without degrading grassland quality. The most widely used way to prevent overgrazing is to control the **stocking rate,** the number of a particular kind of animal grazing on a given area, so that it doesn't exceed the carrying capacity. But determining the carrying capacity of a range site is difficult and costly. Even when the carrying capacity is known, it can change due to drought, invasions by new species, and other environmental factors.

Controlling the distribution of grazing animals over a range is the best way to prevent overgrazing and undergrazing. Ranchers can control distribution by building fences to protect degraded rangeland, rotating livestock from one grazing area to another, providing supplemental feeding at selected sites, and locating water holes and salt blocks in strategic places. Livestock need both salt and water, but not together. If salt blocks are placed in undergrazed areas away from water sources, livestock are forced to spend some time in these areas.

A more expensive and less widely used method of rangeland management is to suppress the growth of unwanted plants by spraying with herbicides, mechanical removal, or controlled burning. A cheaper and more effective way to remove unwanted vegetation is controlled, short-term trampling by large numbers of livestock.

Growth of desirable vegetation can be increased by seeding and applying fertilizer, but this method is usually too costly. On the other hand, reseeding is an excellent way to restore severely degraded rangeland.

Many ranchers still promote the use of poisons, trapping, and shooting to kill rabbits and rodents (such as prairie dogs), which compete with livestock for range vegetation. But this usually gives only temporary relief and is rarely worth the cost because these animals have high reproduction rates and their populations can usually recover in a short time.

For decades U.S. ranchers have shot, trapped, and poisoned predators, such as coyotes, which sometimes kill sheep and goats. However, experience has shown that killing predators is an expensive and temporary solution—and sometimes makes matters worse (see Pro/Con below).

PRO/CON Livestock Predator Control in the United States

Each year sheep and goat raisers in Texas claim they lose 190,000 animals, valued at $9 million, to wild predators. Some ranchers in other western states say they've lost over 25% of their lambs from predation. Conservationists, however, contend that ranchers exaggerate their losses.

Between 1940 and 1972 a controversial and largely unsuccessful control program was waged by western ranchers and the U.S. Department of the Interior against livestock predators, especially the coyote. Because coyotes are too numerous and too crafty to be hunted effectively, emphasis was placed on poisoning them. The most popular poison was sodium fluoroacetate, known as compound 1080. One ounce of this compound is enough to kill 200 people or 20,000 coyotes.

A 1972 report by the government-appointed Advisory Committee on Predator Control recommended that all poisoning of predators by the federal government be halted because poisons can accidentally kill nontarget animals, including eagles, other endangered species, and people. After receiving the report, President Richard M. Nixon issued an executive order banning predator poisoning on public lands or by government employees anywhere. The Environmental Protection Agency then prohibited the use of several poisons, including 1080, even on private land.

Since 1972, western ranchers have tried to have this ban lifted. In 1985, under pressure from ranchers, western congressional representatives, and the Reagan administration, the EPA approved the use of compound 1080 in livestock collars. These poison-filled rubber collars are placed around the necks of sheep, goats, and other livestock. Coyotes and other predators are poisoned when they bite the neck of their prey.

Conservation and environmental groups strongly oppose the use of compound 1080. They argue that the poison dribbling down the neck of a sheep after it's been killed by a coyote could kill golden eagles, vultures, and other scavengers feeding on the sheep carcass. Carcasses of poisoned coyotes could also kill scavengers. Conservationists also fear that some ranchers might illegally extract the poison from collars and use it to bait livestock carcasses.

Because the coyote is so adaptable and prolific, conservationists argue that any poisoning program is doomed to failure and is a waste of tax dollars. It would cost taxpayers less to pay ranchers for each sheep or goat killed by a coyote.

If poisoning or other programs did succeed in killing most coyotes, the populations of rodents and rabbits they eat and keep under control would explode. These small herbivores then would compete with livestock for range-land vegetation, reducing livestock productivity and causing range-land degradation. In the long run, a drastic reduction of coyote populations would cause larger economic losses for ranchers than the losses of livestock killed by these predators.

Conservationists suggest that fences, repellants, and trained guard dogs be used to keep predators away. Using a combination of these methods, sheep producers in Kansas have one of the country's lowest rates of livestock losses to coyotes. The annual cost of their predator control program is only 5% of what neighboring Oklahoma spends on a predator control program of poisoning and trapping.

In 1986 Department of Agriculture researchers reported that predation can be sharply reduced by penning young lambs and cattle together for 30 days and then allowing them to graze together on the same range. When predators attack, cattle butt and kick them and in the process protect themselves and the sheep. Llamas and donkeys, also tough fighters against predators, can be used in the same way to protect sheep.

Conservationists point out that only a few coyotes and other predators prey on livestock. Instead of trying to kill all predators, they suggest concentrating on killing or removing the rogue individuals. What do you think should be done?

Management of U.S. Public Rangelands Government agencies are required by law to manage public rangelands according to the principle of multiple use. The Bureau of Land Management and the Forest Service issue 10-year permits allowing about 2% of the country's private ranchers (17% of those in the West) to graze their herds on public range. For years, ranchers and conservationists have battled over how much ranchers should be charged for the privilege of grazing their livestock on public lands (see Pro/Con below).

13-6 PARKS: USE, AND ABUSE

Threats to Parks The world's first national park, Yellowstone, was set aside by an act of Congress in 1872. It was the first park established for the benefit and enjoyment of the general public. Today there are over 1,000 national parks in more than 120 countries. This is an important achievement in the global conservation movement. In addition to national parks, the U.S. public has access to state, county, and city parks (Figure 9-15, p. 210). Most state parks are located near urban areas and thus are used more heavily than national parks.

But these parks are increasingly threatened. In MDCs many national parks are threatened by nearby industrial development, urban growth, air and water pollution, roads, noise, invasion by alien species, and loss of natural species. Some of the most popular national parks are also threatened by overuse.

In LDCs the problems are worse. Plant and animal life in national parks are being threatened by local people who desperately need wood, cropland, and other resources. Poachers kill animals and sell their parts, such as rhino horns, elephant tusks, and furs. Park services in these countries have too little money and staff to fight these invasions, either through enforcement or public education programs. Also most national parks in MDCs and LDCs are too small to sustain many of their natural species, especially larger animals.

U.S. National Parks The National Park System is dominated by 49 national parks found mostly in the West (Figure 13-10). These repositories of majesty, beauty, and biological diversity have been called America's crown jewels.

During the 1970s several national recreation areas, seashores, lakeshores, and other units, usually located close to heavily populated urban areas, were added to bring national parks closer to the people. Since they opened in the 1970s, the Golden Gate National Rec-

---

PRO/CON Grazing Fees on Public Rangeland

Over 26,000 ranchers lease rights to graze on public range from the BLM and pay a grazing fee for this privilege. In 1981 the Reagan administration set grazing fees at about one-fifth of the average market value of federal grazing lands.

This means that U.S. taxpayers give the small percentage of ranchers with federal grazing permits subsidies amounting to about $75 million a year—the difference between the fees collected and the actual value of the grazing on this land. Each year the government also spends hundreds of millions of tax dollars to maintain these public rangelands. Overall, the government collects only about $1 from ranchers in grazing fees for every $10 spent on range management.

Conservationists call for grazing fees on public rangeland to be raised to the level found by the BLM and the Forest Service to be a fair market value for use of this

land. Higher fees would reduce incentives for overgrazing and provide more money for improvement of range conditions, wildlife conservation, and watershed management.

Conservationists contend that any rancher with a permit who can't stay in business without government subsidies shouldn't be in the ranching business. The 96% of the country's ranchers without federal permits have to survive without such subsidies. Earl Sandvig, formerly administrator of the grazing program for the Forest Service, has suggested that grazing rights be sold by competitive bidding, as is the case with timber cutting rights in national forests.

Ranchers with permits fiercely oppose higher grazing fees and competitive bidding. Grazing rights on public land raise the value of their livestock animals by $1,000 to $1,500 per head. This means that a permit to graze 500

cattle on public land can be worth $500,000 to $750,000 a year to the rancher. The economic value of a permit is considered a rancher's private property. It's included in the overall worth of the ranches and can be used as collateral for a loan.

Ranchers contend that overgrazing on public rangeland is also caused by increasing numbers of elk and other grazing wildlife. The ranchers resent the fact that the government is forcing them to reduce cattle numbers to reduce overgrazing but is not requiring game and fish departments to reduce excessive wildlife numbers.

Most ranchers who can't get a grazing permit favor open bidding for grazing rights on public land. They believe that the permit system gives politically influential ranchers an unfair economic advantage at the expense of taxpayers. What do you think should be done?

reation Area near San Francisco and the Gateway National Recreation Area near New York City have been two of the most widely used units in the National Park System.

Nature walks, guided tours, and other educational services provided by Park Service employees have provided many Americans with a better understanding of how nature works. Some conservationists urge that this effective educational program be expanded to show citizens ways to work with nature in their own daily lives. They have proposed that all park buildings and other facilities be designed as or converted to systems that demonstrate energy-efficient, low-polluting methods of heating, cooling, water purification, waste handling, transportation, and recycling.

Stresses on Parks The major problems of national and state parks stem from their spectacular success. Because of more roads, cars, and affluence, annual recreational visits to National Park System units increased twelvefold and visits to state parks sevenfold between 1950 and 1988.

The recreational use of state and national parks is expected to increase even more in the future, putting additional stress on many already overburdened parks. Under the onslaught of people during the peak summer season, the most popular national and state parks are often overcrowded with cars and trailers and plagued by noise, traffic jams, litter, vandalism, deteriorating trails, polluted water, drugs, and crime. The theft of timber and cacti from national parks is a growing problem. At Grand Canyon National Park 50,000 small-plane and helicopter flights per year for tourists have turned the area into a noisy flying circus. Park Service rangers now spend an increasing amount of their time on law enforcement instead of resource conservation and management.

Populations of wolves, bears, and other large predators in and near various parks have dropped sharply or disappeared because of excessive hunting, poisoning by ranchers and federal officials, and the limited size of some parks. This decline has allowed populations of remaining prey species to increase sharply, destroy vegetation, and crowd out other native animal species. Currently no park in the lower 48 states is large enough to support minimum viable natural populations of large mammals over the long term.

The movement of alien species into parks is also a threat. Wild boars are a major threat to vegetation in part of the Great Smoky Mountains National Park. The Brazilian pepper tree has invaded Florida's Everglades National Park. Mountain goats in Washington's Olympic National Park trample native vegetation and accelerate soil erosion.

The greatest danger to many parks today is from human activities in nearby areas. Wildlife and recreational values are threatened by mining, timber harvesting, grazing, coal-burning power plants, water diversion, and urban development. In 1988 the Wilderness Society identified the 10 most endangered national park units (Figure 13-24). Within your lifetime the greatest threat to many of the world's parks will be shifts in regional climate caused by an enhanced greenhouse effect.

Park Management: Combining Conservation and Sustainable Development Some park managers, especially in LDCs, are developing integrated management plans that combine conservation and sustainable development of the park and surrounding areas (Figure 13-25). In such a plan the inner core and especially vulnerable areas of the park are protected from development and treated as wilderness. Controlled numbers of people are allowed to use these areas for hiking, nature study, ecological research, and other nondestructive recreational and educational activities.

In other areas controlled commercial logging, sustainable grazing by livestock, and sustainable hunting and fishing by local natives are allowed. Money spent by park visitors adds to local income. By involving local people in developing park management plans, managers help them see the park as a vital resource they need to protect and sustain rather than degrade.

Park managers can also survey the land surrounding a park to identify areas that threaten the park's wildlife. Sometimes these areas can be added to the park. If not, managers may be able to persuade developers or local people to use less critical areas for certain types of development.

An Agenda for U.S. National Parks The National Park Service has two goals that increasingly conflict. One is to preserve nature in parks. The other is to make nature more available to the public. The Park Service must accomplish these goals with a small budget at a time when park usage and external threats to the parks are increasing.

In 1988 the Wilderness Society and the National Parks and Conservation Association published the results of studies they had made of the National Park System. Their blueprint for the future of this system included the following proposals:

- Educate the public about the urgent need to protect, mend, and expand the system.

- Establish the National Park Service as an independent agency responsible to the president and Congress. This would make it less vulnerable to the shifting political winds of the Interior Department.

- Block the mining, timbering, and other threats that are taking place near park boundaries on land

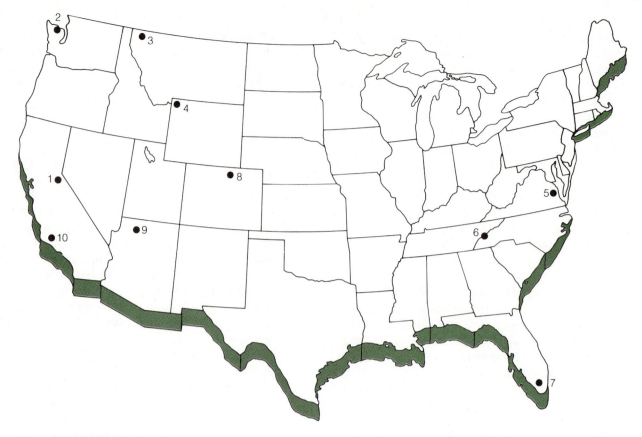

1 Yosemite
- Logging and road building in nearby national forests
- Nearby mining and geothermal energy development
- Nearby urban development

2 Olympic
- Offshore oil drilling
- Logging and road building in surrounding national forest
- Non-native goats

3 Glacier
- Nearby residential and commercial development
- Oil drilling, logging, and road building in nearby national forests
- Wolf-killing program

4 Yellowstone
- Logging and road building, oil and gas drilling, and geothermal energy development in nearby national forests
- Nearby residential development and ski runs
- Building up to 9 dams on Clarks Fork River

5 Manassas National Battlefield
- Proposed adjacent shopping mall

6 Great Smoky Mountain
- Logging and road building in nearby national forests
- Air pollution
- Non-native wild boars

7 Everglades
- Nearby urban development
- Water pollution
- Military use

8 Rocky Mountain
- Nearby condominiums and urban sprawl
- Overcrowding
- Logging and road building on nearby national forest

9 Grand Canyon
- Tourist planes
- Nearby uranium mining
- Damage to beaches and fish from upstream Glen Canyon Dam

10 Santa Monica Recreation Area
- Only one third of proposed recreation area purchased within last 10 years
- Increasing private development within the area

Figure 13-24 The 10 most endangered units of the National Park System. (Data from the Wilderness Society)

managed by the U.S. Forest Service and the Bureau of Land Management.

- Acquire new parkland near threatened areas and add at least 75 new parks within the next decade.

- Locate commercial park facilities (such as restaurants) *outside* park boundaries.

- Wherever feasible, place visitor parking areas outside the park areas. Use low-polluting vehicles to

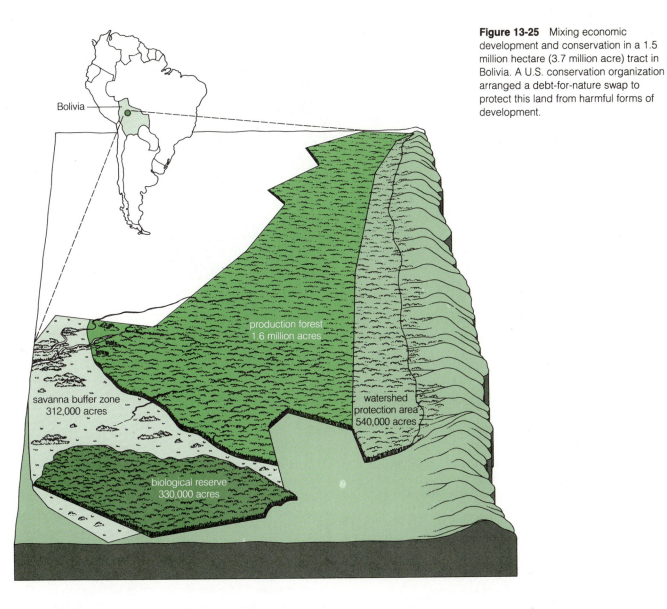

Figure 13-25 Mixing economic development and conservation in a 1.5 million hectare (3.7 million acre) tract in Bolivia. A U.S. conservation organization arranged a debt-for-nature swap to protect this land from harmful forms of development.

Bolivia

production forest
1.6 million acres

savanna buffer zone
312,000 acres

watershed
protection area
540,000 acres

biological reserve
330,000 acres

carry visitors to and from parking areas and for transportation within the park.

- Greatly expand the Park Service budget for maintenance and science and conservation programs.

- Require the Park Service and the Forest Service to develop integrated management plans so that activities in nearby national forests don't degrade national parklands.

13-7 WILDERNESS PRESERVATION

How Much Wild Land Is Left? According to the Wilderness Act of 1964, **wilderness** consists of those areas "where the earth and its community of life are untrammeled by man, where man himself is a visitor who does not remain." The Wilderness Society estimates that a wilderness area should contain at least 405,000 hectares (1 million acres). Otherwise, the area can be degraded by air pollution, water pollution, and noise pollution from nearby mining, oil and natural gas drilling, timber cutting, industry, and urban development.

A 1987 survey sponsored by the Sierra Club revealed that only about 34% of the earth's land area is undeveloped wilderness in blocks of at least 405,000 hectares (Figure 13-26). About 30% of these remaining wild lands are forests. Much of this is tropical forests, which are being rapidly cleared and degraded. Tundra and desert make up 64% of the world's remaining wild lands. If they were not so hot and dry or cold, these biomes would have been intensely developed.

Why Preserve Wilderness? There are many reasons. We need wild places where we can experience majestic beauty and natural biological diversity. We need places where we can enhance our mental health by getting away from noise, stress, and large numbers of people. Wilderness preservationist John Muir advised:

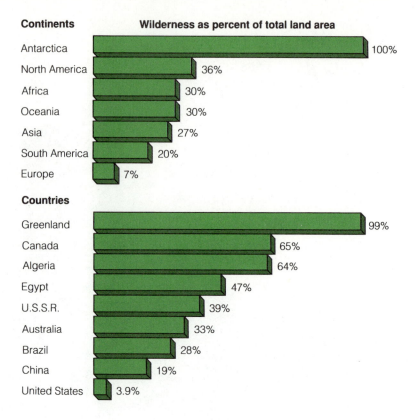

Figure 13-26 Wilderness areas by major geographical areas. (Data from J. Michael McCloskey and Heather Spalding, "A Reconnaissance-Level Inventory of the Wilderness Remaining in the World," Sierra Club, 1987)

Continents

Wilderness as percent of total land area

Continent	Percent
Antarctica	100%
North America	36%
Africa	30%
Oceania	30%
Asia	27%
South America	20%
Europe	7%

Countries

Country	Percent
Greenland	99%
Canada	65%
Algeria	64%
Egypt	47%
U.S.S.R.	39%
Australia	33%
Brazil	28%
China	19%
United States	3.9%

Climb the mountains and get their good tidings. Nature's peace will flow into you as the sunshine into the trees. The winds will blow their freshness into you, and the storms their energy, while cares will drop off like autumn leaves.

Even if individuals do not use the wilderness, many want to know it is there, a feeling expressed by novelist Wallace Stegner:

Save a piece of country . . . and it does not matter in the slightest that only a few people every year will go into it. This is precisely its value . . . we simply need that wild country available to us, even if we never do more than drive to its edge and look in. For it can be a means of reassuring ourselves of our sanity as creatures, a part of the geography of hope.

Wilderness areas provide recreation for growing numbers of people. They produce economic benefits for the booming outdoor-gear and tourist industries. They also are a savings account of resources that can be used later in a true emergency, rather than now for short-term economic gain.

Wilderness also has important ecological values. It provides undisturbed habitats for wild plants and animals, maintains diverse biological reserves protected from degradation, and provides a laboratory in which we can discover how nature works. It is an ecological insurance policy against eliminating too much of the earth's natural biological diversity. In the words of Henry David Thoreau (Figure 2-8, p. 37): "In wild-

ness is the preservation of the world." On ethical grounds wilderness should be preserved because the wild species it contains have a right to exist without human interference (Section 24-2).

U.S. Wilderness Preservation System In the United States, preservationists have been trying to keep wild areas from being developed since 1900 (Section 2-4). They have fought timber, mining, oil, and natural gas companies, as well as scientific conservationists (see Spotlight on p. 41).

Mostly they have fought a losing battle. It was not until 1964 that Congress passed the Wilderness Act. It allows the government to protect undeveloped tracts of public land from development as part of the National Wilderness Preservation System. Establishing this system was a vital step in wilderness preservation. But by 1964 much of the country's land was already developed. And since then resource developers have vigorously fought almost every proposal for adding more land to the system.

Only 3.9% of U.S. land area is protected as wilderness. Almost two-thirds of this is in Alaska. Even in Alaska only 9 of 43 wilderness areas consist of more than 405,000 hectares. Only 1.8% of the land area of the lower 48 states is protected in the wilderness system. Of the 413 wilderness areas there, only 4 consist of more than 405,000 hectares. Also the present wilderness preservation system includes only 81 of the country's 233 distinct ecosystems.

There remain almost 40.5 million hectares (100 million acres) of public lands that could qualify for designation as wilderness. But resource developers lobby elected officials and government agencies to build roads in these areas so that they can't be designated wilderness.

Conservationists believe that two of the country's most urgent priorities should be to permit no more development of any virgin lands and to begin a massive program to protect and restore large areas of degraded lands as wilderness. The long-term goal would be to have 30% of the country's land area protected as wilderness. This would require that virtually all Forest Service and Bureau of Land Management public lands be reclassified as wilderness and restored as natural wildlife habitat.

Use and Abuse of Wilderness Areas In 1988 people made an estimated 145 million recreational visits to U.S. wilderness areas—about three times the number in 1970. Popular wilderness areas, especially in California, North Carolina, and Minnesota, are visited by so many people that their wildness is threatened. Fragile vegetation is damaged, soil is eroded from trails and campsites, water is polluted from bathing and dishwashing, and litter is scattered along trails. Instead of quiet and solitude, visitors sometimes face the noise and congestion they are trying to escape.

Wilderness areas are also being degraded by air, water, and noise pollution from nearby grazing, logging, oil and gas drilling, factories, power plants, and urban areas. In 1985 the National Park Service reported that scenic views in 64 wilderness areas within national parks were obscured by haze from air pollutants at least 90% of the time.

Global warming from the greenhouse effect is expected to be the biggest threat to wilderness, parks, forests, rangelands, croplands, estuaries, and inland wetlands during your lifetime. In a warmer world, vegetation zones will shift away from the equator and toward the poles. Many inland wetlands will dry up, while many coastal wetlands will be flooded. This will disrupt wilderness areas and other protected areas. Then they will no longer be able to serve the purpose for which they were established, even with the best management possible.

Wilderness Management To protect the most popular areas from damage, wilderness managers have had to limit the number of people hiking or camping at any one time. They have also designated areas where camping is allowed. Managers have increased the number of wilderness rangers to patrol vulnerable areas and enlisted volunteers to pick up trash discarded by thoughtless users.

Historian and wilderness expert Roderick Nash suggests that wilderness areas be divided into three categories. The easily accessible, popular areas would be intensively managed and have trails, bridges, hiker's huts, outhouses, assigned campsites, and extensive ranger patrols. Large, remote wilderness areas would not be intensively managed. They would be used only by people who get a permit by demonstrating their wilderness skills. A third category would consist of large, biologically unique areas. They would be left undisturbed as gene pools of plant and animal species, with no human entry allowed.

In addition to setting aside more wilderness areas, conservationists believe that many areas need to be reclaimed as wilderness by restoring and rehabilitating native ecosystems (see Enrichment Study on p. 151) and reintroducing native wildlife species. In the West many logging and other roads on public lands would be closed, ravaged clearcuts rehabilitated, and livestock grazing phased out to create preserves of 405,000 hectares (1 million acres) or more.

National Wild and Scenic Rivers System In 1968 Congress passed the National Wild and Scenic Rivers Act. It allows rivers and river segments with outstanding scenic, recreational, geological, wildlife, historical, or cultural values to be protected in the National Wild and Scenic Rivers System.

These waterways are to be kept forever free of development. They cannot be widened, straightened, dredged, filled, or dammed along the designated lengths. The only activities allowed are camping, swimming, nonmotorized boating, sport hunting, and sport and commercial fishing. New mining claims, however, are permitted in some areas.

By 1988 the Wild and Scenic Rivers System protected 116 rivers and river segments. They make up about 0.2% of the country's 5.6 million kilometers (3.5 million miles) of rivers. Conservationists have urged Congress to add 1,500 additional eligible river segments to the system by the year 2000. If this goal is achieved, about 2% of the country's unique rivers would be protected from further development. Conservationists also urge that a permanent federal administrative body be established to manage the Wild and Scenic Rivers System.

Sustaining forests, rangelands, wilderness, and parks is an urgent task. It will cost a great deal of money and require strong support from the public. But it will cost our civilization much more if we do not protect these resources from degradation and destruction.

Forests precede civilizations, deserts follow them.
François-Auguste-René de Chateaubriand

Chapter Summary

Forests, which cover about one-third of the earth's surface, supply us with lumber, fuelwood, paper pulp, medicines, and many other valuable products. Forests also perform vital ecological functions by helping control climate, adding oxygen to the atmosphere, providing habitats for wildlife, absorbing noise and some air pollutants, and holding and releasing water gradually, thus helping reduce soil erosion, the severity of flooding, and the amount of sediment washing into rivers and reservoirs.

The world's remaining forests, especially tropical moist forests, are being cut and degraded at a rapid rate by poor people clearing land for fuelwood and to grow food, by ranchers to graze cattle and produce low-cost beef mostly for export to MDCs, and by commercial logging companies to provide timber used mostly in MDCs. These incredibly diverse forests are of immense economic and ecological importance to everyone on earth and to the at least 50% of the world's species that live in these biomes. If clearing and degradation of tropical forests continues at the current rate, almost all of them will be gone or severely damaged within your lifetime. There is an urgent need to establish an internationally funded program to slow down this destruction and degradation and to restore degraded tropical forest areas. This will also help solve the shortage of fuelwood used for cooking and heating by 70% of the people in LDCs and help slow down global warming.

Over one-third of all U.S. land consists of public lands owned jointly by all citizens and managed for them by various agencies of the federal government. These public lands have been divided by Congress into National Forests, National Resource Lands (mostly rangeland), National Wildlife Refuges, National Parks, and the National Wilderness Preservation System.

Forests are managed by either of two methods. With *even-aged management*, trees in a given stand are maintained at about the same age and size, harvested all at once, and replanted naturally or artificially so that a new

---

GUEST ESSAY Tropical Forests and Their Species: Going, Going . . . ?

Norman Myers

Norman Myers is an international consultant in environment and development with emphasis on conservation of wildlife species and tropical forests. He has served as a consultant for many development agencies and research organizations, including the U.S. National Academy of Sciences, the World Bank, the Organization for Economic Cooperation and Development, various UN agencies, and the World Resources Institute. Among his recent publications (see Further Readings) are The Sinking Ark *(1979),* Conversion of Tropical Moist Forests *(1980),* A Wealth of Wild Species *(1983),* The Primary Source *(1984), and* The Gaia Atlas of Planet Management *(1985).*

Tropical forests still cover an area roughly equivalent to the "lower 48" United States. Climatic and biological data suggest they could have once covered an area at least twice as large. So we have already lost half of them, mostly in the recent past. Worse, remote-sensing surveys show that we are now destroying the forests at a rate of at least 1.25% a year, and we are grossly degrading them at a rate of at least another 1.25% a year—and both rates are accelerating rapidly. Unless we act now to halt this loss, within just another few decades at most, there could be little left, except perhaps a block in central Africa and another in the western part of the Amazon basin. Even these remnants may not survive the combined pressures of population growth and land hunger beyond the middle of the next century.

This means that we are imposing one of the most broad-scale and impoverishing impacts on the biosphere that it has ever suffered throughout its 4 billion years of existence. Tropical forests are the greatest celebration of nature to appear on the face of the planet since the first flickerings of life. They are exceptionally complex ecologically, and they are remarkably rich biotically. Although they now account for only 7% of the earth's land surface, they still are home for half, and perhaps three-quarters or more, of all the earth's species of plant and animal life. Thus, elimination of these forests is by far the leading factor in the mass extinction of species that appears likely over the next few decades.

Already, we are certainly losing several species every day because of clearing and degradation of tropical forests. The time will surely come, and come soon, when we shall be losing many thousands every year. The implications are profound, whether they be scientific, aesthetic, ethical—or simply economic. In medicine alone, we benefit from myriad drugs and pharmaceuticals derived from tropical forest plants. The commercial value of these products worldwide can be reckoned at $20 billion each year.

By way of example, the rosy periwinkle from Madagascar's tropical forests has produced two potent drugs against Hodgkin's disease, leukemia, and other

even-aged stand will grow. Such intensively managed stands containing only one or a few tree species are called *tree farms*. With *uneven-aged management*, trees in a given stand are maintained at many ages and sizes to permit continuous natural regeneration. The major steps in both types of forest management are making an inventory of the site, developing a forest management plan, preparing the site for harvest, harvesting commercially valuable timber, and regenerating and managing the site before the next harvest.

Trees are harvested and regenerated by five main methods: *selective cutting, shelterwood cutting, seed-tree cutting, clearcutting,* and *whole-tree harvesting.* The method used for harvesting depends on whether uneven-aged or even-aged forest management is being used, the tree species involved, the nature of the site, and the objectives of the owner. Forest management also involves protecting forests from disease, insects, fires—especially highly destructive *crown fires*—and air pollution.

In the United States commercial timber companies want to increase the amount of timber harvested from the national forests, which presently provide about 15% of the country's annual timber harvest. Conservationists, however, believe that present timber harvest levels in national forests should be cut in half, clearcutting should be reduced, some older diverse forests should remain uncut, and no timber in these public forests should be sold at a loss to taxpayers.

Presently about 42% of the world's rangelands, mostly grasslands, are used for grazing by about 3 billion domesticated animals. *Overgrazing* by livestock can kill the root system of rangeland grass so that little if any grass is left. *Undergrazing* can also damage rangeland by causing shifts from grasses to woody plants and forbs.

Throughout the world most rangelands used extensively for livestock show signs of overgrazing. Presently 64% of public rangeland in the United States is in poor to fair quality.

Rangeland management involves controlling the number and kinds of animals grazing on a given area by using

blood cancers. Madagascar has—or used to have—at least 8,000 plant species, of which more than 7,000 could be found nowhere else. Today Madagascar has lost 93% of its virgin tropical forest. The U.S. National Cancer Institute estimates that there could be many other plants in tropical forests with potential against various cancers—provided pharmacologists can get to them before they are eliminated by chain saws and bulldozers.

We benefit in still other ways from tropical forests. Elimination of these forests disrupts certain critical environmental services, notably their famous "sponge effect" by which they soak up rainfall during the wet season and then release it in regular amounts throughout the dry season. When tree cover is removed and this watershed function is impaired, the result is a yearly regime of floods followed by droughts, which destroys property and reduces agricultural production. There is also concern that if tropical deforestation becomes wide enough, it could trigger local, regional, or even global changes in climate. Such climatic upheavals would affect the lives of billions of people, if not the whole of humankind.

All this raises important questions about our role in the biosphere and our relations with the natural world around us. As we proceed on our disruptive way in tropical forests, we—that is, political leaders and the general public alike—give scarcely a moment's thought to what we are doing. We are deciding the fate of the world's tropical forests unwittingly, yet effectively and increasingly.

The resulting shift in evolution's course, stemming from the elimination of tropical forests, will rank as one of the greatest biological upheavals since the dawn of life. It will equal, in scale and significance, the development of aerobic respiration, the emergence of flowering plants, and the arrival of limbed animals, taking place over eons of time. But whereas these were enriching disruptions in the course of life on this planet, the loss of biotic diversity associated with tropical forest destruction will be almost entirely an impoverishing phenomenon brought about entirely by human actions. And it will all have occurred within the twinkling of a geologic eye.

In short, our intervention in tropical forests should be viewed as one of the most challenging problems that humankind has ever encountered. After all, we are the first species ever to be able to look upon nature's work and to decide whether we should consciously eliminate it or leave much of it untouched.

So the decline of tropical forest is one of the great sleeper issues of our time. Yet we can still save much of these forests, and the species they contain. Should we not consider ourselves fortunate that we alone among all generations are being given the chance to preserve tropical forests as the most exuberant expression of nature in the biosphere—and thereby to support the right to life of many of our fellow species and their capacity to undergo further evolution without human interference?

Guest Essay Discussion

1. What obligation, if any, do you as an individual have to preserve a significant portion of the world's remaining tropical forests?

2. Should MDCs provide most of the money to preserve remaining tropical forests in LDCs? Explain.

3. What can you do to help preserve some of the world's tropical forests? Which, if any, of these actions do you plan to carry out?

fences, rotating livestock from one area to another, providing supplemental feeding at selected sites, and strategically locating water holes and supplies of salt. Other methods for managing rangeland include removing unwanted vegetation, planting desired vegetation, and killing animals that compete with livestock for range vegetation or that prey on livestock.

Today there are over 1,000 national parks in more than 120 countries. In the United States and other MDCs many national parks are threatened by nearby industrial development, urban growth, air and water pollution, roads, noise, invasion by alien species, loss of natural species, overuse by visitors, crime, noise, and vandalism. In LDCs plant and animal life in national parks are being threatened by wildlife poachers and by local people who desperately need wood, cropland, and other resources.

The key to protecting existing parks is to develop management plans that combine conservation and sustainable development of the park and, if possible, surrounding areas. Greatly increased funding is also needed to maintain and expand existing parks and to establish new ones.

Since 1900 conservationists have fought a largely losing battle to protect undeveloped tracts of public land in the United States from development by making them part of the National Wilderness Preservation System. Only 3.9% of the U.S. land area (1.8% in the lower 48 states) is presently protected in this system. About 0.2% of the total length of U.S. rivers has also been protected from development as part of the Wild and Scenic Rivers System.

Wilderness areas provide wild places where one can experience natural beauty and solitude. They provide recreational experiences, economic benefits for the outdoor-gear and tourist industries, and undisturbed habitats for wildlife, and they serve as an ecological laboratory for studying how nature works. It is also argued that wilderness areas should be preserved because their plant and animal species have an inherent right to exist without human interference.

Conservationists believe that remaining roadless areas and undeveloped river segments, especially in the lower 48 states, should be added to the wilderness and river systems. But representatives of timber, mining, energy, and other resource industries generally oppose expansion of these systems.

Discussion Topics

1. What difference could the loss of essentially all the remaining tropical forests have on your life and on the life of any child you might have?

2. Explain how eating a hamburger in some U.S. fast-food chains indirectly contributes to the destruction of tropical moist forests. What, if anything, do you believe should be done about this?

3. Should private companies cutting timber from national forests continue to be subsidized by federal payments for reforestation and for building and maintaining access roads? Explain.

4. Should a much larger percentage of the world's uneven-aged, old-growth and secondary forests be converted into even-aged tree farms? Explain. What are the alternatives?

5. Should fees for grazing on public rangelands in the United States be (a) eliminated and replaced with a competitive bidding system, (b) increased to the point where they equal the fair market value estimated by the Bureau of Land Management and the Forest Service? Explain your answers.

6. Should compound 1080 or other poisons be used in livestock collars to poison coyotes that prey on livestock? Explain. What are the alternatives?

7. Should trail bikes, dune buggies, and other off-road vehicles be banned from public rangeland to reduce damage to vegetation and soil? Explain.

8. Explain why you agree or disagree with each of the proposals listed on page 309 concerning the U.S. national park system.

9. Should more wilderness areas and wild and scenic rivers be preserved in the United States, especially in the lower 48 states? Explain.

10. Should virtually all U.S. Forest Service and Bureau of Land Management public land be reclassified as wilderness and restored as natural wildlife habitat? Explain.

11. Brazil's president has denounced the criticism of his country (by the United States and other MDCs) for developing some of its tropical forests, calling it environmental imperialism. He points out that the U.S. and other industrialized countries achieved their economic growth by ruthlessly exploiting natural resources—including cutting down most of their native forests and fouling the environment in the process. He calls for direct negotiations, not preaching, by what he calls the world's greatest environmental sinner. He raises several issues. How can Brazil be expected to control its economic development when it is staggering under a $111 billion foreign debt and must raise cash quickly to pay the billions of dollars of interest on this debt each year? By what right does the U.S., which is destroying its own ancient forests in the Pacific Northwest, Alaska, and Hawaii, and which spews out more pollutants than any other nation, lecture poor countries like Brazil on their responsibilities for sustaining the earth? Why aren't Americans banning all destruction of their remaining old-growth forests and greatly increasing the small amount of land protected from development in their wilderness system? Within the next few decades Brazil will have much more land protected from development than the United States. Why aren't Americans greatly increasing fuel-economy standards for new cars and emission standards for coal-burning power plants to reduce energy waste, pollution, forest degradation, and global warming? Why haven't Americans discouraged gasoline waste by increasing federal gasoline taxes to bring U.S. fuel prices closer to those in Brazil and the rest of the world? Are American banks and international lending agencies willing to relieve Brazil of much of its foreign debt in exchange for protecting large areas of its tropical forests from harmful development? How can Americans expect us to think of development in our sparsely populated tropical forests as our most urgent environmental problem when the 15 million people in the city of São Paulo experience some of the worst air and water pollution in the world and many of our other cities face serious environmental problems that we don't have the funds to deal with? How would you respond to these questions? What should the United States do? What should you do?

CHAPTER 14

Wild Plant and Animal Resources

General Questions and Issues

1. Why are wild species of plants and animals important to us and to the ecosphere?

2. What human activities and natural traits cause wild species to become depleted, endangered, and extinct?

3. How can endangered and threatened wild species be protected from premature extinction caused by human activities?

4. How can populations of large game species be managed to have enough animals available for sport hunting without endangering the long-term survival of the species?

5. How can populations of species of freshwater and marine fish be managed to have enough available for commercial and sport fishing without endangering the long-term survival of the species?

The mass of extinctions which the Earth is currently facing is a threat to civilization second only to the threat of thermal nuclear war.

National Academy of Sciences

In the 1850s Alexander Wilson, a prominent ornithologist, watched a single migrating flock of passenger pigeons darken the sky for over four hours. He estimated that this flock consisted of more than 2 billion birds and was 240 miles long and 1 mile wide.

By 1914 the passenger pigeon (Figure 14-1) had disappeared forever. How could the species that was once the most numerous bird in North America become extinct in only a few decades?

The answer is people. The major reasons for the extinction of this species were uncontrolled commercial hunting and loss of habitat and food supplies as forests were cleared for farms and cities.

Passenger pigeons were good to eat and were widely used for fertilizer. They were easy to kill because they flew in gigantic flocks and nested in long, narrow colonies. People captured one pigeon alive and tied it to a perch called a stool. Soon a curious flock landed beside this "stool pigeon." They were then shot or trapped by nets that might contain more than 1,000 birds.

Beginning in 1858, the massive killing of passenger pigeons became a big business. Shotguns, fire, traps, artillery, and even dynamite were used. Birds were also suffocated by burning grass or sulfur below their roosts. Live birds were used as targets in shooting galleries. In 1878 one professional pigeon trapper made $60,000 by killing 3 million birds at their nesting grounds near Petoskey, Michigan.

By the early 1880s commercial hunting ceased because only several thousand birds were left. Recovery of the species was essentially impossible because these birds laid only one egg per nest. Many of the remaining birds died from infectious disease and from severe storms during their annual fall migration to Central and South America.

By 1896 the last major breeding colony had vanished, and by 1900 only a few small, scattered flocks were left. In 1914 the last known passenger pigeon on earth—a hen named Martha after Martha Washington—died in the Cincinnati Zoo. Her stuffed body is now on view at the National Museum of Natural History in Washington, D.C.

Sooner or later all species become extinct. However, we have become a major factor in the premature extinction of an increasing number of species. Over the next three decades our activities are expected to hasten the extinction of as many as 1 million species. Reducing this premature loss of the earth's biological

Figure 14-1 The extinct passenger pigeon. The last known passenger pigeon died in the Cincinnati Zoo in 1914.

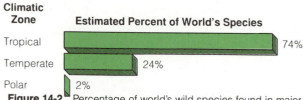

Figure 14-2 Percentage of world's wild species found in major climatic zones. (Data from International Union for Conservation of Nature and Natural Resources and World Resources Institute)

Figure 14-3 The nine-banded armadillo is used in research to find a cure for leprosy.

diversity and restoring species that we have helped deplete are vital tasks. As conservationist Aldo Leopold said, "To keep every cog and wheel is the first precaution of intelligent tinkering."

14-1 WHY PRESERVE WILD PLANT AND ANIMAL SPECIES?

How Many Species Exist? We share this planet with 5 million to 30 million different wild species of plants and animals, most of them insects. So far scientists have identified only about 1.8 million species, two-thirds of them insects.

Almost three-fourths of the world's known and unknown wild plant and animal species are believed to live only in areas with tropical climates (Figure 14-2). Biologists estimate that at least 50% of the world's species live in tropical forests, which are being rapidly cleared and degraded (Figure 13-3, p. 287).

These millions of wild species are a giant genetic library of successful survival strategies developed over several billion years. The biological diversity—*biodiversity* for short—found in these species is the foundation of the ecosystem services upon which we and other species depend and the source of future biological evolution and genetic engineering. In addition to their ecological importance, there are also economic, aesthetic, recreational, and ethical reasons for not hastening the extinction of any wild species.

Economic and Medical Importance Wild species that are actually or potentially useful to people are called

wildlife resources. They are potentially renewable resources, if not driven to extinction or near extinction by our activities.

Most of the plants that supply 90% of the world's food today were domesticated from wild plants found in the tropics. Existing wild plant species, most of them still unclassified and unevaluated, will be needed by agricultural scientists to develop new crop strains that have higher yields and increased resistance to diseases, pests, heat, salinity, and drought.

Wild animal species are a largely untapped source of food. In some parts of the world insects are eaten as a source of protein. They may become an even more important food source in the future.

About 80% of the people in LDCs rely on natural herbs and other plants for most of their health care. Roughly half of the prescription and nonprescription drugs used in the world and 25% of those used in the United States today have active ingredients extracted from wild organisms. About one-fourth of these ingredients are extracted from plants found only in tropical forests.

Materials extracted from an endangered species of evening primrose have the potential to treat coronary heart disease, multiple sclerosis, schizophrenia, eczema, and possibly alcoholic hangovers. A chemical that causes leaves to change color in the fall is being studied as a possible cure for colon cancer.

Many wild animal species are used to test drugs, vaccines, chemical toxicity, and surgical procedures and to increase our understanding of human health and disease. Elephants under stress are used to study the causes of heart disease. The nine-banded armadillo (Figure 14-3) is being used to study leprosy and prepare a vaccine for this disease. Mice, rats, chimpanzees, and rhesus monkeys are used to test for possible cancer-causing agents and toxic chemicals. The endangered Florida manatee is being used in hemophilia research. However, animal rights advocates are protesting the use of animals in medical and biological research and teaching (see Pro/Con below).

Aesthetic and Recreational Importance   Wild plants and animals are a source of beauty, wonder, joy, and recreational pleasure for large numbers of people. Observing leaves change color in autumn, smelling wildflowers, seeing a robin feeding its young, watching an eagle soar overhead or a porpoise glide through the water are only a few of the pleasurable experiences provided for us by wild species.

Wild **game species** provide recreation in the form of hunting and fishing. Each year, almost one of every two Americans participates in some form of outdoor recreational activity involving wildlife, and in the process these people spend $37 billion.

Wildlife tourism is important to the economy of some LDCs, such as Kenya. One wildlife economist estimated that one male lion living to seven years of age in Kenya leads to $515,000 of expenditures by tourists. If the lion were killed for its skin, it would be worth only about $1,000.

Scientific and Ecological Importance   Each species has scientific value because it can help scientists understand how life has evolved and will continue to evolve on this planet. Wild species also perform vital ecosystem services. They supply us and other species with food from the soil and the sea, recycle nutrients essential to agriculture, and help produce and maintain fertile soil. Wild species also produce and maintain oxygen and other gases in the atmosphere, moderate the earth's climate, help regulate water supplies, and store solar energy as chemical energy in food, wood, and fossil fuels. They also filter and detoxify poisonous substances, decompose wastes, control most potential crop pests and carriers of disease, and make

---

PRO/CON Should Animals Be Used for Research and Teaching?

Members of animal rights groups fall into two categories: "no animal research," and "necessary research yes, cruelty no." Some believe that all use of animals for research and teaching is inhumane and should be replaced with other methods.

Others recognize that some use of animals for research and teaching is necessary. They support efforts to halt the unnecessary use of animals for such purposes. They also call for much stricter laws and better enforcement of existing laws requiring comfortable and considerate treatment for all test animals.

Most scientists favor laws requiring considerate treatment for lab animals. However, they also believe that some animal experimentation in medicine and science is vital for human welfare.

They argue that animals would benefit more if animal rights advocates concentrated on preventing people from abandoning 200,000 dogs and cats *each week* in the United States. Each year U.S.

pounds and animal shelters have to kill about 12 million unwanted cats and dogs because of pet overpopulation and a throwaway mentality. By contrast about 200,000 dogs and cats—most obtained from shelters and pounds where they would be put to death—are killed each year for research and teaching purposes.

Scientists point out that animals people cherish as companions can now have cataracts removed, undergo open-heart surgery, or wear a pacemaker because of animal research performed to benefit humans. Animals also benefit from vaccines for rabies, distemper, anthrax, tetanus, feline leukemia, and rinderpest (a virus that kills millions of cattle slowly and painfully)—all developed by animal experiments.

Under intense pressure from animal rights groups, scientists are trying to find testing methods that do not cause animals to suffer, or better yet, do not use animals at

all. Promising alternatives include the use of cell and tissue cultures, simulated tissues and body fluids, and bacteria. Computer-generated models can also be used to estimate the toxicity of a compound from knowledge of its chemical structure and properties.

Computer simulations of animals under anesthesia can be used to teach veterinary medical students. Videotapes can replace live demonstrations on animals for biology and veterinary medical students.

But researchers point out that such techniques cannot replace all animal research. Cell cultures, for example, do not have bones and therefore cannot be used to test treatments for arthritis or other bone and joint diseases. Researchers argue that live animals are still needed to help perfect new surgical techniques and to test many lifesaving drugs and vaccines. What do you think?

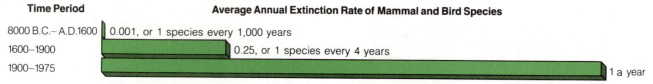

Time Period	Average Annual Extinction Rate of Mammal and Bird Species
8000 B.C.–A.D.1600	0.001, or 1 species every 1,000 years
1600–1900	0.25, or 1 species every 4 years
1900–1975	1 a year

Figure 14-4 Estimated average annual extinction rate of mammal and bird species between 8000 B.C. and 1975 A.D. (Data from E.O. Wilson and Norman Myers)

up a vast gene pool from which we and other species can draw.

Ethical Importance So far, the reasons given for preserving wildlife are based on the actual or potential usefulness of wild species as resources for people. This view is based on the human-centered (anthropocentric) belief that we are the most important species on the planet. According to this worldview, we have the right, and, according to some, the duty to use the world's resources as we please.

Many ecologists and conservationists believe that wild species will continue to disappear at an alarming rate until we replace this human-centered view of wildlife and the environment either with a life-centered (biocentric) view or with an ecosystem-centered (ecocentric) view. According to the biocentric worldview, each wild species has an inherent right to exist or at least the right to struggle to exist equal to that of any other species. Thus, it is ethically wrong for us to hasten the extinction of any species. Some go further and believe that each individual wild creature—not just a species— has a right to survive without human interference, just as each human being has the right to survive.

Some distinguish between the survival rights of plants and those of animals. The poet Alan Watts once commented that he was a vegetarian "because cows scream louder than carrots." Many people make ethical distinctions among various types of animals. For instance, they think little about killing a fly, mosquito, cockroach, or sewer rat, or about catching and killing fish they don't eat. Unless they are strict vegetarians, they also think little about having others kill cows, calves, lambs, and chickens in slaughterhouses to provide them with meat, leather, and other animal products. The same people, however, might deplore the killing of game animals such as deer, squirrels, or rabbits.

The ecocentric worldview stresses the importance of preserving biodiversity by preserving or not degrading entire ecosystems, rather than focusing only on individual species or an individual organism. It is based on Aldo Leopold's ethical principle that something is right when it tends to maintain the earth's life-support systems for us and other species and wrong when it tends otherwise.

14-2 HOW SPECIES BECOME DEPLETED AND EXTINCT

Extinction Before the Dawn of Agriculture The species found on earth today are the result of two biological processes taking place since life emerged on earth several billion years ago. One is **speciation,** the formation of new species from existing ones through natural selection in response to changes in environmental conditions (Figure 6-9, p. 141 and Figure 6-10, p. 142). The other is **extinction,** the process in which a species ceases to exist because its members cannot adapt and reproduce under new environmental conditions.

During the last 4.6 billion years the earth has been home for an estimated 500 million species of plants and animals. Only 5 million to 30 million of those species exist today. This means that 94% to 99% of the earth's species have either become extinct or have evolved into a form different enough to be identified as a new species.

Fossil remains and other evidence suggest that over the past 500 million years there have been five or six catastrophic extinctions of life, mostly numerous species of animals. We probably will never know the exact cause of these past mass extinctions. We do know, however, that humans caused none of them.

Extinction of Species Today Extinction is a natural process. However, since agriculture began about 10,000 years ago, the rate of species extinction has increased sharply as human settlements have expanded worldwide.

Rough estimates indicate that between 8000 B.C. and 1975 A.D. the average extinction rate of mammal and bird species increased about 1,000-fold (Figure 14-4). If the extinction rates of plant and insect species are included, the estimated extinction rate in 1975 was several hundred species a year (Figure 14-5). Since then the rate of extinction has accelerated. Biologist Edward O. Wilson estimated that by 1985 the extinction rate had increased at least 10-fold to several thousand species per year.

Edward Wilson, Norman Myers (see Guest Essay on p. 314), and other biologists are alarmed at this situation. They warn that if deforestation (especially of tropical forests), desertification, and destruction of wetlands and coral reefs continue at their present rates,

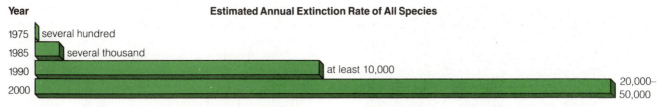

Figure 14-5 Estimated annual extinction rate of all species between 1975 and 2000. These estimates assume that there are 10 million species worldwide. If there are at least 30 million insect species in tropical forests alone, then the extinction rates for 1990 and 2000 will be much higher. (Data from E.O. Wilson and Norman Myers)

then at least 500,000 and perhaps 1 million species will become extinct because of human activities between 1975 and 2000. Most of these species will be plants and insects that have yet to be classified and evaluated for their value to humans and their roles in ecosystems.

Using the lower estimate of 500,000 extinctions, by the year 2000 an average of 20,000 species a year would become extinct because of our activities. This is an average of 1 species every 30 minutes—a 200-fold increase in the extinction rate in only 25 years. Even if the average extinction rate is only 1,000 per year by the end of this century, the total loss will still rival the great mass extinctions of the past.

Animal extinctions get the most publicity. But plant extinctions are more important ecologically because most animal species depend directly or indirectly on plants for food. It is estimated that about 10% of the world's plant species are threatened with extinction today. By the year 2000, from 16% to 25% of all plant species face extinction.

There are important differences between the present mass extinction and those in the past. First, the present "extinction spasm" is being caused by us. Second, it is taking place in only a few decades rather than over several million years. Such extinction cannot be balanced by speciation because it takes between 2,000 and 100,000 generations for new species to evolve. Third, plant species are disappearing as rapidly as animal species, thus threatening many animal species that otherwise would not become extinct at this time.

Threatened and Endangered Species Today Private conservation organizations and government conservation agencies often classify species heading toward extinction as either endangered or threatened. An **endangered species** is one having so few individual survivors that the species could soon become extinct over all or most of its natural range. Examples are the white rhinoceros in Africa (100 left), the California condor in the United States (none left in the wild), the giant panda in central China (1,000 left), and the snow leopard in central Asia (2,500 left).

A **threatened species** is still abundant in its natural range but is declining in numbers and likely to become endangered. Examples are the African elephant, Utah prairie dog, bald eagle, and grizzly bear.

The International Union for the Conservation of Nature (IUCN) regularly compiles lists of the world's threatened and endangered species. In 1988 the IUCN listed 4,600 species as threatened or endangered. Many thousands of others are being evaluated for listing. Some will become extinct before this process is completed. Thousands of other species—mostly plants and insects—disappear before they are even found and recognized as species by biologists.

Endangered and threatened species in the United States and other parts of the world are listed and given federal protection by the Office of Endangered Species of the U.S. Department of the Interior's Fish and Wildlife Service. By June 1989 the Office of Endangered Species had listed 1,046 species as endangered or threatened, with 539 of them found only in the United States. About 3,000 of the 25,000 plant species in the United States have been identified by scientists as endangered. Only 204 of these were under federal protection by 1989. Up to 700 native plant species may become extinct in the United States by the year 2000.

Many wild species are not in danger of extinction, but their populations have been sharply reduced locally or regionally. Because such number losses are occurring much faster and more frequently than extinctions, they may be a better sign of the condition of wildlife and entire ecosystems. They can serve as early warnings so that scientists can prevent species extinction rather than responding mostly to emergency situations.

Habitat Loss and Disturbance The greatest threat to most wild species is destruction, fragmentation, and degradation of their habitats. As the human population increases, we increase our use of the earth's land and water resources at the expense of other creatures.

We build cities and suburbs, clear forests, drain and fill wetlands, plow up grasslands and plant them with crops, and strip the land by mining. Such dis-

Figure 14-6 The whooping crane is an endangered species in North America. Their low reproduction rates and fixed migration pattern make these birds vulnerable to extinction. Mostly because of illegal shooting and loss of habitat, the number of whooping cranes in the wild dropped to only 15 by 1941. Because of a $5 million-a-year habitat protection and captive breeding program directed by the U.S. Fish and Wildlife Service, about 200 birds survive today.

ruption of natural communities threatens wild species by destroying migration routes, breeding areas, and food sources. Deforestation, especially of tropical forests, is probably the single greatest cause of the decline in global biological diversity (Section 13-2).

A UN study found that two-thirds of the original wildlife habitat in tropical Africa and in much of Southeast Asia has been lost or severely degraded. Bangladesh, the world's most densely populated large country, has lost 95% of its wildlife habitat.

In the United States forests have been reduced by one-third, tall-grass prairies by 98%, and wetlands by 50%. Furthermore, much of the remaining wildlife habitat is being fragmented and polluted at an alarming rate. Loss or degradation of habitat is the key factor in the extinction of American bird species such as the heath hen and the near extinction of Atwater's prairie chicken, the whooping crane (Figure 14-6), and the California condor.

Many rare and threatened species live in vulnerable, specialized habitats such as small islands or single trees in tropical forests. About 75% of the mammals and birds that have become extinct in recent history were island-dwelling species. Human alterations of ecosystems fragment wildlife habitats into patches, which are often too small to support the min-

imum number of individuals needed to sustain a population. Fragmenting of habitat can also cause inbreeding, which produces genetically inferior offspring that are vulnerable to extinction. Remaining individuals and species in isolated patches are also highly vulnerable to being killed by human activities, floods, and other disasters.

The removal of large dead and dying trees from forests, city parks, and suburban areas eliminates important wildlife habitats. The holes and cavities in such trees are nesting sites for hundreds of bird species and for squirrels, raccoons, and other animals. Most cavity-nesting birds help control nuisance insects such as mosquitoes and flies. They also help protect forests from being ravaged by insects such as gypsy moths and wood-boring beetles.

Many species of insect-eating, migratory songbirds in North America are being threatened with extinction. Their summer habitats in North America and their winter habitats in the tropical forests of Mexico, Central America, South America, and the Caribbean islands are being destroyed, degraded, or fragmented.

Commercial Hunting   There are three major types of hunting: commercial, subsistence, and sport. **Commercial hunting** involves killing animals for profit from sale of their furs or other parts. The killing of animals to provide enough food for survival is called **subsistence hunting. Sport hunting** is the killing of animals for recreation.

Subsistence hunting once caused the extinction of many animal species. Today, however, subsistence hunting has declined sharply in most parts of the world because of the decrease in hunting-and-gathering societies.

Sport hunting is now closely regulated in most countries. Game species are endangered by such hunting only when protective regulations do not exist or are not enforced. No animal in the United States, for instance, has become extinct or endangered because of regulated sport hunting.

Worldwide, legal and illegal commercial hunting threatens many species of large animals. The jaguar, tiger, snow leopard, and cheetah are hunted for their furs. It is not surprising that Bengal tigers face extinction, since a coat made from their fur sells for $100,000 in Tokyo. Rhinoceros are hunted for their horns (see Case Study on p. 323) and elephants for their tusks. The African elephant, though not officially an endangered species, could be wiped out within 10 years, if widespread poaching is not halted.

Commercial hunting in the United States was an important factor in the extermination of the American passenger pigeon. It also played a key role in the near extermination of the American bison (Figure 2-9, p. 39) and the snowy egret (Figure 2-7, p. 37).

Today commercial hunting is not legal in the United States, except for fur trapping, mostly of raccoon, muskrat, and beaver. Illegal hunting, however, does occur. In 1989 U.S. Fish and Wildlife officials arrested 66 people for allegedly killing black bears in Appalachia and several northeastern states. The bears were killed for their tennis-ball-sized gallbladders, sold for $50 to $150 each for use in Asia as an alleged aphrodisiac.

Predator and Pest Control Extinction or near extinction can also occur when people attempt to extermi-nate pest and predator species that compete with humans for food and game. Fruit farmers exterminated the Carolina parakeet in the United States around 1914 because it fed on fruit crops. The species was easy to exterminate because when one member of a flock was shot, the rest of the birds hovered over its body, making themselves easy targets.

As animal habitats have shrunk, farmers have killed large numbers of African elephants to keep them from trampling and eating food crops. Carnivore predators that sometimes kill livestock and game are shot, trapped, and poisoned (see Pro/Con on p. 307).

CASE STUDY Near Extinction of the Rhinoceros

The rhinoceros is one of the earth's oldest animals, dating back some 55 million years. There are five surviving wild rhino species. Two of these—black rhinos (Figure 14-7) and white rhinos—live in northern and southern African grasslands. The other three—Sumatran, great Indian, and Javan—inhabit rain forests in Asia. All five species are threatened with extinction because of loss of habitat and poachers, who kill them for their horns.

Importing rhino horn is illegal in most countries. However, an illegal $3-million-a-year trade flourishes in the Middle East and eastern Asia. In the Middle East, Asian rhino horn, the most prized, can fetch as much as $13,000 a pound—33 times the price of gold.

In North Yemen the horns are carved into dagger handles that sell for $500 to $12,000. These ornate daggers are worn as a sign of masculinity and virility. North Yemen has been responsible for about half of the world's consumption of rhino horn since 1970.

In China and other parts of Asia rhino horns are ground into a powder and used for reducing fever and other medicinal purposes for which its effectiveness has not been verified by medical science. Some Asians believe the powder is an aphrodisiac. If this were true, human hair and fingernails, which consist of the same substance (keratin) as rhino horn, would be a much cheaper, readily available sexual stimulant.

Africa's wildlife poachers were once local tribesmen armed with machetes and spears. Today's poachers use military tactics, AK-47s, and large-caliber machine guns. If poaching continues at present rates, no rhinos will be left in the wild within a decade.

In Zimbabwe government park rangers patrol around the clock to protect the remaining black rhinos from extinction. They have orders to shoot poachers on sight. Since 1985 they have killed more than 30 poachers and taken over 20 prisoners. But poachers have also killed several park rangers and civilians.

Private and government conservationists are trying to protect rhinos from further poaching by creating fenced or heavily guarded sanctuaries and private ranches, relocating some animals to protected areas, and building up captive breeding populations for all species. These efforts have led to a slow increase in numbers in protected areas and in captivity. But it is an expensive and dangerous uphill fight.

North Yemen, Hong Kong, and Singapore, once major markets for rhino horn and elephant ivory, have cracked down on the illegal trade of these items in response to international pressure. But the illegal trade continues, especially in Taiwan, where government enforcement is lax.

Figure 14-7 Only about 3,500 black rhinos are left in Africa. This and other species of rhinoceros face extinction because they are illegally killed for their valuable horns.

Figure 14-9 The black-footed ferret is one of the most endangered mammals in North America, with none left in the wild.

Figure 14-8 Black-tailed prairie dog at its burrow entrance. Once found in large numbers on western rangeland, these rodents usually live in "towns" containing several hundred individuals. Their underground passages aerate grassland soils and their droppings add fertilizer to the soil. Sometimes cattle and horses trip on prairie dog burrow mounds and break their legs. For this reason, livestock ranchers have used poisons to eliminate prairie dogs from most rangeland in the western United States.

Since 1929, ranchers and government agencies have poisoned prairie dogs (Figure 14-8) because their mounds sometimes cause horses and cattle to stumble and break their legs. This poisoning has killed 99% of the prairie dog population in North America. It has also led to the near extinction of the black-footed ferret (Figure 14-9), which preyed on the prairie dog. Other species whose populations have been greatly reduced by prairie dog poisoning campaigns include burrowing owls, swift foxes, and prairie falcons. These species help control rodents such as ground squirrels, which also compete with livestock for range grass.

Pets, Decorative Plants, and Medical Research   Each year large numbers of threatened and endangered species are smuggled into the United States, Great Britain, West Germany, and other countries. Most are sold as pets.

Worldwide, over 3.5 million live wild birds are captured and sold legally each year. Another 2.5 million are captured and sold illegally. For example, exotic-bird collectors may pay $10,000 for a threatened hyacinth macaw smuggled out of Brazil. For every bird that reaches a pet shop legally or illegally, at least one other dies in transit. After purchase many of these animals are mistreated, killed, or abandoned by their owners.

Some species of exotic plants, especially orchids and cacti, are also endangered because they are gathered, often illegally. They are then sold to collectors and used to decorate houses, offices, and landscapes. A collector may pay $5,000 for a single rare orchid.

Nearly one-third of the cactus species native to the United States, especially those in Texas and Arizona, are thought to be endangered because they are collected and sold for use as potted plants. For example, a rare, mature crested saguaro cactus removed illegally from an Arizona site turned up in a Las Vegas nursery with a $15,000 price tag. To reduce losses from cactus rustlers, Arizona has put 222 species under state protection with penalties of up to $1,000 and jail sentences up to one year. However, only seven people are assigned to enforce this law over the entire state and fines are too small to discourage poaching.

Most animal species used for medical research are not endangered. However, research and habitat loss are serious threats to endangered wild primates such as the chimpanzee and the orangutan. As many as six chimpanzees die during capture and shipment for each one that ends up in a laboratory.

Pollution   Chemical pollution is a growing threat to wildlife. Toxic chemicals degrade wildlife habitats, including wildlife refuges, and kill some plants and animals.

Industrial wastes, mine acids, and excess heat from electric power plants have wiped out some species of fish, such as the humpbacked chub, in local areas. Slowly degradable pesticides, especially DDT and dieldrin, have caused populations of some bird species to decline (see Spotlight on p. 325).

Wildlife in even the best protected and best managed wildlife reserves throughout the world may be depleted in a few decades because of climatic change caused by the greenhouse effect. Changes in vegetation, especially in temperate and boreal forests, will eliminate or degrade key wildlife habitats and cause the extinction of many species. Wildlife in subpolar and polar regions may also be harmed by the greatly increased ultraviolet radiation caused by the depletion of the ozone layer. Altering our lifestyles to slow down global warming and ozone depletion (Section 19-5) is probably the most important thing we must do to protect wildlife as well as our future supplies of food, timber, and fuelwood.

Introduction of Alien Species As p▨▨ around the world, they sometimes pick up p▨▨ animals intentionally or accidentally and introduce these species to new geographical regions. Many of these alien species have provided food, game, and beauty and have helped control pests in their new environments.

SPOTLIGHT **Biological Amplification of Pesticides in Food Chains and Webs (continued)**

brown pelicans (Figure 2-11, p. 40), and bald eagles (Figure 2-16, p. 43) declined drastically. These birds feed mostly on fish at the top of long aquatic food chains and webs and thus ingest large quantities of biologically amplified DDT in their prey.

Populations of predatory birds such as prairie falcons, sparrow hawks, Bermuda petrels, and peregrine falcons also dropped when they ate animal prey containing DDT. These birds control populations of rabbits, ground squirrels, and other crop-damaging small mammals. Only about 1,000 pere-

grine falcons are left in the lower 48 states. Most of them were bred in captivity and then released into the wild.

Research has shown that these population declines occurred because DDE, a chemical produced by the breakdown of DDT, accumulated in the bodies of the affected bird species. This chemical reduces the amount of calcium in the shells of their eggs. As a result, the shells are so thin that many of them break, and the unborn chicks die.

Since the U.S. ban on DDT in 1972, populations of most of these

bird species have made a comeback. In 1980, however, it was discovered that levels of DDT and other banned pesticides were rising in some areas and in some species such as the peregrine falcon and the osprey.

These species may be picking up biologically amplified DDT and other chlorinated hydrocarbon insecticides in Latin American countries, where the birds live during winter. In those countries the use of such chemicals is still legal. Illegal use of DDT and other banned pesticides in the United States may also play a role.

CASE STUDY **Effects of Importing Wild European Hares to Australia**

In 1859 a farmer in southern Australia imported a dozen pairs of wild European hares as game animals. Within six years the 24 hares had mushroomed to 22 million and by 1907 had reached every corner of the continent. By the 1930s their population had reached an estimated 750 million.

The hares competed with sheep for the best grass and in many areas cut the sheep population in half. They also competed with native species, such as kangaroos and wallabies, for vegetation. The hares devoured food crops, gnawed young trees, fouled water holes (Figure 14-11), and accelerated soil erosion.

In the early 1950s about 90% of the hare population was killed by a viral disease deliberately introduced by humans. Now scientists are concerned that succeeding

generations of the remaining hare population will develop immunity to this disease through natural

selection. Then the hares could again become the scourge of Australian farmers and ranchers.

Figure 14-11 European wild hares around a water hole in Australia.

A factor affecting the survival of some individual organisms and populations of organisms is **biological amplification,** a condition in which concentrations of certain chemicals soluble in the fatty tissues of organisms feeding at high trophic levels in a food chain or web are drastically higher than concentrations of these chemicals found in organisms feeding at lower trophic levels.

Some synthetic chemicals, such as the pesticide DDT, PCBs, some radioactive materials, and some toxic mercury and lead compounds, have the three properties needed for biological amplification. They are insoluble in water, solu-

ble in fat, and are slowly degraded or not degraded by natural processes. This means that they become more concentrated in the fatty tissues of organisms at successively higher trophic levels in food chains and webs.

Figure 14-10 shows the biological amplification of DDT in a five-step food chain of an estuary ecosystem. If each phytoplankton in such a food chain concentrates one unit of water-insoluble DDT from the water, a small fish eating thousands of phytoplankton will store thousands of units of fat-soluble DDT in its fatty tissue. Then a large fish that eats 10 of the smaller fish will receive and store

tens of thousands of units of fat-soluble DDT. A bird or a person that eats several large fish can ingest hundreds of thousands of units of DDT.

High concentrations of DDT or other slowly degraded, fat-soluble chemicals can reduce populations of species in several ways. It can directly kill the organisms, reduce their ability to reproduce, or weaken them so that they are more vulnerable to diseases, parasites, and predators.

During the 1950s and 1960s, populations of ospreys, cormorants, eastern and California

(continued)

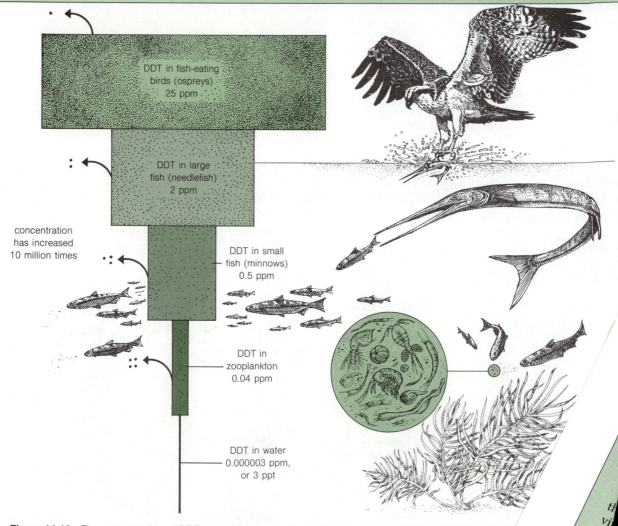

DDT in fish-eating
birds (ospreys)
25 ppm

DDT in large
fish (needlefish)
2 ppm

concentration
has increased
10 million times

DDT in small
fish (minnows)
0.5 ppm

DDT in
zooplankton
0.04 ppm

DDT in water
0.000003 ppm,
or 3 ppt

Figure 14-10 The concentration of DDT in the fatty tissues of organisms was biologically amplified about 10 million times in this food chain of an estuary adjacent to Long Island Sound near New York City. Dots repres[ent] DDT and arrows show small losses of DDT through respiration and excretion.

A factor affecting the survival of some individual organisms and populations of organisms is **biological amplification,** a condition in which concentrations of certain chemicals soluble in the fatty tissues of organisms feeding at high trophic levels in a food chain or web are drastically higher than concentrations of these chemicals found in organisms feeding at lower trophic levels.

Some synthetic chemicals, such as the pesticide DDT, PCBs, some radioactive materials, and some toxic mercury and lead compounds, have the three properties needed for biological amplification. They are insoluble in water, solu-

ble in fat, and are slowly degraded or not degraded by natural processes. This means that they become more concentrated in the fatty tissues of organisms at successively higher trophic levels in food chains and webs.

Figure 14-10 shows the biological amplification of DDT in a five-step food chain of an estuary ecosystem. If each phytoplankton in such a food chain concentrates one unit of water-insoluble DDT from the water, a small fish eating thousands of phytoplankton will store thousands of units of fat-soluble DDT in its fatty tissue. Then a large fish that eats 10 of the smaller fish will receive and store

tens of thousands of units of fat-soluble DDT. A bird or a person that eats several large fish can ingest hundreds of thousands of units of DDT.

High concentrations of DDT or other slowly degraded, fat-soluble chemicals can reduce populations of species in several ways. It can directly kill the organisms, reduce their ability to reproduce, or weaken them so that they are more vulnerable to diseases, parasites, and predators.

During the 1950s and 1960s, populations of ospreys, cormorants, eastern and California

(continued)

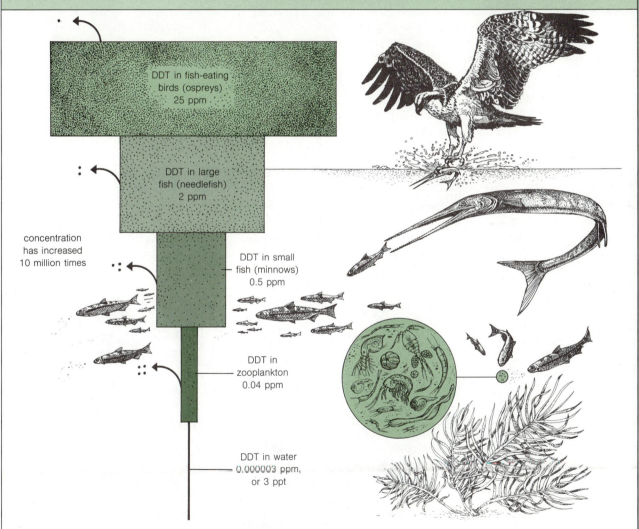

DDT in fish-eating birds (ospreys)
25 ppm

DDT in large fish (needlefish)
2 ppm

concentration has increased 10 million times

DDT in small fish (minnows)
0.5 ppm

DDT in zooplankton
0.04 ppm

DDT in water
0.000003 ppm, or 3 ppt

Figure 14-10   The concentration of DDT in the fatty tissues of organisms was biologically amplified about 10 million times in this food chain of an estuary adjacent to Long Island Sound near New York City. Dots represent DDT and arrows show small losses of DDT through respiration and excretion.

and polar regions may also be harmed by the greatly increased ultraviolet radiation caused by the depletion of the ozone layer. Altering our lifestyles to slow down global warming and ozone depletion (Section 19-5) is probably the most important thing we must do to protect wildlife as well as our future supplies of food, timber, and fuelwood.

Introduction of Alien Species As p[...] around the world, they sometimes pick up pl[...] animals intentionally or accidentally and introduce these species to new geographical regions. Many of these alien species have provided food, game, and beauty and have helped control pests in their new environments.

SPOTLIGHT **Biological Amplification of Pesticides in Food Chains and Webs (continued)**

brown pelicans (Figure 2-11, p. 40), and bald eagles (Figure 2-16, p. 43) declined drastically. These birds feed mostly on fish at the top of long aquatic food chains and webs and thus ingest large quantities of biologically amplified DDT in their prey.

Populations of predatory birds such as prairie falcons, sparrow hawks, Bermuda petrels, and peregrine falcons also dropped when they ate animal prey containing DDT. These birds control populations of rabbits, ground squirrels, and other crop-damaging small mammals. Only about 1,000 pere-

grine falcons are left in the lower 48 states. Most of them were bred in captivity and then released into the wild.

Research has shown that these population declines occurred because DDE, a chemical produced by the breakdown of DDT, accumulated in the bodies of the affected bird species. This chemical reduces the amount of calcium in the shells of their eggs. As a result, the shells are so thin that many of them break, and the unborn chicks die.

Since the U.S. ban on DDT in 1972, populations of most of these

bird species have made a comeback. In 1980, however, it was discovered that levels of DDT and other banned pesticides were rising in some areas and in some species such as the peregrine falcon and the osprey.

These species may be picking up biologically amplified DDT and other chlorinated hydrocarbon insecticides in Latin American countries, where the birds live during winter. In those countries the use of such chemicals is still legal. Illegal use of DDT and other banned pesticides in the United States may also play a role.

CASE STUDY **Effects of Importing Wild European Hares to Australia**

In 1859 a farmer in southern Australia imported a dozen pairs of wild European hares as game animals. Within six years the 24 hares had mushroomed to 22 million and by 1907 had reached every corner of the continent. By the 1930s their population had reached an estimated 750 million.

The hares competed with sheep for the best grass and in many areas cut the sheep population in half. They also competed with native species, such as kangaroos and wallabies, for vegetation. The hares devoured food crops, gnawed young trees, fouled water holes (Figure 14-11), and accelerated soil erosion.

In the early 1950s about 90% of the hare population was killed by a viral disease deliberately introduced by humans. Now scientists are concerned that succeeding

generations of the remaining hare population will develop immunity to this disease through natural

selection. Then the hares could again become the scourge of Australian farmers and ranchers.

Figure 14-11 European wild hares around a water hole in Australia.

However, some alien species have no natural predators and competitors in their new habitats. Thus, they can dominate their new ecosystem and reduce the populations of many native species. Eventually, they can cause the extinction, near extinction, or displacement of native species (see Table 14-1 and the Case Study on p. 326).

The kudzu vine was imported into the southeastern United States from Africa to help control soil erosion. It does control erosion, but it is so prolific that it has also covered hills, trees, houses, roads, stream banks, and even entire patches of forest. It has displaced some natural plant species. People have dug it up, cut it up, burned it, and tried to kill it with herbicides, all without success.

Population Growth, Affluence, and Poverty The underlying causes of wildlife extinction and popula-

---

Table 14-1 Damage Caused by Plants and Animals Imported Into the United States

Name	Origin	Mode of Transport	Type of Damage
Mammals			
European wild boar	Russia	Intentionally imported (1912), escaped captivity	Destruction of habitat by rooting; crop damage
Nutria (cat-sized rodent)	Argentina	Intentionally imported, escaped captivity (1940)	Alteration of marsh ecology; damage to levees and earth dams; crop destruction
Birds			
European starling	Europe	Intentionally released (1890)	Competition with native songbirds; crop damage; transmission of swine diseases; airport interference
House sparrow	England	Intentionally released by Brooklyn Institute (1853)	Crop damage; displacement of native songbirds
Fish			
Carp	Germany	Intentionally released (1877)	Displacement of native fish; uprooting of water plants with loss of waterfowl populations
Sea lamprey	North Atlantic Ocean	Entered via Welland Canal (1829)	Destruction of lake trout, lake whitefish, and sturgeon in Great Lakes
Walking catfish	Thailand	Imported into Florida	Destruction of bass, bluegill, and other fish
Insects			
Argentine fire ant	Argentina	Probably entered via coffee shipments from Brazil (1918)	Crop damage; destruction of native ant species
Camphor scale insect	Japan	Accidentally imported on nursery stock (1920s)	Damage to nearly 200 species of plants in Louisiana, Texas, and Alabama
Japanese beetle	Japan	Accidentally imported on irises or azaleas (1911)	Defoliation of more than 250 species of trees and other plants, including many of commercial importance
Plants			
Water hyacinth	Central America	Intentionally introduced (1884)	Clogging waterways; shading out other aquatic vegetation
Chestnut blight (a fungus)	Asia	Accidentally imported on nursery plants (1900)	Destruction of nearly all eastern American chestnut trees; disturbance of forest ecology
Dutch elm disease, *Cerastomella ulmi* (a fungus, the disease agent)	Europe	Accidentally imported on infected elm timber used for veneers (1930)	Destruction of millions of elms; disturbance of forest ecology

From *Biological Conservation* by David W. Ehrenfeld. Copyright © 1970 by Holt, Rinehart and Winston, Inc. Modified and reprinted by permission.

tion reduction are population growth, affluence, and poverty. As the human population grows, it occupies more land and clears and degrades more land to supply food, fuelwood, timber, and other resources.

Increasing affluence in MDCs is a key factor because it leads to greatly increased average resource use per person (Figure 1-13, p. 20). In LDCs the combination of rapid population growth and poverty push the poor to cut forests, grow crops on marginal land, and poach endangered animals. This unsustainable use of potentially renewable resources destroys wildlife habitats and decreases wildlife populations.

Characteristics of Extinction-Prone Species Some species have natural traits that make them more vulnerable than others to premature extinction (Table 14-2). Species with low reproductive rates, such as the California condor (see Case Study below), are particularly vulnerable.

CASE STUDY The California Condor: A Highly Endangered Species

On April 19, 1987, for the first time in 600,000 years, no wild California condors (Figure 14-12) soared through California skies. In 1967, when this species was placed on the endangered species list, 40 wild individuals remained, living mainly in a mountainous sanctuary north of Los Angeles. Despite considerable efforts to protect the species, by 1986 only 9 wild birds were left.

In 1987 the U.S. Fish and Wildlife Service, the California Fish and Game Department, and the Audubon Society decided to take the few remaining birds into protective custody at the San Diego Wild Animal Park.

By July 1989 there were 32 condors in captivity. Most of them were hatched in the San Diego Wild Animal Park and the Los Angeles Zoo from eggs removed from nests in the wild. Several one-year-old chicks were also taken from the wild and are being reared in the zoos. On April 29, 1988, the first California condor conceived in captivity hatched. Another hatched in 1989. The goal of this $200,000-a-year program is to breed at least 200 condors so that some can be returned to the wild in 20 to 40 years.

Why is the California condor on the brink of extinction? Part of the answer is that the condor's large size made it an easy target for shooters, who prized its long feathers. Many birds were also killed by ranchers and farmers, who wrongly blamed them for the deaths of lambs, calves, and chickens, not knowing that these birds fed only on animal carcasses.

Another characteristic that makes the California condor vulnerable is its low reproduction rate. Condor pairs are monogamous partners for life and usually produce only one offspring every two years. Chicks fail to hatch when human activities and noise scare the parents away from the nest during the 42-day incubation period. A newborn chick depends on its parents for up to two years and dies if prematurely abandoned. It also takes a condor six to seven years to reach reproductive age.

Condors need a large, undisturbed habitat and often fly 161 kilometers (100 miles) a day between nesting and feeding areas. In 1987 the federal government bought several thousand acres of condor habitat to be added to a national wildlife refuge in California. Conservationists hope there will be a large enough, undisturbed habitat left when some of the captive birds are ready to be returned to the wild.

Figure 14-12 California condor breeding pair in captivity at the San Diego Zoo. None of these birds are left in the wild.

Each animal species has a critical population density and size, below which survival may be impossible because males and females have a hard time finding each other. Once the population reaches its critical size, it continues to decline even if the species is protected, because its death rate exceeds its birth rate. The remaining small population can easily be wiped out by fire, flood, landslide, disease, or some other catastrophic event.

Some species, such as bats, are vulnerable to extinction for a combination of reasons (see Case Study on p. 330).

14-3 PROTECTING WILD SPECIES FROM EXTINCTION

The Species Approach: Treaties and Laws Organizations such as the International Union for the Conservation of Nature and Natural Resources (IUCN), the International Council for Bird Preservation (ICBP), and the World Wildlife Fund (WWF) have identified threatened and endangered species and led efforts to protect them. The IUCN, for example, compiles lists of threatened and endangered species and publishes them in *The Red Data Book*.

Several international treaties and conventions help protect wild species. One international conservation agreement is the 1979 Convention on Conservation of Migratory Species of Wild Animals, now signed by 23 countries. One of the most far-reaching treaties is the 1975 Convention on International Trade in Endangered Species (CITES), developed by the IUCN and administered by the UN Environment Program (see Spotlight on p. 331).

Many countries have passed laws to protect endangered or threatened species. Canada, the United States, and the Soviet Union have the most strictly enforced wildlife protection laws.

The United States controls imports and exports of endangered wildlife and wildlife products with two important laws. One is the Lacey Act of 1900, which prohibits transporting live or dead wild animals or their parts across state borders without a federal permit. The other law is the Endangered Species Act of 1973, including amendments in 1982 and 1988 (see Spotlight on p. 331).

The federal government has the main responsibility for managing migratory species, endangered species, and wildlife on federal lands. States are responsible for the management of all other wildlife.

Funds for state game management programs are

Table 14-2 Characteristics of Extinction-Prone Species

Characteristic	Examples
Low reproduction rate	Blue whale, polar bear, California condor, Andean condor, passenger pigeon, giant panda, whooping crane
Specialized feeding habits	Everglades kite (eats apple snail of southern Florida), blue whale (krill in polar upwelling areas), black-footed ferret (prairie dogs and pocket gophers), giant panda (bamboo), Australian koala (certain types of Eucalyptus leaves)
Feed at high trophic levels	Bengal tiger, bald eagle, Andean condor, timber wolf
Large size	Bengal tiger, African lion, elephant, Javan rhinoceros, American bison, giant panda, grizzly bear
Limited or specialized nesting or breeding areas	Kirtland's warbler (nests only in 6- to 15-year-old jack pine trees), whooping crane (depends on marshes for food and nesting), orangutan (now found only on islands of Sumatra and Borneo), green sea turtle (lays eggs on only a few beaches), bald eagle (prefers habitat of forested shorelines), nightingale wren (nests and breeds only on Barro Colorado Island, Panama)
Found in only one place or region	Woodland caribou, elephant seal, Cooke's kokio, and many unique island species
Fixed migratory patterns	Blue whale, Kirtland's warbler, Bachman's warbler, whooping crane
Preys on livestock or people	Timber wolf, some crocodiles
Certain behavioral patterns	Passenger pigeon and white-crowned pigeon (nest in large colonies), redheaded woodpecker (flies in front of cars), Carolina parakeet (when one bird is shot, rest of flock hovers over body), Key deer (forages for cigarette butts along highways—it's a "nicotine addict")

provided by the sale of hunting and fishing licenses and federal taxes on hunting and fishing equipment. Two-thirds of the states also have checkoffs on state income tax returns that allow individuals to contribute money to state wildlife programs.

Most of these funds are spent on the management of game species. Only 10% of all federal and state wildlife dollars are spent to study or benefit the non-game species that make up nearly 90% of the country's wildlife species.

CASE STUDY Bats: Misunderstood, Feared, and Vulnerable

The world's nearly 1,000 species of bats make up one-fourth of all mammal species. These small, nocturnal creatures form the largest populations of any warm-blooded animal. They are found in all but the most extreme polar and desert areas of the earth.

Despite their variety and distribution, bats have several traits that make them vulnerable to extinction from human activities. They reproduce very slowly compared to other mammals and nest in huge breeding colonies in accessible places such as caves, where people can easily destroy them by blocking the entrances.

They are also specialized feeders. Some bats feed only on certain types of nectar, others on certain types of fruit, and others on various night-flying insects.

People kill bats in large numbers because of misinformed fears based on vampire movies and folklore. Most people also falsely believe that bats are dangerous creatures that attack and infect humans and livestock with rabies and other diseases and destroy fruit crops.

Because of such fears and misinformation, some countries have begun massive bat eradication programs, and others are considering such programs. A number of species have been driven to extinction and others are threatened in Australia, Southeast Asia, and the South Pacific.

Most bat species are harmless to people, livestock, and crops. Less than half of one percent of bats get rabies, and these individuals rarely become aggressive and transmit rabies to wildlife or people. The few people who are bitten by a bat are those who foolishly pick up a sick bat, which bites in self-defense, as almost any sick wild animal would.

In all of Asia, Europe, Australia, and the Pacific Islands, only two people have been suspected of dying from bat-transmitted rabies. No people in these areas are known to have died of any other bat-transmitted disease. By comparison, in India some 15,000 people die each year from rabies transmitted by other animals, mostly dogs.

In the United States only 10 people have died of bat-transmitted disease in four decades of record keeping. More Americans die each year from dog attacks, falling coconuts, or food poisoning contracted at church picnics.

Because of such unwarranted fear and misunderstanding of the ecological roles of bats, Americans spend millions of dollars annually to have pest control companies exterminate them. In Europe and the USSR, where there is greater recognition of their benefits, bats receive legal protection.

In fact, bats are of great ecological and economic importance to us. Bats disperse seeds and pollinate tropical trees and shrubs and thus are crucial to the survival of tropical rain forests. In Thailand, for example, a cave-dwelling, nectar-eating bat species is the only known pollinator of durian trees, whose fruit crops are worth $90 million per year.

Many people are unaware that bananas, guavas, mangoes, avocados, dates, figs, and many other tropical fruits are pollinated and seeded by nectar-eating and fruit-eating bats. Only fruit that is too ripe to harvest and worthless to farmers is consumed by fruit-eating bats. Removal of this ripe fruit by bats also eliminates food for the larvae of the Mediterranean fruit fly that can devastate commercial fruit crops.

The pollinating and seeding activities of bats also play an important role in the production of many other materials we get from tropical forests: prized timber used for furniture, kapok filler used for life preservers and surgical bandages, hemp fibers for rope, beads for jewelry, and hundreds of other commercially important materials.

Insectivorous bats are the only major predators of night-flying insects. They help control many insects that damage human crops. A single cave colony of insect-eating bats can devour 250,000 pounds or more of insects each night.

In parts of Asia families earn a living by periodically scraping bat droppings, or guano, from bat caves and selling it for fertilizer. Bats are also valuable to medicine and science. Research on bats has contributed to the development of birth control and artificial insemination methods, drug testing, studies of disease resistance and aging, production of vaccines, and development of navigational aids for the blind.

We need to see bats as valuable allies—not enemies—before we destroy them and lose their important benefits. The extinction of these keystone species can trigger a cascade of extinction of other species dependent on the ecological services they provide.

By 1988 the CITES treaty had been signed by 96 countries. It now lists 675 species that cannot be commercially traded as live specimens or wildlife products because they are endangered or threatened. Another 27,000 species can be traded commercially only under certain conditions and with special permits.

This treaty has reduced illegal traffic in some endangered wild species, especially crocodiles, turtles, and some large cat species whose skins are used for furs. But enforcement is spotty, and con-victed violators often pay only small fines. In 1979, for example, a Hong Kong fur dealer illegally imported 319 Ethiopian cheetah skins valued at $43,900. The dealer was caught, but was fined only $1,540.

Much of the $1-billion- to $2-billion-a-year illegal trade in wildlife and wildlife products goes on in countries, such as Singapore, that have not signed CITES. Some countries—Bolivia, for example—have signed the treaty but do little to enforce its provisions. Many Bolivian dealers use forged and stolen CITES permits to export wildlife smuggled into Bolivia from other countries.

Another problem is that countries can exclude certain species when they sign the treaty. For example, Japan exempted itself from the prohibition against taking the endangered hawsbill sea turtle to convert its shell into jewelry and figurines. Despite these drawbacks, CITES is considered one of the most successful international wildlife treaties because it is so vigorously enforced.

The Endangered Species Act of 1973 is one of the world's toughest environmental laws. This act makes it illegal for the United States to import or to carry on trade in any product made from an endangered species unless it is used for an approved scientific purpose or to enhance the survival of the species.

To make control more effective, all commercial shipments of wild-life and wildlife products must enter or leave the country through one of nine designated ports. But many illegal shipments of wildlife slip by. The 60 Fish and Wildlife Service inspectors are able to physically examine only about one-fourth of the 90,000 shipments that enter and leave the United States each year (Figure 14-13).

Permits have been falsified and some government inspectors have been bribed. Even if caught, many violators are not prosecuted, and convicted violators often pay only a small fine.

The law also provides protection for endangered and threatened species in the United States and abroad. It authorizes the

(continued)

Figure 14-13 Confiscated products derived from endangered species. Because of a lack of funds and too few inspectors, probably no more than one-tenth of the illegal wildlife trade in the United States is discovered. The situation is much worse in most other countries.

Steve Hildebrand/U.S. Fish and Wildlife Service

The Species Approach: Wildlife Refuges In 1903 President Theodore Roosevelt established the first U.S. federal wildlife refuge at Pelican Island on the east coast of Florida to protect the endangered brown pelican (Figure 2-11, p. 40). By 1988 the National Wildlife Refuge System had 437 refuges (Figure 13-10, p. 293). About 85% of the area included in these refuges is in Alaska.

Over three-fourths of the refuges are wetlands for protection of migratory waterfowl. Many other species are also protected in these refuges. Most of the species on the U.S. endangered list have habitats in the refuge system. Some refuges have been set aside for specific endangered species. These have helped the key deer, the brown pelican of southern Florida, and the trumpeter swan to recover. Conservationists complain that there has been too little emphasis on establishing refuges for endangered plants.

Congress has not established guidelines (such as multiple use or sustained yield) for management of the National Wildlife Refuge System, as it has for other public lands. As a result, the FWS has allowed many refuges to be used for hunting, fishing, trapping, timber cutting, grazing, farming, oil and gas development, mining, and recreational activities. The Reagan administration encouraged expansion of commercial activities in refuges to provide some of the money for their operation. By 1988 more than 60% of the refuges were open to hunting and almost 50% were open to fishing.

Development of oil, gas, and other resources can destroy or degrade wildlife habitats through road building, well and pipeline construction, oil and gas leaks, and pits filled with brine or drilling muds (see Pro/Con on p. 333).

Pollution is also a problem in a number of refuges. A 1986 study by the FWS estimated that one in five federal refuges is contaminated with toxic chemicals. Most of this pollution comes from old toxic-waste dump sites and runoff from nearby agricultural land. A 1983 FWS survey showed that 86% of the federal refuges had water quality problems and 67% had air quality and visibility problems.

Private groups also play an important role in conserving wildlife in refuges and other protected areas. For example, since 1951 the Nature Conservancy has been able to preserve over 1 million hectares (2.5 million acres) of forests, marshes, prairies, islands, and other areas of unique ecological or aesthetic significance in the United States. The preserved areas are either maintained by the Nature Conservancy and managed by volunteers or donated to government agencies, universities, or other conservation groups.

The Species Approach: Gene Banks, Botanical Gardens, and Zoos Botanists preserve genetic information and endangered plant species by storing their seeds in gene banks—refrigerated environments with low humidity. Gene banks of most known and many potential varieties of agricultural crops and other plants now exist throughout the world (Figure 12-5, p. 264). Scientists have urged that many more be established. Despite their importance, gene banks have drawbacks (see Spotlight on p. 272).

SPOTLIGHT **The Endangered Species Act (continued)**

National Marine Fisheries Service (NMFS) of the Department of Commerce to identify and list endangered and threatened marine species. The Fish and Wildlife Service (FWS) identifies and lists all other endangered and threatened species. These species cannot be hunted, killed, collected, or injured in the United States.

Any decision by either agency to add or remove a species from the list must be based only on biological grounds without economic considerations. The act also prohibits federal agencies from carrying out, funding, or authorizing projects that would jeopardize endangered or threatened species

or destroy or modify their critical habitats.

Once a species is listed as endangered or threatened in the United States, the FWS or the NMFS is supposed to prepare a plan to help it recover. However, because of a lack of funds, recovery plans have been developed and approved for only 45% of the endangered or threatened species native to the United States, and half of these plans exist only on paper. Only a handful of species have recovered sufficiently to be removed from protection.

Between 1978 and 1988 the annual federal budget for endangered species stayed around $25 million when adjusted for infla-

tion—about equal to the cost of 12 Army bulldozers. In 1988 Congress reauthorized the Endangered Species Act. New provisions authorize funding to more than double to $56 million in 1989 and rise to $66 million by 1992. It also includes stiffer penalties for violators and more protection for endangered plants.

Even at these increased funding levels, it will take the FWS 20 years to evaluate the species presently under consideration for listing. Many species will probably disappear before they can be protected. What do you think should be done?

The world's botanical gardens also help preserve some of the genetic diversity found in the wild. However, the gardens have too little storage capacity and too little money to maintain all of the world's threatened plants.

Zoos and animal research centers are increasingly being used to preserve a representative number of individuals of critically endangered animal species. Two techniques for preserving such species are egg pulling and captive breeding.

Egg pulling involves collecting eggs produced in the wild by the remaining breeding pairs of a critically endangered bird species and hatching them in zoos or research centers. Removing these eggs sometimes causes parents to nest again and lay more eggs, increasing the number of eggs that can be hatched in the wild and in captivity. In 1983 scientists began an egg-pulling program to help save the critically endangered California condor (Figure 14-12).

For captive breeding some or all of the individuals

Should There Be Oil and Gas Development in the Arctic National Wildlife Refuge?

The Arctic National Wildlife Refuge on Alaska's North Slope near the Canadian border is the second largest in the system (Figure 14-14), covering an area the size of South Carolina. It is home for a herd of over 180,000 caribou and many other species, including polar bears, grizzly bears, musk oxen, wolves, snow geese, golden eagles, and peregrine falcons.

Its coastal plain—the most biologically productive part of the refuge–is the only stretch of Alaska's Arctic coast that has not been opened to oil and gas development. That could change. Energy companies have asked Congress to open 607,000 hectares (1.5 million acres) of the coastal plain of the refuge to drilling for oil and natural gas. In 1987 the secretary of the interior joined forces with energy developers in this request. They argue that the area might contain oil and natural gas deposits that would reduce U.S. reliance on foreign oil.

Conservationists oppose this plan and want Congress to designate the entire coastal plain as wilderness. They point to Interior Department estimates that there is only a 19% chance of finding any economically recoverable large deposits of oil in this area. They do not believe that it's worth degrading a priceless and irreplaceable wildlife resource for the remote possibility of providing the United States with a six-month supply of oil. We could save twice as much oil in only two years merely by raising the average gas

mileage requirements for new cars from 27.5 mpg in 1989 to 30 mpg by 1991.

Officials of oil companies claim they have developed the Prudhoe Bay oil fields, just 60 miles west of the Arctic National Wildlife Refuge, without significant harm to wildlife. They argue that their 15 years of experience with this project should enable them to do an even better job of protecting wildlife in the Arctic Refuge. But the massive 1989 oil spill from the *Exxon Valdez* tanker in Alaska's Prince William Sound cast serious doubt on such promises (see Case Study in Chapter 20).

Also, according to a study leaked from the FWS in 1988, oil drilling at Alaska's Prudhoe Bay has caused much more air and

water pollution than was estimated before drilling began in 1972. The drilling activity also destroyed 4,450 hectares (11,000 acres) of vegetation used by wildlife—almost double the amount predicted. This has caused decreases in the populations of bears, wolves, other predators, and 100 bird species.

According to the FWS, oil development in the coastal plain could cause the loss of 20% to 40% of the area's caribou herd, 25% to 50% of the musk oxen still left, 50% or more of the wolverines, and 50% of the snow geese that winter in this area. Do you think that oil and gas development should be allowed in the Arctic National Wildlife Refuge?

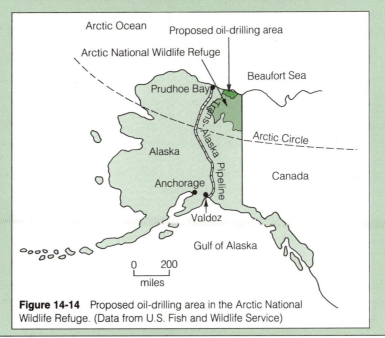

Figure 14-14 Proposed oil-drilling area in the Arctic National Wildlife Refuge. (Data from U.S. Fish and Wildlife Service)

of a critically endangered species still in the wild are captured and placed in zoos or research centers to breed in captivity. Scientists hope that after several decades of captive breeding and egg pulling, the captive population of an endangered species will be large enough that some individuals can be successfully reintroduced into protected wild habitats.

Captive breeding programs at zoos in Phoenix, San Diego, and Los Angeles saved the nearly extinct Arabian oryx (Figure 14-15). This large antelope species once lived throughout the Middle East. However, by the early 1970s it had disappeared from the wild after being hunted by people using jeeps, helicopters, rifles, and machine guns. Since 1980 small numbers of these animals bred in captivity have been returned to the wild in protected habitats in the Middle East.

Keeping populations of endangered animal species in zoos and research centers is limited by lack of space and money. The captive population of each species must number 100 to 500 to avoid extinction through accident, disease, or loss of genetic variability through inbreeding. Moreover, caring for and breeding captive animals is very expensive. For example, maintaining the 700 Siberian tigers now in the world's zoos costs almost $2.4 million a year. Because of a lack of space and money, the world's zoos now contain only 20 endangered species of animals with populations of 100 or more individuals. Probably no more than 900 species of endangered animals could be protected and bred in zoos and research centers. It is doubtful that the more than $6 billion needed to take care of these animals for 20 years will be available.

Limitations of the Species Approach The species approach has been successful in protecting and allowing populations of a number of species to increase, especially in the United States (Table 14-3).

Because of limited money and trained personnel, however, only a few of the world's endangered and threatened species can be saved by treaties, laws, wildlife refuges, and zoos. This means that wildlife experts must decide which species out of thousands of candidates should be saved. Many experts suggest that the limited funds for preserving threatened and endangered wildlife be concentrated on those species that **(1)** have the best chance for survival, **(2)** have the most ecological value to an ecosystem, and **(3)** are potentially useful for agriculture, medicine, or industry.

The Ecosystem Approach: Protecting Habitats Most wildlife biologists believe that the best way to prevent the loss of wild species is to establish and maintain a worldwide system of reserves, parks, and other protected areas. The system would consist of at least 10% of the world's land area. The goal would be to conserve and manage entire ecosystems instead of the

Figure 14-15 The Arabian oryx barely escaped extinction in 1969 after being overhunted in the deserts of the Middle East. Captive breeding programs in zoos in Arizona and California have been successful in saving this antelope species from extinction.

present species-centered approach to wildlife preservation.

This ecosystem approach would prevent many species from becoming endangered by human activities and reduce the need for human intervention to prevent extinction. It would also be cheaper than managing endangered species one by one. The reserves would be natural habitats for endangered species now in zoos and other artificial habitats. Reserves could also be used for wildlife research and education.

By 1988, there were more than 3,600 major protected areas throughout the world, totaling almost 4.4 million square kilometers (1.7 million square miles). This is an important beginning, but it represents only about 3.2% of the earth's land area and 7.2% of the land in the United States. Less than 5% of the world's remaining virgin forests are protected within parks and reserves. Furthermore, many of the world's ecosystem types have not been included in reserves, or reserve ecosystems are too small to protect their populations of wild species.

UNESCO, the IUCN, and the President's Council on Environmental Quality have proposed that the world's MDCs set up an international fund to help LDCs protect and manage biosphere reserves. The program would cost $100 million a year—about what the world spends on arms every 90 minutes. Establishing a global network of protected areas is an exciting challenge. If this can be done, it will be a major way to preserve some of the world's rapidly vanishing biodiversity.

In the United States, conservationists urge Congress to pass an Endangered Ecosystems and Biolog-

Table 14-3 Animal Wildlife Conservation Successes in the United States (data from U.S. Fish and Wildlife Service)

Species	Populations	
	1900	1988
Trumpeter swan	73	10,000
American bison	1,000	75,000
Sea otters	nearly extinct	100,000
Pronghorn antelope	13,000	1 million
Wild turkey	30,000	3.8 million
Rocky Mountain elk	41,000	1 million
White-tailed deer	500,000	15 million
Canada goose	1 million	2.3 million

ical Diversity Protection Act as an important step toward preserving the country's biodiversity. The 21% of the major terrestrial ecosystems not protected in federal lands and another 29% that are underrepresented would be added to the country's public land system as protected wilderness areas. Funds would also be provided for restoration of degraded ecosystems.

Such an act would also require environmental impact studies to assess the effects of any federal activity on biological diversity. It should also establish and support a National Center for Biological Diversity and Conservation Research. Financial support for carrying out the act would be provided from the federal Land and Water Conservation Fund, which is funded largely from receipts from offshore oil and gas leases.

World Conservation Strategy In 1980 the IUCN, the UN Environment Program, and the World Wildlife Fund developed the *World Conservation Strategy*, a long-range plan for conserving the world's biological resources. The goals of this plan:

- Maintain essential ecological processes and life-support systems on which human survival and economic activities depend.

- Preserve species diversity and genetic diversity.

- Ensure that any use of species and ecosystems is sustainable.

This strategy is not based on protecting large parts of the earth from use by humans. Instead, it is based on combining wildlife conservation with sustainable development (see Figure 13-25 on p. 311).

By 1988 forty countries had planned or established national conservation programs. In 1988 a new global conservation strategy, *World Conservation Strategy II*, was being developed for publication in 1990. Some proposals for this strategy:

- Include women and indigenous people in the development of conservation plans.

- Monitor the sustainability of development.

- Promote an ethic that includes protection of plants and animals as well as people.

- Encourage recognition of the harmful environmental effects of armed conflict and economic insecurity.

- Encourage rehabilitation of degraded ecosystems upon which humans depend for food and fiber.

If MDCs provide enough money and scientific assistance, this conservation strategy offers hope for preserving much of the world's vanishing biological and genetic diversity.

14-4 WILDLIFE MANAGEMENT

Management Approaches **Wildlife management** is the manipulation of wildlife populations (especially game species) and habitats for their welfare and for human benefit, the preservation of endangered and threatened wild species, the introduction of exotic wild species into ecosystems, and wildlife law enforcement. The first step in wildlife management is to decide which species or groups of species are to be managed in a particular area. Difficult choices must be made; in any wildlife management scheme; some wildlife species will benefit and others will be harmed.

Ecologists stress preservation of biological diversity. Wildlife conservationists are concerned about endangered species. Bird watchers want the greatest

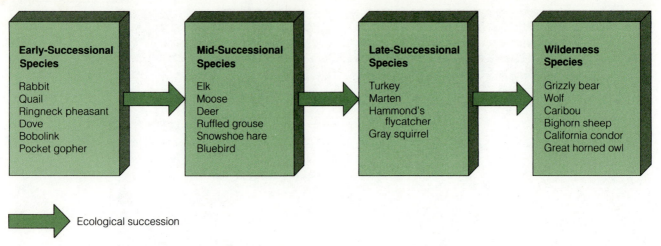

Early-Successional Species

Rabbit
Quail
Ringneck pheasant
Dove
Bobolink
Pocket gopher

Mid-Successional Species

Elk
Moose
Deer
Ruffled grouse
Snowshoe hare
Bluebird

Late-Successional Species

Turkey
Marten
Hammond's
 flycatcher
Gray squirrel

Wilderness Species

Grizzly bear
Wolf
Caribou
Bighorn sheep
California condor
Great horned owl

Ecological succession

Figure 14-16 Preferences of some wildlife species for habitats at different stages of ecological succession.

diversity of bird species. Hunters want large populations of game species for harvest each year during hunting season.

One management option is to protect a wilderness or other undisturbed area from most human activities. Another approach is to control population sizes and habitats to maintain a diversity of species in an area. A third option is to manipulate population sizes and habitats to favor a single species, usually a game species or an endangered species. In the United States most wildlife management is devoted to the production of harvestable surpluses of game animals and game birds.

After goals have been set, the wildlife manager must develop a management plan. Ideally, the plan should be based on principles of ecological succession (Section 6-3), wildlife population dynamics (Section 6-2), and an understanding of the cover, food, water, space, and other habitat requirements of each species to be managed. The manager must also consider the number of potential hunters, their success rates, and the regulations available to prevent excessive harvesting.

This ecological information is difficult, expensive, and time consuming to get. Often it is not available or reliable. That is why wildlife management is as much an art as a science. In practice it involves much guesswork and trial and error. Management plans must also be adapted to political pressures from conflicting groups and to lack of money.

Manipulation of Habitat Vegetation and Water Supplies Wildlife managers can encourage the growth of plant species that are the preferred food and cover for a particular animal species by controlling the ecological succession of vegetation in various areas (Figure 6-11, p. 145).

Animal wildlife species can be classified into four types according to the stage of ecological succession at which they are most likely to be found: wilderness, late-successional , midsuccessional, and early-successional (Figure 14-16). **Wilderness species** flourish only in fairly undisturbed, climax vegetational communities, such as large areas of old-growth forest, tundra, grasslands, and deserts. Their survival depends largely on the establishment of large wilderness areas and wildlife refuges.

Late-successional species need old-growth and mature forest habitats to produce the food and cover on which they depend. These animals require the establishment and protection of moderate-sized, old-growth forest refuges.

Midsuccessional species are found around abandoned croplands and partially open areas. Such areas are created by the logging of small stands of timber, controlled burning, and clearing of vegetation for roads, firebreaks, gas pipelines, and electrical transmission lines.

Such openings of the forest canopy promote the growth of vegetation favored as food by midsuccessional mammal and bird species. It also increases the amount of edge habitat, where two communities such as a forest and field come together. This transition zone allows animals such as deer to feed on vegetation in clearings and quickly escape to cover in the nearby forest.

Early-successional species find food and cover in weedy pioneer plants. These plants invade an area that has been cleared of vegetation for human activities and then abandoned.

Various types of habitat improvement can be used to attract and encourage the population growth of a desired species. Improvement techniques include artificial seeding, transplanting certain types of vegetation, and building artificial nests. Wildlife managers often create or improve ponds and lakes in wildlife refuges to provide water, food, and habitat for waterfowl and other wild animals.

Prescribed burning is widely used to encourage the growth of vegetation preferred by game species such as deer and elk. Prescribed burns are also carried out on grasslands to promote the growth of taller plants useful as habitat for nesting ducks, quails, prairie chickens, and other wild species.

Population Management by Controlled Sport Hunting Wildlife managers usually use controlled hunting to manipulate the number, gender distribution, and age distribution of populations of wild game species. Deer, rabbits, squirrels, quails, ducks, and several other game animals reproduce rapidly. Without effective control by natural predators or hunting by human predators, such species will exceed the carrying capacity of their habitat.

For example, a deer population can more than double every two years. As the number of deer exceeds the carrying capacity of their range, vegetation is destroyed and their habitat deteriorates. Without enough food many deer weaken and die of diseases or starvation during winter. People have eliminated most natural predators of deer, but carefully regulated hunting can keep the populations of game animals within the carrying capacity of the available habitat.

The United States and most MDCs use sport hunting laws to manage populations of game animals. These laws

- require hunters to have a license
- allow hunting only during certain months of the year to protect animals during mating season
- allow hunters to use only certain types of hunting equipment, such as bows and arrows, shotguns, and rifles
- set limits on the size, number, and sex of animals that can be killed and on the number of hunters allowed in a game refuge

But close control of sport hunting is often not possible. Accurate data on game populations may not exist and may cost too much to get. People in communities near hunting areas, who benefit from money spent by hunters, may push to have hunting quotas raised. On the other hand, some individuals and conservation groups are opposed to sport hunting and exert political pressure to have it banned or sharply curtailed (see Pro/Con below).

PRO/CON Sport Hunting Controversy

Sport hunters, hunting groups, and state game officials believe that Americans should be free to hunt as long as they obey state and local game regulations and don't damage wildlife resources. They argue that carefully regulated sport hunting by human predators is needed because we have eliminated most of the natural predators of deer and other large game animals. Without hunting, populations of game species will exceed the carrying capacity of their habitats and destroy vegetation they and other species need.

Sport hunting also provides recreational pleasure for millions of people (17 million in the United States) and stimulates local economies. Defenders of sport hunting also point out that sales of hunting licenses and taxes on firearms and ammunition have provided more than $1.6 billion since 1937. This money has been used to buy, restore, and maintain wildlife habitats and to support wildlife research in the United States.

Conservation groups such as the Sierra Club and Defenders of Wildlife consider hunting an acceptable management tool to keep numbers of game animals in line with the carrying capacity of their habitats. They see this as a way of preserving biological diversity by helping prevent depletion of other native species of plants and animals.

But some individuals and groups such as the Humane Society oppose sport hunting. They believe that it inflicts unnecessary pain and suffering on animals, few of which are killed to supply food needed for survival. In the 1970s statewide and nationwide surveys showed that about half of the American public opposed hunting.

The Humane Society also points out that sport hunting tends to reduce the genetic quality of remaining wildlife populations because hunters are most likely to kill the largest and strongest trophy animals. In contrast, natural predators tend to improve population quality by eliminating weak and sick individuals.

Hunting opponents also argue that game managers deliberately create a surplus of game animals by eliminating their natural predators such as wolves. Then, having created the surplus, game managers claim that the surplus must be harvested by hunters to prevent habitat degradation. Instead of eliminating natural predators, say opponents, wildlife managers should reintroduce them to eliminate the need for sport hunting.

But hunting supporters point out that populations of many game species such as deer are so large that predators such as the wolf cannot possibly control them. Also, because most wildlife habitats are fragmented, introduction of predators can lead to the loss of nearby farm animals. What do you think?

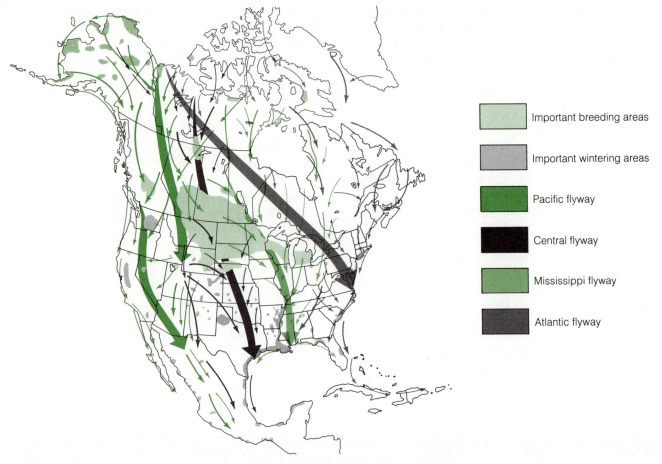

Figure 14-17 Major breeding and wintering areas and fall migration flyways used by migratory waterfowl in North America.

Legend:
- Important breeding areas
- Important wintering areas
- Pacific flyway
- Central flyway
- Mississippi flyway
- Atlantic flyway

Management of Migratory Waterfowl In North America, migratory waterfowl such as ducks, geese, and swans nest in Canada during the summer. During the fall hunting season they migrate to the United States and Central America along generally fixed routes called **flyways** (Figure 14-17).

Canada, the United States, and Mexico have signed agreements to prevent habitat destruction and overhunting of migratory waterfowl. However, since 1979 the estimated breeding populations of ducks in North America have been declining. The major reasons for this decrease are prolonged drought in key breeding areas and degradation and destruction of wetland and grassland breeding habitats by farmers.

So far there has been little destruction of waterfowl habitats in the far north of Canada, where much of the waterfowl breeding occurs. However, more than half of the original coastal and inland wetlands in the United States has been lost to farming and other development (see Spotlight on p. 128 and Enrichment Study on p. 129). About 90% of the wetlands once found along the Pacific flyway has been drained and converted to cropland and human settlements.

The remaining wetlands are used by dense flocks of ducks and geese. This crowding makes them more vulnerable to diseases and predators such as skunks, foxes, coyotes, minks, raccoons, and hunters. Waterfowl in wetlands near croplands (Figure 5-21, p. 127) are also exposed to pollution from pesticides and other chemicals in the irrigation runoff they drink. For example, toxic selenium leached from the soil by irrigation water in California's San Joaquin Valley has caused birth defects in young birds hatched in the nearby Kesterson National Wildlife Refuge.

Each year hunters in Canada and the United States kill about 20 million ducks (12 million in the United States). Another 20 million ducks die each year from disease, predation, and accidents. Hunting also causes lead poisoning of an estimated 2 million to 3 million ducks and geese, which die when they ingest the lead shotgun pellets that fall into the bodies of water where waterfowl feed. By 1992 the use of lead shot for waterfowl hunting in the United States will be banned. However, lead shot already deposited in wetlands will continue to kill waterfowl for decades.

Wildlife officials manage waterfowl by regulating hunting, protecting existing habitats, and developing new habitats. More than 75% of the federal wildlife refuges in the United States are wetlands used for migratory birds. Other waterfowl refuges have been

14-5 FISHERY MANAGEMENT

Freshwater Fishery Management The goals of freshwater fish management are to encourage the growth of populations of desirable commercial and sport fish species and to reduce or eliminate populations of less desirable species. Several techniques are used:

- regulating the timing and length of fishing seasons
- establishing the minimum-size fish that can be taken
- setting catch quotas
- requiring that commercial fishnets have a large enough mesh to ensure that young fish are not harvested
- building reservoirs and farm ponds and stocking them with gamefish
- fertilizing nutrient-poor lakes and ponds with commercial fertilizer, fish meal, and animal wastes
- protecting and creating spawning sites and cover spaces
- protecting habitats from buildup of sediment and other forms of pollution and removing debris
- preventing excessive growth of aquatic plants to prevent oxygen depletion
- using small dams to control water flow
- controlling predators, parasites, and diseases by habitat improvement, breeding genetically resistant fish varieties, and using antibiotics and disinfectants
- using hatcheries to restock ponds, lakes, and streams with species such as trout and salmon (Figure 14-18).

Figure 14-18 Trout hatcheries and farms, like this one in Moscow, Idaho, use aquacultural methods to raise trout for food or for release in local streams for anglers to catch.

established by local and state agencies and private conservation groups such as Ducks Unlimited, the Audubon Society, and the Nature Conservancy.

Building artificial nesting sites, ponds, and nesting islands is another method of establishing protected habitats for breeding populations of waterfowl. Solar-powered electric fences are being used to keep predators away from nesting waterfowl.

In 1986 the United States and Canada agreed on a plan to spend $1.5 billion over a 15-year period, with the goal of almost doubling the continental duck breeding population. The key elements in this program will be the purchase, improvement, and protection of an additional 2.3 million hectares (5.6 million acres) of waterfowl habitat in five priority areas.

Since 1934 the Migratory Bird Hunting and Conservation Stamp Act has required waterfowl hunters to buy a duck stamp each season they hunt. Revenue from these sales goes into a fund to buy land and easements for the benefit of waterfowl.

The Federal Farm Act of 1985 contains a provision designed to reduce the conversion of wetlands to cropland. Under this law's so-called swampbuster provision, farmers who convert wetlands to cropland that produces a cash crop lose federal farm benefits on all their land. But verifying and enforcing this provision is difficult.

Marine Fishery Management The history of the world's commercial marine fishing and whaling industry is an excellent example of the tragedy of the commons—the abuse and overuse of a potentially renewable resource (see Spotlight on p. 12). Users of the marine fisheries tend to maximize their catch for short-term economic gain, risking long-term economic collapse from overfishing (see Case Study on p. 341). As a result, many species of commercially valuable fish and whales in international and coastal waters have been overfished to the point of commercial extinction. At that point the stock of a species is so low that it's no longer profitable to hunt and gather the remaining individuals in a specific fishery.

Managers of marine fisheries can use several techniques to prevent commercial extinction and allow depleted stocks to recover. Without some form of governmental or international regulation, users have little

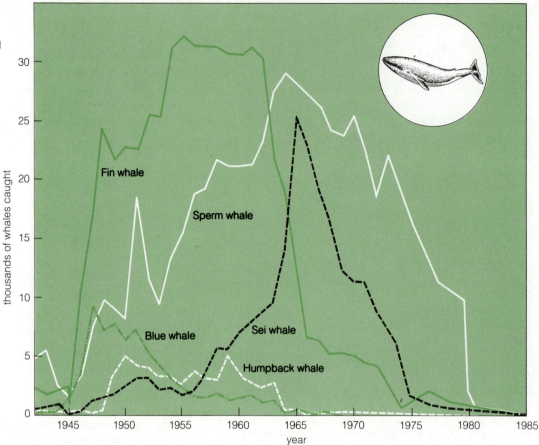

Figure 14-19 Whale harvests, showing the signs of overfishing. (Data from International Whaling Commission)

incentive to protect these common-property resources for future generations.

Fishery commissions, councils, and advisory bodies with representatives from countries using a fishery can be established. They can set annual quotas for harvesting fish and marine mammals and establish rules for dividing the allowable annual catch among the countries participating in the fishery.

These groups may also also limit fishing seasons and regulate the type of fishing gear that can be used to harvest a particular species. For example, the size of the mesh in fishing nets may have to be large enough to let smaller, younger individuals escape so that they can reach sexual maturity and reproduce. Fishing techniques such as dynamiting and poisoning are outlawed. Fishery commissions may also enact size limits that make it illegal to keep fish above or below a certain size, usually the average length of the particular fish species when it first reproduces.

As voluntary associations, however, fishery commissions don't have any legal authority to compel member states to follow their rules. Nor can they compel all countries fishing in a region to join the commission and submit to its rules.

International and national laws have been used to extend the offshore fishing zone of coastal countries to 370 kilometers (200 nautical miles or 230 statute miles) from their shores. Foreign fishing vessels can take cer-

tain quotas of fish within such zones—called exclusive economic zones—only with government permission.

Ocean areas beyond the legal jurisdiction of any country are known as the high seas. Any limits on the use of the living and mineral common-property resources in these areas are set by international maritime law and international treaties.

Food and game fish species, such as the striped bass along the Pacific and Atlantic coasts of the United States, can be introduced. Artificial reefs can be built from boulders, construction debris, and automobile tires to provide food and cover for commercial and game fish species. About 400 such reefs have been established off U.S. coasts, and Japan has set aside $1 billion to create 2,500 of them.

Decline of the Whaling Industry Whales are mammals ranging in size from the 0.9-meter (3-foot) porpoise to the giant, 15- to 30-meter (50- to 100-foot) blue whale. They can be divided into two major groups, toothed whales and baleen whales. Toothed whales, such as the porpoise, sperm whale, and killer whale, bite and chew their food. They feed mostly on squid, octopus, and other marine animals.

Baleen whales, such as the blue, gray, humpback, and finback, are filter feeders. Instead of teeth, several hundred horny plates made of baleen, or whalebone, extend downward from their upper jaw. These plates filter small plankton organisms, especially shrimplike krill about the size of your thumb, from seawater. Baleen whales are the most abundant group of whale species.

The pattern of the whaling industry has been to hunt the most commercially valuable species until it becomes too scarce to be of commercial value and then turn to another species. In 1900 an estimated 4.4 million whales swam the ocean. Today only about 1 million are left. Overharvesting has caused a sharp drop in the populations of almost every whale species of commercial value (Figure 14-19). The populations of 8 of the 11 major species of whales once hunted by the whaling industry have been reduced to commercial extinction. This devastation has happened because of the tragedy of the commons and because whales are more vulnerable to biological extinction than are fish species (see Case Study below).

In 1946 the International Whaling Commission (IWC) was established to regulate the whaling industry. Since 1949 the IWC has set annual quotas to prevent overfishing and commercial extinction. However, these quotas often were based on inadequate scientific information or were ignored by whaling countries. Without any powers of enforcement, the IWC has been unable to stop the decline of most whale species.

The discovery in the 1960s that the blue whale was in danger of extinction led to an international "Save the Whales" movement. In the late 1960s conservationist and other groups began pressuring the IWC to

ban all commercial whaling. Greenpeace, the largest international environmentalist group, and the Sea Shepherd Society have used bold, commandolike tactics to embarrass whaling countries, stop pirate whalers who ignore the quotas, and gain worldwide publicity and support for whale protection.

In 1970 the United States stopped all commercial whaling and banned all imports of whale products into the country. Since then conservation groups and the governments of many countries, including the United States, have called for a ban on all commercial whaling. Annual whale quotas have been reduced sharply, but most cutbacks came only after a species had already been hunted to commercial extinction.

In 1982, after 10 years of meetings and delays, the IWC established a five-year halt on commercial whaling, between 1986 and 1992. However, the Soviet Union and Norway did not agree to end commercial hunting of whales until 1987. Japan, the world's largest whaling nation, refused to honor the ban until 1988. It only agreed to this under harsh criticism and a threat by the United States to limit fishing in U.S. waters.

Japan announced, however, that it will take 875 whales each year for "scientific" purposes. Norway and Iceland announced similar plans. Then they sold most of the meat from whales they had captured for "research" to Japan. Roger Payne and Sidney Holt, two of the world's most prominent marine mammal scientists, view these actions as a thinly disguised continuation of commercial whaling. In 1988 the IWC rejected requests from Japan, Iceland, and Norway for permits to harvest whales for scientific purposes. But

---

CASE STUDY Near Extinction of the Blue Whale

The blue whale is the world's largest animal. Fully grown, it's more than 30 meters (100 feet) long and weighs 136 metric tons (150 tons). The heart of an adult is as big as a Volkswagen "bug" and pumps 7.3 metric tons (8 tons) of blood. Some of its arteries are big enough for a child to swim through. Its brain weighs four times more than yours. The blue whale shows signs of great intelligence.

Blue whales spend about eight months of the year in Antarctic waters. There they find an abundant supply of shrimplike krill, which they filter from seawater. During the winter months they migrate to warmer waters, where their young are born.

Once an estimated 200,000 blue whales roamed the Antarctic waters. Today the species has been hunted to near biological extinction for its oil, meat, and bone. The annual catch of blue whales reached a peak of almost 30,000 in 1930. After that the annual catch dropped sharply and fell nearly to zero by 1964. Less than 1,000 blue whales may be left today.

This decline was caused by a combination of prolonged overfishing and certain natural traits of the blue whale. Their huge size made them easy to spot. They were caught in large numbers because they grouped together in their Antarctic feeding grounds. Also, they take 25 years to mature

sexually and have only one offspring every 2 to 5 years. This low reproduction rate makes it hard for the species to recover once its population has been reduced to a low level.

Blue whales haven't been hunted commercially since 1964 and are classified as an endangered species. Despite this protection, some marine experts believe that not enough blue whales are left for the species to recover. If so, each year there will be fewer blue whales until they disappear forever.

all three countries defied the ruling and harvested about 600 whales for "scientific" purposes.

In 1987 the United States opposed scientific whaling. This policy changed in 1988, when the United States supported limited scientific whaling by Iceland because the U.S. wanted building permits for the air base at Keflavik, Iceland. This weakening of the U.S. antiwhaling stance was a key factor leading Japan, Iceland, and Norway to defy the IWC and continue "scientific" whaling in 1988 and 1989.

It appears that commercial whaling will stop for a few years, although some whales are still being taken illegally for "research" purposes. But large-scale commercial whaling may resume when the present moratorium ends.

Individual Action We are all involved, at least indirectly, in the destruction of wildlife any time we buy or drive a car, build a house, consume almost anything, and waste electricity, paper, water, or any other resource. All these activities contribute to the destruction or degradation of wildlife habitats or to the killing of one or more individuals of some plant or animal species. Modifying our consumption habits is a key goal in protecting wildlife, the environment, and ourselves. This also involves supporting efforts to reduce global warming and ozone depletion—two of the greatest threats to the earth's wildlife and the human species (Section 19-4).

To help protect and heal the earth, we can try to improve the habitat on a patch of the earth in our immediate environment. We can improve our backyards, abandoned city lots, campus areas, and streams clogged with debris. We can develop a wildlife protection and management plan for any land that we own.

We can also support politicians and groups that fight for wildlife conservation (Appendix 1). One goal should be to pressure Congress to pass a national biological diversity act and another goal should be to encourage the development of an international treaty to preserve biological diversity at the ecosystem, species, and gene levels. The United States should also develop a national conservation program as part of the World Conservation Strategy.

It is the responsibility of all who are alive today to accept the trusteeship of wildlife and to hand on to posterity, as a source of wonder and interest, knowledge, and enjoyment, the entire wealth of diverse animals and plants. This generation has no right by selfishness, wanton or intentional destruction, or neglect, to rob future generations of this rich heritage. Extermination of other creatures is a disgrace to humankind.

World Wildlife Charter

CHAPTER SUMMARY

Wildlife resources provide people with a variety of economic benefits as sources of food, fuel, paper, fibers, leathers, medicines, natural insecticides, and biological control of various weeds and insect pests. Many wild species are also sources of beauty and recreational pleasure. Their most important contribution, however, is their role in maintaining the health and integrity of the world's ecosystems.

Most people believe that wildlife should be protected only because of their actual or potential uses for people—known as the *anthropocentric (human-centered)* worldview. Some people hold the *biocentric (life-centered)* belief that it is wrong for humans to hasten the extinction of any species because humans are no more important than any other species on earth. Others hold the *ecocentric (ecosystem-centered)* belief that something is right when it tends to maintain the earth's life-support systems for us and other species and wrong when it tends otherwise.

At least 94% of the half a billion or so different species estimated to have lived on earth have become extinct or have evolved into new species. Mass extinctions in the distant past resulted from unknown natural causes. However, since agriculture began about 10,000 years ago, the rate of species extinction increased a millionfold as a result of human activities and is expected to rise sharply in coming decades. Species that may soon become extinct are classified as *endangered species* and those likely to become endangered are classified as *threatened species*.

The major human-related factors that can lead to a species becoming threatened, endangered, or extinct are **(1)** habitat elimination and disturbance, **(2)** commercial hunting, **(3)** pest and predator control for protection of livestock, crops, and game, **(4)** collecting specimens as pets, decorative plants, for medical research, and for zoos, **(5)** pollution, **(6)** accidental or deliberate introduction of a competing or predatory alien species into an ecosystem, and **(7)** population growth, affluence, and poverty.

Some species have natural characteristics that make them more susceptible to extinction by human activities and natural disasters than other species. Examples include low reproductive rates, large size, limited or specialized nesting or breeding areas, specialized feeding habits, fixed migratory patterns, and certain behavioral patterns.

Three main strategies are used to protect endangered and threatened wild species and to prevent other wild species from becoming endangered: **(1)** establishing treaties, passing laws, and setting aside refuges; **(2)** using gene banks, zoos, research centers, botanical gardens, and aquariums to preserve a small number of individuals of wild species; and **(3)** preserving and protecting a variety of unique and representative ecosystems throughout the world.

Wildlife management involves manipulating populations of wild species and their habitats for human benefit, the welfare of other species, and the preservation of endangered and threatened species. Three approaches are used to meet these often conflicting goals: **(1)** protect relatively undisturbed areas from harmful human activities, **(2)** manipulate the population size, habitat vegetation, and water supplies to maintain a diversity of species in an area, or **(3)** manipulate population size, habitat vegetation, and water supply of an area to favor a single species.

In the United States and most MDCs, populations of game animals are managed by laws that govern how and when certain species can be hunted for sport. Migratory waterfowl can be managed by **(1)** protecting existing grassland and wetland habitats in their summer and winter homes and along the flyways they use during migration, (2) developing new habitats, and (3) regulating hunting.

Laws and regulations are also used to manage populations of desirable commercial and sport freshwater and marine fish species. However, many commercially important species of marine fish and whales have been exploited for short-term economic gain to the point where they are so rare that it no longer pays to hunt them (*commercial extinction*).

DISCUSSION TOPICS

1. Discuss your gut-level reaction to this statement: "It doesn't really matter that the passenger pigeon is extinct and the blue whale, whooping crane, bald eagle, grizzly bear, and a number of other plant and animal species are endangered mostly because of human activities." Be honest about your reaction, and give arguments for your position.

2. Make a log of your own consumption and use of food and other products for a single day. Relate your consumption to the increased destruction of wildlife and wildlife habitats in the United States and in tropical forests.

3. Do you accept the ethical position that each species has the inherent right to survive without human interference, regardless of whether it serves any useful purpose for humans? Explain.

4. Do you believe that the species listed below have an inherent right to exist? Explain.
   a. Anopheles mosquitoes, which transmit malaria
   b. tigers that roam the jungle along the border between India and Nepal and have killed at least 105 persons between 1978 and 1983

   c. bacteria that cause smallpox or other infectious diseases
   d. rats, which compete with humans for food
   e. rattlesnakes, which sometimes kill people

5. Do you believe that each individual of an animal cies has an inherent right to survive? Explain. Wo you extend such rights to individual plants and m organisms? Explain.

6. Use Table 14-2 to predict a species that may soon endangered. What, if anything, is being done for species? What pressures is it being subjected to? work up a plan for protecting it.

7. Since 1981 funds available to federal agencies cha with protecting and managing wildlife on publicl owned lands have been sharply decreased. Do yc agree or disagree with this action? Explain. If you believe that funding for these programs should b sharply increased, then what federal expenditures would you cut in order to provide more money for wildlife protection and management?

8. Make a survey of your campus and local community to identify examples of habitat destruction or degradation that have had harmful effects on the populations of various wild plant and animal species. Develop a management plan for the rehabilitation of these habitats and wildlife.

9. Are you for or against sport hunting? Explain.

10. Should sport hunting be allowed on federal wildlife refuges? Explain.

11. Why have the populations of most whale species been severely depleted? What natural biological factors make the blue whale so vulnerable to commercial and biological extinction?

CHAPTER 15

Nonrenewable Mineral Resources and Solid Waste

General Questions and Issues

1. How are minerals formed and distributed?
2. How are mineral deposits found and extracted from the earth's crust?
3. What harmful environmental impacts occur from mining, processing, and using minerals?
4. How long will affordable supplies of key minerals last for the world and the United States?
5. How can we increase the supplies of key minerals?

6. How can we make supplies of key minerals last longer by reducing the production of solid waste?

Mineral resources are the building blocks on which modern society depends. Knowledge of their physical nature and origins and the web they weave between all aspects of human society and the physical earth can lay the foundations for a sustainable society.

Ann Dorr

W hat do cars, spoons, glasses, dishes, beverage cans, coins, electrical wiring, bricks, and sidewalks have in common? Few of us stop to think that these products and many others we use every day are made from nonrenewable minerals we have learned to extract from the earth's solid crust—the upper layer of the lithosphere (Figure 4-1, p. 77).

A **mineral** is a nonmetallic or metallic solid that occurs naturally in the earth's crust. Examples of nonmetallic minerals are salt, clay, silicates (to make glass), and sand, gravel, limestone, and gypsum (to make concrete). Iron, aluminum, copper, and gold are some of the important metallic minerals. An **ore** is a mineral deposit containing enough of a metallic element to permit it to be extracted and sold at a profit.

The more than 100 nonfuel minerals we extract from the earth's crust are worth billions. At least 75% of these minerals are used by 33 MDCs with only 23% of the world's population. The other 25% are used by 142 LDCs with 77% of the world's people.

If LDCs are to become MDCs, the supplies of nonfuel minerals vital to industry and modern lifestyles will have to increase dramatically and we will have to greatly increase the recycling and reuse of these nonrenewable resources. We will also have to reduce the environmental impact from mining, processing, and using more of these resources.

15-1 ORIGIN AND DISTRIBUTION OF MINERAL RESOURCES

The Rock Cycle A **rock** is a naturally occurring solid that contains one or more minerals. The largest and slowest of the earth's cyclical processes is the **rock cycle** (Figure 15-1). In this cycle three major types of rocks—igneous, sedimentary, and metamorphic (Figure 15-2)—in the earth's crust and mantle are formed and modified by geologic processes over millions of years.

Igneous rocks, such as granite and basalt, are formed when magma (molten rock) wells up from the earth's upper mantle, cools, and solidifies below the earth's surface or on the surface (cooled lava spewed from volcanoes or fractures in the earth's crust). They are the most abundant type of rock and are the major source of the nonfuel minerals we use.

Exposed mounds and mountains of igneous rock are gradually broken into smaller pieces by water, wind, ice, plant roots, and acid secretions from lichens and mosses that grow on rocks. The resulting sediments are transported by wind, water, gravity, and ice to basins at lower elevations. Gradually accumulated sediments are compacted to form **sedimentary rocks,** such as sandstone from compacted sand.

Over millions of years deposits of sedimentary and

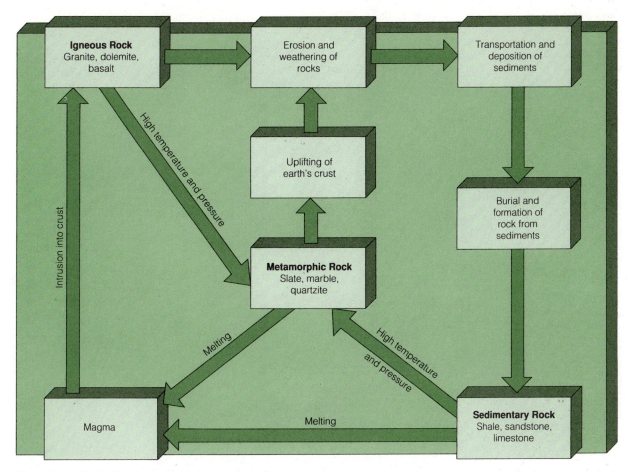

Figure 15-1 The rock cycle.

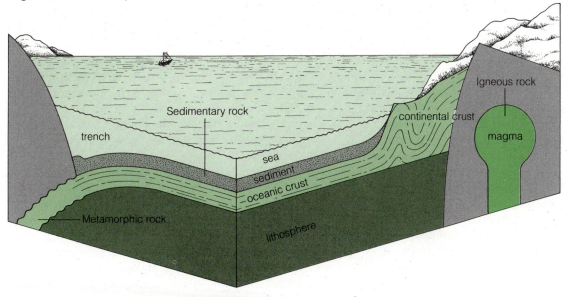

Figure 15-2 Major rock types.

igneous rocks are buried deeper and deeper in the earth's crust, where intense heat and great pressures change them into **metamorphic rocks,** such as shale. Some metamorphic rocks then melt or are uplifted to the earth's surface to start the rock cycle again (Figure 15-1).

Mineral Abundance and Formation We know how to find and mine more than 100 minerals. We convert these nonrenewable minerals into many everyday items we use and then discard, reuse, or recycle (Figure 15-3). A few minerals, such as gold and silver, occur as free elements. But most minerals are compounds of

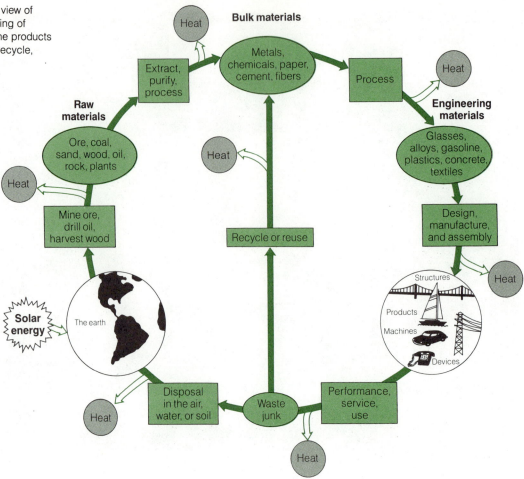

Figure 15-3 Generalized view of the extraction and processing of raw materials to produce the products we use and then discard, recycle, or reuse.

only ten elements that make up 99.3% of the earth's crust (Figure 15-4).

Plate tectonics, poorly understood movements of parts of the earth's crust downward, upward, and across one another, is important in the formation of some mineral deposits (Figure 15-5). Plate tectonics theory also explains how the continents have drifted together and apart over hundreds of millions of years.

Some of the richest deposits of metallic ores, called *hydrothermal deposits*, are formed at the boundaries where tectonic plates separate or come together. Where tectonic plates separate along the ocean floor, molten igneous rock (magma) contacts cold ocean water. This hot, mineral-laden water rises through fractured rocks and spews out of *hydrothermal vents* on the ocean floor along a ridge where the plates separate. When the water cools, metal sulfides are deposited around the vents.

Where tectonic plates come together, igneous rocks saturated with seawater are forced together. The resulting high temperatures and pressures melt the rocks in the mantle to form magma, which may force its way upward into the crust and cool, allowing minerals to crystallize out.

Mineral deposits also form where plate movements allow magma to penetrate the earth's surface and form volcanos. As the molten igneous rock inside the volcano cools, minerals with high densities crystallize first and sink to the bottom. Less dense minerals crystallize later and are found near the top of the rock deposit.

Sedimentary processes also concentrate minerals in deposits. The processes that weather and erode igneous rocks and deposit them as sediments can remove unwanted materials and leave behind deposits of useful minerals.

Weathering and erosion also deposit materials in ocean and stream beds at lower elevations. Sand and gravel, for example, are sedimentary deposits of fine-grained rock. Mineral deposits called *placers* are formed when flowing water separates heavier mineral particles (such as gold) from sediment and drops them on stream beds with little water flow and turbulence.

Some mineral deposits are formed when minerals dissolve in water and then crystallize out as the water evaporates. For example, above-ground salt deposits form when the sun evaporates water from shallow pools of saltwater.

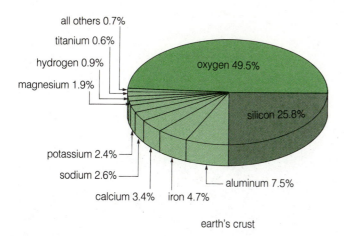

all others 0.7%
titanium 0.6%
hydrogen 0.9%
magnesium 1.9%
oxygen 49.5%
silicon 25.8%
potassium 2.4%
sodium 2.6%
aluminum 7.5%
calcium 3.4%
iron 4.7%
earth's crust

Figure 15-4 Percentage by weight of elements in the earth's crust.

Figure 15-5 Plate tectonics. The earth's crust is divided into rigid plates which move in relation to each other because of movements in the underlying mantle.

15-2 LOCATING AND EXTRACTING MINERAL RESOURCES

Making Mineral Resources Available Several steps are involved in making a mineral resource available:

- A deposit with enough mineral to make removing it profitable must be found.
- Mining extracts the mineral from the deposit.
- Processing removes impurities (gangue).
- In some cases (especially metallic ores) the purified mineral is converted to a different chemical form by smelting or other chemical processes. Usually these processes free a metallic element from the oxygen, sulfur, or other elements with which it is combined in an ore. For example, aluminum is found in ore form as aluminum oxide (Al_2O_3). After the ore is purified and melted, electrical current is passed through the molten oxide to convert it to aluminum metal (Al) and oxygen gas (O_2). Copper and zinc often are found combined with sulfur, which is removed in smelters by heat or chemical reactions. Scientists are also experimenting with using natural and bioengineered microorganisms to separate metals from other elements in ores.

Finding and Mining Mineral Deposits Deposits of useful minerals are difficult and expensive to find. Mining companies use several methods to find promising deposits. Geological information about crustal movements and mineral formation helps mining companies find areas for closer study. Photos taken from airplanes or images relayed by satellites sometimes reveal geological features such as mounds or rock formations often associated with deposits of certain minerals. Other instruments on aircraft and satellites can detect deposits by effects on the earth's magnetic or gravitational fields.

Mineral deposits near the earth's surface are removed by **surface mining.** Mechanized equipment strips away the overlying layer of soil and rock—known as **overburden**—and vegetation. Surface mining is used to extract about 90% of the minerals in the United States.

The type of surface mining used depends on the type of mineral and the local topography. In **open-pit surface mining,** machines dig holes and remove the deposits, primarily stone, sand, gravel, iron, and copper. Sand and gravel are removed from thousands of small pits in many parts of the country. Building rocks such as limestone, granite, and marble are taken from larger pits called quarries. After the stone is removed, these sites often fill with water. Iron and copper are usually removed from huge open-pit mines (Figure 15-6).

Strip mining is surface mining in which bulldozers, power shovels, or stripping wheels remove large chunks of the earth's surface in strips. It is used mostly for mining phosphate rock, especially in Florida, North Carolina, and Idaho, and for extracting about two-thirds of the coal mined in the United States, as discussed in Section 16-3. Another form of surface mining is **dredging,** in which chain buckets and draglines scrape up surface deposits covered with water. It removes sand from streambeds and gravel from placer deposits in streams.

Some mineral deposits lie so deep that surface mining is too expensive. These deep beds or veins are removed by **subsurface mining.** For some metallic ores, miners dig a deep vertical shaft, blast tunnels and rooms, and haul the ore to the surface.

Certain soluble minerals such as salt are removed from underground deposits by *solution subsurface min-*

Figure 15-6 This open pit copper mine in Bingham, Utah, is the largest human-made hole in the world. It is 4.0 kilometers (2.5 miles) in diameter and 0.8 kilometer (0.5 mile) deep. This mine produces 227,000 metric tons (250,000 tons) of copper a year along with fairly large amounts of gold, silver, and molybdenum.

ing. A well is drilled into the deposit, water is pumped into the well to dissolve the mineral, and the solution is brought back to the surface through another well. Groundwater contamination is often a problem with this type of subsurface mining.

15-3 ENVIRONMENTAL IMPACT OF MINING, PROCESSING, AND USING MINERAL RESOURCES

Overall Environmental Impact and Economics   The mining, processing, and use of any nonfuel mineral resource or a fuel mineral such as coal (Section 16-3) cause land disturbance, erosion, air pollution, and water pollution (Figure 15-7). The degree to which these harmful effects are reduced depends mostly on whether their costs are included in the initial prices we pay for items.

To keep their costs and product prices low, mining companies and manufacturers prefer to pass pollution and other social costs of resource extraction and

processing and product manufacture on to the general public. We end up paying all of these so-called *external costs* in the form of poorer health, higher medical and health insurance bills, and higher taxes for pollution control, land restoration, and health care. Most of these costs are not included in the market prices we pay for items, which gives us no way to relate our consumption habits to unnecessary resource waste, pollution, and environmental degradation.

Mining companies and manufacturers also have little incentive to find ways to reduce resource waste and pollution as long as they can pass many of the harmful environmental costs of their production on to society. Changing this situation is a major way to reduce pollution, environmental degradation, and resource waste, as discussed more fully in Section 22-3.

Mining Impacts   Mining involves removing material from the surface or subsurface of the earth and dumping unwanted rock and other waste materials, called **spoils,** somewhere else—usually near the mining site. The harmful environmental effects of such land disturbance depend on the type of mineral mined, the

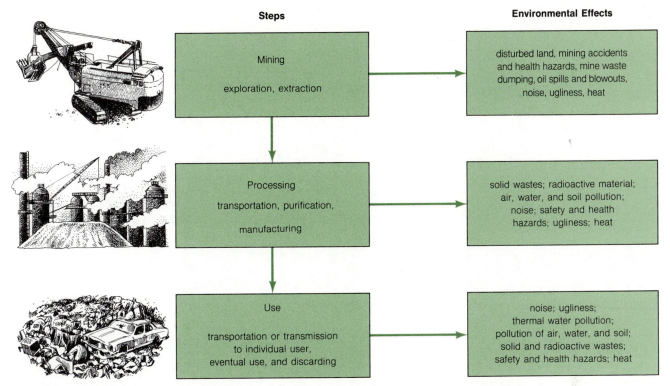

Steps	Environmental Effects
Mining exploration, extraction	disturbed land, mining accidents and health hazards, mine waste dumping, oil spills and blowouts, noise, ugliness, heat
Processing transportation, purification, manufacturing	solid wastes; radioactive material; air, water, and soil pollution; noise; safety and health hazards; ugliness; heat
Use transportation or transmission to individual user, eventual use, and discarding	noise; ugliness; thermal water pollution; pollution of air, water, and soil; solid and radioactive wastes; safety and health hazards; heat

Figure 15-7 Some harmful environmental effects of resource extraction, processing, and use. The energy used to carry out each step causes further pollution and environmental degradation. Most of the harm is caused by not having mining, processing, and manufacturing companies pay the full costs of the pollution and environmental degradation they cause. Instead, many of these "external" costs are passed on to society in the form of poorer health, increased health and insurance costs, and increased taxes to deal with pollution and environmental degradation. Requiring these external costs to be internalized and included in the market cost of raw materials and manufactured goods would eliminate most of these harmful effects or reduce them to acceptable levels.

deposit size, the method used, and the local topography and climate.

Mining uses only a small amount of the earth's surface. For example, between 1930 and 1988, only 0.3% of the total land area of the United States was used for extraction and processing of nonfuel mineral resources and fuel resources (mostly coal). About 70% of this land was excavated, while the rest was used for disposal of waste from mining and mineral processing.

However, mining has a severe local (and sometimes regional) environmental impact on the land, air, and water. Bare land created when vegetation and topsoil are removed by surface mining and the waste piles created by surface and subsurface mining are eroded by wind and water; harmful materials run off into nearby rivers and streams and some toxic compounds in mining spoils percolate into groundwater (Figure 15-8). The air can be contaminated with dust and toxic substances.

Surface mining disrupts the landscape more than subsurface mining. One way to reduce the severe environmental impact of surface mining is to pass and strictly enforce laws that require mining companies to

restore land after minerals have been removed. Restoration costs range from $2,470 to $12,350 per hectare ($1,000 to $5,000 an acre). In the United States only about one-third of all mined land (including coal mining) has been restored.

The success of restoration efforts depends on average precipitation, slope of the land, the existence of surface-mining regulations, and how well they are enforced. Restoration is simpler and more effective in areas with more than 25 centimeters (10 inches) of rainfall a year and with flat or slightly rolling terrain.

For each unit of mineral produced, subsurface mining disturbs less than one-tenth as much land as surface mining. Usually subsurface mining also produces less waste material.

But subsurface mining is more dangerous and expensive than surface mining. Roofs and walls of underground mines collapse, trapping and killing miners. Explosions of dust and natural gas kill and injure them. Prolonged inhalation of mining dust causes lung diseases. Underground fires sometimes cannot be put out. Land above underground mines caves in or subsides: roads buckle, houses crack, railroad tracks

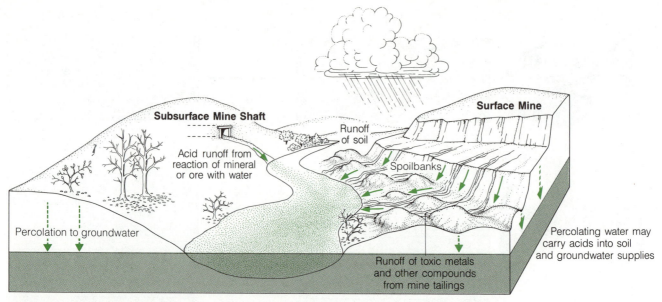

Figure 15-8 Degradation and pollution of a stream and groundwater by runoff of acids—called *acid mine drainage*—and toxic chemicals from surface and subsurface mining operations.

bend, sewer lines crack, gas mains break, and groundwater systems disrupt. Blasting damages property.

Another environmental problem of mining, especially subsurface mining, is *acid mine drainage* when aerobic bacteria convert sulfide compounds in minerals in mine wastes left in mines to sulfuric acid. Rainwater seeping through the mine or mine wastes transfers the acid to nearby rivers and streams (Figure 15-8), destroying aquatic life and contaminating water supplies. Other harmful materials running off or leached from underground mines or above ground mining wastes are iron oxides (called yellow boy), radioactive uranium compounds, and compounds of toxic metals such as lead, arsenic, or cadmium.

Large-scale mining operations also have social impacts. When mining begins, many workers and their families move into the area and add to the local economy. But existing schools, water supplies, rental housing, and sewage and solid waste disposal are often unable to meet the needs of the rapid increase in people.

Communities may adjust to the increased growth. But a mine-dependent local economy can have cycles of booms and bust because of fluctuating mineral prices and demand. Eventually the mines are depleted and shut down. Then communities that depended on them for most of their income become ghost towns.

Processing Impacts Some ores contain no more than a few tenths of a percent of the desired metal, and few contain more than 30%. Processing extracted mineral deposits to remove impurities produces huge quantities of rock and other waste materials. That is why most processing takes place near mine sites.

The waste materials, called **tailings,** usually are piled on the ground or dumped into ponds near mining and processing sites. Unless covered and stabilized, tailings can contaminate the water and air. Wind blows particles of dust, toxic metals, and radioactive substances (from uranium mines) from tailings into the atmosphere, and water leaches toxic and radioactive substances into nearby surface water or groundwater (Figure 15-8).

As lower-grade ores are mined and processed, the quantity of tailings rises sharply. Laws have forced mining companies to reduce contamination from tailings in the United States, but enforcement is weak. In many countries, especially LDCs, such laws don't exist.

Without effective pollution control equipment, mineral-smelting plants emit massive quantities of air pollutants that damage vegetation and soils in the surrounding area. Pollutants include sulfur dioxide, soot, and tiny particles of arsenic, cadmium, lead, and other toxic elements and compounds found as impurities in many ores. Decades of uncontrolled sulfur dioxide emissions from copper-smelting operations near Copperhill and Ducktown, Tennessee, killed all vegetation for miles around (see Case Study on p. 351).

Smelting plants also cause water pollution and produce liquid and solid hazardous wastes, which must be disposed of safely or converted into less harmful substances. Workers in some smelting industries have an increased risk of cancer.

Solid Waste The United States is the world's trashiest country. It leads the world by far in total and per capita production of nonhazardous and hazardous solid, liquid, and gaseous waste. Currently the U.S. produces at least 10 billion metric tons (11 billion tons), an average of 40 metric tons (44 tons) per American, of nonhazardous **solid waste**—any unwanted or discarded material that is not a liquid or a gas.

About 98.5% of this nonhazardous solid waste comes from mining, oil and natural gas production, and industrial activities. Most mining waste is left piled near mine sites and pollutes the air, surface water, and groundwater. Most industrial solid waste such as scrap metal, plastics, paper, fly ash from electrical power plants, and sludge from industrial waste treatment plants is disposed of at the plant site where it is produced.

Municipal solid waste from homes and businesses in or near urban areas makes up the remaining 1.5% of the nonhazardous solid waste produced in the United States. Between 1960 and 1988, the amount of municipal solid waste in the U.S. increased by 89%. The 204 metric tons (227 million tons) produced in 1988—about 0.9 metric tons (1 ton) per American—would fill a bumper-to-bumper convoy of garbage trucks that would encircle the earth almost eight times.

The average amount of municipal solid waste thrown away per person in the United States is two to five times that in most other MDCs. Only Australia, Canada, and New Zealand come close to U.S. per capita levels. Unless massive waste reduction and recycling programs are put into operation, the EPA projects that the average American's daily output of garbage will almost double between 1988 and the year 2000.

Roughly 56% of the total weight the typical American throws away as garbage and rubbish is paper, paperboard, and yard waste from potentially renewable resources (Figure 15-10). Most of the rest is products made from glass, plastic, aluminum, iron, steel, tin, and other nonrenewable mineral resources. Only about 10% of these potentially usable resources are recycled. The rest is hauled away and dumped or burned at a cost of almost $5 billion a year. Each year these wasted solids have enough aluminum to rebuild the country's entire commercial air fleet every three months, enough iron and steel to continuously supply the nation's automakers, and enough wood and paper to heat 5 million homes for 200 years.

Another source of solid waste is the litter that people throw down almost anywhere. When a climbing team reached the peak of Alaska's Mount McKinley,

---

CASE STUDY The Deaths of Ducktown and Copperhill, Tennessee

Between 1855 and 1907 a large copper smelter operated near the towns of Ducktown and Copperhill, Tennessee. Sulfur dioxide and other fumes from the smelter killed the forest once growing on this land, leaving a desert of dry, red-clay hills with no signs of life (Figure 15-9).

Between 1930 and 1970 efforts to restore vegetation on the 145-square-kilometer (56-square-mile) area were unsuccessful. In the 1970s, however, new reforestation techniques were used, and today about two-thirds of what used to be desert sprouts some kind of vegetation. With an expenditure of $6 million the remaining desert could be covered with vegetation in 10 to 20 years.

Copper mines continued to operate in the area until 1986 and were the leading employer of the almost 1,000 people living in Ducktown and Copperhill. As the ecological health of the area slowly improves, the towns now face eco-nomic death from closure of the depleted mines.

In Sudbury, Ontario, an area three times larger than that in Tennessee has been ravaged by copper mining and metal smelting since 1886. Like Ducktown and Copperhill, this land is slowly being revived and reforested. Meanwhile, new ecologically devastated areas are being created around mining and smelting operations in Mexico, Brazil, and other LDCs without adequate environmental controls.

Figure 15-9 Sulfur dioxide and other fumes from a copper smelter that operated for 52 years near Ducktown and Copperhill, Tennessee, killed the forest once found on this land and left a desert in its place. After decades of replanting, some vegetation has returned to the area.

A. Keith, U. S. Geological Survey

the highest peak in North America, they found a pile of partially eaten food, foil wrappers from freeze-dried meals, plastic bags, and other trash left behind by previous climbers.

Ways to deal with nonhazardous solid waste are discussed in Sections 15-6 and 15-7. Hazardous wastes are discussed in Chapter 18.

15-4 WILL THERE BE ENOUGH MINERAL RESOURCES?

How Much Is There?   How much of a particular non-renewable mineral resource exists? How much of it can be found and extracted at an affordable price and with acceptable environmental harm? Answering these questions is difficult and controversial.

The term **total resources** refers to the total amount of a particular material that exists on earth. It's hard to make useful estimates of total resources because the entire world has not been explored for each resource.

The U.S. Geological Survey estimates actual and potential supplies of a mineral resource by dividing the estimated total resources into two broad categories: identified and undiscovered (Figure 15-11). **Identified resources** are deposits of a particular mineral-bearing material of which the location, quantity, and quality are known or have been estimated from geological evidence and measurements.

Undiscovered resources are potential supplies of a particular mineral. They are believed to exist on the basis of geologic knowledge and theory, though specific locations, quality, and amounts are unknown.

These two categories are subdivided into reserves and resources. **Reserves,** or **economic resources,** are identified resources from which a usable mineral can be extracted profitably at present prices with current mining technology. **Resources** are all identified and undiscovered deposits, including those that can't be recovered profitably with present prices and technology. They may become reserves when prices rise or mining technology improves.

Reserves are like the money you now have available to spend. Resources are the total income you expect to have during your lifetime. Your cash reserves are certain. But the resources you expect to have may or may not become available for many reasons.

Most published estimates of the available supply of a particular nonrenewable mineral refer to reserves, not resources or total resources. Supplies of a mineral are usually higher than estimates of reserves. Some deposits classified as resources will be converted to reserves. However, a large portion of potentially recoverable resources will not become available. Usually the first deposits of a mineral to be exploited are high grade ores found near the earth's surface and near the point of use. Once these deposits are depleted,

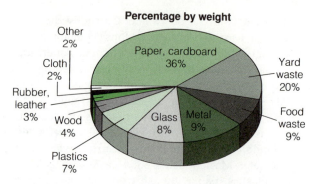

Percentage by weight

Figure 15-10   Composition by weight of urban solid waste thrown away in a typical day by each American in 1988. Because plastic containers are replacing many glass containers, plastics are expected to make up 10% of urban solid waste by the year 2000. (Data from Office of Technology Assessment).

the industry must turn to deeper, more remote, and lower-grade deposits. Eventually extracting, transporting, and processing the remaining lower-quality deposits costs more than they are currently worth.

How Fast Are Supplies Being Depleted?   Worldwide demand for mineral commodities is increasing exponentially due to increasing population and rising average per capita consumption (Figure 1-12, p. 19). The future supply of a nonrenewable mineral resource depends on two factors: its actual or potential supply and how rapidly this supply is being depleted. We never completely run out of any mineral. Instead of becoming physically depleted, a mineral becomes *economically depleted*. When this economic limit is reached, we have four choices: recycle or reuse what has already been extracted, cut down on unnecessary waste of the resource, find a substitute, or do without.

Depletion time is how long it takes to use a certain portion—usually 80%—of the known reserves or estimated resources of a mineral at an assumed rate of use. Resource experts project depletion times and plot them on a graph by making different assumptions about the resource supply and its rate of use (Figure 15-12).

We get one estimate of depletion time by assuming that the resource is not recycled or reused, that its estimated reserves will not increase, and that its price increases over time (curve A, Figure 15-12). We get a longer depletion time estimate by assuming that recycling will extend the life of existing reserves and that improved mining technology, price rises, and new discoveries will expand present reserves by some factor, say 2 (curve B). We get an even longer depletion time estimate by assuming that new discoveries, recycling, reuse, and reduced consumption will expand reserves even more, perhaps five or ten times (curve C).

Finding a substitute for a resource cancels all these curves and requires a new set of depletion curves for

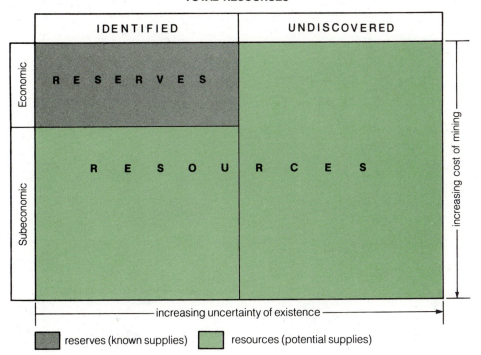

TOTAL RESOURCES

| IDENTIFIED | UNDISCOVERED |

Economic — RESERVES

Subeconomic — RESOURCES

increasing cost of mining

increasing uncertainty of existence

■ reserves (known supplies) ■ resources (potential supplies)

Figure 15-11 General classification of mineral resources by the U.S. Geological Survey.

the new resource. Figure 15-12 shows why cornucopians and neo-Malthusians disagree over projected supplies of nonrenewable nonfuel and fuel resources (see Pro/Con on p. 22). We get optimistic or pessimistic projections of the depletion time for a nonrenewable resource by making different assumptions.

Who Has the World's Nonfuel Mineral Resources?
Five countries—the Soviet Union, the United States, Canada, Australia, and South Africa—supply most of the 20 minerals that make up 98% of all nonfuel minerals consumed in the world. The United States and the Soviet Union are the world's two largest producers and consumers of nonfuel mineral resources.

No industrialized country is self-sufficient in mineral resources, although the Soviet Union comes close. The United States, Japan, and western European countries are heavily dependent on imports for most of their critical nonfuel minerals.

Minerals essential to the economy of a country are called **critical minerals** and those necessary for national defense are called **strategic minerals**. Despite its rich resource base, the United States is dependent on a steady supply of imports from 25 other countries for 24 of its 42 most critical and strategic nonfuel minerals (Figure 15-13).

Some of these minerals are imported because they are consumed more rapidly than they can be produced from domestic supplies. Others are imported because other countries have higher-grade ore deposits that are cheaper to extract than lower-grade U.S. reserves.

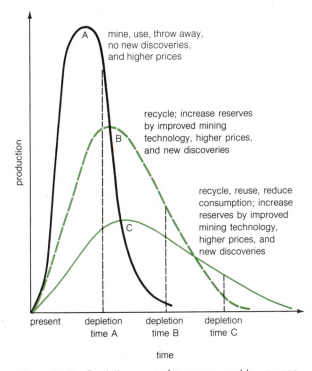

A mine, use, throw away, no new discoveries, and higher prices

B recycle; increase reserves by improved mining technology, higher prices, and new discoveries

C recycle, reuse, reduce consumption; increase reserves by improved mining technology, higher prices, and new discoveries

present | depletion time A | depletion time B | depletion time C

time

Figure 15-12 Depletion curves for a nonrenewable resource, such as aluminum or copper, using three sets of assumptions. Dashed vertical lines show when 80% depletion occurs.

The U.S. Situation Figure 15-14 shows the projected deficiency in U.S. reserves for 20 critical nonfuel minerals to the year 2000 and the major foreign sources of these minerals. Most U.S. mineral imports come

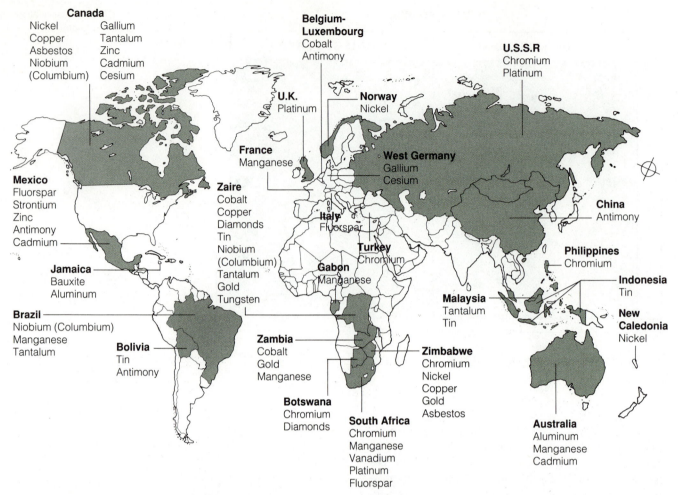

Figure 15-13 The United States is dependent on imports from 25 other countries for more than 50% of its supply of 24 critical and strategic minerals. (Data from American Chemical Society)

from reliable and politically stable countries. There is particular concern over embargoes or sudden cutoffs of supplies of four strategic minerals for which the United States has essentially no reserves and depends on imports from potentially unstable countries or the Soviet Union. These minerals are

- manganese (imports, mostly from politically unstable South Africa, provide 99% of U.S. needs)

- cobalt (imports, especially from politically unstable Zambia and Zaire, provide 95% of U.S. needs)

- platinum (imports, especially from South Africa and the Soviet Union, provide 91% of U.S. needs)

- chromium (imports, mostly from South Africa, Zimbabwe, and the Soviet Union, provide 82% of U.S. needs)

Helium (He), a nonmetal gaseous element, is a rare and irreplaceable resource found only in trace amounts in the atmosphere (0.0005%) and natural gas (0.4%). Normally it is extracted from air, but this takes

a lot of energy. This lighter-than-air gas makes balloons float, does not react chemically with other elements, and has a very low freezing point (-270°C). Because of these unique properties, helium has several uses for which there are no satisfactory substitutes:

- lifting balloons more safely than hydrogen, which can burn

- creating an unreactive atmosphere for welding and similar processes

- cooling to very low temperatures in nuclear fusion reactors, supercomputers, and other devices requiring superconductivity

- testing for leaks.

Helium-filled weather balloons are useful, but huge amounts of helium are wasted to fill millions of balloons released into the atmosphere at sporting events and celebrations. For example, the city of Cleveland once released 1.5 million helium-filled balloons and Disneyworld released 1.1 million. Japan once launched 384,000 balloons to advertise a brand of instant noo-

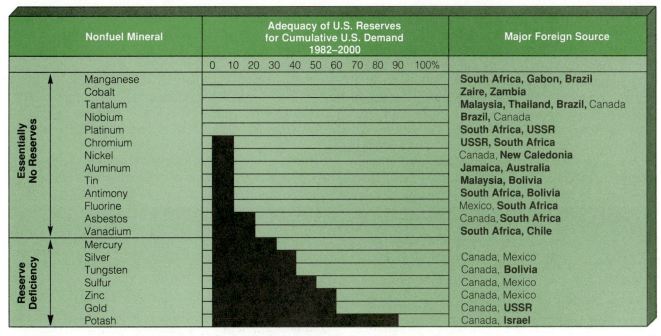

Figure 15-14 Estimated deficiencies of selected nonfuel mineral elements in the United States, 1982–2000, and major foreign sources of these minerals. Foreign sources subject to potential supply interruption by political, economic, or military disruption are shown in boldface print. (Data from U.S. Geological Survey)

dles. It's not unusual for 20,000 balloons to be released during the halftime show at a football game. Even environmentalists have released thousands of balloons to illustrate potential radioactive fallout patterns from a nuclear power plant!

Besides wasting helium, such balloon releases are just like tossing plastic sandwich bags out of an airplane. When the helium escapes or the balloons burst, the plastic balloons fall back to the earth as long-lasting litter. Fish, turtles, seals, whales, and other aquatic animals die when they ingest balloons falling into oceans and lakes. This practice also suggests to children and adults that it is acceptable to litter, waste helium, and kill wildlife. Environmentalists now urge states, localities, and universities to ban balloon releases except for essential scientific purposes.

The United States has stockpiles of most of its critical and strategic minerals to cushion against short-term supply interruptions and sharp price rises. These stockpiles are supposed to last through a three-year conventional war, after subtracting the amounts available from domestic sources and secure foreign sources. However, stockpiles for most of these minerals are far below this level.

Will There Be Enough? Cornucopians and neo-Malthusians disagree whether there will be enough affordable supplies of key nonfuel minerals to meet the projected future needs of the world's MDCs and LDCs (see Pro/Con on p. 22). Many LDCs fear that most of these resources will be used to sustain increas-

ingly greater economic growth by the MDCs, so that many LDCs will never become developed (see Pro/Con on p. 356).

15-5 INCREASING MINERAL RESOURCE SUPPLIES: THE SUPPLY-SIDE APPROACH

Economics and Resource Supply Geologic processes determine how much there is of a mineral resource. Economics determines what part of the total supply will be used.

According to standard economic theory, a competitive free market should control the supply and demand of goods and services. If a resource becomes scarce, its price rises. If there is an oversupply, the price falls. Cornucopians believe that increased demand will raise mineral prices and stimulate new discoveries and development of more efficient mining technology. Higher prices will also make it profitable to mine ores of increasingly lower grades and stimulate the search for substitutes.

Many economists argue that this theory does not apply to nonfuel mineral resources in most MDCs. In the United States and many other MDCs, industry and government have gained so much control over supply, demand, and prices of mineral raw materials and mineral products that a competitive free market does not exist.

Another problem is that the costs of nonfuel mineral resources make up only a small part of the total cost of most goods. A major reason for this is that the cost of a mineral resource does not include most of the harmful external costs caused by its extraction, processing, and use (Figure 15-7). As a result, scarcities of nonfuel minerals do not raise the market price of products very much.

Because market prices of products don't reflect dwindling mineral supplies, consumers have no incentive to reduce demand soon enough to avoid economic depletion of the minerals. Low mineral prices caused by failure to include the external costs of mining and processing them also encourages resource waste, faster depletion, and more pollution and environmental degradation.

Another economic factor that can limit production of nonfuel minerals is lack of investment capital. In today's fluctuating mineral markets and rising costs it is increasingly difficult to attract investors who are willing to have their money tied up for long periods of time with no assurance of a reasonable return.

PRO/CON Are Rich Nations Exploiting the Mineral Resource Base of Poor Nations?

To LDCs and some resource analysts the question of whether we will have enough affordable supplies of nonrenewable minerals can be viewed as asking whether the world's 33 MDCs with 23% of the world's population will run out of such resources. They believe that there is little concern over meeting the mineral resource needs of the 142 LDCs that contain 77% of the world's people but presently use only about 25% of the world's mineral resources.

MDCs argue that when they buy nonfuel minerals from LDCs, they provide funds that the LDCs need for their own economic development. Multinational companies point out that mines they develop in LDCs are a source of jobs and income for these countries. It is also argued that when MDCs depend on LDCs for critical minerals the rich countries have an interest in helping preserve economic and political stability in these countries.

LDCs agree that selling their resources at any price helps stimulate their economic development. But for short-term economic survival they feel they have little choice but to sell their resources at prices they believe to be too low. They charge that MDCs and multinational companies based in MDCs do this by controlling the technology, capital, and markets for mineral resources.

Companies based in MDCs end up with most of the profits and in the process often cause severe environmental degradation and pollution in LDCs. Economic growth in mineral-exporting LDCs is stunted when these countries borrow money from MDCs to buy expensive imported finished products made from minerals they feel they had to sell too cheaply. The low mineral prices also encourage unnecessary resource waste in MDCs and rapidly depletes supplies of key resources that the LDCs will need for their own future economic growth.

Geologist Eugene Cameron points out that, contrary to popular opinion, the United States has not developed its industrial economy using the nonfuel mineral resources of the rest of the world. Data shows that as late as 1979 the United States was still producing about 97% of its mineral consumption from domestic supplies. Today mineral imports have increased but about 62% of these imports come from other MDCs.

However, critics counter U.S. mineral use is so high that the 38% of its imports from LDCs amounts to huge quantities. This gives the U.S. or other large volume buyers, such as Japan and Western European countries, considerable influence over the market price of such resources. As the United States increases its import dependence in the future (Figure 15-14), LDCs fear its influence over mineral prices will grow.

Politics also plays a key role in mineral prices. If an LDC fails to go along with foreign policy decisions of a mineral-importing MDC, the MDC may stop importing resources from that LDC (assuming other sources are available) or reduce or cut off foreign aid. Such countries feel they are victims of economic blackmail by importing MDCs.

Currently LDCs owe MDCs over $1 trillion. Each year, LDCs pay MDCs $43 billion in interest on this debt. LDCs have called for a new international economic order, in which a larger and fairer share of the world's wealth would be shifted from MDCs to LDCs. This proposal calls for

- a substantial increase in aid from industrialized countries to LDCs
- relieving LDCs of some of their massive indebtedness to MDCs
- removal of trade barriers that restrict LDCs from selling some of their products to MDCs
- increasing the prices paid for minerals, timber, and other resources exported from LDCs to MDCs
- giving LDCs with greater influence in the decision making of international lending institutions, such as the World Bank and the International Monetary Fund

So far MDCs have generally opposed this program. What do you think should be done?

Finding New Land-Based Mineral Deposits Geologic exploration—guided by better geologic knowledge, satellite surveys, and other new techniques—will increase present reserves of most minerals. However, in MDCs and many LDCs, most of the easily accessible, high-grade deposits have already been discovered. Thus, geologists believe that most new concentrated deposits will be found in unexplored areas in LDCs.

Exploration for new resources requires a large capital investment and is a risky financial venture. Typically, if geologic theory identifies 10,000 sites where a deposit of a particular resource might be found, only 1,000 sites are worth costly exploration; only 100 justify even more costly drilling, trenching, or tunneling; and only 1 out of the 10,000 will probably be a producing mine.

Even if large new supplies are found, no nonrenewable mineral supply can stand up to continued exponential growth in its use. For example, a 1-billion-year supply of a resource would be exhausted in only 584 years if its rate of use increased at 3% a year.

Improving Mining Technology and Mining Low-Grade Deposits Cornucopians assume that all we have to do to increase supplies of any mineral is to mine increasingly lower grades of ore. They point to the development of large earth-moving equipment, impurity removal techniques, and other advances in mining technology during the past few decades.

For example, these and other technological changes have allowed the average grade of copper ore mined in the United States to fall from about 5% copper in 1900 to 0.4% today with a drop in the inflation-adjusted copper price. Technological improvements also led to a 500% increase in world copper reserves between 1950 and 1980.

Since 1950 known reserves of most other minerals have also increased, despite growing consumption. Also inflation-adjusted prices for most industrial minerals have fallen. However, such price drops are not inevitable. Mineral prices are the results of a race between falling extraction costs and falling ore quality. Since 1975 the prices of most nonfuel minerals have been declining at a decreasing rate, and the prices of some, such as iron, nickel, and tin, have started to increase.

Neo-Malthusians point out that several factors limit the mining of lower-grade deposits. As increasingly poorer ores are mined, energy costs increase sharply. We eventually reach a point where it costs more to mine and process such resources than they are currently worth unless we have a virtually inexhaustible source of cheap energy. Most energy experts believe that in the future energy will neither be unlimited nor cheap.

Available supplies of fresh water also may limit the supply of some mineral resources, because large amounts of water are needed to extract and process most minerals. Many areas with major mineral deposits are poorly supplied with fresh water.

Finally, exploitation of lower grades of ore may be limited by the environmental impact of waste material produced during mining and processing. The mining and processing of low-grade ores increases the amount of disturbed land and the amount of air and water pollution. At some point, land restoration and pollution control costs exceed the current value of the minerals.

Getting More Minerals from Seawater and the Ocean Floor Ocean resources are found in three areas: seawater, sediments and deposits on the shallow continental shelf and slope, and sediments and nodules on the deep-ocean floor. Most of the 90 chemical elements found in seawater occur in such low concentrations that recovering them takes more energy and money than they are worth. Only magnesium, bromine, and sodium chloride are abundant enough in seawater to be extracted profitably at present prices with current technology.

Offshore seabed deposits and sediments in shallow waters are already significant sources of sand, gravel, phosphates, and nine other nonfuel mineral resources. Offshore wells also supply large amounts of oil and natural gas.

Ocean crusts at various sites, some near shore, may be a future source of manganese and other metallic minerals whose domestic supplies are unable to meet present or projected future needs (Figure 15-14). Most seabed deposits of minerals of interest to the United States are believed to lie within 200 nautical miles (230 miles) of the coast, where the United States has legal ownership of mineral, fish, and other marine resources.

There are also deposits of metal sulfides of iron, manganese, copper, cobalt, lead, chromium, zinc, gold, and nickel around hydrothermal vents found at certain locations on the deep-ocean floor. However, concentrations of metals in most of these deposits are too low to be valuable mineral resources.

Environmentalists recognize that seabed mining would probably cause less harm than mining on land. They are concerned, however, that removing seabed mineral deposits and dumping back unwanted material will stir up ocean sediments. This could destroy seafloor organisms and have unknown effects on poorly understood ocean food webs. Surface waters might also be polluted by the discharge of sediments from mining ships and rigs.

At a few sites on the deep-ocean floor, manganese-rich nodules have been found in large quantities. These potato-size rocks contain 30% to 40% manganese, used in certain steel alloys. They also contain small amounts of other strategically important metals such as nickel and cobalt. These nodules could be scooped up or sucked up from the muds of the ocean floor and transported by pipe or by a continuous cable with buckets to a mining ship above.

However, most of these modules are found in seabed sites in international waters. Development of these resources has been put off indefinitely because of squabbles between countries over who owns these resources. According to the 1982 United Nations Law of the Sea Treaty, mineral resources or profits from mineral deposits in international waters are to be shared by all countries. This treaty has been signed by 159 countries but the United States and many other MDCs disagree with this provision and have refused to sign the treaty.

Economic and political uncertainties make it doubtful whether significant amounts of minerals will be obtained from seabed nodules, ocean crusts, and deep sedimentary basins in the near future. Ample and much cheaper onshore supplies of most of these minerals are expected to be available for many decades. Faced with legal and economic uncertainties and lack of knowledge, private ocean-mining companies have halted most exploration and research and development of seabed minerals since 1984.

Finding Substitutes Cornucopians believe that even if supplies of key minerals become very expensive or scarce, human ingenuity will find substitutes. They point out that new developments by scientists are already leading to a materials revolution in which materials made of silicon and other abundant elements are being substituted for most scarce metals (see Spotlight below). In 1980 Japan's government saw the development of new materials as a key technology of the future and launched a ten-year, $400 million program of research.

In the 1970s supplies of the critical mineral cobalt from Zaire were cut off because of war. The sharp rise in prices led to a search for new technologies and substitutes. Cobalt-free magnets were developed and ceramic blades were developed to replace metal turbine blades.

Substitutes can probably be found for many scarce mineral resources. But finding or developing a substitute is costly and phasing it into a complex manufacturing requires a long lead time. While an increasingly scarce mineral is being replaced, people and businesses dependent on it may suffer economic hardships as the price rises sharply.

Finding substitutes for some key materials may be extremely difficult, if not impossible. Examples are helium, phosphorus for phosphate fertilizers, manganese for making steel, and copper for wiring motors and generators.

Also some substitutes are inferior to the minerals they replace. For example, aluminum could replace copper in electrical wiring but the energy cost of producing aluminum is much higher than that of copper. And aluminum wiring is more of a fire hazard than copper wiring. The materials revolution is an important advance, but it will not meet all of our mineral needs.

15-6 WASTING RESOURCES: THE THROWAWAY APPROACH

Ways to Deal with Solid Waste There are several options for dealing with the mountains of solid waste we produce in mining, processing, manufacturing, and

---

SPOTLIGHT The Materials Revolution

Scientists and engineers are rapidly developing new materials that can replace many of the metals we now rely on. Ceramic materials are being used in engines, knives, scissors, batteries, fish hooks, and artificial limbs.

Ceramics are harder, stronger, lighter, and longer-lasting than many metals. Also, they withstand enormous temperatures, and they do not corrode. Because they can burn fuel at higher temperatures than metal engines, ceramic engines can boost fuel efficiency by 30% to 40%.

High-strength plastics and composite materials strengthened by carbon and glass fibers are likely to transform the automobile and aerospace industries. Many of these new materials are stronger and lighter than metals. They cost less to produce because they require less energy. They don't need painting and can easily be molded into any shape.

Many cars now have plastic body parts, which reduce weight and boost fuel economy. Planes and cars made almost entirely of plastics—held together by new superglues—may be common in the next century.

The materials revolution is also transforming medicine. So-called biomaterials, made of new plastics, ceramics, glass composites, and alloys, are being used in artificial skin, arteries, organs and joints.

using resources. One is a *throwaway* or *high-waste approach* in which these wastes are left where they are produced, buried, or burned. The other is a *conservation* or *low-waste approach* based on greatly increased waste reduction, recycling, and reuse.

In the United States about 89% of the municipal solid waste is hauled away and buried in landfills (80%) or burned in municipal incinerators (9%) (Figure 15-15). Only 10% is recycled. This throwaway attitude explains why the U.S. is No. 1 in trash (see Spotlight below).

Burying Solid Waste in Landfills   Until 1976, when the Resource Conservation and Recovery Act (RCRA) was enacted, some trash in the United States was thrown into open dumps or burned in crude incinerators. The open dumps created health hazards, polluted nearby surface water and groundwater, and often caught fire and polluted the air. Unregulated incinerators also polluted the air.

The RCRA banned all open dumps and required landfills to be upgraded to sanitary landfills. A **sanitary landfill** is a land waste disposal site in which wastes are spread out in thin layers, compacted, and covered with a fresh layer of soil each day (Figure 15-16). No open burning is allowed, odor is seldom a

problem, and rodents and insects cannot thrive. Sanitary landfills should be located so as to reduce water pollution from runoff and leaching, but this is not always done.

A sanitary landfill can be put into operation quickly, has low operating costs, and can handle a massive amount of solid waste. After a landfill has been filled and allowed to settle for a few years, the land can be graded and used as a park, a golf course, a ski mountain, an athletic field, a wildlife area, or other recreation area.

However, while landfills are in operation, there is much traffic, noise, and dust. Wind can scatter litter

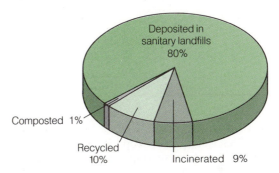

Figure 15-15   Fate of solid waste in the United States. (Data from Environmental Protection Agency)

SPOTLIGHT Waste: An Outmoded and Dangerous Concept

For plants and nonhuman animals there is virtually no waste. The wastes or dead bodies of one form of life are food or nutrients for other forms of life. Sooner or later everything is recycled through natural processes.

Our challenge is to imitate these natural processes in our economic systems and lifestyles. *We need to recognize that most of what we call solid wastes are really wasted solids. They are potential resources that we are too dumb to recycle, reuse, or convert to useful raw materials or products.* Garbage is presently one of America's most abundant unused resources. Some U.S. trash dumps are richer in resources than some of the country's mines.

We should be teaching small children and adults to view trash cans and dumpsters as resource containers, trash as concentrated urban ore, and landfills as urban mines. Schools can be collection points for recycled materials as

they were during World War II. Profits from school and university recycling centers run by students could be used to fund school activities. Students should also take field trips to recycling centers to see how the resources they collect are put back into use.

We can also make products that last longer and are easy to repair, recycle, and remanufacture. We should also recognize that each unit of energy that we waste unnecessarily harms the environment and sooner or later costs us money.

The basic problem is that we use economic systems to reward those who produce waste instead of those who try to use resources more efficiently. We give timber, mining, and energy companies tax write-offs and other subsidies to cut trees and to extract copper, oil, and coal from the earth's crust. But we give few if any such subsidies to companies and businesses

that recycle copper or paper, use oil or coal more efficiently, or develop renewable alternatives to using nonrenewable fossil fuels.

This means that the market prices of nonfuel minerals, oil, gasoline, electricity, and water are much lower than their total costs to us and to society. You and I will buy products that unnecessarily waste energy and other resources and produce more pollution than necessary as long as the market prices we pay for them don't include the costs of the harmful effects from their extraction, production, and use.

Using our economic and political systems to reward resource conservation instead of resource waste is the key to making the transition from a throwaway society to a sustainable earth society. What are you doing to help bring about this shift?

Figure 15-16 A sanitary landfill. Wastes are spread in a thin layer and then compacted with a bulldozer. A scraper (foreground) covers the wastes with a fresh layer of soil at the end of each day. Portable fences catch and hold windblown debris.

and dust before each day's load of trash is covered with soil. That is why most people do not want a landfill nearby, even if it is eventually used as a recreation site.

The underground anaerobic decomposition of organic wastes at landfills produces explosive methane gas and toxic hydrogen sulfide gas. These gases can get into utility lines and seep into basements as far as a quarter mile from the landfill. The buildup of these gases can cause asphyxiation or one spark can cause a methane explosion.

This problem can be prevented by equipping landfills with vent pipes to collect these gases so that they can be burned or allowed to escape into the air. At the Fresh Kills landfill on Staten Island enough methane gas is collected to heat 50,000 homes a year. Besides saving energy, collecting and burning methane gas from all large landfills worldwide would lower atmospheric emissions of methane by 6% to 18%. This would help reduce depletion of the ozone layer and global warming from greenhouse gases.

Contamination of groundwater below and nearby surface water is also a problem, especially for thousands of older filled and abandoned landfills. At least 180 of the almost 1,200 worst hazardous waste sites to be cleaned up by the EPA are abandoned landfills. Also at least 25%—some say 80%—of the sanitary landfills in operation today in the United States may be polluting surface water and groundwater.

Within the next five to ten years half of existing U.S. landfills, especially in the East and Midwest, will be filled and closed. For example, the Fresh Kills landfill in Staten Island is one of only two used to handle waste from New York City. By 1997, when it is expected to be 153 meters (500 feet) high, it will have to be

closed because it is in the flight path of Newark International Airport.

Most cities are not building new landfills. Either there are no acceptable sites or construction is prevented by citizens who want their trash hauled away but don't want a landfill anywhere near them—the not in my backyard (NIMBY) attitude toward dealing with the wastes we all help create.

Some cities without enough landfill space are shipping their trash elsewhere. Philadelphia ships part of its solid waste to a waste-to-energy incinerator in Baltimore, Maryland. The rest goes to rural areas in Pennsylvania, Ohio, West Virginia, and Kentucky and by boat to Panama. Officials in southern states with large areas for landfills are mobilizing to restrict garbage imports from other states. LDCs are also rebelling against garbage dumping by MDCs. Increasingly, people, businesses, and communities will have to accept responsibility for the wastes they produce instead of trying to make them somebody else's problem.

Even where landfill space is available, operating costs are rising sharply and will rise even more because of new EPA regulations. By 1991 landfill operators will have to

- close landfills near airports, flood plains, wetlands, and earthquake zones

- monitor nearby surface and groundwater supplies for contaminants

- install a liner at the bottom of a new landfill to control runoff of contaminated water and a system to collect liquid (leachate) that does run off (environmentalists believe that landfills should have double liners and double leachate collection systems)

- monitor release of methane gas and install vent pipes to collect methane or vent it to the atmosphere

- monitor a landfill for at least 30 years after it is closed

Burning Solid Waste Burning solid waste in incinerators kills disease-carrying organisms and reduces the volume of solid waste by 90% and its weight by 75%. In *waste-to-energy incinerators*, heat released when combustible solid trash is burned can be used to run the incinerator or heat nearby buildings, or it can be sold to generate electricity. This income helps reduce waste management costs. Denmark and Sweden burn about half of their waste to produce energy, compared to 6% in the United States.

Incinerators do not pollute groundwater and add little pollution to the air if equipped with effective pollution control devices that are properly maintained. Sweden requires devices that remove 99% of the pollutants emitted.

Incinerators built in the 1960s and 1970s in the United States caused severe air pollution because of a lack of effective pollution controls and poor maintenance. If controls proposed by the EPA in 1988 are approved by Congress, all new U.S. incinerators will have to use the best available technology to remove 95% or more of the air pollutants. Also states would be required to have plans for adding more effective air pollution control equipment to existing incinerators. Including these external costs will cost incinerator operators $450 million to $500 million per year, explaining why they oppose such regulations.

Even with advanced air pollution control devices, incinerators emit small amounts of hydrochloric acid, highly toxic dioxins and furans, and tiny particles of lead, cadmium, mercury, and other toxic substances into the atmosphere. Without continuous maintenance and good operator training and supervision, the air pollution control equipment on incinerators often fails and the pollution exceeds emission standards. Employees at incinerator plants in Japan, West Germany, and Switzerland are generally much better trained than those in the United States.

Incineration leaves about 25% of the original waste in the form of toxic ash residues. This ash, currently disposed of in ordinary landfills, is usually contaminated with hazardous substances such as dioxins and lead, cadmium, mercury, and other toxic metals. Environmentalists want the EPA to classify incinerator ash as hazardous waste and allow it to be disposed of only in landfills designed to handle hazardous waste.

Incinerator sites are hard to find because of citizen opposition—the NIMBY attitude. But as urban areas run out of acceptable landfills, incineration will become more economically attractive. By the end of this century incinerators are projected to be burning 30% of the solid waste in the United States.

Incinerators, especially trash-to-energy incinerators, will play some role in a waste management system. But conservationists oppose very much dependence on incinerators because it is still a throwaway approach that wastes resources and pollutes the air. It encourages people to continue tossing away paper, plastics, and other burnable materials rather than looking for ways to conserve, recycle, and reuse these resources and to reduce waste production.

15-7 EXTENDING RESOURCE SUPPLIES: THE CONSERVATION APPROACH

The Low-Waste Approach Environmentalists and conservationists believe we should begin shifting from the high-waste, throwaway approach (Figure 3-18, p. 71) to a low-waste, sustainable-earth approach for dealing with nonfuel solid resources (Figure 3-19, p. 74). This will require much more emphasis on conserving wasted solids by composting, recycling, reuse, and waste reduction instead of dumping, burying, and burning them.

A 1988 study by solid-waste experts concluded that recycling and composting could reduce the amount of solid waste going to U.S. landfills by 70% and save $110 million a year compared to incineration. Japan has the world's most comprehensive waste management and recycling program (see Case Study on p. 362).

Composting Degradable solid waste from slaughterhouses, food-processing plants, and kitchens and yard waste, manure, and muncipal sewage sludge can be mixed with soil and decomposed by aerobic bacteria to produce **compost,** a soil conditioner and fertilizer. Composting cannot be used for mixed urban waste because sorting out the glass, metals, plastic, and organic waste is too expensive.

But organic waste produced by food-processing, animal feedlots, muncipal sewage treatment plants, and various industries can be collected and degraded in large composting plants, bagged, and sold. This approach is used in many European countries, including the Netherlands, West Germany, France, Sweden, and Italy. Sweden, for example, composts 25% of its municipal solid waste.

Paper, leaves, and grass clippings can be decomposed in backyard compost bins and used in gardens and flower beds (Figure 10-22, p. 232). Composting yard waste would reduce the amount of solid waste

Japan is a pioneer in developing an integrated waste management program in which 50% of its municipal solid waste is recycled. About 34% is incinerated, 16% is disposed of in landfills, and only 0.2% is composted. Japan's program is partly imposed by geography and heavy dependence on imported raw materials. For example, between 1980 and 1985, Japan imported 99.8% of its oil, 95% of its iron ore, 95% of its copper ore, 92% of its coal, 75% of its aluminum ore, 65% of its timber, and 18% of its pulp for making paper.

Japan is a small, densely populated country the size of California with only 21% of this land habitable. The rest is mountainous and forested. About 77% of its population—about half that of the United States—is crowded into urban areas. About 45% of its population lives in the three metropolitan areas of Tokyo, Osaka, and Nagoya, which occupy only 3% of the country's land area. The Japanese have over 1,400 people per square kilometer of habitable area compared to 50 in the United States. The country ran out of adequate landfill space 35 years ago.

Japan's divides its waste into four categories. The first includes glass, metals, paper, some plastics, other naturals that can be recycled, and bulky objects such as books, furniture, toys, appliances, and bicycles that can be repaired and reused. For over 100 years the Japanese have referred to these materials as resources, not wastes.

The second category consists of hazardous materials such as batteries and certain plastics that are detoxified or disposed of in landfills designed only for such wastes. The third category is non-combustible, non-toxic materials such as ceramics, some plastics, and construction debris that can't be recycled. They are placed in conventional landfills. These two categories make up about 16% of the country's municipal solid waste.

The remaining 34% of the country's solid waste output are combustible materials that are too soiled to be recycled. It includes some kitchen wastes, yard waste, some plastics, and soiled paper and wood. Most of this waste is burned in the country's almost 2,000 incinerators, with 362 of these incinerators recovering energy. The government provides 25% of the construction costs—50% in high pollution areas—for new incinerators.

Each household and business in about 90% of Japanese cities separates its wastes into these four categories for collection. Hundreds of volunteer civic groups and private resource recovery dealers pick up recyclables and sell them to companies.

Municipal employees and civic groups collect bulky objects and take them to cultural centers where they are repaired and resold. Much of this work is done by senior citizens and handicapped persons. Municipal employees also collect soiled combustibles to be incinerated several times a week and pick up hazardous material from homes and businesses upon request.

From their earliest school years on, Japanese children are taught about recycling and waste management. They often tour their local recycling centers and incinerators.

Japanese incinerators are strictly controlled. Noncombustible materials that would upset furnace operations and increase air pollution are removed before wastes are incinerated. This plus earlier separation of hazardous wastes greatly reduces the amount and toxicity of the ash left after incineration. To protect workers this ash is removed by conveyor belts and transported to carefully designed and monitored hazardous waste landfills in sealed trucks. Before disposal the ash is often solidified in cement blocks.

The newer incinerators are equipped with air pollution control devices that remove 95% to 99% of potential air pollutants. Plant operations and emissions are carefully monitored and violations of air standards are punishable by large fines, plant closings, and in some cases jail sentences for company officials. Incinerator workers spend 6 to 18 months learning how the incinerator works, must have an engineering degree, and undergo closely supervised on-site training.

Despite these precautions there is widespread opposition to the building of new incinerators throughout Japan. This is caused by concern about harmful emissions (especially traces of dioxins), inadequate emission controls on older plants, truck traffic, and lower property values—the same NIMBY attitude found almost everywhere.

But even this highly effective program can be improved. Japan could probably recycle 70% to 80% of its municipal solid waste by instituting municipal and household composting programs for much of the yard and food waste it now burns. Composting has declined because of increased use of inorganic fertilizers, although this may change as harmful effects of such fertilizers become more apparent. Better standards for reducing toxic materials in urban compost would encourage more farmers to use compost.

The average amount of waste generated per person in Japan is half that of the average American but the Japanese output can be reduced further. Recently Japan has begun a national campaign to reduce solid waste production.

Japanese officials are also worried that the younger generation of urban dwellers brought up on throwaway lifestyles are backsliding in their participation in waste recovery. Littering of soft-drink containers and illegal dumping is increasing.

[*]Based mostly on material in Allen Hershkowitz and Eugene Salerni, 1987, *Garbage Management in Japan: Leading the Way* (New York: INFORM).

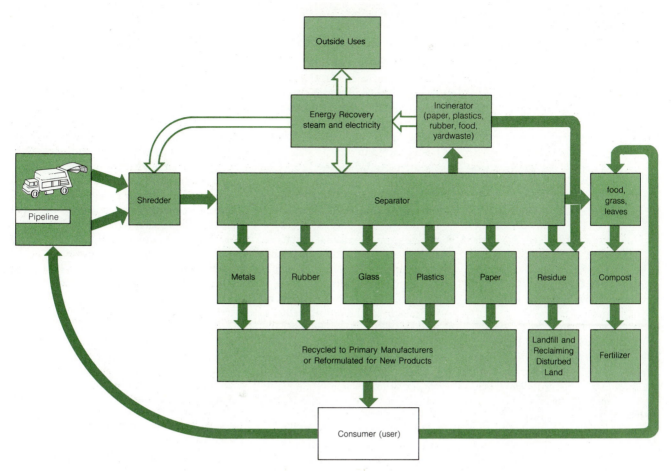

Figure 15-17 Generalized urban resource recovery system. Very few of this type of resource recovery plant exist today.

in the U. S. by almost 18%. Presently only 1% of solid waste in the United States is composted.

But this could change because of a lack of landfill space, mandatory composting programs, and use of economic incentives to encourage composting. For example, locating a city compost heap next to a landfill would reduce the waste going to the landfill and extend its life. The compost can then be used as landfill cover and used by public works departments for fertilizing parks, forests, roadway medians, and the grounds around public buildings.

Seattle plans to recycle 65% of its urban solid waste by 1993. This strategy includes curbside collection and composting of yard wastes and promotion of backyard composting.

Resource Recovery The salvaging of usable metals, paper, plastic, and glass from municipal solid waste and selling them to manufacturing industries for recycling or reuse is called **resource recovery.** This extends the supply of minerals by reducing the amount of virgin materials that must be extracted from the earth's crust to meet demand. Recycling and reuse usually save energy, cause less pollution and land disruption

than use of virgin resources, cut waste disposal costs, and prolong the life of landfills by reducing the volume of solid waste.

Resources can be recycled by using high- or low-technology approaches. In *high-technology resource recovery plants*, machines shred and automatically separate mixed urban waste to recover glass, iron, aluminum, and other valuable materials (Figure 15-17). These materials are then sold to manufacturing industries as raw materials for recycling. The remaining paper, plastics, and other combustible wastes are recycled or incinerated. The heat given off is used to produce steam or electricity to run the recovery plant and for sale to nearby industries or residential developments.

Currently the United States has only a few plants that recover some iron, aluminum, and glass for recycling. However, by 1989 there were 111 trash-to-energy incinerators operating in 40 states, and 210 others were being built or planned.

Environmentalists oppose the widespread use of trash-to-energy incinerators. Unless strictly controlled and monitored, they emit hazardous air pollutants and create toxic ash. They also encourage people to keep

Every day Americans purchase nearly 200 million aluminum cans of beer and soda and many millions of glass and plastic bottles. About 56% of the new aluminum beverage cans used in the United States were recycled in 1988 at more than 5,000 recycling centers set up by the aluminum industry, other private interests, and local governments.

People who returned the cans got about a penny a can for their efforts, earning about $900 million in 1989. Within six weeks the average recycled aluminum has been melted down and is back on the market as a new can.

Despite this progress, about 44% of the 80 billion aluminum cans produced each year in the United States are still thrown away—more aluminum in discarded cans than most countries use for all purposes. If the cans Americans throw away in one year were laid side by side, the cans would wrap around the earth at the equator more than 164 times. Each discarded aluminum can is almost-indestructible solid waste. The electricity needed to produce an aluminum can from virgin ore would keep a 100-watt light bulb burning for 100 hours. Recycling that can takes only 5% as much energy and saves the energy equivalent of six ounces of gasoline.

Beverage container deposit laws can be used to decrease litter and encourage recycling of nonrefillable glass, metal, and plastic containers (refillable containers are discussed later in this chapter). Consumers pay a deposit (usually five to ten cents) on each beverage container they buy. The deposits are refunded when empty containers are turned in to retailers, redemption centers, or reverse vending machines, which return cash when consumers put in empty beverage cans and bottles.

Container deposit laws have been adopted in Sweden, Norway, the Netherlands, the Soviet Union, and parts of Australia, Canada, Japan, and Ecuador (where the deposit is 15 cents). Such laws have been proposed in almost every state in the U.S., but have been enacted in only 11 states with about one-fourth of the U.S. population.

Experience in the United States has shown that 90% of cans and bottles are turned in as long as refunds are at least five cents a container (refunds of only one cent a container, as in California, are not as effective). Litter is decreased by 35% to 70%, depending mostly on the refund value. Also, expensive landfills don't fill up as quickly, energy and mineral resources are saved, and jobs are created. Environmentalists and conservationists believe a nationwide deposit law should be passed by Congress.

So far such a law has been effectively opposed in all but 11 states by a well-funded lobby of steel, aluminum, and glass companies, metalworkers' unions, supermarket chains, and most major brewers and soft drink bottlers. Merchants don't like to have returned bottles and cans piling up in their stores.

Labor unions are afraid that some workers in bottle and can manufacturing industries will lose their jobs. Beverage makers fear the extra nickel deposit per container will hurt sales and cause a shift to refillable glass containers. Some people support deposit laws, but believe that this problem should be dealt with by each state.

Ad campaigns financed by Keep America Beautiful and other groups opposing deposit laws have helped prevent passage of such laws in a number of states. These groups favor litter-recycling laws, which levy a tax on industries whose products may end up as litter or in landfills. Revenues from the tax are used to set up and maintain statewide recycling centers. By 1988 seven states, containing about 14% of the U.S. population, had this type of law.

Environmentalists point out that according to surveys, litter taxes are not as effective as container deposit laws. Litter laws are output approaches that provide some money to clean up litter. By contrast, container deposit laws are input approaches that reward consumers who return containers and can also make people aware of the need to shift to refillable containers. This is a major reason that companies making nonrefillable containers oppose such laws.

Surveys have also shown that a national container deposit law is supported by 73% of the Americans polled. EPA and General Accounting Office studies estimate that such a law would

- save consumers at least $1 billion annually

- reduce overall outdoor litter by 35% and beverage container litter by 60% to 70%

- reduce urban solid waste by at least 1%, saving taxpayers about $50 million a year in waste disposal costs

- decrease mining and processing of aluminum ore by 53% to 74% and the use of iron ore by 45% to 83%

- reduce air, water, and solid waste pollution from the beverage industry by 44% to 86%

- save energy in one year that equals the electricity used by a city the size of Milwaukee for four years

- create 80,000 to 100,000 new jobs because collecting and recycling beverage containers requires more labor than producing new ones

Do you favor passage of such a law?

on creating solid waste and can discourage recycling of paper, plastics, and other burnable trash and waste reduction. Cogeneration in industrial plants can produce electricity and heat much cheaper and more efficiently than incinerators.

Low-technology resource recovery is used to recycle most waste materials in the United States and other countries. Homes and businesses place various kinds of waste materials—usually glass, paper, metals, and plastics—into separate containers. Compartmentalized city collection trucks, private haulers, or volunteer recycling organizations pick up the segregated wastes and sell them to scrap dealers, compost plants, and manufacturers. Studies have shown that household trash separation takes only 16 minutes a week for the average American family. Composting is also a low-technology approach for recovering and recycling nutrients to the land.

A comprehensive low-technology recycling program could save 5% of annual U.S. energy use—more than the energy generated by all U.S. nuclear power plants—at perhaps one-hundredth of the capital and operating costs. By contrast, burning all combustible urban solid waste in waste-to-energy plants would supply only 1% of the country's annual energy use.

The low-technology approach produces little air and water pollution and has low start-up costs and moderate operating costs. It also saves more energy and provides more jobs for unskilled workers than high-technology resource recovery plants. Recycling creates three to six times more jobs per unit of material than landfilling or incineration. Another advantage is that collecting and selling cans, paper, and other materials for recycling is an important source of income for many people (especially the homeless and the poor) and for volunteer service organizations. In densely populated and resource-poor countries such as Japan and the Netherlands, 33% to 65% of urban waste materials are recycled mostly by the low-technology approach (see Case Study on p. 362).

Recycling rates are also high in some LDCs, including Mexico, India, and China. Small armies of poor people go through urban garbage disposal sites by hand. They remove paper and sell it to paper mills. They sell metal scrap to metal-processing factories, bones to glue factories, and rags to furniture factories for use in upholstery.

Recycling Iron, Aluminum, Wastepaper, Plastics, and Tires Items containing iron and aluminum account for 94% of all metals used. Using scrap iron instead of iron ore to produce steel conserves iron ore and the coal needed to process the ore. It requires 65% less energy and 40% less water, and produces 85% less air pollution and 76% less water pollution. Recycling aluminum produces 95% less air pollution and 97% less water pollution and requires 95% less energy than mining and processing aluminum ore. In the United States the recycling rate for aluminum is only 29% (see Case Study on p. 364).

In many MDCs the use of throwaway paper products is hastening the deforestation of softwood forests and adding to the growing problem of solid waste. Sharply increasing the recycling of paper is a key to preventing the clearing and degradation of forests (Section 13-2) and reducing the unnecessary waste of timber resources (see Case Study below) and water and air pollution.

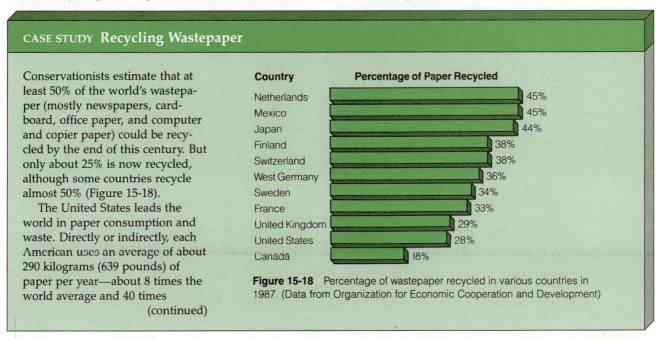

CASE STUDY Recycling Wastepaper

Conservationists estimate that at least 50% of the world's wastepaper (mostly newspapers, cardboard, office paper, and computer and copier paper) could be recycled by the end of this century. But only about 25% is now recycled, although some countries recycle almost 50% (Figure 15-18).

The United States leads the world in paper consumption and waste. Directly or indirectly, each American uses an average of about 290 kilograms (639 pounds) of paper per year—about 8 times the world average and 40 times (continued)

Figure 15-18 Percentage of wastepaper recycled in various countries in 1987. (Data from Organization for Economic Cooperation and Development)

Plastics now account for about 7% of the weight and 30% of the volume of municipal solid wastes in the United States and are the fastest-growing type of waste in landfills. We are being swamped by throwaway plastic bags, milk jugs, bottles, lids, diapers, and other products. By 2000, plastics are expected to make up 10% of the weight and 66% of the volume of these wastes, unless more of these wastes are recycled or, better yet, not produced (see Case Study on p. 367).

Efforts are under way to recycle some of the 200 million tires that are thrown away each year in the United States and other MDCs. Some are dumped in landfills, but most are piled in junkyards where they are fire hazards and breeding grounds for mosquitoes.

Some paper and cement companies are shredding tires and mixing the rubber with coal to burn in their boilers. In Modesto, California, a power plant burns tires to generate enough electricity for 15,000 homes. Next to the plant sits the world's largest pile of tires.

Other companies are using pulverized tires to make resins for a number of products, including car bumpers and garbage cans. A Canadian firm has developed a process that converts used tires into heating oil and high-octane compounds that can substitute for lead in gasoline. Used tires have also been used to build artificial reefs to attract fish.

So far, however, only a tiny fraction of the tires thrown away each year are recycled. In addition to

CASE STUDY Recycling Wastepaper (continued)

the average in LDCs. During World War II, when paper drives and recycling were national priorities, the United States recycled about 45% of its wastepaper. In 1988 only about 29% was recycled, up from 26% in 1987.

Product overpackaging is a major contributor to paper use and waste. Packages inside packages and oversized containers are designed to trick consumers into thinking they're getting more for their money. Product packaging uses 65% of the paper and 15% of the wood produced in the United States. Nearly $1 of every $10 spent for food in the United States goes for throwaway packaging.

Recycling paper saves trees (17 trees per ton of recycled paper), and reduces the harmful environmental effects of tree farms (p. 295). Recycling the press run of just one Sunday edition of the New York Times saves 75,000 trees. Recycling paper also saves 30% to 55% of the energy needed to produce paper from virgin pulpwood, reduces air pollution from pulp mills by 74% to 95%, lowers water pollution by 35%, conserves 7,000 to 20,000 gallons of water per ton of paper, and saves landfill space. Recycling paper also helps prevent groundwater contamination from the toxic ink left after paper biodegrades in landfills.

Recycling half the wastepaper discarded in the United States would save enough energy to supply 10 million people with electrical power each year. In 1988 American Telephone and Telegraph earned more than $360,000 in revenue and saved close to $1 million in disposal costs by collecting and recycling high-grade office paper.

Requiring people to separate paper from other waste materials is a key to increased recycling. Otherwise, paper becomes so contaminated with other trash that wastepaper dealers won't buy it. Slick paper magazines and glossy newspaper and advertising supplements cause contamination and must not be included.

Currently, only one-third of the 600 paper mills in the United States run solely on recovered paper. Thus, much of the wastepaper collected in the United States is exported to other countries. Cardboard cartons collected from 2,000 wastepaper dealers and 100,000 scavengers are the port of New York's number-one export. The cardboard is sent mostly to paper mills in Japan, Taiwan, South Korea, Mexico, Italy, and other countries to be recycled.

Tax subsidies and other financial incentives that make it cheaper to produce paper from trees than from recycling hinder wastepaper recycling in the United States. Widely fluctuating prices and a lack of demand for recycled paper products also make recycling wastepaper a risky financial venture.

If the demand for recycled paper products increased, recycled paper would be cheaper and the price paid for wastepaper would rise. One way to increase demand is to require federal and state governments to use recycled paper products as much as possible. The federal government alone uses 2% of all paper products sold in the United States. Half of the trash the government throws away is paper.

In the mid-1970s Congress passed a law calling for federal agencies to buy as many recycled products as practical. But this law has failed because it contains so many exemptions that almost nothing has to be recycled. In 1977 Maryland enacted a similar but better law. Since then recycled paper stock bought by the state has increased by 25%. Five other states have similar laws.

Simple measures like asking teachers to instruct their students to write on both sides of the paper would also reduce unnecessary paper waste and increase environmental awareness. Conservationists call for national, state, and local policies designed to recycle half of the wastepaper in the United States by 2000. What do you think?

Most plastics used today are non-degradable or take some 200 to 500 years to degrade. When these plastics are buried in landfills they take up lots of space.

Scientists are hard at work trying to develop degradable plastics. Some are *photodegradable plastics* that disintegrate after a few weeks' exposure to sunlight. Others are *partially biodegradable* plastics made with a combination of plastic and corn starch. The corn starch can be broken in the soil by aerobic bacteria and moisture, leaving behind a fine powder of plastic. A number of companies are making partially degradable plastic garbage bags, grocery bags, six-pack yokes, and fast-food containers.

Photodegradable and biodegradable plastics make sense for products and containers likely to end up as outdoor litter. But without sunlight, photodegradable plastics take decades to hundreds of years to break down when covered in landfills. Biodegradable plastics take decades to break down partially in landfills because of a lack of aerobic bacteria and moisture.

We also need to know more about what degradable plastics degrade to. The residues that remain after many plastics break down could contaminate groundwater supplies. They also may be hazardous to animals that ingest them. Of particular concern is possible pollution from toxic metal compounds of lead and cadmium used as pigments and stabilizers in some plastics and chlorine compounds from polyvinyl chloride (PVC) plastic.

To many environmentalists, degradable plastics are a sham. Saying a plastic product is degradable doesn't tell us how long it takes to degrade in nonlaboratory conditions and what it degrades into. And adding degradable plastics to other plastics being recycled can gum up recycling equipment.

To environmentalists it makes more sense to recycle plastics instead of burying slowly degradable plastics in landfills and even better sense to reduce the amount of plastic we use. Recycling plastics saves landfill space and also saves twice as much energy as burning them in a waste-to-energy incinerator.

Currently only 1% of all plastic wastes and 4% of plastics packaging used in the United States are recycled. One problem is that plastics rarely can be recycled to make the same products because of health and manufacturing problems. Also, unlike glass or aluminum, plastics aren't all alike. Trash contains several types, and some plastic products contain several types.

Recycling plastics may increase significantly because it is a way to make money. Plastics have become the second most valuable recyclable material after aluminum. Nine states have bottle deposit bills for plastic bottles.

The Plastic Pollution Control Act of 1988 requires that by 1992 all plastic items deemed recyclable by the EPA and the Commerce Department must be recycled. All remaining plastic items would have to be biodegradable.

With proper economic and political incentives, about 43% of the plastic wastes produced in the United States could be recycled by the year 2000. Since most of the raw materials used to make plastics come from petroleum and natural gas, recycling would help reduce unnecessary waste of these energy resources. So far, East Germany is the only country that collects and recycles household plastics on a nationwide scale.

The plastics industry has set up the Council for Solid Waste Solutions which runs ads promoting plastics recycling. But the main purpose of this organization is to keep us buying more plastics. To conservationists the best solution is simply to use less plastic in the first place and pressure elected officials to ban the use of plastics in products where other less harmful alternatives are available.

Consumers are urged to substitute other materials—reusable glass bottles, paper packaging, wax paper for wrapping food, and cloth diapers, for example—for plastics. For example, the 18 million disposable diapers that are dumped into U.S. landfills each year make up about 4% of all household solid waste and take 500 years to decompose.

Disposable diapers cost about $1,716 a child during the 30-month period an infant typically uses diapers. Another $360 million of tax revenues are spent each year for landfill disposal of these diapers. Their disposal also exposes sanitation workers to viral diseases, including hepatitis, polio, and AIDS. By contrast, a diaper service that picks up dirty cloth diapers and leaves clean ones costs about $975 per infant. Washing cloth diapers at home costs only about $299 per infant.

But big oil companies supply the basic ingredients of plastic resins and also own some of the largest trash and grocery bag companies. Thus, they oppose use of degradable plastics containing nonpetroleum products, plastics recycling, and reduced use of plastics. Less use of plastics would reduce the profits of oil companies from the multibillion-dollar-a-year plastic bag, packaging, disposable diaper, and other plastic products businesses.

Companies making plastics, however, point to some of the benefits of plastic containers. They are generally lighter than glass or metal ones so that less energy is required to transport them. Generally they also require less energy to make than glass or metal containers. But environmentalists contend that the energy inputs vary with different types of plastics. They also point out that chlorine-containing plastics, such as polyvinyl chloride (PVC), can contaminate the air and water when produced, incinerated, or decomposed in the environment. What do you think should be done?

Figure 15-19 Evidence of the throwaway mentality at the site of an outdoor rock concert.

UPI/Bettmann Newsphotos

recycling tire rubber, conservationists call for requiring tire companies to use known methods to make only tires that last for an average of 49,700 to 62,100 kilometers (80,000 to 100,000 miles) instead of 18,360 to 24,800 kilometers (30,000 to 40,000 miles).

Obstacles to Recycling in the United States

Hundreds of U.S. cities are recycling 15% to 50% of their municipal solid waste. The recycling honor role includes San Francisco, Seattle, Chicago, Philadelphia, Minneapolis, San Jose and Davis, California, Woodbury, New Jersey, and Hamburg, New York.

Eight states—Connecticut, Florida, Maryland, New Jersey, New York, Oregon, Pennsylvania, and Rhode Island—have comprehensive recycling programs with goals of recycling 25% to 50% of their solid waste sometime before 1995. But more than half of the states currently recycle less than 5% of their municipal solid waste. What are your state and community doing?

Several factors hinder recycling in the United States. One is the failure of many U.S. metals industries to modernize. Since 1950, countries such as Japan and West Germany have built modern steel plants that use large amounts of scrap steel, much of it bought from the United States.

During the same period, the U.S. steel industry did not invest much of its profits in modernizing and replacing older plants. Instead, it continued to rely heavily on older processes that require virgin iron ore. The industry has now lost much of its business to foreign competitors and no longer has the capital to modernize. This shows how overemphasis on short-term economic gain can lead to long-term economic

pain, decline, and loss of jobs for thousands of Americans.

Another problem is that Americans have been conditioned by advertising and example to a throwaway lifestyle (Figure 15-19). The emphasis is on making, using, and replacing more and more items to increase short-term economic growth regardless of the long-term environmental and economic costs. Also, because the true costs of items are not reflected in their market prices, consumers have little incentive to recycle and conserve recoverable resources.

The growth of the recycling, or secondary-materials, industry in the United States is hindered by several factors. One is that primary mining and energy industries get huge tax breaks, depletion allowances, and other tax-supported federal subsidies to encourage them to get virgin resources out of the ground as fast as possible. In contrast, recycling industries get few tax breaks and other subsidies. The lack of large, steady markets for recycled materials also makes recycling a risky business. It is typically a boom-and-bust financial venture that attracts little investment capital.

Overcoming the Obstacles   In 1988 the EPA set a goal of recycling 25% of municipal solid waste by 1992. By the year 2000, the United States could easily recycle and reuse 35% of the municipal solid waste resources it now throws away. Some analysts believe that by 2012 at least 50% and perhaps 80% of these resources could be recycled or reused. Regardless of the percentage, any increase in recycling benefits the economy and the environment.

Greatly increased recycling and reuse in the United States could be accomplished through the following measures:

- Enact a national beverage container law (see Case Study on p. 364).

- Ban use of disposable plastic items.

- Include waste disposal costs in the price of all disposable items rather than in local taxes, so market prices of items directly reflect what it cost to dispose of them. This is now done in Florida, Massachusetts, Michigan, and Minnesota.

- Provide economic incentives for recycling waste oil, plastics, tires, and CFCs used as coolants in refrigerators and air conditioners. Twenty-four states have oil recycling programs, but few are fully implementing them. Only eight states have programs to recycle tires.

- Require labelling of products made with recyclable materials and the percentages used—now done in only eight states.

- Provide federal and state subsidies for secondary-materials industries and for municipal recycling and waste reduction programs. New York, North Carolina, Florida, Oregon, and Wisconsin give tax breaks to businesses that use secondary materials or buy recycling equipment.

- Decrease federal and state subsidies for primary-materials industries.

- Guarantee a large market for recycled items and stimulate the recycling industry by encouraging federal, state, and local governments to require the highest feasible percentage of recycled materials in all products they purchase. Twenty-two states have such laws, but their effectiveness varies widely.

- Use advertising and education to discourage the throwaway mentality.

- Require consumers to sort household wastes for recycling, or give them financial incentives for recycling. For example, garbage separated for recycling can be picked up free while people who don't separate their trash are charged a fee per bag or pound. Also, households can be provided with free reusable containers for separating recyclable trash.

- Encourage municipal composting and back-yard composting by banning the disposal of yard wastes in landfills.

Many U.S. communities are rapidly moving toward recycling, not because it saves energy, resources, or the environment, but because it saves money on solid waste disposal and adds to the local economy (see Guest Essay on p. 371). Based on current costs, it is estimated that an average suburban community with landfill or incineration charges of $45 a ton or more would save money by recycling much of its solid waste. What is your community doing?

Reusable Products   Reuse involves using the same product again and again in its original form. An example is glass beverage bottles that can be collected, washed, and refilled by bottling companies. Until 1975 most beverage containers in the United States were refillable glass. Today they make up only 15% of the market, with nonrefillable aluminum and plastic containers making up the rest.

Another reusable container is the metal or plastic lunch box that most workers and school children once used. Today many people carry their lunches in paper or plastic bags that are thrown away. If you must use plastic bags, reuse baggies by washing them out. Use empty bread bags to carry your lunch and to wrap food for storage in the refrigerator. Reusable cloth diapers can be used instead of disposable ones (see Case Study on p. 367).

Reuse extends resource supplies and reduces energy use and pollution even more than recycling. Refillable glass bottles are the most energy-efficient beverage container on the market. Three times more energy is needed to crush and remelt a glass bottle to make a new one than to clean and refill it. Cleaning and refilling a bottle also takes much less energy than melting a used aluminum can and making a new one.

If reusable glass bottles replaced the 82 billion throwaway beverage cans produced annually in the United States, enough energy would be saved to supply the annual electricity needs of 13 million people. Denmark has led the way by banning all nonreusable beverage containers.

Reuse is much easier if containers for products that can be packaged in reusable glass are available in only a few sizes. In Norway and Denmark, less than 20 sizes of reusable containers for beer and soft drinks are allowed. In Ecuador there are only two sizes of bottles, and with a 15 cent deposit most bottles are reused and many stay in circulation for more than 10 years.

Waste Reduction   Reducing unnecessary waste of nonrenewable mineral resources, plastics, and paper can extend supplies even more dramatically than recycling and reuse. Reducing waste generally saves more energy than recycling and reduces the environmental impacts of extracting, processing, and using resources (Figure 15-7). Table 15-1 compares the throwaway resource system of the United States, a resource recovery and recycling system, and a sustainable-earth, or low-waste, resource system.

Manufacturers can conserve resources by using less material per product. Smaller, lighter cars, for example, save nonfuel mineral resources as well as energy.

Solid-state electronic devices and microwave transmissions greatly reduce materials requirements. Optical fibers drastically reduce the demand for copper wire in telephone transmission lines.

Another low-waste approach is to make products that last longer. The economies of the United States and most industrial countries are built on the principle of planned obsolescence. With planned obsolescence, product lives are designed to be much shorter than they could be so that people will buy more things to stimulate the economy and raise short-term profits. Many things appear to be designed to break down or fall apart after the warranty runs out or after the loan has been paid off. Many consumers can empathize with Willy Loman in Arthur Miller's *Death of a Salesman*: "Once in my life I would like to own something outright before it's broken! I'm always in a race with the junkyard." Much of the more than $45 billion Americans spend each year on clothing is to replace perfectly good clothes that manufacturers tell consumers are no longer in style.

Products should also be easy to repair. Today many items are intentionally designed to make repair impossible or too expensive. Manufacturers should adopt the principle of modular design which allows circuits in computers and other electronic devices to be easily and quickly replaced without replacing the entire item. We also need to develop remanufacturing industries that would disassemble, repair, and reassemble used and broken items.

What Can You Do to Help? Each of us must understand and accept our role in both creating solid waste and in conserving these vital matter resources. The most important thing we need to do is to make a conscious effort to produce less waste mostly by not using disposable products when other alternatives are available. Since both paper and plastic products cause pollution during their manufacture and make up much of the solid waste, the best solution is to avoid paper and plastic products if possible. Also push for mandatory trash separation and recycling programs in your community and schools. Use rechargeable batteries.

Write to manufacturers and tell them what you like or dislike about their package or product. Buy food items in large cans or bulk to reduce packaging. Don't put fruits and vegetables in plastic bags. Choose items that have the least packaging or, better yet, no packaging. When enough people do this, producers of packaged materials will get the message.

Carry small loads of groceries and other items in a reusable basket, string or canvas bag, or small cart. BYOC (bring your own container) is one reason why Europeans, Africans, and Asians produce so much

Table 15-1 Three Systems for Handling Discarded Materials

Item	For a High-Waste Throwaway System	For a Moderate-Waste Resource Recovery and Recycling System	For a Low-Waste Sustainable Earth-System
Glass bottles	Dump or bury	Grind and remelt; remanufacture; convert to building materials	Ban all nonreturnable bottles and reuse (not remelt and recycle) bottles
Bimetallic "tin" cans	Dump or bury	Sort, remelt	Limit or ban production; use returnable bottles
Aluminum cans	Dump or bury	Sort, remelt	Limit or ban production; use returnable bottles
Cars	Dump	Sort, remelt	Sort, remelt; tax cars lasting less than 15 years, weighing more than 818 kilograms (1,800 pounds), and getting less than 13 kilometers per liter (30 miles per gallon)
Metal objects	Dump or bury	Sort, remelt	Sort, remelt; tax items lasting less than 10 years.
Tires	Dump, burn, or bury	Grind and revulcanize or use in road construction; incinerate to generate heat and electricity.	Recap usable tires; tax or ban all tires not usable for at least 96,000 kilometers (60,000 miles)
Paper	Dump, burn, or bury	Incinerate to generate heat	Compost or recycle; tax all throwaway items; eliminate overpackaging
Plastics	Dump, burn, or bury	Incinerate to generate heat or electricity	Limit production; use returnable glass bottles instead of plastic containers; tax throwaway items and packaging
Yard wastes	Dump, burn, or bury	Incinerate to generate heat or electricity	Compost; return to soil as fertilizer; use as animal feed

less solid waste per person than most people in the United States.

Skip the bag when you buy only a quart of milk, a loaf of bread, or anything you can carry out with your hands. Tell store clerks and managers why you are doing this and increase their sensitivity to unnecessary waste.

Buy beverages in reusable glass bottles instead of metal and plastic containers and again explain to store clerks and managers why you are doing this. If you can't find a reusable container, use one that is recyclable. Ask stores, communities, and colleges to install reverse vending machines that give you cash for each reusable or recyclable container you put in. If a product isn't recyclable or reusable, ask yourself if you really need it.

Use cloth napkins and dish towels instead of paper ones, and don't use throwaway paper and plastic plates and cups. If you have an infant, use a cloth diaper service instead of disposable diapers. Don't buy helium-filled plastic balloons, and urge elected officials and university administrators to ban balloon releases except for atmospheric research and monitoring.

At work don't use throwaway coffee and drink cups, forks, spoons, and paper towels. Instead, have your own reusable coffee cup, glass, spoon, fork, and cloth napkin and towel and encourage others to do this.

Pressure managers of businesses and schools to separate valuable ledger and computer paper for recycling. Ask heads of companies to switch their letterhead and paper stock to recycled products. Join a local environmental group and urge it to identify suppliers of recycled products in your area. Consider going into the recycling business as a way to make money. And of course, don't litter.

We owe our children, future generations, and the other species that live on this planet with us a better environmental future. Each of our acts—no matter how small—that helps sustain rather than destroy the earth contributes to this goal.

Solid wastes are only raw materials we're too stupid to use.

Arthur C. Clarke

GUEST ESSAY Materials Recovery and the Wealth of a Nation

Neil Seldman

Neil Seldman is co-founder and President of the Institute for Local Self Reliance (ILSR). Since 1974 this organization has promoted use, recovery, and reuse of local resources to enhance local self-reliance. He has worked with the World Bank, the National Science Foundation, several cities, and numerous private industries and citizens groups to implement projects that support local self-reliance. Among the books he has written or co-authored are: Proven Profits from Pollution Prevention: Case Studies in Resource Conservation and Waste Reduction *(1986, ILSR);* Waste to Wealth: A Business Guide for Community Recycling Enterprises *(1985, ILSR);* An Environmental Review of Incineration Technologies *(1985, ILSR);* Garbage in Europe: Technologies, Economics, and Trends *(1984, ILSR); and* Proven Profits *(1984, ILSR).*

Today, it is impossible for city officials to ignore the demand for reevaluating decisions to bury and burn waste. The costs of these approaches is now simply too high. By 1988 landfill costs had shot up to over $100 a ton on the East Coast and other areas of the country are facing costs of over $50 a ton. Ten years ago typical landfill costs were $10 a ton. To meet the increased costs, such cities must sharply raise property or other taxes.

The cost of building and operating incinerators is also rising. These costs will increase more as new air pollution control devices and hazardous ash disposal procedures are adopted at the state and federal levels. Also, these plants will become the single largest source of pollution from toxic metals, particulate matter, and acid-forming gases in most of the communities where they are located. One incinerator plant, even with all the presently required air pollution control devices, adds as much sulfur dioxide to the air as 186,000 additional cars driving 34 miles per day.

Happily, grassroots citizens organizations and recycling groups have shifted solid waste management procedures away from bury or burn in many cities. Between 1985 and 1989 over 30 incinerators, which would have cost $4 billion, were cancelled because of actions by informed local citizens. In Austin, Texas, the city council cancelled a plant after

(continued)

CHAPTER SUMMARY

People mine more than 100 nonrenewable nonfuel minerals from mineral deposits in the earth's crust. Minerals are formed and modified as a result of processes taking place over millions of years in the earth's rock cycle.

Using a mineral resource involves several steps: locating a rich-enough deposit, extracting the mineral by some form of mining, processing the mineral to remove impurities and to convert it to the desired chemical form, and then using the mineral to make various products.

Mineral deposits located near the earth's surface are removed by *surface mining* such as open-pit mining, strip mining, or dredging. When a mineral deposit lies deep in the ground it is extracted by *subsurface mining*.

The mining, processing, and use of any nonfuel mineral resource cause land disturbance, erosion, air pollu- tion, and water pollution. Subsurface mining is more dangerous and expensive than surface mining but disturbs far less land. Subsurface mining can also pollute water from acid mine drainage. Surface-mined land can be restored in most cases, but the process is expensive. The production of minerals and the throwaway approach to use of products made from minerals and timber also create massive amounts of solid waste.

Estimating how much of a particular nonrenewable mineral resource exists and how much of it can be located and extracted at an affordable price is a complex and controversial process. Supplies of mineral resources are divided into *identified resources* and *undiscovered resources*. These categories are each then subdivided into *reserves* (identified resources that can be extracted profitably at present prices with current mining technology) and *resources* (all identified and unidentified resources, including those that cannot be recovered profitably with present

---

GUEST ESSAY Materials Recovery and the Wealth of a Nation (continued)

spending $23 million, because it discovered it could save $150 million by adopting a recycling program. New York City would save $456 million a year if it recycled half of its solid waste.

Recycling is at the take-off stage in the United States. Since 1968, drop-off, curbside pickup, and buy-back recycling programs have flourished. From 1989 on there will be major new investments in recycling.

Households that separate and recycle wastes will be given lower rates than those that still discard their solid waste. Haulers will be given "shared savings" payments for helping cities save money through recycling. They will also be given low-interest loans to buy new recycling equipment. "Recycling literacy" programs will teach students how and why to recycle.

Seattle has set a 65% recycling goal and Philadelphia a 50% goal. Some towns in the United States and Europe have achieved a 70% recycling rate, primarily by adding composting to their recycling programs.

As cities and counties move from 10% or 20% recycling to over 50% recycling, millions of tons of usable materials they are now throwing away will be recovered. This will create jobs and stimulate the local economy. By contrast, the outdated burn and bury strategy creates far fewer jobs and imposes large costs and higher taxes on a community. Materials recovery can also significantly reduce energy use and thus also reduce carbon dioxide emissions and other forms of atmospheric pollution.

The percentage of paper recycled in the United States could easily be raised from today's 26% rate to 80%. About 30% to 40% of U.S. urban waste consists of organic matter—food, yard waste, and sewage— that could be composted and used to displace commercial fertilizer that pollutes the air and water and takes lots of energy to produce.

Collecting and using discarded paper, plastics, and metals as raw materials for small-scale local manufac- turing plants adds jobs, increases the tax base, and recycles dollars to the local community. Wasting these potential resources by burying or burning them costs the community huge amounts of money.

New small-scale technologies in plastic, glass, metal, and glass manufacturing make it possible for cities to produce much of what its government, citizens, and businesses need from recycled local materials, without having to import these goods from outside the city. Development of such plants can be stimulated by government procurement policies which favor products with recycled material content and economic development programs to attract such industries.

The potential economic rewards for cities that recycle and manufacture new products from these materials are huge. For example, tire disposal alone costs Newark, New Jersey $700,000 a year. But, if Newark built a rubber recycling plant with a combination of loans from state, county, and city sources over $3 million would be injected into the local economy annually. With the money saved from tire disposal that's a $3.7 million boost for the economy each year.

People who recycle are rewarded by knowing that they are helping improve their local community, state, and country and making the world more sustainable for future generations. I hope you will join the recycling and reuse revolution and encourage such economically and environmentally beneficial programs in your local community.

Guest Essay Discussion

1. How is solid waste handled in your community? Would you favor a mandatory waste separation and recycling program for your community? Explain.

2. How much of what you use do you recycle or reuse? Why don't you recycle or reuse more?

prices and technology). Most published estimates of a particular nonrenewable mineral refer to reserves.

When 80% of the reserves or estimated resources of a mineral have been extracted and used, the resource is said to be depleted because removing the remaining 20% is usually not profitable. The amount available and thus the depletion time can be increased by an increase in the estimated reserves when higher prices lead to new discoveries, new mining technology, increased recycling and reuse, or reduced consumption. Substitutes can be found for some economically depleted resources.

The United States depends on imports from 25 other countries for more than 24 of its 42 most critical and strategic nonfuel minerals. U.S. reserves for 20 critical nonfuel minerals are projected to be inadequate by the year 2000.

To extend supplies, environmentalists favor greatly increasing recycling and reuse of nonrenewable mineral resources and reducing unnecessary waste of such resources. Recycling, reuse, and waste reduction also require less energy resources and produce less land degradation and air and water pollution than use of virgin resources.

Despite these advantages, currently only about 10% of the municipal solid waste is recycled in the United States, compared to rates of 50% in Japan and several European countries. Most of the solid waste in the United States is buried in landfills or burned in incinerators.

Factors hindering recycling in the United States include (1) failure of U.S. industries to install new processes that make use of recycled iron, steel, paper, and other materials, (2) a throwaway lifestyle in which wastes are not viewed as potential resources, (3) tax breaks, depletion allowances, and other tax-supported federal subsidies designed to encourage mining industries to get virgin resources out of the ground as fast as possible, (4) lack of similar incentives for recycling and reuse of materials, and (5) lack of large, steady markets for recycled materials.

Environmentalists call for the United States and other MDCs to shift from high-waste, throwaway societies to low-waste, sustainable-earth societies. This will require greatly increased composting, recycling, reuse, and reduction of resources we now think of as wastes. It will also require economic incentives, action by governments and individuals, and changes in attitudes and lifestyles.

DISCUSSION TOPICS

1. So far only about 0.3% of the land area of the United States has been surface mined. Why then should we be concerned about the environmental impact from increasing surface mining?

2. What resources are mined in your local area? What mining methods are used? Do local, state, or federal laws require restoration of the landscape after mining is completed? If so, how well are these laws enforced?

3. Do you believe that the United States is an overdeveloped country that uses and unnecessarily wastes too many of the world's resources relative to its population size? Explain.

4. Debate each of the following propositions:
   a. The competitive free market will control the supply and demand of mineral resources.
   b. New discoveries will provide all the raw materials we need.
   c. The ocean will supply all the mineral resources we need.
   d. We will not run out of key mineral resources because we can always mine lower-grade deposits.
   e. When a mineral resource becomes scarce, we can always find a substitute.
   f. When a nonrenewable resource becomes scarce, all we have to do is recycle it.

5. Use the second law of energy (thermodynamics) to show why the following options are usually not profitable:
   a. extracting most minerals dissolved in seawater
   b. recycling minerals that are widely dispersed
   c. mining increasingly lower-grade deposits of minerals
   d. using inexhaustible solar energy to mine mineral
   e. continuing to mine, use, and recycle minerals at increasing rates.

6. Explain why you support or oppose the following:
   a. eliminating all tax breaks and depletion allowan for extraction of virgin resources by mining industries
   b. passing a national beverage container deposit law
   c. requiring that all beverage containers be reusable

7. Why is it difficult to get accurate estimates of mineral resource supplies?

8. Compare the throwaway, recycling, and sustainable-earth (or low-waste) approaches to waste disposal and resource recovery and conservation for (a) glass bottles, (b) "tin" cans, (c) aluminum cans, (d) plastics, and (e) leaves, grass, and food wastes (see Table 15-1). Which approach do you favor? Which approach do you use in your own lifestyle?

9. Keep a list for a week of the solid waste materials you dispose of. What percentage is composed of materials that could be recycled, reused, or burned as a source of energy?

10. Would you favor requiring all households and businesses to sort recyclable materials for curbside pickup in separate containers? Explain.

11. Determine whether (a) your college and your city have recycling programs; (b) your college sells soft drinks in throwaway cans or bottles; (c) your college bans release of helium-filled balloons at sporting events and other activities, and (d) your state has, or is contemplating, a law requiring deposits on all beverage containers.

CHAPTER 16

Nonrenewable Energy Resources:
Fossil Fuels, Geothermal Energy,
and Nuclear Energy

General Questions and Issues

1. How can we evaluate present and future energy alternatives?

2. What are the uses, advantages, and disadvantages of oil and natural gas as energy resources?

3. What are the uses, advantages, and disadvantages of coal as an energy resource?

4. What are the uses, advantages, and disadvantages of geothermal energy as an energy resource?

5. What are the advantages and disadvantages of using conventional nuclear fission, breeder nuclear fission, and nuclear fusion to produce electricity?

We are an interdependent world and if we ever needed a lesson in that, we got it in the oil crisis of the 1970s.

Robert S. McNamara

U seful high-quality energy is the lifeblood of the ecosphere and human societies. About 99% of the energy we and other living organisms use comes from the sun and costs us nothing. As we have shifted from hunting-and-gathering societies to agricultural societies to industrialized societies, creative people have found ways to supplement this input of solar energy (Figure 2-3, p. 34).

These supplemental energy resources now supply 1% of the energy we use. Supplemental energy resources—mostly oil, coal, and natural gas—have supported most of the world's economic growth, especially since 1950. Their use has also greatly increased pollution and environmental degradation.

Most analysts agree that the era of cheap oil is coming to an end. This means we must find substitutes for the oil that now supplies one-third of the world's supplemental energy (40% in the United States and 55% in Japan) and 90% of the energy we use for transportation.

Some say we should burn more coal and synthetic liquid and gaseous fuels made from coal. Some believe natural gas is the answer. Others think nuclear power is the answer (see Guest Essay on p. 406). Others believe that a combination of energy conservation and increased energy from the sun, wind, flowing water, biomass, and heat from the earth's core (geothermal energy) is the solution (see Guest Essay on p. 408). Each of these energy choices has certain advantages and disadvantages, as discussed in this and the next chapter.

16-1 EVALUATING ENERGY RESOURCES

Experience has shown that it takes about 50 years to develop and phase in new supplemental energy resources on a large scale (Figure 16-1). In deciding which combination of energy alternatives we should use to supplement solar energy in the future, we need to plan for three time periods: the short term (1991 to 2001), the intermediate term (2001 to 2011), and the long term (2011 to 2041).

First we must decide how much we need, or want, of different kinds of energy, such as low-temperature heat, high-temperature heat, electricity, and fuels for transportation. This involves deciding what type and quality of energy (Figure 3-7, p. 59) can best perform each energy task (see Guest Essay on p. 408). Then we decide which energy sources can meet these needs at the lowest cost and environmental impact by answering four questions about each alternative:

- How much will probably be available during the short term, intermediate term, and long term?
- What is the estimated net useful energy yield (Figure 3-17, p. 69)?
- How much will it cost to develop, phase in, and use?
- What are its potentially harmful environmental, social, and military and economic security impacts and how can they be reduced?

After answering these questions, we will be ready to develop personal, local, national, and global energy strategies.

We can use geologic analysis to project how long nonrenewable energy resources such as oil, coal, natural gas, uranium (used to fuel nuclear reactors), and some forms of geothermal energy might last (Figure 15-12, p. 353). The first and second laws of energy can help us evaluate the net useful energy we can get from each energy option (Section 3-5).

We can use economic analysis to help us decide which energy choices are the most cost-effective so that we can make wise use of our limited financial capital (Section 22-4). Ecology and environmental science can help us evaluate the environmental impacts of each energy alternative. This is crucial because most of the world's air pollution, water pollution, and land disruption comes from mining, processing, and using fossil fuels (Figure 15-7, p. 349). For example, nearly 80% of all U.S. air pollution is caused by burning fossil fuels in cars, furnaces, industries, and power plants.

Politics also plays a major role in our energy choices. The political influence of energy companies and individuals helps determine how tax dollars are allocated to subsidize the development and use of various energy resources. The choices we make as individuals about the types and amounts of energy we consume as individuals are political and economic acts that help shape national energy policy as well as our own economic well-being. Because we have limited funds and little time to develop and phase in replacements for oil, making the wrong choices could lead to economic and environmental chaos and increase the threat of conventional and nuclear wars.

Ethics derived from our world view should be the bedrock for making national and individual energy decisions (Chapter 24). The most important question decision makers should ask is: What energy choices will do the most to sustain the earth for us, for future generations, and for the other species living on this planet? In choosing a lifestyle each person should ask: How can I live in a way that sustains rather than degrades the earth's life-support systems?

Despite their importance, these ethical questions are rarely considered by government officials, energy company executives, and most people. Changing this

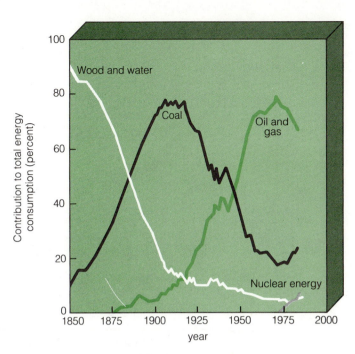

Figure 16-1 Shifts in use of energy resources in the United States since 1850. Shifts from wood to coal and then from coal to oil and natural gas have each taken about 50 years. (Data from U.S. Department of Energy)

situation is probably the most important and difficult challenge we face.

16-2 OIL AND NATURAL GAS

Conventional Crude Oil **Petroleum**, or **crude oil**, is a gooey liquid consisting mostly of hydrocarbon compounds and small amounts of compounds containing oxygen, sulfur, and nitrogen. Crude oil and natural gas are often trapped together deep within the earth's crust on land (Figure 16-2) and beneath the sea floor. Usually the crude oil is dispersed in pores and cracks of these underground rock formations.

The most valued petroleum, known as light or sweet crude, contains few sulfur impurities and large amounts of components that can be easily refined into gasoline. The lower the sulfur content of oil, the less sulfur dioxide emitted into the atmosphere when the oil is burned. The least valued petroleum is heavy or sour crude. It has higher levels of sulfur impurities and is more difficult and more costly to refine into gasoline than sweet crude.

If there is enough pressure from water and natural gas under the dome of rock, some of the crude oil will be pushed to the surface when a well is drilled. Such wells, called gushers, are rare. **Primary oil recovery** involves pumping out the oil that flows by gravity into the bottom of the well. Thicker, slowly flowing heavy oil is not removed.

After the flowing oil has been removed, water can be injected into adjacent wells to force some of the

Figure 16-2 Oil and natural gas are usually found together beneath a dome of impermeable cap rock.

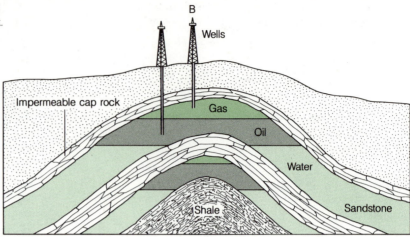

Wells

Impermeable cap rock

Gas

Oil

Water

Shale

Sandstone

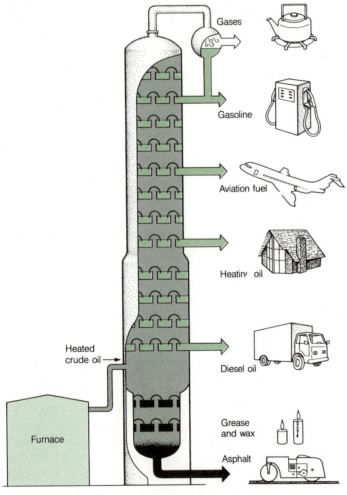

Gases

Gasoline

Aviation fuel

Heating oil

Diesel oil

Grease and wax

Heated crude oil

Asphalt

Furnace

Figure 16-3 Refining of crude oil. Major components are removed at various levels, depending on their boiling points, in a giant distillation column.

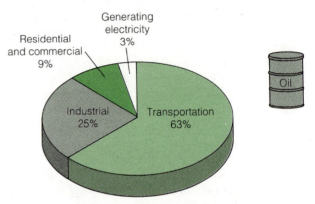

Generating electricity 3%

Residential and commercial 9%

Industrial 25%

Transportation 63%

Oil

Figure 16-4 How oil was used in the United States in 1987. About 60% of the 16.5 million barrels of oil consumed *each day* in 1987 came from domestic sources. The rest was imported, with about 18% coming from OPEC countries (8% from Arab OPEC countries) and 22% from non-OPEC countries. (Data from U. S. Department of Energy)

ical well. As oil prices rise, it may become economical to remove about 10% of the heavy oil by **enhanced oil recovery**. One method is to force steam into the well to soften the heavy oil so that it can be pumped to the surface. Carbon dioxide gas can also be pumped into a well to force some of the heavy oil into the well cavity for pumping to the surface.

The problem is that enhanced oil recovery is expensive. The net useful energy yield is low because we have to use the energy equivalent of one-third of a barrel of oil to soften and pump each barrel of heavy oil to the surface. Additional energy is needed to increase the flow rate and to remove sulfur and nitrogen impurities before the heavy oil can be pumped through a pipeline to an oil refinery. Recoverable heavy oil from known U.S. crude oil reserves could supply U.S. oil needs for only about seven years at current usage rates.

Once it is removed from a well, most crude oil is sent by pipeline to a refinery. There it is heated and distilled to separate it into gasoline, heating oil, diesel oil, asphalt, and other components. Because these

remaining thicker crude oil into the central well and push it to the surface. This is known as **secondary oil recovery**. Usually primary and secondary recovery remove only one-third of the crude oil in a well.

For each barrel removed by primary and secondary recovery, two barrels of heavy oil are left in a typ-

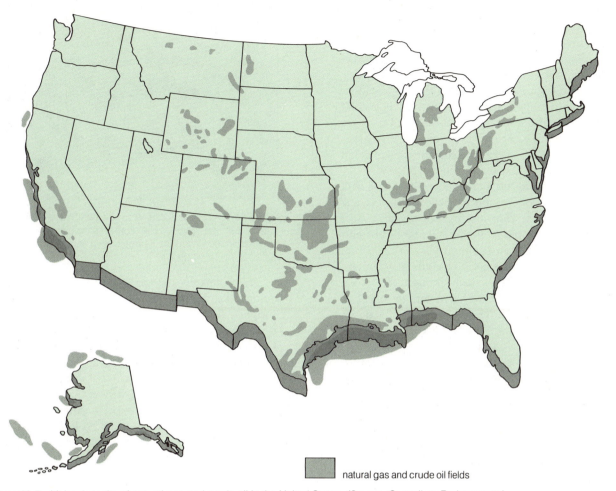

Figure 16-5 Major deposits of natural gas and crude oil in the United States. (Source: Council on Environmental Quality)

components boil at different temperatures, they are removed at different levels of giant distillation columns (Figure 16-3).

Some components called **petrochemicals** are used as raw materials in industrial chemicals, fertilizers, pesticides, plastics, synthetic fibers, paints, medicines, and many other products. About 3% of the crude oil extracted throughout the world (7% in the U.S.) is used in this way. Thus, the prices of many items we use go up after crude oil prices rise.

How Long Will Supplies of Conventional Crude Oil Last? Almost two-thirds of the world's proven oil reserves are in just five countries: Saudi Arabia, Kuwait, Iran, Iraq, and the United Arab Emirates. OPEC countries have 67% of these reserves, with Saudi Arabia having 25%. The Middle East also contains most of the world's undiscovered oil. This explains why OPEC is expected to have long-term control over world oil supplies and prices.

There are also imbalances between oil reserves and where oil is extracted and consumed. The Soviet Union is presently the world's largest oil extractor, with an annual output triple that of Saudi Arabia. The United

States has only 3% of the world's oil reserves but uses nearly 30% of the oil extracted each year. Transportation uses almost two-thirds of the 17 million barrels of oil consumed each day in the United States (Figure 16-4).

Although the United States is the world's second largest oil extractor, it has imported oil since 1950 to help meet its enormous demand. Most oil deposits in the Middle East are large and cheap to extract; most in the United States are small and more expensive to tap. Therefore, it has generally been cheaper for the United States to buy oil from other countries than to extract it from its own deposits (Figure 1-9, p. 14).

U.S. military intervention in the Persian Gulf by the Reagan and Bush administrations since 1985 means that U.S. oil imports from Arab OPEC countries cost $495 a barrel when the military costs are included. Thus, Americans are buying the world's most expensive oil—costing about 28 times the average market price for oil—to meet about 8% of their consumption. They are also footing most of the bill for protecting the much larger amounts of Arab OPEC oil going to Japan and western European countries.

Figure 16-5 shows the locations of the major crude oil and natural gas fields in the United States. U.S. oil extraction has declined steadily since 1970 despite greatly increased exploration and test drilling. Because of much unsuccessful exploratory drilling, in 1989 the U.S. Geological Survey lowered its estimate of undiscovered oil in the United States by 58%.

Experts disagree over how long the world's identified and unidentified crude oil resources will last. At present consumption rates, world crude oil reserves will be economically depleted in 33 years. U.S. reserves will be depleted by 2005 at the current consumption rate and by 2001 if oil use increases by 2% a year.

Cornucopians argue that higher oil prices will stimulate the discovery and extraction of large new crude oil resources. They also believe we can extract and upgrade heavy oils from oil shale, tar sands, and enhanced recovery from existing wells.

Some believe that the earth's mantle may contain 100 times more oil than usually thought. But such deposits, if they exist, lie 10 kilometers (6 miles) or more below the earth's surface—about twice the depth of today's deepest wells. New and expensive drilling technology would have to be developed to find and tap these deposits. Most geologists do not believe these deposits exist. But if they do, and if they could be tapped at an affordable price compared to other energy options, they would meet human oil needs for centuries.

Neo-Malthusians argue that cornucopians misunderstand the arithmetic and consequences of exponential growth in the use of any nonrenewable resource. Consider the following facts about the world's exponential growth in oil use, assuming that we continue to use crude oil at the current rate:

- Saudi Arabia, with the world's largest known crude oil reserves, could supply all the world's oil needs for only ten years if it were the world's only source.

- Mexico, with the world's sixth largest crude oil reserves, could supply the world's needs for only about three years.

- The estimated crude oil reserves under Alaska's North Slope—the largest deposit ever found in North America—would meet world demand for only six months or U.S. demand for three years.

- The oil that oil companies have a one-in-five chance of finding by drilling in Alaska's Arctic Wildlife Refuge would meet world demand for only one month and U.S. demand for six months.

- All estimated undiscovered, recoverable deposits of oil in the United States would meet world demand for only 1.7 years and U.S. demand for 10 years.

- Cornucopians who believe that new discoveries will solve world oil supply problems must figure out how to discover the equivalent of a new Saudi Arabian deposit *every ten years* just to keep on using oil at the current rate.

Figure 16-6 Sample of oil shale rock and the shale oil extracted from it. Major oil shale projects have now been canceled in the United States because of excessive cost.

U.S. Department of Energy

The ultimately recoverable supply of crude oil is estimated to be three times today's proven reserves. Suppose all this new oil is found and developed—which most oil experts consider unlikely—and sold at a price of $50 to $95 a barrel, compared to the 1988 price of about $18 a barrel. About 80% of this oil would be depleted by 2073 at the current usage rate and by 2037 if oil use increased 2% a year.

We can see why most experts expect little of the world's affordable crude oil to be left by the 2059 bicentennial of the world's first oil well. Oil company executives have known this for a long time, which explains why oil companies have become diversified energy companies. To keep making money after oil runs out, these international companies now own much of the world's natural gas, coal, and uranium reserves and have bought many of the companies producing solar collectors and solar cells.

Advantages and Disadvantages of Oil   Oil has been and still is fairly cheap (Figure 1-10, p. 15), can easily be transported within and between countries, and has a high net useful energy yield (Figure 3-17, p. 69). It is also a versatile fuel that can be burned to propel vehicles, heat buildings and water, and supply high-temperature heat for industrial processes and electricity production.

Oil also has some disadvantages. Its burning releases carbon dioxide gas, which could alter global climate, and other air pollutants such as sulfur oxides and nitrogen oxides which damage people, crops, trees, fish, and other wild species. Oil spills and leakage of toxic drilling muds cause water pollution, and the brine solution injected into oil wells can contaminate groundwater. The crucial disadvantage of oil is that affordable supplies are expected to be depleted within 40 to 80 years.

Heavy Oil from Oil Shale   **Oil shale** is a fine-grained sedimentary rock (Figure 16-6) that contains varying amounts of a solid, waxy mixture of hydrocarbon

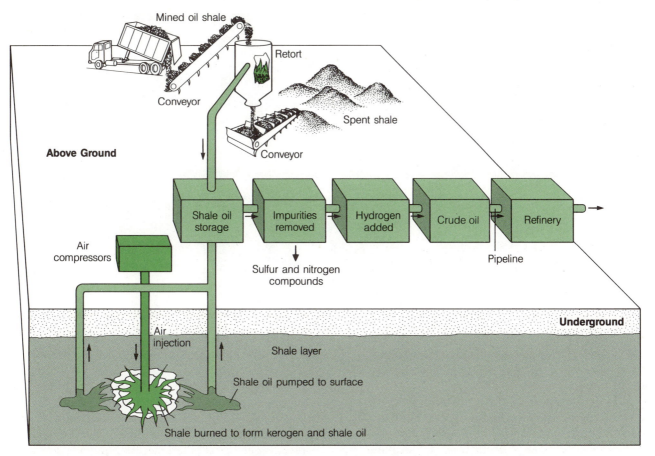

Figure 16-7 Aboveground and underground (in situ) methods for producing synthetic crude oil from oil shale.

compounds called **kerogen**. After being removed by surface or subsurface mining, shale rock is crushed and heated to a high temperature to vaporize the kerogen (Figure 16-7). The kerogen vapor is condensed, forming a slow-flowing, dark brown, heavy oil called **shale oil**. Before shale oil can be sent by pipeline to a refinery, it must be processed to increase its flow rate and heat content and to remove sulfur, nitrogen, and other impurities.

The world's largest known deposits of oil shale are in Colorado, Utah, and Wyoming. Because 80% of this rock is below public lands, energy companies must get leases from the federal government to exploit these resources. In 1987 conservationists were outraged when the Reagan administration leased 33,000 hectares (82,000 acres) of prime public grazing and recreation land in Colorado to an oil-shale consortium for a mere $2.50 an acre.

It is estimated that the potentially recoverable heavy oil from oil shale deposits in the United States could meet the country's crude oil demand for 41 years if consumption remains at the current level, and for 32 years if consumption rises 2% a year. Large oil shale deposits are also found in Canada, China, and the Soviet Union.

Environmental problems may limit shale oil production. Shale oil processing requires large amounts of water, which is scarce in the semiarid areas where the richest deposits are found. The conversion of kerogen to processed shale oil and its burning release more carbon dioxide per unit of energy than conventional oil. Nitrogen oxides and sulfur dioxide are also released. There would be massive land disruption from the mining and disposal of large volumes of shale rock, which breaks up and expands like popcorn when heated. Also various salts, cancer-causing substances, and toxic metal compounds can be leached from the processed shale rock into nearby water supplies.

One way to avoid some of these environmental problems is to extract oil from shale underground—known as *in situ* (in-place) *processing* (Figure 16-7). But this method is too expensive with present technology and produces more sulfur dioxide emissions than surface processing.

The net useful energy yield of shale oil is much lower than that of conventional oil because the energy equivalent of almost one-half of a barrel of conventional crude oil is needed to extract, process, and upgrade one barrel of shale oil (Figure 3-17, p. 69). Also shale oil does not refine as well as crude oil and yields fewer useful products.

In 1987, scientists at Lawrence Livermore Laboratory developed a process they claim might produce shale oil for $25 a barrel. But some analysts believe that shale oil may never be economically feasible because it takes so much energy (derived mostly from

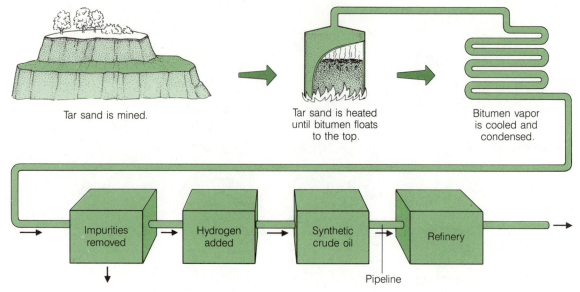

Figure 16-8 Generalized summary of how synthetic crude oil is produced from tar sand.

crude oil) to extract, process, upgrade, and refine. If so, each increase in the price of crude oil would also raise the price of shale oil.

Heavy Oil from Tar Sand **Tar sand** (or oil sand) is a deposit of a mixture of fine clay, sand, water, and varying amounts of **bitumen**, a gooey, black, high-sulfur, heavy oil. Tar sand is usually removed by surface mining and heated with steam at high pressure to make the bitumen fluid enough to float to the top. The bitumen is removed and then purified and chemically upgraded into a synthetic crude oil suitable for refining (Figure 16-8). So far it is not technically or economically feasible to remove deeper deposits of tar sand by underground mining or to remove bitumen by underground extraction.

The world's largest known deposits of tar sands lie in a cold, desolate area in northern Alberta, Canada. Heavy oil in these deposits is estimated to exceed the proven oil reserves of Saudi Arabia. Other large deposits are in Venezuela, Colombia, and the Soviet Union. Smaller deposits exist in the United States, mostly in Utah. If all these were developed, they would supply all U.S. oil needs at the current usage rate for only about three months at a price of $48 to $62 a barrel.

Since 1985 two Canadian plants have been supplying almost 12% of Canada's oil demand by extracting and processing heavy oil from tar sands at a cost of $12 to $15 a barrel—below the average world oil price between 1986 and 1988. By 2000 tar sands should be supplying 20% of Canada's oil demand. Economically recoverable deposits of heavy oil from tar sands can supply all of Canada's projected oil needs for about 33 years at the current consumption rate. These deposits are an important source of oil for Canada, but they

would meet the world's present oil needs for only about 2 years.

Producing synthetic crude oil from tar sands has several disadvantages. The net useful energy yield is low because it takes the energy equivalent of almost one-half of a barrel of conventional oil to extract and process one barrel of bitumen and upgrade it to synthetic crude oil before it can be sent to an oil refinery. Other problems include the need for large quantities of water for processing and the release of air and water pollutants. Upgrading bitumen to synthetic crude oil releases sulfur dioxide, hydrogen sulfide, and particulates of toxic metals such as lead, cadmium, nickel, and chromium.

Environmentalists charge that synthetic crude oil is produced from tar sand at a low price only because Canada's plants are not required to control air pollution emissions. The plants have also created huge waste disposal ponds. Cleaning up these toxic waste dump sites is another external cost not included in the price of crude oil produced from Canadian tar sand.

Natural Gas In its underground gaseous state, **natural gas** is a mixture of 50% to 90% methane gas and smaller amounts of heavier gaseous hydrocarbon compounds such as propane and butane. *Conventional natural gas* lies above most deposits of crude oil (Figure 16-2). *Unconventional natural gas* is found by itself in other underground deposits.

When a natural gas deposit is tapped, propane and butane gases are liquefied and removed as **liquefied petroleum gas (LPG)**. LPG is stored in pressurized tanks for use mostly in rural areas not served by natural gas pipelines. The rest of the gas (mostly methane) in the deposit is dried, cleaned of hydrogen sul-

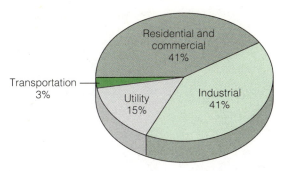

Figure 16-9 How natural gas was used in the United States in 1987. About 95% of this supply came from domestic sources and the other 5% was imported by pipeline from Canada. (Data from U. S. Department of Energy)

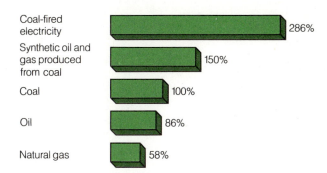

Figure 16-10 Carbon dioxide emissions per unit of energy produced by other fossil fuels as percentages of those produced by coal.

fide and other impurities, and pumped into pressurized pipelines for distribution.

At a very low temperature natural gas can be converted to **liquefied natural gas (LNG)**. This liquid form of natural gas can then be shipped to other countries in refrigerated tanker ships.

How Long Will Natural Gas Supplies Last? The Soviet Union has 40% of the world's proven reserves and is the world's largest natural gas extractor. Other countries with large proven natural gas reserves are Iran (14%), the United States (6%), Qatar (4%), Algeria (4%), Saudi Arabia (3%), and Nigeria (3%). Geologists expect to find more conventional natural gas deposits, especially in LDCs that have not been widely explored for this resource.

Most U.S. reserves of natural gas are located with the country's deposits of crude oil (Figure 16-5). America's largest known deposits of conventional natural gas lie in Alaska's Prudhoe Bay, thousands of miles from natural gas consumers in the lower 48 states.

About 95% of the natural gas used in the United States comes from domestic sources; the other 5% is imported by pipeline from Canada. California gets 40% of its natural gas from Canada. Algeria and the Soviet Union use pipelines to supply many eastern and western European countries with natural gas and are planning more pipelines.

In 1987 about 82% of the natural gas consumed in the United States was used for space heating of residential and commercial buildings and for drying and other purposes in industry (Figure 16-9). New natural gas or LPG furnaces have energy efficiencies of 90% to 95%.

Between 1981 and 1989, estimated U.S. reserves of natural gas dropped 56%. Known reserves and undiscovered, economically recoverable conventional natural gas deposits in the United States are projected to last 35 years and world supplies 59 years at present consumption rates.

As the price of natural gas from conventional sources rises, it may become economical to get natural gas from unconventional sources. Such sources include coal seams, Devonian shale rock, deep underground deposits of tight sands, and deep geopressurized zones that contain natural gas dissolved in hot water. New technology for extracting gas from these resources is being developed rapidly.

In 1988 the Department of Energy estimated that technically recoverable natural gas from both conventional and unconventional sources in the lower 48 states would meet domestic needs for 50 years at current usage rates. The world's identified reserves of conventional natural gas are projected to last until 2045 at the current usage rates and until 2022 if consumption rises 2% a year.

Estimated supplies of conventional and unconventional supplies available at higher prices would last about 200 years at the current rate and 80 years if usage rose 2% a year. If these estimates are correct, natural gas could become the most widely used fuel for space heating, industrial processes, producing electricity, and transportation.

Advantages and Disadvantages of Natural Gas
Natural gas burns hotter and produces less air pollution than any fossil fuel. It produces virtually no sulfur dioxide and particulate matter and about one-sixth as much nitrogen oxides per unit of energy as burning coal, oil, and gasoline. Burning natural gas produces carbon dioxide, but the amount per unit of energy produced is lower than that of other fossil fuels (Figure 16-10). Methane, the major component of natural gas, is a greenhouse gas, but most of the methane in the atmosphere does not come from extraction and use of natural gas.

So far the price of natural gas has been low. It can be transported easily over land by pipeline and has a high net useful energy yield (Figure 3-17, p. 69). It is a versatile fuel that can be burned cleanly and efficiently in furnaces, stoves, water heaters, dryers, boilers, incinerators, fuel cells, heat pumps, air conditioners, refrigerators, and dehumidifiers. It can also be used as a clean-burning fuel in modified conventional

Figure 16-11 Stages in the formation of coal over millions of years. Peat is a humus soil material. Lignite and bituminous coal are sedimentary rocks, and anthracite is a metamorphic rock.

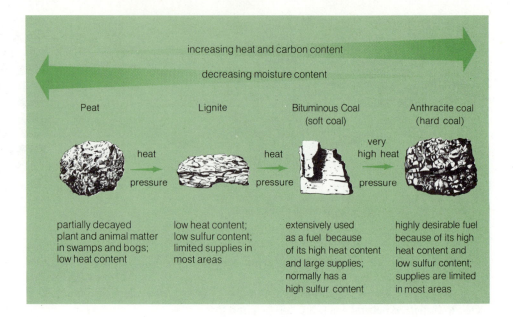

increasing heat and carbon content

decreasing moisture content

| Peat | Lignite | Bituminous Coal (soft coal) | Anthracite coal (hard coal) |

heat pressure → heat pressure → very high heat pressure →

partially decayed plant and animal matter in swamps and bogs; low heat content

low heat content; low sulfur content; limited supplies in most areas

extensively used as a fuel because of its high heat content and large supplies; normally has a high sulfur content

highly desirable fuel because of its high heat content and low sulfur content; supplies are limited in most areas

and diesel engines, especially for large fleets of buses, taxis, and trucks that can be refueled in centralized facilities.

Burning compressed natural gas in retrofitted older vehicles instead of gasoline would lower smog-forming hydrocarbon emissions by 50% to 80% and by as much as 90% in new engines designed for this fuel. Also carbon monoxide emissions would be reduced by 50% to 90%. But emissions of nitrogen oxides would increase slightly.

New natural gas burning turbines, working like jet engines, can be used to produce electricity. They cost half as much to build as a coal-fired system and are cheaper to operate. They can be put into operation within 12 to 18 months and are 47% efficient, compared to 38% for the best coal plants and only 30% for nuclear plants. Natural gas can also be burned cleanly and efficiently in cogenerators to produce high-temperature heat and electricity and burned with coal in boilers to reduce air pollution emissions.

One problem is that natural gas must be converted to liquid natural gas before it can be shipped by tanker from one country to another. Shipping LNG in refrigerated tankers is expensive and dangerous. Massive explosions could kill many people and cause much damage in urban areas near LNG loading and unloading facilities. Conversion of natural gas to LNG also reduces the net useful energy yield by one-fourth.

If large amounts of natural gas can be extracted from nonconventional deposits at affordable prices, natural gas will be a key option for making an acceptable and orderly transition to solar and other energy options as oil is phased out over the next 50 years.

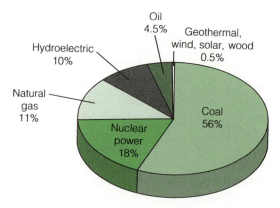

Figure 16-12 Electricity generation methods in the United States in 1987. (Data from U. S. Department of Energy)

16-3 COAL

Types and Distribution Coal is a solid formed in several stages as the remains of plants are subjected to intense heat and pressure over millions of years. It consists mostly of carbon with varying amounts of water and small amounts of nitrogen and sulfur. Four types of coal are formed at different stages: peat, lignite, bituminous coal, and anthracite (Figure 16-11). The last three types are the most widely used. Low-sulfur coal produces less sulfur dioxide when burned than high-sulfur coal. The most desirable type of coal is anthracite because of its high heat content and low sulfur content.

About 60% of the coal extracted in the world and 70% in the United States is burned in boilers to pro-

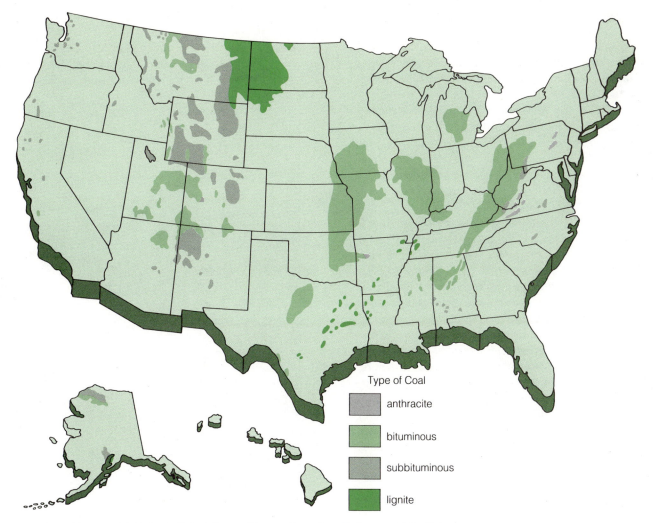

Figure 16-13 Major coal fields in the United States. (Source: Council on Environmental Quality)

Type of Coal

- anthracite
- bituminous
- subbituminous
- lignite

duce steam to generate electrical power. The rest is converted to coke used to make steel and burned in boilers to produce steam used in various manufacturing processes. Coal is burned to supply 56% of the electricity generated in the United States (Figure 16-12).

Coal is the world's most abundant fossil fuel. About 68% of the world's proven coal reserves and 85% of the estimated undiscovered coal deposits are located in three countries: the United States, the USSR, and China. These countries extract 60% of the coal used today. China, which recently passed the USSR as the world's largest coal extractor, plans to double its coal consumption between 1987 and 2000.

Most major U.S. coalfields are located in 17 states (Figure 16-13). Anthracite, the most desirable form of coal, makes up only 2% of U.S. coal reserves. About 45% of U.S. coal reserves is high-sulfur, bituminous coal with a high fuel value. It is found in the East,

mostly in Kentucky, West Virginia, Pennsylvania, Ohio, and Illinois.

About 55% of U.S. coal reserves are found west of the Mississippi River. Most of these are deposits of low-sulfur, bituminous, and lignite coal. Currently, about one-third of the country's coal is extracted from these deposits, mostly by surface mining. The problem is that these deposits are far from the heavily industrialized and populated East, where most coal is consumed.

Extracting Coal Surface mining is used to extract almost two-thirds of the coal used in the United States. Most surface-mined coal is removed by area strip mining or contour strip mining, depending on the terrain.

Area strip mining involves stripping away the overburden and digging a series of parallel trenches to remove a mineral deposit found in an area with flat or gently rolling terrain (Figure 16-14). After the coal deposit is removed from a trench, that trench is filled with overburden from the next parallel trench. This process is repeated for the entire deposit. If the land is not restored, this type of mining leaves a wavy series of highly erodible hills of rubble called *spoil banks* (Figure 16-15).

Contour strip mining is a form of surface mining used in hilly or mountainous terrain. A power shovel cuts a series of terraces into the side of a hill or mountain. The overburden from each new terrace is dumped onto the one below. Unless the land is restored, a wall of dirt is left in front of a highly erodible bank of soil and rock called a *highwall* (Figure 16-16). In the United States, contour strip mining is used mostly for extracting coal in the mountainous Appalachian region. If the land is not restored, this type of surface mining has a devastating impact on the land (Figure 16-17).

Subsurface mining is used to remove coal too deep to be extracted by surface mining. Miners dig a deep vertical shaft, blast subsurface tunnels and rooms to get to the deposit, and haul the coal or ore to the surface. In the *room-and-pillar method* as much as half the coal is left in place as pillars to prevent the mine from collapsing. In the *longwall method* a narrow tunnel is created and then supported by movable metal pillars. After a cutting machine has removed the coal or ore from part of the mineral seam, the roof supports are moved forward, allowing the earth behind the supports to collapse. No tunnels are left behind after the mining operation has been completed. Sometimes giant augers are used to drill horizontally into a hillside to extract underground coal.

Environmental Impact of Extracting and Burning Coal
Surface mining of coal causes severe land disturbance and destroys natural vegetation and habitats

for many types of wildlife (Figures 16-15 and 16-17). Soil erosion from unrestored or poorly restored land that has been surface mined is up to 1,000 times that from the same area under natural conditions. Also sediment and toxic minerals and salts leached from

Figure 16-14 Area strip mining of coal in Oak Creek, Colorado. This type of surface mining is used on flat or gently rolling terrain.

USDA/Soil Conservation Service

Figure 16-15 Effects of area strip mining of coal in Missouri. Restoration of newly strip-mined areas is now required in the United States, but many previously mined areas have not been restored. In arid areas, full restoration isn't possible and enforcement of surface mining laws is often lax.

National Archives

overburden pollute nearby streams and kill aquatic life and can contaminate groundwater aquifers located near coal seams (Figure 15-8, p. 350).

In some areas land disturbed by surface mining of coal has been restored (Figure 16-18) as required by law in the United States (see Spotlight on p. 387). But about three-fourths of the coal in the United States that can be surface mined is in the West, in arid and semiarid regions. There the climate and soil usually prevent full restoration of surface-mined land.

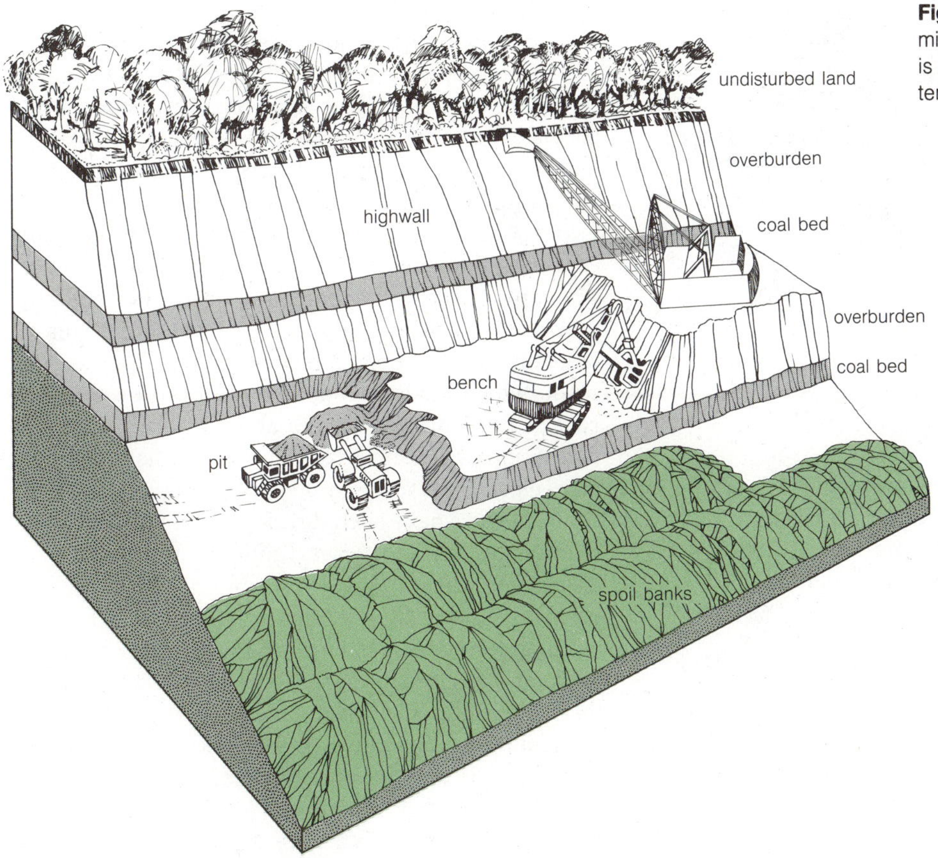

Figure 16-16 Contour strip mining of coal. This type of surface mining is used in hilly or mountainous terrain.

undisturbed land

overburden

highwall

coal bed

overburden

coal bed

bench

pit

spoil banks

Figure 16-17 Severely eroded hillsides on Bolt Mountain, West Virginia, as a result of contour strip mining of coal without proper restoration.

U.S. Department of Agriculture

Figure 16-18 With the land returned to its original contour and grass planted to hold the soil in place, it is hard to tell that this was once a surface coal-mining site in West Virginia.

Coal mining, especially underground mining, is a dangerous occupation. Since 1900 underground mining in the United States has killed more than 100,000 miners and permanently disabled at least 1 million. At least 250,000 retired U.S. miners suffer from black lung disease, a form of emphysema caused by prolonged breathing of coal dust and other particulate matter. Past failures to enact and enforce stricter mine safety laws now cost U.S. taxpayers over $1 billion a year in federal disability benefits paid to coal miners with black lung disease.

Coal mining in the United States is safer than in most other countries, but it could be made safer by stricter enforcement of existing laws and by enactment of tougher new laws. An estimated one-third of all underground mines in the United States still have conditions that subject miners to a high risk of black lung disease.

Acids and toxic metal compounds flushed from abandoned underground coal mines can kill fish and many other forms of aquatic life (Figure 15-8, p. 350). In the United States, acid mine drainage has degraded over 11,300 kilometers (7,000 miles) of streams—90% of them in Appalachia.

Underground coal mining can also cause subsidence—a depression in the earth's surface—when a mine shaft partially collapses during or after mining. Over 800,000 hectares (2 million acres) of land, much of it in central Appalachia, has subsided because of underground coal mining.

Without effective air pollution control devices, burning coal causes much more air pollution than burning other fossil fuels. About 70% of the sulfur dioxide emissions and almost one-fourth of the emissions of nitrogen oxides in the United States are produced by coal burning, mostly in electric power plants. These emissions are major contributors to the acid deposition that damages many forests and aquatic ecosystems in the eastern United States and parts of Canada (Section 19-3).

Each year these and other air pollutants emitted when coal is burned kill about 5,000 people in the United States. They also cause 50,000 cases of respiratory disease and several billion dollars in property damage each year. Since 1978 federal law has reduced allowable emissions of sulfur dioxide, nitrogen oxides, and particulate matter by all new coal-burning power and industrial plants in the United States.

But to avoid expensive investments in air pollution control equipment, utilities and industries have patched up many old coal-burning plants instead of building new ones. Requiring all older coal-burning plants to meet the same air pollution emission standards as new plants would reduce the deaths caused by burning coal in the United States to about 500 per year. Air pollution laws in most other countries that burn coal are weaker than those in the United States.

New ways have been developed to burn coal more cleanly and efficiently (see Spotlight on p. 388).

To environmentalists, one of the most serious problems with coal is that burning it gives off much more carbon dioxide per unit of energy produced than burning other fossil fuels (Figure 16-10). This means that burning more coal to meet energy needs can accelerate the greenhouse effect (Section 19-4). Presently there is no effective and affordable method for preventing carbon dioxide released by fossil-fuel burning from reaching the atmosphere. This problem by itself may prevent much of the world's coal reserves from being mined and burned.

How Long Will Supplies Last? Identified world reserves of coal should last about 220 years at current usage and 65 years if usage rises 2% a year. The world's unidentified coal resources are projected to last about 900 years at the current rate and 149 years if usage increases 2% a year.

Identified coal reserves in the United States should last about 300 years at the current usage rate. Unidentified U.S. coal resources could extend these supplies at the current rate for perhaps 100 years, at a much higher average cost.

Advantages and Disadvantages of Solid Coal Coal is the most abundant conventional fossil fuel in the world and in the United States. It also has a high net useful energy yield for producing high-temperature heat for industrial processes and for generating electricity (Figure 3-17, p. 69). In countries with adequate coal supplies, burning solid coal is the cheapest way to produce high-temperature heat and electricity. But these low costs do not include requiring the best air pollution control equipment on all plants and requiring effective reclamation of all land surface mined for coal.

Coal is dangerous to mine. Surface mining causes severe land disturbance (Figures 16-15 and 16-17), and surface mined land in arid and semiarid areas can only be partially restored. Underground mining is very dangerous and causes subsidence. Surface and subsurface mining of coal can cause severe water pollution from acids and toxic metal compounds (Figure 15-8, p. 350).

Once coal is mined it is expensive to move from one place to another and cannot be used in solid form as a fuel for cars and trucks. Currently most coal is transported by railroad. A cheaper method is to transport coal in pipelines as a coal slurry, made by suspending powdered coal in water. But this method requires enormous amounts of water, a scarce resource in the semiarid regions where some major coal deposits are found.

Coal is the dirtiest fossil fuel to burn. Without expensive air pollution control devices, burning coal produces larger amounts of sulfur dioxide, nitrogen oxides, and particulate matter than other fossil fuels. These pollutants contribute to acid deposition, corrode metals, and harm trees, crops, wild animals, and people. Burning coal also produces more carbon dioxide per unit of energy than other fossil fuels (Figure 16-10).

Synfuels: Converting Solid Coal to Gaseous and Liquid Fuels Solid coal can also be converted to gaseous or liquid fuels, called **synfuels.** They are more useful than solid coal in heating homes and powering vehicles, and burning these fuels produces much less air pollution than burning solid coal.

Coal gasification (Figure 16-20) is the conversion of solid coal to synthetic natural gas (SNG). **Coal liquefaction** is the conversion of solid coal to a liquid hydrocarbon fuel such as methanol or synthetic gasoline. A commercial coal liquefaction plant supplies 10% of the liquid fuel used in South Africa at a cost

---

SPOTLIGHT Surface Mining Legislation in the United States

More than 405,000 hectares (1 million acres) of American land disturbed by surface mining have been abandoned by coal companies and not restored. To control such land disturbance, Congress enacted the Surface Mining Control and Reclamation Act of 1977. Among its requirements:

- Surface-mined land must be restored as closely as possible to its original contour.
- Surface mining is banned on some prime agricultural lands in the West, and farmers and ranchers can veto mining under their lands even though they do not own the mineral rights.
- Mining companies must reduce the effects of their activities on local watersheds and water quality by using the best available technology, and they must prevent acid from entering local streams and groundwater.
- Surface-mined land not reclaimed before 1977 is to be

restored with money provided by a fee on each ton of coal mined.

- States are responsible for enforcing the law except on federally owned lands.
- The Department of the Interior has enforcement power when states fail to act and on federally owned lands.
- The public has the right to observe federal mine inspections and to sue if the law is not followed.

Many surface-mined areas have been restored as required by this law, but some coal companies found ways to get around it. One strategy was to divide a strip mine into plots too tiny to be covered by the law and connect them by dirt roads. More than 4,000 of these "string-of-pearl" mines were dug and abandoned without reclamation before Congress closed this loophole in 1987.

Some coal companies have

ignored the law and not reclaimed strip-mined land. Others have left a mess and called it reclamation.

How do they get away with such flagrant violations? For one thing, the Reagan administration cut the federal inspection and enforcement staff by 70%. Also, the Office of Surface Mining has failed to collect $200 million in fines owed by mining companies breaking the law.

Lack of money has also limited enforcement in many states. For example, in 1983 Utah state officials were carrying out fewer than half the inspections required by law.

In 1988 fifteen conservation groups accused West Virginia of having the worst strip mining enforcement program of any state. They filed suit against the Department of the Interior and West Virginia's Department of Energy for failure to enforce the federal surface mining law. What do you think should be done?

---

equal to paying $35 a barrel for oil. When two new plants are completed, the country will be able to meet half of its oil needs from this source. Engineers hope to get the cost down to $25 a barrel.

Synfuels can be transported through a pipeline, burn more cleanly than solid coal, and are more versatile than solid coal. Besides being burned to produce high-temperature heat and electricity as solid coal does, synfuels can be burned to heat houses and water and to propel vehicles.

But a synfuel plant costs much more to build and run than an equivalent coal-fired power plant fully

---

SPOTLIGHT Burning Coal More Cleanly and Efficiently

A mixture of powdered coal and water or a mixture of powdered coal and natural gas can be burned more cleanly and efficiently than coal alone. One of the most promising methods for burning coal more efficiently, cleanly, and cheaply than in conventional coal boilers is **fluidized-bed combustion (FBC)** (Figure 16-19). Crushed coal is burned on a bed of limestone suspended on a cushion of high-pressure air, which increases energy efficiency by 5%. Gaseous sulfur dioxide produced when the coal burns reacts with the limestone to produce solid calcium sulfate, which can be disposed of in a landfill.

FBC removes 90% to 98% of the sulfur dioxide gas produced during combustion and also reduces emissions of nitrogen oxides. FBC boilers also can burn many other fuels. Power plants can convert to FBC by modifying their conventional boilers.

Successful small-scale FBC plants have been built in Great Britain, Sweden, Finland, the Soviet Union, West Germany, and China. In the United States, commercial FBC boilers are expected to begin replacing conventional coal boilers in the mid-1990s.

Figure 16-19
Fluidized-bed combustion of coal. A stream of hot air is blown into a boiler to suspend a mixture of powdered coal and crushed limestone. This removes most of the sulfur dioxide, sharply reduces emissions of nitrogen oxides, and burns coal more efficiently and cheaply than conventional combustion methods.

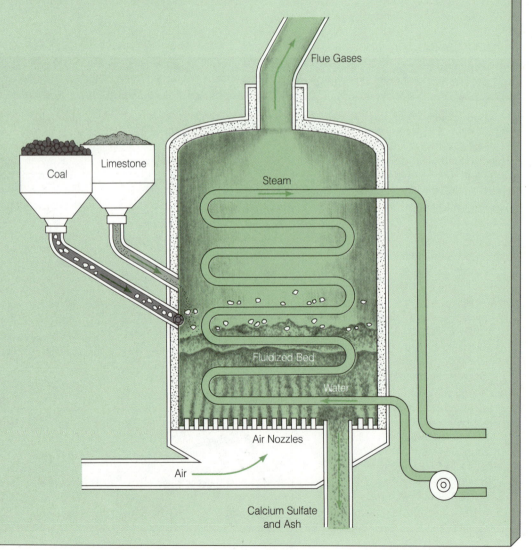

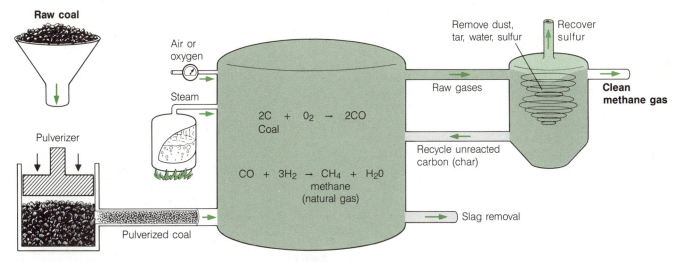

Figure 16-20 Coal gasification. Generalized view of one method for converting solid coal into synthetic natural gas (methane).

equipped with air pollution control devices. Synfuels also have low net useful energy yields (Figure 3-17, p. 69). The widespread use of synfuels would accelerate the depletion of world coal supplies because 30% to 40% of the energy content of coal is lost in the conversion process. It would also lead to greater land disruption from surface mining because producing synfuels uses more coal per unit of energy produced than burning solid coal.

Producing synfuels requires huge amounts of water, and burning synfuels releases large amounts of carbon dioxide per unit of energy (Figure 16-10). Converting coal to SNG underground would solve or reduce some of these problems (except carbon dioxide emissions, high costs, and low net energy yields). But currently underground coal gasification is not competitive with conventional coal mining and aboveground coal gasification.

The major factor holding back large-scale production of synfuels in the United States is their high cost compared to conventional oil and natural gas. Producing synfuels with current technology is the equivalent of buying oil at $50 to $100 a barrel. The U.S. Department of Energy has a goal of supporting development of new processes that will reduce the cost to $25 per barrel by 1995, but most analysts expect synfuels to play only a minor role as an energy resource in the next 30 to 50 years.

16-4   GEOTHERMAL ENERGY

Nonrenewable Geothermal Energy   Heat from the earth's molten core is also a source of energy. At various places in the earth's crust this **geothermal energy** is transferred over millions of years to nonrenewable or very slowly renewable underground deposits of dry steam (steam with no water droplets), wet steam (a mixture of steam and water droplets), and hot water.

If these geothermal deposits are close enough to the earth's surface, wells can be drilled to extract the dry steam, wet steam, or hot water (Figure 16-21). This thermal energy can be used for space heating and to produce electricity or high-temperature heat for industrial processes.

Currently about 20 countries are tapping geothermal deposits. This energy heats over 2 million homes in cold climates and supplies electricity for over 1.5 million homes with an output equal to five large coal-fired or nuclear power plants. The United States accounts for 44% of the electricity produced by geothermal power plants in 18 countries. Figure 16-22 shows that most accessible, high-temperature geothermal deposits in the United States lie in the west, especially in California and the Rocky Mountain states.

Dry-steam deposits are the preferred geothermal resource, but also the rarest. A large dry-steam well near Larderello, Italy, has been producing electricity since 1904 and is a major source of power for Italy's electric railroads. Two other major dry-steam sites are the Matsukawa field in Japan and the Geysers steam field about 145 kilometers (90 miles) north of San Francisco.

The Geysers field has been producing electricity since 1960. Currently it supplies more than 6% of northern California's electricity—enough to meet all the electrical needs of a city the size of San Francisco—at less than half the cost of a new coal or nuclear plant and largely without government subsidies. New units can be added every 2 to 3 years (compared to 6 years for a coal plant and 10 to 12 years for a nuclear plant). By 2000 this field may supply one-fourth of California's electricity.

Underground *wet-steam deposits* are more common but harder and more expensive to convert to electricity. The world's largest wet-steam power plant is in Wairaki, New Zealand. Others operate in Mexico, Japan, El Salvador, Nicaragua, and the Soviet Union. Currently geothermal plants in El Salvador and Nicaragua produce 17% of the electric power generated in Central America. Four small-scale wet-steam demonstration plants in the United States are producing electricity at a cost equal to paying $40 a barrel for oil.

Hot-water deposits are more common than dry-steam and wet-steam deposits. Almost all the homes, buildings, and food-producing greenhouses in Reykjavik, Iceland, a city with a population of about 85,000, are heated by hot water drawn from deep geothermal deposits under the city. At 180 locations in the United States, mostly in the West, hot-water deposits have been used for years to heat homes and farm buildings and to dry crops.

The hot salty water (brine) pumped up from such wells can also be used to produce electricity. A demonstration plant has been operating in California's Imperial Valley since 1984. The main problem is that the brine corrodes metal parts and clogs pipes. An underground system is being tested as a means to reduce corrosion and wastewater problems. It also leaves water and steam in the well for continual reheating rather than depleting the resource.

A fourth potential source of nonrenewable geothermal energy and natural gas is *geopressurized zones*. These are underground reservoirs of water at a high temperature and pressure, usually trapped deep under ocean beds of shale or clay. With present drilling technology, they would supply geothermal energy and natural gas at a cost equal to paying $30 to $45 a barrel for oil.

Advantages and Disadvantages The major advantages of nonrenewable geothermal energy include a 100- to 200-year supply of energy for areas near deposits, moderate net useful energy yields for large and easily accessible deposits, and no emissions of carbon dioxide. The cost of producing electricity in geothermal plants is about half the cost of power from new coal plants and one-fourth the cost of power from new nuclear plants.

Two limitations of nonrenewable geothermal energy are the scarcity of easily accessible deposits and inability to use this energy to power vehicles. Without pollution control, geothermal energy production causes moderate to high air pollution from hydrogen sulfide, ammonia, and radioactive materials. It also causes moderate to high water pollution from dissolved solids (salinity) and runoff of several toxic compounds. Noise, odor, and local climate changes can also be problems. Most experts, however, consider the environmental effects of geothermal energy to be less or

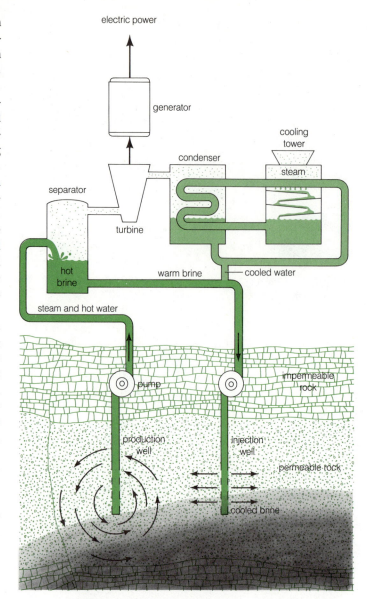

Figure 16-21 Tapping the earth's heat—geothermal energy—to produce electricity.

no greater than those of fossil fuel and nuclear power plants.

Perpetual Geothermal Energy There are also three types of vast, virtually perpetual sources of geothermal energy: *molten rock* (magma) found near the earth's surface; *hot dry-rock zones*, where molten rock has penetrated the earth's crust from below and heats subsurface rock to high temperatures; and low- to moderate-temperature *warm-rock deposits*, useful for preheating water and running geothermal heat pumps for space heating and air conditioning. According to the National Academy of Sciences, the amount of potentially recoverable energy from such deposits would meet U.S. energy needs at current consumption levels for 600 to 700 years.

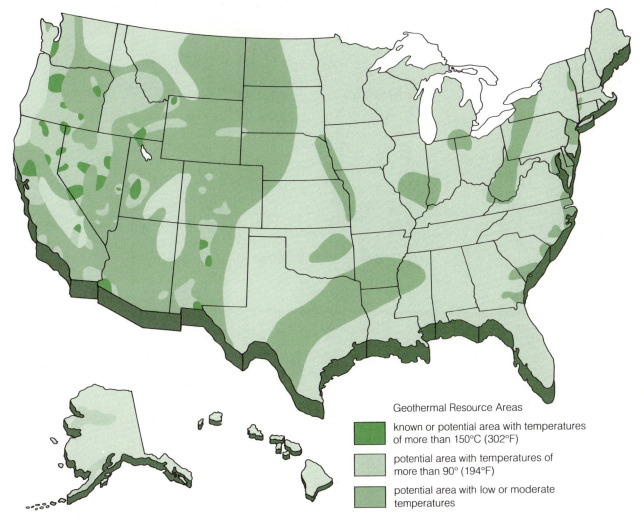

Figure 16-22 Major deposits of geothermal resources in the United States. (Source: Council on Environmental Quality)

Geothermal Resource Areas

known or potential area with temperatures of more than 150°C (302°F)

potential area with temperatures of more than 90° (194°F)

potential area with low or moderate temperatures

The problem is developing methods to extract this energy economically. Several experimental projects are in progress, but so far none has been able to produce energy at a cost competitive with other energy sources.

16-5 CONVENTIONAL NONRENEWABLE NUCLEAR FISSION

A Controversial Fading Dream Originally nuclear power was envisioned as a clean, safe, and cheap source of energy. By the end of this century 1,800 nuclear power plants were supposed to supply 21% of the world's supplemental energy and 25% of that used in the United States.

These rosy forecasts turned out to be an example of unrealistic high-tech intoxication. By 1988, after 41 years of development, 417 commercial nuclear reactors in 33 countries were producing only 17% of the world's electricity—equal to only about 4.5% of the

world's supplemental energy (Figure 16-23). The percentage of the world's electricity produced by nuclear power will probably drop between 1990 and 2010 as aging nuclear plants are retired faster than new ones are built.

Industrialized countries like Japan and France, which have few fossil fuel resources, officially believe that using nuclear power is the best way to reduce their dependence on imported oil. France plans to get 90% of its electricity from nuclear power by the early 1990s. However, both Japan and France already are producing more electricity than they can use, and nuclear power cannot be used to run vehicles—the main use of oil (see Guest Essay on p. 408).

Since the Chernobyl nuclear accident in 1986 (see Spotlight on p. 397), many countries have scaled back or eliminated their plans to build nuclear power plants. Denmark, Norway, Australia, Greece, Luxembourg, the Netherlands, New Zealand, Italy, and Switzerland have decided not to build any nuclear power plants. Sweden plans to shut down 2 of its 12 nuclear reactors

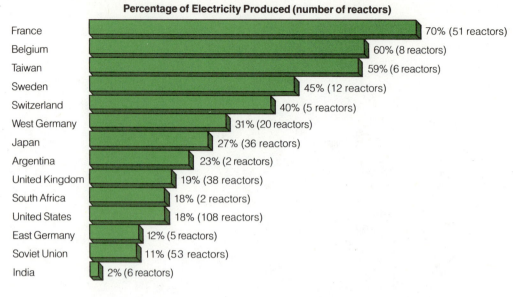

Figure 16-23 Use of nuclear fission reactors to produce electricity in various countries in 1987. (Data from Atomic Industrial Forum and International Atomic Energy Agency)

Percentage of Electricity Produced (number of reactors)

France	70% (51 reactors)
Belgium	60% (8 reactors)
Taiwan	59% (6 reactors)
Sweden	45% (12 reactors)
Switzerland	40% (5 reactors)
West Germany	31% (20 reactors)
Japan	27% (36 reactors)
Argentina	23% (2 reactors)
United Kingdom	19% (38 reactors)
South Africa	18% (2 reactors)
United States	18% (108 reactors)
East Germany	12% (5 reactors)
Soviet Union	11% (53 reactors)
India	2% (6 reactors)

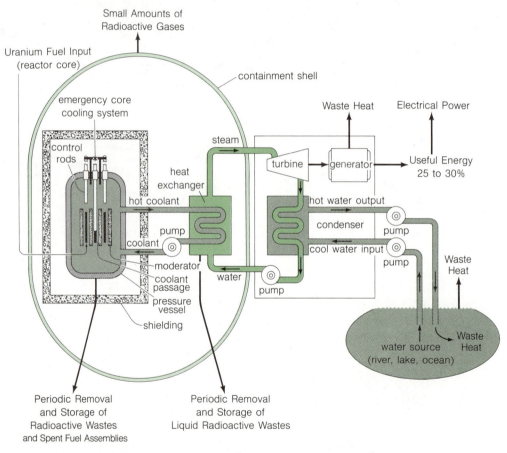

Figure 16-24 Light-water-moderated-and-cooled nuclear power plant with a pressurized water reactor.

by 1996 and close the other 10 by 2010. Austria and the Philippines have decided to dismantle their single nuclear plants.

In 1988 the United States, with 114 reactors licensed to operate in 34 states, produced 31% of the world's nuclear power and used it to supply only 20% of the country's electricity and 5% of its supplemental energy. Since 1975, no new nuclear power plants have been ordered in the United States and 108 previous orders have been canceled. By the year 2000 fifteen of these reactors will be retired and by 2010 another 55 will be eligible for retirement. Thus, if no new reactors are built, the U.S. will have only about 41 reactors operating in 2010.

What happened to nuclear power? The answer is that the nuclear industry has been crippled by high and uncertain costs of building and operating plants, shoddy construction, billion-dollar cost overruns, frequent malfunctions, false assurances and coverups by government and industry officials, overproduction of

Figure 16-25 Bundles of fuel rods filled with pellets of enriched uranium-235 oxide serve as the fuel core for a conventional nuclear fission reactor.

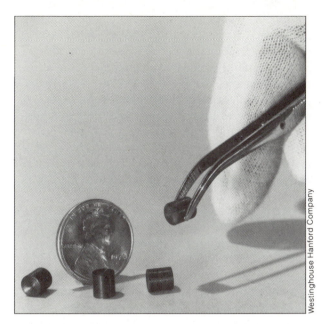

Figure 16-26 Fuel pellets of uranium oxide. They contain about 3% fissionable uranium-235.

electricity, poor management, and lack of public acceptance because of mistrust and concerns about safety, cost, radioactive waste disposal, and nuclear weapons proliferation.

Polls show that public opposition to nuclear power in the United States rose from 30% in 1979 to 60% in 1989. To better understand some of the problems with nuclear power, we need to know how a nuclear power plant works.

How Does a Nuclear Fission Reactor Work? When the nuclei of atoms such as uranium-235 and plutonium-239 are split by neutrons, energy is released and converted mostly to high-temperature heat in a nuclear fission chain reaction (Figure 3-10, p. 62). The rate at which this happens can be controlled in the nuclear fission reactor in a nuclear power plant, and the high-temperature heat released can be used to spin a turbine and produce electrical energy.

Light-water reactors (LWRs) now generate about 85% of the electricity generated worldwide (98% in the U.S.) by nuclear power plants. Key parts of an LWR are the core, fuel assemblies, fuel rods, control rods, moderator, and coolant (Figure 16-24). The core of an LWR typically contains about 40,000 long, thin fuel rods bundled in 180 fuel assemblies of around 200 rods each (Figure 16-25). Each fuel rod is packed with eraser-sized pellets of uranium oxide fuel (Figure 16-26).

About 97% of the uranium in each fuel pellet is uranium-238, an isotope that cannot be fissioned. The other 3% is uranium-235, which can be fissioned. This fuel is produced by increasing (enriching) the uranium-235 found in natural uranium ore (Figure 3-2, p. 54) from 0.7% to 3%. The uranium-235 in each fuel rod produces energy equal to that of three railroad carloads of coal and lasts about three to four years (Figure 16-26).

When the fuel in the rods can no longer sustain nuclear fission, the intensely radioactive spent fuel rods are removed. About 4% of the weight of a spent rod is composed of extremely radioactive plutonium, strontium, cesium, and other isotopes created during the fission reaction in the reactor. If these rods are processed to remove plutonium and other very long-lived radioactive isotopes, they must be safely stored for at least 10,000 years. Otherwise, they must be stored safely for at least 240,000 years—about six to eight times longer than *homo sapiens sapiens* has been around.

Control rods made of materials that absorb neutrons are moved in and out of the reactor core to regulate the rate of fission and the amount of power the reactor produces. All reactors place or circulate some type of material between the fuel rods and the fuel assemblies. This material, known as a moderator, slows down the neutrons emitted by the fission process so that the chain reaction can be kept going.

Three-fourths of the world's commercial reactors use ordinary water, called light water, as a moderator. The moderator in about 20% of the world's commercial reactors (50% of those in the Soviet Union, including the ill-fated Chernobyl reactor) is solid graphite, a form of carbon. Graphite-moderated reactors can also be used to produce fissionable plutonium-239 for use in nuclear weapons.

A coolant circulates through the reactor's core. It removes heat to keep fuel rods and other materials from melting and to produce steam that spins generators to produce electricity. Most water-moderated and graphite-moderated reactors use water as a coolant; a few gas-cooled reactors use an unreactive gas such as helium or argon for cooling.

A typical LWR has an energy efficiency of only 25% to 30% compared to 40% for a coal-burning plant. Graphite-moderated, gas-cooled reactors are widely used in the United Kingdom. Although they are more expensive to build and operate, they are more energy-efficient (38%) than LWRs because they operate at a higher temperature.

Nuclear power plants, each with one or more reactors, are only one part of the nuclear fuel cycle necessary for using nuclear energy to produce electricity (Figure 16-27). *In evaluating the safety and economy of*

nuclear power, we need to look at the entire cycle—not just the nuclear plant itself.

After about three to four years in a reactor, the concentration of fissionable uranium-235 in a fuel rod becomes too low to keep the chain reaction going, or the rod becomes damaged from exposure to ionizing radiation. Each year about one-third of the spent fuel elements in a reactor are removed and stored in large, concrete-lined pools of water at the plant site.

After they have cooled for several years and lost some of their radioactivity, the spent fuel rods are sealed in shielded, supposedly crash-proof casks. These casks can be loaded onto a truck or train and transferred to storage pools away from the reactor or to a permanent nuclear waste repository or dump. Because neither of these options exists in the United States, spent fuel is stored at plant sites, where storage space is rapidly running out.

A third option is to send spent fuel to a fuel-reprocessing plant (Figure 16-27). There, remaining fissionable uranium-235 and plutonium-239 (produced as a by-product of the fission process) are removed and sent to a fuel fabrication plant.

Figure 16-27 The nuclear fuel cycle.

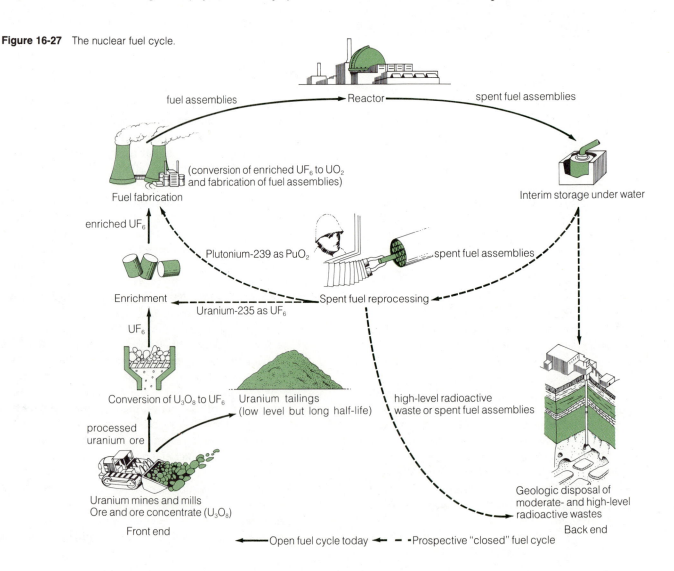

Two small commercial fuel-reprocessing plants in operation (one in France and one in Great Britain) have had severe operating and economic problems. Two others are under construction—one in Japan and one in West Germany. The United States has delayed development of commercial fuel-reprocessing plants because of technical difficulties, high construction and operating costs, and adequate domestic supplies of uranium. Also, such plants would handle and ship nuclear fuel in a form that could be used to make nuclear weapons.

The fission products produced in a nuclear reactor give off radioactivity and heat even after control rods have been inserted to stop all nuclear fission in the reactor core. To prevent a *meltdown* of the fuel rods and the reactor core after a reactor is shut down, huge amounts of water must be kept circulating through the core. A meltdown could release massive quantities of highly radioactive materials into the environment.

How Safe Are Nuclear Power Plants? To greatly reduce the chances of a meltdown and other serious reactor accidents, commercial reactors in the United States (and most countries) have many safety features:

- thick walls and concrete and steel shields surrounding the reactor vessel

- a system for automatically inserting control rods into the core to stop fission under emergency conditions

- a steel-reinforced concrete containment building to keep radioactive gases and materials from reaching the atmosphere after an accident (ineffective in a complete core meltdown or a massive gas explosion like the one at the Chernobyl plant in 1986)

- large filter systems and chemical sprayers inside the containment building to remove radioactive dust from the air and further reduce chances of radioactivity reaching the environment

- systems to condense steam released from a ruptured reactor vessel and prevent pressure from rising beyond the holding power of containment building walls

- an emergency core-cooling system to flood the core automatically with massive amounts of water within one minute to prevent meltdown of the reactor core

- two separate power lines servicing the plant and several diesel generators to supply backup power for the massive pumps in the emergency core-cooling system

- X-ray inspection of key metal welds during construction and periodically after the plant goes into operation to detect possible sources of leaks from corrosion

- an automatic backup system to replace each major part of the safety system in the event of a failure

Such elaborate safety systems make a complete reactor core meltdown very unlikely. However, a partial or complete meltdown is possible through a series of equipment failures, operator errors, or both. In 1979 a reactor at the Three Mile Island plant in Pennsylvania underwent a partial meltdown because of equipment failures and operator errors (see Spotlight below).

SPOTLIGHT Some Significant Nuclear Accidents

Winter 1957
Perhaps the worst nuclear disaster in history occurred in the Soviet Union in the southern Ural Mountains near the city of Kyshtym, believed to then be the center of plutonium production for Soviet nuclear weapons. The cause of the accident and the number of people killed and injured remain a secret. However, in 1989 Soviet officials admitted that several hundred square miles were contaminated with radioactivity when a tank containing radioactive wastes exploded. Today the area is deserted and sealed off and the names of 30 towns and villages in the region have disappeared from Soviet maps.

October 7, 1957
A water-cooled, graphite-moderated reactor used to produce plutonium for nuclear weapons north of Liverpool, England, caught fire as the Chernobyl nuclear plant did 29 years later. By the time the fire was put out, 516 square kilometers (200 square miles) of countryside had been contaminated with radioactive material. Exposure to high levels of radiation caused an estimated 33 people to die prematurely from cancer.

March 22, 1975
Against regulations, a maintenance worker used a candle to test for air leaks at the Brown's Ferry commercial nuclear reactor near Decatur, Alabama. It set off a fire that knocked out five emergency core-cooling systems. Although the reactor's cooling water dropped to a dangerous level, backup systems prevented any radioactive material from escaping into the environment. At the same plant in 1978, a worker's rubber boot fell into a reactor and led to an unsuccessful search costing $2.8 million. Such incidents,

(continued)

caused mostly by unpredictable human errors, are common in most nuclear plants.

March 28, 1979

The worst accident in the history of U.S. commercial nuclear power happened at the Three Mile Island (TMI) nuclear plant near Harrisburg, Pennsylvania (Figure 16-28). One of its two reactors lost its coolant water because of a series of mechanical failures and human operator errors not anticipated in safety studies. The reactor's core became partially uncovered. At least 70% of the core was damaged, and about 50% (62 tons) of it melted and fell to the bottom of the reactor. Unknown amounts of ionizing radiation escaped into the atmosphere and 144,000 people were evacuated. Investigators found that if a stuck valve had stayed opened for just another 30 to 60 minutes, there would have been a complete meltdown. No one is known to have died because

of the accident, but its long-term health effects on workers and nearby residents are still being debated because data published on the radiation released during the accident are contradictory and incomplete.

Partial cleanup of the damaged TMI reactor will cost more than $1 billion, more than the $700 million construction cost of the reactor, and won't be completed until 1990 or later. Also, about $187 million of taxpayers' money has been spent by the Department of Energy on the TMI cleanup. Plant owners have also payed out $25 million to over 2,100 people who filed lawsuits for damages. The TMI cleanup is only partial. Probably in 1991 the plant will be sealed and some radioactive debris will be left in the plant (called in nuclear jargon "post-defueling monitored storage") for 20 to 90 years.

Confusing and misleading statements about the accident issued by Metropolitan Edison

(which owned the plant) and by the Nuclear Regulatory Commission (NRC) eroded public confidence in the safety of nuclear power. Nuclear power critics contend that it is mostly luck that has prevented the TMI accident and hundreds of serious incidents since then from leading to a complete meltdown and breach of a reactor's containment building. Nuclear industry officials claim that a catastrophic accident has not happened because the industry's multiple-backup safety systems work.

April 26, 1986

At 1:23 A.M. there were two massive explosions inside one of the four graphite-moderated, water-cooled reactors at the Chernobyl nuclear power plant north of Kiev in the Soviet Union. The blasts blew the 909-metric-ton (1,000-ton) roof off the reactor building, set the graphite core on fire, and flung radioactive debris several thou-

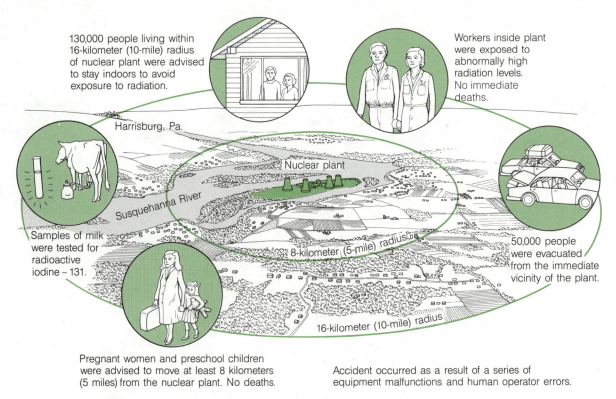

130,000 people living within 16-kilometer (10-mile) radius of nuclear plant were advised to stay indoors to avoid exposure to radiation.

Workers inside plant were exposed to abnormally high radiation levels. No immediate deaths.

Harrisburg, Pa.

Nuclear plant

Susquehanna River

Samples of milk were tested for radioactive iodine – 131.

8-kilometer (5-mile) radius

50,000 people were evacuated from the immediate vicinity of the plant.

16-kilometer (10-mile) radius

Pregnant women and preschool children were advised to move at least 8 kilometers (5 miles) from the nuclear plant. No deaths.

Accident occurred as a result of a series of equipment malfunctions and human operator errors.

Figure 16-28   Three Mile Island (TMI) in eastern Pennsylvania, where a nuclear accident occurred on March 28, 1979.

sand feet into the air (Figure 16-29). Over the next several days winds carried some of these radio-active materials over parts of the Soviet Union and much of eastern and western Europe as far as 2,000 kilometers (1,250 miles) from the plant. The accident happened because engineers turned off most of the reactor's automatic safety and warning systems to keep them from interfering with an unauthorized safety experiment (Figure 16-29).

About 135,000 people living within 29 kilometers (18 miles) of the plant were eventually evacuated by an armada of 1,100 buses and trucks. According to Soviet officials, most of these people will never be able to return to their contaminated homes and farms.

By 1989 exposure to high levels of ionizing radiation at the accident site had killed 36 plant workers, fire fighters, and rescuers. Another 237 people were hospitalized with acute radiation sickness.

Many of these people will probably die prematurely from cancer in coming years.

Soviet and Western medical experts estimate that 5,000 to 100,000 people in the Soviet Union and the rest of Europe will die prematurely over the next 70 years from cancer caused by exposure to the ionizing radiation release at Chernobyl. Thousands of others will be afflicted with thyroid tumors, cataracts, and sterility. The death toll would have been much higher if the accident had happened during the day, when people were not sheltered in houses, and if the wind had been blowing toward Kiev and its 2.4 million people.

Records of radiation levels have been classified top secret, casting doubt on whether the true effects of the accident will ever be known. In 1989 the governing body of the area in which the accident occurred suggested to the central government that another 106,000

people be relocated. This is an indication that the severity of the accident and the risk it posed to human life were either suppressed or greatly underestimated.

In 1988 Soviet officials revealed that the Chernobyl accident cost $14.4 billion, almost four times their original estimate of damages. Today the reactor is entombed in concrete and metal.

In 1987 the United States permanently shut down a graphite-moderated military reactor at Hanford, Washington; 54 serious safety violations had occurred at the plant during 1985 and 1986. The Chernobyl accident eroded public support for nuclear power worldwide and showed people that they need to be concerned about the safety of nuclear plants within and outside the borders of their countries.

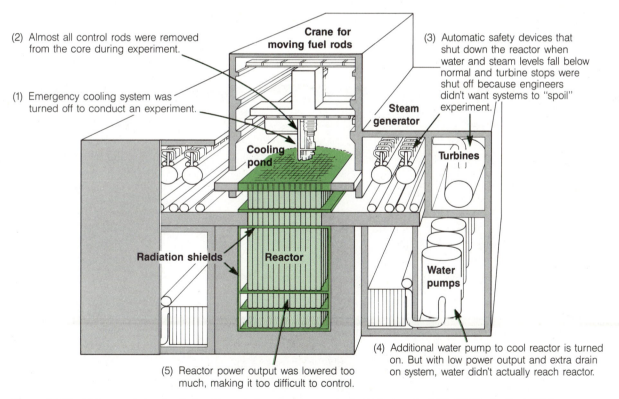

(2) Almost all control rods were removed from the core during experiment.

(1) Emergency cooling system was turned off to conduct an experiment.

Crane for moving fuel rods

(3) Automatic safety devices that shut down the reactor when water and steam levels fall below normal and turbine stops were shut off because engineers didn't want systems to "spoil" experiment.

Steam generator

Cooling pond

Turbines

Radiation shields

Reactor

Water pumps

(4) Additional water pump to cool reactor is turned on. But with low power output and extra drain on system, water didn't actually reach reactor.

(5) Reactor power output was lowered too much, making it too difficult to control.

Figure 16-29 Major events leading to the Chernobyl nuclear power plant accident on April 26, 1986 in the Soviet Union.

Another highly unlikely but possible danger is a powerful hydrogen gas or steam explosion inside the reactor containment vessel. This could split the containment building open and spew highly radioactive materials high into the atmosphere. Winds could spread this cloud of radioactive materials for thousands of miles as happened at Chernobyl. A worst-case accident could kill and injure hundreds of thousands of people and contaminate large areas with radioactive isotopes for thousands of years.

Many studies of nuclear safety have been made since 1957 when the first commercial nuclear power plant began operating in the United States. However, there is still no officially accepted study of just how safe or unsafe these plants are and no study of the safety of the entire nuclear fuel cycle. Even if engineers can make the hardware 100% reliable, human reliability can never reach 100% (Section 18-1). To be human is to err, and human behavior is highly unpredictable, as the TMI and Chernobyl accidents showed.

Less than a year after Chernobyl, an NRC engineer found operators at a number of nuclear plants turning off key safety systems, unknowingly or through carelessness. In 1987 operators at the Peach Bottom plant in Pennsylvania were found sleeping in the control room with the reactor running at full power. The NRC shut the plant down.

The Nuclear Regulatory Commission estimated that there is a 15% to 45% chance of a complete core meltdown at a U.S. reactor during the next 20 years. The commission also found that 39 U.S. reactors have an 80% chance of containment failure from a meltdown or massive gas explosion. Scientists in West Germany

and Sweden project that, worldwide, there is a 70% chance of another serious core-damaging accident within the next 5.4 years.

A 1982 study by the Sandia National Laboratory estimated that a worst-case accident in a reactor near a large U.S. city might cause 50,000 to 100,000 immediate deaths, 10,000 to 40,000 later deaths from cancer, and $100 billion to $150 billion in damages. Most citizens and businesses suffering injuries or property damage from a major nuclear accident would get little if any financial reimbursement. Since the beginnings of commercial nuclear power in the 1950s, insurance companies have refused to cover more than a small part of the possible damages from an accident.

In 1957 Congress enacted the Price-Anderson Act, which until 1988 limited insurance liability from a nuclear accident in the United States. In 1988 Congress extended the law for 20 years and raised the insurance liability to $7 billion—still only 7% of the possible damage from a severe accident.

Without this law the U.S. nuclear power industry would never have developed. Critics charge that the law is an unfair subsidy of the nuclear industry, and that if nuclear power plants are not safe enough to operate with adequate insurance, then they are not safe enough to operate at all. Nuclear critics also contend that nuclear accident plans in the United States are inadequate (see Pro/Con below).

There is also widespread lack of confidence in the NRC's ability to enforce nuclear safety. In 1989 NRC documents revealed that four out of five licensed U.S. reactors had failed to make all of the new safety changes

PRO/CON How Large Should the Evacuation Zone Around a Nuclear Plant Be?

After the TMI accident, 16-kilometer (10-mile) evacuation zones were set up around all U.S. commercial reactors. In 1986 nuclear power critics called for extending the evacuation zone to at least the 30 kilometers (19 miles) Soviet officials found necessary after the Chernobyl accident.

Another problem is that areas around many U.S. reactors are up to ten times more densely populated than those around most Soviet reactors. For example, whereas 135,000 had to be evacuated because of the Chernobyl accident, about 1.5 million people would have to be evacuated if a similar accident occurred at the

Indian Point plant near New York City.

Many urban areas near U.S. reactors would be impossible to evacuate; most Americans would get into their cars and clog exit routes. At Chernobyl few people had cars.

Instead of increasing the evacuation zone, the U.S. nuclear industry has been pushing the NRC to *reduce* the evacuation area around reactors to as low as 1.6 kilometers (1 mile). Industry officials contend that new safety studies show that less radiation would escape in the event of an accident than previously thought.

Environmentalists charge that the industry wants to reduce the size of evacuation zones to prevent state and local governments from blocking the licensing of new nuclear plants whose evacuation plans are inadequate.

In 1988, just before leaving office, President Reagan issued an executive order allowing the NRC to give operating permits for nuclear power plants without states or localities approving or participating in emergency evacuation plans they believe to be inadequate. Do you agree with this executive decision?

required in 1979 after the TMI accident. None of these plants were shut down by the NRC. According to a 1987 General Accounting Office report, the NRC has also allowed plants to continue operating even after a record of repeated safety violations.

Congressional hearings in 1987 uncovered evidence that high-level NRC staff members have destroyed documents and obstructed investigations of criminal wrongdoing by utilities, suggested ways utilities can evade commission regulations, and provided utilities and their contractors with advance warnings of surprise inspections. Some NRC field supervisors have also harassed and intimidated lower-level NRC inspectors who cite utilities for too many violations.

Disposal and Storage of Radioactive Wastes Each part of the nuclear fuel cycle for military and commercial nuclear reactors produces solid, liquid, and gaseous radioactive wastes (Figure 16-27). Some of these, called *low-level radioactive wastes*, give off small amounts of ionizing radiation, usually for a short time. Others are *high-level radioactive wastes*, which give off large amounts of ionizing radiation for a long time.

From the 1940s to 1970 most low-level radioactive waste produced in the United States (and most other countries) was dumped into the ocean in steel drums. Since 1970 low-level radioactive wastes from military activities have been buried at government-run landfills. Three of these have been closed because of leakage.

Low-level waste materials from hospitals, universities, industries, and other producers are put in steel drums and shipped to regional landfills run by federal and state governments. By 1989 three of the six commercial landfills had been closed due to radioactive contamination of groundwater and nearby property.

Most high-level radioactive wastes are spent fuel rods from commercial nuclear power plants and an assortment of wastes from nuclear weapons plants. According to the EPA, spent fuel rods must be stored safely for 10,000 years—longer than recorded history—before they decay to acceptable levels of radioactivity. However, unless plutonium and other very long-lived radioactive isotopes are removed by expensive reprocessing, high-level wastes would have to be stored safely for at least 240,000 years. In 1986 U.S. citizens learned that since the mid-1950s there was serious disregard for the safety of workers and nearby residents in the country's nuclear weapons production facilities (see Spotlight below).

After 37 years of research and debate, scientists still don't agree on a safe method of storing these wastes (see Spotlight on p. 400). Regardless of the storage method, most U.S. citizens strongly oppose the location of a low- or high-level nuclear waste disposal facility anywhere near them. Many citizens are also trying to find ways to ban shipments of radioactive wastes through their communities.

In 1982 Congress passed the Nuclear Waste Policy Act. It set a timetable for the Department of Energy

---

SPOTLIGHT Safety at U.S. Nuclear Weapons Facilities: The Government Lied to Its Citizens

Since 1986 government studies and once-secret documents have revealed that most of the nuclear weapons production facilities supervised by the Department of Energy have been operated with gross disregard for the safety of their workers and people in nearby areas. Since 1957 these facilities have released huge quantities of radioactive particles into the air and dumped tons of potentially cancer-inducing radioactive waste and toxic substances into flowing creeks and leaking pits without telling local residents.

Between 1957 and 1985 at least 30 serious incidents were kept secret while government officials repeatedly assured local residents that there was no danger from radioactive contamination. DOE

officials also admit that the government ignored repeated requests from private contractors running weapons facilities to provide funds for improving safety and handling procedures at these plants.

No one will ever know how many workers and innocent people living near weapons facilities have been or will be afflicted with cancer, birth defects, and thyroid problems because of releases of radioactive and toxic materials from these plants. Ohio's Senator John Glenn summed up the situation: "We are poisoning our own people in the name of national security."

It is difficult and costly for afflicted individuals to prove in court that their ailments and the deaths of loved ones were caused

by radioactivity from weapons facilities. Even if this can be done, contractors running these facilities and the federal government are largely immune from lawsuits to recover damages. No one, it appears, is liable or accountable.

The General Accounting Office and Department of Energy estimate that it will cost taxpayers $84 billion to $270 billion over 60 years to get these facilities cleaned up and in safe working order. Short-term economic greed leads to long-term grief. Without loud and constant pressure from citizens, Congress may not appropriate enough money to do the job. In 1989 the Department of Energy proposed that Congress provide $21.5 billion as a five-year down payment for the clean-up.

---

to choose a site and build the country's first deep underground repository for storage of high-level radioactive wastes from commercial nuclear reactors. In 1985 the Department of Energy announced plans to build the first repository, at a cost of $6 billion to $10 billion, based on the design shown in Figure 16-30.

The repository is to be built in a volcanic rock formation called tuff on federal land in the Yucca Mountain desert region, 161 kilometers (100 miles) northwest of Las Vegas, Nevada. Final tests and studies are to be made to determine the likelihood of earthquakes and water penetration at the site over the next 10,000 years.

Construction is supposed to begin in 1998 and the facility is scheduled to open by 2003, but few observers expect this schedule to be met. Before 2003, at least 73 nuclear plants will run out of space for storing their highly radioactive spent fuel rods. By 2010 the Department of Energy is to report to Congress on the need for a second repository, probably in the eastern United States.

If all goes well—a big if—in 2003 or sometime after, the first shipments of spent intensely radioactive fuel rods and other wastes will begin arriving at the Nevada storage site from more than 100 operating nuclear reactors around the country (Figure 16-31). If all waste is transported by truck, there will be about 6,405 shipments every year passing through parts of 45 states—an average of 17 shipments a day for 30 years. If all waste is transported by rail, there will be about 830 shipments annually.

Citizens in cities and states along the proposed routes for transporting these highly radioactive wastes to the Nevada repository are becoming increasingly concerned about the possibility of accidents that would release radioactive materials. Many cities are passing laws to ban shipments of radioactive materials through their areas, but such laws may be overridden by the federal government.

CASE STUDY What Can We Do with High-Level, Long-Lived Radioactive Waste?

Some scientists believe that the long-term safe storage or disposal of high-level radioactive wastes is technically possible. Others disagree, pointing out that it is impossible to show that any method will work for the 10,000 years of fail-safe storage needed for reprocessed wastes and the 240,000 years needed for unreprocessed wastes. The following are some of the proposed methods and their possible drawbacks:

1. *Bury it deep underground.* The currently favored method is to package unreprocessed spent fuel rods and bury them in a deep underground salt, granite, or other stable geological formation that is earthquake resistant and waterproof (Figure 16-30). A better method would be to reprocess the waste to remove very long-lived radioactive isotopes and convert what is left to a dry solid. The solid would then be fused with glass or a ceramic material and sealed in metal cannisters for burial. This would reduce burial time from 240,000 years to 10,000

years, but is expensive. Some geologists question the idea of burying nuclear wastes. They argue that the drilling and tunneling to build the repository might cause water leakage and weaken resistance to earthquakes. They also contend that with present geological knowledge scientists cannot make meaningful 10,000 to 240,000-year projections about earthquake probability and paths of groundwater flows in underground storage areas.

2. *Shoot it into space or into the sun.* Costs would be very high and a launch accident, such as the explosion of the space shuttle Challenger, could disperse high-level radioactive wastes over large areas of the earth's surface.

3. *Bury it under the Antarctic ice sheets or the Greenland ice caps.* The long-term stability of the ice sheets is not known. They could be destabilized by heat from the wastes, and retrieval of the wastes would be difficult

or impossible if the method failed.

4. *Dump it into downward-descending, deep-ocean sediments.* The long-term stability of these sediments is unknown. Wastes could eventually be spewed out somewhere else by volcanic activity. Waste containers might leak and contaminate the ocean before being carried downward, and retrieval would probably be impossible if the method did not work.

5. *Change it into harmless or less harmful isotopes.* Presently there is no way to do this. Even if a method were developed, costs would probably be extremely high. Resulting toxic materials and low-level but very long-lived radioactive wastes would have to be disposed of safely.

6. *Use it in shielded batteries to run small electric generators.* Researchers claim that a waste-basket-sized battery using spent fuel could produce enough electricity to run five homes for 28 years or longer at about half the current price of electricity. But

The U.S. government has spent $700 million building the Waste Isolation Pilot Plant (WIPP) for the underground storage of radioactive wastes from nuclear weapons plants. It has been carved out in salt beds 7,050 kilometers (2,150 feet) below the desert near Carlsbad, New Mexico. In 1988 its opening was delayed indefinitely because of failure to pass safety and environmental reviews.

DOE engineers have questioned the facility's safety and the quality of its construction. There is concern that water already seeping into the storage area could corrode steel barrels containing waste and form a slurry of brine and radioactive materials that could contaminate the nearby Pecos River, a tributary of the Rio Grande. Scientists also worry that radioactive gas given off by the wastes might breach the plugs in the facility's access and ventilation shafts and escape into the atmosphere.

Another safety concern is that the container to be used to transport waste to the WIPP has repeatedly failed to pass impact tests. Also, there is not enough money to train and equip emergency response teams along shipping routes that cross more than 20 states. Critics fear that the facility will be used despite many safety concerns because the DOE has already invested $700 million and desperately needs to clean up its nuclear weapons plants.

Decommissioning Nuclear Power Plants and Weapons Facilities The useful operating life of today's nuclear power plants is hoped to be 30 to 40 years, but many plants are aging faster than expected. Because the core and many other parts contain large amounts of radioactive materials, a nuclear plant cannot be abandoned or demolished by a wrecking ball like a worn-out coal-fired power plant.

Decommissioning nuclear power plants and nuclear weapons plants is the last step in the nuclear fuel cycle. Three ways have been proposed:

leakage could contaminate homes and communities. Dispersing high-level radioactive waste throughout a country would probably be politically unacceptable. Also, this method would use only a small portion of the nuclear waste.

Critics of nuclear power are appalled that after 41 years there has been so little effort to solve the serious problem of what to do with nuclear waste while plunging ahead and building hundreds of nuclear reactors and weapons facilities. They liken the situation to telling people to jump out of airplanes without parachutes, while assuring them that scientists will find some way to save them before they hit the ground. What do you think should be done?

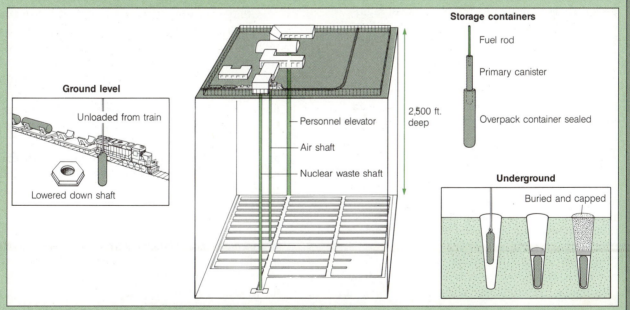

Figure 16-30 Proposed general design for deep underground permanent storage of high-level radioactive wastes from commercial nuclear power plants in the United States. (Source: U.S. Department of Energy)

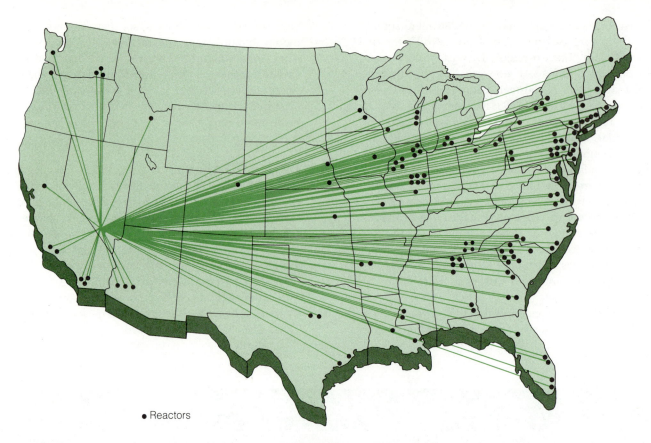

● Reactors

Figure 16-31 Proposed routes for shipping intensely radioactive wastes, mostly as spent fuel rods, from more than 100 operating nuclear reactors to the nuclear waste repository in Nevada sometime after 2003. Citizens in communities along these routes are concerned about radioactive contamination if trucks or trains carrying these wastes should have a serious accident. Ironically, Nevada has no commercial nuclear plants.

■ *immediate dismantlement:* decontaminating and taking the reactor apart after shutdown and shipping all radioactive debris to a radioactive-waste burial facility. This promptly rids the plant site of radioactive materials and is the least expensive option. But it exposes work crews to the highest level of radiation and results in the largest volume of radioactive waste.

■ *mothballing:* putting up a barrier and setting up a 24-hour security guard system to keep out intruders for several decades before dismantlement. This permits short-lived radioactive isotopes to decay, which reduces the threat to dismantlement crews and the volume of contaminated waste.

■ *entombment:* covering the reactor with reinforced concrete and putting up a barrier to keep out intruders. This allows for radioactive decay but passes a dangerous legacy to future generations.

Each method involves shutting down the plant, removing the spent fuel from the reactor core, draining all liquids, flushing all pipes, and sending all radioactive materials to an approved waste storage site yet to be built.

Worldwide, more than 20 commercial reactors (4 in the United States) have been retired and are await-

ing decommissioning. Another 225 large commercial reactors (70 in the United States) will probably be retired between 2000 and 2010.

Utility company officials estimate that dismantlement of a typical large reactor should cost about $170 million and mothballing $225 million. Most analysts consider the dismantlement figure too low and put the dismantlement cost at $1 billion to $3 billion per large reactor—roughly equal to the initial construction cost. Decommissioning costs will add to the already high price of electricity produced by nuclear fission. Politicians and nuclear industry officials in the U.S. and other countries may be tempted to mothball retired plants and pass dismantlement costs and problems on to the next generation.

Proliferation of Nuclear Weapons Since 1958 the United States has been giving away and selling to other countries various forms of nuclear technology. Today at least 14 other countries sell nuclear technology in the international marketplace.

For decades the U.S. government denied that the information, components, and materials used in the nuclear fuel cycle could be used to make nuclear weapons. In 1981, however, a Los Alamos National Laboratory report admitted: "There is no technical demarcation between the military and civilian reactor and there never was one"—something environmentalists had been saying for years.

Today 134 countries have signed the 1968 Nuclear-Nonproliferation Treaty. They have agreed to forego building nuclear weapons in return for help with commercial nuclear power. The International Atomic Energy Agency (IAEA) was established to monitor compliance.

But the system is not tight enough. Nuclear facilities belonging to India, Israel, South Africa, Pakistan, and other countries that have not signed the treaty are not monitored. Also, nuclear facilities in countries such as China, France, Great Britain, the Soviet Union, and the United States that have signed the treaty are generally not monitored by the IAEA.

There is clear evidence that the governments of Israel, South Africa, Pakistan, and India have made almost 200 nuclear weapons, mostly by diverting weapons-grade fuel from research reactors and commercial power plants. At least seven other countries—Argentina, Brazil, Libya, Syria, Iraq, Iran, and Kuwait—are actively seeking to make nuclear weapons or to buy them from black-market sources. It takes only about 10 kilograms (22 pounds) of plutonium to make a Nagasaki-sized nuclear bomb.

Sophisticated terrorist groups can also make a small atomic bomb by using about 2.2 kilograms (5 pounds) of plutonium or uranium-233, or about 5 kilograms (11 pounds) of uranium-235. Such a bomb could blow up a large building or a small city block and would contaminate a much larger area with radioactive materials for centuries. For example, a crude 10-kiloton nuclear weapon placed properly and detonated during working hours could topple the World Trade Center in New York City. This could easily kill more people than those killed by the atomic bomb the United States dropped on Hiroshima in 1945.

Spent reactor fuel is so highly radioactive that theft is unlikely, but plutonium separated at commercial and military reprocessing plants is easily handled. Although plutonium shipments are heavily guarded, they could be stolen from nuclear weapons or reprocessing plants, especially by employees. Each year about 3% of the 142,000 people working in 127 U.S. nuclear weapons facilities in 23 states are fired because of drug use, mental instability, or other security risks. By the mid-1990s hundreds of shipments of plutonium separated from reprocessing facilities in France, Great Britain, West Germany, Japan, and India will be traveling by land, sea, and air within and between countries.

Bomb-grade plutonium fuel or highly enriched fissionable uranium could also be stolen from one of the more than 150 research and test reactors operating in 30 countries. Also, simple and fairly cheap technologies are now available for concentrating 3% uranium-235 to weapons-grade material.

Those who would steal plutonium need not bother to make atomic bombs. They could simply use a conventional explosive charge to disperse the plutonium into the atmosphere from atop any tall building. Dispersed in this way, 1 kilogram (2.2 pounds) of plutonium oxide powder theoretically would contaminate 8 square kilometers (3 square miles) with dangerous levels of radioactivity for several hundred thousand years.

An analysis of government reports indicated that by 1988 at least 4.4 metric tons (4.8 tons) of bomb-grade plutonium from commercial power plants and government-run weapons and reprocessing plants throughout the world was unaccounted for. This is enough to make 190 to 360 blockbuster nuclear bombs or many much larger nuclear weapons. These materials, however, are not officially "missing" because officials don't know whether they were stolen, miscounted, or stuck in plant pipes.

One way to reduce the diversion of plutonium fuel from the nuclear fuel cycle is to contaminate it with other substances that make it not useful as weapons material. But so far no one has come up with a way to do this and most nuclear experts doubt that it can be done.

The best ways to slow down the spread of bomb-grade material are to abandon civilian reprocessing of power plant fuel, develop substitutes for highly enriched uranium in research reactors, and tighten international safeguards.

Soaring Costs   After the United States dropped atomic bombs on Hiroshima and Nagasaki, ending World War II, the scientists who developed the bomb and the elected officials responsible for its use were determined to show the world that the peaceful uses of atomic energy would outweigh the immense harm it had done. One part of this "Atoms for Peace" program was to use nuclear power to produce electricity. American utility companies were skeptical but began ordering nuclear power plants in the late 1950s for four reasons:

- The Atomic Energy Commission and builders of nuclear reactors projected that nuclear power would produce electricity at a very low cost compared to using coal and other alternatives.

- The nuclear industry projected that nuclear reactors would have an 88% *capacity factor*—a measure of the time a reactor would operate each year at full power.

- The first round of commercial reactors was built with the government paying about one-fourth of the cost and with the reactors provided to utilities at a fixed cost with no cost overruns allowed. (The builders lost their shirts but knew they could make big profits on later rounds of plants.)

- Congress passed the Price-Anderson Act, which protected the nuclear industry and utilities from significant liability to the general public in case of accidents.

It was an offer utility company officials could not resist. Today many wish they had.

Experience has shown that nuclear power is a very expensive way to produce electricity, even when it is heavily subsidized and enjoys partial protection from free market competition with other energy sources. According to the Department of Energy, commercial nuclear power received $1 trillion in research and development and other federal subsidies between 1952 and 1988—an average of $9 billion per reactor. Yet after 37 years of subsidies and development, commercial nuclear reactors in the United States now deliver less of the country's energy than that provided by wood and crop wastes with hardly any subsidies.

In 1987 new nuclear power plants in the United States produced electricity at an average of 13.5 cents per kilowatt-hour—equal to buying oil at $216 per barrel. These already high costs do not include most of the costs of storing radioactive wastes and decommissioning worn-out plants.

In contrast, new coal plants with the latest air pollution control equipment produced electricity at an average cost of six cents per kilowatt-hour in 1987. Producing electricity by cogeneration costs only five cents per kilowatt-hour, and saving electricity by improving energy efficiency costs only about one cent to four cents per kilowatt-hour. Sometime in the 1990s wind power and solar photovoltaic cells will be able to produce cheaper electricity than nuclear plants.

Operating costs of nuclear plants have been higher than projected because U.S. pressurized water reactors operate at an average of only about 60% of their full-time, full-power capacity—far below the 88% capacity projected by proponents of nuclear power in the 1950s. The average capacity factor for PWRs in the United Kingdom is only 51% and those in Sweden 54%. Those in other countries are higher: Japan and Canada (71%), France (74%), West Germany (82%), and Switzerland (87%), mostly because of standardized design and better management.

New nuclear plants in France and Japan cost about half as much per kilowatt of power to build as those in the United States because they are better planned and use standardized designs, but France ran up an enormous $39 billion debt to finance its nuclear industry. Also, France and Japan already produce more electricity than they need (see Guest Essay on p. 408).

In the United States, where almost every nuclear plant has a different design, poor planning and management and stricter safety regulations since the TMI accident have increased costs and lengthened construction time. Currently, new nuclear power plants cost three times as much to build as equivalent coal-fired plants with the latest air pollution control equipment. A 1989 Department of Energy study also found that operating costs for American nuclear plants are rising so fast that electric utilities may find it cheaper to close many of them before the end of their useful lives.

Banks and other lending institutions have become skeptical about financing new U.S. nuclear power plants. The Three Mile Island accident showed that utility companies could lose $1 billion or more of equipment in an hour, and at least $1 billion more in cleanup costs, even without any known harmful effects on public health. Lender confidence in nuclear power was eroded further in 1988 when it was decided not to open the completed Shoreham nuclear plant in New York (see Spotlight at left).

The business magazine *Forbes* has called the failure of the U.S. nuclear power program "the largest managerial disaster in U.S. business history." It involves perhaps $1 trillion in wasted investments, cost over-

SPOTLIGHT New York's Shoreham Nuclear Plant

The Shoreham nuclear power plant on Long Island near New York City was completed in 1984 but probably will never operate. It cost $5.3 billion to build—three times what it was supposed to cost.

Local and state officials have opposed putting the plant into operation. They believe it would not be possible to evacuate most of the people on Long Island in a major nuclear accident.

In 1988 the executives of the almost bankrupt utility company that built the plant and state officials worked out a plan for dismantlement. The utility executives agreed to sell the plant to the state for $1. The state agreed to spend at least $400 million to dismantle the plant if it can figure out what to do with the radioactive core. (Even though the NRC knew the plant had little chance of getting a full operating license, it allowed the utility to load radioactive fuel into the plant.)

As part of the deal, the state will grant the utility company a series of rate increases to help save the company from bankruptcy. This will force the company's customers to pay part of the $2.5 billion that the utility still owes for construction and to pay for dismantling. In 1989 the Bush administration filed suit to prevent the plant from being dismantled. What do you think should be done?

runs, and unnecessarily high electricity costs, and production of more electricity than the country needs. In 1989 citizens of Sacramento, California voted to close the Rancho Seco nuclear power plant mostly because of its poor operating record, expensive repairs, and utility rates that nearly doubled between 1984 and 1988.

Is nuclear power dead in the United States and most other MDCs? You might think so because of its high costs and massive public opposition. But powerful economic and political forces strive to maintain and expand the world's nuclear power industry (see Pro/Con below). Also, the U.S. Department of Energy and energy agencies in many other MDCs are heavily staffed with officials who continue to push for nuclear power at the expense of other safer and more cost-effective alternatives.

PRO/CON Should More Nuclear Power Plants Be Built in the United States?

Since the Three Mile Island accident, the U.S. nuclear industry and utility companies have financed a massive advertising campaign by the U.S. Council for Energy Awareness. This campaign, with a $340 million budget in 1988, is designed to improve the industry's image, resell nuclear power to the American public, and downgrade the importance of solar energy, conservation, geothermal energy, wind, and hydropower as alternatives to nuclear power.

The campaign's magazine and television ads do not tell readers and viewers that the ads are paid for by the nuclear industry. Most ads use the argument that more nuclear power is needed in the United States to reduce dependence on imported oil.

The truth is that since 1979 only about 5% (3% in 1988) of the electricity in the United States has been produced by burning oil and 95% of this is residual oil that can't be used for other purposes. Thus, *building more nuclear plants will not save the country any significant amount of domestic or imported oil.*

The nuclear industry points out correctly that nuclear power, unlike coal burning, does not add any carbon dioxide to the atmosphere. They argue that replacing coal-burning power plants with nuclear plants would help delay major climate changes from the greenhouse effect. They hope to convince governments and utility companies to build hundreds of new "second-generation" plants using standardized designs (see Guest Essay on p. 406). They are supposed to be safer, quicker to build (3 to 5 years), operate at full power 85% of the time, and last 60 years. Nuclear critics say that these promises are basically the same ones that nuclear advocates made for the present generation of reactors.

Nuclear advocates call these new designs, still only on drawing boards, *inherently safe.* One design is even named Passive Inherent Ultimate Safe (PIUS). But Robert Pollard, a former safety engineer with the NRC, points out that any scheme for fissioning atoms is inherently dangerous. You can build new reactors that are safer than existing ones, but you can't make them inherently safe.

Also, none of the new designs solve the problem of what to do with nuclear waste and the problem of the use of nuclear technology and fuel to build nuclear weapons. Indeed, these problems would become more serious as the number of nuclear plants increased from a few hundred to the many thousands needed to slow global warming only a little.

Also, the largest amounts of CO_2 are emitted into the atmosphere by motor vehicles—a problem that is not affected by building nuclear or any kind of power plant. If half of the U.S. use of coal used to produce electricity was displaced by building 200 large new nuclear plants at a cost of $1.2 trillion or more, this would reduce the world's greenhouse effect by only 2%. Just to make this small dent in the CO_2 problem would require completing a new large nuclear reactor in the U.S. every 3 days for the next 37 years. To do this worldwide, we would have to build *one reactor a day* for 37 years at a total cost of $23 trillion!

Improvements in energy efficiency—especially requiring all new cars to get at least 21 kilometers per liter (50 miles per gallon) of gasoline—would result in much greater and faster reductions of carbon dioxide emissions at a fraction the cost of building new nuclear plants. Improving energy efficiency by 2% a year could cut CO_2 emissions in half in the next 40 years and cut the nation's energy bill by $220 billion a year.

According to the Rocky Mountain Institute, each dollar put into improving energy efficiency reduces seven times more CO_2 than a dollar spent on nuclear power. If we hope to reduce CO_2 emission using the least-cost methods, then investing in energy efficiency and renewable energy resources is at the top of the list and nuclear power is at the bottom. Using the least-cost approach is not only more effective, it also frees capital for reforestation and other activities for reducing greenhouse warming.

Nuclear power critics believe that we do not need much of the electricity we already produce, and even if we did, there are better, quicker, and cheaper ways to produce it (see Guest Essay on p. 408). They also believe that we should not spend trillions of dollars to produce electricity, which cannot replace oil for transportation and would do little to delay global warming. What do you think?

Advantages and Disadvantages of Conventional Nuclear Fission Using nuclear fission to produce electricity has many advantages. Nuclear plants don't release carbon dioxide, particulate matter, sulfur dioxide, or nitrogen oxides into the atmosphere as do coal-fired plants. Water pollution and disruption of land are low to moderate if the entire nuclear fuel cycle operates normally. Multiple safety systems greatly decrease the likelihood of a catastrophic accident releasing deadly radioactive material into the environment. But the Chernobyl accident showed this can happen because of inability to control human errors.

Nuclear power also has many disadvantages. It produces electricity, which cannot be used to run vehicles without the development of affordable, long-lasting batteries to propel electric cars. Construction and operating costs for nuclear power plants in the United States and most countries are high and rising, even with massive government subsidies.

Standardized design and mass production can bring costs down, but electricity can still be produced by safer methods at a cost equal to or lower than that of nuclear power. Although large-scale accidents are infrequent, a combination of mechanical failure and human errors, sabotage, or shipping accidents could again release deadly radioactive materials into the environment.

The net useful energy yield of nuclear-generated electricity is low (Figure 3-17, p. 69). Scientists disagree greatly over how high-level radioactive wastes should be stored, and some doubt that an acceptably safe method can ever be developed.

Today's military and commercial nuclear energy programs commit future generations to storing dan-

---

GUEST ESSAY: Nuclear Power: A Faustian Bargain We Should Accept

Alvin M. Weinberg

Alvin M. Weinberg was a member of the group of scientists that developed the first experimental fission reactors at the University of Chicago in 1941. Since then he has been a leading figure in the development of commercial nuclear power. From 1948 to 1973 he served as director of the Oak Ridge National Laboratory. In 1974 he was director of the Office of Energy Research and Development in the Federal Energy Administration (now the Department of Energy). From 1975 to 1985 he was director of the Institute for Energy Analysis of the Oak Ridge Associated Universities, where he is now a Distinguished Fellow. He has written numerous articles and books on nuclear energy (see Further Readings) and has received many awards for his contributions to the development of nuclear energy.

There are two basically different views of the world's future. The one most popular in recent years holds that the earth's resources are limited. According to this neo-Malthusian view, nothing except drastic reduction in population, affluence, and certain types of technology can prevent severe environmental degradation.

The other view, held by cornucopians, holds that as scarce materials are exhausted there will always be new, more expensive ones to take their place. According to this view, Spaceship Earth has practically infinite supplies of resources, but it will cost more and more to stay where we are as we use up those resources that are readily available.

The cornucopian view seems to me to be the more reasonable, especially since all of our past experience has shown that as one resource becomes scarce, another takes its place. We do not use whale oil for lighting anymore, yet we have better lighting than our ancestors who burned this oil in lamps.

In the long run humankind will have to depend on the most abundant and almost infinitely abundant elements in the earth's crust: iron, sodium, carbon, nitrogen, aluminum, oxygen, silicon, and a few others. Glass, cement, and plastics will perform many more functions than they do now. Our average standard of living will be diminished, but probably no more than by a factor of 2.

Thus, in contrast to what seems to be the prevailing mood, I retain a certain basic optimism about the future. My optimism, however, is predicated on certain assumptions:

1. Technology can indeed deal with most of the effluents of this future society. Here I think I am on firm ground, for, on the whole, where technology has been given the task and been given the necessary time and funding, it has come through with very important improvements such as reducing air pollution emissions by cars. On the other hand, CO_2, which is the major greenhouse gas, cannot be controlled; this may place a limit on the rate at which we burn fossil fuels.

gerous radioactive wastes for thousands of years even if nuclear fission power is abandoned tomorrow. Perhaps even more dangerous, the existence of nuclear power technology helps spread knowledge and materials that can be used to make nuclear weapons. For these reasons, many people feel that it is unethical to use nuclear power to produce electricity.

16-6 BREEDER NUCLEAR FISSION AND NUCLEAR FUSION

Nonrenewable Breeder Nuclear Fission At the present rate of use, the world's supply of uranium should last for at least 100 years and perhaps 200 years. However, some nuclear power proponents project a sharp rise in the use of nuclear fission to produce electricity after the year 2000. They urge the development and widespread use of breeder nuclear fission reactors (see Guest Essay below).

Conventional fission reactors use fissionable uranium-235, which makes up only 0.7% of natural uranium ore. **Breeder nuclear fission reactors** convert nonfissionable uranium-238 into fissionable plutonium-239. Since breeders would use over 99% of the uranium in ore deposits, the world's known uranium reserves would last 1,000 years and perhaps several thousand years.

Under normal operation a breeder reactor is considered by its proponents to be much safer than a conventional fission reactor. But if the reactor's safety system should fail, the reactor could lose some of its liquid sodium coolant. This could cause a runaway fission chain reaction and perhaps a small nuclear

2. Phosphorus, though essentially infinite in supply in the earth's crust at various locations, has no substitute. Will we be able to so revolutionize agriculture that we can eventually use the "infinite" supply of phosphorus at acceptable cost? This technological and economic question is presently unresolved, although I cannot believe it to be unresolvable.

3. All of this presupposes that we have at our disposal an inexhaustible, relatively cheap source of energy. As I and others now see the technological possibilities, there is only one energy resource we can count on—and this is *nuclear fission*, based on *breeder reactors* to extend the world's supply of fissionable uranium far into the future. This is not to say that nuclear fusion, geothermal energy, or solar energy will never be economically available. We simply do not know now that any of these will ever be available in sufficient quantity and at affordable prices. We know, however, that conventional nuclear fission and breeder reactors are already technologically feasible, and that standardized, improved, and inherently safer reactor designs already being tested or on the drawing boards should bring costs down in the future.

In opting for nuclear fission breeders—and we hardly have a choice in the matter—we assume a moral and technological burden of serious proportion. A properly operating nuclear reactor and its subsystems are environmentally a very benign energy source. In particular, a reactor emits no carbon dioxide.

The issue hangs around the words *properly operating*. Can we ensure that henceforth we shall be able to maintain the degree of intellectual responsibility, social commitment, and stability necessary to maintain this energy form so as not to cause serious harm? This is basically a moral and social question, though it does have strong technological components.

It is a Faustian bargain that we strike: in return for this essentially inexhaustible energy source, which we must have if we are to maintain ourselves at anything like our present numbers and our present state of affluence, we must commit ourselves and generations to come—essentially forever—to exercise the vigilance and discipline necessary to keep our nuclear fires well behaved.

As a nuclear technologist who has devoted his career to this quest for an essentially infinite energy source, I believe the bargain is a good one, and it may even be an inevitable one, especially if our concerns about the greenhouse effects are justified. It is essential that the full dimension and implication of this Faustian bargain be recognized, especially by the young people who will have to live with the choices that are being made on this vital issue.

Guest Essay Discussion

1. Do you agree that the resources of the earth are practically infinite? Explain.

2. The author bases his optimism on three assumptions. Do you believe that these assumptions are reasonable? Explain. Are there any other assumptions that should be added?

3. Do you agree that we should accept the Faustian bargain of conventional and breeder nuclear fission? Explain.

4. Do you agree with the author that "we hardly have any choice" in opting for nuclear fission breeder reactors? Explain.

explosion with the force of several hundred pounds of TNT. Such an explosion could blast open the containment building, releasing a cloud of highly radioactive gases and particulate matter. Leaks of flammable liquid sodium can also cause fires, as has happened with all experimental reactors built so far.

Since 1966, small experimental breeder reactors have been built in the United Kingdom, the Soviet Union, West Germany, Japan, and France. In December 1986 France began operating a commercial-size breeder reactor, the Superphenix. It cost three times the original estimate to build. The little electricity it has produced is twice as expensive as that generated by France's conventional fission reactors. In 1987, shortly after the reactor began operating at full power, it began leaking liquid sodium coolant and was shut down. Repairs may be so expensive that the reactor may not be put back into operation.

Tentative plans to build full-size commercial breeders in West Germany, the Soviet Union, and the United Kingdom may be canceled because of the excessive cost of France's reactor and an excess of electric generating capacity. Also, experimental breeders built so far produce only about one-fourth of the plutonium-239 each year needed to replace their own fissionable material—much less produce enough fuel to start up another breeder. If this serious problem is not solved, it would take 100 years to 200 years at best for breeders to begin producing enough plutonium to fuel a significant number of other breeders.

Nuclear Fusion Scientists hope someday to use controlled nuclear fusion (Figure 3-11, p. 63) to provide an almost limitless source of energy for producing high-temperature heat and electricity. For 40 years research has focused on the D-T nuclear fusion reaction in which two isotopes of hydrogen-deuterium (D) and tritium (T) fuse at about 100 million degrees—ten times as hot as the sun's interior.

Another possibility is the D-D fusion reaction in which the nuclei of two deuterium atoms fuse together at much higher temperatures. If developed, it would run on virtually unlimited heavy water (D_2O) fuel obtained from seawater at a cost of about ten cents a gallon.

After 40 years of research, high-temperature nuclear fusion is still at the laboratory stage. Deuterium and tritium atoms have been forced together by using electromagnetic reactors the size of 12 locomotives, 120-trillion watt laser beams, and bombardment with high-

GUEST ESSAY: Technology Is the Answer (But What Was the Question?)

Amory B. Lovins

Physicist and energy consultant Amory B. Lovins is recognized as one of the world's leading experts on energy strategy. Alvin Weinberg (see previous Guest Essay) has called him "the most articulate writer on energy in the world today." In 1989 he was the first recipient of the Delphi Prize, one of the world's top environmental awards. He is director of research at the Rocky Mountain Institute in Old Snowmass, Colorado, which he and his wife Hunter cofounded in 1982. He has briefed five heads of state and served as a consultant to several United Nations agencies, the U.S. Department of Energy, the Congressional Office of Technology Assessment, the U.S. Solar Energy Research Institute, and many state and local governments. He is active in energy affairs in 20 countries and has published several hundred papers and a dozen books, including the widely discussed Soft Energy Paths *(New York: Harper Colophon, 1979), and the nontechnical version of this work with coauthor L. Hunter Lovins,* Energy Unbound: Your Invitation to Energy Abundance *(San Francisco: Sierra Club Books, 1986).*

The answers you get depend on the questions you ask. But sometimes it seems so important to resolve a crisis that we forget to ask what problem we're trying to solve.

It is fashionable to suppose that we're running out of energy, and that the solution is obviously to get lots more of it. But asking how to get more energy begs the question of how much we need. That depends not on how much we used in the past but on what we want to do in the future and how much energy it will take to do those things.

How much energy it takes to make steel, run a sewing machine, or keep you comfortable in your house depends on how cleverly we use energy, and the more it costs, the smarter we seem to get. It is now cheaper, for example, to double the efficiency of most industrial electric motor drive systems than to get more electricity to run the old ones. (Just this one saving can more than replace the entire U.S. nuclear power program.) We know how to make lights five times as efficient as those presently in use and how to

speed particles. But so far none of these approaches have produced more energy than they use.

If researchers eventually can get more energy out than they put in, the next step is to build a small fusion reactor and then scale it up to commercial size. This task is considered one of the most difficult engineering problems ever undertaken. The estimated cost of a commercial fusion reactor is at least four times that of a comparable conventional fission reactor. If everything goes right—a very big if—high-temperature fusion might be in widespread commercial use sometime after 2100.

In 1989 two chemists announced what might be either a spectacular energy breakthrough or merely a fascinating scientific experiment. Preliminary results suggest that they were able to bring about some D-D nuclear fusion at room temperature using a simple apparatus. But it is not clear whether some of this energy is coming from unexpected chemical reactions or other nonfusion processes. It will probably take two to three decades to evaluate the commercial feasibility, if any, of cold nuclear fusion.

If feasible, a commercial cold nuclear fusion plant, one of the most complicated machines ever built, would create hundreds of times less radioactive waste than a nuclear fission power plant. Also, it wouldn't emit the greenhouse gases and harmful sulfur and nitrogen oxides and particulate matter that coal plants do.

If everything goes right—another very big if—a commercial cold fusion power plant might be built as early as 2030. But even if everything goes right, energy experts don't expect cold or high-temperature nuclear fusion to be a significant source of energy until 2100, if then. Meanwhile, several other quicker, cheaper, and safer ways can produce more electricity than we need, as discussed in the next chapter and in the guest essay below.

Nuclear fission energy is safe only if a number of critical devices work as they should, if a number of people in key positions follow all their instructions, if there is no sabotage, no hijacking of the transport, if no reactor fuel processing plant or repository anywhere in the world is situated in a region of riots or guerrilla activity, and no revolution or war—even a "conventional one"—takes place in these regions. No acts of God can be permitted.

Hannes Alfvén, Nobel Laureate in Physics

make household appliances that give us the same work as now, using one-fifth as much energy (saving money in the process).

Eight automakers have made good-sized, peppy, safe prototype cars averaging 30 to 52 kilometers per liter (70 to 120 miles per gallon). We know today how to make new buildings and many old ones so heat-tight (but still well ventilated) that they need essentially no energy to maintain comfort year-round, even in severe climates.

These energy-saving measures are uniformly cheaper than going out and getting more energy. Detailed studies in over a dozen countries have shown that supplying energy services in the cheapest way—by wringing more work from the energy we already have—would let us increase our standard of living while using several times less total energy (and electricity) than we do now. Those savings cost less than finding new domestic oil or operating existing power plants.

But the old view of the energy problem included a worse mistake than forgetting to ask how much energy we needed: It sought more energy, in any form, from any source, at any price—as if all kinds of energy were alike. This is like saying, "All kinds of food are alike; we're running short of potatoes and turnips and cheese, but that's OK, we can substitute sirloin steak and oysters Rockefeller."

Some of us have to be more discriminating than that. Just as there are different kinds of food, so there are many different forms of energy, whose different prices and qualities suit them to different uses (Figure 3–7, p. 59). There is, after all, no demand for energy as such; nobody wants raw kilowatt-hours or barrels of sticky black goo. People instead want energy services: comfort, light, mobility, ability to bake bread, ability to make cement. We ought therefore to start at that end of the energy problem: to ask, "What are the many different tasks we want energy for, and what is the amount, type, and source of energy that will do each task *in the cheapest way?*"

Electricity is a particularly special, high-quality, expensive form of energy. An average kilowatt-hour delivered in the United States in 1987 was priced at about eight cents, equivalent to buying the heat content of oil costing $128 per barrel—over seven times the average world price during 1987. The average cost of electricity from nuclear plants (including fuel and operating expenses) beginning operation in 1987 was 13.5 cents per kilowatt-hour, equivalent on a heat basis to buying oil at about $216 per barrel.

Such costly energy might be worthwhile if it were used only for the premium tasks that require it, such as lights, motors, electronics, and smelters. But those special uses, only 8% of all delivered U.S. energy

(continued)

CHAPTER SUMMARY

The major factors determining the degree of use of any energy alternative are its **(1)** estimated short-, intermediate-, and long-term supplies, **(2)** net useful energy yield, **(3)** cost, and **(4)** potentially harmful environmental, social, and security impacts. Each energy alternative has certain advantages and disadvantages.

Conventional crude oil can be easily transported throughout the world, is a relatively cheap and versatile fuel, and has a high net useful energy yield. However, affordable supplies may be depleted in 40 to 80 years, burning oil releases carbon dioxide into the atmosphere which could alter global climate, and its use has other moderate environmental impacts.

Unconventional heavy oils left in conventional and obtained from oil shale and tar sands could extend oil supplies. But they are costly, have low net useful energy yields, produce carbon dioxide, require large quantities of water for processing, and have a higher environmental impact than conventional oil.

Conventional natural gas burns hotter and cleaner than any other fossil fuel, is versatile and relatively cheap, and has a high net useful energy yield. But supplies may be depleted in 40 to 100 years, and burning of natural gas produces carbon dioxide. Various unconventional sources

---

GUEST ESSAY, Continued

needs, are already met twice over by today's power stations. Two-fifths of our electricity is already spilling over into uneconomic, low-grade uses such as water heating, space heating, and air conditioning. Yet no matter how efficiently we use electricity (even with heat pumps), we can never get our money's worth on these applications. Electricity is far too expensive to be worthwhile for the 58% of the delivered energy needed in the form of heat in the United States and for the 34% needed to run nonrail vehicles. But these tasks are all that additional electricity could be used for without wasting energy and money, because today's power stations already supply our real electric needs twice over.

Thus, *supplying more electricity is irrelevant to the energy problem that we have.* Even though electricity accounts for almost all of the federal energy research and development budget and for at least half of national energy investment, it is the wrong kind of energy to meet our needs economically. Arguing about what kind of new power station to build—coal, nuclear, solar—is like shopping for the best buy in antique Chippendale chairs to burn in your stove or brandy to put in your car's gas tank. *It is the wrong question.*

Indeed, *any kind of new power station is so uneconomical that if you have just built one, you will save the country money by writing it off and never operating it.* Why? Because its additional electricity can be used only for low-temperature heating and cooling (the premium, "electricity-specific" uses being already filled up) and is the most expensive way of supplying these services.

The real question is what is the cheapest way to do low-temperature heating and cooling. That means weatherstripping, insulation, heat exchangers, greenhouses, superwindows, window shades and overhangs, trees, and so on. These measures generally cost about half a penny per kilowatt-hour, whereas the running costs *alone* for a new nuclear plant will be nearly four cents per kilowatt-hour, so it is cheaper not to run it. In fact, under our crazy U.S. tax laws, the extra saving from not having to pay the plant's

future subsidies is probably so big that society can also recover the capital cost of having built the plant by shutting it down!

If we want more electricity, we should get it from the cheapest sources first. In approximate order of increasing price, these include:

1. Converting to efficient lighting equipment. This would save the U.S. electricity equal to the output of 120 large power plants plus $30 billion a year in fuel and maintenance costs.

2. Eliminating pure waste of electricity, such as lighting empty offices at headache level. Each kilowatt-hour saved can be resold without having to generate it anew.

3. Displacing with good architecture, and with passive and some active solar techniques, the electricity now used for water heating and space heating and cooling. Some U.S. utilities now give low- or zero-interest weatherization loans, which you need not start repaying for ten years or until you sell your house—because it saves them millions of dollars to get electricity that way compared with building new power plants. Most utilities also offer rebates for buying efficient appliances.

4. Making lights, motors, appliances, smelters, and the like cost-effectively efficient.

Just these four measures can quadruple U.S. electrical efficiency, making it possible to run today's economy, with no changes in lifestyles, using no thermal power plants, whether old or new, and whether fueled with oil, gas, coal, or uranium. We would need only the present hydroelectric capacity, readily available small-scale hydroelectric projects, and a modest amount of windpower. But if we still wanted more electricity, the next cheapest sources would include:

5. Industrial cogeneration, combined-heat-and-power plants, low-temperature heat engines run by industrial waste heat or by solar ponds, filling empty turbine bays and upgrading equipment in existing big dams, modern wind machines or

of natural gas could extend supplies for several hundred to a thousand years but are presently costly to locate and extract and have a lower net useful energy yield than conventional natural gas.

Coal is the world's most abundant conventional fossil fuel, has a high net useful energy for producing electricity and high-temperature heat for industrial processes, and is fairly cheap. But coal is **(1)** an extremely dirty, hazardous, and environmentally harmful fuel to mine and burn without adequate and costly air pollution control devices, improved mine safety, and reclamation of strip-mined land, **(2)** releases more carbon dioxide per unit of energy produced than other fossil fuels, and **(3)** cannot conve-

niently be used to fuel vehicles and heat homes unless converted to gaseous or liquid fuels. Gaseous and liquid fuels produced from coal burn more cleanly, are more versatile, and can be transported more conveniently than solid coal. But they have low net energy yields and large water requirements for processing, release large quantities of carbon dioxide, and lead to greatly increased land disruption from surface mining.

Heat from the earth's core, or *geothermal energy,* is transferred to *nonrenewable* underground deposits of dry steam, wet steam, and hot water at various places. When these deposits are close enough to the earth's surface, their heat can be extracted and used for space heating and to pro-

small-scale hydroelectric turbines in good sites, steam-injected natural gas turbines, and perhaps recent developments in solar cells with waste heat recovery.

It is only after we had clearly exhausted all these cheaper opportunities that we would even consider:

6. Building a new central power station of any kind—the slowest and costliest known way to get more electricity (or to save oil).

To emphasize the importance of starting with energy end uses rather than energy sources, consider a sad little story from France, involving a "spaghetti chart" (or energy flowchart)—a device energy planners often use to show how energy flows from primary sources via conversion processes to final forms and uses. In the mid-1970s energy conservation planners in the French government started, wisely, on the right-hand side of the spaghetti chart. They found that their biggest single need for energy was to heat buildings, and that even with good heat pumps, electricity would be the most uneconomic way to do this. So they had a fight with their nationalized utility; they won; and electric heating was supposed to be discouraged or even phased out because it was so wasteful of money and fuel.

But meanwhile, down the street, the energy supply planners (who were far more numerous and influential in the French government) were starting on the left-hand side of the spaghetti chart. They said: "Look at all that nasty imported oil coming into our country! We must replace that oil. Oil is energy. . . . We need some other source of energy. Voila! Reactors can give us energy; we'll build nuclear reactors all over the country." But they paid little attention to what would happen to that extra energy, and no attention to relative prices.

Thus, the two sides of the French energy establishment went on with their respective solutions to two different, indeed contradictory, French energy problems: *more energy of any kind,* versus *the right kind to do each task cheapest.* It was only in 1979 that these conflicting perceptions collided. The supply side planners

suddenly realized that the only way they would be able to *sell* all that nuclear electricity would be for electric heating, which they had just agreed not to do.

Every industrial country is in this embarrassing position (especially if we include in "heating" air conditioning, which just means heating the outdoors instead of the indoors). Which end of the spaghetti chart we start on, or *what we think the energy problem is,* is not an academic abstraction: It *determines what we buy.* It is the most fundamental source of disagreement about energy policy.

People starting on the left side of the spaghetti chart think the problem boils down to whether to build coal or nuclear power stations (or both). People starting on the right realize that *no* kind of new power station can be an economic way to meet the needs for low- and high-temperature heat and for vehicular liquid fuels that are 92% of our energy problem.

So if we want to provide our energy services at a price we can afford, let's get straight what question our technologies are supposed to provide the answer to. Before we argue about the meatballs, let's untangle the strands of spaghetti, see where they're supposed to lead, and find out what we really need the energy for!

Guest Essay Discussion

1. List the energy services you would like to have, and note which of these must be furnished by electricity.

2. The author argues that building more nuclear, coal, or other electrical power plants to supply electricity for the United States is unnecessary and wasteful. Summarize the reasons for this conclusion and give your reasons for agreeing or disagreeing with this viewpoint.

3. Do you agree or disagree that increasing the supply of energy, instead of concentrating on improving energy efficiency, is the wrong answer to U.S. energy problems? Explain.

duce electricity or high-temperature heat. They can provide a 100- to 200-year supply of energy for areas near the deposits at a moderate cost. They have a moderate net useful energy yield and don't emit carbon dioxide. But there is not an abundance of easily accessible deposits, the energy cannot be used to power vehicles, and without pollution control its use results in moderate to high air and water pollution.

There are also vast, essentially *perpetual* sources of geothermal energy in the form of molten rock, dry hot rock, and warm rock deposits, but these deposits lie so deep under the earth's crust that with present technology they are too costly to develop on a large scale.

During the 1950s and 1960s it was projected that by the year 2000 almost one-fourth of the world's commercial energy would be produced by *conventional nuclear fission*. However, by 1988 nuclear power was providing only 4.5% of the world's commercial energy, and high and increasing costs had led many countries to abandon their plans to increase their use of this energy alternative.

Major advantages of conventional nuclear fission are **(1)** nuclear reactors do not release air pollutants such as carbon dioxide, particulate matter, and sulfur and nitrogen oxides like coal-fired plants, and **(2)** water pollution and disruption of land are low to moderate if the entire nuclear fuel cycle operates normally.

Major disadvantages are **(1)** construction and operating costs of nuclear plants have been much higher than projected, even with massive government and consumer subsidies; **(2)** conventional nuclear power plants can be used only to produce electricity; **(3)** although large-scale accidents are extremely unlikely, some have already occurred as a result of mechanical and human errors, and these have eroded public confidence; **(4)** the net useful energy yield of nuclear power is low; **(5)** safe methods for storing high-level radioactive waste for ten to several hundred thousand years have not been developed; and **(6)** its use spreads knowledge and materials that could be used to make nuclear weapons.

Some experts project that *breeder nuclear fission* could greatly extend the world's supply of uranium fuel, but experimental plants built so far indicate that this is too costly, and it also has some safety problems.

Some experts hope that high-temperature or cold *nuclear fusion* will eventually be able to provide an inexhaustible supply of energy. However, after 45 years of research, high-temperature nuclear fusion is still at the laboratory stage and no one has been able to get more energy out of the process than must be put in to initiate the fusion reaction. Preliminary experiments in 1989 suggested that cold nuclear fusion might be possible. If so, it will take several decades to determine whether it can be used on a commercial basis. Even if everything goes right—a very big if—nuclear fusion is not expected to be a significant source of commercial energy until between 2050 and 2150, if ever.

DISCUSSION TOPICS

1. Explain why you agree or disagree with the following statements:
   a. We can get all the oil we need by extracting and processing heavy oil left in known oil wells.

   b. We can get all the oil we need by extracting and processing heavy oil from oil shale deposits.
   c. We can get all the oil we need by extracting heavy oil from tar sands.
   d. We can get all the natural gas we need from unconventional sources.

2. Coal-fired power plants in the United States cause an estimated 10,000 deaths a year, mostly from atmospheric emissions of sulfur oxides, nitrogen oxides, and particulate matter. These emissions also damage many buildings and some forests and aquatic systems. Should air pollution emission standards for *all* new and existing coal-burning plants be tightened significantly? Explain.

3. Should all coal-burning power and industrial plants in the United States be required to convert to fluidized-bed combustion? Explain. What are the alternatives?

4. Do you favor a U.S. energy strategy based on greatly increased use of coal-burning plants to produce electricity? Explain. What are the alternatives?

5. List the energy services you would like to have, and note which of these must be furnished by electricity.

6. Explain why you agree or disagree with the following statements:
   a. Dry-steam, wet-steam, and hot-water geothermal deposits can supply most needs for electricity in the United States by the year 2010.
   b. Molten rock (magma) geothermal deposits should be able to supply the United States with all the electricity and high-temperature heat it needs by 2025.
   c. Although geothermal energy may not be a major source of energy for the United States over the next few decades, it can supply a significant fraction of energy needs in areas where high-quality deposits are found.

7. Do you favor a U.S. energy strategy based on building a large number of new, better-designed, conventional nuclear fission reactors to produce electricity? Explain.

8. Explain why you agree or disagree with each of the following proposals made by the nuclear power industry and currently supported by the Bush administration:
   a. The licensing time of new nuclear power plants in the United States should be halved (from an average of 12 years) so they can be built at less cost and compete more effectively with coal and other renewable energy alternatives.
   b. A large number of new nuclear power plants should be built in the United States to reduce dependence on imported oil and slow down global warming.
   c. Large federal subsidies (already totaling $1 trillion) should continue to be given to the commercial nuclear power industry so it does not have to compete in the open marketplace with other energy alternatives receiving less or little federal subsidies.

9. A major program for developing the nuclear breeder fission reactor should be developed and funded largely by the federal government to conserve uranium resources and keep the United States from being dependent on other countries for uranium supplies.

Renewable and Perpetual Energy Resources: Conservation, Sun, Wind, Water, and Biomass

General Questions and Issues

1. What are the advantages and disadvantages of improving energy efficiency as a way to reduce unnecessary energy waste?

2. What are the advantages and disadvantages of capturing and using some of the sun's direct input of solar energy for heating buildings and water and for producing electricity?

3. What are the advantages and disadvantages of using indirect solar energy stored in falling and flowing water (hydropower) for producing electricity?

4. What are the advantages and disadvantages of using indirect solar energy in the form of heat stored in water for producing electricity and heating buildings and water?

5. What are the advantages and disadvantages of using indirect solar energy stored in winds to produce electricity?

6. What are the advantages and disadvantages of using renewable, indirect solar energy stored in plants and organic waste (biomass) for heating buildings and water and for transportation (biofuels)?

7. What are the advantages and disadvantages of producing and using hydrogen gas and fuel cells to produce electricity, to heat buildings and water, and to propel vehicles when oil runs out?

8. What are the best present and future energy options for the United States, and what should be the country's long-term energy strategy?

If the United States wants to save a lot of oil and money and increase national security, there are two simple ways to do it: stop driving Petropigs and stop living in energy sieves.

Amory B. Lovins

What is our best energy option? Cut out unnecessary energy waste. What is our next best energy option? Here there is much disagreement.

Some say find and burn more conventional and unconventional forms of oil, natural gas, and coal. Some say build more and better conventional nuclear power plants and increase efforts to develop breeder nuclear fission and nuclear fusion. These choices, based on using more of the earth's nonrenewable resources, were evaluated in the last chapter.

Others say get more of the energy we need from the sun, wind, flowing water, biomass, and renewable forms of geothermal energy. They urge us to make more use of locally available energy supplies instead of building more large fossil-fuel and nuclear plants and having them send energy to us. These energy choices, based on using the earth's perpetual and renewable energy resources, are evaluated in this chapter.

17-1 IMPROVING ENERGY EFFICIENCY: DOING MORE WITH LESS

Reducing Energy Waste: An Offer We Can't Afford to Refuse The easiest and cheapest way to make more energy available with the least environmental impact is to reduce or eliminate unnecessary energy use and waste. There are three general ways to do this:

- Reduce energy consumption by changing energy-wasting habits. Examples of such changes include walking or riding a bicycle for short trips, using mass transit instead of cars, wearing a sweater indoors in cold weather to allow a lower thermostat setting, turning off unneeded lights, and reducing our use of throwaway items.

- Improve energy efficiency by using less energy to do the same amount of work. Examples include adding more insulation to houses and buildings, keeping car engines tuned, and switching to more energy-efficient cars, houses, heating and cooling systems, appliances, lights, and industrial processes.

- Use less energy to do more work by developing devices that waste less energy than existing ones. Examples include solar cells that convert solar energy directly to electricity, aerodynamic vehicle designs that reduce fuel consumption, and more efficient heating and cooling systems, appliances, and vehicle engines.

Improving energy efficiency has the highest net useful energy yield of all energy alternatives. It reduces the environmental impacts of using energy because less of each energy resource is used to provide the same amount of energy. It adds no carbon dioxide to the atmosphere and is the best, cheapest, and quickest way to slow global warming by reducing wasteful use of fossil fuels (see Pro/Con on p. 405).

Reducing the amount of energy we use and waste makes domestic and world supplies of nonrenewable fossil fuels last longer, buys time for phasing in perpetual and renewable energy resources, and reduces dependence on imported oil. It also reduces international tensions and improves national and global military and economic security by reducing dependence on oil imports and the need for military intervention to protect sources of oil, especially in the Middle East. Furthermore, it usually provides more jobs and promotes more economic growth per unit of energy than other energy alternatives. By contrast, each big new power plant loses the economy about 4,000 jobs by starving other sectors of the capital they need.

Improving energy efficiency also has fewer disadvantages than any energy alternative. One disadvantage is that improving energy efficiency by replacing houses, industrial equipment, and cars as they wear out with more energy-efficient ones takes a long

SPOTLIGHT The World's Biggest Energy User and Waster

As the world's largest energy user and waster, the United States has more impact on fossil fuel depletion, global warming, and acid deposition than any country. At least 41% of all energy used in the United States is unnecessarily wasted. This waste equals all the energy consumed by two-thirds of the world's population.

The largest untapped supplies of energy in the United States are in its energy-wasting buildings, factories, and vehicles, not in Alaska or offshore areas. This source of energy can be found almost everywhere, can be exploited cheaply and fairly quickly, strengthens rather than weakens the economy and national security, improves rather than damages the environment, and leaves no harmful wastes. Had the United States vigorously pursued a least-cost, high-energy-efficiency energy policy since 1973 instead of its high-cost, mostly fruitless search for new domestic deposits of oil, the country would have no need to import any oil today.

The Alaska oil pipeline is a much greater threat to national security than not being able to move oil by tankers through the Persian Gulf. There are now other oil suppliers and several alternate ways to get oil from the Middle East, but only one way to get oil from Alaska. Sabotage of the highly vulnerable Alaska oil pipeline could disrupt the entire American economy. The Department of Defense admits that it is impossible to protect this pipeline.

The good news is that since 1979 the U.S. has gotten more than seven times as much energy from improvements in energy efficiency as from all net increases in the supply of all forms of energy with little help from federal and state governments. This reduction of energy waste has cut the country's annual energy bill by about $150 billion—about equal to the current annual national deficit.

On the average, American houses now use 20% less space-heating energy per square foot than they did in 1972. The average

new home being built today is 35% more energy efficient than the typical house before 1973 and some new houses are 75% more efficient. In 1988 new U.S. autos averaged about 26.5 miles per gallon, nearly double that of new cars in 1973. New refrigerators are now about 72% more efficient than they were in 1972.

The bad news is that despite these improvements, energy efficiency in the United States is half what it could be. Average gas mileage for new cars and for the entire fleet of cars is below that in most other MDCs. Most U.S. houses and buildings are still underinsulated and leaky. Electric resistance heating is the most wasteful and expensive way to heat a home, yet it is installed in over half the new homes in the United States. Today, the energy unnecessarily wasted in the United States costs about twice as much as the annual federal budget deficit, or more than the entire $10,000-a-second military budget.

Some more good news is that the untapped energy available by

time. For example, replacing most buildings and industrial equipment takes several decades, and replacing the older cars on the road with new ones takes 10 to 12 years. Some of the improvements in automobile gas mileage depend mainly on driving smaller and lighter cars, which some drivers don't like.

Because the United States uses more energy than any country and has only moderate energy efficiency, it wastes more energy than any country (see Spotlight below).

Improving Industrial Energy Efficiency In the United States, industrial processes consume more energy than transportation, residences, and commercial buildings (Figure 17-2).

Today American industry uses 70% less energy to produce the same amount of goods as it did in 1973. But American industry still wastes enormous amounts of energy.

Japan has the highest overall industrial energy efficiency in the world. Denmark, France, Italy, Spain, and West Germany also have high industrial energy efficiencies. Japanese products have a 5% average price advantage over American goods simply because of the higher average energy cost of U.S. goods.

Industries that use large amounts of high-temperature heat and electricity can save energy and money by installing *cogeneration units,* which produce both of these types of energy. Today industrial cogeneration in the United States supplies electricity equal to the output of 16 large (1,000-megawatt) power plants. By 2000 cogeneration has the potential to produce more electricity than all of the country's nuclear power plants.

Industry uses almost half of the world's electricity. For example, massive amounts are used to convert aluminum ore to aluminum metal. A new process for doing this uses 25% less electricity. Using recycled aluminum reduces electricity use by 95%. Despite such enormous savings, the average world aluminum-recycling rate is only 25%. This could easily be doubled or tripled.

About 70% of the electricity used in U.S. industry drives electric motors. Most of these motors run at fixed speeds and voltages regardless of the tasks they perform. Adding variable-speed drives, light dimmers, and other devices that match the output of a

---

improving energy efficiency in the United States at low cost is over three times that from developing remaining nonrenewable energy resources at a very high cost (Figure 17-1). Full use of the best available oil- and natural-gas saving technologies would save about three-fourths of the oil now used, at a cost equivalent to buying oil at around $6 a barrel—three times less than the average market price in 1988.

Improving the efficiency of electricity use in inefficient motors, lights, appliances, and industrial equipment in the United States by using technologies already on the market would save about 75% of all electricity now used. This can be done at a cost of about 0.6 cents per kilowatt-hour—one-tenth the average price of electricity from a coal burning power plant and one-twentieth that from a nuclear plant. Using these energy-efficient technologies would replace the electricity produced by 250 large power plants and cut the country's

annual electricity bill by $100 billion.

The amount the United States spends each year to buy energy would be reduced by $200 billion a year if it used energy as efficiently as Japan or Sweden. Bringing about a low-cost energy efficiency revolution would stimulate the economy and save $2 trillion between 1990 and 2000—enough to pay off the entire national debt.

The bad news is that the United States is not vigorously pursuing this least-cost approach. Why? Mostly because of undue influence by energy companies and failure of citizens to demand that elected officials change the direction of U.S. energy policy. This would involve switching from the present *worst-buys-first* approach to a *best-buys-first* approach based on improving energy efficiency and greatly increasing the use of perpetual and renewable sources of energy. What do you think should be done?

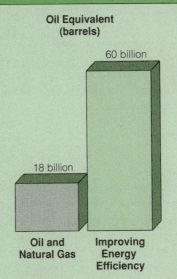

Figure 17-1 Improving energy efficiency in the United States using available technologies will produce over three times as much energy at a low cost by 2020 than finding and developing all new oil and natural gas deposits believed to exist in the United States at a very high cost. (Data from Natural Resources Defense Council and Rocky Mountain Institute)

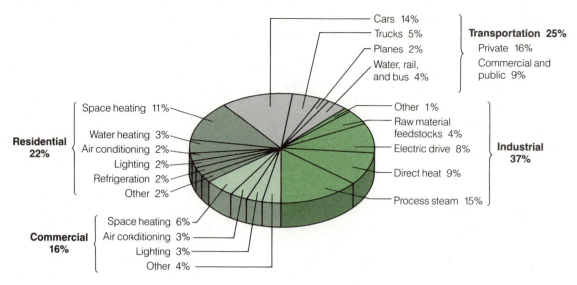

Figure 17-2 Distribution of commercial energy use in the United States among various sectors in 1984. (Data from U.S. Department of Energy)

motor or other electrical device to power needs would cut U.S. electricity use by one-sixth. This would eliminate the need for all existing U.S. nuclear power plants and save hundreds of millions of dollars a year.

Switching to high-efficiency lighting is another way to save energy in industry. Industries can also use computer-controlled energy management systems to turn off lighting and equipment in nonproduction areas and make adjustments in periods of low production.

Within 20 years newly discovered superconductors could save energy and money. Another major way to save energy in industry is to greatly reduce the production of throwaway products. This can be done by increasing recycling and reuse and by making products that last longer and are easy to repair and recycle (Section 15-7).

Improving Transportation Energy Efficiency One-fourth of the supplemental energy consumed in the United States is used to transport people and goods (Figure 17-2). With 4.8% of the world's people, the United States has 35% of the world's cars and trucks. Each year these vehicles travel almost as many miles as the rest of the world's motor vehicles taken together.

The increased use of the automobile, especially in the United States, has decreased the use of railroads and buses and has led to energy-wasting urban sprawl. About one-tenth of the oil consumed in the world each day is used by American motorists on their way to and from work, 69% of them driving alone.

Today transportation consumes 63% of all oil used in the United States—up from 50% in 1973. Transportation also uses much of the oil consumed in other countries: 39% in Japan, 44% in western Europe, and 49% in LDCs.

Thus, the best way to reduce world oil consump-

tion and to slow global warming is to improve vehicle fuel efficiency (Figure 17-3), make greater use of mass transit (Figure 17-4), and haul freight more efficiently. Denmark has the highest average fuel efficiency for new and existing cars, followed closely by West Germany, Italy, Japan, and the United Kingdom. Canada and the United States have the lowest. Between 1973 and 1988 the average fuel efficiency of new American cars nearly doubled, and the average fuel efficiency of all the cars on the road increased from 13 miles per gallon (mpg) to 20 mpg. Between 1975 and 1988 these fuel-efficiency improvements saved American consumers about $285 billion in fuel costs.

This is an important gain, but it is well below the 30 to 33 mpg fuel efficiency of new cars and the 22 to 25 mpg fuel efficiency of car fleets in Japan and western Europe. Because of lower fuel efficiency and more driving, the average car in the United States and Canada burns twice as much gasoline each year as the average car in Japan and western Europe.

New U.S. cars were supposed to average 27.5 mpg by 1985, but Congress caved in to pressure from car-makers and the Reagan administration and between 1985 and 1988 rolled back the average required for new cars from 27.5 mpg to 26 mpg. Environmentalists call this "use oil faster and save it slower" policy a tragic economic, environmental, and strategic mistake. Each year this rollback has wasted oil equal to all U.S. imports from the Persian Gulf or the average annual output of oil the Interior Department hopes to get over 30 years from beneath the Arctic National Wildlife Refuge (see Pro/Con on p. 333). The rollback has cost the U.S. Treasury more than $1 billion as a gift from taxpayers to Ford and GM shareholders and also penalized Chrysler for meeting the original standards. In 1990 the 27.5 mpg standard was reinstated, five years late.

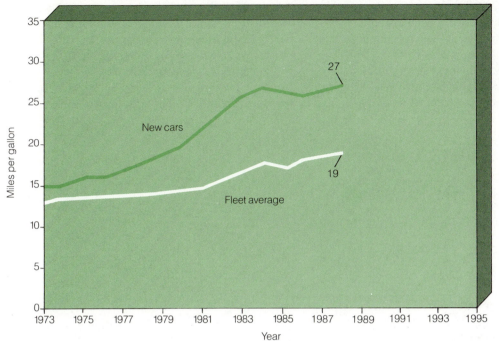

Figure 17-3 Increase in average fuel efficiency of new cars and the entire fleet of cars in the United States between 1973 and 1988. (Data from U.S. Department of Energy and Environmental Protection Agency)

According to the U.S. Office of Technology Assessment, new cars produced in the United States could easily average between 38 and 55 mpg by 1992, with only $50 to $90 added to the cost of a car. By the year 2000 new U.S. cars could average 51 to 78 mpg for an additional cost of $120 to $330 a car. Replacing the U.S. car and light truck fleet (4-wheel drive vehicles, pickup trucks, and minivans) with 60-mpg vehicles would save over 5 million barrels of oil per day, eliminating the need to import any oil.

By 1988 the three leading American car companies had discontinued much of their research and development on small, more fuel-efficient cars. The major reasons for this were the higher profits to be made on larger cars and declining consumer interest in improved fuel efficiency because of the temporary oil glut of the 1980s (see Case Study on p. 14).

Meanwhile, Japan and some western European countries have increased their research in this area. They want to have fuel-efficient cars ready when the oil crisis of the 1990s replaces the oil glut of the 1980s.

The Chevrolet Geo built in Japan by Suzuki has a fuel efficiency of 57 mpg. Prototype models built by Volvo, Volkswagen, Toyota, Peugeot, and Renault get 71 to 124 mpg. The Volvo LCP-2000 gets 63 mpg in the city and 81 mpg on the highway. It seats four, weighs half as much as the average American car, exceeds U.S. crash safety standards, meets U.S. air pollution limits, and has better acceleration than the average American car. It is ready for production and could be mass produced at about the same cost as today's subcompacts. Widespread use of these new designs could raise the average fuel economy of new cars and trucks to between 70 and 120 mpg over the next 20 years.

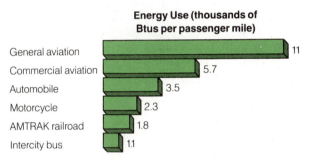

Figure 17-4 Energy efficiency of various types of domestic transportation.

There are several other ways to make the world's diminishing supply of oil last longer. One is to shift more freight from trucks and airplanes to trains (Figure 17-4). Manufacturers can increase the energy efficiency of transport trucks by improving their aerodynamic design and using turbocharged diesel engines and radial tires. Truck companies can reduce waste by not allowing trucks to return empty after reaching their destination. The energy efficiency of today's commercial jet aircraft fleet could be doubled by improved designs.

Improving the Energy Efficiency of Commercial and Residential Buildings Most commercial and residential buildings in the United States consume much more energy than necessary (Figure 17-5). With existing technology the United States could save 40% to 60% of the energy used in existing buildings and 70% to 90% of the energy used in new buildings.

Sweden and South Korea have the world's toughest standards for energy efficiency in buildings and houses. For example, the average home in Sweden, the world's leader in energy efficiency, consumes about one-third as much energy as an average American home of the same size.

A monument to energy waste is the 110-story, twin-towered World Trade Center in Manhattan, which uses as much electricity as a city of 100,000 persons. Windows in its walls of glass cannot be opened to take advantage of natural warming and cooling. Its heating and cooling systems must run around the clock, chiefly to take away heat from its inefficient lighting.

By contrast, Atlanta's 17-story Georgia Power Company building uses 60% less energy than conventional office buildings. The largest surface of the build-

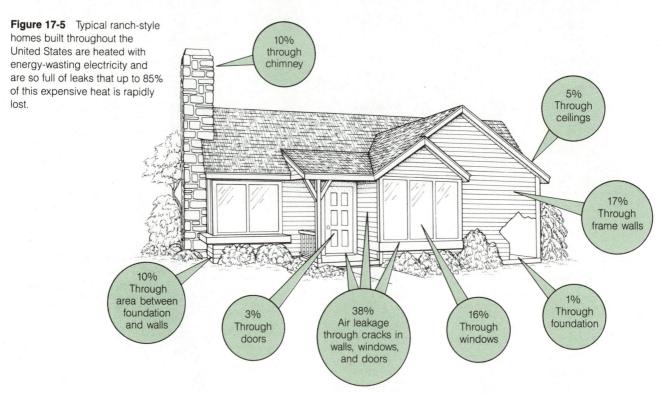

Figure 17-5 Typical ranch-style homes built throughout the United States are heated with energy-wasting electricity and are so full of leaks that up to 85% of this expensive heat is rapidly lost.

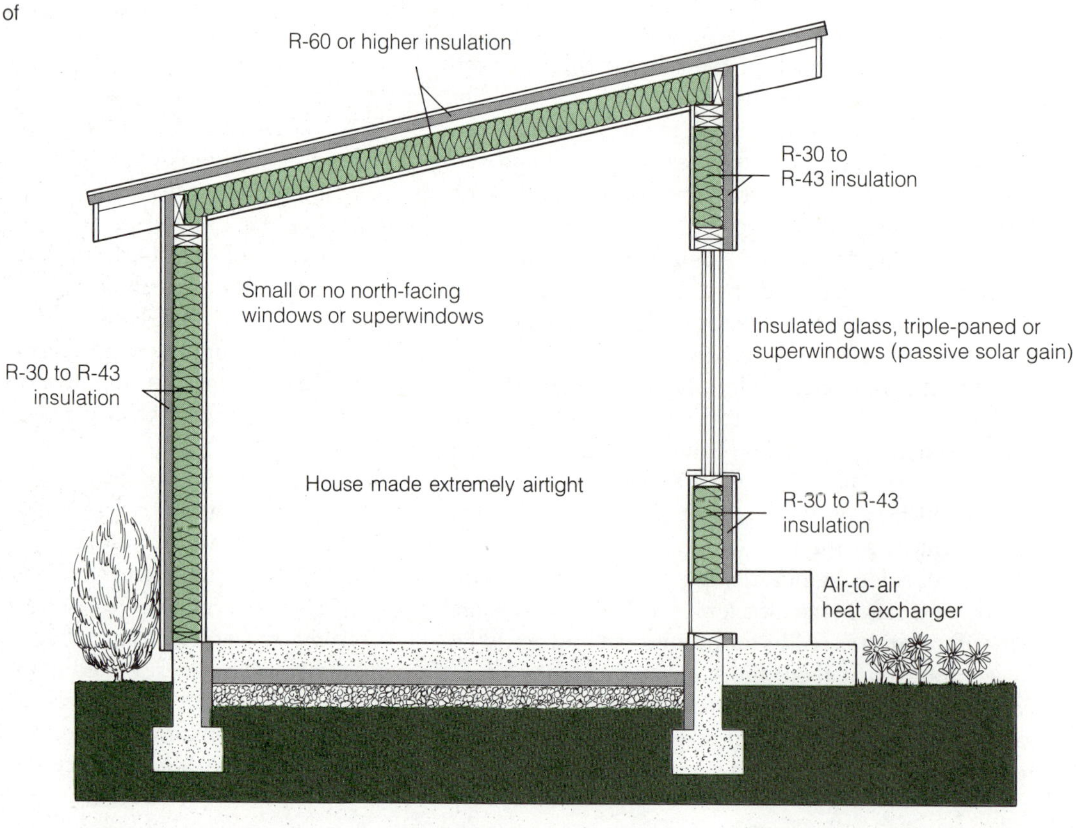

10% through chimney

5% Through ceilings

17% Through frame walls

10% Through area between foundation and walls

3% Through doors

38% Air leakage through cracks in walls, windows, and doors

16% Through windows

1% Through foundation

Figure 17-6 Major features of a superinsulated house.

R-60 or higher insulation

R-30 to R-43 insulation

Small or no north-facing windows or superwindows

Insulated glass, triple-paned or superwindows (passive solar gain)

R-30 to R-43 insulation

House made extremely airtight

R-30 to R-43 insulation

Air-to-air heat exchanger

ing is oriented to capture solar energy. Each floor extends over the one below, allowing heating by the low winter sun and blocking out the higher summer sun to reduce air conditioning costs. Energy-efficient lights focus on desks rather than illuminating entire rooms. Employees working at unusual hours use an adjoining three-story building so that the larger structure doesn't have to be heated or cooled when few people are at work.

Building a *superinsulated house* is the best way to improve the efficiency of residential space heating and save on lifetime energy costs, especially in cold climates (Figure 17-6). Such a house is heavily insulated and made extremely airtight. Heat from direct solar gain, people, and appliances warms the house, requiring little if any auxiliary heating. An air-to-air heat exchanger prevents buildup of humidity and indoor air pollution.

Most home buyers look only at the initial price, not the more meaningful lifetime cost. A superinsulated house costs about 5% more to build than a conventional house. But this extra cost is paid back by energy savings within five years and can save a homeowner $50,000 to $100,000 over a 40-year period. Combining energy efficiency measures with existing and emerging technology could greatly increase the energy efficiency of new houses (see Spotlight below).

Many energy-saving features can be added to existing homes, a process called *retrofitting*. Simply increasing insulation above ceilings can drastically reduce heating and cooling loads. The home owner usually recovers initial costs in two to six years and then saves money each year. Caulking and weatherstripping around windows, doors, pipes, vents, ducts, and wires save energy and money quickly. Switching to new gas furnaces with energy efficiencies of 90% to 95%, compared to 60% to 65% for most conventional gas furnaces, also saves energy and money on a lifetime-cost basis (Figure 3-16, p. 68).

One-third of the heat in U.S. homes escapes through closed windows—an energy loss equal to the energy in all the oil flowing through the Alaskan pipeline each year. This is because a single-pane glass window has an insulating value of only R-1. The R-value of a material indicates its insulating ability. Even double-glazed windows have an insulating value of only R-2 and a typical triple-glazed window has an insulating value of R-4 to R-6.

Two U.S. firms now sell "superinsulating" R-10 to R-12 windows, about the insulating value of a normal outside wall (R-11), that pay for themselves in two to four years. These superwindows, which cost about the same as conventional triple-glazed windows, combine triple glazing, heat-reflecting films that let light in without letting much heat out, and inert insulating gases such as argon. If everyone in the United States used these windows, it would save more oil and natural gas each year than Alaska now supplies. The cost of saving this energy is equivalent to buying oil at $2 to $3 a barrel.

Today American homes are responsible for 14% of the carbon dioxide emitted into the atmosphere from

SPOTLIGHT The Energy-Efficient House of the Near Future

Amory and Hunter Lovins (see Guest Essay on p. 408) have built a large passively heated, superinsulated, partially earth-sheltered home and office combination in Old Snowmass, Colorado, where winter temperatures can drop to −40°F. This structure, which also houses the research center for the Rocky Mountain Institute, gets all of its heat from the sun, uses one-tenth the normal amount of electricity, and uses less than half the normal amount of water. Electricity bills run about $30 a month, while those of conventional structures of this size in the same area run $330 to $1,000 per month.

Some energy-efficient houses of the near future will be controlled by microprocessors (computer chips), each programmed to do a different job. These microprocessors will monitor indoor temperatures, sunlight angles, and the location of people and will then send heat or cooled air where it is needed. Some will automatically open and close windows and insulated shutters to take advantage of solar energy and breezes and to reduce heat loss from windows at night and on cloudy days.

Windows will have a coating like the light-sensitive glass in some sunglasses, automatically becoming opaque to keep the sunlight out when the house gets too hot. Superinsulating windows (R-10 to R-12) already available mean that a house can have as many windows as the owner wants in any climate without much heat loss. Thinner insulation material will allow roofs to be insulated to R-100 and walls to R-43, far higher than today's best superinsulated houses (Figure 17-6).

Small-scale cogeneration units that run on natural gas or LPG are already available. They can supply a home with all its space heat, hot water, and electricity needs. The units are no larger than a refrigerator and make less noise than a dishwasher. Except for an occasional change of oil filters and spark plugs, they are nearly maintenance-free. Typically, this home-sized power and heating plant will pay for itself in four to five years.

Soon home owners may be able to get all the electricity they need from rolls of solar cells attached like shingles to a roof or applied to window glass as a coating (already developed by Arco).

burning all fossil fuels. Home energy use also accounts for 25% of sulfur dioxide emissions and 13% of nitrogen oxides emissions—both key causes of acid deposition. Cutting average home energy use in half would also cut these emissions in half.

Communities can use laws to increase energy conservation in homes and buildings. Building codes can be changed to require that all new houses use 80% less energy than conventional houses of the same size, as has been done in Davis, California (see Spotlight on p. 209). Laws can require that any existing house be insulated and weatherproofed to certain standards before it can be sold, as required in Portland, Oregon, for example. If the energy efficiency standards now required for all new homes in California were applied nationwide, the United States would save more oil by 2020 than the projected total to be found by drilling under Alaska's Arctic Wildlife Refuge, the Florida Keys, and the California coast.

Using the most energy-efficient appliances available can also save energy and money.* About one-third of the electricity generated in the United States and other industrial countries is used to power household appliances.

At least 20% of the electricity produced in the United States is used for lighting—about equal to the output of 100 large power plants. Since conventional incandescent bulbs are only 5% efficient, their use wastes enormous amounts of energy and adds to the heat load of houses during hot weather.

Socket-type fluorescent light bulbs that use one-fourth as much electricity as conventional bulbs are now available. Although they cost about $20 a bulb, they last about 13 times longer than conventional bulbs and save 3 times more money than they cost.

Switching to these bulbs and other improved lighting equipment would save one-third of the electric energy now produced by all U.S. coal-fired plants or eliminate the need for all electricity produced by the country's 111 nuclear power plants.

The amount of electricity used for lighting could be cut in half by installing more efficient ballasts that regulate the flow of electricity in fluorescent lights and by installing automatic dimmer switches to turn down lights when there is enough sunlight to illuminate building interiors. This would eliminate the need for 50 large power plants.

A few utilities in the United States are beginning to realize that it is much cheaper for them to save electricity than to generate it. For example, Southern

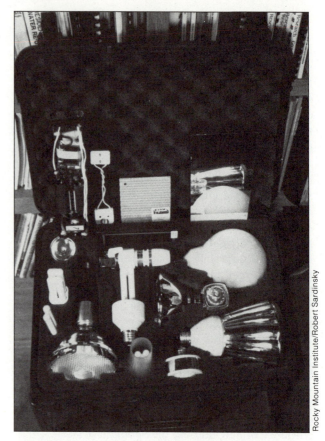

Figure 17-7 Amory Lovins' briefcase of available energy-saving lights, superinsulating window glass, water-flow restrictors, and other devices. Using these throughout the United States would save energy equal to that from 200 large electric power plants, save hundreds of billions of dollars, and sharply reduce pollution and environmental degradation.

California Edison has given away 450,000 fluorescents to poor residents in the Los Angeles area. This helps those who have little if any money to invest in saving energy and also saves the utility money. Unfortunately, most state commissions that regulate utilities have policies that reward companies with higher rates when they sell electricity produced by almost any method other than least-cost methods.

U.S refrigerators consume about 7% of the country's electricity, roughly the output of 26 large power plants. If all U.S. households had the most efficient 17-cubic-ft. frost-free refrigerators now available, they would save enough electricity to eliminate the need for 18 large nuclear or coal-fired power plants. New prototype refrigerators being built in Denmark and Japan cut electricity use by another 50%.

Similar savings are possible with high-efficiency models of other energy appliances such as stoves, hot water heaters, and air conditioners. If the most energy-efficient appliances now available were installed in all U.S. homes over the next 20 years, we would save fuel equal to all the oil produced by Alaska's North Slope fields over their 25-year lifetime.

---

*Each year the American Council for an Energy-Efficient Economy publishes a list of the most energy-efficient major appliances mass-produced for the U.S. market. For a copy, send $2 to the council at 1001 Connecticut Ave., N.W., Suite 530, Washington, D.C. 20036.

Table 17-1 Energy Use and Conservation in the United States and Sweden

Use or Method	United States	Sweden
Average per capita use	230,000 kcal/day	150,000 kcal/day
Transportation energy use	High	One-fourth of U.S.
Country size	Large	Small
Cities	Dispersed	Compact
Mass transit use	Low	High
Average car fuel economy	Poor	Good
Gasoline taxes	Low	High to encourage conservation
Tariffs on oil imports	Low	High to encourage conservation
Industrial energy efficiency	Fairly low	High
Nationwide energy-conserving building codes	No	Yes
Municipally owned district heating systems	None	30% of population
Emphasis on electricity for space heating	High (one-half of new homes)	High (one-half of new homes)
Domestic hot water	Most kept hot 24 hours a day in large tanks	Most supplied as needed by instant tankless heaters
Refrigerators	Mostly large, frost-free	Mostly smaller, non-frost-free using about one-third the electricity of U.S. models
Long-range national energy plan	No	Yes
Government emphasis and expenditures on energy conservation and renewable energy	Low	High
Government emphasis and expenditures on nuclear power	High	Low (to be phased out)

Energy expert Amory Lovins (see Guest Essay on p. 408) carries around a small briefcase that contains examples of fluorescent lightbulbs, a low-flow shower head, superinsulated window glass, and other devices that save energy and money (Figure 17-7). Using these devices throughout the United States would save energy equal to the output of 200 large electric power plants. This would also save enough money to pay off the national debt, eliminate the need to import any oil, sharply reduce pollution and environmental degradation, and slow global warming.

The 1987 National Appliance Energy Conservation Act set minimum energy efficiency standards for 13 household appliances including refrigerators and air conditioners. If enforced, within 20 years this law should save energy equal to that in 1.5 billion barrels of oil plus the output of 40 large power plants.

Developing a Personal Energy Conservation Plan

Each of us can develop an individual plan for saving energy and money (see inside back cover for suggestions). Four basic guidelines:

- Don't use electricity to heat space or water.

- Insulate new or existing houses heavily, and caulk and weatherstrip to reduce air infiltration and heat loss.

- Get as much heat and cooling as possible from natural sources—especially sun, wind, geothermal energy, and trees for windbreaks and natural shading.

- Buy the most energy-efficient homes, cars, and appliances available, and evaluate them only in terms of lifetime cost.

Energy Efficiency Differences Between Countries

Japan, Sweden, and most industrialized western European countries have average standards of living at least equal to and in some cases greater than that in the United States. Yet people in these countries use an average of one-third to two-thirds less energy per person than Americans.

One reason for this difference is that these countries put greater emphasis on improving energy efficiency than the United States does (Table 17-1). Another

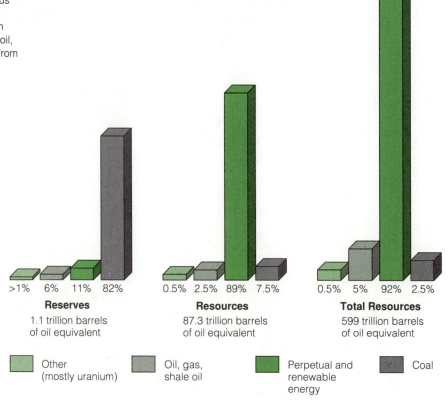

Figure 17-8 U.S. energy resource estimates. The estimated total resources (reserves plus resources) available from perpetual and renewable energy sources is more than ten times that from domestic supplies of coal, oil, natural gas, shale oil, and uranium. (Data from U.S. Department of Energy)

| >1% | 6% | 11% | 82% |

Reserves
1.1 trillion barrels
of oil equivalent

| 0.5% | 2.5% | 89% | 7.5% |

Resources
87.3 trillion barrels
of oil equivalent

| 0.5% | 5% | 92% | 2.5% |

Total Resources
599 trillion barrels
of oil equivalent

Other (mostly uranium)   Oil, gas, shale oil   Perpetual and renewable energy   Coal

is that most cities in these countries are more compact than U.S. cities. This means that the average person in these countries drives fewer miles per year than the average American.

17-2 DIRECT SOLAR ENERGY FOR PRODUCING HEAT AND ELECTRICITY

The Untapped Potential of Perpetual and Renewable Energy Resources The largest, mostly untapped sources of energy for all countries are perpetual and renewable energy from the sun, wind, flowing water, biomass, and the earth's internal heat (geothermal energy). Currently the United States gets about 11% of its energy from perpetual and renewable energy resources but could easily get much more using available technology. California currently gets roughly 30% of its electricity from perpetual and renewable sources of energy; by the year 2000 this figure could rise to 50%.

According to the U.S. Department of Energy, reserves and potential supplies of perpetual and renewable energy sources of energy in the United States make up 93% of the country's total energy resources (Figure 17-8). Developing these untapped resources could meet up to 80% of the country's projected energy needs by 2010 and virtually all energy needs if coupled with improvements in energy efficiency (Figure

17-1). Doing this would save money, eliminate the need for oil imports, produce less pollution and environmental degradation per unit of energy used, and increase economic, environmental, and military security. The rest of this chapter evaluates the various perpetual and renewable energy resources available to us.

Passive Solar Systems for Space Heating A **passive solar heating system** captures sunlight directly within a structure and converts it to low-temperature heat for space heating (Figure 17-9). It has several design features. Insulating windows or a greenhouse or solarium face the sun to collect solar energy by direct gain. Thermal mass such as walls and floors of concrete, adobe, brick, stone, or tile store collected solar energy as heat and release it slowly throughout the day and night. Some designs also use water-filled glass or plastic columns, black-painted barrels, and panels or cabinets containing heat-absorbing chemicals to store heat.

Besides collecting and storing solar energy as heat, passive systems must also reduce heat loss. Such structures are heavily insulated and caulked and have insulating windows. Movable, insulated shutters or curtains on windows or superwindows reduce heat loss at night and on days with little sunshine.

Houses with passive solar systems often have an open design to allow the collected and stored heat to be distributed by natural airflow or fans. Buildup of

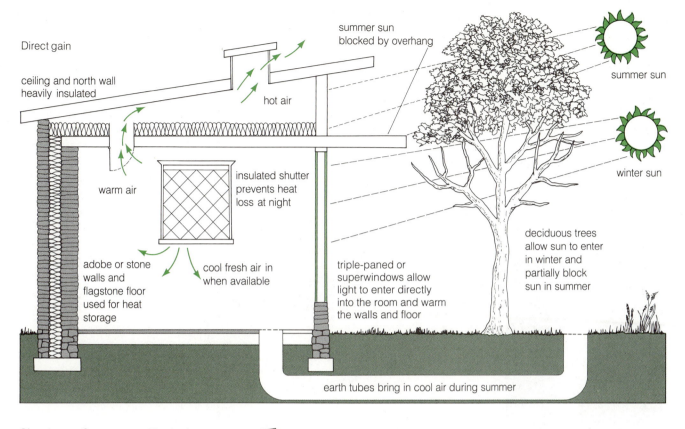

Direct gain

ceiling and north wall heavily insulated

hot air

warm air

insulated shutter prevents heat loss at night

adobe or stone walls and flagstone floor used for heat storage

cool fresh air in when available

triple-paned or superwindows allow light to enter directly into the room and warm the walls and floor

summer sun blocked by overhang

summer sun

winter sun

deciduous trees allow sun to enter in winter and partially block sun in summer

earth tubes bring in cool air during summer

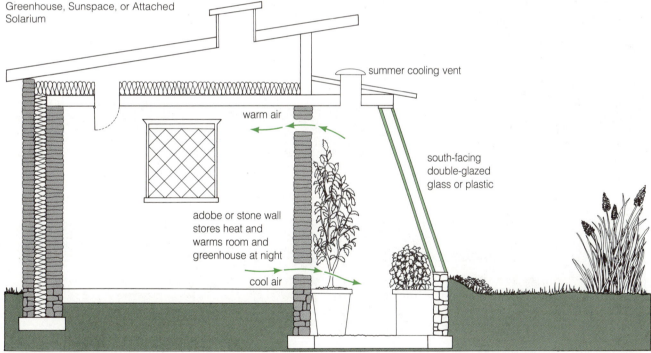

Greenhouse, Sunspace, or Attached Solarium

summer cooling vent

warm air

south-facing double-glazed glass or plastic

adobe or stone wall stores heat and warms room and greenhouse at night

cool air

Figure 17-9 Three examples of passive solar design. (Continues on next page.)

moisture and indoor air pollutants is prevented by an air-to-air heat exchanger, which supplies fresh air without much heat loss or gain. A small backup heating system may be used but is not necessary in a well-designed passively heated and superinsulated house in most climates. A passive solar system can be even more efficient in an earth-sheltered house (see Figure 17-9 and Spotlight on p. 424). Today almost 500,000 homes and 17,000 nonresidential buildings in the United States have passive solar designs.

A series of roof-mounted passive solar water heaters (Figure 17-10) can also supply hot water for a house.

The installed cost is $1,800 to $4,000 in the United States and $1,000 in Israel and Japan.

Passively heated buildings must also be designed to stay cool in hot weather. Passive cooling can be provided by deciduous trees, window overhangs, or awnings to block the high summer sun (Figure 17-9). Think of a mature deciduous tree between a house and the summer sun as five window-mounted air conditioners. Windows and fans take advantage of breezes and keep air moving. A foil sheet can be suspended in the attic to block heat from radiating heat down into the house.

At a depth of 3 to 6 meters (10 to 20 feet), the temperature of the earth stays about 13°C (55°F) all year long in cold northern climates and about 19°C (67°F) in warm southern climates. Earth tubes buried at this depth can pipe cool and partially dehumidified air into an energy efficient house at a cost of several dollars a summer (Figure 17-9). For a large space, two to three of these geothermal cooling fields running in different directions from the house should be installed. Then when the added heat degrades the cooling effect from one field, homeowners can switch to another field. Each winter all fields are renewed for using dur-

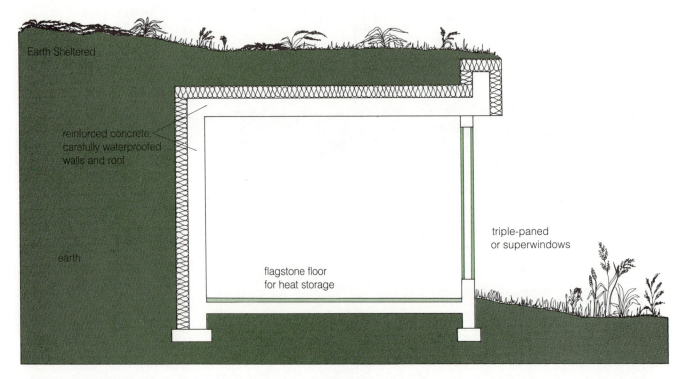

Figure 17-9 (continued)

SPOTLIGHT Earth-Sheltered Houses

Some people in the United States are building passively heated and cooled houses (Figure 17-9) and commercial buildings partially or completely underground. Such earth-sheltered buildings cost about 15% more to build than comparable above-ground structures.

The extra cost comes from the large amount of concrete needed to bear the heavy load of earth and the need for careful waterproofing to prevent leaks that would be dif-ficult and expensive to repair. However, a new design using insulated, curved wooden panels that form underground arches has reduced the cost to that of a comparable aboveground structure.

Earth-sheltered houses have much lower heating and cooling requirements. They need no exterior maintenance and painting, and they provide more privacy, quiet, and security from break-ins, fires, hurricanes, tornadoes, earthquakes, and storms than conven-tional buildings. Thus, they have lower insurance rates. Even with higher initial costs, earth-sheltered houses are cheaper than aboveground houses of the same size on a lifetime-cost basis.

The interior of an earth-sheltered house looks like that of an ordinary house. South-facing, solar-collecting windows, an attached greenhouse, and skylights can provide more daylight than is found in most conventional dwellings.

ing the following summer. Initial construction costs (mostly digging) are high, but operating and maintenance costs are extremely low. People allergic to pollen and molds should add an air purification system but would also need to do this with a conventional cooling system.

In areas with dry climates, such as the southwestern United States, evaporative coolers can remove interior heat by evaporating water. In hot and humid areas a small dehumidifier or a solar-assisted geothermal heat pump may be needed to lower humidity to acceptable levels. Solar-powered air conditioners

Active Solar Hot Water Heating System

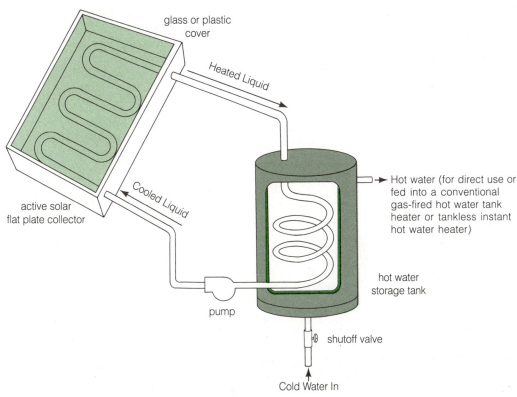

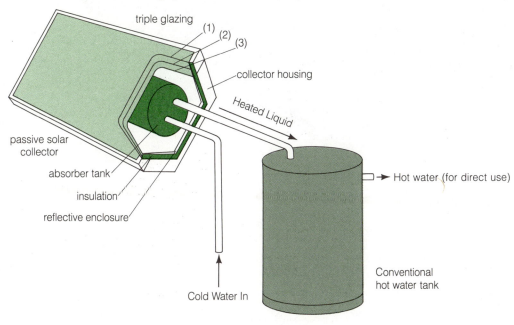

Figure 17-10 Active and passive solar water heaters.

have been developed but so far are too expensive for residential use.

Some office buildings in Sweden collect and store so much heat given off by people and equipment that they require little if any auxiliary heating. In Reno, Nevada, some buildings stay cool throughout the hot summer without air conditioning; large, insulated tanks of water chilled by cool nighttime air keep indoor temperatures comfortable during the day.

Active Solar Systems for Heating Space and Water   In an **active solar heating system,** specially designed collectors concentrate solar energy and store it as heat for space heating and heating water. Several connected collectors are usually mounted on a roof with an unobstructed exposure to the sun (Figure 17-10).

Solar energy collected as heat is transferred to water, an antifreeze solution, or air pumped through copper pipe inside the collector. The heated solution or air is pumped through and stored in an insulated tank containing water or rocks. Thermostat-controlled fans or pumps distribute this stored heat as needed, usually through conventional heating ducts. In middle and high latitudes with cold winter temperatures and moderate levels of sunlight (Figure 17-11), a small backup heating system is needed during prolonged cold or cloudy periods.

Active solar collectors can also supply hot water. Over 1 million active solar hot-water systems have been installed in the United States, especially in California, Florida, and southwestern states with ample sunshine. They save more than 3 million barrels of oil per year. The main barrier to their widespread use in the United States is an initial cost of $2,500 to $5,000.

Solar water heaters are used in 90% of all households in Cyprus. In Israel 65% of all domestic water heating is supplied by simple active solar systems that cost less than $500 per residence. About 12% of the houses in Japan and 37% in Australia use such systems.

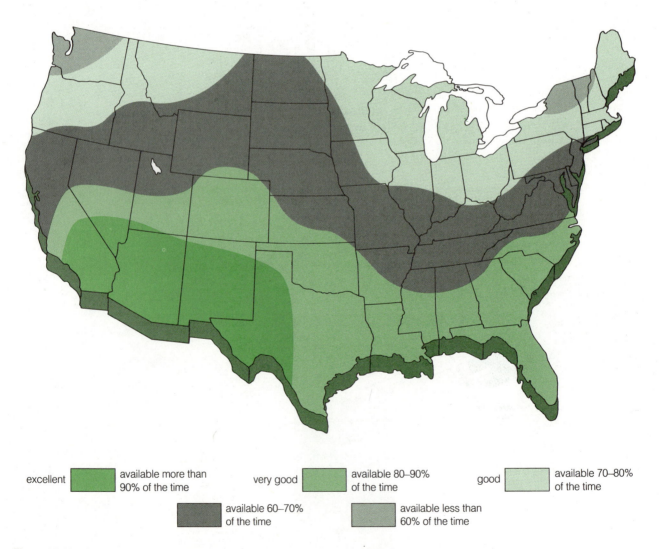

excellent	available more than 90% of the time	very good	available 80–90% of the time	good	available 70–80% of the time
	available 60–70% of the time		available less than 60% of the time		

Figure 17-11   Availability of solar energy during the day in the continental United States. (Data from U.S. Department of Energy and National Wildlife Federation)

Between 1984 and 1988, sales of active solar collectors in the United States dropped by 75%, and 28,000 of the industry's 30,000 employees lost their jobs. This happened because of low oil and natural gas prices and the elimination of federal and most state tax credits for installation of renewable energy systems in residences and businesses (see Spotlight below).

In 1989 Bomin-Solar Company in West Germany developed a new active solar-energy system that may provide heat for homeowners, apartment buildings, and small villages or housing developments at an affordable price. The key to this new design is a core of magnesium hydride used to store collected solar energy and produce temperatures as high as 400°C (752°F). The stored heat can be used to heat space and water, cook, and produce electricity.

Advantages and Disadvantages of Solar Energy for Heating Space and Water Using active or passive systems to collect solar energy for low-temperature heating of buildings and water has many advantages. The energy supply is free and naturally available on sunny days, and the net useful energy yield is moderate to high. The technology is well developed and can be installed quickly. No carbon dioxide is added to the atmosphere, and environmental impacts from air pollution and water pollution are low. Land disturbance is also low because passive systems are built into structures and active solar collectors are usually placed on rooftops.

On a lifetime-cost basis, good passive solar and superinsulated design is the cheapest way to provide 50% to 100% of the space heating for a home or small building in regions with enough sunlight. Such a system usually adds 5% to 10% to the construction cost but lowers the lifetime cost of a house by 30% to 40% of the cost of conventional houses.

Active systems cost more than passive systems on a lifetime basis because they require more materials to build, they need more maintenance, and eventually they deteriorate and must be replaced. However, retrofitting an existing house with an active solar system is often easier than adding a passive system.

In areas with enough sunlight, an active solar system is a cost-effective way to supply hot water for most homes and buildings. In such areas it may also be a cost-effective way to provide all or most of the space heating for homes, moderate-size and large buildings with unshaded rooftops, and small villages or developments using the new magnesium hydride storage system.

However, there are disadvantages. The energy supply is not available at night and on cloudy days. This means that heat storage systems and small backup heating systems are usually needed. Higher initial costs discourage buyers not used to considering lifetime costs and buyers who move every few years.

With present technology, active solar systems usually cost too much for heating most homes and small buildings. Better design and mass production techniques could change this. Many people also believe that active solar collectors sitting on rooftops or in yards are ugly.

Most passive solar systems require that owners open and close windows and shades to regulate heat flow and distribution, but this can be done by cheap microprocessors. Owners of solar systems also need laws that prevent others from building structures that block a user's access to sunlight. Such legislation is often opposed by builders of high-density developments.

SPOTLIGHT Are Solar Energy Subsidies a Good Idea?

You may be surprised to learn that some of the strongest supporters and most innovative people in the solar energy industry oppose giving federal and state subsidies and tax credits to the solar industry and to all other sources of energy.

These critics within the solar industry point out that most of the federal and state tax credits used for a few years were not designed to reward manufacturers who developed new, lower-cost, more energy efficient solar technologies. Also profits from inflated prices made possible by the tax credits brought many fast-buck artists into the business. These charlatans gave the industry a bad name before most went out of business when the tax credits dried up.

Also people and companies who used low-cost, energy-efficient passive solar systems were ineligible for tax credits. Instead of revising the tax credits to encourage energy savings and stimulate innovation, Congress (under pressure from oil, coal, and nuclear power interests) eliminated them.

These critics believe that the best approach would be to phase out subsidies and tax breaks for all energy resources and allow them to compete in the marketplace on an even playing field. But this appears to be virtually impossible because of the political power of the large energy companies.

If this can't be done, they suggest giving subsidies on an equal basis to all major energy resources based on their ability to get the highest energy efficiency for the lowest cost. What do you think should be done?

Figure 17-12 Solar furnace near Odeillo in the Pyrenees Mountains of southern France.

Peter Menzel/Stock, Boston

Figure 17-13 Solar I power tower used to generate electricity in the Mojave Desert near Barstow, California. This approach is an expensive way to produce electricity compared to other alternatives.

Sandia National Laboratories, Livermore, California

Concentrating Solar Energy to Produce High-Temperature Heat and Electricity In experimental systems, huge arrays of computer-controlled mirrors track the sun and focus sunlight on a central heat collection point, usually atop a tall tower. This concentrated sunlight can produce temperatures high enough for industrial processes or for making high-pressure steam to run turbines and produce electricity.

The world's largest *solar furnace*, the Odeillo Furnace, has been operating high in the Pyrenees Mountains in southern France since 1970 (Figure 17-12). This system, which produces temperatures up to 2,760°C (5,000°F) is used in the manufacture of pure metals and other substances; the excess heat is used to produce steam and generate electricity fed into the public utility grid. Smaller units are being tested in France, Italy, Spain, and Japan.

Several private and government-financed experimental *solar power towers*, which produce electricity, have been built in the United States. Five 30-megawatt power towers have been built in the Mojave Desert in southern California and supply enough electricity for 10,000 homes (Figure 17-13). By 1992, at least 14 more of these units are expected to be in operation. New, more efficient designs have also been developed. A 200-megawatt plant in the Mojave Desert near Los

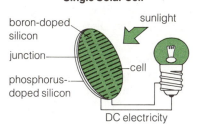

Single Solar Cell

boron-doped silicon

sunlight

junction

cell

phosphorus-doped silicon

DC electricity

Panel of Solar Cells

Figure 17-14 Use of photovoltaic (solar) cells to provide DC electricity for an energy efficient home; any surplus can be sold to the local power company. Prices should be competitive sometime in the 1990s.

Array of Solar Cell Panels on a Roof

photovoltaic panels

power lines

panel wire

to breaker panel (inside house)

inverter (converts DC to AC)

battery bank (located in shed outside house, due to explosive nature of battery gases)

Angeles produces enough electricity to supply enough electricity for 270,000 people.

The towers take only a year to build and cost about the same per kilowatt as new nuclear plants. The main use of these small plants will be to supply reserve power to meet daytime peak electricity loads, especially in sunny areas with large air conditioning demands.

Some analysts believe that these systems will make little contribution to overall energy supplies. They have a low net useful energy yield and cost more to build and operate than several other energy alternatives. Other analysts believe that new designs and innovations will make them economically competitive.

Their impact on air and water is low, but their disruption of land is significant because they need large areas for solar collection. Also, they are usually built in sunny, arid, ecologically fragile desert biomes, where there may not be enough water for use in cooling towers to recondense spent steam.

Converting Solar Energy Directly to Electricity: Photovoltaic Cells Solar energy can be converted by **photovoltaic cells**, commonly called *solar cells*, directly into electrical energy. A solar cell consists of a thin wafer of purified silicon, which can be made from inexpensive, abundant sand. Trace amounts of other substances (such as gallium arsenide or cadmium sulfide) are added so that the wafer emits electrons and produces a small amount of electrical current when struck by sunlight (Figure 17-14).

Today solar cells supply electricity for at least 15,000 homes worldwide (6,000 in the United States plus 6,000 villages in India). Most of these buildings are in isolated areas where it costs too much to bring in electric power lines. Solar cells are also used to switch railroad tracks and to supply power for water wells, irrigation pumping, battery charging, calculators, portable lap-top computers, ocean buoys, lighthouses, and offshore oil-drilling platforms in the sunny Persian Gulf. Some scientists have proposed putting billions of solar cells on large orbiting satellites and beaming the energy back to earth as microwaves. Such schemes, however, are considered far too costly.

Because the amount of electricity produced by a single solar cell is very small, many cells must be wired together in a panel to provide 30 to 100 watts of electric power (Figure 17-14). Several panels are wired together and mounted on a roof or on a rack that tracks the sun to produce electricity for a home or building.

Massive banks of such cells can also produce electricity at a small power plant. But this is expensive and has a low net useful energy yield. It involves spending a lot of money and energy to collect dispersed sunlight in a concentrated form and then disperse it again as electricity fed to homes, businesses, and factories.

Homeowners can sell excess electricity produced during daylight to the local utility company. It can also be stored for use at night and on cloudy days in long-lasting, rechargeable DC batteries like those used in boats and golf carts.

The electricity produced by solar cells is direct current (DC), not the alternating current (AC) commonly used in households. One option is to use this electricity to power lights and appliances that run on DC, such as those in most recreational vehicles. Another is to use an electronic inverter to convert direct current to alternating current. In the future, DC electricity produced by solar cells could be used to decompose water to produce hydrogen gas, which would be used as a fuel for cars and burned in fuel cells to provide space heat, hot water, and electricity (Section 17-7). However, it is extremely wasteful of energy and money to use solar cells (or any form of energy) to supply electricity for space heating, heating water, and energy inefficient lights and appliances (see p. 59).

To produce electricity competitively, commercial solar cells must have an energy efficiency of about 15%, enabling them to produce electricity at about six cents per kilowatt hour. In 1988 commercially available solar cells, with an efficiency of 7% to 12%, could produce electricity at about 25 to 30 cents per kilowatt-hour. A new type of solar cell tested under laboratory conditions had an efficiency of 31%, and researchers in Israel developed a solar cell that can store energy.

In 1990 Arco is expected to market new solar cells that can produce electricity at about 13 cents per kilowatt hour—cheaper than electricity produced by a new nuclear power plant. The development of more energy-efficient (at least 15%) cells and cost-effective mass-production techniques should allow solar cells to produce electricity at about six cents per kilowatt hour by the mid-1990s or shortly after the turn of the century. The potential market for these cells would be $100 billion a year.

Since 1981 the U.S. federal research and development budget for solar cells has been cut by 90%, while Japanese government expenditures in this area have tripled. Between 1980 and 1988 Japan's share of the worldwide solar cell market grew from 15% to 37% and the U.S. share dropped from 75% to 32%. By 1989 Japan, West Germany, and Italy were spending more on solar cell research than was the United States.

Federal and private research efforts on photovoltaics in the United States need to be increased sharply. Otherwise, the United States may find much of its capital being drained to pay for imports of photovoltaic cells from Japan and other countries. The United States would also lose out on a major global economic market.

Advantages and Disadvantages of Photovoltaic Cells Solar cells have many advantages. If present projections are correct, they could supply 20% to 30% of the world's electricity by 2050. This would eliminate the need to build large-scale power plants of any type and allow many existing nuclear and coal-fired power plants to be phased out.

Solar cells are also reliable and quiet, have no moving parts, and should last 30 years or more if encased in glass or plastic. They can be installed quickly and easily and need little maintenance other than occasional washing to prevent dirt from blocking the sun's rays.

Most solar cells are made from silicon, the second most abundant element in the earth's crust. They do not produce carbon dioxide during use. Air and water pollution during operation is low, air pollution from manufacture is low, and land disturbance is very low for roof-mounted systems. The net useful energy yield is fairly high and rising with new designs.

However, solar cells have some drawbacks. The present costs of solar cell systems are high but are projected to become competitive in 7 to 15 years. Many people find racks of solar cells on rooftops or in yards ugly. Without tough plastic coating, solar cells can be damaged by hail storms. The use of solar cells could be limited by an insufficient amount of gallium and cadmium. Without effective pollution control, the manufacture of solar cells can produce moderate water pollution from chemical wastes.

17-3 INDIRECT SOLAR ENERGY: PRODUCING ELECTRICITY FROM FALLING AND FLOWING WATER

Types of Hydroelectric Power Since the 1700s, kinetic energy in the falling and flowing water of rivers and streams has been used to produce electricity in small- and large-scale hydroelectric plants. In *large-scale hydropower projects*, high dams are built across large rivers to create large reservoirs (Figure 5-19, p. 126). The stored water is then allowed to flow at controlled rates, spinning turbines and producing electricity as it falls downward to the river below the dam.

The electricity produced by water flowing over large dams is an indirect form of the perpetual solar energy that drives the hydrologic cycle. However, the reservoirs behind the dams usually fill with silt and become useless in 30 to 300 years, depending on the rate of natural and human-accelerated soil erosion from land above the dam. This means that large hydroelectric plants are nonrenewable sources of energy.

In *small-scale hydropower projects*, a low dam with no reservoir or only a small one is built across a small river or stream. The natural water flow is used to generate electricity. However, electricity production can vary with seasonal changes in stream flow. Under drought conditions there may not be enough water flow to produce any electricity.

Falling water can also be used to produce electricity in *pumped-storage hydropower systems*. Their main use is to supply extra power during times of peak electrical demand. When electricity demand is low, usually at night, electricity from a conventional power plant pumps water uphill from a lake or reservoir to another reservoir at a higher elevation, usually on top of a mountain. When a power company temporarily needs more electricity than its plants can produce, water in the upper reservoir is released. On its downward trip to the lower reservoir, the water flows through turbines and generates electricity. But this is a very expensive way to produce electricity. Much cheaper alternatives, such as natural gas turbines, are available. Another possibility may be the use of solar-powered pumps to raise the water to the upper reservoir.

Present and Future Use of Hydropower In 1987 hydropower supplied 21% of the world's electricity and 6% of the world's total supplemental energy Countries or areas with mountainous or plateau regions have the greatest hydropower potential.

Much of the hydropower potential of North America and Europe has been developed. Hydropower supplies Norway with essentially all its electricity, Switzerland 74%, and Austria 67%. Canada gets more than 70% of its electricity from hydropower and exports electricity to the United States.

Africa has harnessed only 5% of its hydropower potential, Latin America 8%, and Asia 9%. In 1987, LDCs got almost 50% of their electricity from hydropower. Between 1981 and 1995, LDCs are projected to add large hydropower plants that will produce electricity equal to that of 225 large nuclear or coal-burning power plants. Half of this new hydropower capacity will be added in Brazil, China, and India.

China, with one-tenth of the world's hydropower potential, is likely to become the world's largest producer of hydroelectricity. There is a controversial proposal to build a massive hydropower dam across the Yangtze River that could produce electricity equal to that of 25 large nuclear or coal power plants. This project, however, would force 2 million people to leave their homes. China has also built almost 100,000 small dams to produce electricity for villages.

The United States is the world's largest producer of electricity from hydropower. Today hydropower produced at almost 1,600 sites supplies 12% of the electricity and 5% of all supplemental energy used by the United States.

U.S. hydroelectric power plants produce electricity more cheaply than any other source. One reason is that most large-scale projects were built from the 1930s to the 1950s, when costs were low and were subsidized by all taxpayers. Another reason is that hydroelectric energy efficiency is high (83% to 93%) and the plants produce full power 95% of the time, compared to 55% for nuclear plants and 65% for coal plants, which are shut down for repairs and maintenance more frequently. This explains why regions such as the Pacific Northwest, where most of the electricity is produced by hydropower, have the lowest electric rates in the country.

But the large dam-building era in the United States is drawing to a close because of high construction costs and lack of suitable sites. Any new large supplies of hydroelectric power in the United States will be imported from Canada.

By 1988 almost 1,500 small-scale hydroelectric power plants were operating or under construction, mostly in the West and Northeast. They were generating electricity equal to that of three large coal or nuclear power plants. According to the U.S. Corps of Engineers, retrofitting abandoned small and medium-size hydroelectric sites and building new small-scale hydroelectric plants on suitable sites could supply the United States with electricity equal to that of 45 large power plants.

However, since 1985 the development of small-scale hydropower in the United States has fallen off sharply because of low oil prices and the loss of federal tax credits. Many projects have been opposed by local residents and conservationists because the dams reduce stream flow, disrupting aquatic life and preventing some types of recreation.

Advantages and Disadvantages of Hydropower

Hydropower has a number of advantages. Many LDCs have large, untapped potential sites, although many are far from where the electricity is needed. Hydropower has a moderate to high net useful energy yield and fairly low operating and maintenance costs.

Hydroelectric plants rarely need to be shut down, and they produce no emissions of carbon dioxide or other air pollutants during operation. They have life spans two to ten times those of coal and nuclear plants. In addition to producing electricity, large dams help control flooding and supply a regulated flow of irrigation water to areas below the dam.

Developing small-scale hydroelectric plants by rehabilitating existing dams has little environmental impact, and once rebuilt, the units have a long life. Only a few people are needed to operate them and they need little maintenance.

But hydropower has some drawbacks. Construction costs for new large-scale systems are high, and few suitable sites are left in the United States and Europe. Large-scale projects flood large areas to form reservoirs, destroy wildlife habitats, uproot people, decrease natural fertilization of prime agricultural land in river valleys below the dam, and decrease fish harvests below the dam (see Case Study on p. 248). Without proper land-use control, large-scale projects can greatly increase soil erosion and sediment water pollution near the reservoir above the dam. This reduces the effective life of the reservoir.

By reducing stream flow, small hydroelectric projects threaten recreational activities and aquatic life, disrupt scenic rivers, and destroy wetlands. During drought periods these plants produce little if any power. Most of the electricity produced by these projects can be supplied at a lower cost and with less environmental impact by industrial cogeneration and by improving the energy efficiency of existing big dams.

Tidal Power Twice a day a large volume of water flows in and out of inland bays or other bodies of water near the coast to produce high and low tides because of gravitational attraction between the earth and the moon. In a few places tides flow in and out of a bay with an opening narrow enough to be obstructed by a dam with gates that can be opened and closed. If the difference in water height between high and low tides is large enough, the kinetic energy in these daily tidal flows based on moon power can be used to spin turbines to produce electricity. But only about two dozen places in the world have these conditions.

Using tidal energy to produce electricity has several advantages. The energy source (tides from gravitational attraction) is free, operating costs are low, and the net useful energy yield is moderate. No carbon dioxide is added to the atmosphere, air pollution is low, and little land is disturbed.

Most analysts, however, expect tidal power to make only a tiny contribution to world electricity supplies. There are few suitable sites and construction costs are high. The output of electricity varies daily with tidal flows, and there must be a backup system. The dam and power plant can be damaged by storms, and metal parts are easily corroded by seawater.

Wave Power The kinetic energy in ocean waves, created primarily by wind, is another potential source of energy. Japan, Norway, Great Britain, Sweden, the United States, and the Soviet Union have built small experimental plants to evaluate this form of hydropower. None of these plants have produced electricity at a competitive price, but some designs show promise.

Most analysts expect this alternative to make little contribution to world electricity production except in a few coastal areas with the right conditions. Construction costs are moderate to high and the net useful energy yield is moderate. Equipment could be damaged or destroyed by saltwater corrosion and severe storms.

17-4 INDIRECT SOLAR ENERGY: PRODUCING ELECTRICITY FROM HEAT STORED IN WATER

Ocean Thermal Energy Conversion Ocean water stores huge amounts of heat from the sun. Japan and the United States have been conducting experiments to evaluate the technological and economic feasibility of using the large temperature differences between the cold bottom waters and the sun-warmed surface waters of tropical oceans to produce electricity.

If feasible, a gigantic floating **ocean thermal energy conversion (OTEC)** power plant would be anchored in a tropical ocean area no more than 81 kilometers (50 miles) offshore. Warm surface water would be pumped through a large heat exchanger and used to evaporate and pressurize a low-boiling fluid such as liquid ammonia. The pressurized ammonia gas would drive turbines to generate electricity. Then, cold bottom water as deep as 900 meters (3,000 feet) below the plant would be pumped to the surface through massive pipes 30 meters (100 feet) in diameter. The water would be used to cool and condense the ammonia back to a liquid state to begin the cycle again. Pumps in a medium-size plant would pump more water than the average flow rate of the Mississippi River.

A large cable would transmit the electricity to shore. Other possibilities include using the electricity produced to desalinate ocean water, extract minerals and chemicals from the sea, or decompose water to produce hydrogen gas, which could be piped or transported to shore for use as a fuel.

The source of energy for OTEC is limitless at suitable sites, and a costly energy storage and backup system is not needed. No air pollution except carbon dioxide is produced during operation, and the floating power plant requires no land area. Nutrients brought up when water is pumped from the ocean bottom might be used to nourish schools of fish and shellfish.

However, most energy analysts believe that the large-scale extraction of energy from ocean thermal gradients may never compete economically with other energy alternatives. Construction costs are high—two to three times those of comparable coal-fired plants. Operating and maintenance costs are also high because of corrosion of metal parts by seawater and fouling of heat exchangers by algae and barnacles. Plants could also be damaged by hurricanes and typhoons.

Other problems include a limited number of sites and a low net useful energy yield. Pumping large volumes of deep-ocean water to the surface could disrupt aquatic life and releases lots of dissolved carbon dioxide into the atmosphere.

Inland Solar Ponds   A **solar pond** is a solar energy collector consisting of at least 0.5 hectare (1 acre) of a lined cavity filled with salt water or with fresh water enclosed in black plastic bags. *Saline solar ponds* can be used to produce electricity and are usually located near inland saline seas or lakes, near deserts with ample sunlight. The bottom layer of water in such ponds stays on the bottom when heated because it has a higher salinity and density (mass per unit volume) than the top layer. Heat accumulated during daylight in the bottom layer can be used to produce electricity in a manner similar to the OTEC process in a tropical ocean.

An experimental saline solar pond power plant on the Israeli side of the Dead Sea has been operating successfully for several years. By 2000, Israel plans to build several plants around the Dead Sea to supply electricity for air conditioning and desalinating water. By 1986, more than a dozen experimental saline solar ponds had been built in the United States. Most were in desert areas near the Salton Sea in California and the Great Salt Lake in Utah.

Freshwater solar ponds can be used as a source of hot water and space heating. A very shallow hole is dug, lined with concrete, and covered with insulation. A number of large, black plastic bags, each filled with several inches of water, are placed in the hole. The top of the pond is then covered with fiberglass panels, which let sunlight in and keep most of the heat stored in the water during daylight from being lost to the atmosphere.

When a computer-controlled monitoring system determines that the water in the bags has reached its peak temperature in the afternoon, the computer turns on pumps to transfer the hot water to large, insulated tanks for distribution as hot water or for space heating. The world's largest freshwater solar pond went into operation at Fort Benning, Georgia, in 1985. This $4 million, 4-hectare (11-acre) pond supplies hot water for 6,500 service personnel and is expected to save up to $10 million over a 17-year period.

Saline and freshwater solar ponds have the same advantages as OTEC systems. In addition, they have a moderate net useful energy yield, have moderate construction and operating costs, and need little maintenance. Freshwater solar ponds can be built in almost any sunny area. They may be useful for supplying hot water and space heating for large buildings and small housing developments. Enthusiasts project that with adequate research-and-development support, solar ponds could supply 3% to 4% of U.S. supplemental energy by the year 2000.

Saline solar ponds are feasible in areas with moderate to ample sunlight, especially ecologically fragile deserts. Operating costs can be high because of saltwater corrosion of pipes and heat exchangers. Unless lined, the ponds can become ineffective when compounds leached from bottom sediment darken the water and reduce sunlight transmission.

17-5   INDIRECT SOLAR ENERGY: PRODUCING ELECTRICITY FROM WIND

Wind Power: Past and Present   Since the 1600s prevailing winds, produced indirectly by solar energy, have been used to propel ships, grind grain, pump water, and power many small industrial shops. In the 1700s settlers in the American West used small windmills to pump groundwater for farms and ranches (Figure 17-15). In the 1930s and 1940s, small farms beyond the reach of electric utility lines used small wind turbines to produce electricity. By the 1950s cheap hydropower, fossil fuels, and rural electrification had replaced most of these wind turbines.

Since the 1970s small-to-large modern wind turbines have been developed and are used in 95 countries (Figure 17-15). Experience has shown that these machines can produce electricity at a reasonable cost for small communities and large utility companies in areas with average wind speeds of 14 to 24 miles per hour, often found in mountain passes and along coastlines.

Since 1974 more than 20,000 wind turbines have been installed, especially in California and Denmark. Small (10- to 50-kilowatt) and intermediate-size (60- to 1,000-kilowatt) wind turbines are the most widely used. They are easier to mass-produce, are less vulnerable to stress and breakdown, and can produce more power in light winds than large wind turbines.

Use of wind power in the United States has grown more rapidly since 1981 than any other new source of electricity. More than 70% of the electricity produced by wind energy worldwide, and 90% of that in the United States, is generated in California in three windy mountain passes. Between 1981 and 1988 almost 17,000 small to intermediate-size wind turbines were installed in California, mostly by private companies. They are grouped together in clusters called *wind farms* (Figure 17-16). In 1989 these turbines produced electricity equal to that of 1.6 large power plants, enough to meet 16% of San Francisco's electrical demand. Economically, it makes more sense to build wind farms to serve entire communities or groups of houses than for individual home owners to install wind power systems.

The California Energy Commission projects that wind power will supply 8% of the state's electricity by 2000. The island of Hawaii gets about 8% of its electricity from wind, and the use of wind power is spreading to the state's other islands. However, the development of this energy resource in the United States has slowed since 1986, when federal tax credits and most state tax credits for wind power were eliminated. Also, the federal budget for research and development of wind power was cut by 90% between 1981 and 1988. Other countries planning to make increasing use of wind energy include Denmark, China, India, Canada, Spain, Greece, Argentina, the United Kingdom, Sweden, West Germany, Australia, the Netherlands, and the Soviet Union.

Advantages and Disadvantages of Wind Power

Wind power is an unlimited source of energy at favorable sites, and large wind farms can be built in three to six months. Wind power systems have a moderate to fairly high net useful energy yield, emit no carbon dioxide or other air pollutants during operation, and need no water for cooling. They operate 80% to 98% of the time the wind is blowing. Their manufacture and use produce little water pollution. The land occupied by wind farms can be used for grazing and other purposes. They don't require water to operate, making

Figure 17-15 An old windmill and a modern 200-kilowatt wind turbine in Clayton, New Mexico.

U.S. Department of Energy

Figure 17-16 A California wind farm consisting of an array of modern wind turbines in a windy mountain pass. Such farms can produce electricity at competitive prices.

George Gerster/Photo Researchers, Inc.

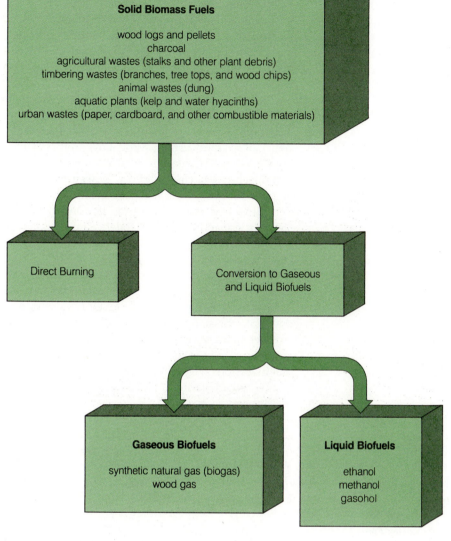

Figure 17-17 Major types of biomass fuel.

Solid Biomass Fuels

wood logs and pellets
charcoal
agricultural wastes (stalks and other plant debris)
timbering wastes (branches, tree tops, and wood chips)
animal wastes (dung)
aquatic plants (kelp and water hyacinths)
urban wastes (paper, cardboard, and other combustible materials)

Direct Burning

Conversion to Gaseous
and Liquid Biofuels

Gaseous Biofuels

synthetic natural gas (biogas)
wood gas

Liquid Biofuels

ethanol
methanol
gasohol

them especially well suited for arid and semiarid areas. Wind farms are expected to have an economic advantage over coal and nuclear power plants in the United States and the world by the 1990s, and already do at good sites.

But wind power can be used only in areas with sufficient winds. Backup electricity from a utility company or from an energy storage system is necessary when the wind dies down, but this is not a problem at suitable sites. Backup could also be provided by linking wind farms with a solar cell or hydropower system, or both. Building wind farms in mountain passes and along shorelines can cause visual pollution. Noise and interference with local television reception have been problems with large turbines but can be overcome with improved design and use in isolated areas. Large wind farms might also interfere with the flight patterns of migratory birds in certain areas.

17-6   INDIRECT RENEWABLE SOLAR ENERGY: BIOMASS

Renewable Biomass as a Versatile Fuel   Biomass is organic plant matter produced by solar energy through photosynthesis. Some of this plant matter can be burned as solid fuel or converted to more convenient gaseous or liquid *biofuels* (Figure 17-17). In 1987, biomass, mostly from the burning of wood and manure to heat buildings and cook food, supplied about 15% of the world's supplemental energy (4% to 5% in Canada and the United States).

All biomass fuels have several advantages in common. They can be used in solid, liquid, and gaseous forms for space heating, water heating, producing electricity, and propelling vehicles. Biomass is a renewable energy resource as long as trees and plants are not harvested faster than they grow back—something that is not being done in most places (Section 13-2).

There is no net increase in atmospheric levels of carbon dioxide as long as the rate of removal and burning of trees and plants and loss of below-ground organic matter does not exceed their rate of replenishment. Burning of biomass fuels adds much less sulfur dioxide and nitric oxide to the atmosphere per unit of energy produced than the uncontrolled burning of coal and thus requires fewer pollution controls.

Biomass fuels also share some disadvantages. Without effective land-use controls and replanting, widespread removal of trees and plants can deplete soil nutrients and cause excessive soil erosion, water pollution, flooding, and loss of wildlife habitat. Biomass resources also have a high moisture content (15% to 95%), which lowers their net useful energy. The added weight of the moisture makes collecting and hauling wood and other plant material fairly expensive. Each type of biomass fuel has other specific advantages and disadvantages.

Burning Wood and Wood Wastes   About 80% of the people living in LDCs heat their dwellings and cook their food by burning wood or charcoal made from wood. However, about 1.1 billion people cannot find or are too poor to buy enough fuelwood to meet their needs, and this number may increase to 2.5 billion by 2000 (Figure 13-7, p. 291).

In MDCs with adequate forests, the burning of wood, wood pellets, and wood wastes to heat homes and produce steam and electricity in industrial boilers increased rapidly during the 1970s because of price increases in heating oil and electricity. Sweden leads the world in using wood as an energy source, mostly for district heating plants.

The forest products industry (mostly paper companies and lumber mills) consumes almost two-thirds of the fuelwood used in the United States. Homes and small businesses burn the rest. In 1985 one of every ten single-family homes (one in six in nonmetropolitan areas) relied entirely on wood for space heating. Almost one-third of other U.S. homes burned wood for some of their space heating.

The largest use of fuelwood is in New England, where wood is plentiful. However, because of market saturation, loss of tax credits, and low oil prices, annual sales of wood stoves in the United States dropped from 3 million to 450,000 between 1980 and 1987.

Wood has a moderate to high net useful energy yield when collected and burned directly and efficiently near its source. But in urban areas where wood must be hauled long distances, it can cost home owners more per unit of energy produced than oil and electricity.

Harvesting and burning wood can cause accidents. Each year in the United States over 10,000 people are injured by chain saws. Also several hundred Americans are killed each year in house fires caused mostly by improperly located or poorly maintained wood stoves.

Burning fuelwood releases carbon monoxide, solid particulate matter, and unburned residues that pollute indoor and outdoor air. According to the EPA, wood burning causes as many as 820 cancer deaths a year in the United States.

This air pollution can be reduced 75% by a $100 to $250 catalytic combustion chamber in the stove or stovepipe. These units also increase the energy efficiency of a typical airtight wood stove from 55% to as high as 81% and reduce the need for chimney cleaning and the chance of chimney fires. However, they must be replaced every four years at a cost of about $100. Recently wood stoves have been developed that are 65% efficient and that emit 90% less air pollution than conventional wood stoves without using catalytic combustion.

In London and in South Korean cities, wood fires have been banned to reduce air pollution. Oregon, Colorado, and Montana have passed laws setting air pollution emission standards for all wood stoves, and 20 other states were considering similar laws. In some areas, especially valleys suffering from frequent thermal inversions (Figure 19-8, p. 493), wood burning is banned when particulate matter in the atmosphere reaches certain levels.

Since 1990 the EPA has required all new wood stoves sold in the United States to emit at least 70% less particulate matter than earlier models. Some new stoves meet these standards by using catalytic combustion devices, others by better design or by using clean-burning wood pellets for fuel.

Energy Plantations   One way to produce biomass fuel is to plant large numbers of fast-growing trees in *biomass-energy plantations* to supply fuelwood. Plantations of oil palms and varieties of Euphorbia plants, which store energy in hydrocarbon compounds (like those found in oil), can also be established. After these plants are harvested, their oil-like material can be extracted and either refined to produce gasoline or burned directly in diesel engines. Both types of energy plantations can be established on semiarid land not needed to grow crops, although lack of water can limit productivity.

This industrialized approach to biomass production usually requires heavy use of pesticides and fertilizers, which can pollute drinking supplies and harm wildlife. Conversion of large areas to monoculture energy plantations also reduces biodiversity. In some areas biomass plantations might compete with food crops for prime farm land. Also, they are likely to have low or negative net useful energy yields, as do most conventional crops grown by industrialized agricultural methods.

Burning Agricultural and Urban Wastes In agricultural areas, crop residues (the inedible, unharvested parts of food crops) and animal manure can be collected and burned or converted to biofuels. By 1985 Hawaii was burning a residue (called *bagasse*) left after sugarcane harvesting and processing to supply almost 10% of its electricity (58% on the island of Kauai and 33% on the island of Hawaii). Power plants burning rice husks are operating in India, Malaysia, the Philippines, Thailand, Suriname, and India. Other crop residues that could be burned include coconut shells, peanut and other nut hulls, and cotton stalks. This approach makes sense when residues are burned in small power plants located near areas where the residues are produced.

In most areas, however, plant residues are widely dispersed. Unless they are harvested along with crops, they require large amounts of energy to collect, dry, and transport to large centralized power plants. Also, ecologists argue that it makes more sense to use crop residues to feed livestock, retard soil erosion, and fertilize the soil.

An increasing number of cities in Japan, western Europe, and the United States have built incinerators that burn trash and use the heat released to produce electricity or to heat nearby buildings (Section 15-6). Some analysts argue that more energy is saved by composting or recycling paper and other organic wastes than by burning them.

Converting Solid Biomass to Liquid and Gaseous Biofuels Plants, organic wastes, sewage, and other forms of solid biomass can be converted by bacteria and various chemical processes into gaseous and liquid biofuels (Figure 17-17). Examples are *biogas* (a mixture of 60% methane and 40% carbon dioxide), *liquid methanol* (methyl, or wood alcohol), and *liquid ethanol* (ethyl, or grain alcohol).

In China, bacteria in an estimated 7 million *biogas digesters* convert organic plant and animal wastes into methane fuel for heating and cooking. After the biogas has been removed, the solid residue left behind is used as fertilizer on food crops or, if contaminated, on nonedible crops such as trees. India has about 750,000 biogas digesters in operation, half of them built since 1986.

When they work, biogas digesters are very efficient. However, they are slow and unpredictable. They don't work well at low temperatures or when contaminated by acids, heavy metals, synthetic detergents, and other industrial effluents. Development of new, more reliable models could change this.

Methane fuel is also produced by underground decomposition of organic matter in the absence of air (anaerobic digestion) in active and closed landfills. The gas is collected by pipes inserted into landfills, purified, and burned as a fuel. By 1988 almost 50 landfill gas recovery systems were operating in the United States (mostly in California) and 35 others were under construction. Some 2,000 to 3,000 large U.S. landfills have the potential for large-scale methane recovery. Because methane is a greenhouse gas, this recovery also helps slow global warming.

Methane can also be produced by anaerobic digestion of manure and sludge produced at sewage treatment plants. Converting to methane all the manure that U.S. livestock produce each year could provide nearly 5% of the country's total natural gas consumption at the current level. But collecting and transporting manure for long distances to large centralized power plants takes energy.

It is more economical to digest manure or sludge near sites where it is produced, collect the methane produced, and then burn it at farms, feedlots, or small nearby power plants. In California's Imperial Valley a private entrepreneur has built a power plant that produces electricity by burning cattle manure bought from nearby feedlot owners. The plant operates at full capacity 85% of the time, produces little air pollution, and its incinerator ash is sold to fertilize soils, pave roads, and soak up toxic waste. The power, which is sold to Southern California Edison, supplies electricity for as many as 20,000 homes. However, conservationists believe that in most cases recycling manure to the land to replace commercial inorganic fertilizer, which requires large amounts of natural gas to produce, would probably save more natural gas than burning the manure.

Some analysts believe that methanol and ethanol can be used as liquid fuels to replace gasoline and diesel fuel when oil becomes too scarce and expensive. Both alcohols can be burned directly as fuel without requiring additives to boost octane ratings.

Currently, emphasis is on using ethanol as an automotive fuel. It can be made from sugar and grain crops (sugarcane, sugar beets, sorghum, and corn) by fermentation and distillation. Pure ethanol can be burned in today's cars with little engine modification. Gasoline can also be mixed with 10% to 23% ethanol to make *gasohol*. It burns in conventional gasoline engines and is sold as super unleaded or ethanol-enriched gasoline.

By 1988 ethanol made by fermentation of sugarcane accounted for about 62% of the automotive fuel consumption in Brazil. Almost one-third of existing cars and 90% of all new cars produced in Brazil can run on pure ethanol. The rest can run on an unleaded gasoline mixture containing 20% ethanol. The use of ethanol helped Brazil cut its oil imports in half between 1978 and 1984. It also created an estimated 575,000 full-time jobs. But the government has spent $8 billion

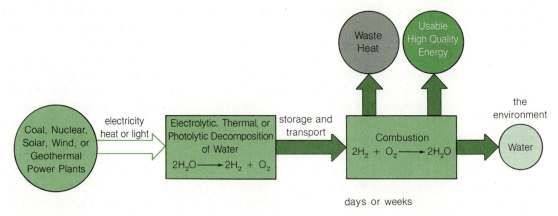

Figure 17-18 The hydrogen energy cycle. The production of hydrogen gas requires electricity, heat, or solar energy to decompose water, thus leading to a negative net useful energy yield.

to prop up the country's ethanol industry. Also, without catalytic converters, cars burning ethanol fuels produce more aldehydes and PANs that kill plants and cause eye irritation than do cars burning gasoline.

Super unleaded gasoline containing 90% gasoline and 10% ethanol now accounts for about 8% of gasoline sales in the United States—25% to 35% in Illinois, Iowa, Kentucky, and Nebraska. The ethanol used in gasohol is made mostly by fermenting corn in 150 ethanol production plants built between 1980 and 1985. Excluding federal taxes, it costs about $1.60 to produce a gallon of ethanol, compared to about 50 cents for a gallon of gasoline. However, new, energy-efficient distilleries are lowering the production costs. Soon this fuel may be able to compete with other forms of unleaded gasoline without federal tax breaks, which are scheduled to expire in 1992.

The distillation process to make ethanol produces large volumes of a waste material known as swill, which if allowed to flow into waterways, kills algae, fish, and plants. Another problem is that the net useful energy yield for producing ethanol fuel is low in older oil- or natural-gas-fueled distilleries. However, the yield is moderate at new distilleries using modern technology and powered by coal, wood, or solar energy.

Some experts are concerned that growing corn or other grains to make alcohol fuel could compete for cropland needed to grow food. For example, 40% of the entire U.S. annual harvest of corn would be needed to make enough ethanol to meet just 10% of the country's demand for automotive fuel.

Another alcohol, methanol, can be produced from wood, wood wastes, agricultural wastes, sewage sludge, garbage, coal, and natural gas at a cost of about $1 to $2 per gallon. High concentrations of methanol corrode conventional engines, but in a properly modified engine methanol burns cleanly without any problems.

A fuel of 85% methanol and 15% unleaded gaso-line could reduce emissions of ozone-forming hydrocarbons 20% to 50%. Running cars on pure methanol would reduce these emissions by 85% to 95% and carbon monoxide emissions by 30% to 90%. However, cars burning pure methanol emit two to five times more formaldehyde, a suspected carcinogen, than those burning gasoline. Methanol-powered cars emit less carbon dioxide than gasoline-powered cars. But producing the methanol from coal would double carbon dioxide emissions.

Diesohol, a mixture of diesel fuel with 15% to 20% methanol by volume, is being tested and could lower emissions of nitrogen oxide pollutants, a drawback of regular diesel fuel. Another alternative fuel for diesel engines is vegetable oil, particularly soybean oil. The oil can be treated chemically to produce a diesel fuel, or it can be blended with ethanol and a touch of detergent.

Growing more soybeans in the United States could replace as much as 88% of the diesel fuel used by agriculture. The chief problem is cost. Diesel fuel made from soybean oil costs about $1.60 a gallon, almost twice as much as regular diesel fuel. More research could bring the cost down to $1 a gallon and make this a competitive fuel when gasoline prices rise, probably in the 1990s.

17-7 HYDROGEN AS A POSSIBLE REPLACEMENT FOR OIL

Some scientists have suggested that we use hydrogen gas (H_2) to fuel cars, heat homes, and provide hot water when oil and natural gas run out. Hydrogen gas does not occur in significant quantities in nature. However, it can be produced by chemical processes from nonrenewable coal or natural gas or by using heat, electricity, or perhaps sunlight to decompose fresh water or seawater (Figure 17-18).

Hydrogen gas can be burned in a reaction with oxygen gas in a power plant, a specially designed automobile engine, or a fuel cell that converts the chemical energy produced by the reaction into direct-current electricity. Fuel cells running on a mixture of hydrogen and air have efficiencies of 60% to 80%.

Hydrogen burns cleanly in pure oxygen, yielding only water vapor and no air pollutants. When burned in air, it produces only small amounts of nitrogen oxides, 200 times less than current vehicles. Hydrogen gas can be stored in porous carbon granules or be combined with various metals to produce solid compounds that can be heated to release hydrogen as needed in a specially designed automobile motor. Unlike gasoline, the solid metallic hydrogen compounds would not explode or burn if the tank is ruptured in an accident. Hydrogen gas can also be absorbed on activated carbon granules which can be heated to release hydrogen as needed.

The major problem with hydrogen as a fuel is that only trace amounts of the gas occur in nature. Producing it uses high-temperature heat or electricity from another energy source, such as nuclear fission, direct solar power, or wind, to decompose water. This is expensive.

Because of the first and second energy laws, hydrogen production by any method will take more energy than is released when it is burned. Thus, its net useful energy yield will always be negative. This means that its widespread use depends on having an abundant and affordable supply of some other type of environmentally acceptable energy.

Another problem is that hydrogen gas is highly explosive. However, most analysts believe we could learn how to handle it safely, as we have for highly explosive gasoline and natural gas. Over two dozen experimental hydrogen-fueled cars are operating in the world today.

Burning hydrogen does not add carbon dioxide to the atmosphere. However, carbon dioxide would be added to the atmosphere if electricity or high-temperature heat from coal or other fossil-fuel-burning power plants were used to decompose water and produce hydrogen. No carbon dioxide would be added if photovoltaic, wind, hydroelectric, geothermal, or nuclear power were used to produce hydrogen.

Scientists are trying to develop cells that use ordinary light or solar energy to split water molecules into hydrogen and oxygen gases with reasonable efficiency. In 1988 construction began on an experimental solar-hydrogen plant in Bavaria, West Germany. In 1989 an American scientist developed a cell that uses sunlight to produce hydrogen gas from seawater. If everything goes right, affordable commercial cells for using solar energy to produce hydrogen could become available sometime after 2000.

17-8 DEVELOPING AN ENERGY STRATEGY FOR THE UNITED STATES

Overall Evaluation of U.S. Energy Alternatives Table 17-2 summarizes the major advantages and disadvantages of the energy alternatives discussed in this and the preceding chapter, with emphasis on their potential in the United States. Energy experts argue over these and other projections, and new data and innovations may change some information in this table. But it does provide a useful framework for making decisions based on presently available information. Four major conclusions can be drawn:

- The best short-term, intermediate, and long-term alternative for the United States and other countries is improving the efficiency of energy use (Section 17-1).

- Total systems for future energy alternatives in the world and the United States will probably have low to moderate net useful energy yields and moderate to high development costs. Since there is not enough financial capital to develop all energy alternatives, projects must be chosen carefully. Otherwise, limited capital will be depleted on energy alternatives that yield too little net useful energy or prove to be economically or environmentally unacceptable.

- We cannot and should not depend mostly on one nonrenewable energy resource like oil, coal, natural gas, or nuclear power. Instead, the world and the United States should rely more on improving energy efficiency and a mix of perpetual and renewable energy resources.

- We should decrease dependence on using coal and nuclear power to produce electricity at large, centralized power plants. Individuals, communities, and countries should get more of their heat and electricity from locally available renewable and perpetual energy resources.

Economics and National Energy Strategy Cost is the major factor determining which commercial energy resources are widely used by consumers. Governments throughout the world use three major economic and political strategies to stimulate or dampen the short- and long-term use of a particular energy resource:

- *not attempting to control the price*, so that its use depends on open, free-market competition (assuming all other alternatives also compete in the same way)

- *keeping prices artificially low* to encourage its use and development

- *keeping prices artificially high* to discourage its use and development

Energy Resources	Estimated Availability			Estimated Net Useful Energy of Entire System	Projected Cost of Entire System	Actual or Potential Overall Environmental Impact of Entire System
	Short Term (1990–2000)	Intermediate Term (2000–2010)	Long Term (2010–2040)			
Nonrenewable Resources						
Fossil fuels						
Petroleum	High (with imports)	Moderate (with imports)	Low	High but decreasing	High for new domestic supplies	Moderate
Natural gas	High (with imports)	Moderate (with imports)	Moderate (with imports)	High but decreasing	High for new domestic supplies	Low
Coal	High	High	High	High but decreasing	Moderate but increasing	Very high
Oil shale	Low	Low to moderate	Low to moderate	Low to moderate	Very high	High
Tar sands	Low	Fair? (imports only)	Poor to fair (imports only)	Low	Very high	Moderate to high
Biomass (urban wastes for incineration)	Low	Moderate	Moderate	Low to fairly high	High	Moderate to high
Synthetic natural gas (SNG) from coal	Low	Low to moderate	Low to moderate	Low to moderate	High	High (increases use of coal)
Synthetic oil and alcohols from coal and organic wastes	Low	Moderate	High	Low to moderate	High	High (increases use of coal)
Nuclear energy						
Conventional fission (uranium)	Low to moderate	Low to moderate	Low to moderate	Low to moderate	Very high	Very high
Breeder fission (uranium and thorium)	None	None to low (if developed)	Moderate	Unknown, but probably moderate	Very high	Very high
Fusion (deuterium and tritium)	None	None	None to low (if developed)	Unknown	Very high	Unknown (probably moderate)
Geothermal energy (trapped pockets)	Poor	Poor	Poor	Low to moderate	Moderate to high	Moderate to high
Perpetual and Renewable Resources						
Improving energy efficiency	High	High	High	Very high	Low	Decreases impact of other sources

Each approach has certain advantages and disadvantages.

Free Market Competition Leaving it to the marketplace without any government interference is appealing in principle. However, a free market rarely exists in practice because business people are in favor of it for everyone but their own companies.

Most energy industry executives work hard to get control of supply, demand, and price for their particular energy resource, while urging free-market competition for any competing energy resources. They try

Energy Resources	Estimated Availability			Estimated Net Useful Energy of Entire System	Projected Cost of Entire System	Actual or Potential Overall Environmental Impact of Entire System
	Short Term (1990–2000)	Intermediate Term (2000–2010)	Long Term (2010–2040)			
Perpetual and Renewable Resources (continued)						
Water power (hydroelectricitiy)						
New large-scale dams and plants	Low	Low	Very low	Moderate to high	Moderate to very high	Low to moderate
Reopening abandoned small-scale plants	Moderate	Moderate	Low	High	Moderate	Low
Tidal energy	None	Very low	Very low	Unknown (moderate?)	High	Low to moderate
Ocean thermal gradients	None	Low	Low to moderate (if developed)	Unknown (probably low to moderate)	Probably high	Unknown (probably moderate)
Solar energy						
Low-temperature heating (for homes and water)	High	Moderate to high	High	Moderate to high	Moderate to fairly high	Low
High-temperature heating	Low	Moderate	Moderate to high	Moderate	Very high initially (but probably declining fairly rapidly)	Low to moderate
Photovoltaic production of electricity	Low to moderate	Moderate	High	Fairly high	High initially but declining fairly rapidly	Low
Wind energy						
Home and neighborhood turbines	Low	Moderate	Moderate to high	Fairly high	Moderate	Low
Large-scale power plants	None	Very low	Probably low	Low	High	Low to moderate?
Geothermal energy (low heat flow)	Very low	Very low	Low to moderate	Low to moderate	Moderate to high	Moderate to high
Biomass (burning of wood, crop, food, and animal wastes)	Moderate	Moderate	Moderate to high	Moderate	Moderate	Variable
Biofuels (alcohols and natural gas from plants and organic wastes)	Low to moderate?	Moderate	Moderate to high	Low to fairly high	Moderate to high	Moderate to high
Hydrogen gas (from coal or water)	None	Low	Moderate	Variable	Variable	Variable

to influence elected officials and help elect those who will give their businesses the most favorable tax breaks and other government subsidies. Such favoritism distorts and unbalances the marketplace.

An equally serious problem with the open marketplace is its emphasis on today's prices to enhance short-term economic gain. This inhibits long-term development of new energy resources, which can rarely compete in their development stages without government support.

One effort to increase free-market competition among energy alternatives in the United States is the

1978 Public Utility Regulatory Policies Act (PURPA). This law forces utilities to buy electricity at favorable rates from private firms and individuals producing power by using conventional fuels, cogeneration, or renewables such as wind and hydropower.

Power companies bitterly fought this law in Congress and the courts. But in 1983 the Supreme Court upheld the law. By 1988 a variety of privately owned firms were generating electricity equal to that from 12 large nuclear power plants. This output is expected to double between 1988 and 1993. Eventually these sources could supply electricity equal to the output of 62 nuclear power plants. This would eliminate the need to build any new nuclear power plants as older ones are retired.

Keeping Energy Prices Artificially Low: The U.S. Strategy

Many governments give tax breaks and other subsidies, pay for long-term research and development, and use price controls to keep prices for a particular energy resource artificially low. This is the main approach used by the United States and the Soviet Union.

This approach encourages the development and use of energy resources getting favorable treatment. It also helps protect consumers (especially the poor) from sharp price increases, and it can help reduce inflation. Because keeping prices low is popular with consumers, this practice often helps leaders in democratic societies get reelected and helps keep leaders in nondemocratic societies from being overthrown.

But this approach also encourages waste and rapid depletion of an energy resource (such as oil) by making its price lower than it should be compared to its true value and long-term supply. This strategy discourages the development of energy alternatives not getting at least the same level of subsidies and price control. Once energy industries such as the fossil fuel and nuclear power industries get government subsidies, they usually have enough clout to maintain this support long after it becomes unproductive. And they often fight efforts to provide equal or higher subsidies for the development of new energy alternatives that would allow more equal competition in the marketplace.

In 1984 federal tax breaks and other subsidies for the development of energy conservation and perpetual solar-based energy resources in the United States amounted to $1.7 billion. But these tax breaks were eliminated a year later and have not been restored.

By contrast, during 1984 the nuclear power industry received $15.6 billion, the oil industry $8.6 billion, the natural gas industry $4.6 billion, and the coal industry $3.4 billion in federal tax breaks and subsidies. These subsidies, unlike those for energy conser-

vation and renewable energy, have not been eliminated. Thus, the marketplace is distorted in favor of fossil fuels and nuclear power.

Conservationists are alarmed that an increasing share of the Department of Energy's annual budget is being used to develop nuclear weapons instead of new energy alternatives. Between 1981 and 1989 the share of the Department's budget used for making nuclear weapons and developing new ones increased from 38% to 65%. Thus, almost two-thirds of the DOE budget is actually an addition to the Defense Department's budget. Critics call for these activities to be shifted from the Department of Energy to the Department of Defense.

Most of the remaining 35% of the DOE budget is used for research and development of energy resources. Only 7% of the 1990 DOE budget was for research and development to improve energy efficiency and to develop perpetual and renewable sources of energy. The remaining 93% of the proposed R&D budget was mostly for continued development of fossil fuels and nuclear fission and fusion. Yet, according to the Department of Energy, reserves and potential supplies of perpetual and renewable energy resources make up 92% of the total energy resources potentially available to the United States and could meet up to 80% of the country's projected energy needs by 2010. Conservationists call for an entirely new national energy strategy in the 1990s (see Spotlight on p. 443).

Keeping Energy Prices Artificially High: The Western European Strategy

Governments keep the price of an energy resource artificially high by withdrawing existing tax breaks and other subsidies or by adding taxes on its use. This encourages improvements in energy efficiency, reduces dependence on imported energy, and decreases use of an energy resource (like oil) whose future supply will be limited.

However, increasing taxes on energy use contributes to inflation and dampens economic growth. They also put a heavy economic burden on the poor unless some of the energy tax revenues are used to help low-income families offset increased energy prices and to stimulate labor-intensive forms of economic growth such as improving energy efficiency. High gasoline and oil import taxes have been imposed by many European governments. That is one reason why those countries use less energy per person and have greater energy efficiency than the United States (Table 17-1).

One popular myth is that higher energy prices would wipe out jobs. Actually, low energy prices increase unemployment because farmers and industries find it cheaper to substitute machines run on cheap energy for human labor. On the other hand, raising energy prices stimulates employment because building solar collectors, adding insulation, and carrying out other forms of improving energy efficiency are labor-intensive activities.

Why the U.S. Has No Comprehensive Long-Term Energy Strategy   After the 1973 oil embargo, Congress was prodded to pass a number of laws (see Appendix 3) to deal with the country's energy problems. Most energy experts agree, however, that these laws do not represent a comprehensive energy strategy. Indeed, analysis of the U.S. political system reveals why the United States has not been able and will probably never be able to develop a coherent energy policy.

One reason is the complexity of energy issues as revealed in this and the preceding chapter. But the major problem is that the American political process produces laws—not policies—and is not designed to deal with long-term problems. Each law reflects political pressures of the moment and a maze of compromises between competing groups representing industry, conservationists, and consumers. Once a law is passed, it is difficult to repeal or modify drastically until its long-term consequences reach crisis proportions.

SPOTLIGHT A New Energy Strategy for the United States

Conservationists and environmentalists believe that the present U.S. energy strategy could lead to economic and environmental disaster and greatly increase the chances of nuclear and conventional war. They call for greatly increased research-and-development spending on energy conservation and renewable energy in the 1990s.

They also believe that energy conservation and renewable energy alternatives should get at least the same level of federal subsidies as fossil fuels and nuclear power. Another way to allow energy alternatives to compete on a more equal footing would be to eliminate all energy subsidies. However, this would be nearly impossible to do because of the political and economic power of the fossil fuel and nuclear industries.

Conservationists call for Congress to raise the average fuel efficiency requirement of new cars and light trucks to 60 miles per gallon by 2000. Incentives could also be established to encourage consumers to scrap older cars early and buy more efficient ones.

Some conservationists believe that the government should phase in a $1 per gallon gasoline tax over the next five years. This would bring U.S. gasoline prices closer to world levels and help discourage the use of fuel-inefficient vehicles. It would also raise $100 billion of revenue each year to help reduce the national debt, provide funds for energy research aimed at reducing dependence on oil and reducing carbon dioxide emissions, and for giving energy assistance to the poor.

Another conservation measure the government can take is to give tax write-offs for consumers who buy new energy efficient homes or who make older ones more energy efficient. The goal would be to cut in half the consumption of oil, gas, and electricity for heating space and hot water over the next 20 years. Much tougher energy efficiency standards should also be set for all major appliances.

Experts also suggest that a climate protection tax be levied on all fossil fuels based on the basis of their relative emission rates of carbon dioxide to the atmosphere (Figure 16-10, p. 381). Such a tax could delay climate changes from the greenhouse effect and raise at least $53 billion a year for encouraging energy conservation and the development of renewable energy resources.

Department of Energy expenditures on research and development of more energy efficient cars, building designs, appliances, and industrial processes should be greatly increased. The DOE spends a piddling $50 million a year on all transportation research and development, while the country is spending $100 billion a year on gasoline. The annual utility bill for the country's buildings is $160 billion, while the government spends almost nothing on research and development in this area.

Present policies regulating most utility companies encourage them to sell more electricity than is needed and not penalize them for using high-cost options (such as nuclear power) by having consumers pay for poor management decisions. Conservationists urge state utility commissions to change this by

- Decoupling electricity sales by utilities from their profits, as is now being done in California. Then there would be no incentive for utilities to promote increased consumption of electricity.

- Giving higher rates to utility companies that produce their power at the lowest cost and lower rates to those that don't, as has been proposed in Maine.

- Ammending the Public Utilities Regulatory Policy Act of 1978 to require all states to implement least-cost planning regulations.

Federal and state governments could also lead the way by requiring all of their buildings to have super-efficient lights and motors. What do you think should be done?

Taking Energy Matters into Your Own Hands While elected officials, energy company executives, and conservationists argue over the key components of a national energy strategy, many individuals localities have gotten fed up and taken energy matters into their own hands. With or without tax credits, they are insulating, weatherizing, and making other improvements to conserve energy and save money.

Some are building passively heated and cooled solar homes. Others are building superinsulated dwellings or are adding passive solar heating to existing homes. Each of us can develop a personal energy strategy that improves personal and national security and saves money (see Spotlight below and inside back cover).

Similarly, local governments in a growing number of cities are developing successful programs to improve

SPOTLIGHT Working with Nature: A Personal Progress Report

I am writing this book deep in the midst of some beautiful woods in Eco-Lair, a structure that Peggy, my wife and earthmate, and I designed to work with nature. First, we purchased a 1954 school bus from a nearby school district and sold the tires for the same price that we paid for the bus. We built an insulated foundation, rented a crane for two hours to lift and set the gutted bus on the foundation, placed heavy insulation around the bus, and added a wooden outside frame.

We attached a paneled solar room—a passive solar collector with double-paned conventional sliding glass windows (for ventilation)—to the entire south side of the bus structure (Figure 17-19).

The solar room serves as a year-round sitting and work area and contains a small kitchen with a stove and refrigerator that run on liquefied petroleum gas (LPG).

The room collects enough solar energy to meet about 60% of our heating needs during the cold months. A solar-assisted water stove in a small building outside provides backup heat as needed by burning wood. During sunny days active solar collectors store heat in a 1,900-liter (500-gallon) insulated tank with a built-in firebox. Wood is burned in the firebox in very cold weather to supplement the stored solar energy.

Placing this system in a separate shed eliminates indoor smoke and soot. A pump connected to

the water tank circulates heated water through insulated underground pipes to a heat exchanger before the water is returned to the tank. A fan transfers the heat in the water to air, which is blown through ducts connected to the house. With a conventional thermostat to control indoor temperature, the system eliminates the uneven heating provided by a conventional wood stove. A tankless, instant water heater fueled by LPG is attached to the water-stove tank as a backup.

Our hot water is supplied by active solar collectors connected to the water stove. In winter the solar-heated water is heated further as needed by a tankless, instant heater fueled by LPG. Most of our light bulbs we use last an average of six years and use about 60% less electricity than conventional bulbs.

For the time being we are buying electricity from the power company. But we plan to get our electricity from roof-mounted panels of photovoltaic cells (Figure 17-14, p. 429) when their price is lower, probably sometime in the 1990s. We hope to be able to sell any excess power we produce back to the power company. Our present monthly electricity bills run around $35.

We cool in moderate weather by opening windows to capture breezes during hot and humid North Carolina summers. We get additional cooling from earth tubes, or cool tubes (Figure 17-9, p. 423). Four plastic pipes were buried about 5.5 meters (18 feet) underground, extending down a

Ron Seils

Figure 17-19 Eco-Lair is where I work. A south-facing solar room collects solar energy passively and distributes it to a well-insulated recycled school bus. Backup heat is provided by a solar-assisted water stove housed in the separate structure on the left. Cooling is provided by buried tubes (earth tubes) at a cost of about $1 a summer. Electricity bills run about $35 a month.

energy efficiency and to rely more on locally available energy resources. Across the country, towns are realizing that paying for energy is bleeding them to death economically, with 80% to 90% of the money they spend on energy leaving the local economy forever (see Case Study on p. 446). Instead of creating local jobs and income this money goes to wealthy Saudi Arabians, Texas oil barons, and New York investors.

Each of these individual and local initiatives are crucial political and economic actions that are bringing about change from the bottom-up. Multiplied across the country, such actions can shape a sane national energy strategy with or without help from federal and state governments.

Most LDCs can also improve energy efficiency and use renewable and perpetual energy resources to meet

gently sloping hillside until their ends emerge some 31 meters (100 feet) away. The other ends of the tubes come up into the foundation of the bus and connect to a duct system containing a small fan whose speed can be varied by a rheostat. When the fan is turned on, outside air at a temperature of 35°C (95°F) is drawn slowly through the buried tubes (which are surrounded by earth at about 16°C (60°F) and enters the structure at about 22°C (72°F). This natural air conditioning costs about $1 per summer for running the fan.

Several large oak trees and other deciduous trees in front of the solar room give us additional passive cooling during summer and drop their leaves to let the sun in during winter. Because of allergies, we have had to install a recycled conventional air conditioning unit. We turn it on for short periods (typically no more than 30 minutes a day) when excessive pollen or heat and humidity overwhelm our immune systems and the earth tubes. Life always involves some trade-offs.

Eco-Lair is surrounded by natural vegetation including flowers and low-level ground cover. This means we have no grass to cut and no lawnmower to repair, feed with gasoline, and listen to. To the natural diversity of the landscape we have added plants that repel various insects, so we have few insect pest problems. The surrounding trees and other vegetation also provide habitats for various species of insect-eating birds. When ants, mice, and other creatures find their way inside we repel and

control them using various natural alternatives (see p. 564).

We have reduced water use by installing water-saving faucets and low-flush toilets. We have also experimented with a waterless composting toilet that gradually converts waste and garbage scraps to a dry, odorless powder that can be used as a soil conditioner. Kitchen wastes are composted and recycled to the soil and paper is carried to a recycling center. We store extra furniture, clothes, and other items in three other old school buses and recycle these items to family, friends, and people in need.

Eco-Lair lies near the end of a narrow, one-mile-long dirt road that at times can be traversed only by a four-wheel-drive vehicle. As a result, we have to drive a vehicle that consumes much more gasoline than we would like.

As soon as they become available, we plan to buy a car that gets 34 to 43 kilometers per liter (80 to 100 miles per gallon) and use it for most trips. If the technology becomes available and economically feasible in the future, we hope to have one that runs on hydrogen gas produced by solar photovoltaic cells that decompose water into hydrogen and oxygen gas. Because of laziness and allergies, we get most of our food from the grocery store rather than growing it ourselves.

We feel a part of the piece of land we live on and love. To us, ownership of this land means that we are ethically driven to defend and protect it from degradation. We feel that the trees, flowers,

deer, squirrels, hummingbirds, songbirds, and other forms of wildlife we often see are a part of us and we are a part of them. As temporary caretakers of this small portion of the biosphere, we feel obligated to pass it on to future generations with its ecological integrity and sustainability preserved.

Most of our political activities involve thinking globally but acting locally. They include attempts to prevent an economically unnecessary nuclear power plant from opening about 24 kilometers (15 miles) away (it opened anyway), to prevent an ecologically unsound development along a nearby river that is already badly polluted (we've been successful so far), to prevent the building of a large, conventional housing development that would double the size of the closest town (successful).

We also financially support numerous environmental and conservation organizations working at the national and global levels (see Appendix 1). We are not opposed to all forms of development, only those that are ecologically unsound and destructive.

We find that working with nature gives us great joy and a sense of purpose. It also saves us money. We are trying to work with nature in a rural area. But people in cities can also have high-quality lifestyles that conserve resources and protect the environment (see Further Readings).

essary economic and environmental hardships and increased human suffering.

In the long run, humanity has no choice but to rely on renewable energy. No matter how abundant they seem today, eventually coal and uranium will run out. The choice before us is practical: We simply cannot afford to make more than one energy transition within the next generation.

Daniel Deudney and Christopher Flavin

CHAPTER SUMMARY

The easiest and cheapest way to make more energy available and reduce the environmental impact of present use is to reduce or eliminate unnecessary energy waste in industry, transportation, and commercial and residential buildings. This can be done by changing energy-wasting habits, increasing energy efficiency by using less energy to do the same amount of work, and developing new devices that waste less energy than existing ones. Improving energy efficiency makes supplies of nonrenewable fossil fuels last longer, buys time for phasing in perpetual and renewable energy resources, reduces dependence on imported oil, and improves national and global military and economic security.

The largest, mostly untapped energy sources for all countries are perpetual and renewable energy from the sun, wind, flowing water, and biomass. Direct solar energy can be used to provide low-temperature heat for space heating and heating water. A passive solar system in a superinsulated or well-insulated and weatherized house is the cheapest and most energy-efficient way to heat a residence on a lifetime cost basis with a very low environmental impact. An active solar system is a cost-effective way of providing hot water for a residence on a lifetime cost basis.

Direct solar energy can also be concentrated to produce high-temperature heat for industrial processes and to produce electricity in solar power plants, but with present technology costs are high. Direct solar energy can also be converted directly to electricity in photovoltaic cells; environmental impact is low and costs should be competitive sometime in the 1990s.

New large and small hydroelectric projects can greatly increase electricity production in many LDCs and some MDCs with moderate to high costs and moderate to low environmental impact. New large-scale hydroelectric projects in the United States are limited by lack of suitable and environmentally acceptable sites. However, many existing large hydroelectric plants could be upgraded and many abandoned small hydroelectric plants could be reopened at moderate cost with relatively low environmental impact.

Producing electricity by tapping into the energy in twice-daily ocean tides (tidal power) and ocean waves (wave power) is expected to make little contribution to world energy resources because of limited suitable sites and high costs.

Electricity can also be produced from solar energy stored as heat in seawater at tropical ocean sites and in inland solar ponds containing either salt water or fresh water. Suitable sites for large floating ocean thermal electric power plants are limited and technological problems

much of their energy needs. Most renewable-energy projects have short construction times and provide large numbers of jobs. Countries and communities that depend on energy from locally available renewable resources are less vulnerable to disruptions of fuel supplies and price rises, and their economies are stronger because they spend less on energy imports.

This will require greatly increased aid to LDCs from MDCs and international aid agencies. Currently the U.S. Agency for International Development, the World Bank, and other international development banks are allocating only 1% of all energy project funds for improving energy efficiency.

A few countries are leading the way in making the transition from the age of oil to the age of energy efficiency and renewable energy. Sweden leads the world in energy efficiency, followed by Japan. Brazil and Norway get more than half their energy from hydropower, wood, and alcohol fuel. Israel, Japan, the Philippines, and Sweden plan to rely on renewable and perpetual sources for most of their energy.

Countries that have the vision to change from an unsustainable to a sustainable energy strategy will be rewarded with increased security—not just military security but also economic, energy, and environmental security. Those that do not will experience unnec-

and high costs may severely limit the use of this energy resource. Solar ponds on inland saltwater seas and lakes can be used to produce electricity at a few limited sites, but costs are high. Building freshwater inland solar ponds may be a quick and cost-effective effective way to provide low-temperature heat for providing hot water and space heating for large buildings and groups of houses.

Electricity primarily for local utilities can be produced by large numbers of modern wind turbines in wind farms at numerous suitable sites in the United States and the world at competitive prices. Environmental impact is low and installation time is short (three to five months).

Energy can be obtained from a number of biomass fuels. Wood is a widely used fuel for cooking, space heating, and water heating throughout the world, especially in LDCs. However, fuelwood supplies are decreasing in many LDCs as forests are being stripped of trees without adequate replanting. Burning wood and wood wastes can be a cost-effective way for the forest products industry to cogenerate steam and electricity and for individuals to heat residences. However, without adequate air pollution control, burning wood to heat houses produces unacceptable levels of indoor and outdoor air pollution.

Large quantities of fast-growing plants and trees on biomass-energy plantations may become a source of biomass fuel. However, the environmental impact from increased soil erosion could be high without careful controls.

Agricultural and urban wastes can be burned to cogenerate steam and electricity for nearby industries, homes (district space heating), and local utility companies. Some analysts argue, however, that more energy would be saved by recycling or composting such organic wastes.

Useful but limited amounts of methane-rich biogas fuel can be produced by bacterial decomposition of plants, organic wastes buried in large landfills, manure collected from animal feedlots, and sludge from sewage treatment plants.

Ethanol, produced from sugar and grain crops, is being used in automobiles in Brazil and is mixed with gasoline to produce super unleaded gasoline in the United States. But prices are fairly high without government tax breaks. Another liquid biofuel, methanol, can be produced from wood, agricultural wastes, sludge from sewage treatment plants, garbage, coal, and natural gas. With present technology, however, it is far too expensive and can be burned only in modified automobile engines.

Some believe that hydrogen gas may be used to fuel cars, heat homes, and produce electricity when oil runs out sometime in the next century. Although hydrogen is a very clean-burning fuel, it is rare in nature and must be produced by decomposition of water. The resulting negative net useful energy yield means that its widespread use depends on having a large and affordable supply of energy available from some other source—perhaps from special cells powered by solar energy.

In the United States (and in most countries) the best energy options are improving energy efficiency and getting much more energy from the sun, wind, flowing water, and biomass. Emphasis should be on small, decentralized systems that make use of locally available perpetual and renewable sources of energy.

Governments can stimulate or dampen the use of a particular energy resource by not controlling prices (free-market competition), by keeping prices artificially high, or by keeping prices artificially low. Each approach has certain advantages and disadvantages.

Because of the complexity of energy problems and the nature of the American political system, it is virtually impossible for elected federal officials to develop a coherent energy plan for the United States. As a result, many individuals and local communities are developing their own plans to save energy and money and to make increased use of locally available sources of energy.

DISCUSSION TOPICS

1. What are the ten most important things an individual can do to save energy in the home and in transportation (see table inside the back cover)? Which, if any, of these do you do? Which, if any, do you plan to do? When?

2. Make an energy use study of your school, and use the findings to develop an energy conservation program.

3. Should the United States institute a crash program to develop solar photovoltaic cells? Explain.

4. Explain why you agree or disagree with each of the following statements:

   a. The United States can get most of the electricity it needs by developing solar power plants.

   b. The United States can get most of the electricity it needs by using direct solar energy to produce electricity in photovoltaic cells.

   c. The United States can get most of the electricity it needs by building new, large hydroelectric plants.

   d. The United States can get most of the electricity it needs by building ocean thermal electric power plants.

   e. The United States can get most of the electricity it needs by building wind farms.

   f. The United States can get most of the electricity it needs by building power plants fueled by wood, crop wastes, trash, and other biomass resources.

5. Explain why you agree or disagree with the following propositions suggested by various energy analysts:

   a. The United States should cut average per capita energy use by at least 50% between 1990 and 2010.

   b. A mandatory energy conservation program should form the basis of any U.S. energy policy t provide economic, environmental, and mi security.

   c. To solve world and U.S. energy supply pr all we need do is recycle some or most of we use.

   d. Federal subsidies for all energy alternative be eliminated so that all energy choices ca in a true free-enterprise market system.

   e. All government tax breaks and other subsi conventional fuels (oil, natural gas, coal), s natural gas and oil, and nuclear power sho removed and replaced with subsidies and for improving energy efficiency and developing solar, wind, geothermal, and biomass energy alternatives.

   f. Development of solar and wind energy should be left to private enterprise without help from the federal government, but nuclear energy and fossil fuels should continue to receive large federal subsidies (present U.S. policy).

g. To solve present and future U.S. energy problems, all we need do is find and develop more domestic supplies of conventional and unconventional oil, natural gas, and coal and increase our dependence on nuclear power (present U.S. policy).

h. The United States should not worry about heavy dependence on foreign oil imports because they improve international relations and help prevent depletion of domestic supplies (the "don't drain America first" approach).

i. A heavy federal tax should be placed on gasoline and imported oil used in the United States.

j. Between 2000 and 2020, the U.S. should phase out all nuclear power plants.

6. The present government policy in the United States is to keep heating oil, gasoline, natural gas, coal, and electricity prices artificially low by giving massive tax-supported subsidies to the fossil-fuel and nuclear industries and not imposing higher taxes on gasoline and imported oil. Explain how this policy can (a) discourage exploration for domestic supplies of fossil fuels, (b) increase or at least not significantly decrease dependence on imported oil, (c) lead to higher than necessary unemployment, (d) discourage development of direct and indirect sources of solar energy, and (e) discourage improvements in energy efficiency.

PART FIVE

Pollution

I am utterly convinced that the great environmental struggles will
either be won or lost in the 1990s, and that by the next century it will
be too late to act.

Thomas E. Lovejoy

CHAPTER 18

Environment, Health, and Risk

General Questions and Issues

1. What are common physical, chemical, and biological hazards that people face and what are their effects?

2. What are the major health risks for people living in LDCs and in MDCs?

3. How can the risks and benefits associated with using a particular technology or product be estimated and managed?

4. What are the major risks that can lead to cancer and how can they be reduced?

5. What are the risks from food additives found in processed foods?

6. What are the major types, sources, and effects of hazardous waste and how should it be managed?

7. What are the major types of sexually transmitted diseases and how can the risks be reduced?

Though their health needs differ drastically, the rich and the poor do have one thing in common: both die unnecessarily. The rich die of heart disease and cancer, the poor of diarrhea, pneumonia, and measles. Scientific medicine could vastly reduce the mortality caused by these illnesses. Yet, half the developing world lacks medical care of any kind.

William U. Chandler

Almost everything we do and every form of technology involves some degree of risk to our health and the health of other species. In LDCs poverty is the major cause of premature death. It leads to overcrowding, unsafe drinking water, poor sanitation, malnutrition, living in areas subject to flooding and other physical hazards, and the spread of transmissible diseases that rarely kill people in MDCs.

In MDCs premature death could be greatly reduced if people chose to eat properly, exercise more, not smoke or abuse alcohol, stay out of the sun and tanning booths, drive safely, reduce stress, not use toxic chemicals around the house, and practice safe sex. In evaluating risks the key questions are do the risks of damage from each hazard outweigh the benefits and how can we minimize the risks?

18-1 HAZARDS: TYPES AND EFFECTS

Common Hazards A **hazard** is something that can cause injury, disease, economic loss, or environmental damage. Most hazards come from exposure to various factors in our environment:

- *Physical hazards*: ionizing radiation (see Spotlight on p. 451), noise, earthquakes, hurricanes, tornados, fires, floods (see Case Study on p. 244), and drought (see p. 243)

- *Chemical hazards:* harmful chemicals in air (Chapter 19), water (Chapter 20), and food (Section 18-5 and Chapter 21)

- *Biological hazards:* disease-causing bacteria and viruses, pollen, parasites, and attacks by hungry or vicious animals

- *Cultural hazards:* working and living conditions, smoking, diet, drugs, excessive drinking, driving, criminal assault, unsafe sex, and poverty

Chemical Hazards A **toxic substance** is a chemical that is harmful to people or other living organisms. The effects from exposure to a toxic substance may be acute or chronic. **Acute effects** are those that appear shortly after exposure, usually to a large concentration or dose over a short time. Examples are skin burns or rashes, eye irritation, chest pains, kidney damage, headache, convulsions, and death.

Effects that are delayed and usually long-lasting are called **chronic effects.** They may not appear for months to years after exposure and usually last for years. Examples are cancer, lung and heart disease, birth defects, genetic defects, and nerve and behavioral disorders. Chronic effects often occur as a result of prolonged exposure to fairly low concentrations or doses of a toxin. However, they may also occur as the delayed effects of short-term exposure to high doses.

Determining Toxicity Levels Determining the toxicity levels of substances is difficult, costly, and controversial. It is neither ethical nor practical to use people to test toxicity. Thus, toxicity is usually determined by carrying out tests on laboratory animals (mostly mice and rats), bacteria, and cell and tissue cultures and by studying the effects on human populations exposed to high levels at work or by accidents.

Tests are run to develop a **dose-response curve**, which shows the effects of high doses of a toxic substance on a group of test organisms (Figure 18-2). Using high dose levels reduces the number of test animals needed, cuts the time needed for results to show up, and lowers costs. Even then testing a single chemical for toxicity or other harmful effects can cost $200,000 to $1 million and take two to five years.

The goal is to determine the lethal, mean lethal, and no-effect doses of a substance. The **lethal dose** is the amount of material per unit of body weight of the test animals that kills all of the test population in a certain time. Then the dose is reduced until an exposure level is found that kills half the test population

---

SPOTLIGHT Effects of Ionizing Radiation on the Human Body

Ionizing radiation, a form of electromagnetic radiation (Figure 4-3, p. 78), has enough energy to dislodge one or more electrons from the atoms it hits to form positively charged ions, which can react with and damage living tissue. Examples of ionizing radiation are ultraviolet radiation from the sun and sun lamps, X rays, neutrons emitted by nuclear fission (Figure 3-9, p. 61) and nuclear fusion (Figure 3-11, p. 63), and alpha, beta, and gamma radiation emitted by radioactive isotopes (Figure 3-8, p. 61).

Exposure to ionizing radiation can damage cells in the human body in two ways. One is genetic damage, which alters genes and chromosomes. This can show up as a genetic defect in immediate offspring or several generations later. The second type is somatic damage, which can cause harm during the victim's lifetime. Examples are burns, some types of leukemia, miscarriages, eye cataracts, and bone, thyroid, breast, skin, and lung cancers.

The effects from ionizing radiation depend on the amount and frequency of exposure, the type of ionizing radiation, its penetrating power (Figure 3-8, p. 61), and whether it comes from outside or inside the body. Most damage occurs in tissues with rapidly

Table 18-1 Probable Effects on Humans of Various Doses of Radiation to the Whole Body in a Short Period of Time

Dose (rems)	Effects
0–50	No consistent symptoms
50–200	Decreased white blood cells, nausea, vomiting; about 10% die within months at 200 rems
200–400	Loss of blood cells, fever, hemorrhage, hair loss, nausea, vomiting, diarrhea, fatigue, skin blotches; about 20% die within months
400–500	Same symptoms as 200–400 rems but more severe, increased infections due to lack of white blood cells; 50% death rate within months at 450 rems
500–1,000	Severe gastrointestinal damage, cardiovascular collapse, central nervous system damage; doses above 700 rems fatal within a few weeks
10,000	Death in hours
100,000	Death in minutes

dividing cells, such as the bone marrow (where blood cells are made), spleen, digestive tract (whose lining must be constantly renewed), reproductive organs, and lymph glands. Rapidly growing tissues of the developing embryo are also extremely sensitive, so pregnant women should avoid all unnecessary exposure to radioactivity and X rays unless they are essential for health or diagnostic purposes.

Small doses of ionizing radiation (often measured in *rems*) over a long period of time cause less damage than the same total dosage given all at once, because the body apparently has some ability to repair itself. Exposure to a large dose of ionizing radiation over a short time, however, can be fatal within a few minutes to a few months later, depending on the dose (Table 18-1).

(continued)

in a certain time. This is the **median lethal dose** or **LD₅₀**. Table 18-2 compares the estimated LD_{50} values on humans for various chemicals. One of the most toxic substances is the dioxin TCDD (see Case Study on p. 454).

Then the dose is slowly reduced until the entire test population shows undetectable adverse effects. This **no-effect dose** on test animals is then extrapolated to humans. Regulators then usually include a safety factor by setting the allowable human dose at some fraction, perhaps 1/10 or 1/100, of the estimated no-effect dose.

In most cases, the evidence suggests that any exposure can have some harmful effect and that the effect increases as the dose is raised (Figure 18-2, left). However, there is some evidence that some toxic agents may have a threshold dose below which no detectable harmful effects occur (Figure 18-2, right).

There are several problems with animal testing. Except in industrial and other accidents, humans are rarely exposed to the high dose levels per unit of body weight given to test animals. The high doses given to test animals also don't detect whether threshold levels exist at low doses. Extrapolating from high dose to low dose levels is uncertain and controversial. Many scientists also question the validity of extrapolating data from test animals to humans because human metabolism is different from that of the test animals.

Another approach to toxicity testing and determining the agents causing diseases such as cancer is **epidemiology**—the study of patterns of disease or effects from toxic exposure within defined groups of people. Typically the effects on people exposed to a particular toxic chemical from an industrial accident, people working under high exposure levels, or people in certain geographic areas are compared with groups of people not exposed to these conditions to see if there are statistically significant differences.

This approach also has limitations. For many toxic agents not enough people have been exposed to high

---

It is impossible to avoid all exposure to ionizing radiation, but we can reduce unnecessary risk. Each of us is continually exposed to small amounts of ionizing radiation, known as **natural,** or **background, ionizing radiation.** Sources include cosmic rays (a high-energy form of ionizing electromagnetic radiation) from outer space, radioactive radon-222 in soil and rock (see Case Study on p. 489), and natural radioactivity in our bodies from intakes of air, water, and food (Figure 18-1). Background radiation from radon-222 alone is equivalent to having two Chernobyl nuclear accidents every year.

We get additional exposure to ionizing radiation as a result of various human activities (Figure 18-1). Most of this comes from medical X rays and diagnostic tests and treatment using radioactive isotopes. These important tools save many thousands of lives each year and reduce human misery. But sometimes they are done primarily to protect doctors and hospitals from liability suits. The federal government estimates that one-third of the 600 million X rays taken each year in the United States are unnecessary. If your doctor or dentist proposes an X ray or diagnostic test involving radioisotopes, ask why it is necessary, how it will help find what is wrong and influence possible treatment, and what alternative tests are available with less risk.

Each year Americans are exposed to an average of 0.23 rems of ionizing radiation from background sources and human activities. According to the National Academy of Sciences, this exposure over an average lifetime causes about 1% of all fatal cancers and 5% to 6% of all normally encountered genetic defects in the U.S. population. Any unnecessary increase in the exposure to ionizing radiation from human activities should be avoided.

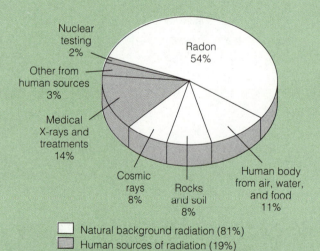

Figure 18-1 Contribution of natural sources and human activities to the average dose of ionizing radiation received by the population of the United States. (Data from National Council on Radiation Protection and Measurements)

enough levels to detect statistically significant differences. Also, people are exposed to many different toxic chemicals and disease-causing factors throughout their lives. Thus, it is not possible to say with much certainty that an observed epidemiological effect is caused only by exposure to a particular toxic agent or other hazardous condition.

Despite their shortcomings, animal testing and epidemeology are the best practical methods we have for estimating the acute effects of toxic agents on humans. However, animal tests are coming under increasing fire from animal rights groups and scientists are trying to find other methods (see Pro/Con on p. 319).

Carcinogens Tumors are growths of cells that enlarge and reproduce at abnormal rates. Tumors are classified as benign or malignant. A **benign tumor** is one that remains within the tissue where it develops and often grows slowly. A **malignant tumor** or **cancer** is one in which cells multiply uncontrollably and invade the surrounding tissue. If not detected and treated in time, many cancerous tumors undergo **metastasis**; that is, they release malignant (cancerous) cells that travel in body fluids to various parts of the body, making treatment much more difficult. Any cell is capable of becoming cancerous, but most cancer cells are found in tissues undergoing rapid cellular division. Examples are the cells in the lungs, bone marrow, ovaries, testes, skin, and intestinal lining.

Cancers are caused or promoted by poorly understood interactions between genes and environmental factors such as ionizing radiation, certain chemicals, and certain viruses. Environmental agents that can cause or promote the growth of malignant tumors or cancers are called **carcinogens.**

The three major ways of testing for carcinogens are animal tests, epidemiological studies, and bacterial tests. Only about 10% of the 70,000 chemicals in commercial use have been adequately tested to deter-

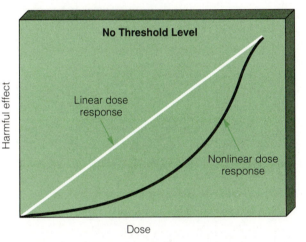 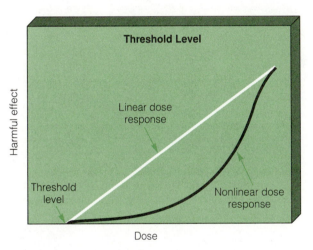

Figure 18-2 Different hypothetical dose-response curves. The curves on the left represent harmful effects that increase with increasing doses of a toxic substance. The curves on the right show a substance with harmful effects that appear only when the dose is above a certain value or threshold level.

Agent	LD$_{50}$ milligrams per kilogram of body weight	General Toxicity rating	Approximate Lethal Dose for Humans
Ethyl Alcohol	10,000	Slightly Toxic	Between pint and quart
Sodium Chloride (table salt)	4,000		
Morphine Sulfate	1,500	Moderately Toxic	Between ounce and pint
DDT	100	Very Toxic	Between teaspoonful and ounce
Strychnine Sulfate	2		Few drops
Nicotine	1		
Curare	0.5	Super Toxic	One drop
Dioxin (TCDD)	0.001		1/500th of a drop
Botulinus Toxin	0.00001		1/50,000th of a drop

Table 18-2 Approximate Toxicity of a Variety of Chemical Agents for Humans

mine whether they are carcinogens. Each year about 1,000 new chemicals are introduced into the marketplace. With only limited testing more than 400 toxic chemicals, most of which cumulate in the body, have been conclusively linked to human cancers. Examples are asbestos, arsenic, cadmium, benzene, aflatoxins (chemicals produced by certain molds found in wheat, corn, and nuts and in milk from cows that eat moldy grain), carbon tetrachloride, benzo (α) pyrene (found in cigarette and coal smoke), vinyl chloride, soot, and coal tar. Several hundred other chemicals are known to cause various cancers in laboratory animals and thus may cause cancers in humans.

Establishing strong evidence that a chemical or other agent does or does not cause or promote cancer in humans is difficult and costly. It is virtually impossible to isolate the effects of the thousands of chemicals and other factors in the environment that people are exposed to during the 10 to 40 years that may elapse before a cancer reaches detectable size. Also, we still know fairly little about how cancers are induced.

Mutagens and Teratogens Individuals in a population of a species don't have exactly the same genetic structure because of **mutations:** inheritable changes in the DNA molecules in the genes found in chromosomes. These altered genes transmit these traits from parent to offspring. Some mutations are beneficial, but most are harmful. The harmful ones can cause some types of cancer or various inheritable diseases

---

CASE STUDY Dioxins

Dioxins are a family of more than 100 different chlorinated hydrocarbon compounds formed as unwanted by-products in chemical reactions involving chlorine and hydrocarbons, usually at high temperatures. One form in particular, usually referred to as TCDD, is the most toxic dioxin (Table 18-2). In test animals it causes liver cancer, birth defects, and death at extremely low levels. TCDD and other dioxins also persist in the environment, especially in soil and fatty tissue in the human body, and can apparently be biologically amplified to higher levels in food webs. Although TCDD is extremely toxic to test animals, limited studies on humans give mixed results ranging from no effect to highly toxic.

Dioxins are unwanted by-products in the manufacture of chlorinated compounds such as the wood preservative pentachlorophenol (PCP) and herbicides such as silvex, 2,4-D, and 2,4,5-T. Agent Orange (a 50-50 mixture of 2,4-D and 2,4,5-T) was widely sprayed to defoliate trees during the Vietnam War (Section 21-3). TCDD and several other dioxins and their toxic cousins, furans, are always formed in trace amounts when chlorinated organic compounds are burned in municipal and hazardous waste incinerators and other combustion processes.

Researchers generally consider tainted foods such as fish, mother's milk, milk from cows eating grass growing in contaminated soil, and crops grown in contaminated soil the most important sources of exposure to dioxins and furans for the general population. The average American currently receives an average daily dose of TCDD that is 166 times the level the EPA uses to classify a substance as a cancer-causing agent.

In 1988 individuals and the environmental organization Greenpeace used the Freedom of Information Act to learn that there may be unacceptable levels of dioxins and furans in bleached paper products produced by paper mills that use chlorine as a bleaching agent. This limited information suggests that unacceptable levels of dioxins and furans may be leaching into food and beverages from chlorine bleached paper used in coffee filters (especially dangerous because of exposure to a hot liquid), milk cartons, frozen food cartons, paper towels, paper plates, toilet paper, sanitary napkins, disposable baby diapers, and other paper products. Leaching from each paper source may give a level of dioxins and furans below that believed to be unsafe, but cumulative exposure from multiple sources can exceed safe levels.

To reduce the threat from dioxins and furans environmentalists call for

- banning the use of chlorine for bleaching wood pulp and substituting oxygen or other nonchlorine bleaching processes. Sweden, for example, has banned the sale of chlorine-bleached disposable diapers.
- increasing recycling of paper (see Case Study on p. 365)
- increasing use of unbleached (slightly brown) paper in coffee filters, food containers, paper plates, and other products and educating consumers to understand that demanding white paper products is unnecessary and potentially hazardous to their health and the environment. Unbleached coffee filters, toilet paper, milk cartons, and other paper products are widely used in Austria and Sweden.
- banning incineration of chlorinated plastics and other chlorinated wastes
- setting up comprehensive recycling and waste reduction programs (Section 15-7)
- banning production and use of chlorinated phenols such as the wood preservative PCP

What do you think should be done?

---

such as manic depression, cystic fibrosis, hemophilia, sickle cell anemia, and Down's syndrome.

Some mutations result from exposure to various environmental factors, such as ionizing radiation, heat, and certain environmental agents, called **mutagens.** Examples of mutagens are aflatoxin, benzo (α) pyrene, caffeine, ozone, and most glue solvents. Nearly all carcinogens are also mutagens, and most mutagens are carcinogens.

Birth defects occur in about 2% to 3% of all live births. This means that every two minutes a baby is born in the United States with a birth defect. About 5% to 10% of all birth defects are caused by chemicals called **teratogens** (from the French word *terat* meaning monster). Examples of teratogens known to cause birth defects in laboratory animals are caffeine, DES, PCBs, and heavy metals such as arsenic, cadmium, lead, and mercury. Birth defects can also be caused by ionizing radiation and some types of viruses.

One of the most publicized teratogens is thalidomide, a sedative used widely in West Germany and Great Britain in the late 1950s. Based on animal studies, this chemical was considered to be so safe that it was sold without a prescription in West Germany. However, in the early 1960s it was discovered that women who had taken this drug during the first 12 weeks of pregnancy had babies with flipperlike arms, shortened arms, no arms or legs, and other birth defects (Figure 18-3). The use of this drug resulted in over 5,000 surviving malformed babies in: West Germany (4,000), Great Britain (1,000), and the United States (20 whose mothers took the drug while in Europe).

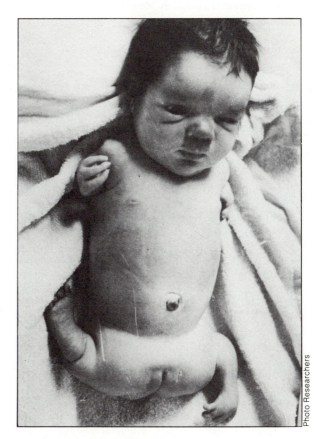

Figure 18-3 Birth defects on a baby whose mother took thalidomide during pregnancy.

18-2 BIOLOGICAL HAZARDS: DISEASE, ECONOMICS, AND GEOGRAPHY

Types of Disease Human diseases can be broadly classified as transmissible and nontransmissible. A **transmissible disease** is caused by living organisms such as bacteria, viruses, and parasitic worms and can be spread from one person to another by air, water, food, body fluids, and in some cases by insects and other nonhuman transmitters (called vectors). Examples are malaria, schistosomiasis, elephantiasis, sleeping sickness, measles, AIDS, and other sexually transmitted diseases (see Enrichment Study on p. 480).

A **nontransmissible disease** is not caused by living organisms and does not spread from one person to another. Examples include cardiovascular (heart and blood vessel) disorders, most cancer, diabetes, chronic respiratory diseases (bronchitis and emphysema), and malnutrition (p. 269). Many of these diseases have several often unknown causes and tend to develop slowly and progressively over time.

Diseases can also be classified according to their effect and duration. An **acute disease** is a disease such as measles or typhoid fever from which the victim either recovers or dies in a relatively short time. A **chronic disease** lasts for a long time (sometimes for life). Although this type of disease may go into remission, it may flare up periodically (malaria), become progressively worse (cancers and cardiovascular disorders), or disappear with age (childhood asthma).

Disease in LDCs Poverty is the underlying cause of the lower average life expectancy in LDCs. It increases the spread of transmissible diseases which account for about 40% of all deaths in LDCs. In LDCs, about 15 million children under the age of 5 die every year from: diarrhea (5 million); pneumonia, bronchitis, and other respiratory infections (4 million); measles (2 million); malaria (1 to 2 million, see Case Study on p. 456); and other diseases frequently associated with the combination of poverty, overcrowding, unsafe drinking water, poor sanitation, and malnutrition (Figure 12-9, p. 268). The hot, wet climates of tropical and subtropical countries also increase the chances of infection, because organisms that cause or carry disease can thrive year round.

Fortunately, major improvements in human health in LDCs can be made with primary preventive health care measures at a relatively low cost. These include providing

- contraceptive supplies and family planning counseling

- better nutrition, prenatal care, and birth assistance for pregnant women. At least 500,000 women in LDCs die each year of mostly preventable pregnancy-related causes, compared to only 6,000 in MDCs.

CASE STUDY Malaria

More than half the world's population live in malaria-prone regions in about 100 different countries in tropical and subtropical regions, especially West Africa and Southeast Asia (Figure 18-4). Malaria, spread by various species of the water-breeding *Anopheles* mosquito, afflicts 500 million people worldwide. Each year it kills at least 2.5 million (some sources say 5 million) people. At least half of its victims are children under age 5.

Each year there are 200 to 400 million new cases. Even in the United States, each day an average of four people discover they have malaria. Malaria's symptoms come and go; they include fever and chills, anemia, an enlarged spleen, severe abdominal pain and headaches, extreme weakness, and greater susceptibility to other diseases.

Malaria is caused by one of four species of protozoa (one-celled organisms) of the genus *Plasmodium*. The disease is transmitted from person to person by a bite from the female of about 60 of the 400 different kinds of *Anopheles* mosquito. When an infected mosquito bites a person, *Plasmodium* parasites move into the bloodstream, multiply in the liver, and then enter blood cells to continue multiplying. When an uninfected mosquito bites an infected person, the cycle starts over (Figure 18-5). Malaria can also be transmitted when a person receives the blood of an infected donor or when a drug user shares a needle with an infected user.

Since the 1950s the spread of malaria has been reduced by draining swamplands and marshes and by spraying breeding areas with DDT, dieldrin, and other pesticides. Also drugs like chloro-

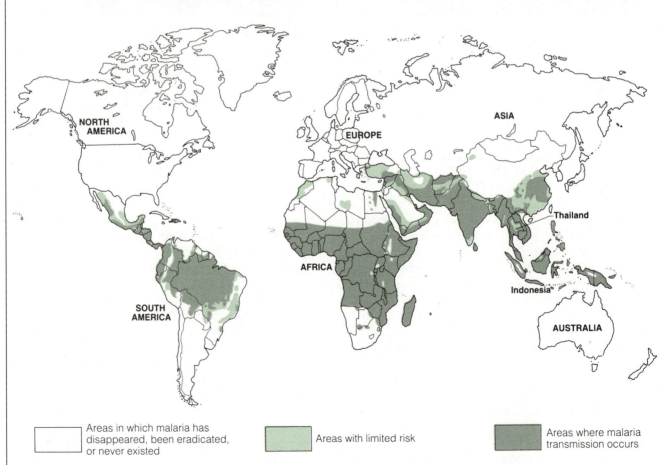

Areas in which malaria has disappeared, been eradicated, or never existed

Areas with limited risk

Areas where malaria transmission occurs

Figure 18-4 Malaria threatens half the world's population. (Data from the World Health Organization)

- greatly improved postnatal care (including the promotion of breast-feeding) to reduce infant mortality
- immunization against tetanus, measles, diphtheria, typhoid, and tuberculosis
- oral rehydration for diarrhea victims by feeding them a simple solution of water, salt, and sugar
- antibiotics for infections
- clean drinking water and sanitation facilities to the third of the world's population that lacks them

quine have been used to kill the *Plasmodium* parasites in the bloodstream.

This strategy worked for two decades but since 1970 malaria has made a dramatic comeback in many parts of the world. Because of repeated spraying, most of the malaria-carrying species of *Anopheles* mosquitoes have become genetically resistant to most of the insecticides used. Also the protozoa have become genetically resistant to chloroquine and other widely used antimalarial drugs. Other factors increasing the incidence of malaria are the spread of

irrigation ditches that provide new mosquito breeding grounds and reduced budgets for malaria control due to the belief that the disease was under control.

In 1989 U.S. Department of Agriculture researchers found that mice fed a diet high in fish oils (which contain omega-3 fatty acids) and then injected with malaria parasites were free of the parasites within four weeks. If this works in humans, this dietary approach could be combined with antimalarial drugs, such as the Chinese herbal remedy ginghaosu, now being evaluated for malaria

treatment by the World Health Organization.

Research is also being carried out to develop biological controls for *Anopheles* mosquitoes and to develop antimalarial vaccines. But such approaches are in the early stages of development and lack adequate funding. The World Health Organization estimates that only 3% of the money spent worldwide each year on biomedical research is devoted to malaria and other tropical diseases, even though more people suffer and die worldwide from these diseases than from all others combined.

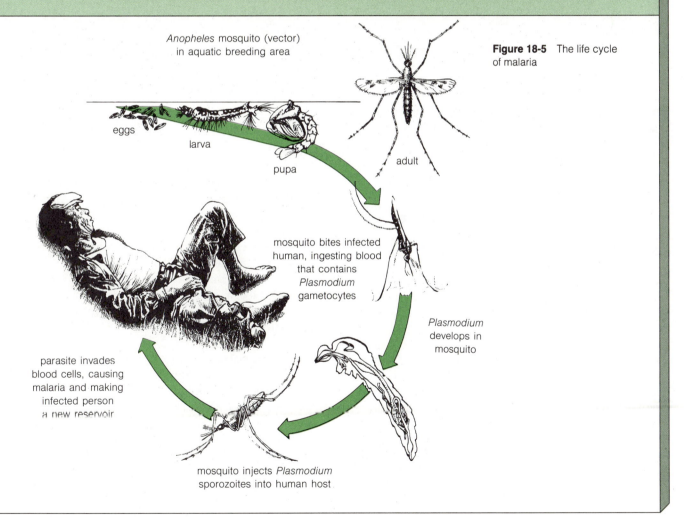

Anopheles mosquito (vector) in aquatic breeding area

Figure 18-5   The life cycle of malaria

eggs

larva

pupa

adult

mosquito bites infected human, ingesting blood that contains *Plasmodium* gametocytes

Plasmodium develops in mosquito

parasite invades blood cells, causing malaria and making infected person a new reservoir

mosquito injects *Plasmodium* sporozoites into human host

Extending such primary health care to all the world's people would cost an additional $10 billion a year, one twenty-fifth as much as the world spends each year on cigarettes. In addition, relatively small expenditures on research and control of tropical diseases by MDCs and governments of LDCs would greatly reduce death rates and suffering from tropical diseases.

Disease in MDCs In most MDCs, safe water supplies, public sanitation, adequate nutrition, and immunization have nearly stamped out many transmissible diseases. In 1900 pneumonia, influenza, tuberculosis, and diarrhea and other intestinal infections were the leading causes of death in MDCs. By contrast, the four leading causes of death in MDCs today are heart disease and stroke, cancer, respiratory infections, and accidents, especially automobile accidents (see Pro/Con on p. 201).

These deaths are largely a result of environmental and lifestyle factors rather than infectious agents invading the body. Except for auto accidents, these deaths result from chronic diseases that take a long time to develop, have multiple causes, and are largely related to the area in which people live (urban or rural), their work environment, their diet, whether they smoke, how much exercise they get, and the amount of alcohol they consume.

Changing these harmful lifestyle factors could prevent 40% to 70% of all premature deaths, a third of all cases of acute disability, and two-thirds of all cases of chronic disability. Another area of growing concern in both MDCs and LDCs is the spread of AIDS and other sexually transmitted diseases, mostly because of ignorance, drug abuse, and failure to practice safe sex (see Enrichment Study on p. 480).

In 1988 about 11% of the GNP of the United States was spent on health care—an average of $2,000 per American. But more than 95% of this money was used to treat rather than prevent disease. Clearly, a much better balance between treatment and prevention is needed.

18-3 RISK ASSESSMENT AND RISK MANAGEMENT

Determining Risks **Risk** is the probability that something undesirable will happen from deliberate or accidental exposure to a hazard. Most expressions of risk describe both the possibility of harm and its severity. Everything we do involves some degree of risk from one or more types of hazards.

Risk assessment is the process of gathering data and making assumptions to estimate the short- and long-term harmful effects on human health or the environment from exposure to environmental hazards associated with the use of a particular technology or product. Professional risk analysts use scientific experiments, models, and statistical methods to evaluate risks. But most ordinary citizens rely on intuitive risk judgments based on past experience, media information, and perceptions about how risky something is.

Formal risk assessment is difficult, imprecise, and controversial. It involves determining the types of hazards involved, estimating the number of people likely to be exposed to the hazard and the number likely to suffer serious consequences, and estimating the probability of each hazard occurring. Probabilities based on past experience are used to estimate risks from older technologies and products. For new technologies, much more uncertain statistical probabilities, based on models rather than actual experience, must be calculated.

The potential dangers from the use of food additives, drugs, pesticides, and other chemicals can be evaluated by using test animals, bacteria, computer-generated models, and epidemiology studies. As discussed earlier, estimating risks in these ways is filled with uncertainty but these methods are all we have.

The more complex a technological system, the more difficult it is to make realistic calculations of risks based on statistical probabilities of the failure of equipment and people. The total reliability of any technological system is the product of two factors:

$$\text{system reliability (\%)} = \text{technology reliability} \times \text{human reliability} \times 100$$

With careful design, quality control, maintenance, and monitoring, a high degree of technology reliability can usually be obtained in complex systems such as a nuclear power plant, space shuttle, or early warning system for nuclear attack. However, human reliability is almost always much lower and virtually impossible to predict; to be human is to err.

For example, suppose that the technology reliability of a system such as a nuclear power plant is 95% (0.95) and the human reliability is 65% (0.65). Then the overall system reliability is only 62% (0.95 x 0.65 = 0.62 x 100 = 62%). Even if we could increase the technology reliability to 100% (1.0), the overall system reliability would still be only 65% (0.65) (1.0 x 0.65 = 0.65 x 100 = 65%).

This crucial dependence of even the most carefully designed systems on unpredictable human reliability helps explain the occurrence of extremely unlikely events that risk analysts consider almost impossible. Examples are the Three Mile Island and Chernobyl nuclear power plant accidents (see Spotlight on p. 395), the tragic explosion of the space shuttle *Challenger,* and the far too frequent false alarms given by early warning defense systems on which the fate of the entire world depends.

Figure 18-6 Control room of a nuclear power plant. Watching these indicators is such a boring job that government investigators have found some operators asleep and in one case found no one in the control room. Most nuclear power plant accidents have resulted primarily from human errors.

Department of Energy

Poor management, training, and supervision increase the chances of human errors. Maintenance workers or people who monitor warning panels in complex systems such as the control rooms of nuclear power plants (Figure 18-6) become bored and inattentive because most of the time nothing goes wrong. They may fall asleep while on duty (as has happened at several U.S. nuclear plants); they may falsify maintenance records, because they believe that the system is safe without their help; they may be distracted by personal problems or illness; or they may be told by managers to take shortcuts to increase short-term profits or to make the managers look more efficient and productive.

One way to improve system reliability is to move more of the potentially fallible elements from the human side to the technical side, making the system more foolproof or "fail-safe." But chance events such as a lightning bolt can knock out automatic control systems. And no machine or computer program can replace all the skillful human actions and decisions involved in seeing that a complex system operates properly and safely. Also the parts in any automated control system are manufactured, assembled, tested, certified, and maintained by fallible human beings.

Risk-Benefit Analysis The key question is whether the estimated short- and long-term benefits of using a particular technology or product outweigh the estimated short- and long-term risks compared to other alternatives. One method for making such evaluations is **risk-benefit analysis**. It involves estimating the short- and long-term societal benefits and risks involved and then dividing the benefits by the risks to find a **desirability quotient**:

$$\text{desirability quotient} = \frac{\text{societal benefits}}{\text{societal risks}}$$

Assuming that accurate calculations of benefits and risks can be made (a big assumption), here are several possibilities:

1. large desirability quotient $= \dfrac{\text{large societal benefits}}{\text{small societal risks}}$

Example: *X rays.* Use of ionizing radiation in the form of X rays to detect bone fractures and other medical problems has a large desirability quotient. But this is true only if X rays are not overused to protect doctors from liability suits, the dose is no larger than needed, and less harmful alternatives are not available. Other examples in this category are mining, most dams, and airplane travel.

2. very small desirability quotient $= \dfrac{\text{very small societal benefits}}{\text{very large societal risks}}$

Example: *Nuclear war.* Global nuclear war has no societal benefits (except the short-term profits made by companies making weapons and weapons defense systems) and involves totally unacceptable risks to the earth's present human population and to many future generations. Global nuclear war is the single greatest threat to the human species and the earth's life-support systems for all species (see p. 15).

We already live in a world with enough nuclear weapons to kill everyone on earth 67 times. By the end of this century 60 countries—one of every three in the world—will either have nuclear weapons or the knowledge and capability to build them. In addition to the health and ecological threats, the buildup of nuclear and conventional weapons drains funds and creativity that could be used to solve most of the world's population, food, health, resource, and environmental problems. For example, about 40% of the world's research and development expenditures and 60% of its physical scientists and engineers are devoted to developing weapons to improve our ability to kill one another.

3. small desirability = $\dfrac{\text{large societal benefits}}{\text{much larger societal risk}}$

Example: *Coal-burning power plants* (Section 16-3) *and nuclear power plants* (Section 16-5). Nuclear and coal-burning power plants provide society with electricity—a highly desirable benefit. But many analysts contend that the short- and long-term societal risks from widespread use of these technologies outweigh the benefits. They believe that many other more economically and environmentally acceptable alternatives exist for producing electricity with less severe societal risks (see Guest Essay on p. 408 and Table 17-2, p. 440).

4. uncertain desirability = $\dfrac{\text{large benefits}}{\text{large risks}}$

Example: *Genetic engineering* (see Pro/Con on p. 148). Some see this new biotechnology as a way to increase food supplies, degrade toxic wastes, eliminate certain genetic diseases and afflictions, and make enormous amounts of money. Others fear that its use, without strict controls, could cause many unpredictable, possibly harmful effects, as have many other forms of technology.

Limitations of Risk-Benefit Analysis   Calculation of desirability quotients is extremely difficult, filled with uncertainty, and controversial. For example, many people—especially those who make their living or earn profits from the technologies involved—would disagree with the general estimates of desirability quotients just given.

Some technologies benefit one group of people (population A) while imposing a risk on another (pop-

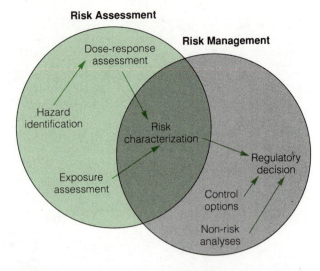

Figure 18-7   Summary of risk assessment and risk management (Environmental Protection Agency)

ulation B). Some people making the estimates emphasize short-term risks while others put more weight on long-term risks. Which type of risk should get the most emphasis and who decides this?

There is also the problem of who carries out a particular risk-benefit analysis. Should it be the corporation or government agency involved in developing or managing the technology, or some independent laboratory or panel of scientists? If it involves outside evaluation, who chooses the persons to do the study? Who pays the bill and thus has the potential to influence the outcome by refusing to give the lab, agency, or experts future business?

Once the study is done, who reviews the results—a government agency, independent scientists, the general public—and what influence will outside criticism have on the final decisions? Clearly, politics, economics, and value judgments that can be biased in either direction are involved at every step of the risk-benefit analysis process.

The difficulties in making risk-benefit assessments does not mean that they should not be made or that they are not useful. Despite the inevitable uncertainties involved, risk assessment and risk-benefit analysis are useful ways to organize available information, identify significant hazards, focus on areas that need more research, and stimulate people to make decisions about health goals and priorities.

But scientists, politicians, and the general public who must evaluate such analyses and make decisions based on them should be aware of their serious limitations. At best they can only be expressed as a range of probabilities and uncertainties based on different assumptions—not the precise bottom-line numbers that decision makers want. The present uncertainty in risk assessment is so great that we need to understand that regulatory decisions are based primarily on political analysis rather than scientific analysis.

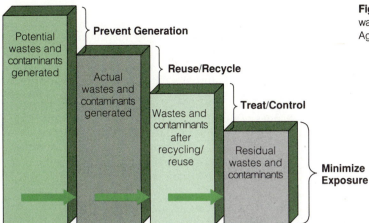

Table 18-3 Examples of Risk Reduction Strategies (Environmental Protection Agency)

Strategy	Individuals	Communities and Community Groups	Industry	Federal and State Governments
Prevent Pollutant Generation	Conserve energy	Reduce pesticide use	Substitute raw materials and redesign processes	Ban certain materials
Recycle and Reuse	Return wastes to recycling centers	Promote and operate recycling centers	Reclaim solvents	Purchase recycled products
Treat and Control	Inspect and remove asbestos	Treat water supplies	Treat hazardous waste	Mandate air and wastewater treatment standards
Reduce Residual Exposure	Avoid fishing and swimming in polluted waters	Operate clean sanitary landfills	Operate clean chemical landfills	Establish high-level radiation and toxic disposal facilities

Deciding How and What Risks to Manage **Risk management** includes the administrative, political, and economic actions taken to decide how, and if, a particular societal risk is to be reduced to a certain level and at what cost. It is integrated with risk assessment (Figure 18-7). Risk management involves trying to answer the following questions:

- Which of the vast number of risks facing society should be evaluated and managed with the limited funds available?

- In what sequence or priority should the risks be evaluated and managed?

- How reliable is the risk-benefit analysis carried out for each risk?

- How much risk is acceptable? How safe is safe enough?

- How much money will it take to reduce each risk to an acceptable level?

- How much will each risk be reduced if sufficient funds are not available, as is usually the case?

- How will the risk management plan be communicated to the public, monitored, and enforced?

Risk managers must make difficult decisions involving inadequate and uncertain scientific data and understanding, potentially grave consequences for human health and the environment, and large economic effects on industry and consumers. Thus, each step in this process involves value judgments and trade-offs to find some reasonable compromise between conflicting political and economic interests.

So far most risk reduction from pollutants has focused on output or end-of-pipe pollution control techniques. Very little emphasis has been placed on reducing risks by using input methods for waste and pollution prevention and reduction. Beginning with pollution prevention instead of end-of-pipe pollution control is the key to risk reduction (Figure 18-8). Table 18-3 shows how such strategies can be applied at various levels of society.

Risk-benefit analysis attempts to find some acceptable level of pollution or other risk. By contrast, pollution prevention aims at reducing the risk to health to the lowest possible level. If a pollutant or risky technology is eliminated, the elaborate and uncertain system of risk assessment, standard setting, and the resulting controversy and legal challenges become irrelevant.

Risk Perception and Communication Risk management involves comparing the estimated risk and harm of a particular technology or product with the risk and harm perceived by the general public. This comparison helps the risk manager develop a management program that is politically acceptable to the public but that does not cause economic ruin of the businesses involved or require excessive expenditure of tax dollars.

The public generally perceives that a technology or product has a greater risk than the risk estimated by experts when it:

- is relatively new or complex (genetic engineering, nuclear power) rather than a familiar one (dams, automobiles, peanut butter)

- is mostly involuntary (nuclear power plants, nuclear weapons, industrial pollution, food additives) instead of voluntary (smoking, drinking alcohol, driving).

- is viewed as beneficial and necessary (cars) rather than unnecessary (CFCs in aerosol spray cans, food additives used to increase sales appeal)

- involves a large number of deaths and injuries from a single catastrophic accident (severe nuclear power plant accident, industrial explosion, or plane crash) rather than the same or larger number of deaths spread out over a longer time (coal-burning power plants, automobiles, malnutrition in LDCs). For example, U.S. citizens tolerate 45,000 deaths from automobile accidents each year—equivalent to a fully loaded passenger jet crashing with no survivors every day—because these deaths are distributed in space and time. If these deaths all occurred at one place and at the same time, like a plane crash, they would be considered a monstrous catastrophe and would not be tolerated. People also view flying in an airplane as more hazardous than riding in a car even though the number of deaths per passenger mile is ten times higher in a car than in a plane.

- involves unfair distribution of the risks. Citizens are outraged when government officials decide to put a hazardous waste dump or incinerator in or near their neighborhood under the guise of scientific analysis. This is usually viewed as politics not science.

- is poorly communicated. Does the decision making agency or company come across as trustwor-

thy and concerned or dishonest, unconcerned, or arrogant (as Exxon was viewed after the Valdez oil spill and the NRC and the nuclear industry have been viewed since the Three Mile Island accident)? Does it involve the community and tell it what's going on before the real decisions are made? Does it listen and respond to community concerns?

- does not take into account ethical and moral concerns. Spewing out numbers and talking about cost-risk trade-offs seems very callous when the risk involves moral issues such as the health of people and environmental quality.

To the risk experts, risk means expected annual mortality. But to the public it also involves the other factors just listed. And the public becomes outraged at risk experts and managers who fail to take these factors into account.

Some observers contend that when it comes to evaluation of large-scale, complex technologies, the public often is better at seeing the forest than are the risk-benefit specialists, who look primarily at the trees. This commonsense wisdom does not usually depend on understanding or even caring about the details of scientific risk-benefit analysis. Instead, it is based on the average person's understanding that science and technology have limits and that the people responsible for potentially hazardous technological systems and products are fallible just like everyone else.

18-4   RISK FACTORS AND CANCER

Cancer Incidence, Cure Rates, and Geographic Distribution Cancer will strike about 985,000 Americans this year and one of every three Americans now living will eventually have some type of cancer (see Spotlight on p. 464). Every 66 seconds an average of one person dies from cancer in the United States. But the good news is that almost half of all Americans who get cancer can now be cured—defined as being alive and cancer-free five or more years after treatment—compared to only a 38% cure rate in 1960. Survival rates for some types of cancers now range from 66% to 88%. This has happened mostly because of a combination of early detection and improved use of surgery, radiation, and drug treatments.

The frequency of various cancers varies in different parts of the world. Higher than normal incidences of certain types of cancer in various parts of the world indicate the effects of diet, industrialization, and other environmental factors such as soil and water contamination on cancer rates (Figure 18-9). Breast cancer occurs more frequently in the United States and Europe than it does in Japan. Cancer of the stomach, especially in males, is more common in Japan than in the United States. The incidence of lung cancer is much

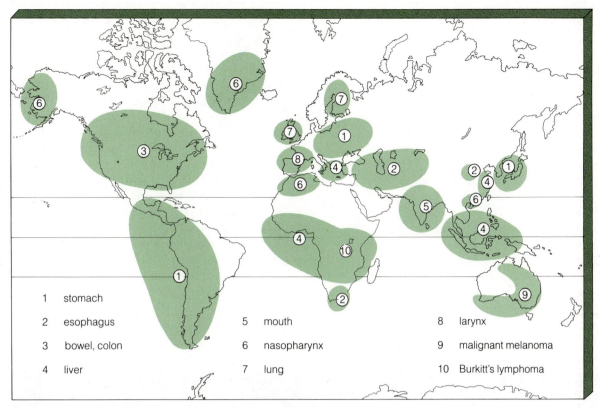

Figure 18-9 Areas around the world where incidence rates of certain types of cancer are much higher than in other countries. These differences are believed to be caused primarily by environmental factors such as diet, smoking, and pollution. (Data from the American Cancer Society)

1	stomach
2	esophagus
3	bowel, colon
4	liver
5	mouth
6	nasopharynx
7	lung
8	larynx
9	malignant melanoma
10	Burkitt's lymphoma

higher in the industrialized world than in the nonindustrialized world.

In the United States, cancer death rates for men are much higher in large cities and in the heavily urbanized and industrialized Northeast, Great Lakes region, Gulf Coast, and West Coast. U.S. states or territories with the highest number of cancer deaths per 100,000 population in 1988 were in order the District of Columbia, Delaware, Maryland, New Jersey, Ohio, and Rhode Island. Those with the lowest rates were Utah, Wyoming, Colorado, Puerto Rico, and Texas. Studies show that U.S. Mormons, who do not smoke or drink alcohol, have one-fourth the incidence of lung, esophagus, and larynx cancers compared to the average U.S. white population.

Cancer Risk Factors   Cancers are caused by poorly understood interactions between genes and environmental factors. According to the World Health Organization, environmental and lifestyle factors play a key role in causing or promoting 80% to 90% of cancers. Major sources of carcinogens are cigarette smoke (40%), dietary factors (25% to 30%), occupational exposure (10% to 15%), and environmental pollutants (5% to 10%) such as radioactive radon-222 gas (see Case Study on p. 489) and asbestos (see Pro/Con on p. 491). About 10% to 20% of cancers are believed to be caused by inherited genetic factors and some viruses.

Thus the risks of developing cancer can be greatly reduced by working and living in a less hazardous environment, not smoking, drinking in moderation (no more than two beers or drinks a day) or not at all, adhering to a healthful diet, and shielding oneself from the sun. According to experts, 60% of all cancers could be prevented by such lifestyle changes.

But many people don't make such changes. One problem is that usually 10 to 40 years elapse between the initial cause or causes of a cancer and the appearance of detectable symptoms. For instance, healthy high school and college students and young adults have difficulty accepting the fact that their smoking, drinking, eating, and other lifestyle habits today will be major influences on whether they will die prematurely from cancer before they reach age 50.

Cancer and Smoking   Smoking tobacco causes more death and suffering by far among adults than any other environmental factor. More than a billion of the world's people—one of every five—smoke 5 trillion cigarettes a year. Worldwide, cigarette use has doubled since 1960 and is projected to double again in 30 years. While cigarette smoking has dropped somewhat in the United States and many MDCs, it is rising rapidly in most LDCs.

Worldwide, at least 3 million smokers die prematurely each year from heart disease, lung cancer, bronchitis, emphysema, other cancers, and stroke—all related to smoking. In 1988 smoking killed about 390,000 Americans—an average of 1,068 a day. This annual death toll in the United States is equal to three fully loaded jumbo jets crashing every day with no survivors, almost eight times the number of people killed in traffic accidents each year, and seven times the number of American soldiers killed in the nine-year Vietnam War.

Nicotine is not classified as an illegal drug for political and economic reasons. Yet, it kills and harms more people each year in the United States than all illegal drugs and alcohol (the second most harmful drug), automobile accidents, suicide, and homicide combined (Figure 18-10). In 1988 Surgeon General C. Everett Koop said, "Our nation has mobilized enormous resources to wage a war on illicit drugs. We should also give priority to the one addiction—tobacco addiction—that is killing more than 390,000 Americans a year. . . . Smoking is the greatest preventable cause of death in the United States."

Numerous studies have shown that the nicotine in tobacco is a highly addictive drug that, like heroin and cocaine, can quickly and strongly hook its victims. A British government study showed that adolescents who smoke more than one cigarette have an 85% chance of becoming smokers. An inhaled hit of nicotine takes only 5 to 10 seconds to reach the brain—twice as fast as intravenous drugs and three times faster than alcohol. The typical smoker has a 200 to 400 hit a day legalized habit.

Smokers develop tolerance to nicotine and experience withdrawal symptoms when they try to stop. Some recovering heroin addicts report they had a much harder time quitting smoking than quitting heroin. National surveys reveal that 75% to 85% of the 51 million smokers in the United States would like to quit

---

SPOTLIGHT The Cancer You Are Most Likely to Get

Normally nonfatal skin cancer is by far the most common form of cancer; about one in seven Americans get it sooner or later. Cumulative exposure to ultraviolet ionizing radiation in sunlight over a number of years is the major cause of basal-cell and squamous cell skin cancers. These two types of cancer can be cured if detected early enough, although their removal may leave disfiguring scars. I have had three basal-cell cancers on my face because of too much sun exposure in my younger years.

Evidence suggests that just one severe, blistering burn as a child or teenager is enough to double the risk of contracting deadly malignant melanoma later in life, regardless of the skin type or the amount of cumulative exposure to the sun. This form of skin cancer of the cells that produce the skin's pigment spreads rapidly to other organs and can kill its victims. Each year it kills about 6,000 Americans and 100,000 people worldwide. The number of cases of this type of cancer is increasing at a rapid rate.

Virtually anyone can get skin cancer but those with very fair and freckled skin run the highest risk. White Americans who spend long hours in the sun or in tanning booths (which are even more hazardous than direct exposure to the sun) greatly increase their chances of developing skin cancer and also tend to have wrinkled, dry skin by age 40. Blacks with darker skin are almost immune to sunburn but do get skin cancer, although at a rate ten times lower than whites. A dark suntan also doesn't prevent skin cancer. Outdoor workers are particularly susceptible to cancer of the exposed skin on the face, hands, and arms.

The safest thing to do is to stay out of the sun and tanning booths. Avoid direct exposure between 10 AM and 3 PM when the sun's ultraviolet rays are strongest. Sitting under an umbrella does not protect against the sun because of sunlight reflected from sand, cement, or water. Clouds are deceptive because they admit as much as 80% of the sun's harmful ultraviolet radiation.

When you are in the sun wear tightly woven protective clothing and a wide-brimmed hat and apply a sunscreen with a protection factor of 15 or more (25 if you have light skin) to all exposed skin. Reapply sunscreen after swimming or excessive sweating. Children using a sunscreen with a protection factor of 15 anytime they are in the sun from birth to age 18 decrease their chance of skin cancer by 80%.

Get to know your moles and examine your skin surface at least once a month for any changes. The warning signs are a change in the size, shape, or color of a mole or wart (the major sign of malignant melanoma, which needs to be treated quickly), sudden appearance of dark spots on the skin, or a sore that keeps oozing, bleeding, and crusting over but does not heal. You should also be on the watch for precancerous growths that appear as reddish brown spots with a scaly crust. If any of these signs are observed, you should immediately consult a doctor. What are you doing to protect your skin?

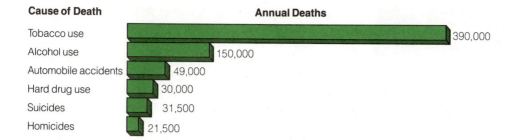

Cause of Death	Annual Deaths
Tobacco use	390,000
Alcohol use	150,000
Automobile accidents	49,000
Hard drug use	30,000
Suicides	31,500
Homicides	21,500

Figure 18-10 Annual deaths in the United States related to tobacco use and other causes in 1988. (Data from National Center for Health Statistics)

but so far have been unable to do so. About 70% of smokers who quit start smoking again within six months, about the same relapse rate as recovering alcoholics and heroin addicts.

Smokers are not the only ones harmed by smoke from cigarettes and other tobacco products. About 86% of nonsmoking Americans involuntarily inhale smoke from other people's cigarettes, amounting to an average of about one cigarette a day. Several studies indicate that passive smoke causes 3,000 to 15,000 premature deaths of Americans a year. According to a 1986 study by the National Research Council, nonsmoking spouses of smokers have a 30% greater chance of getting lung cancer than spouses of nonsmokers. Women exposed to passive smoke three hours or more a day appear to have a three-fold increased risk for cervical cancer.

There is some good news, however. In the United States the percentage of the population that smokes dropped from 42% in 1966 to 20% in 1989. But this still means that one of every four Americans smokes. After about one year, an ex-smoker's chances of developing heart disease are about the same as a nonsmoker's assuming all other heart disease risk factors are equal. Studies also show that 10 to 15 years after smokers quit, they have about the same risk of dying from lung cancer as those who never smoked.

Tobacco's harmful costs to American society exceed its economic benefits to tobacco farmers and employees and stockholders of tobacco companies by more than two to one. In the United States, smoking costs society at least $49 billion (some estimate $95 billion) a year in premature death, disability, medical treatment, increased insurance costs, and lost productivity because of illness. Thus, smoking costs every American man, woman, and child an average of at least $205 a year. These external costs amount to an average cost to society of at least $2.10 per pack of cigarettes sold.

The American Medical Association and numerous health experts have called for:

- a total ban on cigarette advertising in the United States

- prohibition of the sale of cigarettes and other tobacco products to anyone under 21 with strict penalties for violations

- a ban on all cigarette vending machines

- classifying nicotine as a drug and placing the manufacture, distribution, sale, and promotion of tobacco products under the jurisdiction of the Food and Drug Administration

- eliminating all federal subsidies to U.S. tobacco farmers and tobacco companies.

- tax cigarettes at about $2.10 a pack to discourage smoking and to make smokers pay for the harmful effects of smoking now borne by society as a whole

- prohibit elected and appointed government officials from exerting any influence on other governments to enhance the export of tobacco from the United States to other countries

But enacting such restrictions is very difficult because of the immense political clout of the $35 billion a year U.S. tobacco industry. The American tobacco industry's response to the drop in the percentage of Americans who smoke is to sell more of its products overseas, primarily to LDCs—especially those in Asia. Because of increased tobacco use the World Health Organization predicts that LDCs will face a cancer epidemic by the year 2000.

In 1985 the tobacco industry persuaded the Reagan administration and influential members of Congress to threaten trade sanctions against foreign countries that did not lift tariffs and other restrictions on American tobacco products. Environmentalists point out that this means that the U.S. government is coercing other governments into allowing imports of a very hazardous, addictive drug from America while trying to halt the flow of illicit drugs from other countries into the United States.

Cancer and Diet Improper diet plays a key role in an estimated 25% to 30% of all cancer deaths. The major factors—especially in cancers of the breast, bowel (colon and rectum), liver, kidney, stomach, and prostate—seem to be fats, nitrosamines, and nitrites. The incidence of cancers of the colon, rectum, and female breast is about five times higher in Americans than in Japanese, who have low-fat diets. Third-generation offspring of Japanese immigrants, however, have about the same incidence of these types of cancer as other

The National Academy of Sciences and the American Heart Association advise that the risk of certain types of cancer—lung, stomach, colon, breast, and esophagus—heart disease, and diabetes can be significantly reduced by a daily diet that cuts down on certain foods and includes others. Such a diet limits

- total fat intake to 30% or less of total calories, with no more than 10% from saturated fats, and the remaining 20% divided about equally between polyunsaturated fats (like safflower oil and corn oil) and monosaturated fats (such as olive oil)
- protein (particularly meat protein) to 15% of total calories or about 171 grams (6 ounces) a day (about the amount in one hamburger)
- alcohol consumption to 15% of total caloric intake—no more than two drinks, glasses of wine, or beers a day
- cholesterol consumption to no more than 300 milligrams a day with the goal of keeping blood cholesterol levels below 200 milligrams per deciliter
- sodium intake to no more than 6 grams (about 1 teaspoon) a day to help lower blood pressure, which should not exceed 140 over 90

Also each of us should achieve and maintain the ideal body weight for our frame size and age by a combination of diet and exercise for 20 minutes a day at least three days a week.

Our diet should include fruits (especially vitamin C-rich oranges, grapefruit, and strawberries), minimally cooked orange, yellow, and green leafy vegetables such as spinach and carrots, and cabbage-family vegetables such as cauliflower, cabbage, kale, brussels sprouts, and broccoli. It should also incorporate starches and other complex carbohydrates, 10 to 15 grams of whole-grain fiber a day (from bran and fibers in vegetables and fruits), and a daily intake of selenium not exceeding 200 micrograms.

Preliminary evidence suggests that eating cold-water fish such as bluefish, salmon, herring, and sardines, which are rich in omega-3 fish oils, two or three times a week may help prevent heart disease and help prevent and arrest the growth of breast, colon, and prostate cancers. Salt-cured, nitrate-cured, and smoked ham, bacon, hot dogs, sausages, bologna, salami, corned beef, and fish should not be eaten or eaten only rarely.

Americans. A high-fat, high-protein diet may also be a factor in cancers of the breast, prostate, testis, ovary, pancreas, and kidney.

High levels of nitrate and nitrite food preservatives, found in smoked and cured meats and in some beers, may increase the risk of stomach cancer because the body converts them to carcinogenic compounds known as nitrosamines. These compounds have been implicated in the very high incidence of stomach cancer in Japan (Figure 18-9), where large amounts of dried, salted, pickled, and smoked fish are consumed. Despite the uncertainty in linking specific cancers to excessive consumption of specific foods, enough evidence exists to suggest a diet that should reduce cancer risks (see Spotlight at left).

Cancer and the Workplace Occupational exposure to carcinogens and radiation accounts for about 10% to 15% of cancer deaths. Roughly one-fourth of U.S. workers run the risk of some type of illness from routine exposure to one or more toxic compounds. The National Institute for Occupational Safety and Health estimates that as many as 100,000 deaths a year—with at least half from cancer—are linked to workplace diseases in the United States (Table 18-4).

Most work-related deaths could be prevented by stricter laws and enforcement of existing laws governing exposure of workers to ionizing radiation and dangerous chemicals. If enforced, the Occupational Safety and Health Act of 1970 and the Toxic Substances Control Act of 1975 could establish such controls. However, political pressure by industry officials has hindered effective enforcement of these laws.

Cancer and Pollution A fourth cause of cancer is pollution of the air we breathe (Chapter 19), the water we drink (Chapter 20), and the food we eat (Section 18-5 and Chapter 21). Pollution is estimated to contribute from 5% to 10% (some say 2%) of cancer deaths in the United States.

The risks are higher for residents of airtight, energy-efficient housing without air-to-air heat exchangers, because of abnormally high levels of indoor air pollution (Section 19-2); nonsmokers who work or live in an environment that exposes them to cigarette smoke; and residents of cities whose drinking water is contaminated with one or more toxic metals or carcinogenic organic compounds (Sections 18-6 and Chapter 20).

18-5 RISKS FROM FOOD ADDITIVES

Use and Types of Food Additives In LDCs, many rural and urban dwellers consume harvested crops directly. In MDCs and in a growing number of cities

Table 18-4 Cancer Risks in the Workplace in the United States*

Substance	Workers Exposed (millions)	Industries	Cancer Risks
Asbestos	2.5	Asbestos, textiles, insulation, mining, shipyards	Lung, larynx, mesothelioma, bowel, stomach
Vinyl chloride	3.5	Vinyl chloride and vinyl plastic	Liver, brain, breast
Benzene	3.0	Tire, shoe, paint, rubber cement, glue, varnish, chemicals	Leukemia (bone marrow)
Arsenic	1.5	Pesticides, copper, leather tanning, mining, vineyards, oil refining	Lung, skin, liver, testis
Chromium	1.5	Bleaching, glass, pottery, batteries, linoleum	Lung, nasal, larynx
Nickel	1.4	Nickel ore processors and refiners	Lung, nasal, larynx
Cadmium	1.4	Electrical, paint, metal alloys	Prostate, renal, respiratory
Carbon tetrachloride	1.4	Dry cleaning, machinists	Liver
Formaldehyde	1.3	Wood finishing, plastics, synthetic resins	Nasal

*Data from Occupational Safety and Health Administration and the AFL-CIO

in LDCs, harvested crops are used to produce processed foods for sale in grocery stores and restaurants. A large and increasing number of natural and synthetic chemicals, called **food additives**, are deliberately added to such processed foods to retard spoilage, to enhance flavor, color, and texture, and to provide missing amino acids and vitamins.

Some food additives are useful in extending shelf life and preventing food poisoning, but most are added to improve appearance and sales. For example, the following letter to the editor of the Albany *Times-Union* lists only a few of the 93 chemicals that may be added to the "enriched" bread you buy in a grocery store:

Give us this day our daily calcium propionate (spoilage retarder), sodium diacetate (mold inhibitor), monoglyceride (emulsifier), potassium bromate (maturing agent), calcium phosphate monobasic (dough conditioner), chloramine T (flour bleach), aluminum potassium sulfate acid (baking powder ingredient), sodium benzoate (preservative), butylated hydroxyanisole (antioxidant), monoisopropyl citrate (sequestrant); plus synthetic vitamins A and D.
Forgive us, O Lord, for calling this stuff BREAD.

*J. H. Read, Averill Park**

---

*Used by permission of the *Times-Union*, Albany, New York.

All food, of course, is a mixture of chemicals, but today at least 2,800 chemicals are deliberately added to processed foods in the United States. Each year, the average American consumes about 4 kilograms (9 pounds) of food additives, excluding sugar and salt, the two most widely used additives. Table 18-5 lists major classes of food additives. Many of the foods we buy also have trace amounts of various contaminants such as mouse hairs and droppings, hormones, and pesticides (Chapter 21).

Natural versus Synthetic Foods The presence of synthetic chemical additives does not necessarily mean that a food is harmful, and the fact that a food is completely natural is no guarantee that it is safe. A number of natural or totally unprocessed foods contain potentially harmful toxic substances.

Polar bear or halibut liver can cause vitamin A poisoning. Aflatoxins produced by fungi sometimes found on corn, wheat, and peanuts are extremely toxic to human beings and are not legal in U.S. foods at levels above 20 parts per billion. Clams, oysters, cockles, and mussels can concentrate natural and artificial toxins in their flesh.

In addition, natural foods can be contaminated with food-poisoning bacteria, such as *Salmonella* and the deadly *Clostridium botulinum* (Table 18-2) through improper processing, food storage, or personal hygiene. Each year, more than 20 million Americans get food poisoning and 9,000 of these people die. The

Table 18-5 Commonly Used Food Additives and Food Processes

Class	Function	Examples	Foods Typically Treated
Preservatives	To retard spoilage caused by bacterial action and molds (fungi)	Processes: drying, smoking, curing, canning (heating and sealing), freezing, pasteurization, refrigeration Chemicals: salt, sugar, sodium nitrate, sodium nitrite, calcium and sodium propionate, sorbic acid, potassium sorbate, benzoic acid, sodium benzoate, citric acid, sulfur dioxide	Bread, cheese, cake, jelly, chocolate syrup, fruit, vegetables, meat
Antioxidants (oxygen interceptors, or freshness stabilizers)	To retard spoilage of fats (excludes oxygen or slows down the chemical breakdown of fats)	Processes: sealing cans, wrapping, refrigeration Chemicals: lecithin, butylated hydroxyanisole (BHA), butylated hydroxytoluene (BHT), propyl gallate	Cooking oil, shortening, cereal, potato chips, crackers, salted nuts, soup, toaster tarts, artificial whipped topping, artificial orange juice, many other foods
Nutritional supplements	To increase nutritive value of natural food or to replace nutrients lost in food processing*	Vitamins, essential amino acids	Bread and flour (vitamins and amino acids), milk (vitamin D), rice (vitamin B_1), cornmeal, cereal
Flavoring agents	To add or enhance flavor	Over 1,700 substances, including saccharin, aspartame (NutraSweet®), monosodium glutamate (MSG), essential oils (such as cinnamon, banana, vanilla)	Ice cream, artificial fruit juice, toppings, soft drinks, candy, pickles, salad dressing, spicy meats, low-calorie foods and drinks, most processed heat-and-serve foods
Coloring agents	To add aesthetic or sales appeal, to hide colors that are unappealing or that show lack of freshness	Natural color dyes, synthetic coal tar dyes	Soft drinks, butter, cheese, ice cream, cereal, candy, cake mix, sausage, pudding, many other foods
Acidulants	To provide a tart taste or to mask undesirable aftertastes	Phosphoric acid, citric acid, fumaric acid	Cola and fruit soft drinks, desserts, fruit juice, cheese, salad dressing, gravy, soup
Alkalis	To reduce natural acidity	Sodium carbonate, sodium bicarbonate	Canned peas, wine, olives, coconut cream pie, chocolate eclairs
Emulsifiers	To disperse droplets of one liquid (such as oil) in another liquid (such as water)	Lecithin, propylene glycol, mono- and diglycerides, polysorbates	Ice cream, candy, margarine, icing, nondairy creamer, dessert topping, mayonnaise, salad dressing, shortening
Stabilizers and thickeners	To provide smooth texture and consistency; to prevent separation of components; to provide body	Vegetable gum (gum arabic), sodium carboxymethyl cellulose, seaweed extracts (agar and algin), dextrin, gelatin	Cheese spread, ice cream, sherbet, pie filling, salad dressing, icing, dietetic canned fruit, cake and dessert mixes, syrup, pressurized whipped cream, instant breakfasts, beer, soft drinks, diet drinks
Sequestrants (chelating agents, or metal scavengers)	To tie up traces of metal ions that speed up oxidation and other spoilage reactions in food; to prevent clouding in soft drinks; to add color, flavor, and texture	EDTA (ethylenediaminetetraacetic acid), citric acid, sodium phospate, chlorophyll	Soup, desserts, artificial fruit drinks, salad dressing, canned corn and shrimp, soft drinks, beer, cheese, frozen foods

*Adding small amounts of vitamins to breakfast cereals and other "fortified" and "enriched" foods in America is basically a gimmick used to raise the price. The manufacturer may put vitamins worth about 5¢ into 340 grams (12 ounces) of cereal and then add 45% to the retail price. Vitamin pills are normally a much cheaper source of vitamins than fortified foods. The best way to get vitamins, however, is through a balanced diet.

most frequent victims are elderly people with weakened immune systems and the very young. An increasing number of food-poisoning cases—more than a quarter million each year—are caused by germs that have become genetically resistant to antibiotics and are found in meat from cows, pigs, and chickens raised on antibiotic-laden feed.

Several environmentalists have suggested that people who read Orville Schell's book *Modern Meat* (see Further Readings) would probably become vegetarians. According to the General Accounting Office, 500 to 600 chemicals probably end up in the meat we eat, with 143 of them in amounts above the tolerance levels set by the government. Many of these are suspected of causing cancer. Yet the government monitors only 60 of these residues, and meat inspections have declined since 1981.

In 1989 Bush administration officials proposed ending all government inspections at the country's meat- and poultry-processing plants and relying mostly on the plants to keep their products clean and safe. But even with inspection the number of cases of salmonella caused by contaminated meat products doubled between 1981 and 1988. Instead of eliminating federal meat inspections, environmentalists believe they should be increased. Also fish, which is not federally inspected, should be inspected. Only about 2% of the food imported into the United States is tested by the Food and Drug Administration.

The good news is that some natural foods contain chemicals that help prevent some types of cancer. Ground beef contains some substances that inhibit the onset of skin cancer in mice. Fermented soy sauce and a wide variety of fruits and vegetables contain various unidentified anticarcinogens. Adding a gravy containing two well-known amino acids reduces the formation of carcinogens when meat or fish is fried or broiled.

Consumer Protection: FDA and the GRAS List In the United States, the safety of foods and drugs has been monitored by the Food and Drug Administration (FDA) since its establishment by the Pure Food and Drug Act of 1906. However, it was not until 1958 that federal laws required that the safety of any new food additive be established by the manufacturer and approved by the FDA before the additive was put into common use.

Today the manufacturer of a new additive must carry out extensive toxicity testing, costing up to a million dollars per item, and submit the results to the FDA. The FDA itself does no testing but merely evaluates data submitted by manufacturers. The FDA can also use the Delaney clause to ban any food additives shown to cause cancer in test animals (see Pro/Con below).

However, these federal laws did not apply to the hundreds of additives in use before 1958. Instead of making expensive, time-consuming tests, the FDA drew up a list of the food additives in use in 1958 and asked several hundred experts for their professional opinions on the safety of these substances. A few substances were deleted, and in 1959 a list of the remaining 415 substances was published as the "generally recognized as safe," or GRAS (pronounced "grass"), list. Since 1959, further testing has led the FDA to ban several substances on the original GRAS list.

PRO/CON **The Delaney Clause**

In 1958 an amendment, known as the Delaney clause, was added to U.S. food and drug laws. It was named after Representative James J. Delaney of New York, who fought to have this amendment passed despite great political pressure and heavy lobbying by the food industry.

This amendment prohibits the deliberate use of any food additive shown to cause cancer in test animals or people. The amendment is absolute, allowing for no extenuating circumstances or consideration of benefits versus risks. But, between 1958 and 1988, the FDA used this amendment to ban only nine chemicals.

Critics say the Delaney clause is too rigid and not needed because the FDA already has the power to ban any chemical it finds unsafe. In general, the food industry would like to see the amendment removed and some scientists and politicians want it modified to allow a consideration of benefits versus risks. Some critics also argue that cancer tests using high doses on test animals don't necessarily apply to human beings.

Supporters of the Delaney clause say that because people can't serve as guinea pigs, animal tests are the next best thing. Such tests don't prove that a chemical will cause cancer in human beings, but they do strongly suggest that a risk is present.

It is also argued that because the clause is absolute, it protects FDA officials from undue pressure from the food industry and politicians. If the FDA had to weigh benefits versus risks, political influence and lobbying by the food industry could delay banning a dangerous chemical while it underwent years of study.

Indeed, instead of revoking the Delaney clause, some scientists feel it should be strengthened and expanded to include mutagens and teratogens. Some argue that the clause gives the FDA too much discretion, including the right to reject the validity of well-conducted animal experiments that show carcinogenicity. These critics cite the FDA's infrequent use of the clause as evidence that the law is too weak. What do you think?

Table 18-6 Suggested Food Additives to Avoid

Additive	Major Uses	Possible Problems
Coal tar dyes (reds no. 3, 8, 9, 19, and 37, and orange no. 17)	Cherries in fruit cocktail, candy, beverages	May cause cancer; poorly tested
Citrus red no. 2	Skin of some Florida oranges	May cause cancer
Yellow no. 5	Gelatin dessert, candy, baked goods	May cause cancer; allergic reaction in some people; widely used
BHA	Antioxidant in chewing gum, potato chips, oils	May cause cancer; stored in body fat; can cause allergic reaction; safer alternatives available
BHT	Same as BHA	Appears safer than BHA, but needs better testing; safer alternatives available
Propyl gallate	Antioxidant in oils, meat products, potato stock, chicken soup base, chewing gum	Not adequately tested; use is frequently unnecessary
Quinine	Flavoring in tonic water, quinine water, bitter lemon	Poorly tested; may cause birth defects
Saccharin	Noncaloric sweetener in diet foods	Causes cancer in animals
Sodium nitrite, sodium nitrate	Preservative and flavoring agent in bacon, ham, hot dogs, luncheon meats, corned beef, smoked fish	Prevents formation of botulism bacteria but can lead to formation of cancer-causing nitrosamines in stomach
Sodium bisulfite, sulfur dioxide	Preservative and bleach in wine, beer, grape juice, dehydrated potatoes, imported shrimp, dried fruit, cake and cookie mixes, canned and frozen vegetables, breads, salad dressings, fruit juices, soft drinks, some baked goods and snacks, some drugs	Causes severe allergic reaction in about 500,000 Americans; implicated in 12 deaths between 1982 and 1986

*Data from Center for Science in the Public Interest.

What Can the Consumer Do? Avoiding all food additives is virtually impossible for a consumer in an affluent country. Indeed, many additives perform important functions, and there is no guarantee that natural foods will always be better and safer. But to minimize risk, individuals can follow a prudent diet (see Spotlight on p. 466) and avoid or use with caution those additives that have come under suspicion (Table 18-6). Many of these additives are used primarily to increase sales appeal.

18-6 RISKS FROM HAZARDOUS WASTE

What Is Hazardous Waste? According to the EPA, **hazardous waste** is any solid, liquid, or containerized gas that has one or more of the following properties:

- *Ignitability*. A waste that catches fire easily. Examples are waste oils, most used organic solvents, and PCBs from leaking or burning electrical transformers (see Case Study on p. 471).

- *Corrosivity*. A highly acidic (low pH) or highly basic (high pH) waste or one that corrodes steel easily.

- *Reactivity*. A highly unstable waste that can cause explosions or toxic fumes or vapors. Examples are liquid wastes from TNT operations and used cyanide solvents.

- *Toxicity*. A waste in which hazardous concentrations of toxic materials can leach out. Examples are toxic mercury and lead compounds (see Case Study on p. 472). In 1984 Congress ordered the EPA to also include carcinogenic and mutagenic materials in this category, but by mid-1989 the EPA had not done this.

Environmentalists consider the EPA definition of hazardous wastes much too narrow. It does not include radioactive wastes, hazardous materials discarded by households, mining wastes, oil and gas drilling wastes, cement kiln dust, municipal incinerator ash, and wastes from thousands of small businesses and factories that generate less than 100 kilograms (220 pounds) of hazardous waste per month.

Since 1966, scientists have found widespread contamination from a widely used group of 209 different toxic, oily, synthetic chlorinated hydrocarbon compounds known as **polychlorinated biphenyls (PCBs)**. The biggest use of these stable, nonflammable compounds is to dissipate heat produced in electrical capacitors and transformers.

Most PCBs are insoluble in water, soluble in fats, and resistant to biological and chemical degradation. This means that the concentration of PCBs can be greatly increased, or biologically ampli-

fied, in food chains and webs (Figure 18-11). Traces of PCBs have been found all over the world in soil, surface water and groundwater, fish, human breast milk, human fatty tissue, and even in Arctic snow.

The major source of PCBs in humans appears to be our food, beginning with milk from nursing mothers. The long-term health effects on people exposed to low levels of PCBs and their more toxic furan impurities are unknown. But in laboratory animals, high doses of PCBs produce liver and kidney damage, gastric disorders, birth

defects, bronchitis, miscarriages, skin lesions, and tumors. Some studies indicate that most of these harmful effects are caused by polychlorinated dibenzofurans (commonly called furans) found as contaminants in some PCBs.

In 1976 Congress banned further manufacture and use of PCBs in the United States, except those in existing electrical transformers, capacitors, and other electrical equipment. However, the EPA estimated that at least 68,200 metric tons (75,000 tons) of PCBs had entered the environment before the ban because of dumping at

(continued)

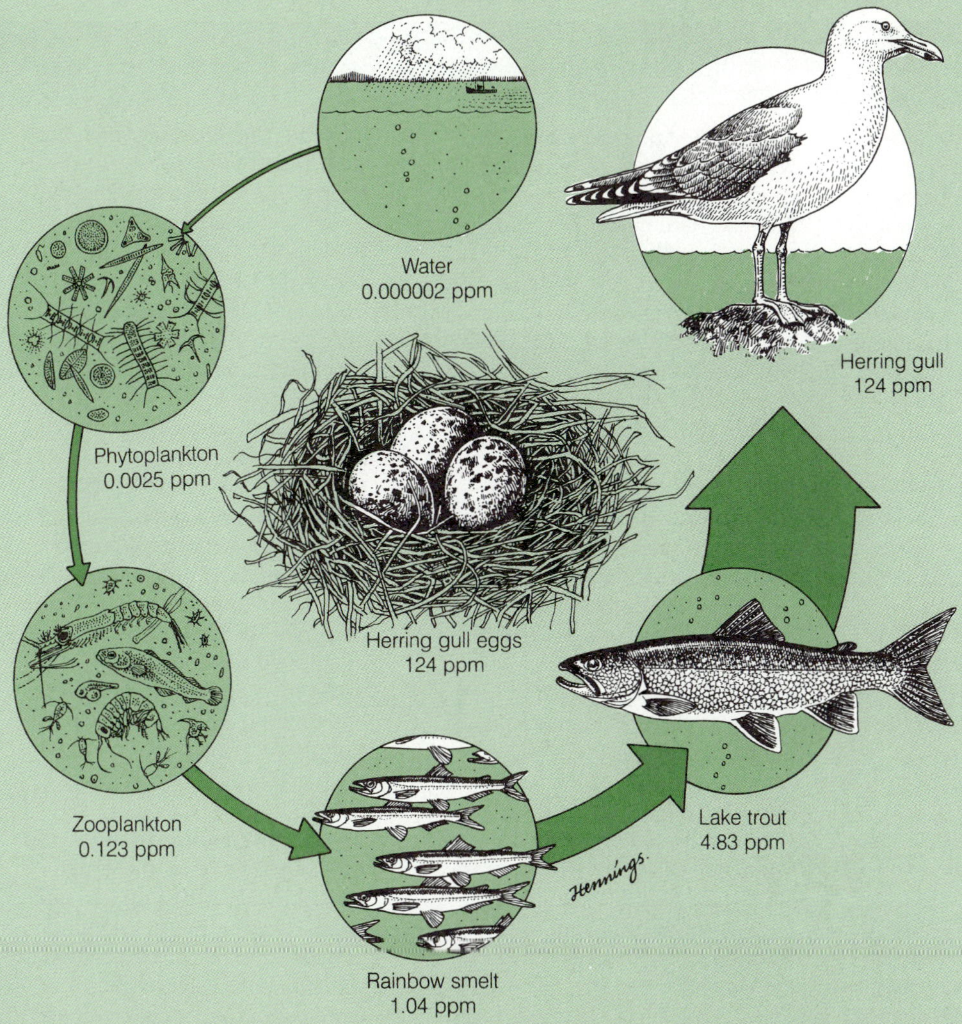

Figure 18-11 Biological amplification of PCBs in an aquatic food chain in the Great Lakes. Because PCBs are insoluble in water and soluble in fats, they are stored in the fatty tissues of animals. This means that their concentrations are greatly increased, or amplified, at each subsequent trophic level in a food chain or web.

landfills and fields, into sewers, and along roadsides.

Most of these discarded PCBs are believed now to be in soil and in bottom sediments of rivers, lakes, reservoirs, and oceans. In 1988 researchers reported that some newly evolved forms of anaerobic bacteria found in river sediments break down PCBs into harmless compounds. But since the bacteria work only in an oxygen-free environment, they won't degrade PCBs in soil.

Since 1981, fires involving PCB-filled electrical transformers have exposed people in office buildings, apartment complexes, shopping malls, and train and subway stations to much more severe risks. During a transformer fire highly toxic furans and dioxins (see Case Study on p. 454) produced by the combustion of PCBs can spread throughout a building. They are also flushed into storm sewers and surface waters by water used to extinguish the fire.

The EPA has ordered that all PCBs must be removed from electrical transformers in U.S. apartment and office buildings, hospitals, and shopping malls by 1990. Further installation of PCB-filled transformers in or near commercial buildings is banned. This will still leave about 140,000 sealed electrical transformers and capacitors (owned mostly by utility companies).

PCBs can be 99.9% detoxified by high-temperature burning in specially designed toxic-waste incinerators. But this is very expensive and cannot be used for large quantities of contaminated soil or pure PCB oils.

CASE STUDY Lead in the Environment

Levels of lead in the environment have been increasing throughout the world since humans began mining and using lead, about 800 B.C. As a result the typical body burden of lead today is 500 to 1,000 times higher than it was in people living before the industrial age. An exception is lead poisoning linked to lead pipes and beverage vessels used by upper-class Romans.

We take in small amounts of lead in the air we breath, the food we eat, and the water we drink. Once lead enters the blood, about 10% is excreted and the rest is stored in the bones. Children up to about age 9 are particularly vulnerable to lead poisoning because their bodies absorb lead very readily. Pregnant women can also transfer dangerous levels of lead to unborn children.

A 1986 EPA study revealed that 77% of the U.S. population—including 88% of all children under 5—have unsafe lead levels in their blood. About 200 American children die each year from lead poisoning, especially from ingesting large quantities of leaded paint chips.

Another 12,000 to 16,000 children each year are treated for lead poisoning. About 30% of those who survive suffer from palsy, partial paralysis, blindness, and mental retardation. According to the National Institute of Health Sciences, up to 45% of U.S. children may be exposed to lead at levels that can damage the brain and central nervous system, lower IQ scores, lower the ability to absorb iron and calcium and metabolize vitamin D, and cause partial hearing loss, hyperactivity, and behavior problems.

Studies have also indicated that low levels of lead in the blood of children and adults can lead to high blood pressure and irritability. An EPA researcher estimates that 60,000 to 70,000 heart attacks per decade might be prevented if the mean blood lead level of Americans were reduced by a third. Lead-industry officials, however, call these nonscientific accusations by extremist environmentalists and pseudoscientists.

In order of estimated total exposure the major sources of lead in the United States are:

- paint in houses built before 1976. Until 1977 lead oxide and other lead compounds were added to interior and exterior paint to make it shinier and last longer, and to fix colors. In the United States it is estimated that 40 million houses built before 1950 and 20% of those built between 1960 and 1975 have lead paint. These houses are a major source of lead poisoning for children between ages 1 and 3, who crawl around the floor and inhale lead dust from cracking and peeling paint or ingest it by sucking their thumbs, putting toys in their mouth, or gnawing on window sills or furniture. Dust in yards and streets around such houses where children play also contains particles of chipped lead paint. People living in houses or apartments built before 1977 should chip off samples of paint and have them analyzed for lead by the local health department.

- drinking water. According to the EPA, nearly one in five Americans (including 10.4 million children) drinks tap water containing excess levels of lead, when acidic or soft water leaches lead from copper pipes that contain lead solder and lead connectors found in most plumbing (from the Latin *plumbum*, for lead) sys-
(continued)

There was little concern over hazardous waste until 1977. Then it was discovered that hazardous chemicals leaking from an abandoned waste dump had contaminated a suburban development known as Love Canal, located in Niagara Falls, New York (see Case Study on p. 474). The publicity surrounding this event made the public and elected officials aware of dangers from the large amounts of hazardous waste we produce each day, as well as from wastes buried in the soil in the past.

Hazardous Waste Production: Present and Past   The total quantity of hazardous wastes produced throughout the world or even in one country is nearly impossible to estimate accurately. For the United States, estimates range from 240 million metric tons (264 million tons) by the EPA to 509 million metric tons (400 million tons) by the Office of Technology Assessment. With either of the estimates, it is clear that the United States leads the world in hazardous waste production.

About 95% of this waste is generated and either

CASE STUDY Lead in the Environment (continued)

tems and drinking water fountains. Since 1987, the use of pipes and solder containing lead in public water systems has been banned, but a large percentage of existing houses, buildings, and drinking fountains have pipes and solder joints containing lead. Homeowners with copper pipes or joints should have the local water department or private laboratory (cost about $20 to $30) test their tap water for lead. Also have the local water department test the pH and hardness of your water. If the ph is less than 7 or the hardness is less than 60, your water is likely to leach out lead. Running tap water and drinking fountains two to three minutes before drinking may help, but this wastes water. Never use water from the hot tap for drinking or cooking and especially for making baby formula because heat greatly increases the rate of leaching of lead. Most home water filtration systems don't remove lead or other toxic metals. An alternative is to drink bottled spring water but be sure that it is regularly tested for lead content by the bottler. In building or remodeling, homeowners should use plastic or galvanized pipes or ask plumbers to use lead-free solder (which costs only a few dollars more) on copper pipes. Before buying a house, have its water (that has been standing in pipes for at least 12 hours) and its paint tested for lead.

■ lead particles in air, dust, and soil in areas with heavy traffic

and where lead has been and continues to be released into the atmosphere by incinerators and various industrial plants. Tiny particles of lead compounds are emitted into the atmosphere from the burning of leaded gasoline (which contains tetraethyl lead as an antiknock additive) and from lead smelters, foundries, steel mills, incinerators, and waste recovery plants. Even though emissions have been reduced by air pollution control laws, there is a toxic legacy of nondegradable lead compounds from the past, especially in some low-income areas. Since 1975 atmospheric emissions of lead have dropped sharply due to the gradual reduction by 91% of the lead allowed in gasoline in the United States. Since 1972 environmentalists and many health officials have been pushing for a complete ban of lead in gasoline. But by late 1989 this had not been done, primarily because of vigorous lobbying and legal challenges by the gasoline additives industry and because some older vehicles and farm machinery cannot run on unleaded fuel without engine modifications.

■ lead solder used to seal the seams on food cans, especially in acidic foods such as tomatoes and citric juices. This type of solder has been sharply reduced in U.S. food cans but may be found in cans of imported foods. Health officials estimate that solder in cans still accounts

for 24% of low-level lead poisoning.

■ imported cups, plates, pitchers, and other types of ceramic ware used to cook, store, or serve food, especially acidic foods and hot liquids and foods. Lead can be leached or chipped from the glaze of imported ceramic ware (that makes up 60% of U.S. ceramic dinnerware sales) and older items made in the United States. Many of these items weren't fired at the high temperatures now legally required in the United States to prevent chipping, flaking, and leaching of lead particles into food. Before using such items, consumers should test them for lead content.*

■ vegetables and fruits grown on soil contaminated for many years by lead, especially cropland or home gardens near highways, incinerators, and smelters. Careful washing should remove at least half of this lead.

■ burning certain types of paper in woodstoves and fireplaces. Homeowners should not burn comic strips, Christmas wrapping paper, or painted wood, which can be a source of lead contamination indoors and outdoors.

---

*A simple home test for lead content of up to 100 items of dishware is available for $24.50 from Frandon Enterprises, 511 N. 48th St., Seattle, Washington 98103.

stored or treated on site by large companies—chemical producers, petroleum refineries, and manufacturers. Much of this waste is injected into deep wells theoretically drilled beneath aquifers sometimes tapped for drinking water and irrigation. The remaining 4% is handled by commercial facilities that take care of hazardous waste generated by others.

A serious problem facing the United States and most industrialized countries is what to do with thousands of dumps where large quantities of hazardous

In 1977, residents of a suburb of Niagara Falls, New York, discovered that "out of sight, out of mind" often does not apply. Hazardous industrial waste buried decades earlier bubbled to the surface, found its way into groundwater, and ended up in backyards and basements.

Between 1942 and 1953, Hooker Chemicals and Plastics Corporation dumped almost 20,000 metric tons (22,000 tons) of highly toxic and cancer-causing chemical wastes (mostly in steel drums) into an old canal excavation, known as the Love Canal. In 1953 Hooker Chemicals covered the dump site with clay and topsoil and sold the site to the Niagara Falls school board for one dollar. The deed specified that the company would have no future liability for any injury or property damage caused by the dump's contents.

An elementary school, playing fields, and a housing project, eventually containing 949 homes, were built in the Love Canal area. Residents began complaining to city officials in 1976 about chemical smells and chemical burns received by children playing in the canal, but these complaints were ignored. In 1977 chemicals began leaking from the badly corroded steel drums into storm sewers, gardens, and basements of homes next to the canal.

Informal health surveys conducted by alarmed residents revealed an unusually high incidence of birth defects, miscarriages, assorted cancers, and nerve, respiratory, and kidney disorders among people who lived near the canal. Complaints to local officials had little effect.

Continued pressure from residents and unfavorable publicity eventually led state officials to conduct a preliminary health survey and tests. They found that pregnant women in one area near the canal had a miscarriage rate four times higher than normal. They also found that the air, water, and soil of the canal area and the basements of nearby houses were contaminated with a number of toxic and carcinogenic chemicals.

In 1978 the state closed the school, permanently relocated the 238 families whose homes were closest to the dump, and fenced off the area around the canal. On May 21, 1980, after protests from the outraged 711 families still living fairly close to the landfill, President Jimmy Carter declared Love Canal a federal disaster area and had these families relocated. Federal and New York state funds were then used to buy the homes of those who wanted to move permanently.

Since that time the school and the homes within a block and a half of the canal have been torn down and the state has purchased 570 of the remaining homes. About 45 families have remained in the desolate neighborhood, unwilling or unable to sell their houses and move.

The dump site has been covered with a clay cap and surrounded by a drain system that pumps leaking wastes to a new treatment plant. Local officials have pressed the federal government for a clean bill of health so that the state can resell the homes it bought from fleeing home owners and begin rehabilitating the neighborhood.

But cleanup proved to be difficult and expensive, with total costs of more than $140 million. Two-thirds of the area is supposed to be safe enough to live in again by 1990. The rest of the neighborhood near the old dump site may never be safe.

As yet no conclusive study has been made to determine the long-term effects on former Love Canal residents of exposure to hazardous chemicals. All studies made so far have been criticized on scientific grounds. In 1988 an informal survey was made of families that once lived in a group of ten houses next to the canal. All but one had some cancer cases; there were also two suicides and three cases of birth defects among grandchildren.

The psychological damage to evacuated families is enormous. For the rest of their lives they will wonder whether a disorder will strike and will worry about the possible effects of the chemicals on their children and grandchildren.

In 1985 former Love Canal residents received payments from a 1983 out-of-court settlement from Occidental Chemical Corporation (which bought Hooker Chemicals in 1968), the city of Niagara Falls, and the Niagara Falls school board. The payments ranged from $2,000 to $400,000 for claims of injuries ranging from persistent rashes and migraine headaches to cancers and severe mental retardation.

In 1979 the EPA filed a suit against Occidental Chemical to recover cleanup costs. In 1988 a U.S. district court ruled that Occidental must pay the cleanup costs, but the company is expected to appeal the case.

The Love Canal incident is a vivid reminder that we can never really throw anything away, that wastes don't stay put, and that preventing pollution is much safer and cheaper than cleaning it up.

wastes were disposed of in an unregulated manner in the past. Even with adequate funding, effective cleanup is difficult because officials don't know what chemicals have been dumped and where all sites are located. West Germany alone is estimated to have 35,000 problem sites.

Control and Management of Hazardous Waste

There are three basic ways of dealing with hazardous waste, as outlined by the National Academy of Sciences: **(1)** waste prevention by waste reduction, recycling, and reuse, **(2)** conversion to less hazardous or nonhazardous material, and **(3)** perpetual storage (Figure 18-12). The first and most desirable method is an input, or waste prevention, approach. Its goal is to reduce the amount of waste produced by modifying industrial or other processes and by reusing or recycling the hazardous wastes that are produced. So far no country has implemented an effective program for achieving this goal.

The EPA estimates that at least 20% of the hazardous materials currently generated in the United States could be recycled, reused, or exchanged so that one industry's waste becomes another's raw material. Presently, however, only about 5% of such materials are managed in this manner. Yet, the EPA's 1988 budget request for waste reduction, recycling, and reuse was less than 1% of its total budget. Table 18-7 compares the preferred priorities for management of hazardous waste with the actual U.S. government priorities based upon budget allocations.

Firms trying the waste prevention approach have found that waste reduction and pollution prevention save them money. Since 1975 the Minnesota Mining and Manufacturing Company (3M) has had a program that by 1987 had cut its waste production in half and saved over $300 million.

However, most firms have little incentive to reduce their output of waste because waste management makes up only 0.1% of the total value of the products they ship. Placing a tax of only about $1 on each ton of hazardous waste generated would provide enough money to support a strong program for reducing, recycling, and reusing hazardous waste.

North Carolina has taken the lead in encouraging waste reduction. The state's $600,000-a-year Pollution

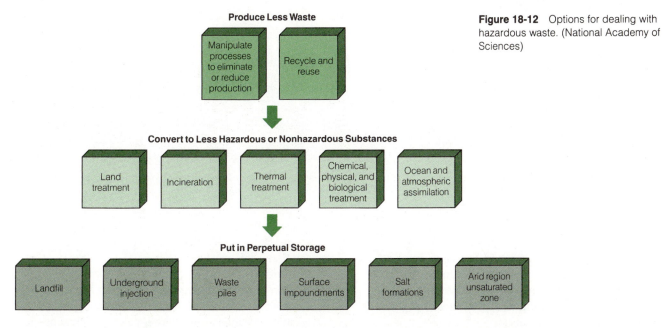

Figure 18-12 Options for dealing with hazardous waste. (National Academy of Sciences)

Table 18-7 Preferred Priorities for Management of Hazardous Wastes and Actual U.S. Government Policies Based on Budget Allocations

Preferred Priorities	Actual Priorities
1. Waste prevention	1. Burial
2. Waste reduction	2. Incineration without energy utilization
3. Waste reuse within production process	3. Incineration with energy utilization
4. Waste reuse off-site	4. Waste reuse off-site
5. Incineration with use of energy derived from waste	5. Waste reuse on-site
6. Burial	6. Waste reduction
	7. Waste prevention

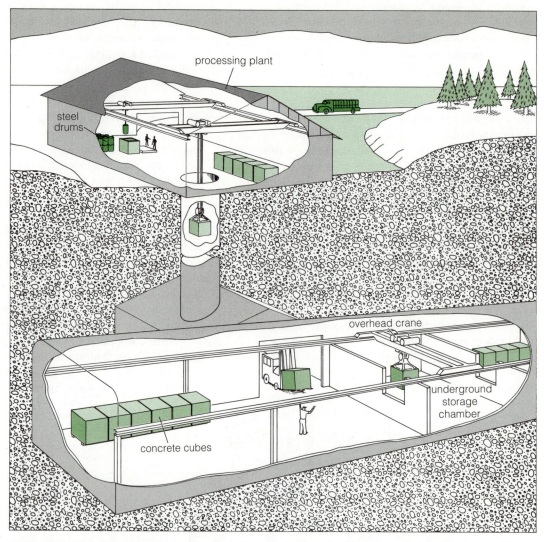

Figure 18-13 Swedish method for handling hazardous waste. Hazardous materials are placed in drums, which are stored in concrete cubes. The cubes are then placed in an underground vault.

Prevention Pays Program offers technical assistance, a database of information, and matching grants to small and large companies and communities wanting to implement waste reduction and recycling projects. California, New York, Pennsylvania, Illinois, Wisconsin, Minnesota, and Tennessee also have waste reduction programs. Developing such programs in all states would be an important step.

The second phase of a hazardous waste management program is to convert any waste remaining after waste reduction, recycling, and reuse to less hazardous or nonhazardous materials (Figure 18-12). Conversion methods include spreading degradable wastes on the land, burning them on land or at sea in specially designed incinerators, thermally decomposing them, or treating them chemically or physically.

The Netherlands incinerates about half its hazardous waste. The EPA estimates that about 60% of all U.S. hazardous waste could be incinerated. With proper air pollution controls, incineration is potentially the safest method of disposal for most types of hazardous waste. But it is also the most expensive method. The ash that is left must be disposed of and often contains toxic metals, and the gaseous and particulate combustion products emitted can be health hazards if not controlled. Another problem is that not all hazardous wastes are combustible. Moreover, most citizens vigorously oppose locating a hazardous waste incinerator anywhere near their community—summarized by the "not-in-my-backyard" (NIMBY) slogan.

Some countries have been incinerating some of their hazardous wastes at sea in incinerator ships. But because of lack of controls and fear of contaminating ocean ecosystems, most MDCs (including the United States) have agreed to end at-sea incineration of hazardous wastes by 1994.

Denmark, which relies almost exclusively on groundwater for drinking water, has the most comprehensive and effective program for detoxifying most of its hazardous waste. Each municipality has at least one facility that accepts paints, solvents, and other hazardous wastes from households. Toxic waste from industries is delivered to 21 transfer stations scattered throughout the country. All waste is then transferred to a large treatment facility in the town of Nyborg on the island of Fyn near the country's geographic center. There about 75% of the waste is detoxified and the rest is buried in a carefully designed and monitored landfill. The West German state of Bavaria has a similar system in operation and South Korea is developing a system based on the Danish approach.

The third phase of waste management involves placing any waste left after detoxification in containers and storing them in specially designed *secured landfills* or *underground vaults* (Figure 18–13). Ideally, such landfills should be located in a geologically and environmentally secure place that is carefully monitored for leaks. In 1983, however, the Office of Technology Assessment concluded that sooner or later any secured landfill will leak hazardous chemicals into nearby surface water and groundwater.

Citizens vigorously oppose the location of a hazardous waste landfill or incinerator in their communities. Often elected officials locate these facilities in areas where the poor and minority groups live. A study showed that three of the five largest hazardous waste landfills—accounting for 40% of the estimated U.S. landfill capacity—are in predominantly black or Hispanic communities.

There is also growing concern about accidents during some of the 500,000 shipments of hazardous wastes in the United States each year. Between 1980 and 1988 there were 11,048 toxic-chemical accidents, causing 309 deaths, 11,000 injuries, and evacuation of 500,000 people. Most communities do not have the equipment and trained personnel to deal adequately with most types of hazardous waste spills.

With disposal costs running from $60 to $200 per 55-gallon drum, toxic waste disposal and management firms can make huge profits. The industry is expanding by 20% to 30% a year. Law enforcement officials warn that large profits and generally lax law enforcement have led to increased involvement of organized crime in the hazardous waste disposal industry, especially in New York, New Jersey, Ohio, and Florida.

Another growing source of illegally dumped toxic wastes is illegal drug labs set up in rented houses, motel rooms, farm buildings, and remote forests. Also waste disposal firms in the United States and several other industrialized countries have shipped hazardous wastes to other countries, especially LDCs in Asia, Africa, and Latin America (see Spotlight on p. 478).

U.S. Hazardous Waste Legislation In 1976 Congress passed the Resource Conservation and Recovery Act, amending it in 1984. This law requires the EPA to identify hazardous wastes, set standards for their management, and provide guidelines and financial aid to establish state waste management programs. The law also requires all firms that store, treat, or dispose of more than 100 kilograms (220 pounds) of hazardous wastes per month to have a permit stating how such wastes are to be managed.

To reduce illegal dumping, hazardous waste producers granted disposal permits by the EPA must use a "cradle-to-grave" manifest system to keep track of waste transferred from point of origin to approved offsite disposal facilities. EPA administrators, however, point out that this requirement is impossible to enforce effectively. The EPA and state regulatory agencies do not have enough personnel to review the documentation of more than 750,000 hazardous waste generators and 15,000 haulers each year, let alone to verify them and prosecute offenders. If caught, however, violators are subject to large fines.

The 1980 Comprehensive Environmental Response, Compensation, and Liability Act, known as the Superfund program, and amendments in 1986 established a $10.1 billion fund, financed jointly by federal and state governments and taxes on chemical and petrochemical industries, for the cleanup of abandoned or inactive hazardous waste dump sites and leaking underground tanks.

The EPA is authorized to collect fines and sue the owners of abandoned sites and tanks (if they can be found and held responsible) to recover up to three times the cleanup costs.

In 1989, the EPA estimated that there are over 31,500 sites in the United States containing potentially hazardous wastes, with this number increasing at a rate of about 2,500 a year. The General Accounting Office estimates that there are 130,00 to 425,000 sites.

By July 1989 the EPA had placed 1,224 sites on a priority cleanup list because of their threat to nearby populations. The priority list is expected to grow by about 180 sites a year. The largest number of these sites are in New Jersey, followed by New York, Pennsylvania, Michigan, and California. Many are located over major aquifers and pose a serious threat to groundwater. Also about 56% of U.S. black, Hispanic, and American Indian minorities live in communities with toxic waste sites on the priority list.

By mid-1989 the EPA had spent $4.5 billion to start cleanups at 257 priority sites. But only 50 sites had been cleaned up and only 27 declared clean enough to be removed from the list. EPA officials estimate that the agency can complete only about 25 to 30 cleanups a year. At that rate it would take 41 to 50 years to clean up the 1,224 priority sites listed in 1989. In 1985 the Office of Technology Assessment estimated that the final list may include at least 10,000 sites, with cleanup costs amounting to as much as $300 billion over the next 50 years. Cleanup funds provided by taxes on industries that generate waste has amounted to about $1 billion a year—far short of the need.

In 1984 Congress amended the 1976 Resource Conservation and Recovery Act to make it national policy to minimize or eliminate land disposal of 450 regulated hazardous wastes by 1990 unless the EPA has determined that it is an acceptable or the only feasible approach for a particular hazardous material. Even then, each chemical is to be treated to the fullest extent possible to reduce its toxicity before land disposal of any type is allowed. If strictly enforced, this policy represents a much more ecologically sound approach to dealing with hazardous waste.

What Can You Do? You can help reduce inputs of hazardous waste into the environment. Use pesticides and other hazardous chemicals only when absolutely

---

SPOTLIGHT The International Hazardous Waste Trade

To save money and avoid regulatory hurdles, cities and waste disposal companies in the United States and other MDCs legally ship large amounts of hazardous waste to other countries. West Germany exports about one-fourth of its hazardous waste to East Germany. Great Britain is a major importer of hazardous waste from many MDCs, especially the Netherlands, Ireland, and Belgium.

Most legal U.S. exports of hazardous waste go to Canada and Mexico. All U.S. firms have to do to ship hazardous waste to other countries is notify the EPA of their intent to ship, get written permission from the recipient country, and file an annual report with the EPA.

Legal shipments of hazardous wastes from one country to another may be only the tip of the "sludgeberg." There is evidence of a growing trade in illegal shipments of hazardous wastes across international borders.

It is often easy to ship hazardous wastes illegally. Customs officials in the United States and other countries are not trained to detect illegal shipments. Sometimes exported wastes are labelled as materials to be recycled and then dumped after reaching their destination. Hazardous wastes have also been mixed with wood chips or sawdust and shipped legally as burnable material.

Waste disposal firms can charge high prices, running as much as $2,000 per ton, for picking up hazardous wastes. If they can then dispose of them legally or illegally in other countries at low costs, they pocket huge profits. Officials and individuals in poor countries, especially in Africa, Latin America, and the Caribbean, find it hard to resist the income (often in the form of bribes) from receiving these wastes.

In 1987 an Italian businessman worked out a scheme to make a $4.3 million profit in the illegal toxic waste trade. He paid a retired timber worker $100 a month to store thousands of barrels of PCBs and other hazardous wastes in his backyard in Koko, Nigeria, a remote port town with about 5,000 inhabitants. Since then 19 people have died from rice contaminated by chemicals from leaking barrels. In 1988 outraged Nigerian officials arrested 54 people and made Italy take back the wastes. Several Nigerian workers repacking and loading the wastes for the return shipment suffered severe chemical burns and one worker was partially paralyzed. This incident prompted the country to pass a law which requires life imprisonment for anyone found guilty of dumping or aiding the dumping of hazardous waste in Nigeria.

More countries are beginning to realize how importing hazardous waste can threaten their environment and the health of their people and weaken their long-term economic growth. More are beginning to adopt the slogan "Not In Our Country" (NIOC) and a "return to sender" policy when illegal waste shipments are discovered.

In 1989 leaders from 116 countries drafted an international treaty to help control the export of hazardous wastes. It would ban such exports unless the government of a receiving country gives prior written permission to receive the wastes. Instead of signing the treaty, President Bush proposed that Congress pass a law giving the U.S. government authority to ban all exports of hazardous waste "except where we have an agreement with the country providing for the safe handling and management of those wastes."

Many environmentalists and some members of Congress go further and call for the United States to ban all exports of hazardous waste to other countries. They believe that the U.S. has an ethical obligation to take care of any hazardous waste it produces within its own borders. It is wrong to export Love Canals to other countries.

But even the most stringent regulations will not end legal and illegal trade of these wastes. The profits to be earned are simply too great. What do you think should be done?

necessary and in the smallest amount possible. Use less hazardous (and usually cheaper) cleaning products (Table 18-8).

Don't mix household chemicals because many of them react and produce deadly chemicals. For example, when ammonia and household bleach are combined or even get near one another, they react to produce deadly poisonous chloramine gas. Hazardous household chemicals should also not be flushed down the toilet, poured down the drain, buried in the yard, or dumped down storm drains.

Also don't throw such chemicals away in the garbage because they will end up in a landfill, where they can contaminate drinking water supplies. Instead, contact your local health department or environmental agency for information on what to do with leftover pesticides, paint solvents, cleaning compounds, wood preservatives, and other hazardous chemicals. Take used motor oil, transmission fluid, brake fluid, and car batteries to a local auto service center for recycling. Return broken smoke detectors, which contain radioactive materials, to the manufacturer or retailer. Encourage your local community to set up a hazardous waste collection center.

Health and a good state of body are above all gold, and a strong body above infinite wealth.
Ecclesiastes 40:15

Table 18-8 Alternatives for Some Hazardous Household Chemicals

Chemical	Alternative
Deodorant	Sprinkle baking soda on a damp wash rag and wipe skin. Baking soda also is excellent for cleaning teeth.
Oven cleaner	Use baking soda for scouring. For baked-on grease, apply 1/4 cup of ammonia in oven overnight to loosen; scrub the next day with baking soda; sprinkle salt on spills when warm, then scrub.
Drain cleaner	Pour 1/2 cup salt down drain, followed by boiling water; flush with hot tap water; or pour 1 handful baking soda and 1/2 cup white vinegar and cover tightly for one minute.
Glass polish	Use ammonia and soap.
Wall and floor cleaners containing organic solvents	Use detergents to clean large areas and then rinse with water.
Toilet bowl, tub, and tile cleaner	Mix borax and lemon juice in a paste. Rub on paste and let set two hours before scrubbing.
Mirrors	Use one-to-one mixture of vinegar and water
General surface cleaner	Use mixture of vinegar, salt, and water
Bleach	Use baking soda or borax to whiten
Mildew stain remover and disinfectant cleaner	Chlorine bleach
Furniture polish	Melt 1 pound carnauba wax into 1 pint of mineral oil. For lemon oil polish, dissolve 1 teaspoon of lemon oil into 1 pint of mineral oil.
Shoe polish	Use polishes that do not contain methylene chloride, trichloroethylene, or nitrobenzene.
Spot removers	Launder fabrics when possible to remove stains. Also try cornstarch, vinegar, lemon juice, club soda, or cornmeal-and-water paste.
Carpet and rug shampoos	Sprinkle cornstarch on and vacuum
Detergents and detergent boosters	Washing soda and soap powder
Water softeners	Washing soda
Pesticides (indoor and outdoor)	Use natural biological controls (Section 21-5); sprinkle boric acid for roaches, for ants pour a line of red chili powder, cayenne pepper, paprika, or dried peppermint at points of entry or wipe surface with vinegar.
Mothballs	Soak dried lavender, equal parts of rosemary and mint, dried tobacco, whole peppercorns, and cedar chips in real cedar oil and place in a cotton bag

CHAPTER SUMMARY

We are constantly exposed to risks from various physical (such as ionizing radiation), chemical (toxic substances), biological (disease-causing agents), and cultural hazards (lifestyle factors) in the environment. Determining the toxicity levels of substances is difficult, costly, and controversial. It is done by carrying out tests on laboratory animals (mostly mice and rats), bacteria, and cell and tissue cultures and by studying the effects on human populations exposed to high levels at work or by accidents (epidemiology). All of these methods have serious shortcomings, but they are all we have.

Poverty is the underlying cause of the lower average life expectancy in LDCs. The overcrowding, unsafe drinking water, poor sanitation, and malnutrition that accompanies poverty increases the spread of transmissible diseases (such as malaria, schistosomiasis, and measles) which account for about 40% of all deaths in LDCs. Major improvements in human health in LDCs can be made with preventive and primary health care measures at a relatively low cost, but efforts and funding lag far behind the need.

ENRICHMENT STUDY Sexually Transmitted Diseases

Sexually transmitted diseases (STDs) have reached epidemic proportions during the 1980s. The disease agents are mostly bacteria and viruses that usually are transmitted from infected to uninfected persons during sexual activity.

Worldwide estimates of the number of people infected with STDs are difficult to make because of underreporting and lack of adequate health care in most LDCs. In the United States at least 10 million adults have been officially diagnosed as having some form of STD and the number of new reported cases of most STDs has been rising each year since 1981. Each year one out of every seven sexually active teenagers in the United States contracts a sexually transmitted disease.

No one knows the number of unreported cases of STDs in the United States, but the Centers for Disease Control estimate that total infections are at least twice the number reported. Here are some basic facts about some of the most common sexually transmitted diseases.

Chlamydia

- **Cause:** *Chlamydia trachomatis* bacteria
- **Symptoms:** None in 40% to 50% of men and up to 80% of women. But can include painful urination, genital itching, and watery discharge in men. In women: itching, burning, discharge, dull pelvic pain, bleeding between periods. As many as 45% of sexually active teenagers and college students get the infection.
- **Complications:** In women may cause 50% of the cases of pelvic inflammatory disease, which can result in abnormal pregnancies and infertility. Can also cause infertility in men.
- **Treatment:** Antibiotics (mostly tetracycline and sulfonamides).

Gonorrhea

- **Cause:** *Neisseria gonorrhoea* bacteria
- **Symptoms:** Usually none in women but men may have burning discharge from penis three to five days after contact.
- **Complications:** Inflammation and scarring of tissue, which can lead to infertility in both men and women; eye infections and pneumonia in newborns of infected mothers; arthritis.
- **Treatment:** Antibiotics, but antibiotic resistant strains are appearing more frequently.

Genital Warts

- **Cause:** Human *papillomavirus* (HPV). Spreads rapidly.
- **Symptoms:** None for many people; others get warts in or around the anal and genital areas. Infects about one-third of all sexually active teenagers.
- **Complications:** Greatly increases the risk of cervical cancer that kills 7,000 American women each year. Women most at risk of warts becoming cancerous are those who smoke or whose immune systems have been weakened by illness or other infections. May have infected 10 to 12 million Americans.
- **Treatment:** No cure; warts can be removed with chemicals, surgery, or other methods but they can return. Women with this disease should have yearly or semi-annual Pap smears to detect early stages of cervical cancer.

Genital Herpes

- **Cause:** Usually herpes simplex virus 2; sometimes herpes simplex virus 1, which more commonly causes cold sores on the mouth. Highly contagious.
- **Symptoms:** None in some people. Others may suffer from an initial outbreak of painful genital sores, which usually go away in about a week. The outbreaks usually recur throughout the lifetime of the victim, and are sometimes accompanied by headaches, fever, and fatigue. May have infected 20% of sexually active men and women in the United States. Most cases apparently go unreported.
- **Complications:** Virus can be transferred to the eye, causing blindness, or to a newborn during childbirth.
- **Treatment:** No cure, but an antiviral prescription drug called acyclovir can prevent or lessen severity and frequency of outbreaks.

In most MDCs, safe water supplies, public sanitation, adequate nutrition, and immunization have nearly stamped out many transmissible diseases. The four leading causes of death in MDCs today are heart disease and stroke, cancer, respiratory infections, and accidents. These deaths are largely a result of environmental and lifestyle factors rather than infectious agents invading the body. However, more than 95% of the massive amount of money spent on health care in the United States is used to treat rather than prevent disease.

Risk-benefit analysis involves estimating and comparing the short- and long-term benefits and risks to individuals and society of a technology or product to determine its desirability. *Risk management* encompasses all the administrative, political, and economic actions taken to decide how, and if, a particular societal risk is to be reduced to a certain level and at what cost. Both risk-benefit analysis and risk management are important, difficult, and controversial processes that involve many uncertainties, value judgments, and trade-offs. Often there are major differences between the degree of risk estimated by experts and the risk perceived by the general public.

One of the major killers in MDCs is *cancer*, a name for a group of more than 120 diseases characterized by the

Syphilis

- **Cause:** *Treponema pallidium* bacteria

- **Symptoms:** First, a painless sore that disappears. Later, fever, sore throat, hair loss, itchy rash. In final stage (two or more years after infection), lesions on skin and internal organs and brain and spinal cord damage.

- **Complications:** Transmission to newborn infants; if untreated, final stage can lead to insanity, blindness, paralysis, even death.

- **Treatment:** Antibiotics

AIDS (Acquired Immune Deficiency Syndrome)

- **Cause:** Human immunodeficiency virus (HIV). Transmitted by sexual activity, sharing of drug needles, infected blood, or by infected mothers to babies before or during birth.

- **Symptoms:** May not appear for 5 to 10 years after infection. Then the body immune system is progressively weakened, making victims easy prey for certain infections and cancers; these include a rare cancer (*Kaposis Sarcoma*) and a rare form of pneumonia (*pneumocystis carinii*)

- **Complications:** Eventually leads to death from repeated infections by various diseases; transmitted to infants before or during birth.

- **Treatment:** Incurable; an expensive ($6,000 a year) drug, AZT, has prolonged the lives of some victims; scientists are hoping to develop additional treatments that prolong life; they also hope to develop a vaccine to prevent uninfected people from getting the disease, but this may take many years.

AIDS currently has the lowest incidence of the major STDs, but it is spreading rapidly. By mid-1989, officials of the World Health Organization estimated that 480,000 people worldwide had AIDS. At least another 5 million people are believed to be infected with the HIV virus. More than 1 million of those infected with the virus are expected to develop AIDS by 1992 and by then 50 to 100 million people may be infected with the virus. If present trends continue, 3 to 5 million new cases will be diagnosed in 2010 and 1.5 to 2 million people will have died from AIDS.

In the United States over 104,200 Americans had officially reported cases of AIDS and 62,000 of these victims had died by mid-1989. Currently AIDS strikes someone in the United States every 14 minutes and there is no letup in sight. By 1989 from 1 million to 1.5 million Americans were believed to be infected with the AIDS virus, including 2 to 3 out of every 1,000 college students. The Centers for Disease Control estimate that by the end of 1992, 365,000 Americans will have come down with AIDS, and 263,000 of those will have died.

The AIDS epidemic can affect anyone anywhere in the world who takes unnecessary risks in engaging in sexual activity or in shooting drugs. But its greatest long-term toll is expected to be among poor people in LDCs and in MDCs. Large numbers of this global underclass cannot afford condoms or new needles (if they shoot drugs), are not reached by health prevention and education programs, have little or no access to health clinics, and are more vulnerable to AIDS (and other STDs) because of their weakened condition from malnutrition and repeated illnesses.

Preventing Sexually Transmitted Diseases

The risk of getting an STD can be greatly reduced in several ways:

- not having sex with another person (not a popular solution for most people)

- having sex only with one mutually faithful, uninfected partner

- having sex using a good quality latex condom plus the spermicide nonoxynol-9 smeared on the outside and inside the condom tip. But this is not failsafe since condoms have a failure rate of 10% to 15% and it is only *assumed* that the AIDS virus (and other sexually transmitted disease organisms) cannot pass through the walls of a latex condom.

- not shooting drugs and if drugs are shot always using a clean needle that has not been used by anyone else and that is never reused.

uncontrolled growth and multiplication of certain cells. Most cancers take 10 to 40 years to develop. Environmental and lifestyle factors such as smoking, diet, and occupation play a key role in causing or promoting 80% to 90% of cancers, mostly by exposure to ionizing radiation and various carcinogens. Changing these lifestyle factors is the key to sharply reducing the risks of premature death and poor health from cancer.

In MDCs and in many cities in LDCs large numbers of chemicals, known as *food additives,* are added to processed foods to retard spoilage, to enhance flavor, color, and texture, and to provide missing amino acids and vitamins. Although most food additives are probably safe, some are harmful. So far there has been inadequate testing to determine which of the 2,800 different chemicals added to food in the United States do not increase the risks of cancer, birth defects, and other disorders.

The production and improper handling of *hazardous waste* is a serious and growing problem. There is also the problem of what to do with hazardous wastes improperly stored in thousands of dumps in the past. The basic ways of dealing with hazardous waste in order of priority are **(1)** waste prevention by waste reduction, recycling and reuse, **(2)** conversion to less hazardous or nonhazardous material, and **(3)** perpetual storage. So far few countries have a comprehensive program based on this strategy. Each of us has an important role to play by reducing our own use of hazardous materials, seeing that those we use are properly disposed of, and pressuring elected officials to establish a hazardous waste management system built around waste prevention, reduction, recycling, and reuse.

There is growing concern over the spread of AIDS, gonorrhea, genital herpes, and other sexually transmitted diseases. Dealing with this will require much better sex education at an early age and massive public education about the need to practice safe sex by using condoms plus a spermicide and having sex with only one safe partner.

DISCUSSION TOPICS

1. Considering the benefits and risks involved, do you believe that
   a. nuclear power plants should be controlled more rigidly and gradually phased out?
   b. coal-burning power plants should be controlled more rigidly and gradually phased out?
   c. genetic engineering should be prohibited?
   d. genetic engineering should be rigidly controlled?
   e. air bags or other automatic passenger protection systems should be made mandatory on all vehicles?
   In each case defend your position.

2. What are the major limitations of risk-benefit analysis and risk management? Does this mean that these processes are useless? Explain.

3. Explain why you agree or disagree with each of the following proposals:
   a. All advertising of cigarettes and other tobacco products should be banned.
   b. All smoking should be banned in public buildings and commercial airplanes, buses, subways, and trains.
   c. All government subsidies to tobacco farmers and the tobacco industry should be eliminated.

   d. Cigarettes should be taxed at about $2.10 a pack so that smokers—not nonsmokers—pay for the health and productivity losses now borne by society as a whole.

4. Explain why you agree or disagree with each of the following proposals:
   a. All new and presently used food additives should be reviewed and tested not only for toxicity and carcinogenicity but also for their ability to induce birth defects and harmful genetic effects.
   b. All testing of food additives should be performed by a third party, completely independent of the food industry.
   c. All food additives, including specific flavors, colors, and sodium content (for people on salt-free diets), should be listed on the label or container of all foods and drugs.
   d. All food additives should be banned unless extensive testing establishes that they are not toxic, carcinogenic, mutagenic, or teratogenic.
   e. All food additives should be banned except those that enhance the nutritive content of foods or prevent food spoilage or contamination by harmful bacteria and molds.

5. Compare brands of various foods found in a grocery store. See if there are some that contain *none* of the controversial additives listed in Table 18-6.

6. Explain the fallacies in the following statements:
   a. All synthetic food additives should be banned, and we should all return to eating only natural foods.
   b. All foods are chemicals, so we shouldn't worry about artificial additives.
   c. Because some natural foods contain harmful chemicals, we should not be so concerned about synthetic food additives.
   d. Food additives are essential; without them we would suffer from malnutrition, food poisoning, and spoiled food.

7. Would you oppose locating a hazardous waste landfill or incinerator in your community? Explain. If you oppose both of these alternatives, how would you propose that the hazardous waste generated in your community and state be managed?

8. Explain why you agree or disagree with each of the following proposals for dealing with hazardous waste:
   a. Reduce the production of hazardous waste and encourage this and recycling and reuse of hazardous materials by levying a tax or fee on producers for each unit of waste generated.
   b. Ban all land disposal of hazardous waste to encourage recycling, reuse, and treatment and to protect groundwater from contamination.
   c. Provide low-interest loans, tax breaks, and other financial incentives to encourage industries that produce hazardous waste to recycle, reuse, treat, destroy, and reduce generation of such waste.
   d. Ban the shipment of hazardous waste from the United States to any other country.

9. What hazardous wastes are produced at your college or university? What happens to these wastes?

CHAPTER 19

Air Pollution

General Questions and Issues

1. What are the major types and sources of air pollutants?
2. What is smog and acid deposition?
3. What undesirable effects can air pollutants have on people, other species, and materials?
4. What undesirable effects can certain air pollutants have on the ozone layer and global climate?

5. What legal and technological methods can be used to reduce air pollution?

I thought I saw a blue jay this morning. But the smog was so bad that it turned out to be a cardinal holding its breath.

Michael J. Cohen

Take a deep breath. About 99% of the air you inhaled is gaseous nitrogen and oxygen. You also inhaled trace amounts of other gases, minute droplets of various liquids, and tiny particles of various solids. Studies have detected up to 2,800 compounds in urban air. Many of these chemicals are classified as air pollutants. Most come from cars, trucks, power plants, factories, cigarettes, cleaning solvents, and other sources related to human activities.

Repeated exposure to trace amounts of many of these chemicals can damage lung tissue, plants, buildings, metals, and other materials. The changes in the chemical content of the atmosphere from air pollutants can also alter local, regional, and global climates and increase the amount of the sun's harmful ultraviolet radiation reaching the earth's surface. These problems are considered as planetary emergencies that we must deal with now.

19-1 TYPES AND SOURCES OF OUTDOOR AND INDOOR AIR POLLUTION

Our Air Resources The **atmosphere**, a thin envelope of gases surrounding the earth, is divided into several spherical layers—much like the successive layers of skin on an onion (Figure 19-1). About 95% of the mass

of the air is found in the innermost layer, known as the **troposphere**, extending only about 17 kilometers (11 miles) above the earth's surface. If the earth were an apple, our vital air supply would be no thicker than the apple's skin.

About 99% of the volume of clean, dry air in the troposphere consists of two gases: nitrogen (78%) and oxygen (21%). The remaining volume of air in the troposphere has slightly less than 1% argon and about 0.035% carbon dioxide. Air in the troposphere also holds water vapor in amounts varying from 0.01% by volume at the frigid poles to 5% in the humid tropics.

Large masses of air in the troposphere are constantly churning and swirling as air heated by the sun rises and is replaced by cooler air. The physical processes causing these movements throughout the troposphere are a key factor determining the earth's climate and weather (Section 5-1). They also affect the types and distribution of harmful chemicals in the troposphere.

As clean air moves across the earth's surface, it collects trace amounts of various chemicals produced by natural events and human activities. Once in the troposphere, these potential air pollutants mix vertically and horizontally and often react chemically with each other or with natural components of the atmosphere. Air movements and turbulence help dilute potential pollutants, but long-lived pollutants are transported great distances before they return to the

Figure 19-1 The earth's atmosphere. About 95% of the planet's mass of air circulates in the troposphere, where temperatures decrease rapidly with altitude. Most ultraviolet radiation from the sun is absorbed by small amounts of ozone (O_3) in the stratosphere, where temperatures rise with increasing altitude. Most of this ozone is found in what is called the ozone layer between 17 and 26 kilometers (11 and 16 miles) above sea level.

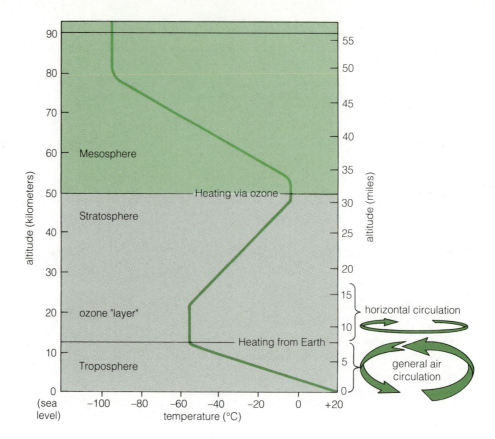

earth's surface as solid particles, liquid droplets, or chemicals dissolved in precipitation.

The second layer of the atmosphere, extending from about 17 to 48 kilometers (11 to 30 miles) above the earth's surface, is called the **stratosphere** (Figure 19-1). It contains small amounts of gaseous ozone (O_3) that filters out about 99% of the incoming harmful ultraviolet (UV) radiation (Figure 4-3, p. 78). This filtering action by the thin gauze of ozone in the stratosphere protects us from increased sunburn, skin cancer, eye cancer, and eye cataracts. This global sunscreen also prevents damage to some plants and aquatic organisms.

By filtering out high-energy UV radiation, stratospheric ozone also keeps much of the oxygen in the troposphere from being converted to ozone. The trace amounts of ozone that do form in the troposphere as a component of urban smog damage plants, the respiratory systems of people and other animals, and materials such as rubber. Thus, our good health depends on having enough "good" ozone in the stratosphere and as little as possible "bad" ozone in the troposphere. Unfortunately, our activities are decreasing ozone in the stratosphere and increasing it in the troposphere.

The composition, temperature, and self-cleansing ability of the earth's atmosphere have all varied since the planet first formed. However, during the past two centuries and especially during the past fifty years the atmosphere's composition has undergone significant change because of our activities. Such activities include the combustion of fossil fuels, burning wood and other vegetation, deforestation, and various industrial and agricultural activities.

Major Types of Outdoor Air Pollutants When the concentration of a normal component of air, or a new chemical added to or formed in the air, builds up to the point of causing harm to humans, other animals, vegetation, metals, stone, or other materials, that chemical is classified as an **air pollutant**.

There are hundreds of air pollutants in the troposphere. However, nine major classes of pollutants cause most outdoor air pollution:

1. *carbon oxides.* carbon monoxide (CO) and carbon dioxide (CO_2)

2. *sulfur oxides.* sulfur dioxide (SO_2) and sulfur trioxide (SO_3)

3. *nitrogen oxides.* nitric oxide (NO), nitrogen dioxide (NO_2), and nitrous oxide (N_2O)

4. *volatile organic compounds (VOCs).* hundreds of compounds such as methane (CH_4), benzene (C_6H_6), chlorofluorocarbons (CFCs), and bromine-containing halons

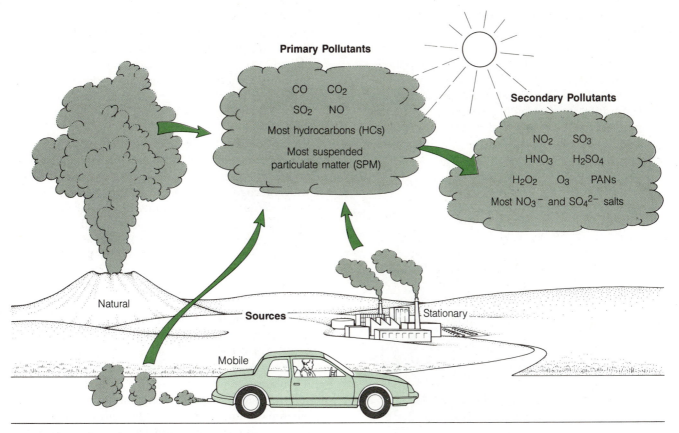

Figure 19-2 Primary and secondary air pollutants.

5. *suspended particulate matter (SPM)*: thousands of different types of *solid particles* such as dust (soil), soot (carbon), asbestos, and lead, arsenic, cadmium, nitrate (NO_3^-) and sulfate (SO_4^{2-}) salts and *liquid droplets* of chemicals such as sulfuric acid (H_2SO_4), oil, PCBs (see Case Study on p. 471), dioxins (see Case Study on p. 454), and various pesticides (Chapter 21)

6. *photochemical oxidants*. ozone (O_3), PANs (peroxyacyl nitrates), hydrogen peroxide (H_2O_2), hydroxy radicals (OH), and aldehydes such as formaldehyde (CH_2O) formed in the atmosphere by the reaction of oxygen, nitrogen oxides, and volatile hydrocarbons under the influence of sunlight

7. *radioactive substances*. radon-222, iodine-131, strontium-90, plutonium-239, and other radioisotopes that enter the atmosphere as gases or suspended particulate matter

8. *heat*. produced when any kind of energy is transformed from one form to another, especially when fossil fuels are burned in cars, factories, homes, and power plants (see p. 196)

9. *noise*. produced by motor vehicles, airplanes, trains, industrial machinery, construction machinery, lawn mowers, vacuum cleaners, food blenders, sirens, earphones, radios, cassette players, and live concerts (see p. 198)

Each of these chemicals or forms of energy (heat and noise) can be classified as either a primary or secondary air pollutant. A **primary air pollutant**, such as sulfur dioxide, directly enters the air as a result of natural events or human activities. A **secondary air pollutant**, such as sulfuric acid, is formed in the air through a chemical reaction between a primary pollutant and one or more air components (Figure 19-2).

Pollutants such as suspended particulate matter remain in the atmosphere for different lengths of time depending mostly on the relative size of the particles (Figure 19-3) and on the climate. Large particles, with diameters greater than 10 micrometers (about 0.000039 inches) normally remain in the troposphere only a day or two before being brought to earth by gravity or precipitation. Medium-sized particles, with diameters between 1 and 10 micrometers, are lighter and tend to remain suspended in the air for several days.

Fine particles, with diameters less than 1 micrometer, may remain suspended in the troposphere for one to two weeks and in the stratosphere for one to five years—long enough to be transported all over the world. These fine particles are the most hazardous to human health because they are small enough to penetrate the lung's natural defenses; they can also bring with them droplets or other particles of toxic or cancer-causing pollutants that become attached to their surfaces.

Sources of Outdoor Air Pollution Natural sources of air pollutants include forest fires started by lightning, pollen dispersal, wind erosion of soil, volcanic eruptions, evaporation of volatile organic compounds from leaves (mostly terpene hydrocarbons responsible for the odors of pines and other plants), bacterial decomposition products of organic matter, sea spray (sulfate and salt particles), and natural radioactivity (radon-222 gas from deposits of uranium, phosphate, and granite).

Most atmospheric emissions from widely scattered natural sources are diluted and dispersed throughout the world and rarely reach concentrations high enough to cause serious damage. Exceptions are massive injections of sulfur dioxide and suspended particulate matter into the atmosphere from large volcanic eruptions and buildup of radioactive radon-222 gas inside buildings.

Air pollution is not new (see Spotlight on p. 487), but since the industrial revolution the types and quantities of air pollutants have increased. Much of the widely recognized outdoor air pollution in the United States comes from five groups of pollutants: carbon monoxide, nitrogen oxides, sulfur oxides, volatile organic compounds (mostly hydrocarbons), and suspended particulate matter (Figure 19-4). Other key pollutants are ozone and lead (see Case Study on p. 472).

In MDCs most of these pollutants are emitted into the atmosphere from the burning of fossil fuels in power and industrial plants (*stationary sources*) and in motor vehicles (*mobile sources*). The combustion of fossil fuels injects carbon dioxide, nitrogen oxides (which form when nitrogen and oxygen in the air are heated), and sulfur dioxide (expecially from coal and some types of oil) into the atmosphere. If the burning is incomplete, it also yields carbon monoxide, soot (carbon particles), and a variety of hydrocarbons (including methane). In LDCs, especially in rural areas where over half of the world's people live, most air pollution (especially CO_2, CO, and nitrogen oxides) is produced by the burning of wood, dung, and crop residues in crude stoves and open fires.

The burning of forests and savanna grasslands in tropical and subtropical regions to create cropland and pastures injects large quantities of carbon dioxide, carbon monoxide, nitrogen oxides, and methane into the atmosphere. Also, when forests are cleared the exposed soil emits nitrous oxide. It is also emitted when nitrogen-rich fertilizers are spread on cropland. Significant amounts of methane are emitted into the atmosphere

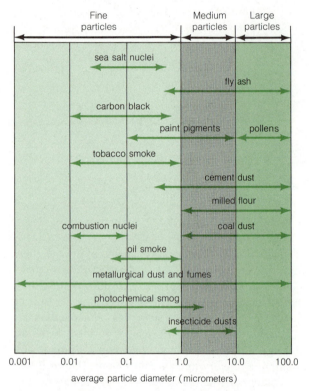

Figure 19-3 Suspended particulate matter is found in a wide variety of types and sizes. (1 micrometer = 0.001 millimeter = 0.00004 in.)

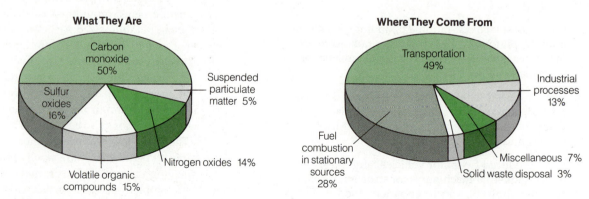

Figure 19-4 Emissions of major outdoor air pollutants in the United States. (Data from Environmental Protection Agency)

from the stomachs of livestock and by anaerobic decomposition from wet rice paddies.

Recently it has been recognized that hundreds of *unconventional outdoor air pollutants* may be a long-term threat to human health when inhaled over long periods. These toxic compounds include various volatile organic compounds (especially chlorinated hydrocarbons such as chloroform, carbon tetrachloride, and methylene chloride) and different types of SPM (especially fine particles of toxic metals and asbestos) found in the atmosphere in trace amounts.

A 1989 report by the EPA revealed that in 1987 1.1 million metric tons (1.2 million tons) of 329 potentially toxic chemicals were emitted into the atmosphere in the United States. These chemicals were emitted mostly by various industries, especially oil refineries and plants producing chemicals, metals, and paper. These emissions are legal because these chemicals are not controlled by existing air pollution control laws. Actual emissions are much higher because this survey did not include toxic chemicals emitted by cars, trucks, and toxic waste dumps and by thousands of small businesses such as dry cleaners and gas stations.

Not all of the chemicals are necessarily harmful and some are presumably diluted or transformed so that they pose no significant risk to human health. However, based on just 20 chemicals, not the 329 included in the survey, the EPA estimates that these pollutants cause up to 3,000 cases of cancer every year.

People working in or living near chemical, metals, paper, oil refineries, and other various industrial plants have the highest risk from exposure to these chemicals. So far little effort has been made to control these pollutants.

Types and Sources of Indoor Air Pollution High concentrations of toxic air pollutants can also build up indoors, where most people spend 70% to 98% of their time (Figure 19-5). Indeed, scientists recently have found that the air inside many homes, schools, office buildings, factories, cars, and airliners in the United States (and presumably most MDCs) is more polluted and dangerous than outdoor air on a smoggy day. Indoor air pollution poses an especially high risk for the elderly, the very young, the sick, and factory workers who spend a large amount of time indoors.

Indoor air pollution shows why the total air pollution emissions from various sources (Figure 19-4) do not always correlate with harmful impacts on human health (Table 19-1). The key factor affecting human health is not total emissions but how long people spend exposed to each pollutant. Note that the major exposure from the pollutants shown in Table 19-1 comes from indoor sources.

Many people associate air pollution with urban areas of industrialized countries. While these areas do have serious air pollution problems, the most severe exposure to air pollution, especially particulate matter,

---

SPOTLIGHT Air Pollution in the Past

Humans probably first experienced harm from air pollution when they built fires in poorly ventilated caves. As cities grew during the agricultural revolution, air pollution from the burning of wood and later of coal became an increasingly serious problem. In 1273 A.D. King Edward I of England banned the burning of coal in order to reduce air pollution.

In 1911, at least 1,150 Londoners died from the effects of coal smoke. The author of a report on this disaster coined the word *smog* for the mixture of smoke and fog that often hung over London. An even worse London air pollution incident killed 4,000 people in 1952, and further disasters in 1956, 1957, and 1962 killed a total of about 2,500 people. As a result, London has taken strong measures

against air pollution and has much cleaner air today.

In the United States the Industrial Revolution brought air pollution as coal-burning industries and homes filled the air with soot and fumes. In the 1940s air in industrial centers like Pittsburgh and St. Louis became so thick with coal smoke that automobile drivers sometimes had to use their headlights at midday. The rapid rise of the automobile, especially since 1940, brought new forms of pollution such as photochemical smog, which causes the eyes to sting, and toxic lead compounds from the burning of leaded gasoline.

The first known U.S. air pollution disaster occurred in 1948, when fog laden with sulfur dioxide vapor and suspended particulate matter stagnated over the

town of Donora in Pennsylvania's Monongahela Valley for five days. About 6,000 of the town's 14,000 inhabitants fell ill and 20 of them died. This killer fog resulted from a combination of mountainous terrain surrounding the valley and stable weather conditions that trapped and concentrated deadly pollutants emitted by the community's steel mill, zinc smelter, and sulfuric acid plant.

In 1963, high concentrations of air pollutants accumulated in the air over New York City, killing about 300 people and injuring thousands. Other episodes during the 1960s in New York, Los Angeles, and other large cities led to much stronger air pollution control programs in the 1970s.

occurs inside the dwellings of poor rural people in LDCs. Most of these people use simple unvented stoves for cooking, and in temperate and cold areas, for heating. The burning of wood, dung, and crop residues in these unvented or poorly vented stoves exposes these people, especially women and young children, to very high levels of indoor air pollution. This helps explain why respiratory illnesses are the chief cause of death and illness in most LDCs. By contrast, wood stoves and fireplaces used by most people in MDCs have chimneys or flues.

In 1985 the EPA reported that toxic chemicals found in almost every American home are three times more likely to cause some type of cancer than outdoor air pollutants. Other air pollutants found in buildings produce dizziness, head aches, coughing, sneezing, burning eyes, and flulike symptoms in many people— a health problem called the "sick building syndrome."

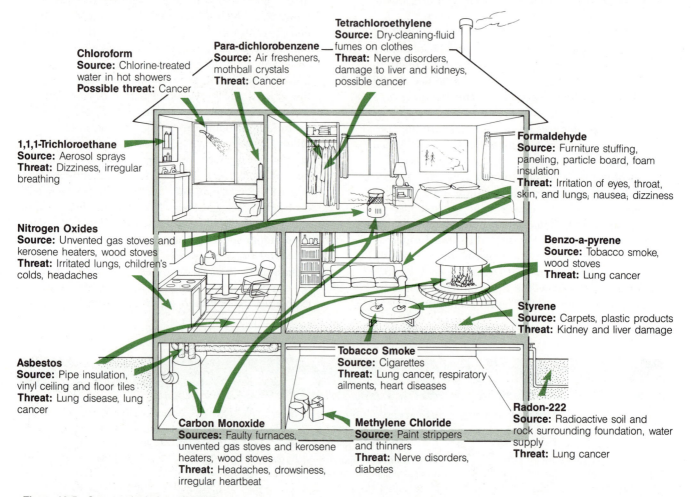

Chloroform
Source: Chlorine-treated water in hot showers
Possible threat: Cancer

Para-dichlorobenzene
Source: Air fresheners, mothball crystals
Threat: Cancer

Tetrachloroethylene
Source: Dry-cleaning-fluid fumes on clothes
Threat: Nerve disorders, damage to liver and kidneys, possible cancer

1,1,1-Trichloroethane
Source: Aerosol sprays
Threat: Dizziness, irregular breathing

Formaldehyde
Source: Furniture stuffing, paneling, particle board, foam insulation
Threat: Irritation of eyes, throat, skin, and lungs; nausea; dizziness

Nitrogen Oxides
Source: Unvented gas stoves and kerosene heaters, wood stoves
Threat: Irritated lungs, children's colds, headaches

Benzo-a-pyrene
Source: Tobacco smoke, wood stoves
Threat: Lung cancer

Styrene
Source: Carpets, plastic products
Threat: Kidney and liver damage

Asbestos
Source: Pipe insulation, vinyl ceiling and floor tiles
Threat: Lung disease, lung cancer

Tobacco Smoke
Source: Cigarettes
Threat: Lung cancer, respiratory ailments, heart diseases

Carbon Monoxide
Sources: Faulty furnaces, unvented gas stoves and kerosene heaters, wood stoves
Threat: Headaches, drowsiness, irregular heartbeat

Methylene Chloride
Source: Paint strippers and thinners
Threat: Nerve disorders, diabetes

Radon-222
Source: Radioactive soil and rock surrounding foundation, water supply
Threat: Lung cancer

Figure 19-5 Some major indoor air pollutants.

Table 19-1 Comparison of Sources of Selected Pollutants by Emissions and Exposure		
Pollutant	Major Emission Sources	Major Exposure Sources
Benzene	Industry; automobiles	Smoking
Tetrachloroethylene	Dry-cleaning shops	Dry-cleaned clothes
Chloroform	Sewage treatment plants	Showers
p-Dichlorobenzene	Chemical manufacturing	Air deodorizers
Particulates	Industry; automobiles; home heating	Smoker at home
Carbon monoxide	Automobiles	Driving; gas stoves
Nitrogen dioxide	Industry; automobiles	Gas stoves

An estimated one-fifth to one-third of all U.S. buildings, including the EPA headquarters, are now considered "sick." The EPA has found that the air in some office buildings is 100 times more polluted than the air outside. Each year exposure to pollutants inside factories and businesses in the United States kills from 100,000 to 210,000 workers prematurely.

Poor ventilation causes about half of the indoor air pollution problems. The rest come from specific sources such as copying machines, electrical and telephone cables, mold and microbe-harboring air conditioning systems and ducts, cleaning fluids, cigarette smoke, carpet, latex caulk and paint, vinyl molding, linoleum tile, and building materials and furniture that emit air pollutants such as formaldehyde.

A study of commuter autos on a Los Angeles freeway found levels of carbon monoxide, benzene, and 14 other air pollutants inside cars three to five times higher than levels outside. According to the EPA and public health officials, cigarette smoke (see p. 463), radioactive radon-222 gas (see Case Study below), and asbestos (see Pro/Con on p. 491) are the three most dangerous indoor air pollutants in the United States.

CASE STUDY Is Your Home Contaminated with Radioactive Radon Gas?

Radon-222 is a colorless, odorless, tasteless, naturally occurring radioactive gas produced by the radioactive decay of uranium-238. Small amounts of radon-producing uranium-238 are found in most soil and rock. But this isotope is much more concentrated in underground deposits of uranium, phosphate, granite, and shale rock.

When radon gas from such deposits percolates upward to the soil and is released outdoors, it disperses quickly in the atmosphere and decays to harmless levels. However, when the gas seeps or is drawn into buildings through cracks and drains in basements or into water in underground wells over such deposits, it can build up to high levels (Figure 19-6). Stone and other building materials obtained from radon-rich deposits can also be a source of indoor radon contamination.

Radon-222 gas quickly decays into solid particles of other radioactive elements that can be inhaled, exposing lung tissue to a large amount of ionizing radiation from alpha particles. Smokers are especially vulnerable because the inhaled radioactive particles tend to adhere to tobacco tar deposits in the lungs and upper respiratory tract. Repeated exposure to these radioactive particles over 20 to 30 years can cause lung cancer.

Data from a sampling of indoor radon levels taken mostly from basements or crawlspaces of houses in 30 states indicate that at least one of every ten American homes—perhaps as many as one of every three—may contain harmful levels of this gas. In Pennsylvania radon levels in the home of one family created a cancer risk equal to having 455,000 chest X rays a year. So far the highest radon levels in well water were found in Maine.

According to studies by the EPA and the National Research Council, prolonged exposure to high levels of radon over a 70-year life span is second to smoking as a cause of lung cancer. It causes up to 20,000 of the 136,000 lung cancer deaths each year in the United States, with 85% of these caused by a combination of radon and smoking. Radon released from groundwater found near radon-laden rock and later heated and used for showers and washing clothes may be responsible for 50 to 400 of these premature deaths.

Because radon hot spots can occur almost anywhere, it is impossible to know which buildings have unsafe levels of radon without carrying out tests. In 1988 the EPA and the U.S. Surgeon General's Office recommended that everyone living in a detached house, townhouse, mobile home, or first three floors of an apartment building test for radon.

Unsafe levels can build up easily in a superinsulated or airtight home unless the building has an air-to-air heat exchanger to change indoor air without losing much heat. Some tests also indicate higher levels in houses with electric heat. Homeowners with wells should also have their water tested for radon.

Fortunately, radon is neither difficult to test for nor costly to correct. Individuals can measure radon levels in their homes or other buildings with radon detection kits that can be bought in many hardware stores and supermarkets or from mail-order firms for $10 to $50. Pick one that is EPA approved. Leave detectors in basement and first-floor levels for a few days—ideally during winter when houses are sealed up. Mail them to an EPA-certified testing laboratory to get the test results.[*]

If testing reveals an unacceptable level (over four picocuries of radiation per liter of air), the EPA recommends several ways to reduce radon levels and health risks.[†] The first is to stop all indoor smoking or at least confine it to a well-ventilated room. The next corrective measure is natural ventilation, especially leaving basement

(continued)

[*] For information see the article, "Radon Detectors: How To Find Out if your House Has a Radon Problem," in the July, 1987 issue of *Consumer Reports.*

[†] A free copy of *Radon Reduction Methods* can be obtained from the Environmental Protection Agency, 401 M St., S.W., Washington, D.C. 20460. A free copy of *Radon Reduction in New Construction* is available from state radiation-protection offices or the National Association of Home Builders, Attention: William Young, 15th and M Streets, N.W., Washington, D.C. 20005. You can also call the EPA's radon hotline at 1–(800) 334–8571.

windows partially open or crawl-space vents open. Also cracks in basement walls and floors and around pipes and joints between floors and walls should be sealed.

Air-to-air heat exchangers ($1,200 to $2,500) can be installed to remove radon if radiation levels are not above 10 picocuries per liter of air. These devices also remove most other indoor air pollutants.

For houses with serious radon gas problems, special venting systems usually have to be installed below the foundations at a cost of $700 to $2,500. To remove radon from contaminated well water, a special type of activated carbon filter can be added to holding tanks at a cost of about $1,000. Contact the state radiological health office or regional EPA office to get a list of approved contractors and avoid unscrupulous radon testing and repair firms.

In Sweden no house can be built until the lot has been tested for radon. If the reading is high, the builder must follow government-mandated construction procedures to ensure that the house won't be contaminated.

Environmentalists urge enactment of a similar building-code program for all new construction in the United States. They also suggest that before buying a lot to build a new house, individuals should have the soil tested for radon.

Similarly, no one should buy an existing house unless it has been tested for radon by certified personnel, just as houses must now be inspected for termites. People building a new house should insist that the contractor use relatively simple construction practices that prevent harmful buildup of radon and add only $100 to $1,000 to the construction cost. Has the building where you live been tested for radon?

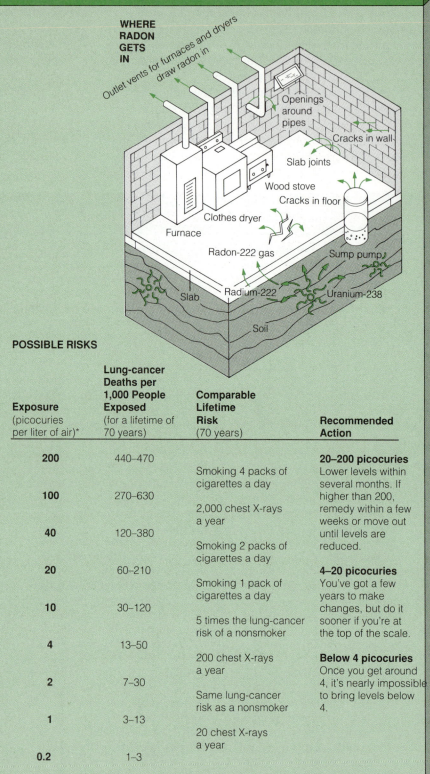

POSSIBLE RISKS

Exposure (picocuries per liter of air)*	Lung-cancer Deaths per 1,000 People Exposed (for a lifetime of 70 years)	Comparable Lifetime Risk (70 years)	Recommended Action
200	440–470		**20–200 picocuries** Lower levels within several months. If higher than 200, remedy within a few weeks or move out until levels are reduced.
100	270–630	Smoking 4 packs of cigarettes a day	
		2,000 chest X-rays a year	
40	120–380	Smoking 2 packs of cigarettes a day	
20	60–210	Smoking 1 pack of cigarettes a day	**4–20 picocuries** You've got a few years to make changes, but do it sooner if you're at the top of the scale.
10	30–120	5 times the lung-cancer risk of a nonsmoker	
4	13–50	200 chest X-rays a year	**Below 4 picocuries** Once you get around 4, it's nearly impossible to bring levels below 4.
2	7–30	Same lung-cancer risk as a nonsmoker	
1	3–13	20 chest X-rays a year	
0.2	1–3		

*A picocurie is a trillionth of a curie, a standard measure of ionizing radiation.

Figure 19-6 Sources of indoor radon-222 gases and comparable risks of exposure to various levels of this radioactive gas for a life span of 70 years. Levels are those in an actual living area, not a basement or crawlspace where levels are much higher. Smokers have the highest risk of getting lung cancer from a combination of prolonged exposure to cigarette smoke and radon-222 gas. (Data from Environmental Protection Agency)

19-2 SMOG AND ACID DEPOSITION

Smog: Cars + Sunlight = Tears A mixture of certain primary pollutants and secondary pollutants formed in the lower troposphere when some of the primary pollutants (particularly nitrogen oxides and hydrocarbons from vehicle exhausts) interact under the influence of sunlight is called **photochemical smog** (Figure 19-7). Virtually all modern cities have photochemical smog, but it is much more common in those with sunny, warm, dry climates and lots of motor vehicles. Cities with serious photochemical smog include Los Angeles, Denver, Salt Lake City (see photo on p. 449), Sydney, Mexico City, and Buenos Aires. The worst episodes of photochemical smog tend to occur in summer. Photochemical smog is also appearing in regions of the tropics and subtropics where savanna grasses are periodically burned.

The major product of such photochemical reactions is ozone, which causes eye irritation, impaired lung function, and damage to trees and crops. Thus, the severity of smog is generally associated with atmospheric concentrations of ozone at ground level. Other harmful compounds in photochemical smog are aldehydes, peroxyacyl nitrates (PANs), and nitric acid (Figure 19-7).

PRO/CON What Should Be Done about Asbestos?

Asbestos is a group of minerals made up of tiny fibers. Unless completely sealed into a product, asbestos can easily crumble into a dust of tiny fibers small enough to become suspended in the air and inhaled into the lungs, where they remain for many years.

Considerable evidence indicates that exposure to even a small amount of asbestos fibers can cause lung cancer, mesothelioma (a cancer of the lung and abdominal lining), or asbestosis (a chronic lung condition that eventually makes breathing nearly impossible) 15 to 40 years later. Children are especially vulnerable.

The EPA estimates that exposure to asbestos in U.S. schools, shopping malls, office buildings, and apartment buildings causes 3,000 to 12,000 deaths a year from cancer and other illnesses. Workers who smoke and are exposed to asbestos have a much greater chance of dying from lung cancer than those who don't smoke.

Between 1900 and 1986, over 28 million metric tons (31 million tons) of asbestos were used in the United States for hundreds of purposes. Much of it was sprayed on ceilings and other parts of schools and public and private buildings for fireproofing, sound deadening, insulating heaters and pipes, and decorating walls and ceilings, until these uses were banned in 1974.

In 1989 the EPA ordered a ban on almost all other uses of asbestos such as brake linings, roofing shingles, and water pipes by 1997. This ban will eliminate 94% of the asbestos used in the United States. EPA officials estimate that the proposed ban would prevent at least 1,900 cancer deaths over the next 15 years. Higher costs for products made with asbestos substitutes would cost each consumer on the average a total of $10 during this period. Representatives of the asbestos industry in the United States and Canada (which produces most of the asbestos used in the United States) oppose the EPA ban and may challenge it in court. They contend that with proper precautions asbestos products can be safely used and that the costs of the ban outweigh the benefits.

In 1988 the EPA estimated that one of every seven commercial and public buildings in the United States contains easily broken asbestos. These buildings include Manhattan's World Trade Center, Chicago's John Hancock Building, Houston's Astrodome, and possibly a building you live or work in. In two-thirds of these buildings the asbestos has been so damaged that it is likely to become airborne and be inhaled. This is a potential threat to millions of people, including 15 million students and 1.4 million employees in elementary and secondary schools, especially those built between 1945 and 1978.

In 1986 Congress passed the Asbestos Hazards Emergency Response Act. It required all schools to have a qualified inspector check for asbestos and submit plans for containment or removal by May 8, 1989.* It is estimated that removing asbestos from schools will cost $3.2 billion and cleanup of all buildings will cost $51 billion. Financially strapped schools cannot afford such expenditures without increased local taxes or help from state and federal governments.

Some analysts argue that the benefits of asbestos removal from schools are not worth the costs, except in clear cases where ceilings and walls are deteriorating and releasing asbestos fibers. They call for sealing and other forms of containment instead of removal of most asbestos and point out that improper removal can release more hazardous fibers than sealing off asbestos that is not crumbling.

But some leading U.S. health experts, such as Dr. Irving Selikoff, contend that even the best available containment methods leave an unacceptable margin of risk for those exposed to asbestos fibers. What do you think should be done?

*For information on the control or removal of asbestos call the EPA's Toxic Substances Control Hotline at 1-(202) 554-1404 or write the EPA. You can also get a copy of *Asbestos in the Home* from the U.S. Government Printing Office, Washington, D.C. 20402.

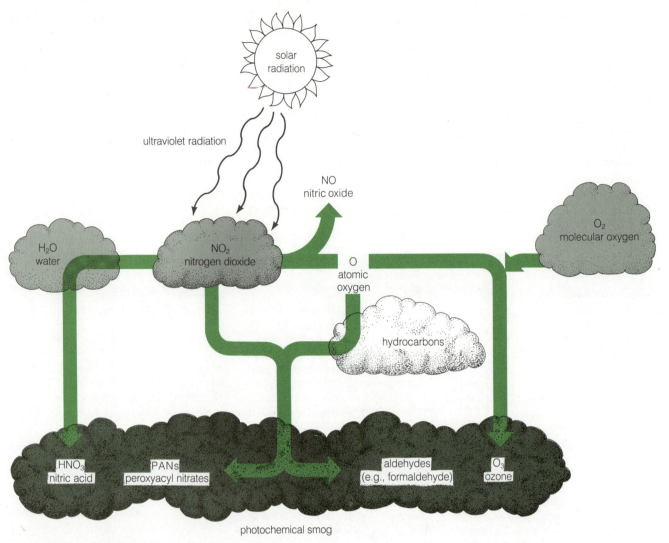

Figure 19-7 Simplified scheme of the formation of photochemical smog.

Traces of these secondary pollutants in photochemical smog build up to peak levels by early afternoon on a sunny day, irritating people's eyes and respiratory tracts. People with asthma and other respiratory problems and healthy people who exercise outdoors between 11 a.m and 4 p.m. are especially vulnerable. The hotter the day, the higher the levels of ozone and other components of photochemical smog.

Thirty years ago cities like London, Chicago, and Pittsburgh burned large amounts of coal and heavy oil, which contain sulfur impurities, in power and industrial plants and for space heating. During winter such cities suffered from **industrial smog** consisting mostly of a mixture of sulfur dioxide, suspended droplets of sulfuric acid formed from some of the sulfur dioxide, and a variety of suspended solid particles. Today coal and heavy oil are burned only in large boilers and with reasonably good control or tall smokestacks so that industrial smog is rarely a problem. However, this is not the case in China and in some eastern European countries, such as Poland (see Case

Study on p. 18) and Czechoslovakia, where large quantities of coal are burned with inadequate controls.

Local Climate, Topography, and Smog The frequency and severity of smog in an area depend on the local climate and topography, the density of population and industry, and the major fuels used in industry, heating, and transportation. In areas with high average annual precipitation, rain and snow help cleanse the air of pollutants. Winds also help sweep pollutants away and bring in fresh air, but may transfer some pollutants to distant areas (Figure 9-9, p. 196).

Hills and mountains tend to reduce the flow of air in valleys below and allow pollutant levels to build up at ground level. Buildings in cities also slow wind speed and reduce dilution and removal of pollutants.

During the day the sun warms the air near the earth's surface. Normally this heated air expands and rises, diluting low-lying pollutants and carrying them higher into the troposphere. Air from surrounding high-pressure areas then moves down into the low-

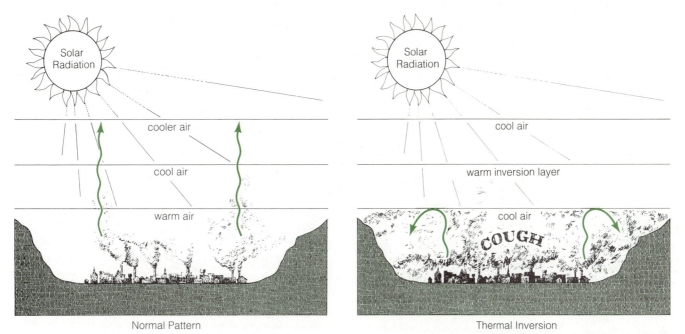

Normal Pattern   Thermal Inversion

Figure 19-8 Thermal inversion traps pollutants in a layer of cool air that cannot rise to carry the pollutants away.

Figure 19-9 Two faces of New York City. The almost clear view was photographed on a Saturday afternoon (November 26, 1966). The effect of more cars in the city and a thermal inversion is shown in the right photograph, taken the previous day.

pressure area created when the hot air rises (Figure 19-8, left). This continual mixing of the air helps keep pollutants from reaching dangerous levels in the air near the ground.

But sometimes weather conditions trap a layer of dense, cool air beneath a layer of less dense, warm air in an urban basin or valley. This is called a **temperature inversion**, or **thermal inversion** (Figure 19-8, right, and Figure 19-9). In effect, a warm-air lid covers the region and prevents pollutants from escaping in upward-flowing air currents. Usually these inversions last for only a few hours, but sometimes they last for several days when a high-pressure air mass stalls over an area. Then air pollutants at ground level build up to harmful and even lethal levels (see Spotlight on p. 487). Thermal inversions also enhance the harmful

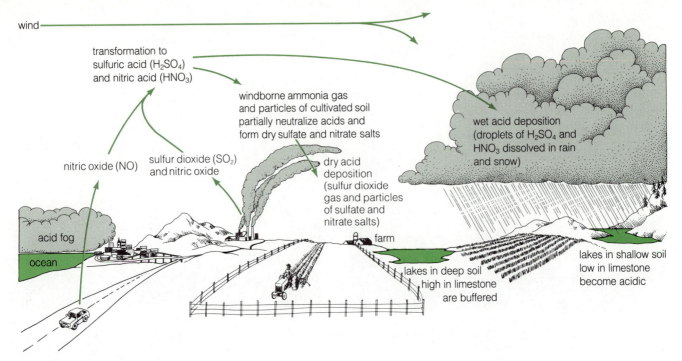

wind

transformation to
sulfuric acid (H₂SO₄)
and nitric acid (HNO₃)

windborne ammonia gas
and particles of cultivated soil
partially neutralize acids and
form dry sulfate and nitrate salts

wet acid deposition
(droplets of H₂SO₄ and
HNO₃ dissolved in rain
and snow)

nitric oxide (NO)

sulfur dioxide (SO₂)
and nitric oxide

dry acid
deposition
(sulfur dioxide
gas and particles
of sulfate and
nitrate salts)

acid fog

ocean

farm

lakes in shallow soil
low in limestone
become acidic

lakes in deep soil
high in limestone
are buffered

Figure 19-10 Acid deposition.

effects of urban heat islands and dust domes that build up over urban areas (Figure 9-9, p. 196).

Thermal inversions occur more often and last longer over towns or cities located in valleys surrounded by mountains (Donora, Pennsylvania, p. 487), on the leeward sides of mountain ranges (Denver), and near coasts (New York City). A city with several million people and automobiles in an area with a sunny climate, light winds, mountains on three sides, and the ocean on the other, has the ideal conditions for photochemical smog worsened by frequent thermal inversions. This describes the Los Angeles basin. It has almost daily inversions, many of them prolonged during the summer months, 12 million people, 8 million cars, and thousands of factories. Despite having the world's toughest air pollution control program, Los Angeles is the air pollution capital of the United States.

Acid Deposition When electric power plants and industrial plants burn coal and oil, their smokestacks emit large amounts of sulfur dioxide, suspended particulate matter, and nitrogen oxides. Power plants and factories emit 90% to 95% of the sulfur dioxide and 57% of the nitrogen oxides in the United States. Almost 60% of the SO₂ emissions are released by tall smokestacks, enabling them to travel long distances.

As emissions of sulfur dioxide and nitric oxide from stationary sources are transported long distances by winds, they form secondary pollutants such as nitrogen dioxide, nitric acid vapor, and droplets containing solutions of sulfuric acid and sulfate and nitrate salts. These chemicals descend to the earth's surface in wet form as acid rain or snow and in dry form as gases,

fog, dew, or solid particles. Gases in this mixture can be absorbed directly by leaves. The combination of dry and wet deposition and absorption of acids and acid-forming compounds at or near the earth's surface is known as **acid deposition**, commonly called acid rain (Figure 19-10). Other contributions to acid deposition come from emissions of nitric oxide from massive numbers of automobiles in major urban areas. This form of pollution can affect urban and rural areas. Because water droplets and most solid particles are removed from the atmosphere fairly quickly, acid deposition is a regional or continental rather than a global problem.

Different levels of acidity and basicity of water solutions of substances are commonly expressed in terms of pH (Figure 10-7, p. 221). A neutral solution has a pH of 7; one with a pH greater than 7 is basic, or alkaline; and one with a pH less than 7 is acidic. The lower the pH below 7, the more acidic the solution. Each whole-number decrease in pH represents a tenfold increase in acidity.

Natural precipitation varies in acidity but has an average pH of 5.6. Acid deposition with a pH value less than 5.6 has a number of harmful effects, especially when the pH falls below 5.1:

- damaging statues, buildings, metals, and car finishes

- killing fish, aquatic plants, and microorganisms in lakes and streams

- reducing the ability of salmon and trout to reproduce when the pH falls below 5.5

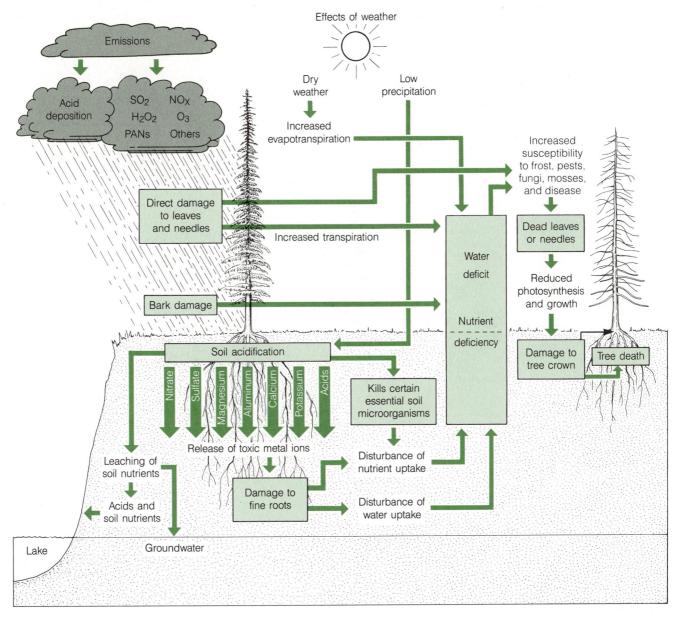

Figure 19-11 Harmful effects of air pollutants on trees.

- killing and reducing productivity of many species of phytoplankton when the pH is below their optimum range of 6 to 8

- disrupting the nitrogen cycle in lakes with a pH of 5.4 to 5.7

- weakening or killing trees, especially conifers at high elevations, by leaching calcium, potassium, and other plant nutrients from soil (Figure 19-11).

- damaging tree roots and killing many kinds of fish by releasing ions of aluminum, lead, mercury, and cadmium from soil and bottom sediments (Figure 19-11)

- weakening trees and making them more suscepti- ble to attacks by diseases, insects, drought, and fungi and mosses that thrive under acidic condi- tions (Figure 19-11)

- stunting the growth of crops such as tomatoes, soybeans, snap beans, tobacco, spinach, carrots, broccoli, and cotton

- increasing populations of giardia, a protozoan that is associated with a severe gastrointestinal disease that afflicts hikers and mountain climbers who drink water from seemingly clear mountain- stream waters

- leaching toxic metals such as copper and lead from city and home water pipes into drinking water

- causing and aggravating many human respiratory diseases and leading to premature death

Acid deposition illustrates the threshold effect (Figure 18-2, p. 453). Most soils, lakes, and streams

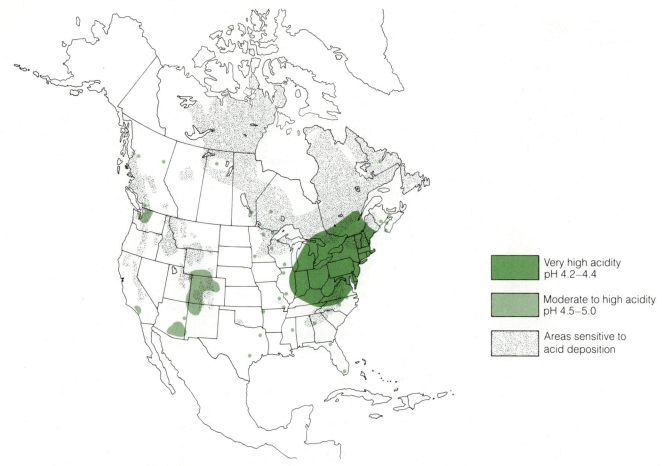

■ Very high acidity	pH 4.2–4.4
■ Moderate to high acidity	pH 4.5–5.0
⬚ Areas sensitive to	acid deposition

Figure 19-12 Average acidity of acid deposition and areas with soils sensitive to acid deposition in North America in 1984. (Data from Environmental Protection Agency)

contain alkaline or basic chemicals that can react with a certain amount of acids and thus neutralize them. But repeated exposure to acids year after year can deplete most of these acid-buffering chemicals. Then suddenly large numbers of trees start dying and most fish in a lake or stream die when exposed to the next year's input of acids. By the time this happens it is 10 to 20 years too late to prevent serious damage.

Acid deposition is already a serious problem in northern and central Europe, the northeastern United States, southeastern Canada, and parts of China, Brazil, and Nigeria. It is emerging as a problem in heavily industrialized parts of Asia, Latin America, and Africa and in parts of the western United States (mostly from dry deposition). It is also occurring in parts of the largely unindustrialized tropics, mostly from the release of nitrogen oxides by biomasss burning. A large portion of the acid-producing chemicals produced in one country is exported to others by prevailing surface winds. Over three-fourths of the acid deposition in Norway, Switzerland, Austria, Sweden, the Netherlands, and Finland is blown to these countries from industrialized areas of western and eastern Europe.

More than half the acid deposition in heavily pop-

ulated southeastern Canada and in the eastern United States originates from emissions from the heavy concentration of coal-and oil-burning power and industrial plants in seven central and upper midwestern states—Ohio, Indiana, Pennsylvania, Illinois, Missouri, West Virginia, and Tennessee (Figure 19-12). The acidity of the precipitation falling over much of eastern North America has a pH of 4.0 to 4.2. This is 30 to 40 times greater than the acidity of the normal precipitation that fell on these areas several decades ago. Overall the states that emit the largest amounts of chemicals leading to acid deposition are California, Indiana, Ohio, and Texas.

About 75% of the acid deposition falling on Canada originates in the United States; only 15% of the acid deposition falling on the northeastern states originates from Canada. This large net flow of acid deposition from the United States to Canada is straining relations between the two countries. Canadian scientists and officials and many U.S. scientists criticize the U. S. government for not moving fast enough to reduce harmful emissions from industrial and power plants by at least 50%. The Ontario Ministry of the Environment estimates that acid deposition threatens

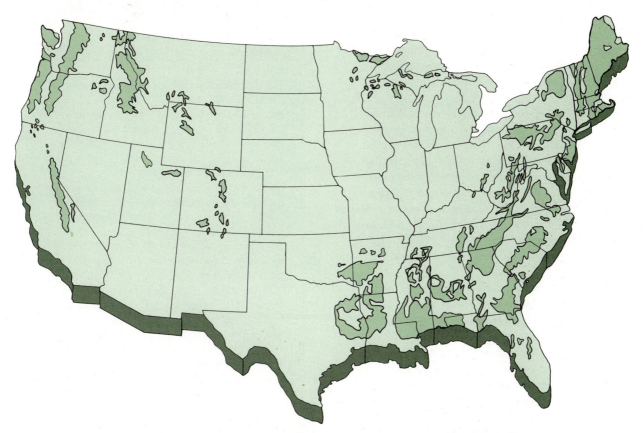

Figure 19-13 Areas in which U.S. lakes and streams are especially vulnerable to acid deposition because they have low concentrations of alkaline substances, such as bicarbonate ions, that can help neutralize acid inputs. Compare these areas with the levels of high acid deposition shown in Figure 19-12. (Data from the Environmental Protection Agency)

48,000 Canadian lakes, endangering the $1.1-billion-a-year sport fishing industry and $10 billion-a-year tourism industry. Canadians are also worried that acid deposition will harm the forestry and related industries, which provide jobs for one in every ten Canadians and earn $14 billion a year.

According to the National Academy of Sciences, damage from acid deposition already costs the United States at least $6 billion a year, and costs will rise sharply unless action is taken now. The cost of reducing these pollutants would run from $1.2 billion to $20 billion, depending on the extent of cleanup and the technology used.

Soils in some areas contain limestone and other alkaline substances that can neutralize the acids. But acidic, thin soils in other areas have little ability to neutralize acids (Figure 19-12). Also repeated exposure of any soil to large inputs of acids can eventually deplete its acid-neutralizing chemicals. Acid runoff in these sensitive areas can kill many forms of aquatic life in nearby lakes and streams. As with soils, some lakes and streams are especially vulnerable because of low alkalinity (especially a low content of bicarbonate ions) which can help neutralize acid inputs (Figure 19-13).

19-3 EFFECTS OF AIR POLLUTION ON LIVING ORGANISMS AND MATERIALS

Damage to Human Health Your respiratory system has a number of mechanisms that help protect you from air pollution. Hairs in your nose filter out large particles. Sticky mucus in the lining of your upper respiratory tract captures small particles and dissolves some gaseous pollutants. Automatic sneezing and coughing mechanisms expel contaminated air and mucus when your respiratory system is irritated by pollutants. Your upper respiratory tract is lined with hundreds of thousands of tiny, mucus-coated hairs, called cilia. They continually wave back and forth, transporting mucus and the pollutants they trap to your mouth, where it is either swallowed or expelled.

But years of smoking and exposure to air pollutants can overload or deteriorate these natural defenses, causing or contributing to a number of respiratory diseases such as lung cancer, chronic bronchitis, and emphysema. Elderly people, infants, pregnant women, and persons with heart disease, asthma, or other respiratory diseases are especially vulnerable to air pollution.

Fine particles are particularly hazardous to human health because they are small enough to penetrate the lung's natural defenses. Smoking is the leading cause of lung cancer, but the disease has also been linked to inhalation of a number of other air pollutants, such as asbestos fibers (see Pro/Con on p. 491).

Inhaling the ozone found in photochemical smog (Figure 19-7) causes coughing, shortness of breath, nose and throat irritation, and discomfort, and aggravates chronic diseases such as asthma, bronchitis, emphysema, and heart trouble. Animal studies also show that ozone damages lung tissue and weakens the immune system. Outdoor exercise in areas where ozone levels exceed safe levels (0.12 parts per million per hour) amplifies these effects. Many U.S. cities frequently exceed these levels, especially during warm weather.

Bronchitis and emphysema are marked by coughing, wheezing, and shortness of breath. Emphysema is an incurable condition that reduces the ability of the lungs to transfer oxygen to the blood so that the slightest exertion causes acute shortness of breath. Prolonged smoking and exposure to air pollutants can cause emphysema in anyone. However, about 2% of emphysema cases are caused by a defective gene that reduces the elasticity of the air sacs of the lungs. Anyone with this hereditary condition, for which testing is available, should not smoke and should not live or work in a highly polluted area.

The World Health Organization estimates that worldwide nearly 1 billion urban dwellers—almost one of every five people on earth—are being exposed to health hazards from air pollutants. Cities with high levels of air pollution include Milan, Italy; Paris, France; Seoul, South Korea; Mexico City, Mexico (see Case Study on p. 190), New Delhi and Calcutta, India; Athens, Greece; and Rio de Janeiro, Cubatao, and São Paulo, Brazil (see Spotlight to right). An estimated 60% of the people living in Calcutta suffer from respiratory diseases related to air pollution. Breathing the air in Mexico City is roughly equivalent to smoking two packs of cigarettes a day (see Case Study on p. 190). In Athens air pollution kills as many as six people a day.

In 1988 the EPA estimated that 102 million Americans—42% of the population—were breathing unsafe air. The congressional Office of Technology Assessment estimates that some 50,000 people in the United States may die prematurely each year as a result of diseases caused or worsened by inhalation of airborne sulfates. Scientists at the University of California at Davis estimate that the use of gasoline and diesel fuel in the United States causes up to 30,000 premature deaths a year, especially among those suffering from respiratory ailments. Between 1970 and 1987 deaths in the United States from chronic lung diseases, such as emphysema and cancer, increased 36%.

SPOTLIGHT **The World's Most Polluted City**

The air pollution capital of the world may be Cubatao, an hour's drive south of São Paulo, Brazil. This city of 100,000 people lies in a coastal valley that has frequent thermal inversions. Residents call the area "the valley of death."

In this heavily industrialized city scores of plants spew thousands of tons of pollutants a day into the frequently stagnant air. More babies are born deformed there than anywhere else in Latin America.

In one recent year 13,000 of the 40,000 people living in the downtown core area suffered from respiratory disease. One resident says, "On some days if you go outside, you will vomit." The mayor refuses to live in the city.

Most residents would like to live somewhere else, but they need the jobs available in the city and cannot afford to move. The government has begun some long overdue efforts to control air pollution but has far to go. Meanwhile the poor continue to pay the price of this form of economic progress: bad health and premature death.

Air pollution costs the United States at least $110 billion annually in health care and lost work productivity. About $100 billion of this is caused by indoor air pollution.

Damage to Vegetation   Some gaseous pollutants, such as sulfur dioxide, nitrogen oxides, ozone, and PANs, cause direct damage to leaves of crop plants and trees when they enter leaf pores (stomata) (Figure 19-11). Chronic exposure of leaves and needles to air pollutants can also break down the waxy coating that helps prevent excessive water loss and damage from diseases, pests, drought, and frost. In the midwestern United States crop losses of wheat, corn, soybeans, and peanuts from damage by ozone and acid deposition amount to about $5 billion a year.

Chronic exposure to air pollutants interferes with photosynthesis and plant growth, reduces nutrient uptake, and causes leaves or needles to turn yellow or brown and drop off. Coniferous trees, especially at high elevations, are highly vulnerable to the effects of air pollution because of their long life spans and the year-round exposure of their needles to polluted air.

In addition to causing direct leaf and needle damage, acid deposition can leach vital plant nutrients such as calcium, magnesium, and potassium from the soil and kill essential soil microorganisms. It also releases aluminum ions, which are normally bound to soil par-

Figure 19-14 Tree death and damage in this coniferous forest in West Germany is believed to be the result of long-term exposure to multiple air pollutants, which made the trees more vulnerable to disease and drought.

Phototake/Bernd Uhlig

ticles, into soil water. There they damage fine root filaments, reduce uptake of water and nutrients from the soil, and make trees more vulnerable to drought, frost, insects, fungi, mosses, and disease (Figure 19-11). This indirect damage that weakens trees is believed to be much more threatening than the direct damage from air pollution. Prolonged exposure to high levels of multiple air pollutants can eventually kill all trees and vegetation in an area (see the Case Study on p. 351).

The effects of chronic exposure of trees to multiple air pollutants may not be visible for several decades. Then suddenly large numbers begin dying because of soil nutrient depletion and increased susceptibility to pests, diseases, fungi, mosses, and drought.

That is what is happening to almost one-fourth of the forests in Europe. The phenomenon, known as *waldsterben* (forest death), turns whole forests into stump-studded meadows. For example, 8% of the trees in some West German forests were found to be dead or damaged in 1982. One year later the figure was 34%, and by 1987 the toll stood at about 52% (Figure 19-14). Today about a third of West Germany's trees show heavy damage. This has caused a $10 billion loss of commercially important trees, such as spruce, fir, pine, beech, and oak. The diebacks have also eliminated habitats for many types of wildlife. Similar damage is occurring in at least 15 other European countries.

Similar diebacks in the United States have occurred mostly in coniferous forests on higher-elevation slopes facing moving air masses. The most seriously affected areas are the Appalachian Mountains from Georgia to New England. In New York, Vermont, and New Hampshire, air pollution has killed 60% of high-elevation red spruce trees. By 1988 most spruce, fir, and other conifers atop North Carolina's Mt. Mitchell, the highest peak in the East, were dead from being bathed in ozone and acid fog for years. The soil was so acidic that new seedlings could not survive.

Plant pathologist Robert Bruck warns that damage to mountaintop forests is an early warning that many tree species at lower elevations may soon die or be damaged by prolonged exposure to air pollution, as has happened in Europe. Many scientists fear that elected officials in the United States will continue to delay establishing stricter controls on all major forms of air pollution until it is too late to prevent a severe loss of valuable forest resources like that happening in Europe.

Damage to Aquatic Life Acid deposition has a severe harmful impact on the aquatic life of freshwater lakes and streams, especially in areas where surrounding soils or bodies of water have little acid-buffering capacity (Figure 19-12, Figure 19-13). The first signs of excess acidity are a decline in the numbers of leeches, mollusks, and insects that are important to a lake's overall health. This sets the stage for the loss of various fish species, such as trout, pike, and sunfish.

Much of the damage to aquatic life in the Northern Hemisphere is a result of *acid shock*. Acid shock is caused by the sudden runoff of large amounts of highly acidic water (along with toxic aluminum leached from the soil) into lakes when snow melts in the spring or when heavy rains follow a period of drought. The aluminum leached from the soil and lake sediment kills fish by clogging their gills.

In Norway and Sweden at least 68,000 lakes either contain no fish or have lost most of their acid-buffering capacity because of excess acidity. In Canada the

Figure 19-15 This marble monument in Rome has been damaged by exposure to acidic air pollutants.

Harry Lloyd/Peter Arnold

Department of the Environment reports some 14,000 lakes are almost fishless, and another 150,000 are in peril because of excess acidity.

In the United States acidified lakes are concentrated in the Northeast and Upper Middle West (mostly in parts of Minnesota, Michigan, Wisconsin, and the upper Great Lakes). About one-fourth of the lakes and ponds in New York's Adirondack Mountains are too acidic to support fish. Another 20% have lost most of their acid-neutralizing capacity. Half the streams of the mid-Atlantic coastal plain are also threatened.

A 1988 study by the Environmental Defense Fund indicated that excess nitrate input from acid deposition is a major threat to many types of aquatic plants and fish in lakes and estuaries, such as the Chesapeake Bay. Nitrate plant nutrients stimulate the over-growth of algae and other phytoplankton, which cloud the water and prevent light from filtering down to plants on the lake bottom. When the algae die, their decomposition by oxygen-consuming bacteria depletes the water of dissolved oxygen, suffocating fish and other aerobic organisms.

Damage to Materials Each year air pollutants cause millions of dollars in damage to various materials (Table 19-2). The fallout of soot and grit on buildings, cars, and clothing requires costly cleaning. Irreplaceable marble statues, historic buildings, and stained-glass windows throughout the world have been pitted and discolored by air pollutants (Figure 19-15).

Unless they are painted or maintained properly, metals such as iron and steel used in railroad tracks and to support bridges and expressways are corroded and weakened by air pollutants. Various air pollutants also damage leather, rubber, paper, paint, and fabrics such as cotton, rayon, and nylon (Table 19-2).

19-4 EFFECTS OF AIR POLLUTION ON STRATOSPHERIC OZONE AND GLOBAL AND REGIONAL CLIMATE

Depletion of Ozone in the Stratosphere In 1974 chemists Sherwood Roland and Mario Molina theorized that human-made chlorofluorocarbons (CFCs)—better known as Freons—are lowering the average concentration of ozone in the stratosphere. No one suspected such a possibility when CFCs were developed in 1930.

These stable, odorless, nonflammable, nontoxic, and noncorrosive chemicals were a chemist's dream. Soon they were widely used as coolants in air conditioners and refrigerators and as propellants in aerosol spray cans. They are also used to clean electronic parts, as hospital sterilants, and as blowing agents to puff liquid plastic into styrofoam and other plastic foams used for insulation and packaging. Since 1945 the use of the four major types of CFCs has increased sharply. Bromine-containing compounds, called *halons*, are also widely used, mostly in fire extinguishers. Industrial countries account for 84% of CFC production, with the United States being the top producer, followed by western European countries and Japan.

Since 1978 the use of CFCs in aerosol cans has been banned in the U.S., Canada, and most Scandinavian countries. But worldwide nonaerosol uses have risen sharply, along with aerosol use in western Europe. Aerosols are still the largest use, accounting for 25% of global CFC use. Spray cans, discarded or leaking refrigeration and air conditioning equipment, and the burning of plastic foam products release the CFCs into the atmosphere. Depending on the type, CFCs stay in the atmosphere for 22 to 111 years.

Over several decades they gradually move up to the stratosphere. There, under the influence of high-energy UV radiation, they break down and release chlorine atoms, which speed up the breakdown of ozone into oxygen gas. Over time a single chlorine atom can convert as many as 100,000 molecules of O_3 to O_2. Bromine atoms released in the stratosphere from halons also convert ozone into oxygen gas. CFCs are also greenhouse gases that contribute to global warming.

In 1988 the National Aeronautics and Space Administration (NASA) released a study showing that stratospheric ozone has decreased by as much as 3% over the most populous areas of North America, Europe, China, and Japan since 1969 (Figure 19-16).

Over Scandinavia and Alaska the average loss during winter months is 6%.

In the 1980s researchers were shocked to find that each year up to 50% of the ozone in the upper stratosphere over the Antarctic is destroyed from September through November. In 1987, this Antarctic ozone hole covered an area the size of the continental United States. Measurements indicate that this large annual decrease in ozone over the South Pole is caused by the presence of ice clouds that make ozone-destroying CFCs more active. In 1989 measurements revealed the presence of the same destructive chlorine compounds in the stratosphere over the North Pole. Thus, very little stands in the way of the formation of another ozone hole over the Arctic for a few months each year.

Large volcanic eruptions and natural climatic processes such as cyclic changes in solar output can alter stratospheric ozone levels. However, there is considerable and growing evidence that CFCs, halons, and other chlorine-containing chemicals (such as carbon tetrachloride and methyl chloroform used as cleaners and degreasers) are a major cause of ozone depletion in the stratosphere.

Effects of Ozone Depletion With less ozone in the stratosphere, more UV radiation will reach the earth's surface (see cartoon on p. 501). The EPA estimates that a 5% ozone depletion would cause the following effects in the United States:

- an additional 940,000 cases annually of basal-cell and squamous-cell skin cancers, both disfiguring but usually not fatal cancers if treated in time (see Spotlight on p. 464)

- an additional 30,000 cases annually of often-fatal melanoma skin cancer, which now kills almost 9,000 Americans each year

- a sharp increase in eye cataracts and severe sunburn in people and eye cancer in cattle

- suppression of the human immune system, which would reduce our defenses against a variety of infectious diseases

- an increase in eye-burning photochemical smog, highly damaging ozone, and acid deposition in the troposphere

- decreased yields of important food crops such as corn, rice, soybeans, and wheat

- damage to some aquatic plant species essential to ocean food webs

- a loss of perhaps $2 billion a year from degradation of plastics and other polymer materials

- increased global warming (greenhouse effect) leading to changes in climate, agricultural and forest productivity, and wildlife survival

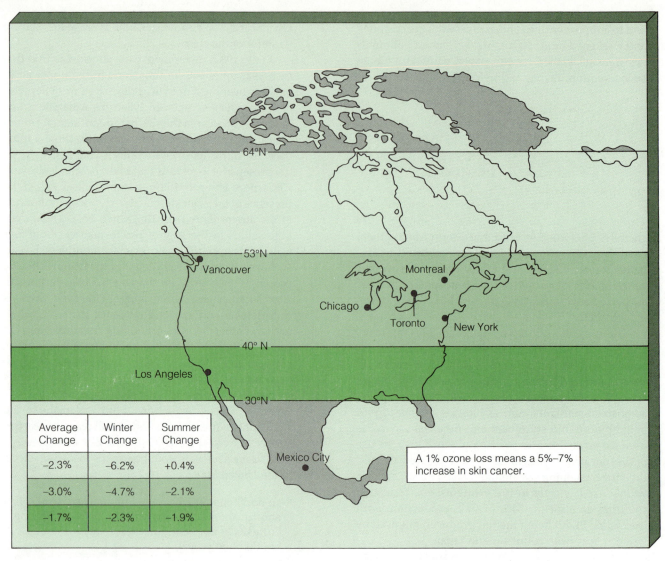

Average Change	Winter Change	Summer Change
−2.3%	−6.2%	+0.4%
−3.0%	−4.7%	−2.1%
−1.7%	−2.3%	−1.9%

A 1% ozone loss means a 5%–7% increase in skin cancer.

Figure 19-16 Average drops in ozone levels in the stratosphere above parts of the earth between 1969 and 1986, based on data gathered from satellites and ground stations. (Data from NASA)

" I MISS THE OZONE LAYER...."

Protecting the Ozone Layer Models of atmospheric processes indicate that just to keep CFCs at 1987 levels would require an immediate 85% drop in total CFC emissions throughout the world. Analysts believe that the first step toward this goal should be an immediate worldwide ban on the use of CFCs in aerosol spray cans and in producing plastic foam products. Cost-effective substitutes are already available for these uses. Also automotive service shops should be required to recycle CFCs from automobile air conditioners and the sale of small cans of CFCs used by consumers to charge leaky auto air conditioners should be banned by 1992.

The next step would be to phase out all other uses of CFCs, halons, methyl chloroform, and carbon tetrachloride by 1995. Substitute coolants in refrigeration and air conditioning will probably cost more. But compared to the potential economic and health consequences of ozone depletion, such cost increases would be minor. However, there is concern that substitutes for CFCs that damage the ozone layer may still make a significant contribution to atmospheric warming.

Some progress has been made. In 1987 46 countries producing CFCs developed a treaty to reduce production of the eight most widely used and most damaging CFCs. By 1989, thirty-nine countries had ratified the treaty. If carried out, it will reduce total emissions of CFCs into the atmosphere by about 35% between 1989 and 2000. According to the EPA this would prevent about 137 million cases of skin cancer, 27 million skin-cancer deaths, and 1.2 million eye cataracts.

However, the treaty makes no provisions for the retrieval and destruction of the millions of tons of CFCs that will escape from presently running refrigerators and air conditioners when they wear out or develop leaks. Also it does not decrease use of halons, carbon tetrachloride, and methyl chloroform that can also deplete ozone.

Most scientists agree that the treaty is an important symbol of global cooperation but that it does not go far enough to prevent significant depletion of the ozone layer. They call for phasing out all uses of these chemicals by 1995, as Sweden has agreed to do. In 1989 delegates from 81 countries meeting in Helsinki agreed to halt all use and production of certain CFCs by the year 2000 and agreed on the need to phase out or reduce the use of other ozone-depleting substances such as halons, carbon tetrachloride, and methyl chloroform.

Even if all CFCs and halons were banned tomorrow, it would take about 100 years for the planet to recover from the present ozone depletion and that to come from CFCs and halons already in the atmosphere. The key question is whether MDCs can agree to sacrifice short-term economic gain by quickly kicking their present addiction to CFCs and halons to protect life on earth in coming decades.

Global Warming from an Enhanced Greenhouse Effect

A buildup of one or several greenhouse gases in the atmosphere would cause the average temperature of the earth's lower atmosphere to rise as a result of an enhanced greenhouse effect (Figure 5-5, p. 110). This appears to be what is happening, mostly because of gases we are putting into the atmosphere (Figure 19-17).

Between 1860 and 1988 the average global level of carbon dioxide in the atmosphere increased 25%, with a sharp rise since 1958 (Figure 19-17a). About 80% of this rise is due to the burning of fossil fuels, with 75% of this CO_2 coming from MDCs. About 22% of the world's carbon dioxide emissions are produced by the United States. This comes from burning fossil fuels in industries (29%), electric power plants (28%), trans-

portation (27%), and homes and businesses (16%). Burning forests produce CO_2, whereas growing forests convert CO_2 into wood. Average annual emissions of CO_2 per American total 4.5 metric tons (5 tons), the world's highest. Deforestation, especially the wholesale clearing and burning of tropical forests, is believed to account for about 20% of the increase in carbon dioxide levels. Levels of other heat-trapping, greenhouse gases have also been increasing (Figure 19-17 b, c, d).

Since 1880 average global temperatures have risen about 0.7°C (1.2°F) (Figure 19-18). Climate experts believe that normal climatic fluctuations caused about one-third of this increase, with the greenhouse effect causing the rest. Many climate experts expect the enhanced greenhouse effect caused mostly by our activities to begin accelerating in the 1990s.

Climatic models project that the earth's average atmospheric temperature will rise 1.5°C to 4.5°C (2.7°F to 18.1°F) between 2030 and 2050, if greenhouse gases continue to rise at the current rate. Temperatures at middle and high latitudes will rise two to three times the average increase. If these changes take place, the atmosphere will be warmer than it has been at any time during the past 150,000 years. Changes caused by this warming could last for hundreds to thousands of years.

Effects of Global Climate Changes

At first glance a warmer average climate might seem desirable. It could lead to lower heating bills and longer growing seasons in middle and high latitudes. Crop yields might increase 60% to 80% in some areas because more carbon dioxide in the atmosphere can increase the rate of photosynthesis. Increased warming of the troposphere may cause some cooling in the stratosphere, thereby slowing down reactions that destroy ozone.

But other factors could offset these effects. Air conditioning bills would be higher. Potential gains in crop yields could be wiped out by increased damage from insect pests because warmer temperatures would boost insect breeding. Higher temperatures would also increase plant aerobic respiration rates and reduce water availability. Also soils in some of the new food-growing areas would not be useful for growing key crops. Much of Canada, for example, does not have the optimum type of soil for growing wheat and corn.

A 4°C (7°F) rise in temperature would change worldwide patterns of precipitation, winds, storms, and ocean currents. There would be major shifts in areas where crops could be grown, with each 1°C (1.8°F) rise pushing climatic zones 100 to 150 kilometers (62 to 93 miles) northward. Iowa could become a desert and Alberta, Canada a breadbasket. Severe droughts may occur in southern Canada where most of the population lives, while increased flooding may occur in

Figure 19-17 Increases in average concentrations of greenhouse gases in the atmosphere. They are projected to increase the global warming trend shown in Figure 19-18. (Data from Electric Power Research Institute. Adapted by permission from Cecie Starr and Ralph Taggart, *Biology: The Unity and Diversity of Life*, 5th ed., Belmont, Calif.: Wadsworth, 1989).

a. Carbon dioxide (CO_2) Currently this gas is responsible for 57% of the global warming trend. Major sources are fossil fuel burning (80%) and deforestation (20%). CO_2 remains in the atmosphere for 2 to 4 hundred years. Industrial countries account for 65% of CO_2 emissions with the United States and the Soviet Union responsible for 50%. LDCs, with 80% of the world's people, are responsible for 35% of CO_2 emissions but may contribute 50% by 2020. CO_2 emissions are increasing by 4% a year.

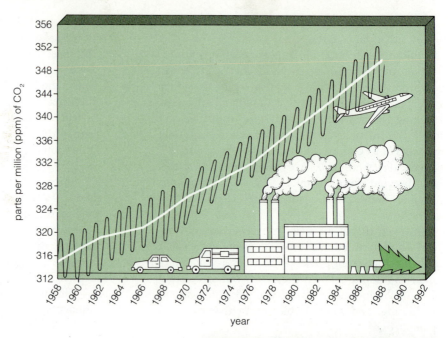

b. Chlorofluorocarbons (CFCs) Currently these gases are responsible for about 25% of the global warming trend. Major sources are leaking air conditioners and refrigerators, evaporation of industrial solvents, production of plastic foams, and propellants in aerosol spray cans (in some countries). CFCs remain in the atmosphere for 22 to 111 years, depending on the type. These chemicals are about 15,000 times more effective in causing warming than a CO_2 molecule. CFC emissions are increasing by 5% a year.

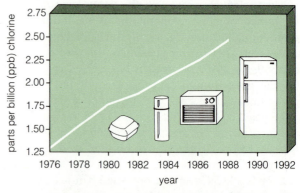

c. Methane (CH_4) Currently this gas is responsible for 12% of the global warming trend. It is produced by anaerobic bacterial decay processes in swamps, bogs, rice fields, and landfills, in the stomachs of cows and sheep, and in the guts of termites. Some also leaks from natural gas wells, pipelines, storage tanks, furnaces, dryers, and stoves. Natural sources produce an estimated one-third of the methane in the atmosphere, and human activities produce the rest. CH_4 remains in the troposphere for about 11 years. Each molecule of methane is about 25 times more effective than a carbon dioxide molecule in greenhouse warming. CH_4 emissions are increasing by 1% a year.

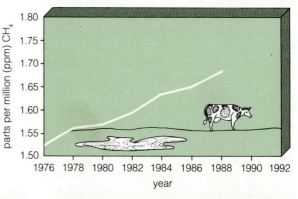

d. Nitrous oxide (N_2O) Currently this gas is responsible for 6% of the global warming. It is released from the breakdown of nitrogen fertilizers in soil, livestock wastes, and nitrate-contaminated groundwater, and by biomass burning. Its average stay in the troposphere is 150 years. Each molecule of N_2O is 230 times more effective than a carbon dioxide molecule in greenhouse warming. N_2O also depletes ozone in the stratosphere. Nitrous oxide emissions are increasing by 0.2% a year.

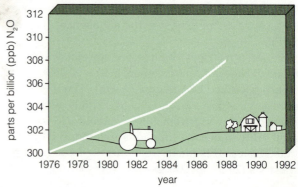

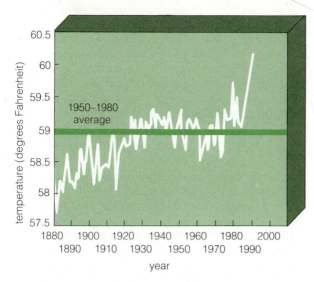

Figure 19-18 Average global temperatures, 1880–1988. Note the general increase since 1880 and the sharp rise in the 1980s. The baseline is the global average temperature from 1950 to 1980. (Data from National Academy of Sciences and National Center for Atmospheric Research.)

the north. Lower water levels in the Great Lakes would concentrate existing pollutants. The Gulf Stream might stop flowing northeastward as far as Europe, leading to a much colder climate in that part of the world.

Global warming would probably speed up the decay of organic matter in the soil, which would increase the release of carbon dioxide and methane into the atmosphere and accelerate greenhouse warming. Warmer air could also speed up the decay of peat in tundra soils, which would allow flowing water to erode large areas of these soils. The spread of tropical climates from the equator would bring malaria (see Case Study on p. 456) and other insect-borne diseases to formerly temperate zones.

The frequency and intensity of weather extremes such as heat waves, droughts, and hurricanes would increase in many parts of the world. For example, giant hurricanes with 50% more destructive potential than those today, would hit farther north and during more months of the year. Rainfall would increase in Africa and India but probably drop in the Midwest of the United States. The mountain snow that supplies much of California's water would dwindle. Rain instead of snow in the mountains would cause winter floods followed by summer droughts that would disrupt food production and water supplies, especially for already arid southern California (Figure 11-3, p. 247).

The growth rates of commercially important tree species might be lowered by a rise in average temperature. The range of most tree species in the eastern United States would shift northward. But to do this many species such as beech, birch, and sugar maple would have to migrate northward at a speed ten times greater than they have been able to do so in the past and somehow leap over cities and other barriers in

their way. Stress to trees from pests and disease microorganisms would increase because they are able to adapt to climate change faster than trees. The number of devastating fires in drier forest areas and grasslands would increase. Many wildlife species would disappear. Least affected would be tropical rainforests, if we don't cut most of them down.

Higher temperatures would warm the oceans, expanding water volume and raising average sea levels. Partial melting of mountain glaciers would raise levels further. Warmer water temperatures would probably devastate most coral reefs because most of their species already live close to their temperature limits.

Present models indicate that raising the average atmospheric temperature by 4°C (7°F) would raise the average global sea level by between 0.5 to 1.5 meters (1.6 to 5 feet) over the next 50 to 100 years, assuming no breakup of the West Antarctic ice sheet (which would lead to much greater increases). This would cause havoc for many of the one-third of the world's people that live in low-lying coastal cities, ports, river deltas, and wetlands. If most of the Greenland and West Antarctic ice sheets melted, as happened during a warm period 120,000 years ago, sea levels would gradually rise as much as 6 meters (20 feet) over several hundred years.

With only modest rises in sea level, major cities such as Shanghai and Cairo and large areas of agricultural lowlands and deltas in Bangladesh (see Case Study on p. 244), India, and China, where much of the world's rice is grown, would be flooded. Other threatened cities include Rotterdam, Venice, Bangkok, and Taipei. Low-lying islands like the Marshall Islands in the Pacific, the Maldives (a series of 1,800 islands in the Indian Ocean off the west coast of India) and some Caribbean nations would disappear.

Coastal wetlands that are nurseries for most commercially important fish and shellfish species (see Spotlight on p. 122) would also be flooded. This would decrease world food supplies and decimate migratory bird populations and other wildlife. The EPA projects that a sea level rise of 1 meter (3 feet) would destroy 26% to 65% of the coastal wetlands in the United States. If bulkheads and levees were built to protect coastal cities, 50% to 82% of U.S. wetlands would be lost because these structures keep the sea from moving inland and creating new wetlands. Even a 0.5-meter (1.6-foot) rise would drown about one-third of U.S. coastal wetlands. The salinity of rivers, bays, and coastal aquifers would also increase.

Most barrier islands would be underwater along with the Florida Keys and the present beaches of Malibu, California. Low-lying cities such as New Orleans, New York, Atlantic City, Galveston, Charleston, and Miami (which lies at or just above sea level on swampland reclaimed from the Everglades) would be threatened by flooding unless billions of dollars were spent to build massive systems of dikes and levees. In Washington, D.C. water levels would almost reach the Capitol steps and the White House. In the United States even a modest 0.3-meter (1-foot) rise would flood major portions of Louisiana and Florida and erode Atlantic and Gulf Coast beaches at least 30 meters (98 feet) inland. A comedian joked that he was planning to buy land in Kansas because it would probably become valuable beach front property.

Tanks storing hazardous chemicals along the Gulf and Atlantic coasts would also be flooded and saltwater would intrude into groundwater supplies (Figure 11-16, p. 251) in many coastal areas. Aquifers that supply water for large numbers of people in Florida and Long Island would become too salty to use.

Dealing with Global Warming   Most climate experts agree that we will experience global warming for several hundred years mostly because of the massive amounts of long-lived chemicals we have been pouring into the atmosphere for decades (Figure 19-17). The only debate at this point is how large the rise in average global temperature will be, how fast it will climb, and what the regional effects will be. There is no way we can quickly remove greenhouse gases, cool the atmosphere, or lower the average sea level.

There is also widespread agreement that any significant change in world climate would cause a sharp increase in food prices, massive famines, severe economic losses, and economic, ecological, and social chaos. The faster the climate change, the greater these problems. Thus, global warming caused by our activities is a genuine planetary emergency.

Basically we have two options for dealing with the global warming we have helped set in motion: slow it down or adjust to its effects. Many atmospheric scientists believe that past emissions of greenhouse gases will automatically raise average atmospheric temperatures 0.6°C to 1.7°C (1.1°F to 3.1°F), even if we stop burning fossil fuels tomorrow. But slowing down the rate of change can help prevent economic and social chaos and buy time to switch to other energy alternatives.

We can slow down the rate of global warming by

- banning emissions of CFCs and halons
- cutting fossil fuel use by at least 20% by 2000 and 50% by 2015, mostly by placing heavy taxes on gasoline and emissions fees on fossil fuels and using the revenue to develop energy alternatives to replace fossil fuels, improve energy efficiency, plant trees worldwide, and give energy subsidies to the poor. The key question is no longer how much oil, gas, and coal we have (Chapter 16), but how much we can afford to burn.
- sharply reducing the use of coal, which emits 60% more carbon dioxide per unit of energy produced

than any other fossil fuel (Figure 16-10, p. 381). As an interim measure, we could switch power plants from coal to natural gas, which produces only half as much CO_2 per unit of energy and also sharply reduces emissions of other air pollutants. But to power its industrialization program, China plans to nearly double coal use in the next decade.

- using scrubbers to remove carbon dioxide from the smokestack emissions of coal-burning power and industrial plants and from vehicle exhausts; present methods remove only about 30% of the CO_2 and are too expensive, but chemists at the Solar Energy Research Institute have developed specialized molecules that can remove CO_2 from the air more efficiently. It could then be pumped into oil wells to recover heavy oil from wells or converted to methanol and used as a fuel for cars.
- improving energy efficiency (Section 17-1). A recent World Resources Institute study concluded that MDCs could halve fossil-fuel usage by improving energy efficiency using existing technology.
- raising average gas mileage in new cars from 27.5 miles per gallon to 60 miles per gallon by 2005 to cut lifetime CO_2 emissions from vehicles in half
- requiring new homes to have the most efficient heating and cooling systems available (Figure 3-16, p. 68)
- greatly increasing use of solar energy, wind power, and geothermal energy (Chapter 17)
- increasing use of natural gas during the transition from the present fossil fuel age to a new solar age (Section 16-2)
- greatly slowing down the clearing and degradation of tropical forests (Section 13-2)
- planting trees worldwide; 0.4 hectare (1 acre) of trees absorbs enough carbon dioxide each year to offset that produced by driving a car 42,000 kilometers (26,000 miles)
- slowing population growth (Chapter 8)

Achieving these goals will require countries to draw up and abide by a Global Law of the Atmosphere.

We could also increase use of nuclear power if a new generation of much safer reactors can be developed and the problem of how to store nuclear waste safely for thousands of years can be solved. But to make a real contribution to slowing global warming we would need thousands of reactors (see Pro/Con on p. 405). Also using nuclear energy to produce electricity is very inefficient (Figure 3-17, p. 69) and electricity cannot be used to run cars unless much better batteries are developed. This would also be an expensive way to go compared to other options. Improving energy efficiency is quicker and reduces emissions of CO_2 per dollar invested 2.5 to 10 times more than nuclear power.

Many observers doubt that countries will agree to reduce fossil fuel use and deforestation in time to prevent significant global warming. Countries likely to have a more favorable climate after global warming will resist severe restrictions, whereas countries likely to suffer from reduced food-growing capacity may favor taking immediate action. Sharply restricting fossil fuel use, no matter how desirable from a long-term environmental and economic viewpoint, would cause major short-term economic and social disruptions that most countries would find unacceptable.

Thus, some analysts suggest that while attempting to reduce fossil fuel use and deforestation to buy time, we should also begin to prepare for the effects of long-term global warming. Their suggestions include

- increasing research on the breeding of food plants that need less water and plants that can thrive in water too salty for ordinary crops
- building dikes to protect coastal areas from flooding, as the Dutch have done for hundreds of years
- moving storage tanks of hazardous materials away from coastal areas
- banning new construction on low-lying coastal areas
- storing large supplies of key foods throughout the world as insurance against disruptions in food production
- expanding existing wilderness areas, parks, and wildlife refuges northward in the Northern Hemisphere and southward in the Southern Hemisphere and creating new wildlife reserves in these areas
- developing management plans for existing parks and reserves that take into account possible climate changes

But making such changes would take 20 years and cost hundreds of billions of dollars. For example, adjusting the world's irrigation systems alone could take $200 billion. There is no free lunch.

Changing the global climate by our activities can be viewed as the ultimate tragedy of the commons. In 1975, anthropologist Margaret Mead said, "The atmosphere is the key symbol of global interdependence. If we can't solve some of our problems in the face of threats to this global commons, then I can't be very optimistic about the future of the world." Perhaps the challenge posed by the greenhouse effect can be a catalyst for worldwide awareness of the urgent need to start working with the earth.

19-5 CONTROLLING AIR POLLUTION

U.S. Air Pollution Legislation Air pollution or any other type of pollution can be controlled by laws to establish desired standards and by technology to achieve the standards. In the United States, Congress passed the Clean Air Acts of 1970 and 1977, which gave the federal government considerable power to control air pollution.

These laws required the EPA to establish **national ambient air quality standards (NAAQS)** for seven major outdoor pollutants: suspended particulate matter, sulfur oxides, carbon monoxide, nitrogen oxides, ozone, hydrocarbons, and lead. Each standard specifies the maximum allowable level, averaged over a specific time period, for a certain pollutant in outdoor (ambient) air.

The EPA was required to set two types of NAAQS without taking into consideration the cost of meeting them. *Primary ambient air quality standards* were set to protect human health, with a margin of safety for the elderly, infants, and other vulnerable persons, and deadlines were set for their attainment. *Secondary ambient air quality standards* were set to maintain visibility and to protect crops, buildings, and water supplies; no deadlines were set for their attainment.

Each of the 247 air quality control regions established by the EPA across the country was supposed to meet all primary standards by 1982 with some extensions possible to 1987, but many areas failed to meet these deadlines. To meet this requirement, any new plant or significant expansion of an existing one must have pollution control equipment that will lead to the lowest rate of emissions achieved by any similar plant anywhere in the country regardless of cost. There must also be a drop in the total emissions in the area. To meet this second requirement, a company can buy and close down an existing plant or buy equipment to reduce emissions from an existing plant. Another option is to buy emissions credits from another company in the area that has reduced its emissions below that required in its permit.

The EPA has also established a policy of *prevention of significant deterioration*. It is designed to prevent a decrease in air quality in regions where the air is cleaner than required by the NAAQS for suspended particulate matter and sulfur dioxide. Otherwise, industries could move into these areas and gradually degrade air quality to the national standards for these two major pollutants.

The Clean Air Acts of 1970 and 1977 required each state to develop an EPA-approved state implementation plan showing how it would achieve federal standards fully by 1982, with extensions possible until 1987. Congress gave the EPA the power to halt the construction of major new plants or expansions of existing ones and to cut off federal funds for construction of highways for any state not submitting an acceptable plan, but this has not been done because of political pressures.

The Clean Air laws also required the EPA to set uniform national maximum emission standards, known

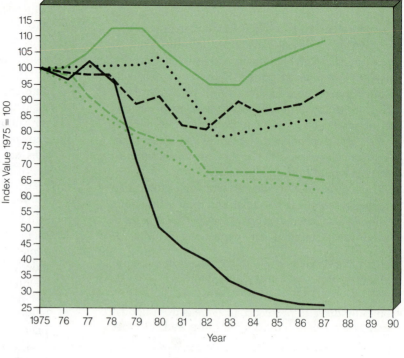

Figure 19-19 Trends in U.S. outdoor air quality for six pollutants, 1975–1987. (Data from Environmental Protection Agency)

Carbon monoxide · · · · · · · · · · · · · · ·

Lead ——————————————

Nitrogen oxides ——————————————

Ozone – – – – – – – – – – – –

Sulfur dioxide – – – – – – – – – – – –

Suspended particulate · · · · · · · · · · · ·
matter

as *new source performance standards*, on an industry-by-industry basis for newly built plants or major expansions of existing plants. Unlike NAAQS, costs and energy requirements can be considered in setting these standards.

Congress set a timetable for achieving certain percentage reductions in emissions of carbon monoxide, hydrocarbons, and nitrogen oxides from motor vehicles. Although significant progress has been made, a series of legally allowed extensions has pushed deadlines for complete attainment of most of these goals into the future.

Trends in U.S. Outdoor Air Quality In the United States between 1975 and 1987 average outdoor concentrations of most major pollutants, except nitrogen oxides, dropped as a result of air pollution control laws, economic recession, and higher energy prices (Figure 19-19). Lead made the sharpest drop because of the 91% drop in the amount of lead allowed in leaded gasoline (see Case Study on p. 473).

However, from 1986 to 1987 levels of ozone and suspended particulate matter increased and nitrogen dioxide levels stayed the same, mostly because of auto emissions. Environmentalists allege that these increases are the result of budget cutbacks, efforts by the Reagan administration to relax enforcement of air pollution control regulations, and emphasis on pollution control instead of pollution prevention.

Averages of air pollutants in several hundred EPA measuring stations across the country do not reveal the severity of air pollution in different major urban areas. The EPA uses a pollution standards index (PSI) to indicate how frequently and to what degree the air quality in a particular city exceeds one or more of the primary health standards. Daily PSI indexes are often reported by the media to alert the public to air pollution levels (Figure 19-20).

Between 1976 and 1987 there was a sharp drop in the number of days in which the air was classified as hazardous, very unhealthful, or unhealthful in most major urban areas. New York, Chicago, and Cleveland showed considerable improvement, while Los Angeles, Houston, and Dallas-Fort Worth showed relatively little improvement. However, in 1989 the EPA was charged with deliberately falsifying and underreporting these data.

Except for Sweden, the United States has made more progress in reducing levels of the six major outdoor pollutants shown in Figure 19-19 than other

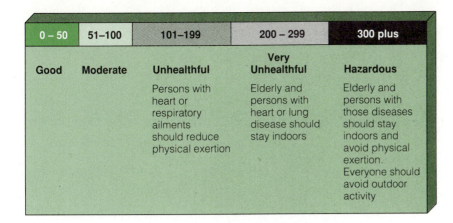

0 – 50	51–100	101–199	200 – 299	300 plus
Good	Moderate	Unhealthful	Very Unhealthful	Hazardous
		Persons with heart or respiratory ailments should reduce physical exertion	Elderly and persons with heart or lung disease should stay indoors	Elderly and persons with those diseases should stay indoors and avoid physical exertion. Everyone should avoid outdoor activity

countries. However, there is still much to be done because the increase in new vehicles and other emission sources gradually overwhelms pollution control efforts.

In 1988 one out of three Americans lived in 101 major cities where average ozone levels regularly exceed safe levels. The worst was Los Angeles where ozone levels exceeded the standard for 148 days during 1988. Other areas where the ozone standard was exceeded 15 to 54 days a year in 1988 were New York, Baltimore, Parkersburg, Pittsburgh, Philadelphia, Sacramento, Bakersfield, Sheboygan (Wisconsin), Worchester, Steubenville (Ohio), and Knox County (Maine). One out of four Americans lives in 59 cities with too much carbon monoxide.

Although new cars emit much less pollution than 1970 models, smog levels are still high mostly because there are now 55% more cars on the road, traveling more net miles. Also because of ineffective inspection and enforcement, the emission control systems on about 60% of the U.S. car fleet have been disconnected or are not working properly.

In the 1970s most western European countries, Canada, Australia, Japan, and South Korea established automobile emissions standards similar to those in the United States, although some European countries lag behind. Brazil will have similar standards by 1997. Little, if any, attempt is made to control vehicle emissions in India, Mexico, Argentina, China, the Soviet Union, and eastern European countries.

Methods of Pollution Control Once a pollution control standard has been adopted, two general approaches can be used to prevent levels from exceeding the standard. One is *input control*, which prevents or reduces the severity of the problem (see Guest Essay on p. 515). The other is *output control*, which treats the symptoms. Output control methods, especially those that attempt to remove the pollutant once it has entered the environment, tend to be expensive and difficult.

Input methods are usually easier and cheaper in the long run. The five major input control methods

for reducing the total amount of pollution of any type from reaching the environment are

- regulating population growth (Chapter 8)
- reducing unnecessary waste of metals, paper, and other matter resources through increased recycling and reuse and by designing products that last longer and are easy to repair (Section 15-7)
- reducing energy use
- using energy more efficiently (Section 17-1)
- switching from coal to natural gas, which produces less pollution and carbon dioxide when burned (Section 16-2 and Figure 16-10, p. 381)
- switching from fossil fuels to energy from the sun, wind, and flowing water (Chapter 17) or nuclear power (Section 16-5)

These input methods are the most effective and least costly ways (except nuclear power) to reduce air, water, and soil pollution. They are the only cost-effective methods for reducing the rate of buildup of carbon dioxide and other greenhouse gases in the atmosphere. However, they are rarely given serious consideration in national and international strategies for pollution control.

Control of Sulfur Dioxide Emissions from Stationary Sources Environmentalists in the United States and Canada call for a 50% reduction in sulfur dioxide emissions from U.S. coal-burning plants over the next ten years. The cost of doing this is estimated at $2 billion to $7 billion a year. In addition to the general input control methods mentioned above, the following approaches can lower sulfur dioxide emissions or reduce their effects:

Sulfur Dioxide Input Control Methods

1. *Burn low-sulfur coal.* Especially useful for new power and industrial plants located near deposits

Figure 19-21 Limestone injection multiple burning (LIMB). Crushed limestone is injected into a boiler burning powdered coal at a lower temperature than normal burners. The limestone combines with sulfur dioxide to produce a solid material (gypsum).

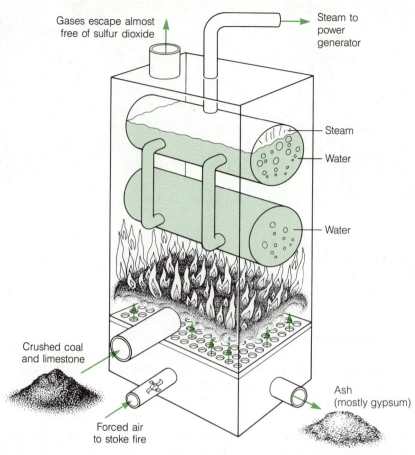

Gases escape almost free of sulfur dioxide

Steam to power generator

Steam

Water

Water

Crushed coal and limestone

Forced air to stoke fire

Ash (mostly gypsum)

of such coal; Midwest power plants could switch to low-sulfur coal strip-mined in the West. This would put 23,000 to 60,000 miners in eastern states out of work, but would result in a net creation of 195,000 jobs from mining low-sulfur coal, transporting coal, and constructing and operating emission control and monitoring devices in other geographical areas.

2. *Remove sulfur from coal.* Fairly inexpensive; present physical and chemical methods remove only 20% to 50%; scientists eventually hope to find or genetically engineer bacteria that will remove sulfur in coal more efficiently and cheaply than present physical and chemical methods; bacteria used so far remove only about 40% of the organic sulfur and take four to six weeks to do this.

3. *Convert coal to a gas or liquid fuel* (Figure 16-20, p. 389). Low net energy yield.

4. *Remove sulfur during combustion by fluidized-bed combustion (FBC) of coal* (Figure 16-19, p. 388). Removes up to 90% of the SO_2, reduces CO_2 by 20%, and increases energy efficiency by 5%; should be commercially available for small to medium plants in the mid-1990s.

5. *Remove sulfur during combustion by limestone injection multiple burning (LIMB)* (Figure 19-21). Still in the development and testing stage.

Sulfur Dioxide Output Control Methods

1. *Use smokestacks tall enough to pierce the thermal inversion layer.* Can decrease pollution near power or industrial plants but increases pollution levels in downwind areas.

2. *Remove pollutants after combustion by using flue gas desulfurization (FGD), or scrubbing* (Figure 19-22d, p. 512). Removes up to 95% of SO_2 and 99.9% of SPM (but not the more harmful fine particles); can be used in new plants and added to most existing large plants but is very expensive.

3. *Add a tax on each unit emitted.* Encourages development of more efficient and cost-effective methods of emissions control; opposed by industry because it costs more than tall smokestacks and requires polluters to bear more of the harmful costs now passed on to society.

In 1985 the Soviet Union and 21 European countries signed a treaty agreeing to reduce their annual emissions of sulfur dioxide from 1980 levels by at least 30% by 1993; 4 countries agreed to 70% cuts. Sweden set a goal of reducing its sulfur dioxide emissions by 65% and nitrogen oxides emissions by 95% by 1995. The United States and Great Britain refused to participate in this historic agreement, citing scientific uncertainty over the harmful effects of sulfur dioxide.

U.S. air pollution control laws encourage emissions of SO_2 and SPM by allowing tall smokestacks and by not requiring coal-burning power and industrial plants built before 1972 to install effective pollution control devices. This gives corporations an incentive to keep old, polluting plants in operation rather than build new advanced plants.

Today U.S. smokestacks still spew out some 18 million metric tons (20 million tons) of sulfur dioxide a year. Cutting these emissions by about one-third will cost an estimated $3.7 billion and cutting them by about two-thirds about $89 billion.

Control of Emissions of Nitrogen Oxides from Stationary Sources

About half the emissions of nitrogen oxides in the United States come from the burning of fossil fuels at stationary sources, primarily electric power and industrial plants. The rest comes mostly from motor vehicles.

So far little emphasis has been placed on reducing emissions of nitrogen oxides from stationary sources because control of sulfur dioxide and particulates was considered more important. Now it is clear that nitrogen oxides are a major contributor to acid deposition and that they increase tropospheric levels of ozone and other photochemical oxidants that can damage crops, trees, and materials. The following approaches can be used to decrease emissions of nitrogen oxides from stationary sources:

Input Control Methods for Nitrogen Oxides

1. *Remove nitrogen oxides during fluidized bed combustion* (Figure 16-19, p. 388). Removes 50% to 75%.

2. *Remove during combustion by limestone injection multiple burning (LIMB)* (Figure 19-21). Removes 50% to 60% but is still being developed.

3. *Reduce by decreasing combustion temperatures.* Well-established technology that reduces production of these gases by 50% to 60%.

Output Control Methods for Nitrogen Oxides

1. *Use tall smokestacks.*

2. *Add a tax for each unit emitted.*

3. *Remove after combustion by reburning.* Removes 50% or more but is still under development for large plants.

4. *Remove after burning by reacting with isocyanic acid (HCNO).* Removes up to 99% and breaks down into harmless nitrogen and water; will not be available commercially for at least ten years.

In 1988 representatives from 24 countries, including the United States, signed an agreement that would freeze emissions of nitrogen oxides at 1987 levels by 1995. Twelve western European countries agreed to cut emissions of nitrogen oxides by 30% between 1987 and 1997.

Control of Suspended Particulate Matter Emissions from Stationary Sources

The only input control method for suspended particulate matter is to convert coal to a gas or liquid, a method that is expensive and low in net energy yield. The following output approaches can be used to decrease emissions of suspended particulate matter from stationary sources:

Suspended Particulate Matter Output Control Methods

1. *Use tall smokestacks.*

2. *Add a tax on each unit emitted.*

3. *Remove particulates from stack exhaust gases.* The most widely used method in electric power and industrial plants. Several methods are in use: **(a)** electrostatic precipitators (Figures 19-22a and 19-23); **(b)** baghouse filters (Figure 19-22b); **(c)** cyclone separators (Figure 19-22c); and **(d)** wet scrubbers (Figure 19-22d). Except for baghouse filters, none of these methods removes many of the more hazardous fine particles; all produce hazardous solid waste or sludge that must be disposed of safely; except for cyclone separators, all methods are expensive.

Control of Emissions from Motor Vehicles

The following approaches can be used to decrease emissions of carbon monoxide, nitrogen oxides, SPM, and lead from motor vehicles:

Motor Vehicle Input Control Methods

1. *Rely more on mass transit, bicycles, and walking* (Section 9-4).

2. *Shift to less-polluting automobile engines* such as steam or electric engines. Presently these engines are not as good as the internal combustion engine in performance, fuel economy, durability, and cost.

3. *Shift to less-polluting fuels* such as natural gas, alcohols (p. 437), and hydrogen gas (p. 438).

4. *Improve fuel efficiency.* A quick and cost-effective approach. Present U.S. fuel-efficiency standards for new cars should be increased from 27.5 miles per gallon in 1990 to at least 40 miles per gallon by 2000.

5. *Modify the internal combustion engine to reduce emissions.* Burning gasoline using a lean, or more air-rich, mixture reduces carbon monoxide and hydrocarbon emissions but increases emissions of nitrogen oxides; a new lean-burn engine that reduces emissions of nitrogen oxides by 75% to 90% may be available in about ten years.

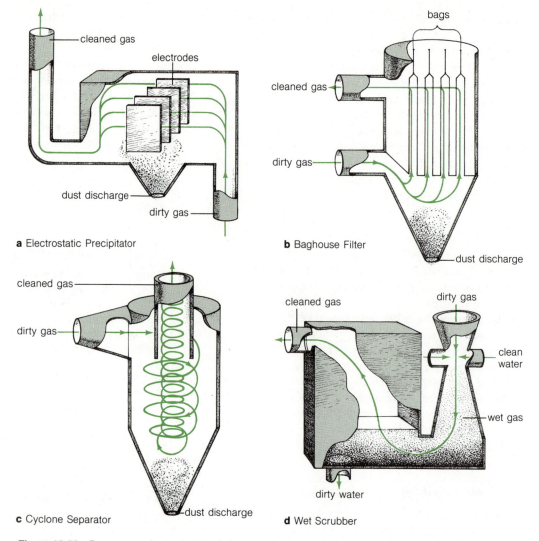

cleaned gas

electrodes

dust discharge

dirty gas

a Electrostatic Precipitator

bags

cleaned gas

dirty gas

dust discharge

b Baghouse Filter

cleaned gas

dirty gas

dust discharge

c Cyclone Separator

cleaned gas

dirty gas

clean water

wet gas

dirty water

d Wet Scrubber

Figure 19-22   Four commonly used methods for removing particulates from the exhaust gases of electric power and industrial plants. The wet scrubber is also used to reduce sulfur dioxide emissions.

6. *Raise annual registration fees on older, more polluting cars or offer owners an incentive to retire such cars.*

7. *Add a charge on all new cars based on the amount of the three major pollutants emitted by the engine according to EPA tests.* This would prod manufacturers to reduce emissions and encourage consumers to buy less-polluting cars.

Motor Vehicle Output Control Methods

1. *Use emission control devices.* Most widely used approach; engines must be kept well-tuned for such devices to work effectively; three-way catalytic converters now being developed can decrease pollutants by 90% to 95% and should be available within a few years.

2. *Require car inspections twice a year and have drivers exceeding the standards pay an emission charge based on the grams emitted per mile and the number of miles driven since the last inspection.* This would encour-

age drivers not to tamper with emission control devices and to keep them in good working order.

3. *Establish emission standards for light-duty trucks and minivans* (presently not effectively regulated by U.S. air pollution control laws).

Control of Troposphere Ozone Levels   Ozone levels in the troposphere are affected primarily by emissions of nitrogen oxides and hydrocarbons coupled with sunlight (Figure 19-7). Thus, decreasing ozone levels involves combining the input and output methods already discussed for nitrogen oxides and for motor vehicles.

It also involves decreasing hydrocarbon emissions. In 1989 California's South Coast Air Quality Management District Council proposed a drastic program to reduce ozone and photochemical smog in the Los Angeles area. If approved by the state environmental agency and the EPA this plan would require

Figure 19-23 The effectiveness of an electrostatic precipitator in reducing particulate emissions is shown by this stack, with the precipitator turned off (left) and with the precipitator operating.

- strict control or relocation of petroleum refining, dry cleaning, auto painting, printing, baking, trash-burning plants, and other industries that release large quantities of hydrocarbons and other pollutants; bias-ply tires that release particulate matter would be banned

- finding substitutes or banning use of aerosol propellants, paints, household cleaners, barbecue starter fluids, and other consumer products that release hydrocarbons

- gradual elimination of gasoline burning engines over two decades by converting 40% of cars and 70% of trucks, buses, and all gas-powered lawnmowers to alternate fuels such as methanol, ethanol, natural gas, or electricity by 1998; bus fleets would have to do this by 1991 and taxis and rental cars by 1993; by 2009 all vehicles and boats that burned gasoline would be banned

- gas stations to use a hydrocarbon vapor recovery system on gas pumps and sell alternative fuels

- much higher parking fees to discourage automobile use and encourage car pooling and use of mass transit

- banning 70% of any fleet's trucks from streets during weekday morning and evening rush hours

The plan will cost $2.8 billion to $15 billion a year and may be defeated by public opinion when residents begin to feel the pinch from such drastic changes. But proponents argue that the alternative of continuing degradation of air quality in the country's air pollution capital will cost consumers and businesses much more.

Controlling Toxic Emissions The Clean Air Act of 1970 ordered the EPA to evaluate the health hazards posed by the hundreds of toxic compounds, some of them known carcinogens, emitted into the atmosphere and then set standards to control each chemical. But by 1989 the EPA had issued regulations for only seven of the hundreds of potentially toxic air pollutants.

Part of the problem is the difficulty of getting accurate scientific data on the effects of specific pollutants on human health (Section 18-1) and in estimating risks and benefits (Section 18-3). Economic and political pressures also hamper the EPA's work. Since 1981, Congress has slashed EPA budgets and the Reagan administration reduced enforcement of air pollution laws.

Because setting standards for each toxic pollutant is so difficult and time consuming, it has been proposed that this chemical-by-chemical approach be replaced by an industry-by-industry approach using technological standards instead of emissions standards. First, the EPA would rank industries according to the amount of toxics they emit. Then the industrial plants emitting the largest amounts would be given deadlines to reduce their emissions to certain levels using the best available technology.

Control of Indoor Air Pollution For most people, indoor air pollution poses a much greater threat to their health than outdoor air pollution. Yet, the EPA spends $200 million a year trying to reduce outdoor air pollution and only $2 million a year on indoor air pollution.

To sharply reduce indoor air pollution it is not necessary to establish mandatory indoor air quality standards and monitor the more than 100 million homes and buildings in the United States. Instead this can be done by

■ modifying building codes to prevent radon infiltration, require use of air-to-air heat exchangers or other devices to change indoor air at certain intervals

■ removing up to 90% of the hazardous materials in furniture and building materials in new and older homes, apartments, and workplaces by keeping people out, baking the materials out at 38°C (100°F) for three to four days, and then using a fan to exhaust and replace the contaminated air several times

■ requiring exhaust hoods or vent pipes for stoves, refrigerators, dryers, kerosene heaters, or other appliances burning natural gas or other fossil fuels

■ setting emission standards for building materials such as particleboard and plywood (that emit formaldehyde), insulation, and materials used in furniture, carpets, and carpet backing

■ finding substitutes for potentially harmful chemicals in aerosols, cleaning compounds, paints, and other products used indoors and requiring all such products to have labels listing their ingredients

■ requiring employers to provide safe indoor air for employees

Meanwhile people can prevent buildup of most indoor air pollutants by installing air-to-air heat exchangers, which maintain a flow of fresh air without causing major heating or cooling losses. Purchase building materials labelled "low-emitting formaldehyde" or use nonformaldehyde materials. Indoor levels of formaldehyde and several other toxic gases can be sharply reduced by house plants such as the spider or airplane plant (the most effective), golden pathos, syngonium, and philodendron. Houses can also be baked out at 68°C (100°F) for three to four days.

Other remedies include changing air filters regularly, cleaning air conditioning systems, emptying humidifier water trays frequently, and not storing gasoline, solvents, and other volatile hazardous chemicals inside a home or attached garage. Also consumers can use cheaper and safer substitutes for many household hazardous chemicals (Table 18-8, p. 479).

People building and remodeling homes should not use particleboard and plywood—found in roughly 80 million houses and mobile homes in the United States. These materials can emit high levels of formaldehyde for several months to several years. Consumers should not use room deodorizers and air fresheners, and they should properly dispose of or store partially used containers of paints, solvents, cleaners, cosmetics, and pesticides.

Smokers can reduce exposure to others by smoking outside or in a closed room vented to the outside. If many indoor pollution sources cannot be eliminated, whole-house electrostatic air cleaners and charcoal filters can be attached to central heating and air conditioning equipment. Humidifiers, however, can load indoor air with bacteria, mildew, and viruses.

In LDCs major reductions in respiratory illnesses would occur if governments gave rural residents and poor people in cities simple stoves that burn biofuels more efficiently (which would also reduce deforestation) and that are vented outside.

What Needs To Be Done In 1981 the 1977 Clean Air Act was up for revision. Between 1981 and 1988 industry officials and the Reagan administration pushed hard to ease federal auto emission standards, relax industrial cleanup goals, allow more pollution in regions with low pollution levels, and extend nationwide EPA deadlines for meeting primary air pollution standards. They claimed that the benefits of existing air pollution control laws are not worth their high costs, that these laws threaten economic growth, and that they are implemented too inflexibly by the EPA.

Environmentalists, on the other hand, have proposed stricter limits on all polluting emissions, a ban on CFCs and other ozone-destroying chemicals, and a program for prevention and control of key indoor air pollutants in homes, factories, and office buildings. A comprehensive approach is made necessary by the multiple interactions of different pollutants and should replace the present "one-pollutant-at-a-time" approach. Some health scientists also believe that the emphasis in air pollution control laws should shift from controlling emissions to reducing total exposure (Table 19-1, p. 488).

Environmentalists recognize that the costs of implementing a much stricter and more comprehensive air pollution control program will be high. But they argue, the long-term costs of not doing so could be astronomical: massive damage to humans, livestock, crops, materials, forests, soils, and lakes.

At the international level, countries, especially MDCs, need to develop agreements to ban CFCs to reduce global ozone depletion (and delay atmospheric warming), reduce emissions of sulfur dioxide and nitrogen oxides to control acid deposition, and reduce emissions of carbon dioxide and other greenhouse gases to delay global warming.

What Can You Do? The most important thing you can do to reduce air pollution and ozone depletion, slow global climate change, and save money is to improve energy efficiency (see suggestions inside the back cover). Drive a car that gets at least 35 miles a gallon, drive fewer miles, and walk, bicycle, or use mass transit when possible. Replace incandescent light bulbs with compact fluorescent bulbs, make your home energy efficient, and buy only energy-efficient appliances. Recycle newspapers, aluminum, and other materials. Plant trees and avoid purchasing products such as styrofoam that contain CFCs. If you have an auto air conditioner, have it serviced at a shop that recycles CFCs. Lobby for much stricter clean air laws and enforcement and development of international treaties to reduce ozone depletion and slow global warming.

From this chapter's overview of the earth's air resources, we see that any human activities that affect the physical properties or chemical composition of the atmosphere can cause serious problems. Changing our resource consumption patterns to prevent long-term climate changes and to make indoor and outdoor air healthier for people, other animals, and plants is one of the greatest political, economic, and ethical challenges we face.

There is the very real possibility that the human race—through ignorance or indifference or both—is irreversibly altering the ability of the atmosphere to support life.

Sherwood Rowland

GUEST ESSAY: Don't Forget To Take Your Umbrella!*

Donald G. Barnes

Donald G. Barnes is Staff Director of the Science Advisory Board of the U.S. Environmental Protection Agency. In this position he oversees and coordinates more than 60 top grade scientists and engineers and more than 200 consultants who act as advisors to the EPA. For ten years prior to this appointment, he served as Senior Science Advisor to the Assistant Administrator for Pesticides and Toxic Substances. He is considered one of the world's experts on the toxic effects of the dioxin TCDD (see Case Study on p. 451).

I am increasingly convinced that a proper aim of education should be leading students to see the wisdom embodied in longstanding sayings and slogans and applying it to new situations. Consider, for example, a number of "old saws" which people recite with ease, and ignore with even greater ease:

"A stitch in time saves nine."
"An ounce of prevention is worth a pound of cure."
"Leave your campsite cleaner than you found it."

and a less-familiar home-spun favorite of mine:

"Don't forget to take your umbrella."

These sayings and slogans cause the hearer to take some foresighted action now in order to prevent the need for greater, more costly action in the future.

The truth of these sayings is attested to by numerous situations in the past where we have failed to heed this advice. For example, when I was a child, medicine's answer to the scourge of polio was to put a victim who could not breathe because of paralysis into an iron lung (arguably a ton, rather than a pound of cure!), rather than a polio vaccine (developed later) weighing about an ounce. In the 1960s a stitch called "Head Start" held the promise of preventing the need for the "nine" of today's adult remedial reading and learning programs. Since the dawn of the environmental movement in the 1950s, public pressure, social consciousness, and governmental regulations have combined to encourage us to leave this campsite (the Earth) cleaner than we found it.

Historically, it seems that we are forever "coming from behind" when it comes to the stewardship of the Earth, ignoring these easily quoted truths. For example, we took action to make the air "safe" to breathe for people (even susceptible populations) only *after* the pollution was clearly visible to all. We adopted the modest goal of making our surface waters "fishable and swimmable" (hardly a radical notion) only *after*

(continued)

*DISCLAIMER: This essay expresses the personal opinions of the author. It has not been reviewed by either the U.S. Environmental Protection Agency or its Science Advisory Board and should not be construed as representing the opinions or policies of either.

rivers caught fire (Figure 2-14, p. 00) and fish populations disappeared. We took actions about dumpsites only *after* thousands of locations across the country had become potential problems to public health and the environment (see Case Study on p. 000).

The after-the-fact strategy of cleaning up after the mess was created has certain inevitable consequences, some of which are related to the Second Law of Thermodynamics described elsewhere in this book (see p. 62). The cleanup of the mess we have created will cost a ton more money and require ninety-nine stitches more than if we had thought about the consequences of our actions ahead of time. Once you forget your umbrella and it rains, you are going to get wet! Such a strategy is expensive, at best, and losing, at worst.

An alternative strategy is to follow the advice of the old slogans and anticipate problems *before* they show up, and take action to prevent their occurrence in the first place. Increasingly, we are becoming aware of the *absolute necessity* of such a strategy based on prevention rather than cure—taking an umbrella, rather than hoping it won't rain.

This imperative is more obvious in some of the emerging environmental problems that are more global in character and irreversible in outcome. For example, while evidence about "ozone holes" in the earth's polar regions continues to mount and production of the indicted agents—mostly chlorofluorocarbons (CFCs)—is being restricted somewhat, the question of the long-term effects of the CFCs *already in the environment* remains. Atmospheric loadings of fossil fuel emissions pose possible long-term consequences in the form of acid deposition and global climate change. On all of these issues we are "coming from behind," hoping that conditions are reversible and we still have time—and the wherewithal—to correct the situations.

Over the past decade we have begun to adopt a preventive strategy. For example, manufacturers who are about to introduce a new chemical into the marketplace are required to supply the EPA with available information, on the basis of which the Agency can make some judgment as to whether or not the substance is likely to pose an unreasonable risk to human health or the environment. Also, producers of new pesticides are required by law to supply massive amounts of environmental and toxicity data which help the Agency determine whether the intended uses of the pesticide are likely to cause problems. Recently, the Agency has established an Office of Pollution Prevention, with the goal of focusing on "front end" prevention, rather than "end-of-pipe" controls.

But much more needs to be done to anticipate adequately future problems so that preventive steps can be taken before situations become too expensive or irreversible to correct. As a part of this effort for foreseeing these emerging problems, we need to gather background information on the major ecosystems of the world. These data will give us good "background" data on current conditions (which, surprisingly, are not well-known) and allow us to make accurate and early detection of any changes or trends in the status of major ecosystems, when they occur, and what their associated causes might be.

There is already enough information in one emerging problem area that the wise student will be contemplating appropriate action today. Specifically, demographic and educational data show that with the current number of capable, motivated people going into environmental science and environmental studies it is unlikely that our future needs will be easily met. Therefore, many challenges and opportunities, coupled with service and satisfaction, will await those who learn the wisdom inherent in the longstanding advice, "Don't forget to take your umbrella!"

Guest Essay Discussion

1. Why is it so difficult to get individuals, elected officials, and government agencies to develop and implement prevention strategies?

2. List ten prevention strategies that you could use to reduce your personal risks from various hazards. How many of these strategies do you seriously follow?

3. Have you considered a career in environmental science, environmental law, environmental medicine, responsible forestry, wildlife conservation, or some other field related to sustaining the earth?

CHAPTER SUMMARY

Air pollution occurs when the concentration of a normal component of the air or a new chemical added to or formed in the air builds up to the point of causing harm to humans, other animals, vegetation, or materials. Some air pollutants are *primary pollutants*, added directly to the air, and others are *secondary pollutants*, formed in the air.

Although there are natural sources of some outdoor air pollutants, most are a result of the burning of fossil fuels at *stationary sources* (power and industrial plants) or *mobile sources* (motor vehicles). High concentrations of certain air pollutants such as tobacco smoke, radioactive radon gas, and formaldehyde can also build up indoors, especially in airtight houses.

Air pollutants can build up to dangerous levels when a layer of dense, cool air is trapped beneath a layer of less dense, warm air. Such *thermal inversions* occur more frequently over towns or cities located in valleys surrounded by mountains, on the leeward side of a mountain range, or near a coast.

Some of the sulfur dioxide and nitric oxide emitted by tall smokestacks and other sources can be transported long distances, in the process forming a variety of secondary pollutants: sulfuric and nitric acids and sulfate and nitrate salts. *Acid deposition* occurs when these liquid acid droplets (wet deposition) and solid acid-forming particles and gases (dry deposition) return to the earth's surface.

The human respiratory system has a number of defenses that filter, dilute, or expel air pollutants. However, these defenses can be overwhelmed by exposure to high levels of one or more air pollutants or exposure to low or moderate concentrations of some air pollutants over a long period. Effects include watery eyes, coughing, heart disease, and respiratory diseases such as chronic bronchitis, emphysema, and lung cancer.

Prolonged exposure to multiple air pollutants such as ozone and acid deposition can damage leaves of trees and other plants and kill large numbers of trees by leaching plant nutrients from the soil, killing essential soil microorganisms, damaging roots, and increasing susceptibility to drought, pests, and disease. Air pollutants also severely damage statues, buildings, metals, rubber, paint, paper, fabrics, and other materials, causing huge economic losses.

There is considerable evidence a group of widely used chemicals known as chlorofluorocarbons (CFCs) and halons which remain in the atmosphere for as long as 111 years are depleting ozone in the stratosphere. Ozone filters out most of the sun's harmful ultraviolet radiation. Attempts are being made to get countries to limit or ban the production and use of these chemicals but so far efforts are not enough to prevent serious depletion of stratospheric ozone.

There is also growing concern that human activities such as fossil fuel burning and deforestation may lead to a gradual warming of the earth's atmosphere as a result of an enhanced *greenhouse effect*. This is caused by increased atmospheric levels of carbon dioxide and other greenhouse gases. Such a change in global climate would disrupt food production and cause flooding of low-lying areas. This potentially serious long-range problem can be dealt with by reducing emissions of greenhouse gases, improving energy efficiency, reducing deforestation, planting trees, and making long-term preparations for changes in climate.

Air pollution control laws enacted in the 1970s set standards for the maximum allowable levels of several key air pollutants in outdoor air. Meeting these standards involves using pollution control methods to prevent all or most of a pollutant from being formed (*input control*) or reducing the amount emitted to the atmosphere (*output control*).

As a result of this legislation, levels of most major outdoor air pollutants in the U.S. have either decreased or not risen significantly since the laws were enacted. However, considerably more needs to be done to reduce levels of numerous hazardous outdoor pollutants, CFCs, greenhouse gases, and indoor pollutants, with greatly increased emphasis on pollution prevention.

DISCUSSION TOPICS

1. Rising oil and natural gas prices and environmental concerns over nuclear power plants could force the U.S. to depend more on coal, its most plentiful fossil fuel, for producing electric power. Comment on this in terms of air pollution. Would you favor a return to coal with strict air pollution controls instead of increased use of nuclear power? Explain.

2. Evaluate the pros and cons of the statement, "Since we have not proven absolutely that anyone has died or suffered serious disease from nitrogen oxides, present federal emission standards for this pollutant should be relaxed."

3. Why is air pollution from fine particulate matter a serious problem? What should be done about this problem?

4. Should all uses of CFCs be banned in the U.S., including their use in refrigeration and air conditioning units? Explain.

5. Should MDCs set up a world food bank to store several years' supply of food to reduce the harmful effects of a loss in food production caused by a change in climate? How would you decide who gets this food in times of need?

6. What topographical and climate factors either increase or help decrease air pollution in your community?

7. Do you favor or oppose requiring a 50% reduction in emissions of sulfur dioxide and nitrogen oxides by fossil-fuel-burning electric power and industrial plants and a 50% reduction in emissions of nitrogen oxides by motor vehicles in the U.S. over the next ten years? Explain.

8. Should all tall smokestacks be banned? Explain.

9. Do buildings in your college or university contain asbestos? If so, what is being done about this potential health hazard?

10. Should standards be set and enforced for most major indoor air pollutants? Explain.

11. Has the U.S. Clean Air Act been reauthorized and amended since this book was written? If so, evaluate the changes in this law.

CHAPTER 20

Water Pollution

General Questions and Issues

1. What are the major types, sources, and effects of water pollutants?

2. What are the major pollution problems of rivers and lakes?

3. What are the major pollution problems of the world's oceans?

4. What are the major pollution problems of groundwater aquifers?

5. What technological and legal methods can be used to reduce water pollution?

6. What can you do to reduce your contribution to water pollution?

Brush your teeth with the best toothpaste. Then rinse your mouth with industrial waste.

Tom Lehrer

lthough fresh water is a renewable resource (Figure 4-25, p. 99) it can become so contaminated by human activities that it is no longer useful for many purposes and can be harmful to living organisms using the water. The level of purity required for water depends on its use. Water too polluted to drink may be satisfactory for washing steel, producing electricity at a hydroelectric power plant, or cooling the steam and hot water produced by a nuclear or coal-fired power plant. Water too polluted for swimming may not be too polluted for boating or fishing.

Water pollution is a local, regional, and global environmental problem and is connected with air pollution and how we use the land. When air pollutants fall back to the earth they can become water pollutants (Figure 19-10, p. 494). Some of the fertilizers and pesticides we apply to croplands runoff into nearby surface waters or leach into aquifers. Poor land use accelerates the erosion of soil that pollutes surface waters with sediment. Some of the sludge and other wastes we produce on land are dumped into the oceans.

The natural flows of rivers and ocean currents carry water pollutants far from their point of origin, frequently across international borders. As with air pollution, we need to shift our emphasis from using output methods to clean up polluted waters to input methods that prevent aquatic systems from becoming seriously polluted. This requires that we view the global environment as an interconnected web.

20-1 TYPES, EFFECTS, AND SOURCES OF WATER POLLUTION

Major Types and Effects of Water Pollutants The following are eight common types of water pollutants.

disease-causing agents. bacteria, viruses, protozoa, and parasitic worms that enter water from domestic sewage and animal wastes and cause diseases (Table 20-1). In LDCs, they are the major cause of sickness and death—killing an average of 25,000 people each day (Section 18-2).

oxygen-demanding wastes. organic wastes, which when degraded by oxygen-consuming bacteria, can deplete water of dissolved oxygen gas (Figure 20-1).

water-soluble inorganic chemicals. acids, salts, and compounds of toxic metals such as lead and mercury (Table 20-2). High levels of such dissolved solids can make water unfit to drink, harm fish and other aquatic life, depress crop yields, and accelerate corrosion of equipment that uses water.

Table 20-1 Common Diseases Transmitted to Humans Through Contaminated Drinking Water

Type of Organism	Disease	Effects
Bacteria	Typhoid fever	Diarrhea, severe vomiting, enlarged spleen, inflamed intestine; often fatal if untreated
	Cholera	Diarrhea, severe vomiting, dehydration; often fatal if untreated
	Bacterial dysentery	Diarrhea; rarely fatal except in infants without proper treatment
	Enteritis	Severe stomach pain, nausea, vomiting; rarely fatal
Viruses	Infectious hepatitis	Fever, severe headache, loss of appetite, abdominal pain, jaundice, enlarged liver; rarely fatal but may cause permanent liver damage
	Polio	High fever, severe headache, sore throat, stiff neck, deep muscle pain, severe weakness, tremors, paralysis in legs, arms, and body; can be fatal
Parasitic protozoa	Amoebic dysentery	Severe diarrhea, headache, abdominal pain, chills, fever; if not treated can cause liver abscess, bowel perforation, and death
	Giardia	Diarrhea, abdominal cramps, flatulence, belching, fatigue
Parasitic worms	Schistosomiasis	Abdominal pain, skin rash, anemia, chronic fatigue, and chronic general ill health

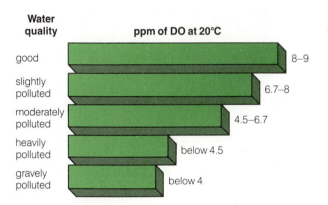

Figure 20-1 Water quality and dissolved oxygen (DO) content in parts per million (ppm).

- *inorganic plant nutrients.* water-soluble nitrate and phosphate compounds that can cause excessive growth of algae and other aquatic plants, which then die and decay, depleting water of dissolved oxygen and killing fish. Excessive levels of nitrates in drinking water can reduce the oxygen carrying capacity of the blood and kill unborn children and infants, especially those under three months old. Nitrates in wastewater can seep through soil into the groundwater, where bacteria transform them into nitrous oxide that escapes into the atmosphere and contributes to the greenhouse effect (Figure 19-17, p. 504).

- *organic chemicals.* oil, gasoline, plastics, pesticides, cleaning solvents, detergents, and many other water-soluble and insoluble chemicals that threaten human health and harm fish and other aquatic life. Some of the more than 700 synthetic organic chemicals found in trace amounts in sur- face and underground drinking-water supplies in the United States can cause kidney disorders, birth defects, and various types of cancer in laboratory test animals (Table 20-2). It is not known what levels of these chemicals in drinking water can cause such chronic effects in humans (Section 18-1).

- *sediment or suspended matter.* insoluble particles of soil, silt, and other solid inorganic and organic materials that become suspended in water and that in terms of total mass are the largest source of water pollution. Many rivers and streams have always carried high sediment loads because of natural erosion occurring in their watersheds. But in most rivers sediment loads have risen sharply because of accelerated erosion from cropland, rangeland, forestland, and construction and mining sites (Section 10-2). Suspended particulate matter clouds the water, reduces the ability of some organisms to find food, reduces photosynthesis by aquatic plants, disrupts aquatic food webs, clogs the gills of fish and the filters of clams and other filter feeders, and carries pesticides, bacteria, toxic metals, and other harmful substances. Bottom sediment destroys feeding and spawning grounds of fish and clogs and fills lakes, reservoirs, river and stream channels, and harbors.

- *radioactive substances.* radioisotopes that are water soluble or capable of being biologically amplified in food chains and webs. Ionizing radiation from such isotopes can cause DNA mutations, leading to birth defects, cancer, and genetic damage (see Spotlight on p. 451).

Table 20-2 Health Effects on Common Chemical Contaminants in Drinking Water

Contaminant	Effects*
Inorganic Substances	
Arsenic	Cancer; liver, kidney, blood, and nervous system damage
Cadmium	Kidney damage, anemia, pulmonary problems, high blood pressure, possible fetal damage, and cancer
Chromium	Suspected cancer from some forms such as chromate
Lead	Headaches, anemia, nerve disorders, birth defects, and cancer; mental retardation, learning disability, and partial hearing loss in children (see Case Study on p. 473)
Mercury	Nervous system and kidney damage; biologically amplified in food webs
Nitrates	Respiratory distress and possible death in infants and the unborn; possible formation of carcinogenic nitrosamines
Synthetic Organic Substances	
Aldicarb (Temik)	High toxicity to nervous system
Benzene	Chromosomal damage, anemia, blood disorders, and leukemia
Carbon tetrachloride	Cancer; liver, kidney, lung, and central nervous system damage
Chloroform	Liver and kidney damage and suspected cancer
Dioxins (especially TCDD)	Skin disorders, cancer, and genetic mutations (see Case Study on p. 454)
Ethylene dibromide (EDB)	Cancer and male sterility
Polychlorinated biphenyls (PCBs)	Liver, kidney, and pulmonary damage (see Case Study on p. 471)
Trichloroethylene (TCE)	In high concentrations, liver and kidney damage, central nervous system depression, skin problems, and suspected cancer and mutations
Vinyl chloride	Liver, kidney, and lung damage; pulmonary, cardiovascular, and gastrointestinal problems; cancer and suspected mutations

*Based primarily on studies of laboratory animals.

■ *heat.* excessive inputs of heated water used to cool electric power plants. The resulting increases in water temperatures lower dissolved oxygen content and make aquatic organisms more vulnerable to disease, parasites, and toxic chemicals.

Point and Nonpoint Sources For purposes of control and regulation it is useful to distinguish between point sources and nonpoint sources of water pollution from human activities. **Point sources** discharge pollutants at specific locations through pipes, ditches, or sewers into bodies of surface water (Figure 20-2). Examples include factories, sewage treatment plants (which remove some but not all pollutants), active and abandoned underground coal mines (Figure 15-8, p. 350), and offshore oil wells. Because point sources are at specific places, they are fairly easy to identify, monitor, and regulate.

Nonpoint sources are big land areas that discharge pollutants into surface and underground water over a large area and parts of the atmosphere where pollutants are deposited on surface waters (Figure 20-2). Examples include runoff into surface water and seepage into groundwater from croplands, livestock feedlots, logged forests, urban and suburban lands, septic tanks, construction areas, parking lots, roadways, and acid deposition (Figure 19-10, p. 494). In the United States nonpoint pollution from agriculture is responsible for an estimated 64% of the total mass of pollutants entering rivers and 57% of those entering lakes.

Little progress has been made in the control of nonpoint water pollution because of the difficulty and expense of identifying and controlling discharges from so many diffuse sources. Controlling these inputs requires emphasis on prevention by better land use (Section 9-5), soil conservation (Section 10-3), reducing resource waste (Section 15-7), controlling air pollution (Section 19-5), and regulating population growth (Chapter 8).

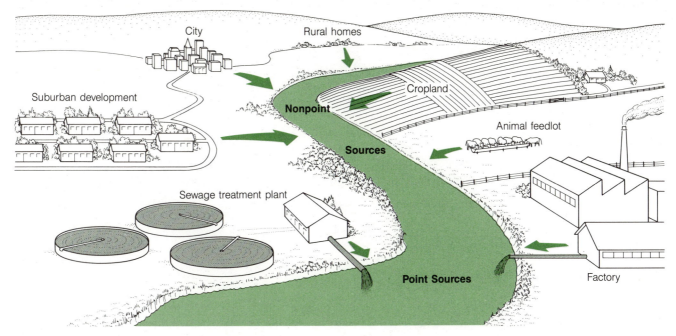

Figure 20-2 Point and nonpoint sources of water pollution.

20-2 POLLUTION OF RIVERS, LAKES, AND RESERVOIRS

Natural Processes Affecting Pollution Levels in Surface Water In a large, rapidly flowing river, relatively small amounts of pollutants are quickly diluted to low concentrations and the supply of dissolved oxygen needed for aquatic life and for biodegradation of oxygen-consuming wastes is rapidly renewed. However, such rivers can be overloaded with pollutants. In addition, dilution and biodegradation are sharply reduced when flow is decreased during dry spells or when large amounts of water are withdrawn for irrigation or cooling and returned at high temperatures, decreasing its dissolved oxygen content. High temperatures increase the rate of biodegradation by aerobic bacteria and can transfer volatile chemicals to the atmosphere.

In lakes, reservoirs, estuaries, and oceans dilution is often less effective than in rivers because these bodies of water frequently contain stratified layers that undergo little vertical mixing (Figure 5-14, p. 121 and Figure 5-16, p. 123). But in some cases mixing occurs because of waves and currents. Stratification also reduces the levels of dissolved oxygen, especially in the bottom layer which is not exposed to the atmosphere except during fall and spring turnovers (Figure 5-18, p. 125). In addition, lakes and reservoirs have little flow, further reducing dilution and replenishment of dissolved oxygen.

Another problem with relying on dilution to disperse pollution is that some substances, especially synthetic organic chemicals, can have harmful effects on aquatic life and humans at extremely small concentrations (Table 18-2, p. 453). Biodegradation is ineffective in removing slowly degradable or non-biodegradable pollutants and some of these chemicals (such as DDT, PCBs, some radioactive isotopes, and some mercury compounds) are biologically amplified to higher concentrations as they pass through food webs (Figure 14-10, p. 325 and Figure 18-11, p. 471).

Sedimentation can remove trace amounts of some organic and inorganic pollutants, which become attached to particles that settle and accumulate in the mud at the bottom of lakes, reservoirs, and slow-flowing rivers. But toxic substances stored in bottom sediments can become suspended again if the bottom is dredged or if it is stirred up by high flow rates during flooding.

Rivers and Oxygen-Consuming Wastes Every day the world's rivers receive enormous amounts of natural sediment runoff, industrial discharges, human sewage, and surface runoff from urban and agricultural uses of the land. Because they flow, most rivers recover rapidly from some forms of pollution—especially excess heat and degradable oxygen-demanding wastes—as long as the rivers are not overloaded (Figure 20–3). Slowly degradable and nondegradable pollutants, however, are not eliminated by these natural purification processes.

The depth and width of the *oxygen sag curve* (Figure 20-3) and thus the time and distance a river takes to recover depend on the river's volume, flow rate,

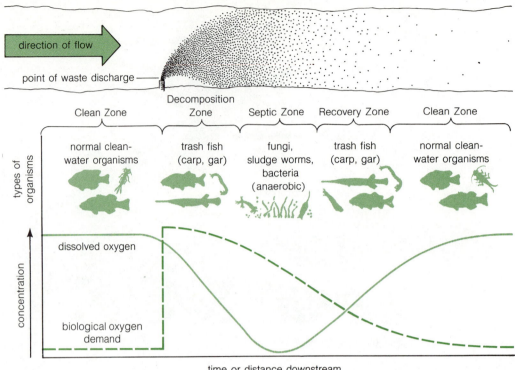

Figure 20-3 The oxygen sag curve (solid) versus oxygen demand (dashes). Depending on flow rates, water temperature, pH, and the amount of pollutants, rivers recover from oxygen-demanding wastes and heat if given enough time and if they are not overloaded.

temperature, pH, and the volume of incoming degradable wastes. Slow-flowing rivers can easily be overloaded with oxygen-demanding wastes, as can normally rapid-flowing rivers whose volume and flow-rate are reduced during hot summer months or drought. Similar oxygen sag curves occur when heated water from power plants is discharged into rivers.

Along many rivers, water for drinking is removed *upstream* from a city, and the city's industrial and sewage wastes are discharged *downstream*. The river can then become overloaded with pollutants as this pattern is repeated hundreds of times along the river as it flows toward the sea.

Requiring each city to withdraw its drinking water downstream rather than upstream would dramatically improve the quality of river water. Each city would be forced to clean up its own waste outputs rather than passing them on to downstream areas. However, political and economic pressures work against using this input approach for pollution prevention. It is fought by upstream users, who have the use of fairly clean water without high cleanup costs.

River Water Quality in the United States Water pollution control laws enacted in the 1970s have greatly increased the number and quality of wastewater treatment plants in the United States. Laws have also required industries to reduce or eliminate point source discharges into surface waters.

Since 1972 these efforts have enabled the United States to hold the line against increased pollution of most of its rivers and streams by disease-causing agents and oxygen-demanding wastes. National water quality surveys indicate that by 1985 about 73% of monitored stream miles fully supported their designated uses, mainly fishing, boating, and swimming. This is an impressive accomplishment, considering the rise in economic activity and population since 1972.

But there is still much to be done in improving the water quality of many of the country's rivers and streams. Inputs of nitrates, phosphates, pesticides, and other toxic chemicals have increased in many rivers since 1972 and still contaminate drinking water and cause large fish kills (Figure 20-4).

Further improvements in the quality of U.S. rivers will require stricter monitoring and enforcement of existing standards for discharges from point sources and massive efforts to reduce inputs from nonpoint sources. But this can lead to social and economic conflicts (see Case Study on p. 524).

River Water Quality in Other Countries Pollution control laws have also led to improvements in dissolved oxygen content in many rivers and streams in Canada, Japan, and most western European countries since 1970. Many rivers in the Soviet Union, however, have become more polluted with industrial wastes as

Figure 20-4 Fish killed by pesticide runoff in Arrowhead Lake, North Dakota.

industries have expanded without adequate pollution controls.

A spectacular river cleanup has occurred in Great Britain. In the 1950s the river Thames was little more than a flowing anaerobic sewer. But after more than 30 years of effort, $250 million of British taxpayers' money, and millions more spent by industry, the Thames has made a remarkable recovery. Dissolved oxygen levels have risen to the point where the river now supports increasing populations of at least 95 species of fish, including the pollution-sensitive salmon. Commercial fishing is thriving, and many species of waterfowl and wading birds have returned to their former feeding grounds.

Available data indicate that pollution of rivers and streams from massive discharges of untreated or inadequately treated sewage and industrial wastes is a serious and growing problem in most LDCs. Most of Poland's rivers are severely polluted (see Case Study on p. 18). More than two-thirds of India's water resources are polluted. Of India's 3,119 towns and cities, only 218 have any type of sewage treatment facilities. India's Ganges River, in which millions of Hindus regularly immerse themselves to wash away their sins, is highly contaminated. It receives untreated sewage and industrial wastes from millions of people

in 114 cities along with pesticide and fertilizer runoff. It has even caught fire twice.

In China only about 2% of the wastewater is treated. Of the 78 rivers monitored in China, 54 are seriously polluted. In Latin America and Africa many rivers are severely polluted.

Pollution Problems of Lakes and Reservoirs Lakes and reservoirs act as natural traps, collecting nutrients, suspended solids, and toxic chemicals in their growing amounts of bottom sediments. The flushing and changing of water in lakes and large reservoirs can take from one to a hundred years, compared to several days to several weeks for rivers.

Thus, lakes are more vulnerable than rivers to contamination with plant nutrients, oil, pesticides, and toxic substances that can destroy bottom life and kill fish. Atmospheric fallout and runoff of acids into lakes is a serious problem in lakes vulnerable to acid deposition (Figure 19-13, p. 497). In the Soviet Union, Lake Baikal—the world's largest and deepest body of fresh water—is threatened with pollution (see Guest Essay on p. 54).

In 1985 the EPA reported that the water quality in 78% of the area of 3,755 U.S. lakes and reservoirs monitored fully support their designated uses such as boating, commercial and sport fishing, and swimming. Despite this encouraging news, significant water pollution problems remain, especially as a result of runoff of plant nutrients and toxic wastes from nonpoint sources.

Eutrophication of lakes is a natural process (Figure 5-17, p. 124). But the stepped-up addition of phosphates and nitrates as a result of human activities can produce in a few decades the same degree of plant nutrient enrichment that takes thousands to millions of years by natural processes. Such cultural eutrophication is a major pollution problem for shallow lakes and reservoirs, especially near urban or agricultural centers (Figure 20-5).

Overloading shallow lakes with plant nutrients during the summer produces dense growths of rooted

---

CASE STUDY Jobs Versus the Environment: Cleanup of the Pigeon River

Since 1908 Champion International has operated a paper mill at Canton, a town in western North Carolina about 64 kilometers (40 miles) from the Tennessee border. In 1908 when the mill first opened, black, smelly water flowed down the Pigeon River into Tennessee and through the town of Newport.

To the people in Canton whose economy was built around the plant, the paper-mill odor of rotten eggs that hung over the town and river smelled liked money. But the people downstream in Tennessee were forced to accept the stench, the foul-tasting fish, and the low land values along the river's banks.

In 1912 Champion officials promised that wastes from the plant would soon be recycled within the plant. Since then the company has periodically updated its wastewater treatment facilities, spending more than $24 million since 1960. Today the water discharged from the plant ranges from the color of strong tea when the river runs high in the winter to dark coffee in summer when river flow is low.

Champion is currently the largest employer in western North Carolina with an annual payroll of $100 million. In addition to 1,800 workers in Canton (pop. 4,800), the mill's payroll supports thousands of other workers in local and nearby businesses. Currently, the plant produces one-third of all the nation's paper for milk and juice cartons and a quarter of the paper used for envelopes.

In 1985 the Environmental Protection Agency ruled that North

Carolina's water discharge permit for the Canton mill was invalid because it did not force the mill to comply with either Tennessee or North Carolina water standards, especially the one for color used to measure sediment in water. Champion appealed this ruling with strong support from the governor, U. S. senators, and other elected officials of North Carolina.

But environmentalists, citizens, and the governor of Tennessee favored requiring the mill to meet their state's water quality standards. In 1988 the EPA held public hearings on the problem in Asheville, North Carolina and Knoxville, Tennessee. Some 11,000 angry citizens—the greatest number attending any hearing in the history of the EPA—turned out to vent their strong feelings about both sides of this issue. EPA officials also received over 160,000 letters concerning this dispute and several threats of violence.

In 1988 the environmental organization Greenpeace supplied evidence that the river was polluted with the deadly dioxin TCDD, produced by the chlorine bleaching process used at the mill (see Case Study on p. 454). Some fish taken from the Pigeon had levels of TCDD three times the Food and Drug Administration's safe level for food items. North Carolina health officials have closed the river to fishing from Canton to the Tennessee border. But for decades all but the poorest residents had refused to eat fish taken from the river.

In 1989 EPA officials announced they would require the mill to

comply with Tennessee water quality standards as mandated in the Clean Water Act by 1992. Champion could meet these standards by installing expensive ultrafiltration equipment that produces a black tarry sludge. Rather than do this and find a way to dispose of the sludge, Champion officials announced in 1989 that they would probably shut down four of the mill's six papermaking machines and lay off 1,000 workers over the next three years.

Some analysts charge Champion officials with using this controversy as a way to lay off large numbers of union workers. Although the mill's payroll would be cut by half, its projected daily papermaking capacity would drop by only about 6%. The most modern sections of the mill will remain open and be further automated to reduce labor costs.

Jobs will be lost in North Carolina. But for decades jobs have been lost in Tennessee because industries won't locate in towns along the river because of the smell. Also people in Tennessee can't build homes on beautiful sites along the river, can't enjoy the river for recreation, and can't use the water for irrigation because of dioxin contamination.

Regardless of the outcome, this case provides a preview of what might lie ahead as the world tries to solve cross-border pollution conflicts between people in geographical areas with different standards and priorities. What do you think should be done?

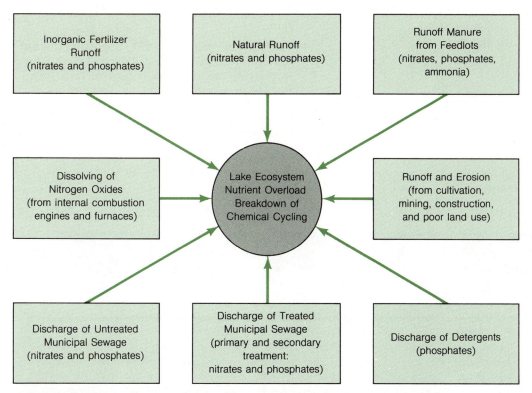

Figure 20-5 Major sources of nutrient overload, or cultural eutrophication, in lakes, slow-flowing rivers, and estuaries. The amount of nutrients from each source varies depending on the types of human activities taking place in various watersheds and airsheds.

Figure 20-6 Mass of dead and dying algae from cultural eutrophication of Lake Minnetonka in Minnesota.

plants and floating plants (such as water hyacinths) near the shore. It also causes algal blooms—population explosions of floating algae, especially the blue-green species. They make the water look like green soup and release substances that make the water taste and smell bad and that are toxic to some aquatic organisms (Figure 20-6).

Dissolved oxygen in the surface layer of water near the shore and in the bottom layer is depleted when large masses of algae die, fall to the bottom, and are decomposed by aerobic bacteria (Figure 20-6). Then important game fish such as lake trout and small-mouth bass die of oxygen starvation, leaving the lake populated by carp and other less desirable species that need less oxygen. If excess nutrients continue to flow into a lake, the bottom water becomes foul and almost devoid of animals, as anaerobic bacteria take over and produce their smelly decomposition products such as hydrogen sulfide and methane.

About one-third of the 100,000 medium to large lakes and about 85% of the large lakes near major population centers in the United States suffer from some degree of cultural eutrophication. The Great Lakes, for example, receive massive inputs of plant nutrients, as well as numerous toxic water pollutants, from point and nonpoint sources and from the atmosphere (see Case Study on p. 526).

Control of Cultural Eutrophication The solution to cultural eutrophication is to use input control methods to reduce the flow of nutrients into lakes and reservoirs and output control methods to clean up lakes suffering from excessive eutrophication.

Input Control Methods

- Use advanced waste treatment (Section 20-5) to remove 90% of phosphates from effluents of sewage treatment and industrial plants before they reach a lake.

- Ban or set low limits on phosphates in household detergents and other cleaning agents to reduce the amount of phosphate reaching sewage treatment plants.

- Control land use (Section 9-5), use sound soil conservation practices (Section 10-3), and clean streets regularly to reduce runoff of fertilizers, manure, and soil from nonpoint sources. Farmers can be required to plant buffer areas of trees or other vegetation between their fields and nearby lakes or other surface waters.

- Protect coastal and inland wetlands that filter and retain nutrients flowing off the land (see Case Studies on pp. 122 and 128).

CASE STUDY The Great Lakes

The five interconnected Great Lakes contain at least 95% of the surface fresh water in the United States and 20% of the world's fresh water (Figure 20-7). The massive watershed around these lakes has thousands of industries and over 60 million people—one-third of Canada's population and one-eighth of the U.S. population. The lakes supply drinking water for 26 million people. About 40% of U.S. industry and half of Canada's industry are located in this watershed.

Despite their enormous size, these lakes are especially vulnerable to pollution from point and nonpoint sources because less than 1% of the water entering the Great Lakes flows out the St. Lawrence River each year. Although Lake Erie is flushed out once about every 2.7 years, the flushing time for Lake Superior is 182 years and that for Lake Michigan is 105 years. The Great Lakes also receive large quantities of acids, pesticides, and other toxic chemicals by deposition from the atmosphere.

By the 1960s many areas of the Great Lakes were suffering from severe cultural eutrophication, massive fish kills, and contamination with bacteria and other wastes. Many bathing beaches had to be closed, and there was a sharp drop in commercial and sport fishing.

Although all five lakes were affected, the impact on Lake Erie was particularly intense. It is the shallowest of the Great Lakes and has the smallest volume of water. Also, its drainage basin is heavily industrialized and has the largest population of any of the lakes. At one time in the mid-1960s, massive algal blooms choked off oxygen to 65% of Lake Erie's bottom. By 1970 the lake had lost nearly all its native fish. Lake Ontario's small size and shallowness also made it vulnerable to cultural eutrophication and other forms of water pollution.

Since 1972 a joint $15 billion pollution control program has been carried out by Canada and the United States. It has led to significant decreases in levels of phosphates, coliform bacteria, and many toxic industrial chemicals. Algal blooms have also decreased, and dissolved oxygen levels and sport and commercial fishing have increased. By 1988 only 8 of 516 swimming beaches remained closed because of pollution.

These improvements were mainly the result of decreased point source discharges, brought about by new or upgraded sewage treatment plants and improved treatment of industrial wastes. Also, phosphate detergents, household cleaners, and water conditioners were banned or their phosphate levels were lowered in many areas of the Great Lakes drainage basin.

The runoff of phosphates from nonpoint sources is still a problem in some areas of the basin. But the most serious problem today is contamination from toxic wastes flowing into the lakes from land runoff, rivers, and atmospheric deposition. Most toxic "hot spots" are found in harbors or near the mouths of tributaries emptying into the lakes, especially Lake Erie and Lake Ontario. For example, there are 164 toxic-waste disposal sites in a 4.8 kilometer (3 mile) strip along the U.S. side of the Niagara River. Sores and liver cancers are common among many fish in these areas. Children under age 16 and pregnant women are advised not to eat any trout, salmon, or other fatty fish from many areas of the Great Lakes. Other people are advised not to eat such fish more than once a week.

In 1978 the U.S. and Canada signed a new agreement with the goal of virtual elimination of discharges of about 360 toxic chemicals. However, recent studies indicate that much of the input of toxic chemicals—more than 50% in Lake Superior—comes from the atmosphere, a source not covered by the agreement. Practically any long-lived chemical discharged into the atmosphere in the Northern Hemisphere can end up in the Great Lakes.

Solving these problems will be quite expensive and take many years. But not dealing with the problems will cost far more.

Output Control Methods

- Dredge bottom sediments to remove excess nutrient buildup. Impractical in large, deep lakes and not very effective in shallow lakes; often reduces water quality by resuspending toxic pollutants and can increase water salinity; dredged material must go somewhere and is often dumped into the ocean; changes wildlife habitats.

- Remove or harvest excess weeds. Disrupts some forms of aquatic life and is difficult and expensive in large lakes.

- Control nuisance plant growth with herbicides and algicides. Can pollute water and kill off animals and other plants (Section 21-3).

- Pump air through lakes and reservoirs to avoid oxygen depletion. Expensive.

- Control or eliminate bottom-feeding fish such as carp which stir up nutrients in sediments.

As with other forms of pollution, input or prevention approaches are the most effective and usually the cheapest in the long run. Input control methods have

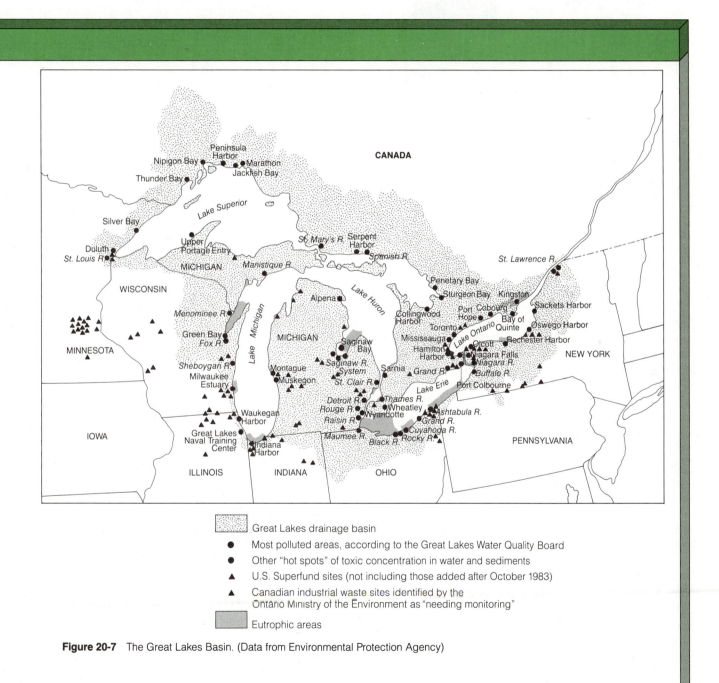

Figure 20-7   The Great Lakes Basin. (Data from Environmental Protection Agency)

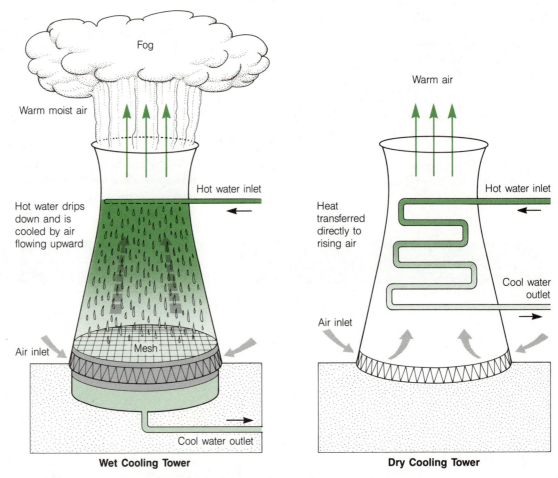

Figure 20-8 Wet and dry cooling towers transfer heat from cooling water to the atmosphere.

to be tailored to each situation based on the limiting factor principle (p. 86). When a number of nutrients are needed for the growth of various plant species, the one in smallest supply will limit or stop growth. For example, because phosphorus is the limiting factor in most freshwater lakes, its control should be emphasized. It is also easier to control than nitrogen.

But there is disagreement over whether phosphorus inputs should be lowered by banning or limiting phosphates in laundry detergents and other cleaning agents, by removing phosphates from wastewater at sewage treatment plants, or both. Studies of over 400 bodies of water indicate that a reduction of 20% in the total phosphate load must be achieved to produce a detectable effect on water quality.

Currently, eight states—Indiana, Maryland, Michigan, Minnesota, New York, Vermont, Virginia, and Wisconsin—many cities, and many parts of Canada have banned the use of phosphate detergents. Such bans have made a major contribution to reducing cultural eutrophication in the Great Lakes and other areas and have saved consumers and taxpayers money.

In some lakes and in coastal waters and estuaries, emphasis should be on reducing inputs of nitrogen because it is the limiting factor. Fortunately, if excessive inputs of limiting plant nutrients stop, the lake will usually return to its previous state. But it is much harder to control nitrogen than phosphorus because nitrates are more water soluble and run off from large areas of land.

Thermal Pollution of Rivers and Lakes Almost half of all water withdrawn in the United States each year is for cooling electric power plants. The cheapest and easiest method is to withdraw cool water from a nearby body of surface water, pass it through the plant, and return the heated water to the same body of water.

Small amounts of heat have no serious effects on aquatic ecosystems. Large rivers with rapid flow rates can dissipate heat rapidly (Figure 20-3) and suffer little ecological damage unless their flow rates are sharply reduced during summer months or prolonged drought. However, large inputs of heated water from a single plant or a number of plants using the same lake or slow-moving river can have harmful effects on aquatic life. This is called **thermal pollution**.

Warmer temperatures lower dissolved oxygen content by decreasing the solubility of oxygen in water. Warmer water also causes aquatic organisms to increase their respiration rates and consume oxygen faster, and

Figure 20-9 A 2,400-hectare (6,000-acre) canal system is used to transfer heat from cooling water into the atmosphere at the Turkey Point power plant site near Miami, Florida rather than discharging the heated water into Biscayne Bay. One of the four units—two nuclear and two fossil fuel—is located at the upper right.

Florida Power and Light Company

it increases their susceptibility to disease, parasites, and toxic chemicals. Discharge of heated water into shallow water near the shore also may disrupt spawning and kill young fish.

Fish and other organisms adapted to a particular temperature range can also be killed from **thermal shock**: sharp changes in water temperature when new power plants open up or when plants shut down for repair. Many fish die on intake screens used to prevent fish and debris from clogging the heat exchanger pipes. Pumping large volumes of cold, nutrient-rich water from the bottom layer of moderate-size lakes also speeds up the eutrophication process.

While some scientists call the addition of excess heat to aquatic systems thermal pollution, others talk about using heated water for beneficial purposes, calling it **thermal enrichment**. They point out that heated water results in longer commercial fishing seasons and reduction of winter ice cover in cold areas.

Warm water from power plants could also be used for irrigation to extend the growing season in frost-prone areas and cycled through aquaculture pens to speed the growth of commercially valuable fish and shellfish. For example, waste hot water is used to cultivate oysters in aquaculture lagoons in Japan and in New York's Long Island Sound and to cultivate catfish and redfish in Texas.

Heated water could also be used to heat nearby buildings and greenhouses, melt snow, desalinate ocean water, and provide low-temperature heat for some industrial processes. However, because of dangers from air pollution and release of radioactivity, most coal-burning and electric power plants are usually not located near enough to aquaculture operations, buildings, and industries to make thermal enrichment economically feasible.

Reduction of Thermal Water Pollution   There are a number of ways to minimize the harmful effects of excess heat on aquatic ecosystems:

- use and waste less electricity (Section 17-1)
- limit the number of power and industrial plants discharging heated water into the same body of water
- return the heated water at a point away from the ecologically vulnerable shore zone
- transfer the heat in the water to the atmosphere by means of wet or dry cooling towers (Figure 20-8). Most new power plants use wet cooling towers, but they have several drawbacks: larger withdrawals of surface water to replace water lost by evaporation, visual pollution from the gigantic cooling towers, high construction and operating costs, and excessive fog and mist in nearby areas. Dry towers are seldom used because they cost two to four times more to build than wet towers.
- discharge the heated water into shallow cooling ponds or canals, allow the water to cool, and withdraw it for reuse as cooling water (Figure 20-9). This method is useful where enough affordable land is available (about 1,000 acres for a 1,000-megawatt plant).

20-3   OCEAN POLLUTION

Our Ultimate Trash Dump   Marine explorer Jacques Cousteau has warned that "the very survival of the human species depends upon the maintenance of an ocean clean and alive, spreading all around the world. The ocean is our planet's life belt."

Oceans are the ultimate sink for much of the waste matter we produce. In addition to natural runoff, the world's oceans receive agricultural and urban runoff, atmospheric fallout, garbage and untreated sewage from ships, accidental oil spills from tankers and offshore oil drilling platforms, and intentional discharges of oil by tankers when they empty or clean their bilges. Barges and ships also dump industrial wastes, sludge from sewage plants, and materials dredged or scraped from the bottoms of harbors and rivers to maintain shipping channels into the oceans.

Oceans can dilute, disperse, and degrade large amounts of sewage, sludge, and some types of industrial waste, especially in deep-water areas. Marine life

The Chesapeake Bay (Figure 20-10) on the east coast is the largest estuary in the United States and one of the world's most productive estuaries. It is home for about 200 species of fish and shellfish. It is the largest single source of oysters in the United States and the largest producer of blue crabs in the world. The bay is also important for shipping, recreational boating, and sport fishing. Between 1940 and 1987 the number of people living close to the bay grew from 3.7 million to 13.2 million and is projected to reach 15 million by 2000.

The estuary receives wastes from point and nonpoint sources scattered throughout a vast drainage basin that includes 9 large rivers and 141 smaller rivers and creeks in parts of six states. It has become a massive pollution sink because only 1% of the waste entering the bay is flushed into the Atlantic Ocean.

Levels of phosphate and nitrate plant nutrients have risen sharply in many parts of the bay, causing algal blooms and oxygen depletion. Studies have shown that point sources, primarily sewage treatment plants, contribute most of the phosphates. Nonpoint sources, mostly runoff from urban and suburban areas and agricultural activities and acid deposition, are the major sources of nitrates.

Additional pollution comes from nonpoint runoff of large quantities of pesticides from cropland and urban lawns. Point source discharge of numerous toxic wastes by industries, often in violation of their discharge permits, is also a problem.

Commercial harvests of oysters, crabs, and several commercially important fish have fallen sharply since 1960. However, populations of bluefish, menhaden, and other species that spawn in salt water and feed around algae blooms have increased. In many areas of the bay underwater grasses have virtually disappeared. These plants help control erosion, filter pollutants, and are a vital link in the bay's food webs.

Since 1983 over $650 million in federal and state funds have been spent on a Chesapeake Bay cleanup program that will ultimately cost several billion dollars. Between 1980 and 1987, discharges of phosphates from point sources dropped by about 20%, but there is a long way to go to reverse severe eutrophication and oxygen depletion in many areas (Figure 20-10).

Bans on phosphate-containing detergents and cleaning agents will probably have to be enacted throughout the six-state drainage basin. Forests and wetlands around the bay must also be protected from development. Halting the deterioration of this vital estuary will require the prolonged, cooperative efforts of citizens, officials, and industries.

Figure 20-10 The Chesapeake Bay. The largest estuary in the United States is severely degraded as a result of pollution from point and nonpoint sources in six states.

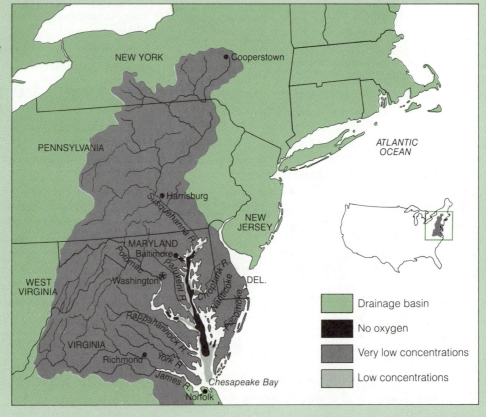

Figure 20-11 Surveys in the North Sea show that half of the individuals of some bottom-dwelling species have pollution-induced cancers or other lesions. This flounder, caught in coastal water near the mouth of the Elbe River, West Germany, has lesions due to bacterial or viral infections caused by living in polluted water.

Figure 20-12 Sea lions (seen here) and seals die by the thousands each year after becoming entangled in plastic debris, especially broken and discarded fishing nets.

has also proved to be more resilient than some scientists had expected.

But coastal areas, especially vital estuaries and wetlands (see Spotlight on p. 122), in the United States and other coastal countries bear the brunt of our massive inputs of wastes into the ocean. This can overwhelm the natural dilution and degradation processes of these areas and destroy vital sources of food and recreational pleasure (see Enrichment Study on p. 129).

Pollution problems of one type or another occur virtually anywhere along the coastlines of the continental United States, as the country is increasingly becoming "megalopolis-by-the-sea" (see Enrichment Study on p. 129). The list of notoriously polluted areas includes Boston Harbor, New York Harbor, Chesapeake Bay, Puget Sound, San Francisco Bay, Santa Monica Bay, and the Gulf of Mexico. In Great Britain at least 56% of the coastal areas are seriously polluted along with much of the Mediterranean and Baltic seas. The list could go on.

Scientists warn that there are limits to any natural cleansing processes and that we know less about the deep ocean than outer space. There is concern that we have exceeded threshold levels of pollution in some coastal areas and are approaching these levels in many other areas. Biologist Albert Manville of Defenders of Wildlife warns: "We're running out of time. We cannot continue to use the ocean as a garbage dump."

Toxic Chemicals and Plastics Another problem is that natural processes can't readily degrade many of the plastics, pesticides, and other synthetic organic chemicals (many of them toxic to some forms of aquatic life) that end up in the ocean. There is little life in ocean areas where large amounts of toxic sewage sludge is dumped. Lobsters and crabs caught in some areas have mysterious burn holes. And fish caught in some areas have tumors and lesions, mostly from exposure to toxic chemicals (Figure 20-11).

By 1988 about 27% of U.S. coastal waters around the lower 48 states was closed to shellfish harvesters because of pollution and habitat disruption. This loss of marine resources costs the United States about $80 million a year.

Studies indicate that each year as many as 2 million seabirds and more than 100,000 marine mammals, including whales, seals, dolphins, and sea lions (Figure 20-12) die when they ingest or become entangled in plastic cups, bags, six-pack yokes, fishing gear, and other forms of plastic trash thrown or washed into the ocean.

Merchant ships dump at least 450,000 plastic containers overboard every day. The United States is responsible for approximately one-third of all the trash thrown into the world's oceans.

Ocean Dumping by the United States Every year barges and ships legally dump more than 172 million metric tons (189 million tons) of solid waste off the Atlantic, Pacific, and Gulf Coasts, where they mingle with vast amounts of agricultural and urban runoff. This dumping is permitted by the Ocean Dumping Act of 1972. This law also called for efforts to end all ocean dumping by 1977.

But large-scale ocean dumping is still going on. About 80% of these wastes are **dredge spoils**, materials scraped from the bottoms of harbors and rivers to maintain shipping channels. Typically about one-third of these dredged materials are contaminated with toxic effluents from industries and urban areas and runoff from farmlands.

Most of the remaining 20% of the wastes barged out and dumped into the ocean are industrial wastes and **sewage sludge**, a gooey mixture of toxic chemicals, infectious agents, and settled solids removed from wastewater at sewage treatment plants. There are four ways to dispose of sludge: burn it, bury it, dump it in the ocean, or treat it to remove toxic materials and spread it on the land as a soil conditioner.

As a result of the Ocean Dumping Act of 1972, the volume of industrial wastes dumped at sea in U.S.

coastal waters declined by about 75% between 1975 and 1985. However, the volume of sewage sludge dumped into U.S. coastal waters increased by almost 60% during the same period. This happened because of the greatly increased levels of sewage treatment required by water pollution control laws enacted in the 1970s and the lack of suitable and affordable land dumping sites. Everything is connected to everything.

Sewage sludge from two New York communities (including New York City) and eight New Jersey communities is dumped at a deep-water site 170 kilometers (106 miles) east of New York City, just beyond the con-

PRO/CON Should Ocean Dumping of Sewage Sludge Be Banned?

During the summer of 1988 hypodermic needles, IV tubing, blood sample vials, and other medical wastes washed ashore on beaches from Maine to North Carolina. Beaches in several states, especially New York and New Jersey, had to be closed.

In an election year the resulting public outcry prompted Congress to pass the Ocean Dumping Ban Act of 1988 banning all ocean sludge dumping by 1992. In 1988 New Jersey ordered an end to all ocean dumping of sludge by 1991, with the goal of protecting its $7 billion coastal tourism industry and its $100 million a year fishing industry.

Some elected officials and scientists oppose this ban. They argue that ocean disposal is safer and cheaper than land dumping and incineration, especially for areas such as New York City where there are not enough suitable sites for landfills or incinerators.

It is also argued that banning ocean sludge dumping will do little to prevent pollution of beaches because sewage sludge and the floatable solid waste that fouls beaches are two different things.

Proponents of ocean sludge dumping argue that debris found on beaches comes from

■ combined sewers that mix storm runoff with municipal wastewater and overflow during periods of heavy rain
■ sewage treatment plants that occasionally malfunction

■ illegal dumping of medical and other wastes
■ floatable material that collects in streets and drains and is washed out by big storms or high tides
■ garbage dumped at sea by commercial and pleasure boats
■ debris thrown away by beach users

Potentially harmful medical waste represents less than 1% of beach litter. Most of the rest is plastic and paper debris dropped by beachgoers. Thus, if we want clean and safe beaches all of us will have to change our disposal-oriented lifestyles.

There is general agreement that the deep ocean is better equipped than land to handle sewage and some forms of industrial waste. But most scientists believe that the ocean should not be used for the dumping of slowly degradable or nondegradable pollutants like PCBs, some pesticides and radioactive isotopes, and toxic mercury compounds that can be biologically amplified in ocean food webs. Many of these materials are mixed with some types of sewage sludge and industrial waste being dumped into the ocean in large quantities.

There is concern that the site where sludge is dumped off the East Coast is the prime migratory path for species like tuna and marlin. The suspended sludge particles can also threaten the offshore spawning area for the bluefish, the

region's number-one sport fish.

A 1988 study by NOAA scientists warned that because of the Gulf Stream currents at the deep-water site off the coast of New York, hazardous suspended solids dumped there could spread all the way to Cape Hatteras off North Carolina. Some NOAA scientists propose drilling 1.4 million 122-meter- (400 foot-) deep holes in a 26-square-kilometer (10-square-mile) section of the Atlantic floor and filling the holes with sludge from New York City.

Other scientists argue that the battering rams used to drill the holes and the debris produced would have harmful effects on shellfish and other aquatic life. Some NOAA officials argue that seabed burial is not the same as at-sea dumping and thus is not subject to the Ocean Dumping Ban Act.

Environmentalists favor requiring that sludge be treated to remove PCBs, toxic metals and other hazardous substances. Then the sludge would be safer to dispose of on the land or at sea or better yet could be used as a soil conditioner for forests, parks, and other areas not used to grow food. The small volume of highly toxic chemicals removed from the sludge could be disposed of in landfills designed for such wastes (Figure 18-13, p. 476). What do you think should be done with sewage sludge?

tinental shelf. But in 1989 the EPA reduced the permitted dumping rate at the new site after finding that the sludge was not dispersing as quickly as expected.

This is the only place in U. S. waters where the ocean dumping of sludge is still permitted, a practice that violates the international London Dumping Convention. Some politicians and environmentalists believe there should be a ban on using the ocean as a sludge dumping ground. Other politicians and some scientists believe that ocean disposal is safer than other alternatives (see Pro/Con on p. 532).

Ships also dump large amounts of garbage at sea. Countries could ban such dumping in waters under their control and an international treaty could ban garbage dumping in international waters. But such bans would be hard to enforce. Garbage that can be dumped at sea free of charge can cost 25 cents to 50 cents a pound to dispose of at a port—costing a typical ship $500 to $1,000 each time it docks. Most shipowners would continue dumping at sea and risk getting caught and paying small fines to avoid such costs.

Ocean Oil Pollution   Crude petroleum (oil as it comes out of the ground) and refined petroleum (Figure 16-3, p. 376) are accidentally or deliberately released into the environment from a number of sources. Tanker accidents and blowouts (oil escaping under high pressure from a borehole in the ocean floor) at offshore drilling rigs receive most of the publicity. However, almost half (some experts estimate 90%) of the oil reaching the oceans comes from the land as a result of runoff and dumping of waste oil by cities and industries.

In 1979 the largest blowout occurred at the *Ixtoc I* oil well in the southern Gulf of Mexico. During the eight months it took to cap the borehole over 694 million liters (184 million gallons) of oil leaked into the gulf. But releases of oil from offshore wells during normal operations and during transport of the oil to shore add a much larger volume of oil to the oceans than occasional blowouts. Natural oil seepages also release large amounts of oil into the ocean at some sites.

Tanker accidents account for only 10% to 15% of the annual input of oil into the world's oceans, but such spills can have severe ecological and economic impacts on coastal areas. The largest accident took place in 1983 when the tanker *Castillow de Bellver* caught fire and released 296 million liters (78.5 million gallons) of oil into the ocean off the coast of Capetown, South Africa. Since 1973 there has been a decrease in the average annual number of major oil tanker accidents due mostly to improved safety measures, better navigational equipment, and better training.

However, environmentalists charge that the lower number of accidents and lack of effective supervision and enforcement of federal and state regulations has

Figure 20-13   A seabird coated with crude oil from an oil spill. Such birds die unless the oil is removed with a detergent solution. Many die even when the oil is removed.

led oil companies to relax their standards and sharply reduce their research on methods for containing and cleaning up oil spills to save money. The Valdez oil spill in 1989 provided evidence backing up these charges (see Case Study on p. 534).

Effects of Oil Pollution   The effects of oil on ocean ecosystems depend on a number of factors: type of oil (crude or refined), amount released, distance of release from shore, time of year, weather conditions, average water temperature, and ocean and tidal currents. Crude oil and refined oil are collections of hundreds of substances with widely differing properties. After an oil spill, low-boiling, aromatic hydrocarbons such as benzene and toluene are the primary cause of the immediate killing of a number of shellfish and nonmigratory fish, especially in their more vulnerable larval forms. In warm waters most of these toxic chemicals evaporate into the atmosphere within a day or two but in cold waters this may take up to a week.

Some other chemicals remain on the surface and form floating tarlike globs that range from the size of marbles to the size of tennis balls. This very sticky material adheres to marine birds (Figure 20-13), sea otters, seals, sand, rocks, and almost all objects that it encounters. This oily coating destroys the animals' natural insulation and buoyancy, and most drown or die of exposure from loss of body heat. These globs are gradually broken down by bacteria over several weeks or months, although they persist much longer in cold polar waters.

Heavy oil components that sink to the ocean floor or wash into estuaries are believed to have the greatest long-term impact on marine ecosystems. These components can kill bottom-dwelling organisms such as crabs, oysters, mussels, and clams or make them unfit for human consumption because of their oily taste and smell. In general, oil chemicals are not biologically amplified in food webs.

Studies of some previous spills have indicated that most forms of marine life recover from exposure to large amounts of crude oil within three years. However, recovery of marine life from exposure to refined

CASE STUDY Valdez: The Predicted Oil Spill

Crude oil extracted from fields in Alaska's North Slope near Prudhoe Bay is carried by pipeline to the port of Valdez and then shipped by tanker to the West Coast (Figure 20-14). Since the opening of the Alaskan pipeline in 1977, nearly 9,000 tankers with a trillion dollars worth of oil have made the trip from Valdez without any major accidents.

This changed on March 24, 1989. Just after midnight the *Exxon Valdez* tanker, more than three football fields long, went off course in Prince William Sound near Valdez and hit submerged rocks on a reef. About 42 million liters (11 million gallons) of oil—22% of its cargo—gushed from several gashes in the hull, creating the worst oil spill in U.S. waters and spoiling one of America's most beautiful and richest wildlife areas.

Blood tests after the accident indicated that the captain, with a history of alcohol abuse known to Exxon officials, was drunk on duty. When the accident happened, he had retired to his cabin and had turned over the ship to an inexperienced third mate. Since 1984 the captain had been arrested for drunken driving three times and had lost his license to drive a car, but Exxon officials still kept him in charge of one of their largest tankers.

The rapidly spreading oil slick coated and killed more than 34,000 birds (Figure 20-13), at least 1,000 sea otters, and untold numbers of fish, jeopardized the area's $100 million-a-year fishing industry, and covered hundreds of kilometers of shoreline with tar-like goo. The final toll on wildlife will never be known because most of the animals killed sink and decompose without being counted. Clean-up workers were exposed to health risks from breathing toxic fumes. These losses can't be measured in dollars. How do you measure a sea otter's death or a shoreline slimed with oil?

Some biologists predict recovery in three to five years. But others believe that recovery will take at least a decade because the spill took place in an enclosed body of cold water where biological decomposition of oil is slow.

In the early 1970s conservationists predicted that a large, damaging spill might occur in these treacherous waters with icebergs, submerged reefs, and violent storms. Conservationists urged that Alaskan oil be brought to the lower 48 states by pipeline over land to reduce potential damage.

But officials of Alyeska, a company formed by the seven oil companies extracting oil from Alaska's North Slope, said that a pipeline would take too long to build and that a large spill was "highly unlikely." They assured Congress that they would be at the scene of any accident within five hours and have enough equipment and trained people to clean up any spill. The oil companies won when the 49-to-49 tie vote in the U.S. Senate was broken by Vice President Spiro Agnew under orders from President Richard M. Nixon.

But when the Valdez spill occurred, Alyeska and Exxon officials did not have enough equipment and personnel and did too little too late. To save a few dollars, in the mid-1980s Alyeska had disbanded a full-time, highly trained emergency clean-up crew of 20, and replaced it with part-time inexperienced people. The first cleanup crew arrived 14 hours after the spill, rather than 5.

A few days after the accident an Exxon official announced that its costs would be passed on to American consumers like any other normal cost of doing business. After hearing this, over 1,000 outraged consumers cut up their Exxon credit cards, mailed them back to the company, and began buying their gas from other companies.

There is probably not enough equipment or trained personnel at any place in the world to deal with a spill of this size. But Alyeska clearly did not have the ability to deal with spills even half this size. This $1.5 billion accident and an immeasurable loss of wildlife could probably have been prevented by not allowing a captain with a history of alcohol abuse to command an oil tanker and by spending $22.4 million to have the tanker built with a protective second hull to keep oil from most accidents from reaching the ocean.

According to Jay Hair, president of the National Wildlife Federation: "This is a classic example of corporate greed. Big oil, big lies. Big lie number one was, 'Don't worry, be happy, be happy, nothing's going to happen at Valdez.' Big lie number two was, 'We're doing such a

oil, especially in estuaries, may take ten years or longer. The effects of spills in cold, polar waters generally last longer.

Oil slicks that wash onto beaches can have serious economic effects on coastal residents, who lose income from fishing and tourist activities. Oil-polluted beaches washed by strong waves or currents are cleaned up fairly rapidly, but beaches in sheltered areas remain contaminated for several years.

Controlling Ocean Oil Pollution   The best way to deal with oil pollution is to use various input approaches to prevent it from happening in the first place. Output rategies can be used to deal with oil pollution once has occurred, but they have not been very effective.

Input Control Methods

■ Use and waste less oil (Section 17-1).

good job with the environment at the North Slope we ought to be allowed into the Arctic National Wildlife Refuge, the finest Arctic sanctuary for wildlife in the world, and Bristol Bay."

Others must also share the blame for this tragedy. State officials had been lax in monitoring Alyeska and pretty much took the word of oil company officials that they were prepared to deal with any oil spills. Two years before the spill, the Coast Guard, suffering from budget cuts, had replaced its already inadequate radar system with a less powerful unit.

American consumers must also share some of the blame. Their enormous and unnecessarily

wasteful use of oil and gasoline is the driving force for trying to find more domestic oil without adequate environmental safeguards. For example, insisting that Congress raise the fuel-economy standards for new automobiles and light trucks from 27.5 miles per gallon to 40 miles per gallon by the year 2000 would save twice as much oil spilled in the Prince William Sound every day. It would also save more oil than is expected to be found in new searches for oil in Alaska and in U.S. coastal waters.

The Valdez spill seriously damaged the credibility of the oil companies in Alaska and elsewhere. Citizens and some elected officials

are now looking more closely at oil company proposals to drill for oil in Alaska's Arctic National Wildlife Refuge (see Pro/Con on p. 333), in Bristol Bay, and in offshore areas along all U.S. coasts.

The Valdez spill highlights an important issue: What degree of environmental risk should be accepted to provide a fairly small amount of domestic oil for U.S. consumers and elected officials who are unwilling to get serious about curbing their enormous and wasteful consumption of oil? What do you think should be done?

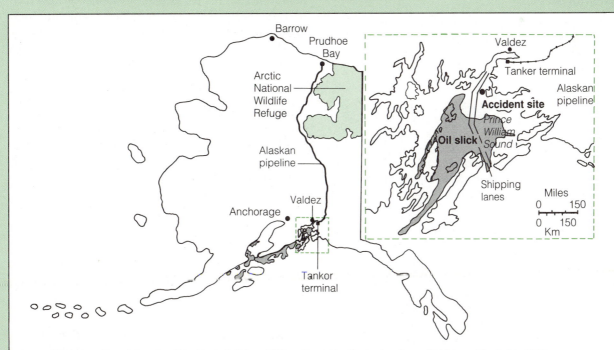

Figure 20-14   Site of the oil spill in Alaska's Prince William Sound by the tanker *Exxon Valdez* on March 24, 1989.

- Collect used oils and greases from service stations and other sources and reprocess them for reuse.

- Strictly regulate the building, maintenance, loading and unloading procedures, training of crews, and routing of oil tankers to reduce accidents.

- Require new and existing tankers to have double hulls to lessen chances of severe leaks.

- Require larger and better trained tanker crews.

- Require oil companies to routinely test employees for drug and alcohol abuse and ban convicted drunken drivers from tanker commands and offshore drilling rig management positions.

- Require the Coast Guard to have state-of-the-art radar equipment linked to tankers using harbors and sounds and sound an alarm automatically if a tanker wanders off course.

- Require updated and stringent oil spill cleanup plans with large and strict penalties for non-compliance.

- Ban the rinsing of sludge from empty oil tankers and dumping it into the sea.

- Require oil tankers to load and unload oil on platforms several miles offshore to keep tankers out of sensitive coastal zones. Oil would be piped to and from the platforms.

- Strictly regulate safety, training, and operation procedures for offshore wells.

- Strictly regulate safety, operation, and disposal procedures for oil refineries and industrial plants.

Output Control Methods

- Treat spilled oil with chemical dispersants sprayed from aircraft within a day after a spill so that it will disperse, dissolve, or sink. Not effective after one or two days. Some biologists contend that the dispersants kill more marine life than the oil does.

- Use helicopters equipped with lasers to ignite and burn off much of the oil, especially the more toxic, volatile components. Cheaper and more effective than dispersants for small spills, and the only effective method in ice-congested seas; must be done very soon after the spill; creates air pollution and the ashes may be toxic to fish.

- Use mechanical barriers (inflatable booms) to prevent oil from reaching the shore. Ineffective in high seas and bad weather conditions, in ice-congested water, or for large spills.

- Pump the oil-water mixture into small boats called skimmers where special machines separate the oil from the water and pump the oil into storage tanks. Pillows containing chicken feathers can also be used to absorb oil from small spills; ineffective in high seas and for large spills and the collected oil must be disposed of or reprocessed.

- Use genetic engineering techniques to develop bacterial strains that can degrade compounds in oil faster and more efficiently than natural bacterial strains. Possible ecological side effects of such "superbugs" should be carefully investigated before widespread use (see Pro/Con on p. 148).

- Clean up polluted beaches by use of straw (Figure 2-15, p. 43), detergents, high-pressure hoses, spreading nitrogen and phosphorus fertilizers to accelerate growth of natural bacteria that break down oil, and other methods; time-consuming and too expensive for cleaning up large areas.

- Greatly increase government and oil company research on methods for containing and cleaning up oil spills. The Valdez spill revealed how little research the oil companies have done in this area since the mid-1970s, mostly because it wasn't required by law.

20-4 GROUNDWATER POLLUTION

Is It Safe to Drink the Water? Groundwater is a vital resource that provides drinking water for one out of two Americans and 95% of those in rural areas. About 75% of American cities depend on groundwater for all or most of their supply of drinking water. Water seeping from underground aquifers provides nearly a third of the flow in U.S. streams and supplies much of the nation's other surface water (Figure 11-3, p. 240). This increases the risk that surface water may be polluted by contaminated groundwater.

Little is known about the quality of groundwater in the United States and other countries, despite the importance of this resource. Only limited testing has been done. By 1988 only 38 of the several hundred chemicals found in groundwater were covered by federal water quality standards and routinely tested for in municipal drinking water supplies.

In a 1982 survey the EPA found that 45% of the large public water systems served by groundwater were contaminated with synthetic organic chemicals that posed potential health threats. The most common are solvents such as trichloroethylene (TCE), carbon tetrachloride, and chloroform. The EPA has documented groundwater contamination by 74 pesticides in 38 states.

Another EPA survey in 1984 found that two-thirds of the rural household wells tested violated at least one federal health standard for drinking water. The most common contaminants were nitrates from fertilizers and pesticides used to kill nematode worms. In Florida, where 90% of the population relies on groundwater, more than 1,000 wells have been closed due to pollution by a cancer-causing worm killer.

Vulnerability of Groundwater to Pollution Some bacteria and most suspended solid pollutants are removed as contaminated surface water percolates

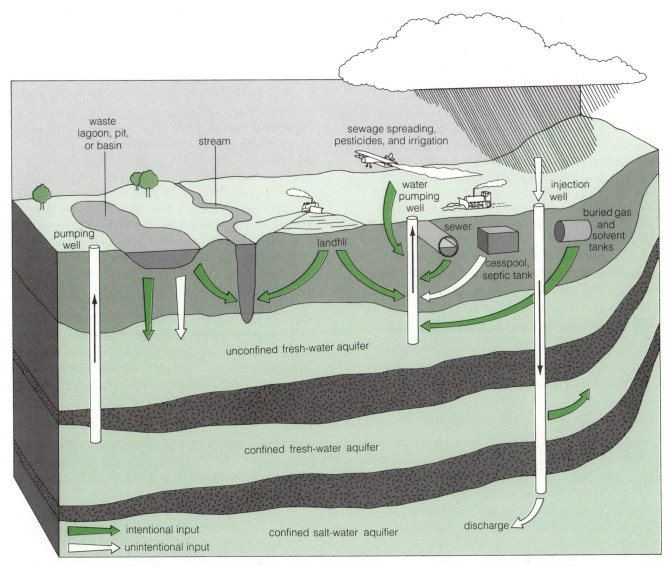

Figure 20-15 Major sources of groundwater contamination in the United States.

The figure labels include: waste lagoon, pit, or basin; stream; sewage spreading, pesticides, and irrigation; water pumping well; injection well; pumping well; buried gas and solvent tanks; sewer; landfill; cesspool, septic tank; unconfined fresh-water aquifer; confined fresh-water aquifer; confined salt-water aquifer; discharge; intentional input; unintentional input.

through the soil into aquifers. But this process can be overloaded by large volumes of wastes, and its effectiveness varies with the type of soil. For example, these pollutants are not effectively filtered out in porous, sandy soils such as those in much of Florida.

No soil is effective in filtering out viruses and some synthetic organic chemicals. Bacterial degradation of oxygen-demanding wastes reaching aquifers does not occur readily because of the lack of dissolved oxygen and sufficient microorganisms in groundwater.

Once contaminants reach groundwater, they are usually not effectively diluted and dispersed because the movement of water in most aquifers is slow and not turbulent. Degradable organic wastes are not broken down as readily as in rapidly flowing surface waters exposed to the atmosphere because groundwater has little dissolved oxygen and fairly small populations of anaerobic decomposing bacteria. This means that it can take hundreds to thousands of years for contaminated groundwater to cleanse itself of degradable

wastes. Slowly degradable and nondegradable wastes can permanently contaminate aquifers.

Because groundwater flows so slowly, contamination being discovered in wells today may be the result of pollutants that seeped into an aquifer many years ago. And water from a well may test pure one day and then be contaminated the next day by water that has been flowing toward the well for years. You can see why most analysts believe that groundwater pollution is the most serious U.S. water quality problem today and why they expect it to get much worse.

Sources of Groundwater Contamination Groundwater can be contaminated from a number of point and nonpoint sources (Figure 20-15). Two major sources of groundwater contamination are leaks of hazardous organic chemicals from underground storage tanks (see Pro/Con on p. 538) and seepage of hazardous organic chemicals and toxic heavy metal compounds from landfills, abandoned hazardous waste dumps, and industrial waste storage lagoons located above or near aquifers (Section 18-6).

Another concern is accidental leaks into groundwater aquifers from wells used to inject almost 60% of the country's hazardous wastes deep underground. Such wells are bored through aquifers and separated from them by an impermeable layer of rock that theoretically seals the waste in an underground tomb. In practice, however, liquid wastes from some wells have migrated into aquifers and surface waters. Migration occurs through abandoned and unplugged gas and oil wells, blowouts, and cracks caused by earth tremors and by dynamite used to expand the disposal area. Wastes can also escape through faulty well casings and joints.

Laws regulating well injection of hazardous wastes are weak and poorly enforced. Reporting of the types of wastes injected is not required and no national inventory of active and abandoned wells is kept. Operators are not required to monitor nearby aquifers and are not liable for any damages from leaks once a disposal well is abandoned and plugged. Environmentalists believe that all well disposal of hazardous waste in the United States should be banned, since

there are safer ways to deal with such waste (Section 18-6).

20-5 CONTROLLING WATER POLLUTION

Nonpoint Source Pollution Although most U.S. surface waters have not declined in quality since 1970, they have also not improved. The primary reason has been the absence until recently of any national strategy for controlling water pollution from nonpoint sources. Such a strategy would require greatly increased efforts to control soil erosion through conservation and land-use control for farms, construction sites, and suburban and urban areas (Sections 9-5 and 10-3).

The leading nonpoint source of water pollution is agriculture (see Spotlight on p. 271). Farmers can sharply reduce fertilizer runoff into surface waters and leaching into aquifers in several ways. They should avoid using excessive amounts of fertilizer and use none on steeply sloped land. They can use no-till cultivation (Figure 10-17, p. 227) and slow-release fertilizers, and knife the fertilizer or liquid manure into the

---

PRO/CON What Should Be Done About Leaking Underground Tanks?

Leaks of gasoline, home-heating oil, industrial-cleaning solvents, and other hazardous chemicals from 2 million to 7 million underground storage tanks may be responsible for as much as 40% of the country's groundwater contamination. About 95% of these tanks contain motor fuel and 10% contain other hazardous chemicals.

In 1988 the EPA estimated that 15% of the country's underground storage tanks were leaking and that by 1990 up to 58% may be leaking. Leaks occur from improper installation, corrosion (most are bare steel tanks designed to last only 15 to 20 years), cracking (fiberglass tanks), and overfilling.

A gasoline leak of just one gallon a day can seriously contaminate the water supply for 50,000 persons. Such slow leaks usually remain undetected until someone discovers that a well is contaminated. Determining the extent of a leak can cost $25,000 to $250,000.

Cleanup costs from $10,000 for a small spill to $250,000 and up if the chemical reaches an aquifer. Replacing a leaking tank adds an additional $10,000 to $60,000, and damages to injured parties and legal fees can run into the millions.

Most gasoline tanks are owned by independent operators or local petroleum suppliers and distributors, who tend not to report leaks for fear of going bankrupt. By 1986 only two states, Florida and Connecticut, required monitoring of underground tanks. In 1986 Congress passed legislation placing a tax on motor fuel to create a $500 million fund for cleaning up leaking underground tanks.

The EPA requires that all tanks installed after 1993 have a leak detection system and that discovered leaks must be stopped right away. By 1998 tanks that contain petroleum products or any of 701 hazardous chemicals listed under the Superfund law must have

overfill and spill prevention devices and double-walls or concrete vaults to help prevent leaks into groundwater (already required in 13 states for some or all tanks).

Environmentalists believe this is too little too late. They call for faster phasing in of these regulations and requiring much stricter training and certification for tank installers, as is done in Maine and Massachusetts. Also, monitoring systems should be required for all underground tanks, not just new ones. Operators should also be required to carry enough liability insurance to cover cleanup and damage costs and be liable for leaks from abandoned tanks.

In West Germany such a program has been quite successful in reducing underground tank leaks for 20 years. Most business owners oppose such regulations, believing they are too costly and increase government regulation. What do you think should be done?

ground. Fields can be periodically planted with soybeans or other nitrogen-fixing plants to reduce the need for fertilizer. Farmers should also be required to have buffer zones of permanent vegetation between cultivated fields and nearby surface water.

Similarly, farmers can reduce pesticide runoff and leaching by applying no more pesticide than needed and by applying it only when needed. They can reduce the need for pesticides by using biological methods of pest control (Section 21-5).

Livestock growers can control runoff and infiltration of animal wastes from feedlots and barnyards by several methods. They should control animal density, plant grassway buffers, and not locate feedlots on land sloping toward nearby surface water. They can divert runoff of animal wastes into detention basins or wastewater lagoons from which the nutrient-rich water can be pumped and applied as fertilizer to cropland or forestland (Figure 20-16).

Point Source Pollution: Wastewater Treatment In many LDCs and some parts of MDCs, sewage and waterborne industrial wastes from point sources are not treated. Instead, they are discharged into the near-est waterway or into a storage basin such as a cesspool or lagoon.

In MDCs, however, most of the wastes from point sources are purified to varying degrees. In rural and suburban areas with suitable soils, sewage and wastewater from each house is usually discharged into a **septic tank** (Figure 20-17). It traps greases and large solids and discharges the remaining wastes over a large drainage field. As these wastes percolate downward, the soil filters out some potential pollutants, and soil bacteria decompose biodegradable materials. Bacteria in the tank also decompose some of the waste.

In the United States, septic tanks are regulated by all states to ensure that they are installed in soils with adequate drainage, not placed too close together or too near well sites, and installed properly. In most states, systems must be reinspected whenever a house is sold. To prevent backup and overflow, grease and solids must be periodically pumped out of the tank.

In many small urban areas and throughout many LDCs, sewage is transported to a series of **wastewater lagoons** where air, sunlight, and microorganisms break down wastes, allow solids to settle out, and kill some disease-causing bacteria. Water typically remains in a

Figure 20-16 A detention basin or wastewater lagoon such as this one in Cass County, Michigan can be used to capture runoff from animal feedlots. Nutrient-rich water can be pumped out and used to fertilize cropland.

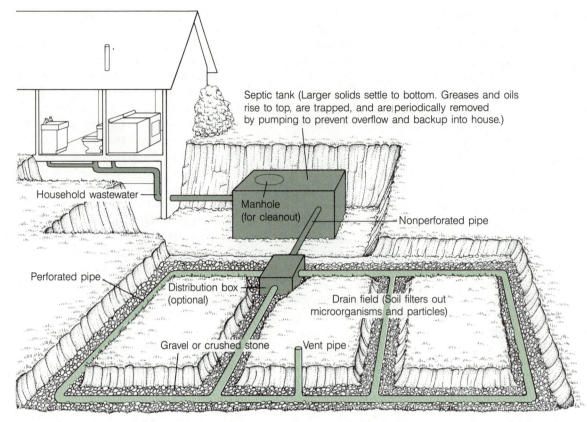

Figure 20-17 Septic tank system used for disposal of domestic sewage and wastewater in rural and suburban areas.

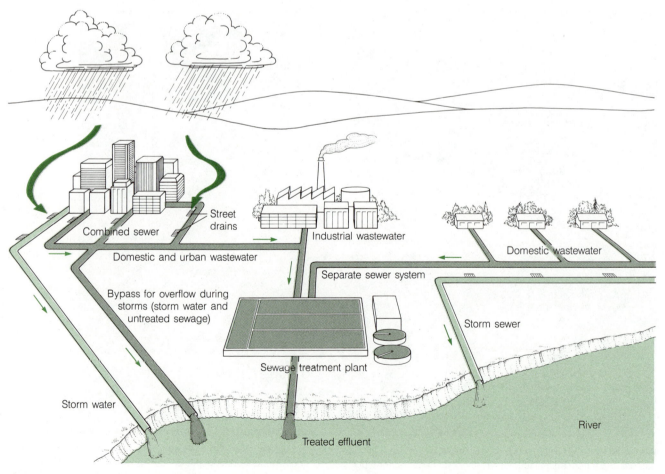

Figure 20-18 Separated and combined storm and sewer systems used in cities.

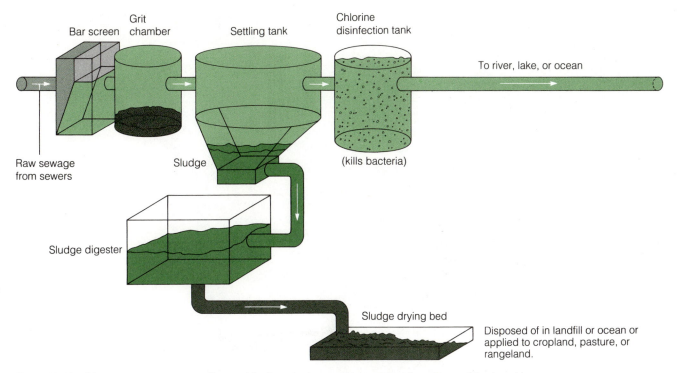

Grit chamber · Bar screen · Settling tank · Chlorine disinfection tank

To river, lake, or ocean

Raw sewage from sewers

Sludge

(kills bacteria)

Sludge digester

Sludge drying bed

Disposed of in landfill or ocean or applied to cropland, pasture, or rangeland.

Figure 20-19 Primary sewage treatment. If a combination of primary and secondary (or advanced) treatment is used, the wastewater is not disinfected until the last step.

lagoon for 30 days. Then it is treated with chlorine and pumped out for use by a city or farms. Lagoons are also widely used to handle wastes from animal feedlots (Figure 20-16).

In larger urban areas in MDCs most waterborne wastes from homes, businesses, factories, and storm runoff flow through a network of sewer pipes to wastewater treatment plants. Some urban areas have separate lines for sewage and storm water runoff, but in other areas (such as parts of Boston) lines for these two sources are combined because it is cheaper (Figure 20-18). The problem with a combined sewer system is that during heavy rains the total volume of wastewater and storm runoff flowing through the system usually exceeds—by as much as 100 times—the amount that can be handled by the sewage treatment plant. The overflow, which contains untreated sewage, is discharged directly into surface waters.

When sewage reaches a treatment plant, it can undergo up to three levels of purification, depending on the type of plant and the degree of purity desired. The three possible levels of sewage treatment are classified as primary, secondary, and advanced. Once the desired level is achieved the wastewater is disinfected before being released into the environment.

Primary sewage treatment is a mechanical process that uses screens to filter out debris like sticks, stones, and rags. Then suspended solids settle out as sludge in a sedimentation tank (Figure 20-19). Chemicals are sometimes added to speed up sedimentation.

Secondary sewage treatment is a biological process that uses aerobic bacteria as a first step to remove bio-

degradable organic wastes (Figure 20-20). This removes up to 90% of the oxygen-demanding wastes. Some plants use trickling filters, where aerobic bacteria degrade sewage as it seeps through a large vat bed filled with crushed stones covered with bacteria and protozoa. Others use an activated sludge process, in which the sewage is pumped into a large tank and mixed for several hours with bacteria-rich sludge and air bubbles to increase degradation by microorganisms. The water then goes to a sedimentation tank, where most of the suspended solids and microorganisms settle out as sludge. The sludge is removed and then is broken down in an anaerobic digestor, disposed of by incineration, dumped in the ocean or a landfill, or applied to land as fertilizer.

In the United States, combined primary and secondary treatment must be used in all communities served by wastewater treatment plants. Combined primary and secondary treatment, however, still leaves about 3% to 5% of the oxygen-demanding wastes, 3% of the suspended solids, 50% of the nitrogen (mostly as nitrates), 70% of the phosphorus (mostly as phosphates), and 30% of most toxic metal compounds and synthetic organic chemicals in the wastewater discharged from the plant. Virtually none of any long-lived radioactive isotopes and persistent organic substances such as pesticides are removed by these two processes.

Advanced sewage treatment is a variety of specialized chemical and physical processes that lower the quantity of specific pollutants still left after primary and secondary treatment (Figure 20-21). Types

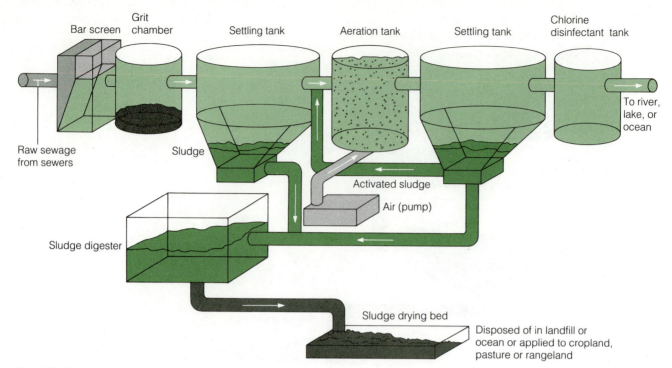

Figure 20-20 Secondary sewage treatment.

of advanced treatment vary depending on the contaminants in specific communities and industries. Except in Sweden, Denmark, and Norway, advanced treatment is rarely used because the plants cost twice as much to build and four times as much to operate as secondary plants.

Preliminary experiments have shown that wastewater from secondary treatment can be purified further by allowing it to flow slowly through long canals filled with plants such as water hyacinths or bullrushes. These plants also remove toxic organic chemicals and metal compounds not removed by conventional primary and secondary treatment. But the masses of contaminated plants must be disposed of.

One of the last steps in any form of wastewater treatment is to disinfect the water before it is discharged into nearby waterways or applied to land for further filtering and use as fertilizer. Disinfection removes water coloration and kills disease-carrying bacteria and some (but not all) viruses. The usual method is chlorination, with one out of two Americans drinking chlorinated water. A problem is that chlorine reacts with organic materials in the wastewater or in surface water to form small amounts of chlorinated hydrocarbons. Some of these, such as chloroform, are known carcinogens. Preliminary evidence also suggests that drinking chlorinated water can cause a 1% increase in blood cholesterol, which gives a small added risk of getting heart disease. Several other disinfectants, such as ozone and UV light, are being used in some places, but are more expensive than chlorination.

According to health scientists, no disinfection process can guarantee complete removal or destruction of pathogens, especially viruses. But a combination of methods working properly can control up to 98% of all pathogens.

Alternatives to Large-Scale Treatment Plants

Small-scale, *package wastewater treatment plants* are sometimes used for secondary treatment of small quantities of wastes from shopping centers, apartment complexes, villages, and small housing subdivisions. However, many of these do not work properly and require considerable attention and maintenance. Often they are put in by developers and then abandoned or poorly run and maintained.

Some small rural villages and suburban developments where groundwater used for drinking is being polluted by large numbers of septic tanks are using an alternative to building expensive wastewater treatment plants. They have installed a small-diameter, gravity flow sewer system to link the septic tanks of all residences and carry wastewater to large soil-absorption drainage fields or beds of sand several feet thick. Such systems cost about one-third to one-half as much as conventional sewage treatment plants used in larger cities, but sufficient land must be available for the drainage fields.

There are also some promising experiments using aquatic plants and bacteria in solar greenhouses to purify wastewater. Scientists at the Sandia National Laboratory are experimenting with using the UV light in sunlight to reduce levels of organic pollutants to

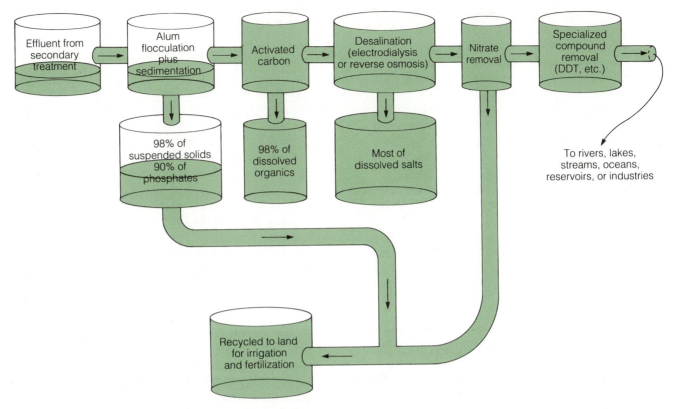

Figure 20-21 Advanced sewage treatment. This diagram shows several different types of advanced treatment. Often only one or two of these processes are used to remove specific pollutants in a particular area.

several parts per billion by passing contaminated water through long glass tubes exposed to sunlight.

Land Disposal of Sewage Effluent and Sludge

Sewage treatment also produces large volumes of sludge that must be disposed of, usually by incineration or dumping in the ocean or a landfill. Nutrient-rich effluents discharged by sewage treatment plants are usually discharged into nearby surface waters, where the nutrients can contribute to cultural eutrophication (Figure 20–5, p. 525).

An alternative is to apply the sludge and effluent to the land as fertilizers. The EPA estimates that sludge produced in the United States has a nutrient content worth $1 billion a year if these nutrients were applied to the land. Currently more than 25% of all U.S. municipal sludge and sewage plant effluent is returned to the land as fertilizer at more than 2,600 sites.

One problem with land disposal of sewage plant effluents and sludge is that they contain bacteria, viruses, toxic metals, and hazardous synthetic organic chemicals which can contaminate crops and groundwater. Several ways have been used to avoid or minimize the problem. Before it is applied, sludge can be heated to kill harmful bacteria, as is done in West Germany and Switzerland, or composted. Sludge and effluents can also be treated to remove toxic metals and organic chemicals before application, but this can

be expensive. Untreated sludge and effluent can be applied to land not used for crops or livestock or to land where groundwater is already contaminated or is not used as a source of drinking water. Examples include forests, surface-mined land, golf courses, lawns, cemeteries, and highway medians.

Purification of Drinking Water Treatment of water for drinking by urban residents is much like wastewater treatment. The degree of treatment required varies with the purity of the water coming into the treatment plant. Areas depending on surface water usually store it in a reservoir for several days to improve clarity and taste by allowing the dissolved oxygen content to increase and suspended matter to settle out.

The water is then pumped to a purification plant and given the degree of treatment needed to meet federal drinking water standards. Usually it is run through sand filters, then through activated charcoal, and then disinfected. In areas with very pure sources of groundwater, little if any treatment is necessary.

Control of Groundwater Pollution Groundwater pollution is much more difficult to detect and control than surface water pollution. Monitoring groundwater pollution is expensive (up to $10,000 per monitoring well), and many monitoring wells must be sunk.

Because of its location deep underground, pumping polluted groundwater to the surface, cleaning it up, and returning it to the aquifer is usually too expensive—$5 million to $10 million for a single aquifer. Even cleaning up a small contaminated area can cost $250,000 and up.

Some scientists propose that genetic engineering techniques be used to develop strains of anaerobic bacteria that could be injected into polluted aquifers to break down specific pollutants under low-oxygen conditions. Other scientists, however, are concerned about the possible side effects of such bacteria, including mutations into other strains (see Pro/Con on p. 148).

Preventing contamination is generally viewed as the only effective way to protect groundwater resources. In 1984 the EPA suggested that each state classify its groundwater resources into one of three categories for different degrees of protection:

- *Class I* contains irreplaceable sources of drinking water and ecologically vital sources that should be given the highest protection.

- *Class II* includes all other groundwater currently in use or potentially available for drinking water or for other beneficial uses. These areas would be given the next highest level of protection.

- *Class III* groundwater is not a potential source of drinking water and is of limited beneficial use, usually because it is already too contaminated, too salty, or too high in dissolved minerals (such as iron) from natural sources.

Protecting groundwater will require enacting and enforcing many unpopular laws at the federal and state levels. Any potentially polluting activities would have to be banned in Class I and II areas, but they could be allowed in Class III areas. Essentially all disposal of hazardous wastes in landfills and deep wells would have to be banned except perhaps in Class III areas. Expensive monitoring would be required for aquifers near existing landfills, underground tanks, and other potential sources of groundwater contamination.

Much stricter controls would have to be placed on the application of pesticides and fertilizers by millions of farmers and homeowners. People using private wells for drinking water would probably have to have their water tested once a year.

By 1988 thirteen states had enacted laws pertaining to statewide groundwater protection strategies, groundwater classification, or appropriated funds for groundwater cleanup. Unless nationwide federal standards are enacted, states that take such measures to protect their water supplies and the health of their citizens might lose industries and jobs to states with less regulation.

20-6 U.S. WATER POLLUTION CONTROL LAWS

Protecting Drinking Water   Currently about 89% of the U.S. population get their drinking water from approximately 200,000 public water supply systems. The other 11%, mainly in rural areas, get their drinking water from private wells.

Before 1974 the United States had no enforceable national standards for drinking water from public supply systems. Each state set its own standards, and these varied in range and rigor from state to state.

This began changing with passage of the Safe Drinking Water Act of 1974. This law required the EPA to establish national drinking water standards, called *maximum contaminant levels*, for any pollutants that "may" have adverse effects on human health. The EPA must also require the country's public water supply systems to regularly test drinking water to be sure federal standards are being met.

Environmentalists and health officials, however, have criticized the EPA for being slow in implementing this law. By 1986—12 years after the original legislation was passed—the EPA had set maximum contaminant levels for only 26 of the at least 700 potential pollutants found in municipal drinking water supplies. In 1986 amendments to the Safe Drinking Water Act required the EPA to regulate 83 contaminants by June 1989 and develop a list of an additional 25 contaminants every 3 years thereafter for possible regulation. Other amendments require use of granular activated carbon for removal of synthetic organic chemicals, ban the use of lead pipe and solder in any new public water system, and require the EPA to establish regulations for monitoring deep waste-injection wells.

Privately owned wells for millions of individual homes in suburban and rural areas are not required to meet federal drinking water standards. The major reasons are the cost (at least $1,000) of testing each well regularly and political opposition to mandatory testing and compliance by some homeowners.

Since 1974 the Safe Drinking Water Act has helped improve drinking water in much of the United States, but there is still a long way to go. A study by the National Wildlife Federation cited 101,000 violations of drinking-water laws by public-water systems in 1987 alone. Based on these data, it was estimated that 26 million Americans drank water contaminated with too many bacteria in 1987. About 10 million drank water contaminated with excessive radioactivity and 7 million drank water contaminated with other chemicals, mostly pesticides.

Contaminated wells and concern about possible contamination of public drinking water supplies have created a boom in the number of Americans drinking bottled water or adding water purification devices to their home systems. This has created enormous profits for legitimate companies and hucksters in these businesses.

In 1988 about 1 in 17 Americans spent $2 billion to buy bottled water, at an average cost 700 times the average price of tap water. Water bottling companies can legally get their water from springs, wells, and even public water right from the tap. More than one-third of the bottled water sold in the United States comes from the same groundwater and surface water sources which provide tap water. Sellers are not required to identify on their labels the source of their water or the type of purifying equipment, if any, used.

Bottled water is regulated by the Food and Drug Administration (FDA), not the EPA. But only bottled water marketed over state lines must meet federal drinking water standards and the FDA generally relies on tests by the bottling companies. Mineral water is not regulated by the FDA or any other agency.

To be safe consumers should purchase bottled water only from companies that have their water regularly tested and certified, ideally by EPA-certified laboratories. Obtain copies of their tests and ask them to give you the source of their water in writing. *Consumer Reports* magazine tested 50 brands of bottled water and reported the results in their January 1987 issue. Look at dates and buy the freshest batch available and store the water in a refrigerator.

Several processes are used in devices for treating home drinking water, each with certain advantages and disadvantages:

- *activated-charcoal filters* ($200 to $2,500). Remove most synthetic organic chemicals if filters are changed regularly, but are not effective in removing bacteria, viruses, nitrates, and other dissolved salts. Only a few models remove toxic metals.

- *reverse osmosis* ($500 to $1,000). Removes toxic metals and radioactive contamination, but generally wastes several gallons of water for every good one produced and some models don't do well in removing bacteria and viruses.

- *distillation* ($200 to $700). Removes toxic metals, radioactive contamination, and some organic contaminants. Expensive to operate and produces flat-tasting water.

- *ultraviolet light*. Kills most bacteria and some viruses but does not remove other pollutants.

- *water softeners*. Remove dissolved minerals but don't remove bacteria, viruses, and most other hazardous substances.

Machines that combine several approaches can remove most pollutants if they are properly maintained at a cost of at least $100 a year. But before buying expensive purifiers, consumers should get their water tested by local health authorities or private labs to find out what contaminants, if any, need to be removed. Then buy a unit that does the job. Buyers should be suspicious of door-to-door salespeople, telephone appeals, and scare tactics. They should check out companies selling such equipment carefully and demand to see certification of purifying claims by EPA-certified laboratories.

U.S. Water Pollution Control Efforts The Federal Water Pollution Act of 1972, renamed the Clean Water Act of 1977 when it was amended (along with amendments in 1981 and 1987), and the 1987 Water Quality Act form the basis of U.S. efforts to control pollution of the country's surface waters. The goal of these laws is to make all U.S. surface waters safe for fishing and swimming.

These acts require the EPA to establish *national effluent standards* and to set up a nationwide system for monitoring water quality. These effluent standards limit the amounts of certain conventional and toxic water pollutants that can be discharged into surface waters from factories, sewage treatment plants, and other point sources. Each point source discharger must get a permit specifying the amount of each pollutant that facility can discharge.

By 1988 87% of the country's publicly owned sewage treatment plants, which handle 95% of the total volume of municipal wastewater, used at least secondary treatment for the wastewater they received. Also about 80% of all industrial dischargers were officially in compliance with their discharge permits. But studies by the General Accounting Office have shown that most industries periodically violate their permits. Also 500 cities ranging from Boston to Key West, Florida have failed to meet federal standards for sewage treatment plants. In 1988 34 East Coast cities, including Boston and two sections of New York City, were still not doing anything more to their sewage than screening out large floating objects and discharging the rest into coastal waters.

Between 1972 and 1987 water quality has improved, in some cases dramatically, in 11% of the miles of streams and rivers surveyed for levels of several conventional pollutants. During the same period, however, roughly two-thirds of the stream miles and lakes surveyed showed no change in water quality. And about 2% of the stream miles and 10% of the lake areas monitored have deteriorated since 1972. According to a 1987 survey by the Fund for Renewable Energy and the Environment the three states with the best surface water protection programs were North Carolina, Georgia, and Iowa.

Scientists point out, however, that many rivers, streams, and lakes are polluted to an unknown degree by a variety of unconventional toxic pollutants not monitored and controlled by present laws. Even the data on conventional surface water pollutants are inadequate because measurements are made at widely separated, fixed points.

Current water pollution control laws also require states to establish local and regional planning to reduce water pollution from nonpoint sources. But no goals and standards have been established, and relatively little funding has been provided to reduce water pollution from nonpoint sources. The country also has no comprehensive legislation, goals, or funding designed to protect its groundwater supplies from contamination.

Future Water Quality Goals Environmentalists and conservationists believe that future water pollution control efforts in the United States should focus on four major goals. First, existing laws controlling discharge of conventional and toxic pollutants into surface waters from point sources should be strictly enforced and not weakened. Second, new legislation

sharply reducing runoff of conventional and toxic pollutants into surface waters from nonpoint sources should be enacted and funded. Third, new laws should be enacted, funded, and strictly enforced to protect the country's groundwater drinking supplies from pollution by point and nonpoint sources. Finally, water pollution control needs to be integrated with air pollution control, soil conservation, and land use.

What Can You Do? As individuals we can reduce pollution of water by safely disposing of products containing harmful chemicals, as discussed on p. 479. We can also reduce water pollution by using less water (see table inside the back cover) and by using low-phosphate or nonphosphate detergents and cleaners.

Commercial inorganic fertilizers, pesticides, detergents, bleaches, and other chemicals should be used only if necessary and then in the smallest amounts possible. Better yet use less harmful substances for most household cleaners (see Table 18-8, p. 479). We can also support tougher water pollution control laws

---

GUEST ESSAY: Economics Versus Ecology in the USSR: The Case of Lake Baikal

Philip R. Pryde

Philip R. Pryde is a specialist in land-use planning, water resources, energy resources, and environmental impact analysis in the Department of Geography at San Diego State University. He is also a leading U.S. expert on environmental problems and resource conservation in the USSR. He has served on the San Diego County Planning Commission and San Diego's Growth Management Review Task Force, and he is a director of the San Diego County Water Authority. In addition to numerous articles, he is the author of Nonconventional Energy Resources *(Wiley, 1983) and* Conservation in the Soviet Union *(Cambridge University Press, 1972).*

Lake Baikal is perhaps the most remarkable lake in the world. It is located in the Soviet Union just north of the border with Mongolia and contains the world's largest volume of fresh water. At 1,620 meters (5,311 feet), it is also the world's deepest body of fresh water. It stretches for about 700 kilometers (435 miles) between steep mountain ranges, in a geological depression called a *graben*. The geological faults that produced the graben also subject the entire region to severe earthquakes.

However, the lake's uniqueness is not limited to just its size. In Lake Baikal's unusually clear waters can be found about 800 species of plants and 550 species of animal life. Nearly three-quarters of these species occur nowhere else on earth. Because of its uniqueness and scientific value, controversy over the potential pollution of Lake Baikal has drawn considerable interest, not just within the Soviet Union, but throughout the world.

Timber cutting and small industrial facilities have existed in the Lake Baikal basin for decades. But in the 1960s, plans were prepared for two new wood-processing plants to be built on its shores. To keep them supplied with timber, large increases were planned in the logging activities on the surrounding mountain slopes. This would not only be an eyesore but could also result in considerable erosion of soil into the lake.

Wood-processing plants of the type proposed produce large amounts of potential water pollutants. A debate began almost immediately over whether the proposed wastewater treatment plants at the two factories would be adequate to preserve the quality of Lake Baikal's waters. This debate was noteworthy, as it was the first major

and their enforcement at the local, state, and federal levels.

The reason we have water pollution is not basically the paper or pulp mills. It is, rather, the social side of humans—our unwillingness to support reform government, to place into office the best-qualified candidates, to keep in office the best talent, and to see to it that legislation both evolves from and inspires wise social planning with a human orientation.

Stewart L. Udall

CHAPTER SUMMARY

The major types of water pollutants are disease-causing agents, oxygen-demanding wastes, water-soluble inorganic chemicals, inorganic plant nutrients (mostly nitrates and phosphates), insoluble and water-soluble organic chemicals, sediment, radioactive substances, and heat. These pollutants come from identifiable *point sources* such as industrial plants and scattered and diffuse *nonpoint sources* such as crop fields and urban and suburban lands.

Concentrations of pollutants entering surface waters such as rivers, lakes, and oceans can be decreased by *dilution*, *biodegradation* (oxygen-demanding wastes), and *sedimentation* (settling out). These natural cleaning processes work much better in large, fast-flowing rivers than in slow-flowing rivers and lakes but can be overloaded in any body of water by excessive waste inputs. They also don't take care of persistent and slowly degradable or nondegradable synthetic compounds that we dump into aquatic systems.

Treatment of sewage and industrial wastes has reduced point source inputs of many pollutants—especially oxygen-demanding wastes—into many rivers and lakes in the United States and other MDCs. Most rivers and lakes near population centers in LDCs, however, receive massive loads of untreated sewage and industrial wastes.

Contamination with toxic metals and synthetic organic chemicals is a major problem in many rivers and lakes in the United States and other MDCs. Many lakes and reservoirs located near urban and agricultural areas in these countries suffer from *cultural eutrophication* caused by massive inputs of nitrate and phosphate plant nutrients from human activities. Slow-moving rivers and lakes can also

environmental issue to be widely publicized in the Soviet press.

Despite the pleas of many leading Soviet scientists, artists, and writers, there was at that time little likelihood that the plans for the factories would be abandoned. The most feasible goal of the protesters was to ensure that the highest possible degree of protection would be provided for the lake. And indeed, in addition to more advanced wastewater treatment plants, several other safeguards to protect the lake were adopted.

A special decree was passed on the need to protect Lake Baikal, and a commission was appointed to monitor water quality in the lake. A later decision required that the wood pulp manufactured by the plants be transported to other industrial centers for processing to prevent further addition of pollutants to Lake Baikal. Finally, natural reserves and other types of protected areas have been established around the lake.

As a result of all this controversy, planning, and replanning, could people feel confident that Lake Baikal had been saved from pollution? Unfortunately, the differences of opinion went on. The industrial planners continued to defend their operations, claiming no serious harm had come to the lake, that the treatment facilities were adequate, and that the lake itself could act as a purifier of pollutants.

But in the early 1980s, the chief Soviet scientist in charge of protecting the lake stated that he still had serious doubts that the steps taken were sufficient. The problem is that even a small amount of pollution, an amount that might be acceptable in an ordinary lake or river, could do irreversible harm in such a unique water body as Lake Baikal. Not all of the pollutants discharged into the lake are degradable and some are highly toxic. Further, it is known that wastewater purification facilities at the wood-processing plants have been closed down on more than one occasion for improvements.

Finally, in 1987, another decree was enacted that converted one pulp mill to furniture manufacturing, which involves much less pollution. A closed-cycle water system was required at the other pulp mill. Further reductions in timber cutting were also ordered. Thus, after decades of controversy, Lake Baikal's amazing storehouse of biotic treasures, including many that are quite rare, may today be in somewhat less jeopardy.

The Lake Baikal saga shows clearly that environmental pollution is a worldwide phenomenon inherent in any country experiencing large-scale industrial development. Its cure involves a combination of increased funding for improved pollution abatement facilities and the political determination to see that they are used effectively.

Guest Essay Discussion

1. Do you think that Soviet officials have done enough to protect Lake Baikal? Explain.

2. Compare these efforts with those to protect the Great Lakes in the United States (see Case Study on p. 526).

suffer from oxygen depletion and fish kills from *thermal pollution*—large inputs of heated water used to cool electric power and industrial plants.

Vast quantities of waste materials flow or are dumped into the oceans and are especially damaging to aquatic life living around the edges in estuaries, wetlands, and small inland seas. Large quantities of sewage sludge containing toxic metals and organic compounds are dumped into the ocean with unknown long-term consequences. Fish, shellfish, and diving birds can be killed and beaches can be contaminated by oil reaching the ocean from urban and river runoff, routine discharges by tankers and refineries, and occasional tanker accidents and blowouts of offshore oil rigs.

A serious and growing water pollution problem is contamination of groundwater that serves as a source of drinking water for 50% of the U.S. population. Dilution, dispersion, and biodegradation of wastes are not very effective in cleansing groundwater because of its slow flow and lack of aerobic bacteria; thus, a contaminated aquifer remains that way for decades to centuries. Because cleanup of a contaminated aquifer is usually too costly, pollutants must be prevented from entering groundwater from point and nonpoint sources.

Waterborne wastes from households, industries, and businesses are collected by sewer systems and sent to sewage treatment plants for *primary and secondary treatment* and, in some cases, *advanced treatment*. The solids or sludge removed from treated sewage can be disposed of by incineration or dumping in the ocean or a landfill. With proper precautions, it can also be applied to land as a fertilizer. Household wastes in rural areas can be filtered and biodegraded in soil through the use of *septic tank systems*. Water drawn from surface water or groundwater sources can also be purified by similar treatment at water treatment plants. Such practices are widely used in MDCs but not in LDCs.

Since 1972 the United States and most MDCs have passed laws requiring municipalities and industries to install facilities for the secondary treatment of household and industrial wastewater and purification of drinking water in order to meet certain national standards. In the United States this control of discharges from point sources has prevented deterioration of most of the country's rivers and lakes in terms of dissolved oxygen and loss of aquatic life. However, little attention and funding have been devoted to reducing runoff of conventional and toxic pollutants into surface waters from nonpoint sources or to protecting groundwater drinking supplies from pollution by point and nonpoint sources.

DISCUSSION TOPICS

1. Explain why dilution is not always the solution to water pollution. Give examples and conditions for which this solution is, and is not, applicable.

2. Explain how a river can cleanse itself of oxygen-demanding wastes. Under what conditions will this natural cleansing system fail?

3. In your community:
   a. What are the major nonpoint sources of contamination of surface water and groundwater?
   b. What is the source of drinking water?
   c. How is it purified?
   d. What contaminants are tested for?
   e. Has drinking water been analyzed recently for the presence of synthetic organic chemicals, especially chlorinated hydrocarbons? If so, were any found and are they being removed?
   f. How many times during each of the past five years have levels of tested contaminants violated federal standards and how was the public notified about the violations?

4. Give your reasons for agreeing or disagreeing with the idea that we should deliberately dump most of our wastes in the ocean because it is a vast sink for diluting, dispersing, and degrading wastes, and if it becomes polluted, we can get food from other sources.

5. Should all dumping of wastes in the ocean be banned? Explain. If so, where would you put these wastes? What exceptions, if any, would you permit? Under what circumstances? Explain why banning ocean dumping alone will not stop ocean pollution.

6. Contact local officials to determine whether during the past 10 years any swimming areas in your area have been closed because of high coliform bacteria counts. How often are swimming areas tested for coliform bacteria?

7. Should the injection of hazardous wastes into deep underground wells be banned? Explain.

CHAPTER 21

Pesticides and Pest Control

General Questions and Issues

1. Why has pesticide use increased and what major types of pesticides are being used?
2. What are the major advantages of using insecticides and herbicides?
3. What are the major disadvantages of using insecticides and herbicides?
4. How is pesticide usage regulated in the United States?
5. What alternatives are there to using pesticides?

A weed is a plant whose virtues have not yet been discovered.

Ralph Waldo Emerson

A **pest** is any unwanted organism that directly or indirectly interferes with human activity. Pests compete with people for food and some spread disease. Weeds or pioneer plants play an important role in ecological succession (Figure 6-11, p. 145). But we don't like it when they invade gardens, cropfields, and other areas and compete for soil nutrients and water. In a forest termites hasten the decay of wood and speed up the natural regeneration of trees. But in a house they threaten the physical structure we live in.

In diverse natural ecosystems it is difficult for one species to take over because the sizes of the populations of species are usually limited by other organisms and the availability of nutrients, sunlight, and other limiting factors (Section 4-2). For example, only about 100 of the at least 1 million catalogued insect species cause about 90% of damage to food crops. In diverse ecosystems their populations are kept in control by a variety of natural enemies.

But instead of working with nature to keep pest populations down, our approach has generally been to work against nature. Since 1945 vast fields planted with only one crop or only a few crops, as well as homes, home gardens and lawns, have been treated with a variety of chemicals called **pesticides** (or *biocides*)—substances that can kill organisms that we consider to be undesirable. The most widely used types of pesticides are

- **herbicides,** to kill weeds, unwanted plants that compete with crop plants for soil nutrients
- **insecticides,** to kill insects that consume crops and food and transmit diseases to humans and livestock
- **fungicides** to kill fungi that damage crops
- **rodenticides** to kill rodents, mostly rats and mice

There is much controversy over whether the harmful effects of these chemicals outweigh their benefits compared to other alternatives, as discussed in this chapter.

21-1 PESTICIDES: TYPES AND USES

First-Generation Pesticides The ideal pest-killing chemical would

- kill only the target pest
- have no short- or long-term health effects on non-target organisms, including people
- be broken down into harmless chemicals in a fairly short time
- prevent the development of genetic resistance in target organisms
- save money compared to making no effort to control pest species

Unfortunately, no known pest control method meets all these criteria.

Before 1940 there were only a few dozen chemical pesticides on the market. Many of these *first-generation pesticides* were nonpersistent organic compounds made or extracted from insect poisons found naturally in plants. For example, pyrethrum, a powder obtained from the heads of chrysanthemums (Figure 21-1), was used by the Chinese 2,000 years ago and is still in use today. Caffeine is also an excellent insecticide that can be used to control tobacco hornworms, mealworms, milkweed bugs, and mosquito larvae. Other insecticides derived from natural plant sources include nicotine (as nicotine sulfate) from tobacco, rotenone from the tropical derris plant, red pepper (for ant control), and garlic oil and lemon oil, which can be used against fleas, mosquito larvae, houseflies, and other insects.

A second type of first-generation commercial pesticide in use before 1940 consisted of persistent inorganic compounds made from toxic metals such as arsenic, lead, and mercury. Most of these compounds are no longer used because they are highly toxic to people and animals, they contaminate the soil for 100 years or more, and they tend to accumulate in soil to the point of inhibiting plant growth. Traces of some of these persistent toxic chemicals are still being taken up by tobacco, vegetable, and other crops grown on soil that received heavy doses of these pesticides decades ago.

Second-Generation Pesticides A major revolution in insect pest control occurred in 1939 when it was discovered that DDT (dichlorodiphenyltrichloroethane), a chemical known since 1874, was a potent insecticide. Since 1945, chemists have developed many varieties of such synthetic organic chemicals known as *second-generation pesticides.*

Worldwide, about 2.3 million metric tons (2.5 million tons) of second-generation pesticides are used each year—an average of 0.45 kilogram (1 pound) for each person on earth. About 85% of all pesticides are used in MDCs, but use in LDCs is growing rapidly and is projected to increase at least fourfold between 1985 and 2000. An estimated 20% of the pesticides used in LDCs is for cosmetic purposes on pineapples, oranges, bananas, coffee, and other luxury crops exported to MDCs.

In the United States about 700 biologically active ingredients and 1,200 inert (presumably biologically inactive) ingredients are mixed to make some 50,000 individual pesticide products. Each year an average of 2.3 kilograms (5 pounds) of these products is used for each American. Various classes of pesticides are used in different ways in the United States, with 77% of them applied to commercial cropland. The rest are applied to government and industrial lands (11%), households (11%), and forest lands (1%).

Figure 21-1 The heads of these pyrethrum daisy flowers being harvested in Kenya, Africa, are ground into a powder used as a commercial insecticide or converted into other pyrethroid insecticides.

Herbicides account for 85% of all pesticide use in the United States and 88% of the pesticides used by farmers. Insecticides make up about 10% of pesticide use in the United States and fungicides about 5%. Four crops—corn, cotton, wheat, and soybeans—account for about 70% of the insecticides and 80% of the herbicides used on crops in the United States.

About 20% of the pesticides used each year in the United States are applied to lawns, gardens, parks, and golf courses. According to the EPA, 91% of all U.S. households use pesticides indoors (for example, bug sprays and ant, roach, and rat poisons) and outdoors on lawns and gardens and to preserve wood. The average home owner in the United States applies about five times more pesticide per unit of land area than do farmers.

Major Types of Insecticides and Herbicides Most of the thousands of different insecticides used today fall into one of four classes of compounds: chlorinated hydrocarbons, organophosphates, carbamates, or pyrethroids (Table 21-1). Most of these chemicals kill target and nontarget insects in the sprayed area by disrupting their nervous systems. These chemicals vary widely in their persistence, the length of time they remain active in killing insects (Table 21-1).

By the mid-1970s most slowly degradable, chlorinated hydrocarbon insecticides shown in Table 21-1 (except lindane) were banned or severely restricted in the United States and most MDCs. However, many of these compounds are still produced in the United

Table 21-1 Major Types of Insecticides

Type	Examples	Persistence
Chlorinated hydrocarbons	DDT, aldrin, dieldrin, endrin, heptachlor, toxaphene, lindane, chlordane, kepone, mirex	High (2–15 years)
Organo-phosphates	Malathion, parathion, monocrotophos, methamidophos, methyl parathion, DDVP	Low to moderate (normally 1–12 weeks, but some can last several years)
Carbamates	Carbaryl, maneb, priopoxor, mexicabate, aldicarb, aminocarb	Usually low (days to weeks)
Pyrethroids	Pemethrin, decamethrin	Usually low (days to weeks)

Table 21-2 Major Types of Herbicides

Type	Examples	Effects
Contact	Triazines such as atrazine and paraquat	Kills foliage by interfering with photosynthesis
Systemic	Phenoxy compounds such as 2,4-D, 2,4,5-T, and Silvex; substitutes ureas such as diuron, norea, fenuron, and other nitrogen-containing compounds such as daminozide (Alar), glyphosate	Absorption creates excess growth hormones; plants die because they cannot obtain enough nutrients to sustain their greatly accelerated growth
Soil sterilants	Trifluralin, diphenamid, dalapon, butylate	Kills soil microorganisms essential to plant growth; most also act as systemic herbicides

States and exported to other countries, mostly LDCs, where they have not been banned.

In the United States and most MDCs these chemicals have been replaced by a number of more rapidly degradable pesticides, especially organophosphates and carbamates (Table 21-1). But some of these compounds (such as parathion) are more toxic to birds, people, and other mammals than the chlorinated hydrocarbon insecticides they replaced. They are also more likely to contaminate surface water and groundwater because they are water soluble, whereas chlorinated hydrocarbon insecticides are insoluble in water but soluble in fats. Furthermore, to compensate for their fairly rapid breakdown, farmers usually apply nonpersistent insecticides at regular intervals to ensure more effective insect control. This means they are often present in the environment almost continuously, like the slowly degradable pesticides they replaced. Use of pyrethroids (Table 21-1) is growing rapidly because they are generally nonpersistent, effective at low doses, and not highly toxic to mammals.

Herbicides can be placed into three classes based on their effect on plants: contact herbicides, systemic herbicides, and soil sterilants (Table 21-2). Most herbicides are active for only a short time. In the United States and most MDCs the use of 2,4,5-T has been banned.

Why the Need for Pest Control Has Increased Over the past 200 years, an increasing number of insects and other pests have become serious threats to crops that feed the world's rapidly increasing population. A major reason for this is industrialized agriculture. To grow food we take diverse ecosystems, typically containing small populations of many species, and replace with greatly simplified agricultural ecosystems and lawns that contain large populations of only one or two desired plant species (Figure 6-13, p. 147).

In such biologically simplified ecosystems, some organisms that are controlled naturally in more diverse systems can grow in number and achieve pest status. As a result, people have had to spend an increasing amount of time, energy, and money to control pests in crop fields, lawns, tree farms (Figure 13-12, p. 295), homes, and other simplified ecosystems (Table 6-3, p. 149). The increased use of no-till cultivation (Figure 10-17, p. 227) reduces soil erosion and runoff, but requires an increased used of herbicides to control weeds that were formerly plowed under.

21-2   THE CASE FOR PESTICIDES

Proponents of pesticides believe that the benefits of pesticides outweigh their harmful effects. They point out the following benefits:

- *Pesticides save lives.* Since World War II, DDT and other chlorinated hydrocarbon and organophosphate insecticides have probably prevented the premature deaths of at least 7 million people from insect-transmitted diseases such as malaria (carried by the *Anopheles* mosquito), bubonic plague (rat fleas), typhus (body lice and fleas), and sleeping sickness (tsetse fly) (Section 18-2). Thus, DDT and other insecticides have probably saved more human lives than any other synthetic chemicals since people have inhabited the earth.

- *They increase food supplies and lower food costs.* Each year about 55% of the world's potential food supply is lost to pests before (35%) and after harvest (20%). This amounts to a loss of $20 billion a year. Proponents argue that without pesticides these losses would be much higher and food prices would increase (for example, by 30% to 50% in the United States). For example, the U.S. Department of Agriculture estimates that if the triazine herbicides, widely used on corn, were banned, corn yields would decrease by an average of 8%, raising prices about 31%.

- *They increase profits for farmers.* In the United States 42% of the annual potential food supply is destroyed by pests before and after harvest. Pesticide companies estimate that every $1 spent on pesticides leads to an increase in crop yield worth $3 to $5 to farmers.

- *They work faster and better than other alternatives.* Compared to alternative methods of pest control, pesticides can control most pests quickly and at a reasonable cost, have a relatively long shelf life, are easily shipped and applied, and are safe when handled properly. When genetic resistance occurs in pest insects and weeds, farmers can usually keep them under control by using stronger doses or switching to other pesticides.

- *Safer and more effective products are continually being developed.* Pesticide company scientists are continually developing pesticides that are safer to use and that cause less ecological damage. For exam-

ple, pyrethroid insecticides (Table 21-1) are not highly toxic to mammals and are effective at low doses, thus slowing the rate at which genetic resistance develops. Their use in small quantities helps compensate for their high cost. New herbicides are being developed that are effective at very low dosage rates. Genetic engineering biotechnology also holds promise (see Pro/Con on p. 148). For example, genes that are not resistant to widely used pesticides or genes that are resistant to key pest organisms could be inserted into strains of major crops.

21-3   THE CASE AGAINST PESTICIDES

Development of Genetic Resistance   The most serious drawback to using chemicals to control pests is that most pest species, especially insects, can develop genetic resistance to any chemical poison through natural selection. When an area is sprayed with a pesticide, most of the pest organisms are killed. However, a few organisms in a given population of a particular species survive because by chance they already had genes that made them resistant or immune to a specific pesticide.

Because most pest species—especially insects and disease organisms—have short generation times, a few surviving organisms can reproduce a large number of similarly resistant offspring in a short time. For example, the boll weevil (Figure 21-2), a major cotton pest, can produce a new generation every 21 days.

When populations of offspring of resistant parents are repeatedly sprayed with the same pesticide, each succeeding generation contains a higher percentage of resistant organisms. Thus, eventually all widely used pesticides (especially insecticides) fail because of genetic resistance and usually lead to even larger populations of pest species, especially insects with large numbers of offspring and short generation times. In temperate regions most insects develop genetic resistance to any chemical poison within five years and much sooner in tropical areas. Weeds and plant disease organisms also develop genetic resistance, but not as quickly as most insects.

Between 1950 and 1989 almost 500 major insect pest species have developed genetic resistance to one or more insecticides and at least 20 insect species are now apparently immune to all insecticides. It is estimated that by the year 2000 virtually all major insect pest species will show some form of genetic resistance.

By 1989 genetic resistance to one or more pesticides had also appeared in strains of 70 species of weeds treated with herbicides, 50 species of fungi treated with fungicides, and 10 species of small rodents (mostly rats) treated with rodenticides. Because half of all pesticides applied worldwide are herbicides,

Figure 21-2 The cotton boll weevil accounts for at least 25% of the pesticides used in the United States, but farmers are now increasing their use of natural predators to control this major pest.

U.S. Department of Agriculture

genetic resistance in weeds is expected to increase significantly.

Because of genetic resistance, most widely used insecticides no longer protect people from insect-transmitted diseases in many parts of the world, leading to even more serious disease outbreaks. By 1986 at least 50 of the 61 species of malaria-carrying *Anopheles* mosquitoes had become resistant to the three chlorinated hydrocarbon insecticides—DDT, lindane, and dieldrin—most commonly sprayed inside houses. At least ten of these species are also resistant to the organophosphates malathion and fenitrothion and four species are resistant to the carbamate propoxur. This is major reason for the almost 40-fold increase in malaria between 1970 and 1988 in 84 tropical and subtropical countries (see Case Study on p. 456).

Killing of Natural Pest Enemies and Conversion of Minor Pests to Major Pests
Most insecticides are broad-spectrum poisons that kill not only the target pest species but also a number of natural predators and parasites that may have been maintaining the pest species at a reasonable level. Without sufficient natural enemies, and with much food available, a rapidly reproducing insect pest species can make a strong comeback a few days or weeks after being initially controlled.

The use of broad-spectrum insecticides also kills off the natural enemies of many minor pests. Then their numbers can increase greatly and they become major pests.

The Pesticide Treadmill
When genetic resistance develops, pesticide sale representatives usually recommend more frequent applications, stronger doses, or switching to new (usually more expensive) chemicals to keep the resistant species under control, rather than suggesting nonchemical alternatives. This puts farmers on a **pesticide treadmill**, in which they pay more and more for a pest control program that becomes less and less effective. For example, between 1940 and 1984 crop losses to insects in the United States increased from 7% to 13%, while there was a 12-fold increase in insecticide use.

Worldwide, insects and weeds reduce crop production by about 30%, about the same as before modern pesticides were used. The development of new chemicals by pesticide companies to reduce the spread of genetic resistance lags far behind the development of such resistance, especially in insects and plant pathogens.

David Pimentel, an expert in insect ecology (see his Guest Essay on p. 235), estimates that when the environmental and other external costs of insecticides are included, they end up saving U.S. farmers somewhere between nothing and $2.40 for each $1 invested. This is much lower than the pesticide companies' estimate of $3 to $5 saved for each $1 invested. Because of this an increasing number of farmers are reducing pesticide use and increasing their use of other alternatives (Section 21-5).

Mobility and Biological Amplification of Persistent Pesticides
Pesticides don't stay put. No more than 10% of the pesticides applied to crops by airplane spraying (Figure 21-3) or ground spraying reaches the target pests. The remaining 90% or more ends up in the soil, air, surface water, groundwater, bottom sediment, food, and nontarget organisms, including people and even penguins in the Antarctic. According to pesticide expert David Pimentel (see Guest Essay on p. 235), often less than 0.1% of insecticides and 5% of herbicides applied to crops reaches target pests.

Pesticides reaching the atmosphere, especially those applied by airplane, can be carried long distances. In the United States the EPA has found small levels of

Figure 21-3 Crop duster spraying a Florida orange grove with fungicide. No more than 10% and often as little as 0.1% of the chemical being applied reaches the target organisms. Aircraft are used to apply 60% of the pesticides used on cropland in the United States.

U.S. Department of Agriculture

74 pesticides in groundwater tested at various sites in 38 states. In Iowa 75% of the wells tested were contaminated with pesticides. Some pesticides, such as Alachlor, have been found in groundwater at high concentrations.

Concentrations of fat-soluble, slowly degradable insecticides such as DDT and other chlorinated hydrocarbons (Table 21-1) can be biologically amplified thousands to millions of times in food chains and webs (Figure 14-10, p. 325). High levels can kill forms of wildlife feeding at high trophic levels or interfere with their reproduction (see Spotlight on p. 325).

Threats to Wildlife Each year an estimated 20% of all honeybee colonies in the U.S. are killed by pesticides and another 15% of the colonies are damaged—causing annual losses of at least $206 million from reduced pollination of vital crops. Pesticide runoff from cropland is a major cause of fish kills in the United States (Figure 20-4, p. 523) and in other countries.

During the 1950s and 1960s there were drastic declines in populations of fish-eating birds such as the osprey, cormorant, brown pelican (Figure 2-11, p. 40), and bald eagle (Figure 2-16, p. 43). There were also sharp declines in population of predatory birds such as the prairie falcon, sparrow hawk, Bermuda petrel, and peregrine falcon; these birds help control populations of rabbits, ground squirrels, and other crop-damaging small mammals (see Spotlight on p. 325).

Short-Term Threats to Human Health from Pesticide Use and Manufacture The World Health Organization estimates that each year at least 1 million people are poisoned by pesticides and 3,000 to 20,000 of them die. At least half of those poisoned and 75% of those killed are farm workers in LDCs, where educational levels are low, warnings are few, and pesticide regulation and control methods are often lax or nonexistent.

In the United States it is estimated that at least 313,000 of the 7 million U.S. farm workers become seriously ill from exposure to pesticides each year and at least 25 of them die. The actual number of pesticide-related illness among farm workers in the United States and throughout the world is probably greatly underestimated because of poor records, lack of doctors and reporting in rural areas, and faulty diagnosis. Some researchers estimate up to 2 million pesticide poisonings and 40,000 deaths a year.

Each year at least 20,000 Americans, the majority children, become sick because of unsafe use or storage of pesticides in and around the home. In the United States pesticides are the second most frequent cause of poisoning in young children, following medicines. Also, accidents and unsafe practices in pesticide plants can expose workers, their families, and sometimes the general public to harmful levels of pesticides or chemicals used in their manufacture (see Case Study on p. 555).

In the 1960s a controversy began over the possible health effects from the use of the herbicides 2,4,5-T and 2,4-D (Table 21-2). Between 1962 and 1970, large amounts of Agent Orange, a 50-50 mixture of 2,4-D and 2,4,5-T, were sprayed to defoliate swamps and forests in Southeast Asia during the Vietnam War.

In 1965 and 1966 a study commissioned by the National Cancer Institute found that low levels of 2,4,5-T caused high rates of birth defects in laboratory animals. This report was not released to the public until 1969. Because of the resulting pressure from environmentalists and health officials, however, the Vietnam

In 1984 the world's worst industrial accident occurred at a Union Carbide pesticide plant located in Bhopal, India. Over 3,300 people were killed when about 36 metric tons (40 tons) of highly toxic methyl isocyanate gas, used in the manufacture of carbamate pesticides, leaked from a storage tank. Up to 20,000 people suffered from blindness, sterility, kidney and liver infections, tuberculosis, brain damage, and other serious disorders, and another 200,000 people suffered some sort of illness. The death toll is projected to reach almost 5,000 by 1991. Union Carbide could probably have prevented this tragedy by spending no more than a million dollars to improve plant safety.

India sued Union Carbide for $3.1 billion in damages in a district court in Bhopal. In 1989 India's supreme court agreed to a $470 million settlement from Union Carbide. This set off a storm of protest. Lawyers estimated that if the case had been filed in the U.S. court system the settlement would have been much higher—perhaps ten times more. Some lawyers also charge that the settlement sends a message to the chemical industry worldwide that they need not bother to spend money on the safety of their plants in many LDCs. San Francisco lawyer Melvin Belli also charged that after the Indian government skims off much of the funds, each surviving victim will receive an average of less than $100.

defoliation program was halted in 1970. Investigations revealed that the birth defects in laboratory animals were probably caused by TCDD, a highly toxic dioxin (see Case Study on p. 454), formed in minute quantities as a contaminant during the manufacture of 2,4,5-T.

More than 31,000 Vietnam veterans have filed claims with the Veterans Administration for disabilities allegedly caused by exposure to Agent Orange. The Veterans Administration and chemical manufacturers of Agent Orange, however, continue to deny any connection between the medical disorders and Agent Orange and attribute the problems to the post-Vietnam stress syndrome. In 1984, the companies making Agent Orange agreed to a $180 million out of court settlement with the Vietnam veterans, without admitting any guilt or connection between the disorders and the use of the herbicide.

In 1988 an epidemiologic study provided evidence strongly linking many of the health problems of military veterans with exposure to dioxin-tainted Agent Orange. In 1989 a federal court ordered the Veterans Administration to reconsider the claims of the veterans exposed to Agent Orange.

In 1986 a National Cancer Institute study found that U.S. farmers who used 2,4-D—a component of Agent Orange and the active ingredient in more than 1,500 herbicide products used by farmers and home gardeners—were more than twice as likely as non-farmers to develop a rare form of cancer known as non-Hodgkin's lymphoma. Earlier, Swedish researchers had shown an association between 2,4,5-T and 2,4-D and two other cancers—soft-tissue sarcoma and Hodgkin's disease.

Long-Term Threats to Human Health A number of scientists are concerned about possible long-term health effects of continuous, long-term exposure to very low levels of pesticides. Such chronic effects, if any, won't be known for several decades because the people who have carried these chemicals in their bodies the longest were only 45 years old by 1990.

Traces of almost 500 of the 700 active ingredients used in pesticies in the United States show up in the food most people eat. Pesticide residues are especially likely to be found in tomatoes, grapes, apples, lettuce, oranges, potatoes, beef, and dairy products. The results of this long-term worldwide experiment, with people involuntarily playing the role of guinea pigs, may never be known, because it is almost impossible to determine that a specific chemical caused a particular cancer or other harmful effect (Section 18-1).

However, some disturbing but inconclusive evidence has emerged. DDT, aldrin, dieldrin, heptachlor, mirex, endrin, and 19 other pesticides have all been found to cause cancer in test animals, especially liver cancer in mice. In addition, autopsies have shown that the bodies of people who died from cancers, cirrhosis of the liver, hypertension, cerebral hemorrhage, and softening of the brain contained fairly high levels of DDT or its breakdown products DDD and DDE.

In 1987 the National Academy of Sciences reported that the active ingredients in 90% of all fungicides, 60% of all herbicides, and 30% of all insecticides in use in the United States may cause cancer in humans. According to the worst-case estimate in this study, exposure to pesticides in food causes up to 20,000 cases of cancer a year in the United States. In 1987 the EPA ranked pesticide residues in foods as the third most serious environmental problem in the U.S. (after worker exposure and indoor radon) in terms of cancer risk. In 1989 the Natural Resources Defense Council released a controversial study suggesting that most U.S. children under age six are being exposed to levels of pesticides that could increase their risk of getting various types of cancer (see Pro/Con on p. 556).

Is the Public Adequately Protected? Because of the potentially harmful effects of pesticides on wildlife and people, Congress passed the Federal Insecticide, Fungicide, and Rodenticide Act (FIFRA) in 1972. This act, amended in 1975, 1978, and 1988, requires that all commercial pesticides be approved for general or restricted use by the Environmental Protection Agency.

Approval is based primarily on an evaluation of the safety of the 700 chemicals that pesticide companies designate as biologically active ingredients. These data are submitted to the EPA by the companies seeking approval and must include test data on the potential to cause adverse short- and long-term effects in

---

PRO/CON Are Kids in the United States Being Exposed to Unsafe Levels of Pesticides?

In 1989 the Natural Resources Defense Council released a study projecting that between 5,200 and 6,200 of the current population of 22 million American preschool children may eventually get cancer solely as a result of their exposure before age six to eight pesticides (daminozide, mancozeb, Captan, methamidophos, parathion, methyl parathion, diazinon, and aldicarb) commonly found in fruits and vegetables. The highest cancer risks are believed to come from two pesticides—daminozide (trade name, Alar), a growth regulator used primarily on apples and peanuts, and Captan, a fungicide widely used on apples, almonds, peaches, and seeds.

The study estimated that preschoolers receive four times the exposure, on average, than adults to the eight pesticides cited because preschoolers eat more relative to their weight and consume, on the average, much larger quantities of fresh fruit, fruit juices, and other fruit products than do adults. The report also charged the EPA with disregard for children because the agency has failed to adequately factor in children's greater exposure to pesticides when setting standards for permissible residues in food.

The study also estimated that at least 3 million preschoolers are exposed to unsafe levels of organophosphates that may cause neurological damage. Among the crops treated with these chemicals are tomatoes, green beans, and cucumbers.

EPA officials denied these charges, saying it routinely takes into account the potentially higher exposure of children and infants when evaluating the risk from exposure to pesticides. However, a scientist serving as a member of a National Academy of Sciences panel studying this issue (with a report due in 1990) agreed that the pesticide limits allowed by the EPA need to be tightened and that the EPA had not been giving the potentially higher exposure levels in young children enough weight.

EPA officials also noted that the risks from pesticides in the diet are small and that these risks are outweighed by the benefits of pesticides to society. They pointed out that in a population of 22 million preschool kids, some 5.5 million would be expected to get cancer from all causes during their lifetime. The Natural Resources Defense Council's estimate of 6,000 excess cancers represents just a blip in the total cancer risk, from 25% to 25.025%.

Also, EPA officials reported that they had been investigating the safety of Alar, which causes an estimated 90% of the risk, and would probably ban the chemical sometime before 1991. Because of the publicity most uses of Alar by growers had ceased by mid-1989. EPA officials also announced that they were banning the use of the fungicide Captan on 42 crops.

The health risk from pesticide residues can be reduced by

- Buying organically grown produce that has not been grown using synthetic fertilizers, pesticides, or growth regulators. Purchase only organic produce that is certified to be free of pesticide residues by independent testing laboratories, and urge your supermarket manager to carry only organic produce that meets these standards.*

- Not buying imported produce, which generally contains more pesticide residues than domestic fruits and vegetables. Show your concern and influence supermarket buying decisions by asking managers where their produce comes from.

- Not buying perfect-looking fruits and vegetables, which are more likely to contain higher levels of pesticide residues.

- Buying produce in season because it is less likely to be treated with fungicides and other chemicals to preserve its appearance during storage.

- Carefully washing and scrubbing all fresh produce in soapy water.

- Removing and not using the outer leaves of lettuce and cabbage and peeling fruits that have thick skins.

- Growing your own fruits and vegetables using organic methods.

What do you think should be done about this problem?

*For a list of more than 100 sources of organically grown and processed fruits, vegetables, grains, and meats, send a self-addressed business envelope with 50 cents postage to Mail-Order Organic, The Center for Science in the Public Interest, 1501 16th St., N.W., Washington, D.C. 20036.

humans, fish, wildlife, and endangered species. Data must also be included on the environmental fate of the active ingredients so that the EPA can evaluate, among other things, whether these chemicals pose a threat to surface or groundwater.

Data on the safety of the 1,200 inert (presumably biologically inactive) ingredients in pesticide products is normally not required. However, in 1986, after years of pressure from environmentalists, the EPA began to review the safety of these ingredients—a process that may take at least two decades.

Since 1972 the EPA has used this law to ban the use, except for emergency situations, of over 40 pesticides because of their potential hazards to human health. The banned chemicals include most chlori-nated hydrocarbon insecticides, several carbamates and organophosphates, and several herbicides such as 2,4,5-T and Silvex.

However, according to a 1988 report by the National Academy of Sciences, federal laws regulating the use of pesticides in the United States are inadequate and poorly enforced by the Food and Drug Administration (FDA) and the EPA (see Spotlight below). According to another National Academy of Science study, by 1984 only 10% of the 700 active ingredients and none of the 1,200 inert ingredients used in U.S. pesticide products had been tested well enough to determine their potential for producing cancer, genetic mutations, birth defects, and neurological damage in humans.

SPOTLIGHT Inadequate Federal Regulation of Pesticides in the United States

Numerous studies by the National Academy of Sciences and the General Accounting Office have shown that the weakest and most poorly enforced U.S. environmental law in the United States is the Federal Insecticide, Fungicide, and Rodenticide Act of 1972 and its subsequent amendments. It is the only U.S. environmental law that allows a chemical known to cause cancer or other harmful effects on people and the environment to be used when its economic benefits (estimated by the pesticide manufacturer) exceed its estimated harmful health and environmental effects (also estimated in test data provided by the pesticide manufacturer).

This act required the EPA to reevaluate the 600 active ingredients approved for use in pesticide products before 1972 to determine whether any of these substances caused cancer, birth defects, or other health risks. The EPA was supposed to complete this analysis by 1975, yet by 1989 the EPA had developed data on only 192 of these chemicals and had completed its review on only two of them. In 1987 Congress extended the deadline for completing this review to 1997. The EPA claims that Congress has not appropriated enough money for it to do the job.

According to the National Academy of Sciences, up to 98% of the potential risk of developing cancer from pesticide residues on food grown in the United States would be eliminated if the EPA set the same standards for pesticides registered for use before 1972 as the stricter standards for those registered after 1972.

It has also become clear that many of the so-called inert or biologically inactive ingredients in pesticide products are in fact biologically active and can cause harm to people and some forms of wildlife. At least 100 of these chemicals pose known or suspected health hazards to people, and 800 have not been tested. So far none of these chemicals have been banned, mostly because they are not covered by the present pesticide law.

This law also allows the EPA to leave inadequately tested pesticides on the market and to license new chemicals without full health and safety data. It also gives the EPA unlimited time to remove a chemical when its health and environmental effects are shown to outweigh its economic benefits. The appeals and procedures built into the law often allow a dangerous chemical to remain on the market for up to ten years.

The EPA can immediately can-cel the use of a chemical on an emergency basis. But the law requires the EPA to use its already severely limited funds to compensate pesticide manufacturers for their remaining inventory and for all the costs of storing and disposing of the banned pesticide. Emergency cancelling of just one or two chemicals could consume the entire EPA budget for all aspects of pesticide regulation. In 1989 the agency spent more on pesticide disposal than on pesticide regulation.

Between 1978 and 1988 environmentalists made repeated attempts to have this provision of the law removed. They pointed out that it amounts to an insurance policy for the pesticide industry paid for by taxpayers—something not provided for any other product regulated by the government. In 1988 Congress passed several new amendments to the federal pesticide law. One of these amendments shifts some—but not all—of the costs of banning and disposing of banned pesticides from the EPA to companies making the chemicals.

Environmentalists consider the 1988 amendments better than nothing. But they point out that the law still has numerous weaknesses and loopholes. One loop-

(continued)

21-5 ALTERNATIVE METHODS OF INSECT CONTROL

Modifying Cultivation Procedures   Opponents of the widespread use of pesticides argue that there are many safer, and in the long-run cheaper and more effective, alternatives to the use of pesticides by farmers and home owners. For centuries farmers have used cultivation methods that discourage or inhibit pests. Examples are

- *crop rotation*, in which the types of crops planted in fields are changed from year to year so that populations of pests that attack a particular crop don't have time to multiply to uncontrollable sizes

- *planting rows of hedges or trees in and around crop fields* to act as barriers to invasions by insect pests, provide habitats for their natural enemies, and serve as windbreaks to reduce soil erosion (Figure 10-20, p. 229)

- *adjusting planting times* to ensure that most major insect pests starve to death before the crop is available or are consumed by their natural predators

- *growing crops in areas where their major pests do not exist*

- *switching from monocultures to modernized versions of intercropping, agroforestry, and polyculture* that use plant diversity to help control pests

Unfortunately, to increase profits and in some cases to avoid bankruptcy, many farmers in MDCs such as the United States have abandoned these cultivation methods.

Artificial Selection, Crossbreeding, and Genetic Engineering   Varieties of plants and animals that are genetically resistant to certain pest insects, fungi, and diseases can be developed. New varieties usually take a long time (10 to 20 years) to develop by conventional methods and are costly. The new strains must also produce high yields (Figure 12-6, p. 264).

Also, insect pests and plant diseases can develop new strains that attack the once-resistant varieties, forcing scientists to continually develop new resistant strains. In the future, genetic engineering techniques

---

SPOTLIGHT   Inadequate Federal Regulation of Pesticides in the United States (continued)

hole allows the sale in the United States of a number of insecticide products containing as much as 15% DDT by weight, classified as an impurity. These products, along with others illegally smuggled into the United States (mostly from Mexico), are believed to be responsible for increases in DDT levels in some vulnerable forms of wildlife and on some fruits and vegetables grown and sold in the United States (especially in California).

Each year the Food and Drug Administration inspectors check less than 1% (about 12,000 samples) of domestic and imported food each year for pesticide contamination. Furthermore, the routine testing procedures used by FDA laboratories cannot detect 40% of the pesticides classified by the EPA as having moderate to high health hazards. At least half of the food found to be contaminated has been sold and consumed during the average of 28 days it takes FDA laboratories to complete the analysis.

But the FDA has only a $48 million budget and 1,000 inspectors checking everything from blood banks and drugs to food safety. The agency's repeated requests for funds have been denied and the general public has put little pressure on elected officials to improve food safety.

Pesticide companies can make and export to other countries pesticides that have been banned in the United States or that have not been submitted to the EPA for approval. The U.S. leads the world in pesticide exports, followed by West Germany and the United Kingdom. In what environmentalists call a *circle of poison*, residues of some of these exported pesticides often return to the United States on imported coffee, fruits, and vegetables. Many LDCs encourage the importation and overuse of pesticides by not controlling pesticide use and by subsidizing as much as 89% of the cost of pesticides for farmers.

In 1983, the United Nations

passed a resolution calling for stringent restrictions on the export of pesticides and other products whose use has been banned or severely restricted in the exporting nation; in addition, the U.N. asked for widespread publication of a list of such products.

Under orders from President Reagan, the United States was the only country opposing this resolution. It was argued that countries receiving exports of banned or unregistered pesticides, drugs, and other chemicals from the United States should be free to use these chemicals if they so desire and that if U.S. companies do not sell these substances to them, someone else will. What, if anything, do you think should be done to provide more protection for the public from contamination of food and drinking water by traces of numerous pesticides?

Figure 21-4 The praying mantis (left) and the ladybug (eating an aphid) are used to control insect pests. The praying mantis, however, has a high mortality rate and may also devour other beneficial insects.

may be used to develop resistant crops and animals more rapidly (see Pro/Con on p. 148).

Biological Control Various natural predators (Figure 21-4), parasites, and pathogens (disease-causing bacteria and viruses) can be introduced or imported to regulate the populations of various pests. Worldwide, more than 300 biological pest control projects have been successful, especially in China and the Soviet Union. Recently a tiny wasp was used to stop devastation of cassava crops in Africa by a mealybug. The wasps saved this crucial crop for 200 million people in 35 countries. The use of fungi, bacteria, and other disease-causing agents has great potential to sharply reduce the use of herbicides for controlling weeds.

A bacterial agent (*Bacillus thuringiensis*) is a registered pesticide sold commercially as a dry powder. It is effective in controlling many strains of leaf-eating caterpillars, mosquitoes, black flies, and gypsy moths. As conventional pesticide prices continue to climb, it will become economically feasible to mass produce many biological control agents.

Other examples of biological control include the use of

- *Guard dogs* to protect livestock from predators. Guard dogs are more effective and cost less than erecting fences and shooting, trapping, and poisoning predators, which sometimes kill nontarget organisms, including people (see Pro/Con on p. 307).

- *Ducks* to devour insects and slugs. However, ducks sometimes damage vegetables, especially leafy greens, and should be kept out of these parts of gardens.

- *Geese* for weeding orchards, eating fallen and rotting fruit (often a source of pest problems), and controlling grass in gardens and nurseries. Geese also warn of approaching predators or people by honking loudly.

- *Chickens* to control insects and weeds and to increase the nitrogen content of the soil in orchards or in gardens after plants have become well established.

- *Birds* to eat insects. Farmers and home owners can provide habitats and nesting sites that attract woodpeckers, purple martens, chickadees, barn swallows, nuthatches, and other insect-eating species.

- *Spiders* to eat insects. Spiders are insects' worst enemies, devouring enough bugs worldwide in a single day to outweigh the entire human population. Leaving strips of weeds around soybean and cotton fields provides habitats for wolf spiders, which devour most insect pests for free. One type of banana spider, harmless to humans, can keep a house clear of cockroaches. Most spiders, except the brown recluse and the black widow, are harmless to humans.

- *Allelopathic plants* that naturally produce chemicals that are toxic to their weed competitors or that repel or poison their insect pests. For example, certain varieties of barley, wheat, rye, sorghum, and Sudan grass can be grown in gardens or orchard trees to suppress weeds. Plant combinations that help protect against various insect pests include cassavas and beans, potatoes and mustard greens, and a mixture of sunflowers, maize, oats, and sesame. Peppermint can be planted around houses to repel ants and to be used as a natural mouth freshener (pull off leaf, wash it, and chew it) and cooking spice.

Biological control has a number of advantages. It normally effects only the target species and is nontoxic to other species, including people. Once a population of natural predators or parasites is established, control of pest species is often self-perpetuating. Development of genetic resistance is minimized because both pest and predator species usually undergo natural selection to maintain a stable interaction (coevolution).

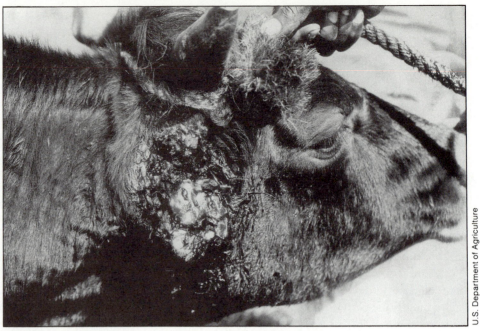

Figure 21-5 Infestation of screwworm fly larvae in the ear of a steer. A fully grown steer can be killed in ten days from thousands of maggots feeding on a single wound.

U.S. Department of Agriculture

In the United States biological control has saved farmers an average of $25 for every $1 invested, compared to the estimated maximum of $2.40 saved for every $1 invested in pesticides. For example, spending about $750,000 in the 1940s to find and introduce a European beetle to control a toxic range weed in California has saved livestock ranchers more than $100 million.

No method of pest control, however, is perfect. Typically, 10 to 20 years of research may be required to understand how a particular pest interacts with its various enemies and to determine the best biological control agent. Mass production of biological agents is often difficult and farmers find that they are slower to act and harder to apply than pesticides. Biological agents must also be protected from pesticides sprayed in nearby fields, and there is a chance that some can also become pests. In addition, some pest organisms can develop genetic resistance to viruses and bacterial agents used for biological control and some (such as praying mantises) may also devour other beneficial insects.

Insect Control by Insect Sterilization Males of some insect pest species can be raised in the laboratory and sterilized by radiation or chemicals. Then they can be released in large numbers in an infested area to mate unsuccessfully with fertile wild females.

If sterile males outnumber fertile males by 10 to 1, a pest species in a given area can be eradicated in about four generations, provided reinfestation does not occur. This technique works best if the females mate only once, if the infested area is isolated so that it can't be periodically repopulated with nonsterilized males, and if the insect pest population has already been reduced to a fairly low level by weather, pesticides, or other factors. Success is also increased if only the sexiest—the loudest, fastest, and largest—males are sterilized.

The screwworm fly is a major livestock pest in South America, Central America, and the southeastern and southwestern United States. This metallic blue-green insect, about two to three times the size of the common housefly, deposits its eggs in open wounds of warm-blooded animals such as cattle and deer. Within a few hours the eggs hatch into parasitic larvae that feed on the flesh of the host animal (Figure 21-5). A severe infestation of this pest can kill a mature steer within ten days.

The Department of Agriculture used the sterile-male approach to essentially eliminate the screwworm fly from the southeastern states between 1962 and 1971. In 1972, however, the pest made a dramatic comeback, infesting 100,000 cattle and causing serious losses until 1976, when a new strain of the males was developed, sterilized, and released to bring the situation under temporary control. To prevent resurgences of this pest, new strains of sterile male flies have to be developed, sterilized, and released every few years. This approach is also being used in an attempt to reduce populations of fruit flies in Florida.

Major problems with this approach include ensuring that sterile males are not overwhelmed numerically by nonsterile males, knowing the mating times and behavior of each target insect, preventing reinfestation with new nonsterilized males, and high costs.

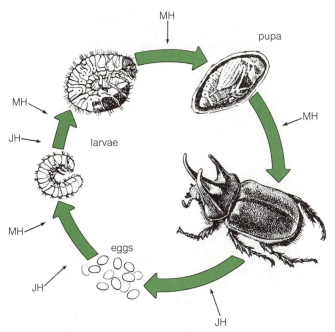

Figure 21-6 For normal growth, development, and reproduction certain juvenile hormones (JH) and molting hormones (MH) must be present at genetically determined stages in the typical life cycle of an insect. If applied at the right time, synthetic hormones can be used to disrupt the life cycle of insect pests.

Figure 21-7 Chemical hormones can prevent insects from maturing completely and make it impossible for them to reproduce. Compare the normal mealworm (left) with one that failed to develop an adult abdomen after being sprayed with a synthetic hormone.

Insect Sex Attractants Various pheromones and hormones can be used to control populations of insect pest species. Some scientists believe that these two new types of chemical agents, sometimes called *third-generation pesticides*, may eventually replace the present use of less desirable second-generation pesticides.

In many insect species, when a virgin female is ready to mate she releases a minute amount (typically about one-millionth of a gram) of a species-specific chemical sex attractant called a *pheromone*. Males of the species up to a half-mile away can detect the chemical and follow the scent upwind to its source.

Pheromones are extracted from an insect pest species or synthesized in the laboratory. They are then used in minute amounts to lure pests into traps containing toxic chemicals or to attract natural predators of insect pests into crop fields. An infested area can also be sprayed with the appropriate pheromone or covered with millions of tiny cardboard squares impregnated with the substance so that the males become confused and are unable to find a mate because they detect the smell of virgin females everywhere.

Recent research indicates that instead of using pheromones to trap pests it is more effective to use them to lure the pests' natural predators into fields and gardens. Sex attractants are now commercially available for use against 30 major pests.

These chemicals work only on one species, are effective in trace amounts, have little chance of causing genetic resistance, and are not harmful to nontarget species. However, it is costly and time consuming to identify, isolate, and produce the specific sex attractant for each pest or natural predator species. Pheromones have also failed for some pests because only adults are drawn to the traps; for most species, the juvenile forms—such as caterpillars—do most of the damage.

Insect Hormones Hormones are chemicals produced in an organism's cells that travel through the bloodstream and control various aspects of the organism's growth and development. Each step in the life cycle of a typical insect is regulated by the timely release of juvenile hormones (JH) and molting hormones (MH) (Figure 21-6).

These chemicals can be extracted from insects or synthesized in the laboratory. When applied at certain stages in an insect's life cycle (Figure 21-6), they produce abnormalities that cause the insect to die before it can reach maturity and reproduce (Figure 21-7).

They have the same advantages as sex attractants, but they take weeks to kill an insect, are often ineffective with a large infestation, and sometimes break down before they can act. Also, they must be applied at exactly the right time in the life cycle of the target insect. They sometimes affect natural predators of the target insect species and other nonpest species and can kill crustaceans if they get into aquatic ecosystems.

Like sex attractants, they are difficult and costly to produce.

Irradiation of Foods Exposing certain foods to various levels of radiation is being touted by the nuclear industry and the food industry as a means of killing and preventing insects from reproducing in certain foods after harvest, extending the shelf life of some perishable foods, and destroying parasitic worms (such as trichinae) and bacteria (such as salmonella that each year kill 2,000 Americans).

In 1986 the FDA approved use of low doses of ionizing radiation on spices, fruits, vegetables, and fresh pork and it may soon be approved for use on poultry and seafood. Irradiated foods are already sold in 33 countries including the Soviet Union, Japan, Canada, Brazil, Israel, and many west European countries.

Because tests show that consumers will not buy food if it is labeled as being irradiated, foods exposed to radiation sold in the United States bear a characteristic logo and a label stating that the product has been *picowaved*. This information is meaningless to many consumers, but it is better than no labelling. The label, however, is only required on foods that have been directly irradiated, not on those that contain irradiated components such as various spices used in processed foods, cheese spreads, and luncheon meats.

Exposure to higher doses—generally those above what is presently allowed by the FDA—also could extend the shelf life of some perishable foods. A food does not become radioactive when it is irradiated, just as being exposed to X rays does not make the body radioactive. There is controversy, however, over irradiating food (see Pro/Con at right).

Integrated Pest Management Pest control is basically an ecological problem, not a chemical problem. That is why using large quantities of broad-spectrum chemical poisons to kill and control pest populations eventually fails and ends up costing more than it is worth.

The solution is to replace this ecologically and economically unsustainable chemical approach with an ecological approach. An increasing number of pest control experts believe that in most cases the best way to control crop pests is a carefully designed **integrated pest management (IPM)** program. In this approach each crop and its pests are evaluated as an ecological system. Then a pest control program is developed that uses a variety of cultivation, biological, and chemical methods in proper sequence and timing.

The overall aim of integrated pest management is not eradication but keeping pest populations just below the size at which they cause of economic loss (Figure 21-8). Fields are carefully monitored to check whether

---

PRO/CON Should Food Be Irradiated?

According to the FDA and the World Health Organization, over 1,000 studies show that foods exposed to low radiation doses are safe for human consumption. However, critics of irradiation argue that not enough animal studies have been done and that tests of the effects of irradiated foods on people have been too few and brief to turn up any long-term effects, which typically require 30 to 40 years to be evaluated.

The focus of this controversy is the fact that irradiation produces trace amounts of at least 65 chemicals in foods, some of which cause cancer in test animals. The FDA estimates that 58 of these chemicals are also found in nonirradiated foods and assumes that the concentrations of all 65 chemicals in irradiated food is too small to affect human health. Opponents of food irradiation say this assumption is unwarranted until these chemicals have been identified and thoroughly tested.

Opponents also fear that more people might die of deadly botulism in irradiated foods. Present levels of irradiation do not destroy the spore-enclosed bacteria that cause this disease but they do destroy the microbes that give off the rotten odor that warns of the presence of botulism bacteria. Critics also note that irradiation can be expensive, adding as much as five cents a pound to the price of some fresh vegetables.

Proponents, however, respond that irradiation of food is likely to reduce health hazards to people by decreasing the use of some potentially damaging pesticides and food additives (Section 18-5). What do you think?

---

pests have reached an economically damaging level. When such a level is reached, farmers first use biological and cultural controls. Small amounts of pesticides are applied only when absolutely necessary, and a variety of chemicals are used to retard development of genetic resistance. This approach allows farmers to escape from the pesticide treadmill and to minimize the hazards to human health, wildlife, and the environment from the widespread use of chemical pesticides.

Over the past 35 years, there have been almost 50 successful integrated pest management programs. China, Brazil, Indonesia, and the United States have led the world in the use of this approach, especially to protect cotton and soybeans. By 1984, integrated pest management programs were being used for nearly 40 crops in 15 states on about 8% of U.S. harvested

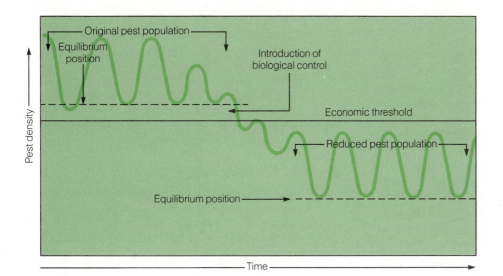

Figure 21-8 The goal of biological control and integrated pest management is to keep each pest population just below the size at which it causes economic loss.

cropland. Farmers using these programs saved $579 million more than they would have otherwise.

These experiences have shown that a well-designed integrated pest management program can

- reduce inputs of fertilizer and irrigation water
- reduce preharvest pest-induced crop losses by 50%
- reduce pesticide use and control costs by 50% to 90%
- increase crop yields and reduce crop production costs

However, there are some drawbacks to integrated pest management. It requires expert knowledge about each pest-crop situation and is slower acting and more labor intensive (but this creates jobs) than the use of conventional pesticides. Methods developed for a given crop in one area may not be applicable to another area with slightly different growing conditions. Although long-term costs are typically lower than those using conventional pesticides, initial costs may be higher.

So far the potential of integrated pest management has barely been tapped. Switching to this approach on a large scale in the United States is very difficult. First, it is strongly opposed by the politically and economically powerful agricultural chemical companies, who would suffer from a sharp drop in pesticide sales ($12.5 billion in 1987). They see little profit to be made from most alternative pest control methods, except insect sex attractants and hormones.

Second, farmers get most of their information about pest control from pesticide sales people. They also get information from U.S. Department of Agriculture county farm agents, who have supported pesticide use for decades and rarely have adequate training in the design and use of integrated pest management.

Integrated pest management methods will have to be developed and introduced to farmers by federal and state agencies. However, current federal funding of integrated pest management in the United States is only about $20 million a year—about half of what it costs to develop just one new chemical pesticide. Only about 2% of the Department of Agriculture's budget is spent on integrated pest management.

Environmentalists urge the USDA to promote integrated pest management by

- adding a 2% sales tax on pesticides and using all of these revenues to greatly expand the federal budget for integrated pest management
- setting up a federally supported demonstration project on at least one farm in every county
- training Department of Agriculture field personnel and all county farm agents in integrated pest management so they can help farmers use this alternative
- providing federal and state subsidies and perhaps government-backed crop-loss insurance to farmers who use integrated pest management or other approved alternatives to pesticides
- gradually phasing out federal and state subsidies to farmers who depend almost entirely on pesticides, once effective integrated pest management methods have been developed for major pest species

Indonesia has led the way in the no-chemical pesticide revolution. In 1986 the Indonesian government banned the use of 57 pesticides on rice and launched a nationwide program to switch to integrated pest management. By 1988 extension workers had trained over 31,000 farmers in integrated pest management techniques. This should have far-reaching benefits for

Indonesia and serve as a model for other rice-growing countries.

In 1987 Sweden adopted a program with the goal of cutting risks from pesticides in half by 1992. In 1987 the Danish government began a program with the goal of cutting pesticide use by 25% by 1997 and added a 3% tax on pesticide sales to provide funds for increased research and development and educational efforts on alternatives to chemical pesticides.

Changing the Attitudes of Consumers and Farmers

Two attitudes tend to increase the use of pesticides and lock us into the pesticide treadmill. First, many people believe that the only good bug is a dead bug. Second, most consumers insist on buying only perfect, unblemished fruits and vegetables, even though a few holes or frayed leaves do not significantly affect the taste, nutrition, or shelf life of such produce. Educating farmers and consumers to change these attitudes would significantly help reduce pesticide use.

Homeowners can also reduce the dangers of pesticides by using the smallest amount possible only when absolutely necessary and by disposing of unused pesticides in a safe manner (contact your local health department or environmental agency for safe disposal methods). The president and members of Congress should be pressured to significantly strengthen the Federal Insecticide, Fungicide, and Rodenticide Act in order to better protect human health and the environment from the harmful effects of pesticides.

Use the following natural alternatives to pesticides for controlling common household pests.*

- *Ants.* Make sure firewood and tree branches are not in contact with the house; caulk common entry points such as windowsills, door thresholds, and baseboards (also saves energy and money); keep ants out by planting peppermint at entrances and by putting coffee grounds or crushed mint leaves around doors and windows; sprinkle cayenne, red pepper, or boric acid along ant trails inside your house and wipe off counter tops with vinegar. After about four days of such treatments, ants usually go somewhere else.

- *Mosquitoes.* Establish nests and houses for insect-eating birds; eliminate sources of stagnant water in or near your yard; plant basil outside windows and doors; use screens on all doors and windows and a yellow light bulb outside entryways; reduce bites by not using scented soaps and not wearing perfumes, colognes, and other scented products

outdoors during mosquito season; repel them by rubbing a bit of vinegar on exposed skin; don't use no-pest strips for control of flying insects, especially in bedrooms or areas where food is prepared or eaten, because most contain DDVP, an organophosphate that some environmentalists have been trying unsuccessfully to have banned; don't use electric zappers to kill mosquitoes and other flying insects because these devices are noisy, waste electricity, and the light attracts insects rather than repelling them.

- *Weevils and flour beetles.* Sprinkle sage in kitchen cabinets where you keep such staples as flour and cornmeal; put a bay leaf in a small cheesecloth bag for each container of cereal, flour, and other grain products; then tightly seal each container and store them in a cool cabinet or the refrigerator.

- *Roaches.* Caulk or otherwise plug small cracks around wall shelves, cupboards, baseboards, pipes, sinks, and bathroom fixtures (also saves energy); eliminate folded up grocery sacks and newspapers which are favorite hiding places for roaches; don't leave out dirty dishes, food spills, dog or other indoor pet food, or uncovered food or garbage overnight; kill roaches by sprinkling boric acid under sinks and ranges, behind refrigerators, in cabinets and closets and other dark, warm places; repel roaches by sprinkling a mixture of bay leaves and cucumbers or a mixture of 1 cup borax, $\frac{1}{2}$ cup flour, $\frac{1}{4}$ cup confectioner's sugar, and 1 cup cornmeal; establish populations of banana spiders.

- *Flies.* Dispose of garbage and clean garbage pails regularly; eat or remove overripened fruit; don't leave moist, uneaten pet food out for more than an hour; repel flies by planting sweet basil and tansy near doorways and patios; put a blend of equal amounts of bay leaf pieces, coarsely ground cloves, clover blossoms, and eucalyptus leaves in several small bags or mosquito netting or other mesh material and hang them just inside entrance doors; grow sweet basil in the kitchen; place sweet clover in small bags made of mosquito netting and hang them around the room.

- *Termites.* Make sure soil around and under your home is well drained and that crawl spaces are dry and well ventilated; remove scrap wood, stumps, sawdust, cardboard, firewood, and other sources of cellulose close to your house; replace heavily damaged or rotted sills, joists, or flooring; fill voids in concrete or masonry with cement grout; in new construction install a termite shield between the foundation and floor joists and don't let untreated wood touch soil; inspect for damage each year, and if infestation is discovered apply a heat lamp at 60°C (140°F) for 10 minutes to any infested area; for a large infestation have your house treated by a professional using one of the

---

*For further information on safe control of insect pests, contact the National Coalition Against the Misuse of Pesticides, 530 7th St., N.E., Washington D.C. 20003.

new termicides such as Dursban, Torpedo, or Dragnet; safer treatments that may soon be available are freezing termites to death by pouring liquid nitrogen into walls and infested areas, a growth regulator that transforms young termites into soldiers instead of workers needed to feed a colony, and antibiotics that eliminate the wood-digesting microorganisms that live inside termites.

Homeowners should seriously consider allowing plants native to an area to grow on all or most of the land around a house site not used for gardening. These plants can be supplemented by a mix of wildflowers, herbs (for cooking), low-growing ground cover, small bushes, and other vegetation natural to the area. Create paths covered with wood chips, stones, or strips of discarded carpet through the area so that little, if any, mowing is required.

This approach, based on natural diversity rather than the traditional monoculture of grass, saves time, energy, and money (no lawn mower, gasoline, or mower repairs). This type of yard also reduces infestations by mosquitoes and other insects by providing a diversity of habitats for their natural predators.

The largest homesite infestations by insect pests and weeds such as crabgrass usually occur in yards planted with grass kept cut below 8 centimeters (3 inches). Taller grass provides more habitats for natural predators of many pest species, shades weeds out, and holds moisture in the soil.

If you fertilize your lawn, reduce insect and plant disease problems by using compost (Figure 10-22, p. 232) instead of commercial inorganic fertilizers. If you hire a company to take care of your lawn, use one that relies only on organic methods.* If a company claims to use only organic methods, get this in writing. If such a company is not in your area, encourage existing companies to provide this alternative or start up such a company yourself. This business has tremendous growth potential.

We need to recognize that pest control is basically an ecological, not a chemical problem.

Robert L. Rudd

CHAPTER SUMMARY

In a diverse natural ecosystem insects and vegetation considered pests are usually kept in check by natural predators, disease organisms, and parasites. Because such natural controls are sharply reduced in simplified croplands and gardens, people have increasingly used a variety of chemicals called *pesticides*.

Pesticide manufacturers and a number of agricultural scientists argue that the benefits of pesticides far exceed their threats to wildlife and human health. Pesticides have reduced outbreaks of insect-transmitted diseases such as malaria and saved millions of people from illness and premature death. They have also increased crop yields by reducing losses to pests. This increase in food production has reduced illness and premature deaths from malnutrition, kept food prices low, and increased profits for farmers.

Environmentalists and conservationists, however, contend that the harmful effects of these chemicals outweigh their benefits. Pesticides eventually cause larger, more damaging outbreaks of the pests they are supposed to control when the pests develop genetic resistance to the pesticides and their natural predators are wiped out. The widespread killing of predator species allows prey species that were not pests or were only minor pests to multiply rapidly and become major pests. This puts farmers on a *pesticide treadmill*, in which the cost of using pesticides increases while their effectiveness decreases. Widespread use of pesticides also threatens wildlife and human health.

Pesticides in the United States are regulated by the Federal Insecticide, Fungicide, and Rodenticide Act of 1972, which requires all commercial pesticides to be approved by the EPA. Although the EPA has used this act to ban or restrict the use of a number of pesticides, environmentalists consider it a weak law that does not adequately protect human health and the environment.

Alternatives to reliance on pesticides include (1) modified cultivation procedures (such as crop rotation); (2) biological control by natural predators; (3) breeding or genetic engineering to create crop and animal varieties resistant to insect pests and plant pathogens; (4) raising sterilized male insect pests and releasing them in infested areas to mate unsuccessfully with fertile wild females; (5) insect sex attractants to lure pests into traps containing toxic chemicals or to attract natural predators of insect pests into crop fields; (6) application of insect hormones at certain stages in the pest's life cycle to produce abnormalities that cause the insect to die before it can reach maturity and reproduce; (7) irradiation of certain foods to kill insects and pathogens after harvest and to extend shelf life; and (8) integrated pest management in which a variety of biological, chemical, and cultivation methods are used in proper sequence and timing to keep pest populations just below the economic loss level.

Consumers should not demand perfect-looking fruits and vegetables because appearance has no effect on the food's nutritional value and demand for perfect appearance increases pesticide use. Whenever possible, individuals should use natural alternatives to pesticides for household gardens and to control outdoor and indoor pests, and should also use pesticides only when absolutely necessary in the smallest amounts possible.

---

*For names of lawn companies that don't use toxic chemicals, write Lorens Tronet, Executive Director of Lake Country Defenders, Box 911, Lake Zanich, Illinois 60047, and the Bio-Integral Resource Center, Box 7414, Berkeley, Calif. 94707. Also consult *Success with Lawns Starts with Soil*, Ringer Research Corp., 6860 Flying Cloud Drive, Eden Prairie, Minn. 55344.

DISCUSSION TOPICS

1. Should DDT and other pesticides be banned from use in malaria control throughout the world? Explain. What are the alternatives?

2. Environmentalists argue that because essentially all pesticides eventually fail, their use should be phased out and farmers should be given economic incentives for switching to integrated pest management. Explain why you agree or disagree with this proposal.

3. Explain how the use of insecticides can actually increase the number of insect pest problems and threaten some carnivores and omnivores, including people.

4. How does genetic resistance to a particular pesticide develop? What major advantages do insects have over humans in this respect?

5. Debate the following resolution: Because DDT and the other banned chlorinated hydrocarbon pesticides pose no demonstrable threat to human health and have probably saved more lives than any other chemicals in history, they should again be approved for use in the United States.

6. Should certain types of foods used in the United States be irradiated? Explain.

7. What changes, if any, do you believe should be made in the Federal Insecticide, Fungicide, and Rodenticide Act regulating pesticide use in the United States?

8. Should U.S. companies continue to be allowed to export pesticides, medicines, and other chemicals that have been banned or severely restricted in the United States to other countries? Explain.

PART SIX

Environment and Society

When it is asked how much it will cost to protect the environment, one more question should be asked: How much will it cost our civilization if we do not?

Gaylord Nelson

We do not have generations, we only have years, in which to turn things around.

Lester Brown

CHAPTER 22

Economics and Environment

General Questions and Issues

1. What are the major types of economic goods and resources?

2. What types of economic systems are found throughout the world?

3. What is economic growth and how can it be redirected and managed to sustain the earth's life-support systems?

4. How can economics be used to regulate resource use and reduce environmental degradation and pollution?

As important as technology, politics, law, and ethics are to the pollution question, all such approaches are bound to have disappointing results, for they ignore the primary fact that pollution is primarily an economic problem, which must be understood in economic terms.

Larry E. Ruff

You were born wanting to have all your needs and wants satisfied and to have complete control over what you do. There are several problems with this. One is that the planet has 5.2 billion other people with the same goals. Another is that the earth's resources are limited.

The basic economic problem is that we cannot use the world's limited resources to produce enough material goods and services to satisfy everyone's unlimited wants. Therefore, individuals, businesses, and societies must make **economic decisions** about what goods and services to produce, how to produce them, how much to produce, and how to distribute them. **Economics** is the study of how individuals and groups make economic decisions about how to meet their needs and wants. Because producing and using anything has some harmful impact on the environment, economic decisions also affect the quality of the environment. In this chapter we will see how individual and group economic decisions affect resource use and environmental quality.

22-1 ECONOMIC GOODS AND RESOURCES

Economic Goods, Needs, and Wants An **economic good** is any material item or service that gives people satisfaction and whose present or ultimate supply is limited. Some of these goods are *material items* like food, gasoline, cars, and TV sets. Others are *services*—intangible things such as medical care, education, defense, and cleaning. An **economy** is a system of production, distribution, and consumption of economic goods.

The types and amounts of certain economic goods—food, clothing, water, oxygen, shelter—that you must have to survive and to stay healthy are your **economic needs**. Anything beyond this is an **economic want**. Each year well over $100 billion is spent in the United States on advertising and sales promotion largely to increase economic wants. What you believe you need and want is influenced by the customs and conventions of the society you live in and your level of affluence (see Spotlight on p. 569).

Private and Public Goods Any economic good that can be owned and enjoyed on a private, or exclusive, basis is a **private good.** Such goods can be produced and sold in units. Most things you buy in the marketplace are private goods.

On the other hand, **public goods** cannot be divided and sold in units and can be enjoyed by anybody. National defense is an example. Once provided for any citizen by a given level of expenditure, it is available to all. Other examples are police forces, fire departments, courts of law, public parks, public education, clean air, clean water, beautiful scenery, flood control projects, and wild plants and animals.

Private producers have little, or sometimes, no incentive to provide public goods and will undersupply them. Thus, governments step in and use tax revenues to provide public goods or to pay others to supply these goods. With limited tax revenues the government can't satisfy all needs and wants for public goods. Also, because there are no market prices to govern supply and demand, public goods are often provided in an inefficient manner.

Scarcity and Price All private economic goods are scarce. Otherwise they would cost us nothing. The *price* of a good usually reflects how scarce it is and how much it is valued by people.

But price is not always a good indicator of how scarce a good is. A producer of a good who has complete control over its supply—a **monopoly**—can reduce the supply to create artificial scarcity and raise its price. When a few large firms dominate the market for a good, they have an **oligopoly.** If these firms agree to set the price for the good they produce, they have the same effect as a monopoly. When countries that are the major suppliers of a good get together to regulate the supply and determine the price of a good, such as oil, they form a **cartel.** OPEC is an example.

In some cases the prices of goods are lower than their values. Examples are trees on public land (see Pro/Con on p. 304), water (Section 11-3), and clean air.

Governments can use taxpayer dollars to encourage production or conservation of a good. They can do this by giving suppliers of a good tax breaks, payments, and other *subsidies.* Subsidies reduce production costs, encourage suppliers to produce the good, and can lower the price consumers pay. But this artificially low price reduces consumers' incentive to conserve this resource.

A government can also add taxes to the price of a good that is being overproduced or that is causing unacceptable environmental problems. This encourages consumers to conserve, extends the supply, and stimulates the search for a substitute.

Economic Resources The things used in an economy to produce material goods and services are called **economic resources** or **factors of production.** They are usually divided into three groups:

1. **Natural resources:** resources produced by the earth's natural processes. These include the actual area of the earth's solid surface, nutrients and minerals in the soil and deeper layers of the earth's crust, wild and domesticated plants and animals, water, air, and nature's waste disposal and recycling services.

2. **Capital or intermediate goods:** manufactured items made from natural resources and used as inputs to produce and distribute final economic goods and services bought by consumers. These include tools, machinery, factory buildings, and transportation and distribution facilities.

3. **Labor:** the physical and mental talents of people. *Workers* sell their time and talents for *wages.*

SPOTLIGHT What Is Poverty?

Poverty is usually defined as not being able to meet basic economic needs. But people in different societies differ in what they think are their basic needs. Poverty is relative to the average standards of living in each country. At the top of the economic ladder about 10% of the world's people get about 50% of the world's income. At the bottom, 60% of the world's population get only 10% of the world's income.

In the United States anyone with an average annual income of less than $6,024 ($12,092 for a family of four) in 1988 was classified by the government as living in poverty. In 1988, 31.9 million Americans were living at or below this level. About 55% of these people were too young, too old, too sick, or too disabled to make enough money to escape poverty. Most others classified as poor are employed and underpaid or would like to work.

In 1960 one in five Americans were classified as living in poverty. By 1988 the figure had risen to one in eight. Some of the poor get income from food stamps and government housing subsidies. When this aid is included one in ten Americans were poor in 1988.

Poor people in a less developed country with an annual income of only several hundred dollars would not consider most Americans living in poverty as poor.

Poverty in an LDC may mean sleeping in the streets or on a dirt floor, going hungry for days, drinking polluted water, having too little fuel to keep warm and cook food, and having little if any access to medical care.

Poverty begets poverty. Avenues of escape are hard to find. Bright, capable, and healthy people have a good chance of finding their way out, but only a certain percentage of people born have these characteristics. Many of the poor without these qualities feel trapped and beaten and give up. What do you think should be done?

Entrepreneurs and *investors* assume the risk. *Managers* take responsibility for combining natural resources, capital goods, and workers to produce an economic good. *Profit* is the reward entrepreneurs and investors get for taking the risks for supplying an economic good they believe people need or want. If they guess wrong, they lose the time and money they have invested and earn no profit.

Note two important characteristics of economic resources. First, using and combining them depends on the ability of people to discover ways to extract raw materials from the earth and convert them to economic goods. Second, virtually everything we have or will have comes ultimately from the sun and the earth to produce three kinds of wealth: material, cultural, and biological. But our economic systems often refuse to treat the earth's natural resources as capital. Instead, we spend them as income and then are surprised when nature begins bouncing our checks.

Private, Common, and Public Property Resources

Any resource owned by individuals or groups of individuals is a **private property resource**. People tend to maintain and improve resources they own. If you own a house, you have a strong incentive to paint, repair, and improve it. These improvements help maintain or increase the economic value of the house.

A **common property resource** is one to which people have virtually free and unmanaged access. Most are potentially renewable resources. Examples are air, fish in international waters, migratory birds, wildlife in areas where there are no controls on hunting and harvesting, the carbon dioxide content of the lower atmosphere, and the ozone content of the stratosphere.

Anyone has a right to use or abuse common property resources. Thus, they can easily be polluted (air, international waters) or overharvested (whales, tropical forests) and converted from renewable to slowly renewable or nonrenewable resources. This is sometimes referred to as the tragedy of the commons (see Spotlight on p. 12).

Other resources, called **public property resources**, fall somewhere between private and common property resources. Such resources are owned jointly by all people of a country, state, or locality but are managed for them by the government. Examples are public lands such as national and state forests, wildlife refuges, parks, and areas protected from most uses except hiking and camping in the national wilderness preservation system (see Spotlight on p. 294).

22-2 ECONOMIC SYSTEMS

Traditional Economic System: Custom Decides In a **traditional economic system** people use past customs and traditions to answer the basic economic ques-

tions. Often these systems are **subsistence economies,** where families, tribes, or other groups produce only enough goods to meet their basic survival needs, with little or no surplus left over for sale or trade.

Traditional systems are found in tribal communities, which are rapidly disappearing. Decisions about what plants to gather, what crops to plant, what animals to hunt, who will do each of these tasks, and how food will be distributed are based on what the tribe has done in the past. Everyone's role is understood and fixed by custom. Upward economic mobility by individuals is discouraged and is rare. Technological changes and innovations that clash with tradition and threaten social order are also discouraged.

Societies with nontraditional economies also make some economic decisions based on tradition. For example, so far male domination has been a tradition in almost all economies.

Pure Market Economic System: The Market Decides In a **pure market economic system,** also known as **pure capitalism,** all economic decisions are made in *markets,* where buyers (demanders) and sellers (suppliers) of economic goods freely interact without government or other interference.

In its pure form this is a *produce-or-die distribution system.* Only those who receive wages and produce can afford to buy goods. Those who don't produce anything have no income and can't buy anything. They starve to death.

This system is based on private property, freedom of choice, and pure competition. All economic resources are owned by private individuals and private institutions, rather than by the government.

All buying and selling is based on **pure competition,** in which many small buyers and many small sellers act independently. No seller or buyer is large enough to control the supply, demand, or price of a good. Anyone is allowed to produce a product and attempt to sell it to others. But to participate, sellers and buyers must accept the going market price.

The major argument for the pure market system is that its resources are distributed among those who can afford them as cheaply as possible. A second argument for this system is that it emphasizes personal freedom. No one can tell you what you must buy or what you can and cannot have if you can afford the going market price.

Supply, Demand, and Market Equilibrium in the Pure Market System Economic decisions in the pure market system are governed by interactions of demand, supply, and price. In a pure market system buyers want to pay as little as possible for an economic good and sellers want to get as high a price as possible. **Market equilibrium** occurs when the quantity supplied equals the quantity demanded and the price is no higher than buyers are willing to pay and no lower

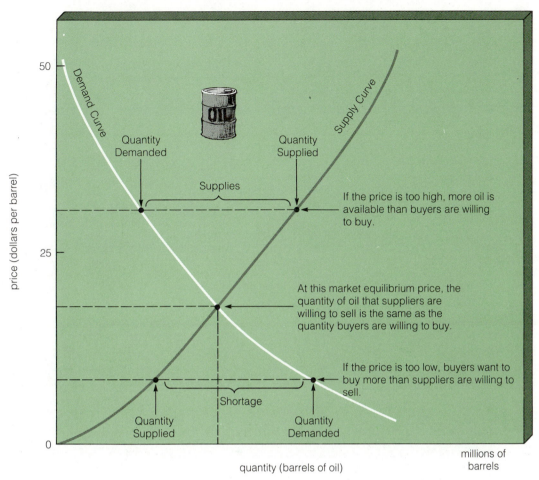

Figure 22-1 Monthly supply, demand, and market equilibrium for gasoline in a pure market system. If price, supply, and demand are the only factors involved, the market equilibrium point occurs where the demand and supply curves intersect.

than sellers are willing to accept. If price, supply, and demand are the only factors involved, the demand and supply curves for an economic good intersect at the *market equilibrium point* (Figure 22-1). This point gives the price buyers are willing to pay for an economic good and the amount suppliers are willing to supply at this price.

But things are not this simple. Factors other than price affect the supply of and demand for a good. These factors shift the original supply and demand curves to the right or the left, upsetting the market equilibrium and establishing new equilibrium points.

Factors that increase demand shift the demand curve to the right (Figure 22-2), and those that decrease demand shift it to the left. Examples are changes in the number of buyers, in buyer taste, in average income, and in prices of related goods. The supply curve for an economic good like gasoline can be shifted to the right or left by changes in technology, in production costs, in taxes, in prices of related goods, and in number of suppliers (Figure 22-3).

The general operation of a pure market economy can be represented by a **circular flow model** (Figure 22-4). It shows how the factors of production and the

economic goods produced flow between households, businesses, and the environment and how money flows between households and businesses to produce and buy economic goods.

Pure Command Economic System: The Government Decides In a **pure command economic system,** or **totally planned economy,** all economic decisions are made by the government. It determines what economic goods are produced, how they are produced, how much of each is produced, how much each will cost, and how they are distributed.

The pure command economy is based on the belief that government control is the most efficient way to produce, use, and distribute scarce resources. Socialism and its purer form, communism, are types of command economic systems.

Mixed Economic Systems: The Real World None of the world's countries have a pure market economy or a pure command economy. Instead they have **mixed economic systems** that fall somewhere between the pure market and pure command systems and have some elements of tradition (Figure 22-5).

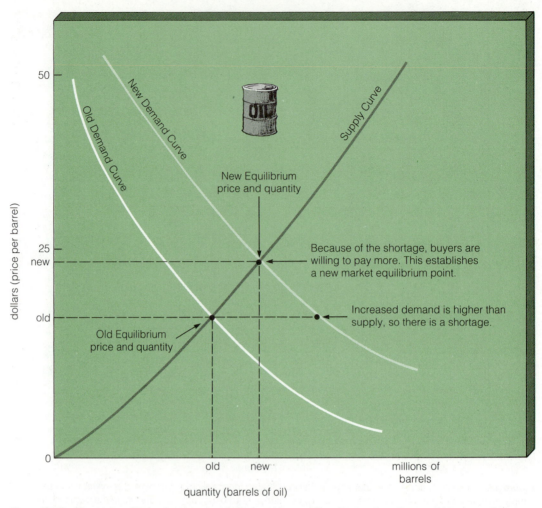

Figure 22-2 Short-term effects of an increase in demand for gasoline. Demand can increase because of more drivers, a switch to bigger cars with lower fuel efficiency, more spendable income for travel, or decreased use of mass transit. The original demand curve shown in Figure 22-1 shifts to the right. The increased demand creates a temporary shortage. Buyers are then willing to pay more. This establishes a new market equilibrium point. A similar situation occurs if the demand for gasoline decreases because of fewer drivers, a switch to more fuel-efficient cars, less spendable income for travel, or increased use of mass transit. In that case the original demand curve shifts to the left. Decreased demand creates a temporary surplus. Then competition stimulates sellers to charge less, until the price reaches a new market equilibrium point.

Why? Because pure markets are not able to provide all community needs. Government intervention is needed to

- promote and maintain competitive markets by preventing formation of monopolies
- provide national security and other public goods
- promote fairness (equity) through the redistribution of income and wealth, especially to people unable to meet their basic needs
- ensure economic stability by preventing cycles of boom and depression that commonly occur in a pure market system
- help compensate owners for large-scale destruction of assets by floods, earthquakes, hurricanes, and other disasters

- prevent or reduce pollution
- manage public land resources (Chapter 13)

Most western countries have mixed economies that blend socialism and capitalism with an emphasis on capitalism. Government intervention into the market place varies, with government spending absorbing over 50% of the GNP in West Germany and about 30% in the United States.

The Soviet Union, China, Cuba, and most eastern European countries have mixed economies that blend socialism and capitalism with emphasis on socialism (Figure 22-5). In these countries the central government owns most resources and makes most economic decisions.

Some government regulation of an economy is needed. But too much can stifle innovation and com-

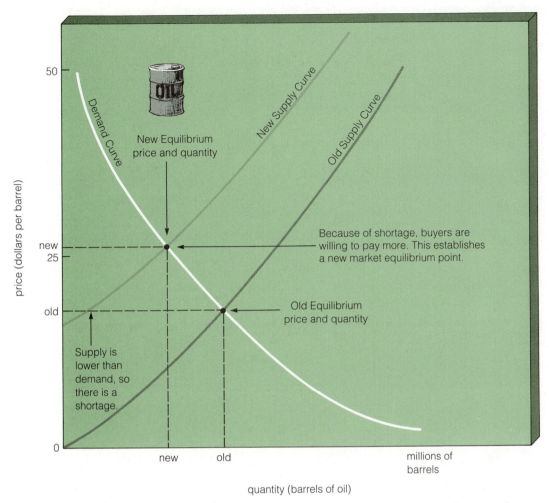

Figure 22-3 Short-term effects of a decrease in the supply of gasoline. A decrease can occur if the cost of finding, extracting, and refining oil increases or if existing oil deposits are economically depleted and not replaced by new discoveries. Also, if oil producers expect higher prices in the future, they may lower present production with the hope of making larger profits later. The original supply curve shown in Figure 22-1 shifts to the left. During the temporary shortage buyers are willing to pay more for gasoline. Thus, the price reaches a higher market equilibrium point. A similar situation occurs if the supply increases. In that case the original supply curve shifts to the right, reflecting a temporary surplus. Then competition stimulates sellers to charge less, and the price moves down to a new market equilibrium point.

petition, increase inefficiency, and waste money. Black (illegal) markets are also found in countries with strict government control. These are major reasons most command economic systems mix in some capitalism.

22-3 ECONOMIC GROWTH, PRODUCTIVITY, AND EXTERNAL COSTS

Gross National Product and Economic Growth The **gross national product (GNP)** is the market value in current dollars of all goods and services, for final use, produced by an economy during a year (Figure 22-6). To get a better idea of how much economic output is actually growing or declining, economists use the **real GNP:** the gross national product adjusted for *inflation*—any increase in the average price level of goods and services for final use.

All market and centrally planned mixed economies in the world today seek to increase their economic growth. **Economic growth** is an increase in the capacity of the economy to provide goods and services for final use. It is almost always identified with an increase in real GNP. Economic growth creates a larger economic pie. However, most people care little about how much bigger the pie is if they are not getting a bigger slice.

To show how the average person's slice of the economic pie is changing, economists often calculate the **average per capita real GNP:** the real GNP divided by the total population. If population expands faster than

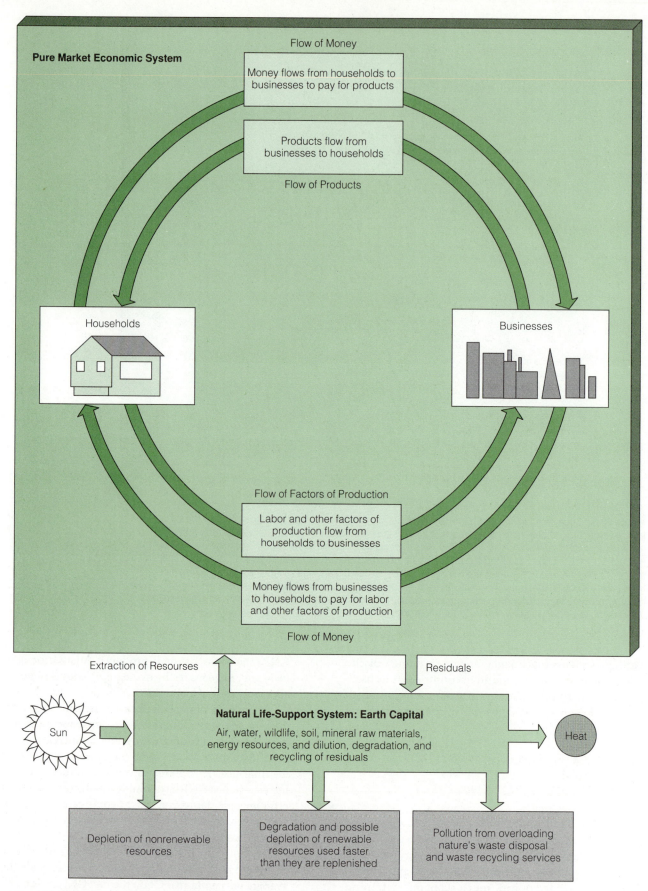

Figure 22-4 The circular flow model between households, businesses, and the environment in a pure market economy. The factors of production and the economic goods produced flow between households, businesses, and the environment. Money flows between households and businesses to pay for the economic goods produced and consumed. In most economics texts the vital bottom portion of this figure is not shown.

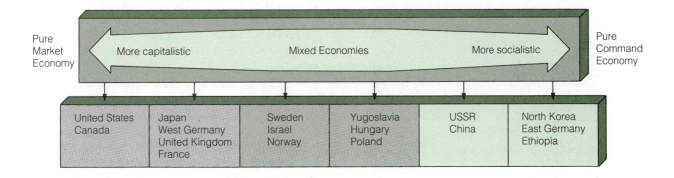

| United States Canada | Japan West Germany United Kingdom France | Sweden Israel Norway | Yugoslavia Hungary Poland | USSR China | North Korea East Germany Ethiopia |

Figure 22-5 Countries throughout the world have mixed economic systems that fall somewhere between the extremes of a pure market system and a pure command system.

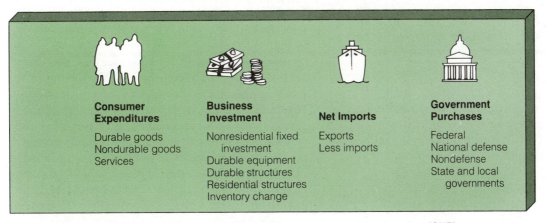

Consumer Expenditures

Durable goods
Nondurable goods
Services

Business Investment

Nonresidential fixed
investment
Durable equipment
Durable structures
Residential structures
Inventory change

Net Imports

Exports
Less imports

Government Purchases

Federal
National defense
Nondefense
State and local
governments

Figure 22-6 Major factors included in a country's expenditures on gross national product (GNP).

economic growth, the average per capita (per person) GNP falls. The pie has grown but the average slice per person has shrunk.

Between 1972 and 1988 the average per capita GNP in the United States has increased more than threefold. But adjusted for inflation, the average real per capita GNP (in 1972 dollars) rose only slightly during this period. The average slice has stayed about the same.

In the United States, the 20% of the people with the lowest incomes get only 5% of the country's total income. The highest 20% get 43% of the total income. Since 1950 the United States has had rapid economic growth. But the distribution of income today is about the same as it was in 1950.

GNP, Quality of Life, and Environmental Degradation

Since 1942 most governments have used real GNP and average per capita real GNP as measures of their society's well-being. But these indicators do not and were never intended to measure social welfare or quality of life. Instead, they measure the speed at which an economy is running.

Real GNP and real per capita GNP can give a general picture of the relative wealth of countries and in

some cases the average living standards of their people. But this picture is distorted. Why? One reason is that these indicators include the values of both beneficial and harmful goods and services. They lump together goods and bads, anything that can be assigned a monetary value, and nothing that cannot.

For example, producing more cigarettes raises real GNP. But it also causes more cancer and heart disease (Figure 18-10, p. 465). Ironically, these diseases increase the real GNP by increasing health and insurance costs. But the real GNP figure tell us nothing about the deaths and decreased quality of life suffered by the disease victims.

GNP indicators also don't tell us how resources and income are distributed among the people in a country—how many people have a large slice and how many have only a few crumbs of the economic pie. Also depletion of natural resources upon which all economies ultimately depend (Figure 22-4) are not subtracted from GNP. This means that a country can exhaust its mineral resources, erode its soils, deplete its forests, and hunt its wildlife and fisheries to extinction and this would not be reflected as a loss of an asset and future income in its GNP while these resources were being depleted.

Table 22-1 The 10 Highest and Lowest Countries on the Human Suffering Index in 1987. This index combines measures of per capita GNP, inflation, food sufficiency, literacy, access to drinking water, energy consumption, and political freedom (Data from Population Crisis Committee)

10 Highest		10 Lowest	
1. East Timor	183	1. Japan	5.5
2. Afghanistan	182	2. Iceland	5.7
3. Sierra Leone	176	3. Finland	6.5
4. Mali	175	4. Sweden	6.8
5. Gambia	169	5. Switzerland	6.9
6. Kampuchea	160	6. Hong Kong	7.5
7. Malawi	157	7. Canada	7.9
8. Guinea	153	8. Denmark	7.9
9. Ethiopia	152	9. Netherlands	8.0
10. Somalia	150	10. France	8.1

This distortion gives policymakers very misleading signals. This leads policymakers to ignore or destroy natural resources and environmental quality in the name of economic development. When depletion of the natural resource base is not included in GNP, a country can have illusory short-term gains in income and permanent loss in long-term national wealth.

Indicators of Social Well-being What we need are indicators that distinguish between good and bad economic goods and indicate who receives the "goods" and who receives the "bads." Economists William Nordhaus and James Tobin have developed an indicator called **net economic welfare (NEW)** to estimate the annual change in quality of life in a country.

Nordhaus and Tobin calculate the NEW by putting a price tag on pollution and other "negative" goods and services included in GNP—those that do not improve the quality of life. The costs of these negative factors are then subtracted from GNP to give NEW. Things such as household services—cleaning, cooking, repairs—that people do without pay are also added. These services contribute to life quality but do not show up in GNP.

The net economic welfare can then be divided by a country's population to estimate the **average per capita net economic welfare.** These indicators can then be adjusted for inflation. Applying this indicator to the United States shows that since 1940 average real NEW per person has risen at about half the rate of the average real GNP per person.

The net economic welfare indicator was developed in 1972, but is still not widely used. One reason is that putting a price tag on the "bads" is not easy and is

controversial. Another reason is that some politicians prefer using the real GNP per person because it can make people think they are better off than they are.

Social factors can also be used to evaluate average life quality in a country or part of a country. The Overseas Development Council has devised the *physical quality of life indicator (PQLI)*, based on three social indicators—average life expectancy, infant mortality, and literacy. But this indicator is less widely used than GNP.

Another indicator, called the *human suffering index*, has been developed by the Population Crisis Committee. It adds together ratings on 10 different scales, including GNP per capita, inflation rate, access to clean water, food sufficiency, literacy, energy consumption, urbanization, and political freedom. A score of 0 means essentially no suffering, and a score of 100 is as bad as you can get. Table 22-1 compares the 10 countries with the highest and lowest human suffering indices in 1987.

Economist Kenneth Boulding (see his Guest Essay on p. 153) has suggested that indicators be used to measure progress toward a sustainable-earth society. One indicator would measure the value of goods and services based on sustainable use of perpetual and renewable resources and on increased recycling and reuse of nonrenewable resources. A second indicator would represent the value of goods and services based on the throwaway use of nonrenewable resources with little or no recycling or reuse. Progress toward a sustainable-earth society would be indicated by an increase in the first indicator over the value of the second indicator.

In 1989 Robert Repetto and other researchers at the World Resources Institute proposed that the depletion of natural resources be included as a factor in GNP. This would give a *gross sustainable productivity (GSP)*. They have developed a fairly simple model for doing this and have applied it to Indonesia, which during the last decade has increased its annual GNP by severely depleting its once-rich natural resource base of oil, timber, and soil.

These indicators, like all indicators, are not perfect. But they provide more information than GNP, which is not designed to measure life and environmental quality and resource depletion.

Without accurate indicators we know too little about what is happening to people, the environment, and the planet's natural resource base, the lost value of depleted resources, what needs to be done, and what types of policies work. Unless we incorporate better indicators of what we are doing to ourselves and the earth, we will continue to act like a blind captain piloting a rudderless ship.

Productivity Growth: Doing More with Less There are several ways to increase economic growth. One is to produce more goods and services by using more of the factors of production (natural resources, capital, labor). This is the supply-side, or produce-more, approach.

A production increase can be brought about by an increase in population size—more people means more potential workers and consumers. It will also occur if there is an increase in average output and consumption of goods by each person. To conservationists this "growth-mania," based on the idea that all economic growth is good, is wasteful and harmful. It does not distinguish between the production of "bads" and "goods" and depletion of the earth's natural resource base (see Pro/Con at right).

Another way to increase production is to increase productivity by finding more efficient ways to use the factors of production. **Productivity** is a measure of the output of economic goods and services produced by the input of the factors of production (natural resources, capital goods, and labor).

Increasing productivity means getting more output from the same or less input of the factors of production by making better use of what we have—doing more with what we have. This allows lower prices, more effective competition, higher profits, and a higher average standard of living.

Improving productivity without increasing consumption conserves more resources and helps protect the environment more than simply increasing production or output. Nevertheless, increasing productivity will not solve our resource and environmental problems. We also need to emphasize increasing the production of goods and services that benefit the health and well-being of people and the earth. Also increases in productivity must include any decreases this causes in natural resources. Otherwise we get false information, like a ship captain operating in polar waters whose radar doesn't detect icebergs.

New technology is one key to increasing economic productivity. Such innovations require large investments in research and development and education. A high national savings rate is also needed to provide for investment to increase productivity.

Another key factor is a low interest rate on borrowed capital. Any country with a large national debt tends to have high interest rates. A large part of the government's tax income must be used to pay interest on the debt. This leaves less money for investment in productivity. Interest rates remain high to encourage domestic and foreign investors to keep lending the government money to make up the difference between what it takes in and spends each year.

Internal and External Costs The price you pay for a car reflects the costs of building and operating the factory, raw materials, labor, marketing, shipping, and company and dealer profits. After you buy the car,

---

PRO/CON Should Economic Growth Be Unlimited or Redirected?

Proponents of unlimited economic growth argue that it is

- The best way to increase material abundance and raise average standards of living. If the pie keeps growing, there is a better chance that the size of each person's slice will also grow.

- The best cure for poverty. As long as the economic pie is growing, more wealth can "trickle down" to the world's poor.

- Needed to provide money for environmental protection and more efficient development and use of the earth's resources. The best way to reduce pollution is to control pollution, not economic growth.

Most critics of unlimited economic growth are not against all economic growth. Instead, they believe growth should be redirected to produce things that reduce environmental pollution and degradation, that conserve resources, and that improve life quality. At the same time, we should move toward a stable world population through improved education, infant care, health, status of women, and family planning (Chapter 8).

These critics counter some of the conventional arguments for unlimited economic growth as follows:

- Directed—not unlimited—economic growth is the best way to raise average living standards and help the poor.

- The "trickle down" idea may sound good on paper, but much too little trickles down. Despite decades of worldwide economic growth, the gap in average GNP per person between the rich and the poor is growing (Figure 1-7, p. 10).

- We need to maximize the average real per capita net economic welfare, not the average real per capita GNP. We also need to add depletion of natural resources as a factor in evaluating national annual income.

What do you think?

---

you also have to pay for gasoline, maintenance, and repair. All these direct costs, paid for by the seller and buyer of an economic good, are called **internal costs**.

Making, distributing, and using any economic good also involve what economists call **externalities**. These are social benefits ("goods") and social costs ("bads") outside the market process. They are not included in the market price of an economic good or service. For example, if a car dealer builds an aesthetically pleasing sales building, this is an **external benefit** to other people who enjoy the sight at no cost to them.

On the other hand, when a factory or other business emits pollutants into the environment, their harmful effects are an **external cost** passed on to society and in some cases future generations. The external costs of our love affair with the automobile are many. Pollution from making cars and driving them and accidents caused by unsafe cars harm people and kill some of them unnecessarily. This means that car insurance, health insurance, and medical bills go up for everyone. Air pollution from cars also kills or weakens some types of trees, raising the price of lumber, paper, and this textbook (see Pro/Con on p. 201).

Taxes may also go up. Why? Because the public may demand that the government spend a lot of money to regulate the land, air, and water pollution and degradation caused by producing and using cars and by mining and processing the raw materials used to make them.

Because these harmful costs are external and hence aren't included in the market price, you don't connect them with the car or type of car you are driving. But as a consumer and taxpayer, you pay these hidden costs sooner or later.

If you use a car, you can pass other external costs on to society. You increase these costs when you throw trash out of a car, drive a car that gets poor gas mileage and thus adds more air pollution per mile than a more efficient car, dismantle or don't maintain a car's air pollution control devices, drive with a noisy muffler, and don't keep your motor tuned. You don't pay directly for these harmful activities. But you and others pay indirectly in the form of higher taxes, higher health costs, higher health insurance, and higher cleaning bills.

Internalizing External Costs   As long as it pays to pollute, deplete, degrade, and waste resources, few people are going to volunteer to change—to commit economic suicide. Suppose you own a company and believe that it is wrong to pollute the environment any more than can be handled by the earth's natural processes. If you voluntarily install expensive pollution controls and your competitors don't, your product will cost more. Your profits would decline and sooner or later you'll probably go bankrupt and your employes will lose their jobs.

A general way to deal with the problem of external costs is for the government to force producers to include all or most of them in the market price of all economic goods. Then the market price of an economic good would be its **true cost**: its internal costs plus its short- and long-term external costs. This is what economists call *internalizing the external costs.*

Internalizing external costs requires government action. Why? Because few people are going to increase their cost of doing business unless their competitors have to do it. Government intervention since 1968 has helped internalize some of the external costs of pollution. For example, factories are now required to install equipment to reduce their discharges and cars now have to have air pollution control equipment. But this job is only partly done and we keep discovering new harmful external costs.

What would happen if we internalized enough of the external costs of pollution and waste to achieve more optimum levels of pollution and resource use? Economic growth would be redirected. We would increase the beneficial parts of the GNP, decrease the harmful parts, increase production of beneficial goods, raise the net economic welfare, and help sustain the earth.

On the other hand, some things you like would not be available any more because they would cost producers so much to make that few people could afford to buy them. You would pay more for most things because their market prices would be closer to their true costs. But everything would be "up front." External costs would no longer be hidden. You would have the information you need to make informed economic decisions.

Moreover, real market prices wouldn't always be higher. Some things could even get cheaper. Internalizing external costs stimulates producers to find ways to cut costs by increasing productivity. Doing so helps them compete with producers in countries where external costs are not internalized.

Internalizing external costs makes so much sense you might be wondering why it's not more widely done. One reason is that many producers of harmful and wasteful goods fear they would have to charge so much that they couldn't stay in business or would have to give up government subsidies that have helped hide the external costs.

Another problem is that it's not easy to put a price tag on all the harmful effects of making and using an economic good. People disagree on the values they attach to various costs and benefits. But making difficult choices about resource use is what economics and politics is all about.

22-4   ECONOMIC APPROACHES TO IMPROVING ENVIRONMENTAL QUALITY AND CONSERVING RESOURCES

How Far Should We Go?   You, like most people, are probably in favor of a clean environment and resource conservation. But how clean do you want the environment to be? How far do you believe we should go in requiring resource conservation? How much money are you willing to spend to achieve these goals? What changes in your lifestyle are you willing to make to reach these goals? Are we spending too much on environmental protection (see Pro/Con below)?

Shouldn't our goal always be zero pollution? For most pollutants the answer is no. First, because everything we do produces some potential pollutants, and nature can handle some of our wastes. The trick is not to destroy, degrade, or overload these natural processes. Exceptions are harmful products that cannot be degraded by natural processes or that break down very slowly in the environment. They should neither be produced nor used except in small amounts with special permits.

Second, we can't afford to have zero pollution for any but the most harmful substances. Removing a small percentage of the pollutants in air, water, or soil is not too costly, but when we remove more, the price per unit multiplies. The cost of removing pollutants follows a J curve of exponential growth (Figure 22-7).

For example, in 1972 the EPA estimated that removing 85% of the pollutants from all industrial and municipal effluents between 1971 and 1981 would cost $62 billion. But to remove all the pollutants would have cost at least $317 billion. It costs five times as much to remove the last 15% as it does to remove the first 85%.

How far do we go? If we go too far in cleaning up, the costs of pollution control will be greater than its harmful effects. This may cause some businesses to go bankrupt. You and others may lose jobs, homes, and savings (see Spotlights on pp. 16 and 524). If we don't go far enough, however, the harmful external effects will cost us more than reducing the pollution to a lower level would cost. Then you and others may get sick or even die. Getting the right balance is crucial.

How do we do this? We plot a curve of the estimated social costs of cleaning up pollution and a curve of the estimated social costs of pollution. We then add the two curves to get a third curve showing the total costs. The lowest point on this third curve is the optimum level of pollution (Figure 22-8).

On a graph this looks neat and simple. But environmentalists and business leaders often disagree in their estimates of the social costs of pollution. Furthermore, the optimum level of pollution is not the same in different areas. Areas with lots of people and industry have lower optimum pollution levels. Soils and lakes in some areas are more sensitive to acid deposition than those in other places.

Improving Environmental Quality and Reducing Resource Waste You have seen why preventing pollution and reducing unnecessary resource use and

---

PRO/CON Is Environmental Protection Costing Too Much in Money and Jobs?

Is the United States spending too much on environmental protection? Have our environmental protection standards caused massive unemployment?

Industrialists often argue that the costs of reducing pollution will make their businesses unprofitable and force them to close down plants and lay off employees. They argue that the economic benefits of jobs outweigh the need for stricter environmental control (see Spotlight on p. 524). Environmentalists and conservationists argue that we are spending too little on pollution control.

What are the facts? By 1985 environmental damage was costing the United States an estimated 4% of its GNP. But the country was spending only about 1.6% of its GNP on environmental protection. U.S. businesses were spending only 2.7% of their capital

investments on pollution control. The average annual rate of U.S. spending for pollution control and abatement between 1972 and 1980 was 4.7%, but between 1980 and 1985 the expenditures increased by an average of only 0.8% a year.

Moreover, pollution control itself is a rapidly growing beneficial form of economic activity, amounting to $70 billion in 1988. The pollution control business is growing at about 18% per year—twice the annual growth rate for all U.S. manufacturing.

Pollution control also creates far more jobs than it eliminates. Between 1971 and 1985, U.S. air and water pollution control laws created over 300,000 new jobs. According to the Environmental Protection Agency, during this same period fewer than 52,000 workers were alleged to have lost

their jobs because of environmental regulations.

Pollution control expenditures create more jobs and help reduce unemployment more than most other expenditures. Studies have shown that 60,000 to 70,000 jobs are created for each $1 billion spent on pollution control. By comparison, each $1 billion of GNP generates an average of 50,000 jobs, and each $1 billion of military spending creates only 28,000 jobs.

Pollution control also saves industry money in the long run. For example, an $8 million pollution control system installed by the Great Lakes Paper Company reduced the plant's operating cost by $4 million a year and paid for itself in only two years. Hundreds of industries are finding that pollution prevention pays.

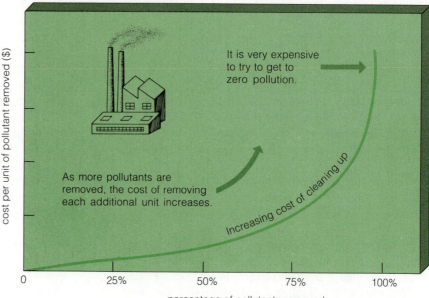

Figure 22-7 The cost of removing each additional unit of pollution rises exponentially.

cost per unit of pollutant removed ($)

It is very expensive to try to get to zero pollution.

As more pollutants are removed, the cost of removing each additional unit increases.

Increasing cost of cleaning up

0   25%   50%   75%   100%

percentage of pollutants removed

waste require government intervention in the free market. There are four ways the government can intervene:

- *Make harmful actions illegal.* Pass and enforce laws that set pollution standards, regulate harmful activities, and require that certain resources be conserved.

- *Penalize harmful actions.* Levy taxes on each unit of pollution discharged into the air or water and each unit of unnecessary resource waste.

- *Market pollution rights and resource use rights.* Sell rights that allow pollution up to the estimated optimum level; sell the right to harvest or extract a certain amount of resources from public lands or common property resources.

- *Reward beneficial actions.* Use tax dollars to pay subsidies to businesses and individuals that install pollution control equipment and reduce unnecessary resource use and waste by recycling and reusing resources and by inventing more efficient processes and devices.

Often several or all of these methods are needed to deal with environmental and resource problems.

The first three are *polluter-or-resource-waster-pays* approaches that internalize some or most external costs of pollution and resource waste. Because the internalized costs are passed on to consumers, these measures make each of us pay directly for the unnecessary pollution added to the environment and the resources wasted in the production of the economic goods we choose to buy.

Most economists prefer the second and third methods because they use the marketplace to control pollution and resource waste and do a better job of internalizing the external costs. Most conservationists favor a combination of the first three methods.

The first three approaches share several disadvantages. Because pollution costs are internalized, the initial cost of products may be higher unless new, more cost-effective and productive technologies are developed. This can put a country's products at a disadvantage in the international marketplace. Higher initial costs also mean that the poor are left out unless they are given tax relief or other subsidies from public funds. Also, fines and other punishments must be severe enough and enforced quickly enough to deter violations.

The fourth approach is a *taxpayer-pays* approach that does little to internalize external costs. It leads to higher-than-optimum levels of pollution and resource waste. It is not surprising that polluting industries and resource wasters usually prefer this approach, which has taxpayers pay them not to pollute or waste resources.

All four approaches are limited by incomplete and disputed information about the short- and long-term effects of pollutants and require greatly increased environmental monitoring to determine how well they work. Widespread monitoring is also necessary to catch violators of antiwaste and antipollution laws.

We need to greatly increase research and monitoring to get better information about environmental quality and resource depletion and degradation. But we will never have enough. Lack of information may cause us to make mistakes in our attempts to reduce pollution and resource waste. But not dealing with these problems will be much more harmful and costly in the long run.

Another problem with all four approaches is the potential for international economic blackmail for controlling global pollution costs. Multinational companies are based in one country but operate in many countries. If it costs too much to control pollution or conserve resources in one country, a company can

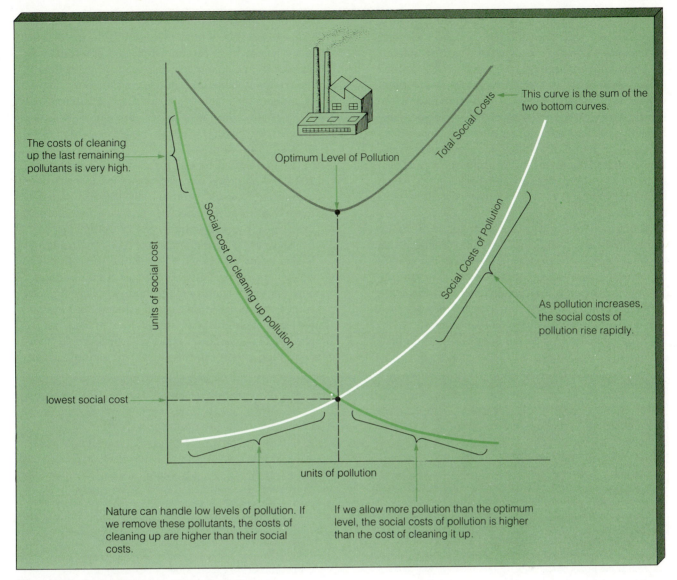

The costs of cleaning up the last remaining pollutants is very high.

Optimum Level of Pollution

Total Social Costs

This curve is the sum of the two bottom curves.

Social cost of cleaning up pollution

units of social cost

Social Costs of Pollution

As pollution increases, the social costs of pollution rise rapidly.

lowest social cost

units of pollution

Nature can handle low levels of pollution. If we remove these pollutants, the costs of cleaning up are higher than their social costs.

If we allow more pollution than the optimum level, the social costs of pollution is higher than the cost of cleaning it up.

Figure 22-8 Finding the optimum level of pollution.

close down plants there and open up new ones in countries with less strict environmental and resource use regulations or higher subsidies.

But governments should not use economic blackmail as an excuse for not dealing with environmental and resource problems. Since many of these problems are regional and global, governments must begin to recognize the need for global policies. Table 22-2 summarizes other advantages and disadvantages of the four approaches governments can use to intervene in the marketplace to control pollution and reduce resource depletion and degradation.

Cost-Benefit Analysis Comparing the estimated short-term and long-term costs (losses) and benefits (gains) of an economic decision is called **cost-benefit analysis.** If the estimated benefits exceed the estimated costs, the decision to produce or buy an economic good or provide a public good is considered worthwhile. You intuitively make such evaluations when you decide to buy a particular economic good or service.

More formal cost-benefit analysis is often used in evaluating whether to build a large hydroelectric dam, to clean up a polluted river, or to reduce air pollution emissions to an optimum level. Cost-benefit analysis is widely used by government agencies, but its use is controversial.

One problem is that present costs may be fairly easy to estimate, but putting a price tag on future benefits and costs is difficult. Because the future is unknown, all we can do is make educated guesses based on various assumptions about what the future value of a resource might be. Different assumptions give different estimates.

These assumptions are a major source of disagreement between conservationists and business people. Business people give more weight than conservationists do to immediate profits and values over possible future profits and values: "A bird in hand is worth two in the bush." They worry that inflation will make the value of their earnings less in the future than now. They also fear that innovation or changed consumer preferences will make a product or service obsolete.

Many business leaders and economists also assume that economic growth through technological progress will automatically raise average living standards in the future. So why should the current generation pay higher prices and taxes to benefit future generations who will be better off anyhow? Cost-benefit analyses have a built-in bias against future environmental protection and resource conservation because they weigh future benefits and costs lower than current benefits and costs.

Conservationists put greater emphasis on the future value of resources. They are also not convinced that future economic growth will raise average living standards unless we redirect this growth to reduce the "bads" and increase the "goods" and start including depletion of natural resources in the indicators such as GNP we use to measure national incomes.

Another problem is determining who gets the ben-efits and who is harmed by the costs. For example, suppose a cost-benefit analysis concludes that it is too expensive to meet certain safety and environmental standards in a manufacturing plant. The owners of the company benefit by not having to spend money on making the plant less hazardous. Consumers may also benefit from lower prices. But the workers are harmed by having to work under hazardous and unhealthful conditions.

In the United States, for example, an estimated 100,000 Americans die from exposure to hazardous chemicals at work. Another 400,000 are seriously injured from such exposure. Is this a necessary or unnecessary (and unethical) cost of doing business?

The most serious limitation of cost-benefit analysis is that many things we value cannot be reduced to dollars and cents. Some of the costs of air pollution, such as extra laundry bills, house repainting, and ruined crops, are fairly easy to estimate. But how do we put meaningful price tags on human life, clean air and water, beautiful scenery, a wilderness area, whooping cranes, and the ability of natural systems

Table 22-2 Evaluation of Ways to Improve Environmental Quality and Conserve Resources

Advantages	Disadvantages
Direct Government Regulation	
Helps keep pollution and resource waste below a certain level; internalizes some external costs; having the same emission and resource recycling standards everywhere prevents polluters and resource wasters from moving to parts of the country with lower standards; leaves firms free to decide how best to meet standards; encourages innovation and development of new pollution control and resource conservation technology but this is often not done; only effective way to control emissions and resource waste from cars and home furnaces; easier to get through Congress than other methods	Requiring all pollution emitters and resource wasters to meet the same standards internalizes only part of the external costs; does not take into account differences in the capacity of the local or regional environment to dilute or degrade some pollutants; requiring all producers to use the same control technology discourages development of better and cheaper pollution control and resource conservation technology; can force small producers without enough capital to install new equipment out of business; standards tend to be ones that are enforceable rather than optimum; unfair because polluters do not pay for damages
Pollution Emission and Resource Use Charges	
Internalizes external costs if charges are close to estimated external costs; encourages producers to reduce pollution and resource waste to optimum levels; generates tax revenue rather than having taxpayers pay for external costs; fair because polluters pay	May take several trials and errors to find right level of fees; inflation can lead to an increase in pollution and resource waste unless charges automatically rise with inflation; hard to get through Congress
Pollution and Resource Use Rights	
Encourages producers to reduce pollution and resource waste to optimum levels; environmental and conservation groups can buy up and hold rights to protect vulnerable areas; generates tax revenue rather than having taxpayers pay for external costs; inflation would automatically raise prices of rights and keep pollution and resource waste from rising	Requires extensive monitoring and enforcement to make sure that those not buying rights do not pollute, degrade, and waste resources
Economic Incentives	
Decreases production costs and can lead to higher profits, keep prices of goods down, and improve competitiveness in the international marketplace	Does little to internalize external costs; producers tend to lobby for and receive subsidies to increase their output rather than conserve resources and improve pollution control; uses tax revenues instead of generating them; subsidies often go to those with the most influence; difficult to discontinue when no longer needed; takes tax dollars away from other uses

to degrade and recycle some of our wastes and replenish timber, fertile soil, and other vital potentially renewable resources? According to agriculturalist Wendell Berry, "We do not know how to place a market value on soil, and we are not going to be able to learn how. Its value is inestimable. We must value it beyond whatever price we put on it, by *respecting* it, by taking good care of it."

We can assign dollar values to such items, but the values we assign will vary widely because of different assumptions and value judgments. This can lead to a wide range of projected costs and benefits. For example, in 1984 the EPA did a cost-benefit analysis on a proposed revision of the Clean Air Act. The analysis concluded that the net benefits (after deducting the projected costs) ranged from a loss of $1.4 billion to a gain of $110 billion—depending mostly on the monetary value assigned to human life, human health, and a cleaner environment.

Values assigned to a human life in various cost-benefit studies vary from nothing to about $7 million. The most frequently assigned values range from $200,000 to $500,000. If you were asked to put a price tag on your life, you might say it is infinite, or you might contend that making such an estimate would be impossible or even immoral.

You may not want others to place a low monetary value on your own life. But you place a low value on your life if you choose to smoke cigarettes, not eat properly, drive without a seat belt, drive while impaired by alcohol or some other drug, or refuse to pay more for a safer car. In each case you decide that the benefits—pleasure, convenience, or a lower purchase price—outweigh the potential costs—poorer health, injury, or death.

Critics of cost-benefit analysis argue that because estimates of many costs and benefits are so uncertain, they can easily be weighted to achieve the desired outcome by proponents or opponents of a proposed project or action. The experts making or evaluating such analyses have to be paid by somebody, so they often represent the point of view of that somebody.

The difficulty in making cost-benefit analyses does not mean that they should not be made or that they are not useful. At best they are crude estimates and sometimes they are deliberately distorted. But they can be useful as long as decision makers and the public are aware that they give only rough estimates and guidelines for resource use and management based on assumptions. They should never be thought of as precise, "bottom-line" numbers. And we should understand that they represent assigning market price values to things that cannot be valued in this way.

There have been successes in using cost-benefit analysis for environmental protection and resource conservation. Much of today's environmental protection legislation is based on cost-benefit analyses by John Krutilla, Anthony Fisher, Lester Lave, Charles Chicchetti, Eugene Seskin, and other economists (see Case Study below).

CASE STUDY Preservation Versus Development: The Hell's Canyon Case*

Hell's Canyon is on the Snake River, which separates Idaho and Oregon. The deepest canyon in North America, it provides a spectacular view for visitors and is a habitat for a variety of wildlife. It is also one of the best remaining sites in the United States for a hydroelectric power plant.

During the 1970s a major controversy arose over whether a dam should be built across this canyon to produce hydroelectric power or the canyon should be preserved in its natural state. The dam would create a large lake behind and change the character of the canyon.

Congress asked Resources for the Future, Inc., a respected Washington think tank, to make a cost-benefit analysis of this project. Economists Anthony Fisher, John Krutilla, and Charles Chicchetti carried out the study.

They found that the demand for recreational use of this unique canyon area was increasing rapidly. Construction of the dam would diminish the value of the site for recreation. On the other hand, electricity produced by the dam would be valuable. They found that the projected electricity demand could be met by other methods, but these methods would be more expensive.

The economists found that the current potential net benefits from producing hydroelectricity were greater than the current recreational benefits of preservation. However, the net benefits from preservation were rising more rapidly over time than the projected net benefits of producing electricity.

The analysis concluded that if the current annual value of recreational benefits at the canyon site

exceeded $80,000, the site should be preserved. The economists estimated that the current annual value of recreational activities at the site was $900,000—over ten times the value needed to justify preservation. They admitted that the $900,000 estimate may have been too high, but they thought it unlikely to be ten times too high.

Thus, they recommended preservation. On the basis of this recommendation and other considerations, Congress voted to protect Hell's Canyon from development.

*Based on material in Tietenberg, Tom. 1988. *Environmental and Resource Economics*, 2nd ed., Glenview, Ill.: Scott, Foresman.

Conservationists and economists have suggested ways to improve cost-benefit analysis:

- require all studies to use a uniform set of standards
- clearly state all assumptions
- show all projected costs with their estimated range of values based on each set of assumptions
- estimate the short- and long-term benefits and costs to all affected population groups
- estimate the effectiveness of the project or form of regulation, instead of assuming (as is often done)

SPOTLIGHT Characteristics of a Sustainable-Earth Economy

A sustainable-earth economy discourages certain types of economic growth and encourages other types to prevent overloading and degradation of the earth's life-support systems now and in the future.

Discourages

- throwaway and nondegradable products, oil and coal use, nuclear energy, deforestation, overgrazing, groundwater depletion, soil erosion, resource waste, and output pollution control
- creating and satisfying wants that cause high levels of pollution, environmental degradation, and resource waste

Does this by

- using fees and marketable permits to internalize the external costs of goods and services
- removing government subsidies from highly pollution-producing, resource-depleting, and resource-wasting economic activities

Encourages

- recycling, reuse, solar energy, energy conservation, education, prevention of health problems, ecological restoration, input pollution control (pollution prevention), appropriate technology, and long-lasting, easily repaired products
- consumption of goods and services that satisfy essential needs, not artificially created wants
- growth in productivity—not mere production—of beneficial goods and services (do more with less)

- encouraging sustainable development that rejects policies and practices that support current living standards by depleting the earth's natural resource capital and that leave future generations with poorer prospects and greater risks than our own
- use of renewable resources at a sustainable rate
- use of locally available matter and energy resources
- decentralization of some production facilities to reduce transportation costs, make better use of locally available resources, enhance national security by spreading out targets, and increase employment
- preservation of biological diversity at local, national, and global levels by setting aside and controlling the use of forests, wetlands, grasslands, soil, and wildlife
- self-sufficiency of families, urban areas, rural areas, and countries
- regulation of human population growth
- global economic and political cooperation to promote peace and sustain the earth's life-support systems for everyone now and in the future
- fairer distribution of the world's resources and wealth

Does this by

- integrating economics and ecology in decision making (the most important condition)
- using government subsidies to encourage pollution reduction and prevention and resource-conserving activities and selling marketable permits for resource

extraction

- educating people to understand and value the earth's life-sustaining processes for present and future generations and for all species; follow the advice given by a Chinese poet in 500 B.C.: "If you are thinking a year ahead, sow a seed. If you are thinking ten years ahead, plant a tree. If you are thinking a hundred years ahead, educate the people."
- increasing aid from rich countries to poor countries that helps LDCs become more self-reliant rather than more dependent on MDCs (since 1982 the traditional flow of capital from MDCs to LDCs has been reversed, with more than $43 billion annually transferred to MDCs from LDCs mostly to pay interest on their massive debt; this causes such countries to deplete their ecological capital even faster to pay the interest and the debt)
- eliminating much of the trillion dollar debt that LDCs owe to MDCs and international lending agencies through a combination of debt forgiveness and debt-for-nature swaps in which debts are forgiven in exchange for countries agreeing to set aside and use areas as wilderness or for sustainable development (Figure 13-25, p. 311)

Determines progress with indicators that measure

- changes in the quality of life
- sustainable use of renewable resources
- recycling and reuse of nonrenewable resources

---

that all projects and regulations will be executed with 100% efficiency and effectiveness

- open such evaluations to public review and challenge

A Sustainable-Earth Economy Conservationists and a few economists, including Herman Daly, Kenneth Boulding (see Guest Essay on p. 152), and Nicholas Georgescu-Roegen, have proposed that the world's countries make a transition to a **sustainable-earth economy** (see Spotlight on p. 584 and Guest Essay below).

They believe that in its present form, the industrial economy is not a sustainable economy because it is based on depleting and degrading the earth's natural capital. We are running up a massive earth debt—the ultimate debt—that can't be ignored any longer. They call for us to move from an earth-plundering economy to a more sustainable ecological economy.

They see the processes that sustain the earth as the best model for any human economy. The earth's processes use, conserve, and recycle resources with virtually no waste and with far greater efficiency and productivity than any economy we have invented.

Making a transition to such a new economic order is not a utopian dream. In fact, two highly respected international bodies have moved to incorporate such ideas in their work. In 1987 the World Commission on Environment and Development published a report entitled *Our Common Future*. The commission stated

The time has come to break out of our past patterns. . . . Economics and ecology must be completely integrated in decision-making and in lawmaking processes. . . . This integration would

be best secured by decentralizing the management of resources upon which local communities depend, and giving all those communities an effective say over the use of these resources.

Also, the World Health Organization has urged local communities to recycle more of their flows of food, energy, materials, and waste and to get more of their matter and energy resource needs from local sources. The more this is done the more each community will be able to keep its money circulating within its boundaries and the more self-reliant and healthy it will be.

According to the Worldwatch Institute, making the transition to a sustainable-earth economy will cost about $150 billion a year—about one-sixth of the world's annual military budget—over the next decade. The reward will be a sustainable resource base and a stable global economy.

Doing this will require government intervention into the marketplace using policies and laws that integrate economics and ecology (Chapter 23). But the necessary political intervention into the marketplace won't happen unless enough people adopt a sustainable-earth worldview (Chapter 24) and live their lives and base their consumption patterns on this understanding of how the world works. This begins with the realization that the most important things that sustain us and other creatures cannot be assigned a dollar value.

There is something fundamentally wrong in treating the earth as if it were a business in liquidation.

Herman E. Daly

GUEST ESSAY **The Steady State Economy in Outline**

Herman E. Daly

Herman E. Daly is currently Senior Environmental Economist at the World Bank. He is also Alumni Professor of Economics at Louisiana State University. He has been a member of the Committee on Mineral Resources and

Environment of the National Academy of Sciences and has served on the boards of advisors of numerous environmental organizations. He is also co-editor of the journal Environmental Economics *(Elsevier). His interest in economic development, population, resources, and environment has resulted in some 75 professional articles, as well as four books including* Steady-State Economics *(Freeman, 1977),* Economics, Ecology, Ethics *(Freeman, 1980), and* Economics for Community *(with John Cobb, Beacon Press, 1989). He is one of a small number of economists seriously thinking about sustainable-earth economics.*

The steady state economy is basically a physical concept with important social and moral implications. It is defined as a constant stock of physical wealth and people. This wealth and population size is maintained at some desirable, chosen level by a low rate of

(continued)

throughput of matter and energy resources so the longevity of people and goods is high.

Throughput is roughly equivalent to GNP, the annual flow of new production. It is the cost of maintaining the stocks of goods and services by continually importing high-quality matter and energy resources from the environment and exporting waste matter and low-quality heat energy back to the environment (Figure 3-18, p. 71).

Currently we attempt to maximize the growth of the gross GNP. But the reasoning just given suggests that we should relabel it gross national cost or GNC. We should minimize it, subject to maintenance of a chosen level of stocks of essential items. For example, if we can maintain a desired, self-sufficient stock of items such as cars with a lower throughput of iron, coal, petroleum, and other resources, we are better off, not worse off.

To maximize GNP throughput for its own sake is absurd. Physical and ecological limits to the volume of throughput imply the eventual necessity of a steady state economy. Less recognizable but probably more stringent social and moral limits imply the desirability of a steady state economy long before it becomes a physical necessity.

For example, the development and use of nuclear reactors to produce electricity is heavily subsidized by the government. Since the mid-1970s the growth of this technology has declined sharply. This decline is not due to a shortage of uranium fuel. Instead it is due to social and economic limits. Poor management, excessive costs, and serious accidents such as the one at the Chernobyl nuclear plant have seriously undermined public support of this technology.

These plants exist only because of massive government subsidies. If the nuclear power industry was forced to operate in an open market without government subsidies, it would probably not be developed because of too low an economic return on the investment. Attempts to revive the nuclear industry by providing more subsidies based on the argument that nuclear power is needed to reduce the rate of global warming will further waste massive amounts of limited economic and human resources and do little to slow global warming compared to other more cost-effective alternatives (see Pro/Con on p. 405).

Once we have attained a steady state economy at some level of stocks, we are not forever frozen at that level. Moral and technological changes may make it both possible and desirable to grow (or decline) to a different level. But growth will be seen as a temporary process necessary to move from one steady state level to another, not as an economic norm. This requires a substantial shift in present economic thought. It will require that most current economic ideas and models be replaced or drastically modified. Most economists strongly resist this radical change in the way they think and act.

The major challenges facing us today are

- For physical and biological scientists to define more clearly the limits and interactions within ecosystems and the ecosphere (which determine the feasible levels of the steady state) and to develop technologies more in conformity with such limits,
- For social scientists to design the institutions that will bring about the transition to a steady state and permit its continuance, and
- For philosophers, theologians, and educators to stress the neglected traditions of stewardship and distributive justice that exist in our cultural and religious heritage.

The latter is of paramount importance because the problem of sharing a fixed amount of resources and goods is much greater than that of sharing a growing amount. Indeed, this has been the major reason for giving top priority to growth. If the pie is always growing there will be crumbs for the poor. This avoids the moral question of a more equitable distribution of the world's resources and wealth.

The kinds of economic institutions needed to make this transition follow directly from the definition of a steady state economy. We need an institution for maintaining a constant population size within the limits of available resources. For example, economic incentives can be used to encourage each woman or couple to have no more than a certain number of children. Or each woman or couple could be given a marketable license to have a certain number of children, as economist Kenneth Boulding has suggested.

We also need an institution for maintaining a constant stock of physical wealth and limiting resource throughput. For example, the government could set and auction off transferable annual depletion quotas for key resources. Finally, there must be an institution to limit inequalities in the distribution of the constant physical wealth among the constant population in a steady state economy. For example, there might be minimum and maximum limits on personal income and maximum limits on personal wealth.

Many such institutions could be imagined. The problem is to achieve the necessary global and societal (macro) control with the least sacrifice of freedom at the individual (micro) level.

Guest Essay Discussion

1. Does a steady state economy imply the end of technological growth? Explain.

2. Why does the concept of the steady state economy force us to face up to the moral issue of the distribution of wealth?

3. Should minimum and maximum limits on personal income and wealth be established? Explain.

CHAPTER SUMMARY

The basic economic problem is that we cannot use the world's limited resources to produce enough material goods and services to satisfy everyone's unlimited wants. Therefore, individuals, businesses, and societies must make *economic decisions* about what goods and services to produce, how to produce them, how much to produce, and how to distribute them. Because producing and using anything has some harmful impact on the environment, economic decisions also affect the quality of the environment.

Any material item or service that gives people satisfaction and whose present or ultimate supply is limited is an *economic good*. The natural resources, capital or intermediate goods, and labor used in an economy to produce material goods and services are called *economic resources* or *factors of production*.

There are four major types of economic systems that a group of people use to choose what goods and services to produce, how to produce them, how much to produce, and how to distribute them to people: *traditional* (past custom decides), *pure market* (the market decides), *pure command* (the government decides), and *mixed* (various combinations of the other three systems). Virtually all nations have some form of mixed economic system.

Economic growth is an increase in the real value of all final goods and services produced by an economy. It is measured by an increase in the *real gross national product (real GNP)*—the market value in current dollars of all final goods and services produced by an economy during a year adjusted for inflation. In other words, it is an increase in real GNP. To show how the average person's slice of the economic pie is changing, economists calculate the *average per capita real GNP:* the real GNP divided by the total population.

Although these indicators do not and were never intended to measure social welfare or quality of life, they are widely used in this way. These indicators include the values of both beneficial and harmful goods and services, don't indicate how resources and income are distributed among the people in a country, and don't include the depletion of natural resources and ecological services upon which ultimately all economies depend. Conservationists urge that other currently available indicators that include these factors be widely used.

In making or using anything, there are direct internal *costs* paid for by the seller and buyer of an economic good. There are also *external costs* not included in the market price of an economic good that are passed on to society and in some cases to future generations. Examples of such external costs are environmental pollution and resource depletion and degradation.

A general way to deal with the problem of external costs is for the government to force producers to include all or most of them in the market price of all economic goods. When external costs are internalized the market price of an economic good becomes its *true cost:* its internal costs plus its short- and long-term external costs.

There are four ways that governments can intervene in the marketplace to improve environmental quality and reduce resource waste: **(1)** make harmful actions illegal, **(2)** penalize harmful actions, **(3)** sell rights to produce certain acceptable levels of pollution and to use certain amounts of resources, and **(4)** use tax dollars to reward or subsidize beneficial actions by individuals and businesses. The first three are *polluter-or-resource-waster-pays* approaches that internalize some or most external costs of pollution and resource waste. The fourth approach is a *taxpayer-pays* approach that does little to internalize external costs.

Cost-benefit analysis is widely used to evaluate economic choices. It involves estimating the short-term and long-term costs (losses) and benefits (gains) of an economic decision. The assumptions made in such analyses are a major source of disagreement between conservationists and business people. A serious limitation of cost-benefit analysis is that many things we value—such as human life, clean air and water, a wilderness area, and the ability of natural systems to degrade and recycle some of our wastes and replenish renewable resources—cannot be reduced to dollars and cents. Therefore, there is a built-in bias to undervalue them so that they are depleted or degraded.

Most conservationists and environmentalists and some economists believe that in its present form, the industrial economy is not a sustainable economy in the long run because it is based on depleting and degrading the earth's natural capital. They call for a transition to a *sustainable-earth economy* that uses economic and political systems to discourage harmful types of economic growth and encourages other types to prevent overloading and degradation of the earth's life-support systems now and in the future.

DISCUSSION TOPICS

1. Some economists argue that only by increasing economic growth will we have enough money to eliminate poverty and protect the environment. Explain why you agree or disagree with this view. If you disagree, how should we deal with these problems?

2. Do you believe that cost-benefit analysis should be used to make all decisions about how limited federal, state, and local government funds are to be used? Explain. If not, what decisions should not be made in this w[ay]? How should these decisions be made?

3. What are the major advantages and disadvantage[s of] the present mixed economic system in the Unite[d] States? What major changes, if any, would you m[ake in] this system?

4. What are the major advantages and disadvantage[s of a] sustainable-earth economy? Do you favor makin[g a] gradual shift to such a system? Explain.

5. What good and bad effects would internalizing t[he] external costs of pollution and unnecessary reso[urce] waste have on the U.S. economy? Do you favor [doing] this? Explain. How might it affect your lifestyle? [The] lifestyle of the poor? Wildlife?

6. If you wanted to develop an index of gross national quality (GNQ), what specific items would you include?

7. What are the social and environmental costs associated with **(a)** smoking cigarettes, **(b)** driving a car, and **(c)** living or working in an air-conditioned building? Do you believe that the benefits outweigh the costs in each case? Explain.

CHAPTER 23

Politics and Environment

General Questions and Issues

1. How can political systems be used to regulate resource use and reduce environmental degradation and pollution?
2. How are environmental and resource laws and policies made in the United States?
3. What are some of the major achievements of environmental law in the United States?
4. What political actions can you take to help sustain the earth?

A technological society has two choices. First, it can wait until catastrophic failures expose systemic deficiencies, distortions, and self-deceptions. . . . Second, a culture can provide social checks and balances to correct for systemic distortions prior to catastrophic failures.

Mahatma Gandhi

Politics is concerned with the distribution of resources in an orderly fashion. Because resources such as food, water, air, land, minerals, and energy are provided by the ecosphere through the efforts of people, politics—like economics (Figure 22-4, p. 574)—rests on an ecological foundation.

Public politics is the process by which individuals and groups try to influence or control the policies and actions of governments of the local, state, national, or international community. Public politics is concerned with the distribution of resources and benefits—who gets what, when, and how. Thus, it plays a major role in regulating the world's economic systems and influencing economic decisions. Public political decisions can also help prevent the degradation of commonly owned or shared resources such as air, water, wildlife, and public land.

23-1 INFLUENCING PUBLIC ENVIRONMENTAL AND RESOURCE POLICY

Groups Involved in Influencing Public Policy Decisions about environmental and resource use policies are influenced by a mixture of governmental and nongovernmental organizations operating at the global, regional, national, and subnational (state and local) levels (Table 23-1).

At the global level the United Nations plays an important role in highlighting global and regional environmental and resource problems and in negotiating solutions and treaties. Major efforts began in 1972 when the UN sponsored the Stockholm Conference on the Human Environment. The government delegates to this conference agreed on a number of principles concerning the environment, which are expressed in the Declaration on the Human Environment, and recommended that the General Assembly establish the UN Environment Program (UNEP).

Since its formation in 1972 the UNEP has made substantial contributions to the development and use of sustainable development. The UN has also sponsored a number of international conferences designed to increase awareness and establish action plans for various environmental and resource problems. These include conferences on population (Bucharest, 1974), food (Rome, 1974), women (Mexico City, 1974), human settlements (Vancouver, 1976), water (Mar del Plata, 1977), desertification (Nairobi, 1977), renewable energy (Nairobi, 1981), human environment (1982), law of the sea treaty negotiations (1973–1982), and the ozone layer (1987, 1989).

In 1976 the Man and the Biosphere Program (MAB) was established through the UN Educational, Scientific, and Cultural Organization (UNESCO). The goal of this program is to focus research, technical training, and public education on the need to know more about how the biosphere works. This program includes the

Table 23-1 Groups Influencing Environmental and Resource Use Public Policy

Levels	Governmental	Nongovernmental	
		Nonprofit	Profit Making
Global	Intergovernmental organizations such as the UN Food and Agriculture Organization, UN Environment Program, International Atomic Energy Agency	International Union for the Conservation of Nature and Natural Resources, Friends of the Earth, Greenpeace (see Appendix 1)	Mutinational businesses such as Dole, Mobil Oil, Mitsubishi
Regional	European Economic Community, Joint Commission on the Great Lakes (Canada and the United States)	European League for Economic Cooperation	Business operating in a region such as North America or the Mediterranean basin
National	National governments, agencies such as the U.S. Environmental Protection Agency and the U.S. Forest Service	American Forestry Association, Sierra Club, Natural Resources Defense Council (see Appendix 1)	Businesses operating within a country
Subnational	State and local governments and agencies	State and local citizen groups	Businesses operating within a state or local area

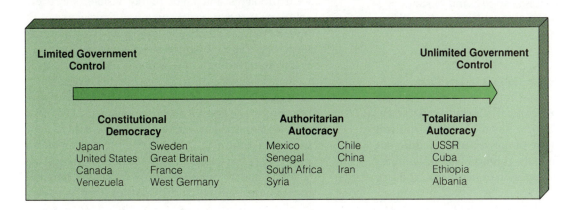

Figure 23-1 Current types of governments in selected countries.

Biosphere Reserve Program with the goal of establishing, protecting, and studying reserves representing several examples of each of the earth's ecosystems.

Basic Functions and Types of National Governments

The basic functions of governments are protection against external and internal enemies, enforcement of law and order, economic management, and cultural reinforcement of shared beliefs. Elites, the relatively few people who form the groups who have power, not the masses, govern all societies. But governments differ in the way elites carry out the major functions of government. There are two broad types of government:

- *Constitutional democracy* in which an effective constitution provides the basis of governmental authority and restraints on governmental power through free elections and freely expressed public opinion. A democracy is government "by the people" through elected elites who are supposed to follow a constitution.

- *Autocracy* in which governmental power is concentrated in a self-authorized, self-directing, self-perpetuating elite. In an *authoritarian autocracy* the ruling elite allow individuals and societal groups significant independent activity as long as such activity does not threaten the power or policies of the ruling elite. In a *totalitarian autocracy* nothing is permitted unless it is specifically authorized by the ruling elite.

Figure 23-1 shows the general types of governments in selected countries today. The major mechanism for change in autocratic governments is for the people or some portion of the government (often military leaders) to overthrow the ruling elite and establish a new governing elite.

Constitutional democracies are run by elected elites drawn largely from the upper socioeconomic strata of society. These government officials are strongly influenced by other elites running corporations, the media, educational institutions, and other organized special interest groups. Individuals and organized groups influence and change government policies in constitutional democracies mainly by

- voting

- contributing money and time to candidates running for office

- lobbying and writing elected representatives to pass certain laws, establish certain policies, and fund various programs (see Enrichment Study on p. 606)

- using the formal education system and the media to influence public opinion

- filing lawsuits asking the courts to overturn, enforce, or interpret the meaning of existing laws

- carrying out nonviolent demonstrations such as marches, mass meetings, sit-ins, and blocking logging trucks and entrances to nuclear power plants

- rioting

Reaction-to-Crisis Public Politics in Democracies

Political systems in constitutional democracies are designed to bring about gradual or incremental change, not revolutionary change. Rapid change is difficult because of distribution of power among different branches of government, conflicts among interest groups, conflicting information from experts, and lack of money.

Because there is always competition for scarce resources to satisfy unlimited wants, decision makers in democratic governments must deal with an array of conflicting groups. Each special-interest group is asking for resources or money or relief from taxes to help purchase or control more of certain resources. Interest groups that are highly organized and well funded usually have the most influence.

Because tax income is limited, developing and adopting a budget is the most important thing decision makers do. This involves answering two key questions: What resource use and distribution problems will be addressed? How much of limited tax income will be used to address each problem? Someone once said that the way to understand human history is to study budgets.

Politics has been called the *art of compromise*—finding ways to balance competing interests. Most political decisions are made by bargaining, accommodation, and compromise between leaders of competing elites within a society. Most politicians who remain in power become good at finding compromises and making trade-offs that give a little to each side. They play an important role in holding society together, preventing chaos and disorder, and making incremental changes.

Politicians would like to solve problems with *win-win solutions*, where everyone comes out ahead. But most political decisions about resource distribution are *win-lose situations*, in which some people benefit and some are hurt (see Case Studies on pp. 16 and 524).

For example, suppose the government bans the use of high-sulfur coal in electric power plants in the United States to reduce the harmful effects of acid deposition. This will benefit people, forests, and streams and lakes in the eastern United States and southeastern Canada. But coal miners in West Virginia, Illinois, Pennsylvania, and other states where high-sulfur coal is mined will be out of work. They and their families will suffer hardship from this political decision.

Successful politicians usually practice *pressure-and-crisis politics*. To stay in power, they focus on short-term problems and favor highly visible, short-term solutions that may make some problems worse in the future. Politicians who call for the public to make short-term sacrifices in the interests of projected long-term gains often find it hard to win or hold office.

For example, suppose a presidential candidate ran on a platform calling for the federal tax on gasoline to be raised to the point where gasoline would cost about three dollars a gallon—an approach now used in many European countries. The candidate argues that this tax raise is necessary to encourage conservation of oil and gasoline and to enhance future economic, environmental, and military security. Would you vote for a candidate who promises to triple the price of gasoline?

Elected representatives have great difficulty in dealing with long-range problems. Like the rest of us, they are usually overwhelmed with a multitude of daily problems, stresses, and pressures that must be dealt with now. It is easy to say that elected officials should take the long range into account, but this is far easier said than done.

In the United States, the term of a representative is only two years, the president four, and a senator's six. Those hoping to get reelected must devote much of their time and energy during the last year of their term to this task. Thus, you can see why the time horizon is only about one year for a representative, three years for a president, and five years for a senator. Yet, preventing or dealing with most of the environmental, economic, and social problems we face today requires a time horizon of 10 to 50 years.

Business leaders can take a longer view, but many don't. Why? Because far too often their salary, bonuses, and jobs are tied to the profits made during the past

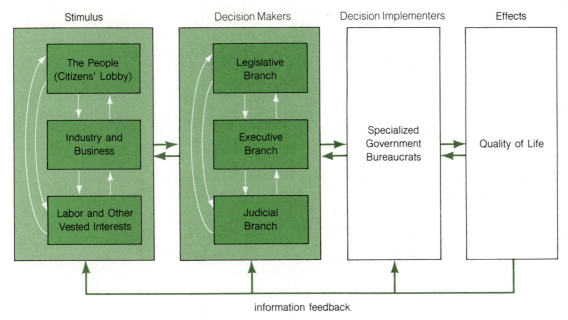

Figure 23-2 Crude model of the U.S. political system.

year. Focusing on this year's economic bottom line is a major driving force behind resource depletion, environmental degradation, and pollution through resistance to including the external costs of goods and services in their market prices (Sections 22-3 and 22-4). But all other bottom lines are irrelevant if we don't build our actions around the earth's bottom line of natural capital that supports all life and economic activity (Figure 22-4, p. 574).

23-2 ENVIRONMENTAL AND RESOURCE POLICY IN THE UNITED STATES

Structure and Major Tools of the Government The writers of the U.S. Constitution wanted to develop a political system strong enough to provide security and order and to protect liberty and property but without giving too much power to the federal government. This was done by dividing political power between the federal and state governments and within the three branches of the federal government—legislative, executive, and judicial (Figure 23-2). These branches are connected and controlled by a series of checks and balances to prevent one branch from gaining too much power. Once federal laws are passed, they are supposed to be implemented and enforced by various bureaucratic agencies in the executive branch of the federal government (Figure 23-3) and by delegation of certain responsibilities to state governments.

The federal government influences the economy, regulates resource use, protects the environment, and helps the poor by using several major devices:

- *establishing monetary policy:* putting more or less money into the economy by controlling the amount of money printed and influencing the supply of credit by raising or lowering the interest rate

- *passing statutory laws:* passing laws that regulate various industries, encourage some types of resource use, and discourage other types of resource use, tax undesirable resource use, and provide subsidies for desirable forms of resource use (Table 22-2, p. 582)

- *establishing fiscal policy:* establishing income and other taxes and deciding what programs will be funded by tax revenues and how much each program will receive

The last two devices are also the major tools used by state and local governments.

Major Factors in Federal Environmental Policy Making Actions that affect environmental quality and resource use are controlled by an elaborate network of laws and regulations at the federal, state, and local levels. Figure 23-4 summarizes the major forces involved in environmental policy making at the federal level. The first step in establishing environmental or other policies is to persuade lawmakers that a problem exists and that the government has a responsibility to find solutions to the problem. This must be accomplished by a combination of public concern, media coverage, and scientific and economic judgements (Figure 23-4).

Once this hurdle is passed lawmakers try to pass laws to deal with the problem (Figure 23-5). Most pro-

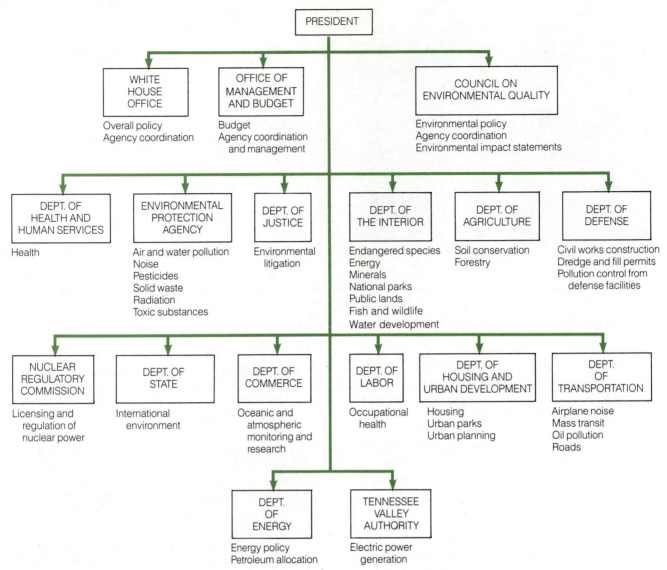

Figure 23-3 Major agencies of the executive branch of the federal government with responsibilities for environmental protection and resource management. (Data from U.S. General Accounting Office)

posed environmental laws are evaluated by as many as ten committees in each chamber because no single committee has complete responsibility for all environmental issues. Effective proposals are inevitably weakened by this fragmentation and the accompanying intense pressure and lobbying from groups supporting or opposing the law.

The end result is usually a compromise that satisfies no one but muddles through, mostly by making short-term incremental changes. Even if a tough environmental law is passed, the next hurdle is to see that Congress appropriates enough funds to see that the law is adequately enforced (Figure 23-5). Often environmental laws contain glowing rhetoric about goals but only vague, unrealistic, or indirect guidance about how these goals are to be achieved. The details of

implementation are left up to a regulatory agency such as the EPA and the courts.

Almost every major environmental regulation is challenged in court, as discussed in Section 23-3. Some suits charge that the law is unconstitutional. Others charge the regulatory agency with exceeding its authority in administering the law, not following the law, or misinterpreting the law.

U.S. Environmental Legislation Environmentalists, with backing from many other citizens and members of Congress, have pressured Congress to enact a number of important federal environmental and resource protection laws, as discussed throughout this text and listed in Appendix 3. Similar laws, and in some cases even stronger laws, have been passed by most states.

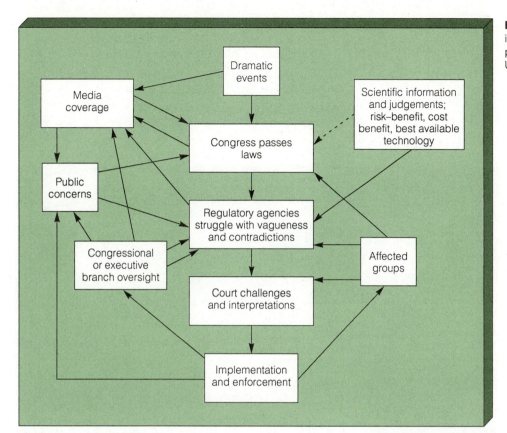

Figure 23-4 Major forces involved in making environmental policy at the federal level in the United States.

These laws attempt to provide environmental protection using five major approaches:

1. setting pollution level standards or limiting emissions or effluents for various classes of pollutants: Federal Water Pollution Control Act and the Clean Air Act

2. screening new substances before they are widely used in order to determine their safety: Toxic Substances Control Act of 1976

3. requiring a comprehensive evaluation of the environmental impact of an activity before it is undertaken: National Environmental Policy Act (see Case Study on p. 595)

4. setting aside or protecting various ecosystems, resources, or species from harm: Wilderness Act and Endangered Species Act

5. encouraging resource conservation: Resource Conservation and Recovery Act and National Energy Act

A major problem with the present approach to environmental laws is that they treat environmental and resource problems in isolation. In nature, environmental and resource problems interact through processes taking place in the atmosphere, hydrosphere, lithosphere, and biosphere. This explains why treating these problems in piecemeal fashion may solve a problem in one part of the ecosphere but intensify a problem in another part of the ecosphere. Every-

thing is intermingled. To help correct this situation the Conservation Foundation has drafted a "model" law, called the Environmental Protection Act, which attempts to develop an integrated approach to environmental protection in the United States.

Implementing Environmental Laws The Environmental Protection Agency, created by administrative reorganization in 1970, has the responsibility for enforcing most federal environmental laws, for administering the Superfund to clean up abandoned toxic waste sites, and for awarding grants for local sewage treatment plants. These laws give the EPA broad powers, including the imposition of jail terms for criminal pollution violations and fines of up to $25,000 a day for polluters, and the power to sue almost any U.S. citizen or company for violation of antipollution laws. Laws governing the use of national forests, wilderness areas, wildlife refuges, and other public lands are enforced by the managing departments (Interior and Agriculture) working through the Department of Justice.

However, responsibility for managing the nation's environmental and resource policy is widely fragmented among many different agencies within the executive branch of the federal government (Figure 23-3) and among state agencies. This often leads to contradictory policies, duplicated efforts, and wasted funds, while prohibiting an effective integrated approach to interrelated problems.

Typically Congress guides regulatory agencies by specifying general mechanisms for setting regulations. Examples are:

- *no unreasonable risk:* food regulations in the Food, Drug, and Cosmetic Act (Section 18-5)

- *no-risk:* the Delaney clause for food additives (see Pro/Con on p. 469) and the goals of the Safe Drinking Water Act and the Clean Water Act

- *risk-benefit balancing* (Section 18-3): pesticide regulations (see Spotlight on p. 558)

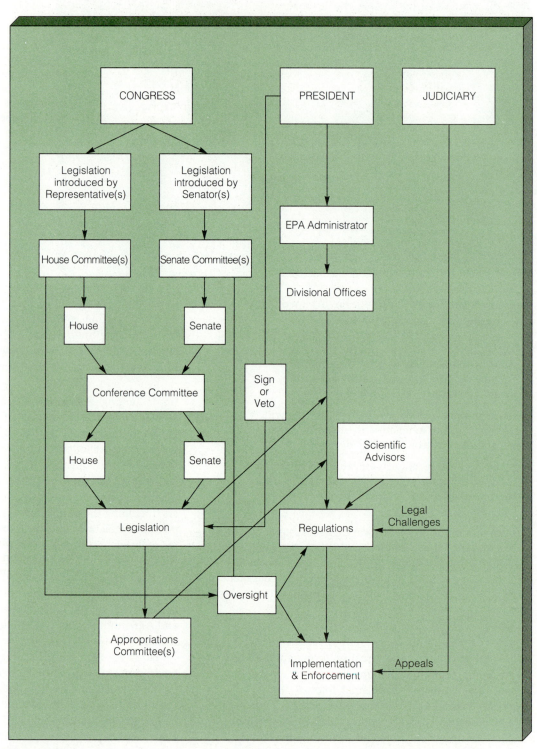

Figure 23-5 Interaction of the branches of the federal government involved in environmental laws and regulations.

- *standards based on best available technology:* Clean Air Act, Clean Water Act, and Safe Drinking Water Act

- *cost-benefit balancing* (Section 22-4): Toxic Substances Control Act and Executive Order 12291, which gives the Office of Management and Bud-

get the power to delay indefinitely, and in some cases veto, any federal regulation that is not proved to have the least cost to society

A regulatory agency such as the EPA should establish a firm scientific base for pollution control regu-

---

CASE STUDY NEPA and Environmental Impact Statements

One important environmental law is the National Environmental Policy Act of 1969 (NEPA). This landmark legislation declared that the federal government has a responsibility to restore and maintain environmental quality. One section of this law, designed to put this policy into action, requires that all federal agencies (except the EPA) file an *environmental impact statement (EIS)* or an *Environmental Assessment (EA)* for any proposed legislation or project having a significant effect on environmental quality. Environmental assessments are prepared for projects with minimal environmental impacts, and more comprehensive environmental impact statements are prepared for those that an agency views as having significant environmental impacts.

A draft environmental impact statement must be made public for review by the EPA, other appropriate federal, state, and local agencies, and the general public at least 90 days before a proposed action. A final statement, incorporating all comments and objections to the draft statement, must be made public at least 30 days before the proposed action is undertaken. Each environmental impact statement must include:

1. the purpose and need for the proposed action
2. the probable environmental impacts (positive, negative, direct, and indirect) of the proposed action and of possible alternatives, including doing nothing
3. any adverse environmental effects that could not be

avoided should the project be implemented
4. relationships between the probable short-term and long-term impacts of the proposal on environmental quality
5. irreversible and irretrievable commitments of resources that would be involved should the project be implemented
6. objections raised by reviewers of the preliminary draft of the statement
7. the names and qualifications of the people primarily responsible for preparing the EIS
8. references to back up all statements and conclusions

Each year about 10,000 environmental assessments and several hundred environmental impact statements are filed by federal agencies. The EPA serves as a central clearinghouse for the review process. If the EPA determines that a proposal is "unsatisfactory from the standpoint of public health or welfare or environmental quality," the agency must make this determination public. Often the EPA uses consultation and negotiation to resolve conflicts. If this fails to meet the EPA's concerns, the agency may refer the matter to the Council on Environmental Quality, which oversees the executive branch's implementation of NEPA, for resolution.

For example, in the spring of 1986 the Department of Agriculture proposed that outbreaks of grasshoppers on public rangelands be controlled by spraying with three pesticides: malathion, Carbyl, and acephate. The agency prepared an environmental impact

statement for the project and submitted it to review by the EPA.

EPA reviewers recognized the need for grasshopper control but expressed concerns that the three pesticides to be used had the potential for contaminating surface waters, threatening wildlife (especially endangered species), and contaminating the meat of cattle feeding on the sprayed forage. They asked the Department of Agriculture to consider using integrated pest management (Section 21-5) as an alternative, including the use of nontoxic biological pest control.

The first major step in this reevaluation was the appointment of an interagency scientific and technical committee. It included representatives from the EPA, the Department of Agriculture, the Department of Interior, the U.S. Forest Service, the Bureau of Land Management, the Fish and Wildlife Service, the Agricultural Research Service, and the National Park Service.

After considerable study, consultation, and negotiation the Department of Agriculture agreed to develop a new EIS in 1987 that included evaluation of alternatives to pesticides. The program's managers also decided to establish a five-year, multi-agency, 40,500 hectare (100,000-acre) demonstration and research project to examine the potential of integrated pest management techniques for grasshopper control.

Having to prepare EAs or EISs has forced government agencies to think more seriously about the effects of proposed projects and in (continued)

lations. But in practice this is a difficult, time-consuming, expensive and controversial process (Section 18-1). The EPA is responsible for implementing a range of environmental laws with limited resources so that priorities must be set. Ideally, these priorities should be based on items that pose the greatest risk to the largest number of people. But often priorities are dominated by short-term, dramatic events that attract the attention of the public and elected officials. This can cause the agency to use its limited funds for "firefighting" dramatic problems rather than establishing a solid base of regulations based on risk priorities.

For example, EPA experts rate indoor air pollution (especially radon) and hazardous outdoor air pollutants as having a high health risk and active and inactive hazardous waste sites and radioactive waste as having a low to medium risk. But the public perceives hazardous waste sites and radioactive waste as having a very high risk and indoor air pollution and hazardous outdoor air pollution as having a moderate to low risk.

Enforcement of Environmental Laws and Conflict Resolution
When environmental laws are violated regulators must decide whether to take the violators to court or try to resolve the dispute through negotiation. The latter approach is usually quicker and cheaper for government agencies. It is also widely used to resolve conflicts over policy between different policymaking government agencies. There are several different types of conflict resolution:

- *Conflict anticipation:* Identification of potential disputes before a project gets under way and opposing positions are solidified.

- *Joint problem solving:* Bringing together interested parties to clarify issues and resolve differences through informal agreements.

- *Mediation:* Formal negotiations between representatives of both sides of a dispute with a third party serving as a mediator to facilitate but not impose a settlement.

- *Policy dialogues:* Interagency advisory committees or meetings between representatives of different government agencies to resolve policy conflicts between agencies.

- *Binding arbitration:* Each party in a dispute presents formal arguments to an arbitrator who imposes settlement that the parties have agreed to abide by.

State Governments
The U.S. Constitution distributes power between national and federal governments. Over time, however, more of the country's political power has become centralized in Washington. Federal grants now provide more than 20% of all state and local revenue.

Before 1972 most federal laws established general environmental goals and provided research, technical assistance, and funding for states to carry out the programs. Since 1972, however, as new problems have arisen and progress has sometimes lagged federal laws have been more specific. Some have established federal environmental standards and compulsory deadlines for states and localities to meet certain environmental goals.

In most cases states have modelled their environmental and resource conservation laws after federal laws and established environmental and state agen-

---

CASE STUDY NEPA and Environmental Impact Statements (continued)

many cases to consider and develop alternatives more carefully. Despite its many successes, the EIS process has been abused in some cases. Problems include

- Using an EIS to justify a decision that has already been made rather than to make it a key part of the decision making process.

- Trying to avoid the process by filing a Finding of Insignificant Impact statement denying that a given project will have a significant environmental impact.

- Reporting impacts in such general terms (for example, "loss of wildlife," "elimination of vegeta-

tion," "increase in turbidity") that they are meaningless.

- Filling documents with massive amounts of irrelevant or highly technical information to obscure serious impacts, overwhelm reviewers, and absorb the limited time and funds of the EPA and public citizen environmental and conservation groups.

- Using the process to delay and raise the costs of legitimate projects. For example, the Pentagon proposed closing a Nebraska air base to save money. But local residents wanted to keep it open and demanded that an environmental impact statement be filed

before any action was taken. Then when the Pentagon prepared an EIS local residents challenged it in court. This kept an expensive and unnecessary base in operation for three years or so before the courts ruled it could be shut down.

Today 36 states also have laws or executive orders requiring environmental impact statements for state projects. Australia, Canada, France, Ireland, New Zealand, Sweden, and several other countries also require environmental impact statements for projects carried out by government agencies.

cies similar to those at the federal level. Because of local or state-wide problems, public pressure, and lack of action at the federal level, some states have initiated solid waste, noise control, groundwater protection, coastal zone management, land use, and other programs on their own. Some of these state programs such as coastal zone management are partially funded by the federal government. Other states, such as California, have adopted air pollution laws and standards that are more stringent than those at the federal level.

Each year an environmental organization, *Renew America* (see Appendix 1), publishes a report summarizing and rating the states on various aspects of environmental protection and resource conservation. The 1988 and 1989 state winners in the categories evaluated were:

- Forest management: Washington (1989)
- Surface water protection: North Carolina (1988)
- Drinking water protection: Maine (1989)
- Reducing pesticide contamination: California (1988)
- Food safety: Iowa (1989)
- Land-use planning and growth management: Oregon (1988 and 1989)
- Solid waste recycling: Oregon (1989)
- Eliminating indoor pollution: New Jersey (1988)
- Highway safety: Maryland (1988)
- Energy pollution control: Massachusetts (1988)

Local Governments The federal government and state governments use much of the revenues they raise from taxes to influence local government policies. Elites running local governments typically concern themselves primarily with increasing local economic growth. These elites are usually dominated by banks, builders, large land owners, and real estate developers who benefit directly from increasing the value of land. Members of local elites make major use of zoning and other forms of land use management (Section 9-5). Usually they mobilize public support for local economic growth policies by promising more jobs or the need to protect existing jobs.

However, a few communities such as Davis, California (see Case Study on p. 209) have emphasized sustainable development and ecological land-use planning (see Spotlight on p. 205). Some communities have also used zoning to protect open space and agricultural land. Others have restricted growth by requiring that a certain amount of land in a development project be kept as open space and by limiting the spread of water lines and sewer hookups.

Hundreds of communities have developed recycling programs for economic and environmental reasons (see Guest Essay on p. 372). Some local governments have also developed successful programs to improve energy efficiency, rely more on locally available energy resources, and keep the dollars saved circulating in the local economy (p. 446).

Most local governments, however, still pursue programs emphasizing unsustainable economic development and wasteful uses of the matter, energy, and economic resources. Changing this is an important key to improving local environmental and economic security. This can be brought about by local citizens organizing and acting to protect and improve the environment where they live.

23-3 ENVIRONMENTAL LAW

Some Principles of Environmental Law There are two types of laws: statutory and common. A **statutory law** is one passed by a state legislature or Congress. Environmental laws, many of which are listed in Appendix 3, govern how the environment and human health should be protected and how resources are to be managed. Many of these laws have been discussed throughout this book. **Common law**, a large body of unwritten principles and rules based on thousands of past legal decisions, is used by judges to resolve disputes in the absence of applicable statutory law.

In any court case the **plaintiff** is the individual, group of individuals, corporation, or government agency bringing the charges, and the **defendant** is the individual, group of individuals, corporation, or government agency being charged. Civil and class action suits are the major types of lawsuits used in environmental law. In a **civil suit**, the plaintiff seeks to collect damages for injuries to health or for economic loss, have the court issue a permanent injunction against any further wrongful action, or both. In this case the plaintiff makes a civil complaint alleging that he or she has been harmed by the defendant. If the court decides that harm has occurred, it orders the defendant to pay the plaintiff to offset the damage and may also issue an injunction forbidding any further harm. Such suits may be brought by an individual plaintiff or a group of clearly identified plaintiffs.

Another type of civil suit is the **class action suit**, in which a group, often a public interest or environmental group such as the Environmental Defense Fund, the Natural Resources Defense Council, or the Sierra Club, files a suit on behalf of a larger number of citizens who allege similar damages but who need not be listed and represented individually. The class, for example, might consist of all people who worked in a certain chemical plant between certain dates when pollution was known to have caused a number of illnesses. A public notice of the intention to file the class action suit is published in a local newspaper. Unless people who believe they are in the class request that they be excluded from the suit, they are automatically included in the class and the lawsuit.

Environmental groups specializing in environmental law have a professional staff with legal and scientific expertise and can obtain help from outside experts on the often complex issues involved in environmental cases. This allows them to carry out a more evenly matched legal contest against large corporations and government agencies.

Problems with Environmental Lawsuits   To use the courts for a civil action the plaintiff must

- allege that an act forbidden by a specific law has been committed or that the plaintiff has suffered injuries to health or economic loss as a result of actions by the defendant

- file the complaint in the court that has jurisdiction over the alleged action

- demonstrate that he or she has standing—the right to bring the case to court

Then, of course, the plaintiff must prove that the actions of the accused caused the alleged damage. As in a criminal case, the accused is presumed innocent until proven guilty.

Unfortunately, there are problems with this procedure:

- A plaintiff may not have standing to file a suit against a defendant. Standing for damage suits is granted only if it is clear that the harm to an individual plaintiff is unique and different enough to be distinguished from that to the general public. For example, you could not sue the Department of the Interior for actions leading to the commercialization of a wilderness area on the grounds that you do not want your taxes used to bring about environmental harm. The harm to you could not be distinguished from that to the general public. However, if the government damaged property you own, you would have standing to sue.

- Bringing any suit is expensive. Often the defendant in an environmental suit is a large corporation or government agency with ample funds for legal and scientific advice. In contrast, the plaintiffs in such cases usually use volunteer legal and scientific talent and rely on donation. According to EPA employee and whistle-blower Hugh Kaufman, "The citizens are armed with rubber bands and chewing gum against major polluters armed with the best-paid engineers and lawyers in the country. It ain't a fair fight."

- It is often difficult for the plaintiff to prove that the accused is liable and responsible for a harmful action. Generally, the plaintiff must be able to **(1)** identify the harmful substance, **(2)** prove that identifiable damages occurred because of the pres-

ence of that substance, and **(3)** demonstrate that the substance came from the defendant. For example, suppose that one company is charged with bringing harm to individuals by polluting a river. If hundreds of other industries and cities dump waste into that river, establishing that the defendant company is the culprit will be very difficult, requiring extensive, costly scientific testing, research, and expert testimony.

- The court, or series of courts if the case is appealed, may take years to reach a decision. During this time, the defendant may continue the alleged damage unless the court issues a temporary injunction forbidding the allegedly harmful actions until the case is decided.

- With large-scale damage a plaintiff may win the case but not be able to collect awarded damages because the company may have gone into bankruptcy.

- Plaintiffs sometimes abuse the system by bringing frivolous suits that delay and run up the costs of legitimate projects

Despite these handicaps, proponents of environmental law have accomplished a great deal since the 1960s. Now there are more than 100 public interest law firms specializing partially or totally in environmental and consumer law, and hundreds of other lawyers and scientific experts participate in environmental and consumer law cases as needed. Major public interest law groups concerned with environmental issues include the Environmental Defense Fund, the Sierra Club's Legal Defense Fund, the National Resources Defense Council (see Case Study on p. 599), the Center for Science in the Public Interest, and others listed in Appendix 1.

Environmental and public interest lawyers and groups, however, are limited by lack of money. In 1976 environmental lawyers received a serious setback when the Supreme Court ruled that public interest law firms cannot recover attorneys' fees unless Congress has specifically authorized such recovery in the law they have sued to enforce.

23-4   WHAT CAN YOU DO?

Anticipatory Public Politics   Emphasis on short-term rewards is natural because no one knows what the future holds. "Take what you can get now and worry about the future later," we say. Psychologically we tend to choose small, but immediate rewards over a larger delayed rewards. We are usually driven to action only by dramatic events or sudden crises that have actually been building for a long time. But short-term, reaction-to-crisis politics is like putting a bunch of Band-Aids on a gaping wound and hoping they will hold.

For some things Band-Aids work. But in an interconnected world facing serious environmental and resource problems and potential nuclear annihilation, we need more than Band-Aids. *Perhaps the greatest challenge we face is to use or modify existing national political and economic systems to anticipate and prevent serious long-term problems, many of them global.*

The motivation for balancing short- and long-term interests may come from a rare type of political leader who has the vision and ability to inspire and mobilize people to see and take new paths. Throughout history key acts of political leadership have been those in which the seemingly impossible—or the highly improbable —is made possible.

To paraphrase George Bernard Shaw, "Some see things as they are and say why? I dream of things that never were and say why not?" These rare individuals practice *anticipatory public politics.* They try to change our institutions and individual actions to prevent anticipated crises. Or they react to crises in ways that may keep them from recurring.

President Abraham Lincoln did this when he led the country to abolish slavery. President Theodore Roosevelt led the first wave of resource conservation (Section 2-4). To many the most inspirational moral and political leader in this century was Mahatma Gandhi, who showed us how to bring about change by using nonviolent tactics.

Such leaders challenge and prod us to do more than we think we can. They bring out the best in us. This is also what a good teacher does. Such leaders and teachers may not always be appreciated or liked

---

CASE STUDY The Natural Resources Defense Council

The Natural Resources Defense Council (NRDC) was founded in 1970. Since then its teams of scientists, lawyers, and resource specialists have been working on critical environmental and resource problems. These efforts are supported by membership fees and contributions from about 100,000 individuals. The following are some of the many accomplishments of the NRDC:

■ 1973—compelled the EPA to establish regulations restricting lead additives in gasoline

■ 1975—forced the Nuclear Regulatory Commission to adopt tougher regulations for storage and disposal of radioactive wastes from uranium mining and processing (mill tailings)

■ 1976—led the successful fight to ban the use of chlorofluorocarbons (CFCs) in aerosol products

■ 1983—filed a lawsuit that forced the National Steel Company to comply with air pollution control laws and pay $2.5 million in back penalties; spearheaded a successful campaign to protect 40 million acres of fragile coastal areas in Florida, California, and Massachusetts from an offshore oil leasing program pushed by the Reagan administration

■ 1984—filed a lawsuit compelling oil refineries to tighten pollution control and reduce toxic discharges; won a Supreme Court case giving the public the right to obtain chemical industry data on the health effects of pesticides

■ 1985—led a coalition of citizen groups in successful negotiations with the chemical industry to strengthen safety provisions of the federal pesticide law; won an appeal against the U.S. Forest Service's 50-year management plans that would have increased environmentally damaging logging in four Colorado national forests

■ 1986—launched a history-making agreement with the Soviet Academy of Sciences that will allow scientists to monitor nuclear test sites in both countries; led negotiations with the oil industry to protect environmentally sensitive areas in Alaska's Bering Sea

■ 1987—won an environmental penalty of $1.5 million against the Bethlehem Steel Company for polluting the Chesapeake Bay; played a key role in promoting the International Ozone Treaty designed to cut worldwide use of CFCs at least 35% by the end of this century; years of lobbying led to new appliance energy-efficiency standards that will save energy equal to that of 40 large coal-fired or nuclear plants and 1.5 billion barrels of oil and natural gas; won a lawsuit on the disposal of radioactive waste from government and commercial nuclear facilities

■ 1988 and 1989—published a research study projecting increased cancer rates among preschool children from exposure to pesticides in their food (see Pro/Con on p. 556); pressured Congress to pass tough legislation to protect the ozone layer; filed a lawsuit to force the EPA to phase out all production and use of CFCs in the United States; mounted a consumer education and action program against CFC products; petitioned the President to declare 1989 as the "International Year of the Climate" and convene an International Summit Meeting of world leaders on global warming; lobbied Congress for legislation that would cut U.S. fossil fuel use by 50% by 2015, increase the use of renewable energy resources (Chapter 17), sharply reduce sulfur dioxide emissions, and set new deadlines for cities to control smog (Chapter 19); worked with the Soviet Academy of Sciences on demonstration projects to combat global warming

because we have a built-in resistance to change. But later we often realize that these people helped make the world and us better by inspiring us to convert our ideals to realities. Instead of saying something can't be done because it's too idealistic, they say, "Let's do it!"

Writer Kurt Vonnegut has suggested a prescription for choosing leaders:

I hope you have stopped choosing abysmally ignorant optimists for positions of leadership. . . . The sort of leaders we need now are not those who promise ultimate victory over Nature, but those with the courage and intelligence to present what appear to be Nature's stern, but reasonable surrender terms:
1. Reduce and stabilize your population:
2. Stop poisoning the air, the water, and the topsoil;
3. Stop preparing for war and start dealing with your real problems:
4. Teach your kids, and yourselves too, while you're at it, how to inhabit a small planet without killing it.
5. Stop thinking science can fix anything, if you give it a trillion dollars.
6. Stop thinking your grandchildren will be OK no matter how wasteful or destructive you may be, since they can go to a nice new planet on a spaceship. That is really mean and stupid.

The American Political System: Muddling Through

We might be disappointed in the ability of the government to anticipate, prevent, and react to environmental and resource problems with the sense of urgency and vision that we believe is needed. But we should not be surprised at this because incremental decision making and compromise are built into the system.

The government established by the Constitution was not designed for efficiency. Instead it was designed for consensus and accommodation to promote survival and adaptation through gradual change. By staying as close to the middle of the road as possible, the government attempts to steer its way through crises. Ralph Waldo Emerson once said, "Democracy is a raft which will never sink, but then your feet are always in the water."

Despite these limitations environmental and resource conservation laws and agencies have produced measurable improvement in environmental quality and prevented some forms of resource degradation in the United States. Many streams, rivers, and lakes are less polluted and air pollutant levels in some metropolitan areas are lower than they were in the 1960s and 1970s. Strip-mined areas must now be restored, and we are slowly beginning to clean up thousands of abandoned hazardous waste dumps. The U.S. national park, wilderness, wildlife refuge, and forest systems and endangered species programs are among the best in the world. On a per capita basis, few other countries spend as much as the United States does to protect the environment. Thus, the system is muddling through.

But new environmental problems keep arising, often as by-products of solutions to old problems treated in isolation rather than as an interacting system. Also there has been too little emphasis on establishing policies that emphasize pollution prevention and reducing resource waste.

Some analysts believe that the U.S. political-economic system is working reasonably well and no fundamental changes need to be made. "If it's not broken, don't fix it," they say. Others think that the system must undergo changes that will improve its ability to deal with, anticipate, or prevent the growing number of regional, national, and global environmental and resource problems we face today.

Sustaining the Earth in the 1990s: The Second Environmental Decade

Effective anticipatory political leaders don't come along very often. When they do, many people are too scared of change to elect and support them. Indeed, change in a world that is always changing is so threatening that many inspirational leaders, such as Abraham Lincoln, Mahatma Gandhi, John Kennedy, and Martin Luther King, have been assassinated. But their challenges to us to make the world a better place continue to haunt and inspire us.

So we can't sit around and wait for such leadership to inspire us to sustain the earth or for elected leaders to stick their necks out. We have to lead the leaders.

For example, the enactment of environmental and resource conservation laws since the mid-1960s (Appendix 3) did not happen primarily because of leadership by elected officials. Instead, the alarm had been sounded in terms that people could understand by a few scientists such as Rachel Carson, Paul Ehrlich, Barry Commoner, and Garrett Hardin. Then the media further explained and showed graphic pictures of environmental damage (Section 2-4).

This led large numbers of citizens to insist that the government do something. Many joined or supported the Sierra Club, Friends of the Earth, the Wilderness Society, Greenpeace, Environmental Defense Fund, Natural Resources Defense Council (see Case Study on p. 599), and other environmental and resource conservation groups. This public support helped elected leaders like Senators Gaylord Nelson and Edmund Muskie, and Representative Morris Udall who led the way in drafting and passing environmental and conservation legislation in the 1970s.

Without the grassroots political actions of millions of individual citizens and organized groups, the air you breathe and the water you drink today would be much more polluted. Leading leaders is not easy. But history shows that it can be done. You can make a difference.

Redefining National Security

Many people call for the United States, the Soviet Union, and other countries to expand the concept of national security to include economic and environmental security rather than defining it only in military terms. They agree with President Dwight D. Eisenhower's warning in the 1960s:

Every gun that is made, every warship launched, every rocket fired, signifies in the final sense a theft from those who are hungry and are not fed, those who are cold and not clothed. This world in arms is not spending money alone. It is spending the sweat of its laborers, the genius of its scientists, and the hopes of its children.

Ozone depletion, global warming, deforestation, desertification, acid deposition, population growth, and other environmental and resource problems clearly affect national, regional, and global economic and political security. Nations spend nearly $1 trillion a year on military security—more than $2.7 billion a day. Countries must begin to treat the integrity of the environment and the sustainability of the earth's resources as vital national and foreign policy issues.

The Worldwatch Institute estimates that spending just 10% of what we now spend on military activities over the next decade could reverse major adverse trends by preventing further erosion of soil from croplands, reforesting the earth, increasing energy efficiency, and shifting to renewable energy resources. Accomplishing this is an urgent priority. Governments, especially those of the superpowers, will have to engage in environmental diplomacy to form regional and global environmental coalitions to sustain the earth. Each of us will also have to look at and change our own environmentally destructive actions and consumption patterns (see Spotlight on p. 48).

Working from the Bottom Up   In recent years an increasing numbers of citizens have been acting individually and in organized groups to bring about political change from the bottom up. Worldwide there are several thousand environmental organizations whose membership now numbers in the hundreds of millions. These grassroots nongovernmental organizations (NGOs) are working against powerful economic and political forces to bring about fundamental changes in the way we are abusing the life-support systems that keep us and other species alive. In this ecological revolution people are insisting that preserving the conditions for human and other life on this planet is more important than increasing national power and private wealth at the expense of the earth's life-support systems.

These organized groups of earth citizens range from a small group of people who go into a forest in India or Brazil and link their hands around trees to prevent them from being cut down to Greenpeace, the world's largest environmental organization with 1.3 million members worldwide and 435,000 in the United States.

The basic mechanism in this grassroots movement is for individual citizens and organized groups to *think globally and act locally* from the bottom up to protect the earth. Some work within the existing system to bring about change while others often risk their lives to protect various patches of the earth and various species from being devastated (see Pro/Con on p. 602). Others work to restore or rehabilitate degraded areas (see Enrichment Study on p. 151).

One of the major advances toward sound environmental policy has been the solidification of public opinion behind environmental protection. Since the mid-1960s polls have shown that the public supports environmentalism. A 1988 international Harris poll conducted in 14 countries for the UN Environment Program found support for environmental protection both wide and deep. Majorities (typically 60% to 70%) in every country said they would be willing to make personal sacrifices, choose a lower standard of living, and pay higher taxes to improve environmental quality in their country.

Environmental concern has even stimulated the emergence of political parties in Western European nations, the Greens. Although their numbers are small compared to established political parties, membership in the Greens has grown rapidly. They serve to maintain environmental pressure on the established parties, which have themselves become more committed to environmental protection, though not nearly as much as the Greens would like. Elections in 1989 gave the Greens 37 of the 518 seats in the European Parliament formed by 12 Western European nations. In every West European country, except Greece, there are now Greens in local government.

Since 1970 numerous polls have revealed that an overwhelming majority of Americans are strongly committed to environmental protection. A 1989 Harris poll found that

- 82% of those polled believe that the federal government must become more involved in solving environmental problems

- 79% believed that too often the government gives in to business interests when it comes to protecting the environment

- 68% favored increasing government spending for environmental protection even if it meant raising their taxes

According to pollster Lou Harris, "the issue of the environment has now become the explosive and cutting edge in mainstream politics." He predicts that in the 1990s politicians in Western Europe and the United States who don't recognize and join this powerful trend will be toppled from office as organized earth citizens lead the leaders into making the 1990s the second environmental decade. Denis Hayes, national coordinator of the first Earth Day in 1970, is directing efforts to organize an international Earth Day on April 22, 1990 for people around the world to demonstrate their support for sustaining the earth.

You Can Make a Difference Can we sustain the earth at the global, regional, and local levels? Yes—if we care enough to make the necessary commitment and in the process discover that understanding and caring for the earth is a never-ending source of joy and inner peace. We must become *earth conservers*, not *earth degraders*.

No goal is more important, more urgent, and more worthy of our time, energy, creativity, and money. In

---

PRO/CON How Far Should We Go in Protecting the Environment?

Members of the Sierra Club, Friends of the Earth, the National Wildlife Federation, and other nongovernment environmental groups lobbying and working within the system have helped bring about improvements in environmental quality. But in the United States and other parts of the world many environmentalists have grown increasingly impatient with the compromise and deal-making carried on by such larger, established environmental organizations.

They say the earth can't wait for the beneficial but much too slow pace of change accomplished by working only within the system. Members of established, mainline environmental groups point to successes and contend that they increase their clout and credibility with politicians and regulatory agencies by negotiating reasonably.

Since the 1970s these hard-line environmental activists have been stepping up their efforts to intervene directly to protect forests and wild creatures from environmental destruction. They refer to their tactics as monkeywrenching or ecotage. Examples include chaining themselves to the tops of trees to keep loggers from cutting them down, driving spikes in trees to prevent them from being cut into lumber (the spikes don't hurt the trees but shatter sawblades), blocking bulldozers with their bodies, blocking or ramming illegal whaling ships, and taking photos and videos of illegal or brutal commercial fishing and hunting activities.

Two such activist groups are Earth First! led by Dave Foreman and the Sea Shepherd Conservation Society led by Paul Watson. Earth First! (with about 10,000

members) concentrates on saving patches of land ecosystems and their wild species from destruction. The Sea Shepherd group (with about 12,000 members) devotes most of its efforts to protecting whales, seals, and other marine mammals.

Dave Foreman was a Washington, D.C. lobbyist for the Wilderness Society. But in 1980 he became fed up with what he considered to be political compromising and quit to form Earth First! and write *Ecodefense: A Field Guide to Monkeywrenching*, a how-to book of ecotage techniques.

In 1983 Foreman was hit and dragged by a logging truck he was blocking to keep a logging road from being cut into a stand of old-growth trees in the Siskiyou National Forests near Grants Pass, Oregon that would prevent the area from being included in the National Wilderness System. His knees suffered permanent damage but three more blockades bought enough time for a lawsuit to lead to a temporary injunction against the roadbuilding and cutting proposed by the Forest Service.

Paul Watson was one of the founders of Greenpeace but left in 1977 after his colleagues objected to his proposals for the organization to use bolder intervention tactics. Since his founding of the Sea Shepherd Conservation Society in 1977 the group

- protected baby harp seals in Eastern Canada by spraying a harmless but indelible dye onto their white fur to destroy the economic value of their pelts
- sank two illegal Spanish whaling boats in 1980
- went to Soviet Siberia in 1981

and documented illegal Russian whaling activities
- saved 76,000 seal pups from being killed in 1983 by blockading the Canadian sealing fleet
- shut down the grey seal hunt in Scotland in 1984 by buying two of the islands on which the seals were being killed
- engineered the sinking of half of Iceland's illegally operated whaling fleet in 1986, thus helping enforce the international moratorium on killing whales
- saved thousands of seals, whales, dolphins, sea birds, and sea turtles in 1987 by forcing the Japanese driftnet fishing fleet to retreat from fishing grounds in the North Pacific

Environmentalists disagree over the use of such tactics. Some applaud and join or financially support such groups. Others don't support such radical efforts and fear that any illegal or violent actions could cause a public backlash against other environmental efforts and groups.

Other environmentalists such as David Brower, past executive director of the Sierra Club and founder of Friends of the Earth and the Earth Island Institute, recognize the need for both types of groups—those who lobby for change and those who put their bodies where their mouths are. They contend it is important to protect forests, wetlands, and wildlife from being ravaged before they can be protected by the slow place of political change. Such direct action also raises the awareness of other people, especially if it involves nonviolent intervention and civil disobedience. What do you think?

sustaining the earth we should be guided by historian Arnold Toynbee's observation: "If you make the world ever so little better, you will have done splendidly, and your life will have been worthwhile," and by George Bernard Shaw's reminder that "indifference is the essence of inhumanity."

The ultimate test of our conscience is our willingness to sacrifice something today for future generations whose words of thanks will never be heard.

Gaylord Nelson

Feeling Edgy

John H. Gibbons

Since 1979 Jack Gibbons has been Director of the Congressional Office of Technology Assessment (OTA). This think tank was formed in 1972 to provide Congress with information on issues involving technology and public policy that is nonpartisan, objective, expert, and anticipatory. He is an internationally recognized scientist and an expert in energy and environmental issues.

Robert Louis Stevenson once observed that "the obscurest epoch is today"; that is, it is sometimes much easier to understand the past, and even envision the future, than it is to see clearly the present. Yet we must today give our understanding and attention to such urgent problems as global warming, acid rain, urban and regional air pollution, species extinction, water and soil degradation, human dislocation, and capital shortages and debt.

The paradigm of the "Cowboy Economy" described years ago by Kenneth Boulding (see Guest Essay on p. 153) effectively captured the dominant traditional Western attitude toward resource use and efficiency. Our tendency to exploit resources causes some people to characterize the sensible response to many of our environmental problems—the wise use of resources, or "conservation"—as weakness. Yet enlightened economic self-interest increasingly compels the United States and other nations to be more thoughtful in the way we use resources.

Energy technologies have enormously enriched the quality of human life. To name a few, they have enabled comfortable living, the lighting of our lives, ease of communication and transportation, and treat-ment of pollution. But energy use also lies at the heart of many of our environmental problems—global warming, acid rain, nuclear waste, deforestation. Fortunately, many opportunities exist to decrease energy use without sacrificing energy services (Section 17-1). In fact, the United States held energy consumption at 1973 levels while expanding the economy by nearly 40%, largely because it costs less to improve energy efficiency than it does to supply new energy. Although U.S. efficiency gains made between 1973 and 1988 pale beside those of Japan and Sweden, they still equate to discovery of an oil field that yields more than 9 million barrels a day—which will never run dry.

There are still plenty of opportunities left for cost-effective increases in energy efficiency in the United States. For example, new automobile designs—using four valves per cylinder and multi-point fuel injection engines, improved lubricants and friction reducing materials, electronic emissions controls, continuously variable transmissions, improved tires, improved aerodynamics, and efficient accessories—can create a much more energy-efficient fleet of American cars. Cost-effective conservation measures are available to reduce the amount of energy consumed in buildings by 30% to 50% (Section 17-1). Minimum efficiency standards for lighting could save consumers $1.9 billion per year by the year 2000, at the same time cutting peak electric demand by 5,000 megawatts. The environmental benefits from improving energy efficiency are enormous, but neither market signals nor government regulation are being used to provide the kind of mutual coercion we seem to need to effect action.

The many opportunities for cost-effective improvements in energy efficiency in the United States can buy some transition time in the shift away from fossil fuels and their inherent environmental problems. But energy demand growth in the developing countries could offset any improvements made in the industrialized world unless we include them in our efforts. As Gro Bruntland tells us, "Poor people must not be condemned to remain in poverty." Economic growth requires energy use. But increasing energy efficiency can reduce the urgent energy import needs and capital investment needs in developing countries, stimulate their economic growth, raise living standards,

(continued)

and improve environmental conditions. Cost-effective improvements are available, particularly in avoided electric-demand and power supply expansion costs.

Shifting away from fossil fuels and addressing our environmental problems requires much more than the "technical fix" envisioned earlier in this century. *Human* activities—from rice growing, animal husbandry, and forest clearing, to complex industrial processes—are changing the globe on which we live. And *humane* solutions—recognizing cultural differences, stages of economic development, and political realities—must be sought for the problems that arise from our activities. The technological potential for improvements is real, but capital investment and international political accommodation will play just as critical a role, and in many ways these are shorter in supply. Consider, for example, what would have to

happen to achieve (at some future time) an equilibrium where accumulations of greenhouse gases (Figure 19-17, p. 504) are no greater than today. It's an interesting analytical question and a fascinating, traumatic political challenge (see p. 506) that I leave for you to think about.

We voyagers on planet earth are almost certainly headed for uncharted waters of global environmental change, driven by our own power as well as by natural forces. That should be enough to make any thinking person "edgy." In the past we've charted our course in a manner less visionary and conservative than we might have been in using resources. We already owe some apologies to future generations, and to people alive today because of our inputs into regional and global climate change, but we can't stop there. *We must accelerate growth of understanding* of the

---

Richard D. Lamm

Richard D. Lamm is Professor and Director of the Center for Public Policy and Contemporary Issues at the University of Denver. Prior to this he served as Governor of Colorado from 1975 to 1987 and as a member of the Colorado House of Representatives from 1966 to 1974. Throughout his career he has been actively concerned about environmental and population problems, peace, and bringing about social change. Among his several books are Megatraumas: America in the Year 2000 *(Houghton Mifflin, 1985) and* The Immigration Time Bomb *(with Gary Imhoff, E. P. Dutton, 1985).*

Schopenhauer once said that "every man confuses the limits of the mind for the limits of the world." How true. None of us is smart enough or perceptive enough to even come close to fully understanding all of the dynamics of the world. We do however have to go forward and make public policy, guided by the

best perceptions that we can bring to where the world is going.

Let me be a public policy Columbus and try to describe the new world into which I see us sailing. It is a world as new and different as Columbus discovered. It is a world where yesterday's virtues become today's vices and where some of the guiding tenets and principles of our society no longer apply. I believe that when the history of these new times is written, the two overriding issues to humankind will be population growth and the abuse of the environment.

The world is living at the upper end of some awesome exponential (geometric) curves. Just as no tree can grow to the sky, we cannot continue to chase exponential curves. I see no public policy restraint on the awesome curves of population growth (Figure 1-1, p. 4) and environmental abuse. There are of course small gains here and there, but overall, decade after decade, our problems outrun our solutions. There are no practical restraints on these galloping curves. They will likely grow until they eventually crash (Figure 6-4, p. 138).

James Gleick in his book *Chaos* says "The world awaits the right metaphor." No matter how smart we are, we can't fully perceive something until we have the right metaphor. Let me relate two metaphors by Garrett Hardin (see Guest Essay on p. 180) that speak to me about two dilemmas the world faces.

The first is the story of St. Martin of Tours, who outside the city gate on a cold and rainy evening meets a beggar. In an act that has lived through the centuries, St. Martin dismounted and cut his cloak in

global effects of human activities, *broaden awareness* of the need to commence conservative actions to lessen future problems, and *improve technology* to provide more options for action.

I would substitute for the "Cowboy Economy" a paradigm of the "Conservator Society" [referred to in this book as the sustainable-earth society]. In such a society, progress is measured not in growth of human numbers and amount of resources annually consumed, but in the extent to which human potential is fulfilled and resources are efficiently used (less input, less waste) in providing goods and services. The big opportunities to be better earth stewards and live fuller, more interesting lives derive from human ingenuity, through increased knowledge, and technology development. It is up to those of us in the industrial nations of the world to lead the way for all human-kind to a post-fossil fuel age and vastly improved efficiency with which we convert resources into goods and services.

One of the most important places for each of us to start is to educate ourselves and others about what is known, diligently pursue understanding, and then try to figure out how to put it to work. There is no more noble or exciting way to commit one's life.

Guest Essay Discussion

1. List five existing technologies that would improve environmental quality and resource efficiency that we are not using effectively. Why?
2. What limitations, if any, would you impose on technology development? Why?

---

half and shared his cloak and food with the cold and starving beggar. It was an act of generosity that lives in our ethical code.

Garrett Hardin postulates that the modern day equivalent to this metaphor is St. Martin of Tours riding down the same road and at the same city gate, he meets not one but 35 cold and starving beggars. What is his ethical duty now? How do we apply the old wisdom to the new reality of a crowded and increasingly poverty stricken world? From my own experience, being in government today is like dividing a cloak that is inadequate to meet all the needs. Human expectations exceed the ability of the political system to deliver. Infinite needs have run into finite resources.

But we cannot come to grips with these problems because of a second Garrett Hardin metaphor. In his well known work "The Tragedy of the Commons," Hardin points out the dilemma of anyone interested in trying to bring environmental sanity to the world. We all individually benefit from our excesses and yet the costs of those excesses are spread out among a much larger group. Thus the pleasure of present excesses, be it energy consumption, resource consumption, too many children, etc., will outweigh the threat of future peril. None of us can fully see our place in the ecological whole because we get the direct pleasure of our environmentally harmful conduct while the indirect costs are spread out among the population as a whole.

We thus inhabit a world without breaks. Our modern civilization is like a rock rolling downhill, gaining momentum all the time, heading for chaos. We often think ourselves immune from nature's laws but, alas, we are not. Our mother earth can only absorb so many people and so much environmental abuse. Then it will teach us a harsh lesson.

The great crusade that we must now embrace is to bring human reason and a sense of environmental awareness to a world rapidly spinning out of control. There is still a door of opportunity; yet it is fast closing. Science teaches us that no species can multiply indefinitely and that every finite space has a "carrying capacity" which cannot be exceeded.

There is hope. There is still "world enough and time." But the hour is late.

Guest Essay Discussion

1. If you meet 35 starving beggars and you only have enough food for five of them, what do you do? How does this relate to the quantity and types of foreign aid that MDCs should give to LDCs?
2. What political actions and changes are needed to deal with the problem of the tragedy of the commons? What changes are needed in your own lifestyle and political actions to deal with this problem?

How to Write Elected Officials

Do you write your congressional representatives and senators opposing or supporting environmental legislation or complimenting them for a particular stand? You may be thinking, "What can my one letter or one vote do?" But if written correctly, letters supporting or opposing a particular position can slowly accumulate. When this happens elected officials are forced to recognize that if they don't vote in a certain way for the people they represent, they may not be reelected.

The following are guidelines for communicating with elected officials effectively:[*]

1. Address the letter properly:
   a. The President
      The White House
      1600 Pennsylvania Avenue, N.W.
      Washington, D.C. 20500 (Telephone: 202 456-1414)
      Dear Mr. President:

   b. Your senators:
      The Honorable _____
      Senate Office Building
      Washington, D.C. 20510 (Telephone: 202 224-3121)
      Dear Senator _____:

   c. Your representative:
      The Honorable _____
      House Office Building
      Washington, D.C. 20515 (Telephone: 202 224-3121)
      Dear Representative _____

2. Always concentrate on your own representatives, but also write the chair or members of the committee holding hearings on legislation that interests you. Try to write the committee chair and members, the conference committee members, and the chair and members of the correct appropriations committee.

3. Be brief (a page or less), cover only one subject, and come to the point quickly. Write the letter in your own words and express your own views—don't sign and send a form or mimeographed letter. Make the letter personal, and don't say that you are writing for an organization (elected officials usually know the positions of organizations).

4. If possible, identify the bill by number (for example, "H.R. 123" or "S. 313") or name, and ask the representative or senator to do something specific (cosponsor, support, or oppose it). You can get a free copy of any bill or committee report by writing to the House Document Room, U.S. House of Representatives, Washington, D.C. 20515, or the Senate Document Room, U.S. Senate, Washington, D.C. 20510.

5. Give specific reasons for your position and give the impact of the legislation on you and your district.

6. If you have expert knowledge, share it. You may give your representative much-needed information.

7. Be courteous and reasonable. Don't be rude, threaten, or berate. Don't pretend that you have vast political influence. Don't begin on a righteous note ("as a citizen and taxpayer . . .").

8. Don't become a constant penpal. Quality at the right time, rather than quantity, is what counts.

9. Include your name and return address.

10. If you don't have time to write a letter, send a telegram or make a phone call. Telegrams are particularly useful in the last few days before a vote. You can send a Western Union mailgram of 50 words or less with overnight delivery or a Public Opinion Message of 20 words or less to the president or any member of Congress for $7.95 which is billed to your home or office phone (call 800-325-6600) at a fairly low cost. A member of Congress (or his or her staff) can also be reached by telephone through the Capitol switchboard: (202) 224-3121. As with letters, be polite, concise, and specific. Introduce yourself as a constituent, and ask to speak to the staff member who works on the issue you are concerned about.

11. Use positive reinforcement. After the vote write your representative a short note of thanks. A general rule here (as well as for life in general) is to give at least two earned compliments for every criticism.

12. If you are going to Washington, D.C., consider visiting your representative to lobby for your position. But go prepared or you risk destroying your credibility and effectiveness. It helps to call or write ahead to ask for an appointment, but you can prob-

[*]A list of the elected federal officials for your state and district is usually available at the local post office. Each year the League of Women Voters publishes a pamphlet, "When You Write to Washington," which lists all elected officials and includes a list of all committee members and chairpersons. This pamphlet can be obtained from the League of Women Voters, 1730 M St., N.W., Washington, D.C 20036.

ably get an appointment (at least with a staff member) by calling after you arrive in Washington. You can also talk with your elected congressional representative when he or she is in your district. Phone the field office for an appointment.

13. Become a contributing member of Common Cause, the Sierra Club, the League of Women Voters, the Environmental Defense Fund, the Natural Resources Defense Council, or other groups (see the list of organizations in Appendix 1), which have full-time professional lobbyists working for you. These organizations exist only by individual support.

14. Remember that getting a bill passed is only the first step. You need to follow up by writing the president to be sure that the bill isn't vetoed or, once the bill has been signed, that the money appropriated by Congress is spent as required. Finally, write the federal agency (see addresses in Appendix 1) charged with carrying out the program, asking it to establish effective regulations or to be more active in enforcing the law. It is even more important to monitor and influence action at the state and local levels, where all federal and state laws are either ignored or enforced. As Thomas Jefferson once said, "The execution of laws is more important than the making of them."

Rules for Effective Political Action

Writing letters is essential. But you also need to support national lobbying organizations to counteract the massive lobbying activities of industry and other vested interests. Join or form local organizations or temporary task forces on particular issues. The late John W. Gardner, former cabinet official and founder of Common Cause (see *In Common Cause*, 1972), has summarized the basic rules for effective political action:

1. Have a full-time continuing organization.

2. Limit the number of targets and hit them hard. Most groups dilute their efforts by taking on too many issues.

3. Get professional advisers to provide you with accurate, effective information and arguments.

4. Form alliances with other organizations on a particular issue.

5. Have effective communication that will state your position in an accurate, concise, and moving way.

6. Persuade and use positive reinforcement—don't attack. Confine your remarks to the issue; do not make personal attacks on individuals. Try to find allies within the institution, and compliment individuals and organizations when they do something you like. Do your homework and then approach public officials whose support you need privately, without lecturing them or using high pressure tactics. In most cases it is best not to bring up something at a public meeting unless you have the votes lined up ahead of time. Most political influence is carried on behind the scenes through one-on-one conversations.

7. Organize for action—not just for study, discussion, or education. Minimize regular meetings, titles, and minutes. Have a group coordinator, a series of task forces with a project leader, a press and communications contact, legal and professional advisers, and a small group of dedicated workers. A small cadre can accomplish more than a large unwieldy group. Work in groups but always keep in mind that people in groups will tend to act collectively in ways they individually know to be stupid.

8. Don't work exclusively at the national level. Concentrate much of your efforts at the state and particularly at the local level (see Further Readings for guidelines).

9. Be honest, accessible, and on good terms with your local press.

CHAPTER SUMMARY

Politics is concerned with the distribution of resources in an orderly fashion. Social change can be brought about by education and persuasion, legal action, enacting laws, and revolution.

Since the 1960s environmental law has played an important role in protecting the environment. Citizens, scientists, and public interest groups have successfully lobbied to see that a number of important *statutory laws* have been passed and enforced. The system of *common law* based on past legal precedents has also been used to prevent environmentally harmful projects from being implemented.

The U.S. and other constitutional democratic political systems have a number of checks and balances (especially elections) designed to promote sustainability through gradual rather than revolutionary change. The system is designed primarily to focus on short-term responses to problems through negotiation and compromise between groups competing for increased economic and political power.

Many people have been working together to sustain the earth and educate people to see themselves as members of a global community with ultimate loyalty to the planet or biosphere, not merely to a particular country. They urge individuals and organized groups to *think globally and act locally to bring about change* by making the 1990s the second environmental decade.

DISCUSSION TOPICS

1. What major trends do you see in society today? Which ones are desirable and which are undesirable? Use various combinations of these trends to construct three scenarios of what the world might be like in 2020. Identify the scenario you favor and outline a program for achieving this alternative future.

2. What do you believe are the major strengths and weaknesses of the form of government in the United States (or in any country where you live) for protecting the environment and sustaining the earth? What major changes, if any, would you make in this system?

3. Explain why you agree or disagree with the idea that the most important form of patriotism is primary loyalty to sustaining the earth. Any action that harms the earth is unpatriotic and wrong.

4. Do you believe that activist environmental groups such as Earth First! and the Sea Shepherd Conservation Society serve a useful role? Explain. What type of environmentalist, if any, are you?

5. List ten things that you plan to do during the 1990s to help sustain the earth. Which of these are you already doing?

CHAPTER 24

Worldviews, Ethics, and Environment

General Questions and Issues

1. What worldview leads to a throwaway society?
2. What worldview leads to a sustainable-earth society?
3. What can you do to help protect the earth?

So long as we are under the illusion that we know best what is good for the earth and for ourselves, then we will continue our present course, with its devastating consequences on the entire earth community. . . . We need not a human answer to an earth problem, but an earth answer to an earth problem. . . . We need only listen to what the earth is telling us. . . . The time has come when we will listen, or we will die.

Thomas Berry

Your individual and public economic and political decisions are built around your **worldview**—how you think the world works and what you think the role of humans is—and your **ethics**—what you believe to be right or wrong behavior. Regardless of what you say you believe, how you act in the world reveals your true beliefs. If we have a throwaway worldview it should not be surprising that we end up with throwaway economic systems and throwaway lifestyles.

You are living at an incredibly exciting time—the most important turning point since the Agricultural Revolution. For several decades we have used our brains to degrade the earth's life support systems at an accelerating pace. Our power to destroy life, including our own species, is now so great that we must use our brains and our hearts to protect and heal the earth. Making this crucial transition requires that we change our human-centered view of the world to a nature-centered one.

24-1 THE THROWAWAY WORLDVIEW

According to E. F. Schumacher, "Environmental deterioration does not stem from science or technology, or from a lack of information, trained people, or money for research. It stems from the lifestyle of the modern world, which in turn arises from its basic beliefs." Or as Gregory Bateson put it, "The major problems in the world are the result of the difference between the way nature works and the way man thinks."

Many people, especially in industrialized countries, have a throwaway worldview based on several beliefs:

- We are apart from nature.
- We are superior to other species.
- Our role is to conquer and subdue wild nature to further our goals by humanizing the earth's surface.
- Resources are unlimited because of our ingenuity in making them available or in finding substitutes—there is always more.
- The more we produce and consume, the better off we are.
- The most important nation is the one that can command and use the largest fraction of the world's resources.
- The ideal person is the self-made individualist who does his or her own thing and hurts no one.

You may not accept all these statements, but most of us act as if we did. And that's what counts.

The frontier or throwaway worldview sees the earth as a place of unlimited room and resources, where ever-increasing production, consumption, and technology inevitably lead to a better life for everyone. If we pollute one area, we merely move to another or eliminate or control the pollution through technology. If we mess up and deplete the earth, we move to the new frontier of space for habitats and minerals.

This worldview is based on dominating nature. It emphasizes and justifies short-term self-interest to satisfy as many of our unlimited wants as possible. Short-term self-interest is natural and motivating. It's why most things have been invented, why we work, and why we survive. But there are 5.2 billion people trying to survive and satisfy as many of their unlimited wants as possible. In your lifetime there may be twice this many people trying to do this.

Many analysts fear that continuing devotion to this seductive worldview will turn out to be a fatal attraction. Theologian Thomas Berry calls the industrial-consumer society built upon this worldview the "supreme pathology of all history."

We can break the mountains apart; we can drain the rivers and flood the valleys. We can turn the most luxuriant forests into throwaway paper products. We can tear apart the great grass cover of the western plains and pour toxic chemicals into the soil and pesticides onto the fields until the soil is dead and blows away in the wind. We can pollute the air with acids, the rivers with sewage, the seas with oil—all this in a kind of intoxication with our power for devastation. . . . We can invent computers capable of processing ten million calculations per second. And why? To increase the volume and speed with which we move natural resources through the consumer economy to the junk pile or the waste heap. Our managerial skills are measured by our ability to accelerate this process. If in these activities the topography of the planet is damaged, if the environment is made inhospitable for a multitude of living species, then so be it. We are, supposedly, creating a technological wonderworld. . . . But our supposed progress toward an ever-improving human situation is bringing us to a wasteworld instead of a wonderworld.

24-2 THE SUSTAINABLE-EARTH WORLDVIEW

Sustainable-Earth Worldview Many possible sustainable-earth economies, political systems, and individual lifestyles are possible. But all are based on the following general beliefs and guidelines that make up the sustainable-earth worldview:

■ We are part of nature (*principle of oneness*).

■ We are a valuable species, but we are not superior to other species; in the words of Aldo Leopold, each of us is "to be a plain member and citizen of nature" (*principle of humility*).

■ Our role is to understand and work with the rest of nature, not conquer it (*principle of cooperation*).

■ Every living thing has a right to live, or at least to struggle to live, simply because it exists; this right is not dependent on its actual or potential use to us (*respect-for-nature principle*).

■ Something is right when it tends to maintain the earth's life-support systems for us and other species and wrong when it tends otherwise; the bottom line is that the earth is the bottom line (*principle of sustainability*).

■ Our primary purposes should be to share the earth's finite resources, care for other people and other species, and interfere with nonhuman species only to satisfy vital needs—not frivolous wants; success is based on the degree to which we achieve these goals (*principle of love, caring, and joy*).

■ It is wrong for humans to cause the premature extinction of any wild species and the elimination and degradation of their habitats (*preservation of wildlife and biodiversity principle*).

■ We have a right to protect ourselves against harmful and dangerous organisms but only when we cannot avoid being exposed to such organisms or safely escape from the situation; in protecting ourselves we should do the least possible harm to such organisms (*principle of self-defense*).

■ We have a right to kill other organisms to provide enough food for our survival and good health and to meet other basic survival and health needs, but we do not have such rights to meet nonbasic or frivolous wants (*principle of survival*).

■ When we alter nature to meet what we consider to be basic or nonbasic needs, we should choose the method that does the least possible harm to other living things; in minimizing harm it is in general worse to harm a species than an individual organism, and still worse to harm a community of living organisms (*principle of minimum wrong*).

■ Resources are limited and must not be wasted; there is a lot, but there is not always more (*principle of limits*).

■ No individual, corporation, or nation has a right to an ever-increasing share of the earth's finite resources. As the Indian philosopher and social activist Mahatma Gandhi said, "The earth provides enough to satisfy every person's need but not every person's greed" (*principle of enoughness*).

■ People are entitled to a fair share of the world's resources as long as they are assuming their responsibility for sustaining the earth (*principle of equity*).

■ We can never completely "do our own thing"; everything we do has mostly unpredictable present and future effects on other people and other species (*first law of ecology* or *principle of ecological backlash*).

- It is wrong to treat people and other living things primarily as factors of production, whose value is expressed only in economic terms; as Aldo Leopold said, "We abuse land because we regard it as a commodity belonging to us. When we see land as a community to which we belong, we may begin to use it with love and respect" (*economics-is-not-everything principle*).

- Everything we have or will have ultimately comes from the sun and the earth; the earth can get along without us, but we can't get along without the earth; an exhausted planet is an exhausted economy (*respect-your-roots* or *earth-first principle*).

- Don't do anything that depletes the physical, chemical, and biological capital which supports all life and human economic activities; the earth deficit is the ultimate deficit (*balanced earth budget principle*).

- We must leave the earth in as good a shape as we found it, if not better (*rights-of-the-unborn principle*).

- All people must be held responsible for their own pollution and environmental degradation; wastes we create should be put in our own backyard and then we'll see the need for recycling, reuse, and waste reduction (*responsibility-of-the-born principle*).

- We must protect the earth's remaining wild ecosystems from our activities, rehabilitate or restore ecosystems we have degraded, use ecosystems only on a sustainable basis, and allow many of the ecosystems we have occupied and abused to return to a wild state (*principle of ecosystem protection and healing*).

- In protecting and sustaining nature, go further than the law requires (*ethics-often-exceeds-legality principle*).

- To prevent excessive deaths of people and other species, people must prevent excessive births (*birth-control-is-better-than-death-control principle*).

- To love, cherish, celebrate, and understand the earth and yourself, take time to experience and sense the air, water, soil, trees, animals, bacteria, and other parts and rhythms of the earth directly; learning about the earth indirectly from books, TV images, and ideas is not enough (*experience-is-the-best-teacher principle*).

- Learn about and love your local environment and live gently within that place; walk lightly on the earth (*love your neighborhood principle*).

A sustainable-earth worldview does not reject technology. But it does insist that technology be used in just and humane ways to protect—not to degrade and destroy—all forms of life on earth. It also rejects the idea that a technology should be developed and encouraged just because it is possible.

A sustainable-earth or deep ecology wordview is not new. It has been practiced by various groups of people throughout human history, as revealed by a Wintu Indian woman:

The white people never cared for the land or deer or bear. When the Indians kill meat, we eat it all up. When we dig roots we make little holes. When we build houses we make little holes. . . . We don't chop down trees. We only use dead wood. But the white people plow up the ground, pull down the trees, kill everything. The tree says: "Don't. I am sore. Don't hurt me." But they chop it down and cut it up. The spirit of the land hates them. . . . The white people destroy all. They blast rocks and scatter them on the ground. The rock says: "Don't. You are hurting me." But the white people pay no attention. . . . How can the spirit of the earth like the white man? . . . Everywhere the white man has touched the earth it is sore.

Our challenge is to relearn this way of viewing the world, as urged by deep ecologists such as Arne Naess and George Sessions (see Guest Essay on p. 616). This means we must distinguish between our unlimited wants and our true needs. Some affluent people in MDCs are adopting a lifestyle of *voluntary simplicity,* based on doing and enjoying more with less. They are learning that buying more products and luxuries to satisfy artificially created wants doesn't provide security, freedom, or joy. Instead it can lead to insecurity and reduced freedom because *the more things you own, the more you are owned by things* (principle of overconsumption or thing tyranny). You have to spend a lot of time and money buying, protecting, repairing, or replacing them. However, voluntary simplicity by those who have more than they really need should not be confused with the forced simplicity of the poor, who do not have enough to meet their most basic needs for food, clothing, shelter, and health.

Voluntary simplicity does not mean deprivation and hardship. Quite the opposite, it gives one a sense of joy and purpose, as I have found in struggling to find ways to walk lightly on the earth (see Spotlight on p. 444).

The key is to find a *sense of place*—a river, mountain, or piece of the earth that you feel truly at one with. It can be a place where you live or where you occasionally visit and experience in your inner being. When you become part of a place it becomes a part of you. Then you are driven to defend it against damage and to heal its ecological wounds.

Once you have a personal commitment to a place or bioregion you can apply this understanding and these feelings to other parts of your life, to other places, and to other forms of life. As Aldo Leopold pointed out, "All ethics rest upon a single premise that the individual is a member of a community of interdependent parts."

Achieving a Sustainable-Earth Worldview Achieving a sustainable-earth worldview involves working our way through four levels of environmental awareness summarized in the Spotlight below.

We cannot achieve a sustainable-earth worldview merely by reading and thinking about it. To achieve this level of understanding and feelings we must directly listen to and experience the earth with our senses (see Spotlight on p. 614).

But the sustainable-earth worldview by itself is not enough. It is unrealistic to expect poor people living at the margin of existence to think about the long-term

---

SPOTLIGHT Four Levels of Environmental and Conservation Awareness

First Awareness Level: Pollution and Environmental Degradation

Environmental problems are seen as essentially pollution problems that threaten human health and welfare. Acid deposition, toxic waste, global warming, air pollution, ozone depletion, soil erosion, desertification, wildlife extinction, and resource waste and depletion are seen mostly as separate and isolated problems. Each problem can be solved in isolation by waiting until it reaches a crisis level and then dealing with it by the use of legal, technological, and economic methods. Examples include more restrictive laws administered by environmental bureaucracies, developing technologies for output control of pollution, and mostly feeble attempts to include the external effects of pollution and environmental degradation in the market prices of goods and services (Section 22-4). At this level it is assumed that the growth-oriented technological society can continue indefinitely if the "externalities" of our collective lifestyles can somehow be minimized and controlled at "acceptable levels of risk" to the public. There are three major problems with staying at this awareness level. First, it is exclusively a human-centered view, not a life-centered view. Second, individuals see their own impacts as too tiny to matter, not realizing that billions of individual impacts acting together threaten the life-support systems for us and other species. Third, this approach seduces people into thinking that environmental and resource problems can be solved by quick technological solutions: "Have technol-

ogy fix us up, send me the bill at the end of the month, but don't expect me to change my way of living." Relying only on this human-centered approach for solving our problems is like trying to use Band-Aids to stop a rapidly spreading cancer.

Second Awareness Level: Consumption Overpopulation (Shallow Ecology I)

We recognize that the causes of pollution, environmental degradation, and resource depletion are a combination of people overpopulation in LDCs and consumption overpopulation in MDCs (Figure 1-13, p. 20), with the most environmentally damaging populations living in industrialized societies devoted to very high rates of resource consumption and waste production (Figure 3-18, p. 71). At this level the answers seem obvious. Stabilize and then reduce population sizes in LDCs and MDCs. Reduce wasteful consumption of matter and energy resources—especially in MDCs, which, with less than 26% of the world's population, account for about 80% of the world's resource consumption and environmental pollution. At this level there is little emphasis on reforming societies in ecological ways and in setting aside or restoring much larger areas of the earth's ecosystems as wilderness areas, parks, and wildlife preserves. There is little awareness that most protected natural areas are too small to be ecologically viable and are being rapidly overwhelmed and biologically impoverished by the pollutants and unsustainable use of resources

and the pollutants produced by technological, growth-oriented societies. This second level of awareness still views humans as above or outside nature and as more important than other species. Using this shallow understanding of ecology as the basis for our actions is like trying to stop a rapidly spreading cancer by cutting off various parts of the body.

Third Awareness Level: New Age/Spaceship Earth (Shallow Ecology II)

The goal at this level is to use technology and existing economic and political systems to control population growth, pollution, and resource depletion to prevent environmental overload. This is to be done by converting the world's current industrial societies to "post-industrial" high technology societies. The earth is viewed as a spaceship—a machine that we have the capacity and the duty to steer by using computers, advanced pollution control, and other sophisticated technologies to grow more food and mine more of the earth's mineral resources. If the earth becomes too crowded, we will build stations in space for the excess population. If the earth becomes depleted of mineral resources, we will mine other planets. Bioengineering will be used to control the evolution of life forms and produce organisms that produce more food, clean up oil spills and toxic wastes, and satisfy more of our unlimited wants. This view of the earth as spaceship is a sophisticated expression of our arrogance toward nature—the idea that through technology and

survival of the planet. When people need to burn wood to keep from freezing, they will cut down trees. When their livestock and their families face starvation, they will overgraze grasslands.

Analysts argue that an equally important element in the transition to a sustainable-earth society is gen-erous and effective aid and technical advice from MDCs to LDCs that leads to sustainable use of resources, protection of wild ecosystems, and healing of degraded ecosystems. Such aid should help poorer nations become more self-reliant rather than making them more dependent on MDCs for goods and services.

human ingenuity we can control nature and create artificial environments and life forms to avoid environmental overload. Also, astronauts in a spaceship must give up individual freedom in order to survive; they lead lives directed by ground control, constricted by the need for continual monitoring and maintenance of the artificial technological systems that keep them alive. Living in a spaceship or space station may be an exciting adventure at first, but only because the astronauts believe or hope they can return to earth and regain some control over their lives. Thus, as the earth's human density and control bureaucracy increases there will be a steady decrease in human freedom and biodiversity. Instead of novelty, spontaneity, joy, freedom, and biological and cultural diversity, the spaceship model is based on cultural sameness, social regimentation, greatly reduced biodiversity, and gadgetry. This approach can also cause environmental overload and resource depletion in the long run because it is based on the false idea that we understand how nature works. This human-centered awareness level does not seriously question the throwaway worldview that is the basis of modern industrial society and the major cause of our environmental and resource problems. This spaceship worldview, like the throwaway worldview it is built upon, is inadequate for dealing with an overpopulated, environmentally stressed, and globally interconnected world. This view believes that our task is to learn how to pilot spaceship earth by

attempting to extend our technical and managerial skills into every sphere of existence. This human-centered approach believes that we can cure a rapidly spreading cancer by developing some magic machine or form of genetic manipulation.

Fourth Awareness Level: Sustainable Earth (Deep Ecology)

The first three levels of understanding are human-centered views in which we shape the world to meet our needs. They do not recognize that the solution to our problems lies in giving up our destructive fantasies of omnipotence based on our arrogance toward nature. Instead we must develop an earth-centered or life-centered worldview. Somehow we must tune our senses to the beat of existence, sensing in nature fundamental rhythms we can trust even though we will never fully understand them. We must learn anew that it is we who belong to the earth and not the earth to us. At this level we realize that

- all living species are interconnected and interdependent
- we are part of—not apart from—nature
- we are just one particular strand in the web of life
- every living thing has a right to live, or at least to struggle to live, simply because it exists
- our role is not to dominate and control nature but to work with the rest of nature and to meet our needs on the basis of ecological understanding and doing as little harm to other species as possible

- our attempts at excessive control of the earth will sooner or later backfire because the earth's organisms and their interactions are so diverse that we will never even come close to fully understanding how the earth works and maintains itself
- our major goal should be to preserve the ecological integrity, sustainability, and diversity of the life-support systems for all species
- the forces of biological evolution, not technological control, should determine which species live or die
- we have no right to interfere destructively with nonhuman life except to satisfy essential needs
- we must work toward a much lower human population to allow for the flourishing of non-human species and sustainable ecosystems
- we should protect all remaining wild ecosystems not disturbed by our activities from development
- existing ecosystems or bioregional areas that have been degraded by unsustainable human use should be rehabilitated or restored and used only on a sustainable basis
- as the human population decreases and ecosystems are used on a sustainable basis, many of the human-occupied ecosystems should be allowed to return to wild ecosystems

24-3 WHAT CAN YOU DO?

Avoiding Some Common Traps Sustaining the earth requires each of us to make a personal commitment to live an environmentally ethical life. We must do this not because it is required by law but because it is right. It is our responsibility to ourselves, our children, our neighbors, and the earth.

Start by being sure that you have not fallen into some common traps or excuses that lead to indifference and inaction:

■ *Gloom-and-doom pessimism:* the belief that the world is doomed by nuclear war or environmental catastrophe, so we should enjoy life while we can.

■ *Blind technological optimism:* the belief that human ingenuity will always be able to come up with technological advances that will solve our problems. This is the most seductive and dangerous trap. It is something that we would like to believe: Don't worry, be happy, don't change your lifestyle, there are no limits, and technology will save us.

■ *Fatalism:* the belief that whatever will be will be, and we have no control over our actions and the future.

■ *Extrapolation to infinity:* the belief that "If I can't change the entire world quickly, I won't try to change any of it." This rationalization is reinforced by modern society's emphasis on instant gratification and quick results with as little effort as possible.

All of these traps represent various forms of *denial*. To avoid facing up to problems and the need for change,

---

SPOTLIGHT Listening to the Earth and Ourselves

The essence, rhythms, and pulse of the earth within and around us can only be experienced at the deepest level by our senses and feelings—our emotions. We must tune our senses into the flow of air and water into our bodies that are absolute needs provided for us by nature at no charge.

We must listen to the soft, magnificent symphony of billions of organisms expressing their interdependency. We must pick up a handful of soil and try to sense its teeming microscopic life forms that keep us alive. We must look at a tree, a mountain, a rock, a bee and try to sense how they are a part of us and we are a part of them.

We must learn to cherish and listen to the gentle sounds of silence within and around us instead of identifying any lack of frantic activity as boredom and loneliness. We must tune in to our urgent yearning to understand and experience ourselves and the rest of nature. Instead, we often cover up this need by seeking a frantic life of motion and artificial things and sensations that only deepen our emotional separation from our inner selves and from the earth.

Michael J. Cohen urges each of us to recognize who we really are by saying,

I am a desire for water, air, food, love, warmth, beauty, freedom, sensations, life, community, place, and spirit in the natural world. These pulsating feelings are the Planet Earth, alive and well within me. I have two mothers: my human mother and my planet mother, Earth. The planet is my womb of life.

We need to stop attaching more feelings of survival and happiness to dollars that we can't eat, breathe, and drink than to the sun, land, air, water, plants, bacteria, and other organisms that really keep us alive. We need to recognize that our technological cocoon and our feeling of self-importance as a species has given us an incredibly distorted picture of what is really important and joyful.

If we think of nature as separate from us and made up of disjointed parts to be manipulated by us, then we will tend to become people whose main motivation with regard to each other and to nature is also manipulation and control. This is an unsatisfying, empty, and joyless way to live.

We need to understand that formal education is important but is not enough. Much of it is designed to cut us off from the sense of wonder, joy, and communion with nature within and around us that we had at birth. Much of it is designed to socialize and homogenize us so that we will accept and participate in the worldview that our role is to conquer nature and to suppress and deny the deep feelings of guilt we have about doing this.

The way to break out of this mental straight jacket is to experience nature directly so that you truly feel that you are part of nature and it is part of you. When this happens you will be able to hear within yourself the sound of the earth crying at what you and the rest of us are doing to it.

This allows you to get in touch with your deepest self that has sensed from birth that when you destroy and degrade natural systems to insulate yourself from nature, you are attacking yourself. Then you will love the earth as an inseparable part of yourself and live your life in ways that sustain and replenish the earth and thus yourself.

Discovering ourselves means discovering the earth. This is true progress. This is not sacrifice and deprivation. This is living life at its fullest.

we stick our heads in the sand and engage in activities that divert us from facing up to reality. With our present power to destroy ourselves and most other species, denial is a recipe for disaster.

Becoming Earth Citizens The good news is that we can sustain the earth and lead more meaningful and joyful lives. To do this begin with yourself.

1. **Evaluate the way you think the world works and sensitize yourself to your local environment.** Look around, experience what is going on in the environment around you, compare what is with what could and should be. Examine your room, your home, your school, your place of work, your street, and your city, state, country, and world. What things around you improve and what things detract from the quality of your life and that of other people? Where do the water you drink and the air you breathe come from? What kind of soil is around your home? Where does your garbage go? What forms of wild plants and animals live around you? What species have become extinct in your area and what ones are threatened with extinction? What is the past history of land use in your area and what are the projected future uses of this land? What are your environmental bad habits? What is your worldview? Do the assumptions on which it is based represent a valid view of the real world?

2. **Become ecologically informed.** Give up your throwaway thinking and immerse yourself in sustainable-earth thinking. Specialize in one particular area of environmental knowledge and awareness, relate this to sustainable-earth thinking, and share your knowledge and understanding with others (networking). Consider going into an environmental profession or starting or working in an environmentally responsible business. Everyone doesn't need to be an ecologist or a professional environmentalist, but you do need to "ecologize" your lifestyle. Keep in mind Norman Cousins' statement: "The first aim of education should not be to prepare young people for careers but to enable them to develop respect for life."

3. **Become emotionally involved in caring for the earth by experiencing nature directly and by trying to find a place that you love and must defend because you are part of it and it is part of you.** Intellectual ecological knowledge of how the world works is vitally important. But it will not be enough to bring about a change in the way you live unless it is combined with a sense of place—a feeling of oneness with and thankfulness for some piece of the earth that you truly love and respect. Poet-philosopher Gary Snyder urges us to "find our place on the planet, dig in, and take responsibility from there."

4. **Choose a simpler lifestyle by reducing resource consumption and waste and pollution production.** Do this by distinguishing between your true needs and your wants and by using trade-offs. For every high energy, high waste, or highly polluting thing you do (buying a car, living or working in an air-conditioned building), give up a number of other things. Such a lifestyle will be less expensive and should bring you joy as you learn how to break through the technological barriers that artificially separate most of us from other people, from other parts of nature, and from our true selves.

5. **Become more self-sustaining by trying to unhook yourself from dependence on large, centralized systems for your water, energy, food, and livelihood.** You can do this in the country or in the city (see Further Readings). Use organic, intensive gardening techniques to grow some of your own food in a small plot, roof garden, or windowbox planter. Get as much of your energy as possible from renewable sources such as the sun, wind, water, or biomass. An organic garden of any size, a solar house, or solar window collectors in an apartment save energy and money on a lifetime cost basis. They also put you in direct contact with nature by bringing the sun, soil, and plants into your life.

6. **Remember that environment begins at home.** Before you start trying to convert others, begin by changing your own living patterns. If you become an earth citizen, be prepared to have everyone looking for and pointing out your own environmental sins because your actions force people to look at what they are doing—a threatening process. People are most influenced by what we do, not by what we say.

7. **Avoid the four do-nothing traps: gloom-and-doom pessimism, blind technological optimism, fatalism, and extrapolation to infinity.** Jump in and become a doer, not a bench sitter or toe dipper.

8. **Become politically involved on local and national levels.** Start or join a local environmental group, and also join and financially support national and global environmental and conservation organizations whose causes you believe in (see Appendix 1). Learn how to cooperate with others to amplify or synergize your efforts (see p. 607). Work to elect sustainable-earth leaders and to influence officials once they are elected to public office (see Enrichment Study on p. 606).

9. **Do the little things based on thinking globally and acting locally.** Environmental problems are caused by quadrillions of small, unthinking actions by billions of people. They'll be cured by quadrillions of small actions in which you and others substitute environmentally beneficial

actions for thoughtless and wasteful ones. Recycle and reuse things, improve the **energy efficiency** of your house, plant trees, **have a compost pile**, help restore a damaged **part of the earth**, eat lower on the food **chain, grow food** organically, drive a car that **gets at least 40 miles** per gallon, join a carpool, **use mass transit**, ride a bicycle to work, replace incandescent lights with fluorescent lights, **turn off unnecessary** lights, use low-flow shower heads, choose to have no more than one or at most two children, write on both sides of a piece of paper, don't discard useful clothing and other items just to be fashionable, don't buy overpackaged products, **distinguish between your needs and your wants** before you buy anything, and buy products from and invest in companies that are **working** to sustain the environment (see Susan Meeker-Lowry, *Economics as If the Earth Really Mattered*). Each of these small acts sensitizes you to ecologically sound practices and leads to more such acts. Each of these acts is also an individual economic and political decision that when coupled with those of others leads to larger scale political and economic changes.

10. **Work on the big polluters and big problems, primarily through political action.** Individual actions help reduce pollution and environmental degradation, give us a sense of involvement, and help us develop a badly needed earth consciousness. Our awareness must then expand to recognize that large-scale pollution and environmental degradation are caused by industries, governments, and big agriculture. The ethic of the international Greenpeace movement, for example, is "not only to personally bear witness to atrocities against life; it is to take direct nonviolent action to prevent them." Start by taking direct action to improve your local environment. Provide financial support and where possible some of your time to organizations working on various environmental and resource problems at the local, regional, national, and global levels (see Appendix 1).

11. **Start a movement of awareness and action.** You can change the world by changing the two people next to you. For everything, big or little, that you decide to do to help sustain the earth, try to convince two others to do the same thing and persuade them in turn to convince two others.

GUEST ESSAY The Deep Ecology Movement

George Sessions

George Sessions teaches philosophy at Sierra College in California and is one of the leading interpreters of the deep ecology movement. He has been involved in mountaineering and conservation activities since the mid-1950s and has been doing research in ecophilosophy since 1970. He has written a number of professional papers in ecophilosophy and is co-author (with Bill Devall) of the important book Deep Ecology *(Peregrine Smith Books, 1985).*

The year 1988 marked the second great global environmental awakening of this century. *Time* chronicled this event by naming endangered Earth as the Planet of the Year. As I think back to Earth Day 1970, an event that celebrated the first great environmental awakening, I see that we face the same problems today: exponential human population growth and overcrowding, starvation, air and water pollution, toxic and nuclear waste disposal, pesticide and other chemical poisoning, the death of lakes and oceans, desertification, destruction of the world's forests, wildlife habitat destruction, and rising rates of species extinction. In short, the death of the planet.

These problems have greatly intensified in the 1970s and 1980s. At the same time more globally staggering problems have emerged: acid rain, accelerating destruction of tropical rainforests where most species live, the greenhouse effect, and ozone layer depletion.

Professional ecologists, such as Stanford's Paul Ehrlich, warned of these problems in the 1960s and 1970s, but they were dismissed as "doomsayers" and pessimistic neo-Malthusians by industrialists, conventional economists, and other professional apologists for the modern industrial state.

Unfortunately, a deep ecological perspective did not penetrate to society-at-large in the 1970s and 80s even after the awakening of the first Earth Day. Rather, a human-centered (anthropocentric), shallow environmentalism was adopted which legally tinkered with the existing political and economic systems instead of altering society's anthropocentric view and overall direction in the fundamental ways called for by ecology. In the 1980s we opted for the business-as-usual, anti-ecological economic growth and development policies of the Reagan administration in the

Carrying out this doubling or exponential process (see Spotlight on p. 4) only 28 times would convince everyone in the United States. But it is only necessary to have about 5% to 10% of the people in a community, state, or country actively involved in order to bring about change. The national and global environmental movement is nearing this critical mass and needs your help.

12. **Don't make people feel guilty.** If you know people who are overconsuming or carrying out environmentally harmful acts, don't make them feel bad. Instead, find the things that each individual is willing to do to sustain the earth. There is plenty to do, and no one can do everything. Use positive rather than negative reinforcement. We need to nurture, reassure, understand, and love rather than to threaten one another.

Make a difference by caring. Care about the air, water, soil. Care about wild plants, wild animals, wild places. Care about people—young, old, black, white, brown—in this generation and generations to come.

Let this caring be your guide for doing. Live your life caring about the earth and you will be fulfilled. Live your life this way and know that if the earth that bore and sustains you could speak, it would say, Thank you for caring, thank you for making a difference.

Envision the world as made up of all kinds of matter cycles and energy flows. See these life-sustaining processes as a beautiful and diverse web of interrelationships—a kaleidoscope of patterns and rhythms whose very complexity and multitude of potentials remind us that cooperation, honesty, humility, and love must be the guidelines for our behavior toward one another and the earth.

The main ingredients of an environmental ethic are caring about the planet and all of its inhabitants, allowing unselfishness to control the immediate self-interest that harms others, and living each day so as to leave the lightest possible footprints on the planet.

Robert Cahn

United States. We essentially "played ostrich" and buried our heads in the sand while the world's environmental problems became tragically worse and more difficult to solve.

The value system of modernism is oriented to technological/economic/legalistic solutions to problems, to continual growth and development on a finite planet, to an expanding economic system and a constantly growing GNP as a measure of social well-being, and to expanding luxury consumerism as a way of life.

As traditional cultures and values have been destroyed or abandoned, modern people have been socialized to these values and ways of seeing the world. But this entire world view is in direct conflict with the healthy ecological functioning of the Earth. We in the overdeveloped industrial countries are looting ecosystems worldwide. We are trading the gorgeous ecosystems and species of the world and mortgaging the future biological diversity of the planet for superfluous technological toys and overly luxurious, extravagant lifestyles while at the same time suffering from an overcrowded, polluted environment, technological overkill, and dying from preventable, environmentally related cancers and toxic waste poisoning. At the same time, the poor in Third World countries live in unbelievably overcrowded squalor with exploding populations which destroy ecosystems and other species just to stay alive. Both extremes are degrading and demeaning to the full potentialities of

humans and the planet, as summarized by the leading Catholic eco-theologian Thomas Berry on p. 610.

John Muir, Rachel Carson, David Brower, Paul Ehrlich, and many other earth citizens have helped us enter the emerging Age of Ecology, as summarized in Section 2-4 of this book. The development of environmental concerns in the 1960s prompted the prominent Norwegian philosopher Arne Naess to articulate the philosophical worldview of the Age of Ecology in his 1972 paper "The Shallow and the Deep Long-Range Ecology Movements." His major ideas, drawn from the science of ecology and from ecological intuitions based on experiencing nature, are awareness of:

- The total *interrelatedness* and intermingling of all components of ecosystems and the biosphere. There are no isolated individuals or species. We all share a common fate. This insight has recently been expressed in an updated version of the Gaia hypothesis that the Earth is a living organism (see Pro/Con on p. 143).

- *Ecological equality.* From an ecological perspective, no species on earth is privileged; all individuals and species have an "equal right to live and blossom."

- *Biological diversity and symbiosis.* Naess claimed that the ecologist "acquires a deep seated respect, or even veneration, for ways and forms of life."

- *Cultural diversity and anti-class posture.* An awareness of ecological equality also heads to an awareness of

(continued)

CHAPTER SUMMARY

The *throwaway worldview* upon which modern industrial societies are based assumes that we are apart from and above nature and that our role is to conquer and subdue nature to further our goals. Matter and energy resources are assumed to be unlimited because of human ingenuity, and endlessly rising production and consumption of material goods is considered to be the primary goal of humans.

The *sustainable-earth worldview* is based on the beliefs that we are part of nature and that our primary purposes are to share the earth's finite resources, care for all people and all nonhuman species, interfere with nonhuman species only to satisfy vital human needs, and work with—not against—nature. Matter and energy resources are finite and must not be wasted, and production and consumption of material goods need not increase endlessly.

Achieving a sustainable-earth world view involves working through four levels of awareness: *pollution and environmental degradation* (the symptoms), *consumption overpopulation* (shallow ecology I), *new age/spaceship earth* (shallow ecology II), and *sustainable earth* (deep ecology). Reaching the sustainable earth level requires us to directly listen to and experience the earth so we sense how the earth is part of us and we are part of the earth. This is accomplished by finding a *sense of place*—a piece of the earth that we love and become a part of and it a part of us so that we are driven to defend it against damage and to heal its ecological wounds.

Deep ecology calls for us to distinguish between our wants and our true needs by making our lifestyles more harmonious with natural cycles and by adopting a philosophy of *voluntary simplicity* based on doing more with less. We must also not fall into the traps of *gloom and doom pessimism, blind technological optimism, fatalism,* and *extrapolation to infinity* as excuses to avoid change and to avoid becoming involved in caring for the earth.

To accomplish this each of us needs to become sensitized to the way the world works and our local environment, ecologically informed, and emotionally involved in caring for the earth by experiencing nature directly. We can also choose a simpler lifestyle to reduce resource consumption and waste and pollution production, become more self-reliant, avoid do-nothing rationalizations, become politically involved on local and national levels, do the little things based on thinking globally and acting locally, work on big problems and big polluters through

---

GUEST ESSAY The Deep Ecology Movement (continued)

human social equality and the need to preserve a diversity of nondestructive human cultures.

- *The need to fight against pollution and resource depletion.* But this fight should not favor rich industrial nations and individuals over the poor. And we should think of resources for all species, not just for humans.

- *Complexity not complication.* An appreciation of the complexity of ecological systems makes us humble concerning our knowledge of how these systems work, and more careful about disturbing these systems unnecessarily.

- *Local autonomy and decentralization.* From an ecological understanding of interrelatedness, ecocentric equality, the importance of biological and cultural diversity and symbiosis, it is understood that social changes are needed to bring humanity into balance with the wider cycles of Nature. These changes lead in the direction of decentralized and locally autonomous societies using appropriate small-scale technology, a concept now referred to as bioregionalism.

Arne Naess was instrumental in developing a Deep Ecology Platform in 1984 which expands upon the above points (a detailed discussion of this platform appears in Devall and Sessions, *Deep Ecology*, 1985). This platform also stresses the importance of human population stabilization and reduction by humane means to allow for the flourishing of nonhuman species and human cultural diversity. Also stressed is the ecological importance of protecting wilderness and "free nature" habitats for nonhuman species. A key point is the need to develop an anti-consumerist way of life by concentrating on satisfying our *vital needs* in contrast with our superfluous wants and desires.

There have been many encouraging developments toward the emergence of a post-modern ecological society since Earth Day 1970. Support for environmental reform legislation has remained exceptionally strong over the years. Interest in the deep long-range ecology movement has grown in the 1980s. There is a rise of the international Green political movement, the international bioregional movement, the animal rights movement which has raised popular consciousness about the treatment of both domestic and wild animals, ecofeminism, and direct action groups such as Earth First! which intervene to protect old growth forests and wild species and ecosystems.

Also innovative ideas have been advanced to transform our cities in ecological ways. The outstanding ecologist Paul Ehrlich, together with his wife Anne, have analyzed our current environmental situation in their book *Earth* (1987) and proposed realistic solutions to our problems. They claim that the most important step to ecological sanity is "to permit no development of any more virgin lands." All of the Earth's areas which have not been developed or modified in major ways by humans must be protected at this point. Paul Ehrlich has also claimed that "the main hope for changing humanity's course may lie . . . in the deep ecology movement."

There is also a strong movement now underway involved with ecosystem restoration and rehabilitation (see Enrichment Study on p. 151). Many religious groups are now actively concerned with the environmental crisis as evidenced by the recent North Ameri-

political action, bring about change by changing the two people next to us, and not make people feel guilty. Cooperation, honesty, humility, and love must be the guidelines for our behavior toward one another and the earth.

DISCUSSION TOPICS

1. What obligations, if any, concerning the environment do you have to future generations? List the major environmental benefits and harmful conditions passed on to you by the last two generations.

2. What is your worldview? Has taking this course changed your worldview? How?

3. Do you feel that you are alienated from the earth and without a sense of place? If not, describe the place you love and feel a part of to other members of your class. If you do not have a sense of place, try to explain why and identify changes in your lifestyle that might enable you to have a sense of place.

4. Do you agree with the cartoon character Pogo that "we have met the enemy and he [or she] is us"? Explain.

Criticize this statement from the viewpoint of th[e] From the viewpoint that large corporations and [govern]ment are the really big polluters and resource d[egraders] and degraders.

5. Do you agree with the principles and guideline[s] sustainable-earth worldview given in Section 24[?] Explain. Can you add others? Which ones do y[ou] follow?

6. If you won 10 million dollars in a sweepstakes, [would you] would you live your life differently? Why?

7. Would you work on a project you knew would [cause] harm people? Degrade or destroy a wild habitat? Explain.

8. Rank the following in decreasing order of importance to you: world, self, United States or other birth country, parents, work, state, local community, wildlife.

9. What things are you now doing to help sustain the earth? What things do you plan to do in the future? When? List the excuses you give yourself for not doing more.

can Conference on Christianity and Ecology. The Quakers have developed a checklist calling for a reverence for Nature and wilderness areas and showing individuals how to reduce destructive patterns of consumption at home and in the workplace. They recommend supporting environmental groups from Zero Population Growth to Greenpeace and Friends of the Earth. Some colleges now encourage graduates to sign a voluntary pledge not to accept employment with companies which engage in environmentally destructive practices.

In naming Earth as Planet of the Year and by calling for "a universal crusade to save the planet," *Time* has performed a crucial service to humanity and outlined many useful and far-reaching proposals. But there is no serious critical evaluation of the role of consumerism, current growth-driven economic policies, or the industrial society in our contemporary environmental crisis.

Many of their proposals hinge on conventional economic solutions to our problems. Improved nuclear plants are proposed as a partial solution to our energy problems and global warming. There is also an uncritical endorsement of genetic engineering as a solution to some of our agricultural problems (see Pro/Con on p. 405). Many environmentalists, such as Jeremy Rifkin, have taken a stand against biotechnology on ecological grounds. You may want to read Rifkin's *Algeny* and *Declaration of a Heretic* before making up your mind on this issue. There is also uncritical endorsement of the modern environmental slogan "sustainable development" when the real issue is whether the Earth's ecosystems can stand any more development.

Actually *Time's* treatment of the environmental crisis appears to be a transitional mixture of shallow and deep ecological thinking, of being caught between these two worldviews or cultural paradigms. Many people have recognized that the throwaway worldview is outmoded and dangerous but have been unable to give it up completely and shift to a worldview based on deep ecology.

There is always a danger that the second great environmental awakening that began in 1988 will go the way of Earth Day 1970. That it will become, as the news media called Earth Day, a "passing fad." There is also a danger that this awakening will also turn into a legalistic reform movement which does not address the crucial deep issues. To avoid this ultimate tragedy, we must all develop our ecological consciousness and our sense of connectedness and identification with the ecological processes around and within us and then translate this into effective individual and social/political action.

Guest Essay Discussion

1. Do you agree or disagree with the major principles of the deep ecology movement summarized in this essay? Explain.

2. What role, if any, do you intend to play in the second great environmental awakening of this century? What roles, if any, are you playing?

3. If the throwaway worldview prevails and this second environmental awakening becomes a throwaway fad, many deep ecologists believe it will be the last fad. Do you agree?

Epilogue

Where there is no dream, the people perish.

Proverbs 29:18

his book is based on nine deceptively simple theses:

1. The ecosphere is not only more complex than we think but more complex than we can ever think.

2. In Garrett Hardin's terms, the basic principle of ecology is "that everything and everyone are all interconnected." Because we can never completely know how everything is connected, we must function in the ecosphere with a sense of humility and cooperation with rather than blind domination of nature. Truly accepting this will require that our patterns of living become life-centered or earth-centered instead of human-centered.

3. On earth there are no consumers, only users of materials. We can never really throw anything away, and natural resources are so interdependent that the use or misuse of one will affect others, often in unpredictable ways. This is a threat to a throwaway society, but an opportunity for reuse, recycling, and conservation of matter resources in a sustainable-earth society.

4. Because of the first law of thermodynamics, we can't get anything for nothing, and because of the second law of thermodynamics, virtually every action we take has some undesirable present or future impact on the environment. As a result, there can be no completely technological solution to pollution and environmental degradation, although using appropriate forms of technology can help.

5. The earth's resources and matter recycling systems can support only a limited number of people living at a particular average level of affluence. There is considerable evidence that we have surpassed the earth's capacity for humans (Table 1-1, p. 13).

6. Because we have rounded the bend on the J-shaped curves of exponentially increasing population, resource use, pollution, and environmental degradation, we now have the power to disrupt the earth's life-support systems for us and for most of the earth's other species.

7. Our primary task must be to move from a simplistic, unsustainable throwaway society to a diverse, adaptable, sustainable earth society that is more harmonious with the ecological cycles and fundamental rhythms of life that sustain us and other species.

8. Informed individual and collective action based on a combination of realistic hope, ecological understanding, and becoming a part of rather than apart from nature offers humanity the opportunity to make the transition to a sustainable-earth society.

9. It is not too late. There is time to deal with the complex, interacting problems we face and to make an orderly rather than catastrophic transition to a sustainable-earth society if enough of us really care. It's not up to "them," it's up to "us." Don't wait.

Publications, Environmental Organizations, and Federal and International Agencies

Publications

The following publications can help you keep well informed and up to date on environmental and resource problems. Subscription prices, which tend to change, are not given.

Acid Precipitation Digest, Acid Rain Information Clearinghouse, 33 S. Washington St., Rochester, NY 14608. Summarizes current news and research related to acid deposition.

Acres USA, P.O. Box 9547, Kansas City, MO. Monthly newspaper on sustainable agriculture.

Alternate Sources of Energy, Alternate Sources of Energy, Inc., 107 S. Central Ave., Milaca, MN 56353. Source of information on renewable energy alternatives.

American Demographics, American Demographics, Inc., P.O. Box 68, Ithaca, NY 14851. Basic information.

American Forests, American Forestry Association, 1516 P St. NW, Washington, DC 20005. Popular treatment of forest and conservation issues.

Amicus Journal, Natural Resources Defense Council, 122 E. 42nd St., New York, NY 10168. Useful summary of activities and issues.

Annual Review of Energy, Department of Energy, Forrestal Building, 1000 Independence Ave. SW, Washington, DC 20585. Basic data.

Audubon, National Audubon Society, 950 Third Ave., New York, NY 10022. Popular summaries of conservation and wildlife issues.

Audubon Wildlife Report. National Audubon Society, 950 Third Ave., New York, NY 10022. Annual summary of wildlife agencies, problems, and species; published since 1985; excellent source of data.

BioScience, American Institute of Biological Sciences, 730 11th St. NW, Washington, DC 20001. Popular and technical coverage of biological aspects of conservation and environmental issues.

Bulletin of the Atomic Scientists, 935 E. 60th St., Chicago, IL 60637. Covers some environmental issues, particularly those related to nuclear power and nuclear weapons.

Buzzworm, P.O. Box 6853, Syracuse, NY 13217-7930. Discussions of controversial environmental issues and what individuals can do.

Ceres, Food and Agriculture Organization of the United Nations (FAO), UNIPUB, Inc., P.O. Box 433, New York, NY 10016. Articles on population-food problems.

The CoEvolution Quarterly, P.O. Box 428, Sausalito, CA 94965. Covers a wide range of environmental and self-sufficiency topics.

Conservation Biology, Blackwell Scientific Publications, Inc., 52 Beacon St., Boston, MA 02108. Excellent coverage of wildlife conservation.

Conservation Foundation Letter, The Conservation Foundation, 1250 24th St. NW, Washington, DC 20037. Good summaries of key issues.

Conservation News, National Wildlife Foundation, 1400 16th St. NW, Washington, DC 20036. Popular coverage of wildlife issues.

Demographic Yearbook, Department of International Economic and Social Affairs, Statistical Office, United Nations Publishing Service, United Nations, NY 10017. Basic population data.

Earth Island Journal, Earth Island Institute, 300 Broadway, Suite 28, San Francisco, CA 94133. Nontechnical summaries of national and global conservation and environmental issues.

Ecological Economics, Elsevier Science Publishers, P.O. Box 882, Madison Square Station, New York, NY 10159. Professional journal.

The Ecologist, Ecosystems Ltd., 73 Molesworth St., Wadebridge, Cornway PL27 7DS, United Kingdom. Wide range of articles on environmental issues from an international viewpoint.

Ecology, Ecological Society of America, Dr. Duncan T. Patten, Center for Environmental Studies, Arizona State University, Tempe, AZ 85281. Professional journal.

Ecology Law Quarterly, University of California, Boalt Hall School of Law, Berkeley, CA 94720. Latest developments in environmental law.

Ekistics, Athens Center of Ekistics, 24 Strat Syndesmou, Athens 136, Greece. Reviews the problems and science of human settlements. Reflects ideas of such planners as Constantine Doxiadis, R. Buckminster Fuller, and John McHale.

E Magazine, P.O. Box 5098, Westport, CN 06881. Popular coverage of environmental and resource issues.

Endangered Species UPDATE, School of Natural Resources, The University of Michigan, Ann Arbor, MI 48109. Monthly reprint of the latest U.S. Fish and Wildlife endangered species technical bulletin, a feature article, and technical notes.

Environment, Heldref Publications, 4000 Albemarle St. NW, Washington, DC 20016. Nontechnical articles on environmental and resource issues.

Environment Abstracts, Bowker A & I Publishing, 245 W. 17th St., New York,

NY 10011. Basic bibliographic tool; in most libraries.

Environmental Action, 1525 New Hampshire Ave. NW, Washington, DC 20036. Popular coverage of environmental and resource issues; emphasis on political and social action.

Environmental Defense Letter, Environmental Defense Fund, 257 Park Ave. South, New York, NY 10010. Summaries of efforts to devise practical economically sustainable solutions to a wide range of environmental problems.

Environmental Ethics, Department of Philosophy, The University of Georgia, Athens, GA 30602. Major journal in the field.

The Environmental Professional, Editorial Office, Department of Geography, University of Iowa, Iowa City, IA 52242. Semi-technical discussion of environmental and resource issues.

Environmental Quality, Council on Environmental Quality, 722 Jackson Place NW, Washington, DC 20006. Annual report on environmental problems and progress in environmental protection in the United States.

EPA Journal, Environmental Protection Agency. Order from Government Printing Office, Washington, DC 20402. Nontechnical coverage of environmental issues and updates on EPA activities.

Environmental Science & Technology, American Chemical Society, 1155 16th St. NW, Washington, DC 20036. Mostly technical articles on water, air, and solid waste chemistry.

Everyone's Backyard, Citizens' Clearing House on Hazardous Waste, P.O. Box 926, Arlington, VA 22216. Research, information, and action on hazardous waste.

Family Planning Perspectives, Planned Parenthood-World Population, Editorial Offices, 666 Fifth Ave., New York, NY 10019. Coverage of population issues and latest information on birth control methods.

FDA Consumer, U.S. Department of Health and Human Services, Public Health Service, 5600 Fishers Lane, Rockville, MD 20857. Useful source of information on health issues and food additives.

Fisheries. American Fisheries Society, 5410 Grosvenor Lane, Bethesda, MD 20814. Professional journal.

The Futurist, World Future Society, P.O. Box 19285, Twentieth Street Station, Washington, DC 20036. Popular coverage of environmental, resource, and social issue with emphasis on the future.

Garbage: The Practical Journal for the Environment, P.O. Box 56520, Boulder, Co 80321-6520. Popular coverage of what individuals can do to reduce their environmental impacts.

Greenpeace Magazine, Greenpeace USA, 1436 U St. NW, Washington, DC 20009. Coverage of key issues with emphasis on individual and political action.

INFORM Reports, INFORM, 381 Park Ave. South, New York, NY 10016. Information key environmental and resource issues.

International Environmental Affairs, University Press of New England, 17½ Lebannon St., Hanover, NH 03755. Covers key international issues.

International Journal of the Air Pollution Control, Air Pollution Control Association, P.O. Box 2861, Pittsburgh, PA 15230. Technical research articles.

International Wildlife, National Wildlife Federation, 1400 16th St. NW, Washington, DC 20036. Popular coverage of global wildlife and other resource conservation issues.

Issues in Science and Technology, National Academy of Sciences, 2101 Constitution Ave. NW, Washington, DC 20077–5576. Covers key issues.

Journal of the American Public Health Association, 1015 18th St. NW, Washington, DC 20036. Some coverage of environmental health issues.

Journal of Environmental Education, Heldref Publications, 4000 Albemarle St. NW, Suite 504, Washington, DC 20016. Useful information for teachers.

Journal of Environmental Health, National Environmental Health Association, 720 S. Colorado Blvd., South Tower 970, Denver, CO 80222. Professional journal.

Journal of Forestry. Society of American Foresters, 5400 Grosvenor Lane, Betheseda, MD 20814. Professional journal.

Journal of Range Management, Society for Range Management, 1839 York St., Denver, CO 80206. Professional journal.

Journal of Soil and Water Conservation, Soil and Water Conservation Society, 7515 NE Ankeny Rd., Ankeny, IA 50021. Professional journal.

Journal of the Water Pollution Control Federation, 601 Wythe St., Alexandria, VA 22314. Technical research articles

Journal of Wildlife Management, Wildlife Society, 5410 Grosvenor Lane, Bethesda, MD 20814. Covers basic issues and information.

National Geographic, National Geographic Society, P.O. Box 2895, Washington, DC 20077–9960. Popular coverage of wildlife and environmental issues; beautiful photographs.

National Parks and Conservation Magazine, National Parks and Conservation Association, 1015 31st St. NW Washington, DC 20007. Popular coverage of parks and wildlife issues.

National Wildlife, National Wildlife Federation, 1400 16th St. NW, Washington, DC 20036. Popular coverage of wildlife and other resource conservation issues in the United States.

Natural History, American Museum of Natural History, Central Park West at 79th St., New York, NY 10024. Popular coverage of a broad range of topics including environmental and resource issues.

Natural Resources Journal, University of New Mexico School of Law, 1117 Stanford NE, Albuquerque, NM 87131. Articles on basic issues and policies.

Nature, 711 National Press Building, Washington, DC 20045. Summaries of latest research in a range of scientific fields.

New Scientist, 128 Long Acre, London, WC 2, England. Nontechnical coverage of environmental and other issues related to science.

Newsline, Natural Resources Defense Council, 122 E. 42nd St., New York, NY 10168. Newsletter summarizing research and legal actions taken by the Natural Resources Defense Council to protect the environment.

Not Man Apart, Friends of the Earth, 530 Seventh St. SE, Washington, DC 20003. Nontechnical summaries and articles on national and international conservation and environmental issues.

Organic Gardening & Farming Magazine, Rodale Press, Inc., 33 E. Minor St., Emmaus, PA 18049. Guide to organic gardening.

Pollution Abstracts, Cambridge Scientific Abstracts, 7200 Wisconsin Ave., Bethesda, MD 20814. Basic bibliographic tool; in many libraries.

Population and Vital Statistics Report, UN Publications Sales Section, New York, NY 10017. Basic population data.

Population Bulletin, Population Reference Bureau, 777 Fourteenth St. NW, Suite 800, Washington, DC 20005. In-depth nontechnical articles on population issues.

PV News, PV Energy Systems, 2401 Childs Lane, Alexandria, VA 22308. Monthly newsletter summarizing developments in solar photovoltaic cell technology.

Renewable Energy News, Solar Vision, Inc., 7 Church Hill, Harrisville, NH 03450. Useful summary of latest technological and political developments.

Rocky Mountain Institute Newsletter, 1739 Snowmass Creek Road, Snowmass, CO 81654. Summaries of the latest developments in ways to save energy, water, and other resources.

Science, American Association for the Advancement of Science, 1333 H St. NW, Washington, DC 20005. Technical articles and popular summaries of scientific issues.

Science News, Science Service, Inc., 1719 N St. NW, Washington, DC 20036. Popular weekly summaries of scientific developments, including environmental topics.

Scientific American, 415 Madison Ave., New York, NY 10017. Semi-technical articles on science with some coverage of environmental and resource issues.

Sierra, 730 Polk St., San Francisco, CA 94108. Popular coverage of conservation and environmental issues with emphasis on political action.

Solar Age, Solar Vision, Inc., 7 Church Hill, Harrisville, NH 03450. Summary of advances in solar technology.

State of the States, Renew America, 1001 Connecticut Ave. NW, Suite 719, Washington, DC 20036. Annual summary and rating of the states in various categories of environmental protection.

State of the World, Worldwatch Institute, 1776 Massachusetts Ave. NW, Washington, DC 20036. Annual summary of environment and resource issues.

Statistical Yearbook, Department of International Economic and Social Affairs, Statistical Office, United Nations Publishing Service, United Nations, NY 10017. Annual summary of data on population, food production, resource production and consumption, energy, housing, and forestry.

Technology Review, Room E219–430, Massachusetts Institute of Technology, Cambridge, MA 02139. Popular discussion of scientific and engineering issues, with about half its pages devoted to environment and resource issues.

Transition, Laurence G. Wolf, ed., Department of Geography, University of Cincinnati, Cincinnati, OH 45221. Quarterly journal of the Socially and Ecologically Responsible Geographers.

The Trumpeter Journal of Ecosophy, P.O. Box 5883 Stn. B, Victoria, B.C., Canada V8R 6S8. Basic journal of the deep ecology movement.

Wilderness, The Wilderness Society, 1400 I St. NW, 10th Floor, Washington, DC 20005. Nontechnical articles on wilderness and wildlife conservation.

World Development Report, World Bank, Publications Department, 1818 H St. NW, Washington, DC 20433. Annual summary.of economic development.

World Rainforest Report, Rainforest Action Network, 300 Broadway, Suite 29, San Francisco, CA 94133. Excellent summary of problems and progress in protecting rainforests.

World Resources, World Resources Institute, 1735 New York Ave. NW, Washington, DC 20006. Summary of environment and resource problems published every two years; useful source of data.

World Watch, Worldwatch Institute, 1776 Massachusetts Ave. NW, Washington, DC 20036. Bimonthly magazine covering major envirnmental and resource issues.

Worldwatch Papers, Worldwatch Institute, 1776 Massachusetts Ave. NW, Washington, DC 20036. Series of nontechnical reports designed to serve as an early warning system on major environmental and resource problems.

Yearbook of World Energy Statistics, Department of International Economic and Social Affairs, Statistical Office, United Nations Publishing Service, United Nations, NY 10017. Annual summary of data on worldwide energy production.

Environmental and Resource Organizations: United States and Canada

For a more detailed list of national, state, and local organizations, see *Conservation Directory,* published annually by the National Wildlife Federation, 1400 16th St. NW, Washington, DC 20036.

Advanced Agriculture, Box 138, Demolite, IN 46310. Provides help to farmers who want to switch from industrialized agriculture to sustainable agriculture.

Air Pollution Control Association, P.O. Box 2861, Pittsburgh, PA 15230. Education on air pollution and its control. Publishes *Journal of the Air Pollution Control Association.*

Alliance for Environmental Education, Inc., Box 1040, 3421 M St. NW, Washington, DC 20007. Works to further environmental education activities at all levels.

American Association for World Health, 515 22nd St. NW, Washington, DC 20037. Provides general information on national health problems and publishes a quarterly newsletter.

American Council For An Energy Efficient Economy, 1001 Connecticut Ave. NW, Suite 535, Washington, DC 20013. Conducts research and development of energy efficient technologies, policy research, and advocacy of energy policy.

American Farmland Trust, 1920 N St. NW, Washington, DC 20036. Acts to save farmland from development.

American Fisheries Society, 5410 Grosvenor Lane, Bethesda, MD 20014. Professional society to promote conservation of fisheries.

American Forestry Association, 1516 P St. NW, Washington, DC 20005. Promotion of management and use of forests, soil, water, wildlife, and all natural resources. Publishes *American Forests.*

American Geographical Society, 156 Fifth Ave., Suite 600, New York, NY 10010. Sponsors research and publishes scientific and popular books and periodicals.

American Institute of Biological Sciences, Inc., 730 11th St. NW, Washington, DC 20001. Professional organization. Publishes *BioScience.*

American Society for Environmental Education, P.O. Box 800, Hanover, NH 03755. Education of teachers and the public concerning environmental issues. Publishes *Environmental Education Report.*

American Solar Energy Society, 2400 Central Ave., Boulder, CO 80301. Information on solar energy.

American Water Resources Association, 5410 Grosvenor Lane, Suite 220, Bethesda, MD 20814. Disseminates information on water resources science and technology. Publishes *Water Resources Bulletin.*

Animal Protection Institute of America, P.O. Box 22505, Sacramento, CA 95822. Provides education and information on the humane treatment of animals.

Association of American Geographers, 1710 16th St. NW, Washington, DC 20009. Professional association.

Bat Conservation International, P.O. Box 162603, Austin, TX 78716. Dedicated to conservation and protection of bats and their habitats worldwide.

Bioregional Project (North American Bioregional Congress), Turtle Island Office, 1333 Overhulse Rd. NE, Olympia, WA 98502. Publications and information about reinhabiting and restoring bioregions in the United States.

Canadian Coalition on Acid Rain, 112 St. Clair Ave. West, Toronto, Ontario M4V 2Y3. Research, education, and action on acid deposition.

Canadian Coalition on Nuclear Responsibility, CP 236, Saccursale, Snowden, Montreal, Quebec H3X 3T4. Nuclear energy.

Canadian Environmental Law Association, 234 Queen St. West, Toronto, Ontario M5V 1Z4. Research, education, and litigation on environmental and conservation issues.

Center for Marine Conservation, 1725 DeSales St. NW, Suite 500, Washington, DC 20036. Concerned with conservation of endangered and threatened species and marine habitats. Also sponsors the Whale Protection Fund.

Center for Science in the Public Interest, 1501 16th St. NW, Washington, DC 20036. National consumer advocacy organization that focuses on health and nutrition issues. Publishes *Nutrition Action Newsletter*.

Chesapeake Bay Foundation, Inc. 162 Prince George St., Annapolis, MD 21401. Research, education, and litigation on environmental problems and management of the Chesapeake Bay and surrounding land.

Citizens' Clearinghouse for Hazardous Waste, P.O. Box 926, Arlington, VA 22216. Research, information, and organizing on this issue. Publishes *Everyone's Backyard*.

Clean Water Action Project, 317 Pennsylvania Ave. SE, Washington, DC 20003. National citizen action organization lobbying for strict water pollution control and safe drinking water.

Climatic Institute, 316 Pennsylvania Ave. SE, Suite 403, Washington, DC 20003 Sponsors scientific and policy conferences and publishes a quarterly newsletter, *Climate Alert*.

Common Cause, 2030 M St. NW, Washington, DC 20036. Citizens' lobby with over 100,000 members, who work hard on a broad range of political issues including nuclear freeze, arms control, and campaign financing reform.

Congress Watch, 215 Pennsylvania Ave. SE, Washington, DC 20003. Lobbying group concerned with corporate responsibility, nuclear energy, and campaign financing.

Conservation Foundation, 1250 42nd St. NW, Washington, DC 20076. Affiliated with World Wildlife Fund–US. Active in conservation, analysis of the ecological impact of foreign aid, and conservation education in the schools. Publishes *Conservation Foundation Letter*.

Conservation International, 1015 18th St. NW, Suite 1002, Washington, DC 20036. Works on conservation of ecosystems and wildlife in tropical areas, especially Costa Rica.

Consumer Federation of America, 1424 18th St. NW, Washington, DC 20009. Works on consumer and environmental safety issues.

Cousteau Society, 930 W. 21st St., Norfolk, VA 23517. Research and education with emphasis on preservation of the world's oceans.

Defenders of Wildlife, 1244 19th St. NW, Washington, DC 20036. Works for preservation of all forms of wildlife. Research, education, lobbying.

Ducks Unlimited, One Waterfowl Way, Long Grove, IL 60047. Has acquired or protected over 2 million acres of vital breeding habitats for migrating waterfowl.

Earth First!, P.O. Box 2358, Lewiston, ME 04241. Activist environmental organization.

Ecology Action Center, 1657 Barrington St., Suite 520, Halifax, Nova Scotia B3J 2A1. Research, education, and action on environmental and conservation issues.

Ecological Society of America, Dr. Hazel R. Delcourt, Secretary, Department of Botany, University of Tennessee, Knoxville, TN 37996. Professional society.

Energy Conservation Coalition, 1725 I St. NW, Suite 610, Washington, DC 20036. Education and lobbying.

Energy Probe, 100 College St., Toronto, Ontario M5G 1L5. Research and education on energy alternatives.

Environmental Action Foundation, Inc., 1525 New Hampshire Ave., Washington, DC 20036. Research and education on a broad range of environmental issues.

Environmental Action, Inc., 1525 New Hampshire Ave. NW, Washington, DC 20036. Nonprofit organization that evolved from Earth Day 1970. Lobbies for effective legislation for environmental reform. Publishes *Environmental Action*.

Environmental Defense Fund, Inc., 257 Park Ave. South, New York, NY 10010. A public benefit organization composed of scientists, lawyers, and laypersons; works to link law and science in defense of the environment before courts and regulatory agencies.

Environmental Law Institute, 1616 P St. NW, Suite 200, Washington, DC 20036. Conducts a wide program of research and education in environmental law.

Environmental Policy Institute, 218 D St. SE, Washington, DC 20003. An environmental public interest law group that emphasizes research, education, lobbying, and legal aid on a range of environmental issues.

Farralones Institute, 15920 Coleman Valley Road, Occidental, CA 95465. Provides information on ecological living in urban environments and urban agriculture.

Food and Agriculture Organization of the United Nations, Via delle di Caracalla, Rome 00100 Italy. Conducts surveys and research and provides information on world food problems and nutrition.

Food First, 1885 Mission St., San Francisco, CA 94103. Research and education on agriculture, especially in LDCs.

Friends of the Earth, Inc. 530 Seventh Ave. SE, Washington, DC 20003. Education, lobbying, and litigation on a variety of environmental issues. Its political arm, the League of Conservation Voters, raises funds for congressional candidates with sound environmental records.

Friends of the Earth (CANADA), 53 Queen St., Room 16, Ottawa, Ontario. Research, education, and lobbying on environmental and conservation issues.

Friends of Trees, P. O. Box 1466, Chelan, WA 98816. Forest and wildlife conservation.

Fund for Animals, Inc., 200 W. 57th St., New York, NY 10019. Education, lobbying, and litigation on animal rights, endangered species, and wildlife conservation.

Global Greenhouse Network, 1130 17th St. NW, Suite 530, Washington, DC 20036. Facilitation of international cooperation on the greenhouse crisis at government and grass root levels.

Global Tomorrow Coalition, 1325 G Street NW, Suite 915, Washington, DC 20005. Research and education on environmental and conservation issues.

Green Party, 831 Commercial Drive, Vancouver, British Columbia. Political party built around environmental and conservation issues.

Greenpeace, USA, Inc., 1436 U St. NW, Washington, DC 20009. Lobbying, organizing, and direct action with emphasis on whales, seals, nuclear energy, and toxic wastes.

Greenpeace (CANADA), 427 Bloor St., West Toronto, Ontario M5S 1X7. Lobbying, organizing, and nonviolent direct action with emphasis on whales, seals, nuclear energy, and toxic wastes.

Household Hazardous Waste Project, Box 87, 901 South National Ave., Springfield, MO 65804. Information on household toxins and safe alternatives.

Humane Society of the United States, Inc. 2100 L St. NW, Washington, DC 20037. Dedicated to protection of domestic and wild animals.

INFORM, 381 Park Ave. South, New York, NY 10016. Research and education on major environmental and resource issues. Publishes *INFORM Reports.*

Institute for Alternative Agriculture, 9200 Edmonston Rd., Suite 117, Greenbelt, MD. Research and promotion of sustainable agriculture.

Institute for Local Self-Reliance, 1717 18th St. NW, Washington, DC 20009. Research and education; dedicated to helping communities become more self-reliant in resources and economic development.

International Association of Fish and Wildlife Agencies, 444 North Capitol St. NW, Suite 534, Washington, DC 20001. Promotes conservation, protection, and management of wildlife and related natural resources.

International Fund for Animal Welfare, Inc., P.O. Box 193, Yarmouth Port, ME 02675. Dedicated to protection of wild and domestic animals.

International Planned Parenthood Federation, 105 Madison Ave., 7th Floor, New York, NY 10016. Provides information, education, and services; attempts to persuade governments to establish family planning programs.

International Union for the Conservation of Nature and Natural Resources (IUCN), Avenue du Mont Blanc, CH-1196 Gland, Switzerland (022.64 71 81). Promotes scientifically based action for the conservation of wildlife.

Izaak Walton League of America, 1401 Wilson Blvd., Level B, Arlington, VA 22209. Research and education on wildlife conservation, renewable natural resources, and water quality.

John Muir Institute for Environmental Studies, 743 Wilson St., Napa, CA 94558. Research and education on a wide range of environmental issues.

Keep America Beautiful, 9 West Broad St., Stamford, CT 06902. Education to combat litter as a necessary first step toward solving broader environmental problems and a program to increase knowledge of solid waste disposal techniques.

League of Conservation Voters, 2000 L St. NW, Suite 804, Washington, DC 20036. Political action and national campaign committee working to promote the election of legislators pledging to seek a healthy environment. Publicizes roll call votes on environmental issues. Political arm of Friends of the Earth.

League of Women Voters of the U. S., 1730 M St. NW, Washington, DC 20036. Lobbies for a wide range of environmental issues; local and state leagues work for political responsibility through an informed and active citizenry. Research and education by the League of Women Voters Education Fund (same address).

National Audubon Society, 950 Third Ave., New York, NY 10022. Research and lobbying on a wide range of environmental issues. Operates 40 wildlife sanctuaries across the country and provides a wide variety of ecology education services. Publishes *Audubon* and *Audubon Wildlife Report.*

National Center for Policy Alternatives, 2000 Florida Ave. NW, Washington, DC 20003. Works to develop environmentally and socially responsible public policy.

National Coalition Against the Misuse of Pesticides, 530 7th St. SE, Washington, DC 20003. Devoted to improving pesticide safety.

National Geographic Society, 17th and M Sts. NW, Washington, DC 20036. Promotes diffusion of knowledge about geography, environmental problems, and resource conservation.

National Parks and Conservation Association, 1015 31st St. NW, Washington, DC 20007. Research and education designed to improve the US park system. Publishes *National Parks Magazine.*

National Recreation and Park Association, 3101 Park Center Drive, 12th Floor, Alexandria, VA 22302. Promotes recreation and park conservation and development.

National Science Teachers' Association, 1742 Connecticut Ave. NW, Washington, DC 20009. Educational affiliate of the American Association for the Advancement of Science. Dedicated to improving the teaching of science (including environmental issues) from preschool through college.

National Solid Waste Management Association, 1730 Rhode Island Ave. NW, Suite 100, Washington, DC 20036. Compiles statistics and provides information on waste management and resource recovery.

National Wildlife Federation, 1400 16th St. NW, Washington, DC 20036. Research and education. Encourages citizen and governmental action for conservation. Publishes *International Wildlife, National Wildlife,* and an annual directory of conservation organizations.

Natural Resources Defense Council, 122 East 42nd St., New York, NY 10168. Research, organizing, and litigation on a wide range of environmental issues.

The Nature Conservancy, 1800 N. Lynn St., Arlington, VA 22209. Research and preservation of natural areas. Acquires and manages a system of over 1,000 ecologically significant sanctuaries.

New Alchemy Institute, 237 Hatchville Road, East Falmouth, MA 02536. Research and education with emphasis on self-sufficient agriculture, aquaculture, passive solar energy, wind power, and energy conservation.

Nuclear Awareness Project, 730 Bathurst St., Toronto, Ontario M5S 2R4. Research and education on nuclear energy.

The Oceanic Society, Executive Offices, 1536 16th St. NW, Washington, DC 20036. Promotes protection and sensible management of ocean and coastal resources.

Ontario Environment Network, P.O. Box 125, Station P, Toronto, Ontario M5S 2Z7. Research and education on environmental and conservation issues.

Ontario Public Interest Research Group, 229 College St., Toronto, Ontario K1P 5C5. Research and education on environmental issues.

Organization of Tropical Studies, P.O. Box DM, Duke Station, Durham, NC 27706. Supports research on tropical ecosystems.

Permaculture Association, P.O. Box 202, Orange, MA 01364. Research and education on sustainable agriculture.

Permaculture Institute of North America, 6488 South Maxwelton Rd., Clinton, WA 98236. Information on sustainable agriculture.

Physicians for Social Responsibility, 639 Massachusetts Ave., Cambridge, MA 02139. Research and education on the health effects of nuclear weapons and nuclear war.

Planet/Drum Foundation, P.O. Box 31251, San Francisco, CA 94131. Research and education on bioregionalism with emphasis on wise use of land and watersheds.

Planned Parenthood Federation of America, 810 Seventh Ave., New York, NY 10019. Education and research on fertility control and family planning.

Pollution Probe, 12 Madison Ave., Toronto, Ontario M5R 2S1. Research and education on environmental issues.

Population Institute, 110 Maryland Ave. NE, Suite 207, Washington, DC 20002. Education on need to control global population growth.

Population Reference Bureau, 777 14th St. NW, Suite 800, Washington, DC 20005. Publishes information on the social, economic, and environmental implications of U.S. and international population dynamics. Publishes *Population Bulletin*.

Probe International, 100 College St., Toronto, Ontario M5G 1L5. Research and education on environmental and resource issues.

Public Citizen, 215 Pennsylvania Ave. SE, Washington, DC 20003. Research and education on environmental issues.

Rachel Carson Council, Inc., 8940 Jones Mill Road, Chevy Chase, MD 20815. Education on dangers of pesticides and toxic substances.

RAIN, 2270 NW, Irving, Portland, OR 97210. Research and education on appropriate technology and community and regional self-reliance.

Rainforest Action Network, 300 Broadway, Suite 29A, San Francisco, CA 94133. Works internationally to protect rainforests.

Rainforest Foundation, Department 0101, Los Angeles, CA 90084. Works to raise funds to preserve a rainforest national park about the size of Great Britain in the Amazon basin. This park would be used as model showing how tropical rainforests can be used on a sustainable basis.

Rainforest Information Centre, P.O. Box 368, Lismore, New South Wales 2480, Australia. Provides information on rainforest issues worldwide.

Recycling Council of Ontario, P.O. Box 310, Station P, Toronto, Ontario M8S 2S8. Research and education on resource conservation and pollution.

Renew America, 1001 Connecticut Ave. NW, Suite 719, Washington, DC 20036. Research and education on solar energy and key environmental problems. Publishes *The State of the States*, an annual report summarizing progress and rating the states on environmental and resource issues.

Resources for the Future, 1616 P St. NW, Washington, DC 20036. Research and education on environmental problems and resource conservation.

Rocky Mountain Institute, 1739 Snowmass Creek Road, Snowmass, CO 81654. Research and education on environmental and resource issues with special emphasis on energy. Its mission is to

foster the efficient and sustainable use of resources as a path to global security.

Rodale Research Center, Emmaus, PA 18098. Research on organic farming and sustainable agriculture.

Scientists' Institute for Public Information, 355 Lexington Ave., New York, NY 10017. Utilizes scientists of all disciplines in public information programs for the media relevant to scientific, technological, environmental, and resource issues.

Sea Shepherd Conservation Society, P.O. Box 7000-S, Redondo Beach, CA 90277. International marine conservation action organization.

Sierra Club, 730 Polk St., San Francisco, CA 94109. Lobbying and education on a wide range of environmental issues. Provides films, manuals, exhibits, and speakers; publishes books and *Sierra*. Emphasizes activism by volunteers.

Smithsonian Institution, 1000 Jefferson Drive SW, Washington, DC 20560. Promotes environmental education through a wide variety of programs.

Society for Conservation Biology, Biology Dept., Montana State University, Bozeman, MT 59717. Professional society dedicated to providing information for the preservation of biological diversity.

Society of American Foresters, 5400 Grosvenor Lane, Bethesda, MD 20814. Dedicated to advancing the science, technology, education, and practice of professional forestry.

Soil and Water Conservation Society, 7515 N.E. Ankeny Road., Ankeny, IA 50021. Professional society dedicated to soil and water conservation.

Student Conservation Association, Inc., P.O. Box 550, Charlestown, NH 03603. Promotes and coordinates work and learning opportunities during summer vacations for students at the high school, college, and graduate levels.

Tomorrow Foundation, 10511 Saskatchewan Drive, Edmonton, Alberta T6E 4S1. Research and education on environmental and conservation issues.

Union of Concerned Scientists, 26 Church St., Cambridge, MA 02238. Lobbying, research, education, and litigation with emphasis on nuclear power safety and arms control.

Water Pollution Control Federation, 601 Wythe St., Alexandria, VA 22314. Disseminates technical information. on water quality and water resources. Publishes *Journal of the Water Pollution Control Federation*.

The Wilderness Society, 1400 I St. NW, Washington, DC 20005. Research, education, and lobbying with emphasis on

wilderness, parks, and public lands. Publishes *Wilderness*.

Wildlife Management Institute, Suite 725, 1101 14th St. NW, Washington, DC 20005. Promotes better use of wildlife and related natural resources.

Wildlife Society, 5410 Grosvenor Lane, Bethesda, MD 20814. Scientific and education organization for wildlife research, education, and management. Publishes *The Journal of Wildlife Management*.

Woods Hole Research Center, P.O. Box 296, Woods Hole, MA 02543. Research on environmental issues, especially those relating to oceans and the greenhouse crisis.

World Resources Institute, 1735 New York Ave. NW, Washington, DC 20006. Research center providing analysis and information on environment and resource policy options. Publishes numerous reports including *World Resources*, a summary of resource and environment problems.

Worldwatch Institute, 1776 Massachusetts Ave. NW, Washington, DC 20036. Research, early warning, and education on major environmental problems. Publishes *World Watch*, *Worldwatch Papers*, and *State of the World*.

World Wildlife Fund, 1250 24th St. NW, Washington, DC 20037. Research and education on endangered species and acquisition of wildlife habitats.

World Wildlife Fund (CANADA), 60 St. Clair Ave. East, Suite 201, Toronto, Ontario M4T 1N5. Research and education on wildlife conservation and acquisition of wildlife habitats.

Zero Population Growth, 1601 Connecticut Ave. NW, Washington, DC 20009. Education and lobbying on population and immigration issues.

Federal and International Agencies

Bureau of Land Management, U.S. Department of Interior, 18th and C Sts., Room 5660, Washington, DC 20240

Bureau of the Census, U.S. Department of Commerce, Washington, DC 22161.

Bureau of Mines, 2401 E St. NW, Washington, DC 20241

Bureau of Reclamation, Washington, DC 20240

Congressional Research Service, 101 Independence Ave. SW, Washington, DC 20540

Consumer Product Safety Commission, Washington, DC 20207.

Council on Environmental Quality, 722 Jackson Place NW, Washington, DC 20006

Department of Agriculture, 14th St. and Jefferson Dr. SW, Washington, DC 20250

Department of Commerce, 14th St. between Constitution Ave. and E St. NW, Washington, DC 20230

Department of Energy, Forrestal Building, 1000 Independence Ave. SW, Washington, DC 20585

Department of Health and Human Services, 200 Independence Ave. SW, Washington, DC 20585

Department of Housing and Urban Development, 451 Seventh St. SW, Washington, DC 20410

Department of the Interior, 18th and C Sts. NW, Washington, DC 20240

Department of Transportation, 400 Seventh St. SW, Washington, DC 20590

Environmental Protection Agency, 401 M St. SW, Washington, DC 20460

Federal Energy Regulatory Commission, 825 N. Capitol St. NE, Washington, DC 20426

Fish and Wildlife Service, Department of the Interior, 18th and C Sts. NW, Washington, DC 20240

Food and Drug Administration, Department of Health and Human Services, 5600 Fishers Lane, Rockville, MD 20852

Forest Service, P.O. Box 96090, Washington, DC 20013

Geological Survey, 12201 Sunrise Valley Drive, Reston, VA 22092

Government Printing Office, Washington, DC 20402

International Whaling Commission, The Red House, 135 Station Rd., Histon, Cambridge CB4 4NP England 02203 3971

Marine Mammal Commission, 1625 I St. NW, Washington, DC 20006

National Academy of Science, Washington, DC 20550

National Center for Appropriate Technology, 3040 Continental Dr., Butte, MT 59701

National Center for Atmospheric Research, P.O. Box 3000, Boulder, CO 80307

National Marine Fisheries Service, U.S. Dept. of Commerce, NOAA, 182 Connecticut Ave., Washington, DC 20235

National Oceanic and Atmospheric Administration, Rockville, MD 20852

National Park Service, Department of the Interior, P.O. Box 37127, Washington, DC 20013.

National Science Foundation, 1800 G. St. NW, Washington, DC 20550

National Solar Heating and Cooling Information Center, P.O. Box 1607, Rockville, MD 20850

National Technical Information Service, Department of Commerce, 5285 Port Royal Rd., Springfield, VA 22161

Nuclear Regulatory Commission, 1717 H St. NW, Washington, DC 20555

Occupational Safety and Health Administration, Department of Labor, 200 Constitution Ave. NW, Washington, DC 20210

Office of Ocean and Coastal Resource Management, 1825 Connecticut Ave., Suite 700, Washington, DC 20235

Office of Surface Mining Reclamation and Enforcement, 1951 Constitution Ave. NW, Washington, DC 20240

Office of Technology Assessment, U.S. Congress, 600 Pennsylvania Ave. SW, Washington, DC 20510

Soil Conservation Service, P.O. Box 2890, Washington, DC 20013

Solar Energy Research Institute, 6536 Cole Blvd., Golden, CO 80401

Surface Mining Reclamation and Enforcement, U.S. Department of Interior, 1951 Constitution Ave. NW, Washington, DC 20240

United Nations Environment Programme, New York Liaison Office, Room DC2–0803, United Nations, New York, NY 10017

U.S. International Development Cooperation Agency, 320 21st St. NW, Washington, DC 20523

155 Units of Measurement

Length
Metric
1 kilometer (km) = 1,000 meters (m)
1 meter (m) = 100 centimeters (cm)
1 meter (m) = 1,000 millimeters (mm)
1 centimeter (cm) = 0.01 meter (m)
1 millimeter (mm) = 0.001 meter (m)
English
1 foot (ft) = 12 inches (in)
1 yard (yd) = 3 feet (ft)
1 mile (mi) = 5,280 feet (ft)
1 nautical mile = 1.15 miles
Metric-English
1 kilometer (km) = 0.621 mile (mi)
1 meter (m) = 39.4 inches (in)
1 inch (in) = 2.54 centimeters (cm)
1 foot (ft) = 0.305 meter (m)
1 yard (yd) = 0.914 meter (m)
1 nautical mile = 1.85 kilometers (km)

Area
Metric
1 square kilometer (km^2) = 1,000,000 square meters (m^2)
1 square meter (m^2) = 1,000,000 square millimeters (mm^2)
1 hectare (ha) = 10,000 square meters (m^2)
1 hectare (ha) = 0.01 square kilometer (km^2)
English
1 square foot (ft^2) = 144 square inches (in^2)
1 square yard (yd^2) = 9 square feet (ft^2)
1 square mile (mi^2) = 27,880,000 square feet (ft^2)
1 acre (ac) = 43,560 square feet (ft^2)
Metric-English
1 hectare (ha) = 2.471 acres (ac)
1 square kilometer (km^2) = 0.386 square mile (mi^2)
1 square meter (m^2) = 1.196 square yards (yd^2)
1 square meter (m^2) = 10.76 square feet (ft^2)
1 square centimeter (cm^2) = 0.155 square inch (in^2)

Volume
Metric
1 cubic kilometer (km^3) = 1,000,000 cubic meters (m^3)
1 cubic meter (m^3) = 1,000,000 cubic centimeters (cm^3)
1 liter (L) = 1,000 milliliters (mL) = 1,000 cubic centimeters (cm^3)
1 milliliter (mL) = 0.001 liter (L)
1 milliliter (mL) = 1 cubic centimeter (cm^3)
English
1 gallon (gal) = 4 quarts (qt)
1 quart (qt) = 2 pints (pt)
Metric-English
1 liter (L) = 0.265 gallon (gal)
1 liter (L) = 1.06 quarts (qt)
1 liter (L) = 0.0353 cubic foot (ft^3)
1 cubic meter (m^3) = 35.3 cubic feet (ft^3)
1 cubic meter (m^3) = 1.30 cubic yard (yd^3)
1 cubic kilometer (km^3) = 0.24 cubic mile (mi^3)
1 barrel (bbl) = 159 liters (L)
1 barrel (bbl) = 42 U.S. gallons (gal)

Mass
Metric
1 kilogram (kg) = 1,000 grams (g)
1 gram (g) = 1,000 milligrams (mg)
1 gram (g) = 1,000,000 micrograms (μg)
1 milligram (mg) = 0.001 gram (g)
1 microgram (μg) = 0.000001 gram (g)
1 metric ton (mt) = 1,000 kilograms (kg)
English
1 ton (t) = 2,000 pounds (lb)
1 pound (lb) = 16 ounces (oz)
Metric-English
1 metric ton = 2,200 pounds (lb) = 1.1 tons
1 kilogram (kg) = 2.20 pounds (lb)
1 pound (lb) = 454 grams (g)
1 gram (g) = 0.035 ounce (oz)

Energy and Power
Metric
1 kilojoule (kJ) = 1,000 joules (J)
1 kilocalorie (kcal) = 1,000 calories (cal)
1 calorie (cal) = 4.184 joules (J)
Metric-English
1 kilojoule (kJ) = 0.949 British thermal unit (Btu)
1 kilojoule (kJ) = 0.000278 kilowatt-hour (kW-h)
1 kilocalorie (kcal) = 3.97 British thermal units (Btu)
1 kilocalorie (kcal) = 0.00116 kilowatt-hour (kW-h)
1 kilowatt-hour (kW-h) = 860 kilocalories (kcal)
1 kilowatt-hour (kW-h) = 3,400 British thermal units (Btu)
1 quad (Q) = 1,050,000,000,000,000 kilojoules (kJ)
1 quad (Q) = 2,930,000,000,000 kilowatt-hours (kW-h)
Approximate crude oil equivalent
1 barrel (bbl) crude oil = 6,000,000 kilojoules (kJ)
1 barrel (bbl) crude oil = 2,000,000 kilocalories (kcal)
1 barrel (bbl) crude oil = 6,000,000 British thermal units (Btu)
1 barrel (bbl) crude oil = 2,000 kilowatt-hours (kW-h)
Approximate natural gas equivalent
1 cubic foot (ft^3) natural gas = 1,000 kilojoules (kJ)
1 cubic foot (ft^3) natural gas = 260 kilocalories (kcal)
1 cubic foot (ft^3) natural gas = 1,000 British thermal units (Btu)
1 cubic foot (ft^3) natural gas = 0.3 kilowatt-hour (kW-h)
Approximate hard coal equivalent
1 ton (t) coal = 20,000,000 kilojoules (kJ)
1 ton (t) coal = 6,000,000 kilocalories (kcal)
1 ton (t) coal = 20,000,000 British thermal units (Btu)
1 ton (t) coal = 6,000 kilowatt-hours (kW-h)

Temperature Conversions

Fahrenheit (°F) to Celsius (°C): $°C = \dfrac{(°F - 32.0)}{1.80}$

Celsius (°C) to Fahrenheit (°F): $°F = (°C \times 1.80) + 32.0$

Major U.S. Resource Conservation and Environmental Legislation

General

National Environmental Policy Act of 1969 (NEPA)

International Environmental Protection Act of 1983

Energy

National Energy Act of 1978, 1980

National Appliance Energy Conservation Act of 1987

Water Quality

Water Quality Act of 1965

Water Resources Planning Act of 1965

Federal Water Pollution Control Acts of 1965, 1972

Ocean Dumping Act of 1972

Safe Drinking Water Act of 1974, 1984

Clean Water Act of 1977, 1987

Air Quality

Clean Air Act of 1963, 1965, 1970, 1977, 1989

Noise Control

Noise Control Act of 1965

Quiet Communities Act of 1978

Resources and Solid Waste Management

Solid Waste Disposal Act of 1965

Resources Recovery Act of 1970

Resource Conservation and Recovery Act of 1976

Toxic Substances

Hazardous Materials Transportation Act of 1975

Toxic Substances Control Act of 1976

Resource Conservation and Recovery Act of 1976

Comprehensive Environmental Response, Compensation, and Liability (Superfund) Act of 1980, 1986

Nuclear Waste Policy Act of 1982

Pesticides

Federal Insecticide, Fungicide, and Rodenticide Control Act of 1972, 1988

Wildlife Conservation

Anadromous Fish Conservation Act of 1965

Fur Seal Act of 1966

National Wildlife Refuge System Act of 1966, 1976, 1978

Species Conservation Act of 1966, 1969

Marine Mammal Protection Act of 1972

Marine Protection, Research, and Sanctuaries Act of 1972

Endangered Species Act of 1973, 1982, 1985, 1988

Fishery Conservation and Management Act of 1976, 1978, 1982

Whale Conservation and Protection Study Act of 1976

Fish and Wildlife Improvement Act of 1978

Fish and Wildlife Conservation Act of 1980 (Nongame Act)

Land Use and Conservation

Taylor Grazing Act of 1934

Wilderness Act of 1964

Multiple Use Sustained Yield Act of 1968

Wild and Scenic Rivers Act of 1968

National Trails System Act of 1968

National Coastal Zone Management Act of 1972, 1980

Forest Reserves Management Act of 1974, 1976

Forest and Rangeland Renewable Resources Act of 1974, 1978

Federal Land Policy and Management Act of 1976

National Forest Management Act of 1976

Soil and Water Conservation Act of 1977

Surface Mining Control and Reclamation Act of 1977

Antarctic Conservation Act of 1978

Endangered American Wilderness Act of 1978

Alaskan National Interests Lands Conservation Act of 1980

Coastal Barrier Resources Act of 1982

Food Security Act of 1985

Further Readings

Chapter 1 Population, Resources, Environmental Degradation, and Pollution

Agency for International Development. 1987. *The Environment: Managing Natural Resources for Sustainable Development.* Washington, D.C.: Agency for International Development

Brown, Lester R., et al. Annual. *State of the World.* New York: W. W. Norton.

Cahn, Robert, ed. 1985. *An Environmental Agenda for the Future.* Covelo, Calif: Island Press.

Coalition of Environmental Groups. 1989. *Blueprint for the Environment.* Salt Lake City, Utah: Howe Brothers Press.

Council on Environmental Quality and U.S. Department of State. 1980. *The Global 2000 Report to the President*, Vols. l–3. Washington, D.C.: Government Printing Office.

Council on Environmental Quality. *Annual Report.* Washington, D.C: Government Printing Office.

Dahlberg, Kenneth A., et al. 1985. *Environment and the Global Arena.* Durham, N.C.: Duke University Press.

DocTer Institute. 1989. *European Environmental Yearbook 1987.* Rockville, Md.: BNA.

Durrell, Lee. 1986. *State of the Ark: An Atlas of Conservation in Action.* Garden City, N.Y.: Doubleday.

Eckholm, Erik P. 1982. *Down to Earth: Environment and Human Needs.* New York: W. W. Norton.

Editorial Research Reports. 1986. *Earth's Threatened Resources.* Washington, D.C.: Congressional Quarterly.

Ehrlich, Anne H., and Paul R. Ehrlich. 1987. *Earth.* New York: Franklin Watts.

Ehrlich, Paul R., and John P. Holdren, eds. 1988. *The Cassandra Conference: Resources and the Human Predicament.* Texas Station: Texas A & M University Press.

Goldfarb, Theodore D. 1987. *Taking Sides: Clashing Views on Controversial Environmental Issues.* Guilford, Conn.: Dushkin Publishing Group.

Goldsmith, Edward, and Nicholas Hildyard. 1988. *The Earth Report:The Essential Guide to Global Ecological Issues.* Los Angeles: Price Stern Sloan.

Hardin, Garrett. 1968. "The Tragedy of the Commons." *Science*, vol. 162, 1243–1248.

Hardin, Garrett. 1985. *Filters Against Folly.* East Rutherford, N.J.: Viking.

Henning, Daniel H., and William R. Mangun, 1989. *Managing the Environmental Crisis:* Durham, N.C.: Duke University Press.

Holdren, John P., and Paul R. Ehrlich. 1974. "Human Population and the Global Environment." *American Scientist*, vol. 62, 282–292.

Jacobson, Jodi L. 1988. *Environmental Refugees: A Yardstck of Habitability.* Washington, D.C.: Worldwatch Institute.

Maurice, Charles, and Charles W. Smithson. 1984. *The Doomsday Myth.* Stanford, Calif.: Hoover Institution Press.

McKay, Bonnie J., and James M. Achesos, eds. 1987. *The Question of the Commons.* Tuscon: University of Arizona Press.

Meadows, Donella H., et al. 1972. *The Limits to Growth.* New York: Universe Books.

Meadows, Donella, et al. 1982. *Groping in the Dark: The First Decade of Global Modeling.* New York: Wiley.

Myers, Norman, ed. 1984. Gaia: *An Atlas of Planet Management.* Garden City, N.Y.: Anchor Press/Doubleday.

National Geographic Society. 1988. *Earth '88: Changing Geographic Perspectives.* Washington, D.C.: National Geographic Society.

Office of Technology Assessment. 1987. *U.S. Oil Production: The Effect of Low Oil Prices.* Washington, D.C.: Government Printing Office.

Repetto, Robert. 1986. *World Enough and Time: Successful Strategies for Resource Management.* New Haven, Conn.: World Resources Institute.

Repetto, Robert. 1987. "Population, Resources, Environment: An Uncertain Future," *Population Bulletin*, vol. 42, no. 2, 1–44.

Sampson, Neil, and Dwight Hair, eds. 1989. *Natural Resources for the 21st Century.* Covelo, Calif.: Island Press.

Schumacher, E. F. 1973. *Small Is Beautiful: Economics As If People Mattered.* New York: Harper & Row.

Simon, Julian L. 1981. *The Ultimate Resource.* Princeton, N.J.: Princeton University Press.

Simon, Julian L., and Herman Kahn, eds. 1984. *The Resourceful Earth.* New York: Basil Blackwell.

Watt, K. E. F. 1982. *Understanding the Environment.* Newton, Mass.: Allyn & Bacon.

Wattenberg, Ben J. 1984. *The Good News Is the Bad News Is Wrong.* New York: Simon & Schuster.

Weber, Susan, ed. 1988. *USA by Numbers: A Statistical Portrait of the United States.* Washington, D.C.: Zero Population Growth.

World Resources Institute and International Institute for Environment and Development. Annual. *World Resources.* New York: Basic Books.

Chapter 2 Brief History of Resource Exploitation and Conservation

Borrelli, Peter, ed. 1988. *Crossroads: Environmental Priorities for the Future.* Covelo, Calif.: Island Press.

Bramwell, Anna. 1989. *Ecology in the 20th Century.* New Haven, Conn.: Yale University Press.

Bronowski, Jacob, Jr. 1974. *The Ascent of Man.* Boston: Little, Brown.

Brundtland, G. H. 1987. *Our Common Future: World Commission on Environment and Development.* New York: Oxford University Press.

Carson, Rachel. 1962. *Silent Spring.* Boston: Houghton Mifflin.

Carter, V. G., and T. Dale. 1974. *Topsoil and Civilization.* Norman: University of Oklahoma Press.

Clawson, Marion. 1983. *The Federal Lands Revisited.* Washington, D.C.: Resources for the Future.

Cohen, Michael. P. 1984. *The Pathless Way: John Muir and American Wilderness.* Madison: University of Wisconsin Press.

Congressional Quarterly. 1983. *The Battle for Natural Resources.* Washington, D.C.: Congressional Quarterly, Inc.

Conservation Foundation. 1987. *State of the Environment: A View Toward the Nineties.* Washington, D.C.: Conservation Foundation.

Culhane, Paul J. 1981. *Public Land Politics: Interest Group Influences on the Forest Service and the Bureau of Land Management.* Washington, D.C.: Resources for the Future.

Dunlap, Thomas. 1988. *Saving America's Wildlife.* Princeton, N.J.: Princeton University Press.

Ferguson, Denzel, and Nancy Ferguson. 1983. *Sacred Cows at the Public Trough.* Bend, Ore.: Maverick Publications.

Fox, Stephen. 1981. *John Muir and His Legacy: The American Conservation Movement.* Boston: Little, Brown.

Friends of the Earth et al. 1982. *Reagan and Environment.* San Francisco: Friends of the Earth.

Fund for Renewable Energy and the Environment. Annual. *The State of the States.* Washington, D.C.: Fund for Renewable Energy and the Environment.

Graham, Frank. 1971. *Man's Dominion: The Story of Conservation in America.* New York: M. Evans.

Hartzog, George B., Jr. 1988. *Battling for the National Parks.* Mt. Kisco, N.Y.: Moyer Bell.

Hays, Samuel. 1987. *Beauty, Health, and Permanence: Environmental Politics in the United States: 1955–1985.* New York: Cambridge University Press.

High Country News. 1989. *Reforming the Western Frontier.* Covelo, Calif.: Island Press.

Hughes, J. Donald. 1975. *Ecology in Ancient Civilizations.* Albuquerque, N.M.: University of New Mexico Press.

Hughes, J. Donald. 1983. *American Indian Ecology.* El Paso, Texas: Texas Western Press.

Hyams, Edward. 1976. *Soils and Civilization.* New York: Harper & Row.

Koppes, Clayton R. 1987. "Efficiency/Equity/Esthetics: Towards a Reinterpretation of American Conservation." *Environmental Review,* Summer, 127–146.

Lash, Jonathan, et al. 1984. *A Season of Spoils.* New York: Pantheon.

Leopold, Aldo. 1949. *A Sand County Almanac.* New York: Oxford University Press.

Livingston, John A. 1973. *One Cosmic Instant: A Natural History of Human Arrogance.* Boston: Houghton Mifflin.

Marsh, George Perkins. 1864. *Man and Nature.* New York: Scribners.

McCormick, John. 1989. *Reclaiming Paradise: The Global Environmental Movement.* Bloomington: Indiana University Press.

Meine, Curt. 1988. *Aldo Leopold: His Life and Work.* Madison, Wis.: University of Wisconsin Press.

Mumford, Lewis. 1962. *The Transformations of Man.* New York: Collier.

Nash, Roderick. 1982. *Wilderness and the American Mind.* 3rd ed. New Haven, Conn.: Yale University Press.

Nash, Roderick. 1988. *The Rights of Nature: A History of Environmental Ethics.* Madison: University of Wisconsin Press.

Nicholson, Max. 1987. *The New Environmental Age.* New York: Cambridge University Press.

Odell, Rice. 1980. *Environmental Awakening: The New Revolution to Protect the Earth.* Cambridge, Mass.: Ballinger.

Osborn, Fairfield. 1948. *Our Plundered Planet.* Boston: Little, Brown.

Petulla, Joseph M. 1988. *American Environmental History.* 2nd ed. Columbus, Ohio: Merrill.

Repetto, Robert, ed. 1986. *The Global Possible: Resources, Development, and the New Century.* New Haven, Conn.: Yale University Press.

Repetto, Robert. 1986. *World Enough and Time.* New Haven, Conn.: Yale University Press.

Roe, Frank G. 1970. *The North American Buffalo.* Toronto: University of Toronto Press.

Roth, Dennis M. 1984. *The Wilderness Movement and the National Forests.* Washington, D.C.: Forest Service.

Sabaloff, Jeremy A., and C. C. Lamberg-Karlovsky. 1975. *The Rise and Fall of Civilizations.* Menlo Park, Calif.: Benjamin-Cummings.

Sears, Paul B. 1980. *Deserts on the March.* Norman: University of Oklahoma Press.

Shanks, Bernard. 1984. *This Land Is Your Land.* San Francisco: Sierra Club Books.

Simmons, I. G. 1989. *Changing the Face of the Earth: Culture, Environment, and History.* London: Basil Blackwell.

Speth, James Gustave. 1988. *Environmental Pollution: A Long-Term Perspective.* Washington, D.C.: World Resources Institute.

Stroup, Richard L., and John A. Baden. 1986. *Natural Resources: Bureaucratic Myths and Environmental Management.* San Francisco: Institute for Public Policy Research.

Tanner, Thomas, ed. 1987. *Aldo Leopold: The Man and His Legacy.* Ankeny, Iowa: Soil Conservation Society of America.

Thibodeau, Francis R., and Herman H. Field, eds. 1984. *Sustaining Tomorrow: A Strategy for World Conservation and Development.* Hanover, N.H.: University Press of New England.

U.S. Department of Agriculture, Forest Service. 1976. *Highlights in the History of Forest Conservation.* Washington, D.C.: Government Printing Office.

Udall, Stewart L. 1963. *The Quiet Crisis.* New York: Holt, Rinehart & Winston (1988 reprint and updating: Gibbs Smith, Layton, Utah).

Vig, Norman J., and Michael J. Craft. 1984. *Environmental Policy in the 1980s.* Washington, D.C.: Congressional Quarterly Press.

Williams, Michael. 1989. *Americans and Their Forests: A Historical Account.* New York: Cambridge University Press.

Winner, Langdon. 1986. *The Whale and the Reactor: A Search for Limits in an Age of High Technology*. Chicago: University of Chicago Press.

World Resources Institute. 1989. *The Crucial Decade: The 1990s and the Global Environmental Challenge*. Washington, D.C.: World Resources Institute.

Worster, Donald, ed. 1988. *The Ends of the Earth: Perspectives on Modern Environmental History*. New York: Cambridge University Press.

Worthington, E. B. 1983. *The Ecological Century*. New York: Oxford University Press.

Zaslowsky, Dyan, and Wilderness Society. 1986. *These American Lands*. New York: Henry Holt.

Chapter 3 Matter and Energy Resources: Types and Concepts

American Physical Society. 1975. *Efficient Use of Energy*. New York: American Institute of Physics.

Bent, Henry A. 1971. "Haste Makes Waste: Pollution and Entropy." *Chemistry*, vol. 44, 6–15.

Bent, Henry A. 1977. "Entropy and the Energy Crisis." *Journal of Science Teaching*, vol. 44, no. 4, 25–29.

Carrying Capacity, Inc. 1987. *Beyond Oil*. New York: Ballinger.

Christensen, John W. 1984. *Global Science: Energy, Resources, and Environment*. 2nd ed. Dubuque, Iowa: Kendall/Hunt.

Colorado Energy Research Institute. 1976. *Net Energy Analysis: An Energy Balance Study of Fossil Fuel Resources*. Golden, Colo: Colorado Energy Research Institute.

Cook, Earl. 1976. *Man, Energy, Society*. San Francisco: W. H. Freeman.

Fowler, John M. 1984. *Energy and the Environment*. 2nd ed. New York: McGraw-Hill.

Hirsch, Robert L. 1987. "Impending United States Energy Crisis" *Science*, vol. 235, 1467–1473.

Lovins, Amory B. 1977. *Soft Energy Paths*. Cambridge, Mass.: Ballinger.

Lynch, Michael. 1987. "The Next Oil Crisis." *Technology Review*, Nov./Dec., 39–45.

Miller, G. Tyler, Jr. 1971. *Energetics, Kinetics and Life: An Ecological Approach*. Belmont, Calif.: Wadsworth.

Nash, Hugh, ed. 1979. *The Energy Controversy: Soft Path Questions and Answers*. San Francisco: Friends of the Earth.

Odum, Howard T., and Elisabeth C. Odum. 1980. *Energy Basis for Man and Nature*. New York: McGraw-Hill.

Rifkin, Jeremy. 1980. *Entropy: A New World View*. New York: Viking Press.

Rose, David. 1986. *Learning about Energy*. New York: Plenum.

Schneider, Steven A. 1983. *The Oil Price Revolution*. Baltimore, Md.: Johns Hopkins University Press.

Chapter 4 Ecosystems: What Are They and How Do They Work?

Andrewartha, H. G., and L. C. Birch. 1984. *The Ecological Web*. Chicago: University of Chicago Press.

Bolin, B., and R. B. Cook. 1983. *The Major Biogeochemical Cycles and Their Interactions*. New York: Wiley.

Colinvaux, Paul A. 1978. *Why Big Fierce Animals Are Rare*. Princeton, N.J. Princeton University Press.

Colinvaux, Paul A. 1986. *Ecology*. New York: John Wiley.

Ehrlich, Anne H., and Paul R. Ehrlich. 1987. *Earth*. New York: Franklin Watts.

Ehrlich, Paul R. 1985. "Human Ecology for Introductory Biology Courses." *American Zoologist*, vol. 25, 379–394.

Ehrlich, Paul R. 1986. *The Machinery of Life: The Living World Around Us and How It Works*. New York: Simon & Schuster.

Ehrlich, Paul R., Anne H. Ehrlich, and John P. Holdren. 1977. *Ecoscience: Population, Resources and Environment*. San Francisco: W. H. Freeman.

Gates, David M. 1985. *Energy and Ecology*. Sunderland, Mass.: Sinauer.

Kormondy, Edward J. 1984. *Concepts of Ecology*. 3rd ed. Englewood Cliffs, N.J.: Prentice-Hall.

Krebs, Charles J. 1985. *Ecology*. 3rd ed. New York: Harper & Row.

McIntosh, R. P. 1985. *The Background of Ecology: Concept and Theory*. New York: Cambridge University Press.

O'Neil, R. V., et al. 1986. *A Hierarchial Concept of Ecosystems*. Princeton, N.J.: Princeton University Press.

Odum, Eugene P. 1989. *Ecology and Our Endangered Life-Support Systems*. Sunderland, Mass.: Sinauer.

Ramadé, Francois. 1984. *Ecology of Natural Resources*. New York: John Wiley.

Rickleffs, Robert E. 1976. *The Economy of Nature*. Portland, Ore.: Chiron Press.

Smith, Robert L. 1985. *Elements of Ecology*. 2nd ed. New York: Harper & Row.

Springer, Victor G., and Joy P. Gold. 1989. *Sharks in Question: The Smithsonian Answer Book*. Washington D.C.: Smithsonian.

Tudge, Colin. 1988. *The Environment of Life*. New York: Oxford University Press.

Watt, Kenneth E. F. 1982. *Understanding the Environment*. Newton, Mass.: Allyn & Bacon.

Worster, Donald. 1985. *Nature's Economy: A History of Ecological Ideas*. New York: Cambridge University Press.

Chapter 5 Ecosystems: What Are the Major Types?

See also the readings for Chapter 4.

Attenborough, David. 1984. *The Living Planet*. Boston: Little, Brown.

Brown, J. H., and A. C. Gibson. 1983. *Biogeography*. St. Louis: C. V. Mosby.

Burke, David G., et al. 1989. *Protecting Nontidal Wetlands*. Washington, D.C.: American Planning Association.

Calder, Nigel. 1974. *The Weather Machine: How Our Weather Works and Why It Is Changing*. New York: Viking Press.

Clapham, W. B., Jr. 1984. *Natural Ecosystems*. 2d ed. New York: Macmillan.

Daiber, Franklin C. 1986. *Conservation of Tidal Marshes.* New York: Van Nostrand Reinhold.

Forsyth, A., and K. Miyata. 1984. *Tropical Nature.* New York: Charles Scribner.

Gedzelman, Stanley L. 1980. *The Science and Wonders of the Atmosphere.* New York: Wiley.

Goldman, C., and A. Horne. 1983. *Limnology.* New York: McGraw-Hill.

Greenland, David. 1983. *Guidelines for Modern Resource Management: Soil, Land, Water, Air.* Columbus, Ohio: Charles E. Merrill.

Hynes, H. B. N. 1970. *The Biology of Running Waters.* Toronto: University of Toronto Press.

Kaufman, Wallace, and Orin Pilkey. 1979. *The Beaches Are Moving.* Garden City, N.Y.: Anchor Press/Doubleday.

Mabberly, D. J. 1983. *Tropical Rain Forest Ecology.* London: Blackie.

Maltby, Edward. 1986. *Waterlogged Wealth.* Washington, D.C.: Earthscan.

McArthur, R. H. 1972. *Geographical Ecology.* New York: Harper & Row.

Mitsch, William J., and James G. Gosselink. 1986. *Wetlands.* New York: Van Nostrand Reinhold.

National Wildlife Federation. 1987. *Status Report of Our Nation's Wetlands.* Washington, D.C.: National Wildlife Federation.

National Wildlife Federation. 1989. *A Citizens' Guide to Protecting Wetlands.* Washington, D.C.: National Wildlife Federation.

Navara, John G. 1979. *Atmosphere, Weather, and Climate: An Introduction to Meteorology.* Philadelphia: Saunders.

Office of Technology Assessment. 1984. *Wetlands: Their Use and Regulation.* Washington, D.C.: Government Printing Office.

Parker, Henry S. 1985. *Exploring the Oceans.* Englewood Cliffs, N.J. Prentice-Hall.

Pilkey, Orin H., Jr, and William J. Neal, eds. 1987. *Living With the Shore.* Durham, N.C.: Duke University Press.

Pilkey, Orin H., Jr., et al. 1984. *Coastal Design, A Guide for Builders, Planners, & Homeowners.* New York: Van Nostrand Reinhold.

Simon, Anne W. 1978. *The Thin Edge: Coast and Man in Crisis.* New York: Harper & Row.

Teal, J., and M. Teal. 1969. *Life and Death of a Salt Marsh.* New York: Ballantine.

Tiner, Ralph W., Jr. 1984. *Wetlands of the United States: Current Status and Recent Changes.* Washington, D.C.: U.S. Government Printing Office.

Tudge, Colin. 1988. *The Environment of Life.* New York: Oxford University Press.

Wagner, F. H. 1980. *Wildlife of the Deserts.* New York: Harry N. Abrams.

Wallace, David. 1987. *Life in the Balance.* New York: Harcourt Brace Jovanovich.

Whittaker, R. H. 1975. *Communities and Ecosystems.* 2nd ed. New York: Macmillan.

Chapter 6 Changes in Populations, Communities, and Ecosystems

See also the readings for Chapters 4 and 5.

Anderson, Walter T. 1987. *To Govern Evolution.* New York: Harcourt Brace Jovanovich.

Barrett, G. W., and R. Rosenberg, eds. 1981. *Stress Effects on Natural Ecosystems.* New York: Wiley.

Battra, L. R., and W. Klasen, eds. 1987. *Public Perceptions of Biotechnology.* Bethesda, Md.: Agricultural Research Institute.

Berger, John J. 1986. *Restoring the Earth.* New York: Alfred A. Knopf.

Berger, John J. 1989. *Environmental Restoration: Science and Strategies for Restoring the Earth.* Covelo, Calif.: Island Press.

Boulding, Kenneth E. 1985. *The World as a Total System.* Beverly Hills: Sage.

Bradshaw, A. D., and T. McNeilly. 1981. *Evolution and Pollution.* Baltimore, Md.: Edward Arnold

Cairns, John, ed. 1988. *Rehabilitating Damaged Ecosystems.* (2 vols.) Toledo, Ohio: CRC Press.

Crutzen, Paul J. 1985. "The Global Environment After Nuclear War." *Environment,* vol. 27, no. 8, 6–11, 34–37.

Dotto, Lydia. 1986. *Planet Earth in Jeopardy: Environmental Consequences of Nuclear War.* New York: Wiley.

Ehrlich, Paul R. 1980. "Variety Is the Key to Life." *Technology Review,* Mar./Apr., pp. 599–568.

Ehrlich, Paul R. 1988. "The Ecology of Nuclear War." In Paul R. Ehrlich and John P. Holdren, eds. *The Cassandra Conference: Resources and the Human Predicament.* Texas Station: Texas A & M University Press.

Ehrlich, Paul R., et al. 1984. *The Cold and the Dark: The World After Nuclear War.* New York: W. W. Norton.

Endler, John A. 1986. *Natural Selection in the Wild.* Princeton, N.J.: Princeton University Press.

Erickson, Jon. 1989. *The Living Earth: The Coevolution of Planet and Life.* New York: TAB Books.

Farvar, M. Tagi, and John Milton, eds. 1972. *The Careless Technology.* Garden City, N.Y.: Natural History Press.

Fowle, J. R. III, ed. 1987. *Application of Biotechnology: Environmental and Policy Issues.* Boulder, Colo.: Westview Press.

Freedman, Bill. 1989. *Environmental Ecology. The Impacts of Pollution and other Stresses on Ecosystem Structure and Function.* San Diego, Calif.: Academic Press.

Hardin, Garrett. 1985. "Human Ecology: The Subversive, Conservative Science." *American Zoologist,* vol. 25, 469–476.

Levin, S., and M. Harwell. 1986. "Potential Ecological Consequences of Genetically Engineered Organisms." *Environmental Management,* vol. 10, no. 4, 495–498.

Lovelock, James E. 1979. *Gaia: A New Look At Life on Earth.* New York: Oxford University Press.

Lovelock, James E. 1988. *The Ages of Gaia: A Biography of Our Living Earth.* New York: Norton.

Lugo, Ariel E. 1988. "The Future of the Forest: Ecosystem Rehabilitation in the Tropics." *Environment,* vol. 30, no. 7, 17–44.

Lyman, Francesca. 1989. "What Gaia Hath Wrought: The Story of a Scientific Controversy." *Technology Review,* July, 54–61.

Marx, Jean L,.ed. 1989. *A Revolution in Biotechnology.* New York: Cambridge University Press.

McArthur, Robert H., and E. O. Wilson. 1967. *The Theory of Island Biogeography.* Princeton, N.J.: Princeton University Press.

National Academy of Sciences. 1985. *The Effects on the Atmosphere of a Major Nuclear War.* Washington, D.C.: National Academy Press.

Odum, Eugene P. 1969. "The Strategy of Ecosystem Development," *Science,* vol. 164, 262–270.

Oldfield, Margery. 1984. *The Value of Conserving Genetic Resources.* Washington, D.C.: U.S. Department of Interior, National Park Service.

Olsen, Steve. 1986. *Biotechnology.* Washington, D.C.: National Academy Press.

Piller, Charles, and Keith R. Yamamoto. 1988. *Gene Wars: Military Control over the New Genetic Technologies.* Boston: Beech Tree.

Pimentel, David, et al. 1989. "Benefits and Risks of Genetic Engineering in Agriculture." *Bio Science,* vol. 39, no. 9, 606–614.

Rifkin, Jeremy. 1983. *Algeny.* New York: Viking Penguin.

Rifkin, Jeremy. 1985. *Declaration of a Heretic.* Boston: Routledge & Kegan Paul.

Schell, Jonathan. 1982. *The Fate of the Earth.* New York: Alfred A. Knopf.

Schneider, S. H., and R. S. Londer. 1984. *The Coevolution of Climate and Life.* San Francisco: Sierra Club Books.

Scientific Committee On Problems of the Environment (SCOPE). 1986. *Environmental Consequences of Nuclear War.* (2 vols.) New York: Wiley.

Slobodkin, Laurence B. 1980. *Growth and Regulation of Animal Populations.* New York: Dover Press.

Suzuki, David. 1989. *Genethics: The Clash Between the New Genetics and Human Values.* Cambridge, Mass.: Harvard University Press.

Thompson, Staley L., and Stephen H. Schneider. 1986. "Nuclear Winter Reappraised." *Foreign Affairs,* Summer.

Wilson, E. O. 1984. *Biophilia.* Cambridge, Mass.: Harvard University Press.

Wilson, E. O., ed. 1988. *Biodiversity.* Washington, D.C.: National Academy Press.

Woodwell, G. M. 1970. "Effects of Pollution on the Structure and Physiology of Ecosystems," *Science,* vol. 168, 429–433.

Chapter 7 Population Dynamics

Bouvier, Leon F. 1980. "America's Baby Boom Generation: The Fateful Bulge." *Population Bulletin,* April, 1-35.

Bouvier, Leon F. 1984. "Planet Earth 1984–2034: A Demographic Vision." *Population Bulletin,* vol. 39, no.1, 1–39.

Brown, Lester R., and Jodi Jacobson. 1986. *Our Demographically Divided World.* Washington, D.C.: Worldwatch Institute.

Dickenson, J.P., et al. 1983. *A Geography of the Third World.* New York: Methuen.

Dychtwald, Ken. 1989. *Age Wave: The Challenges and Opportunities of an Aging America.* New York: Tarcher.

Grant, James P. 1989. *The State of the World's Children 1989.* New York: Oxford University Press.

Haub, Carl. 1987. "Understanding Population Projections." *Population Bulletin,* vol. 42, no. 4, 1–41.

Haupt, Arthur, and Thomas T. Kane. 1985. *The Population Handbook: International.* 2nd ed. Washington, D.C.: Population Reference Bureau.

Jones, Elsie F., et al. 1986. *Teenage Pregnancy in Industrialized Countries.* New Haven, Conn.: Yale University Press.

Keyfitz, Nathan. 1989. "The Growing Human Population." *Scientific American,* September, 119–126.

Merrick, Thomas W. 1986. "World Population in Transition." *Population Bulletin,* vol. 41, no. 2, 1–51.

Merrick, Thomas W., and Stephen J. Tordella. 1988. "Demographics: People and Markets." *Population Bulletin,* vol. 43, no. 1, 1–46.

Population Reference Bureau. 1986. *Women in the World: The Women's Decade and Beyond.* Washington, D.C.: Population Reference Bureau.

Population Reference Bureau. Annual. *World Population Data Sheet.* Washington, D.C.: Population Reference Bureau.

Russell, Cheryl. 1987. *100 Predictions For the Baby Boom: The Next 50 Years.* New York: Plenum Press.

Saunders, John, 1988. *Basic Demographic Measures: A Practical Guide for Users.* Lanham, Md.: University Press of America.

Senderowitz, Judith, and John M. Paxman. 1985. "Adolescent Fertility: Worldwide Concerns." *Population Bulletin,* vol. 40, no. 2, 1–51.

Soldo, Beth J., and Emily M. Agree. 1988. "America's Elderly." *Population Bulletin,* vol. 43, no. 3, 1–51.

Teitelbaum, Michael, and Jay M. Winter. 1985. *The Fear of Population Decline.* Orlando, Fla.: Academic Press.

Weber, Susan, ed. 1988. *USA by Numbers: A Statistical Portrait of the United States.* Washington, D.C.: Zero Population Growth.

Weeks, John R. 1989. *Population: An Introduction to Concepts and Issues.* 4th ed. Belmont, Calif.: Wadsworth.

Chapter 8 Population Regulation

Borjas, George J., and Marta Tienda. 1987. "The Economic Consequences of Immigration." *Science,* vol. 235, 645–651.

Brown, Lester R. 1981. *Building a Sustainable Society.* New York: W. W. Norton.

Brown, Lester R., and Edward C. Wolf. 1985. *Reversing Africa's Decline.* Washington, D.C.: Worldwatch Institute.

Callahan, Daniel. 1972. "Ethics and Population Limitation." *Science,* vol. 175, 487–494.

Chandler, William U. 1985. *Investing in Children.* Washington, D.C.: Worldwatch Institute.

Commission on Population Growth and the American Future. 1972. *Population and the American Future.* Washington, D.C.: Government Printing Office.

Crewdson, John. 1983. *The Tarnished Door.* New York: New York Times Books.

Croll, Elisabeth, et al. 1985. *China's One-Child Family Policy.* New York: St. Martin's Press.

Dankelman, Irene, and Joan Davidson. 1988. *Women and the Environment in the Third World.* London: Earthscan.

David, Henry P., and Zdenek Dytrych. 1988. *Born Unwanted: Developmental Effects of Denied Abortion.* New York: Springer.

Djerassi, Carl. 1989. "The Bitter Pill." *Science,* vol. 245, 356–361.

Formos, Werner. 1987. *Gaining People, Losing Ground: A Blueprint for Stabilizing World Population.* Washington, D.C.: Population Institute.

Goliber, Thomas J. 1985. "Sub-Saharan Africa: Population Pressures on Development." *Population Bulletin,* vol. 40, no. 1, 1–45.

Greenhalgh, Susan, and John Bogaarts. 1987. "Fertility Policy in China: Future Options." *Science,* vol. 235, 1167–1172.

Gupte, Pranay. 1984. *The Crowded Earth: People and the Politics of Population.* New York: W. W. Norton.

Hardin, Garrett. 1974. *Mandatory Motherhood: The True Meaning of "Right to Life."* Boston: Beacon Press.

Hardin, Garrett. 1982. *Naked Emperors, Essays of a Taboo Stalker.* San Francisco: William Kaufman.

Hartmann, Betsy. 1987. *Reproductive Rights and Wrongs: The Global Politics of Population Control and Contraceptive Choice.* New York: Harper & Row.

Henshaw, Stanley, and Christopher Tietze. 1986. *Induced Abortion: A World Review.* New York: Alan Guttmacher Institute.

Hernandez, Donald J. 1985. *Success or Failure? Family Planning Programs in the Third World.* Westport, Conn.: Greenwood Press.

International Union for Conservation of Nature and Natural Resources and Planned Parenthood Federation. 1984. *Population and Natural Resources.* Gland, Switzerland: IUCN.

Jacobson, Jodi L. 1983. *Promoting Population Stabilization: Incentives for Small Families.* Washington, D.C.: Worldwatch Institute.

Jacobson, Jodi L. 1987. *Planning the Global Family.* Washington, D.C.: Worldwatch Institute.

Jacobson, Jodi L. 1988. "The Forgotten Resource: Third World Women." *World Watch*, May/June, 35–42.

Jaffe, Frederick S., et al. 1980. *Abortion Politics.* New York: Alan Guttmacher Institute.

Lamm, Richard D., and Gary Imhoff. 1985. *The Immigration Time Bomb.* New York: Dutton.

Loup, Jacques. 1983. *Can the Third World Survive?* Baltimore: Johns Hopkins University Press.

Menken, Jane, ed. 1986. *World Population and U.S. Policy: The Choices Ahead.* New York: W. W. Norton.

Morgan, Robin. 1984. *Sisterhood Is Global.* Garden City, N.Y.: Doubleday.

NARAL Foundation. 1984. *Legal Abortion: Arguments Pro & Con.* Washington, D.C.: National Abortion Rights Action League.

Population Reference Bureau. 1986. *Women in the World: The Women's Decade and Beyond.* Washington, D.C.: Population Reference Bureau.

Rodman, Hyman, et al. 1987. *The Abortion Question.* Princeton, N.J. Princeton University Press.

Simon, Julian L. 1981. *The Ultimate Resource.* Princeton, N.J. Princeton University Press.

van de Kaa, Dirk J. 1987. "Europe's Second Demographic Transition." *Population Bulletin*, vol. 42, no. 1, 1–57.

Wattenberg, Ben J. 1987. *The Birth Dearth.* New York: Pharos Books.

Weber, Susan, ed. 1988. *USA by Numbers: A Statistical Portrait of the United States.* Washington, D.C.: Zero Population Growth.

Wilbur, Amy E. 1986. "The Contraceptive Crisis in the United States." *Science Digest*, Sept., 54–85.

Zero Population Growth. 1977. *The Benefits of Zero Population Growth.* Washington, D.C.: Zero Population Growth.

Chapter 9 Population Distribution: Urbanization and Urban Problems

Barnett, Tony. 1989. *Social and Economic Development.* New York: Guilford Publications.

Brenneman, Russell L., and Sarah M. Bates, eds. 1984. *Land-Saving Action.* Covelo, Calif.: Island Press.

Brown, Lester R., and Jodi Jacobson. 1987. *The Future of Urbanization: Facing the Ecological and Economic Restraints.* Washington, D.C.: Worldwatch Institute.

Butler, Stuart M. 1980. *Enterprise Zones: Pioneering in the City.* Washington, D.C.: Heritage Foundation.

Cassidy, Robert. 1980. *Livable Cities: A Grass-Roots Guide to Rebuilding Urban America.* New York: Holt, Rinehart, & Winston.

Choate, Pat, and Susan Walter. 1981. *America in Ruins: Beyond the Public Works Pork Barrel.* Washington, D.C.: Council on State Planning Agencies.

Coates, Gary. 1981. *Resettling America: Energy, Ecology, and Community.* Andover, Mass.: Brick House.

Daiber, Franklin C. 1986. *Conservation of Tidal Marshes.* New York: Van Nostrand Reinhold.

Daniels, Thomas L., and Jihn W. Keller. 1988. *The Small Town Planning Handbook.* New York: APA Planners.

Dantzig, George B., and Thomas L. Saaty. 1973. *Compact City: A Plan for a Liveable Environment.* San Francisco: W. H. Freeman.

Department of International Economic and Social Affairs, United Nations. 1986. *Population Growth and Policies in Mega-Cities.* New York: Population Division, United Nations.

Exline, Christopher H., et al. 1982. *The City: Patterns and Processes in the Urban Ecosystem.* Boulder, Colo.: Westview Press.

Fabos, Julius Gy. 1985. *Land-Use Planning: From Global to Local Challenge.* New York: Chapman and Hall.

Farallones Institute. 1979. *The Integral Urban House: Self-Reliant Living in the City.* San Francisco: Sierra Club Books.

Jacobs, Jane. 1984. *Cities and the Wealth of Nations.* New York: Random House.

Kaplan, Marshall. 1989. *The Future of National Urban Policy.* Durham, N.C.: Duke University Press

Kemp, Roger L., ed. 1988. *America's Cities: Strategic Planning for the Future.* New York: Interstate Printers and Publishers.

League of Women Voters Education Fund. 1977. *Growth and Land Use: Shaping Future Patterns.* Washington, D.C.: League of Women Voters.

Leckie, Jim, et al. 1975. *Other Homes and Garbage: Designs for Self-Sufficient Living.* San Francisco: Sierra Club Books.

Ledec, George, and Robert Goodland. 1989. *Wildlands: Their Protection and Management in Economic Development.* Washington, D.C.: World Bank Publications.

Lowe, Marcia D. 1989. *The Bicycle: Vehicle for a Small Planet.* Washington, D.C.: Worldwatch Institute.

Luten, Daniel B. 1986. *Progress Against Growth.* New York: Guilford Publications.

Mantrell, Michael L., et al. 1989. *Creating Successful Communities: A Guidebook to Growth Management Strategies.* Covelo, Calif.: Island Press.

Marcus, Clare C., and Wendy Sarkissian. 1986. *Housing as if People Mattered.* Berkeley: University of California Press.

McHarg, Ian L. 1969. *Design with Nature.* Garden City, N.Y.: Natural History Press.

Morris, David. 1982. *Energy and the Transformation of Urban America.* San Francisco: Sierra Club Books.

Mumford, Lewis. l968. *The Urban Prospect*. New York: Harcourt Brace Jovanovich.

National Academy of Sciences. 1983. *Future Directions of Urban Public Transportation*. Washington, D.C.: National Academy Press.

Odum, Eugene P. l969. "The Strategy of Ecosystem Development." *Science*, vol. l64, 262–270.

Register, Richard. 1987. *Ecocity Berkeley: Building Cities for a Healthy Future*. Berkeley, Calif.: North Atlantic Books.

Renner, Michael. 1988. *Rethinking the Role of the Automobile*. Washington, D.C.: Worldwatch Institute.

Replogle, Michael L. 1988. *Bicycles and Public Transportation: New Links to Suburban Transit*. 2nd ed. Washington, D.C.: The Bicycle Federation.

Roszak, Theodore. 1985. *Dwellers in the Land: The Bioregional Vision*. San Francisco: Sierra Club Books.

Ryn, Sin van der, and Peter Calthorpe. 1986. *Sustainable Communities: A New Design Synthesis for Cities, Suburbs, and Towns*. San Francisco: Sierra Club.

Smith, Christopher C. 1988. *Public Problems: The Management of Urban Stress*. New York: Guilford Publications.

Stokes, Samuel N., et al. 1989. *Saving America's Countryside: A Guide to Rural Conservation*. Baltimore, Md.: Johns Hopkins University Press.

Todd, Nancy Jack, and John Todd. 1984. *Bioshelters, Ocean Arks, City Farming: Ecology As the Basis of Design*. San Francisco: Sierra Club Books.

Wachs, Martin. 1989. "U.S. Transit Subsidy Policy: In Need of Reform." *Science*, vol. 244, 1545–1549.

Westman, Walter E. 1985. *Ecology, Impact Assessment and Environmental Planning*. New York: John Wiley.

Whyte, William. 1983. "Design As If People Mattered." *Technology Review*, July, 37–42.

Chapter 10 Soil Resources

Batie, Sandra S. 1983. *Soil Erosion: Crisis in America's Croplands?* Washington, D.C.: Conservation Foundation.

Brady, Nyle C. 1974. *The Nature and Properties of Soils*. New York: Macmillan.

Brown, Lester R., and Edward C. Wolf. 1984. *Soil Erosion: Quiet Crisis in the World Economy*. Washington, D.C.: Worldwatch Institute.

Crosson, Pierre R., and Anthony T. Stout. 1983. *Productivity Effects of Cropland Erosion in the United States*. Washington, D.C.: Resources For the Future.

Dale, Tom, and V. G. Carter. 1955. *Topsoil and Civilization*. Norman: University of Oklahoma Press.

Dregnue, Harold. E. 1983. *Desertification of Arid Lands*. New York: Academic Press.

Dregnue, Harold. E. 1985. "Aridity and Land Degradation." *Environment*, vol. 27, no. 8, 33–39.

Gorse, Jean E., and David R. Steeds. 1987. *Desertification in the Sahelian and Sudanian Zones of West Africa*. Washington, D.C.: World Bank.

Grainger, Alan. 1983. *Desertification: How People Make Deserts, How People Can Stop and Why They Don't*. Washington, D.C.: Earthscan.

Heiser, Charles B., Jr. 1985. *Of Plants and People*. Norman: University of Oklahoma Press.

Kassas, Mohamed A. F. 1988. "Ecology and Management of Desertification." In National Geographic Society, *Earth '88: Changing Geographic Perspectives*. Washington, D.C.: National Geographic Society, pp. 198–211.

Little, Charles E. 1987. *Green Fields Forever: The Conservation Tillage Revolution in America*. Covelo, Calif.: Island Press.

Myers, Norman, ed. 1984. *Gaia: An Atlas of Planet Management*. Garden City, N.Y.: Anchor Press/Doubleday.

National Academy of Sciences. 1986. *Soil Conservation*. (2 vols.) Washington, D.C.: National Academy Press.

Paddock, Joe, et al. 1987. *Soil and Survival: Land Stewardship and the Future of American Agriculture*. San Francisco: Sierra Club Books.

Ramadé, Francois. 1984. *Ecology of Natural Resources*. New York: John Wiley.

Sheridan, David. 1981. *Desertification of the United States*. Washington, D.C.: Resources for the Future.

Sophen, C. D., and J. V. Baird. 1982. *Soils and Soil Management*. Reston, Va.: Reston Publishing.

Tolba, M.K. 1986. "Desertification in Africa." *Land Use Policy*, vol. 3, 260–268.

Tompkins, Peter and Christopher Bird. 1989. *Secrets of the Soil*. New York: Harper & Row.

U. S. Department of Agriculture. 1985. *Analysis of Policies to Conserve Soil and Reduce Surplus Crop Production*. Washington, D.C.: U.S. Department of Agriculture Economic Report 534.

Wilson, G. F., et al. 1986. *The Soul of the Soil: A Guide to Ecological Soil Management*. 2nd ed. Quebec, Canada: Gaia Services.

Chapter 11 Water Resources

Anderson, Terry L., ed. 1986. *Water Rights: Scarce Resource Allocation, Bureaucracy, and the Environment*. San Francisco: Pacific Institute for Public Policy.

Ashworth, William. 1982. *Nor Any Drop To Drink*. New York: Summit Books.

Briscoe, John, and David de Ferrani. 1988. *Water for Rural Communities: Helping People Help Themselves*. Washington, D.C.: World Bank.

Conservation Foundation. 1984. *America's Water: Current Trends and Emerging Issues*. Washington, DC: Conservation Foundation.

Cousteau, Jacques-Yves, et al. 1981. *The Cousteau Almanac: An Inventory of Life on Our Water Planet*. Garden City, N.Y.: Doubleday.

El-Ashry, Mohamed, and Diana C. Gibbons, eds., 1988. *Water and the Arid Lands of the Western United States*. New York: Cambridge University Press.

Falkenmark, M. 1986. "Fresh Water— Time for a Modified Approach." *Ambio*, vol. 15, 192–200.

Fradkin, Phillip L. 1981. *A River No More: The Colorado and the West*. New York: Alfred A. Knopf.

Franco, David A., and Robert G. Wetel. 1983. *To Quench Our Thirst: The Present and Future Status of Freshwater Resources of the United States*. Ann Arbor: University of Michigan Press.

Goldsmith, Edward, and Nicholas Hidyard, eds. 1986. *The Social and Environmental Effects of Large Dams*. (3 vols.) New York: John Wiley.

Golfarb, William. 1988. *Water Law*, 2nd ed. New York: Lewis Publishers.

Golubev, G.N., and A.K. Biswas. 1985. *Large Scale Water Transfers: Emerging Environmental and Social Experiences*. Oxford, England: Tycooly.

Gottlieb, Robert. 1989. *A Life of Its Own: The Politics and Power of Water*. New York: Harcourt Brace Jovanovich.

Hunt, Constance Elizabeth. 1988. *Down by the River: The Impact of Federal Water Projects and Policies on Biological Diversity*. Covelo, Calif.: Island Press.

Kahrl, William L. 1982. *Water and Power*. Berkeley: University of California Press.

Kourik, Robert. 1988. *Gray Water Use in the Landscape*. Santa Rosa, Calif.: Edible Publications.

Marx, Wesley. 1977. *Acts of God, Acts of Man*. New York: McCann & Geohegan.

Mather, J. R. 1984. *Water Resources Distribution, Use, and Management*. New York: Wiley.

Myers, Norman, ed. 1984. *Gaia: An Atlas of Planet Management*. Garden City, N.Y.: Anchor Press/Doubleday.

Okun, Daniel L. 1975. "Water Management in England: A Regional Model." *Environmental Science and Technology*, vol. 9, no. 10, 918–923.

Pimentel, David, et al. 1982. "Water Resources in Food and Energy Production." *BioScience*, vol. 32, no. 11, 861–867.

Postel, Sandra. 1985. *Conserving Water: The Untapped Alternative*. Washington, D.C.: Worldwatch Institute.

Pringle, Laurence. 1982. *Water—The Next Great Resource Battle*. New York: Macmillan.

Ramadé, Francois. 1984. *The Ecology of Natural Resources*. New York: John Wiley.

Reisner, Marc. 1986. *Cadillac Desert: The American West and Its Disappearing Water*. New York: Viking.

Reisner, Marc. 1988. "The Next Water War: Cities Versus Agriculture." *Issues in Science and Technology*, Winter, 98–102.

Reisner, Marc, and Sara Bates. 1990. *Overtapped Oasis: Reform or Revolution for Western Water*. Covelo, Calif.: Island Press.

Rocky Mountain Institute. 1988. *Catalog of Water-Efficient Technologies for the Urban/Residential Sector*. Old Snowmass, Colo.: Rocky Mountain Institute.

Rogers, Peter P. 1986. "Fresh Water." In Robert Repetto, ed., *The Global Possible: Resources, Development, and the New Century*. New Haven, Conn.: Yale University Press, pp. 255–297.

Sheaffer, John, and Leonard Stevens. 1983. *Future Water*. New York: William Morrow.

U.S. Geological Survey. 1988. *Estimated Water Use in the United States in 1985*. Washngton, D.C.: U.S. Geological Survey.

Watson, Lyall. 1988. *The Water Planet*. New York: Crown.

Wijkman, Anders, and Lloyd Timberlake. 1984. *Natural Disasters: Acts of God or Acts of Man?* Washington, D.C.: Earthscan.

World Resources Institute. Annual. *World Resources*. New York: Basic Books.

Worster, Donald. 1985. *Rivers of Empire: Water, Aridity, and the Growth of the American West*. New York: Pantheon.

Chapter 12 Food Resources

Aliteri, Miguel A. 1983. *Agroecology: The Scientific Basis of Alternative Agriculture*. Berkeley, Calif.: Division of Biological Control, University of California, Berkeley.

Bardach, John. 1988. "Aquaculture: Moving from Craft to Industry." *Environment*, vol. 30, no. 2, 7–40.

Bartholomew, Mel. 1987. *Square Foot Gardening*. Emmaus, Pa.: Rodale Press.

Battie, Sandra S., and Robert G. Healy. 1983. "The Future of American Agriculture." *Scientific American*, vol. 248, no. 2, 44–53.

Bennett, Jon. 1987. *The Hunger Machine: The Politics of Food*. New York: Basil Blackwell.

Berry, Wendell. 1986. "Home Economics." *Whole Earth Review*, Summer, 50–56.

Bezdicek, D. F., ed. 1984. *Organic Farming: Current Technology and Its Role in a Sustainable Agriculture*. Washington, D.C.: American Society of Agronomy.

Brown, Larry. 1987. "Hunger in America." *Scientific American*, vol. 256, no. 2, 37–41.

Brown, Lester R. 1988. *The Changing World Food Prospect: The Nineties and Beyond*. Washington, D.C.: Worldwatch Institute.

Brown, Lester R. 1988. "The Vulnerability of Oil-Based Farming." *World Watch*, Mar.-Apr., 24–29.

Brown, Lester R., et al. Annual. *State of the World*. New York: W. W. Norton.

Calder, Nigel. 1986. *The Green Machines*. New York: Putnam.

Clawson, David L. 1985. "Small-Scale Polyculture: An Alternative Development Model." *Philippines Geographical Journal*, vol. 29, nos. 3 & 4, 1–12.

Crosson, Pierre R. 1984. "Agricultural Land: Will There Be Enough?" *Environment*. vol. 26, no. 7, 17–20, 40–45.

Crosson, Pierre R., and Norman J. Rosenberg. 1989. "Strategies for Agriculture." *Scientific American*, September, 128–135.

Douglass, Gordon K., ed. 1984. *Agricultural Sustainability in a Changing World Order*. Boulder, Colo.: Westview Press.

Dover, Michael J., and Lee M. Talbot. 1988. "Feeding the Earth: An Agroecological Solution." *Technology Review*, Feb.-Mar., 27–35.

Doyle, Jack. 1985. *Altered Harvest: Agriculture, Genetics, and the Fate of the World's Food Supply*. New York: Viking.

Dudal, R. 1982. "Land Degradation in a World Perspective." *Journal of Soil and Water Conservation*, vol. 37, no. 5, 245–249.

Editorial Research Reports. 1988. *How the U.S. Got Into Agriculture and Why It Can't Get Out*. Washington, D.C.: Congressional Quarterly.

Editors of *Organic Gardening and Farming Magazine*. 1987. *The Encyclopedia of Organic Gardening*. Emmaus, Pa.: Rodale Press.

Ehrlich, Anne H. 1988. "Development and Agriculture." In Paul R. Ehrlich and John P. Holdren, eds., *The Cassandra Conference: Resources and the Human Predicament*. Texas Station: Texas A & M University Press, pp. 75–100.

Everhart, W. H., et al. 1981. *Principles of Fishery Science*. 2nd ed. Ithaca, N.Y.: Comstock.

Fenzau, C. J., and Charles Walters, Jr. 1979. *An Acres USA Primer*. Raytown, Mo.: Acres USA.

Fletcher, W. Wendell, and Charles E. Little. 1982. *The American Cropland Crisis*. Bethesda, Md.: American Land Forum.

Food and Agriculture Organization of the United Nations. 1988. *1986 Yearbook of Fishery Statistics*. New York: United Nations.

Forbes, Malcolm H., and Lois J. Merrill, eds. 1986. *Global Hunger: A Look at the Problem and Potential Solutions*. Evansville, Ind.: University of Evansville Press.

Fukuoka, Masanobu. 1985. *The Natural Way of Farming: The Theory and Practice of Green Philosophy*. New York: Japan Publications.

Gabel, Medard. 1986. *Empty Breadbasket: The Coming Challenge to America's Food Supply and What We Can Do About It*. Emmaus, Pa.: Rodale.

Gips, Terry. 1987. *Breaking the Pesticide Habit*. Minneapolis, Minn.: IASA.

Goliber, Thomas J. 1985. "Sub-Saharan Africa: Population Pressures on Development." *Population Bulletin*, vol. 40, no. 1, 1–47.

Granatstein, David. 1988. *Reshaping the Bottom Line: On-farm Strategies for a Sustainable Agriculture*. Stillwater, Minn.: Land Stewardship Project.

Grant, James P. 1989. *The State of the World's Children 1989*. New York: Oxford University Press.

Harrison, Paul. 1987. *The Greening of Africa*. New York: Viking/Penguin.

Hellinger, Stephen, et al. 1988. *Aid for Just Development*. Boulder, Colo.: Lynne Rienner.

Hendry, Peter. 1988. "Food and Population: Beyond Five Billion." *Population Bulletin*, Apr., 1–55.

Hrabovszky, Janos P. 1986. "Agriculture: The Land Base." In Robert Repetto, ed., *The Global Possible: Resources, Development, and the New Century*. New Haven, Conn.: Yale University Press.

Huessy, Peter. 1978. *The Food First Debate*. San Francisco: Institute for Food and Development Policy.

Hunger Project. 1985. *Ending Hunger: An Idea Whose Time Has Come*. New York: Praeger.

International Rice Institute. 1988. *Science, Ethics, and Food*. Manila, Philippines: International Rice Institute.

Jackson, Wes, et al., eds. 1985. *Meeting the Expectations of Land: Essays in Sustainable Agriculture and Stewardship*. Berkeley, Calif.: North Point Press.

Jackson, Wes. 1980. *New Roots for Agriculture*. San Francisco: Friends of the Earth.

Klausner, A. 1985. "Food From the Sea." *Biotechnology*, vol. 3, no. 1, 27–32.

Klopenburg, Jack R., ed. 1988. *Seeds and Sovereignty*. Durham, N.C.: Duke University Press.

Lal, Rattan. 1987. "Managing the Soils of Sub-Saharan Africa." *Science*, vol. 236, 1069–1076.

Lappé, Francis M., and Joseph Collins. 1977. *Food First*. Boston: Houghton Mifflin.

Lappé, Francis M., et al. 1988. *Betraying the National Interest*. San Francisco: Food First.

Linburg, Peter R. 1981. *Farming the Waters*. New York: Beaufort Books (Scribner).

Lockeretz, W. G., et al. 1981. "Organic Farming in the Corn Belt." *Science*, vol. 211, 540–547.

Lockeretz, William G., ed. 1987. *Sustaining Agriculture Near Cities*. Ankeny, Iowa: Soil and Water Conservation Society.

Lowe, Marcia D. 1988. "Salmon Ranching and Farming Net Growing Harvest." *World Watch*, Jan.-Feb., 28–32.

Lowrance, Richard, ed. 1984. *Agricultural Ecosystems: Unifying Concepts*. Somerset, N.J.: John Wiley.

McKinney, Tom. 1987. *The Sustainable Farm of the Future*. Old Snowmass, Colo.: Rocky Mountain Institute.

Mollison, Bill. 1988. *Permaculture: A Designer's Manual*. Davis, Calif.: AgAccess.

Molnar, Joesph J., and Henry Kinnucan, ed. 1989. *Biotechnology and the New Agricultural Revolution*. Boulder, Colo.: Westview Press.

Montclair, Susan G. 1977. *How the Other Half Dies: The Real Reasons for World Hunger*. Montclair, N.J.: Allanheld, Osmun, & Co.

Morgan, Dan. 1980. *Merchants of Grain*. New York: Penguin Books.

Murphy, Elaine M. 1984. *Food and Population: A Global Concern*. Washington, D.C.: Population Reference Bureau.

Myers, Norman, ed. 1984. *Gaia: An Atlas of Planet Management*. Garden City, N.Y.: Anchor Press/Doubleday.

National Academy of Sciences. 1989. *Alternative Agriculture*. Washington, D.C.: National Academy Press.

Nicholaides, J. J., et al. 1985. "Agricultural Alternatives for the Amazon Basin." *BioScience*, vol. 35, no. 5, 279–284.

Office of Technology Assessment. 1988. *Enhancing Agriculture in Africa*. Washington, D.C.: Office of Technology Assessment.

Oldfield, Margery L. 1984. *The Value of Conserving Genetic Resources*. Washington, D.C.: U.S. Department of Interior, National Park Service.

Olson, Steve. 1986. *Biotechnology: An Industry Comes of Age*. Washington, D.C.: National Academy Press.

Parr, J. F., et al. 1983. "Organic Farming in the United States: Principles and Perspectives." *Agro-Ecosystems*, vol. 8, 183–201.

Peters, William J., and Leon F. Neuerschwander. 1988. *Farming in the Third World Forest*. Moscow: University of Idaho Press.

Phipps, Tim T., Pierre R. Crosson, and Kent A. Price. 1986, eds. *Agriculture and the Environment*. Washington, D.C.: Resources for the Future.

Pimentel, David, and Carl W. Hall. 1984. *Food and Energy Resources*. Orlando, Fla: Academic Press.

Pimentel, David, and Carl W. Hall. 1989 *Food and Natural Resources*. Orlando, Fla: Academic Press.

Pimentel, David. 1987. "Down on the Farm: Genetic Engineering Meets Ecology." *Technology Review*, Jan., pp. 24–30.

Pimentel, David. 1988. "Industrialized Agriculture and Natural Resources." In Paul R. Ehrlich and John P. Holdren, eds., *The Cassandra Conference: Resources and the Human Predicament*. Texas Station: Texas A & M University Press, pp. 53–74.

Plucknett, D. L. et al. 1987. *Gene Banks and the World's Food*. Princeton, N.J.: Princeton University Press.

Poincelot, Raymond P. 1986. *Toward a Sustainable Agriculture*. Westport, Conn.: AVI Publishing.

Prescott-Allen, Robert and Christine Prescott-Allen. 1983. *Genes From the Wild: Using Wild Genetic Resources for Food and Raw Materials*. Washington, D.C.: Earthscan.

Reichert, Walt. 1982. "Agriculture's Diminishing Diversity." *Environment*, vol. 24, no. 9, 6–11 and 39–43.

Robbins, John. 1987. *Diet for a New America*. Waldpole, N.H.: Stillpoint Publishing.

Rose, Tore, ed. 1985. *Crisis and Recovery in Sub-Saharan Africa*. Paris, France: Organization for Economic Recovery and Development.

Rothschild, B. J. 1981. "More Food From the Sea?" *BioScience*, Mar., 216–220.

Sampson, R. N. 1981. *Farmland or Wasteland: A Time to Choose*. Emmaus, Pa.: Rodale Press.

Sanchez, Pedro A., and Jose R. Benites. 1987. "Low-Input Cropping for Acid Soils of the Humid Tropics." *Science*, vol. 238, 1521–1527.

Sanchez, Pedro A., et al. 1982. "Amazon Basin Soils: Management for Continuous Crop Production." *Science*, vol. 216, 821–827.

Schell, Orville. 1984. *Modern Meat: Antibiotics, Hormones, and the Pharmaceutical Farm*. New York: Random House.

Schriefer, Donald L. 1984. *From the Soil Up*. Des Moines, Iowa: Wallace-Homestead Printing Co.

Solkoff, Joel. 1985. *The Politics of Food*. San Francisco: Sierra Club Books.

Steiner, Frederick. 1981. *Ecological Planning for Farmlands Preservation*. Chicago: A.P.A. Planners Press.

Strange, Marty. 1988. *Family Farming*. Lincoln: University of Nebraska Press.

Timberlake, Lloyd. 1985. *Africa in Crisis*. Washington, D.C.: Earthscan.

Todd, Nancy J., and John Todd. 1984. *Bioshelters, Ocean Arks, City Farming: Ecology as a Basis for Design*. San Francisco: Sierra Club Books.

Tudge, Colin. 1988. *Food Crops for the Future: Development of Plant Resources*. Oxford, UK: Blackwell.

Turner, B. L., and Stephen B. Brush, eds. 1987. *Comparative Farming Systems*. New York: Guilford Publications.

Vietmeyer, Noel D. 1986. "Lesser-Known Plants of Potential Use in Agriculture." *Science*, vol. 232, 1379–1384.

Wijkman, Anders, and Lloyd Timberlake. 1984. *Natural Disasters: Acts of God or Acts of Man?* Washington, D.C.: Earthscan.

Withers, Leslie, and Tom Peterson, eds. 1987. *Hunger Action Handbook: What You Can Do and How To Do It*. Decatur, Ga: Seeds Magazine.

Witter, Sylvan, et al. 1987. *Feeding a Billion: Frontiers of Chinese Agriculture*. East Lansing, Mich: Michigan State University Press.

Wolf, Edward C. 1986. *Beyond the Green Revolution: New Approaches for Third World Agriculture*. Washington, D.C.: Worldwatch Institute.

World Bank and the United Nations Environment Program. 1989. *Africa's Adjustment and Growth in the 1980s*. Philadelphia, Penn.: World Bank Publications.

World Resources Institute and International Institute for Environment and Development. Annual. *World Resources*. New York: Basic Books.

Chapter 13   Land Resources: Forests, Rangelands, Parks, and Wilderness

Allin, Craig W. 1982. *The Politics of Wilderness Preservation*. Westport, Conn.: Greenwood Press.

Anderson, Dennis, and Robert Fishwick. 1985. *Fuelwood Consumption and Deforestation in African Countries*. Washington, D.C.: The World Bank.

Arrandale, Thomas. 1983. *The Battle for Natural Resources*. Washington, D.C.: Congressional Quarterly Books.

Atwood, Charles Lee. 1989. "Restoring the Ravaged Rangeland." In National Audubon Society. *Audubon Wildlife Report 1989/1990*. New York: Academic Press, pp. 330–364.

Beattie, Mollie, et al. 1983. *Working With Your Woodland*. Hanover, N.H.: University Press of New England.

Borman, F. H. 1985. "Air Pollution and Forests: An Ecosystem Perspective." *BioScience*, vol. 35, no. 7, 434–441.

Borman, F. H., and G. E. Likens. 1979. *Pattern and Process in a Forested Ecosystem*. New York: Springer-Verlag.

Brown, Lester R., et al. Annual. *State of the World*. New York: W. W. Norton.

Bruneig, E. F. 1987. "The Forest Ecosystem: Tropical and Boreal." *Ambio*, vol. 16, 68–79.

Camp, Orville. 1984. *The Forest Farmer's Handbook*. Ashland, Oreg.: Sky River Press.

Caras, Roger. 1979. *The Forest*. New York: Holt, Rinehart and Winston.

Caufield, Catherine. 1985. *In the Rainforest*. New York: Alfred A. Knopf.

Chase, Alston. 1986. *Playing God in Yellowstone: The Destruction of America's First National Park*. New York: Atlantic Monthly Press.

Clawson, Marion. 1975. *Forests for Whom and for What?* Baltimore: John Hopkins University Press.

Clawson, Marion. 1983. *The Federal Lands Revisited*. Washington, D.C.: Resources for the Future.

Cohen, Michael P. 1984. *The Pathless Way: John Muir and American Wilderness*. Madison: University of Wisconsin Press.

Collard, Andree, and Joyce Contrucci. 1989. *Rape of the Wild: Man's Violence Against Animals and the Earth*. Bloomington: Indiana University Press.

Connally, Eugenia, ed. 1982. *National Parks in Crisis*. Washington, D.C.: National Parks and Conservation Association.

Conservation Foundation. 1985. *National Parks and the New Generation*. Washington, D.C.: Conservation Foundation.

Dana, Samuel T., and Sally K. Fairfax. 1980. *Forest and Range Policy: Its Development in the United States*. 2nd ed. New York: McGraw-Hill.

Daniel, T.W., et al. 1979. *Principles of Silviculture*. New York: McGraw-Hill.

Deacon, Robert T., and M. Bruce Johnson, eds. 1986. *Forestlands: Public and Private*. San Francisco: Pacific Institute for Public Policy.

Defenders of Wildlife. 1982. *1080: The Case Against Poisoning Our Wildlife*. Washington, D.C.: Government Printing Office.

Dysart, Benjamin III, and Marion Clawson. 1988. *Managing Public Lands in the Public Interest*. Westport, Conn.: Praeger.

Eckholm, Erik, et al. 1984. *Fuelwood: The Energy Crisis That Won't Go Away*. Washington, D.C.: Earthscan.

Eckholm, Erik. 1982. *Down to Earth: Environment and Human Needs*. New York: Norton.

Erwin, Keith. 1989. *Fragile Majesty: The Battle for North America's Last Great Forest*. Seattle, Wash.: Mountaineer's Books.

Feeny, Andy. 1989. "The Pacific Northwest's Ancient Forests: Ecosystems Under Seige." In National Audubon Society, *Audubon Wildlife Report 1989/1990*. New York: Academic Press, pp. 93–153.

Ferguson, Denzel, and Nancy Ferguson. 1983. *Sacred Cows at the Public Trough*. Bend, Ore.: Maverick Publications.

Francis, John G., and Richard Ganzel, eds. 1984. *Western Public Lands: The Management of Natural Resources in a Time of Declining Federalism*. Totowa, N.J.: Rowman & Allanheld.

Friends of the Trees. 1989. *1988 International Green Front Report*. Whelan, Wash.: Friends of the Trees.

Fritz, Edward. 1983. *Sterile Forest: The Case Against Clearcutting*. Austin, Texas: Eakin Press.

Frome, Michael. 1974. *The Battle for the Wilderness*. New York: Praeger.

Frome, Michael. 1983. *The Forest Service*. Boulder, Colo.: Westview Press.

Gradwohl, Judith, and Russell Greenberg. 1988. *Saving the Tropical Forests*. Covelo, Calif.: Island Press.

Hartzog, George B., Jr. 1988. *Battling for the National Parks*. New York: Moyer Bell.

Hazlewood, Peter T. 1989. *Cutting Our Losses: Policy Reform to Sustain Tropical Forest Resources*. Washington, D.C.: World Resources Institute.

Heady, H. F. 1975. *Rangeland Management*. New York: McGraw-Hill.

Hendee, John, et al., eds. 1977. *Principles of Wilderness Management*. Washington, D.C.: Government Printing Office.

Hewett, Charles E., and Thomas E. Hamilton, eds. 1982. *Forests in Demand: Conflicts and Solutions*. Boston: Auburn Publishing House.

Jordan, Carl F. 1982. "Amazon Rain Forests." *American Scientist*, vol. 70, July-August, 394–400.

Kelly, David. 1988. *Secrets of the Old Growth Forest*. Layton, Utah: Gibbs Smith.

Leopold, Aldo. 1949. *A Sand County Almanac*. New York: Oxford University Press.

Libecap, Gary D. 1986. *Locking Up the Range: Federal Land Control and Grazing*. San Francisco: Pacific Institute for Public Policy Research.

MacKinnon, J., and K. MacKinnon. 1986. *Managing Protected Areas in the Tropics*. Gland, Switzerland: International Union for the Conservation of Nature and Natural Resources.

Maser, Chris. 1988. *The Redesigned Forest*. San Pedro, Calif.: R. & E. Miles.

McNeely, Jeffery A., and Kenton R. Miller, eds. 1984. *National Parks, Conservation, and Development*. Washington, D.C.: Smithsonian Institution Press.

Mello, Robert A. 1987. *Last Stand of the Red Spruce*. Covelo, Calif.: Island Press.

Minckler, Leon S. 1980. *Woodland Ecology*. 2nd ed. Syracuse, N.Y.: Syracuse University Press.

Moll, Gary, and Sara Ebennech. 1989. *Shading Our Cities: A Resource Guide for Urban and Community Forests*. Covelo, Calif.: Island Press.

Morgan, F., and J. R. Vincent. 1987. *Natural Management of Tropical Moist Forests: Silvicultural and Management Prospects of Sustained Utilization*. New Haven, Conn.: Yale School of Forestry.

Myers, Norman, ed. 1984. *Gaia: An Atlas of Planet Management*. Garden City, N.Y.: Anchor Press/Doubleday.

Myers, Norman. 1984. *The Primary Source: Tropical Forests and Our Future*. New York: W. W. Norton.

Nash, Roderick. 1982. *Wilderness and the American Mind*. 3rd ed. New Haven, Conn.: Yale University Press.

National Audubon Society. Annual. *Audubon Wildlife Report*. New York: National Audubon Society.

National Parks and Conservation Association. 1988. *Blueprint for National Parks* (9 vols). Washington, D.C.: National Parks and Conservation Association.

Norse, Elliot. 1989. *Ancient Forests of the Pacific Northwest*. Covelo, Calif.: Island Press.

Office of Technology Assessment. 1984. *Technologies to Sustain Tropical Forest Resources*. Washington, D.C.: Government Printing Office.

Office of Technology Assessment. 1989. *Oil Production in the Arctic National Wildlife Refuge*. Washington, D.C.: Government Printing Office.

Olen, Paul M., et al. 1985. "Mining and Wilderness: Incompatible Uses or Justifiable Compromise." *Environment*, vol. 27, no. 3, 13–18.

O'Toole, Randal. 1987. *Reforming the Forest Service*. Covelo, Calif.: Island Press.

Peters, William J., and Leon F. Neuerschwander. 1989. *Farming in the Third World Forest*. Moscow: University of Idaho Press.

Postel, Sandra, and Lori Heise. 1988. *Reforesting the Earth*. Washington, D.C.: Worldwatch Institute.

Postel, Sandra. 1984. *Air Pollution, Acid Rain, and the Future of Forests*. Washington, D.C.: Worldwatch Institute.

Ramadé, Francois. 1984. *Ecology of Natural Resources*. New York: John Wiley.

Raphael, Ray. 1981. *Tree Talk: The People and Politics of Timber*. Covelo, Calif.: Island Press.

Repetto, Robert, ed. 1986. *The Global Possible: Resources, Development, and the New Century*. New Haven, Conn.: Yale University Press.

Repetto, Robert. 1989. *The Forest for the Trees: Government Policies and the Misuse of Forest Resources*. Washington, D.C.: World Resources Institute.

Repetto, Robert, and Malcolm Gillis, eds. 1988. *Public Policy and the Misuse of Forest Resources*. New York: Cambridge University Press.

Robinson, Gordon. 1987. *The Forest and the Trees: A Guide to Excellent Forestry*. Covelo, Calif.: Island Press.

Runte, Alfred. 1987. *National Parks: The American Experience*. 2nd ed. Lincoln: University of Nebraska Press.

Sampson, Neil, and Dwight Hart, eds. 1989. *Natural Resources for the 21st Century*. Covelo, Calif.: Island Press.

Shanks, Bernard. 1984. *This Land Is Your Land*. San Francisco: Sierra Club Books.

Sierra Club. 1982. *Our Public Lands: An Introduction to the Agencies and Issues*. San Francisco: Sierra Club Books.

Simon, David J., ed. 1989. *Our Common Lands: Defending the National Parks*. Covelo, Calif.: Island Press.

Smith, D. M. 1982. *The Practice of Silviculture*. New York: John Wiley.

Society of American Forresters. 1981. *Choices in Silviculture For American Forests*. Washington, D.C.: Society of American Forresters.

Spurr, Stephen H., and Buron V. Barnes. 1980. *Forest Ecology*. 3rd ed. New York: Ronald Press.

Stoddard, Charles H., and Glenn M. Stoddard. 1987. *Essentials of Forestry Practice*. 4th ed. New York: John Wiley.

U.S. Department of Interior. 1984. *50 Years of Public Land Management: 1934–1984*. Washington, D.C.: Bureau of Land Management.

Waring, R. H., and W. R. Schlesinger. 1985. *Forest Ecosystems: Concepts and Management*. Orlando, Fla.: Academic Press.

Wegner, Karl F., ed. 1984. *Forestry Handbook*. 2nd ed. New York: John Wiley.

Wilcove, David S. 1988. *National Forests: Policies for the Future*, vols. 1 & 2. Washington, D.C.: Wilderness Society.

Wilderness Society. 1988. *Ancient Forests: A Threatened Heritage*. Washington, D.C.: The Wilderness Society.

Wilderness Society. 1989. *Old Growth in the Pacific Northwest: A Status Report*. Washington, D.C.; Wilderness Society.

Wilson, Edward O. 1989. "Threats to Biodiversity." *Scientific American*, September, pp. 108–116.

World Resources Institute Annual. *World Resources*. New York: Basic Books.

World Resources Institute, World Bank, and United Nations Development Program. 1985. *Tropical Forests: A Call for Action*. Washington, D.C.: World Resources Institute.

Wright, Henry A., and Arthur W. Bailey. 1983. *Fire Ecology*. New York: John Wiley.

Wuerthner, George. 1989. *Yellowstone and the Fires of Change*. Salt Lake City, Utah: Dream Garden Press.

Zaslowsky, Dyan, and The Wilderness Society. 1986. *These American Lands*. New York: Henry Holt.

Chapter 14   Wild Plant and Animal Resources

Allen, Robert L. 1980. *How to Save the World*. London: Kogan Page.

Anderson, S. H. 1985. *Managing Our Wildlife Resources*. Columbus, Ohio: Charles Merrill.

Bailey, J. A. 1984. *Principles of Wildlife Management*. New York: John Wiley.

Baker, Ron. 1985. *The American Hunting Myth*. New York: Vantage Press.

Blockstein, David E. 1989. "Toward a Federal Plan for Biodiversity." *Issues in Science and Technology*, Summer, 63–67.

Bonner, Nigel. 1989. *Whales of the World*. New York: Facts on File.

Clark, Stephen R.L. 1984. *The Moral Status of Animals*. New York: Oxford University Press.

Credlund, Arthur G. 1983. *Whales and Whaling*. New York: Seven Hills Books.

Dasmann, Raymond F. 1981. *Wildlife Biology*. 2nd ed. New York: John Wiley.

Davis, Steven, et al. 1986. *Plants in Danger: What Do We Know?* Cambridge, U.K.: Conservation Monitoring Centre, International Union for Conservation of Nature and Natural Resources.

Decher, Daniels J., and Gary R. Goff, eds. 1987. *Valuing Wildlife: Economic and Social Perspectives*. Boulder, Colo.: Westview Press.

Disilvestro, Roger L. 1989. *The Endangered Kingdom: The Struggle to Save America's Wildlife*. New York: Wiley.

Dunlap, Thomas R. 1988. *Saving America's Wildlife*. Princeton, N. J.: Princeton University Press.

Durrell, Lee. 1986. *State of the Ark: An Atlas of Conservation in Action*. Garden City, N.Y.: Doubleday.

Ehrlich, Paul, and Anne Ehrlich. 1981. *Extinction*. New York: Random House.

Elliot, David K. 1986. *Dynamics of Extinction*. New York: Wiley.

Elton, Charles S. 1958. *The Ecology of Invasions by Plants and Animals*. London: Methuen.

Gaskin, D. E. 1982. *The Ecology of Whales and Dolphins*. London: Heinemann.

Gilbert, Frederick F., and Donald G. Dodds. 1987. *The Philosophy and Practice of Wildlife Management*. Malabar, Fla.: Robert E. Krieger.

Harrison, R., and M. M. Bryden, eds. 1988. *Whales, Dolphins, and Porpoises*. New York: Facts on File.

Hoage, R. J., ed. 1985. *Animal Extinctions: What Everyone Should Know*. Washington, D.C.: Smithsonian Institution.

Huxley, Anthony. 1984. *Green Inheritance*. Garden City, N.Y.: Anchor/Doubleday.

International Union for Conservation of Nature and Natural Resources. 1980. *World Conservation Strategy*. New York: Unipub.

International Union for Conservation of Nature and Natural Resources. 1985. *Implementing the World Conservation Strategy*. Gland, Switzerland: IUCN.

Kaufman, Les, and Kenneth Mallory, eds. 1986. *The Last Extinction*. Cambridge, Mass: MIT Press.

Kennedy, David M. 1987. "What's New At the Zoo?" *Technology Review*, April, 67–73.

Koopowitz, Harold, and Hilary Kaye. 1983. *Plant Extinctions: A Global Crisis*. Washington, D.C.: Stone Wall Press.

Lackey, R. T., and L. A. Nielson. 1980. *Fisheries Management*. New York: John Wiley.

Leopold, Aldo. 1933. *Game Management*. New York: Charles Scribner's Sons.

Livingston, John A. 1981. *The Fallacy of Wildlife Conservation*. Toronto: McClelland and Stewart.

Luoma, Jon. 1987. *A Crowded Ark: The Role of Zoos in Wildlife Conservation*. Boston: Houghton Mifflin.

McNeely, Jeffery A., et al. 1989. *Conserving the World's Biological Resources: A Primer on Principles and Practice for Development Action*. Washington, D.C.: World Resources Institute.

Myers, Norman. 1983. *A Wealth of Wild Species: Storehouse for Human Welfare*. Boulder, Colo.: Westview Press.

Myers, Norman. 1987. "The Impending Extinction Spasm: Synergisms At Work." *Conservation Biology*, vol. 14, 15–22.

Nash, Roderick F. 1988. *The Rights of Nature: A History of Environmental Ethics*. Madison: University of Wisconsin Press.

National Audubon Society. Annual. *Audubon Wildlife Report*. New York: National Audubon Society.

Norton, B. G., ed. 1986. *The Preservation of Species*. Lawrenceville, N.J.: Princeton University Press.

Norton, B.G., ed. 1986. *Why Preserve Natural Variety?* Lawrenceville, N.J.: Princeton University Press.

Office of Technology Assessment. 1986. *Alternatives to Animal Use in Research, Teaching, and Education*. Washington, D.C.: Government Printing Office.

Office of Technology Assessment. 1987. *Technologies to Maintain Biological Diversity*. Washington, D.C.: Government Printing Office.

Office of Technology Assessment. 1989. *Oil Production in the Arctic National Wildlife Refuge*. Washington, D.C.: Government Printing Office.

Oldfield, Margery. 1984. *The Value of Conserving Genetic Resources*. Washington, D.C.: National Park Service.

Passmore, John. 1974. *Man's Responsibility for Nature*. New York: Charles Scribner's.

Prescott-Allen, Robert, and Christine Prescott-Allen. 1982. *What's Wildlife Worth?* Washington, D.C.: Earthscan.

Reagan, Tom, and P. Singer. 1976. *Animal Rights and Human Obligation*. Englewood Cliffs, N.J. Prentice-Hall.

Reagan, Tom. 1982. *All that Dwell Within: Animal Rights and Environmental Ethics*. Berkeley: University of California Press.

Reagan, Tom. 1983. *The Case for Animal Rights*. Berkeley: University of California Press.

Reid, Walter V. C., and Kenton R. Miller. 1989. *Keeping Options Alive: The Scientific Basis for Conserving Biodiversity*. Washington, D.C.: World Resources Institute.

Rolston, Holmes, III. 1988. *Environmental Ethics: Duties to and Values in the Natural World*. Philadelphia. Temple University Press.

Roots, Clive. 1976. *Animal Invaders*. New York: Universe Books.

Sapontzis, Steve F. 1987. *Morals, Reason, and Animals*. Philadelphia: Temple University Press.

Schweitzer, Albert. 1949. *Out of My Life and Thought: An Autobiography.* New York: Holt, Rinehart & Winston.

Shaw, J. H. 1985. *Introduction to Wildlife Management.* New York: McGraw-Hill.

Singer, Peter. 1975. *Animal Liberation: A New Ethics for Our Treatment of Animals.* New York: New York Review Books.

Soulé, Michael E., and Bruce Wilcox, eds. 1980. *Conservation Biology.* Sunderland, Mass: Sinauer Associates.

Soulé, Michael E., ed. 1987. *Viable Populations for Conservation.* New York: Cambridge University Press.

Soulé, Michael E., and Kathryn A. Kohm, eds. 1989. *Research Priorities for Conservation Biology.* Covelo, Calif.: Island Press.

Sperling, Susan. 1988. *Animal Liberators: Research and Morality.* Berkeley: University of California Press.

Terbough, John. 1989. *Where Have All the Birds Gone?* Lawrenceville, N.J.: Princeton University Press.

Tudge, Colin. 1988. *The Environment of Life.* New York: Oxford University Press.

Tuttle, Merlin D. 1988. *America's Neighborhood Bats: Understanding and Learning to Live in Harmony With Them.* Austin: University of Texas Press.

U.S. Fish and Wildlife Service. 1988. *Endangered and Threatened Wildlife and Plants.* Washington, D.C.: U.S. Fish and Wildlife Service.

Wallace, David Rains. 1987. *Life In the Balance.* New York: Harcourt Brace Jovanavich.

Watkins, T. H. 1988. *Vanishing Arctic: Alaska's National Wildlife Refuge.* New York: Aperature.

Western, David, and Mary C. Pearly. 1989. *Conservation in the Twenty-first Century.* New York: Oxford University Press.

Wilson, E. O., ed. 1988. *Biodiversity.* Washington, D.C.: National Academy Press.

Wilson, E. O. 1984. *Biophilia.* Cambridge, Mass.: Harvard University Press.

Wolf, Edward C. 1987. *On the Brink of Extinction: Conserving the Diversity of Life.* Washington, D.C.: Worldwatch Institute.

World Resources Institute and International Institute for Environment and Development. Annual. *World Resources.* New York: Basic Books.

Yalden, D. W., and P. A. Morris. 1975. *The Lives of Bats.* New York: Quadrangle/New York Times.

Chapter 15 Nonrenewable Mineral Resources and Solid Waste

Allan, Theresa, et al. 1989. *Beyond 25 Percent: Materials Recovery Comes of Age.* Washington, D.C.: Institute for Local Self-Reliance.

Barnet, Richard J. 1980. *The Lean Years: Politics in an Age of Scarcity.* New York: Simon & Schuster.

Blumberg, Louis, and Robert Grottleib. 1988. *War on Waste—Can America Win Its Battle With Garbage?* Covelo, Calif.: Island Press.

Borgese, Elisabeth Mann. 1985. *The Mines of Neptune: Minerals and Metals from the Sea.* New York: Abrams.

Broadus, James M. 1987. "Seabed Minerals." *Science,* vol. 235, 853–860.

Chandler, William U. 1983. *Materials Recycling: The Virtue of Necessity.* Washington, D.C.: Worldwatch Institute.

Clark, Joel P., and Frank R. Field III. 1985. "How Critical Are Critical Materials?" *Technology Review,* Aug./Sept., 38–46.

Cook, Violetta B., and Earl Cook. 1988. "Romance and Resources." In Paul R. Ehrlich, and John P. Holdren, eds., *The Cassandra Conference: Resources and the Human Predicament.* Texas Station: Texas A & M University Press, pp. 299–316.

Council on Economics and National Security. 1981. *Strategic Minerals: A Resource Crisis.* Washington, D.C.: Council on Economics and National Security.

Council on Environmental Quality and U.S. Department of State. 1980. *The Global 2000 Report to the President.* Vols. 1–3. Washington, D.C.: Government Printing Office.

Dorr, Ann. 1984. *Minerals—Foundations of Society.* Montgomery County, Md: League of Women Voters of Montgomery County Maryland.

Environmental Defense Fund. 1988. *Coming Full Circle.* New York: Environmental Defense Fund.

Environmental Protection Agency. 1989. *Solid Waste Disposal in the United States.* Washington, D.C.: Government Printing Office.

Forrester, Tom. 1988. *The Materials Revolution: Superconductors, New Materials, and the Japanese Challenge.* Cambridge, Mass.: MIT Press.

Frosch, Robert A., and Nicholas E. Gallopoulos. 1989. "Strategies for Manufacturing." *Scientific American,* September, 144–152.

Gordon, Robert B., et al. 1988. *World Mineral Exploration: Trends and Issues.* Washington, D.C.: Resources for the Future.

Hamrin, Robert D. 1983. *A Renewable Resource Economy.* New York: Praeger.

Hershkowitz, Allen, and Eugene Salermi. 1987. *Garbage Management in Japan: Leading the Way.* New York: INFORM.

Hershkowitz, Allen. 1987. "Burning Trash: How It Could Work." *Technology Review,* July, pp. 26–34.

Huls, Jon, and Neil Seldman. 1985. *Waste to Wealth.* Washington, D.C.: Institute for Local Self-Reliance.

Husingh, Donald, et al. 1986. *Proven Profits from Pollution Prevention.* Washington, D.C.: Institute for Local Self-Reliance.

Institute for Local Self-Reliance. 1988. *Recycling Goals and Strategies.* Washington, D.C.:Institute for Local Self-Reliance.

Leontief, Wassily, et al. 1983. *The Future of Nonfuel Minerals in the U.S. and World Economy: 1980–2030.* Lexington Mass: Lexington (Heath).

Maurice, Charles, and Charles W. Smithson. 1984. *The Doomsday Myth.* Stanford, Calif.: Hoover Institution Press.

Neal, Homer A., and J. R. Schubel. 1987. *Solid Waste Management and the Environment: The Mounting Garbage and Trash Crisis.* Englewood Cliffs, N.J.: Prentice-Hall.

Newsday. 1989. *Rush to Burn: Solving America's Garbage Crisis?* Covelo, Calif.: Island Press.

Office of Technology Assessment. 1985. *Strategic Materials: Technologies to Reduce U.S. Import Vulnerability.* Washington, D.C.: Government Printing Office.

Office of Technology Assessment. 1987. *Marine Minerals: Exploring Our New Ocean Frontier.* Washington, D.C.: Government Printing Office.

Office of Technology Assessment. 1988. *Advanced Materials By Design: New Structural Materials Technologies.* Washington, D.C.: Government Printing Office.

Office of Technology Assessment. 1989. *Facing America's Trash: What's Next for Municipal Solid Waste.* Washington, D.C.: Government Printing Office.

Pollack, Cynthia. 1987. *Mining Urban Wastes: The Potential for Recycling.* Washington, D.C. Worldwatch Institute.

Polprasert, Chorgrah. 1989. *Organic Waste Recycling.* New York: John Wiley.

Purcell, Arthur H. 1980. *The Waste Watchers: A Citizen's Handbook for Conserving Energy and Resources.* Garden City, N.Y.: Anchor Press/Doubleday.

Seldman, Neil, and Bill Perkins. 1988. *Designing the Waste Stream.* Washington, D.C.: Institute for Local Self-Reliance.

Simon, Julian L. 1981. *The Ultimate Resource.* Princeton, N.J.: Princeton University Press.

Trainer, F. E. 1982. "Potentially Recoverable Resources: How Recoverable?" *Resources Policy,* vol. 8, no. 1, 396–411.

U. S. Geological Survey. 1986. *Subsea Mineral Resources* (Bulletin 1698-A). Denver. Colo.: USGS Federal Center.

U.S. Bureau of Mines. 1983. *The Domestic Supply of Critical Minerals.* Washington, D.C.: Government Printing Office.

Underwood, Joanna D., and Allen Hershkowitz. 1989. *Facts About U.S. Garbage Management: Problems and Practices.* New York: INFORM.

Westing, Arthur H. 1986. *Global Resources and International Conflict.* New York: Oxford University Press.

Chapter 16 Nonrenewable Energy Resources: Fossil Fuels, Geothermal Energy, and Nuclear Energy

See also the readings for Chapter 3.

Allar, Bruce. 1984. "No More Coal-Smoked Skies?" *Environment,* vol. 26, no. 2, 25–30.

American Physical Society. 1985. *Radionuclide Release from Severe Accidents at Nuclear Power Plants.* New York: American Physical Society.

Atomic Industrial Forum. 1985. *Nuclear Power Plant Response to Severe Accidents.* Bethesda, Md.: Atomic Industrial Forum.

Bartlett, Donald L., and James B. Steele. 1985. *Forevermore: Nuclear Waste in America.* New York: W. W. Norton.

Brown, Lester R., et al. Annual. *State of the World.* New York: W. W. Norton.

Burnett, W. M., and S. D. Ban. 1989. "Changing Prospects for Natural Gas in the United States." *Science,* vol. 244, 305–310.

Campbell, John L. 1988. *Collapse of an Industry: Nuclear Power and the Contradictions of U.S. Policy.* Ithaca, N.Y.: Cornell University Press.

Carrigy, Maurice A. 1986. "New Production Techniques for Alberta Oil Sands." *Science,* vol. 234, 1515–1518.

Carter, Luther J. 1987. *Nuclear Imperatives and Public Trust: Dealing With Radioactive Waste.* Baltimore: Resources for the Future.

Clark, Wilson, and Jake Page. 1983. *Energy, Vulnerability, and War.* New York: W. W. Norton.

Cohen, Bernard L. 1983. *Before It's Too Late: A Scientist's Case for Nuclear Power.* New York: Plenum Press.

Congressional Quarterly Editors. 1985. *Energy and Environment: The Unfinished Business.* Washington, D.C.: Congressional Quarterly.

Department of Energy. 1980. *Geothermal Energy and Our Environment.* Washington, D.C.: Department of Energy.

Edmonds, Jae, and John M. Reilly. 1985. *Global Energy: Assessing the Future.* New York: Oxford University Press.

Fesharaki, Fesharki, and Robert Reed, eds. 1989. *The Petroleum Market in the 1990s.* Boulder, Colo.: Westview Press.

Flavin, Christopher. 1980. *The Future of Synthetic Materials.* Washington, D.C.: Worldwatch Institute.

Flavin, Christopher. 1985. *World Oil: Coping with the Dangers of Success.* Washington, D.C.: Worldwatch Institute.

Flavin, Christopher. 1987. *Reassessing Nuclear Power: The Fallout from Chernobyl.* Washington, D.C.: Worldwatch Institute.

Flavin, Christopher. 1988. "The Case Against Reviving Nuclear Power." *World Watch,* July/Aug., 27–35.

Ford, Daniel F. 1983. *Three Mile Island: Thirty Minutes to Meltdown.* New York: Penguin.

Ford, Daniel F. 1986. *Meltdown.* New York: Simon & Schuster.

Fund for Renewable Energy and the Environment. 1987. *The Oil Rollercoaster.* Washington, D.C.: Fund for Renewable Energy and the Environment.

Gates, David M. 1985. *Energy and Ecology.* Sunderland, Mass.: Sinauer.

Hilgartner, Stephen, et al. 1982. *Nukespeak.* San Francisco: Sierra Club Books.

Hippenheimer, T. A. 1984. *The Man-Made Sun: The Quest for Fusion Power.* Boston: Little, Brown.

Hirsch, Robert L. 1987. "Impending United States Energy Crisis." *Science,* vol. 235, 1467–1473.

Holdren, John. 1982. "Energy Hazards: What to Measure, What to Compare." *Technology Review,* April, 32–38.

Hughes, Barry B., et al. 1985. *Energy in the Global Arena: Actors, Values, Policies, and Futures.* Durham, N.C.: Duke University Press.

Humphrey, Craig R., and Frederick R. Buttel. 1982. *Environment, Energy, and Society.* Belmont, Calif.: Wadsworth.

Hunt, Charles B. 1984. "Disposal of Radioactive Wastes." *Bulletin of the Atomic Scientists,* April, 44–46.

Kaku, Michio, and Jennifer Trainer. 1982. *Nuclear Power: Both Sides.* New York: W. W. Norton.

League of Women Voters Education Fund. 1982. *A Nuclear Power Primer: Issues for Citizens.* Washington, D.C.: League of Women Voters.

League of Women Voters Education Fund. 1985. *The Nuclear Waste Primer.* Washington D.C.: League of Women Voters.

Lidsky, Lawrence M. 1983. "The Trouble with Fusion." *Technology Review,* Oct., 32–44.

Lidsky, Lawrence M. 1984. "The Reactor of the Future." *Technology Review,* Feb.-Mar., 52–56.

Lovins, Amory B. 1986. "The Origins of the Nuclear Power Fiasco." *Energy Policy Studies,* vol. 3, 7–34.

Lovins, Amory B., and L. Hunter Lovins. 1980. *Energy/War: Breaking the Nuclear Link*. San Francisco: Friends of the Earth.

Lovins, Amory B., and L. Hunter Lovins. 1982. *Brittle Power: Energy Strategy for National Security*. Andover, Mass.: Brick House.

Marples, David R. 1986. *Chernobyl and Nuclear Power in the USSR*. New York: St. Martin's Press.

Masters, Charles D. 1985. *World Petroleum Resources: A Perspective*. Open-File Report 85–248. Reston, Va.: U.S. Department of Interior Geological Survey.

McCracken, Samuel. 1982. *The War Against the Atom*. New York: Basic Books.

Morone, Joseph G., and Edward J. Woodhouse. 1989. *The Demise of Nuclear Energy?* New Haven, Conn.: Yale University Press.

Mould, Richard F. 1988. *Chernobyl: The Real Story*. New York: Pergamon.

National Academy of Sciences. 1988. *Geothermal Energy Technology*. Washington, D.C.: National Academy Press.

O'Hefferman, Patrick, Amory Lovins, and L. Hunter Lovins. 1984. *The First Nuclear World War*. New York: Morrow Books.

Office of Technology Assessment. 1984. *Managing the Nation's Commercial High-Level Radioactive Waste*. Washington, D.C.: Government Printing Office.

Organization for Economic Cooperation and Development (OECD). 1986. *Decommissioning of Nuclear Facilities: Feasibility, Needs, and Costs*. Washington, D.C.: OECD.

Patterson, Walter C. 1984. *The Plutonium Business and the Spread of the Bomb*. San Francisco, Calif.: Sierra Club Books.

Perry, Harry. 1983. "Coal in the United States: A Status Report." *Science*, vol. 222, no. 4622, 377–394.

Pollock, Cynthia. 1986. *Decommissioning: Nuclear Power's Missing Link*. Washington, D.C.: Worldwatch Institute.

President's Commission on the Accident at Three Mile Island. 1979. *Report of the President's Commission on the Accident at Three Mile Island*. Washington, D.C.: Government Printing Office.

Resnikoff, Marvin. 1983. *The Next Nuclear Gamble: Transportation and Storage of Nuclear Waste*. Washington, D.C.: Council on Economic Priorities.

Resnikoff, Marvin. 1987. *Living Without Landfills*. New York: Radioactive Waste Campaign.

Resnikoff, Marvin. 1988. *Deadly Defense: Military Radioactive Landfills*. New York: Radioactive Waste Campaign.

Schobert, Harold H. 1987. *Coal: The Energy Source of the Past and Future*. Washington, D.C.: American Chemical Society.

Shahinpoor, Mohsen. 1982. "Making Oil From Sand." *Technology Review*, Feb.-Mar., 49–54.

Shea, Cynthia Pollock. 1989. "Decommissing Nuclear Plants: Breaking Up Is Hard to Do." *World Watch*, July/August, 10–16.

Sweet, William. 1989. "Chernobyl: What Really Happened." *Technology Review*, July, 43–52.

Taylor, John J. 1989. "Improved and Safer Nuclear Power." *Science*, vol. 244, 318–325.

U. S. Department of Energy. 1988. *An Analysis of Nuclear Power Operating Costs*. Washington, D.C.: Government Printing Office.

U.S. Office of Technology Assessment. 1984. *Nuclear Power in an Age of Uncertainty*. Washington, D.C.: Government Printing Office.

Union of Concerned Scientists. 1985. *Safety Second: A Critical Evaluation of the NRC's First Decade*. Washington, D.C.: Union of Concerned Scientists.

Watson, Robert K. 1988. *Fact Sheet On Oil and Conservation Resources*. New York: Natural Resources Defense Council.

Weinberg, Alvin M., et al. 1985. *The Second Nuclear Era: A New Start for Nuclear Power*. New York: Praeger.

Weinberg, Alvin M. 1985. *Continuing the Nuclear Dialogue*. La Grange Park, Ill.: American Nuclear Society.

Chapter 17   Renewable and Perpetual Energy Resources: Conservation, Sun, Wind, Water, and Biomass

See also see readings for Chapters 3 and 16.

American Council for an Energy Efficient Economy. 1988. *Energy Efficiency.: A New Agenda*. Washington, D.C.: American Council for an Energy Efficient Economy.

American Institute of Physics. 1985. *Energy Efficiency and Renewable Resources*. New York: American Institute of Physics.

Baer, Steve, and William Shurcliff. 1988. *Subsidizing the Sun*. Albuquerque, N.M.: Zomeworks.

Blackburn, John O. 1987. *The Renewable Energy Alternative: How the United States and the World Can Prosper Without Nuclear Energy or Coal*. Durham, N.C.: Duke University Press.

Bleviss, Deborah Lynn. 1988. *The New Oil Crisis and Fuel Economy Technologies: Preparing the Light Transportation Industry for the 1990s*. Westport, Conn.: Quorum Press.

Bockris, J. O. 1980. *Energy Options: Real Economics and the Solar-Hydrogen System*. London: Taylor & Francis.

Brown, Lester R., and Pamela Shaw. 1982. *Six Steps to a Sustainable Society*. Washington, D.C.: Worldwatch Society.

Brown, Lester R., Annual. *State of the World*. New York: W. W. Norton.

Butti, Ken, and John Perlin. 1980. *A Golden Thread—2500 Years of Solar Architecture*. Palo Alto, Calif.: Cheshire Press.

Chandler, William U., et al. 1988. *Energy Efficiency: A New Agenda*. Washington, D.C.: American Council for an Energy Efficient Economy.

Chapman, Duane. 1983. *Energy Resources and Energy Corporations*. Ithaca, N.Y.: Cornell University Press.

Charlier, Roger Henri. 1982. *Tidal Energy*. New York: Van Nostrand Reinhold.

Davidson, Joel. 1987. *The New Solar Electric Home*. Ann Arbor, Mich: Aatec Publications.

Deudney, Daniel, and Christopher Flavin. 1983. *Renewable Energy: The Power to Choose*. New York: W. W. Norton.

Dinga, Gustav P. 1988. "Hydrogen: The Ultimate Fuel and Energy Carrier." *Journal of Chemical Education*, vol. 65, no. 8, 688–691.

Dostrovsky, I. 1989. *Energy and the Missing Resource*. New York: Cambridge University Press.

Echeverria, John D. 1989. *Rivers at Risk: The Concerned Citizen's Guide to Hydropower*. Covelo, Calif.: Island Press.

Edmonds, Jae, and John M. Reilly. 1985. *Global Energy: Assessing the Future*. New York: Oxford University Press.

Farallones Institute. 1979. *The Integral Urban House: Self-Reliant Living in the City.* San Francisco: Sierra Club Books.

Flavin, Christopher, and Alan B. Durning. 1988. *Building on Success: The Age of Energy Efficiency.* Washington, D.C.: Worldwatch Institute.

Flavin, Christopher. 1980. *Energy and Architecture: The Solar and Conservation Potential.* Washington, D.C.: Worldwatch Institute.

Flavin, Christopher. 1982. *Electricity from Sunlight: The Future of Photovoltaics.* Washington, D.C.: Worldwatch Institute.

Flavin, Christopher. 1984. *Electricity's Future: The Shift to Efficiency and Small-Scale Power.* Washington, D.C.: Worldwatch Institute.

Flavin, Christopher. 1986. *Electricity for a Developing World: New Directions.* Washington, D.C.: Worldwatch Institute.

Fowler, John W. 1984. *Energy and the Environment.* 2nd ed. New York: McGraw-Hill.

Gever, John, et al. 1986. *Beyond Oil.* Cambridge, Mass: Ballinger.

Glasner, David. 1986. *Politics, Prices, and Petroleum: The Political Economy of Energy.* San Francisco: Pacific Institute for Public Policy Analysis.

Gibbons, John H., et al. 1989. "Strategies for Energy Use." *Scientific American,* September, 136–143.

Goldenberg, Jose, et al. 1988. *Energy for a Sustainable World.* New York: Wiley.

Heede, H. Richard, et al. 1985. *The Hidden Costs of Energy.* Washington, D.C.: Center for Renewable Resources.

Hubbard, H. M. 1989. "Photovoltaics Today and Tomorrow." *Science,* vol. 244, 297–304.

Hughes, Barry B., et al. 1985. *Energy in the Global Arena: Actors, Values, Policies, and Futures.* Durham, N.C.: Duke University Press.

Kendall, Henry, and Steven Nadis. 1980. *Energy Strategies: Toward a Solar Future.* Cambridge, Mass.: Ballinger.

Kovarik, Bill. 1982. *Fuel Alcohol: Energy and Environment in a Hungry World.* Washington, D.C.: Earthscan.

Leckie, Jim, et al. 1975. *Other Homes and Garbage: Designs for Self-Sufficient Living.* San Francisco: Sierra Club Books.

Lovins, Amory B. 1989. *Energy, People, and Industrialization.* Old Snowmass, Colo.: Rocky Mountain Institute.

Mazria, Edward. 1979. *The Passive Solar Energy Book: A Complete Guide to Passive Solar Home, Greenhouse, and Building Design.* Emmaus, Pa.: Rodale Press.

Medsker, Larry. 1982. *Side Effects of Renewable Energy Resources.* New York: National Audubon Society.

Meier, James, et al. 1982. *Supplying Energy Through Greater Efficiency.* Berkeley: University of California Press.

Miller, Alan S., et al. 1986. *Growing Power: Bioenergy for Development and Industry.* Washington, D.C.: World Resources Institute.

Morris, James W. 1980. *The Complete Energy Saving Book for Home Owners.* New York: Harper & Row.

Moskovitz, David H. 1989. "Cutting the Nation's Electric Bill." *Issues in Science and Technology,* Spring, 88–93.

National Academy of Sciences. 1983. *Alcohol Fuels: Options for Developing Countries.* Washington, D.C.: National Academy Press.

Nussbaum, Bruce. 1985. *The World After Oil: The Shifting Axis of Power and Wealth.* New York: Simon & Schuster.

Ogden, Joan M., and Robert H. Williams. 1989. *Solar Hydrogen: Moving Beyond Fossil Fuels.* Washington, D.C.: World Resources Institute.

Penny, Terry R., and Desikan Bharathan. 1987. "Power from the Sea." *Scientific American,* vol. 286, no. 1, 86–92.

Pimentel, David, et al. 1984. "Environmental and Social Costs of Biomass Energy." *BioScience,* February, 89–93.

Pryde, Philip R. 1983. *Nonconventional Energy Resources.* New York: John Wiley–Interscience.

Public Citizen. 1989. *Power Surge.* Washington, D.C.: Public Citizen.

Purcell, Arthur. 1980. *The Waste Watchers: A Citizen's Handbook for Conserving Energy and Resources.* Garden City, N.Y.: Anchor Press/Doubleday.

Renner, Michael. 1988. *Rethinking the Role of the Automobile.* Washington, D.C.: Worldwatch Institute.

Rocky Mountain Institute. 1988. *An Energy Security Reader.* 2nd ed. Old Snowmass, Colo.: Rocky Mountain Institute.

Rocky Mountain Institute. 1989. *Resource-Efficient Housing Guide.* Snowmass, Colo.: Rocky Mountain Institute.

Rose, David. 1986. *Learning about Energy.* New York: Plenum.

Rosenbaum, Walter A. 1987. *Energy, Politics, and Public Policy.* 2nd ed. Washington, D.C.: Congressional Quarterly.

Ross, Marc. 1989. "Improving the Efficiency of Electricity Use in Manufacturing." *Science,* vol. 244, 311–317.

Sawyer, Stephen W. 1986. *Renewable Energy: Progress, Prospects.* Washington, D.C.: Association of American Geographers.

Schneider, Claudine. 1989. "Preventing Climate Change." *Issues in Science and Technology.* Summer, 55–62.

Shea, Cynthia Pollack. 1988. "Harvesting the Wind." *World Watch,* Mar./Apr., 12–18.

Shea, Cynthia Pollack. 1988. *Renewable Energy: Today's Contribution, Tomorrow's Promise.* Washington, D.C.: Worldwatch Institute.

Skelton, Luther W. 1984. *The Solar-Hydrogen Economy: Beyond the Age of Fire.* New York: Van Nostrand Reinhold.

Smith, Nigel. 1981. *Wood: An Ancient Fuel with a New Future.* Washington, D.C. Worldwatch Institute.

Smith, Ralph Lee. 1988. *Smart House: The Coming Revolution.* New York: C.P. Publishing.

Solar Energy Research Institute. 1981. *A New Prosperity: Building a Sustainable Energy Future.* Andover, Mass.: Brick House.

Sperling, Daniel. 1989. *New Transportation Fuels.* Berkeley: University of California Press.

Starr, Gary. 1987. *The Solar Electric Book.* Lower Lake, Calif.: Integral Publishing.

Swan, Christopher C. 1986. *Suncell: Energy, Economy, Photovoltaics.* New York: Random House.

U.S. Senate, Committee on Commerce, Science, and Transportation. 1987. *Report on Methanol and Alternative Fuels Promotion Act of 1987.* Washington, D.C.: Government Printing Office.

Underground Space Center, University of Minnesota. 1979. *Earth-Sheltered Housing Design.* Princeton, N.J.: Van Nostrand Reinhold.

Wade, Herb. 1983. *Building Underground: The Design and Construction Handbook for Earth-Sheltered Houses.* Emmaus, Pa. Rodale Press.

Allman, William F. 1985. "Staying Alive in the 20th Century." *Science 85*, October, 31–41.

Amato, Paul R., and Sonia A. Partridge. 1989. *The New Vegetarians: Promoting Health and Protecting Life*. New York: Plenum.

Ames, Bruce N., et al. 1987. "Ranking Possible Carcinogenic Hazards." *Science*, vol. 236, 271–279.

Armstrong, David. 1984. *The Insider's Guide to Health Foods*. New York: Bantam Books.

Bergin, Edward J., and Ronald Grandon. 1984. *The American Survival Guide: How to Survive Your Toxic Environment*. New York: Avon

Bertell, Rosalie. 1986. *No Immediate Danger*. New York: Women's Press.

Block, Alan A., and Frank R. Scarpitti. 1984. *Poisoning for Profit: The Mafia and Toxic Waste in America*. New York: William. Morrow.

Bloom, David E., and Geoffrey Carliner. 1988. "The Economic Impact of AIDS in the United States." *Science*, vol. 239, 604–609.

Bond, Desmond H. 1984. "At-Sea Incineration of Hazardous Wastes." *Environmental Science and Technology*, vol. 18, no. 5, 148A-152A.

Bowen, Otis R., and Robert E. Windom. 1988. *Understanding AIDS*. Washington, D.C.: Government Printing Office.

Chandler, William U. 1986. *Banishing Tobacco*. Washington, D.C: Worldwatch Institute.

Clarke, Lee. 1989. *Acceptable Risk? Making Decisions in a Toxic Environment*. Berkeley: University of California Press.

Cohen, Leonard A. 1987. "Diet and Cancer." *Scientific American*, Nov., 42–48.

Conservation Foundation. 1985. *Risk Assessment and Risk Control*. Washington, D.C.: Conservation Foundation.

Covello, V. T., et al. 1986. *Risk Evaluation and Management*. New York: Plenum.

Crone, Hugh D. 1986. *Chemicals and Society*. Cambridge, Mass.: Cambridge University Press.

Cross, Frank B. 1989. *Environmentally Induced Cancer and the Law: Risks, Regulation, and Victim Compensation*. Westport, Conn.: Greenwood Press.

Curran, James W., et al. 1988. "Epidemeology of HIV Infection and AIDS in the United States." *Science*, vol. 239, 610–616.

Dobbing, John, ed. 1988. *Infant Feeding: Anatomy of a Controversy, 1973–1984*. New York: Springer-Verlag.

Doll, R., and R. Peto. 1981. *The Causes of Cancer*. New York: Oxford University Press.

Douglas, Mary, and Aaron Wildavsky. 1982. *Risk and Culture*. Berkeley: University of California Press.

Dowling, Michael. 1985. "Defining and Classifying Hazardous Wastes." *Environment*, vol. 27, 18–20, 36–41.

Efron, Edith. 1984. *The Apocalyptics: Cancer and the Big Lie*. New York: Simon & Schuster.

Environmental Defense Fund. 1985. *To Burn or Not to Burn*. New York: Environmental Defense Fund.

Environmental Health Watch and Housing Resource Center. 1988. *The 1988 Healthy House Catalog*. Cleveland, Ohio: Environmental Health Watch and Housing Resource Center.

Environmental Protection Agency. 1987. *The Hazardous Waste System*. Washington, D.C.: EPA.

Environmental Protection Agency. 1987. *Unfinished Business: A Comparative Assessment of Environmental Problems*. Washington, D.C.: EPA.

Environmental Protection Agency, Science Advisory Board. 1988. *Future Risk: Research Strategies for the 1990s*. Washington, D.C.: EPA.

Epstein, Samuel S., et al. 1982. *Hazardous Waste in America*. San Francisco: Sierra Club Books.

Eyles, J., and Woods, K.J. 1983. *The Social Geography of Medicine and Health*. New York: St. Martin's Press.

Faber, M. M., and A. M. Reinhardt. 1982. *Promoting Health Through Risk Reduction*. New York: Macmillan.

Fawcett, Howard H. 1984. *Hazardous and Toxic Materials: Safe Handling and Disposal*. Somerset, N.J.: John Wiley.

Fischoff, Baruch, et al. 1984. *Acceptable Risk: Science and Determination of Safety*. New York: Cambridge University Press.

Fortuna, Richard C., and David J. Lennett. 1987. *Hazardous Waste Regulation: The New Era*. New York: McGraw-Hill.

Freedman, Bill. 1989. *Environmental Ecology: The Impacts of Pollution and other Stresses on Ecosystem Structure and Function*. San Diego, Calif.: Academic Press.

Freudenburg, William R. 1988. "Perceived Risk, Real Risk: Social Science and the Art of Probabilistic Risk Assessment." *Science*, vol. 242, 44–49.

Freydberg, N., and W. Gortner. 1982. *The Food Additives Book*. New York: Bantam.

Gibbs, Lois. 1982. *The Love Canal: My Story*. Albany., N.Y.: State University of New York Press.

Gofman, John W. 1981. *Radiation and Human Health*. San Francisco: Sierra Club Books.

Goldman, Benjamin A., et al. 1986. *Hazardous Waste Management: Reducing the Risk*. Washington, D.C.: Island Press.

Gordon, Wendy, and Jane Bloom. 1985. *Deeper Problems: Limits to Underground Injection as a Hazardous Waste Disposal Method*. New York: Natural Resources Defense Council.

Gough, Michael. 1986. *Dioxin, Agent Orange: The Facts*. New York: Plenum Press.

Gough, Michael. 1989. "Estimating Cancer Mortality." *Environmental Science and Technology*, vol. 23, no. 8, 925–930.

Graham, J.D., et al., eds. 1988. *In Search of Safety: Chemicals and Cancer Risk*. Cambridge, Mass.: Harvard University Press.

Grant, James G. 1989. *The State of the World's Children*. New York: Oxford University Press.

Greenberg, M.R. 1987. *Public Health and Environment: The United States Experience*. New York: Guilford Press.

Harrison, R. M., and D. P. H. Laxon. 1981. *Lead Pollution: Causes and Control*. London: Chapman and Hall/Meuthen.

Heise, Lori. 1988. "Unhealthy Alliance: With U.S. Government Help, Tobacco Firms Push Their Goods Overseas." *World Watch*, Sept./Oct., 19–28.

Heise, Lori. 1989. "Responding to AIDS." In Lester R. Brown, et al., *State of the World 1989*. Washington, D.C.: Worldwatch Institute, pp. 114–131.

Hirschorn, Joel S. 1988. "Cutting Production of Hazardous Waste." *Technology Review*, Apr., 52–61.

Holleb, Arthur I., ed. 1986. *The American Cancer Society Cancer Book*. New York: Doubleday.

Howe, G.M. 1986. *Global Geocancerology: A World Geography of Human Cancers*. New York: Churchill Livingstone.

Huisingh, Donald, et al. 1986. *Proven Profits from Pollution Prevention: Case Studies in Resource Conservation and Waste Reduction*. Washington, D.C.: Institute for Local Self-Reliance.

Huisingh, Donald. 1985. *Profits of Pollution Prevention: A Compendium of North Carolina Case Studies in Resource Conservation and Waste Reduction*. Raleigh, N.C.: North Carolina Department of Natural Resources and Community Development.

Hunter, Linda Mason. 1989. *The Healthy House: An Attic-to-Basement Guide to Toxin-Free Living*. Emmaus, Pa.: Rodale Press.

Hurley, Patrick M. 1982. *Living with Nuclear Radiation*. Ann Arbor: University of Michigan Press.

Imperato, P. J., and Greg Mitchell. 1985. *Acceptable Risks*. New York: Viking.

Jacobson, Michael. 1985. *The Complete Eaters Digest and Nutrition Scoreboard*. Garden City, N.Y.: Anchor Press/Doubleday.

Jones, K., and G. Moon. 1987. *Health, Disease, and Society: An Introduction to Medical Geography*. New York: Academic Press.

Kessler, David A. 1984. "Food Safety: Revising the Statute." *Science*, vol. 223, 1034–1040.

Krimsky, Sheldo, and Alonzo Plough. 1988. *Environmental Hazards: Communicating Risks as a Social Process*. Dover, Mass.: Auburn House.

Kupchella, Charles E. 1987. *Dimensions of Cancer*. Belmont, Calif.: Wadsworth.

Lave, Lester B. 1987. *Risk Assessment and Management*. New York: Plenum.

Lowrance, W. W. 1976. *Of Acceptable Risk*. Los Altos, Calif.: William Kaufmann.

Meade, M., et al. 1988. *Medical Geography*. New York: Guilford Press.

Minnesota Mining and Manufacturing. 1988. *Low- or Non-Pollution Technology Through Pollution Prevention*. St. Paul, Minn.: 3M Company.

Morone, Edward J., and Edward J. Woodhouse. 1986. *Averting Catastrophe: Strategies for Regulating Risky Technologies*. Berkeley: University of California Press.

Muir, Warren, and Joanna Underwood. 1987. *Promoting Hazardous Waste Reduction*. New York: INFORM, Inc.

National Academy of Sciences. 1982. *Diet, Nutrition, and Cancer*. Washington, D.C.: National Academy Press.

National Academy of Sciences. 1983. *Risk Assessment in the Federal Government: Managing the Process*. Washington, D.C.: National Academy Press.

National Academy of Sciences. 1983. *Transportation of Hazardous Materials: Toward a National Strategy*. Washington, D.C.: National Academy Press.

National Academy of Sciences. 1984. *Toxicity Testing: Strategies to Determine Needs and Priorities*. Washington, D.C.: National Academy Press.

National Academy of Sciences. 1986. *Environment Tobacco Smoke: Measuring Exposures and Assessing Health Effects*. Washington, D.C.: National Academy Press.

National Academy of Sciences. 1989. *Diet and Health: Implications for Reducing Chronic Disease Risk*. Washington, D.C.: National Academy Press.

National Cancer Institute. 1987. *Atlas of U.S. Cancer Mortality Among Whites*. Bethesda, Md.: National Institutes of Health.

National Cancer Institute. 1988. *Atlas of U.S. Cancer Mortality Among Blacks*. Bethesda, Md.: National Institutes of Health.

National Cancer Institute. 1988. *1988 Annual Cancer Statstics Review*. Bethesda, Md.: National Institutes of Health.

National Council on Radiation Protection and Measurements. 1987. *Ionizing Radiation Exposure of the Population of the United States*. Bethesda, Md.: NCRP Publications.

Nelkin, M. M., and M. S. Brown. 1984. *Workers at Risk: Voices from the Workplace*. Chicago: University of Chicago Press.

Nichols, Alan B. 1988. "Industry Initiates Source Prevention." *Journal WPCF*, vol. 60, no. 1, 36–44.

North Carolina Pollution Prevention Pays Program. 1986. *Accomplishments of North Carolina Industries*. Raleigh, N.C.: North Carolina Department of Natural Resources and Community Development.

Office of Technology Assessment. 1983. *Technologies and Management Strategies for Hazardous Waste Controls*. Washington, D.C.: Government Printing Office.

Office of Technology Assessment. 1985. *Status of Biomedical Research and Related Technology for Tropical Diseases*. Washington, D.C.: Government Printing Office.

Office of Technology Assessment. 1986. *Serious Reduction of Hazardous Waste*. Washington, D.C.: Government Printing Office.

Office of Technology Assessment. 1986. *Transportation of Hazardous Materials*. Washington, D.C.: Government Printing Office.

Office of Technology Assessment. 1987. *From Pollution to Prevention: A Progress Report on Waste Reduction*. Washington, D.C.: Government Printing Office.

Office of Technology Assessment. 1988. *Are We Cleaning Up? 10 Superfund Case Studies*. Washington, D.C.: Government Printing Office.

Perrow, Charles. 1985. *Normal Accidents: Living with High-Risk Technologies*. New York: Basic Books.

Pochin, Edward. 1985. *Nuclear Radiation: Risks and Benefits*. New York: Oxford University Press.

Piaescki, Bruce, ed. 1984. *Beyond Dumping: New Strategies for Controlling Toxic Contamination*. Westport, Conn.: Quorum Books.

Piasecki, Bruce, and Gary Davis. 1987. *America's Future in Toxic Waste Management: Lessons from Europe*. Westport, Conn.: Quorum Books.

Piot, Peter, et al. 1988. "AIDS: An International Perspective." *Science*, vol. 239, 573–579.

Pollack, Stephanie. 1989. "Solving the Lead Dilemma." *Technology Review*, October, 22–31.

Postel, Sandra. 1987. *Defusing the Toxics Threat: Controlling Pesticides and Industrial Waste*. Washington, D.C.: Worldwatch Institute.

Purcell, Arthur H. 1988. "Waste Minimization." *Resources Policy*, June, 144–145.

Regenstein, Lewis. 1982. *America the Poisoned*. Washington, D.C.: Acropolis Books.

Robbins, Anthony, and Phyllis Freeman. 1988. "Obstacles to Developing Vaccines for the Third World." *Scientific American*, Nov., 126–133.

Sandman, Peter M. 1986. *Explaining Environmental Risk*. Washington, D.C.: EPA. Office of Toxic Substances.

Schell, Orville. 1984. *Modern Meat: Antibiotics, Hormones, and the Pharmaceutical Farm*. New York: Random House.

Schneider, Claudine. 1988. "Hazardous Waste: The Bottom Line is Prevention." *Issues in Science and Technology*, Summer, 75–80.

Scott, Ronald M. 1989. *Chemical Hazards in the Workplace*. New York: Lewis Publishers.

Segel, Edward, et al. 1985. *The Toxic Substances Dilemma: A Plan for Citizen Action*. Washington, D.C.: National Wildlife Federation.

Smedley, Howard, et al. 1985. *Cancer: What It Is and How It's Being Treated*. London: Basil Blackwell.

Solomon, Harold. 1986. *Beat the Odds*. New York: Villard Books.

Speth, James Gustave. 1988. *Environmental Pollution: A Long-Term Perspective.* Washington, D.C.: World Resources Institute.

Stackleberg, Peter von. 1989. "White Wash: The Dioxin Coverup." *Greenpeace,* Mar./Apr., 7–11.

Sternglass, Ernest J. 1981. *Secret Fallout: Low-Level Radiation from Hiroshima to Three Mile Island.* New York: McGraw-Hill.

Tschirley, Fred H. 1986. "Dioxin." *Scientific American,* vol. 254, no. 2, 29–35.

United Nations Scientific Committee on the Effects of Atomic Radiation. 1988. *Sources, Effect, and Risks of Ionizing Radiation.* New York: United Nations.

Upton, Arthur C. 1982. "The Biological Effects of Low-Level Ionizing Radiation." *Scientific American,* vol. 246, no. 2, 41–49.

U.S. Department of Health and Human Services. Annual. *The Health Consequences of Smoking.* Rockville, Md.: U.S. Department of Health and Human Services.

U.S. Department of Health and Human Services. 1986. *The Health Consequences of Involuntary Smoking: A Report of the Surgeon General.* Rockville, Md.: U.S.

U.S. Department of Health and Human Services. 1983. *Alcohol and Health.* Washington, D.C.: Government Printing Office.

U.S. Department of Health and Human Services. 1988. *The Health Consequences of Smoking: Nictotine Addiction.* Washington, D.C.: Government Printing Office.

U.S. Department of Health and Human Services. 1988. *The Surgeon General's Report on Nutrition and Health.* Washington, D.C.: Government Printing Office.

Whelan, Elisabeth M. 1985. *Toxic Terror.* Ottawa, Ill.: Jameson Books.

Whelan, Elizabeth M., and Frederick J. Stare. 1983. *The 100% Natural, Purely Organic, Cholesterol-Free, Megavitamin, Low-Carbohydrate Nutrition Hoax.* New York: Atheneum Press.

Wilson, Richard, and E.A.C. Crouch. 1987. "Risk Assessment and Comparisons: An Introduction." *Science,* vol. 236, 267–270.

World Health Organization. 1989. *1989 World Health Statistics Annual.* Geneva, Switzerland: World Health Organization.

Chapter 19   Air Pollution

Abrahamson, Dean E., ed. 1989. *The Challenge of Global Warming.* Covelo, Calif.: Island Press.

Barth, Michael C., and James G. Titus. 1984. *Greenhouse Effect and Sea Level Rise.* New York: Van Nostrand Reinhold.

Bower, John. 1989. *The Healthy House.* New York: Lyle Stuart.

Boyle, Robert H., and R. Alexander Boyle. 1983. *Acid Rain.* New York: Schocken Books.

Brenner, David J. 1989. *Radon: Risk and Remedy.* Salt Lake City, Utah: W. H. Freeman.

Brouder, Paul. 1985. *Outrageous Misconduct: The Asbestos Industry on Trial.* New York: Pantheon Books.

Brown, Michael. 1987. *The Toxic Cloud.* New York: Harper & Row.

Cogan, Douglas G. 1988. *Stones in a Glass House: CFCs and Ozone Depletion.* Washington, D.C.: Investor Responsibility Research Center.

Cohen, Bernie. 1988. *Radon: A Homeowner's Guide to Detection and Control.* Mt. Vernon, N.Y.: Consumer Report Books.

Consumer Product Safety Commission. 1988. *The Inside Story: A Guide to Indoor Air Quality.* Washington, D.C.: Consumer Product Safety Commission.

Dudek, Daniel J. 1988. *Offsetting New CO_2 Emissions.* New York: Environmental Defense Fund.

Ember, Lois R., et al. 1986. "Tending the Global Commons." *Chemistry and Engineering News,* Nov. 24, 14–64.

Environmental Health Watch and Housing Resource Center. 1988. *The 1988 Healthy House Catalog.* 1820 W. 48th St., Cleveland, Ohio: Environmental Health Watch and Housing Resource Center.

Environmental Protection Agency. 1987. *National Air Pollution Estimates, 1940–1986.* Triangle Park, N.C.: Environmental Protection Agency.

Environmental Protection Agency. 1988. *The Potential Effects of Global Climate Change on the United States.* Washington, D. C.: Environmental Protection Agency.

Environmental Protection Agency. 1989. *Policy Options for Stabilizing Global Climate.* Washington, D. C.: Environmental Protection Agency.

Flavin, Christopher. 1988. "The Heat Is On." *World Watch,* Nov./Dec., 10–20

Freedman, Bill. 1989. *Environmental Ecology: The Impacts of Pollution and other Stresses on Ecosystem Structure and Function.* San Diego, Calif.: Academic Press.

Geller, H., et al. 1986. *Acid Rain and Energy Conservation.* Washington, D.C.: American Council for an Energy-Efficient America.

Government Institutes. 1983. *Acid Deposition: Causes and Effects.* Rockville, Md.: Government Institutes.

Graedel, Thomas E., and Paul J. Crutzen. 1989. "The Changing Atmosphere." *Scientific American,* September, 58–68.

Hax, Elizabeth, ed. 1988. *The Home Book: A Guide to Safety, Security, and Savings in the Home.* Washington, D.C.: Center for Study of Responsive Law.

Hileman, Bette. 1989. "Global Warming." *Chemistry & Engineering News,* Mar. 13, 25–44.

Houghton, Richard A., and George M. Woodwell. 1989. "Global Climatic Change." *Scientific American,* vol. 260, no. 4, 36–44.

Hunter, Linda Mason. 1989. *The Healthy House: An Attic-to-Basement Guide to Toxin-Free Living.* Emmaus, Pa.: Rodale Press.

Jacobson, Jodi. 1989. "Swept Away: Rising Waters and Global Warming." *World Watch,* Jan./Feb., 20–26.

Lafavore, Michael. 1987. *Radon: The Invisible Threat.* Emmaus, Pa.: Rodale.

Lester, R.T., and J.P. Myers. 1989. "Global Warning, Climate Disruption, and Biological Diversity." In National Audubon Society. *Audubon Wildlife Report 1989/1990.* New York: Academic Press, pp. 177–221.

Lovins, Amory B., et al. 1989. *Least-Cost Energy: Solving the CO_2 Problem.* 2nd ed. Andover, Mass.: Brick House.

MacKenzie, James J. 1989. *Breathing Easier: Taking Action on Climate Change, Air Pollution, and Energy Efficiency.* Washington, D.C.: World Resources Institute.

MacKenzie, James J., and Mohamed T. El-Ashry. 1988. *Ill Winds: Airborne Pollution's Toll on Trees and Crops.* Holmes, Pa.: World Resources Institute Publishing.

MacKenzie, James J., and Mohamed T. El-Ashry, eds. 1989. *Air Pollution's Toll on Forests and Crops.* New Haven, Conn.: Yale University Press.

McKibben, Bill. 1989. *The End of Nature.* New York: Random House.

McKormick, John. 1985. *Acid Earth: The Global Threat of Acid Pollution.* Washington, D.C.: Earthscan.

Mello, Robert A. 1987. *Last Stand of the Red Spruce*. Covelo, Calif.: Island Press.

Mintzer, Irving M. 1987. *A Matter of Degrees: The Potential for Controlling the Greenhouse Effect*. Washington, D.C.: World Resources Institute.

Mintzer, Irving M. 1989. "Cooling Down a Warmer World: Chlorofluorocarbons, the Greenhouse Effect, and the Montreal Protocol." *International Environmental Affairs*, vol. 1, no. 1, 12–25.

Mintzer, Irving M., et al. 1989. *Protecting the Ozone Shield: Strategies for Phasing Out CFCs During the 1990s*. Washington, D.C.: World Resources Institute.

Mohnen, Volker A. 1988. "The Challenge of Acid Rain. " *Scientific American*, vol. 259, no. 2, 30–38.

Moomaw, William R., and Irving M. Mintzer. 1989. *Strategies for Limiting Global Climate Change*. Washington, D.C.: World Resources Institute.

National Academy of Sciences. 1981. *Indoor Pollutants*. Washington, D.C. National Academy Press.

National Academy of Sciences. 1983. *Changing Climate*. Washington, D.C.: National Academy Press.

National Academy of Sciences. 1986. *Acid Deposition: Long-Term Trends*. Washington, D.C.: National Academy Press.

National Academy of Sciences. 1988. *Air Pollution, the Automobile, and Human Health*. Washington, D.C.: National Academy Press.

National Academy of Sciences. 1989. *Global Environmental Change*. Washington, D.C.: National Academy Press.

National Academy of Sciences. 1989. *Ozone Depletion, Greenhouse Gases, and Climate Change*. Washington, D.C.: National Academy Press.

National Clean Air Coalition. 1983. *The Clean Air Act*. Washington, D.C.: National Clean Air Coalition.

Nero, Anthony V. 1988. "Controlling Indoor Air Pollution." *Scientific American*, vol. 258, no. 5, 42–48.

Office of Technology Assessment. 1985. *Acid Rain and Transported Air Pollutants: Implications for Public Policy*. New York: Unipub.

Pawlick, Thomas. 1986. *A Killing Rain: The Global Threat of Acid Precipitation*. San Francisco: Sierra Club Books.

Postel, Sandra. 1984. *Air Pollution, Acid Rain, and the Future of Forests*. Washington, D.C.: Worldwatch Institute.

Postel, Sandra. 1986. *Altering the Earth's Chemistry: Assessing the Earth's Risks*. Washington, D.C.: Worldwatch Institute.

Postel, Sandra. 1988. "A Green Fix to the Global Warm Up." *World Watch*, Sept./Oct., 29–36.

Regens, James L., and Robert W. Rycroft. 1988. *The Acid Rain Controversy*. Pittsburgh, Pa.: University of Pittsburgh Press.

Renner, Michael G. 1988. "Car Sick." *World Watch*, Nov/Dec., 36–43.

Roan, Sharon L. 1989. *Ozone Crisis*. New York: John Wiley.

Rousseau, David, et al. 1988. *Your Home, Your Health, and Well Being*. Vancouver, B.C.: Enwright, Hartley, and Marks.

Rowland, F. Sherwood. 1989. "Chlorofluorocarbons and the Depletion of Stratospheric Ozone." *American Scientist*, vol. 77, 36–45.

Schmandt, Jurgen, et al., eds. 1989. *Acid Rain and Friendly Neighbors: The Policy Dispute Between Canada and the United States*. Durham, N.C.: Duke University Press.

Schneider, Claudine. 1989. "Preventing Climate Change." *Issues in Science and Technology*. Summer, 55–62.

Schneider, Stephen H. 1987. "Climate Modelling." *Scientific American*, vol. 256, no. 5, 72–80.

Schneider, Stephen H. 1989. *Global Warming: Are We Entering the Greenhouse Century?* New York: Random House.

Schneider, Stephen H. 1989. "The Changing Climate." *Scientific American*, September, 70–79.

Schneider, Stephen H., and R. S. Londer. 1984. *The Coevolution of Climate and Life*. San Francisco: Sierra Club Books.

Shea, Cynthia Pollack. 1988. *Protecting Life on Earth: Steps to Save the Ozone Layer*. Washington, D.C.: Worldwatch Institute.

Shea, Cynthia Pollack. 1989. "Mending the Earth's Shield." *World Watch.*, Jan./Feb.,27–34.

Smith, Kirk R. 1987. *Biofuels, Air Pollution, and Health.: A Global Review*. New York: Plenum.

Stern, Arthur, et al. 1984. *Fundamentals of Air Pollution*. 2nd ed. New York: Academic Press.

Tackett, S. L. 1988. "Lead in the Environment: Effects of Human Exposure." *American Laboratory*, vol. 19, no. 7, 32–41.

Turiel, Issac. 1985. *Indoor Air Quality and Human Health*. Stanford, Calif.: Stanford University Press.

Udall, James R. 1989. "Turning Down the Heat." *Sierra*, July/August, 26–33.

U.N. Environment Program. 1987. *The Ozone Layer*. London: Butterworth.

U. N. Environment Program. 1988. *The Greenhouse Gases*. Washington, D.C.: UNEP.

U.N. Environment Program and World Health Organization. 1987. *Global Pollution and Health*. London: Butterworth.

U.S. Department of Energy. 1988. *Air-to-Air Heat Exchangers*. For a free copy write to Renewable Energy Information, P.O. Box 8900, Silver Spring, Md. 20907.

Waggoner, P. E., ed. 1989. *Climate and Water*. New York: John Wiley.

Wark, K., and C. F. Warner. 1986. *Air Pollution: Its Origin and Control*. 3rd. ed. New York: Harper & Row.

Weisskopf, Michael. 1988. "Lead Astray: The Poisoning of America." *Discover*, Dec., 68–77.

Welburn, Alan. 1988. *Air Pollution and Acid Raid: The Biological Impact*. New York: John Wiley.

Chapter 20 Water Pollution

Aberley, Richard C., and Susan Berg. 1986. "Finding Uses for Sludge." *American City and County*, vol. 101, 38–46.

Ashworth, William. 1986. *The Late, Great Lakes: An Environmental History*. New York: Alfred A. Knopf.

Bastow, Thomas F. 1986. *This Vast Pollution: United States of America v. Reserve Mining Company*. Washington, D.C.: Green Fields Books.

Borgese, Elisabeth Mann. 1986. *The Future of the Oceans*. New York: Harvest House.

Calabrese, Edward J., et al., eds. 1989. *Safe Drinking Water Act: Amendments, Regulations, and Standards*. New York: Lewis Publishers.

Center, Larry W. 1985. *Ground Water Pollution Control*. Chelsea, Mich.: Lewis Publishers.

Conservation Foundation. 1987. *Groundwater Pollution*. Washington, D.C.: Conservation Foundation.

Cousteau, Jacques-Yves, et al. 1981. *The Cousteau Almanac: An Inventory of Life on Our Water Planet*. Garden City, N.Y.: Doubleday.

Crites, R. W. 1984. "Land Use of Wastewater and Sludge." *Environmental Science & Technology*, vol. 18, no. 5, 140A-147A.

D'Elia, Christopher R. 1987. "Nutrient Enrichment of the Chesapeake Bay." *Environment*, vol. 29, no. 2, 6–11, 30–35.

Environmental Policy Institute. 1989. *Bottled Water: Sparkling Hype at a Premium Price*. Washington, D. C.: Environmental Policy Institute.

Environmental Protection Agency. 1984. *A Ground-Water Protection Strategy*. Washington, D.C. Government Printing Office.

Grundlach, Erich R., et al. 1983. "The Fate of Amoco Cadiz Oil." *Science*, vol. 221, 122–129.

Hitteman, Bette. 1988. "The Great Lakes Cleanup Effort." *Chemistry & Engineering News*, Feb. 8, 22–39.

Hunter, Linda Mason. 1989. *The Healthy House: An Attic-to-Basement Guide to Toxin-Free Living*. Emmaus, Penn.: Rodale Press.

King, Jonathan. 1985. *Troubled Water: The Poisoning of America's Drinking Water*. Emmaus, Pa.: Rodale Press.

Lahey, William, and Michael Connor. 1983. "The Case for Ocean Waste Disposal." *Technology Review*, Aug.-Sept., 61–68.

Loer, Raymond C. 1984. *Pollution Control for Agriculture*. 2nd ed. New York: Academic Press.

Loveland, David G., and Beth Reichfield. 1987. *Safety on Tap: A Citizen's Drinking Water Handbook*. Washington, D.C.: League of Women Voters Education Fund.

Lowe, Marcia D.1989. "Down the Tubes: Human Excrement Is Full of Valuable Nutrients." *World Watch*, Mar./Apr., 22–29.

Marx, Wesley. 1981. *The Oceans: Our Last Resource*. San Francisco: Sierra Club Books.

National Academy of Sciences. 1984. *Groundwater Contamination*. Washington, D.C.: National Academy Press.

National Academy of Sciences. 1984. *Disposal of Industrial and Domestic Wastes: Land and Sea Alternatives*. Washington, D.C.: National Academy Press.

National Academy of Sciences. 1985. *Ocean Disposal Systems for Sewage Sludge and Effluent*. Washington, D.C.: National Academy Press.

National Academy of Sciences. 1985. *Oil in the Sea*. Washington, D.C.: National Academy Press.

National Academy of Sciences. 1986. *Drinking Water and Health*. Washington, D.C.: National Academy Press.

Office of Technology Assessment. 1984. *Protecting the Nation's Groundwater from Contamination*. Washington, D.C.: Government Printing Office.

Office of Technology Assessment. 1987. *Wastes in Marine Environments*. Washington, D.C.: Government Printing Office.

Organization for Economic Cooperation and Development. 1986. *Water Pollution by Fertilizers and Pesticides*. Washington, D.C.: OECD.

Patrick, R., E. Ford, and J. Quarles, eds. 1987. *Groundwater Contamination in the United States*. Philadelphia: University of Pennsylvania Press.

Rail, Chester D. 1989. *Groundwater Contamination: Sources, Control, and Preventive Measures*. Lancaster, Penn.: Technomic Publishing Co.

Rice, Rip G. 1985. *Safe Drinking Water: The Impact of Chemicals on a Limited Resource*. Chelsea, Mich.: Lewis Publishers.

Sierra Club Defense Fund. 1989. *The Poisoned Well: New Strategies for Groundwater Protection*. Covelo, Calif.: Island Press.

Simon, Anne W. 1985. *Neptune's Revenge: The Ocean of Tomorrow*. New York: Franklin Watts.

Yates, Steve. 1988. *Adopting a Stream*. Seattle, Wash.: University of Washington Press.

Chapter 21   Pesticides and Pest Control

Aliteri, Miguel A. 1983. *Agroecology: The Scientific Basis of Alternative Agriculture*. Berkeley, Calif.: Division of Biological Control, University of California, Berkeley.

Barrons, Keith C. 1981. *Are Pesticides Really Necessary?* Chicago: Regnery Gateway.

Brown, Joseph E. 1983. *The Return of the Brown Pelican*. Baton Rouge: Louisiana State University Press.

Bull, David. 1982. *A Growing Problem: Pesticides and the Third World Poor*. London: Oxfam.

Carson, Rachel. 1962. *Silent Spring*. Boston: Houghton Mifflin.

Dover, Michael J. 1985. *A Better Mousetrap: Improving Pest Management for Agriculture*. Washington, D.C.: World Resources Institute.

Dover, Michael J., and Brian A. Croft. 1986. "Pesticide Resistance and Public Policy," *BioScience*, vol. 36, no. 2, 78–91

Dunlap, Thomas R. 1981. *DDT: Scientists, Citizens, and Public Policy*. Princeton, N.J.: Princeton University Press.

Flint, M. L., and R. van den Bosch. 1981. *Introduction to Integrated Pest Management*. New York: Plenum Press.

Fukuoka, Masanobu. 1985. *The Natural Way of Farming: The Theory and Practice of Green Philosophy*. New York: Japan Publications.

Gips, Terry. 1987. *Breaking the Pesticide Habit*. Minneapolis, Minn.: IASA.

Gough, Michael. 1986. *Dioxin, Agent Orange: The Facts*. New York: Plenum Press.

Graham, Frank Jr. 1984. *The Dragon Hunters*. New York: E. P. Dutton.

Hallenback, William H., and Kathleen M. Cunningham-Burns. 1985. *Pesticides and Human Health*. New York: Springer-Verlag.

Hileman, B. 1982. "Herbicides in Agriculture." *Environmental Science and Technology*, vol. 16, no. 12, 645A-650A.

Horn, D. J. 1988. *Ecological Approach to Pest Management*. New York: Guilford Press.

Hunter, Linda Mason. 1989. *The Healthy House: An Attic-to-Basement Guide to Toxin-Free Living*. Emmaus, Pa.: Rodale Press.

Hussey, N. W., and N. Scopes. 1986. *Biological Pest Control*. Ithaca, N.Y.: Cornell University Press.

Kurzman, Dan. 1987. *A Killing Wind: Inside Union Carbide and the Bhopal Catastrophe*. New York: McGraw-Hill.

Marco, G. J., et al. 1987. *Silent Spring Revisited*. Washington, D.C.: American Chemical Society.

Metcalf, R. L., and William H. Luckmann, eds. 1982. *Introduction to Insect Pest Management*. New York: John Wiley.

Mollison, Bill. 1988. *Permaculture: A Designer's Manual*. Davis, Calif.: AgAccess.

Morehouse, Ward, and M. Arun Subramaniam. 1986. *The Bhopal Tragedy: What Really Happened and What It Means for American Workers and Communities at Risk*. New York: Council on International and Public Affairs.

Mott, Lawrie, and Karen Snyder. 1988. *Pesticide Alert: A Guide to Pesticides in Fruits and Vegetables.* San Francisco: Sierra Club Books.

Mott, Lawrie. 1984. *Pesticides in Food: What the Public Needs to Know.* San Francisco: Natural Resources Defense Council.

National Academy of Sciences. 1986. *Pesticide Resistance: Strategies and Tactics for Management.* Washington, D.C.: National Academy Press.

Natural Resources Defense Council. 1989. *Intolerable Risk: Pesticides in Our Children's Food.* New York: Natural Resources Defense Council.

Pimentel, David, ed. 1981. *Handbook of Pest Management.* New York: CRC Press.

Pimentel, David, et al. 1980. "Environmental and Social Costs of Pesticides: A Preliminary Assessment." *Oikos,* vol. 34, no. 2, 126–140.

Pimentel, David, and Lois Levitan. 1986. "Pesticides: Amounts Applied and Amounts Reaching Pests." *BioScience,* vol. 36, no. 2, 86–91.

Postel, Sandra. 1987. *Defusing the Toxics Threat: Controlling Pesticides and Industrial Waste.* Washington, D.C.: Worldwatch Institute.

Regenstein, L. 1982. *America the Poisoned.* Washington, D.C.: Acropolis.

Shrivastava, Paul. 1987. *Bhopal: Anatomy of a Crisis.* New York: Harper & Row.

van den Bosch, Robert, and Mary L. Flint. 1981. *Introduction to Integrated Pest Management.* New York: Plenum Press.

van den Bosch, Robert. 1978. *The Pesticide Conspiracy.* Garden City, N.Y.: Doubleday.

Wasserstrom, Robert F., and Richard Wiles. 1985. *Field Duty: U.S. Farmworkers and Pesticide Safety.* Washington, D.C.: World Resources Institute.

Watterson, Andrew. 1988. *Pesticide Users Health and Safety Handbook.* New York: Van Nostrand Reinhold.

Weir, David. 1987. *The Bhopal Syndrome: Pesticides, Environment, and Health.* San Francisco, Calif.: Sierra Club Books.

Yepsen, Roger B., Jr. 1987. *The Encyclopedia of Natural Insect and Pest Control.* Emmaus, Pa.: Rodale Press.

Chapter 22 Economics and Environment

Andrews, Richard N. L. 1981. "Will Benefit-Cost Analysis Reform Regulations?" *Environmental Science and Technology,* vol. 15, no. 9, 1016–1021.

Baram, Michael S. 1980. "Cost-Benefit Analysis: An Inadequate Basis for Health, Safety, and Environmental Regulatory Decision Making." *Ecology Law Quarterly,* vol. 8, 473–479.

Baumol, William J. 1989. "Is There a U.S. Productivity Crisis?" *Science,* vol. 243, 611–615.

Berry, Wendell. 1986. "Home Economics." *Whole Earth Review,* Summer, 50–56.

Boulding, Kenneth E. 1985. *The World as a Total System.* Beverly Hills, Calif.: Sage Publications.

Bowden, Elbert V. 1987. *Principles of Economics: Theory, Problems, Policies.* 4th ed. Cincinatti, Ohio: South-Western.

Boyer, William H. 1984. *America's Future: Transition to the 21st Century.* New York: Praeger.

Brundtland, G. H. 1987. *Our Common Future: World Commission on Environment and Development.* New York: Oxford University Press.

Butlin, John A. 1981. *The Economics of Environmental and Natural Resources Policy.* Boulder, Colo.: Westview Press.

Chandler, William U. 1986. *The Changing Role of the Market in National Economies.* Washington, D.C.: Worldwatch Institute.

Clark, W. C. 1986. *Sustainable Development of the Biosphere.* New York: Cambridge University Press.

Collard, David, et al., eds. 1988. *Economics, Growth, and Sustainable Environments.* New York: St. Martin's Press.

Cyert, Richard M., and David C. Mowery. 1989. "Technology, Employment, and U.S. Competitiveness." *Scientific American,* vol. 260, no. 1, 54–62.

Daly, Herman E. 1977. *Steady-State Economics.* San Francisco: W. H. Freeman.

Daly, Herman E., 1986. "Toward a New Economic Model." *Bulletin of Atomic Scientists,* Apr., 42–44.

Daly, Herman E. 1988. "Moving to a Steady-State Economy." In Paul R. Ehrlich and John P. Holdren, eds., *The Cassandra Conference: Resources and the Human Predicament.* Texas Station: Texas A & M University Press, pp. 271–285.

Daly, Herman E., ed. 1980. *Economics, Ecology, and Ethics.* San Francisco: W. H. Freeman.

Daly, Herman, and John Cobb. 1989. *Economics for Community.* Boston: Beacon Press.

Eisner, Robert. 1987. "The Federal Deficit: How Much Does It Matter?" *Science,* vol. 237, 1577–1582.

Fisher, Anthony C. 1981. *Resource and Environmental Economics.* New York: Cambridge University Press.

Freeman, A. Myrick, III. 1982. *Air and Water Pollution Control: A Benefit-Cost Assessment.* New York: John Wiley.

Gailbraith, John Kenneth. 1988. *Economics in Perspective: A Critical History.* New York: Houghton-Mifflin.

Georgescu-Roegen, Nicholas. 1971. *The Entropy Law and the Economic Process.* Cambridge, Mass.: Harvard University Press.

Georgescu-Roegen, Nicholas. 1977. "The Steady State and Ecological Salvation: A Thermodynamic Analysis." *BioScience,* vol. 27, no. 4, 266–270.

Hamrin, Robert D. 1983. *A Renewable Resource Economy.* New York: Praeger.

Hamrin, R.D. 1988. *America's New Economy: A Basic Guide.* New York: Franklin Watts.

Harrison, Bennett, and Barry Bluestone. 1988. *The Great U-Turn: Corporate Restructuring and the Polarizing of America.* New York: Basic Books.

Kingsley, Michael J. 1988. *Rocky Mountain Institute's Economic Renewal Program: An Introduction.* Old Snowmass, Colo.: Rocky Mountain Institute.

Kolko, Joyce. 1988. *Restructuring the World Economy.* New York: Pantheon.

Krutilla, John V., and Anthony C. Fisher. 1985. *The Economics of Natural Environments.* Washington, D.C.: Resources for the Future.

Maurice, Charles, and Charles W. Smithsonian. 1984. *The Doomsday Myth.* Stanford, Calif.: Hoover Institution Press.

McCay, Bonnie, and James M. Acheson, eds. 1987. *The Question of the Commons: Culture and Ecology of Communal Resources.* Tucson: University of Arizona Press.

McConnell, Campbell R. 1987. *Economics: Principles, Problems, and Policies.* 10th ed. New York: McGraw-Hill.

MacNeill, Jim. 1989. "Strategies for Sustainable Economic Development." *Scientific American*, September, 155–163.

Meeker-Lowry, Susan. 1988. *Economics as If the Earth Mattered: A Catalyst Guide to Socially Conscious Investing*. Philadelphia, Penn.: New Society Publishers.

Mishan, E. J. 1977. *The Economic Growth Debate: An Assessment*. London: Allen & Unwin.

Oden, Michael Dee. 1988. *A Military Dollar Really Is Different: The Economic Impacts of Military Spending Reconsidered*. Lansing, Mich.: Employment Research Associates.

Pierce, David, et al. 1989. *Sustainable Development: Economics and Development in the Third World*. London: Edward Elgar.

Piore, Michael J., and Charles F. Sabel. 1988. *The Second Industrial Divide: Possibilities for Prosperity*. New York: Basic Books.

Repetto, Robert, et al. 1989. *Wasting Assets: Natural Resources in the National Income Accounts*. Washington, D.C.: World Resources Institute.

Riddel, Robert. 1981. *Ecodevelopment: An Alternative to Growth Imperative Models*. Hampshire, England: Gower Publishing.

Sargoff, Mark. 1988. *The Economy of the Earth: Philosophy, Law, and the Environment*. New York: Cambridge University Press.

Smith, V. Kerry. 1979. *Scarcity and Growth Reconsidered*. Baltimore: Johns Hopkins University Press.

Tietenberg, Tom. 1988. *Environmental and Resource Economics*. 2nd ed., Glenview, Ill.: Scott, Foresman.

Wachtel, Paul. 1988. *The Poverty of Affluence*. Santa Cruz, Calif.: New Society.

Ward, Barbara. 1979. *Progress for a Small Planet*. New York: W. W. Norton.

Watt, K. E. F. 1982. *Understanding the Environment*. Newton, Mass.: Allyn & Bacon.

Woodward, Herbert N. 1977. *Capitalism can Survive in a No-Growth Economy*. New York: Brookdale.

Chapter 23   Politics and Environment

Bahro, Rudolf. 1986. *Building the Green Movement*. London: Heretic Books.

Barnet, Richard J. 1980. *The Lean Years: Politics in an Age of Scarcity*. New York: Simon & Schuster.

Benedict, Richard E. 1989. "U.S. Environmental Policy: Relevance to Europe." *International Environmental Affairs*, vol. 1, no. 2, 91–101.

Borrelli, Peter, ed. 1988. *Crossroads: Environmental Priorities for the Future*. Covelo, Calif.: Island Press.

Bureau of National Affairs. 1989. *U.S. Environmental Laws: 1989 Edition*. Washington, D.C.: Bureau of National Affairs Books.

Caldwell, Lynton K. 1984. *International Environmental Policy*. Durham, N.C.: Duke University Press.

Capra, Fritjof, and Charlene Spretnak. 1984. *Green Politics*. New York: E.P. Dutton.

CEIP Fund. 1989. *The Complete Guide to Environmental Careers*. Covelo, Calif.: Island Press.

Chomsky, Norm, and Edward Herman. 1988. *Manufacturing Consent: The Political Economy of the Mass Media*. New York: Pantheon Books.

Chubb, John E., and Paul E. Peterson, eds. 1988. *Can the Government Govern?* Washington, D.C.: Brookings Institute.

Commoner, Barry. 1989. "Why We Have Failed." *Greenpeace*, October, 12–13.

Costanza, Robert. 1987. "Social Traps and Environmental Policy." *BioScience*, vol. 37, no. 6, 407–412.

Dahlberg, Kenneth A., et al. 1985. *Environment and the Global Arena*. Durham, N.C.: Duke University Press.

Day, David. 1989. *The Eco Wars: A Layman's Guide to the Ecology Movement*. London: Harrap.

Durning, Alan B. 1989. *Action at the Grassroots: Fighting Poverty and Environmental Decline*. Washington D.C.: Worldwatch Institute.

Dye, Thomas R., and Harmon Zeigler. 1987. *The Irony of Democracy: An Uncommon Introduction to American Politics*. 7th ed. Pacific Grove, Calif.: Brooks/Cole.

Firestone, David B., and Frank C. Reed. 1983. *Environmental Law for Non-Lawyers*. Woburn, Mass.: Butterworth.

Foreman, Dave., ed. 1980. *Ecodefense: A Field Guide to Monkeywrenching*. Tuscon, Ariz.: Earth First! Books.

Foreman, Dave. 1987. "Whither Earth First!" *Earth First!*, vol. 8, no. 1, 21–21.

Freedman, Leonard, and Roger A. Riske. 1987. *Power and Politics in America*. 5th ed. Pacific Grove, Calif.: Brooks/Cole.

Government Institutes. 1985. *Environmental Statues*. Washington, D.C.: Government Institutes.

Harvey, H., M. Shuman, and D. Arbess. 1989. *Alternative Security: Beyond the Controlled Arms Race*. Old Snowmass, Colo.: Rocky Mountain Institute.

Henderson, Hazel. 1978. *Creating Alternative Futures*. New York: Putnam.

Henderson, Hazel. 1981. *The Politics of the Solar Age*. New York: Anchor/Doubleday.

Henning, Daniel H., and William R. Manguin. 1989. *Managing the Environmental Crisis*. Durham, N.C.: Duke University Press.

Irwin, Frances H. 1989. "Could There Be a Better Law?" *EPA Journal*, July/August, 20–23.

Kormondy, Edward J., ed. 1989. *International Handbook of Pollution Control*. Westport, Conn.: Greenwood Press.

Mathews, Christopher. 1988. *Hardball: How Politics Is Played—Told By One Who Knows the Game*. New York: Summitt Books.

Meier, Kenneth J. 1987. *Politics and the Bureaucracy*. 2nd ed. Pacific Grove. Calif.: Brooks/Cole

Milbrath, Lester. 1984. *Environmentalists: Vangard for a New Society*. Albany: State University of New York Press.

Myers, Norman. 1986. "The Environmental Dimension to Security Issues." *The Environmentalist*, vol. 6, no, 4, 251–257.

Myers, Norman. 1989. "Environmental Security: The Case of South Asia." *International Environmental Affairs*, vol. 2, Spring, 138–151.

Ophuls, William. 1977. *Ecology and the Politics of Scarcity*. San Francisco: W. H. Freeman.

Ornstein, Robert, and Paul Ehrlich. 1989. *New World, New Mind*. New York: Doubleday.

Paehlike, Robert C. 1989. *Environmentalism and the Future of Progressive Politics*. New Haven, Conn.: Yale University Press.

Peaveey, Fran, Myra Levey, and Charles Varon. 1986. *Heart Politics*. Santa Cruz, Calif.: New Society.

Petulla, Joseph M. 1987. *Environmental Protection in the United States: Industry, Agencies, Environmentalists*. San Francisco: San Francisco Study Center.

Porritt, Jonathan. 1984. *Seeing Green: The Politics of Ecology Explained*. Oxford, England: Blackwell.

Rehbinder, Echard. 1989. "U.S. Environmental Policy: Lesson for Europe." *International Environmental Affairs*, vol. 1, no. 1, 3–10.

Renner, Michael. 1989. *National Security: The Economic and Environmental Dimensions*. Washington, D.C.: Worldwatch Institute.

Rosenbaum, Walter A. 1985. *Environment, Politics, and Policy*. Washington, D.C.: Congressional Quarterly.

Ross, Lester. 1989. *Environmental Policy in China*. Bloomington: Indiana University Press.

Ruchelshaw, William D. 1989. "Toward a Sustainable World." *Scientific American*, September, 166–174.

Sargoff, Marc. 1988. *The Economy of the Earth: Philosophy, Law, and the Environment*. New York: Cambridge University Press.

Schneider, Bertrand. 1988. *The Barefoot Revolution: A Report to the Club of Rome*. London: Intermediate Technologies Publications.

Shephard, Mark. 1987. *Ghandi Today: A Report on Mahatma Ghandi's Successors*. Arcata, Calif.: Simple Productions.

Sierra Club. 1989. *The Sierra Club: A Guide*. San Francisco, Calif.: Sierra Club.

Sivard, Ruth. 1989. *World Military and Social Expenditures, 1988–1989*. Cambridge, Mass.: World Priorities, Inc.

Spretnak, Charlene, and Fritjof Capra. 1986. *Green Politics: The Green Pomise*. Santa Fe, New Mexico: Bear and Co.

Stroup, Richard L., and John A. Baden. 1986. *Natural Resources: Bureaucratic Myths and Environmental Management*. San Francisco: Institute for Public Policy Research.

Timberlake, Lloyd. 1987. *Only One Earth: Living for the Future*. New York: Sterling.

Tokar, Michael. 1988. *The Green Alternative: Creating an Alternative Future*. San Pedro, Calif.: R. & E. Miles.

Watt, K. E. F. 1982. *Understanding the Environment*. Newton, Mass.: Allyn & Bacon.

Wenner, Lettie M. 1982. *The Environmental Decade in Court*. Bloomington, Ind.: Indiana University Press.

Westman, Walter E. 1985. *Ecology, Imact Assessment and Environmental Planning*. New York: John Wiley.

Willhoite, Fred H. 1988. *Power and Governments: An Introduction to Politics*. Pacific Grove, Calif.: Brooks/Cole.

Wolf, Sydney. 1988. *Pollution Law Handbook: A Guide to Federal Environmental Laws*. Westport, Conn.: Greenwood Press.

Yandle, Bruce. 1989. *The Political Limits of Environmental Regulation*. Westport, Conn.: Quorum Books.

Chapter 24 Worldviews, Ethics, and Environment

Attfield, Robin. 1983. *The Ethics of Environmental Concern*. New York: Columbia University Press.

Barbour, Ian G., ed. 1973. *Western Man and Environmental Ethics*. Reading, Mass.: Addison-Wesley.

Barbour, Ian G. 1980. *Technology, Environment, and Human Values*. New York: Praeger.

Berg, Peter, ed. 1975. *Reinhabiting a Separate Country: A Bioregional Anthology of Northern California*. San Francisco: Planet Drum Foundation.

Berger, John J. 1986. *Restoring the Earth*. New York: Alfred A. Knopf.

Berman, Morris. 1981. *The Reinchantment of the World*. Ithaca, N.Y.: Cornell University Press.

Berry, Thomas. 1988. *The Dream of the Earth*. San Francisco: Sierra Club Books.

Berry, Wendell. 1977. *The Unsettling of America*. San Francisco: Sierra Club.

Berry, Wendell, Wes Jackson, and Bruce Colemen, eds. 1984. *Meeting the Expectations of the Land*. San Francisco: North Point Press.

Bookchin, Murray. 1982. *The Ecology of Freedom*. Palo Alto, Calif.: Cheshire Books.

Borrelli, Peter. 1988. "The Ecophilosophers." *The Amicus Journal*, Spring, 30–39.

Borrelli, Peter, ed. 1988. *Crossroads: Environmental Priorities for the Future*. Covelo, Calif.: Island Press.

Bowles, Samuel, et al. 1983. *Beyond the Wasteland*. New York: Anchor Press.

Boyer, William H. 1984. *America's Future: Transition to the 21st Century*. New York: Praeger.

Brennan, Andrew. 1988. *Thinking About Nature: An Investigation of Nature, Value, and Ecology*. Athens: University of Georgia Press.

Brown, Lester R. 1981. *Building a Sustainable Society*. New York: W. W. Norton.

Brown, Lester R., et al, 1989. *State of the World 1989*. Washington, D.C.: Worldwatch Institute.

Brundtland, G. H. 1987. *Our Common Future: World Commission on Environment and Development*. New York: Oxford University Press.

Cahn, Robert, ed. 1985. *An Environmental Agenda for the Future*. Covelo, Calif.: Island Press.

Cahn, Robert. 1978. *Footprints on the Planet: A Search for an Environmental Ethic*. New York: Universe Books.

Cailiet, G., et al. 1971. *Everyman's Guide to Ecological Living*. New York: Macmillan.

Caldwell, Lynton K., et al. 1976. *Citizens and the Environment: Case Studies of Popular Action*. Bloomington: Indiana University Press.

Callahan, Daniel. 1973. *The Tyranny of Survival*. New York: Macmillan.

Callenbach, Ernest. 1975. *Ecotopia*. Berkeley, Calif.: Banyan Tree Books.

Callenbach, Ernest. 1981. *Ecotopia Emerging*. Des Plaines, Ill.: Bantam Books.

Callicott, J. Baird. 1988. *In Defense of the Land Ethic: Essays in Environmental Philosophy*. Albany, N.Y.: SUNY Press.

Capra, Fritjof. 1983. *The Turning Point*. New York: Bantam.

Capra, Fritjof. 1987. "Deep Ecology: A New Paradigm." *Earth Island Institute*, Fall, 27–31.

Capra, Fritjof, and Charlene Spretnak. 1986. *The Spiritual Dimensions of Green Politics*. Berkeley, Calif.: University of California Press.

Carson, Rachel. 1962. *Silent Spring*. Boston: Houghton Mifflin.

Clark, Stephen R. L. 1984. *The Moral Status of Animals*. New York: Oxford University Press.

Cohen, Michael, P. 1984. *The Pathless Way: John Muir and American Wilderness*. Madison: University of Wisconsin Press.

Cohen, Michael J. 1988. *How Nature Works: Regenerating Kinship with Planet Earth*. Waldpole, N.H.: Stillpoint.

Council on Economic Priorities. 1988. *Shopping for a Better World*. Washington, D.C.: Council on Economic Priorities.

Daly, Herman E., ed. 1980. *Economics, Ecology, and Ethics*. San Francisco: W. H. Freeman.

de Haes, C. 1986. *The Assisi Declarations: Messages on Man and Nature from Buddhism, Christianity, Hinduism, Islam, and Judaism*. Gland, Switzerland: World Wildlife Fund.

Devall, Bill. 1988. *Simple in Means, Rich in Ends: Practicing Deep Ecology*. Layton, Utah: Peregrine Smith.

Devall, Bill, and George Sessions. 1985. *Deep Ecology: Living As If Nature Mattered*. Salt Lake City, Utah: Gibbs M. Smith.

Drengson, Alan. 1989. *Beyond Environmental Crisis: From Technology to Planetary Person*. Victoria, B.C., Canada: Lightstar.

Earth First!, June, September, and November 1987 issues devoted to deep ecology.

Ehrenfeld, David. 1978. *The Arrogance of Humanism*. New York: Oxford University Press.

Ehrlich, Anne H., and Paul R. Ehrlich. 1987. *Earth*. New York: Franklin Watts.

Elder, Frederick. 1970. *Crisis in Eden: A Religious Study of Man and Environment*. Nashville, Tenn.: Abingdon Press.

Elgin, Duane. 1981. *Voluntary Simplicity: Toward a Way of Life That Is Outwardly Simple, Inwardly Rich*. New York: Morrow.

Elliot, Robery, and Arran Gare, eds. 1983. *Environmental Philosophy: A Collection of Readings*. University Park: Pennsylvania State University Press.

Environmental Ethics Journal. Department of Philosophy, University of Georgia, Athens, Ga. 30602.

Fanning, Odum. 1986. *Opportunities in Environmental Careers*. West Bethesda, Md.: Bradley Hills Books.

Farallones Institute. 1979. *The Integral Urban House: Self-Reliant Living in the City*. San Francisco: Sierra Club Books.

Fox, Stephen. 1981. *John Muir and His Legacy: The American Conservation Movement*. Boston: Little, Brown.

Fritsch, Albert J. 1980. *Environmental Ethics: Choices for Concerned Citizens*. New York: Anchor Books.

Fritsch, Albert J., et al. 1977. *99 Ways to a Simple Lifestyle*. Bloomington: Indiana University Press.

Fromm, Eric. 1968. *The Revolution of Hope: Toward a Humanized Technology*. New York: Harper & Row.

Glacken, Clarence. 1967. *Traces on the Rhodian Shore: Nature and Culture in Western Thought*. Berkeley: University of California Press.

Goldsmith, Edward. 1978. *The Stable Society*. Cornwall, England: Wadebridge Press.

Golley, Frank. 1989. "Deep Ecology: An Analysis from the Perspective of Ecological Science." *Trumpter*, vol. 6, no. 1, 24–29.

Granberg-Michaelson, Wesley. 1984. *A Worldly Spirituality*. New York: Harper & Row.

Gray, Elizabeth. 1982. *Green Paradise Lost*. Wellesley, Mass.: Roundtable Press.

Griffin, Susan. 1978. *Woman and Nature: The Roaring Inside Her*. New York: Harper & Row.

Hardin, Garrett, and John Bardeen, eds. 1977. *Managing the Commons*. San Francisco: W. H. Freeman.

Hardin, Garrett. 1977. *The Limits of Altruism: An Ecologist's View of Survival*. Bloomington: Indiana University Press.

Hardin, Garrett. 1978. *Exploring New Ethics for Survival*. 2nd ed. New York: Viking.

Hardin, Garrett. 1985. "Human Ecology: The Subversive, Conservative Science." *American Zoologist*, vol. 25, 469–476.

Hargrove, Eugene C., ed. 1986. *Religion and Environmental Crisis*. Athens: University of Georgia Press.

Hargrove, Eugene C. 1989. *Foundations of Environmental Ethics*. Englewood Cliffs, N.J.: Prentice-Hall.

Henderson, Hazel. 1978. *Creating Alternative Futures*. New York: Berkley.

Hughes, J. Donald, and Robert Schults, eds. 1981. *Ecological Consciousness*. Washington, D.C.: University Press of America.

Hughes, J. Donald. 1983. *American Indian Ecology*. El Paso, Texas: Texas Western Press.

Johnson, Warren. 1978. *Muddling Toward Frugality*. San Francisco: Sierra Club Books.

LaChapelle, Dolores. 1978. *Earth Wisdom*. Silverton, Colo.: Way of the Mountain Center.

LaChapelle, Dolores. 1989. *Sacred Land, Sacred Sex, Rapture of the Deep: Concerning Deep Ecology and Celebrating Life*. Silverton, Colo.: Finn Hill Arts.

Leckie, Jim, et al. 1975. *Other Homes and Garbage: Designs for Self-Sufficient Living*. San Francisco: Sierra Club Books.

Leopold, Aldo. 1949. *A Sand County Almanac*. New York: Oxford University Press.

Livingston, John A. 1973. *One Cosmic Instant: A Natual History of Human Arrogance* Boston: Houghton Mifflin.

Livingston, John A. 1981. *The Fallacy of Wildlife Conservation*. Toronto: McClelland and Stewart.

McCloskey, H.J. 1983. *Ecological Ethics and Politics*. Totowa, N.J.: Bowman & Littlefield.

McKibben, Bill. 1989. *The End of Nature*. New York: Random House.

Meeker, Joseph W. 1972. *The Comedy of Survival: Studies in Literary Ecology*. New York: Scribner & Sons.

Meeker, Joesph W. 1988. *Minding the Earth: Thinly Disguised Essays on Human Ecology*. Berkeley, Calif.: Latham Foundation.

Meeker-Lowry, Susan. 1988. *Economics as If the Earth Mattered: A Catalyst Gude to Socially Conscious Investing*. Philadelphia, Pa.: New Society Publishers.

Merchant, Carolyn. 1980. *The Death of Nature: Women, Ecology, and the Scientific Revolution*. New York: Harper & Row.

Merchant, Carolyn. 1981. "Earthcare: Women and the Environmental Movement." *Environment*, vol. 23, no. 5, 6–13, 38–42.

Midgley, Mary. 1984. *Animals and Why They Matter*. Athens: University of Georgia Press.

Molesworth, C. 1983. *Gary Snyder's Vison*. Columbia: University of Missouri Press.

Naess, Arne. 1986. "The Deep Ecology Movement." *Philosophical Inquiry*, vol. 8, 10–31.

Naess, Arne. 1989. *Ecology, Community, and Lifestyle*. New York: Cambridge University Press.

Nash, Roderick. 1988. *The Rights of Nature: A History of Environmental Ethics*. Madison: University of Wisconsin Press.

Norton, Bryan G., and Henry Shue, eds. 1986. *The Preservation of Species*. Princeton, N.J.: Princeton University Press.

Ornstein, Robert, and Paul Ehrlich. 1989. *New World, New Mind*. New York: Doubleday.

Partridge, Ernest, ed. 1981. *Responsibilities for Future Generations: Environmental Ethics*. Buffalo, N.Y.: Prometheus Books.

Passmore, John. 1980. *Man's Responsibility for Nature: Ecological Problems and Western Traditions*. New York: Scribner.

Peccei, Aurelio, and Daisaku Ikeda. 1984. *Before It Is Too Late*. Tokyo: Kodansha International.

Potter, Van Renssalaer. 1988. *Global Bioethics: Building on the Leopold Legacy*. East Lansing: Michigan University Press.

Reagan, Tom. 1983. *The Case for Animal Rights*. Berkeley: University of California Press.

Regan, Tom. 1984. *Earthbound: New Introductory Essays in Environmental Ethics.* New York: Random House.

Repetto, Robert. 1986. *World Enough and Time: Successful Strategies for Resource Management.* New Haven, Conn.: Yale University Press.

Rifkin, Jeremy. 1980. *Entropy: A New World View.* New York: Viking.

Rifkin, Jeremy. 1983. *Algeny.* New York: Viking Penguin.

Rifkin, Jeremy. 1985. *Declaration of a Heretic.* Boston: Routledge & Kegan Paul.

Rolston, Holmes, III. 1986. *Philosophy Gone Wild.* Buffalo, N.Y.: Prometheus.

Rolston, Holmes, III. 1988. *Environmental Ethics: Duties to and Values in the Natural World.* Philadelphia: Temple University Press.

Roszak, Theodore. 1978. *Person/Planet.* Garden City, N.Y.: Doubleday.

Roszak, Theodore. 1985. *Dwellers in the Land: The Bioregional Vision.* San Francisco: Sierra Club Books.

Santmire, H. Paul. 1985. *The Travail of Nature: The Ambiguous Ecological Promise of Christian Theology.* Philadelphia: Temple University Press.

Schumacher, E. F. 1973. *Small Is Beautiful.* New York: Harper & Row.

Seed, John, et al. 1988. *Thinking Like a Mountain.* Madison, Wis.: Madison Rainforest Group.

Sessions, George. 1987. "The Deep Ecology Movement: A Review." *Environmental Review,* vol. 11, no. 2, 105–126.

Sessions, George. 1987. "The Deep Ecology, New Age, and Gaian consciousness." *Earth First!* vol. 7, no. 8, 27–30.

Sessions, George. 1988. "Ecocentrism and the Greens: Deep Ecology and the Environmental Task." *The Trumpeter,* vol. 5, no. 2, 65–69.

Sessions, George. 1989. "Ecocentrism, Wilderness and Global Ecosystem Protection." Paper prepared for conference on "The Wilderness Condition," Estes Park, Colorado, August 17–23.

Seymour, John, and Herbert Giradet. 1987. *Blueprint for a Green Planet: Your Practical Guide to Restoring the World's Environment.* Englewood Cliffs, N.J.: Prentice-Hall.

Shrader-Frechette, Kristin, ed. 1981. *Environmental Ethics.* Pacific Grove, Calif.: Boxwood Press.

Shrader-Frechette, Kristin. 1986. "Environmental Ethics and Global Imperatives." In Robert Repetto, ed., *Global Possible: Resources, Development, and the New Century.* New Haven, Conn.: Yale University Press, pp. 97–127.

Shrader-Frechette, Kristin. 1987. "Four Land Use Ethics: An Overview." *Environmental Professional,* vol. 9, 121–132.

Singer, Peter. 1975. *Animal Liberation.* New York: New York Review Books.

Snyder, Gary. 1974. *Turtle Island.* New York: New Directions.

Snyder, Gary. 1977. *The Old Ways.* San Francisco: City Light Books.

Snyder, Gary. 1980. *The Real Work: Interviews and Talks, 1964–1977.* New York: New Directions.

Soloman, Lawrence. 1978. *The Conserver Society.* Garden City, N.Y.: Doubleday.

Squires, Edwin R., ed. 1982. *The Environmental Crisis: The Ethical Dilemma.* Mancelona, Minn.: AuSable Trails Institute

Stivers, Robert L. 1976. *The Sustainable Society.* Philadelphia: Westminster.

Taylor, Paul W. 1986. *Respect For Nature: A Theory of Environmental Ethics.* Lawrenceville, N.J.: Princeton University Press.

Tiger, Lionel. 1979. *Optimism: The Biology of Hope.* New York: Simon & Schuster.

Tobias, Michael. ed. 1985. *Deep Ecology.* San Diego, Calif.: Avant Books.

Todd, Nancy Jack, and John Todd. 1984. *Bioshelters, Ocean Arks, City Farming: Ecology as the Basis of Design.* San Francisco: Sierra Club Books.

The Trumpeter. Fall 1986, Spring and Fall 1987, and Spring 1988 issues devoted to deep ecology.

Valaskakis, Kimon, et al. 1979. *The Conserver Society: A Workable Alternative for the Future.* New York: Harper & Row.

White, Lynn, Jr. 1967. "The Historical Roots of Our Ecologic Crisis." *Science,* vol. 155, 1203–1207.

Wilkinson, Loren, ed. 1980. *Earthkeeping: Christian Stewardship of Natural Resources.* Grand Rapids, Mich.: Erdmans.

Williams, Joy. 1989. "Screw the Whales, Save the Shrimp." *Esquire,* February, 89–95.

Wilson, Edward O. 1975. *Sociobiology.* Cambridge, Mass.: Harvard University Press.

Wilson, Edward O. 1984. *Biophilia.* Cambridge, Mass.: Harvard University Press.

Worster, Donald. 1977. *Nature's Economy: The Roots of Ecology.* San Francisco: Sierra Club Books.

Zimmerman, Michael. 1987. "Feminism, Deep Ecology, and Environmental Ethics." *Environmental Ethics,* vol. 9, 21–44.

Glossary

abiotic Nonliving. Compare *biotic*.

absolute resource scarcity Situation in which there are not enough actual or affordable supplies of a resource left to meet present or future demand. Compare *relative resource scarcity*.

abyssal zone bottom zone of the ocean, consisting of deep, dark, cold water and the ocean bottom (benthos). Compare *bathyal zone, euphotic zone*.

accelerated eutrophication See *cultural eutrophication*.

acid deposition The falling of acids and acid-forming compounds from the atmosphere to the earth's surface. Acid deposition is commonly known as *acid rain*, a term that refers to only wet deposition of droplets of acids and acid-forming compounds.

acidic See *acid solution*.

acid rain See *acid deposition*.

acid solution Any water solution that has more hydrogen ions (H^+) than hydroxide ions (OH^-); any water solution with a pH less than 7. Compare *basic solution, neutral solution*.

active solar heating system System that uses solar collectors to capture energy from the sun and store it as heat for space heating and heating water. A liquid or air pumped through the collectors transfers the captured heat to a storage system such as an insulated water tank or rock bed. Pumps or fans then distribute the stored heat or hot water throughout a dwelling as needed. Compare *passive solar heating system*.

acute disease An infectious disease such as measles or typhoid fever from which the victim either recovers or dies in a relatively short time. Compare *chronic disease*.

acute effect Harmful effect that appears shortly after exposure to a toxic substance or disease-causing organism. Compare *chronic effect*.

advanced sewage treatment Specialized chemical and physical processes that reduce the amount of specific pollutants left in wastewater after primary and secondary sewage treatment. This type of treatment is usually expensive. See also *primary sewage treatment, secondary sewage treatment*.

aerobic organism Organism that needs oxygen to stay alive. Compare *anaerobic organism*.

aesthetic resource Resource valued because of its beauty or ability to give pleasure. Examples are solitude, quiet, and scenic beauty.

age structure (age distribution) Percentage of the population, or the number of people of each sex, at each age level in a population.

agroforestry Planting trees and crops together.

air pollutant See *air pollution, primary air pollutant, secondary air pollutant*.

air pollution One or more chemicals or substances in high enough concentrations in the air to harm humans, other animals, vegetation, or materials. Such chemicals or physical conditions (such as excess heat or noise) are called air pollutants. See *primary air pollutant, secondary air pollutant*.

algae Simple, one-celled or many-celled plants that usually carry out photosynthesis in rivers, lakes, ponds, oceans, and other surface waters.

algal bloom Population explosion of algae in surface waters due to an increase in plant nutrients such as nitrates and phosphates.

alkaline solution See *basic solution*.

alley cropping planting of crops in strips with rows of trees or shrubs on each side.

alpha particle Positively charged matter consisting of two neutrons and two protons that is emitted as a form of radioactivity from the nuclei of some radioisotopes. See also *beta particle, gamma rays*.

ambient Outdoor.

amenity resource See *aesthetic resource*.

anaerobic organism Organism that does not need oxygen to stay alive. Compare *aerobic organism*.

animal manure Dung and urine of animals that can be used as a form of organic fertilizer. Compare *green manure*.

annual rate of natural change Annual rate at which the size of a population changes, usually expressed in percent as the difference between crude birth rate and crude death rate divided by 10.

aquaculture Growing and harvesting of fish and shellfish for human use in freshwater ponds, irrigation ditches, and lakes or in cages or fenced in areas of coastal lagoons and estuaries. See *fish farming, fish ranching*.

aquatic Pertaining to water. Compare *terrestrial*.

aquatic ecosystem Any water-based ecosystem such as a river, pond, lake, or ocean. Compare *biome*.

aquifer Porous layer of underground rock that contains groundwater. See *confined aquifer, unconfined aquifer*.

aquifer depletion Withdrawal of groundwater from an aquifer faster than it is recharged by precipitation.

arable land Land that can be cultivated to grow crops.

area strip mining Cutting deep trenches to remove minerals such as coal and phosphate found near the earth's surface in flat or rolling terrain. Compare *contour strip mining, open-pit surface mining*.

arid Dry. A desert or other area with an arid climate has little precipitation.

artesian aquifer See *confined aquifer*.

atmosphere The whole mass of air surrounding the earth. See *stratosphere, troposphere*.

atoms   Minute particles that are the basic building blocks of all chemical elements and thus all matter.

autotroph   See *producer.*

average life expectancy at birth   See *life expectancy.*

average per capita GNP   Annual gross national product (GNP) of a country divided by its total population. See *average per capita real GNP, gross national product.*

average per capita NEW   Annual net economic welfare (NEW) of a country divided by its total population. See *average per capita real NEW, net economic welfare.*

average per capita real GNP   Average per capita GNP adjusted for inflation.

average per capita real NEW   Average per capita NEW adjusted for inflation. See *average per capita NEW, net economic welfare.*

background ionizing radiation   See *natural ionizing radiation.*

bacteria   One-celled organisms. Some transmit diseases. Most act as decomposers that break down dead organic matter into substances that dissolve in water and are used as nutrients by plants.

basic   See *basic solution.*

basic solution   Water solution with more hydroxide ions (OH$^-$) than hydrogen ions (H$^+$); water solution with a pH greater than 7. Compare *acidic solution, neutral solution.*

bathyal zone   Cold, fairly dark ocean zone below the euphotic zone, in which there is some sunlight but not enough for photosynthesis. Compare *abyssal zone, benthic zone, euphotic zone.*

benign tumor   A growth of cells that are reproducing at abnormal rates but remain within the tissue where it develops. Compare *cancer.*

benthic zone   Bottom of a body of water. Compare *abyssal zone, bathyal zone, euphotic zone, limnetic zone, littoral zone.*

beta particle   Swiftly moving electron emitted by the nucleus of a radioactive isotope. See also *alpha particle, gamma rays.*

bioconcentration   Accumulation of a harmful chemical in a particular part of the body. Compare *biological amplification.*

biodegradable   Material that can be broken down into simpler substances (elements and compounds) by bacteria or other decomposers. Paper and most organic wastes such as animal manure

are biodegradable. Compare *nonbiodegradable.*

biodiversity   See *biological diversity.*

biofuel   Gas or liquid fuel (such as ethyl alcohol) made from plant material (biomass).

biogeochemical cycle   Natural processes that recycle nutrients in various chemical forms from the environment, to organisms, and then back to the environment. Examples are the carbon, oxygen, nitrogen, phosphorus, and hydrologic cycles.

biological amplification   Increase in concentration of DDT, PCBs, and other slowly degradable, fat-soluble chemicals in successively higher trophic levels of a food chain or web.

biological community   See *community.*

biological diversity   Variety of different species and genetic variability among individuals within each species. Compare *genetic diversity, species diversity.*

biological evolution   See *evolution.*

biological magnification   See *biological amplification.*

biological oxygen demand (BOD) Amount of dissolved oxygen needed by aerobic decomposers to break down the organic materials in a given volume of water at a certain temperature over a specified time period.

biological pest control   Control of pest populations by natural predators, parasites, or disease-causing bacteria and viruses (pathogens).

biomass   Total dry weight of all living organisms that can be supported at each trophic level in a food chain; dry weight of all organic matter in plants and animals in an ecosystem; plant materials and animal wastes used as fuel.

biome   Large land (terrestrial) ecosystem such as a forest, grassland, or desert. Compare *aquatic ecosystem.*

biosphere   The living and dead organisms found near the earth's surface in parts of the lithosphere, atmosphere, and hydrosphere. See also *ecosphere.*

biotic   Living. Living organisms make up the biotic parts of ecosystems. Compare *abiotic.*

birth rate   See *crude birth rate.*

bitumen   Gooey, black, high-sulfur, heavy oil extracted from tar sand and then upgraded to synthetic fuel oil. See *tar sand.*

breeder nuclear fission reactor   Nuclear fission reactor that produces more nuclear fuel than it consumes by converting nonfissionable uranium-238 into fissionable plutonium-239.

calorie   Unit of energy; amount of energy needed to raise the temperature of 1 gram of water 1°C. See also *kilocalorie.*

cancer   Group of more than 120 different diseases—one for most major cell types in the human body. Each type of cancer produces a tumor in which cells multiply uncontrollably and invade surrounding tissue.

capitalism   See *pure market economic system.*

capital goods   Tools, machinery, equipment, factory buildings, transportation facilities, and other manufactured items made from natural resources and used to produce and distribute consumer goods and services. Compare *labor, natural resources.*

carbon cycle   Cyclic movement of carbon in different chemical forms from the environment, to organisms, and then back to the environment.

carcinogen   Chemical or form of high-energy radiation that can directly or indirectly cause a cancer.

carnivore   Animal that feeds on other animals. Compare *herbivore, omnivore.*

carrying capacity   Maximum population of a particular species that a given habitat can support over a given period of time.

cartel   Group of countries that work together to control the supply and determine the price of an economic good such as oil. OPEC is an example. See also *monopoly, oligopoly.*

cell   Basic structural unit of all organisms.

cellular aerobic respiration   Complex process that occurs in the cells of plants and animals in which nutrient organic molecules such as glucose ($C_6H_{12}O_6$) combine with oxygen (O_2) and produce carbon dioxide (CO_2), water (H_2O), and energy. Compare *photosynthesis.*

CFCs   See *chlorofluorocarbons.*

chain reaction   Series of nuclear fissions taking place within the critical mass of a fissionable isotope that release an enormous amount of energy in a short time.

chemical   One of the millions of different elements and compounds found in the universe.

chemical change   Interaction between chemicals in which there is a change in the chemical composition of the elements or compounds involved. Compare *physical change.*

chemical reaction   See *chemical change.*

chemosynthesis   Process in which certain organisms (mostly specialized bacteria) convert chemicals obtained from the environment into nutrient molecules without using sunlight. Compare *photosynthesis*.

chlorinated hydrocarbon Organic compound made up of atoms of carbon, hydrogen, and chlorine. Examples are DDT and PCBs.

chlorofluorocarbons (CFCs) Organic compounds made up of atoms of carbon, chlorine, and fluorine. An example is Freon-12 (CCl_2F_2), used as a refrigerant in refrigerators and air conditioners and in plastics such as Styrofoam. Gaseous CFCs can deplete the ozone layer when they slowly rise into the stratosphere and react with ozone molecules.

chromosome A grouping of various genes and associated proteins in plant and animal cells which carry certain types of genetic information. See *gene*.

chronic disease A disease that lasts for a long time (often for life) and that may flare up periodically (malaria), become progressively worse (cancers and cardiovascular disorders), or disappear with age (childhood asthma). Compare *acute disease*.

chronic effect A harmful effect from exposure to a toxic substance or disease-causing organism that is delayed and usually long-lasting. Compare *acute effect*.

circular flow model Model of the general operation of a pure market economy that shows how the factors of production and economic goods flow between household, businesses, and the environment and how money flows between households and businesses that buy economic goods.

class action suit Civil lawsuit in which a group files a suit on on behalf of a larger number of citizens who allege similar damages but who need not be listed and represented individually.

clearcutting Method of timber harvesting in which all trees in a forested area are removed in a single cutting. Compare *selective cutting, seed-tree cutting, shelterwood cutting, whole-tree harvesting*.

climate General pattern of atmospheric or weather conditions, seasonal variations, and weather extremes in a region over a long period—at least 30 years. Compare *weather*.

climax community See *mature community*.

closed forest Forest where the crowns of trees touch and form a closed canopy during all or part of a year. Compare *open forest*.

coal Solid, combustible material containing 55% to 90% carbon mixed with varying amounts of water and small amounts of compounds containing sulfur and nitrogen. It is formed in several stages as the remains of plants are subjected to intense heat and pressure over millions of years.

coal gasification Conversion of solid coal to synthetic natural gas (SNG) or a gaseous mixture that can be burned as a fuel.

coal liquefaction Conversion of solid coal to a liquid fuel such as synthetic crude oil or methanol.

coastal wetland Land along a coastline, extending inland from an estuary that is flooded with salt water all or part of the year. Examples are marshes, bays, lagoons, tidal flats, and mangrove swamps. Compare *inland wetland*.

coastal zone Relatively warm, nutrient-rich, shallow part of the ocean that extends from the high-tide mark on land to the edge of a shelflike extension of continental land masses known as the continental shelf. Compare *open sea*.

cogeneration Production of two useful forms of energy such as high-temperature heat and electricity from the same process.

commensalism An interaction between organisms of different species in which one type of organism benefits while the other type is neither helped or harmed to any great degree. Compare *mutualism*.

commercial extinction Depletion of the population of a wild species used as a resource to a point where it is no longer profitable to harvest the species.

commercial fishing Finding and catching fish for sale. Compare *sport fishing, subsistence fishing*.

commercial hunting Killing of wild animals for profit from sale of their furs or other parts. Compare *sport hunting, subsistence hunting*.

commercial inorganic fertilizer Commercially prepared mixtures of plant nutrients such as nitrates, phosphates, and potassium applied to the soil to restore fertility and increase crop yields. Compare *organic fertilizer*.

common law Large body of legal principles and rules based on past legal decisions; judge-made law. Compare *statutory law*.

common property resource Resource to which people have virtually free and unmanaged access. Examples are air, fish in parts of the ocean not under the control of a coastal country, migratory birds, and the ozone content of the stratosphere. See *tragedy of the commons*. Compare *private property resource, public property resource*.

commons See *common property resource*.

community Populations of different plants and animals living and interacting in an area at a particular time.

competition Two or more individual organisms of a single species (*intraspecific competition*) or two or more individuals of different species (*interspecific competition*) attempting to use the same scarce resources in the same ecosystem.

competitive exclusion principle No two species in the same ecosystem can occupy exactly the same ecological niche indefinitely.

compost Partially decomposed organic plant and animal matter that can be used as a soil conditioner or fertilizer.

composting Partial breakdown of organic plant and animal matter by aerobic bacteria to produce a material (compost) that can be used as a soil conditioner or fertilizer.

compound Combination of two or more different chemical elements held together by chemical bonds. Compare *element*. See *inorganic compound, organic compound*.

concentration Amount of a chemical in a particular volume or weight of air, water, soil, or other medium.

confined aquifer Groundwater between two layers of impermeable rock, such as clay or shale. Compare *unconfined aquifer*.

conifer See *coniferous trees*.

coniferous trees Cone-bearing trees, mostly evergreens, that have needle-shaped or scale-like leaves. They produce wood known commercially as softwood. Compare *deciduous trees*.

conservation Use, management, and protection of resources so that they are not degraded, depleted, or wasted and are available on a sustainable basis for use by present and future generations. Methods include preservation, balanced multiple use, reducing unnecessary waste, recycling, reuse, and decreased use of resources.

conservationists People who believe that resources should be used, managed, and protected so that they will not be degraded and unnecessarily wasted and will be available to present and future generations. See *preservationists, scientific conservationists, sustainable-earth conservationists*.

conservation-tillage farming Crop cultivation in which the soil is disturbed little (*minimum-tillage farming*) or not at all (*no-till farming*) to reduce soil erosion, lower labor costs, and save energy. Compare *conventional-tillage farming*.

constancy   Ability of a living system, such as a population, to maintain a certain size. Compare *inertia, resilience*.

consumer   Organism that cannot produce its own food and must get it by eating or decomposing other organisms; generally divided into *primary consumers* (herbivores), *secondary consumers* (carnivores), and *microconsumers* (decomposers). In economics, one who uses economic goods.

consumption overpopulation   Situation in which people use resources at such a high rate and without sufficient pollution control that significant depletion, pollution, and environmental degradation occur. Compare *people overpopulation*.

consumptive water use   See *water consumption*.

continental shelf   Shallow undersea land adjacent to a continent.

contour farming   Plowing and planting across rather than up and down the slope of land to help retain water and reduce soil erosion.

contour strip mining   Cutting a series of shelves or terraces on the side of a hill or mountain to remove a mineral such as coal from a deposit found near the earth's surface. Compare *area strip mining, open-pit surface mining*.

contraceptive   Physical, chemical, or biological method used to prevent pregnancy.

conventional-tillage farming   Making a planting surface by plowing land, disking it several times to break up the soil, and then smoothing the surface. Compare *conservation-tillage farming*.

cornucopians   People who believe that if present trends continue, economic growth and technological advances will produce a less crowded, less polluted, more resource-rich world in which most people will be healthier, will live longer, and will have greater material wealth. Compare *neo-Malthusians*.

cost-benefit analysis   Estimates and comparison of short-term and long-term costs (losses) and benefits (gains) from an economic decision. If the estimated benefits exceed the estimated costs, the decision to buy an economic good or provide a public good is considered worthwhile.

critical mass   Amount of fissionable isotopes needed to sustain a nuclear fission chain reaction.

critical mineral   A mineral necessary to the economy of a country. Compare *strategic mineral*.

crop rotation   Planting the same field or areas of fields with different crops from year to year to reduce depletion of soil nutrients. A plant such as corn, tobacco, or cotton, which remove large amounts of nitrogen from the soil, is planted one year. The next year a legume such as soybeans, which add nitrogen to the soil, is planted.

crown fire   Extremely hot forest fire that burns ground vegetation and tree tops. Compare *ground fire, surface fire*.

crude birth rate   Annual number of live births per 1,000 persons in the population of a geographical area at the midpoint of a given year. Compare *crude death rate*.

crude death rate   Annual number of deaths per 1,000 persons in the population of a geographical area at the midpoint of a given year. Compare *crude birth rate*.

crude oil   Gooey liquid made up mostly of hydrocarbon compounds and small amounts of compounds containing oxygen, sulfur, and nitrogen. Extracted from underground deposits, it is sent to oil refineries, where it is converted to heating oil, diesel fuel, gasoline, and tar.

cultural eutrophication   Overnourishment of aquatic ecosystems with plant nutrients (mostly nitrates and phosphates) due to human activities such as agriculture, urbanization, and discharges from industrial plants and sewage treatment plants. See *eutrophication*.

DDT   Dichlorodiphenyltrichloroethane, a chlorinated hydrocarbon that has been widely used as a pesticide.

death rate   See *crude death rate*.

deciduous trees   Trees such as oaks and maples that lose their leaves during part of the year. Compare *coniferous trees*.

decomposers   Organisms such as bacteria, mushrooms, and fungi, which get nutrients by breaking down organic matter in the wastes and dead bodies of other organisms into simpler chemicals. Most of these chemicals are returned to the soil and water for reuse by producers. Compare *consumers, detritivores, producers*.

deep ecology   See *sustainable-earth worldview*.

defendant   The individual, group of individuals, corporation, or government agency being charged in a lawsuit. Compare *plaintiff*.

deforestation   Removal of trees from a forested area without adequate replanting.

degradable   See *biodegradable*.

degree of urbanization   Percentage of the population in the world or a country living in areas with a population of more than 2,500 people.

delta   Built-up deposit of river-borne sediments at the mouth of a river.

demand   See *market demand*.

demographic transition   Hypothesis that as countries become industrialized, they have declines in death rates followed by declines in birth rates.

demography   Study of characteristics and changes in the size and structure of the human population in the world or other geographical area.

depletion time   How long it takes to use a certain fraction—usually 80%—of the known or estimated supply of a nonrenewable resource at an assumed rate of use. Finding and extracting the remaining 20% usually costs more than it is worth.

desalination   Purification of salt water or brackish (slightly salty) water by removing dissolved salts.

desert   Type of land ecosystem (biome) where evaporation exceeds precipitation and the average amount of precipitation is less than 25 centimeters (10 inches) a year. Such areas have little vegetation or have widely spaced, mostly low vegetation.

desertification   Conversion of rangeland, rain-fed cropland, or irrigated cropland to desertlike land with a drop in agricultural productivity of 10% or more. It is usually caused by a combination of overgrazing, soil erosion, prolonged drought, and climate change.

desirability quotient   A number expressing the results of risk-benefit analysis by dividing the estimate of the benefits to society of using a particular product or technology by its estimated risks. See *risk-benefit analysis*. Compare *cost-benefit analysis*.

detritivores   Consumer organisms that feed on detritus or dead organic plant and animal matter. The two major types are *detritus feeders* and *decomposers*.

detritus   Dead organic plant and animal matter.

detritus feeders   Organisms that directly consume dead organisms and the cast-off parts and organic wastes of organisms. Examples are vultures, jackals, termites, earthworms, millipedes, ants, and crabs. Compare *decomposers*.

detritus food web   Transfer of energy from one trophic level to another by detritus feeders and decomposers. Compare *grazing food web*.

deuterium (D: hydrogen-2)   Isotope of the element hydrogen with a nucleus containing one proton and one neutron, and a mass number of 2. Compare *tritium*.

developed country See *more developed country*.

differential reproduction Ability of individuals with adaptive genetic traits to outreproduce individuals without such traits. See also *natural selection*.

dissolved oxygen (DO) content (level) Amount of oxygen gas (O_2) dissolved in a certain amount of water at a particular temperature and pressure, often expressed as a concentration in parts of oxygen per million parts of water.

diversity Variety. In biology the number of different species in an ecosystem (*species diversity*) or diversity in the genetic makeup of different species or within a single species (*genetic diversity*).

DNA (deoxyribonucleic acid) Large molecules that carry genetic information in living organisms. They are found in the cells of organisms.

dose-response curve A graph of test data showing the effects of high dose of a toxic substance on a group of test organisms.

drainage basin See *watershed*.

dredge spoils Materials scraped from the bottoms of harbors and rivers to maintain shipping channels. They are often contaminated with high levels of toxic substances that have settled out of the water. See *dredging*.

dredging Type of surface mining in which materials such as sand and gravel are scooped up from seabeds. It is also used to remove sediment from streams, rivers, and harbors to maintain shipping channels. See *dredge spoils*.

driftnet fishing Catching fish in massive nets that drift in the water. Compare *purse-seine fishing, trawler fishing*.

drip irrigation Using small tubes or pipes to deliver small amounts of irrigation water to the roots of plants.

drought Condition in which an area does not get enough water because of lower than normal precipitation, higher than normal temperatures that increase evaporation, or both.

dust dome Dome of heated air that surrounds an urban area and traps pollutants, especially suspended particulate matter. See also *urban heat island*.

early-successional species Wild animal species found in pioneer communities of plants at the early stage of ecological succession. Compare *late-successional species, midsuccessional species, wilderness species*.

ecological land-use planning Method for deciding how land should be used by developing an integrated model that considers geological, ecological, health, and social variables.

ecological niche Description of all the physical, chemical, and biological factors that a species needs to survive, stay healthy, and reproduce in an ecosystem.

ecological succession Process in which communities of plant and animal species in a particular area are replaced over time by a series of different and usually more complex communities. See *primary ecological succession, secondary ecological succession*.

ecology Study of the interactions of living organisms with each other and with their environment; study of the structure and functions of nature.

economic decision Choosing what to do with scarce resources; deciding what goods and services to produce, how to produce them, how much to produce, and how to distribute them to people.

economic depletion Exhaustion of 80% of the estimated supply of a nonrenewable resource. Finding, extracting, and processing the remaining 20% usually costs more than it is worth.

economic good Any service or material item that gives people satisfaction and whose present or ultimate supply is limited.

economic growth Increase in the real value of all final goods and services produced by an economy; an increase in real GNP. Compare *productivity*.

economic needs Types and amounts of certain economic goods—food, clothing, water, oxygen, shelter—that each of us must have to survive and to stay healthy. Compare *economic wants*. See also *poverty*.

economic resources Natural resources, capital goods, and labor used in an economy to produce material goods and services. See *capital goods, labor, natural resources*.

economics Study of how individuals and groups make decisions about what to do with scarce resources to meet their needs and wants.

economic system Method that a group of people uses to choose *what* goods and services to produce, *how* to produce them, *how much* to produce, and *how* to distribute them to people. See *mixed economic system, pure command economic system, pure market economic system, traditional economic system*.

economic wants Economic goods that go beyond our basic economic needs. These wants are influenced by the customs and conventions of the society we live in and by our level of affluence. Compare *economic needs*.

economy System of production, distribution, and consumption of economic goods.

ecosphere Collection of living and dead organisms (biosphere) interacting with one another and their nonliving environment (energy and chemicals) throughout the world. See also *biosphere*.

ecosystem Community of organisms interacting with one another and with the chemical and physical factors making up their environment.

ecotone Transition zone where one type of ecosystem blends into another type. Ecotones contain many of the plant and animal species found in both ecosystems, and often species not found in either. See also *edge*.

edge Area where two different types of plant communities meet.

efficiency Measure of how much output of energy or of a product is produced by a certain input of energy, materials, or labor. See *energy efficiency*.

egg pulling Collecting eggs produced in the wild pairs of a critically endangered species and hatching the eggs in zoos or research centers.

electron Tiny particle moving around outside the nucleus of an atom. Each electron has one unit of negative charge ($-$) and almost no mass.

element Chemical, such as hydrogen (H), iron (Fe), sodium (Na), carbon (C), nitrogen (N), or oxygen (O), whose distinctly different atoms serve as the basic building blocks of all matter. There are 92 naturally occurring elements. Another 15 have been made in laboratories. Two or more elements combine to form compounds that make up most of the world's matter. Compare *compound*.

emigration Migration of people out of one country or area to take up permanent residence in another country or area. Compare *immigration*.

endangered species Wild species with so few individual survivors that the species could soon become extinct in all or most of its natural range. Compare *threatened species*.

energy Ability to do work by moving matter or by causing a transfer of heat between two objects at different temperatures.

energy conservation Reduction or elimination of unnecessary energy use and waste. See *energy efficiency*.

energy efficiency Percentage of the total energy input that does useful work and is not converted into low-temperature, usually useless, heat in an energy conversion system or process. See *net useful energy*.

energy quality Ability of a form of energy to do useful work. High-temperature heat and the chemical energy in fossil fuels and nuclear fuels is concentrated high-quality energy. Low-quality energy such as low-temperature heat is dispersed or diluted and cannot do much useful work. See *high-quality energy, low-quality energy.*

enhanced oil recovery Removal of some of the heavy oil left in an oil well after primary and secondary recovery. Compare *primary oil recovery, secondary oil recovery.*

entropy A measure of disorder or randomness. The higher the entropy of a system, the greater its disorder. See *high-quality energy, high-quality matter, low-quality energy, low-quality matter.*

environment All external conditions that affect an organism or other specified system during its lifetime.

environmental degradation Depletion or destruction of a potentially renewable resource such as soil, grassland, forest, or wildlife by using it at a faster rate than it is naturally replenished. If such use continues, the resource can become nonrenewable on a human time scale or nonexistent (extinct). See also *sustainable yield.*

environmentalists People who are primarily concerned with preventing pollution and degradation of the air, water, and soil. See *conservationists.*

EPA Environmental Protection Agency. It is responsible for managing federal efforts in the United States to control air and water pollution, radiation and pesticide hazards, ecological research, and solid waste disposal.

epidemiology Study of the patterns of disease or other harmful effect from toxic exposure within defined groups of people.

epilimnion Upper layer of warm water with high levels of dissolved oxygen in a stratified lake. Compare *hypolimnion, thermocline.*

erosion See *soil erosion.*

estuarine zone Area near the coastline that consists of estuaries and coastal saltwater wetlands, extending to the edge of the continental shelf.

estuary Zone along a coastline where fresh water from rivers and streams and runoff from the land mix with seawater.

ethics What we believe to be right or wrong behavior.

euphotic zone Surface layer of an ocean, lake, or other body of water which gets enough sunlight for photosynthesis. Compare *abyssal zone, bathyal zone.*

eutrophic lake Lake with a large or excessive supply of plant nutrients—mostly nitrates and phosphates. Compare *mesotrophic lake, oligotrophic lake.*

eutrophication Physical, chemical, and biological changes that take place after a lake, estuary, or slow-flowing river receives inputs of plant nutrients—mostly nitrates and phosphates—from natural erosion and runoff from the surrounding land basin. See also *cultural eutrophication.*

evaporation Physical change in which a liquid changes into a vapor or gas.

even-aged management Method of forest management in which trees, usually of a single species, in a given stand are maintained at about the same age and size and are harvested all at once so a new stand may grow. Compare *uneven-aged management.*

even-aged stand Forest area where all trees are about the same age. Usually, such stands contain trees of only one or two species. See *even-aged management, tree farm.* Compare *uneven-aged management, tree farm, uneven-aged stand.*

evergreen plants Pines, spruces, firs and other plants that keep some of their leaves or needles throughout the year. Compare *deciduous trees.*

evolution Changes in the genetic composition (gene pool) of a population exposed to new environmental conditions as a result of differential reproduction. Evolution can lead to the splitting of a single species into two or more different species. See also *differential reproduction, natural selection, speciation.*

exhaustible resource See *nonrenewable resource.*

exponential growth Growth in which some quantity, such as population size, increases by a constant percentage of the whole during each year or other time period; when the increase in quantity over time is plotted, this type of growth yields a curve shaped like the letter **J**.

external benefit Beneficial social effect of producing and using an economic good that is not included in the market price of the good. Compare *external cost, internal cost, true cost.*

external cost Harmful social effect of producing and using an economic good that is not included in the market price of the good. Compare *external benefit, internal cost, true cost.*

externalities Social benefits ("goods") and social costs ("bads") not included in the market price of an economic good. See *external benefit, external cost.* Compare *internal cost, true cost.*

extinction Complete disappearance of a species from the earth. This happens when a species cannot adapt and successfully reproduce under new environmental conditions. Compare *speciation.* See also *endangered species, threatened species.*

factors of production See *economic resources.*

family planning Providing information, clinical services, and contraceptives to help couples choose the number and spacing of children they want to have.

famine Widespread malnutrition and starvation in a particular area because of a shortage of food, usually caused by drought, war, flood, earthquake, or other catastrophic event that disrupts food production and distribution.

feedlot Confined outdoor or indoor space used to raise hundreds to thousands of domesticated livestock. Compare *rangeland.*

fertilizer Substance that adds inorganic or organic plant nutrients to soil and improves its ability to grow crops, trees, or other vegetation. See *commercial inorganic fertilizer, organic fertilizer.*

first law of ecology We can never do merely one thing. Any intrusion into nature has numerous effects, many of which are unpredictable.

first law of energy See *first law of thermodynamics.*

first law of thermodynamics (energy) In any physical or chemical change, any movement of matter from one place to another, or any change in temperature, energy is neither created nor destroyed but merely transformed from one form to another; you can't get more energy out of something than you put in; in terms of energy quantity you can't get something for nothing, or there is no free lunch. See also *second law of thermodynamics.*

fishery Concentrations of particular aquatic species suitable for commercial harvesting in a given ocean area or inland body of water.

fish farming Form of aquaculture in which fish are cultivated in a controlled pond or other environment and harvested when they reach the desired size. See also *fish ranching.*

fishing Finding and capturing a desirable species of fish or shellfish.

fish ranching Form of aquaculture in which members of an anadromous fish species such as salmon are held in captivity for the first few years of their lives, released, and then harvested as adults when they return from the ocean to their freshwater birthplace to spawn. See also *fish farming*.

fissionable isotope Isotope that can split apart when hit by a neutron or other particle moving at the right speed and thus undergo nuclear fission. Examples are uranium-235 and plutonium-239. Compare *nonfissionable isotope*.

floodplain Land along a river or stream that is periodically flooded when the banks overflow.

fluidized-bed combustion (FBC) Process for burning coal more efficiently, cleanly, and cheaply. A stream of hot air is used to suspend a mixture of powdered coal and limestone during combustion. About 90% to 98% of the sulfur dioxide produced during combustion is removed by reaction with limestone to produce solid calcium sulfate.

flyway Generally fixed route along which waterfowl migrate from one area to another at certain seasons of the year.

food additive A natural or synthetic chemical deliberately added to processed foods to retard spoilage, to provide missing amino acids and vitamins, or to enhance flavor, color, and texture.

food chain Series of organisms, each eating or decomposing the preceding one. Compare *food web*.

food web Complex network of many interconnected food chains and feeding interactions. Compare *food chain*. See *detritus food web, grazing food web*.

forage Vegetation eaten by animals, especially grazing and browsing animals.

forest Terrestrial ecosystem (biome) with enough average annual precipitation (at least 76 centimeters or 30 inches) to support growth of various species of trees and smaller forms of vegetation. See also *closed forest, open forest*.

fossil fuel Buried deposits of decayed plants and animals that have been converted to crude oil, coal, natural gas, or heavy oils by exposure to heat and pressure in the earth's crust over hundreds of millions of years. See *coal, crude oil, natural gas*.

Freons See *chlorofluorocarbons*.

frontier worldview See *throwaway worldview*.

fungicide Chemical used to kill fungi that damage crops.

fungus Type of decomposer; a plant without chlorophyll that gets its nourishment by breaking down the organic matter of other plants. Examples are molds, yeasts, and mushrooms.

Gaia hypothesis Proposal that the earth is alive and can be considered as a gigantic superorganism.

game See *game species*.

game species Type of wild animal that people hunt or fish for fun and recreation.

gamma rays High-energy, ionizing, electromagnetic radiation emitted by some radioisotopes. Like x rays, they readily penetrate body tissues.

gasohol Vehicle fuel consisting of a mixture of gasoline and ethyl or methyl alcohol—typically 10% to 23% ethanol by volume.

gene pool All genetic (hereditary) information contained in a reproducing population of a particular species.

genes The parts of various DNA molecules that control hereditary characteristics in organisms.

genetic adaptation Changes in the genetic makeup of organisms of a species that allows the species to reproduce and gain a competitive advantage under changed environmental conditions.

geothermal energy Heat transferred from the earth's molten core to underground deposits of dry steam (steam with no water droplets), wet steam (a mixture of steam and water droplets), hot water, or rocks lying fairly close to the earth's surface.

GNP See *gross national product*.

grassland Terrestrial ecosystem (biome) found in regions where moderate annual average precipitation (25 to 76 centimeters or 10 to 30 inches) is enough to support the growth of grass and small plants but not enough to support large stands of trees.

grazing food web Food web in which herbivores consume living plant tissue and are then consumed by an array of carnivores and omnivores. Compare *detritus food web*.

greenhouse effect Trapping and buildup of heat in the atmosphere (troposphere) near the earth's surface. Some of the heat flowing back toward space from the earth's surface is absorbed by water vapor, carbon dioxide, ozone, and several other gases in the atmosphere and then reradiated back toward the earth's surface. If the atmospheric concentrations of these greenhouse gases rise, the average temperature of the lower atmosphere will gradually increase.

greenhouse gases Gases in the earth's atmosphere that cause the greenhouse effect. Examples are carbon dioxide, chlorofluorocarbons, ozone, methane, and nitrous oxide.

green manure Freshly cut or still-growing green vegetation that is plowed into the soil to increase the organic matter and humus available to support crop growth. Compare *animal manure*.

green revolution Popular term for introduction of scientifically bred or selected varieties of grain (rice, wheat, maize) that with high enough inputs of fertilizer and water can greatly increase crop yields.

gross national product (GNP) Total market value in current dollars of all final goods and services produced by an economy during a year. Compare *average per capita GNP, average per capita real NEW, real GNP*.

ground fire Fire which burns decayed leaves or peat deep below the ground surface. Compare *crown fire, surface fire*.

groundwater Water that sinks into the soil and is stored in slowly flowing and slowly renewed underground reservoirs called aquifers; underground water in the zone of saturation below the water table. See *confined aquifer, unconfined aquifer*. Compare *runoff, surface water*.

gully erosion Severe soil erosion caused when high-velocity water flow removes enough soil to form miniature valleys. Compare *rill erosion, sheet erosion*.

gully reclamation Restoring land suffering from gully erosion by seeding gullies with quick-growing plants, building small dams to collect silt and gradually fill in the channels, and building channels to divert water away from the gully.

habitat Place or type of place where an organism or community of organisms lives and thrives.

hazard Something that can cause injury, disease, economic loss, or environmental damage.

hazardous waste Any solid, liquid, or containerized gas that can catch fire easily, is corrosive to skin tissue or metals, is unstable and can explode or release toxic fumes, or which has harmful concentrations of one or more toxic materials that can leach out. See also *toxic waste*.

heat Form of kinetic energy that flows from one body to another when there is a temperature difference between the two bodies. Heat always flows spontaneously from a hot sample of matter to a colder sample of matter. This is one way to state the second law of thermodynamics. Compare *temperature*.

heavy oil Black, high-sulfur, tarlike oil found in deposits of crude oil, tar sands, and oil shale.

herbicide Chemical that kills a plant or inhibits its growth.

herbivore Plant-eating organism. Examples are deer, sheep, grasshoppers, and zooplankton. Compare *carnivore, omnivore*.

heterotroph See *consumer*.

high-quality energy Energy that is concentrated and has great ability to perform useful work. Examples are high-temperature heat and the energy in electricity, coal, oil, gasoline, sunlight, and nuclei of uranium-235. Compare *low-quality energy*.

high-quality matter Matter that is organized (low entropy) and contains a high concentration of a useful resource. Compare *low-quality matter*.

host Plant or animal upon which a parasite feeds.

humus Complex mixture of decaying organic matter and inorganic compounds in topsoil. This insoluble material helps retain water and water-soluble nutrients so they can be taken up by plant roots.

hunters-gatherers People who get their food by gathering edible wild plants and other materials and by hunting wild animals and fish.

hydrocarbon Organic compound of hydrogen and carbon atoms.

hydroelectric power plant Structure in which the energy of falling or flowing water spins a turbine generator to produce electricity.

hydrologic cycle Biogeochemical cycle that collects, purifies, and distributes the earth's fixed supply of water from the environment, to living organisms, and back to the environment.

hydropower Electrical energy produced by falling or flowing water. See *hydroelectric power plant*.

hydrosphere All the earth's liquid water (oceans, smaller bodies of fresh water, and underground aquifers), frozen water (polar ice caps, floating ice, and frozen upper layer of soil known as permafrost), and small amounts of water vapor in the atmosphere.

hypolimnion Bottom layer of water in a stratified lake. This layer is colder and more dense than the top or epilimnion layer. Compare *epilimnion, thermocline*.

identified resources Deposits of a particular mineral-bearing material of which the location, quantity, and quality are known or have been estimated from geological evidence and measurements. Compare *total resources*.

igneous rock Rocks that form when magma (molten rock) wells up from the earth's upper crust and cools or crystallizes on or beneath the earth's surface. Compare *metamorphic rocks, sedimentary rocks*.

immature community Community at an early stage of ecological succession. It usually has a low number of species and ecological niches and cannot capture and use energy and cycle critical nutrients as efficiently as more complex, mature ecosystems. Compare *mature community*.

immigration Migration of people into a country or area to take up permanent residence. Compare *emigration*.

industrialized agriculture Using large inputs of energy from fossil fuels (especially oil and natural gas) to produce large quantities of crops and livestock for domestic and foreign sale. Compare *subsistence agriculture*.

industrial smog Type of air pollution consisting mostly of a mixture of sulfur dioxide, suspended droplets of sulfuric acid formed from some of the sulfur dioxide, and a variety of suspended solid particles. Compare *photochemical smog*.

inertia Ability of a living system to resist being disturbed or altered. Compare *constancy, resilience*.

infant mortality rate Annual number of deaths of infants under one year of age per 1,000 live births.

information feedback Process by which information is fed back into a system and causes it to change to maintain a particular equilibrium state. See *negative feedback, positive feedback*.

inland wetland Land away from the coast, such as a swamp, marsh, or bog, that is flooded all or part of the year with fresh water. Compare *coastal wetland*.

inorganic compound Combination of two or more elements other than those used to form organic compounds. Compare *organic compound*.

inorganic fertilizer See *commercial inorganic fertilizer*.

input pollution control Method that prevents a potential pollutant from entering the environment or that sharply reduces the amount entering the environment. Compare *output pollution control*.

insecticide Chemical designed to kill insects.

integrated pest management (IPM) Combined use of biological, chemical, and cultivation methods in proper sequence and timing to keep the size of a pest population below the size that causes economically unacceptable loss of a crop or livestock animal.

intercropping Growing two or more different crops at the same time on a plot. For example, a carbohydrate-rich grain that depletes soil nitrogen and a protein-rich legume that adds nitrogen to the soil may be intercropped. Compare *monoculture, polyculture, polyvarietal cultivation*.

intermediate goods See *capital goods*.

internal cost Direct cost paid by the producer and buyer of an economic good. Compare *external cost*.

interspecific competition Members of two or more species trying to use the same scarce resources in an ecosystem. See *competition, intraspecific competition*.

intraspecific competition Two or more individual organisms of a single species trying to use the same scarce resources in an ecosystem. See *competition, interspecific competition*.

inversion See *thermal inversion*.

ion Atom or group of atoms with one or more positive (+) or negative (−) electrical charges.

ionizing radiation Fast-moving alpha or beta particles or high-energy radiation (gamma rays) emitted by radioisotopes. They have enough energy to dislodge one or more electrons from atoms they hit, forming charged ions that can react with and damage living tissue.

isotopes Two or more forms of a chemical element that have the same number of protons but different mass numbers or numbers of neutrons in their nuclei.

J-shaped curve Curve with the shape of the letter J that represents exponential growth.

kerogen Solid, waxy mixture of hydrocarbons found in oil shale, with a fine-grained sedimentary rock. When the rock is heated to high temperatures, the kerogen is vaporized. The vapor is condensed and then sent to a refinery to produce gasoline, heating oil, and other products. See also *oil shale, shale oil*.

kilocalorie (kcal) Unit of energy equal to 1,000 calories. See *calorie*.

kilowatt (kw) Unit of electrical power equal to 1,000 watts. See *watt*.

kinetic energy Energy that matter has because of its motion and mass. Compare *potential energy*.

kwashiorkor Type of malnutrition that occurs in infants and very young children when they are weaned from mother's milk to a starchy diet low in protein. See also *marasmus*.

labor Physical and mental talents of people used to produce, distribute, and sell an economic good. Labor includes entrepreneurs, who assume the risk and responsibility of combining the resources of land, capital goods, and workers who produce an economic good. Compare *capital goods, natural resources.*

lake Large natural body of standing fresh water formed when water from precipitation, land runoff, or groundwater flow fills a depression in the earth created by glaciation, earthquake, volcanic activity, or a giant meteorite. Compare *reservoir*. See *eutrophic lake, mesotrophic lake, oligotrophic lake.*

landfill See *sanitary landfill.*

land-use planning Process for deciding the best use of each parcel of land in an area. See *ecological land-use planning.*

late-successional species Wild animal species found in moderate-size old-growth and mature forest habitats. Compare *early-successional species, midsuccessional species, wilderness species.*

law of conservation of energy See *first law of thermodynamics.*

law of conservation of matter In any ordinary physical or chemical change, matter is neither created nor destroyed but merely changed from one form to another; in physical and chemical changes existing atoms are either rearranged into different spatial patterns (physical changes) or different combinations (chemical changes).

law of conservation of matter and energy In any nuclear change the total amount of matter and energy involved remains the same. Compare *law of conservation of energy, law of conservation of matter.*

law of demand If price is the only factor affecting the market demand for an economic good, then as its price rises, demand falls, and as its price falls, demand increases. Compare *law of supply*. See *market equilibrium.*

law of energy degradation See *second law of thermodynamics.*

law of supply If price is the only factor affecting the market supply of an economic good, then as its price rises, suppliers will try to supply more, and as its price falls, the supply will drop. Compare *law of demand*. See *market equilibrium.*

law of tolerance The existence, abundance, and distribution of a species are determined by whether the levels of one or more physical or chemical factors fall above or below the levels tolerated by the species. See also *tolerance limit.*

LD$_{50}$ See *median lethal dose.*

LDC See *less developed country.*

leaching Process in which various chemicals in upper layers of soil are dissolved and carried to lower layers and in some cases to groundwater.

less developed country (LDC) Country that has low to moderate industrialization and low to moderate average GNP per person. Most LDCs are located in the tropical (or low) latitudes in Africa, Asia, and Latin America. Compare *more developed country.*

lethal dose Amount of a material per unit of body weight of test animals that kills all the test population in a certain time. Compare *median lethal dose, no-effect dose.*

life-cycle cost Initial cost plus lifetime operating costs of an economic good.

life expectancy Average number of years a newborn infant can be expected to live.

limiting factor Single factor that limits the growth, abundance, or distribution of the population of a particular organism in an ecosystem. See *limiting factor principle.*

limiting factor principle Too much or too little of any single abiotic factor can limit or prevent growth of the populations of particular plant and animal species in an ecosystem even if all other factors are at or near the optimum range of tolerance for the species.

limnetic zone Open water surface layer of a lake, away from the shore, where there is enough sunlight for photosynthesis. Compare *benthic zone, littoral zone, profundal zone.*

liquefied natural gas (LNG) Natural gas converted to liquid form by cooling to a very low temperature.

liquefied petroleum gas (LPG) Mixture of liquefied propane and butane gas removed from a deposit of natural gas.

lithosphere Soil and rock in the earth's upper surface or crust and the earth's upper mantle.

littoral zone Shallow waters near the shore of a body of water, in which sunlight penetrates to the bottom. Compare *benthic zone, limnetic zone, profundal zone.*

low-quality energy Energy such as low-temperature heat that is dispersed or dilute and has little ability to do useful work. Compare *high-quality energy.*

low-quality matter Matter that is disorganized (high entropy), dilute, dispersed, or contains a low concentration of a useful resource. Compare *high-quality matter.*

LPG See *liquefied petroleum gas.*

macronutrient Chemical that a plant or animal needs in large amounts to stay alive and healthy. Compare *micronutrient.*

magma Molten rock material in the earth's core.

malignant tumor See *cancer.*

malnutrition Faulty nutrition. Caused by a diet that does not supply an individual with enough proteins, essential fats, vitamins, minerals, and other nutrients needed for good health. See *kwashiorkor, marasmus*. Compare *overnutrition, undernutrition.*

manure See *animal manure, green manure.*

marasmus Nutritional-deficiency disease caused by a diet that does not have enough calories and protein to maintain good health. See *kwashiorkor, malnutrition.*

market demand How much of an economic good consumers are willing and able to buy at a particular price in a given time period. See *law of demand*. Compare *market supply.*

market equilibrium State in which sellers and buyers of an economic good agree on the quantity to be produced and the price to be paid. See *law of demand, law of supply, market demand, market supply.*

market supply How much of an economic good producers are willing and able to produce and sell at a particular price in a given period of time. See *law of supply*. Compare *market demand.*

mass The amount of stuff in matter.

mass number Sum of the number of neutrons and the number of protons in the nucleus of an atom. It gives the approximate mass of that atom.

mass transit Buses, trains, trolleys, and other forms of transportation that carry large numbers of people.

matter Anything that has mass and occupies space; the stuff the world is made of.

matter quality Measure of how useful a matter resource is based on its availability and concentration. See *high-quality matter, low-quality matter.*

matter-recycling society Society which emphasizes recycling the maximum amount of all resources that can be recycled. The goal is to allow economic growth to continue without depleting matter resources and without producing excessive pollution and environmental degradation. Compare *sustainable-earth society, throwaway society*.

mature community Fairly stable, self-sustaining community in an advanced stage of ecological succession. It usually has a diverse array of species and ecological niches and captures and uses energy and cycles critical chemicals more efficiently than simpler, immature communities. Compare *immature community* .

maximum sustainable yield See *sustainable yield*.

MDC See *more developed country*.

median lethal dose (LD$_{50}$) Amount of material per unit of body weight of test animals that kills half the test population in a certain time. Compare *lethal dose, no-dose effect*.

meltdown The melting of the core of a nuclear reactor.

mesotrophic lake Lake with a moderate supply of plant nutrients. Compare *eutrophic lake, oligotrophic lake*.

metabolic reserve Lower half of range-land grass plants; plants can grow back as long as this part is not consumed by herbivores.

metamorphic rock Rock formed from other types of rocks by high temperatures and high pressures. Some of these rocks may then melt to start the rock cycle over again. Compare *igneous rocks, sedimentary rocks*. See *rock cycle*.

metastasis Spread of malignant (cancerous) cells from a cancer to other parts of the body.

microconsumer See *decomposer*.

micronutrient Chemical that a plant or animal needs in small, or trace, amounts to stay alive and healthy. Compare *macronutrient*.

midsuccessional species Wild species found around abandoned croplands and partially open areas at the middle stages of ecological succession. Compare *early-successional species, late-successional species, wilderness species*.

mineral Any naturally occurring inorganic substance found in the earth's crust as a crystalline solid. See *metallic mineral, nonmetallic mineral*.

mineral resource Nonrenewable chemical element or compound in solid form that is used by humans. Mineral resources are classified as metallic (such

as iron and tin) or nonmetallic (such as fossil fuels, sand, and salt).

minimum-tillage farming See *conservation-tillage farming*.

mixed-economic system Economic system that falls somewhere between pure market and pure command economic systems. Virtually all of the world's economic systems fall into this category, with some closer to a pure market system and some closer to a pure command system. Compare *pure command economic system, pure market economic system, traditional economic system*.

molecule Chemical combination of two or more atoms of the same chemical element (such as O$_2$) or different chemical elements (such as H$_2$O).

monoculture Cultivation of a single crop usually on a large area of land. Compare *polyculture*.

monopoly Complete control over the supply and price of an economic good by a single producer. See also *cartel, oligopoly*.

more developed country (MDC) Country that is highly industrialized and has a high average GNP per person. Compare *less developed country*.

multiple use Principle of managing public land such as a national forest so it is used for a variety of purposes, such as timbering, mining, recreation, grazing, wildlife preservation, and soil and water conservation. See also *sustainable yield*.

municipal solid waste Solid materials discarded by homes and businesses in or near urban areas. See *solid waste*.

mutagen Chemical or form of radioactivity that can increase the rate of genetic mutation in a living organism. See *mutation*.

mutualism An interaction between individuals of different species that benefits each individual. Compare *commensalism*.

mutation An inheritable change in the DNA molecules in the genes found in the chromosomes. See *mutagen*.

nanoplankton Extremely small photosynthetic algae and bacteria. See also *phytoplankton*.

national ambient air quality standards (NAAQS) Maximum allowable level, averaged over a specific time period, for a certain pollutant in outdoor (ambient) air.

natural eutrophication See *eutrophication*.

natural gas Underground deposits of gases consisting of 50% to 90% methane (CH$_4$) and small amounts of heavier gaseous hydrocarbon compounds such as propane (C$_3$H$_8$) and butane (C$_4$H$_{10}$).

natural ionizing radiation Ionizing radiation in the environment from natural sources.

natural radioactivity Nuclear change in which unstable nuclei of atoms spontaneously shoot out "chunks" of mass, energy, or both at a fixed rate.

natural resources Area of the earth's solid surface, nutrients and minerals in the soil and deeper layers of the earth's crust, water, wild and domesticated plants and animals, air, and other resources produced by the earth's natural processes. Compare *capital goods, labor*.

natural selection Process by which some genes and gene combinations in a population of a species are reproduced more than others when the population is exposed to an environmental change or stress. When individual organisms in a population die off over time because they cannot tolerate a new stress, they are replaced by individuals whose genetic traits allow them to cope better with the stress. When these better-adapted individuals reproduce, they pass their adaptive traits on to their offspring. See also *evolution*.

negative feedback Flow of information into a system that counteracts the effects of a change in external conditions on the system. Compare *positive feedback*.

neo-Malthusians People who believe that if present population, resource use, and environmental trends continue, the world will become more crowded and more polluted, and many resources will be depleted or degraded. They believe that competition for scarce resources will lead to greater political and economic turmoil and increase the threat of nuclear and conventional wars. It is an updated and expanded version of the hypothesis proposed in 1789 by Thomas Robert Malthus: Human population growing exponentially will eventually outgrow food supplies and will be reduced in size by starvation, disease, and war. Compare *cornucopians*.

neritic zone See *coastal zone*.

net economic welfare (NEW) Measure of annual change in quality of life in a country. It is obtained by subtracting the value of all final products and services that decrease the quality of life from a country's GNP. See *average per capita NEW*.

net energy See *net useful energy*.

net primary productivity Rate at which all the plants in an ecosystem produce net useful chemical energy. It is equal to the difference between the rate at which the plants in an ecosystem produce useful chemical energy and the rate at which they use some of this energy through cellular respiration.

net useful energy Total amount of useful energy available from an energy resource or energy system over its lifetime minus the amount of energy used (the first energy law), automatically wasted (the second energy law), and unnecessarily wasted in finding, processing, concentrating, and transporting it to users.

neutral solution Water solution containing an equal number of hydrogen ions (H^+) and hydroxide ions (OH^-); water solution with a pH of 7. Compare *acid solution, basic solution*.

neutron (n) Elementary particle in the nuclei of all atoms (except hydrogen-1). It has a relative mass of 1 and no electric charge.

NEW See *net economic welfare*.

niche See *ecological niche*.

nitrogen cycle Cyclic movement of nitrogen in different chemical forms from the environment, to organisms, and then back to the environment.

nitrogen fixation Conversion of atmospheric nitrogen gas into forms useful to plants by lightning, bacteria, and blue-green algae; it is part of the nitrogen cycle.

no-effect dose Amount of a material per unit of body weight of test animals that causes no detectable harmful effects on the entire test population for a certain time. Compare *lethal dose, median lethal dose*.

nonbiodegradable Substance that cannot be broken down in the environment by natural processes. Compare *biodegradable*.

nondegradable See *nonbiodegradable*.

nonionizing electromagnetic radiation Forms of radiant energy such as radio waves, microwaves, infrared light, and ordinary light that do not have enough energy to cause ionization of atoms in living tissue. Compare *ionizing electromagnetic radiation*.

nonmetallic mineral Inorganic substance found in the earth's crust that contains useful nonmetallic compounds. Examples are sand, stone, and nitrate and phosphate salts used as commercial fertilizers. Compare *metallic mineral*.

nonpoint source Large land area such as crop fields and urban areas that discharge pollutants into surface and underground water over a large area. Compare *point source*.

nonrenewable resources Resources available in a fixed amount (stock) in the earth's crust. They can be exhausted either because they are not replaced by natural processes (copper) or because they are replaced more slowly than they are used (oil and coal). Compare *perpetual resource, renewable resource*.

nontransmissible disease A disease that is not caused by living organisms and that does not spread from one person to another. Examples are most cancer, diabetes, cardiovascular disease, and malnutrition. Compare *transmissible disease*.

no-till cultivation See *conservation-tillage farming*.

nuclear change Process in which nuclei of certain isotopes spontaneously change or are forced to change into one or more different isotopes. The three major types of nuclear change are natural radioactivity, nuclear fission, and nuclear fusion. Compare *chemical change*.

nuclear energy Energy released when atomic nuclei undergo a nuclear reaction such as the spontaneous emission of radioactivity, nuclear fission, or nuclear fusion.

nuclear fission Nuclear change in which the nuclei of certain isotopes with large mass numbers (such as uranium-235 and plutonium-239) split apart into two lighter nuclei when struck by a neutron. This process also releases more neutrons and a large amount of energy. Compare *nuclear fusion*.

nuclear fusion Nuclear change in which two nuclei of isotopes of elements with a low mass number (such as hydrogen-2 and hydrogen-3) are forced together at a very high temperature until they fuse to form a heavier nucleus (such as helium-4). This process releases a large amount of energy. Compare *nuclear fission*.

nucleus Extremely tiny center of an atom, making up most of the atom's mass. It contains one or more positively charged protons and one or more neutrons with no electrical charge (except for a hydrogen-1 atom, whose nucleus has one proton and no neutrons).

nutrient Element or compound needed for the survival, growth, and reproduction of a plant or animal. See *macronutrient, micronutrient*.

ocean thermal energy conversion (OTEC) Using the large temperature differences between the cold bottom waters and the sun-warmed surface waters of tropical oceans to produce electricity.

oil See *crude oil*.

oil shale Underground formation of a fine-grained sedimentary rock containing varying amounts of kerogen, a solid, waxy mixture of hydrocarbon compounds. Heating the rock to high temperatures converts the kerogen to a vapor which can be condensed to form a slow-flowing heavy oil called shale oil. See *kerogen, shale oil*.

old-growth forest Uncut, virgin forest containing massive trees that are often hundreds of years old. Examples include forests of Douglas fir, western hemlock, giant sequoia, and coastal redwoods in the western United States. Compare *secondary forest, tree farm*.

oligopoly Domination of the supply of an economic good by a few large firms. If these firms agree to set the price of the good, they become a monopoly. See also *cartel, monopoly*.

oligotrophic lake Lake with a low supply of plant nutrients. Compare *eutrophic lake, mesotrophic lake*.

omnivore Animal organism that can use both plants and other animals as food sources. Examples are pigs, rats, cockroaches, and people. Compare *carnivore, herbivore*.

open forest (woodland) An area where trees are abundant but their crowns do not form a closed canopy. Compare *closed forest*.

open-pit surface mining Removal of materials such as stone, sand, gravel, iron, and copper by digging them out of the earth's surface and leaving a large pit. See also *area strip mining, contour strip mining*.

open sea The part of an ocean that is beyond the continental shelf. Compare *coastal zone*.

ore Mineral deposit containing a high enough concentration of at least one metallic element to permit the metal to be extracted and sold at a profit.

organic compound Molecule that contains atoms of the element carbon, usually combined with itself and with atoms of one or more other elements such as hydrogen, oxygen, nitrogen, sulfur, phosphorus, chlorine, or fluorine. Compare *inorganic compound*.

organic farming Producing crops and livestock naturally by using organic fertilizer (manure, legumes, compost) and natural pest control (bugs that eat harmful bugs, plants that repel bugs, and environmental controls such as crop rotation) instead of using commercial

inorganic fertilizers and synthetic pesticides and herbicides.

organic fertilizer Organic material such as animal manure, green manure, and compost, applied to cropland as a source of plant nutrients. Compare *commercial inorganic fertilizer*.

organism Any form of life.

output pollution control Method for reducing the level of pollution after pollutants have been produced or have entered the environment. Examples are automobile emission control devices and sewage treatment plants. Compare *input pollution control*.

overburden Layer of soil and rock overlying a mineral deposit that is removed during surface mining.

overfishing Harvesting so many fish of a species, especially immature ones, that there is not enough breeding stock left to replenish the species to the point where it is profitable to harvest them.

overgrazing Consumption of rangeland grass by grazing animals to the point that it cannot be renewed or can be only slowly renewed because of damage to the root system.

overnutrition Diet so high in calories, saturated (animal) fats, salt, sugar, and processed foods, and so low in vegetables and fruits that the consumer runs high risks of diabetes, hypertension, heart disease, and other health hazards. Compare *malnutrition, undernutrition*.

overpopulation State in which the life-support systems in the world or geographic area are impaired because people use nonrenewable and renewable resources to such an extent that the resource base is degraded or depleted and air, water, and soil are severely polluted. See *consumption overpopulation, people overpopulation*.

oxygen cycle Cyclic movement of oxygen in different chemical forms from the environment, to organisms, and then back to the environment.

oxygen-demanding wastes Organic materials that are usually biodegraded by aerobic (oxygen-consuming) bacteria if there is enough dissolved oxygen in the water. See also *biological oxygen demand*.

ozone layer Layer of gaseous ozone (O_3) in the stratosphere that protects life on earth by filtering out harmful ultraviolet radiation from the sun.

PANs Peroxyacyl nitrates. Group of chemicals found in photochemical smog.

parasite Consumer organism that feeds on a living plant or animal, known as

the host, over an extended period of time. A parasite harms the host organism but does not kill it—at least not immediately, as most other consumers do. See *ectoparasites, endoparasites*.

particulate matter Solid particles or liquid droplets suspended or carried in the air.

parts per billion (ppb) Number of parts of a chemical found in one billion parts of a particular gas, liquid, or solid mixture.

parts per million (ppm) Number of parts of a chemical found in one million parts of a particular gas, liquid, or solid.

passive solar heating system System that captures sunlight directly within a structure and converts it to low-temperature heat for space heating. Compare *active solar heating system*.

pathogen Organism that produces disease.

PCBs See *polychlorinated biphenyls*.

people overpopulation Situation in which there are more people in the world or a geographic region than available supplies of food, water, and other vital resources can support. It can also occur where the rate of population growth so exceeds the rate of economic growth or the distribution of wealth is so inequitable that a number of people are too poor to grow or buy enough food, fuel, and other important resources. Compare *consumption overpopulation*.

permafrost Water permanently frozen year-round in thick underground layers of soil in tundra.

perpetual resource Resource such as solar energy that comes from a virtually inexhaustible source on a human time scale. Compare *nonrenewable resource, renewable resource*.

persistence See *inertia*.

pest Unwanted organism that directly or indirectly interferes with human activities.

pesticide Any chemical designed to kill or inhibit the growth of an organism that people consider to be undesirable. See *fungicides, herbicides, insecticides*.

pesticide treadmill Situation in which the cost of using pesticides increases while their effectiveness decreases, mostly because the pest species develop genetic resistance to the pesticides.

petrochemicals Chemicals obtained by refining (distilling) crude oil. They are used as raw materials in the manufacture of most industrial chemicals, fertilizers, pesticides, plastics, synthetic fibers, paints, medicines, and many other products.

petroleum See *crude oil*.

pH Numeric value that indicates the relative acidity or alkalinity of a substance on a scale of 0 to 14, with the neutral point at 7. Acid solutions have pH values lower than 7, and basic solutions have pH values greater than 7.

phosphorus cycle Cyclic movement of phosphorus in different chemical forms from the environment, to organisms, and then back to the environment.

photochemical smog Complex mixture of air pollutants produced in the atmosphere by the reaction of hydrocarbons and nitrogen oxides under the influence of sunlight. Especially harmful components include ozone, peroxyacyl nitrates (PANs), and various aldehydes. Compare *industrial smog*.

photosynthesis Complex process that takes place in cells of green plants. Radiant energy from the sun is used to combine carbon dioxide (CO_2) and water (H_2O) to produce oxygen (O_2) and simple nutrient molecules, such as glucose ($C_6H_{12}O_6$). Compare *cellular aerobic respiration, chemosynthesis*.

photovoltaic cell (solar cell) Device in which radiant (solar) energy is converted directly into electrical energy.

physical change Process that alters one or more physical properties of an element or compound without altering its chemical composition. Examples are changing the size and shape of a sample of matter (crushing ice and cutting aluminum foil) and changing a sample of matter from one physical state to another (boiling and freezing water). Compare *chemical change*.

phytoplankton Small, drifting plants, mostly algae and bacteria, found in aquatic ecosystems. See also *nanoplankton*. Compare *plankton, zooplankton*.

pioneer community First integrated set of plants, animals, and decomposers found in an area undergoing primary ecological succession. See *immature community, mature community*.

plaintiff The individual, group of individuals, corporation, or government agency bringing the charges in a lawsuit. Compare *defendant*.

plankton Small plant organisms (phytoplankton and nanoplankton) and animal organisms (zooplankton) that float in aquatic ecosystems.

plantation agriculture Growing specialized crops such as bananas, coffee, and cacao in tropical LDCs, primarily for sale to MDCs.

plate tectonics Widely accepted theory that parts of the earth's crust move horizontally and vertically and in some cases slide over one another.

point source   A single identifiable source that discharges pollutants into the environment. Examples are a smokestack, sewer, ditch, or pipe. Compare *nonpoint source*.

politics   See *public politics*.

pollution   A change in the physical, chemical, or biological characteristics of the air, water, or soil that can affect the health, survival, or activities of humans in an unwanted way. Some expand the term to include harmful effects on all forms of life.

polychlorinated biphenyls (PCBs)   Group of 209 different toxic, oily, synthetic chlorinated hydrocarbon compounds that can be biologically amplified in food chains and webs.

polyculture   Complex form of intercropping in which a large number of different plants maturing at different times are planted together. See also *intercropping*. Compare *monoculture, polyvarietal cultivation*.

polyvarietal cultivation   Planting a plot of land with several varieties of the same crop. Compare *intercropping, monoculture, polyculture*.

population   Group of individual organisms of the same species living within a particular area.

population crash   Large number of deaths over a fairly short time brought about when the number of individuals in a population is too large to be supported by available environmental resources.

population density   Number of organisms in a particular population found in a specified area.

population distribution   Variation of population density over a particular geographical area. For example, a country has a high population density in its urban areas and much lower population densities in rural areas.

population dynamics   Major abiotic and biotic factors that tend to increase or decrease the population size and age and sex composition of a species.

positive feedback   Situation in which a change in a system in one direction provides information that causes the system to change further in the same direction. Compare *negative feedback*.

potential energy   Energy stored in an object because of its position or the position of its parts. Compare *kinetic energy*.

potentially renewable resource   See *renewable resource*.

poverty   Inability to meet basic needs. People in different societies differ in what they consider to be basic needs.

ppb   See *parts per billion*.

ppm   See *parts per million*.

precipitation   Water in the form of rain, sleet, hail, and snow that falls from the atmosphere onto the land and bodies of water.

predation   Situation in which an organism of one species (the predator) captures and feeds on parts or all of an organism of another species (the prey).

predator   Organism that captures and feeds on parts or all of an organism of another species (the prey).

predator-prey relationship   Interaction between two organisms of different species in which one organism called the predator captures and feeds on parts or all of another organism called the prey.

prescribed burning   Deliberate setting and careful control of surface fires in forests to help prevent more destructive crown fires and to kill off unwanted plants that compete with commercial species for plant nutrients; may also be used on grasslands. See *crown fire, ground fire, surface fire*.

preservationists   People who stress the need to limit human use of parks, wilderness, estuaries, wetlands, and other types of ecosystems primarily to nondestructive recreation, education, and research. Compare *scientific conservationists, sustainable-earth conservationists*.

prey   Organism that is captured and serves as a source of food for an organism of another species (the predator).

primary air pollutant   Chemical that has been added directly to the air by natural events or human activities and occurs in a harmful concentration. Compare *secondary air pollutant*.

primary consumer   See *herbivore*.

primary ecological succession   Sequential development of communities in a bare area that has never been occupied by a community of organisms. Compare *secondary ecological succession*.

primary oil recovery   Pumping out the crude oil that flows by gravity into the bottom of an oil well. Compare *enhanced oil recovery, secondary oil recovery*.

primary sewage treatment   Mechanical treatment of sewage in which large solids are filtered out by screens and suspended solids settle out as sludge in a sedimentation tank. Compare *advanced sewage treatment, secondary sewage treatment*.

prime reproductive age   Years between ages 20 and 29, during which most women have most of their children. Compare *reproductive age*.

principle of multiple use   See *multiple use*.

prior appropriation   Legal principle by which the first user of water from a stream establishes a legal right to continued use of the amount originally withdrawn. See also *riparian rights*.

private good   Economic good that can be owned and enjoyed on a private, or exclusive, basis. It can be produced and sold in units. Compare *public good*.

private property resource   Resource owned by an individual or group of individuals other than the government. Compare *common property resource, public property resource*.

producer   Organism that uses solar energy (green plant) or chemical energy (some bacteria) to manufacture its own organic nutrients from inorganic nutrients. Compare *consumer, decomposer*.

productivity   Measure of the output of economic goods and services produced by the input of the factors of production (natural resources, capital goods, labor). Increasing economic productivity means getting more output from less input. Compare *economic growth*.

profundal zone   Deep, open-water region of a lake, a region not penetrated by sunlight. Compare *benthic zone, limnetic zone, littoral zone*.

proton (p)   Positively charged particle in the nuclei of all atoms. Each proton has a relative mass of 1 and a single positive charge.

public good   Economic good that cannot be divided and sold in units, is owned by nobody in particular, and can be enjoyed by anybody. Examples are national defense, clean air, clean water, beautiful scenery, and wild plants and animals (biological diversity). Compare *private good*.

public land resources   Land that is owned jointly by all citizens but is managed for them by an agency of the local, state, or federal government. Examples are state and national parks, forests, wildlife refuges, and wilderness areas. Compare *common property resource, private property resource*.

public politics   Process through which individuals and groups try to influence or control the policies and actions of governments that affect the local, state, national, and international communities.

public property resource   See *public land resource*.

pure capitalism   See *pure market economic system*.

pure command economic system   System in which all economic decisions are made by the government or other central authority. Compare *mixed economic system, pure market economic system, traditional economic system*.

pure competition   State in which there are large numbers of independently acting buyers and sellers for each economic good in a pure market economic system. No buyer or seller is able to control the supply, demand, or price of a good. All buyers and sellers are free to enter or leave the market as they please but must accept the going market price.

pure market economic system   System in which all economic decisions are made in the market, where buyers and sellers of economic goods freely interact with no government or other interference. Compare *mixed economic system, pure command economic system, traditional economic system.*

pyramid of biomass   Diagram representing the biomass, or total dry weight of all living organisms, that can be supported at each trophic level in a food chain. See also *pyramid of energy flow, pyramid of energy loss, pyramid of numbers.*

pyramid of energy flow   Diagram representing the flow of usable, high-quality energy through each trophic level in a food chain. With each energy transfer, only a small part (typically 10%) of the usable energy entering one trophic level is transferred to the next trophic level. See also *pyramid of energy loss.* Compare *pyramid of biomass, pyramid of numbers.*

pyramid of energy loss   Diagram showing the amount of low-quality energy, usually low-temperature heat, lost to the environment at each trophic level in a food chain. Typically 90% of the high-quality energy entering a trophic level is converted to low-quality energy and lost to the environment. See *pyramid of energy flow.* Compare *pyramid of biomass, pyramid of numbers.*

pyramid of numbers   Diagram representing the number of organisms of a particular type that can be supported at each trophic level from a given input of solar energy at the producer trophic level in a food chain. Compare *pyramid of biomass, pyramid of energy flow.*

radiation   Fast-moving particles (particulate radiation) or waves of energy (electromagnetic radiation). See *ionizing radiation, nonionizing radiation.*

radioactive isotope   See *radioisotope.*

radioactive waste   Radioactive waste products of nuclear power plants, research, medicine, weapons production, or other processes involving nuclear reactions.

radioactivity   Nuclear change in which unstable nuclei of atoms spontaneously shoot out "chunks" of mass, energy, or both at a fixed rate. The three major types of radioactivity are gamma rays and fast-moving alpha particles and beta particles.

radioisotope   Isotope of an atom whose unstable nuclei spontaneously emit one or more types of radioactivity (alpha particles, beta particles, gamma rays).

rain shadow effect   Drop in precipitation on the far side (leeward side) of a mountain when prevailing winds flow up and over a high mountain or range of high mountains. This creates semiarid and arid conditions on the leeward side of a high mountain range.

range   See *rangeland.*

range condition   Estimate of how close a particular area of rangeland is to its potential for producing vegetation that can be consumed by grazing or browsing animals.

rangeland   Land, mostly grasslands, whose plants can provide food (forage) for grazing or browsing animals. Compare *feedlot.*

range of tolerance   Range of chemical and physical conditions that must be maintained for populations of a particular species to stay alive and grow, develop, and function normally. See *law of tolerance.*

real GNP   Gross national product adjusted for inflation. Compare *average per capita GNP, average per capita real GNP, gross national product.*

recharge area   Area in which an aquifer is replenished with water by the downward percolation of precipitation through soil and rock.

recycling   Collecting and reprocessing a resource so it can be used again. An example is collecting aluminum cans, melting them down, and using the aluminum to make new cans or other aluminum products. Compare *reuse.*

relative resource scarcity   Situation in which a resource has not been depleted but there is not enough available to meet the demand. This can be caused by a war, a natural disaster, or other events that disrupt the production and distribution of a resource or by deliberate attempts of its producers to lower production to drive prices up. Compare *absolute resource scarcity.*

renewable resource   Resource that normally is replenished through natural processes. Examples are trees in forests, grasses in grasslands, wild animals, fresh surface water in lakes and rivers, most deposits of groundwater, fresh air, and fertile soil. If such a resource is used faster than it is replenished, it can be depleted and converted to a nonrenewa-

ble resource. Compare *nonrenewable resource, perpetual resource.* See also *environmental degradation.*

replacement-level fertility   Number of children a couple must have to replace themselves. The average for a country or the world is usually slightly higher than 2 children per couple (2.1 in the United States and 2.5 in some LDCs) because some children die before reaching their reproductive years. See also *total fertility rate.*

reproductive age   Ages 15 to 44, when most women have all their children. Compare *prime reproductive age.*

reserves (economic resources)   Identified deposits of a particular resource in known locations that can be extracted profitably at present prices and with current mining technology. Compare *resources.*

reservoir   Human-created body of standing fresh water often built behind a dam. Compare *lake.*

resilience   Ability of a living system to restore itself to original condition after being exposed to an outside disturbance that is not too drastic. See also *constancy, inertia.*

resource   Anything obtained from the environment to meet human needs and wants.

resource conservation   See *conservation.*

resource recovery   Salvaging usable metals, paper, and glass from solid waste and selling them to manufacturing industries for recycling.

resources   Identified and unidentified deposits of a particular mineral that cannot be recovered profitably with present prices and mining technology. Some of these materials may be converted to reserves when prices rise or mining technology improves. Compare *reserves.*

respiration   See *cellular aerobic respiration.*

reuse   To use a product over and over again in the same form. An example is collecting, washing, and refilling glass beverage bottles. Compare *recycle.*

rill erosion   Soil erosion caused when small streams of surface water flow at high velocities over the ground and create miniature valleys when the soil is washed away. Compare *gully erosion, sheet erosion.*

riparian rights   System of water law that gives anyone whose land adjoins a flowing stream the right to use water from the stream as long as some is left for downstream users. Compare *prior appropriation.*

risk   The probability that something undesirable will happen from deliberate or accidental exposure to a hazard. See *risk assessment, risk-benefit analysis, risk management.*

risk assessment Process of gathering data and making assumptions to estimate short- and long-term harmful effects on human health or the environment from exposure to hazards associated with the use of a particular product or technology. See *risk, risk-benefit analysis.*

risk-benefit analysis Estimate of the short- and long-term risks and benefits of using a particular product or technology. See *desirability quotient, risk.* Compare *cost-benefit analysis.*

rock Naturally occurring solid that contains one or more minerals and is found in the earth's crust and mantle. See *igneous rock, metamorphic rock, rock cycle, sedimentary rock.*

rock cycle Cyclic processes that form and modify rocks in the earth's crust and mantle. See *igneous rock, metamorphic rock, sedimentary rock.*

rodenticide Chemical designed to kill rodents.

ruminant animals Grazing and browsing herbivores such as cattle, sheep, goats, and buffalo that have a three- or four-chambered stomach which digests the cellulose in vegetation they eat.

runoff Fresh water from precipitation and melting ice that flows on the earth's surface into nearby streams, rivers, lakes, wetlands, and reservoirs. Compare *groundwater.*

rural area Geographical area in the United States with a population of less than 2,500 people. The number of people used in this definition may vary in different countries. Compare *urban area.*

salinity Amount of various salts (especially sodium chloride) dissolved in a given volume of water.

salinization Accumulation of salts that can eventually make the soil unable to support plant growth.

saltwater intrusion Movement of salt water into freshwater aquifers in coastal and inland areas as groundwater is withdrawn faster than it is recharged by precipitation.

sanitary landfill Land waste disposal site in which waste is spread in thin layers, compacted, and covered with a fresh layer of soil each day.

scarcity Situation in which there isn't an unlimited supply of a resource people need or want. See *absolute resource scarcity, relative resource scarcity.*

science Attempts to discover order in nature and then use this knowledge to make projections about what will happen in nature. See *scientific data, scientific hypothesis, scientific law, scientific methods, scientific theory.*

scientific conservationists People who believe that the findings of science and technology should be used to manage resources according to the principle of multiple-use and the principle of sustainable yield so that they are available for future generations. Compare *preservationists, sustainable-earth conservationists.*

scientific data Facts obtained by making observations and measurements. Compare *scientific hypothesis, scientific law, scientific theory.*

scientific hypothesis An educated guess that attempts to explain a scientific law or certain scientific facts. Compare *scientific data, scientific law, scientific theory.*

scientific law Summary of what scientists find happening in nature over and over with the same results. See *first law of thermodynamics, second law of thermodynamics, law of conservation of matter.* Compare *scientific data, scientific hypothesis, scientific theory.*

scientific method The ways scientists gather data and formulate and test scientific laws and theories. See *scientific data, scientific hypothesis, scientific law, scientific theory.*

scientific theory A well-tested and widely accepted scientific hypothesis that explains a scientific law or certain scientific facts. Compare *scientific data, scientific hypothesis, scientific law.*

secondary air pollutant Harmful chemical formed in the atmosphere by reacting with normal air components or other air pollutants. Compare *primary air pollutant.*

secondary consumer See *carnivore.*

secondary ecological succession Sequential development of communities in an area in which natural vegetation has been removed or destroyed, but the soil or sediment is not destroyed. Compare *primary ecological succession.*

secondary forest Stands of trees resulting from secondary ecological succession. Compare *old growth forest, tree farm.*

secondary oil recovery Injection of water into an oil well after primary oil recovery to force out some of the remaining thicker crude oil. Compare *enhanced oil recovery, primary oil recovery.*

secondary sewage treatment Second step in most waste treatment systems, in which aerobic bacteria break down up to 90% of degradable, oxygen-demanding organic wastes in wastewater. This is

usually done by bringing sewage and bacteria together in trickling filters or in the activated sludge process. Compare *advanced sewage treatment, primary sewage treatment.*

second law of ecology Everything is connected to and intermingled with everything else.

second law of energy See *second law of thermodynamics.*

second law of thermodynamics In any conversion of heat energy to useful work, some of the initial energy input is always degraded to a lower-quality, more-dispersed, less useful form of energy, usually low-temperature heat that flows into the environment; you can't break even in terms of energy quality. See *first law of thermodynamics.*

sediment Insoluble particles of soil, silt, and other solid inorganic and organic materials that become suspended in water and eventually fall to the bottom of a body of water.

sedimentary rock Limestone and other rocks that collect as sediments in basins. Compare *igneous rock, metamorphic rock.* See *rock cycle.*

Seed-tree cutting Removal of nearly all trees on a site in one cutting, with a few seed-producing trees left uniformly distributed to regenerate the forest. Compare *clearcutting, selective cutting, shelterwood cutting, whole-tree harvesting.*

selective cutting Cutting of intermediate-aged, mature, or diseased trees in an uneven-aged forest stand either singly or in small groups. This encourages the growth of younger trees and maintains an uneven-aged stand. Compare *clearcutting, seed-tree cutting, shelterwood cutting, whole-tree harvesting.*

septic tank Underground tank for treatment of wastewater from a home in rural and suburban areas. Bacteria in the tank decompose organic wastes and the sludge settles to the bottom of the tank. The effluent flows out of the tank into the ground through a field of drain pipes.

sewage sludge See *sludge.*

shade-intolerant tree species A tree species that needs lots of sunlight in the early growth stages and thrives in forest openings. Compare *shade-tolerant tree species.*

shade-tolerant tree species A tree species that can grow in dim or moderate light under the crown cover of larger trees. Compare *shade-intolerant tree species.*

shale oil Slow-flowing, dark brown, heavy oil obtained when kerogen in oil shale is vaporized at high temperatures and then condensed. Shale oil can be refined to yield gasoline, heating oil, and other petroleum products. See *kerogen, oil shale.*

sheet erosion   Soil erosion caused by surface water moving down a slope or across a field in a wide flow. Because it removes topsoil evenly, it may not be noticeable until much damage has been done. Compare *gully erosion, rill erosion.*

shelterbelt   See *windbreak.*

shelterwood cutting   Removal of mature, marketable trees in an area in a series of partial cuttings to allow regeneration of a new stand under the partial shade of older trees, which are later removed. Typically this is done by making two or three cuts over a decade. Compare *clearcutting, seed-tree cutting, selective cutting, whole-tree harvesting.*

shifting cultivation   Clearing a plot of ground in a forest, especially in tropical areas, and planting crops on it for a few years (typically 2 to 5 years) until the soil is depleted of nutrients or until the plot has been invaded by a dense growth of vegetation from the surrounding forest. Then a new plot is cleared and the process is repeated. The abandoned plot cannot successfully grow crops for 10 to 30 years. See also *slash-and-burn cultivation.*

silviculture   Science and art of cultivating and managing forests to produce a renewable supply of timber.

slash-and-burn cultivation   Cutting down trees and other vegetation in a patch of forest, leaving the cut vegetation on the ground to dry, and then burning it. The ashes that are left add plant nutrients to the nutrient-poor soils found in most tropical forest areas. Crops are planted between tree stumps. Plots must be abandoned after a few years (typically 2 to 5 years) because of loss of soil fertility or invasion of vegetation from the surrounding forest. See also *shifting cultivation.*

sludge   Gooey solid mixture of bacteria- and virus-laden organic matter, toxic metals, synthetic organic chemicals, and solid chemicals removed from wastewater at a sewage treatment plant.

smog   Originally a combination of smoke and fog but now used to describe other mixtures of pollutants in the atmosphere. See *industrial smog, photochemical smog.*

soil   Complex mixture of inorganic minerals (mostly clay, silt, and sand), decaying organic matter, water, air, and living organisms.

soil conservation   Methods used to reduce soil erosion, to prevent depletion of soil nutrients, and to restore nutrients already lost by erosion, leaching, and excessive crop harvesting.

soil erosion   Movement of soil components, especially topsoil, from one place to another usually by exposure to wind, flowing water, or both. This natural process can be greatly accelerated by human activities that remove vegetation from soil. See *gully erosion, rill erosion, sheet erosion.*

soil horizons   Horizontal layers that make up a particular mature soil.

soil porosity   Measure of the volume of pores, or spaces, and the average distances between them in a sample of soil.

soil profile   Cross-sectional view of the horizons in a soil.

soil texture   Relative amounts of the different types and sizes of particles in a sample of soil.

soil water   Underground water that partially fill pores between soil particles and rocks within the upper soil and rock layers of the earth's crust above the water table. Compare *groundwater.*

solar cell   See *photovoltaic cell.*

solar collector   Device for collecting radiant energy from the sun and converting it into heat. See *active solar heating system, passive solar heating system.*

solar energy   Direct radiant energy from the sun. It also includes indirect forms of energy such as wind, falling or flowing water (hydropower), ocean thermal gradients, and biomass, which are produced when direct solar energy interacts with the earth.

solar pond   Fairly small body of fresh water or salt water from which stored solar energy can be extracted because of temperature difference between the hot surface layer exposed to the sun during daylight and the cooler layer beneath it.

solid waste   Any unwanted or discarded material that is not a liquid or a gas.

speciation   Formation of new species from existing ones through natural selection in response to changes in environmental conditions; usually takes thousands to millions of years. Compare *extinction.*

species   All organisms of the same kind; for organisms that reproduce sexually, a species is all organisms that can interbreed.

species diversity   Number of different species and their relative abundances in a given area. Compare *genetic diversity.*

spoils   Unwanted rock and other waste materials produced when a material is removed from the earth's surface or subsurface by mining.

sport fishing   Finding and catching fish mostly for recreation. Compare *commercial fishing, subsistence fishing.*

sport hunting   Finding and killing animals mostly for recreation. Compare *commercial hunting, subsistence hunting.*

S-shaped curve   Leveling off of an exponential, J-shaped curve when a rapidly growing population encounters environmental resistance and ceases to grow in numbers.

stability   Ability of a living system to withstand or recover from externally imposed changes or stresses. See *inertia, resilience.*

statutory law   Law passed by a state or national legislature or other governing body. Compare *common law.*

stocking rate   Number of a particular kind of animal grazing on a given area of grassland.

strategic materials   Fuel and nonfuel minerals vital to the industry and defense of a country. Ideally, supplies are stockpiled to cushion against supply interruptions and sharp price rises.

stratosphere   Second layer of the atmosphere, extending from about 19 to 48 kilometers (12 to 30 miles) above the earth's surface. It contains small amounts of gaseous ozone (O_3), which filters out about 99% of the incoming harmful ultraviolet (UV) radiation.

strip cropping   Planting regular crops and close-growing plants such as hay or nitrogen-fixing legumes in alternating rows or bands to help reduce depletion of soil nutrients.

strip mining   Form of surface mining in which bulldozers, power shovels, or stripping wheels remove large chunks of the earth's surface in strips. See *surface mining.* Compare *subsurface mining.*

subatomic particles   Extremely small particles—electrons, protons, and neutrons—that make up the internal structure of atoms.

subsidence   Sinking down of part of the earth's crust due to underground excavation, such as a coal mine, or removal of groundwater.

subsistence agriculture   Supplementing solar energy with energy from human labor and draft animals to produce enough food to feed oneself and family members; in good years there may be enough food left over to sell or put aside for hard times. Compare *industrialized agriculture.*

subsistence economy   Economic system where the major goal is to produce enough goods to meet basic survival needs with little or no surplus left over for sale or trade. It is often a traditional economic system. See *traditional economic system*. Compare *mixed economic system, pure market economic system, pure command economic system*.

subsistence farming See *subsistence agriculture*.

subsistence fishing Finding and catching fish to get food for survival. Compare *commercial fishing, sport fishing*.

subsistence hunting Finding and killing wild animals to get enough food and other animal material for survival. Compare *commercial hunting, sport hunting*.

subsurface mining Extraction of a metal ore or fuel resource such as coal from a deep underground deposit. Compare *surface mining*.

succession See *ecological succession*.

succulent plants Plants such as cacti that store water and produce the food they need in the thick, fleshy tissue of their green stems and branches.

sulfur cycle Cyclic movement of sulfur in different chemical forms from the environment, to organisms, and then back to the environment.

superinsulated house House that is heavily insulated and extremely airtight. Typically, active or passive solar collectors are used to heat water and an air-to-air heat exchanger is used to prevent buildup of excessive moisture and indoor air pollutants.

supply See *market supply*.

surface fire Forest fire that burns only undergrowth and leaf litter on the forest floor. Compare *crown fire, ground fire*.

surface mining Removal of soil, subsoil, and other strata and then extracting a mineral deposit found fairly close to the earth's surface. See *area strip mining, contour strip mining, open-pit surface mining*. Compare *subsurface mining*.

surface water Precipitation that does not infiltrate into the ground or return to the atmosphere and becomes runoff that flows into nearby streams, rivers, lakes, wetlands, and reservoirs. See *runoff*. Compare *groundwater*.

sustainable agriculture See *sustainable-earth agricultural system*.

sustainable-earth agricultural system Method of growing crops and raising livestock based on organic fertilizers, soil conservation, water conservation, biological control of pests, and minimal use of nonrenewable fossil fuel energy.

sustainable-earth conservationists People who believe that the earth's resources should be protected and sustained not just for human beings but also for other species. They have a life-centered rather than a human-centered

approach to managing and sustaining the earth's resources by working with nature, not wasting resources unnecessarily, and interfering with nonhuman species only to meet important human needs. Compare *preservationists, scientific conservationists*.

sustainable-earth economy Economic system in which the number of people and the quantity of goods are maintained at some constant level. This level is ecologically sustainable over time and meets at least the basic needs of all members of the population.

sustainable-earth society Society based on working with nature by recycling and reusing discarded matter, conserving matter and energy resources by reducing unnecessary waste and use, by not degrading renewable resources, and by building things that are easy to recycle, reuse, and repair. Compare *matter-recycling society, throwaway society*.

sustainable-earth worldview Belief that the earth is a place with finite room and resources so that continuing population growth, production, and consumption inevitably put severe stress on natural processes that renew and maintain the resource base of air, water, and soil that support all life. To prevent environmental overload, environmental degradations and resource depletion, people should work with nature by controlling population growth, reducing unnecessary use and waste of matter and energy resources, and not causing the premature extinction of any other species. Compare *throwaway worldview*.

sustainable yield (sustained yield) Highest rate at which a renewable resource can be used without impairing or damaging its ability to be fully renewed. See also *environmental degradation*.

sustained yield See *sustainable yield*.

synergistic effect Interaction of two or more factors so that the net effect is greater than that expected from adding together the independent effects of each factor.

synfuels Synthetic gaseous and liquid fuels produced from solid coal or sources other than natural gas or crude oil.

synthetic natural gas (SNG) Gaseous fuel containing mostly methane produced from solid coal.

tailings Rock and other waste materials removed as impurities when minerals are mined and mineral deposits are processed. These materials are usually dumped on the ground or into ponds.

tar sand Swamplike deposit of a mixture of fine clay, sand, water, and variable amounts of a tarlike heavy oil known as bitumen. Bitumen can be extracted from tar sand by heating. It is then purified and upgraded to synthetic crude oil. See *bitumen*.

technology Creation of new products and processes that are supposed to improve our survival, comfort, and quality of life. Compare *science*.

temperature Measure of the average speed of motion of the atoms or molecules in a substance or combination of substances at a given moment. Compare *heat*.

temperature inversion See *thermal inversion*.

teratogen Chemical which, if ingested by a pregnant female, causes malformation of the developing fetus.

terracing Planting crops on a long, steep slope that has been converted into a series of broad, nearly level terraces that follow the slope of the land to retain water and reduce soil erosion.

terrestrial Pertaining to land. Compare *aquatic*.

terrestrial ecosystem See *biome*.

tertiary (and higher) consumers Animals that feed on animal-eating animals. They feed at high trophic levels in food chains and webs. Examples are hawks, lions, bass, and sharks. Compare *carnivores, decomposers, herbivores*.

tertiary sewage treatment See *advanced sewage treatment*.

thermal enrichment Beneficial effects in an aquatic ecosystem from a rise in water temperature. Compare *thermal pollution*.

thermal inversion Layer of dense, cool air trapped under a layer of less dense warm air, thus reversing the normal situation. In a prolonged inversion, air pollution in the trapped layer may build up to harmful levels.

thermal pollution Increase in water temperature that has harmful effects on an aquatic ecosystem. See *thermal shock*. Compare *thermal enrichment*.

thermal shock A sharp change in water temperature that can kill or harm fish and other aquatic organisms. See *thermal pollution*. Compare *thermal enrichment*.

thermocline Zone of gradual temperature between warm surface water and colder deep water in a lake, reservoir, or ocean.

threatened species Wild species that is still abundant in its natural range but is likely to become endangered because of a decline in numbers. Compare *endangered species*.

threshold effect   The harmful or fatal effect of a small change in environmental conditions that exceeds the limit of tolerance of an organism, population, or volume of air, water, or soil.

throwaway society   Society found in most advanced industrialized countries, in which ever-increasing economic growth is sustained by maximizing the rate at which matter and energy resources are used with little emphasis on recycling, reuse, reduction of unnecessary waste, and other forms of resource conservation. Compare *matter-recycling society, sustainable-earth society*.

throwaway worldview   Belief that the earth is a place of unlimited resources. Any type of resource conservation that hampers short-term economic growth is unnecessary because if we pollute or deplete resources in one area, we will find substitutes, control the pollution through technology, and if necessary get resources from the moon and asteroids in the "new frontier" of space. Compare *sustainable-earth worldview*.

time delay   Delay between the time information is received by a system regulated by information feedback and the time that the system makes a corrective action by negative feedback.

total fertility rate (TFR)   Estimate of the number of live children the average woman will bear if she passes through all her childbearing years (ages 15 to 44 conforming to the age-specific fertility rates of each year.

total resources   Total amount of a particular resource material that exists on earth. Compare *identified resources, reserves, resources, unidentified resources*.

totally planned economy   See *pure command economic system*.

toxic substance   Chemical that is harmful to people or other organisms.

toxic waste   Form of hazardous waste that causes death or serious injury (such as burns, respiratory diseases, cancers, or genetic mutations) to humans. See *hazardous waste*.

traditional economic system   System in which past customs and traditions are used to make economic decisions. This system is found in most remaining tribal communities and is often a subsistence economic system. Compare *mixed economic system, pure command economic system, pure market economic system*.

tragedy of the commons   Depletion or degradation of a resource to which people have free and unmanaged access. An example is the depletion of commercially

desirable species of fish in the open ocean beyond areas controlled by coastal countries. See *common property resource*.

transmissible disease   A disease that is caused by living organisms such as bacteria, viruses, and parasitic worms and that can spread from one person to another by air, water, food, body fluids, or in some cases by insects. Compare *nontransmissible disease*.

transpiration   Process by which water moves up through a living plant and is transferred to the atmosphere as water vapor from exposed parts of the plant.

tree farm   Site planted with one or only a few tree species in an even-aged stand. When the stand matures, it is usually harvested by clearcutting and replanted. Normally used to grow rapidly growing tree species for fuelwood, timber, or pulpwood. See *even-aged management*. Compare *uneven-aged management, uneven-aged stand*.

tritium (T: hydrogen-3)   Isotope of hydrogen with a nucleus containing one proton and two neutrons, thus having a mass number of 3. Compare *deuterium*.

trophic level   All organisms that consume the same general types of food in a food chain or food web. For example, all producers belong to the first trophic level and all herbivores belong to the second trophic level in a food chain or a food web.

troposphere   Innermost layer of the atmosphere. It contains about 95% of the earth's air and extends about 11 miles above the earth's surface. Compare *stratosphere*.

true cost   Cost of a good when its internal costs and its short- and long-term external costs are included in its market price. Compare *external cost, internal cost*.

unconfined aquifer   Collection of groundwater above a layer of fairly impermeable rock or compacted clay. Compare *confined aquifer*.

undergrazing   Degradation in the quality of rangeland vegetation as a source of food for livestock or wild herbivores because of a lack of grazing. Compare *overgrazing*.

undernutrition   Not taking in enough food to meet one's minimum daily energy requirement for a long enough time to cause harmful effects. Compare *malnutrition, overnutrition*.

undiscovered resources   Potential supplies of a particular mineral resource, believed to exist because of geologic knowledge and theory, though specific

locations, quality, and amounts are unknown. Compare *resources, reserves*.

uneven-aged management   Method of forest management in which trees of different species in a given stand are maintained at many ages and sizes to permit continuous natural regeneration. Compare *even-aged management*.

uneven-aged stand   Stand of trees in which there are considerable differences in the ages of individual trees. Usually, such stands have a variety of tree species. See *uneven-aged management*. Compare *even-aged stand, tree farm*.

upwelling   Movement of nutrient-rich bottom water to the ocean's surface. This occurs along certain steep coastal areas where the surface layer of ocean water is pushed away from shore and replaced by cold, nutrient-rich bottom water.

urban area   Geographic area with a population of 2,500 or more people. The number of people used in this definition may vary in different countries.

urban growth   Rate of growth of an urban population. Compare *degree of urbanization*.

urban heat island   Buildup of heat in the atmosphere above an urban area. This heat is produced by the large concentration of cars, buildings, factories, and other heat-producing activities. See also *dust dome*.

urbanization   See *degree of urbanization*.

wastewater lagoon   Large pond several feet deep where air, sunlight, and microorganisms break down wastes, allow solids to settle out, and kill some disease-causing bacteria. Water typically remains in a lagoon for 30 days. Then it is treated with chlorine and pumped out for use by a city or spread over cropland.

wastewater pond   See *wastewater lagoon*.

water consumption   Water that has been withdrawn from a groundwater or surface water source and is not available for reuse in the area from which it was withdrawn because of seepage, evaporation, or contamination. See *water withdrawal*.

water cycle   See *hydrologic cycle*.

waterlogging   Saturation of soil with irrigation water or excessive precipitation so that the water table rises close to the surface.

water pollution   Any physical or chemical change in surface water or groundwater that can harm living organisms or make water unfit for certain uses.

watershed Land area that delivers run-off water, sediment, and dissolved substances to a major river and its tributaries.

water table Top of the water-saturated part of an unconfined aquifer.

water table aquifer See *unconfined aquifer.*

water withdrawal Removing water from a groundwater or surface water source and transporting it to a place of use. Compare *water consumption.*

watt Unit of power, or rate at which electrical work is done. See *kilowatt.*

weather Short-term changes in the properties of the troposphere from place to place. Compare *climate.*

weathering Process in which rock is gradually broken down into small bits and pieces that make up most of the soil's inorganic material by being exposed to weather and chemicals and invaded by certain organisms.

wetland Land that stays flooded all or part of the year with fresh or salt water. See *coastal wetland, inland wetland.*

whole-tree harvesting Use of machines to cut trees off at ground level or to pull entire trees from the ground and then reduce the trunks and branches to small wood chips.

wilderness Area where the earth and its community of life have not been seriously disturbed by humans and where humans are only temporary visitors.

wilderness species Wild animal species that flourish only in undisturbed mature vegetational communities such as large areas of mature forest, tundra, grassland, and desert. Compare *early-successional species, late-successional species, mid-successional species.*

wildlife All free, undomesticated species of plants, animals, microorganisms.

wildlife conservation Activity of protecting, preserving, managing, and studying wildlife and wildlife resources.

wildlife management Manipulation of populations of wild species (especially game species) and their habitats for human benefit, the welfare of other species, and the preservation of threatened and endangered wildlife species.

wildlife resources Species of wildlife that have actual or potential economic value to people. See also *game species.*

wild species See *wildlife.*

windbreak Row of trees or hedges planted in a north-to-south direction to partially block wind flow and reduce soil erosion on cultivated land.

wind farm Cluster of small to medium-sized wind turbines in a windy area to capture wind energy and convert it to electrical energy.

woodland See *open forest.*

work What happens when a force is used to move a sample of matter over some distance or to raise its temperature. Energy is defined as the capacity to do such work.

worldview How we think the world works and what we think our role is. See *sustainable-earth worldview, throwaway worldview.*

zero population growth (ZPG) State in which the birth rate (plus immigration) equals the death rate (plus emigration) so that population of a geographical area is no longer increasing.

zoning Regulating how various parcels of land can be used.

zooplankton Animal plankton. Small floating herbivores that feed on plant plankton (phytoplankton and nanoplankton). Compare *nanoplankton, phytoplankton.*

Index

Note: Page numbers appearing in **boldface** indicate where definitions of key terms can be found in the text; these terms also appear in the glosssary. Page numbers in *italics* indicate illustrations, tables, and figures.